ENCYCLOPEDIA OF
WORLD BIOGRAPHY

12

ENCYCLOPEDIA OF WORLD BIOGRAPHY

SECOND EDITION

Orozco
/Radisson **12**

GALE

DETROIT · NEW YORK · TORONTO · LONDON

Staff

Senior Editor: Paula K. Byers
Project Editor: Suzanne M. Bourgoin
Managing Editor: Neil E. Walker

Editorial Staff: Luann Brennan, Frank V. Castronova, Laura S. Hightower, Karen E. Lemerand, Stacy A. McConnell, Jennifer Mossman, Maria L. Munoz, Katherine H. Nemeh, Terrie M. Rooney, Geri Speace

Permissions Manager: Susan M. Tosky
Permissions Specialist: Maria L. Franklin
Permissions Associate: Michele M. Lonoconus
Image Cataloger: Mary K. Grimes

Production Director: Mary Beth Trimper
Production Manager: Evi Seoud
Production Associate: Shanna Heilveil
Product Design Manager: Cynthia Baldwin
Senior Art Director: Mary Claire Krzewinski

Research Manager: Victoria B. Cariappa
Research Specialists: Michele P. LaMeau, Andrew Guy Malonis, Barbara McNeil, Gary J. Oudersluys
Research Associates: Julia C. Daniel, Tamara C. Nott, Norma Sawaya, Cheryl L. Warnock
Research Assistant: Talitha A. Jean

Graphic Services Supervisor: Barbara Yarrow
Image Database Supervisor: Randy Bassett
Imaging Specialist: Mike Lugosz

Manager of Data Entry Services: Eleanor M. Allison
Data Entry Coordinator: Kenneth D. Benson

Manager of Technology Support Services: Theresa A. Rocklin
Programmers/Analysts: Mira Bossowska, Jeffrey Muhr, Christopher Ward

Copyright © 1998
Gale Research
835 Penobscot Bldg.
Detroit, MI 48226-4094

ISBN 0-7876-2221-4 (Set)
ISBN 0-7876-2552-3 (Volume 12)

Library of Congress Cataloging-in-Publication Data

Encyclopedia of world biography / [edited by Suzanne Michele Bourgoin and Paula Kay Byers].
    p. cm.
    Includes bibliographical references and index.
    Summary: Presents brief biographical sketches which provide vital statistics as well as information on the importance of the person listed.
    ISBN 0-7876-2221-4 (set : alk. paper)
    1. Biography—Dictionaries—Juvenile literature. [1. Biography.]
I. Bourgoin, Suzanne Michele, 1968- . II. Byers, Paula K. (Paula Kay), 1954- .
CT 103.E56 1997
920′ .003—dc21
                              97-42327
                              CIP
                              AC

Printed in the United States of America
10 9 8 7 6 5 4 3

ENCYCLOPEDIA OF WORLD BIOGRAPHY

12

O

José Clemente Orozco

The Mexican painter José Clemente Orozco (1883-1949) was one of the artists responsible for the renaissance of mural painting in Mexico in the 1920s.

José Clemente Orozco was born on Nov. 23, 1883, in Zapotlán el Grande (now Ciudad Guzmán) in the state of Jalisco. In Mexico City he studied at the School of Agriculture (1897-1899), the National Preparatory School (1899-1908), and the National School of Fine Arts (1908-1914). He exhibited some of his drawings in the Centennial Exposition in 1910 and had his first one-man show in 1916. He visited the United States in 1917-1918.

In 1922 Orozco initiated his mural work. His first murals at the National Preparatory School (1923-1924) are derivative and stiff, but with the work he executed there on the patio walls and staircase vaulting (1926-1927) he began to develop his own style. During this period he also executed the mural *Omniscience* (1925) in the House of Tiles (now Sanborn's Restaurant) and *Social Revolution* (1926) in the Industrial School in Orizaba. His first period as a muralist culminated in the magnificent *Prometheus* (1930) at Pomona College, Claremont, Calif.

In 1931 Orozco did the murals for the New School for Social Research in New York City, and, following a brief trip to Europe in 1932, he painted the frescoes for the Baker Library at Dartmouth College in Hanover, N.H. (1932-1934). There he initiated a new manner of expression, employing brilliant coloring and original forms and ideas. The theme is America, with its Indian and Spanish past, its present filled with wars and atrocities, in which Christ appears destroying everything, even his own cross.

On his return to Mexico City, Orozco painted the mural *Catharsis* in the Palace of Fine Arts (1934). He then executed a series of masterpieces at Guadalajara in the auditorium of the university (1936), the Government Palace (1937), and the Hospicio Cabañas (1938-1939). In 1940 he created new forms in the murals of the Gabino Ortiz Library in Jiquilpan, Michoacán, using themes from the Revolution, and in the six movable panels entitled *Dive Bomber* in the Museum of Modern Art in New York City.

Orozco's mural (1941) in the Supreme Court Building in Mexico City depicts the moral power of justice. His unfinished works in the Hospital de Jesús Nazareno (1942-1944) in Mexico City are unrivaled in their emotional intensity. He also did the mural *National Allegory* for the open-air theater of the National School for Teachers (1948) and *Juárez Resuscitated* for the Museum of History at Chapultepec. His last complete work was the frescoes in the dome of the Legislative Chamber of the Government Palace in Guadalajara (1949).

Orozco was one of the founders of the National College in 1943, and there he presented six exhibitions between 1943 and 1948. In 1946 he was awarded the National Prize in the Arts and Sciences, and that same year a great retrospective exhibition of his works was presented in the Palace of Fine Arts. He died in Mexico City on Sept. 7, 1949.

Further Reading

Orozco's own account is his *An Autobiography*, translated by Robert C. Stephenson (1962). A study of Orozco is MacKinley Helm, *Man of Fire, J. C. Orozco: An Interpretive Memoir* (1953). See also Alma Reed, *The Mexican Muralists* (1960),

and Jon H. Hopkins, *Orozco: A Catalogue of His Graphic Work* (1967).

Additional Sources

Hurlburt, Laurance P. *The Mexican muralists in the United States,* Albuquerque: University of New Mexico Press, 1989.

Rochfort, Desmond. *Mexican muralists: Orozco, Rivera, Siqueiros,* London: Laurence King, 1993. □

Bobby Orr

One of hockey's greats, Bobby Orr (born 1948) was the Boston Bruins' star player in the late 1960s to mid-1970s. He added to the position of defenseman the responsibility of offensive play as well.

Although he played for only nine full seasons (1966-1975) in the National Hockey League, and his name isn't found near the top of the list of all time high scorers, Bobby Orr of the Boston Bruins is widely regarded as one of the greatest hockey players of all time. "The great ones all bear a mark of originality, but Bobby Orr's mark on hockey, too brief in the etching, may have been the most distinctive of any player's. . . . He changed the sport by redefining the parameters of his position. A

defenseman, as interpreted by Orr, became both a defender and an aggressor, both a protector and a producer," wrote E.M. Swift in *Sports Illustrated.*

Robert Gordon Orr was born in 1948 in Parry Sound, Ontario, a resort town on Lake Huron's Georgian Bay. Orr's father, Douglas, was a packer of dynamite at a munitions factory. His mother, Arva, worked as a waitress at a motel restaurant. The family included four other children, Ron, Patricia, Douglas, Jr., and Penny. Like most youngsters in Parry Sound, Orr began skating soon after he had learned to walk. Since, as Orr told *People,* "You don't skate without a stick in your hand," he also began playing hockey at an early age. Orr's extraordinary ability was evident from the start. By the time he was nine years old, he could hold his own in games with adults on his father's amateur team.

Shorter and thinner than most of his peers, the blonde, young blue-eyed Orr dazzled the coaches of Parry Sound's bantam league team with his skill, speed, and tenacity, rather than brute strength (even in his prime years in the NHL Orr was a solid but unprepossessing 5 feet, 11 inches, and weighed 175 pounds). In 1960, at age twelve, he led his bantam team to the final round of the Ontario championship. It was during this game that Orr began attracting the attention of professional hockey scouts. Several organizations showed interest, but the Boston Bruins, then the NHL's worst team, were most aggressive in pursuing Orr. To gain the boy's favor, the Bruins donated money to the Parry Sound youth hockey program, and team representatives made regular visits to the Orr family home. This persistence paid off. In 1962, fourteen-year-old Bobby Orr signed a

contract to play Junior A hockey for the Oshawa (Ontario) Generals, a Bruins farm team. In return, the Orr family received a small cash payment and a new coat of stucco for their house. At Oshawa, Orr's living expenses were paid for and he received $10 a week in pocket money. Realizing that the deal was not to his son's advantage, Douglas Orr retained the services of Alan Eagleson, a savvy young Toronto lawyer, to represent Bobby in future contract negotiations. "Sure I was homesick, and the family I lived with was tougher on me than my own folks," Orr later told *People* about his four years of playing junior hockey in Oshawa. "It was the way you served your apprenticeship. If you were good, you knew you'd turn pro at 18."

Rookie of the Year

Orr played so well in junior hockey that the Bruins would have promoted him to the NHL a year sooner, if not for a league rule against players under 18 years of age. When Orr joined the Bruins in 1966, he arrived as the most highly touted rookie in years. He was also the highest paid rookie in NHL history, rumored to be earning somewhere around $25,000 a year, when the average NHL salary was $17,000 a year and the league's greatest star, the legendary Gordie Howe of the Detroit Red Wings, was earning about $50,000 annually. Showing the team spirit that would earn him the sincere affection and respect of his fellow-players, Orr urged his attorney Alan Eagleson to organize the NHL Players Association, which was instrumental in raising everyone's salary. By the end of his career, Orr was earning $500,000 per year, although this did not compare to the salaries earned by later players such as Wayne Gretzky. "People ask me if I'm upset when I see current players' salaries," Orr told the *Boston Globe* in 1995. "I'm not upset. What upsets me is knowing Player A makes big money and seeing him give you three good games out of ten."

Orr entered the NHL with such hype, it seemed impossible for him to live up to the reputation that preceded him. Often called "unbelievable," Orr did not disappoint his fans. Although the Bruins again finished at the bottom of the then six-team NHL in the 1966-67 season, Orr won the Calder Trophy as Rookie of the Year. The following season the Bruins, enhanced by the acquisition of Phil Esposito, Ken Hodge, and Fred Stanfield from the Chicago Black Hawks, finished third in the Eastern Division of the expanded NHL and earned a place in the Stanley Cup playoffs. Orr won the Norris Trophy, awarded to the NHL's outstanding defenseman (he would win the Norris Trophy for the next seven seasons). The once pitiful Bruins were now among the most competitive teams in the league.

Stanley Cup Champions

In the 1969-70 season, the Bruins won the Stanley Cup for the first time in 29 years, defeating the St. Louis Blues in four straight games in the playoff final. Orr secured the Cup for Boston by scoring a winning goal in an overtime period of the fourth game. In addition to the Norris Trophy, Orr won the Hart Trophy (for most valuable player in the NHL), the Ross Trophy (for Leading Scorer in the NHL), and the Smythe Trophy (for most valuable player in the playoffs). It

was the first time a single player has one all four awards in one season. In the late 1960s and early 1970s, the NHL was expanding rapidly into cities where hockey was not traditionally popular. The unprecedented exploits of Bobby Orr sold tickets in these cities and enabled hockey to become a truly national sport in the United States. "Orr remains the pivot figure in the game, the single charismatic personality around whom the entire sport will coalesce in the decade of the '70s, as golf once coalesced around Arnold Palmer, baseball around Babe Ruth, football around John Unitas," wrote Jack Olsen in the *Sports Illustrated* issue that named Orr the magazine's "Sportsman of the Year" for 1970.

The "Big, Bad Bruins" of the late 1960s and early 1970s, played a tough, messy game of hockey (as opposed to the elegantly classic moves of the Montreal Canadiens, the most frequent possessors of the Stanley Cup). Orr was remarkably polite and well-mannered off the ice but during a game he never shied away from a scrap. "We're not dirty. It's just that we're always determined to get the job done—no matter what it takes," Orr told *Newsweek* in 1969. An older and wiser Orr came to realize that brawling and belligerence set a bad example for children. In 1982, he made a short film called "First Goal" (sponsored by Nabisco Brands for whom he was doing public relations) advising young athletes, and their parents, that having fun is more important than winning.

Announced Retirement at Age 30

After being eliminated by the Montreal Canadiens in the playoffs of the 1970-71 season, the Bruins came back to win the Stanley Cup again in 1971-72. Then the team's fortunes quickly began to fade. At the end of the 1971-72 season several top players, including flamboyant center Derek Sanderson, were lured away to the newly founded World Hockey Association and a number of good second-string players were lost in a further expansion draft. Orr stayed on with the Bruins, but knee injuries, which had plagued him since the start of his professional career, were becoming increasingly serious. "When you are young, you think you can lick the world, that you are indestructible . . . But around 1974-75, I knew it had changed. I was playing, but I wasn't playing like I could before. My knees were gone. They hurt before the game, in the game, after the game. Things that I did easily on the ice I could not do anymore," Orr explained to Will McDonough of the *Boston Globe*.

In 1976, a bitter contract dispute ended Orr's long-time relationship with the Bruins. He signed as a free-agent with the Chicago Black Hawks but knee problems kept him off the ice for all but a handful of games over two seasons. In 1978, he reluctantly announced his retirement. Having left Boston under strained circumstances, Orr was unprepared for the reaction he received from Bruins fans when his number 4 sweater was retired to the rafters of the Boston Garden in 1979. The outpouring of affection left him speechless and on the brink of tears. Similar emotion accompanied the closing ceremonies of the cavernous old Boston Garden in 1995, as Orr took one last skate on the Garden's ice. Perhaps only Ted Williams, the great Boston

Red Sox slugger of the 1940s and 1950s, is held in as high esteem by New England sports fans.

Orr and his wife, Peggy, a former speech therapist, live in suburban Boston (with additional homes on Cape Cod and in Florida). They have two sons, Darren and Brent. Orr spends his time tending to a wide variety of business investments and charitable endeavors. He has no interest in coaching and would like to return to professional hockey as a team owner. "It was good that I retired so young," Orr told Joseph P. Kahn of the *Boston Globe.* "The adjustment period was difficult but at least I had things I could do. I have a great life now."

Further Reading

Fischler, Stan, *Hockey's Greatest Teams,* Henry Regnery Co., 1973.
Dowling, Tom, "The Orr Effect," in the *Atlantic,* April 1971, pp. 62-68.
Boston Globe, May 13, 1990, pp. 43, 57; May 10, 1995, pp. 49, 59; July 13, 1995, pp. 53, 58.
New Yorker, March 27, 1971, pp. 107-114.
Newsweek, March 21, 1969, pp. 64, 67; February 15, 1982, p. 20.
People, March 27, 1978, pp. 62-64.
Sports Illustrated, December 21, 1970, pp. 36-42; October 19, 1971, pp. 28-35; August 5, 1985, pp. 60-64; September 19, 1994, pp. 125-26. □

John Boyd Orr

The Scottish medical scientist John Boyd Orr, 1st Baron of Brechin (1880-1971), pioneered the science of human nutrition and developed new correlations between health, food, and poverty. He was the first director general of the Food and Agricultural Organization.

B orn in Kilmaurs, Ayrshire, on Sept. 23, 1880, to a family of Covenanters, John Boyd Orr overcame the pressures of poverty in his youth by relentless work and the pursuit of greatly varied intellectual aspirations, mainly at Glasgow University. After taking his master's degree in preparation for the ministry, he turned first to science and medicine, finishing a medical degree with the *prix d'honneur* of the medical faculty, and then to research in metabolic diseases, for which he earned a doctoral degree.

Orr's major moral and scientific concern, deepened by close observations of life in Glasgow's slums, was the medical meaning of poverty and ignorance, notably in respect to malnutrition and preventable diseases among schoolchildren in the working population. Convinced of the need for modern research facilities in nutrition, he was instrumental, between 1906 and 1914, in establishing the Rowett Institute. World War I drew him into service as a frontline doctor with the army and the navy. He earned renown for developing a diet that greatly reduced the incidence of disease in his battalion. After the war he resumed the directorate of the

Rowett Institute and extended its researches to agricultural and dietary problems in the colonies and dominions, parts of continental Europe, and the Jewish settlements of Palestine.

In 1931 Orr floated the journal *Nutrition Abstracts and Views.* He published numerous works, among them the report *The Effect of the Wasted Pastures in Kikuyu and Masai Territories upon Native Herds,* which is a classic in nutritional literature, and *Minerals in Pastures and Their Relation to Animal Nutrition* (1928). His pathbreaking survey *Food, Health and Income* (1936) defines the physiological ideal as a state of well-being requiring no improvement by a change of diet, finds that a diet completely adequate for health was reached in the United Kingdom in 1933-1934 at an income level above that of 50 percent of the population, and argues for the need of reconciling the interests of agriculture and public health. For these achievements Orr was elected a fellow of the Royal Society in 1932 and knighted in 1935 for his services to agriculture.

Orr's chief objectives during World War II were the prevention of food shortages in the military and civilian sectors of the nation; the development of world food policies capable of banning the specter of a postwar famine; and the planning of a supranational agency in the context of which food would be removed from international politics and trade by being treated differently from other goods. These aims dominated his term of office (1945-1948) as director general of the Food and Agricultural Organization of the United Nations. Thus he was instrumental in presenting, for the first time in history, a precise appraisal of the

world food situation and in inducing governments to cooperate in the International Emergency Food Council and related common enterprises.

After resigning from the Rowett Institute in 1945, Orr won a Parliament seat, representing the Scottish universities, which he relinquished in 1947, and served at Glasgow University as rector in 1945 and as chancellor in 1946. In 1948 he received a peerage, in 1949 the Harben Medal from the Royal Institute of Public Health, and in 1949 the Nobel Peace Prize in recognition of his efforts to ensure peace by applying science to the removal of hunger and poverty. He died near Edzell, Scotland, on June 25, 1971.

Further Reading

Two books that deal with Orr's life and work are Gove Hambidge, *The Story of FAO* (1955), and Orr's own *As I Recall* (1966). □

Daniel Ortega

Daniel Ortega (born 1945) joined the revolutionary Sandinista National Liberation Front (Frente Sandinista de Liberación National—FSLN) in 1963, helped lead its overthrow of the Somoza dynasty, and was elected president of Nicaragua on November 4, 1984.

Daniel Ortega Saavedra was born on November 11, 1945, in the mining and ranching town of La Libertad, Nicaragua, in the municipality of Chontales. He was the third son of Daniel Ortega Serda, an accountant for a mining firm. The family later moved to Managua, where his father owned a small export-import business.

Ortega received his education in private and Catholic schools. He was an active Catholic during his youth, becoming a catechist and giving Bible studies to those who lived in poor neighborhoods. His seriousness, intelligence, oratorical skills, and religious devotion suggested to many that he would become a priest. He made good grades, but his parents sent him to four different high schools—trying fruitlessly to keep him out of a growing student opposition movement in the late 1950s. Ortega studied law for one year at Managua's Jesuit-run Central American University (c. 1961), but abandoned his formal education for revolutionary politics.

Much of the Ortega family had revolutionary credentials. Father Daniel fought in A.C. Sandino's 1927-1934 rebellion against U.S. occupation of Nicaragua, for which he served three months in prison. Daniel's younger brothers, Humberto (born 1948) and Camilo (born 1950) also became Sandinista revolutionaries. Humberto, a top military strategist, eventually became minister of defense of the revolutionary government, beginning in 1979. Camilo died fighting in the insurrection (1978). Their mother, Lidia Saavedra, became active in the 1970s in protests and went to jail for these actions. Daniel Ortega's wife was poetess Rosario Murillo; they had seven children. She worked with the FSLN after 1969 and was captured by the Somoza regime's security forces in 1979. After the victory she became general secretary of the Sandinista Cultural Workers Association and in 1985 became an FSLN delegate in the National Assembly.

Revolutionary Activity

After the 1956 assassination of Anastasio Somoza Garcia, founder of the Somoza dynasty, Luis Somoza Debayle succeeded his father as president and Anastasio Somoza Debayle assumed command of the National Guard. They terrorized suspected opponents of the regime to avenge their father's death. Repression kindled opposition, which surfaced after Fidel Castro overthrew the Batista regime in 1959. Ortega, still in high school in Managua in 1959, took part in a widespread student struggle against the Somoza regime. The protests of 1959 were organized by the Nicaraguan Patriotic Youth (Juventud Patriótico Nicaragüense—JPN), which Ortega joined in 1960. JPN members later took part in several guerrilla insurgent movements, but only the FSLN survived. In 1960 Ortega was captured and tortured for his role in the protests. Not deterred from his opposition to the Somoza dynasty, he helped establish the Nicaraguan Revolutionary Youth (Juventud Revolucionaria Nicaragüense—JRN), along with the FSLN's Marxist founders Carlos Fonseca Amador and Tomás Borge Martínez. In 1961 Ortega was again arrested and tortured by the regime.

But by 1962 he was again organizing JRN revolutionary cells in Managua's poor barrios.

In 1963 Ortega was recruited into the FSLN, a Marxist-Leninist vanguard revolutionary party committed to the armed overthrow of the Somozas. He helped organize the Federation of Secondary Students (Federación de Estudiantes de Secundaria—FES) and was again arrested and tortured. In 1964 he was captured in Guatemala with other Sandinistas and deported to Nicaragua, again to be imprisoned and tortured. Free in 1965, he cofounded the newspaper *El Estudiante (The Student),* the official paper of the Revolutionary Student Front (Frente Estudiantil Revolucionario—FER), the university support wing of the FSLN. By 1965 he had earned sufficient respect from other top Sandinistas that they named him to the FSLN's Dirección Nacional (National Directorate), the organization's top policy council.

In 1966-1967 Ortega headed the Internal Front, an urban underground that robbed several banks and in 1967 assassinated Gonzalo Lacayo, a reputed National Guard torturer. In November 1967 the security police captured Ortega, and he was given a lengthy sentence for the Lacayo killing. During his seven years in prison he and other Sandinistas exercised, wrote poetry, studied, and continued political activity—including resistance within the prison. During the seven years Ortega spent in jail the FSLN developed and grew. In a December 1974 commando raid in Managua, the FSLN took hostage several top regime officials and Somoza kin. The hostages were freed in exchange for a $5 million ransom, publicity, and the freedom of many Sandinistas, including Ortega and Tomás Borge.

In 1974 President Anastasio Somoza Debayle declared a state of siege (1974-1977) and sharply increased repression of opponents. Under fierce persecution and with many of its elements isolated, the FSLN began to develop different "tendencies" (factions) based on different political-military strategies. In 1975 Ortega rejoined the National Directorate. The next year he resumed clandestine organizing in Managua and Masaya. He helped his brother Humberto and others shape the strategy of the Tercerista (Third Force) tendency of the FSLN. The Terceristas allied with the rapidly growing non-Marxist opposition, and their ranks swelled. Militarily much bolder than the other tendencies in 1977-1978, the Terceristas helped spark a general popular insurrection in September and October of 1978.

Ortega helped form and lead the Terceristas' northern front campaign in 1977, and in 1978-1979 helped lead the rapidly expanding southern front. The FSLN's three tendencies reunited in early 1979 as popular rebellion spread. Daniel and Humberto Ortega became members of the new, joint National Directorate. During the final offensive in June 1979 Ortega was named to the junta of the rebel coalition's National Reconstruction Government. On July 19 the Somoza regime collapsed and the junta took over the shattered nation.

Role in Revolutionary Government

Ortega served on the junta of the National Reconstruction Government from 1979 until its dissolution in January 1985 and was the key liaison between the junta and the National Directorate, which set general policy guidelines for the revolution. In 1981 Ortega became coordinator of the junta, consolidating his leadership role. Within the National Directorate he became a leader of a pragmatic majority faction and emerged as the directorate's and junta's major international representative and domestic policy spokesman. When the FSLN had to choose a nominee for president for the November 4, 1984 election, the directorate selected Ortega. He won with 67 percent of the vote, competing against six other candidates.

The National Directorate and the junta in 1979 adopted, and have since followed, two pragmatic policies that are unusual for a Marxist regime: the economy would be mixed—40 percent in the public sector, 60 percent private—and political parties other than the FSLN (except those linked to the Somozas) could take part in politics and hold cabinet posts. The FSLN quickly consolidated its political advantage in the revolutionary government, fusing itself with the new Sandinista popular army and police and adding new seats to the Council of State in a move denounced by opponents as a power grab.

Ortega exercised no charismatic dominance of the Nicaraguan revolution, but gradually emerged as a first among equals within the top Sandinista leadership. A somewhat gruff and intensely private person, he showed little threat of developing the charismatic mass following that other directorate members feared. Moreover, his ability to concentrate power remained limited by the control of key ministries by other members of the National Directorate.

Ortega's sometimes abrasive or confrontational public style at times caused friction for the revolutionary government, especially with the United States. Members of the U.S. Bipartisan Commission on Central America, for example, reported that Ortega's comments during two 1983 meetings were rather hostile in tone. In contrast, his religious background and longtime acquaintance with Miguel Obando y Bravo, Archbishop of Managua, made him a useful emissary to the Catholic Church hierarchy. But relations with the Catholic Church grew increasingly strained as the Church became an outspoken critic of the Sandinistas in the early 1980s.

As president of Nicaragua, Ortega established a modern team of technical advisers; his cabinet included other top Sandinistas as well as non-Sandinistas. Ortega's rise to the presidency was regarded by many as a commitment by the FSLN's National Directorate to continue the pragmatism of 1979-1985, a sign also reflected in his moderate inaugural speech.

However, daunting problems faced the Ortega administration and the FSLN's National Directorate. Under their leadership Nicaragua expressed solidarity with other Central American rebel movements, built up its military with the help of Cuban advisers, purchased Soviet-bloc arms, increased trade and friendship with the Soviet Union, and sought to increase independence from the United States while remaining friendly with Western Europe and Latin America. U.S. disapproval, however, had severe consequences. The Reagan administration financed a revolt by

10-15,000 anti-Sandinista counterrevolutionary forces sponsored by the Central Intelligence Agency. The civil war severely strained Nicaraguan domestic consensus and resources. U.S. troops maneuvered in neighboring Honduras, fueling Nicaraguans' fear of an invasion. A U.S.-engineered international credit slowdown and trade embargo, begun in May 1985, eroded an economy already shrunken by private sector fears, falling export prices, and management problems. Under such pressures, President Ortega's major task was to struggle for the mere survival of the Nicaraguan revolution in an increasingly hostile international environment.

United States aid to the "contra" forces became increasingly controversial with the 1986 disclosure of "unauthorized" funds being sent to the anti-Sandinistas. It was charged that some of the money realized from the sale of arms to Iran was siphoned off to the contras.

Unsuccessful Bid for Reelection

In February 1990 Ortega's bid for reelection was challenged by Violeta Chamorro. She questioned the Sandinistas' close links with Cuba and the Soviet Union and reached out to center and conservative parties to help defeat Ortega. A second attempt to regain power in 1996 was again unsuccessful. Twenty-three presidential candidates ran in the October 1996 elections, but Ortega and Arnoldo Alemán emerged as favorites. After several days of vote counting, Alemán was declared the winner with 51 percent of the vote; Ortega came in second with 38 percent. Ortega conceded defeat but continued to question the legitimacy of Alemán's government.

Further Reading

Literature on Daniel Ortega is limited. Recommended for background on the Nicaraguan revolution are Thomas W. Walker's *Nicaragua: The Land of Sandino* (1981) and his edited works *Nicaragua in Revolution* (1982) and *Nicaragua: The First Five Years* (1985); George Black, *Triumph of the People: The Sandinista Revolution in Nicaragua* (1981); John A. Booth, *The End and the Beginning: The Nicaraguan Revolution* (1985); Richard Millett, *The Guardians of the Dynasty* (1977); and David Nolan, *The Ideology of the Sandinistas and the Nicaraguan Revolution* (1984). See also Anastasio Somoza with Jack Cox, *Nicaragua Betrayed* (1980), and Bernard Diederich, *Somoza and the Legacy of U.S. Involvement in Central America* (1982). □

José Ortega Y Gasset

The Spanish philosopher and essayist José Ortega y Gasset (1883-1955) is best known for his analyses of history and modern culture, especially his penetrating examination of the uniquely modern phenomenon "mass man."

José Ortega y Gasset was born in Madrid on May 9, 1883. He studied with the Jesuits at the Colegio de Jesuítas de Miraflores del Palo, near Málaga, and from 1898 to 1902 he studied at the University of Madrid, from which he received the degree of *licenciado en filosofía y letras*. In 1904 Ortega earned a doctor's degree at Madrid for a dissertation in philosophy. From 1905 to 1907 he did postgraduate studies at the universities of Leipzig, Berlin, and Marburg in Germany. Deeply influenced by German philosophy, especially the thought of Hermann Cohen, Wilhelm Dilthey, Edmund Husserl, and Martin Heidegger, as well as by the French philosopher Henri Bergson, Ortega sought to overcome the traditional provincialism and isolation of philosophical study in his native Spain.

From 1910 to 1936 Ortega taught philosophy at the University of Madrid. Early in his career he gained a reputation through his numerous philosophical and cultural essays, not only in literary journals but also in newspapers, which were a peculiar and important medium of education and culture in pre-Civil War Spain. Ortega's most famous book, *The Revolt of the Masses* (1930), first appeared in the form of newspaper articles. Throughout his career he was generally active in the cultural and political life of his country, both in monarchist and in republican Spain. In 1923 Ortega founded the journal *Revista de Occidente*, which flourished until 1936.

After the outbreak of the Spanish Civil War in 1936, Ortega left Spain and lived abroad, dwelling in France, Holland, Argentina, and Portugal until the end of World War II. He returned to Spain in 1945, living there and in

Portugal, with frequent trips and stays abroad, until his death. In 1948, together with Julián Marías, Ortega founded the Instituto de Humanidades, a cultural and scholarly institution, in Madrid. In 1949 Ortega lectured in the United States, followed by lectures in Germany and in Switzerland in 1950 and 1951. He received various honorary degrees, including a doctorate *honoris causa* from the University of Glasgow. Ortega died in Madrid on Oct. 18, 1955.

Ortega's numerous and varied writings, in addition to *The Revolt of the Masses,* include *The Modern Theme* (1923), *The Mission of the University* (1930), *On Love* (1940), *History as System* (1941), *Man and People* (1957), *Man and Crisis* (1958), and *What Is Philosophy?* (1958). Often mentioned, as is Miguel de Unamuno, with the existentialists, Ortega expounded a philosophy that has been called "ratiovitalism" or "vital reason," in which he sought to do justice to both the intellectual and passional dimensions of man as manifestations of the fundamental reality, "human life."

Ortega's philosophy is closest to that of Heidegger. He described human life as the "radical reality" to which everything else in the universe appears, in terms of which everything else has meaning, and which is therefore the central preoccupation of philosophy. Man is related to the world in terms of the "concerns" to which he attends. The individual human being is decisively free in his inner self, and his life and destiny are what he makes of them within the "given" of his heredity, environment, society, and culture. Thus man does not so much *have* a history; he *is* his history, since history is uniquely the manifestation of human freedom.

Further Reading

Two studies of Ortega's thought which include biographical material are José Sánchez Villaseñor, *Ortega y Gasset, Existentialist: A Critical Study of His Thought and Its Sources* (1949), and José Ferrater Mora, *Ortega y Gasset: An Outline of His Philosophy* (1957; rev. ed. 1963). Excellent discussions of Ortega's literary theories are in Joseph Frank, *The Widening Gyre: Crisis and Mastery in Modern Literature* (1963), and William H. Gass, *Fiction and the Figures of Life* (1970).

Additional Sources

Gray, Rockwell. *The imperative of modernity: an intellectual biography of José Ortega y Gasset,* Berkeley: University of California Press, 1989.
Ouimette, Victor. *José Ortega y Gasset,* Boston: Twayne Publishers, 1982. □

Abraham Ortelius

The Flemish map maker and map seller Abraham Ortelius (1527-1598) is known for his "Theatrum orbis terrarum," one of the first major atlases. He accelerated the movement away from Ptolemaic geographical conceptions.

braham Ortelius was born Abraham Ortels of German parents in Antwerp on April 14, 1527. He was trained as an engraver, worked as an illuminator of maps, and by 1554 was in the business of selling maps and antiquities. This business involved extensive traveling, which enabled Ortelius to make contacts with the international community of scholars concerned with exploration and cartography and especially with English experts like Richard Hakluyt and John Dee. From these sources Ortelius obtained cartographical materials and information; he also collected and published maps by his fellow Flemish geographer Gerhardus Mercator.

Ortelius began issuing various maps in the 1560s. Among these were maps of Egypt, Asia, and the world. The *Theatrum orbis terrarum* (1570) consisted of 70 maps on 53 sheets. There was a world map and maps of the continents of Africa and Asia. Europe, however, was the area most completely surveyed. In 1573 an *Additamenta* (atlas supplement) was issued. Later editions of both atlas and supplement were revised and expanded. By 1624 the *Theatrum* had run through 40 editions and had grown to 166 maps. It appeared in Latin and translations into Dutch, German, French, Spanish, and English.

The collection deserves to be called an atlas because of its uniform publishing format, critical selection from the existing mass of material, and scholarly citation of authorities whose maps were used (87 in all). Greatly diminished was the influence of Ptolemy's *Geography,* an ancient masterpiece revived for Europeans in the 15th century.

The Ptolemaic influence had itself marked an advance in academic cartography. Medieval geography had registered a profound cleavage between the geographical notions of the Schoolmen, highly abstract and shaped by theological constructs, and the practical activity of the Mediterranean chart makers, whose portolano charts gave an amazingly accurate record of coastlines visited and surveyed by mariners. The coordinates provided by Ptolemy, from which world maps were constructed, helped to undermine the medieval academic outlook and put scholarly cartography on a more scientific basis.

Nevertheless, by the late 16th century the acceleration of the flow of new geographical information produced by the Discoveries had rendered many of Ptolemy's observations obsolete. It was time once more for the printed map to catch up with the manuscript chart, a task facilitated by the work of Ortelius and Mercator. It is significant, however, that both Europe and Southeast Asia received the most accurate rendition from Ortelius, whereas the outlines of South America remained very inadequately portrayed—perhaps a reflection of the real weight of the Discoveries with respect to their lines of economic and geographical attraction. Ortelius died at Antwerp on July 4, 1598.

Further Reading

Ortelius's career and contributions are examined in Lloyd Arnold Brown, *The Story of Maps* (1949); Boies Penrose, *Travel and Discovery in the Renaissance: 1420-1620* (1952); and G. R. Crone, *Maps and Their Makers: An Introduction to the History of Cartography* (1953; 4th rev. ed. 1968). □

Simon J. Ortiz

Simon Ortiz (born 1941) became one the most respected and widely read Native American poets. His work is characterized by a strong storytelling voice that recalls traditional Native American storytelling.

"When I see native people, it assures my existence," expressed Simon J. Ortiz in a 1994 interview. A noted poet and writer with an international following, Ortiz acknowledges his origins from the Acoma Pueblo, or "Aa-co" as it is called in his language. Born on May 27, 1941, he is a member of the Eagle or Dyaamih Clan, his mother's clan—a composition of many individuals including Ortiz's extended family members. As there are no words in his native tongue for "cousin," "aunt" or "uncle," each member is referred to as a "brother," "sister," "mother," or "father." When Ortiz speaks about his family, one senses the deep cultural ties that bind not only the family together, but the people to the land. His father, a woodcarver and elder in the clan, was charged with keeping the religious knowledge and customs of the Acoma Pueblo people. His brother Earl is a graphic artist. Ortiz is the father of three children: a son, Raho Nez,

an attorney for the Tohono O'odham Nation in Sells, Arizona, and two daughters, Rainy Dawn and Sara Marie, both students.

A Young Boy in His Community

Ortiz spent his early childhood years in the village of McCartys, or "Deetzeyaamah" in his language, attending McCartys Day School through the sixth grade. It was customary at that time for Native American children to leave home and attend boarding schools, and Ortiz was no exception; soon after, he was sent to St. Catherine's Indian School in Santa Fe, but his attendance was curtailed as he became homesick for his family and home. Ortiz began to notice cultural distinctions and conflicts in his life; and he began to collect stories and thoughts at an early age, recording them in his diaries. Reading whatever was available became a passion for Ortiz. He was especially interested in dictionaries, which would allow his mind to travel to a "state of wonder."

St. Catherine's, while attempting to provide Native American children with an education, also encouraged the Indian children to abandon their cultural ways and adopt a more "American" lifestyle. "The fear of God was instilled in each child . . . penance and physical duty were the day's rigor," Ortiz recalled, "I spoke and knew only the Acoma world." Disillusioned with St. Catherine's, Ortiz heard that Albuquerque Indian School taught trade classes such as plumbing and mechanics, and decided it would be a good experience to transfer schools. Ortiz's father, a railroad worker in addition to his community activities, was opposed

to his son learning a trade and encouraged his children to get an education and training in a field other than hard, manual labor. Although Ortiz attended sheet metal and woodworking classes, his interest did not remain in those areas. He liked to read and study, to learn about the world. In retrospect, he claimed that it was "an escape from a hard life. Study, dream and read . . . escape to fantasy. It became the food for my imagination." Ortiz did not consider becoming a writer—writing was not something Native Americans practiced. When asked why, he replied that "it is a profession only whites did." His thoughts would later change. If whites could do it, so could he.

In the 1950s, public schools were beginning to receive funding from Johnson-O'Malley legislation, which provided opportunities for greater numbers of Native American students to attend school. Ortiz attended one such school, Grants High School in Grants, New Mexico—the largest non-Indian town near Acoma. Education had always been a significant priority with the people of Acoma Pueblo. It was the means by which they could better their own lives and their community. Ortiz believed this approach stemmed from the "indoctrination" of the Bureau of Indian Affairs (BIA) which tried to make Indians "good American citizens." Yet, in those days Indian children received no further encouragement to pursue an education beyond high school. While attending high school, Ortiz's leadership skills began to emerge. Although he often refers to himself as a "not too social kid," he became a school leader by "default." He disagreed with the manner and treatment accorded to Native American students and advised them that they did not have to accept a subordinate position.

A Search for Meaning in Education

The day after Ortiz graduated from high school, he began work in the uranium industry at Kerr-McGee as a laborer. Wanting to be a chemist, Ortiz applied for a technical position at Kerr-McGee but was employed instead as a clerk-typist because he was "good at typing." He was ultimately promoted "down to the pit" as a crusher, and later to a semi-skilled operator. His work experience as a mining laborer would later provide the material for his writings in *Fight Back: For the Sake of the People, for the Sake of the Land.*

Using his savings and funds from a BIA educational grant, Ortiz left the mining industry to pursue a university education. In 1962, he attended Fort Lewis College majoring in chemistry. While his interest in science prevailed, his grades did not. He was more interested in learning about life and being a part of it. The study of chemistry did not encompass elements about understanding or respecting life. Barely passing his biology and organic chemistry classes, he decided to try English because he had been "remotely" contemplating becoming a teacher. "It was *remotely* because what I really wanted to do was read, think and write," he explained. The prescribed university curriculum did not favor Ortiz's search for knowledge, and he "felt an intuitive resistance to the knowledge being learned." University structure was attempting to change who he was as a natural person. Ortiz began to develop as an artist and expres-

sionist, though. Drama interested him and he auditioned for a part in the university play *Death of a Salesman.* Drama enabled him to express his thoughts visually, and he temporarily found a new form of artistic freedom.

As a leader of the Indian Student Organization, Ortiz found himself confronting many different issues. No matter where he turned, he was surrounded with the inferior treatment of native peoples. Ortiz began to seek something different, something to answer the questions and reasons of life. He found it in alcohol, which provided a false sense of relief. Security soon faded and bouts with alcohol abuse would haunt Ortiz for many years to come.

Ortiz enlisted in the U.S. Armed Forces in 1963 because he wanted something different to experience and write about. Scoring high on verbal aptitude tests, he was assigned to edit the battalion newsletter; however, the army discontinued the publication after its first printing. Following the abrupt end to his journalistic career, Ortiz was sent to Texas as a member of a missile defense technical team. While still in the army, he made plans to return to civilian life and attend the University of New Mexico to study English literature and creative writing. By this time, he considered himself a "writer."

At the University of New Mexico, Ortiz found himself once more confined by the structured curriculum, and he soon discovered that few ethnic writers had entered the semiprivate domain of American literature. He became aware that a new age of Native American writers was beginning to emerge in the midst of political activism. Ortiz credits the political climate and activities of the day as one of the fundamental reasons for altering his writing style. Writing previously from absolute self-expression, he now focused on the unheard Native American voice.

The duration of university life lasted two more years, until 1968, when he received a fellowship for writing at the University of Iowa in the International Writers Program. "I don't have any college degrees," Ortiz explained in a 1993 autobiographical statement. "I've worked at various jobs . . . and had a varied career, including ups and too many downs." Ortiz served as public relations director at Rough Rock Demonstration School from 1969 to 1970, and edited *Quetzal* from 1970 to 1973. He taught at San Diego State University and at the Institute of American Arts in Santa Fe, New Mexico, in 1974, and at Navajo Community College from 1975 to 1977. He also taught at the College of Marin in Kentfield, California, from 1976 to 1979, and the University of New Mexico from 1979 to 1981. Beginning in 1982, he served as consultant editor for the Pueblo of Acoma Press.

Returned to Acoma Pueblo Origins

In 1988 Ortiz was appointed as tribal interpreter, and in 1989 he became First Lieutenant Governor for Acoma Pueblo in New Mexico. Being connected to his Acoma community has been of major importance in his life. "Helping others in the community are the very reasons for purpose and meaning in life," according to Ortiz's interpretation of traditional Acoma ways. "To help or to be helpful . . . is a quality associated with the responsibility each individual has to the community," not only in traditional

Acoma ways, but with Native Americans in general," observed Ortiz, adding that "leadership is a way of showing that each person is meant for some larger or extended purpose, for the true meaning of his existence is to be helpful to his community. Leadership is not a personal choice; you are appointed to serve the people as completely as possible, and you offer to help achieve happiness and wholeness for all the people." For Ortiz there is a certain element of sharing in coming together with elders to hear their stories and wisdom. Under the guidance and direction of their leaders, Ortiz explained that the "coming together of community members is a responsibility we all have to carry out in order to assure the continuance of our community."

In 1988 Ortiz was appointed to be the Acoma tribal interpreter, but he was not sure what responsibilities this task entailed. He learned through family and community members that he was "working for the people and for the land." These leadership roles in the community afforded him the method by which he connected himself spiritually, in wholeness, with the continuance of his culture. In his "What We See: A Perspective on Chaco Canyon and Pueblo Ancestry," Ortiz wrote: "All human construction involves a relationship between the natural and the man-made. That relationship physically shapes the human cultural environment. In historical terms, the character of that relationship is a major indication of the character of a culture as a whole. It tells us how the human beings who made it thought of themselves in relation to the rest of creation."

Writing with a Native Voice

The writings of Ortiz are emotionally charged and complex. His expressions of anger, passion, love, fear, and threats to human existence make the reader question the backdrop of the society in which he or she exists. Essayists have compared his writing to other present-day poets and authors, but Ortiz stands on his own. Pertinent to both Native and non-Native readers, Ortiz's subjects are those that affect daily life. In his *Simon Ortiz*, Andrew Wiget noted that Ortiz has "committed himself to articulating what he saw as a distinctly Native American perspective on fundamental human experiences . . . a consciously assumed purpose which came from a clear sense of the power and function of language derived from Ortiz's immersion in the oral tradition."

Presented with his first collection of poems, *Going for the Rain,* Ortiz's editors found themselves in an unusual position. They favorably accepted the collection, but could not understand how a person of Native American culture could write with such a style of verse. Although Ortiz himself found it interesting that he could write in such a manner using the English language, a language that had usually only served to oppose Indian favor, his work confirms, verifies and affirms the essence of the land and people together, and their existence based on the concept of "wholeness."

In his collections and stories, Ortiz reminds his readers that "there must exist a reciprocal relationship for humanity to take care of itself as well as for the environment." His

storytelling relates traditions of his culture, and conjures visions familiar and foreign to the reader. His second collection of poems, *A Good Journey,* includes the remarkable Ortiz trait of awakening the reader's senses while leaving a message for his children to always be aware of their Native American traditions and the beauty of nature and the environment.

Ortiz demonstrates many examples of blending experience and oral tradition. In his *Stories* selections, he illustrates a deep, personal experience about his not speaking until he was fours years old. He then takes the realistic experience and blends it with an oral tradition story involving his grandfather. Having taken a key from his pocket, the grandfather was referring to speech and its importance to knowing the world; he then "turned the key, unlocking language." Later, Ortiz speaks. Ortiz emphasizes that language provides for the "discovery of one's capabilities and creative thought." Language has many uses, and one of those uses implemented by Ortiz is to convey a message with political overtones. In *A Good Journey,* Ortiz describes his camping trip at Montezuma Castle where he encounters resistance from the National Park Service. Wanting to collect firewood for his camp, he is told that he must first buy a permit. He considers this a ridiculous concept since his grandfathers "ran this place," and ignores the permit request. He cuts his firewood anyway, mumbling along the way, "Sue me."

In considering material for his works, Ortiz relies on the stories that he "likes and believes the most; it's as simple as that." These stories are those that let him know where he has been, or locate for him a place that is distinct, special, and true because everything about it is familiar. Questioned about his subject matter, Ortiz related, "The best stories told are those that provide for me, the listener-reader, a sense of grounding even when I've never been in the locale or setting where the storyteller or writer sets his story." Ortiz often refers to his mother's ability to lead him as a child into envisioning the words of the stories as she told him about days past of gathering and roasting pinion cones. As a child, his father told him stories about the desperation and cold the community had to endure; he knew the essence of those words because "it was the experience of his people and he is part of them." Ortiz further explained that these stories are believable "when we are intimately involved or linked to them because they are who we are, or when we become intimately and deeply involved and linked with them." As a poet, fiction and nonfiction writer, Ortiz captures life on paper. It is not a fancy, superficial life, but one in which words come alive in the heart and mind; they are words that tell the story of Ortiz himself and the world he knows most and loves. Ortiz is a writer of accomplishment who combines the often hurtful knowledge of reality with mythic wholeness.

In each of his travels, he incorporates his journey into his writings. In 1970 he went in search of "Indians." He concluded that Native Americans were not credited with any part of America's history, other than the bare mention of the Native American wars and savagery. He then asked himself if the Native American were a myth. Were there no more Indians? Had the movie industry absorbed Native Americans into savage portrayals? He soon understood that the vanished "Red Man" was vanished only from the public mind; it was intentional, for if Native Americans existed, then there would be claims to the land, water, and all things residing in western civilization. Ortiz traveled to the South where he found 45,000 Lumbee Native Americans living in the North Carolina region, and his writings have debunked the myth of the vanished Indian. Wiget summarizes Ortiz's work with the tribute that "it is not about a race that is vanishing, a way of life that is passing, or a language that is dying, but about a nation of those who have preserved their humor, their love for the land that is their mother, and their sense of themselves as a distinctive people. It is about journeying, about survival, about the many significances of being a veteran."

Ortiz continued writing for both book and television production into the 1990s. His books include 1992's *Woven Stones* and 1994's *After and Before the Lightning.* In reading and listening to Ortiz's work, the reader is left with the indelible printed image in Chaco Canyon and Pueblo ancestry that "from the moment in creation, life moved outward, and from that moment, human consciousness began to be aware of itself. And the 'hanoh,' the people, began to know and use the oral tradition that would depict the story of their journey on the 'hiyaanih,' the road, of life. The oral tradition of Acoma Pueblo, and of all the other Pueblos, is central to the consciousness of who they are, and it is basic to their culture. It is through oral tradition that the journey is told . . . in order that the people may be secure and fully aware within their cultural environment." The works of Simon Ortiz ensure that for generations to come there will be the opportunity to see past life existence as though it were living today.

Further Reading

Ortiz, Simon J., "What We See: A Perspective on Chaco Canyon and Pueblo Ancestry," in *Chaco Canyon: A Center and Its World,* Museum of New Mexico Press, 1994.
Twentieth Century Writers, second edition, edited by Geoff Sadler, St. James Press, 1991.
Wiget, Andrew, *Simon Ortiz,* Boise State University Printing and Graphic Services, 1986.
Ortiz, Simon J., interviews with JoAnn di Filippo during May and June, 1994. □

John Kingsley Orton

John Kingsley Orton (1933-1967) had a meteoric rise in British theater, with three hit plays produced in the 1960s.

John Kingsley (Joe) Orton was born in Leicester on January 1, 1933, the oldest of four children of a working-class family. His father was a low-paid gardener for the city; his mother worked in a hosiery factory until vision problems made it necessary for her to leave that job, after which she became a charwoman.

Although the family was not a close-knit one emotionally, the older son was his mother's favorite, and after Orton completed his required schooling she arranged to have him attend a commercial college, where he was a student from 1945 to 1947.

It was in 1949 that he developed the desire to act, or at least to be involved in the theater in some capacity. He joined the Leicester Dramatic Society and two other local drama groups, but was cast only infrequently and then usually in minor roles. The following year he took private elocution lessons, principally to purge himself of his Leicester accent, and applied to the Royal Academy of Dramatic Art (RADA), where he was accepted. In 1951 he moved to London.

In his first year at RADA Orton met Kenneth Halliwell, a fellow-student there. Halliwell was seven years older and was sophisticated and well-educated, especially in the Greek and Roman classics. They began a homosexual relationship which lasted for 16 years, and Halliwell's influence on the younger man was profound.

From an upper-middle-class family, Halliwell was no stranger to violent death. When he was 11 his mother was stung on the inside of her mouth by a wasp and, highly allergic to the toxin, choked to death. When he was 23 his father committed suicide, leaving him with a modest yearly income.

Orton acted successfully at RADA, but began to have misgivings about a career as an actor. Thus, when he finished his course there in 1953 he took a position for the spring and summer as the assistant stage manager of the Ipswich Repertory Company. He found this work not to his liking either and returned to London.

For most of the next decade he and Halliwell collaborated on a series of novels and literary experiments which were submitted to publishers but not accepted. They included The *Silver Bucket* (1953); The *Mechanical Womb* and *The Last Days of Sodom* (1955); *The Boy Hairdresser,* a satire in blank verse (1956); *Between Us Girls,* a diary novel (1957); and *The Vision of Gombold Proval,* written by Orton alone (1961).

While they were writing these books, they amused themselves in other ways. In 1958 Orton created the fictional Mrs. Edna Welthorpe, a writer of letters to the newspapers whom he used as an outraged critic of his work after he achieved fame; she was joined later by the imaginary Donald H. Hartley, an Orton booster. In the period from 1959 to 1961 he and Halliwell took books from the Islington public libraries, rewrote the blurbs on the inside of the dust jackets to make them either absurd or obscene, and simultaneously stole 1,653 plates from art books from which they constructed a floor-to-ceiling collage in their apartment. Both were arrested, charged with doing 450 English pounds in damage, convicted, and sent to prison for six months. Orton was unrepentant.

Orton achieved his first breakthrough in 1963. His play *The Ruffian on the Stair,* based on the novel *The Boy Hairdresser,* was accepted for television by the BBC, and his first full-length play, *Entertaining Mr. Sloane,* was sent to an agent; both were presented the following year.

The Ruffian on the Stair shows the strong influence of Harold Pinter, one of the few modern dramatists whom Orton admired (along with Oscar Wilde and George Bernard Shaw), and its opening lines, a conversation between the protagonist and his wife, set the tone for all of Orton's work to come:

Joyce: Have you got an appointment today?

Mike: Yes. I'm to be at King's Cross station at eleven. I'm meeting a man in the toilet.

Joyce: You always go to such interesting places.

As John Lahr summarized it in his introduction to the complete plays, "Orton's plays put sexuality back on the stage in all its exuberant, amoral and ruthless excess. He laughed away sexual categories."

This unique perspective was reinforced by *Entertaining Mr. Sloane,* which opened in London on May 6, 1964. It is the story of a handsome young man who has committed a murder and is taken into the home of Kath, the epitome of bourgeois hypocrisy, and her aged father, Kemp. Sex between Sloane and Kath begins at once. Soon there appears on the scene Kath's brother Ed, who also has designs on the young man. Kemp recognizes Sloane as the murderer and Sloane kills him. Kath and Ed agree to cover up the murder

of their father if Sloane consents to spend six months of every year with each of them.

Sloane demonstrates the validity of Maurice Charney's assessment, "All of his most vigorous characters are vulgar in the literary sense of the term: they pretend to a refinement, tact and gentility that they do not at all have." His characters and his play appealed to the British theater-going public. Writing in the *Sunday Telegraph,* Alan Brien observed, "Mr. Orton is one of those rare dramatists who create their own world and their own idiom," while prominent playwright Terence Rattigan wrote, "I fell wildly in love with *Entertaining Mr. Sloan. . . .* I saw style—a style, well, that could be compared with the Restoration comedies. I saw Congreve in it." At season's end, *Sloane* tied for the best new British play in *Variety*'s London Critics' Poll, but, taken to New York, it fared badly and closed after a short run, the *World Telegram and Sun* critic commenting that it "had the sprightly charm of a medieval cesspool."

In the early months of 1964 Orton wrote *The Good and Faithful Servant,* which was televised three years later. His most serious work, it owes something to the lives of his parents as it covers the last working days, the retirement, and the death of a loyal employee of a large corporation. Although it contains some humorous lines, it is essentially a picture of a life pathetically spent.

Later that year he completed his second major work, the full-length play *Loot.* The principal characters are Hal McLeavy and his lover Dennis, who have robbed a bank and are planning to escape to the Continent. Their project is complicated by the death of Hal's mother, whose body is in the house. Also present are the mother's former nurse, Fay, who wants to marry the widower McLeavy, making him her eighth husband in the past ten years, and the stupid, vicious, and venal policeman Truscott. In the end the two boys, Fay, and Truscott split the loot and the innocent elder McLeavy is arrested and taken off to prison.

Loot premiered on September 27, 1966, and was a hit. Ronald Bryden in *The Observer* wrote that it "establishes Orton's niche in English drama," and at season's end it won both the *Evening Standard* award and the *Plays and Players* award for the best play of the year.

In 1965 Orton wrote another television play, *The Erpingham Camp,* strongly influenced by *The Bacchae* of Euripides; it was produced the following year. Another television drama, *Funeral Games,* was written in 1966 and produced two years later.

Late in 1966 Orton began his third full-length play, *What the Butler Saw,* the first draft of which was completed in July of 1967; simultaneously he worked on a comedy, *Up Against It,* based on *The Silver Bucket,* for the Beatles, although eventually their managers rejected it.

But as Orton's celebrity increased, relations between him and Halliwell became more and more strained. As the playwright's exuberance grew, the older man was increasingly depressed and withdrawn and there were indications that Orton planned to leave him. On August 9, 1967, Halliwell bludgeoned Orton to death with a hammer and then committed suicide.

Chief among Orton's works posthumously presented was *What the Butler Saw,* produced in 1969. A farce with a small debt to the French dramatist Georges Feydeau, it takes place in the office of the psychiatrist Dr. Prentice, whose wife is a nymphomaniac, and introduces a girl who is applying for a position as the doctor's secretary and a young hotel page who has arrived to blackmail Mrs. Prentice. The young people are eventually discovered to be the Prentices' children; the question of double incest is raised and the play ends with the holding on high of the genitals of Winston Churchill, taken from a statue which has been blown up.

The play drew highly disparate reviews. Harold Hobson wrote, "Gradually Orton's terrible obsession with perversion, which is regarded as having brought his life to an end and choked his very high talent, poisons the atmosphere. And what should have become a piece of gaily irresponsible nonsense becomes impregnated with evil." On the other hand, Frank Marcus in the *Sunday Telegraph* observed that it "will live to be accepted as a comedy classic of English literature."

Other posthumous works included the sketch "Until She Screams," revised from T*he Patient Dowager* (1970); *Head to Toe,* based on *The Vision of Gombold Proval* (1971), and Up Against It (1979).

The importance of Orton's work seems established. C.W.E. Bigsby calls him "a pivotal figure, a crucial embodiment of the post-modernist impulse," while Charney (quoted earlier) concludes, "Orton no longer seems to be merely a footnote in the history of modern drama but merits at least a significant chapter."

Further Reading

The definitive biography of John (Joe) Orton is *Prick Up Your Ears* (1978) by John Lahr, who also edited *The Orton Diaries* (1986). Excellent analyses of the playwright and his work are *Joe Orton* (1984) by Maurice Charney and *Joe Orton* (1982) by C. W. E. Bigsby. □

George Orwell

The British novelist and essayist George Orwell (1903-1950) is best known for his satirical novels *Animal Farm* and *Nineteen Eighty-four*.

George Orwell was born Eric Arthur Blair at Motihari, Bengal, India. His father, Richard Walmesley Blair, was a minor customs official in the opium department of the Indian Civil Service. When Orwell was 4 years old, his family returned to England, where they settled at Henley, a village near London. His father soon returned to India. When Orwell was 8 years old, he was sent to a private preparatory school in Sussex. He later claimed that his experiences there determined his views on the English class system. From there he went by scholarship to two private secondary schools: Wellington for one term and Eton for 4 1/2 years.

Orwell then joined the Indian Imperial Police, receiving his training in Burma, where he served from 1922 to 1927. While home on leave in England, Orwell made the important decision not to return to Burma. His resignation from the Indian Imperial Police became effective on Jan. 1, 1928. He had wanted to become a writer since his adolescence, and he had come to believe that the Imperial Police was in this respect an unsuitable profession. Later evidence also suggests that he had come to understand the imperialism which he was serving and had rejected it.

Establishment as a Writer

In the first 6 months after his decision, Orwell went on what he thought of as an expedition to the East End of London to become acquainted with the poor people of England. As a base, he rented a room in Notting Hill. In the spring he rented a room in a working-class district of Paris. It seems clear that his main objective was to establish himself as a writer, and the choice of Paris was characteristic of the period. Orwell wrote two novels, both lost, during his stay in Paris, and he published a few articles in French and English. After stints as a kitchen porter and dishwasher and a bout with pneumonia, he returned to England toward the end of 1929.

Orwell used his parents' home in Suffolk as a base, still attempting to establish himself as a writer. He earned his living by teaching and by writing occasional articles, while he completed several versions of his first book, *Down and Out in London and Paris.* This novel recorded his experiences in the East End and in Paris, and as he was earning his

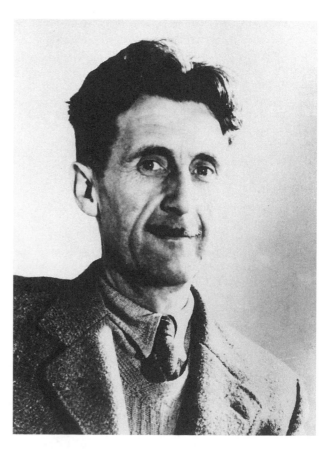

living as a teacher when it was scheduled for publication, he preferred to publish it under a pseudonym. From a list of four possible names submitted to his publisher, he chose "George Orwell." The Orwell is a Suffolk river.

First Novels

Orwell's *Down and Out* was issued in 1933. During the next 3 years he supported himself by teaching, reviewing, and clerking in a bookshop and began spending longer periods away from his parents' Suffolk home. In 1934 he published *Burmese Days*. The plot of this novel concerns personal intrigue among an isolated group of Europeans in an Eastern station. Two more novels followed: *A Clergyman's Daughter* (1935) and *Keep the Aspidistra Flying* (1936).

In the spring of 1936 Orwell moved to Wallington, Hertfordshire, and several months later married Eileen O'Shaughnessy, a teacher and journalist. His reputation up to this time, as writer and journalist, was based mainly on his accounts of poverty and hard times. His next book was a commission in this direction. The Left Book Club authorized him to write an inquiry into the life of the poor and unemployed. *The Road to Wigan Pier* (1937) was divided into two parts. The first was typical reporting, but the second part was an essay on class and socialism. It marked Orwell's birth as a political writer, an identity that lasted for the rest of his life.

Political Commitments and Essays

In July 1936 the Spanish Civil War broke out. By the end of that autumn, Orwell was readying himself to go to Spain to gather material for articles and perhaps to take part in the war. After his arrival in Barcelona, he joined the militia of the POUM (Partido Obrero de Unificacion Marxista) and served with them in action in January 1937. Transferring to the British Independent Labour party contingent serving with the POUM militia, Orwell was promoted first to corporal and then to lieutenant before being wounded in the middle of May. During his convalescence, the POUM was declared illegal, and he fled into France in June. His experiences in Spain had made him into a revolutionary socialist.

After his return to England, Orwell began writing *Homage to Catalonia* (1938), which completed his disengagement from the orthodox left. He then wished to return to India to write a book, but he became ill with tuberculosis. He entered a sanatorium where he remained until late in the summer of 1938. Orwell spent the following winter in Morocco, where he wrote *Coming Up for Air* (1939). After he returned to England, Orwell authored several of his best-known essays. These include the essays on Dickens and on boys' weeklies and "Inside the Whale."

After World War II began, Orwell believed that "now we are in this bloody war we have got to win it and I would like to lend a hand." The army, however, rejected him as physically unfit, but later he served for a period in the home guard and as a fire watcher. The Orwells moved to London in May 1940. In early 1941 he commenced writing "London Letters" for *Partisan Review,* and in August he joined the British Broadcasting Corporation (BBC) as a producer in the Indian section. He remained in this position until 1943.

First Masterpiece

The year 1943 was an important one in Orwell's life for several reasons. His mother died in March; he left the BBC to become literary editor of the *Tribune;* and he began book reviewing on a more regular basis. But the most important event occurred late that year, when he commenced the writing of *Animal Farm.* Orwell had completed this satire by February 1944, but several publishers rejected it on political grounds. It finally appeared in August 1945. This fantasy relates what happens to animals who free themselves and then are again enslaved through violence and fraud.

Toward the end of World War II, Orwell traveled to France, Germany, and Austria as a reporter. His wife died in March 1945. The next year he settled on Jura off the coast of Scotland, with his youngest sister as his housekeeper.

Crowning Achievement

By now, Orwell's health was steadily deteriorating. Renewed tuberculosis early in 1947 did not prevent the composition of the first draft of his masterpiece, *Nineteen Eighty-four.* The second draft was written in 1948 during several attacks of the disease. By the end of 1948 Orwell was seriously ill. *Nineteen Eighty-four* (1949) is an elaborate satire on modern politics, prophesying a world perpetually laid waste by warring dictators.

Orwell entered a London hospital in September 1949 and the next month married Sonia Brownell. He died in London on Jan. 21, 1950.

Orwell's singleness of purpose in pursuit of his material and the uncompromising honesty that defined him both as a man and as a writer made him critical of intellectuals whose political viewpoints struck him as dilettante. Thus, though a writer of the left, he wrote the most savage criticism of his generation against left-wing authors, and his strong stand against communism resulted from his experience of its methods gained as a fighter in the Spanish Civil War.

Further Reading

Collected Essays, Journalism and Letters of George Orwell, edited by Sonia Orwell and Ian Angus (1968), is an invaluable addition to Orwell studies. Probably the most significant work on Orwell is George Woodcock, *The Crystal Spirit: A Study of George Orwell* (1966). Other useful studies of Orwell as man and artist include Tom Hopkinson, *George Orwell* (1953); John Atkins, *George Orwell* (1954); Laurence Brander, *George Orwell* (1954); Christopher Hollis, *A Study of George Orwell* (1956); Richard J. Vorhees, *The Paradox of George Orwell* (1961); Richard Rees, *George Orwell: Fugitive from the Camp of Victory* (1962); Edward M. Thomas, *Orwell* (1965); Ruth Ann Lief, *Home to Oceania: The Prophetic Vision of George Orwell* (1969), particularly for students already familiar with Orwell's writing; and Raymond Williams, *George Orwell* (1971). □

John Osborne

The English playwright John Osborne (1929-1994) was the first of Britain's "Angry Young Men"—a group of social critics and writers. He scathingly attacked many of the establishment's hallowed values in his numerous plays of the 1960s.

John Osborne was born on Dec. 12, 1929, to an advertising writer and a Cockney barmaid. After his father died, when John was a young boy, he attended Belmont College in Devon, but he hated public school. Trying first journalism, then acting, Osborne joined Anthony Creighton's provincial touring company and collaborated with him on two plays.

Osborne's first important work, *The Devil inside Him,* written with Stella Linden, was performed in 1950. It is a melodrama about a Welsh youth who kills a girl after she falsely accuses him of fathering her child. *Personal Enemy* (1955), written with Creighton, concerns the effect upon family and friends of a military prisoner's decision to refuse repatriation from Korea.

A Revolution in Theater

Osborne's *Look Back in Anger* (1956) brought a revolution to English theater as its protagonist, Jimmy Porter, voiced the protests of a generation seething with dissatisfaction. The so-called "angry young men" felt there were no good causes left to die for. In his most famous play, Osborne castigated the hypocrisy of the lower middle class with his excoriating wit. In his obituary on Osborne, Richard Corliss of *Time* called the play "a seismic shock that seemed to signal the birth of a new urgency and the death of the reigning theatrical gentility" and a play that "forever changed the face of theater." *Look Back in Anger,* Corliss wrote, was "drama as rant, an explosion of bad manners, a declaration of war against an empire in twilight" and "a self-portrait of the artist as an angry young man."

That successful play was followed by *The Entertainer* (1957), the story of Archie Rice, a seedy, bitter, middle-aged music hall entertainer who suffers from his inability to communicate with his family or with his audiences. *Look Back in Anger* became a film in 1958, and *The Entertainer* was made into a movie in 1960, starring Laurence Olivier.

A Blooming Career

The central character in *Epitaph for George Dillon* (1958), written earlier with Creighton, is an unsuccessful writer-actor forced to confront his self-dramatizing illusions. *The World of Paul Slickey* (1959), also written earlier, introduces a hero-villain gossip columnist plagued by doubts and depressions in achieving success.

Luther (1961), a historical play, became a popular and critical success. The presentation of Luther was modeled on Bertolt Brecht's *Galileo.* The well-received *Inadmissible Evidence* (1964) portrays a philandering lawyer who fully reveals himself while undergoing a crisis of isolation. *A Patriot for Me* (1965) centers around the career of a homosexual Austrian army colonel as he is blackmailed by Russian intelligence agents into becoming a traitor.

A Bond Honoured (1966) is an adaptation of Lope de Vega's *La fianza satisfecha.* It features an amoral rebel who, after committing atrocities, defiantly refuses payment to Christ. Social and emotional interactions between gifted people of the entertainment world are the distinguishing features of *Time Present* and *The Hotel in Amsterdam* (1968).

Anger Turned Inward

Osborne's own outraged feelings and his provocative honesty charged his best plays with a strident, sometimes desperate note as he attacked the failure of the right and left, both literary and political, to improve the quality of life in modern Britain. His "acid tone, at once comic and desperate," according to Corliss of *Time,* remained sharp throughout his career, reflected in screenplays such as *Tom Jones* (1993). But *Inadmissible Evidence* was his last real hit, and he grew bitter as his audiences grew more scarce.

Osborne's anger was often directed at women, both on stage and in real life. At 21 he married actress Pamela Lane, the first of his five wives (the others were actress Jill Bennett and Mary Ure and writers Penelope Gilliatt and Helen Dawson). He nicknamed Bennett "Adolf," after Hitler, wrote that her voice on stage sounded "like a puppy with a mouthful of lavatory paper," and rejoiced when she committed suicide. He wrote that his only regret at her death was "that I was unable to look down upon her open coffin and, like that bird in the Book of Tobit, drop a good, large mess in her eye.''

Osborne's other favorite target was homosexuals. In *Time Present,* he called them ''uniformly bitchy, envious, self-seeking, fickle and usually without passion.'' A month after Osborne's death in 1994, his friend and fellow playwright Creighton made public a series of letters that documented that he and Osborne had conducted a long-running homosexual affair since the early 1950s.

In Osborne's later years, his misanthropic rage grew tiresome to critics. Reviewing his second volume of memoirs, *Almost a Gentleman* (1991), London's *Economist* magazine said it ''seems to have been written at just that stage of drunkenness when a boor, flailing around with his fists, is about to collapse in tears.'' In his last play, *Dejavu* (1992), a sequel to *Look Back in Anger,* Osborne described himself as ''a churling, grating note, a spokesman for no one but myself; with deadening effect, cruelly abusive, unable to be coherent about my despair.''

Further Reading

Several critical studies of Osborne's work are Ronald Hayman, ed., *John Osborne* (1968), and Simon Trussler, *The Plays of John Osborne: An Assessment* (1969). Osborne figures prominently in a number of works on British drama: George E. Wellwarth, *The Theater of Protest and Paradox: Developments in the Avant Garde Drama* (1964); John Russell Brown, ed., *Modern British Dramatists: A Collection of Critical Essays* (1968); and John Russell Taylor, *The Angry Theatre: New British Drama* (rev. ed. 1969). Frank Magill's *Critical Survey of Drama* (1994) has a profile of Osborne. □

Thomas Mott Osborne

Thomas Mott Osborne (1859-1926), American reformer, helped advance public understanding of prison problems and instituted a number of prison reforms.

Thomas Mott Osborne was born on Sept. 23, 1859, in Auburn, N.Y., the son of a wealthy manufacturer. He enjoyed a pampered and well-traveled youth and won honors at Harvard College. Osborne married happily and succeeded his father in business, maintaining the company until he sold it in 1903.

Osborne's one quirk—which ultimately affected his career—was his flair for masquerades. This publicly expressed itself at costume balls and privately in escapades which took him over the countryside dressed as a vagrant. Later, however, these disguises helped him to see at firsthand public conditions not readily available to one of his social status. He broke family traditions to become a Democrat and was active in upstate New York politics.

His wife's death during childbirth in 1896 turned Osborne intensively to civic affairs. He contributed to the work of the George Junior Republic, which aided needy and delinquent children. Osborne served on several state commissions and in 1913 was appointed chairman of the New York Commission on Prison Reform. He had himself incarcerated in Auburn Prison for a week, under the name of ''Tom Brown.'' In prison clothing, though not disguised, he shared the inmates' experiences, including solitary confinement, and emerged dedicated to prison reform. The experiment was front-page news. His book, *Within Prison Walls* (1914), memorialized the event.

Osborne's major thesis was that prisoners must be treated as human to be human. He instituted his Mutual Welfare League in 1916 at Auburn, based on the then novel principle of prisoners' self-rule—a concept which stirred up critics, who denounced it as a system for ''coddling'' prisoners (an idea which Osborne in fact opposed). In 1914 he was appointed warden of Sing Sing Prison, and he worked to advance his principles there. He achieved both personal and institutional success, although his aggressive deportment and writing style created jealousy and doubt.

Osborne's stormy administration culminated in 1915 with grand-jury charges of malfeasance in office and personal immorality. William J. Fallon, a defender of criminals, led the effort to ruin Osborne. Though he survived the painful and drawn-out assault, which indirectly had positive results—improved penal administration and public interest—he was embittered by the malice he had encountered, and he resigned.

Between 1917 and 1920 Osborne headed the Naval Prison at Portsmouth, N.H., where he instituted further re-

forms. He continued to be penology's most potent weapon, a figure of international fame and influence. He instituted the Welfare League Association (1916) and the National Society of Penal Information (1922), which after his death on Oct. 20, 1926, were merged as the Osborne Association.

Further Reading

Two biographies of Osborne are Frank Tannenbaum, *Osborne of Sing Sing* (1933), and Rudolph W. Chamberlain, *There Is No Truce: A Life of Thomas Mott Osborne* (1935), which better reveals Osborne's personality. □

Osceola

The Seminole Indian war chief Osceola (ca. 1800-1838) led his tribe's fight against being removed from their lands in Florida.

B orn about 1800 on the Tallapoosa River in the present state of Georgia, Osceola was a member of the Creek nation. His mother's second husband was William Powell, a Scottish trader, but Osceola, sometimes called Powell, was a full-blooded Creek.

In 1808 Osceola and his mother moved to Florida. They were associated with the Seminoles, and with them Osceola fought in the War of 1812 and in 1818 against American troops under Andrew Jackson. By 1832 Osceola was living near Ft. King in Florida. Apparently he was not hostile, for he was employed occasionally by the Indian agent to pacify restless tribesmen. Such activities gradually brought him to prominence among the Seminoles.

In 1832, however, the United States government was under pressure to move the Seminoles west of the Mississippi River. Some Seminole chiefs were persuaded to sign a treaty of removal. Osceola opposed this, as he did a similar agreement made in 1835. Most Seminole chiefs signified their disagreement by refusing to touch the pen; Osceola did so by plunging his knife into the paper. He was arrested for this defiance. To secure his release, he pretended that he would work for approval for the treaty. By now a Seminole war chief, once freed, he began gathering warriors for battle.

On Dec. 28, 1835, Osceola and his warriors brutally murdered the agent Wiley Thompson and Chief Charley Emathla, thereby precipitating the Second Seminole War. With Indian followers and fugitive slaves, Osceola overcame many enemies during the next 2 years.

The first of his major battles occurred when Osceola killed Maj. Francis L. Dade and 110 soldiers. Days later, with 200 followers, he fought against Gen. Duncan L. Clinch and 600 soldiers. Wounded, he was forced to retreat. On June 8, 1836, he was repelled at a fortified post, but on August 16 he almost overwhelmed Ft. Drane. Osceola's fight was so successful that it led to widespread public criticism of the U.S. Army, especially of Gen. Thomas S.

Jesup, who ordered Osceola's arrest while under a flag of truce on Oct. 21, 1837.

The captured Seminole chief was imprisoned at Ft. Marion, Fla., then removed to Ft. Moultrie, S.C. He died there on Jan. 30, 1838, of unknown causes.

Further Reading

A full-length biography of Osceola is James B. Ransom, *Osceola* (1838). Information on him is in Theodore Pratt, *Seminole: A Drama of the Florida Indian* (1953), and Alvin Josephy, Jr., *The Patriot Chiefs: A Chronicle of American Indian Leadership* (1961). A good general study of the Seminole problem is Edwin C. McReynolds, *The Seminoles* (1957). For an overview of the war which Osceola commanded see John K. Mahon, *History of the Second Seminole War* (1967). □

Herbert Levi Osgood

The American historian Herbert Levi Osgood (1855-1918) was a leading authority on colonial history in America, especially the origin and development of English-American political institutions.

H erbert Levi Osgood was born on April 9, 1855, in Canton, Maine. He studied at Amherst, and after he graduated he taught for 2 years at Worcester Academy in Massachusetts. He then went on to graduate school at Yale and in 1882-1883 studied in Berlin under Heinrich von Treitschke and consulted frequently with Leopold von Ranke. In general, Osgood adopted Ranke's view of history. Ranke's goal was to reconstruct historical events "as they actually were," avoiding subjective interpretations and moralistic judgments.

Osgood taught at Brooklyn High School from 1883 to 1889, also pursuing his doctorate at Columbia College's faculty of political science, where he received his degree in 1889. Shortly thereafter he decided to concentrate on the political history of the English colonies in America. This area of interest was not an abrupt change from his earlier work. In an article which antedates his doctorate, he urged American scholars to consider British colonial policy more sympathetically. The article, entitled "England and the Colonies" and published in the *Political Science Quarterly,* was of some significance in that it revealed him as one of the first scholars, if not indeed the first, to question the legal justification of the American Revolution, however inevitable it may have been otherwise.

In pursuit of this interest, Osgood spent 15 months in London studying public records. He then received an appointment to the faculty at Columbia, becoming a full professor in 1896. He taught the survey course on European history and the constitutional history of England. However, his primary interest remained the political development of the American colonies. Through his graduate seminar he was responsible for more than 50 dissertations on the early history of every one of the original 13 colonies and Canada and on certain phases of British imperial administration in

London. Both Osgood and his students concentrated for the most part on legal institutions in these works, since he contended that, although social and economic forces contribute to and condition historical development, "the historian must never lose sight of the fact that they operate within a framework of law." Osgood thus abandoned the customary geographical classification of the colonies, substituting instead a legal-political classification (royal, proprietary charters, and corporate charters) that is still commonly used in political science texts.

Osgood's major works were *The American Colonies in the Seventeenth Century* (3 vols., 1904-1907) and *The American Colonies in the Eighteenth Century* (4 vols., 1924). In 1908 he received the Lambat Prize for the best work on early American history published during the previous 5 years, an honor which he gained again, though posthumously, in 1926. Much of the ground covered in these volumes had never before been subjected to scientific historiography. As a whole, the works concern mainly developments between the British Cabinets and the colonial assemblies, which progressively represent the emerging consciousness of the embryo nation.

Osgood edited the eight-volume *Minutes of the Common Council of the City of New York, 1675-1776* (1905), which became a model for subsequent surveys in the area. He was also responsible for reforming the administration of the archives of New York State in 1907. He died on Sept. 11, 1918.

Further Reading

Dixon Ryan Fox, *Herbert Levi Osgood, an American Scholar* (1924), is a biography written by his son-in-law. There is a chapter on Osgood by E. C. O. Beatty in William T. Hutchinson, ed., *The Marcus W. Jernegan Essays in American Historiography* (1937). John Higham and others, *History* (1965), has a biographical sketch of Osgood. □

Sir William Osler

The Canadian physician Sir William Osler (1849-1919) was outstanding in the principles and practice of medicine, contributed writings of classical quality, and collected an impressive library on the history of medicine.

William Osler was born in Tecumseh, Ontario, on July 12, 1849. His father was a clergyman, so his upbringing was in a religious atmosphere. The influence of Thomas Huxley and Charles Darwin, however, turned him toward agnosticism in his days at Trinity College, Toronto. He studied to be a doctor, first at the Toronto School of Medicine and then at McGill University, where he graduated in 1872. Further studies were at University College, London, and at medical centers in Berlin and Vienna. After returning to Canada he accepted the chair of physiology and pathology at McGill, where he continued research in pathology, working on freshwater polyzoa and parasites; he studied hog cholera in 1878-1880.

Osler held the chair of clinical medicine at the University of Pennsylvania from 1884 to 1889, when he went to Baltimore as professor of the principles and practice of medicine and as physician-in-chief at the university hospital. There he joined William H. Welch, William Halsted, and Howard Kelly to form a brilliant medical team sometimes called the "Big Four" of Johns Hopkins. In 1905 Osler was appointed regius professor of medicine at Oxford University, England. However, he remained in constant demand at home and abroad for lectures. The classical flavor of his speech and writing, combined with its wit and insight, has hardly been equaled among medical scholars. He also collected an unusual medical history library of rare books. His library room was transported and restored at the McGill Medical School in Montreal to preserve intact his valuable collection.

Many distinctions and honors came Osler's way, including a baronetcy in 1911. His humanitarianism was exemplified by his criticism of war, which took the life of his only child, Revere, in 1917. Osler died at Oxford on Dec. 29, 1919.

Osler's books include *Principles and Practice of Medicine* (1892), an inimitable textbook for many years because of its thoroughness, style, bits of wisdom, and human touches. It went through numerous editions and was printed in 4 languages. Other significant works were *Science and Immortality* (1904) and *A Way of Life* (1914).

Further Reading

A biography of Osler that won the Pulitzer Prize for its physician-author in 1926 is Harvey Cushing, *The Life of Sir William Osler* (2 vols., 1925). Edith Gittings Reid, *The Great Physician: A Short Life of Sir William Osler* (1931), is largely for popular reading. Other biographies are Walter Reginald Bett, *Osler: The Man and the Legend* (1951); Viola Whitney Pratt, *Famous Doctors: Osler, Banting, Penfield* (1956); and Iris Noble, *The Doctor Who Dared, William Osler* (1959).

Additional Sources

Howard, R. Palmer, *The chief, Doctor William Osler,* Canton, MA, U.S.A.: Science History Publications, 1983.

Wagner, Frederick B., *The twilight years of Lady Osler: letters of a doctor's wife,* Canton, MA: Science History Publications, U.S.A., 1985. □

Osman I

Osman I (1259-1326) was the leader of a tribe of conquering warriors, who formed an independent state out of which arose the great Ottoman Empire.

Born in 1259, Osman I entered a world desperately in need of a leader. In Eastern Europe and the Middle East several great empires were declining. The Byzantine Empire—the eastern Roman Empire based around the capital city of Constantinople (Istanbul)—had endured for nine centuries but was beginning the long process of decline. During the Fourth Crusade of 1204, Constantinople fell for the first time to the Latin knights of the crusade. Impregnable, due to its strategic geographic position and defenses, the fall of the capital city symbolized the declining power of the Byzantine emperor. On the eastern flank of Byzantine lay the Seljuk Empire, consisting of eastern Asia Minor, Syria, Mesopotamia, Armenia, part of Persia, and western Turkestan. But this Empire too began to lose control of its possessions due to the invasions of mongol leader Genghis Khan. After the decisive battle of Kozadagh ended with victory for the Mongol invaders, the Seljuk sultans were reduced to vassals. The Mongol khan, interested only in securing annual payments from his vassal states, did not implement a system of control and government over the former Seljuk territories. With Byzantine control diminishing, Seljuk rule subjugated, and Mongol leadership missing, a power vacuum resulted in Asia Minor.

Situated on the border between the Byzantine and Seljuk empires was a frontier area inhabited by a collection of nomads and city dwellers of many races and religions. Driven up from the east due to political turmoil and the advancing Mongol hordes, many were of Turkoman descent. Caught between feuding and declining empires this area had all the characteristics of a frontier. Beyond the limits of central control, power rested in the hands of inde-

fief in the area of Sogut in northeast Anatolia (roughly, present-day Turkey) to act as a guard and defender of the Seljuk border against the Byzantine forces. In the spirit of a true Ghazi, Ertogrul performed this job for the remainder of his life; he did not acquire any territory beyond the land given him. When he died in 1288, he left his fief and tribal leadership to his son Osman.

Born in 1259 at Sogut, few personal details of Osman's life exist. Legend has it that as a young man, he fell in love with Malkhatun—which apparently means "Treasure of a Woman"—and asked to marry her. But her father, a renowned holy man, refused. Resigned to unhappiness after several more years of refusal, Osman had a dream; he saw himself and a friend sleeping. From his friend's chest arose a full moon (symbolizing Malkhatun) which moved over and sank into the chest of Osman. From this union sprang a great tree which grew, eventually encompassing the world. Supported by the four great mountains—Caucasus, Atlas, Taurus, and Haemus—the tree covered a world of bountiful harvests and gleaming, prosperous cities. Then a wind began to blow, pointing all the leaves of the tree towards Constantinople. As Edward Creasy describes the rest of the dream:

> That city, placed at the junction of two seas and two continents, seemed like a diamond set between two sapphires and two emeralds, to form the most precious stone in a ring of universal empire. Othman thought that he was in the act of placing that visioned ring on his finger, when he awoke.

This dream, so obviously a prophesy of a great and powerful empire that would result from a union of Osman and Malkhatun, caused Malkhatun's father to recant and agree to the marriage. Although this story of Osman's vision of empire is probably only a legend created through hindsight, Osman and his descendants did, indeed, create an empire.

By the time Osman assumed the leadership of his father's tribe in 1288, the stronger Ghazi leaders had begun, through conquest, to form larger principalities. Unlike his father, Osman too began a campaign of conquering the neighboring towns and countryside. In 1299, he symbolically created an independent state when he stopped the payment of tribute to the Mongol emperor. From 1300, there was a period of sustained conquest as he acquired the land west of the Sakarya River, south to Eskishehir and northwest to Mount Olympus and the Sea of Marmara. Osman and his men captured the key forts and cities of Eskishehir, Inonu, Bilejik, and eventually Yenishehir where he established a capital for the new Ottoman state. Still, they were not strong enough to capture the crucial and strongly fortified cities of Bursa, Nicaea, and Nicomedia.

On reaching the Sakarya River and the Sea of Marmara by 1308, Osman had effectively isolated the city of Bursa. An important Byzantine center at the foot of Mount Olympus, Bursa was well fortified, surrounded by a high wall and several small forts and outworks. With all the land around it occupied by Osman, Bursa was still able to receive supplies and communication through the port of

pendent Ghazi leaders who ruled over small tribes and parcels of land. These Ghazis were Turkish warriors fighting for the faith of Islam against the infidel, the Christian settlers in Byzantine areas. On horses, the Ghazis raided and looted Christian villages, securing the goods on which their wealth was based.

One of these leaders was Ertogrul, the father of Osman. There are conflicting stories as to the origin of the Ottomans and their arrival in the frontier area of Anatolia. The most common story is that Ertogrul's father Suleyman Sah, the leader of a tribe of Turkomans, led his people out of northeastern Iran in the late 12th century, just ahead of a Mongol invasion. Fearing death or enslavement, they headed west where Suleyman is said to have drowned crossing the Euphrates. Assuming the leadership, Ertogrul led part of the tribe into Anatolia where they settled. Older versions of the story are more detailed but unsubstantiated.

Historian Edward S. Creasy relates that Ertogrul and his small band, while journeying westward into Asia Minor, came upon two armies engaged in battle. Seeing that one army was much larger than the other, Ertogrul and his followers entered the fray on the side of the smaller force without knowing for whom they fought. Their addition made the difference and the smaller force was victorious. Once the battle was over, Ertogrul learned that the leader of the small force was Alaeddin, the Seljuk sultan, and the army defeated were Mongol invaders. In gratitude, Alaeddin bestowed on Ertogrul a principality on the frontier, bordering the Byzantine state. Regardless of the truth of this part of the story, there is no doubt that Ertogrul was given his

Mudanya. Since Osman's troops could not take the city by force, Osman put Bursa under siege to force a surrender. Then in 1321, Osman took the port of Mudanya, thereby effectively isolating Bursa's inhabitants from the outside world. Incredibly, the siege went on for five more years, the city's stubborn inhabitants refusing to surrender. Inevitably though, the city fell, surrendering to Osman's troops on April 6, 1326.

The surrender of Bursa marked a turning point in the development of Osman's new state. Although Osman had been rapidly acquiring land since 1288, the acquisitions were mainly rural with nomadic peoples. Bursa was a major commercial center which opened up the new state to the rest of the world. From that point on, the Ottoman state was an important player in the events and decisions affecting the Middle East and Eastern Europe.

The year 1326 also marked a turning point with the death of Osman. Due to age and increasing illness, he had placed his eldest son Orhan at the head of his troops. On his deathbed at Sogut, Osman lived long enough to hear from his son of the surrender of Bursa. According to legend, Osman then gave Orhan his final advice:

> My son, I am dying; and I die without regret, because I leave such a successor as thou art. Be just; love goodness, and show mercy. Give equal protection to all thy subjects, and extend the law of the Prophet. Such are the duties of princes upon earth; and it is thus that they bring on them the blessings of Heaven.

In recognition of the importance of the victory, Osman then directed Orhan to bury him at Bursa and to make it the capital city of the new Empire. Shortly after, Osman died at the age of 67. As requested, he was buried at Bursa in a beautiful mausoleum which was to stand as a monument to him for several centuries after.

Unlike his father before him, Osman bequeathed to his son an independent state. It is uncertain whether the minting of coins and the pronouncement of prayers to the house of Osman, the signs of independence, began in the last years of Osman's rule or in the beginning of Orhan's. Still, by the time of his death, Osman had created a state independent of either Byzantine or Mongol control. Recognizing the weakness of the Byzantine Empire, Osman had directed his efforts to acquiring territory at the Byzantine's expense. Crucial to his success was his ability to attract other Ghazi warriors to fight under him. Motivated to fight against the infidel, these Turkish nomads were attracted to Osman's conquest of the Christian towns and cities. Most authors speak of the loyalty and devotion that Osman was able to command from his men.

As a ruler of the people in his dominions, as well as of his troops, Osman had received loyalty and respect. He was reputed to be just in his decisions and in his treatment of all people. All citizens, regardless of ethnicity or religion, were treated equally with respect to property and person. Yet, Osman could also be ruthless in demanding obedience from his followers. One story, whose validity cannot be assured, relates the situation surrounding Osman's decision to attack an important Greek fortress. Osman's uncle, Dundar, who reportedly had been one of the original settlers in Sogut after crossing the Euphrates, opposed the attack as too risky. Perceiving his uncle's actions as a threat to his authority as well as to his rule, Osman said nothing but, raising his bow, shot and killed his uncle instantly. Like his successors, Osman expected obedience and respect from his subjects and soldiers.

Following in his father's footsteps, Orhan continued to expand the new state into Byzantine territory, capturing the cities of Nicaea in 1331 and Nicomedia in 1337. By 1345, the Ottoman state had grown significantly, encompassing all of northwestern Asia Minor from the Aegean to the Black Sea. This expansion was to continue until the late 17th century. From modest beginnings, Osman created the basis for one of the largest and longest-lived empires ever. By 1683, the Ottoman Empire encompassed the Balkans, Greece, Hungary, and Italy in the west, the north shore of the Black Sea, the entire Middle East, Egypt and parts of Arabia along the shores of the Red Sea, as well as all of North Africa, and parts of Morocco and Spain. Although expansion ended after 1683 and decline began, the Ottoman Empire continued to exist until the first World War. Enduring for over 600 years, Osman's state had an enormous effect on the course of historical events in Europe, Asia, the Middle East, and Africa. It is as the founder of this great Empire that Osman acquires his fame.

Further Reading

Creasy, Edward S. *History of the Ottoman Turks: From the Beginnings of their Empire to the Present Time.* Bentley, 1878, repr. Khayats, 1961.

Fisher, Sydney Nettleton. *The Middle East: A History.* 3rd ed. Knopf, 1979.

Shaw, Stanford J. *History of the Ottoman Empire and Modern Turkey,* Vol. 1, *Empire of the Gazis: The Rise and Decline of the Ottoman Empire, 1280-1808.* Cambridge University Press, 1976.

Inalcik, Halil. *The Ottoman Empire: The Classical Age, 1300-1600.* Translated by Norman Itzkowitz and Colin Imber. Praeger, 1973.

Wittek, Paul. *The Rise of the Ottoman Empire.* Royal Asiatic Society, 1938. □

Sergio Osmeña

Sergio Osmeña (1878-1961) was the second president of the Philippine Commonwealth and a distinguished statesman. He led the country in its initial stage of political maturation by his honest and selfless devotion to public service.

Sergio Osmeña was born in Cebu on the island of Cebu on Sept. 9, 1878. He entered the San Carlos Seminary in Cebu in 1889 and then earned his bachelor's degree from San Juan de Letran College. His schooling was interrupted by the 1896 revolution and the Filipino-American War. During the revolution he edited the militantly nationalistic periodical *El Nuevo Dia*. After the revolutionary struggles he continued his studies until he passed the bar examination on Feb. 20, 1903.

On March 5, 1906, Osmeña was elected provincial governor of Cebu at the age of 28. Although he had little political experience, he succeeded in solving the grave problems of public order and community cooperation in his province, cultivating the people's trust in the municipal enforcement officers.

Early Efforts for Independence

In 1902 Osmeña had joined those nationalists who petitioned Governor William Howard Taft to allow the formation of a political party advocating immediate independence for the Philippines. In 1906 Osmeña became president of the first convention of provincial governors, which urged eventual independence. In 1907 he was unanimously elected speaker of the Assembly, a post he held for 9 years. Together with Manuel Quezon, the leader of the majority in the Assembly, and other nationalist leaders, Osmeña formed the Nacionalista party.

In 1918 Osmeña was appointed vice-chairman of the Council of State by Governor Francis B. Harrison. When the Jones Law of 1916 created an elective senate composed of Filipinos, it gave rise to the leadership of Quezon who, in the elections of 1922, replaced Osmeña as the party leader in government. The disagreement between Osmeña and Quezon came from Quezon's description of Osmeña's leadership as "unipersonal" in contrast to Quezon's alleged style of "collective" leadership. However, in April 1924

Quezon and Osmeña fused their factions into the Partido Nacionalista Consolidado in an effort to present a united resistance against the heavy-handed bureaucratic procedures of Governor Leonard Wood.

In 1931 Osmeña, together with Manuel Roxas, headed the Ninth Independence Mission to the United States, which culminated in the passage by the U.S. Congress of the Hare-Hawes-Cutting Act on Jan. 17, 1933, overriding President Herbert Hoover's veto. Quezon led the opposition antis against the Osmeña-Roxas pros for rejection of the bill on Oct. 17, 1933. In 1934 Quezon succeeded in obtaining a modified version of the Hare-Hawes-Cutting Act: the Tydings-McDuffie Act, which provided for complete independence 10 years after the inauguration of the commonwealth.

Inauguration of the Commonwealth

In 1935 Osmeña ran for vice president and won. The commonwealth government was inaugurated on Nov. 15, 1935. Osmeña teamed up with Quezon in a single-party ticket of the Nacionalista party. Osmeña served also as secretary of public instruction and as a member of Quezon's Cabinet. So humble and self-sacrificing was Osmeña that when Quezon's term ended on Nov. 15, 1943, he readily gave up his constitutional right to succeed in office so that the ailing Quezon could indulge his ego in continuing as president of the commonwealth government-in-exile. The operation of the Philippine constitution was temporarily suspended with Osmeña's consent.

On Oct. 25, 1944, after the victorious landing in Leyte, Gen. Douglas MacArthur handed the reins of civil government to Osmeña, who had become president after Quezon's death on Aug. 1, 1944. With his resourceful mind, steadfast purpose, and mature courage in the face of the chaotic conditions of the postwar reconstruction period, Osmeña rallied the Filipinos to unite and fight the remaining Japanese resistance. His first step was to incorporate the guerrilla troops into the reorganized Filipino branch of the U.S. Army. On Feb. 27, 1945, the Commonwealth government was fully reestablished in Manila.

Postwar Years

Immediately thereafter, Osmeña tried to reinstitute the American pattern of education and to get rid of all the residues of Japanese indoctrination. He proposed the creation of the People's Court to investigate all Filipinos suspected of disloyalty or treason. He ordered the post office system reopened and issued a victory currency to stabilize the economy.

Osmeña hoped that Philippine independence would be granted on Aug. 13, 1945, but the U.S. Congress and President Franklin Roosevelt had already fixed the date of independence as July 4, 1946.

Osmeña's perseverance and quiet style of working did not appeal to Gen. MacArthur or to Commissioner Paul V. McNutt, both of whom supported Roxas in his bid for the presidency in the election of April 23, 1945. Roxas won over the weary and self-effacing Osmeña, who refused to campaign for reelection.

Osmeña's situation during the early days of the liberation demanded aggressive tactics and bold policies in order to solve the complicated questions of collaboration, of the domination of the government by feudal landlords, and of the moral rehabilitation of citizens who had been driven to cynicism and pragmatic individualism by the contingencies of war. Osmeña, in spite of his tenacity and astute skill in compromise, yielded to the parasitic oligarchy and acquiesced to the restoration of the prewar semifeudal system, the inherent problems of which could never be solved by parliamentary tact or resiliency. Osmeña retired from public office after his defeat and died on Oct. 19, 1961.

Further Reading

The best sources of facts about Osmeña's career are Joseph Ralston Hayden, *The Philippines: A Study in National Development* (1942), and Theodore Friend, *Between Two Empires: The Ordeal of the Philippines, 1929-1946* (1965). See also Hernando J. Abaya, *Betrayal in the Philippines* (1946), and David Joel Steinberg, *Philippine Collaboration in World War II* (1967), for Osmeña's role in settling the collaboration problem. □

Elisha Graves Otis

The American manufacturer and inventor Elisha Graves Otis (1811-1861) was one of the inventors of the modern elevator and founded a company for their manufacture.

Elisha Otis was born near Halifax, Vt., where his father was for many years a justice of the peace and a state legislator. He received a common education in his hometown and at the age of 19 moved to Troy, N.Y., where he went into the construction trade. Poor health caused him to turn to hauling goods between Troy and Brattleboro, Vt. In a pattern that he was to repeat several times in his life, he saved enough money to start his own operation, in this case a small gristmill.

About 1845 Otis was again forced by ill health to change jobs. He moved to Albany, N.Y., where he became a master mechanic in a bedstead factory. Eventually he opened a small machine shop in that city. Again he was forced to give it up and became a master mechanic in a factory in Bergen, N.J. His son, Charles, then just 15 years old, was so proficient at machine work that he was made an engineer with the same firm.

In 1852 the firm sent Otis to Yonkers, N.Y., to supervise the installation of machinery in a new factory, and there he made some improvements in the elevator with which he was working. He showed the improvements in New York and applied for a patent on the device. The elevator consisted of a platform which was raised by a rope between two vertical posts. On the inside of each post was a rack designed to catch two pawls set in the platform frame when the lifting stopped. In 1854 it was reported that "the pawls are prevented from bearing against the racks during the upwards movement of the frame, and much friction is obviated thereby, and if the rope should break, or be loosened from the driving shaft, or disconnected from the motive power accidentally, the platform will be sustained, and no injury or accident can possibly occur, as the weight is prevented from falling."

Scientific American called the device "excellent" and said that it was "much admired" in New York. Receiving several orders for elevators, Otis again set up his own shop and with the aid of his son began their manufacture. He continued to invent and patent other devices, but his elevator business grew only slowly and was still rather small when he died, a comparatively young man. His son carried on the firm. With the growth of cities and the introduction of the apartment house and the skyscraper in the years after the Civil War, Otis elevators came to lead the field.

Further Reading

There is no adequate biography of Otis. The importance of his work for the growth of American cities is examined in Carl W. Condit, *American Building Art: The Nineteenth Century* (1960). See also Leroy A. Peterson, *Elisah Graves Otis, 1811-1861, and His Influence upon Vertical Transportation* (1945). □

Harrison Gray Otis

Harrison Gray Otis (1765-1848), American states-man, was one of the most important leaders of the Federalist party after 1801. He epitomized both the urbanity and narrowness of the New England Federalist elite.

Harrison Gray Otis was born on Oct. 8, 1765, into a distinguished colonial family. He moved toward political responsibility and power by means of the usual channels for that time and place; he graduated from Harvard in 1783, studied law, and entered the bar prior to the ratification of the Constitution. By the mid-1790s he had assumed his place in the Massachusetts political hierarchy.

The year 1796 saw Otis move swiftly through the political turbulence to prominence. In the spring he established a nationwide reputation as an orator with a speech in defense of Jay's Treaty. During the next 9 months he successively won election to the Massachusetts Legislature, was appointed by President George Washington as U.S. attorney for Massachusetts, stood for election to Congress, and, after winning this seat, resigned his Federal post.

Otis served two terms in the House of Representatives, emerging as a staunch supporter of President John Adams, a fellow Massachusetts man. This loyalty earned him re-appointment to the attorney post in 1801, but President Thomas Jefferson removed him a year later. For many years

thereafter Otis held only minor local offices; he took increasingly greater responsibility for restructuring the out-of-power Federalist party.

Otis believed that for the good of the nation the Federalist party must survive. Thus he was one of a handful of leaders who concluded that it would never do to sacrifice the Federalist party in order to save Federalist theory. He emerged in maturity as a pragmatic political leader and was a party manager who "placed a high premium on loyalty, discipline, and close cooperation."

That potent Massachusetts political oligarchy, the Essex Junto, had long since admitted Otis to membership, and he used this connection to retain a prominent spot within the national structure of the Federalist party prior to the War of 1812. His realization that extreme reaction to the war would hurt the Federalist interest led him to oppose the excesses of the Hartford Convention of 1814, of which he was a member. But his was a lonely voice for moderation.

Otis ended his political career by serving in the U.S. Senate (1817-1822) and as mayor of Boston (1829-1832). Thereafter, disillusioned by the turn American political life had taken, he foreswore public service, although he lived on until Oct. 28, 1848.

Further Reading

Samuel Eliot Morison, *The Life and Letters of Harrison Gray Otis, Federalist, 1765-1848* (2 vols., 1913), was superseded by his excellent one-volume edition, *Harrison Gray Otis, 1765-1848: The Urbane Federalist* (1969). One should also consult David H. Fischer, *The Revolution of American Conservatism: The Federalist Party in the Era of Jeffersonian Democracy* (1965). □

James Otis Jr.

His brilliant defense of American colonial rights at the outset of the struggle between England and its colonies marked James Otis, Jr. (1725-1783), a leading spokesman for the Boston patriots prior to the American Revolution.

At a time when oratory was a powerful political weapon, James Otis's reputation as a defender of colonial rights in the quarrel with Great Britain was unmatched during the decade 1760-1770. While Samuel Adams wrote inflammatory articles at the popular level, Otis appealed to the law and to the logic of Englishmen everywhere. His case rested on the law of nature and the goodness of the British constitution, both terms sufficiently ambiguous for him to convince vast audiences that his arguments were unanswerable. As a leader of the antiadministration party, he worked with the radicals after the Sugar Act and Stamp Act convinced him that the British Empire could not be maintained without some moderation of the old system of parliamentary domination.

James Otis, Jr., was born on Feb. 5, 1725, in West Barnstable, Mass., the eldest of 13 children. His father was a lawyer, judge, and member of the colonial council, and his oldest sister became a talented political writer and observer. Otis graduated from Harvard College in 1743. His legal studies under the distinguished Jeremiah Gridley (1745-1747) and his admission to the bar were the usual approach to power in colonial Massachusetts.

Otis began law practice at Plymouth, Mass., and later moved to Boston. In 1755 he married Ruth Cunningham. The marriage produced three children but cannot be described as a happy union-particularly because of political differences within the family.

The British decision to increase imperial revenues by enforcing old but neglected customs regulations in the Colonies seemed, at first, simply another kind of family quarrel. The Molasses Act of 1733 had not been enforced; indeed, many New England merchants made a comfortable living while evading it. But when the merchants were unable to block the tightening of customs regulations, they turned their wrath upon the general search warrants issued in pursuit of smuggled cargoes. These writs of assistance were issued by the provincial courts, but the merchants insisted that the courts had no such authority.

Independence Is Born

Otis had been appointed a Crown official as advocate general, but he thought that the writs were indefensible and resigned his office to represent the protesting merchants.

The dramatic trial in which Otis confronted his mentor, Gridley (who was the Crown's attorney), was later described by witness John Adams as "the first scene of the first act of opposition to the arbitrary claims of Great Britain. Then and there the child Independence was born." Otis spoke for 5 hours, holding that writs were contrary to both English practice and natural law. Chief Justice Thomas Hutchinson, however, decided against the merchants.

Aided by Oxenbridge Thacher, Samuel Adams, and others of the growing radical element in Boston, Otis helped organize the Boston freeholders to oppose Crown measures. In the general court, he thwarted the plans of Governor Francis Bernard to raise taxes and repeatedly drew all but blood in verbal bouts with Crown officials. Though Otis sidestepped their angry threats with verbal missiles, violence was not far away.

Petty politics and personal squabbles were overshadowed by the new imperial crisis brought on by passage of the Sugar Act in 1764. In a desperate search for revenues, Parliament had reduced the duty on molasses but had made it clear that the new tax would be collected. Otis, Adams, and their radical friends perceived Britain's miscalculation. While Adams began agitation in the popular press, Otis wrote a stirring defense of colonial rights in "The Rights of the British Colonies Asserted and Proved," arguing that even Parliament could not violate the law of nature. His appeal to "a higher authority" shifted the colonial argument to unassailable ground, as Otis saw it, and thousands of colonial Americans agreed. He also urged that America be granted parliamentary representation, without which the colonists were being "taxed without their consent."

A Popular Hero

The pamphlet made Otis a popular hero in America. At this stage, he was inconsistent but still brilliant. He shocked friends by advocating that his archenemy Thomas Hutchinson be sent to England to present the colony's side in the Sugar Act quarrel. However, the appointment of Otis's father as chief justice of the Common Pleas Court set tongues wagging. For a time, Otis's ambivalence cost him some popularity.

When the Stamp Act was announced, in March 1765, colonial tempers soared. The Sugar Act had hurt New England, but the Stamp Act struck at the pocket of every newspaper reader, lawyer, litigant, and businessman—in short—at nearly every adult in all 13 colonies. Otis served on a committee that urged a united colonial front of resistance, and he headed the Massachusetts delegation to the resulting Stamp Act Congress. Here he impressed fellow delegates as a forceful speaker and able committee member.

Otis again turned pamphleteer, and his "A Vindication of the British Colonies" and "Considerations on Behalf of the Colonies" were read by patriots and quoted as unanswerable. In these works he ridiculed the English notion of "virtual representation" in Parliament and attacked the philosophy of the Navigation Acts, which stifled American manufactures. Otis professed a sincere attachment to the empire, however, and insisted that a true rupture with England would lead only to anarchy.

Repeal of the Stamp Act brought a temporary respite to these tensions, but Otis continued to be at odds with the Crown's officials in Boston. When Otis was elected Speaker of the legislature in May 1767, Governor Bernard vetoed the election. Privately, Bernard and Hutchinson blamed most of their problems on the Otis-Adams coterie. The Otis-Adams "Circular Letter" of 1768, urging a general congress for coordinated economic boycotts, further increased friction between governor and legislature. When Bernard demanded that the letter be recalled, Otis informed him that the House stood by its first action by a vote of 92 to 17. Clearly, Otis and Adams were not isolated troublemakers.

The seizure of John Hancock's vessel, the *Liberty,* in 1768 increased tension in Boston and led to a direct clash between Crown officials and a mob. Otis was moderator of the town meeting called to consider effectual ways of preventing another such incident, and he counseled prudent measures. With his influence on the wane, Governor Bernard, trying to have the last word before his recall in 1769, blamed Otis and Adams, "Chiefs of the Faction," for much of the damage done to imperial harmony.

End of a Career

A tragic incident in September 1769 ended Otis's career as a leader of the Boston patriots. He satirized the local commissioners of customs in the *Boston Gazette,* and one of them, John Robinson, confronted Otis the following day. Tempers flared, and Otis was struck in the head. He sued and was awarded £2,000 in damages, but when Robinson offered a public apology, Otis declared that he was satisfied.

Perhaps the blow had only hastened a mental deterioration already begun. Whatever its cause, Otis was thereafter bothered by severe mental lapses, although he was reelected to the General Court. In 1781 an old friend took Otis to Andover, where his mind only occasionally returned to its former brilliance. He was killed by a bolt of lightning on May 23, 1783.

Further Reading

A standard work on Otis remains William Tudor, *Life of James Otis* (1823). Personal comments in the forthcoming *Papers of John Adams,* edited by Lyman Butterfield, should be enlightening. See also Charles F. Mullett, *Fundamental Law and the American Revolution* (1933), and Edmund S. and Helen M. Morgan, *The Stamp Act Crisis* (1953; rev. ed. 1963).

Additional Sources

Galvin, John R., *Three men of Boston,* New York: Crowell, 1976.
□

Philip William Otterbein

Philip William Otterbein (1726-1813), an American clergyman, was one of the founders of the Church of the United Brethren.

William Otterbein was born June 3, 1726, a son of a teacher and minister in Dillenburg, Germany. The elder Otterbein died when William was 16. His mother moved the family to Herborn. In 1748 William graduated from the Reformed Church's school there. He was deeply influenced by the piety at home and the theology taught at Herborn. After his ordination on June 13, 1749, he began zealously and bluntly preaching the necessity of piety and a moral life.

The number of ministers and teachers among the Germans in colonial America was inadequate, so the Dutch Reformed Church attempted to supply the need. Otterbein went to Lancaster, Pa., in 1752 under the auspices of that Church and stayed for 6 years. He decided to take another position but agreed to stay if the members of the congregation accepted the stipulation that he could exercise his pastoral duties according to his conscience and that members of the church would conform more strictly to high moral and spiritual standards and be amenable to church discipline.

Otterbein went next to Tulehocken, Pa. There he introduced regular home visitations and prayer meetings. In 1760 he went to Frederick, Md., and 5 years later to York, Pa. In 1766 Otterbein heard the Mennonite leader Martin Boehm preach to a great meeting, attended by people of many faiths. Although relationships between members of the Reformed Church and the Mennonites were far from cordial, after Boehm's sermon Otterbein embraced him and exclaimed, "We are brethren!"

Otterbein believed in the necessity of education. He advocated the establishment of parochial schools and supported education for the members of the clergy. He was pietistic, evangelistic, ecumenical, and non-predestinarian. He was not narrowly sectarian or denominational. In January 1785 his congregation, calling itself the Evangelical Reformed Church, adopted regulations which emphasized lay activity, family prayers, the necessity of a personal religious experience, and open communion. In 1789 Otterbein assembled a group of ministers, including Boehm, at Baltimore, where they adopted a confession of faith and articles of discipline which he had prepared. The delegates to another conference in 1800 adopted the name Church of the United Brethren in Christ. Otterbein and Boehm were elected superintendents (or bishops), positions they held until death. Otterbein died on Nov. 17, 1813.

Further Reading

Augustus W. Drury, *The Life of Rev. Philip William Otterbein* (1884), is a detailed biography. Arthur C. Core, *Philip William Otterbein, Pastor, Ecumenist* (1968), consists of essays by various authors and a selection of Otterbein's letters. □

Otto I

The Holy Roman emperor Otto I (912-973), called Otto the Great, was the most powerful western European ruler after Charlemagne. He organized a strong German state and expanded his authority over Burgundy and Italy.

Otto I was the son of King Henry I (the Fowler) of Germany. In 929 he married Edith, daughter of Edward the Elder of England; she died in 946. Otto was Duke of Saxony when his father died in 936, and he was at once elected king (which rule he held until 962) at Aix-la-Chapelle by the great magnates. The rulers of the other great duchies caused Otto initial problems. By 947 he had solved them by absorbing the duchy of Franconia into his direct rule and by handing over the others, Lorraine, Swabia, and Bavaria, to members of his family.

By 951 Otto had been drawn into Italy by the fear that its widowed Queen Adelaide, who was having trouble, would be rescued, and her lands absorbed, by the nearby king of Burgundy or his own dukes of Swabia or Bavaria. To forestall these moves, Otto crossed into Italy and married her himself—thus establishing his claims to her lands. Before he could consolidate his position there, however, he was drawn back to Germany by a revolt of his leading dukes, led by his son and heir, and by a serious incursion of the nearby Hungarians. He put down the revolt and crushed the Hungarians at the decisive battle of Lechfeld in 955.

Once these tasks were accomplished, Otto gave the duchy of Lorraine, whose duke had perished at Lechfeld, to his clerical brother Archbishop Bruno of Cologne. At about this time he also began relying increasingly upon churchmen to help him to govern his realm and to furnish him with armed forces. He did so by endowing churchmen, whom he appointed to office, with wide lands and immunities in return for governmental and military services. Since Church offices were not hereditary, this made them a most useful and dependable counterweight to the secular nobles, who often were unreliable and had heirs as well.

While Otto was busy in Germany, however, he did not ignore his neighbors. He intervened in the struggle between the French Capetians and Carolingians and thus assured himself of their acceptance of his absorption of Lorraine into the empire. He kept control over Hedeby in Denmark and over the archbishoprics of that kingdom. He encouraged churchmen and his Saxon subordinates Gero and Herman Billung to begin the conquest of the Slavs beyond the Elbe River, and he forced the Duke of Bohemia to do him homage.

It was as master of much of northern Europe that Otto invaded Italy in 961. A year later, after conquering Rome, Otto was crowned Western emperor by Pope John XII. He and the Pope later quarreled, and Otto with some difficulty replaced him with another candidate, whom he forced upon the clergy and nobles of Rome. Otto's last years were largely spent in Italy, where he tried unsuccessfully to absorb Venice and southern Italy, which were controlled by Byzantium. Before his death, however, Otto was able to secure Byzantine recognition of his imperial title and a Byzantine princess as a bride for his son Otto II.

Finally, Otto deserves credit for supporting learning and culture. His support of learning resulted in the so-called Ottonian Renaissance, which helped to keep learning alive for the future. The churchmen he appointed often proved interested in building and in supporting culture in their church establishments, both monastic and episcopal. Thanks to them, culture continued to flourish there and at the court, making the Age of the Ottos an important intellectual and architectural one for medieval Europe.

Further Reading

Fine accounts of Otto I are in R.H.C. Davis, *A History of Medieval Europe, from Constantine to Saint Louis* (1957); Christopher Brooke, *Europe in the Central Middle Ages, 962-1154* (1964); and Eleanor Duckett, *Death and Life in the Tenth Century* (1967). For Otto's northern European and Eastern policies see Archibald R. Lewis, *The Northern Seas* (1958), and Romilly Jenkins, *Byzantium: The Imperial Centuries, A.D. 610-1071* (1966). □

Otto III

The medieval ruler Otto III (980-1002) was Holy Roman emperor from 996 to 1002 and German king from 983 to 1002. Well educated, brilliant, and filled with hopes of reviving some type of Roman Empire in the West, he died while still a young man.

Otto III (seated on throne)

Otto III was the only son of Emperor Otto II and the Byzantine princess Theophano. He was 3 years of age when his father died, making him German king. Most of Otto's younger years were spent in Germany, where, after a period of difficulty with Duke Henry the Wrangler of Bavaria, his mother served capably as regent. After her death in 991, Otto's grandmother, the dowager empress Adelaide, became regent until, in 994, Otto himself came of age at 14.

During Otto III's minority the empresses Theophano and Adelaide had been relatively successful in keeping peace within Germany itself and in preventing the French kings from annexing Lorraine, which they coveted; but they had been less successful with the Danes, the Slavs beyond the Elbe River, and the Hungarians. The Slavs raided northern Germany constantly; the Danish king had gained control of his Church, which had been in German hands; the Polish ruler Miezko I had been given a crown by the Pope in 990; and the Hungarians remained hostile.

Soon after Otto III assumed personal power, he crossed the Alps into Italy in 996, suppressed a revolt in Rome, and was crowned emperor by his cousin Gregory V, whom he had made pope. Two years later, in 998, he again intervened in Rome, Pope Gregory V having died. Otto made his old friend the scholarly Gerbert of Aurillac pope, with the title of Sylvester II (reigned 998-1003). He and Sylvester collaborated closely until Otto's death in 1002.

The last years of Otto III's reign have caused much controversy among historians, who have been in disagreement as to the Emperor's aims. His mind seemed filled with projects of reviving in some form the Roman Empire in close collaboration with the papacy. His motto, "The Renewal of the Roman Empire," was inscribed on his seal ring, and Otto attempted to make the city of Rome his imperial capital. He also betrothed himself to the niece of the Byzantine emperor Basil II. On the other hand, Otto fully understood the Frankish precedents behind his imperial title, and he did not behave like a sacerdotal ruler. He also felt it important to allow the neighboring rulers of Denmark, Poland, Bohemia, and Hungary a large measure of freedom, control of their local churches, and loose association with his empire, thus conciliating them and helping to integrate their realms into one Western Christendom. Whatever plans Otto III may have had for the future, however, died with him in 1002, and a new and less exalted era ensued for Italy and Germany.

Further Reading

Indispensable to an understanding of Otto III are Geoffrey Barraclough, *Origins of Modern Germany* (1947; rev. ed. 1966), and Eleanor Duckett, *Death and Life in the Tenth Century* (1967). But they should be supplemented by accounts found in Francis Dvornik, *The Making of Central and Eastern Europe* (1949); Christopher Brooke, *Europe in the Central Middle Ages, 962-1154* (1964); Romilly Jenkins, *Byzantium: The Im-*

perial Centuries, A.D. 610-1071 (1966); and Karl Morrison, *Tradition and Authority in the Western Church, 300-1140* (1969). □

Otto of Freising

The German historiographer and philosopher of history Otto of Freising (ca. 1114-1158) was the first chronicler to treat religious and political events with artistic skill and vivid color and to depict them in their temporal as well as their transcendental significance.

Otto of Freising was the son of Margrave Leopold III of Austria (later St. Leopold) and of Agnes, the daughter of Henry IV. He was also a half brother to Emperor Conrad III, the founder of the Hohenstaufen line. Otto studied at the University of Paris and about 1133 entered the French Cistercian monastery of Morimont in Champagne, whose abbot he soon became. In 1137/1138 he was made bishop of Freising. In 1146 Otto took part, under his half brother, Conrad, in the Second Crusade, in which Jerusalem was lost to Saladin. Otto wrote the *Chronicon sive historia de duabus civitatibus* (*Chronicle or History of the Two Cities*), a history of the world in eight books covering events up to 1146. Otto of St. Blaise later continued the history to events through 1209. A moral history of the world, Otto's chronicle depends upon St. Augustine's *On the City of God* and upon Aristotle's philosophy and ranks as one of the most remarkable creations of the Middle Ages.

On the basis of material secured from his nephew Emperor Frederick I and from his chancellery, Otto also wrote the *Gesta Friderici I imperatoris* (*The Deeds of Emperor Frederick I*), the most important source for information concerning the early life of that emperor. Otto's two books were continued with two more books, covering events to 1160, by his notary, Rahewin. Both the *Chronicon* and the *Gesta* were reprinted in edited versions in the German *Monumenta Germaniae historica.*

Otto's writings, all in Latin, reveal a gift for individualization and an ability to penetrate into the spirit of his sources and to treat them in an elegant style. Though not always dependable in details, his works breathe life from their pages. Otto was one of the first German students of Aristotle. A disciple of St. Augustine, he viewed all worldly events as preludes to eternal ones, believing that each temporal happening, however somber, has a happy sequel in eternity. Although he recorded events and their circumstances faithfully, Otto did not slavishly follow the techniques of ancient historians. He enlivened his works with direct address, and he depicted countries, cities, and customs conscientiously. Otto also animated his stories of battles and sieges.

Otto did not gloss over ecclesiastical and theological disputes but deplored them as evils. He practiced scholas-

ticism on its highest level. His account of the illstarred Second Crusade pictures it as starting in a dream of springtime and ending in a nightmare. His presentation, however, employs a modicum of sad detail. An optimistic mood characterizes even more strongly his *The Deeds of Emperor Frederick I,* in which Otto assumed the cheerful disposition of the Emperor and revealed a sure grasp of the spirit of the age of chivalry. Otto died on Sept. 22, 1158.

Further Reading

Otto's works were translated, with useful biographical and critical introductions and annotations, by Charles C. Mierow: *The Two Cities: A Chronicle of Universal History to the Year 1146 A.D.* (1928) and *The Deeds of Frederick Barbarossa* (1953). Discussions of Otto's life and work are in Harry Elmer Barnes, *A History of Historical Writing* (1937), and James Westfall Thompson, *A History of Historical Writing* (2 vols., 1942). □

Louis Karl Rudolf Otto

The German interpreter of religion Louis Karl Rudolf Otto (1869-1937) found a thread of unity among all religions while resisting attempts to account for religion in non-religious terms such as the moral, the rational, and the aesthetic.

Born in Peine (Hanover), Germany, in 1869, Rudolf Otto was educated at Erlangen and Göttingen and taught at the Universities of Göttingen and Breslau before becoming professor of systematic theology at the University of Marburg in 1917. In that same year he published *Das Heilige* (translated as *The Idea of the Holy*), one of the most significant books in religion in the first half of the 20th century. Illness forced his early retirement in 1929, and he died in 1937 of arteriosclerosis and physical/psychological consequences of a serious fall.

His life and work spanned a tempestuous period in the religious and political history of Germany: World War I, the Treaty of Versailles, the Weimar Republic, the rise of the National Socialist movement, and the election of Adolf Hitler as chancellor of Germany. During that period he resisted two strong challenges to religion—evolutionary naturalism and dogmatic, exclusive Christianity. Through that resistance he identified what is "religious" about any religion while recognizing and respecting the peculiar features of specific religions.

Otto is best known for his book on the Holy, which has been translated into Swedish, Spanish, Italian, Japanese, Dutch, French, and English. A British prelate, R. W. Mathews, noted in 1938 the broad impression of the book and suggested that it had an even deeper influence in England and America than in Germany.

Otto always understood himself as a Christian. He grew up in a pious Christian family and in his final lecture before retirement he referred to himself as a "pietistic Lutheran." Yet his thought and his travels both manifested and stimulated his interest in other religions, especially Judaism, Islam, Buddhism, and Hinduism. Judaism provided him the scriptural text (Isaiah 6:3) and the theme of the book on holiness. On a trip to Morocco in 1911 he was moved by a Sabbath service in a synagogue: "I have heard the *Sanctus Sanctus Sanctus* of the Cardinals in St. Peters, the *Swiat Swiat Swiat* in the Cathedral of the Kremlin and the Holy Holy Holy of the Patriarch in Jerusalem. In whatever language they resound, these most exalted words that have ever come from human lips always grip one in the depths of the soul with a mighty shudder, exciting and calling into play the mystery of the other world latent therein."

Development of the Holy

In *The Idea of the Holy,* Otto brought together interests he had pursued earlier: the dominance of the spirit over the letter in a study of Luther (*Die Anschauung vom Heiligen Geiste bei Luther,* 1898), the claim for a source of religion beyond evolutionary naturalism *Naturalistische und religiöse Weltansicht,* 1904), and the rejection of enlightenment rationalism as determinative of religion in favor of "feeling" as more decisive for religious awareness than rational knowledge or faith (*Kantisch-Friessche Religionsphilosophie und ihre Anwendung auf die Theologie* (1909). In this book, Otto isolated the quality of the "religious" which distinguishes it from the moral, the rational, and the aesthetic. He found that quality in the *numen* or, coining a word, in the *numinous*. This quality, he claimed, is present in all religions, usually in connection with other distinct qualities such as the rational and the moral, but it is neither derived from nor reducible to these other qualities. Otto was probably writing to counter explicitly Kant's *Religion within the Bounds of Reason Alone.* Otto spoke of the *numen* as non-rational, implying thereby that the *numen* is, in essence, not "good" or "beautiful."

Having identified the primal quality of the religious as the *numinous,* Otto developed an understanding of the Holy as a complex category, characteristic of all high religions, containing moral, rational, and aesthetic elements along with the *numinous*. Indeed, he traces the main development of religion as successive stages of the interpenetration of the *numen* with rational/moral dimensions, creating a unified fabric in which the warp (rational/moral) and the woof (*numen*) are intertwined. On this base, he suggests as a criterion of religions the extent to which they hold these elements together in harmony. "The degree in which both rational and non-rational elements are jointly present, united in healthy and lovely harmony, affords a criterion to measure the relative rank of religions." This understanding of religion enables Otto to be open to the validity of all religions while holding to the supremacy of Christianity in bringing to mature actuality what is potential in every religion.

Countering Possible Misinterpretations

Otto devoted the intellectual efforts of his later years to show how the *numinous* and reason and morality are positively and essentially conjoined. He did this in two major ways: by showing how the complex qualities of the Holy are

manifest in Christianity (as in *Aufsätze das Numinose betreffend* [1923] and in *Reich Gottes und Menschensohn* [1934] and in Asian religions and their relation to Christianity (as in *West-Östliche Mystik* [1926] and in *Die Gradenreligion Indiens und das Christentum* [1930] and by writing an imposing system of religious (Christian) ethics which he planned to use for the Gifford Lectures at Aberdeen in 1933 under the title "Moral Law and the Will of God" (Sittengesetz and Gotteswille).

Although Otto was not strong enough to deliver the lectures, it is clear that he intended to use the substance of several essays published in different journals for these Gifford lectures. In these ethical essays and his lectures on Christian ethics, Otto showed the inextricable connection between value, personal dignity, and the Holy; between the being of God which places value in and on everything created and the will of God which obligates every person to acknowledge, seek, and preserve value. Hence, there is a divine presence which obligates persons to affirm the value of all things and all persons and thereby to achieve the "dignity" of spontaneously affirming the manifestation of the Holy throughout the creation. Value acknowledgement is the way to God, who alone is altogether Holy, and God supports and sustains value in all things which bear the traces of Holiness. God's will for our salvation includes God's will that we be moral, but salvation is not restricted to morality.

In addition to his teaching Otto started three other kinds of movements: an experimental Christian liturgical community in Marburg, a museum of religious artifacts, and the Inter-religious League. In an essay, "Towards a Liturgical Reform," in his book *Religious Essays,* Otto shows how Holiness, taken seriously, would affect the from of the liturgy. The museum which Otto started with artifacts brought back from his travels in the East is still in Marburg. It is called the *Religionskundliche Sammlung* and is open to visitors along with the Rudolf Otto Archive of the University Library at Marburg. Unfortunately, the religious league is no longer in existence, but Otto's vision for it entailed not an administrative union of religions but the joining together of all religions for moral causes which each religion sustains in its own way. Otto hoped that such a league would unite persons of principle everywhere, "that the law of justice and the feeling of mutual responsibility may hold sway in the relationship between nations, races, and classes, and that the great collective moral tasks facing cultured humanity may be achieved through a closely-knit co-operation." Otto defined some of these common tasks as resisting human exploitation, upholding the position of women and of labor, and solving the problem of race. He called on the religions to become "advocates of religious, national, and social minorities against the force of the existing powers, against the arbitrary victor or the desire for revenge, against oppression and economic slavery, against world banditry and calumniation."

The failure of the league in no way dims the brilliance of Otto's religious and ethical vision nor the relevance of that vision to the way in which different religious groups confront the rational, moral, aesthetic, and religious challenges of contemporary culture. Otto was quite aware of the threat of Nazism and of other forms of brutalization and manipulation of the human spirit. Those things did not shake the central assurance of his life and work, expressed in the words chiseled on his tombstone in the cemetery at Marburg:

"Holy, holy, holy is the Lord of hosts: the whole earth is full of his glory" (Isaiah 6:3)

Further Reading

Most of the writing about Rudolf Otto has been in German, but there are significant essays and a few books in English. Otto influenced Joachim Wach, James Luther Adams, Paul Tillich, Mircea Eliade, Bernard Meland, and David Tracy in significant ways. Wach shows his appreciation of Otto in the essay "Rudolf Otto and the Idea of the Holy" in his book *Types of Religious Experience* (1951). Bernard Meland has a brilliant essay on Otto in *A Handbook of Christian Theologians,* edited by D. G. Peerman and M. E. Marty (1965). John M. Moore considers Otto along with William James and Henri Bergson in his book *Theories of Religious Experience* (1938). John Reeder emphasized Otto's ethics in an essay, "The Relation of the Moral to the Numinous in Otto's Notion of the Holy" in *Religion and Morality* (1973), edited by G. Outka and J. P. Reeder.

There are two excellent books on Otto's life and work in English. Robert F. Davidson published *Rudolf Otto's Interpretation of Religion* in 1947, and this has been an indispensable introduction of Otto to American readers. More recently, Philip C. Almond has written *Rudolf Otto, An Introduction to his Philosophical Theology* (1984). Both of these works identify influences on Otto and present a critical exposition of his thought. Neither one, however, treats adequately the Christian theology and Christian ethics which engaged Otto in the last years of his life. □

Jacobus Johannes Pieter Oud

Jacobus Johannes Pieter Oud (1890-1963) was one of the Netherlands' leading architects of the International Style of the 1920s.

On Feb. 9, 1890, J.J.P. Oud was born in Purmerend in North Holland. He studied at the Quellinus School of Arts and Crafts, the National School of Graphic Arts in Amsterdam, and the Technical University in Delft. His practical training came in the office of Cuijpers and Stuyt in Amsterdam and Theodor Fischer in Munich, but he was influenced as well by the work of H.P. Berlage and Frank Lloyd Wright. Oud's early buildings, those designed between 1906 and 1916, show a nearly total dependence upon the work of Berlage (for example, the design for a bathhouse for Purmerend, 1915). In 1917 Oud joined Theo van Doesburg and others to found de Stijl (the Style), a group of artists and architects that advocated an artistic expression, now best known from the paintings of Piet Mondrian, in which nature is abstracted into an interrela-

tionship of rectangles of primary colors. Its journal (also called *De Stijl*) became the mouthpiece of modernism in the Netherlands. Oud's work now assumed the bleached, cubical forms characteristic of the new architecture of the 1920s (design for row houses, Scheveningen, 1917). He soon broke away from de Stijl.

From his position (1918-1933) as city architect for Rotterdam, where his chief concern was mass housing, Oud became a leader in the European architecture of the International Style, the Dutch counterpart of Walter Gropius in Germany and Le Corbusier in France. For the series of books issued by the Bauhaus, Gropius's school of architecture, Oud produced *Holländische Architektur* (1926), which contains, among other things, an essay on the development of Dutch architecture from P.J.H. Cuijpers through Berlage to Oud himself. Oud contributed a group of low-cost row houses (1927) to the exhibition of the Werkbund, or German association of modern architects and designers, at the Weissenhof in Stuttgart. This exhibition marked the maturation of the International Style. Other outstanding works from this period in Oud's career include the facade design of asymmetrical rectangles for the Café de Unie in Rotterdam (1925; destroyed) and workers' housing quarters in the Hook of Holland (1924-1927) and the Kiefhoek area of Rotterdam (1924-1929). The workers' quarters show the plain stucco cubes, the efficient planning, and the social consciousness characteristic of the progressive architecture of the 1920s in Europe.

From 1933 until his death in Wassenaar on April 5, 1963, Oud practiced as an independent architect. A period of inactivity was closed with the design of the Shell Building in The Hague (1938-1942), but his work of this later period, with an occasional exception such as the Bio Health Resort in Arnhem (1952-1960), failed to go beyond the achievements of the 1920s. In 1955 he was awarded an honorary doctorate by the Technical University in Delft.

Further Reading

The only work in English on Oud is a slight volume by K. Wiekart, *J.J.P. Oud* (1965), with biographical data, bibliography, and illustrations. Oud's writings of the 1920s are discussed in Reyner Banham, *Theory and Design in the First Machine Age* (1960). For his contribution to de Stijl see H.L.C. Jaffé, *De Stijl, 1917-1931* (1956). Henry-Russell Hitchcock, *Architecture: Nineteenth and Twentieth Centuries* (1958), briefly discusses Oud's work in the context of the whole period. □

Sembene Ousmane

The Senegalese writer and film maker Sembene Ousmane (born 1923) was one of Africa's great contemporary novelists. His work is characterized by a concern with ordinary decent people who are victimized by repressive governments and bureaucracies.

Sembene Ousmane was born on Jan. 8, 1923, at Ziguinchor in the southern region of Casamance. Among Francophone African writers, he is unique because of his working-class background and limited primary school education. Originally a fisherman in Casamance, he worked in Dakar as a plumber, bricklayer, and mechanic. In 1939 he was drafted into the colonial army and fought with the French in Italy and Germany. Upon demobilization, he first resumed life as a fisherman in Senegal but soon went back to France, where he worked on the piers of Marseilles and became the union leader of the longshoremen. His first novel, *Le Docker noir* (1956; The Black Docker), is about his experiences during this period.

Well before independence in 1960, Ousmane returned to Senegal, where he became an astute observer of the political scene and wrote a number of volumes on the developing national consciousness. In *Oh pays, mon beau peuple!*, he depicts the plight of a developing country under colonialism. *God's Bit of Wood,* his only novel translated into English, recounts the developing sense of self and group consciousness of railway workers in French West Africa during a strike. *L'Harmattan* focuses upon the difficulty of creating a popular government and the corruption of unresponsive politicians who postpone the arrival of independence (1964).

Ousmane's international reputation was secured by his films based on his stories and directed by himself. He had turned to film to reach that 90 percent of the population of his country that could not read. *Borom Sarat* is remarkable for the cleavages Ousmane reveals in contemporary African society between the masses of the poor and the new African governing class who have stepped into the positions of dominance left by the French. *La Noire de——* is about the tragedy of a Senegalese woman who is lured from her homeland by the promise of wealth and becomes lost in a morass of loneliness and inconsideration. Ousmane's prize-winning work *Le Mandat* (The Money Order) shows what happens to an unemployed illiterate when he is apparently blessed by a large money order; he is crushed by an oppressive bureaucracy and unsympathetic officials.

Sembene Ousmane lived a simple existence in Senegal in a beach-front cottage that he built himself.

Further Reading

The only work by Ousmane thus far translated into English is *God's Bit of Wood* (1960; trans. 1962). A full-length study of Ousmane is not available. The most significant critical assessments are written in French. Claude Wauthier's essentially descriptive summary of a host of black writers, including Ousmane, appeared in English as *The Literature and Thought of Modern Africa* (1964; trans. 1966). A chapter on Ousmane is in A.C. Brench, *The Novelists' Inheritance in French Africa: Writers from Senegal to Cameroon* (1967). For general background see Judith Illsley Gleason, *This Africa: Novels by West Africans in English and French* (1965). □

Ou-yang Hsiu

Ou-yang Hsiu (1007-1072) was a Chinese author and statesman. A Confucian scholar-official, he played a distinguished role in government and also excelled as essayist, poet, and historian. His influence on the development of Sung literature was immense.

Though his ancestral home was Luling, Kiangsi, Ou-yang Hsiu was born in Mienchow, in present-day Szechwan. He lost his father at the age of 4 and was brought up in Suichow, in what is now Hupei, under the protection of an uncle. At the age of 10 he discovered Han Yü, the great T'ang writer whose prose in the "ancient style" (*ku-wen*) and somewhat colloquial poetry were then out of fashion, and aspired to his achievement. In time Ou-yang became the most influential prose writer since Han Yü, establishing *ku-wen* as the dominant style for all prose writers during the Sung and afterward, and one of the shapers of Sung poetry with its distinctive prosaic and philosophic character. In espousing the Confucian orthodoxy of Han Yü, Ou-yang also became one of the forerunners of Neo-Confucianism. His contributions as a political and moral thinker have been traditionally slighted, however, because he was not in the direct line of Confucianists that led to Chu Hsi, the greatest Neo-Confucian philosopher of the Sung times.

In 1030, at the age of 23, Ou-yang passed the metropolitan civil service examination with the highest honors and earned the *chin-shih* degree. In the next year he was assigned to a post in Loyang, where he began to attain fame as an essayist and poet. He made friends with Mei Yao-ch'en, and together they shaped the Sung style of *shih* poetry. During his residence in Loyang he also wrote many *tz'u* poems of a mildly erotic character, which reflect his own experiences with courtesans. In later years his romantic indiscretions served as occasions for his enemies to slander him.

Middle Years

In 1034 Ou-yang returned from Loyang to the capital Kaifeng and served in the Imperial Hanlin Academy. Because he sided with the reformist statesman Fan Chung-yen against the conservative faction at court headed by Lü I-chien, he was exiled from the capital in 1036 as district magistrate of I-ling, in present-day Hupei. While there, he began preparing on his own initiative a *New History of the Five Dynasties* (*Hsin Wu-tai-shih*), which established his reputation as a historian. The history was subsequently adopted as official history—a unique honor for a work not sponsored by the government.

In 1043, with the reformist faction headed by Fan Chung-yen and Han Ch'i back in power, Ou-yang returned to court. He rose in official eminence and helped formulate a series of bureaucratic reforms. These reforms, however, were opposed by the conservatives, and soon Fan and Han were assigned to posts outside the capital. Ou-yang himself was tried for incest; though the charge was dismissed, he was exiled from the capital for 10 years, during which time he served as prefect of Ch'u-chou (in present-day Anhwei), Yangchow, and other cities. While in Ch'u-chou, he styled himself Tsui-weng (the Drunken Old Man) and erected a pavilion known as the Old Drunkard's Pavilion. An essay descriptive of this pavilion and several others written during this period of exile used to be committed to memory by every schoolboy in China.

Recalled to court in 1054, Ou-yang was again appointed to the Hanlin Academy. He was charged with the task of compiling a *New T'ang History* (*Hsin T'ang-shu*), which was completed in 1060. As is the case with most Chinese historiographers, Ou-yang preferred concision to fullness of treatment and adopted a moralistic tone in his interpretation of events. For these reasons neither of his two monumental histories can satisfy the modern historian, but there can be no doubt of his tremendous intellectual energy in being able to prepare two major works of this scope.

Later Years

From 1060 to 1066, during the declining years of Jentsung's reign and the brief reign of his successor Yingtsung (1064-1067), Ou-yang was a highly influential top minister, devising with Han Ch'i a program for orderly, gradual change. The next emperor, Shen-tsung, who ascended the throne in 1067, however, placed his trust in Wang An-shih, who began a drastic program of major reforms in 1067. Ou-yang was opposed to such reforms, though Wang was once his protégé, and he repeatedly requested his resignation.

A malicious censor accused Ou-yang of incest with a daughter-in-law, and though he was cleared, the period of his political power was now over. In 1067 he was made prefect of Pochow, near Yingchow, where he had earlier decided to make his home. In his old age he amused himself with collecting rubbings of ancient writing engraved on stone and metal, thus making for himself a name as an archeologist and classical scholar. In 1071, at 64, he retired from public service, and in the next year he died.

Further Reading

There are selections from Ou-yang's best-known works in prose and poetry in such standard anthologies as Herbert Allen Giles, ed. and trans., *Gems of Chinese Literature* (2 vols., 1884-1898; 2d rev. ed. 1923), and Cyril Birch, ed., *Anthology of Chinese Literature* (1965). The only book-length study of Ou-yang in English is James T. C. Liu, *Ou-yang Hsiu: An Eleventh-century Neo-Confucianist* (1967). While its treatment of Ou-yang as a writer is disappointing, it is a well-balanced critical biography providing thoughtful reconsideration of Ou-yang's many-sided achievements as a statesman, historian, and thinker. □

Ovid

Ovid (43 B.C.-ca. A.D. 18) was a Roman elegiac and epic poet. His verse is distinguished by its easy elegance and sophistication.

Ovid whose full name was Publius Ovidius Naso, was born on March 20, 43 B.C., at Sulmo (modern Sulmona) about 90 miles from Rome. His father, a member of the equestrian order, intended for him to become a lawyer and an official and gave him an excellent education, including study under the great rhetoricians Arellius Fuscus and Porcius Latro. According to Seneca Rhetor, he preferred the *suasoriae,* exercises in giving advice in various historical or imaginary circumstances, to the prescribed debates of the *controversiae,* and his orations seemed nothing but poems without meter. His facility in composition, the content of some of his poems, and the rhetorical nature of much of his work in general all reflect his training with the rhetoricians.

Ovid also studied in Athens, toured the Near East with his friend Macer the poet, and lived for almost a year in Sicily. His father, who frequently pointed out to him that not even Homer had made any money, then apparently prevailed upon him to return to Rome, where he served in various minor offices of a judicial nature; but he disliked the work and lacked further ambition, so he soon surrendered to a life of ease and poetry.

Early Works

Ovid's life in the years after his liberation was that of a poet and man-about-town. He moved in the best literary circles, although never forming part of either of the major coteries of the time, those around Messalla and Maecenas. He had attracted notice as a poet while still in school and in time came to be surrounded by a group of admirers of his own. Ovid's early work was almost all on the theme of love; the residue of this early production, after he had destroyed many poems which he considered faulty, formed three short books of verses known as the *Amores* (*Loves*): the earliest poem of this collection seems to be a lament for Tibullus, who died in 19 B.C., and the latest assignable date for any of these poems is about 2 B.C. Most of these poems concern Ovid's love for a certain Corinna, who is generally considered an imaginary figure: the poems addressed to her form an almost complete cycle of the emotions and situations which a lover might expect to undergo in a love affair. This interest in the psychology of love is also exemplified in his *Heroides,* which dates from roughly the same period and is a series of letters from mythical heroines to their absent husbands or lovers.

This period of Ovid's life seems to have been relatively tranquil as well as productive. Of his private life we know little. In addition to "other company in youth," he was married three times; the last marriage, apparently a very happy one, was to a relative of his patron Paullus Fabius Maximus, a man of great influence. By one of these wives he had a daughter who made him a grandfather. His parents died only shortly before he was suddenly relegated (a form of banishment without the loss of property or civil rights) in A.D. 9 or 8 to Tomi on the Black Sea (the modern Constantsa in Romania).

His Exile

The reasons behind Ovid's exile have been the subject of much speculation. He himself tells us that the reason was "a poem and a mistake." The poem was clearly his *Art of Love.* With this work, its companion piece, *The Remedies for Love,* on how to get over an unsuccessful love affair, and its predecessor, *On Cosmetics,* Ovid had invented a new kind of poetry, didactic and amatory. *The Art of Love* consists of three books which parody conventional love poetry and didactic verse while offering vivid portrayals of contemporary Roman society.

The witty sophistication of this work made it an immediate and overwhelming success in fashionable society and infuriated the emperor Augustus, who was attempting to force a moral reformation on this same society. To the Emperor, this work must have seemed, in the strictest sense, subversive, and he excluded it, along with Ovid's other works, from the public libraries of Rome. What the "mistake" may have been, we do not know. It was, Ovid says, the result of his having eyes, and the most widely accepted suggestion is that he had somehow become aware of the licentious behavior of the Emperor's daughter Julia (who was banished in the same year as he) without his informing Augustus about her.

Upon receiving word of his exile, Ovid dramatically burned the manuscript of his masterpiece, the *Metamorphoses.* The unreality of this gesture can be seen from the fact that his friends already had copies and that he took the unfinished manuscript of his *Fasti* along with him into exile. The journey to Tomi lasted nearly a year, and when he arrived, he found it a frontier post, where books and educated people were not to be found and Latin was practically unknown. Tomi was subject to attack by hostile barbarians and to bitterly cold winters. The production of the last 10 years of his life consists largely of tedious and interminable complaints mingled with appeals for recall, in the *Sorrows* and *Letters from the Black Sea,* but Augustus was too bitterly offended to relent, and the accession of Tiberius in A.D. 14 brought an even more unyielding emperor to the throne.

Ovid's exile was not so unbearable as his letters indicate. He learned the native languages, and his unconquerable geniality and amiability made him a beloved and revered figure to the local citizens, who exempted him from taxes and treated him as well, he said, as he could have expected even in his native Sulmo. He wrote a panegyric to Augustus in the Getic language, the loss of which is a source of regret for philologists; a bitter attack on an unnamed and perhaps imaginary enemy, the *Ibis;* and a work on the fish of the Black Sea, the *Halieutica;* he resumed work on the *Fasti* before his death, which is given by St. Jerome as occurring in A.D. 17, but probably occurred early in the next year.

Ovid's earliest work, in the *Loves and Heroides,* already exhibits his fully developed talent. His verse is facile, smoothly flowing, and rhetorical and artificial without ever being obscure or even very often giving the impression of being other than natural and inevitable. His mastery of Greek literature, from which he draws most of his themes and to which he is continually alluding by direct or indirect quotation, was very great. His faults are those of overfacility and an occasional excessive verbal cleverness.

His Masterpiece

Ovid's masterpiece is generally considered to be his *Metamorphoses.* It is an epic in form, 15 books in length, and devoted to the theme of changes in shape, although some stories not strictly limited to this theme are included. It is arranged in chronological order from the creation of the world to the apotheosis of Julius Caesar, the first 12 books being derived from Greek mythology, and books 13-15 devoted to Roman legends and history, beginning with the story of Aeneas. The transitions between the various stories are managed with great skill.

The metamorphoses are of form only: the character, interests, and activities of the persons transformed remain invariable under transformation. Lycus, for example, in the first metamorphosis in book I, retains his savage cruelty when he is transformed into a wolf; Arachne, changed into a spider for daring to challenge Minerva to a contest in weaving, retains her skill and shows it in her webs; and Baucis and Philemon, transformed into trees, remain inseparable as they were in life and continue to offer hospitality with their shade as they did to Jupiter while they were still in human form. Above all, however, the *Metamorphoses* owes its preservation to the incomparable narrative skill with which Ovid takes the old tales of a mythology which by his time was already hackneyed, and as little an object of belief then as now, and imbues them with sensuous charm and freshness.

The *Fasti* was intended to be a Roman religious calendar in verse, one book for each month. Ovid completed only six books. It is of interest because it contains much antiquarian lore otherwise unknown (probably derived from the works of Marcus Verrius Flaccus, the greatest of Augustan scholars), chosen with Ovid's usual eye for the picturesque and versified with his usual elegance.

Several lost works of Ovid's are recorded, the most important being his tragedy *Medea,* a rhetorical closet drama like the tragedies of Seneca, which is highly praised by Quintilian and Tacitus. Some epigrams are ascribed to him, perhaps correctly.

Later Influence

In antiquity itself the influence of Ovid on all subsequent writers of elegiac and hexameter verse was inescapable, even for those writers who were consciously attempting to return to earlier, Virgilian standards; and his stories, particularly from the *Metamorphoses,* were a major source for the illustrations of artists.

In the Middle Ages, especially the High Middle Ages, when interest in Ovid's works was primarily centered on the *Metamorphoses, Art of Love,* and *Heroides,* Ovid helped to fill the overpowering medieval hunger for storytelling, as exemplified in Chaucer and others, all in greater or lesser degree dependent on Ovid. His frequently exaggerated and romantic tales greatly appealed to the taste of the time; his sensuousness and fantasy fed an age starved for just these elements. The 12th century has been named the *aetas Ovidiana* (the Ovidian age) because of the number of poets writing imitations of Ovidian hexameters on frequently Ovidian themes. In the student songs of the medieval universities and later into the Renaissance, Ovid acts almost as a patron saint for the sensual antinomianism of intellectuals, even if it extended no further than a preference for secular verses over religious literature.

In the Renaissance, Ovid was easily the most influential of the Latin poets. Painters and sculptors used him for themes; writers of all ranks translated, adapted, and plundered him freely. In English literature alone Edmund Spenser and John Milton show a deep knowledge and use of Ovid. William Shakespeare's knowledge of him is also great, for example, his use of the Pyramus and Thisbe legend in the play within the play of *A Midsummer Night's Dream.*

After the Renaissance, Ovid's influence was most often indirect, but among many authors and artists who used him directly, one must mention John Dryden, who translated (with assistance) the *Metamorphoses,* and Pablo Picasso, who illustrated this work.

Further Reading

Two comprehensive recent books on Ovid in English have done much to revive Ovid's reputation as a poet: Hermann Ferdi-

nand Fraenkel, *Ovid: A Poet between Two Worlds* (1945), and L. P. Wilkinson, *Ovid Recalled* (1955; condensed and published as *Ovid Surveyed,* 1962). Also important is Brooks Otis, *Ovid as an Epic Poet* (1966). The bimillenary celebration for the birth of Ovid produced a volume of essays, *Ovidiana,* edited by Niculae I. Herescu, some of them of considerable importance and many of them in English.

The long-disputed question of the cause of Ovid's exile was reopened by John C. Thibault in *The Mystery of Ovid's Exile* (1964). A noteworthy earlier work is the great edition and commentary on the *Fasti* by Sir James George Frazer (1929; repr. 1951). Ovid's place in literary history was extensively studied by Edward Kennard Rand, *Ovid and His Influence* (1925); Mary Marjorie Crump, *The Epyllion from Theocritus to Ovid* (1931); and Wilmon Brewer, *Ovid's Metamorphoses in European Culture* (3 vols., 1933-1957). □

Mary White Ovington

Mary White Ovington (1865-1951) was a civil rights reformer and a founder of the National Association for the Advancement of Colored People.

Mary White Ovington, born in Brooklyn, New York, in 1865, was the daughter of wealthy parents who raised her in the tradition of those men and women who had worked for the abolition of slavery in the United States. Two of the family heroes were abolitionists William Lloyd Garrison and Frederick Douglass. In her youth Ovington was encouraged in the area of racial and civil rights reforms by her Unitarian minister, who was actively involved in social issues. At Radcliffe College Ovington was thoroughly tutored in the socialist school of thought and subsequently felt that racial problems were as much a matter of class as of race.

When she returned to New York in 1891 after her family suffered financial reverses, Ovington lived and worked at the Greenpoint and Lincoln settlement house projects, although she was often the only white person in the neighborhood. While doing this work she became acutely aware of some of the race and class issues faced by African Americans in New York every day. In 1903, after Ovington heard a speech by Booker T. Washington, a prominent African American spokesman of the day, she realized even more forcibly how much discrimination African Americans encountered in the North.

When Ovington became a fellow of the Greenwich House Committee on Social Investigations in 1904 she began a study about African Americans in New York. It was published in 1911 as *Half a Man: The Status of the Negro in New York.* During the time that she was conducting the study Ovington had the opportunity to correspond and talk with W. E. B. DuBois, an African American academician with a doctorate from Harvard University. Later, DuBois invited Ovington to meet with the founding members of the Niagara Movement in 1905. This movement was mostly composed of African American activists who were attempting to find some viable means of combating racial discrimination. After the bloody Springfield, Illinois, race riots of 1908, African Americans and whites from the Niagara Movement and other groups concerned about what seemed to be a deteriorating racial climate met in May 1909 to form the organization that would eventually be called the National Association for the Advancement of Colored People (NAACP).

The mission of the organization was to combat racial violence, especially lynching and police brutality, and to work to eliminate discrimination in the areas of employment, public education, housing, voting, public accommodations, travel, and health services. The NAACP was also concerned with peonage, a system by which African Americans in the South were held in involuntary servitude. The group envisioned a national organization governed by a board of directors with branches all over the United States. NAACP tactics for combatting racial problems would be to publicize acts of racial terrorism in sympathetic newspapers in the United States and abroad and to take cases of obvious discrimination to court in order to establish, hopefully, favorable precedents in the area of civil rights.

The group encountered opposition from without. For example, Booker T. Washington opposed the group because it proposed an outspoken condemnation of racist policies in contrast to his policy of quiet diplomacy behind the scenes. Many newspapers which were owned by or allied with Washington spoke out against the fledgling NAACP. There were also problems within the new association. A chairperson of the board of directors, Oswald Garrison Villiard, grandson of the famous abolitionist William Lloyd Garrison, often clashed with DuBois, the editor of the NAACP journal, *The Crisis,* over matters of policy and control.

Ovington, who was a member of the NAACP's board of directors from the outset and served in almost every capacity until her retirement in 1947, often found that her lot was to be the mediator between various factions on the board. Ovington was a tireless worker who had, it seemed, an innate understanding of organizational power. Villiard described her as a perfect official who was always unruffled and "a most ladylike, refined and cultivated person." DuBois stated that she was one of the few white persons he knew who was totally free of racial prejudice.

Ovington served on a large number of the board's committees and was generally available to fill the vacancies left by departed staff or board members. For example, in 1911 Ovington served without pay as acting secretary for the association even though she still dedicated much of her time to the Lincoln settlement house. In 1912 she was elected as vice president of the board. When some of the board members went to serve in World War I in 1917 Ovington became acting chairperson of the board, and in 1919 she was officially elected to the position and continued to serve in that capacity until 1947. The year that she was elected the NAACP had 220 branches and over 56,000 members and the circulation of *The Crisis* was over 100,000.

The organization continued to grow in numbers and popularity. Sometimes its growth gained its own momentum. In local areas when people were outraged by racial violence or injustice they turned to the NAACP, hoping that something could be done to ensure equal treatment of African Americans. After only minimal success in some areas, Ovington suggested that the NAACP devote most of its efforts to the desegregation of the nation's school systems. Isolated successes in this area finally led to the landmark U.S. Supreme Court decision *Brown* v. *Board of Education* in 1954, which declared that segregated schools were illegal. Unfortunately, Ovington died in 1951, three years before the decision was handed down, but not before she had the opportunity of seeing some of the walls of racial discrimination begin to crumble.

Further Reading

Ovington wrote an autobiography entitled *Walls Came Tumbling Down* (1947). This book is more a history of the NAACP than an autobiography. She wrote a number of other books, including *Half a Man* (1911), *The Shadow* (1920), and *Portraits in Color* (1927). Ovington also wrote articles and newspaper accounts about the work of the NAACP. One of her articles, "The National Association for the Advancement of Colored People," is in the *Journal of Negro History* IX (1924). There is a substantial amount of information about Ovington in Charles Flint Kellogg, *NAACP: A History of the National Association for the Advancement of Colored People. 1909-20* (1967).

Additional Sources

Ovington, Mary White, *Black and white sat down together: the reminiscences of an NAACP founder,* New York: Feminist Press at the City University of New York, 1995. ☐

David Anthony Llewellyn Owen

Lord David Anthony Llewellyn Owen (born 1938), baron of the city of Plymouth, England, was a physician who turned politician and served as peace envoy in former Yugoslavia for the European Community.

David Anthony Llewellyn Owen was born July 2, 1938, in Plymouth, England, the son of a country doctor. He was educated at Bradford College and at Sidney Sussex College of Cambridge University. Deciding to follow in his father's footsteps, Owen studied medicine at St. Thomas Hospital. Earning a Bachelors of Medicine and of Surgery in 1962, Owen was connected with St. Thomas for six years, holding the positions of neurological and psychiatric registrar from 1964 to 1966 and research fellow from 1966 to 1968.

From Medicine to Politics

His interest in medicine, however, took a backseat to a political career. As early as 1964 Owen ran for a seat in the

House of Commons from Torrington as a Labour candidate. Unsuccessful, he ran again two years later to represent the Sutton division of Plymouth and won. He served Sutton until 1974 when he moved to the Devonport division of Plymouth, which he was to serve until 1992 when he received a life peerage. While serving his first two years in the House of Commons, he also was a governor of Charing Cross Hospital. In 1968 he effectively stopped practicing medicine.

His first specialization in political life was in defense. In 1967 he became parliamentary private secretary to the minister of defense for administration. The following year he became parliamentary undersecretary of state for defense for the Royal Navy, a position he held for two years until the Conservatives regained control of the government in 1970. He then became the opposition defense spokesman until 1972, a position from which he resigned because of differences over the Labour Party's stand on the European Economic Community (EEC). His position on defense issues became the subject of his first book, *The Politics of Defence* (1972).

Owen's life, both personal and public, was not a usual one. He married American literary agent Deborah Schabert in 1968, after only a three weeks' acquaintance in Washington, D.C. His positions in the Labour Party were somewhat contradictory, as he was a domestic liberal and a foreign policy conservative. He opposed Harold Wilson in favor of a more right-wing opponent. While he was a highly regarded politician, he never was able to achieve the leading role he desired.

After Labour's return to power in 1974, Owen moved to domestic issues. He served as parliamentary undersecretary of state in the Department of Health and Social Services from March to July of 1974 before being appointed minister of state in that department. He occupied the position for two years before going to the Foreign and Commonwealth Office in 1976. The same year he published his views on the British health system in *In Sickness and in Health—The Politics of Medicine*. He served in the Office of Foreign Affairs for a year when the sudden death of Tony Crosland opened the position of foreign secretary to him. He became the youngest (at age 39) foreign secretary since Anthony Eden assumed the office in 1935. He was foreign secretary for only two years when Margaret Thatcher turned Labour out of office, whereupon Owen became the opposition spokesperson for energy.

Co-Founder of Social Democratic Party

In March of 1981 Owen was co-founder of the Social Democratic Party. Dissatisfied with Labour's position on nuclear weapons, Owen wanted to create a party on the Left that had greater appeal to the British public. He was not particularly successful, although he did move up the ladder in the party hierarchy. He began as chairman of the parliamentary committee (1981-1982), then became deputy leader from 1982 to 1983, and finally leader from 1983 to 1987. The following year he found himself in another awkward party situation. The Social Democrats and the Liberals decided to form an alliance in order to become more effective, a move opposed by Owen because of the Liberals' more leftist stance. He resigned from the merged group but became leader of the Campaign for Social Democracy, a remnant of the original party. The Old Social Democrats were not successful; when Owen left the House of Commons in 1992 the party held only three seats.

Part of Bosnian Peace Process

In 1992 Owen received a life peerage as baron of the city of Plymouth and began another kind of public service. He had always been interested in international peace and was particularly active when he served on the Palme Commission on Disarmament and Security Issues from 1980 to 1989 and on the Independent Commission of International Humanitarian Issues from 1983 to 1988. In 1992 Owen became the EC co-chairman of the International Conference on the Former Yugoslavia as well as its peace envoy in that war-torn region. Together with Cyrus Vance of the United States he developed the Vance-Owen Peace Plan. Though this plan was never accepted by all parties, it helped pave the way for the Dayton Accords, which eventually brought some measure of stability to the region.

Further Reading

Lord Owen evoked much coverage, both positive and negative. On his political career in Britain, see P. Riddell, "Doctor in the House," *New Statesman* (September 7, 1984); "Dr. Owen's Way," *Economist* (September 15, 1984); "A Bad Stumble for a Man in a Hurry," *Newsweek* (August 17, 1987); R. Liddel, "Owen's Legacy," *New Statesman and Society* (September 6, 1991); and N. Malcolm, "Lord Fraud," *New*

Republic (June 14, 1993). For his foreign policy efforts, see "The Future of the Balkans: An Interview with David Owen," *Foreign Affairs* (Spring 1993). For additional insight into Owen's life and thought see *Time To Declare War* (1992), his autobiography, and *Seven Ages* (1992), an anthology of poetry. ☐

Sir Richard Owen

The English zoologist Sir Richard Owen (1804-1892) was one of the greatest comparative anatomists of the 19th century.

Richard Owen was born on July 20, 1804, in Lancaster, where he was apprenticed to a local surgeon in 1820. He studied medicine at the University of Edinburgh from 1824, completing his medical studies at St. Bartholomew's Hospital, London. His interest in anatomy led to his appointment in 1827 as assistant curator of the Hunterian Collection of the College of Surgeons in London. In 1831 he went to Paris to attend the lectures of Baron Cuvier, regarded as the world's foremost authority on comparative anatomy. Owen's 1832 "Memoir on the Pearly Nautilus" established his reputation as an anatomist and was largely responsible for his election as a fellow of the Royal Society in 1834. Owen remained at the College of Surgeons until 1856, being appointed Hunterian professor of comparative anatomy and physiology in 1836.

Owen cataloged and classified the specimens held in the college museum and dissected specimens of new species sent to the Zoological Society of London from Australasia. His private research included work on the fossils found in Britain and Australasia, about which he wrote four major books: *History of British Fossil Mammals and Birds* (1846), *History of British Fossil Reptiles* (1849-1884), *Researches on Fossil Remains of Extinct Mammals of Australia* (1877-1878), and *Memoirs on Extinct Wingless Birds of New Zealand* (1879).

By 1840 Owen was recognized as one of the leading statesmen of British science, and with the passing years he took an increasingly active role in the administration of science. He became the first president of the Microscopical Society (1840) and served on royal commissions on public health (1847). He received many honors in recognition of both his scientific work and his services to the public, including the Wollaston Medal (1838), the Royal Medal (1846), the Copley Medal (1851), and the Prix Cuvier (1857), and was made knight commander of the Bath (1884).

From 1856 until his retirement in 1883, Owen was superintendent of the natural-history collections of the British Museum. He was largely responsible for setting up the new museum buildings in South Kensington.

Owen's original contributions to anatomy and paleontology, besides the original description of many newly found species, included his suggested distinction between homologous and analogous parts of the body. He held to the theory that the structure of all vertebrates could be derived from a common archetype. When Charles Darwin's *Origin of Species* was published, Owen was its leading opponent among biologists. His review of Darwin's work in the *Edinburgh Review* (April 1860) was for many years a source of scientific argument against evolution theory. Owen's opposition to Darwin's theory caused him to lose influence among younger scientists. On Dec. 18, 1892, he died at Sheen Lodge, a residence Queen Victoria gave him in 1852.

Further Reading

Richard S. Owen, *The Life of Richard Owen* (2 vols., 1894), is a biography by Owen's grandson. For a discussion of Owen's contributions to anatomy see Edward Stuart Russell, *Form and Function* (1916).

Additional Sources

Owen, Richard Startin, *The life of Richard Owen,* New York: AMS Press, 1975.
Rupke, Nicolaas A., *Richard Owen: Victorian naturalist,* New Haven, CT: Yale University Press, 1994. ☐

Robert Owen

The attempts of the British socialist pioneer Robert Owen (1771-1858) to reconstruct society widely influenced social experimentation and the cooperative movement.

Robert Owen was born in Newtown, Wales, on May 14, 1771, the son of a shopkeeper. Though he left school at the age of 9, he was precocious and learned business principles rapidly in London and Manchester. By 18 he was manager of one of Manchester's largest cotton mills. In 1799 he purchased the mills at New Lanark, Scotland; they became famous for fine work produced with high regard for the well-being of the approximately 2,000 employees, of whom several hundred were poor children.

A reader and thinker, Owen counted among his acquaintances Robert Fulton, Jeremy Bentham, and the poet Samuel Coleridge. Owen's reforms emphasized cleanliness, happiness, liberal schooling without recourse to punishment, and wages in hard times. As his fame spread, he considered implementing ideas that would increasingly negate competitive economics. His attack on religion at a London meeting in 1817 lost him some admirers. His pioneer papers of the time, including ''Two Memorials on Behalf of the Working Classes'' (1818) and ''Report to the County of Lanark'' (1821), held that environment determined human development.

Owen learned of the religious Rapp colony in America at New Harmony, Ind., and determined to prove his principles in action there. In 1825 he purchased New Harmony and drew some 900 individuals to the community for his experiment. Despite the work of talented individuals, New Harmony did not prosper. By 1828 Owen had lost the bulk of his fortune in New Harmony, and he left it.

Following an unsuccessful attempt to institute a comparable experiment in Mexico that year, Owen returned to England to write and lecture. He propagated ideas first developed in 1826 in *Book of the New Moral World.* A kind, selfless man, he failed to perceive that the industry and responsibility that had made New Lanark great were not present in New Harmony and in other experiments he sponsored. Nevertheless, his views created theoretical bases for developing socialist and cooperative thought.

In *The Crisis* (1832) Owen advocated exchanging commodities for labor rather than money to relieve unemployment. The Equitable Labour Exchange founded that year failed but led to the Chartist and Rochdale movements. Labor unrest further fed on Owenite tenets, and in 1833 the Grand National Consolidated Trades Union was formed. It rallied half a million workers and fostered such new tactics as the general strike but fell apart within a few months, owing to opposition by employers and the government.

Owen continued to write and propagandize. Such experiments as Harmony Hall, in Hampshire, England (1839-45), derived from his theories. But new revolutionary forces and leaders put him out of the main current. His conversion to spiritualism in 1854 and his *New Existence of Man upon the Earth* (1854-1855) seemed to him a broadening of reality, rather than a retreat. His *Autobiography* (1857-1858) is one of the great documents of early socialist experience. He died in Newtown, Wales, on Nov. 17, 1858.

Further Reading

Owen's ideas are attractively presented in his own *A New View of Society* (1813). Full-length studies of Owen are Frank Podmore, *Robert Owen* (1906), and G. D. H. Cole, *Life of Robert Owen* (1925). Cole's *Persons and Periods: Studies* (1938) includes a brief, authoritative statement on Owen. Owen is often considered a utopian, but an immense literature establishes him with socialist founders; see, for example, George Lichtheim, *The Origins of Socialism* (1969). General studies include George B. Lockwood, *The New Harmony Movement* (1905); Arthur E. Bestor, *Backwoods Utopias: The Sectarian and Owenite Phases of Communitarian Socialism in America, 1663-1829* (1950); and J. F. C. Harrison, *Quest for the New Moral World: Robert Owen and the Owenites in Britain and America* (1969).

Additional Sources

Altfest, Karen Caplan, *Robert Owen as educator,* Boston: Twayne Publishers, 1977.

Claeys, Gregory, *Machinery, money, and the millennium: from moral economy to socialism, 1815-1860,* Princeton, N.J.: Princeton University Press, 1987. □

Robert Dale Owen

Robert Dale Owen (1801-1877), Scottish-born American legislator, was conspicuous among radicals in the 1820s and then won stature as an exponent of social legislation.

orn in Glasgow, Scotland, on Nov. 9, 1801, Robert Dale Owen, the eldest son of Robert Owen, attended the school his father had established at New Lanark. After studying for 4 years at Hofwyl, Switzerland, he came home to head his old school, which he celebrated in his *An Outline of the System of Education at New Lanark* (1824).

In 1825 Owen joined his father in his New Harmony, Ind., experiment, where he taught and edited its *Gazette.* He was impressed by the idealism of the social reformer Frances Wright, who was at New Harmony in 1825, and toured Europe with her. When Owen returned to New Harmony he found it in decay; still bent on social change, he organized a group of "Free Enquirers" who repudiated religion, exalted education for all, and urged lenient divorce laws and fairer distribution of wealth. Owen moved to New York City in 1829, and with Frances Wright urged his causes in the *Sentinel* and the Free Enquirer, as well as through the short-lived New York Working Men's party.

In 1832 Owen married Mary Jane Robinson in a ceremony repudiating male dominance. They visited England, where Owen helped his father edit the *Crisis,* and then settled in New Harmony. In 1836 Owen was elected for the first of three terms in the Indiana Legislature. There he advocated liberal causes, including universal education. In 1842 he was sent as a regular Democrat to the U.S. Congress. During his second term in Congress he prepared the bill (1845) creating the Smithsonian Institution.

Defeated for a third term in Congress, Owen helped liberalize rights for women in Indiana. President Franklin Pierce appointed him chargé d'affaires for Naples, Italy, in 1853. Back in America 5 years later, Owen joined other antislavery Democrats in crossing over to the Republican party. He was a moderate on slavery, but the increasing gulf between pro and antislavery forces gave contemporary distinction to such writings as *The Wrong of Slavery* (1864). In Italy, Owen had been converted, like his father, to spiritualism, and he wrote eloquently on its behalf in *Footfalls on the Boundary of Another World* (1860) and *The Debatable Land between This World and the Next* (1872). His last years were hectic, owing to the death of his wife in 1871, embarrassments caused by unscrupulous spiritualists, and his own bout with mental illness in 1875, from which he recovered. He married Lottie W. Kellogg in 1876. Owen died at their summer home at Lake George, N.Y., on June 24, 1877.

Further Reading

Much of the writing on the elder Owen and New Harmony deals also with Robert Dale Owen. His autobiographical chapters in *Threading My Way* (1874; repr. 1967) are excellent, although confined to his early life. Studies of him are Richard W. Leopold, *Robert Dale Owen* (1940), and Elinor Pancoast and Anne E. Lincoln, *The Incorrigible Idealist: Robert Dale Owen in America* (1940). □

Ruth Bryan Owen

Ruth Bryan Owen (1885-1954) was a congresswoman, author, lecturer, world traveler, and the first woman ever to represent the United States as a diplomatic minister to a foreign nation.

ctive in many realms, congresswoman and diplomat Ruth Bryan Owen volunteered as a war nurse and also headed up numerous civic and educational organizations. In addition, she was an advocate for world peace, social reform, and women in politics.

Owen was born in 1885 in Jacksonville, Illinois, the eldest daughter of three-time presidential nominee William Jennings Bryan and the former Mary Baird. The family moved to Nebraska when Ruth was two years old. She attended public schools in Nebraska and, after her father's election to Congress in 1890, in Washington, D.C. At an early age, she was tested by the climate of publicity surrounding her father. Ruth often was seen sitting by his side in the U.S. House of Representatives. She was 12 years old during her father's first campaign for the presidency and a student at the Monticello Seminary in Godfrey, Illinois, when he was nominated the second time.

Moved to London Before World War I

Owen entered the University of Nebraska in 1901. Her college career ended early, however, when she left school to marry William Homer Leavitt in October 1903. She served as her father's traveling secretary during his third presidential campaign, in 1908. The following year, she divorced Leavitt, with whom she had two children. In 1910, Ruth Bryan married Reginald Altham Owen, a British military officer assigned to the Royal Engineers. (They also would have two children.) She accompanied him to his post in Jamaica in the British West Indies and, after three years, the family moved to London at the start of World War I.

When her husband, Reginald Owen, was called to the front, Owen served as secretary-treasurer of the American Women's War Relief Fund, an agency that operated a war hospital in Devonshire and five workrooms in London for unemployed women. She also traveled to the Middle East and served as a nurse with a voluntary aid group attached to the British Army during the Egypt-Palestine campaign of 1915-18. Reginald became ill during the war and, in 1919, the family moved to the States, settling in Miami.

Owen became a popular speaker on the lecture circuit, touring the country and delivering speeches titled "New Horizons for America," "Opening Doors," "Building the Peace," and "After the War—What?" She also taught public speaking at the newly opened University of Miami from 1926 to 1928, using her salary to establish scholarships. She was vice chair of the university's Board of Regents from 1925 to 1928. The school's public speaking fraternity took its name, Rho Beta Omicron, from her initials. Meanwhile, her husband's poor health persevered; he died in 1927.

Elected to Office in 1928

Owen entered Florida politics in 1926, losing the Democratic primary in the state's 4th Congressional District by a mere 770 votes. Two years later she tried again. During the campaign, Owen averaged four speeches a day, nurtured relationships with newspaper editors, and attracted attention by visiting every community in the 18-county district in a Ford coupe that was not yet publicly available. She defeated seven-term incumbent William J. Sears in the primary and followed her father into the U.S. House of Representatives. Her opponent during the general election, Republican William C. Lawson, contested the election results. Lawson contended that Owen was ineligible to hold Congressional office because she had lost her U.S. citizenship when she married an alien and did not recover it under the provisions of the 1922 Cable Act until 1925. Owen successfully defended herself before a House elections committee, while exposing deficiencies in the Cable Act.

Owen entered the 71st Congress on March 4, 1929—the first woman elected to Congress from the Deep South. An enthusiastic advocate of women in politics, Owen was elected in a state that had refused to ratify the Nineteenth Amendment giving women the vote. In a very short time she captivated Washington completely. In Congress, Owen proposed designating the Florida Everglades a national park and creating a cabinet-level department to oversee the health and welfare of families and children. She also served on the Foreign Affairs Committee and surprised observers—who remembered her father's opposition to tariffs—when she supported the 1930 Smoot-Hawley Tariff raising taxes on imports.

Owen was elected to a second term in 1930 but defeated two years later, losing the primary to James M. Wilcox. During the campaign, Wilcox attacked Owen's position supporting Prohibition, on which she had asked for a state referendum. Then, as a lame duck member of Congress, Owen voted to repeal Prohibition—explaining that her views had not changed, but she was representing her constituency's wishes.

Became First Female Diplomat

In 1933, President Roosevelt appointed Owen Minister of Denmark—making her the first American woman to represent the country in such a role. "Her three-year mission in Copenhagen was mainly social," John Findling wrote in the *Dictionary of American Diplomatic History*, "although a minor controversy arose in 1934 when she used a Coast Guard cutter to travel to the United States from Greenland, a trip described as an 'extravagant junket' by congressional opponents."

Owen was forced to resign her post in 1936, after marrying Captain Borge Rohde of the Danish Royal Guards—and a gentleman-in-waiting to King Christian X of Denmark. The marriage made Owen a citizen of both the United States and Denmark, so she could not continue her diplomatic assignment. Upon returning to the States, Owen and Rohde traveled the country in a trailer, campaigning for Roosevelt. In her later years, Owen lived in Ossining, New York, writing and lecturing. At one time, she was the best-paid platform speaker in the country.

Owen was active in several political and world peace organizations and, in 1949, served as an alternate delegate to the United Nations General Assembly. Her involvement in civic, church, and educational movements and organizations was extensive. She served on the Advisory Board of the Federal Reformatory for Women from 1938-54 and was a member of the League of American Penwomen, the Business and Professional Women's Club, Daughters of the American Revolution, Women's Overseas League, Delta Gamma, and Chi Delta Phi. She also was a director of the American Platform Guild from its inception and active in the Parent-Teachers' Association and the National Council on Child Welfare. She received honorary degrees from Rollins College in Florida, Woman's College of Florida, Russell Sage College, and Temple University. Owen died in 1954 while in Copenhagen to accept a Distinguished Service Medal from King Frederik IX.

Works Reflected a Life

In the book *American Women Writers,* Dorothea Mosley Thompson pointed out that Owen's writings reflect the changes in her career, locales, and activities. Her book *Elements of Public Speaking*, published in 1931, emphasized the principles that guided her as a lecturer: Orators are made, not born, she wrote, and clarity and simplicity are crucial elements of an effective speech. *Leaves from a Greenland Diary* and *Caribbean Caravel* recount Owen's travels. *Denmark Caravan,* a children's book, tells of the trailer trip she and her children took through Denmark before she was appointed U.S. minister there. "*Denmark Caravan* sparkles with Owen's warmth and camaraderie with the people she encountered," Thompson wrote. *The Castle in the Silver Wood*, published in 1939, is a collection of fairy tales that perhaps reflect Owen's world view. "Many of the stories concern soldiers on their way home from the wars who meet witches or magical objects that test their courage," Thompson wrote. "All the tales have happy endings, and no one in these fairy tales is really wicked."

The book *Look Forward, Warrior*, published during World War II, outlines Owen's proposal for ensuring world peace—a system heavily based on the Declaration of Independence and U.S. Constitution. Critics called the book fuzzy, unsubstantial, and unpersuasive—although others said it made a valuable contribution. In any event, "the main outlines of her work have found duplication in the actual documents of the United Nations Charter," according to Thompson. "Like her father, Owen believed that political work is visible proof of concern for . . . humanity. This sensible, sensitive love for her fellow human beings is . . . pronounced in Owen's children's books and travel works."

Further Reading

Women in Congress, 1917-1990, U.S. Government Printing Office, 1991, pp. 191-192.
Mainiero, Lina, editor, "A Critical Reference Guide from Colonial Times to the Present," in *American Women Writers,* Vol. 3, Frederick Ungar Publishing Co., 1979, reprinted 1982, pp. 324-325.
Burke, W. J., and Will D. Howe, *American Authors and Books, 1640 to Present,* Crown Publishers, 1972.
Findling, John E., *Dictionary of American Diplomatic History,* Greenwood Press, 1989, p. 415. □

Jesse Owens

American track star Jesse Owens (1913-1980) became the hero of the 1936 Olympic Games in Berlin, as his series of victories scored a moral victory for black athletes.

James Cleveland Owens was born in Oakville, Alabama, on Sept. 12, 1913, the son of a sharecropper. He was a sickly child, often too frail to help his father and brothers in the fields. The family moved to Cleveland, Ohio, in 1921. There was little improvement in their life, but the move did enable young Owens to enter public school, where a teacher accidently wrote down his name as "Jesse" instead of J.C. The name stuck for the rest of his life.

When Jesse was in the fifth grade, the athletic supervisor asked him to go out for track. From a spindly boy he developed into a strong runner. In junior high school he set a record for the 100-yard dash. In high school in 1933 he won the 100-yard dash, the 200-yard dash, and the broad jump in the National Interscholastic Championships.

Owens was such a complete athlete, a coach said he seemed to float over the ground when he ran.

A number of universities actively recruited Owens, but he felt college was a dream. He felt he could not leave his struggling family and young wife when a paycheck needed to be earned. Owens finally agreed to enter Ohio State University in Columbus after officials found employment for his father. In addition to his studies and participating in track, Owens worked three jobs to pay his tuition. He experienced racism while a student at Ohio State, but the incidents merely strengthened his resolve to succeed. At the "Big Ten" track and field championships (at the University of Michigan) in 1935, he broke three world records and tied another. His 26 foot 8 1/4 inch broad jump set a record that was not broken for 25 years.

Owens was a member of the 1936 U.S. Olympic team competing in Berlin. The African-American members of the squad faced the challenges not only of competition but also of Hitler's boasts of Aryan supremacy. Owens won a total of four gold medals at the Olympic games. As a stunned Hitler angrily left the stadium, German athletes embraced Owens and the spectators chanted his name. He returned to America to a hero's welcome, honored at a ticker tape parade in New York. However, within months, he was unable to find work to finance his senior year of college. Owens took work as a playground supervisor, but was soon approached by promoters who wanted to pit him against race horses and

Jesse Owens (center)

cars. With the money from these exhibitions, he was able to finish school.

In 1937 Owens lent his name to a chain of cleaning shops. They prospered until 1939, when the partners fled, leaving Owens a bankrupt business and heavy debts. He found employment with the Office of Civilian Defense in Philadelphia (1940-1942) as national director of physical education for African-Americans. From 1942 to 1946 he was director of minority employment at Ford Motor Company in Detroit. He later became a sales executive for a Chicago sporting goods company.

In 1951 Owens accompanied the Harlem Globetrotters basketball team to Berlin at the invitation of the U.S. High Commission and the Army. He was appointed secretary of the Illinois Athletic Commission (1952-1955), and was sent on a global goodwill tour as ambassador of sport for the United States. Also in 1955, he was appointed to the Illinois Youth Commission. In 1956 he organized the Junior Olympic Games for youngsters in Chicago between the ages of 12 and 17. Owens and his friend Joe Louis were active in helping black youth.

Owens headed his own public relations firm in Chicago and for several years had a jazz program on Chicago radio. He traveled throughout America and abroad, lecturing youth groups. Ideologically moderate, Owens admired Martin Luther King, Jr. Owens and his childhood sweetheart whom he had married in 1931, had three daughters.

Forty years after he won his gold medals, Owens was finally invited to the White House to accept a Medal of Freedom from President Gerald Ford. The following year, the Jesse Owens International Trophy for amateur athletes was established. In 1979, President Jimmy Carter honored Owens with a Living Legend Award.

In the 1970s Owens moved his business from Chicago to Phoenix, but as time progressed, his health deteriorated. He died of cancer on March 31, 1980, after a lengthy stay in a Phoenix hospital. He was buried in Chicago several days later.

The highest honor Owens received came a full ten years after his death. Congressman Louis Stokes from Cleveland lobbied tirelessly to earn Owens a Congressional Gold Medal. The award was finally given to Owens's widow by President Bush in 1990. During the ceremony, President Bush called Owens "an Olympic hero and an American hero every day of his life."

Owens's fabled career as a runner again caught public attention in the 1996 Olympic Games, and 60th anniversary of his Berlin triumph, as entrepreneurs hawked everything from Jesse Owens gambling chips (*Sports Illustrated* August 5, 1996) to commemorative oak tree seedlings (*American Forests* Spring, 1996) reminiscent of one he was awarded as a Gold Medalist in Berlin (*Sports Illustrated* February 20, 1995).

Racism at home had denied Owens the financial fruits of his victory after the 1936 games, but his triumph in what has been called "the most important sports story of the century," continued to be an inspiration for modern day Olympians such as track stars Michael Johnson and Carl Lewis. In *Jet* magazine (August 1996), Johnson credited Owens for paving the way for his and other black athletes' victories.

Further Reading

Owens's ideology and much important biographical information can be found in his own book, *Blackthink: My Life as Black Man and White Man* (1970). John Kieran and Arthur Daley, *The Story of the Olympic Games, 776 B.C. to 1968* (1936; rev. ed. 1969), and Richard Mandell, *The Nazi Olympics* (1971), describe Owens's heroic efforts in 1936. See also Jack Olsen, *The Black Athlete: A Shameful Story—The Myth of Integration in American Sport* (1968). Articles of interest can be found in *Sports Illustrated* (August 5, 1996 and February 20, 1995); *Ebony* (April 1996); and *Jet* (August 26, 1996 and August 15, 1994). An official Jesse Owens Website can be accessed on the Internet at http://www.cmgww.com/sports/owens/owens.html (July 29, 1997). □

Count Axel Gustafsson Oxenstierna

The Swedish statesman Count Axel Gustafsson Oxenstierna (1583-1654) was a major architect of his country's brief rise to greatness among the powers of 17th-century Europe.

Axel Oxenstierna was born at Uppsala on June 16, 1583. His was among the most influential families of the Swedish nobility. His social background, as well as a quick intelligence honed by education in German universities, enabled Oxenstierna to enter top government circles at an early age. He received his first appointment in 1605; by the decade's end he was the leader of the nobility in the Royal Council.

As in other states of eastern and central Europe, the relative weakness of the local bourgeoisie had enhanced the standing of the Swedish nobility. This enabled the aristocracy to wrest concessions from the monarchy, the better to be able to exploit the peasantry. Nevertheless, a dispute within the reigning Vasa dynasty during the 1590s had split the nobility along religious lines, thus shifting the balance of forces back in the King's favor.

King Sigismund Vasa (III), a Catholic who had also been elected King of Poland, tried to bring Lutheran Sweden back into the Roman fold. The result was a coup (1598) which put his uncle into power as Charles IX and led to a purge of the aristocratic minority loyal to Sigismund. Such a purge could only strengthen the incoming King. However, Charles IX and led to contend with Sweden's relatively weak power position with respect to other Baltic states, especially Denmark. Too weak to challenge Denmark's hold over the Baltic Sound (and thus over revenues from the wealthy Baltic commerce), he attacked Muscovy. He was in

1613 Peace of Knäred with that country. This removed the Danish threat and gave some concessions to Sweden with respect to Baltic commerce. Gustavus now resumed the Swedish march to the east. By the time Oxenstierna negotiated the Treaty of Altmark with Poland (1629), his country was in effective command of eastern Baltic commerce. The impetus provided by this aggressive policy, coupled with the outbreak of the Thirty Years War in 1618, sufficed to draw Sweden into the broader conflict in Germany. Oxenstierna now added the duties of war leader to those of administrator and diplomat. In 1630, with financial support from Russia, France, and the Dutch, Gustavus marched into Germany; in 1631 he called Oxenstierna to his side; and when the King was slain at the battle of Lützen (November 1632), his chancellor assumed control of the Swedish war effort.

By that date, Sweden had become the strongest power inside Germany. After Gustavus's death, however, Sweden's position began to slip. Oxenstierna's armies were badly defeated at Nördlingen (1634), and his German allies made their separate Peace of Prague with the emperor in 1635. But the war went on, with France playing a role on the "Protestant" (anti-Hapsburg) side equal to Sweden's. Denmark took Austria's side in 1643 but was handily defeated by the Swedes. In the same year (1645) in which the two countries signed the Treaty of Brömsebro, Swedish armies marched all the way to Vienna. Oxenstierna now retired from the war with profit and honor. After 1648, strengthened by acquisitions from Denmark and the German princes, Sweden emerged as the greatest Baltic power.

Gustavus was succeeded by his daughter, Queen Christina, and Oxenstierna remained the dominant figure in the regime throughout her reign. He died in Stockholm on Aug. 28, 1654.

Further Reading

The leading English-language expert on the period of Oxenstierna and Gustavus Adolphus is Michael Roberts; see his *Gustavus Adolphus: A History of Sweden 1611-1632* (2 vols., 1953-1958). See also I. Anderson, *A History of Sweden* (1956).

Additional Sources

Roberts, Michael, *From Oxenstierna to Charles XII: four studies,* Cambridge; New York: Cambridge University Press, 1991. □

Moscow in 1610 and was planning to add the Czar's domains to his own, when death cut short further expansion.

His youthful heir, Gustavus Adolphus (Gustavus II), now had to face the power of a reunited nobility under Oxenstierna's leadership. A first round of concessions was granted in the charter of 1611; in 1612 Oxenstierna was made the King's chancellor, and a noble monopoly of higher state offices was secured by the formal coronation oath of 1617. Yet, for all this, Sweden did not suffer the fate of Poland and other countries where the nobility ran unchecked. The chancellor and the king found it more convenient to collaborate than quarrel. The pressure to bolster Sweden's security by territorial expansion and to augment its wealth by exploiting its mineral resources and metallurgical industries (chiefly gun manufactures) made for sufficient cooperation among the country's leaders to thrust Sweden dramatically on the stage of European Great Power politics.

At home, succeeding years brought administrative measures similar to those applied by centralizing monarchies to the West. Central and local government, the Estates (Riksdag), and the judiciary were all affected. Oxenstierna played a key role in all decisions taken. Particularly significant was his reorganization of the nobility itself. By the Riddarhusordning of 1626 it was restructured according to criteria for membership in one of three newly formed aristocratic subclasses.

When Gustavus came to power, Sweden was at war with Denmark. Oxenstierna was instructed to conclude the

Amos Oz

Gifted Israeli author, Amos Oz (born 1939), achieved international regard as a novelist and short story writer, as well as the author of political non-fiction.

Born in 1939 to well-read parents who had emigrated from Europe several years earlier, Amos Oz grew up in a working-class neighborhood of Jerusalem. He received his primary education in a modern religious school. Oz was eight years old when Israel was became an independent nation. When he was 12, his mother committed suicide. Three years later, he left his home, at the age of 15, and joined a kibbutz (collective farm) near Tel Aviv. It was at this young age that Oz replaced his family surname, Klausner, with one of his own making: the Hebrew word for strength, ''Oz.'' As a young adult, he studied at the Hebrew University in Jerusalem, where he specialized in literature and philosophy. By the mid-1970s Oz was married with two daughters, living and working on the kibbutz while continuing his fictional and non-fictional writing.

Early Works Receive Critical Acclaim

Oz began publishing short stories in the early 1960s. These were included in his first collection of stories, *Where the Jackals Howl,* which received immediate critical acclaim. In this collection Oz revealed himself as a master craftsman, one who probes the emotional depths of his characters.

Although the collective physical and social structure of the kibbutz are well defined and drawn in his stories, Oz concentrates mostly on the fate of the individuals, their drives, ambitions, and idiosyncrasies. The dividing line between the normal and the pathological is very narrow in much of Oz's fiction, as in one of his first novels, *My Michael.*

In *Elsewhere, Perhaps* and the collection of three stories in the book *The Hill of Evil Counsel* we encounter Israeli pioneers who are dedicated to the land and to the ideal of building a new productive life. On the other hand, we also find that members of the kibbutz passionately crave to return to their native land, even at the price of abandoning their families. In *Elsewhere, Perhaps,* the wife of one of the settlers leaves her husband and returns to Germany with her former lover. In *The Hill of Evil Counsel,* the protagonist escapes with a British admiral, dealing a shocking blow to her family. In both the novel and the three stories, Oz proves himself a keen observer of human nature. He reveals an acute awareness of the turbulent events in the years immediately preceding the establishment of the Israeli state, stressing their impact on the life, ideas, and actions of the characters.

The obsession with time surfaces in Oz's *Late Love,* whose protagonist, perceives his life-mission as warning of Soviet plans to invade Israel. While formerly he was a fanatical believer in Communism and a devotee of the Soviet system, he now transfers his fixation on Israel.

Delusion is the main force prompting the enigmatic Lord Guillaume de Touron in *Crusade,* to set out on his journey to conquer Jerusalem. The crusaders veer from acts of cruelty and complete depravity to yearnings for spiritual salvation. The journey ends with death, as Touron realizes that his men were consumed by the evil spirit within themselves. In these stories and his subsequent novel *Touch the Water, Touch the Wind,* Oz depicts the existential condition of man caught up in the cataclysmic events of World War II, the holocaust and in the highly charged post-war political/social milieu of the Soviet Union and Israel.

The kibbutz is again the setting for *Perfect Peace.* Here Oz deals with the age-old problem of the clash between generations, the gap between ideals and reality and the need to come to terms with a given social and political order. Personal conflicts are the underlying theme in the novel *Black Box.* Oz uses the 18th- and early-19th-century epistolary form to illuminate in the novel the inner lives of the characters and the twists of fate that overtake them.

Peace Without Reconciliation

Although primarily known as an author of fiction, Oz became very politically involved in Israel in the late 1960s, handing out pamphlets that promoted peace with Israel's Arab neighbors. This was not a popular position in Israel at the time, and at one point charges of treason were brought against him. As Christopher Price wrote in the October 20, 1995 *New Statesman & Society,* Israel's Six-Day war caused Oz to develop ''a deep aversion to extremism and fanaticism, which he saw breeding pain and death; and an equally passionate positive belief in compromise. ''One never knows whether compromise will work,'' [Oz] insists, ''but it is better than political and religious fanaticism. Political courage involves the ability and the imagination to realize that some causes are worthwhile whether or not the battle is won or lost in the end.''

Oz's many essays have covered political topics as well as literary ones. He has written extensively about Israel's

Arab and Palestinian conflicts, always advocating a position of peace without reconciliation, i.e. the fighting can stop even while the separate nations remain separate and opposed. First published in 1979 in Hebrew, *Under This Blazing Light,* a collection of essays from 1962-78, was translated into English and published in 1995. As Stanley Poss wrote in *Magill Book Reviews,* these essays "reflect on what it means to live in a nation of five million surrounded by 100 million enemies," and can be regarded as variations on Oz's recurring theme, "Wherever there is a clash between right and right, a value higher than right ought to prevail, and this value is life itself."

Oz wrote an autobiography titled *Panther in the Basement,* published in 1997. Another work, *In the Land of Israel* (1983), describes nationalism as the curse of mankind. In *The Slopes of Lebanon* (1989) Oz looks at Israel's invasion of Lebanon and its reluctance to grant Lebanon statehood, writing "If only good and righteous peoples, with a clean record, deserved self-determination, we would have to suspend, starting at midnight tonight, the sovereignty of three-quarters of the nations of the world."

In 1992 Oz was awarded the German Publishers Peace Prize. In his acceptance speech, titled *Peace and Love and Compromise* and reprinted in the February, 1993, *Harper's Magazine,* Oz stated "Whenever I find that I agree with myself 100 percent, I don't write a story; I write an angry article telling my government what to do (not that it listens). But if I find more than just one argument in me, more than just one voice, it sometimes happens that the different voices develop into characters and then I know that I am pregnant with a story." This way he has kept his expressly political writing separate from his works of fiction.

Author of Irony and Compassion

Throughout his career Oz's fiction has been noted for its compassion, humanism and insight into human nature, as well as for its occasional fantasia and irony. *Unto Death* (1975), *Touch the Water, Touch the Wind* (1974), *Elsewhere, Perhaps* (1973), and *The Hill of Evil Counsel* (1978) each carry the complexity of Oz's themes, style, and form. Oz also tends to explore the dark side of life, exposing human follies and anguish, often in a farcical, grotesque fashion. But Oz's novels are also imbued with humanistic concerns despite the sardonic stance. His humanism pervades all his writings, including his topical essays and critical works, as in his series of Israeli interviews *In the Land of Israel.*

Although fluent in English, Oz has always written in Hebrew. E. E. Goode in the April 15, 1991 *US News & World Report* wrote that Oz "sees the Hebrew language as a volcano in action, a fluid tool for exploring the cracks in the dream." By 1993 his various books had been translated into 26 languages, his place in Israeli and world literature secure.

Further Reading

Amos Oz's works in English include *My Michael* (1972); *Elsewhere, Perhaps* (1973); *Touch the Water, Touch the Wind* (1974); the novellas *Unto Death, Crusade,* and *Late Love*

(1975); *The Hill of Evil Counsel* (1978); *Where the Jackals Howl* (1981); *In the Land of Israel* (1983); and *Perfect Peace* (1985). Critical reviews include Robert Alter, "New Israeli Fiction," *Commentary* (June 1969), and Eisig Silberschlag, "From Renaissance to Renaissance II," *Hebrew Literature in the Land of Israel 1870-1970* (1977).

Additional Sources

Oz, Amos, *To Know a Woman* (1991).
Oz, Amos, *Israel, Palestine and Peace: Essays* (1995).
Balaban, Avraham, *Toward Language and Beyond: Language and Reality in the Prose of Amos Oz* (1988).
Cohen, Joseph, *Voices of Israel: Essays on and Interviews with Yehuda Amichai, A. B. Yehoshua, T. Carmi, Aharon Appelfeld, Amos Oz* (1990). □

Turgut Özal

Under the military regime of 1980-1983, Turgut Özal (1927-1993) began to direct Turkey's economy toward the free market. That process was accelerated after he became prime minister in 1983 and president in 1989. By the time of his death in 1993, Turkey's economy and society had been transformed almost beyond recognition.

Turgut Özal was born in Malatya, Turkey on October 13, 1927 into a humble, provincial family. He was the eldest of three sons, the other two being Korkut and Yusuf Bozkurt. Özal's father was a minor bank official and mother, Hafize, a primary school teacher. Hafize was the strongest influence in the family, constantly emphasizing the importance of education as the way to overcome the family's poverty.

After completing his schooling with honors, Özal enrolled at the Istanbul Technical University in 1946 to study electrical engineering. These were exciting times in Turkey. The country had just created a multi-party regime, an important step in Turkey's democratic development and its integration into the Western world. At the university he met future leaders such as Suleyman Demirel and Necmettin Erbakan who went on to play significant roles in Turkish politics. Both men were instrumental in promoting Özal's career and drawing him into politics.

After graduating in 1950, Özal joined the Office for Electrical Research in Ankara and worked there until 1965. There was little of consequence to report in Özal's life in the 1950s. His arranged marriage in 1952 to a girl from his hometown lasted only a few months. His second marriage to his secretary, Semra Yeyinmen, was of great significance. The latter was a woman of strong ambition, described as the driving force behind her husband's rise to power. They had a daughter, Zeynep, and a son, Ahmet, and both children were figures of controversy once their father rose to power.

Özal went to the United States in 1954 for further studies and there acquired his life-long admiration for American know-how and for the knack of "getting the job

done." Back in Turkey he was placed in the State Planning Organization (SPO) during his military service (1959-1961) and also taught mathematics at the Middle East Technical University.

Entry into Public Service

Özal began his rise to prominence in 1966 when Prime Minister Demirel made him a technical advisor. The following year he was sent to the SPO in order to purge that institution of those elements who were hostile to the private sector. Özal created his own conservative, Islamist team who would continue to serve him faithfully. The military coup of March 12, 1971 against Demirel left Özal out in the cold. However, Özal had made good contacts in the business world, which allowed him to spend two years (1971-1973) in Washington as an advisor at the World Bank.

On his return to Turkey, Özal joined Sabanci Holding, one of the biggest corporations in the country. He left Sabanci in 1975 to work independently as an entrepreneur, and that is when he began to make his fortune. These were good years for the Özals. In 1973, Korkut was elected to Parliament on the religious National Salvation Party's ticket and became minister of agriculture in the coalition government of 1974. Turgut also decided to enter politics and joined his brother's party, but was defeated in the 1977 general election. This turned out to be fortunate, for had he won he would have been disqualified from politics by the military junta that seized power on September 12, 1980.

The 1970s had been years of turmoil in Turkey. The elections of 1973 and 1977 created unstable coalitions that could not cope with the country's many problems. The economy was in tatters, due largely to the crisis in the world, but also because Turkey's invasion of Cyprus in 1974 had left the country isolated even from her allies. The instability was aggravated by terrorism, which seemed designed to provoke military intervention. In these circumstances, Özal was appointed Demirel's economic adviser in November 1979 and given the task of implementing a packet of tough monetary measures. The economic program Özal presented in January 1980 was described by the *Economist* as an "economic earthquake." The program, a radical departure from earlier policies, was designed to create a new economy based on exports rather than the home market. The lira was devalued 30 percent on top of the 43 percent devaluation in 1979, prices were allowed to rise sharply; and wages were tightly controlled, leading to a wave of strikes. The "law of the market" was to prevail so that only the large and efficient enterprises would survive and be competitive.

Such a program could not be implemented without military discipline, and Özal said so. He asked for five years of stability to set the economy straight and that is what the military regime gave him. He was made deputy prime minister and minister of state in charge of the economy in the military government and was described in the foreign press as the "economic supremo." The painful deflationary program was enforced under martial law and inflation of over 100 percent came down as a result. This was part of the success story. However, Özal was forced to resign in July 1982. His policy of freeing interests without adequate controls had led to the "Bankers' scandal"; thousands of middle-class savers lost money on the promise of incredibly high interest rates, that proved impossible to meet.

Özal the Politician

Özal decided to enter politics when political activity was restored in April 1983. He formed the Motherland Party, claiming to unite all the ideological tendencies represented by the parties banned by the junta. His party won the election in November only because its main rivals had not been allowed to run, and Özal became the first civilian prime minister. The local elections of April 1984, confirmed Özal's power and gave him greater confidence.

The party and government were both under Özal's firm control and he brooked no criticism from those around him. The country continued to be ruled by the army under laws passed by the junta while Özal concentrated on the economy. New laws, all designed to create a modern, up-to-date economic structure, were passed during these years. The economy seemed to have turned a corner, especially with the growth of exports, though the foreign debt kept growing.

President Özal

Fortunes were made and a new class of rich emerged for whom money was no object. There was much corruption in government, leading to resignations. That affected Özal's own reputation, especially when his family seemed to be involved. Charges of nepotism flew as Özal's brothers, sons, nephews, and other relatives all moved into prominent government or business posts. Özal helped his wife, Semra, take the helm of the ruling party in Istanbul. As a result of these clouds and his abrupt (some said, sultanic) nature, his popularity declined dramatically. His support slipped from a high of 45 percent in 1983 to the low of 22 percent in April 1989. Opinion polls reported that Özal's popularity had declined to single digits in the early 1990s. There were resignations from the party and few people believed that it would survive the election of 1992. Under these circumstances, Özal decided to have himself elected president of the Republic while his party enjoyed a sufficient majority in the assembly. He became Turkey's eighth president on October 31, 1989, but the opposition promised to oust him as soon as it came to power at the next election.

The 1991 election brought Özal's Motherland Party only 24 percent of the vote. However, Suleyman Demirel was the victor, with the leader of the True Path Party, with only 27 percent. Though Demirel had sworn to run Özal from office upon victory, he could do so only if he was successful in creating a coalition to oppose the president in parliament. Özal's gamble had paid off, and he was to remain president until his death on April 17, 1993.

The years between the 1991 elections and Özal's death proved politically turbulent, as Özal usurped powers unknown to previous presidents and Demirel scrambled to keep up. Though outwardly relaxed and easy-going, Özal the politician was a powerhouse of activity. He "mesmerized members of Turkey's parliament with phone calls to win approval for his hasty decisions," according to David Lawday in U.S. News and World Report. Özal confirmed this perception, saying in Lawday's profile, "I operate by changing people's minds. My style is to move very fast . . . you have to move fast; otherwise, you lose everything while everyone is debating what to do."

The formula worked for Özal, though it involved incredible risks. One of his last and boldest foreign policy moves was to join with the United States and other NATO allies in their opposition to Iraq's invasion of Kuwait in 1990. Though Özal was careful not to provoke war with his neighbor by taking part directly in an invasion, he thrust Turkey into a major role in the conflict, first cutting off oil pipelines from Iraq and then allowing the United States and its allies to use Turkish air bases to launch attacks against Iraq. Özal saw Turkey as a key buffer between the Middle East and Europe, and while wishing to keep one foot in each world, he surmised that helping the United States would pay dividends.

Though Özal's popularity at home slipped to new lows as a result of this action, some dividends came. After Turkey lost billions of dollars in trade through the embargo, Saudi Arabia came forward with over a billion dollars in grants and loans, Japan committed more than $400 million, and the United States threw an extra $200 million on top of an existing $553 million package. Beyond these direct monetary contributions, Turkey's military was treated to an infusion of new hardware. Özal's biggest disappointment resulted from Europe's reluctance, despite Turkey's help, to welcome the country into the European economic union. Observers concluded that discrimination against Turkey's Muslim heritage played a major role in this snub.

Özal's Legacy

Despite his political unpopularity, Özal left Turkey changed forever. His government shattered regulations which inhibited trade and economic growth, his policies attracted new foreign investment and tourism, and his love of technology led to the extension of electricity and telephone wires throughout the entire country. These quick changes came at a price, however: Özal was never able to control galloping inflation.

Özal made no secret of his devotion to his Islamic faith, at once both legitimizing Turkey's heritage with new friends in the West and sidestepping extremist elements which resulted in religious fundamentalist states elsewhere in the region.

In the words of former ambassador, Morton I. Abramowitz, in a Foreign Policy article, the former president "helped change his country like no one since Ataturk, the father of modern Turkey." Even after death, therefore, Özal's impact will continue to remain profound.

Further Reading

Additional information on Turgut Özal and modern Turkey can be found in George Harris, Turkey Coping with Crisis (1985); Dankwart Rustow, Turkey: America's Forgotten Ally (1987); and Feroz Ahmad, The Making of Modern Turkey (1990).
More information about Turgut Özal's final years as president may be found in U.S. News and World Report (August 20, 1990 and July 29, 1991); the New York Times Magazine (November 18, 1990); Time (January 28, 1991; May 13, 1991; and November 4, 1991); Foreign Affairs (Spring, 1991); National Review (April 15, 1991); the New Republic (April 15, 1991); Business Week (April 22, 1991); and Foreign Policy (Summer, 1993). □

Seiji Ozawa

The Japanese musician, Seiji Ozawa (born 1935), was one of the very few non-Westerners able to achieve international renown as a conductor of Western music. His natural musicality, energy, and warmth endeared him to orchestras and public alike.

Seiji Ozawa was born on September 1, 1935, in Fenytien (now Shenjang), in the Manchurian province of Liaoning, China, during the Japanese occupation of that region. When war broke out, his Buddhist father and Presbyterian mother moved the family to Tokyo.

His mother's decision to raise her children as Christians brought Ozawa into early contact with Western church music. This contact was reinforced by his older brother, who became a church organist. From the start Ozawa gravitated toward Western music and only developed an interest in the traditional music of his homeland through association with cross-over composers such as Takemitsu, after his career was well established.

Early Training

Ozawa began piano study at the age of seven and numbered among his teachers Toyomasu, a Bach specialist with whom he studied for ten years. He entered the Toho School in Tokyo at the age of 16 with hopes of becoming a concert pianist. When he broke both index fingers in sports activity Toyomasu suggested he also take up conducting, recommending him to Hideo Saito. Ozawa was awarded first prizes in conducting and composition upon graduation from the Toho School.

Ozawa worked with Saito from 1951 to 1958 and served as his assistant and factotum in order to help pay for lessons. His duties were said to have included everything from orchestrating music to mowing the lawn. Ozawa later considered Saito to be one of the three most important influences in his musical development, the others being Charles Munch and Herbert von Karajan.

His rapid rise through the ranks of conductors may be seen as a chain of increasingly important introductions and fortuitous meetings. This same rapid rise, though, did not allow him time for learning the immense repertoire required to be at the top of his craft. He would spend years catching up.

In 1959 Ozawa left Japan, hoping to further his career in Europe. In Paris he saw an ad for the Bensanáon International Conductor's Competition, which he entered and

won. The judges at Bensanáon included Charles Munch, who invited him to enter another competition at Tanglewood in western Massachusetts, a music camp and summer home of the Boston Symphony Orchestra. There he won the Koussevitsky Prize in 1960.

The same year, while in studying in Berlin with Karajan, he met Leonard Bernstein. Ozawa was invited to accompany Bernstein and the New York Philharmonic Orchestra on a tour of Japan in early 1961 and to be one of three assistant conductors with the same orchestra for the 1961-1962 season. In the 1964-1965 season he held this position alone. He made his debut with the New York Philharmonic Orchestra as one of three conductors needed for Charles Ives' "Central Park in the Dark." Ozawa credits Bernstein's children's concerts as the inspiration for a series he later did for Japanese television, though Ozawa's concerts were aimed at an adult audience.

An enthusiastic recommendation by Bernstein to Ronald Wilford of Columbia Artists' Management led to Ozawa's debut with the San Francisco Symphony Orchestra in 1962. It also secured for him the music directorship (1964-1968) of the Ravinia Festival, summer home of the Chicago Symphony Orchestra. In 1964 he guest conducted the Toronto Symphony Orchestra and became its musical director the following year. This lasted until 1970, when he was appointed to the same position with the San Francisco Symphony Orchestra. Critics commented on his rather lopsided repertoire, which featured very little German or Austrian music from Haydn to Schumann, but much music from the late 19th and early 20th centuries, including Brahms, Schoenberg, Bartok, Ravel, and Debussy.

Long Tenure in Boston

In 1972 he became musical adviser for the Boston Symphony Orchestra and the following year its musical director, still holding his San Francisco appointment. This dual directorship continued until 1976. When this burden became too taxing, he was compelled to give up the West Coast orchestra. His duties with the Boston Symphony Orchestra included directorship of the Tanglewood Festival, a position he had held since 1970, though jointly with Gunther Schuller the first year.

Ozawa retained ties with both Japan and China during his career, serving as musical adviser to the New Japan Philharmonic Orchestra from 1968 and making many guest appearances with orchestras in Osaka and Saporo. When the Peoples Republic of China reestablished cultural ties with the West in 1977, he accepted an invitation to conduct the Beijing Central Philharmonic Orchestra, and the following year led the Boston Symphony Orchestra on a tour of China. Ozawa also retained ties with Japan in his personal life, preferring to settle his wife Vera and their two children in Tokyo and hopping continents to conduct.

While performances in the earlier part of his career were marred by a roughness of sound and did not bear the stamp of a strong musical personality, Ozawa later developed a full, well-rounded tone and distinctive style that were particularly suited to big, coloristic pieces from the late 19th through the 20th centuries, including works by

Mahler, R. Strauss, Sibelius, and Messiaen. He also had surprising success with Stravinsky, Bartok, and Schoenberg, whose "Gurrelieder" ranked among his best recordings. He was criticized on occasion for failing to probe beneath the surface beauty, even in works such as Verdi's "Requiem" which might seem to have been ideally suited to him.

Opera presented further challenges to Ozawa, both in the immense amount of time needed to learn a score and in his additional difficulties with the Italian, German, French, and Russian languages. His opera debut came with Mozart's "Cosi fan tutte" at Salzburg in 1969; others in his repertoire included Tchaikovsky's "Eugene Onegin," Mussorgsky's "Boris Gudonov," and Messiaen's "Saint François d'Assise," of which he conducted the first performance at the Paris Opéra in November 1983. Ozawa's Metropolitan Opera debut came in 1992.

By the late 1990s, Ozawa's extended stay with the Boston Symphony gave him seniority among directors of American orchestras. He made regular guest appearances with the Berlin Philharmonic, the New Japan Philharmonic, the London Symphony, the Orchestre National de France, the Philharmonia of London, and the Vienna Philharmonic and released recordings with the Berlin Philharmonic, the Chicago Symphony, the London Philharmonic, the Orchestre National, the Orchestre de Paris, the Philharmonia of London, the Saito Kinen Orchestra, the San Francisco Symphony, the Toronto Symphony, and the Vienna Philharmonic.

Ozawa recorded over 130 works with the Boston Symphony, representing more than 50 composers. He received two Emmy awards, the first for his television series, "Evening at Symphony," and his second for Individual Achievement in Cultural Programming for the Boston Symphony's "Dvorák in Prague: A Celebration."

In 1992 Ozawa founded the Saito Kinen Festival in Natsumoto, Japan, repaying a debt to the memory of his old master. Honors flowed to Ozawa as well, with the opening of a new concert hall at Tanglewood bearing his name in 1994, and the conferring of honorary doctor of music degrees from the University of Massachusetts, the New England Conservatory of Music, and Wheaton College. In Japan, Ozawa became the first recipient of the Inouye Sho ("Inouye Award").

Ozawa did not forget to pay other debts to the muse: he commissioned several new works of music, including one series commemorating the Boston Symphony's centennial and another celebrating Tanglewood's fiftieth anniversary.

Further Reading

Because Ozawa conducted one of the major orchestras in the United States and continued to record, reviews of his concerts and recordings turn up frequently in all of the well-known music magazines. Articles in *Hi-Fi/Musical America, Stereo Review,* and *American Record Guide* are all indexed in *The Music Index,* as are those in non-music-specific publications such as *Saturday Review,* the *Christian Science Monitor,* and the *Village Voice.* Chapters devoted to Ozawa are found in Helena Matheopoulos' *Maestro: Encounters with Conductors of Today* (1982) and in Philip Hart's *Conductors: A New Generation* (1983). The latter also contains a comprehensive list of recordings. Andrew L. Pincus' *Scenes from Tanglewood* (1989) gives more information about the conductor than is suggested by the title.

General biographical information may also be found on the Internet at sites maintained by BMG Music and the Boston Symphony Orchestra as well as in Michael Walsh's article "What Makes Seiji Run" in *Time* (March 30, 1987). ☐

P

Johann Pachelbel

The German composer and organist Johann Pachelbel (1653-1706) helped to introduce the south German organ style into central and north Germany. Through his close connections to the Bach family, his style influenced and enriched that of Johann Sebastian Bach.

The musical education of Johann Pachelbel began in his childhood. In 1669, while at the University of Altdorf, he was organist in the church of St. Lorenz. The following year, at the gymnasium at Regensburg, and during his employment at St. Stephan's, Vienna, after 1672, he became familiar with the south German musical tradition of J. K. Kerll. In 1677 Pachelbel became court organist at Eisenach, where he met the local branch of the Bach family, in particular Johann Ambrosius Bach, who was one of the municipal musicians.

In 1678 Pachelbel accepted the important post of organist at the Predigerkirche in Erfurt. During this period Johann Christoph Bach studied with him for 3 years. During his stay at Erfurt, Pachelbel produced at least three of the four works listed by J. G. Walther in *Musikalisches Lexikon* (1732) as published during his lifetime: *Musicalische Sterbens-Gedanken* (1683), chorale varitions; *Musicalische Ergetzung* (1691), chamber music; and *Chorale zum Praeambuliren* (1693), an instruction book for organ. Here Pachelbel also composed two cantatas of homage for Karl Heinrich of Metternich-Wenneburg, other cantatas, and possibly other chamber music.

In 1690 Pachelbel accepted employment at the court at Stuttgart, which he fled in 1692 because of the French invasion. He became municipal organist at Gotha, but his activities are uncertain until 1695, when he became organist of the famous church of St. Sebaldus, Nuremberg. Here he was active as a teacher, and Walther speaks of his illustrious reputation. Two of Pachelbel's sons were important musicians: William Hieronymous at Erfurt and Nuremberg, and Carl Theodore at Stuttgart and Charleston, S.C.

Pachelbel was one of the composers of the movement leading to the adoption of equal temperament, making use of as many as 17 different keys in his suites. He applied the variation techniques of the secular suite to the setting for organ of Lutheran chorales (*Musicalische Sterbens-Gedanken*). He introduced to central and north Germany the brief, light keyboard fugue (as in his Magnificat fugues). He is particularly noteworthy for a style of chorale prelude of which he seems to have been the chief protagonist. In it a preliminary imitative passage on each phrase of the melody precedes the statement of the phrase, intact, in one part. His virtuosity as an organist is probably reflected in his toccatas, which emphasize elaborate manual figures and omit the fugal sections typical of the north German style.

Further Reading

Pachelbel's place within the music of his period is discussed in Manfred Bukofzer, *Music in the Baroque Era* (1947). See also Paul Henry Lang, *Music in Western Civilization* (1941). □

Michael Pacher

The Austro-German painter and wood carver Michael Pacher (ca. 1435-1498) amalgamated north Italian perspective and northern realism to produce a uniquely personal style of painting.

Born in a town near the Austro-Italian border, Michael Pacher is recorded in 1467 as an established master in Bruneck (Brunico), where he had a workshop for making altarpieces. He was equally adept at painting and wood carving, and his commissions often were for the German-type altar: sculptured centerpiece, carved Gothic pinnacles above, a predella below, and painted scenes on wing panels. He went to Neustift to paint frescoes in 1471 and worked in Salzburg in 1484 on an altarpiece for the Franciscan church, of which some parts have been preserved.

Pacher traveled in north Italy, studying in Padua the recent frescoes by the noted master of perspective Andrea Mantegna, whose spectacular, low-viewpoint spatial constructions were fundamental to the formation of his own style. With an orientation toward Italy unique among Germanic artists in the late 15th century, Pacher escaped the domination of the Flemish style north of the Alps.

Pacher's masterpiece, the *Altarpiece of St. Wolfgang* (1471-1481), is one of the largest and most impressive carved and painted altar shrines in all of European art. The carved, painted, and gilded centerpiece represents the Coronation of the Virgin, and there are two sets of painted wings with scenes of the Life of Christ and of the local, miracle-working saint, Wolfgang. The whole complex is surmounted by an intricate wooden superstructure containing the Crucifixion. In the central shrine Christ is enthroned, solemnly blessing his mother, whom he has crowned as Queen of Heaven. Angels, beloved in German Gothic art, flutter about, while the life-sized figures of St. Wolfgang and John the Evangelist bear witness. His brittle and agitated sculptural style demanded that each element be freestanding in a space that is deeply recessed.

Pacher's sculpture thus is in stylistic harmony with the perspectival paintings on the wings. Typical of these is the scene of Christ driving the money changers from the Temple, in which an impossibly contorted figure of the Lord, looming in the foreground, wields a cat-o-ninetails as he stands beside a violently receding view into a far-distant, vaulted Gothic cloister. These compositions, in which architectural space is asserted dramatically, anticipate those of Tintoretto.

The painted altarpiece *Four Church Fathers* (ca. 1483) has, once again, on the exterior, scenes of miracles performed by St. Wolfgang. These dramatically reaffirm the fact that Pacher was far in advance of his German contemporaries in depicting forms in space. He died in August 1498 in Salzburg.

Further Reading

There is an outstanding monograph in English on Pacher: Nicolò Rasmo, *Michael Pacher* (1971). It contains excellent reproductions of the sculpture and paintings. □

Pa Chin

Pa Chin (Ba Jin) was the pen name of the Chinese author Li Fei-kan (born 1904). An idealist of humanitarian passion and revolutionary fervor, he was one of China's most prolific and beloved novelists of the 1930s and 1940s.

Born into a large, landowning family in Chengtu, Szechwan, Pa Chin suffered the loss of his parents and many other beloved ones while still a boy. He was active in school and eagerly read the new publications spawned by the May Fourth movement of 1919. His need for love and his vast sympathy determined his course of reading, and an early encounter with a tract by Prince Kropotkin made him a confirmed anarchist. In 1923 he left Chengtu for Shanghai and went on to Nanking to complete his high school education. He returned to Shanghai in 1925 to prepare for a literary career. In January 1927, at the age of 23, he left for France. There he continued to explore his earlier interest in French fiction and the French Revolution and wrote a novel called *Mi-wang* (Destruction), which was serialized in the leading literary journal *Hsiao-shuo Yüeh-pao* (Short Story Magazine). Upon his return to China in 1929, he found himself an acclaimed writer.

From then on Pa Chin wrote prolifically and was also active as a publisher and editor. In most of his early novels and stories, including *Ai-ch'ing ti san-pu-ch'ü* (The Love Trilogy), the characters are flat and rather bookish, but because they speak out for love and revolution, for a new China and a new humanity, they had a tremendous appeal for young readers of that time.

Autobiographically grounded in his youthful experience, *Chieh-liu san-pu-ch'ü* (1933-1940; The Torrent: A Trilogy) is much more impressive for its detailed exposé of the squalor and sickness of a large, tradition-bound Chinese family. The first volume, *Chia* (The Family), has been the most popular of Pa Chin's works because of its great wealth of tear-jerking scenes, but it was the third volume, *Ch'iu* (Autumn), that first evinced his powers as a novelist in his unsentimental portrayal of the clashes between good and bad characters.

Pa Chin continued to mature in the 1940s in such works as *Hsiao-jen hsiao-shih* (Little People and Little Events), a volume of short stories, and *Ti-ssu ping-shih* (Ward Number Four), a novel about patients in a wartime hospital. These prepared for his masterpiece, *Han-yeh* (Cold Nights), written in 1947. This novel, of rare tenderness and psychological truth, studies a trio (son, wife, and mother) against the background of the worsening conditions in wartime Chungking.

Pa Chin's career as a serious novelist was immediately blighted with the establishment of the People's Republic in 1949. Thereafter he wrote mainly as a foreign correspondent and produced slim volumes of reportage about the Korean and Vietnamese wars. As a foreign correspondent Pa Chin spent time in Korea (1952), Japan (1961), and Vietnam (1962). With changes in the Communist regime in the 1960s he was severely persecuted and denounced as a counter-revolutionary. During the Cultural Revolution (1966-1969) he was purged, but was reported to have reappeared during the 1970s. In 1975 Pa Chin was nominated for the Nobel Prize in Literature. As a tribute for his many contributions to Chinese literature, he was awarded a Special Fukuoka Asian Commemorative Prize in 1990.

Further Reading

Only one of Pa Chin's novels is available in English, Sidney Shapiro's translation of *The Family* (1958), sponsored by the Foreign Languages Press of Peking, which also published a volume of the author's sketches of the Korean War, *Living amongst Heroes* (1954). "Dog," in Edgar Snow, ed., *Living China: Modern Chinese Short Stories* (1936), is one of the few stories by Pa Chin available in translation. Olga Lang, *Ba Jin and His Writings: Chinese Youth between the Two Revolutions* (1967), is the most extensive critical biography of the author in any language. It is especially good in relating Pa Chin's literary and intellectual development to Western literature and ideas, particularly Russian and French. C.T. Hsia, *A History of Modern Chinese Fiction, 1917-1957* (1961), includes a succinct study of Pa Chin's achievements and limitations as a writer. See also Oldřich Král, "Ba Jin's Novel The Family," in Jaroslav Prušek, ed., *Studies in Modern Chinese Literature* (1964). Chung-wen Shih, (1982), produced a one-hour video cassette *Return From Silence: China's Revolutionary Writers,* featuring Pa Chin and other Chinese writers. Movies of *The Family* and *Chilly Night,* have been made. □

David Packard

David Packard (1912-1996) was the co-founder and a longtime executive officer of Hewlett-Packard Company, a leading manufacturer of electronic measuring devices, calculators, and computers. He also served as deputy secretary of defense under President Richard Nixon and was a major benefactor to many philanthropic organizations.

David Packard was born September 7, 1912, in Pueblo, Colorado, the son of a lawyer and a high school teacher. He avidly read library books on science and electricity, and built his first radio while still in elementary school. After graduating from his local public high school, Packard enrolled as an electrical engineering student at Stanford University in California. There he met William Hewlett, a fellow student who shared his interest in electronics and the out-of-doors. In college he was a varsity athlete and president of his fraternity. He received a B.A. with honors in 1934.

Packard went to Schenectady, New York, to work in the vacuum tube engineering department of General Electric Company. He returned to Stanford in 1938 to study the theory of the vacuum tube. That year he also married Lucile Salter of San Francisco, whom he had met at Stanford; the Packards had four children.

In 1939 Packard finished his electrical engineering degree under Stanford professor, Frederick Terman. By then he had renewed his friendship with Hewlett, who had developed considerable expertise on negative feedback circuits. Hewlett and Packard set up a laboratory in the Packard family garage and soon were taking orders for apparatus ranging from air conditioning control units to electronic harmonica tuners to exercise machines. In 1939 Hewlett-Packard turned its emphasis from custom orders to mass produced instruments. Particularly important were its audio oscillators, devices that generate a controlled signal at a predetermined frequency. These were generally used to check the performance of amplifiers and broadcast transmitters, but some provided sound effects for Walt Disney's movie *Fantasia.*

During World War II Hewlett-Packard expanded rapidly to meet the needs of various defense projects. Packard ran the company alone, as Hewlett was in the U.S. Army. Business declined sharply at the end of the war, and Hewlett-Packard was forced to lay off employees for the only time in Packard's career. Demand rebounded by 1950; in 1957 the company's stock began to trade on the open market. Hewlett-Packard's product line grew to include not only thousands of electronic measuring devices for a wide

range of frequencies but, beginning in 1972, hand-held scientific calculators. The company had done custom work in computer manufacture as early as the 1940s, but did not begin to market its own computers until the late 1960s. Experienced in supplying engineers and scientists, Hewlett-Packard had some difficulty with wider business and consumer markets. Nonetheless, it developed a wide range of programmable calculators, minicomputers, and microcomputers.

Hewlett-Packard was one of the first and largest electronics companies in the region of California now called Silicon Valley. It gradually expanded its sales force from a handful of representatives into a national and then an international network. Manufacturing facilities also extended out of California, not only to Colorado and Oregon but to Europe, South America, and Asia. At the same time, staff trained at Hewlett-Packard came to have important posts at other electronics firms. For example, Stephen Wozniak, cofounder of Apple Computer, first worked at Hewlett-Packard.

With Packard as manager and Hewlett as technical expert, Hewlett-Packard followed conservative but unconventional business practices. Profits were reinvested in the company so that debt was low. Following General Electric's example, the company preferred to hire employees directly out of school. Staff received generous benefits, were entrusted with considerable responsibility, and rarely were fired. Hewlett and Packard set general objectives, assisted those who carried them out, and chose not to flaunt their wealth and power. Engineering, sales, and management were done by men, while women did much of the actual assembly work. Emphasis was on high quality, not low price. To retain the atmosphere of a small business when the staff came to number thousands, Hewlett and Packard divided the company according to product types, with each division having its own marketing, production, and research groups. Support functions such as sales and advertising often were handled by outside contractors.

In addition to his business activities, Packard took an active interest in civic affairs. From 1948 until 1956 he chaired the Palo Alto School Board; he also gave money to the Republican Party. In 1964 he founded the David and Lucile Packard Foundation in Los Altos, California, to support universities, national institutions, community groups, youth agencies, hospitals, and other organizations that are dependent on private funding and volunteer leadership; he also served as president and chairman of the foundation. When President Richard Nixon was elected, he sought a skilled administrator to serve as deputy secretary for defense. Packard agreed to take the position, decreasing his salary from nearly a million dollars a year to about $30,000. Congressional critics pointed out that Packard owned about one-third of the stock in Hewlett-Packard and that the company did about $100 million in defense-related business each year. To avoid conflicts of interest, Packard put his stock in a trust fund, with all dividends and capital increases going to charity.

In 1971 Packard returned to his post at Hewlett-Packard. Even after he retired from direct administration in 1977, he continued as chairman of the board. He also served on the boards of directors of corporations such as Caterpillar Tractor Co. (1972-83), Chevron Corp. (1972-85), The Boeing Co. (1978-86), Genentech Inc. (1981-92), and Beckman Laser Institute & Medical Clinic (1992-96). He was a trustee of the Herbert Hoover Foundation and of the American Enterprise Institute, conservative research groups. He was a member of The Trilateral Commission from 1973 to 1981 and chaired the U.S.-Japan Advisory Commission from 1983 to 1985. In 1985 he was appointed by President Reagan to chair the Blue Ribbon Commission on Defense Management. He also was a member of the President's Council of Advisors on Science and Technology from 1990 to 1992 and founding vice chairman of the California Roundtable.

In addition to his own foundation, Packard held top positions in many philanthropic organizations. He was chairman of the Monterey Bay Aquarium Foundation; chairman and president of the Monterey Bay Aquarium Research; vice chairman of the California Nature Conservancy in 1983; and director of the Wolf Trap Foundation in Vienna, Virginia, a society dedicated to the performing arts, from 1983 to 1989.

Packard held several patents in the area of electronics measurement and published papers in that field. He received honorary degrees from Pepperdine University, University of Notre Dame, Colorado College, the University of California, Catholic University, and elsewhere. The numerous awards he received in his lifetime for both his contributions to technology and for his philanthropic work include The Gandhi Humanitarian Award in 1988, the Presidential Medal of Freedom in 1988, and induction into the Information Industry Hall of Fame, (presented jointly to Packard and Hewlett) in 1996.

In January 1989 he created the David and Lucile Packard Center for the Future of Children as a part of his foundation. The center was established to target the health and social problems of minority children under seven years old. Packard felt the center was perhaps the most important aspect of his foundation. In September 1993, Packard retired as chairman of the board at Hewlett-Packard and was named chairman emeritus, a position he held until his death at the age of 83.

Packard died on March 26, 1996 at Stanford Medical Center, after being hospitalized for ten days with pneumonia. His entire $6.6 billion fortune was given to the David and Lucile Packard Foundation, making it one of the nation's largest philanthropic organizations.

Further Reading

There is no full-length biography of David Packard. For information about his life see magazine articles such as N.W., "The Maverick of Electronics," *Dun's Review* (August 1967); "Lessons of Leadership: David Packard of Hewlett-Packard," *Nation's Business* (January 1974); and "David Packard—1981 DPMA Distinguished Information Sciences Award Winner," *Data Management* (October 1981). Michael S. Malone discusses Packard, Hewlett, and the Hewlett-Packard Company at some length in his book *The Big Score: The Billion Dollar Story of Silicon Valley* (1985).

Additional Sources

San Jose Mercury News (March 27, 1996).
Hewlett-Packard Homepage, "David Packard 1912-1996," http://www.hp.com/abouthp/packard.htm □

Ignace Jan Paderewski

Ignace Jan Paderewski (1860-1941), Polish pianist, composer, and statesman, was one of the best-known musicians of his time, as well as a very influential statesman who helped create modern Poland after World War I.

Jan Paderewski was born in a rural section of Poland, where his father was an overseer for several large estates. Jan showed an interest in music at an early age and started to compose and to study piano with local teachers. His father sent Jan to Warsaw to enter the conservatory. His progress on the piano was not rapid, and his teacher advised him to study another instrument. He tried the flute, clarinet, bassoon, horn, and finally the trombone, which he played in the conservatory orchestra. The piano remained his chief interest, however.

After graduation Paderewski taught for a few years, then went to Berlin to continue his studies. Once again he was advised that his talent was insufficient to have a career, but undaunted, he went to Vienna to study with Theodor Leschetizky, the most famous teacher of the time. Here too he found little encouragement because the teacher felt that it was too late for the 24-year-old pianist to develop a dependable technique. Paderewski persisted and practiced prodigiously. Finally, his highly successful debut in Paris launched a career that made him for the next 50 years the best-known and best-paid pianist of all time.

Paderewski made his first American tour in 1891 and then returned regularly until the outbreak of World War I. He developed a tremendous following and amassed a fortune estimated at $10 million. His success was due in part to his personal magnetism. He was strikingly handsome, tall, and gracious, crowned with a mane of golden-reddish hair. His audiences felt, it was said, as though they were invited guests to an exclusive soiree. His grand scale of living also made him a glamorous figure. He traveled all over America in his private railway car; besides his piano, his entourage consisted of his piano tuner, secretary, valet, doctor, and chef, as well as his wife, her attendants, and dog. He maintained princely establishments in Switzerland and California, where he entertained continually and lavishly.

Paderewski's repertoire, consisting largely of familiar Beethoven sonatas and compositions by Chopin and Liszt, appealed to unsophisticated audiences as well as musicians. By many standards he was not a great pianist. His technique was limited, and his interpretations were more "poetical" and sentimental than stylistically valid, but this did not matter to his fervent followers.

Early in his career Paderewski wrote a minuet in pseudo-Mozart style. This composition became unbelievably popular. People who did not usually go to concerts went to hear him play it. A spontaneous sigh of recognition and pleasure always swept over the crowd when he started to play. He proved his competence as a composer in several large-scale works. Among these was an opera, *Manru,* successfully produced at the Metropolitan Opera in New York and also in Europe, as well as a symphony and a piano concerto. In these works his use of themes based on Polish folk music classifies him with the other nationalistic composers of the time.

During World War I Paderewski proved to be a Polish nationalist in a wider sense. Concerned with the plight of Polish victims of the war, he raised large sums of money for them through benefit concerts. He also skillfully united various Polish-American groups to work for the same end. Seeing the possibility of rejoining the parts of Poland divided between Germany, Austria, and Russia and making it a modern democracy, he gave up concertizing to implement this project. He became a friend of President Woodrow Wilson and convinced him of the importance of a strong Poland for the future peace of Europe. President Wilson included the idea in his famous Fourteen Points.

Returning to Poland as soon as the war was over, Paderewski was greeted as a national hero. He was elected president and represented Poland at the Paris Peace Conference, where he successfully convinced the other statesmen that a united Poland was necessary. He attended the signing of the Treaty of Versailles and the opening sessions of the

League of Nations. In all, he distinguished himself as a diplomat. He proved to be a masterful orator in French and English, as well as in Polish and German.

His mission accomplished, Paderewski resigned from political activities in 1921 and resumed his concertizing. Everywhere he went he was honored. When he played in Washington, D.C., for instance, he was a houseguest of President Herbert Hoover. When in Rome he always visited the pope, who was a personal friend. He continued to play until 1939, and only his death in New York in 1941 stopped his work for Poland.

Further Reading

The Paderewski Memoirs (1938) covers only the early years of Paderewski's career. A full study is Charlotte Kellogg, *Paderewski* (1956). Interesting insights are in Aniela Strakacz, *Paderewski as I Knew Him: From the Diary of Aniela Strakacz* (1949), covering his life from 1918 to his death. See also the chapter on Paderewski in Harold C. Schonberg, *The Great Pianists* (1963).

Additional Sources

Drozdowski, Marian Marek, *Ignacy Jan Paderewski: a political biography,* Warsaw: Interpress, 1981, 1979.

Landau, Rom, *Ignace Paderewski, musician and statesman,* New York: AMS Press, 1976.

Paderewski, Ignace Jan, *The Paderewski memoirs,* New York: Da Capo Press, 1980, 1938.

Phillips, Charles Joseph MacConaghy, *Paderewski, the story of a modern immortal,* New York: Da Capo Press, 1978, c1933.

Zamoyski, Adam, *Paderewski,* New York: Atheneum, 1982. □

George Padmore

George Padmore (c. 1902-1959) was a Trinidadian leftist political activist and author as well as a noted pan-Africanist ideologue.

George Padmore, whose given name was Malcolm Ivan Meredith Nurse, was educated through secondary school in Trinidad. In 1924 he went to the United States, where he studied at Columbia University, Fisk University, New York University Law School, and Howard University. He had been at first attracted to the study of medicine but then developed an interest in law. In 1927 he joined the Communist party, and his political involvement diverted him from completing his law degree. In 1928, as part of his Communist party activities, Padmore began editing the *Negro Champion,* later called the *Liberator,* in Harlem.

In 1929 Padmore was summoned to the U.S.S.R., where he became the head of the Negro Bureau of the Red International of Labor Unions. In 1931 he was sent to Germany to head the International Trade Union Committee of Negro Workers (ITUC-NW). He edited this organization's journal, *Negro Worker,* and wrote extensively. His first major work appeared at this time, *Life and Struggle of Negro Toilers,* which dealt in some depth with working conditions of blacks around the world. Steeped as he was in Communist ideology, he was very critical of black leaders whom he considered of bourgeois inclination, such as W. E. B. Du Bois and Marcus Garvey, and the political leadership of Liberia and Ethiopia.

In 1933 Padmore's position shifted dramatically. The rise of Hitler forced the termination of ITUC-NW activities in Germany. The threat of fascist Germany also forced the reworking of certain policies in Soviet Russia, including an easing of critical attacks on the imperialism of Britain and France. Padmore soon found the Communist party willing to condemn only the imperialism of Japan. Unable to subscribe to this shift in political tactics, he left the party and in 1934 was officially expelled and denounced.

During the subsequent 20 years Padmore resided primarily in England. Almost immediately after leaving the party, he moved into the pan-Africanist camp, for which he had always shown some affinity. By 1935 he had contacted his former adversary W. E. B. Du Bois and was contributing articles to *Crisis.* From this date he never joined another nonblack organization.

Padmore's *Africa and World Peace* (1937) examines the Ethiopian crisis as well as Hobson's and Lenin's views of African-European relations. That year Padmore organized the International African Service Bureau (IASB), designed to promote the pan-Africanist cause. In 1938 he began editing the IASB's journal, *International African Opinion.* During the latter years of World War II he worked on a new book, *How Russia Transformed Her Colonial Empire: A Challenge to Imperial Powers.* His purpose was to describe the Soviet method in developing the minority nations of the U.S.S.R. as a model for the Western empires. Conceived at a time when the Western powers were closely allied with Russia, the book appeared at the end of the war; and as the developing cold war hardened relations, it was coolly received.

In 1944 Padmore merged the IASB with several other organizations into the Pan-African Federation. The following year he was influential in planning the Fifth Pan-African Congress in Manchester, England. By this time he had formed a close relationship with Kwame Nkrumah. Padmore's *Africa: Britain's Third Empire* (1949), a very critical study, was banned in Kenya and the Gold Coast. By now Nkrumah had returned to the Gold Coast, and Padmore's attention was drawn more and more to the process of the emerging independent state of Ghana. On Nkrumah's invitation he wrote *The Gold Coast Revolution* (1953), a study of that colony's struggle to achieve self-government. *Pan-Africanism or Communism?* (1956) is perhaps his most significant work.

In 1957, when Ghana became fully independent, Padmore moved to Accra to become Nkrumah's personal adviser on African affairs. Padmore's return to a position of political influence was marred by the resentment some Ghanaians held toward non-Ghanaians in government. Despite these difficulties, Padmore remained in Accra in an attempt to press forward his pan-Africanist ideals. During a conference in Liberia in 1959 he was struck with acute dysentery. He flew to London for medical care but died shortly thereafter. He was buried in Christianborg Castle, Accra.

Further Reading

A good account of Padmore's life is James R. Hooker, *Black Revolutionary: George Padmore's Path from Communism to Pan-Africanism* (1967). □

José Antonio Páez

The Venezuelan general and president José Antonio Páez (1790-1873) was one of the leading heroes of Spanish American independence. He continued long afterward to play a dominant role in Venezuelan affairs.

José Antonio Páez was born on June 13, 1790, at Aricagua on the edge of the *llanos,* or plains, of Venezuela's Orinoco Basin. From a poor family, and largely uneducated, he worked for a time as a ranch hand but by the start of the independence movement in 1810 was in the livestock business on his own. He joined the patriot forces at an early date, and after 1814, when the Spaniards reoccupied the major population centers, he was instrumental in keeping resistance alive on the *llanos*. In this he was aided by his instinctive understanding of the tough *llanero* cowboys and his personal mastery of their skills of horsemanship and fighting. After Bolívar transferred his operations to the *llanos,* Páez agreed to serve under his command. But he always retained a degree of independence.

Páez fought beside Bolívar at the victory of Carabobo in 1821, the last major engagement of the war in Venezuela. While Bolívar then carried the struggle as far as Peru and Bolivia, Páez remained in Venezuela, where he exercised a wide, informal personal authority over and above the various subordinate posts entrusted to him. He had become individually wealthy, accumulating a vast amount of land both as a war bonus and through speculation. He was also gradually acquiring a veneer of civilized manners and education, although he remained a rough plainsman at heart, passionately devoted to gambling, horses, and women. He shared the widespread dissatisfaction of Venezuelans with the inclusion of their homeland in the united republic of Gran Colombia, and in 1826 he led a revolt for greater autonomy. He laid down his arms in return for an amnesty from Bolívar, but in December 1829 he agreed to head the movement that was to make Venezuela a separate republic.

Páez served as president of Venezuela from 1830 to 1835 and again in 1839-1843. Whether holding the presidency or not, however, he kept effective control of the country until 1848, ruling through what came to be called the Conservative oligarchy. His power rested ultimately on the military, but he had a close working relationship with the landed and commercial aristocracy, which saw in him a guarantee of stability. Though arbitrary at times, he usually respected legal procedures; and despite the Conservative label of his regime, it carried out such progressive reforms as the introduction of religious freedom and abolition of the state tobacco monopoly.

In 1848 President José T. Monagas, though elected with Páez's blessing, threw off his tutelage and suppressed a revolt launched by Páez in the hope of regaining power. Páez went into exile but returned in time to serve as dictator from 1861 to 1863 in the last stage of the bitter Federal War, fought between Conservatives and Liberals. Defeated in that struggle, Páez left Venezuela for good, traveling in North and South America and in 1867 publishing his autobiography in New York City. He died in New York on May 6, 1873.

Further Reading

A popularly written, not wholly accurate study is Robert Bontine Cunninghame Graham, *José Antonio Páez* (1929), which is largely adapted from the Spanish-language autobiography of Páez. Though it does not focus on Páez personally, there is considerable data on his life and times in Robert L. Gilmore, *Caudillism and Militarism in Venezuela, 1810-1910* (1964). □

Niccolo Paganini

The Italian violinist and composer Niccolo Paganini (1782-1840) inaugurated the century of the virtuoso

and was its brightest star. He laid the foundation of modern violin technique.

Niccolo Paganini was born on Oct. 27, 1782, in Genoa of musically ambitious parents. At the age of 9 he made his debut playing to an enthusiastic audience his own variations on *La Carmagnole.* He studied with Giacomo Costa. When Niccolo was taken to the famous violinist Alessandro Rolla, the latter declared he had nothing to teach him. Nevertheless, Niccolo did study violin for a while, as well as composition and instrumentation. At the age of 14 he freed himself from his father.

Paganini's career was checkered: gambling, love affairs, rumors of his being in league with the devil, and rumors of imprisonment, which he frequently denied in letters to the press. In love with a Tuscan noblewoman, he retired to her palace, where he became completely absorbed in the guitar from 1801 to 1804. On returning to the violin he performed a love duet by using two strings of the violin and then surpassed this by playing a piece for the G string alone.

In 1816 Paganini appeared in a "contest" in Milan with Charles Philippe Lafont and later remarked, "Lafont probably surpassed me in tone but the applause which followed my efforts convinced me that I did not suffer by comparison." Paganini's success in Vienna in 1828 led to a cult in which everything was a *la Paganini.* Similar triumphs followed in Paris and London. In 1833 he invited Hector

Berlioz to write a piece for him for the viola; *Harold en Italie* was the result. Paganini played frequent concerts for the relief of indigent artists. In 1836 he became involved in a Parisian gambling house; government interference led to bankruptcy and permanently damaged his health. He died on May 27, 1840, in Nice.

Even when Paganini was playing Mozart and Beethoven, he could not restrain himself from brilliant embellishments. The violinist made innovations in harmonics and pizzicato and revived the outmoded mistunings. Although he took a giant step forward in scope of technique, he paradoxically did this while holding the violin in the low 18th-century style and using a straight bow of the late Mozart period, which the Parisian violin maker Jean Baptiste Vuillaume persuaded him to give up. Although it is generally assumed that the modern technique is far "superior" to that of the 19th century, this is belied by the fact that many passages in Paganini are still scarcely playable.

Paganini's best pieces—Violin Concertos No. 1 and No. 2, the *Witches' Dance,* and the 24 Caprices—are firmly in the repertoire. Because he jealously guarded his technical secrets for fear they would be stolen, only his 24 Caprices and some music for guitar were published during his lifetime.

Further Reading

Important discussions in English of Paganini's music and playing are in E. van der Straeten, *The History of the Violin* (2 vols., 1933), and G. I. C. de Courcy, *Paganini, the Genoese* (2 vols., 1957).

Additional Sources

Casini, Claudio, *Paganini,* Milano: Electa, 1982.
Courcy, G. I. C. de (Geraldine I. C.), *Paganini, the Genoese,* New York: Da Capo Press, 1977, 1957.
Fetis, Francois-Joseph, *Biographical notice of Nicolo Paganini: with an analysis of his compositions and a sketch of the history of the violin,* New York: AMS Press, 1976.
Kendall, Alan, *Paganini: a biography,* London: Chappell: Elm Tree Books, 1982.
Prod'homme, J.-G. (Jacques-Gabriel), *Nicolo Paganini: a biography,* New York: AMS Press, 1976 1911.
Sugden, John, *Niccolo Paganini, supreme violinist or devil's fiddler?,* Speldhurst, Tunbridge Wells: Midas Books, 1980.
Sugden, John, *Paganini,* London; New York: Omnibus Press, 1986. □

Thomas Nelson Page

The American fiction writer, essayist, and diplomat Thomas Nelson Page (1853-1922), a typical Southern aristocrat, did much to cultivate the popular conception of antebellum plantation life.

orn at Oakland, Va., on an ancestral plantation, Thomas Nelson Page came from a line of leaders in tidewater Virginia: governors, a signer of the Declaration of Independence, army officers, planters, and slaveholders. Page attended Washington (later Washington and Lee) University, then won a law degree from the University of Virginia. He entered law practice in Richmond.

As early as 1877 Page was publishing dialect verses, but it was not until 1884 that he published his first story, "Marse Chan," in the *Century*—"the first Southern writer to appear in print as a Southerner," said a contemporary, one whose stories "showed with ineffable grace that although we were sore bereft, politically, we now had a chance in literature, at least." "Marse Chan" and the stories that followed romantically pictured life on antebellum plantations. Page, often using Negro dialect, set his stories in a glamorous world where "Ole Massa" and "Mistis" and "Mah Lady" rule benevolently over faithful and contented slaves. "For those who knew the old (Hanover) County as it was then, and who can contrast it with what it has become since," Page said, "no wonder it seems that even the moonlight was richer and mellower 'before the war' than it is now." Northerners as well as Southerners enjoyed reading about a region quite different from the uneasy industrialized and urbanized postwar North.

Page's stories were collected in volumes, including *In Ole Virginia* (1887) and *Bred in the Bone* (1924). Novels, similar in setting and theme, include *Two Little Confederates* (1888), a juvenile, and *Red Rock* (1894), picturing the Reconstruction South. Nonfiction works, which urged a more sympathetic understanding of the South, include *Social Life in Old Virginia* (1897) and *The Negro: The Southerner's Problem* (1904).

In 1886 Page married Anne Bruce, who died 2 years later. In 1893 he married Florence Lathrop Field. That same year he abandoned the law for writing and moved to Washington, D.C., where he lived until 1913, when he was made ambassador to Italy. He served with distinction until failing health caused him to resign in 1919; he published *Italy and the World War* in 1920.

Further Reading

Rosewell Page wrote an adulatory, although not particularly informative, biography of his brother, *Thomas Nelson Page: A Memoir of a Virginia Gentleman* (1923). In *Patriotic Gore: Studies in the Literature of the American Civil War* (1962), Edmund Wilson writes more objectively of Page as a sympathetic portrayer of the South and as a reconciler of the North and South. Jay B. Hubbell, *The South in American Literature, 1607-1900* (1954), relates Page to other popular Southern writers of his period.

Additional Sources

Field, Henry, *A memoir of Thomas Nelson Page,* Miami, Fla.: Field Research Projects, 1978. □

Walter Hines Page

The American journalist and diplomat Walter Hines Page (1855-1918) edited several distinguished periodicals and served as ambassador to Great Britain during World War I.

orn in Cary, N.C., on Aug. 15, 1855, Walter Hines Page was educated at Trinity College (now Duke), Randolph-Macon College, and Johns Hopkins University (1871-1878), concentrating his study on the Greek classics. He began his journalistic career in St. Joseph, Mo., as editor of the *Gazette* (1880-1881). He then published a series of articles based on travels in the South and the West, some appearing in the *New York World*.

In 1883 Page returned to the South, hoping to help modernize the region, but his editorial advocacy of social and political reforms in the *State Chronicle* of Raleigh, N.C. (1883-1885), aroused local animosity and he went back to New York. As editor of the *Forum* (1891-1895), *Atlantic Monthly* (1898-1899), and the *World's Work* (1900-1913), he became known as a leader of reform. He helped develop the publishing house of Doubleday, Page and Company in 1899.

Page was one of the earliest political supporters of Woodrow Wilson, and this led to his appointment as ambassador to Great Britain in 1913. He rapidly won the respect and affection of British leaders. After World War I broke out, however, he became estranged from the president. Wilson was an assiduous exponent of neutrality and mediation; Page, convinced of Germany's war guilt, favored diplomatic and economic assistance to the Allies. Occasionally his dealings with British statesmen blunted Wilson's policies. Page strongly criticized the president's measured response to the *Lusitania* sinking of 1915 and opposed the peace mission of Edward M. House in 1916.

When the United States entered the war in 1917, Page immediately urged extensive aid for the Allies, particularly naval and financial assistance. Pleased that his country had finally taken steps he deemed essential, Page remained critical and suspicious of Wilson. In Washington his extensive correspondence was generally dismissed as Anglophile propaganda. Plagued by ill health, the ambassador stayed loyally at his post until August 1918, when he could no longer carry on. He died that year in Pinehurst, N.C., on December 21.

Page wrote two books dealing with his lifelong interest in southern development, *The Rebuilding of Old Commonwealths* (1902) and the novel *The Southerner* (1909), and a third considering his profession, *A Publisher's Confession* (1905).

Further Reading

The principal works on Page are by Burton J. Hendrick, *The Life and Letters of Walter Hines Page* (3 vols., 1922-1925) and *The Training of an American: The Earlier Life and Letters of Walter H. Page, 1855-1913* (1928). For Page's relations with a leading British statesman see Sir Edward Grey, *Twenty-five Years, 1892-1916* (2 vols., 1925). His changing position in the Wilsonian entourage is traceable in Charles Seymour, ed., *The Intimate Papers of Colonel House* (4 vols., 1926-1928). See also Ross Gregory, *Walter Hines Page: Ambassador to the Court of St. James* (1970).

Additional Sources

Cooper, John Milton, *Walter Hines Page: the Southerner as American, 1855-1918,* Chapel Hill: University of North Carolina Press, 1977.

Hendrick, Burton Jesse, *The training of an American: the earlier life and letters of Walter H. Page, 1855-1913,* Atlanta, Ga.: Cherokee Pub. Co., 1990. □

Elaine Hiesey Pagels

Elaine Hiesey Pagels (born 1943), historian of religion, was a leading interpreter of the Nag Hammadi gnostic texts and their implications for understanding the origins and development of Christianity.

Elaine Hiesey Pagels was born on February 13, 1943, in Palo Alto, California, daughter of William McKinley and Louise Sophia (Boogaert) Hiesey. She received both her B.A. (1964) and M.A. (1965) from Stanford University and her Ph.D. from Harvard University (1970). Pagels joined the faculty of the department of religion of Barnard College, Columbia University, as an assistant professor in 1970. She was promoted to associate professor in 1974 and to full professor in 1976. She joined the faculty of Princeton University in 1982 as Harrington Spear Paine Foundation professor of religion. Among the honors and fellowships accorded her were a Rockefeller fellowship (1978-1979), a Guggenheim fellowship (1979-1980), and the MacArthur Prize fellowship (1980-1985).

In 1969 she married Heinz R. Pagels, a theoretical physicist. The couple had two children. In 1987, she suffered the loss of her son and then, in 1988, of her husband.

From the beginning of her academic work Pagels was interested in the implications of the Nag Hammadi gnostic texts for the understanding of the origins of Christianity. Discovered in Egypt in 1945, these texts have been regarded as among the most important archaeological discoveries in this century. They present the world views of early Christian communities which had previously been known chiefly through the refutations made by their opponents. Pagels began studying the texts as a doctoral student at Harvard and wrote her dissertation on the controversies between gnostic and orthodox Christians. In her first two books Pagels examined the ways in which gnostic Christians interpreted scripture, looking first at gnostic interpretations of the Gospel of John *Johannine Gospel in Gnostic Exegesis* (1973) and then at gnostic understandings of the letters of Paul *The Gnostic Paul* (1975). In both books Pagels demonstrated that, far from deriving their ideas solely from "inspiration," these proponents of a tradition of special revelation were

astute interpreters of scripture and used the biblical writings as sources for their own theology.

Following the publication of these works Pagels received several grants that enabled her to study the Nag Hammadi manuscripts at the Coptic Museum in Cairo, and she participated in preparing the first complete edition of the documents in English *The Nag Hammadi Library in English* (1977).

Pagels' later books introduced a general audience to the Nag Hammadi texts and to their implications for understanding the world views of competing groups of Christians during the first four centuries of the Common Era. She sought to place these world views in their socio-political contexts and to explore why certain doctrines gradually won out over others and came to be accepted as characteristic of mainstream Christianity.

In *The Gnostic Gospels* (1988) Pagels presented gnosticism as an interpretation of the life, death, resurrection, and teachings of Jesus which for many years was a powerful alternative to the interpretation set forth by the documents which became the New Testament. In contrast to the majority of early Christians, who saw God primarily through male images and who insisted on the reality of Jesus' human body and his literal (bodily) death and resurrection, gnostic Christians used both male and female metaphors for God. They distrusted the body concept in favor of inner experience, and understood Jesus' death and resurrection in a symbolic way. Each of these doctrines, Pagels argued, had important social and political implications. The views of the majority, which were better suited to the development of an institutional structure, eventually displaced the views of the gnostics, ensuring the survival of New Testament Christianity through the centuries. *The Gnostic Gospels* received the National Book Critics Circle Award in 1979 and the National Book Award in 1980. It has been issued in foreign language editions in nine countries.

In *Adam, Eve, and the Serpent* (1988) Pagels argued that Christian ideas concerning sexuality, moral freedom, and human value were developed during the first four centuries of the Common Era through commentaries on the stories of the creation and fall of human beings in Genesis 1-3. She concluded that Augustine's pessimistic view of human nature—a view shaped by his personal experiences but which he understood as normative—came to prevail as Christianity ceased to be a persecuted religion and became the religion of the emperors. This book provoked a great deal of controversy, most of it focused on Pagels' understanding of Augustine and on the question of the extent to which orthodox Western theology has canonized Augustine's idiosyncrasies.

In 1996 Pagels published *The Origin of Satan,* in which she detailed the evolution of various concepts of Satan, from fallen angel and demon to Prince of Darkness, the embodiment of evil, and the arch-enemy of God. Pagels investigated the conflict between Satan and the followers of Jesus as a parable of the struggle between love and fear or hate in every human being. The idea of Satan, in what was for her one of the weaknesses of Christianity, institutionalizes the demonization of anything strange or disagreeable and legitimizes the concept of "enemy."

In addition to these major works, Pagels published more technical articles on gnosticism and early Christianity in *Harvard Theological Review, Vigiliae Christianae, Journal of the Ancient Near Eastern Society, Journal of Biblical Literature, Signs,* and *Parabola* and in several collections. Pagels was a member of the American Academy of Religion, the Society of Biblical Theologians, and the Society of Biblical Literature. Her work as an historian of religion has shaped the way scholars and the general public understand the origins and development of Christianity.

Further Reading

Elaine Pagels' work was in dialogue with that of other historians investigating gnosticism and the origins of Christianity. Her works on gnosticism, for example, built on and corrected Hans Jonas' classic study of gnosticism, *The Gnostic Religion* (1958). Readers interested in the materials which she studied should see the *Nag Hammadi Library in English* (1977). John Dart provides an engaging narrative of the discovery, content, and importance of the Nag Hammadi texts in *The Jesus of Heresy and History* (1988).

Pagels' discoursed in great depth on her views of Augustine in "The Politics of Paradise," which appeared in the *New York Review of Books* (May 12, 1988). Discussions of her work appeared in *Newsweek* (June 27, 1988) and *Interview* (December 1995). □

Satchel Paige

Long before Jackie Robinson broke the color barrier of "organized baseball," Satchel Paige (1906-1982) was a name well known to the general sports public. As an outstanding performer in "Negro baseball," Paige had become a legendary figure whose encounters with major league players added considerable laurels to his athletic reputation.

L egend and folklore surround the career of pitcher Satchel Paige. Only a single indisputable fact emerges: Paige was one of the very best baseball players to take the mound in the twentieth century. The cruel irony of his life is that his best years were spent not in major league baseball as we know it today, but rather in the Negro Leagues and in numerous exhibition games. Paige, whose fastball was once clocked at 103 miles per hour, never performed for a major league team until he was well into his forties—and past his prime. Even so, the lanky pitcher's talent was such that he became a prominent national athlete, earning as much fame and fortune as most of the major league baseball players of his day.

"There is no question that Satchel Paige was one of the marvels of the century," wrote Robert Smith in *Pioneers of Baseball.* "When he still enjoyed all his youthful strength, Leroy Satchel Paige may well have been the fastest pitcher in the nation, or even in history. It was said that when he really poured a baseball in to the plate with his full strength, it might tear the glove off the catcher.''

Satchel Paige was born Leroy Robert Paige on July 7, 1906, in Mobile, Alabama. The seventh of eleven children of John and Lula Paige, he grew up poor and needy in the segregated South. He spent his childhood days tossing rocks at tin cans and anything that moved, even—occasionally—people. At the tender age of seven, Paige went to work at the Mobile train station, earning tips for carrying travelers' luggage. *Reader's Digest* correspondent John O'Neil noted that the enterprising youngster ''fixed up a rig so he could carry more bags than any other kid, thus earning the name 'Satchel Tree.''' The nickname, a bit shortened, stuck into adulthood.

Paige was ten years old when he began playing organized baseball with his elementary school team. The sport provided the only reason for him to attend school, from his point of view. As Smith put it, ''Books just drove him to playing hooky, as they did many boys that age. But baseball consumed his soul. He loved to throw and he loved to hit and he seemed to do both equally well.'' The love of baseball could not keep Paige out of trouble, however. At twelve he was caught snatching some toy rings from a dime store. That episode and his truancy combined to earn him a sentence to the Industrial School for Negro Children in Mount Meigs, Alabama.

Satchel Paige (right)

Practiced the Skills That Made Him a Master

The industrial school turned out to be just the right place for Paige. Freed from the distractions of his hometown—and under stricter discipline—he became educated *and* played baseball for the school team. He stayed in Mount Meigs until he was seventeen, practicing the baseball skills that would turn his arm into ''the tool that would bring him his fame and fortune,'' to quote O'Neil. After leaving the school, he set out to find work in professional baseball.

Paige had considerable skills at an early age. His principal pitch was the fastball, but he was also known for inventing the crafty ''hesitation pitch.'' What set him apart from other pitchers was his control. As late as the 1950s, a teammate of Paige's from the St. Louis Browns told *Sports Illustrated:* ''You hear about pinpoint control, but Paige is the only man I've ever seen who really has it. Once he threw me six strikes out of 10 pitches over a gum wrapper.'' This precision was not merely a ''gift,'' or natural talent, but was rather the result of Paige's obsessive practice throughout his youth, teen years, and early adulthood. ''We had a lot of players when I came up could throw the ball hard, way harder than I could, as far as that's concerned, but they couldn't gain control,'' Paige told *Sports Illustrated.* ''It's such a thing as I practiced all the time; I just *practiced* control. Anything you practice you begin to come good at, regardless of what it is.''

Paige began his baseball career in 1923 with the Mobile Tigers, an all-black semi-pro team. He earned a dollar a game. He also picked up spare change by pitching batting practice for the local white minor league team. By 1925 Paige had established himself in the fledgling Negro Leagues as a pitcher with the Chattanooga, Tennessee Black Lookouts. From $50 a month his first year, he soon was earning $200 a month with bonuses. Paige discovered that baseball was more than just a game: it was *entertainment,* and it was a *business.* He adapted his methods to meet those challenges. As an entertainer, he clowned and dawdled to and from the mound, saving his seriousness for pitching. As a businessman, he was constantly on the lookout for teams that would pay him more and exhibition games that would bring in extra cash.

A Star in a Segregated Game

Most professional pitchers work only every four or five days and then rest at season's end. Perhaps the most amazing aspect of Paige's career is the fact that he pitched almost every day, all four seasons of the year. It is difficult to chart his career with any sort of precision, because he hopped from team to team in the Negro Leagues and was sent out on ''loan'' to other clubs by his parent team of the moment. These appearances were augmented by numerous exhibition games and barnstorming trips across country, as well as work with winter leagues in Cuba, Venezuela, and Puerto Rico. An *Ebony* magazine contributor estimates that in his career Paige pitched some 2,500 games and won 2,000 of them—with 300 shutouts and 55 no-hitters.

In 1927 Paige pitched in Alabama for the Birmingham Black Barons for $275 a month. The following year he moved to the Nashville Elite Giants and toured in the off-season with a barnstorming group led by Babe Ruth. Barnstorming gave Paige the opportunity to test his mettle against white baseball players—in fact, the very best in the white major leagues. As Smith put it, "Satch pitched against some of the mightiest sluggers in the lily-white major leagues and left them all marveling. But he never had a chance to pitch against Babe Ruth, who seemed to be needed on the bench whenever Satch was scheduled to pitch. In a game on the West Coast, against the Babe Ruth All-Stars, Satch struck out twenty-two major-leaguers—and that would have been a new record in the major leagues."

Such accomplishments assured Paige a national audience of both races for his talents. In the early 1930s he joined the Pittsburgh Crawfords, one of the top Negro League teams, for a salary of $750 per month. In 1934 he served one season at top salary with an all-white independent league team out of Bismarck, North Dakota. It was with the Bismarck team that Paige set a never-to-be-duplicated record of pitching 29 games in a single month. After one year in North Dakota, Paige returned to the Crawfords. He left them again in 1937 to play in the Dominican Republic for the princely wage of $30,000—a salary on par with the best white major leaguers of the time.

At the beginning of the 1940s, Paige was reported to be earning in the neighborhood of $500 per game pitched. The 1941 summer season in the United States found him with the Kansas City Monarchs of the Negro League. With Paige in their ranks, the Monarchs were able to advance to the Negro World Series in 1942 and again in 1946. During the off-season the pitcher again toured the exhibition game circuit, facing everyone from Dizzy Dean to a youngster named Joe DiMaggio. Smith wrote: "The Monarchs hung on to old Satch until the call came for him to try out with the Cleveland club in the American League. Satch pitched Sundays for the Monarchs and weekdays almost anywhere the dollars beckoned. He kept count one year and said he pitched in 134 games."

A Belated Invitation to the Majors

Baseball's "color barrier" was broken in 1946 when Jackie Robinson was signed by the Brooklyn Dodgers. Within a short time, most of the other major league clubs had recruited black players as well. Paige was 40 years old when baseball was integrated. Most owners considered him too old to be a force in the big leagues. During the 1948 season, however, Cleveland Indians owner Bill Veeck approached Paige at mid-year about playing for the Indians. The team was in the midst of a pennant race, and Veeck, for one, thought Paige might help clinch a pennant.

On August 13, 1948, Satchel Paige became the seventh black player recruited into the major leagues when he pitched a 5-0 shutout for Cleveland over the Chicago White Sox. Veeck and Paige combined their talents as entertainers to enliven Paige's appearance in the American League. In a well-orchestrated plot, the two men told reporters that Paige was uncertain of his age and might be as old as fifty. Paige

concocted a story about a goat eating the family Bible that held his birth certificate. Age notwithstanding, Paige pitched to a 4-1 record for the 1948 Indians with a 2.47 earned run average. In the World Series that year, he pitched two-thirds of an inning and did not allow a hit.

Paige was back with the Indians the following year, but his record in 1949 fell to 4-7, and he was released at season's end. He returned to barnstorming until 1951, then signed a contract with the lackluster St. Louis Browns. He stayed with St. Louis, pitching mostly in relief situations, until the team left town in 1954. Smith wrote of Paige: "His incredible stamina had begun to fade." Stomach problems almost forced him to retire, but he staged a comeback—at age fifty—with the minor league Miami Marlins. Once again in Miami he capitalized on his age, requiring a rocking chair in the dugout when he appeared.

A Home in the Hall of Fame

Paige's last hurrah as a pitcher occurred in 1965. He had applied for a pension from major league baseball that year and discovered that he lacked only three innings of work to qualify for the pension. Paige was granted the chance to work his last three innings with the Kansas City Athletics, owned by Charlie Finley. At the age of 59 he took the mound and shut out the Boston Red Sox through the required three innings. As he left the field, the lights went out and the crowd lit 9000 matches and sang songs to him. It was a fitting epilogue to a long and varied career.

Subsequent years found Paige serving as a batting coach with the Atlanta Braves and as an executive for the minor league Tulsa Oilers baseball team. He settled down in Kansas City with his second wife and eight children, completing an autobiography called *Don't Look Back* and adding his recollections to historical accounts of the Negro Leagues. He died of emphysema on June 5, 1982.

Paige rarely expressed any bitterness about his career, although he had every right to feel cheated by a segregated society. Many critics agree that it was actually American baseball that was the loser in the Paige saga. Any number of major league teams would have done better with Paige in their ranks when he was in his prime. Marginal teams might have won pennants; championship teams might have extended their domination. For Paige's part, he earned as much or more money than many major leaguers of his day, and he was among the most famous—if not *the* most famous—of the Negro League baseball stars. *New York Times* correspondent Dave Anderson wrote: "To the end, Satchel Paige had too much dignity to complain loudly about never being in the big leagues when he deserved to be."

At his death Paige was as well known for his "Satchel's Rules for Staying Young" as he was for his sports achievements. The "Rules" were first published in a magazine article in 1948 and were later repeated and quoted widely. The last of them even has made it into *Bartlett's Quotations*. In order, the rules are: 1. Avoid fried meats, which angry up the blood. 2. If your stomach disputes you, lie down and pacify it with cool thoughts. 3. Keep the juices flowing by jangling around gently as you move. 4. Go very light on the vices such as carrying on in society. The social rumble ain't restful. 5. Avoid running at all times. 6. Don't look back; something might be gaining on you.

Satchel Paige was voted into the Baseball Hall of Fame in 1971.

Further Reading

Hotdogs, Heroes and Hooligans: The Story of Baseball's Major League Teams, edited by Michael L. LaBlanc, Visible Ink Press, 1994, pp. 537-57.

Paige, Leroy ''Satchel,'' and David Lipman, *Maybe I'll Pitch Forever,* Grove, 1963.

Ribowsky, Mark, *Don't Look Back: Satchel Paige in the Shadows of Baseball,* Simon and Schuster, 1994.

Smith, Robert, *Pioneers of Baseball,* Little, Brown, 1978, p. 135-49.

Ebony, September 1982, pp. 74-78.

Newsweek, June 1, 1981, p. 12.

New York Times, June 10, 1982, p. D-20.

Reader's Digest, April 1984, pp. 89-93.

Sports Illustrated, June 21, 1982, p. 9. □

John Knowles Paine

John Knowles Paine (1839-1905), American composer and music educator, was especially instrumental in organizing music courses for the college curriculum.

John Knowles Paine was born on Jan. 9, 1839, in Portland, Maine. At 18 he made his debut as an organist and shortly afterward went to Berlin to study organ, composition, and orchestration. Before leaving Europe in 1862, he toured Germany as an organist. Upon his return to America he was made organist and music director of Harvard University. He soon offered to give a series of free lectures at Harvard and, after some debate, was granted permission. Before long Paine was offering, without pay, noncredit courses in musical form, harmony, and counterpoint. His courses eventually were approved for degree credit, and in 1873 Paine was appointed assistant professor. Two years later he was promoted to full professor.

The music school at Harvard evolved largely out of Paine's work, and Harvard's example was shortly followed by other universities. Through his students Paine influenced American composition for decades. He held his chair at Harvard for 30 years, then resigned to devote himself to composition. He died on April 25, 1905, while at work on a symphonic poem dealing with Abraham Lincoln.

Paine was one of the earliest Americans to have his compositions frequently performed. By 1899 the Boston Symphony had played his works more than 18 times. For the Philadelphia Exposition in 1876, Paine was commissioned to write a ''Centennial Hymn,'' and in 1893 he composed ''Columbus March and Hymn'' for the World's Columbian Exposition in Chicago. Paine directed the first performance of his oratorio *St. Peter* in his hometown of Portland in 1873. His cantata *Song of Promise* was presented in 1888 at the Cincinnati Festival. In 1904 his music for Sophocles's *Oedipus Tyrannus* won a gold medal at an international concert in Berlin, and that same year he composed ''Hymn to the West'' for the St. Louis World's Fair.

Paine's First Symphony was premiered in Boston in 1876 but was not published until 1908. His Second Symphony, *Spring,* reflected the composer's fondness for program music. He wrote a number of symphonic poems based on Shakespeare and an overture to *As You Like It.* His opera *Azara* was never staged, although it was given twice in concert form. Paine wrote his own libretto for *Azara,* which did not prove particularly effective theatrically, although his ballet music from the score and the three Moorish dances have been performed occasionally on orchestral programs.

Further Reading

Authoritative accounts of Paine's life and work are contained in John Tasker Howard, *Our American Music* (1931; 4th ed. 1965), and in Gilbert Chase, *America's Music, from the Pilgrims to the Present* (1955; 2d ed. 1966). Irving L. Sablosky, *American Music* (1969), and H. Wiley Hitchcock, *Music in the United States: A Historical Introduction* (1969), discuss Paine briefly.

Additional Sources

Schmidt, John C., *The life and works of John Knowles Paine,* Ann Arbor, Mich.: UMI Research Press, 1980. □

Thomas Paine

Thomas Paine (1737-1809) was an English-born journalist and Revolutionary propagandist. His writings convinced many American colonists of the need for independence.

Thomas Paine came to America in 1774, an unknown and insignificant Englishman. Yet 2 years later he stood at the center of the stage of history, a world figure, an intimate of great men, and a pamphleteer extraordinary.

Paine was born in Thetford, England, on Jan. 29, 1737, the son of a poor farmer and corsetmaker. He attended the local school until, at the age of 13, he withdrew to help his father. For the next 24 years he failed or was unhappy in every job he tried. He went to sea at 19, lived in a variety of places, and was for a time a corsetmaker like his father, then a tobacconist, grocer, and teacher. His first wife died in 1760, a year after their marriage; he married again in 1771 but separated 3 years later. His appointment as excise collector in 1762 was lost in 1765 because of an improper entry in his reports. Reinstated a year later, he was dismissed again in 1774, probably because he wrote a petition to Parliament for higher salaries for excisemen.

Journalist in America

Paine's move to America resulted from a London meeting with Benjamin Franklin, who provided letters of introduction. Paine arrived in Philadelphia in November 1774 and began writing for the *Pennsylvania Magazine,* of which he became editor for 6 months. His contributions included an attack on slavery and the slave trade. His literary eloquence received recognition with the appearance of his 79-page pamphlet titled *Common Sense* (1776). Here was a powerful exhortation for immediate independence. Americans had been quarreling with Parliament; Paine now redirected their case toward monarchy and to George III himself—a "hardened, sullen tempered Pharaoh." The pamphlet revealed Paine's facility as a phrasemaker—"The Sun never shined on a cause of greater worth"; "Oh ye that love mankind . . . that dare oppose not only tyranny but the tyrant, stand forth!"—but it was also buttressed by striking diplomatic, commercial, and political arguments from separation from Britain.

Common Sense was an instantaneous success. Newspapers in other colonies reprinted all or part of it. It was translated into German and reprinted in England, Scotland, Holland, and France. Its American sale of 120,000 copies in 3 months gave it a circulation equivalent to over 6 million today. It was hailed by George Washington for working a "powerful change" in sentiment toward Britain. Clearly, it prepared Americans for the Declaration of Independence a few months later.

For the remainder of the Revolution, Paine's energies remained with the American cause. He served with Washington's army during the retreat across the Jerseys; the sol-

diers' dispiritment lay behind his powerful *The Crisis* papers, 13 of which appeared between December 1776 and April 1783. Again Paine's phrasemaking was impressive: "These are the times that try men's souls. The summer soldier and the sunshine patriot will . . . shrink from the service of his country; but he that stands it now, deserves the love and thanks of man and woman." In later papers Paine attacked Tories, profiteers, inflationists, and counterfeiters.

Paine made little money from his journalistic successes. For 2 years he was secretary to Congress's Committee on Foreign Affairs. When he lost that post in 1779 for disclosing confidential data, Pennsylvania, whose 1776 Constitution he had helped establish, appointed him clerk of the Assembly. In this capacity he wrote the preamble to the state's law abolishing slavery. When Washington appealed for supplies, Paine organized a solicitation, contributed $500 from his own meager salary, and helped organize the Bank of North America to finance the supplies. However, his trip abroad to solicit additional funds lost him his Assembly clerkship.

On April 19, 1783, Paine concluded his *Crisis* series on a note of expectation: "'The times that tried men's souls' are over—and the greatest and completest revolution the world ever knew, gloriously and happily accomplished." Fears for the American union, however, belied Paine's optimism. He had appealed to Virginia in a pamphlet, *Public Good* (1780), to surrender its western land claims to the national government so that Maryland would ratify the Articles of Confederation. In letters in the *Providence Gazette and Country Journal* (November 1782 to February 1783) he urged Rhode Island to approve a national tariff to give Congress adequate financial resources.

England and France

After the Revolution, Paine lived rather quietly on the farm in New Rochelle that Congress had granted him and in Bordentown, N.J. He was working on several inventions. One, a pierless iron bridge to cross the Schuylkill River, took him abroad in 1787 to secure advice from the French Academy of Sciences and English technical assistance. Though he made the warm acquaintance of Edmund Burke, the two fell out when, in 1790, Burke published his attack on the French Revolution and defense of hereditary monarchy. Paine's reply, *The Rights of Man* (1791, 1792), vigorously defended republican principles and virtually called Englishmen to arms to overthrow their monarchy.

The new publication was a journalistic success, with 200,000 copies sold within a year, including French and German translations. The English government proscribed it as seditious and outlawed Paine. He escaped imprisonment by fleeing to France, where he took part in drawing up a new French constitution.

Elected a member of the National Convention, Paine irritated French radicals by protesting the execution of Louis XVI. During the Reign of Terror he was imprisoned. His 11-month confinement was ended by the intercession of the American minister, James Monroe, but Paine publicly expressed bitterness at Washington's failure to secure earlier release in a *Letter to George Washington* (1796).

Paine's most controversial writing was *The Age of Reason* (1794, 1795), a direct attack on the irrationality of revealed religion and a defense of deism. Despite Paine's unequivocal affirmation of a belief in the Creator, the book was denounced as atheistic, was suppressed in England, and evoked countless indignant responses. Like his other writings, its circulation was phenomenal, with French, English, Irish, and American editions. Modern critics recognize the book as one of the clearest expositions of the rationalist theism of the Enlightenment and a reservoir of the ideology of the Age of Reason.

Return to America

When Paine returned to America in 1802, he was attacked for his criticism of Washington and his denunciation of traditional Christianity. He was ostracized by former friends such as Sam Adams and Benjamin Rush, harassed by children in New Rochelle, N.Y., deprived of the right to vote by that city, and even refused accommodations in taverns and on stages. Even his wish to be buried in a Quaker cemetery was denied. He was interred on his farm on June 10, 1809, two days after his death. In a bizarre finale his remains were exhumed by William Cobbett, who planned to rebury them with ceremony in England, but the project failed, and the remains, seized in a bankruptcy proceeding, disappeared.

Posterity did better by Paine. New Rochelle erected a monument on the original gravesite; England hung his picture in the National Portrait Gallery and marked his birthplace with a plaque; France erected a statue of him in Paris;

and Americans placed his bust in the Hall of Fame at New York University. But Paine's real monument was the enormous impact of his writings on his own age and their enduring popularity. Expressive of the Enlightenment's faith in the power of reason to free man from all "tyrannical and false systems . . . and enable him to be free," Paine's vision of universal peace, goodness, and justice appeared even more revolutionary as nationalistic aspirations and bourgeois complacency replaced the enthusiasm and cosmopolitanism of the 18th century.

Further Reading

There is no definitive edition of Paine's writings. Moncure D. Conway, ed., *The Writings of Thomas Paine* (4 vols., 1894-1896), the most scholarly version, omits a great deal. The most complete edition is Philip S. Foner, ed., *The Complete Writings of Thomas Paine* (2 vols., 1945), but it omits several pieces and is inaccurate and incomplete in other respects. The best single volume is Harry H. Clark, ed., *Thomas Paine: Representative Selections* (1944; rev. ed. 1961), which contains Clark's illuminating analysis of Paine's ideas, his literary style, and a critical bibliography of writings about Paine.

Most biographies of Paine are inadequate. Alfred O. Aldridge, *Man of Reason: The Life of Thomas Paine* (1959), is impartial, incorporates the latest scholarship, and corrects many errors which appear in the standard biography, Moncure D. Conway, *Life of Thomas Paine* (2 vols., 1892). Conway's work, upon which most other biographers have drawn, is partisan and adulatory but was extensively researched and contains most of the materials for a reconstruction of Paine's life. Among the later, popular biographies which add little to Conway's work are S.M. Berthold, *Thomas Paine* (1938); Frank Smith, *Thomas Paine* (1938); and William E. Woodward, *Tom Paine* (1945). The semifictionalized *Citizen Tom Paine* (1943) by Howard Fast is one-sided and deals largely with the years 1774 to 1787. Frederick J. Gould, *Thomas Paine* (1925), is brief and reasonably well balanced. Hesketh Pearson, *Tom Paine: Friend of Mankind* (1937), humanizes Paine by accentuating some of his failings. □

Ian K. Paisley

Political leader and minister of religion, Ian K. Paisley (born 1926) played a significant role in the bitter strife that plagued Northern Ireland for decades.

Ian Kyle Paisley, born on April 6, 1926, was reared in the tradition of evangelical Protestantism. His father, a Baptist minister, ordained him in 1946 when he was 20 years old and by 1951 the young Paisley felt able to found his own church, the Free Presbyterian Church of Ulster, and to make himself its moderator.

Publicity was gained by outbursts against Catholicism and the "Romeward" inclinations he attributed to other Protestant churches, and he rose to prominence attacking both ecumenism and the granting of full civil rights to a disadvantaged sector that was largely Roman Catholic. Dismissed as a rabble-rousing bigot in established Unionist and

Orange circles, he eventually challenged these with his own version of both political party and Orange Order.

In 1951 he acquired local notoriety by adopting the cause of Maura Lyons, a 15-year-old Catholic girl who left her home to join his church. His reputation widened when he protested in Rome against the Second Vatican Council in 1962, and the following year he opposed the lowering of the Belfast City Hall flag in respect at the death of Pope John XXIII. With growing momentum his politico-religious drive mounted in the 1960s: against the tricolor of the Irish Republic being used in the 1964 election campaign; against better relations with the Republic on the occasion of Dublin premier Sean Lemass's visit to Belfast in January 1965; against Terence O'Neill's conciliatory and modernizing policies; against the general assembly of the Presbyterian Church in 1966; against the Northern Ireland Civil Rights Association in 1968, and against the Peoples Democracy movement in 1969. In all he mobilized the genuine fears of working people that their traditional safeguards within the United Kingdom and against Catholic clerical influence were being undermined. In 1966 he had founded his Protestant Unionist Party (to become the Democratic Unionist Party in 1971), a couple of shadowy organizations—the Ulster Constitution Defence Committee and the Ulster Protestant Volunteers—and the *Protestant Telegraph,* a publication promoting anti-Catholic and anti-nationalist virulence.

In 1969 he unsuccessfully challenged Terence O'Neill in the latter's Bannside constituency, but after O'Neill's retirement in 1970 Paisley won the seat and held it till the end of the Northern Ireland Parliament in 1972. He also

entered Westminster as Member of Parliament for North Antrim in 1970. After the fall of the Belfast Parliament in March 1972, Paisley became a member of the Northern Ireland Assembly (1973-1975), where he opposed the Sunningdale agreement which provided for a power-sharing executive worked out by Brian Faulkner. He subsequently became a member of the Northern Ireland Constitutional Convention, which he and his United Ulster Unionist Council dominated during its short lifetime, 1975-1976. In 1979 he became Democratic Unionist Member of the European Parliament for Northern Ireland, topping the poll in this three-seat constituency.

These considerable political successes were accompanied by the expansion of his church organization, which grew in numbers and locations. Though his school education did not prepare him for university entrance, his biblical scholarship was respected and his *An Exposition of the Epistle to the Romans Prepared in a Prison Call* is well regarded. A powerful preacher with a dominating physique and voice, he played on traditional anti-Catholicism and emphasized biblical fundamentalism, always being outspoken and always seeing himself in historic roles.

A practiced television performer, quick to make a telling phrase or newsworthy comment, he kept his profile high, bringing his wrath to bear on familiar targets: London-Dublin talks of any kind; Catholic influences in the European Union; Catholic characteristics of the Irish Republic; any power-sharing arrangement with nationalists inside Northern Ireland; and British security policy in Northern Ireland, which he always labeled half-hearted and ineffective. He himself advocated armed preparedness and dabbled with a "Third Force" vigilante movement to protect loyalists.

Paisley helped to make the Northern Ireland Assembly of James Prior work, although he opposed its "cross-community support" requirements and argued for the devolution of increased powers to a majority party. He was able to present a more statesmanlike image, the colorful phrase and witty aside disarming his critics, his firm determination to uphold the Union and biblical truth continuing to inspire his followers. His wife Eileen (married in 1951) and three of their four children played supporting political roles. Yet to many observers he still epitomized the bigotry and violence of Protestant extremism which fueled an equal Catholic extremism. Many pointed to the image of Northern Ireland he helped to create—an image of bitterness and intransigence—which repelled potential friends and served well the propaganda of his avowed enemies. His destructive successes—including a large share in ending the premiership of Terence O'Neill—were visible: positive achievements were harder to discern.

From the mid-1980s through the mid-1990s Paisley's presence continued to make an impact. In 1985 he addressed the founding meeting of Ulster Resistance, whose members were later involved in arms deals. In October 1988 he was beaten and removed from a European Parliament meeting in Strasbourg, France, after displaying a sign that read "John Paul II Antichrist" as the Pope spoke. The Clinton administration in the U.S. prohibited Paisley from visiting the White House due to his militantly anti-Catholic attitudes.

Paisley's uncompromising viewpoints have mostly served him well. His popularity was demonstrated in 1989 when he received more votes to the European Parliament than any politician in United Kingdom electoral history. In the subsequent European Parliament election of 1994, he obtained more than in 1989.

Paisley remained a forceful spokesman and magnet for the right wing, responsible for compelling many of his opponents to become more conservative. Meanwhile, the two extremes in Northern Ireland continued to feed each other. The moderate majority, unable to unite, was condemned to endure their conflict.

Further Reading

There is only one biography, by a Catholic barrister, Patrick Marrinan, *Paisley: Man of Wrath* (1973), though an unpublished Ph.D. thesis of Queen's University Belfast, by D. F. Taylor, "The Lords of Battle: an Ethnographic and Social Study of Paisleyism in N. Ireland" (1983) throws much light on the phenomenon of his movement. Paisley's own political writings include *No Pope Here* (1968), *The Case against Ecumenism* (1971), *United Ireland Never!* (1972), and, with P.D. Robinson and John D. Taylor, *Ulster: the Facts* (1982). C. Carlton, editor, *Bigotry and Blood, Documents on the Ulster Troubles* (1977) contains some of Paisley's views. There is a perceptive short article on Paisley by one of the most tireless European observers of the Northern Ireland situation: René Frechet, "Ian Paisley et L'Irlande du Nord" in *Trema* (1985). For additional information see the Democratic Unionists Web site, http://www.dup.org.uk/paisley.htm; *Irish Voice* (April 12, 1994); and *New Statesman* (November 29, 1996). □

František Palacký

The Czech historian and statesman František Palacký (1798-1876) was the father of 19th-century Czech nationalism. He is known for his monumental *History of Bohemia* and his federalistic concept of *Austro-Slavism*.

František Palacký was born at Hodslavice, Moravia, on June 14, 1798, into a petit bourgeois Protestant family with strong Hussite traditions—a fact of considerable influence on his future outlook. After he attended school in nearby Kunewald (where he learned German), his father, a schoolmaster, sent him to Hungary to study at the Evangelical schools of Trencsén (now Trenčin in Slovakia) and Pozsony (Pressburg, Bratislava). Particularly important was his stay at Pozsony (1812-1820)—then Hungary's administrative center—for there he came into contact with the already powerful Magyar national movement and with the nascent and rising Slavic (Slovak, Czech, pan-Slav) national consciousness, as represented by the works of such intellectuals as J. Palkoviç, J. Benedicti, J. Kollár, and P. Šfařik. From Pozsony he moved to Vienna, where he spent 3 years familiarizing himself with Immanuel Kant's philosophy of

history and publishing a few studies on esthetics and literature. Then he decided to turn to the study of history, driven by the realization that only a clear and scholarly unfolding of the great moments of Czech history could awaken Czech national consciousness and save the nation from total extinction.

In 1823 Palacký moved to Prague, where he was received with great expectations, both by the older Czech scholars (for example, J. Jungmann and J. Dobrovský) and by the patriotic members of the Czech aristocracy, whose patronage (particularly of counts F. and K. Sternberg) permitted him to devote himself fully to scholarly and patriotic activities. After becoming editor of the journal of the Bohemian Museum Society (1827) and completing the publication of medieval Czech annals (1829), Palacký was named Bohemia's official historian. In this capacity he undertook the task of writing the first great synthesis of Czech history.

The first volume of this work (*Geschichte von Böhmen; History of Bohemia*) was printed in German in 1836. Subsequent volumes appeared irregularly in both Czech and German and carried Bohemia's history up to the extinction of its real independence in 1526. Its impact was immediate and phenomenal. It shook Czech national consciousness, particularly by depicting the nation's past as an unceasing struggle against German imperialism and violence. Palacký contrasted this with Czech (Slav) attachment to individual freedom and democracy, and he interpreted the Hussite movement (the central episode of his work) as his nation's effort to liberate the soul from the spiritual bondage of the Romano-Germanic Middle Ages.

Although working for the regeneration of his nation, Palacký did not call for Czech political independence. A nation to him was a kinship group that need not be organized into a state. He felt that small states (such as an independent Bohemia would be) are too much at the mercy of their stronger neighbors. He looked favorably upon the unity of the Austrian Empire and regarded its existence as a European necessity. At the same time, however, he was working for its federative reorganization.

Palacký elaborated his concept of federalism in Austria ("Austro-Slavism") in a plan presented to the Diet of Kroměřiz (Kremsier) in 1848. This plan—calling for the creation of seven autonomous national units in the empire—was in part unrealistic, but with a little goodwill it could have served as a point of departure toward a "new Austria."

Following the failure of the revolutions of 1848, Palacký retired from active political life. Becoming more and more discouraged during the 1860s, he slowly turned to Russia and pan-Slavism. In his *Idea of the Austrian State* (Czech 1865, German 1866), he again offered federalism—now based on the historical provinces—as a solution. Palacký died in Prague on May 26, 1876.

Further Reading

A fine monograph on Palacký, Joseph F. Zaçek's *Palacký: The Historian as Scholar and Nationalist* (1971), is based on primary Czech sources previously unavailable in English. Extensive material on Palacký's life and his influence on the Czech people is in Samuel Harrison Thomson, *Czechoslovakia in European History* (1943; rev. ed. 1953). Robert J. Kerner, ed., *Czechoslovakia* (1940), also considers Palacký. Robert W. Seton, *A History of the Czechs and Slovaks* (1943), briefly surveys his entire career. □

Kostes Palamas

The Greek poet Kostes Palamas (1859-1943) played a dominant role in the development of modern vernacular, or demotic, Greek literature. He drew inspiration from popular mood and expression and gave voice to the aspirations of a people long isolated from their ancient traditions.

Kostes Palamas was born on Jan. 8, 1859, at Patras, the son of a local magistrate, whose death orphaned the boy at the age of 6 and left him in the care of an uncle in Missolonghi. There Palamas received his primary and secondary education, moving to Athens in 1875 with the intention of studying law; he left the University of Athens, however, without completing a degree. In the early 1880s Palamas struggled to support himself as a journalist and literary critic; during these years he became involved with the Demotikistes, moving quickly to the vanguard of this literary school that sought to replace the anachronistic "official" language of government and education with the popular idiom. Palamas published his first collection of lyric verse, entitled *Tragoudia tes Patridos mou* (*Songs of My Fatherland*), in 1886.

The following year Palamas married Maria Valvi, by whom he had three children. The poet wrote perhaps his most moving expression of personal grief in "The Tomb," a poem in memory of his son Alki, who died at the age of 9. During these years filled with struggle and polemic, Palamas produced scores of newspaper articles, and he translated the New Testament and the works of several western European authors into modern Greek. He published a well-known short story, "A Man's Death," in 1895, and issued a collection of poems, *Iambs and Anapaests,* in 1897. That year Palamas was named secretary general of the University of Athens, a position he held until his retirement in 1926.

Asalefte Zoe (*Life Immovable*), Palamas's next collection of verse, appeared in 1904. It exhibited his increasing variety of mood and metrical form. The intensely felt thematic polarities of his work (love of life/mortal anguish; patriotic feeling/bitter denunciation of his homeland; love of past glories/break with any cult of the Greek past; Hellenism/Christianity) became more and more insistent. In 1907 Palamas published *Dodecalogos tou Gyftou* (*The Twelve Lays of the Gypsy*), perhaps his most important work. The Gypsy poet, an outcast possessed only of his vital language, wanders from creative tasks to love and to the death of gods and of the ancients, finally becoming a prophet and uniting at last science, nature, and man. A second work with epic horizons appeared in 1910, *I flogera tou Vasilia* (*The King's Flute*), set in latter-day Byzantine splendor and tracing the pilgrimage of Greek emperor Basil II to Athens and the Shrine of the Virgin Mary.

Palamas is also remembered for a drama, *Trisevgene* (*The Thrice Noble or Royal Blossom*), a highly lyrical piece. The poet, virtually a national hero, died in Athens on Feb. 28, 1943.

Further Reading

Palamas's works were translated by George Thomson as *The Twelve Lays of the Gypsy* (1969) and by Frederic Will as *The King's Flute* (1967), the latter with partial collections of the earlier poems translated by A. E. Phoutrides (1919) and T. Stephanides (1925). Biographical sources in English include R. J. H. Jenkins, *Palamas* (1947), and the "Introduction" to Thomson's translation. □

Giovanni Pierluigi da Palestrina

The Italian composer Giovanni Pierluigi da Palestrina (ca. 1525-1594) was one of the greatest masters of Renaissance music and the foremost composer of the Roman school.

Born Giovanni Pierluigi, the composer is known as Giovanni Pierluigi da Palestrina from the name of his birthplace, a hill town near Rome. It is assumed without historical evidence that Giovanni was a choir singer at the church of St. Agapit in 1532, when he was but 7 years old. When the bishop of Palestrina, Cardinal della Valle, was transferred to the basilica of S. Maria Maggiore in Rome in 1534, the 9-year-old chorister may have followed him, but the earliest cathedral record naming Giovanni carries the date 1537. Except for a brief return to his birthplace, Giovanni served at S. Maria Maggiore until his nineteenth birthday. During this formative period he probably trained with one of the Franco-Flemings in Rome: Robin Mallapert, Firmin Le Bel, or Jacques Arcadelt.

In 1544 Palestrina was summoned to his native town as organist and singing master of the local church. During the following half dozen years he married, fathered the first of his three sons, and began composing. Most important for his future career was the attention accorded his music by the new bishop of Palestrina, Cardinal del Monte. When he became Pope Julius III in 1550, one of his first acts of the following year was to appoint Palestrina choirmaster of the Julian Chapel of St. Peter's.

By 1554 Palestrina had published his first book of Masses and dedicated it to Pope Julius, who rewarded him with a coveted assignment to the Pontifical (Sistine) Choir at St. Peter's. By custom all singers of this choir were unmarried, and they were admitted only after rigorous examination. Since the Pontiff had ignored both traditions, Palestrina's designation was viewed with little enthusiasm. When Pope Julius died a few months later, Paul IV dis-

missed the composer but awarded him a small pension for his services. He also approved Palestrina's appointment as choirmaster at the church of St. John Lateran, where Roland de Lassus had been active only the year before.

Palestrina conducted the chorus at St. John Lateran from 1555 until 1560. But stringent economies and political intrigues made it difficult for him to achieve his artistic aims. After a particularly unpleasant incident about food and lodging for his choirboys, Palestrina left his post without notice. Such bold behavior did not seem to affect adversely his future career, for he became choirmaster at S. Maria Maggiore in 1561. Working conditions in this basilica were considerably better than at the Lateran, and Palestrina remained reasonably content for the next 5 years.

In 1566 Palestrina became music director of the newly formed Roman Seminary. Although he received a smaller salary than at S. Maria Maggiore, he was in part compensated by permission to enroll his sons Rodolfo and Angelo at the institution. What seems to have been initially a suitable arrangement did not, however, work out to his satisfaction, for he left the seminary very soon thereafter. For the next 4 years he was music director for Cardinal Ippolito d'Este II, an outstanding patron of the arts.

In March 1571 Palestrina was appointed choirmaster at the Julian Chapel, where he stayed for the rest of his life. On at least two occasions attempts were made to lure him from Rome. In 1568 Emperor Maximilian had invited him to the imperial court at Vienna. And in 1583 the Duke of Mantua, an amateur musician of talent and frequent correspondent

of the composer, invited Palestrina to his court. To both invitations the master set such a high price on his services that it might be assumed that he never seriously considered leaving the Eternal City.

Reforms in Music

Intermittently from 1545 to 1565 the Council of Trent considered the reform of Church music, even contemplating the ban of all polyphony from the liturgy. According to one report, Palestrina saved the art of music by composing the *Missa Papae Marcelli* according to the requirements of the council. But the role alleged to have been played by this Mass is undoubtedly mythical. Palestrina's reputation makes it likely, however, that he was consulted on decisions about music. We do know that his works were performed before, and approved by, Cardinal Borromeo, who was charged with securing a liturgical music free of secular tunes and unintelligible texts.

Palestrina's influence with the Roman hierarchy is also witnessed by a papal order of 1577. He and a colleague, Annibale Zoilo, were directed to revise the *Graduale Romanum* by purging the old tunes of barbarisms and the excrescences of centuries. Palestrina never did complete this laborious task, and the Medicean Gradual of the early 17th century, sometimes thought to be his work, is actually the labor of others.

His Works

Palestrina's voluminous works encompass the most important categories cultivated in the late Renaissance: Masses, motets, and madrigals. Of these three the madrigals played a small role, for his orientation was overwhelmingly on the side of sacred music. His 250 motets include settings of psalms and canticles, as well as exclusively liturgical items such as 45 hymns, 68 offertories, 13 lamentations, 12 litanies, and 35 Magnificats. Most of these compositions reveal the so-called Palestinian style, in which stepwise melodic movement dominates expansive leaps, and diatonic tones in both horizontal and vertical combinations are preferred to their chromatic counterparts.

Important as are the motets, they are decidedly secondary to the 105 Masses for which Palestrina was justly admired. He essayed various types: the archaic tenor *cantus firmus* Mass; the paraphrase Mass; the Mass erected on hexachord and other contrived subject; and the "parody" Mass, which elaborates a preexistent polyphonic model. True to his preferences Palestrina avoided secular models, opting for the tunes of the Church or at least tunes associated with sacred texts. He was not modern in the same way as his Venetian colleagues with their polychoral pieces. His fuller identification with the older Franco-Flemish masters, however, made him the representative of that illustrious group best remembered by posterity.

Further Reading

The best comprehensive study in English of the life and works of the composer is Henry Coates, *Palestrina* (1938). His style and historical importance are treated in Gustave Reese, *Music in the Renaissance* (1954; rev. ed. 1959), and Knud Jeppesen,

The Style of Palestrina and the Dissonance (1927; 2d rev. ed. 1946). For general historical background, Donald Jay Grout, *A History of Western Music* (1960), is recommended.

Additional Sources

Cametti, Alberto, *Palestrina,* New York: AMS Press, 1979.
Coates, Henry, *Palestrina,* Westport, Conn.: Hyperion Press, 1979. □

William Paley

The English theologian and moral philosopher William Paley (1743-1805) wrote works in defense of theism and Christianity that achieved great popularity in the 19th century. He is acknowledged as one of the founders of the utilitarian tradition.

William Paley was born in Peterborough in July 1743. His father, William, was vicar of Helpston, Northamptonshire, and, later, headmaster of the Giggleswick School. William attended Giggleswick prior to entering Christ's College, Cambridge, in 1759, where he had a brilliant career, excelling in mathematics and debating. After a brief period as a school-teacher Paley was elected a fellow at his college in 1766 and tutor in 1768. He remained at Cambridge until his marriage in 1776. Subsequently Paley, who had been ordained in 1767, accepted a series of ecclesiastical appointments which were less distinguished than his abilities because of his liberal political views.

Paley was the author of four books. He published *The Principles of Moral and Political Philosophy* in 1785. *Horae Paulinae,* a defense of the New Testament, appeared in 1790. *A view of the Evidences of Christianity,* issued in 1794, achieved great fame. *Natural Theology; or Evidences of the Existence and Attributes of the Deity Collected from the Appearances of Nature* was published in 1802. He died in Lincoln on May 25, 1805.

Paley's most successful work was *Natural Theology,* which presented in a clear and lucid manner all of the evidences for the existence of God. Philosophers and theologians have always distinguished between knowledge of the fact that a supreme being exists and knowledge of what such an existence would involve. Paley, as a liberal theologian and thinker, was close to the position of medieval negative theology and 17th-century deism, believing that man can know that the Supreme Being exists but that he can know nothing of His attributes. Thus Paley attempted to establish that the evidence for the existence of God exceeds the objections. Paley's method was analogical reasoning. His most famous illustration was that a reasonable man will admit that experience establishes that the intricate and connected parts of a watch can be produced only by an intelligent designer. If evidence suggests that the workings of the present universe are more complicated and interdependent than those of a watch, then a reasonable man must con-

clude, by analogy, that it is highly probable that God exists as the designer of the universe. Indirectly, said Paley, a reasonable man can attribute personality and power to such a being because these are the experienced conditions of a designer. The weakness of Paley's argument consists in his failure to question the analogy between a watch and a world.

Further Reading

Paley's writings are collected in *The Works of William Paley* (5 vols., 1819). His *Natural Theology: Selections* was edited with a useful and extensive introduction by Frederick Ferré (1963). Paley and his work are discussed in Leslie Stephen, *History of English Thought in the Eighteenth Century* (2 vols., 1876), and less extensively in John Petrow Plamenatz, *The English Utilitarians* (1949).

Additional Sources

LeMahieu, D. L., *The mind of William Paley: a philosopher and his age,* Lincoln: University of Nebraska Press, 1976. □

William S. Paley

Founder and chairman of the Columbia Broadcasting System, William S. Paley (1901-1990) was called alternately a broadcast programmer par excellence, an impresario, a super salesman, and the father of modern broadcasting. Because of his instinctive un-

derstanding of what appeals to the popular taste, Paley was considered by many to be a genius of mass entertainment programming.

William S. Paley was born the son of a prosperous cigar manufacturer in Chicago on September 28, 1901. From an early age his father groomed him to take over the family business, the Congress Cigar Company. Determined that William would be prepared for his future role, Sam Paley sent his son to the Wharton School of Finance and Commerce at the University of Pennsylvania and then had him work at every level within the company. William Paley quickly proved himself to be a knowledgeable tobacco buyer and a gifted salesman. While still a teenager he skillfully resolved a company strike in the absence of his father and uncle, who were away on a business trip.

During the summer of 1925 Paley was again left in charge of the business. This time he decided to experiment with radio advertising. He invested $50 of the company's money to sponsor the ''La Palina Hour'' on a local Philadelphia radio station, WCAU. A singer and an orchestra were included in the price. His uncle Jake was furious when he noticed the expenditure upon his return and abruptly canceled the sponsorship. Listener response to the cancellation was immediate, and a surprised Sam Paley decided to check the books. The sales of La Palina cigars, he found, had risen dramatically during the period that the advertisement had

been on the air. The Congress Cigar Company became one of the largest advertisers on the station.

Building Up CBS Radio

By 1928 WCAU had become affiliated with a new and faltering radio network called the Columbia Broadcasting System (CBS). On the brink of bankruptcy, the CBS owners approached Sam Paley, who decided to buy into the network and secure a position in this promising field for his son. As the new president of CBS, William Paley found his fledgling company in disarray and began the task of reorganization. Paley faced formidable odds. His chief rival, the NBC radio network, was already quite powerful and could draw on the enormous resources of its parent company, RCA.

Unlike NBC, CBS did not own any stations and had only 16 affiliated stations in its network. For Paley the challenge was invigorating. In a brilliant business maneuver he offered stations an irresistible enticement to join his network—free programming. Previously both NBC and CBS had charged affiliated stations for all sustaining (non-sponsored) programs supplied by the network. Under the new contracts affiliated stations would receive these programs free of charge in return for making available to the network certain time blocks for sponsored programs. This disarmingly simple plan revolutionized station-network relations, and CBS doubled the number of its affiliated stations by the year's end. In addition, advertisers found the network's ability to guarantee a fixed lineup of stations for the airing of their programs very attractive.

Within a brief span of time CBS became a viable network, but William Paley would not be satisfied until his company surpassed all of its competitors, particularly NBC. He understood that to accomplish this goal he would need to create the best programs and to attract the best advertisers. His abilities as a salesman were impressive. Paley relentlessly courted George Roy Hill, a tobacco industry executive and one of the largest sponsors on radio at that time, to advertise on CBS. Hill found CBS much more open than NBC to direct advertising. Paley allowed advertisers to say what they wanted about their products, including mentioning prices. As NBC followed suit, radio grew quickly into a full-blown commercial medium.

Paley's powers of persuasion extended to entertainers as well. They soon began to flock to the network. Paley personally discovered and hired singers Bing Crosby and Kate Smith. Realizing the importance of those who represented his network on the air, he carefully cultivated the star system at CBS. He was always well-briefed on the needs of his stars before he met with them. Partly as a result of this lavish treatment, Paley was able to include such vaudeville comedians as Jack Benny, Fred Allen, and George Burns and Gracie Allen in his 1933 CBS lineup.

As a programming strategist, Paley had few equals. Intuitively he knew what would appeal to the general public. Paley also recognized, however, that government watchdogs would hold broadcasters accountable for serving the public interest. He shrewdly devoted a portion of the CBS schedule to developing informative and experimental programs. Since two-thirds of the network's time was unsponsored, this prudent move was not costly and did much to promote the prestige of CBS. Thus, under his stewardship CBS became the center of most creative activity in radio during the late 1930s. A regular program entitled *Columbia Workshop* led the way in generating technical innovations in sound effects and the use of filters. It also produced some of the most critically acclaimed radio dramas of the time, such as Archibald MacLeish's *Fall of the City,* a verse play on the rise of fascism.

Developing the CBS News Team

Since CBS could not for the moment hope to overtake NBC in entertainment programming, Paley gradually built up the CBS news and public affairs division. He sensed that area would be a potential minefield for the network. Biased coverage of the news or the expression of strongly worded opinions on controversial topics might open the door to government intervention. Thus in 1930 Paley hired Ed Klauber, a former newspaperman, to help him define and enforce broadcast news standards. Aside from stressing the importance of objectivity and balanced news reporting, they asserted that reporters were to be news analysts, not news commentators. Paley did not want his news people to express their opinions. As he saw it, their job was to clarify the news, giving equal weight to both sides of every issue. These high standards became the guidelines governing broadcast news coverage in the United States, and upon this basis CBS was able to build a reputation that lured some of the period's most talented journalists to join its news team. Later on, however, these same standards were to prove a source of endless contentions between the network and newspeople who argued that some issues were not always equally balanced.

As World War II broke out in Europe, the popularity and prestige of such exceptional CBS reporters as Edward R. Murrow, Charles Collingwood, Howard K. Smith, and Eric Sevareid raised the CBS image to new heights. Paley's support for his news division was seemingly boundless. When he went to England in 1944 as the chief of radio broadcasting with the Psychological Warfare Division he became a close personal friend of Murrow. Following the war, Paley strongly encouraged Murrow's pioneering efforts as he virtually invented the television documentary. The result was *See It Now,* a program which permitted Murrow to explore a different issue every week. The Murrow-Paley friendship waned as Murrow took on a growing number of controversial topics. When Murrow went after Senator Joseph McCarthy, Paley did not intervene, but was careful to distance himself from the broadcast. By 1957 Paley decided to edge the program out. It occupied a valuable time slot, and he told Murrow that he could not take the stomach pains it gave him anymore. After the game show scandals of 1959, Paley moved to repair the tarnished CBS image by scheduling a similar program called *CBS Reports.* This time, however, Murrow was out. Paley would not allow a strong voice like Murrow's to man the helm again.

The climate of broadcasting had changed after the war and so had Paley. At CBS the number of sponsored pro-

grams had doubled by 1945. Commercial considerations slowly became paramount to Paley. He hired Frank Stanton from the audience research arm of CBS to become its new president, and Paley was named chairman. In 1949, as the shadow of television loomed over radio, Paley raided the NBC Sunday night lineup of stars, a coup which finally gave him the lead in the ratings he had long desired. The news division went into a slow decline at CBS as it was forced to take a back seat to entertainment programs.

Paley also moved to protect his network on other fronts. With the onslaught of the communist scare in the early 1950s, Paley instituted a loyalty oath among his employees. He was the first network executive to bow to the pressures from advertising agencies to establish a blacklist of performers and other artists believed to be communist sympathizers. During this period the agencies were extremely powerful, since they produced a sizable portion of television programs. Paley disliked this dependence on the agencies and was gradually switching the burden of production over to the network. The other networks soon followed his lead.

Success in Television and Recordings

A man with refined taste, Paley collected paintings and art objects from all over the world. He served as president and later chairman of the Museum of Modern Art. When CBS headquarters—or Black Rock, as it is known—was constructed in the mid-1960s, Paley became deeply involved in the choice of materials and the details of design. The dark granite structure later won several architectural awards. In programming, CBS offered some of the most outstanding dramas and documentaries on television and broke new ground in the early 1970s with such daring situation comedies as *All in the Family* and *Maude.* Yet Paley never allowed his personal taste to interfere with his business sense. He believed that the public taste would only accept a limited number of high quality programs. A large percentage of CBS programs, therefore, were aimed at what has been termed the "lowest common denominator," a concept developed by a CBS programming vice-president. The strategy was an enormously successful one, as CBS consistently outdistanced its rivals in the ratings until the mid-1970s when Paley became remote from the details of programming.

Under Paley's leadership CBS Inc. grew from a floundering company in 1928 to a giant corporation that surpassed $4 billion a year in revenue when he retired as chairman in 1983. Acquiring more than 40 other companies during his 50-year tenure as chief executive officer, CBS branched out into various fields of communication and education. Only two years after taking over CBS, Paley formed the Columbia Concerts Corporation, a talent and booking agency that also helped recruit performers for its radio programs.

In 1938 he bought the American Record Corporation, which was to become his most lucrative venture outside of broadcasting. The record company, later known as CBS/Records, received a tremendous boost in its rise to the top of the industry when CBS Laboratories developed the revolutionary 33-1/3 long-playing album in 1948. CBS diversification increased rapidly in the 1960s after Paley agreed to expand the company's base beyond broadcasting as a precaution against government intervention. After that its interests included manufacturing television sets, publishing books and magazines, distributing toys, and for a time CBS owned the New York Yankees baseball team. After his retirement in 1983 Paley continued on as a director and chairman of the executive committee of CBS. His stock holdings in the company amounted to nearly two million shares in 1985. After a corporate shakeup the following year, Paley returned to CBS as interim chairman of the board.

By 1987 Paley's health was failing and his CBS empire was shrinking. The network was losing about $20 million a year and its program ratings were in last place. Laurence Tisch took firm control of the network in January 1987 when he became chief executive officer. Although Paley was infirm, he was determined to remain active at CBS. Until the end of his life he continued to make public appearances and report to his office at Black Rock headquarters.

William S. Paley died of a heart attack on October 26, 1990, at the age of 89. After learning of Paley's death, CBS news anchor Dan Rather said of him, "He was a giant of 20th-century business, a man committed to excellence."

Further Reading

Paley's contribution to broadcasting is best understood within the context offered by the most complete account of the development of radio and television, Eric Barnouw's three volume masterwork *A History of Broadcasting in the United States* (1966, 1968, 1970). For more in-depth biographical information, two books with divergent judgments on many of his decisions as chairman of CBS are David Halberstam's *The Powers That Be* (1977) and William Paley's *As It Happened* (1978). In addition, Fred Friendly's *Due To Circumstances Beyond Our Control . . .* (1967) and Les Brown's *Television: The Business Behind the Box* (1971) are recommended for their insight into television programming at Paley's CBS. An insightful look at Paley and his network is in Lewis J. Paper, *Empire: William S. Paley and the Making of CBS* (1987).

Additional Sources

Smith, Sally Bedell, *In All His Glory: The Life of William S. Paley* (1990).
Macleans (November 5, 1990). □

Andrea Palladio

The buildings of the Italian architect Andrea Palladio (1508-1580) were the most refined of the Renaissance period. Through them and his book on architectural theory he became the most influential architect in the history of Western art.

Roman architecture of the early 16th century had developed a mature classicism in the work of Donato Bramante and his followers. With the sack of Rome in 1527 young architects, such as Michele Sanmicheli and Jacopo Sansovino, brought the style to northern Italy. Andrea Palladio with further study of ancient Roman architecture, refined the classical mode to produce an elegant architecture befitting the opulent culture of the Veneto in the third quarter of the century. The aristocratic, mercantile society of Venice desired a splendid and sumptuous art to express pride in its accomplishments.

Andrea di Pietro dalla Gondola, called Andrea Palladio, was born in Padua on Nov. 30, 1508. In 1521 he was apprenticed for 6 years to a local stonecutter; 3 years later he broke the contract and moved to Vicenza, where he was immediately enrolled in the guild of masons and stonecutters. His first opportunity came about 1538 while he was working as a stone carver on the reconstruction of the Villa Cricoli, near Vicenza, owned by the local humanist Giangiorgio Trissino, who had a classical school for young Vicenzan nobility. Trissino recognized Andrea's ability and took him into his home and educated him. Trissino gave Andrea his humanist name Palladio as a reference to the wisdom of the Greek goddess Pallas Athene.

Early Architecture

Probably Palladio's first independent design was the Villa Godi (ca. 1538-1542) at Lonedo. Its simplified, stripped-down style reveals very little influence of ancient architecture, but its emphasis on clean-cut cubical masses

foreshadows his mature style. The Casa Civena (1540-1546) in Vicenza, with its paired Corinthian pilasters above the ground-floor arcade, is more in the Roman High Renaissance manner, perhaps inspired by the publications of Sebastiano Serlio.

In 1541 Trissino took Palladio to Rome to study the ancient monuments. At this time Palladio began a magnificent series of drawings of ancient buildings. The incomplete Palazzo Thiene (commissioned 1542, constructed ca. 1545-1550) in Vicenza is in the style of Giulio Romano, particularly in its heavy rustication of the ground floor and the massive stone blocks superimposed on the window frames of the main story. As Giulio Romano was in Vicenza in 1542, it is possible that he contributed to the design, since Palladio was still designated as a mason in the contract. The grandiose project, never completed, for the Villa Thiene (before 1550) at Quinto was influenced by Palladio's study of ancient Roman sanctuaries and baths. The only completed pavilion has a temple front facade, his first use of a temple front to decorate a villa, which became a hallmark of his style.

For many years the city of Vicenza had been considering how to refurbish its Gothic law court, the Palazzo della Ragione. In 1546 Palladio's project to surround the old building with loggias was approved, and he was commissioned to erect one bay in wood as a model. In 1547 and 1549 Palladio made further trips to Rome. In 1549 he began to construct two superimposed, arcaded loggias around the Palazzo della Ragione (completed 1617), known ever since as the Basilica Palladiana. Each bay of the loggias is composed of an arch flanked by lintels supported by columns. The motif of the arch flanked by lintels, although it was first used by Bramante and was popularized in Serlio's book, has been called in English the Palladian motif since Palladio used it on the Basilica.

Mature Style

Palladio created on the mainland around Venice a magnificent series of villas for the Venetian and Vicenzan nobility. The most renowned is the Villa Capra, or the Rotonda (1550-1551, with later revisions), near Vicenza. It is a simplified, cubelike mass capped by a dome over the central, round salon and has identical temple front porches on the four sides of the block. The absolute symmetry of the design was unusual in Palladian villas; the architect explained that it permitted equal views over the countryside around the hill on which the villa sits.

The city of Vicenza was almost completely rebuilt with edifices after Palladio's designs. The Palazzo Chiericati (now the Museo Civico) is a two-story structure facing on the square with a continuous Doric colonnade on the ground floor after the idea of an ancient Roman forum; the walled and fenestrated central section of the upper floor is flanked by Ionic colonnades. The facade of the Palazzo Iseppo Porto (ca. 1550-1552) is based on Bramante's Palazzo Caprini in Rome, but the plan is Palladio's version of an ancient Roman house with an entrance atrium and a large peristyle, or court, on the central axis behind the building block.

In 1554 Palladio made his last trip to Rome and in the same year published a fine guidebook to the antiquities of Rome, *Le antichità di Roma*. During the next year a group of Vicenzans, including Palladio, founded the Accademia Olimpica for the furthering of arts and sciences. In 1556 Daniele Barbaro, a Venetian humanist, published a commentary on the architectural treatise of the ancient Roman writer Vitruvius for which Palladio made the illustrations. At the same time Palladio designed for Barbaro and his brother at Maser (ca. 1555-1559) one of the loveliest of all villas. The Villa Barbaro (now Volpi) is set into a gentle hillside. The central, two-storied casino with a temple front of Ionic half-columns and pediment is flanked by single-story arcades connecting it to the service buildings, for the villa also served as a farm. In the 16th century the nobility of the Veneto attempted to improve the agricultural productivity of the land, and their villas served as residences during the periods when they supervised the farming.

Palladio's first architecture in the city of Venice was the commencement of the monastery of S. Giorgio Maggiore, whose refectory he completed (1560-1562). This was followed by the church of S. Giorgio Maggiore (1565-1610), which has a basilical plan with apsidal transept arms and a deep choir. The facade (designed 1565, executed 1607-1610), with its temple front on four giant half columns flanked by two half temple fronts on smaller pilasters, is Palladio's solution to the translation of a Christian church design into the classical mode. He applied a similar facade to the older church of S. Francesco della Vigna (ca. 1565). The Palazzo Valmarana (1565-1566) in Vicenza uses giant Corinthian pilasters, except at the ends, to emphasize the planar aspect of the facade adapted to its urban location.

Late Style

Palladio's treatise on architecture, *I quattro libri dell' architettura* (1570), consists of four books. The first is devoted to technical questions and the classical orders, the second to domestic architecture, the third to civic architecture, and the fourth to ecclesiastical architecture. It is illustrated by ancient architecture and the works of Bramante and Palladio himself.

The truncated Loggia del Capitaniato (1571-1572) in Vicenza has giant half columns with an arcaded loggia below. In many of its details this design reveals an unclassical spirit. The short side, however, is modeled on an ancient triumphal arch and commemorates the victory of Lepanto in October 1571, which occurred while the loggia was being executed. As the chief architect of Venice, Palladio designed the festival triumphal arch and the decorations to welcome the entry of King Henry III of France to Venice in July 1574.

To fulfill a vow of salvation from the disastrous plague of 1575-1576 the Venetian Senate commissioned Palladio to build the Church of the Redentore (1576-1592). Perhaps influenced by the Church of the Gesù in Rome, it is a wide basilica with side chapels and a trilobed crossing with deep choir. The facade, approached by monumental stairs, is a more unified version of his earlier church facades. For the Villa Barbaro at Maser he designed a separate chapel, the

Tempietto (1579-1580), modeled on the ancient Roman Pantheon.

Palladio executed a theater, the Teatro Olimpico (1580), in Vicenza for the Accademia Olimpica. Based on the design of an ancient Roman theater, the auditorium is segmental in plan, facing a stage modeled on a Roman *scaenae frons*. The perspective stage scenery in wood and stucco was added by Vincenzo Scamozzi after Palladio's design. On Aug. 19, 1580, Palladio died in Vicenza.

His Influence

Through his treatise Palladio exerted a dominant influence on architecture for over 2 centuries, particularly in northern Europe. There were two major periods of Palladianism in England. In the first half of the 17th century Inigo Jones converted English architecture to the Italianate Renaissance by introducing Palladio's style, seen best in the Banqueting Hall, Whitehall, London, and the Queen's House, Greenwich. The second wave of Palladianism was fostered in the early 18th century by the Earl of Burlington. Palladio's treatise was published in 1715 in an English translation by Giacomo Leoni. American architecture felt the impact in the late 18th and early 19th century, as seen in Thomas Jefferson's Monticello.

Further Reading

An excellent study of Palladio in English is James S. Ackerman, *Palladio* (1966). For a discussion of the villas see Ackerman's *Palladio's Villas* (1967). The fundamental study of Palladio's theory and its relation to his practice is in parts 3 and 4 in Rudolf Wittkower, *Architectural Principles in the Age of Humanism* (1949; 3d ed. rev. 1962). The Centro Internazionale di Storia dell'Architettura in Vicenza is sponsoring in English a *Corpus Palladianum* of about 30 volumes, the first of which is Camilo Semenzato, *The Rotonda of Andrea Palladio* (trans. 1968).

Additional Sources

Puppi, Lionello, *Andrea Palladio,* Boston: New York Graphic Society, 1975, 1973. □

Ricardo Palma

Ricardo Palma (1833-1919) was a Peruvian essayist and short-story writer. He composed a long series of witty and picaresque tradiciones, or historical prose tales, whose plots and incidents were for the most part derived from the rich wealth of Peruvian literature and history.

Ricardo Palma was born in Lima on Feb. 7, 1833, son of a well-to-do family. He grew up amid turbulent political events and reached adolescence as the romantic tradition in Peru was reaching its zenith. At 15 he published his first verses and became the editor of a political and satiric newssheet called *El Diablo* (The Devil). He was educated in a Jesuit school and went on to the University of San Carlos, where his studies were cut short by a 6-year period of voluntary service in the Peruvian navy.

During these years the young writer was composing romantic dramas (which he later repudiated) and poetry. Palma's first book of verse, *Poems,* appeared in 1855. In 1860 a political reversal sent Palma into exile in Chile, from where he returned to Lima, under an amnesty, in 1863. The colorful *tradiciones* he had published in foreign newspapers and magazines had also now appeared in Peru. His reputation was now established and his literary personality clearly defined.

A trip to Europe in 1864-1865 was marked by the publication of two new volumes of verse, *Harmonies* and *Lyre,* in Paris. Palma returned to Lima in 1865 and became involved in political affairs that engaged him in public service until 1876. Yet during this time he continued to amass an excellent personal library and compose out of the history and legend of Peru's past his charming, spicy, always sprightly *tradiciones.* These were collected in separate volumes during his lifetime, the first selection of his *Peruvian Traditions* appearing in 1872 and the next five at irregular intervals over the next decade. These collections form the nucleus of the six-volume edition of the *Complete Peruvian Traditions,* although from 1883 until his death Palma continued to add new sketches to the original volumes and reordered and revised the individual collections.

The War of the Pacific (1879-1883) between Chile and Peru disrupted Palma's life and resulted in the virtual destruction of his own library as well as that housed in the Peruvian National Library. After the war Palma was named director of the National Library, a post he held until his retirement in 1912. He died in Lima on Oct. 6, 1919.

Further Reading

There is no full-length study of Palma in English. Biographical information is in Harriet de Onis's introduction to Palma's *The Knights of the Cape* (trans. 1945). For background on his life and work see Alfred Coester, *The Literary History of Spanish America* (1916; 2d ed. 1928); Arturo Torres-Rioseco, *The Epic of Latin American Literature* (1942); Enrique Anderson Imbert, *Spanish-American Literature: A History* (trans. 1963; rev. ed. 1969); and Jean Franco, *An Introduction to Spanish-American Literature* (1969). □

Alexander Mitchell Palmer

As U.S. attorney general, Alexander Mitchell Palmer (1872-1936) was instrumental in creating the "red scare" of internal Communist subversion after World War I and was responsible for the illegal arrest of thousands of aliens.

Born in Moosehead, Pa., on May 4, 1872, A. Mitchell Palmer graduated *summa cum laude* in 1891 from Swarthmore College. He then read law for 2 years and became a prominent attorney in Pennsylvania. A moralist and moderate reformer, he was elected to the U.S. Congress as a Democrat in 1908 and again in 1910 and 1912. His personal charm and debating skill, together with his championship of tariff reform, woman's suffrage, and abolition of child labor gave him a considerable reputation. Yet the partisan, dogmatic, and combative qualities which ultimately compromised his career were already evident.

After declining appointment as secretary of war because of his Quaker beliefs, Palmer ran unsuccessfully for the U.S. Senate in 1914. President Woodrow Wilson then named him to a judgeship on the U.S. Court of Claims, but he rejected the appointment because of his unwillingness to abandon active politics. In 1917 Palmer returned to government service as alien property custodian and was soon enveloped in controversy over his partisan appointments and loose construction of the law.

Appointed attorney general in March 1919, Palmer used the office to further his presidential aspirations. He perceived, among other things, that public sentiment was turning against labor, a group he had supported generously in the past. Prompted partly by J. Edgar Hoover, then a division chief in the Department of Justice, Palmer freely issued injunctions against strikers and soon charged striking miners, steelworkers, and railroad workers with promoting economic and social revolution. Meanwhile, influenced partly by the bombing of his own home, and again encouraged by Hoover, he authorized the unconstitutional dragnet arrest of thousands of suspected alien radicals. The action is generally regarded as the most flagrant violation of civil

liberties up to that time. By most estimates, the bitter reaction of liberals and organized labor cost him the presidential nomination in 1920.

Palmer stayed on in Washington and practiced law. He maintained a peripheral interest in politics through the 1920s, and in 1932 he composed the more conservative sections of the Democratic platform. He died in Washington on May 11, 1936.

Further Reading

Stanley Coben, *A. Mitchell Palmer, Politician* (1963), is a full and generally convincing account of Palmer's career. It should be supplemented, for the attorney general years, by Robert K. Murray, *Red Scare: A Study in National Hysteria* (1955), and William Preston, Jr., *Aliens and Dissenters* (1963). □

Arnold Daniel Palmer

Arnold Palmer (born 1929) amassed 92 golf championships in professional competition of national or international stature by the end of 1994. Sixty-one of the victories came on the U.S. PGA Tour. He was the first person to make $1 million playing golf.

Golf legend Arnold Palmer displayed unquestionable skill on the course, but even more importantly, he had much charisma. He almost singlehandedly brought golf out of the elite country clubs and into the consciousness of mainstream America. Throughout his career, Palmer attracted legions of fans—known collectively as "Arnie's Army"—who hung on his every shot, celebrating his successes along with him, and suffering his failures. Even in the twilight of his career, with failures on the links far outnumbering successes, Arnie's Army remained as loyal as ever.

Arnold Palmer was born in Youngstown, Pennsylvania, and grew up in nearby Latrobe, an industrial town not far from Pittsburgh. His family had lived in the area since the early 1800s. Palmer's father, Milfred "Deacon" Palmer, worked at the Latrobe Country Club for more than 40 years, working his way up from grounds keeper to teaching pro. "Deac," as he was called, gave Arnold his first set of golf clubs when he was three years old. Arnold learned the fundamentals of the game on Latrobe's nine-hole course, which he would sneak onto at every opportunity. By the time he was eight, he was playing regularly with the older boys who worked as caddies at the course, and he became a caddie himself at the age of 11.

Attended Wake Forest

Palmer starting winning tournaments while he was still in high school. While starring for the Latrobe High School golf team, he lost only one match in four years. He also won three Western Pennsylvania Junior championships and three Western Pennsylvania Amateur titles during his high school days. During his senior year, Palmer met Bud

would become a household name, and was well on his way to becoming the most popular golfer ever to play on the professional circuit.

1960 Victories Brought Fame

Two spectacular come-from-behind wins in major tournaments cemented Palmer's reputation as a gambler who was never out of contention. In the 1960 Masters, Palmer birdied the final two holes to steal a certain victory from rival Ken Venturi. At the time, golf was just beginning to receive regular television coverage, and Palmer's good looks, combined with his dramatic performance on the course, instantly made him a national hero. Palmer mounted an even more astonishing comeback in the 1960 U.S. Open in Denver, where he scored a 65 in the final round to win the tournament from seven strokes—and 14 players—out of the lead. His fans began to believe that he was never too far behind to win. Palmer's style was an aggressive one. He hit the ball hard, with an awkward-looking swing that often left him careening off-balance, much to the delight of the weekend hacks in the audience whose own swings it resembled.

Those two stunning 1960 victories, along with seven other wins that year, established Palmer as the golden boy of golf. Tournament victories continued to come in droves over the next few years. Wins in major tournaments included the British Open in 1961 and 1962, and the Masters in 1962 and 1964. His galleries became so big that they became an annoyance to fellow players. His fans would stampede to the next fairway before the other players in his group had finished out the hole. They sometimes went so far as to heckle Palmer's opponents, especially archrival Jack Nicklaus. Each of Palmer's trademark mannerisms utterly mesmerized Arnie's Army—the way he hitched up his sagging pants, pitched his half-smoked cigarettes onto the grass, and grimaced at every missed putt.

Palmer quickly became not only the game's biggest star, but one of the nation's biggest celebrities. Never in the past were ordinary people drawn to a golf champion the way they were to Palmer. He became the most sought after person in the world for product endorsements. As his popularity grew, so did his interests outside of golf. Palmer became an avid pilot, and flew his own private jet to tournaments. He also dabbled in television and movie acting, and produced his own golf show. He became an author as well, churning out a new golf book every few years. As money rolled in from both golf and endorsements, Palmer became the richest athlete in the world, with a financial empire that spanned the golf equipment, clothing, printing, insurance, dry cleaning, and investment industries. His companies had branches in Australia, Japan, and Europe. Including earnings from his various businesses, Palmer's income soared to more than $1 million a year.

Named Athlete of the Decade

Although he continued to win the occasional tournament through the rest of the decade, the 1964 Masters was Palmer's last victory in a major event. Dry periods became more frequent and lasted longer. At times, it seemed as if his

Worsham, whose brother Lew was a professional golfer. At Worsham's urging, Palmer accepted a golf scholarship to Wake Forest College in North Carolina. He enrolled at Wake Forest in 1947, and quickly began winning, or coming close to winning, every amateur and intercollegiate tournament in sight.

During Palmer's senior year in college, his best friend and roommate, Bud Worsham, was killed in a car accident. Shaken by Worsham's death, Palmer left school and joined the Coast Guard, where he served for three years. In 1954 Palmer began selling painting supplies for a Cleveland company to support his participation in amateur golf. His victory in the National Amateur championship that year prompted Palmer to begin contemplating the idea of turning professional, making golf a job rather than an expensive and time-consuming hobby. In November of 1954 he turned pro and signed a sponsorship contract with the Wilson Sporting Goods Company. About a month later, he married Winnie Walzer, whom he had met while playing in an amateur tournament and proposed to three days later.

In 1955 Palmer won his first important professional tournament, the Canadian Open, earning $2,400, his first big golf paycheck. He captured three tournaments the following year, and in 1957 took four more. He earned nearly $28,000 that year, making him the number five money-winner on the tour. Palmer won three tournaments during each of the next two seasons. One of his 1958 victories was the prestigious Masters, a tournament held annually in Augusta, Georgia. 1960 was the pivotal year in Palmer's golf career. Before the 1960 season was over, Arnold Palmer involvement in business was distracting him from golf. He sold several of his businesses off to the Radio Corporation of America (RCA) in the mid-1960s, but kept an active role in managing them. In 1969 Palmer was forced to withdraw from the PGA championship because of a hip injury, leading many people to believe that his brilliant career was at an end. After taking several months off to recuperate, however, he came back to win the last two events of the season. After another lengthy drought that lasted for most of the 1970 season—during which the Associated Press named him Athlete of the Decade—Palmer won the 1971 Bob Hope Desert Classic and three other tournaments that year.

Palmer won a couple of minor PGA titles during the 1970s, but overall his play was erratic. His Army, on the other hand, remained huge and loyal. In 1980 Palmer entered the Senior PGA tour, and enjoyed a bit of a career revival. He won the first Senior tournament he ever entered, the 1980 PGA Seniors championship. He also captured the 1981 United States Golf Association (USGA) Senior Open, and took the PGA Seniors again in 1984. In 1985 Palmer won the Senior Tournament Players Championship by 11 strokes, the largest margin of victory ever produced in that event. His last victory on the Senior tour was the 1988 Crestar Classic.

Palmer continued to play regularly, though inconsistently, in the 1990s. In 1994 he made his final appearance at the U.S. Open, fittingly located in Oakmont, Pennsylvania, just a few miles from his hometown. As Palmer finished his final round, the thunderous ovation of his Army brought him to tears. A similarly emotional scene accompanied his last appearance at the British Open in 1995. Fellow players, who call Palmer "the King," realize that the great sums of money they are paid to play the game they love exist largely because of the efforts and charisma of Arnold Palmer. As current golf star Nick Faldo said during Palmer's farewell performance at the British, "If there had been no Arnold Palmer in 1960 . . . it might have been a little shed on the beach instead of these salubrious surroundings. You cannot say what the man has done for the game. It's everything."

Palmer has received countless honors, earning virtually every national award in golf. After his great 1960 season, he won both the Hickock Athlete of the Year and Sports Illustrated's Sportsman of the Year trophies. He is a charter member of the World Golf Hall of Fame, the American Golf Hall of Fame, and the PGA Hall of Fame. He is chairman of the USGA Member Program and served as Honorary National Chairman of the March of Dimes Birth Defects Foundation for 20 years. He played a major role in the fundraising drive that created the Arnold Palmer Hospital for Children and Women in Orlando. A long-time member of the Board of Directors of Latrobe Area Hospital, he established an annual fund-raising golf event for the institution in 1992.

Arnold Palmer underwent surgery for prostate cancer in January of 1997.

Further Reading

McCormack, Mark H., *Arnie: The Evolution of a Legend,* Simon and Schuster, 1967.

Arnold Palmer's Biography, "http://www.sportsline.com/u/fans/celebrity/palmer/bio.htm," July 22, 1997.
Condon, Robert J., *The Fifty Finest Athletes of the 20th Century,* McFarland and Company, 1990, pp. 112-114.
Dorman, Larry, "An Army Bids Palmer One Last Cheerio at Open," in *New York Times Biographical Service,* July 1995, pp. 1058-1059.
Reilly, Rick, "Arnold Palmer," in *Sports Illustrated,* September 19, 1994, p. 70.
Grimsley, Will, editor, *The Sports Immortals,* Prentice Hall, 1972, pp. 306-311.
Seitz, Nick, *Superstars of Golf,* Golf Digest, 1978. □

Nathaniel Brown Palmer

Nathaniel Brown Palmer (1799-1877), American sea captain, sighted the part of the Antarctic Peninsula that came to be known as Palmer Land. In later life he engaged in designing and sailing clipper ships for the China trade.

Nathaniel Palmer was born on Aug. 8, 1799, in Stonington, Conn., the son of a shipyard owner. At the age of 14 he became a seaman on a blockade-runner in the War of 1812. After captaining small coastal vessels, he signed on in 1818 as second mate of a sealing brig that hunted in the newly discovered South Shetland Islands.

In July 1820 Palmer, commanding the 47-foot sloop *Hero,* joined a sealing fleet of five vessels under the command of Benjamin Pendleton. The expedition reached the South Shetlands in November, and Palmer left Deception Island on November 17 to search for seal rookeries that had been seen to the south. He sighted extensive land at 63°S but no seal rookeries. This coastal area was a portion of the Antarctic Peninsula that had been sighted and charted in January 1820 by the British captain Edward Bransfield and had been named Trinity Land. In January 1821 Palmer encountered a Russian exploring expedition and boarded its flagship, the *Vostok.*

Palmer then returned to Stonington, where a new expedition was outfitted; it departed in July 1821 with Palmer commanding the sloop *James Monroe.* Reaching Deception Island in November, he joined British captain George Powell in searching for new sealing grounds. Together they discovered the South Orkney Islands on Dec. 6, 1821. Powell charted them with the name Powell Islands and identified part of the Antarctic Peninsula as Palmer Land.

Palmer spent several years as captain of vessels sailing to the West Indies and South America. In 1829 he again sailed to the Antarctic as part of a Fanning expedition. Two scientists accompanied this expedition. Sealing was poor in the South Shetlands, and his ship returned via the Pacific Ocean, where it was boarded at the Juan Fernández Islands by convicts who forced Palmer to land them in Chile.

In the 1830s Palmer became a packet ship captain and sailed between New York and New Orleans, and New York

and Liverpool. He grew rich and later became involved in the clipper ship trade with China. He designed the prototype clipper ship, the *Houqua* (completed in 1844), and other true clipper ships, all of which he captained at times. After retirement, he became active in pleasure yachting. He died in San Francisco on June 21, 1877, after returning from an Oriental voyage.

Further Reading

A book-length biography of Palmer is John R. Spears, *Captain Nathaniel Brown Palmer: An Old-time Sailor of the Sea* (1922). An accurate analysis of Palmer's Antarctic discoveries is in Philip I. Mitterling, *America in the Antarctic to 1840* (1959). □

3d Viscount Palmerston

The English statesman Henry John Temple, 3d Viscount Palmerston (1784-1865), was the chief architect of British foreign policy in the mid-19th century. His aggressive diplomatic methods symbolized Britain at the zenith of its power.

n the framework of Victorian politics, Lord Palmerston was a liberal because he worked for the independence of constitutional states on the Continent, but he was restrained in the support of liberal programs in England and opposed reform in Ireland.

Henry John Temple was born on Oct. 20, 1784, at Broadlands, Hampshire. His father was Henry Temple, 2d Viscount Palmerston, and his mother was Mary Dee. When he was 8, he went to the Continent with his parents for an extended stay; in the next 2 years he acquired a knowledge of French and Italian. His formal education was at Harrow, the University of Edinburgh, and St. John's College, Cambridge. He succeeded to an Irish viscountcy in 1802 on the death of his father.

Palmerston began his parliamentary career as a Tory representative for a pocket borough (Newport, Isle of Wight) in 1807. As an Irish peer, he was eligible to sit in the House of Commons, and he was to remain in Parliament for 58 years. He served as a junior lord of the Admiralty from 1807 to 1809 in Lord Portland's ministry. Under Spencer Perceval he became secretary of war and held that position for 19 years (1809-1828). He was much influenced by George Canning and thus became committed to a more liberal foreign policy. In 1829, 2 years after Canning's death, Palmerston left the Tory party and joined the Whigs. It was an opportune move, since the Whigs came to office in 1830 under Lord Grey. Palmerston became foreign secretary in the Grey Cabinet. He held this post until 1841 under Grey and then Lord Melbourne except for the 4 months of Sir Robert Peel's ministry of 1834/1835.

Foreign Policy

Palmerston's conduct of foreign policy was popular with the public but irritated the Queen. His bluntness was unheard of in diplomatic circles, and his candid statements that British interests were paramount were not calculated to win allies. Personally, Palmerston was a colorful figure, a bit of a rake who loved horses and fox hunting and who instinctively disliked France and Russia. His energy, wit, and self-confidence were legendary. In 1839 he married Emily Lamb, sister of Lord Melbourne, and Lord Cowper's widow.

The great diplomatic achievement of the 1830s was the establishment and guarantee of the independence of Belgium in the Treaty of London (1839). It was the masterpiece of Palmerston's long career. He also supported efforts to abolish the international slave trade. Not as praiseworthy was his intervention in China and the resultant Opium War (1840-1842), in which British gunboats forcibly opened five Chinese ports to British trade. Crises in the Near East in 1833 and 1839 brought Palmerston's Russophobia into play and Britain to a position of defending the Ottoman Empire. This policy angered France, which had supported Mohammed Ali and Egypt in 1839, but Palmerston was firm and France gave way.

Foreign policy passed into the hands of Lord Aberdeen (1841-1846) in Peel's second ministry, but Palmerston returned to the Foreign Office in 1846 for another 5 years. It was in these years that he was especially outspoken. "England," he said, "is one of the greatest powers of the world and her right to have and to express opinions on matters . . . bearing on her interests is unquestionable." In a speech he said of Britain: "We have no eternal allies and no perpetual enemies. Our interests are eternal and those interests it is our duty to follow." When Don Pacifico, a Portuguese moneylender but a British subject, brought claims of property damage against the Greek government, Palmerston backed him up with the British fleet. He justified his actions in a lengthy speech in which he stated that a British subject, like a Roman citizen of classical times, could count on protection from his government anywhere in the world. This won him extraordinary popular acclaim, but it did not please the court or some of his colleagues. In 1851, when he congratulated the French ambassador on the coup d'etat of Louis Napoleon before consulting other members of the government, Palmerston was dismissed by the prime minister, Lord John Russell.

Prime Minister

Despite this dismissal Palmerston was on the eve of his greatest triumph. He joined the Aberdeen coalition government as home secretary in 1853 but was catapulted into the prime minister's office in 1855, when the disasters of the Crimean War (1854-1856) demanded vigorous leadership. For the next decade, except for the Tory ministry of 1858-1859, Palmerston remained prime minister. The main actions of the Palmerston Cabinet were in foreign affairs; he was disinclined to further reform at home. The Crimean War was ended with the fall of Sevastopol in 1855 and the Treaty of Paris in 1856. Russia had been humiliated, to Palmerston's satisfaction. In 1858 Palmerston was forced to resign as a result of the Orsini attempt to assassinate Napoleon III. Orsini had organized the details of the plot in London. Palmerston's Conspiracy to Murder Bill—to make the plotting of assassinations by foreign refugees a felony—was defeated. A brief Derby government took office, but in June 1859 Palmerston returned as prime minister.

The Cavour-designed unification of Italy met with Palmerston's approval, although no official British intervention was sanctioned. But he became increasingly suspicious of the French role in Italy and went so far as to raise the specter of a new Napoleonic threat to Britain. The Parliament and the public accepted this view and voted new sums for national defense, but Palmerston's panic conclusion was unsound. His reaction to the American Civil War was similarly unwise. He sympathized with the Confederacy, and his old belligerence came to the surface over the *Trent* affair in 1861, in which a British ship had been stopped by an American warship and two Confederate envoys removed. Palmerston's rage was tempered by his colleagues and by Prince Albert, and British neutrality was preserved.

That Palmerston had lost his former dominance in European affairs was clearly evident in a final clash with Bismarck over Schleswig-Holstein. Palmerston failed to carry through a plan to intervene in behalf of Denmark, and Denmark was soundly beaten by Austria and Prussia in a war in 1864. The younger Bismarck had completely outmaneuvered the old master Palmerston. A year later, on October 18, Palmerston died at Brocket Hall, Hertfordshire.

An Evaluation

Palmerston was not a liberal in the Gladstonian sense of the word. He was too narrow in his outlook. He was a nationalist, a British patriot, and an aristocrat who did not favor the franchise for the working classes. He was the spokesman of the British middle classes, who considered themselves God's chosen people in the prosperous years of early Victorian Britain. Palmerston vigorously opposed what he viewed as the two major threats to the British system: absolutism and republicanism. The British *via media,* or middle way, he felt, would avoid both the danger of despotism and the rule of the mob. Consequently, Palmerston spoke against both absolute monarchs and socialist republicans. He favored those Continental liberal movements that sought to imitate Britain.

It was Palmerston's misfortune that, by the time he became prime minister in 1855, he was 70 years old and out of touch with his times. His physical energy remained, but his attitudes were a generation old. His accomplishments at the Foreign Office, working with a notoriously inadequate staff, over a quarter century were, nevertheless, great. He contributed to the preservation of the balance of power in the long period of relative peace from the Napoleonic Wars to the brief Bismarckian conflicts. It was, of course, a British peace, *Pax Britannica,* and a balance of power preserved by the reality of British naval supremacy.

In the final analysis, though, Palmerston's personality was probably more important than his policies. He overawed the Parliament, the nation, and at times all the courts of Europe with his social charm and daring style.

Further Reading

Two excellent studies of Palmerston are Donald Southgate, *"The Most English Minister ...": The Policies and Politics of Palmerston* (1966), and Jasper Ridley, *Lord Palmerston* (1971). Older standard works include Henry Lytton Bulwer, *The Life of Henry John Temple, Viscount Palmerston* (3 vols., 1871-1874); Anthony Evelyn Ashley, *The Life and Correspondence of Henry John Temple, Viscount Palmerston* (2 vols., 1876); and Herbert C. F. Bell, *Lord Palmerston* (2 vols., 1936). The most thorough discussion of Palmerston's foreign policy is Charles K. Webster, *The Foreign Policy of Palmerston, 1830-1841* (2 vols., 1951). Kingsley Martin, *The Triumph of Lord Palmerston* (1924; rev. ed. 1963), sketches the immediate background of public opinion and the Crimean War. Recommended for general historical background are E.L. Woodward, *The Age of Reform, 1815-1870* (1938; 2d ed. 1962); Asa Briggs, *The Age of Improvement, 1783-1867* (1959); and, for the European background to Palmerston's diplomatic activites, A. J. P. Taylor, *The Struggle for Mastery in Europe, 1848-1918* (1954).

Additional Sources

Bourne, Kenneth, *Palmerston, the early years, 1784-1841,* New York: Macmillan, 1982.

Chamberlain, Muriel Evelyn, *Lord Palmerston,* Washington, D.C.: Catholic University of America Press, 1987.

Judd, Denis, *Palmerston,* London: Weidenfeld and Nicolson, 1975.

Trollope, Anthony, *Lord Palmerston,* New York: Arno Press, 1981. □

Vijaya Lakshmi Pandit

Vijaya Lakshmi Pandit (1900-1990) was an Indian diplomat, politician, and a sister of India's first prime-minister, Jawaharlal Nehru. She was active in the Indian freedom movement and held high national and international positions.

Vijaya Lakshmi Pandit was born in Allahabad in what was then the United Provinces (later, Uttar Pradesh) on August 18, 1900, and was given the name Swarup Kumari ("Beautiful Princess") Nehru. She was the eldest daughter of a distinguished Brahmin lawyer, Motilal Nehru, and eleven years younger than her brother, Jawaharlal. Accustomed to luxury and educated at home and in Switzerland, she was greatly influenced by Mohandas Ghandi and became identified with the struggle for independence. She was imprisoned by the British on three different occasions, in 1932-1933, 1940, and 1942-1943.

In May 1921 she married Ranjit Sitaram Pandit, a foreign-educated barrister from Kathiawar. At that time she changed her name to Vijaya Lakshmi Pandit. The Pandit's had three daughters, including the novelist Nayantara (Pandit) Sehgal. Her husband died on January 14, 1944.

In 1934 Pandit's long career in politics officially began with her election to the Allahabad Municipal Board. In 1936 she was elected to the Assembly of the United Provinces, and in 1937 became minister of local self-government and public health—the first Indian woman ever to become a cabinet minister. Like all Congress party officeholders, she resigned in 1939 to protest against the British government's declaration that India was a participant in World War II. Along with other Congress leaders, she was imprisoned after the Congress' "Quit India" Resolution of August 1942.

Forced to reorient her life after her husband's death, Pandit traveled in the United States from late 1944 to early 1946, mainly on a lecture tour. Returning to India in January 1946, she resumed her portfolio as minister of local self-government and public health in the United Provinces. In the fall of 1946 she undertook her first official diplomatic mission as leader of the Indian delegation to the United Nations General Assembly. She also led India's delegations to the General Assembly in 1947, 1948, 1952, 1953, and 1963.

Pandit was elected to India's Constituent Assembly in 1946. Shortly after India's independence in 1947, she joined the foreign service and was appointed India's first ambassador to the Soviet Union. In early 1949 she became ambassador to the United States.

In November 1951 she returned to India to contest successfully for a seat in the Lok Sabha (India's parliament) in the first general elections. In September 1953 she was given the honor of being the first woman and the first Asian to be elected president of the U.N. General Assembly.

For nearly seven years, beginning in December 1954, Pandit served as Indian high commissioner (ambassador) to the United Kingdom, including a tense period in British-Indian relations at the time of the Suez and Hungarian crisis' in 1956. From March 1963 until August 1963 she served as governor of the state of Maharashtra.

Jawaharlal Nehru's death on May 27, 1964 came as a great shock to her. In November, she was elected to the Lok Sabha in a by-election in the Philpur constituency of Uttar Pradesh, which her brother had represented for 17 years. She was re-elected in the fourth general elections in 1967, but resigned the following year for "personal reasons."

Furious at Indira Ghandi's (whose maiden name was Nehru) state-of-emergency suspension of democratic processes from 1975 to 1977, she campaigned against her niece. Her efforts resulted in an electoral defeat for Ghandi.

Pandit had not been politically active for several years when she died in Dehru Dun, India on December 1, 1990. On the occasion of her death, President Ramaswami Venkataraman described Pandit as a "luminous strand in the tapestry of India's freedom struggle. Distinctive in her elegance, courage, and dedication, Mrs. Pandit was an asset to the national movement."

Further Reading

Pandit's own writings include *So I Became a Minister* (1939); *Prison Days* (1946); a touching essay, "The Family Bond," in Rafiq Zakaria, ed., *A Study of Nehru* (1959); many interviews and articles, and innumerable published speeches. Her daughter, Nayantara (Pandit) Sahgal, presented revealing portraits in *Prison and Chocolate Cake* (1954) and *From Fear Set Free* (1963). There is no good biography of Pandit, but three books by professed admirers are interesting: Anne Guthrie *Madame Ambassador: The Life of Vijaya Lakshmi Pandit* (1962); Vera Brittain *Envoy Extraordinary* (1965); and Robert Hardy Andrews *A Lamp for India: The Story of Madame Pandit* (1967). She is often referred to in books on the Nehrus and in biographies of her brother, Jawaharlal Nehru. Obituaries for Pandit appear in the *Chicago Tribune* (December 2, 1990) and the *Washington Post* (December 2, 1990). A brief biography of Pandit appears on-line at the A&E Network Biography site located at www.biography.com. □

Leon E. Panetta

Leon E. Panetta (born 1938) served in the House of Representatives for 16 years before President Bill Clinton appointed him director of the Office of Management and Budget in 1993. In July 1994 Panetta moved into the White House as chief of staff to the president.

Leon E. Panetta was born in Monterey, California, on June 28, 1938, to Italian immigrant parents, Carmelo Frank and Cramelina Maria (Prochilo) Panetta. His parents operated a restaurant until 1947, when they sold it

and bought a walnut ranch in Carmel Valley. It was there that Leon and his older brother lived as teenagers. He attended grammar school at a Catholic mission school and graduated from Monterey High School in 1956. Panetta then enrolled at the University of Santa Clara. Panetta graduated *magna cum laude* in 1960 and received a law degree three years later from the University of Santa Clara Law School. After graduating from law school, he married Sylvia Marie Varni. She bore him three sons: Christopher, Carmelo, and James. During these years Panetta supported Republican Richard M. Nixon in both his presidential and gubernatorial races (1960 and 1962, respectively).

In 1964 Panetta was commissioned in the United States Army, rising from second lieutenant to captain during his three-year stint. He served first at Fort Benning, Georgia and eventually as chief of operations and planning for the intelligence section at Fort Ord, California. He also acted as legal counsel in court-martial cases. It was during his military service that Panetta became sensitized to the evil consequences of prejudice and racial discrimination.

After his discharge from the Army in 1966, the 28-year-old Panetta became an aide to moderate Republican Thomas H. Kuchel, U.S. senator from California. He helped to draft the open housing bill of 1968. When his boss lost his bid for reelection in 1968, Panetta joined the Nixon transition team on matters relating to the Department of Health, Education and Welfare (HEW). Shortly after, he agreed to serve under Nixon's HEW secretary, Robert Finch, as special assistant for civil rights. Several months after that ap-

pointment Finch promoted Panetta to director of the Office of Civil Rights.

In this position Panetta had responsibility for desegregating the 515 southern school districts that had refused to comply with earlier federal orders to do so. However, Nixon's strategy to establish the South as a Republican stronghold worked against Panetta's efforts to enforce the Civil Rights Act of 1964 and led to his forced resignation on February 17, 1970. Disturbed by Panetta's departure, 125 HEW civil rights personnel signed a petition protesting the Nixon administration's actions.

On May 26, 1970, he joined New York City mayor John V. Lindsay as an executive assistant for intergovernmental relations. After serving in that position for five months, Panetta returned to Monterey, where he established the law firm Panetta, Thompson and Panetta. Now as a declared Democrat, Panetta served for six years as counsel for the National Association for the Advancement of Colored People (starting in 1971) and became a member of the Monterey County Democratic Central Committee between 1972 and 1974.

In 1976 he won the Democratic nomination for the 16th (now the 17th) Congressional District and defeated Republican incumbent Burt I. Talcott, receiving 53 percent of the vote. This victory began a 16-year tenure in the House of Representatives, where he won reelection every time by at least 61 percent of the vote. In Congress he developed a reputation as a fiscal conservative, often willing to side with Republicans in decreasing spending on domestic policies. Yet he supported abortion rights and the Equal Rights Amendment for women. In foreign affairs Panetta consistently opposed defense and foreign policy initiatives promoted by President Ronald Reagan, especially financial aid to the Contra rebels in Nicaragua. He also voted against authorizing President George Bush to use armed force to expel Iraqi troops from Kuwait.

During his service in Congress the soft-spoken Californian earned the respect of both Republican and Democratic colleagues for his command of budgetary details, his honesty, and his willingness to forgo politically popular decisions to achieve long-term goals. After serving on the House Budget Committee since 1978, Panetta became chair of that important committee in 1989 and emerged as a key player in the budget negotiations with the Bush administration.

Panetta's constant call for spending constraints differentiated him from most Democrats. His deep knowledge of financial matters, as well as his political courage and unsparing realism, help explain why President Bill Clinton nominated Panetta for director of the Office of Management and Budget (OMB). At the confirmation hearing in January 1993, Panetta stressed that he would make reducing the federal deficit his top priority. The Senate confirmed him on January 21, 1993. In 1993 he was given the Peter Burnett Award for Distinguished Public Service.

As head of OMB Panetta helped the Clinton administration pass the hard-fought budget bill of 1993 (it passed the House by one vote) and the easily passed budget bill of 1994. In July of 1994 Panetta was appointed chief of staff to President Clinton. He served in this position for the next two and one half years, helping to bring order and discipline to the Clinton White House. In November 1996, Panetta announced his resignation as chief of staff. He will be remembered for his many years of service in Congress as well as his integral role in federal budget negotiations.

Further Reading

No biography exists for Panetta, but a book he wrote with Peter Gall, *Bring Us Together: The Nixon Team and the Civil Rights Record* (n.d.), provides material on his conflict with Nixon during his tenure as director of the Office of Civil Rights. □

Emmeline Pankhurst

The English reformer Emmeline Pankhurst (1858-1928) led the movement for women's suffrage in Great Britain, in the process developing agitational tactics still controversial and consequential.

Emmeline Pankhurst was born Emmeline Goulden in Manchester on July 4, 1858. At the age of 14 she accompanied her mother to a women's suffrage meeting. The next few years Emmeline spent in Paris attending school. After her return she married Richard Pankhurst, a barrister and an activist in radical causes, especially in women's suffrage. He died in 1898, leaving her with four children, including daughters Christabel (1880-1958) and Sylvia (1882-1960).

Pankhurst had briefly joined the Fabian Society and then had joined the Independent Labour party. She had held local offices as a Poor Law guardian, as a school board member, and as a paid registrar of births and deaths. In all these experiences she had observed the inferior position of women and their legal and social oppression by men. She concluded that only political rights for women would emancipate women and reform society at large.

In 1903 Pankhurst and Christabel formed the Women's Social and Political Union (WSPU). From its founding, the WSPU held certain policies: Its membership was exclusively female; it was independent of all political parties; it concentrated exclusively on the suffrage issue; and it distrusted all promises and demanded immediate parliamentary action. Another policy, developed in the next few years, was tactical militancy in harassing the Liberals, the political party with the greatest number of sympathizers and after 1905 the party in power, in order to force it to adopt women's suffrage as a party measure.

Pankhurst soon discovered that processions to the Houses of Parliament and hecklings and disruptions of election meetings produced police countermeasures and thus newspaper publicity favorable to her cause. The history of the movement recorded her mounting frustration with Prime Minister Herbert H. Asquith's personal resistance to votes for women and his consequent delaying tactics in Parliament.

Emmeline Pankhurst (center)

In 1908 Pankhurst declared that the suffragettes would either convert the ministry by force or see "the Government themselves destroyed." Soon the WSPU surpassed all other dissident movements, if not in rhetoric, in its violence and in its disruption of public life. The suffragettes organized campaigns of window smashing in central London, burned letters in postboxes, defaced paintings, and burned unoccupied buildings. Pankhurst called this escalation "guerrilla warfare" against property "to make England and every department of English life insecure and unsafe." She stopped short only of endangering human life.

The ministry responded with arrests and imprisonment, of Pankhurst herself for the first time in 1908. The women prisoners then began hunger strikes, which the officials met with brutal forms of forced feeding. In 1913 the "Cat and Mouse" Act allowed the release of fasting prisoners and their rearrest when they had recovered; under these terms Mrs. Pankhurst served only 30 days (of a 3-year sentence) during a calendar year.

Historians have asserted that by 1914 violence had become an end in itself for the WSPU, although Pankhurst always declared it temporary and historically and politically validated. After 1912 Christabel Pankhurst, who had taken sanctuary in Paris, directed the strategy. Yet the movement's objectives, as distinct from its tactics, had become less radical. It accepted a "Conciliation Bill," which excluded working-class women from the vote and which opposed as

impractical the introduction of genuinely universal suffrage. Finally, after Sylvia Pankhurst's expulsion from the movement, on grounds of her socialism and organizational activity among the lower classes, the ministry made her a formal promise of government support. Because of the outbreak of World War I, the pledge could not be redeemed until 1918, when most women over 30 years of age were enfranchised. Later, the Representation Act of 1928 gave women the vote on the same basis as men. Emmeline Pankhurst, who had played little part in the movement after 1914, died on June 14, 1928.

Further Reading

Emmeline Pankhurst's autobiographical account, *My Own Story* (1914), must be read with special caution because of its omissions and rationalizations. Two primary accounts were written by her daughter, Estelle Sylvia Pankhurst: *The Suffragette Movement* (1931) and *The Life of Emmeline Pankhurst* (1935). Another primary account is in Millicent G. Fawcett, *The Women's Victory and After* (1914). A brilliant and lively treatment of the Pankhursts by means of social and psychological analysis is in George Dangerfield, *The Strange Death of Liberal England* (1935). Robert C.K. Ensor, *England, 1870-1914* (1936), is a general history of the period which includes a critical account of the movement. □

Pan Ku

Pan Ku (32-92) was a Chinese historian and man of letters. His name is mainly associated with the *Han-shu,* the standard history of the Western Han period.

At the beginning of the Eastern Han dynasty (25-100) there existed no full historical account of the preceding century, as the *Shih-chi,* which had been compiled by Ssu-ma Ch'ien, ended its record at about 90 B.C. Pan Piao (died A.D. 54), father of Pan Ku attempted to repair this deficiency by continuing the *Shih-chi*'s account to cover those years.

While trying to improve and complete his father's work, Pan Ku was imprisoned on a charge of falsification of the record, but he was later released at the personal order of the Emperor and ordered to finish his work. However, by the time of his death in 92 Pan had not been able to do so; his sister, Pan Chao, was ordered to take responsibility for the task, and the imperial archives were put at her disposal. The process of compiling the history may thus have been protracted over a period of 80 years.

Comparison of Histories

There are several differences in principle between the *Shih-chi* and the *Han-shu,* although both works take as their main theme the history of the Han dynasty. While the *Shih-chi* was compiled as a private venture, the *Han-shu,* though starting likewise as a matter of personal initiative, was finally completed under the patronage of the government. This change set a precedent whereby, from the 7th century onward, Chinese imperial governments regularly assumed responsibility for the compilation of histories as a task which devolved on the state.

In compiling the *Shih-chi,* Ssu-ma Ch'ien had incorporated material on the history of mankind prior to the Han period, whereas the *Han-shu* is, on the whole, restricted to that dynastic period only. For this reason, in place of the five groups in which the chapters of the *Shih-chi* are divided, four suffice for the *Han-shu,* whose 100 chapters are set out as imperial annals, tables, treatises, and biographies.

Although much of the material is identical in these two histories, it cannot be known for certain whether Pan Ku utilized the text of the *Shih-chi* or drew on the original documents on which that work had been based. Stylistically the compilers of the *Han-shu* preferred to retain the archaic expressions of their sources rather than introduce simplifications in the way that was sometimes done in the *Shih-chi.*

While the material that is included uniquely in the *Han-shu* is mostly concerned with the 1st century B.C., some of the information given in respect of those years, for instance, the figures for the population of China in A.D. 1-2 or the list of titles of the books collected in the imperial library, bears a significance of much wider proportions within the whole context of Chinese history.

Other Writings

Pan Ku also wrote other compositions. These included at least one *fu,* a type of rhymed prose that had been developed during the Han dynasty. He also compiled an account of a conference held at court in 79. This was the second occasion that a Chinese emperor had convened a formal meeting of scholars to discuss problems which concerned the authenticity and interpretation of certain versions of early Chinese canonical writings.

Pan Ku's account of the discussions is entitled, in brief, the *Po hu t'ung,* or White Tiger Debate, named after the hall where the meetings were held. The account may be generally accepted as being representative of the discussions which took place and throws considerable light on the intellectual controversies and developments of the 1st century A.D.

The 43 chapters range over a wide variety of subjects, such as cosmology, the workings of heaven and earth, human nature, the relationships between man and his neighbor and the behavior appropriate for certain situations, religious cults and observances, the Five Elements, divination, and the ranks and titles used in the protocol and institutions of state. These matters are discussed in the light of precedent evolved before the Han dynasty and the authority of texts of a similarly early origin.

Further Reading

Critical translations of the 12 chapters of imperial annals and one other chapter were made by Homer H. Dubs, *The History of the Former Han Dynasty* (3 vols., 1938-1955). For annotated editions of two of the treatises see *Food and Money in Ancient China,* edited and translated by Nancy Lee Swann (1950), and A. F. P. Hulsewé, *Remnants of Han Law* (1955). The standard work on the *Po hu t'ung* is Pan Ku's *Po Hu T'ung: The*

Comprehensive Discussions in the White Tiger Hall, edited and translated by Tjan Tjoe Som (2 vols., 1949-1952). Ernest Richard Hughes, *Two Chinese Poets: Vignettes of Han Life and Thought* (1960), contains a brief biography of Pan Ku and an appraisal of his work. For background information consult Charles S. Gardner, *Chinese Traditional Historiography* (1938). □

Wolfhart Pannenberg

While teaching that nothing less than the whole of reality is the proper horizon of theology, Wolfhart Pannenberg (born 1928) insisted that the resurrection of Jesus provides the best key for understanding that reality. His broad interests and creativity distinguished him as one of Germany's most important Protestant theologians of the 20th century.

Wolfhart Pannenberg was born in 1928 in the city of Stettin (today part of Poland). Growing up during the Nazi era, he was pressed into military service during the final days of the Third Reich—an experience which helps account for his wariness of all ideological and political promises. His interest in religion developed after the war as the result of study and reflection during his university days, first at Berlin, then at Gottingen, Basel, and Heidelberg, where he received his doctorate in 1953, writing on the idea of predestination in the thought of Duns Scotus. In 1958 he was appointed professor of systematic theology at Wuppertal, a theological seminary of the Confessing Church. Important university positions followed, first at Mainz (1961) and then at Munich (1968).

Pannenberg insisted that it was rational reflection that led him to Christian faith. He believed that faith should be based, not upon feeling or supposed authority, but upon what is known, most reasonable, or most probable. There is such a thing as revelation through which God becomes known, but revelation is not something selected for a few chosen people or even for a chosen nation. Rather, as G. W. F. Hegel suggested at the dawn of the 19th century, God is revealed through history (or reality) as a whole, and God's revelation can be recognized and understood by reason. Of course, no human being actually knows the whole of history, being limited by time and space. Furthermore, history is not yet complete, and therefore cannot be completely understood. But it is possible for reason to discern in the life, the death, and (especially) the resurrection of Jesus a key to the meaning and an anticipation of the goal of universal history. Pannenberg believed, as Reinhold Niebuhr once argued, that Christianity can be shown to be empirically superior to all alternative interpretations of the meaning of life and history.

One must not, however, begin with supernatural doctrines about the person and work of Jesus—that he was the incarnate Son of God, the Second Person of the Trinity, or the Divine Logos. Rather, this traditional Christology "from above" must be replaced with the conclusions that result from established methods of historical scholarship, or Christology "from below." It is only when one studies the New Testament with such utter honesty that the event of Jesus' resurrection becomes acknowledged as objective historical fact, thereby confirming the high Christology of the New Testament that Jesus was "descended from David according to the flesh," but was "designated Son of God . . . by his resurrection from the dead" (Romans 1:4).

The significance of that fact becomes clear when we ask about the meaning of our own lives. Death would seem to cancel any meaning to life. The promise of a future earthly utopia, so popular among Marxists, leaves past generations out of any participation in the final fulfillment. But the New Testament understands the resurrection of Jesus to be an anticipation of the end and goal of history, the first fruit of a larger harvest, which will be the general resurrection of the dead. Then, as written words only have meaning in relation to a sentence, and as sentences find their meaning in relation to a book, so too the lives of individuals and the history of nations will fulfill their meaning in this transcendent solution, the general resurrection, judgment, and the life everlasting. New Testament eschatology in general, and especially the "Kingdom of God" which Jesus proclaimed, is this retroactive power of a future fulfillment to bring to completion the fragmentary character of life as we know it. In Jesus there pre-occurred what will finally occur for all of us—the consummation of personal life in the eschatological future.

Pannenberg was a brilliant and creative intellect, interested in the broad spectrum of academic knowledge. His thought was far too complex to be easily categorized. In the mid-1960s he was often cited as a leading proponent of the "theology of hope" because of his interest in the future. But Pannenberg disassociated himself from most proponents of that school, both because they were too dependent upon the philosophy of Ernst Bloch rather than on the resurrection of Jesus and because they were too easily deceived by the premature and idolatrous promises of socialism.

These judgments would seem to mark Pannenberg as a conservative. But consider that he bases his faith in the resurrection not upon the authority of the Bible or of the church but upon its demonstrability to rational investigation. Furthermore, he considered authentic religion to be a response to reality as a whole, including world religions, not just parochial and institutional Christianity. Therefore, Pannenberg argues, the proper home for theology is not the institutional church but the university, where the theologian's propositions must be defended and corrected, not just asserted. The church, however, *is* the home of spirituality and community, where both depend upon the Eucharist—received not as a church supper (owned by an institution), but as the Lord's Supper (transcending all denominational boundaries) and anticipating God's plan for the fullness of time to "unite all things" (Ephesians 1:10).

Pannenberg married Hilke Shütte in 1954. He has served as a professor of theology at the University of Heidelberg, Kirchiliche Hochschule Wuppertal, University of Mainz, and the University of Munich. He has had visiting professorships at the University of Chicago, Harvard University, and the Claremont School of Theology. He became the head of the Institute of Ecumenical Theology, Munich, in 1967. Pannenberg has also received honorary doctorates in theology from universities around the world.

Pannenberg's translated works include *What is Man?* (1962); *Jesus: God and Man* (1968); *Revelation as History* (1969); *Theology and the Kingdom of God* (1969); *Basic Questions in Theology, Vol. I* (1970); *Basic Questions in Theology, Vol. II* (1971); *The Apostle's Creed* (1972); *Theology and the Philosophy of Science* (1976); *Human Nature, Election and History* (1977); *Anthropology in Theological Perspective* (1985); *The Theology of Wolfhart Pannenberg: Twelve American Critiques, with an Autobiographical Essay and Response* (1988); *Christianity in a Secularized World* (1989); *Metaphysics and the Idea of God* (1990); *Systematic Theology, Volume I* (1991); *An Introduction to Systematic Theology* (1993); *Toward a Theology of Nature: Essays on Science and Faith* (1993); and *Systematic Theology, Volume II* (1995). Pannenberg has also served as an Erasmus Lecturer and contributor to theology journals.

Further Reading

For Pannenberg's views on Christian political involvement see his *Ethics* (1981). And, for his appreciation of the role of institutional Christianity, see *The Church* (1983). For early evaluative studies see E. Frank Tupper, *The Theology of Wolfhart Pannenberg* (1973), and Don H. Olive, *Wolfhart Pannenberg* (1973). Also see *Contemporary Authors* (1995); and *The International Who's Who* (1993). □

Andreas Papandreou

Founder of the Panhellenic Socialist Party (PASOK), Andreas Papandreou (1919-1996) is credited with introducing a socialist dimension into Greek politics, first as the leader of the opposition and then as prime minister of Greece.

Andreas Papandreou was undoubtedly one of the most controversial political figures of 20th-century Greece. His father, George Papandreou, was known as the "grand old man" of Greek politics. Andreas made his entry into Greek politics through his father who, as head of the Center Union Party, served as prime minister of the country in 1964.

Papandreou was born on February 5, 1919, on the island of Chios. He began his studies as a law student at the University of Athens in 1936. Papandreou displayed an early interest in politics, championing progressive ideas that got him into difficulties with the Metaxas dictatorship. He was arrested and tortured, and after his release left Greece to continue his education in the United States. Papandreou received his Ph.D. in economics from Harvard University in 1943. For the next two decades he made his home in the US, where he held various posts as lecturer and professor of economics at several universities, among them Harvard, Minnesota, Northwestern, and the University of California at Berkeley, where he was dean of faculty from 1956 to 1959.

His experiences with the Metaxas dictatorship in Greece, his progressive or leftist leanings, and his American experience gave Papandreou the dubious distinction of being branded by his political opponents as both a tool of the Kremlin and as an agent of the CIA. These ill-founded allegations contributed to the controversial profile of Andreas Papandreou as he became more involved in Greek politics in the 1960s.

Papandreou's controversial behavior was often exaggerated by those who interpret politics or policy entirely in terms of public statements. Still, his presence in Greek politics brought with it a critical attitude toward United States policy, especially the status of American bases in the country; a reserved attitude toward the European Union; a toughening of his position toward Turkey over the Cyprus issue; a policy of rapprochement toward the (former) Soviet Union; an open-arms' policy toward third world countries; and above all the introduction of socialism as a potentially viable political and economic system for Greece. With the exception of the latter, many of his policies had in fact been initiated by his predecessor, and careful analysis points to remarkably few radical departures despite alarming reports to the contrary. Even Papandreou's "socialism" deserved careful study.

Scholar and Politician

Papandreou was an impressive synthesis of a scholar-statesman. He was articulate and possessed a sharp, analytical mind that served him well in both professions. A prolific writer, he was the author of several scholarly and political monographs and contributed to scores of collaborative volumes, scholarly journals, and encyclopedias. He wrote in both Greek and English and many of his works were translated into Italian, Spanish, French, and Scandinavian languages.

This wide range of interests can be ascertained by a look at his major publications: *A Test of Stochastic Theory of Choice* (1957); *The Course of Economic Thought* (1960); *Planning Resource Allocation for Economic Development* (1962); "Theory Construction and Empirical Meaning in Economics," *American Economic Review* (May 1963); *Fundamentals of Model Construction in Macroeconomics* (1962); *A Strategy for Greek Economic Development* (1962); *An Introduction to Social Science: Personality, Work, Community,* with A. Naftalin, B. Nelson, M. Sibley, D. Calhoun (1953, revised editions 1957, 1961); *Competition and its Regulation,* with J. T. Wheeler (1954); *Economics as a Science* (1958); *Democracy at Gunpoint* (1970); "Greece: Neocolonialism and Revolution," *Monthly Review* (December 1972); "The Multinational Corporation," *The Canadian Forum* (March 1973); "Multinational Corporations and Empire," *Social Praxis* (1973); and "Greece: The November Uprising," *Monthly Review* (February 1974).

It was Papandreou's activities as an economist that first involved him in earnest in Greek politics. In 1959 he left the University of California at Berkeley to return to Greece on an economic development research assignment. In 1961 he was appointed chairman of the board and director general of the Center for Economic Research in Athens, while serving as an adviser to the Bank of Greece (1961-1962).

Papandreou's political career began in 1962 with his election as deputy for Achaia in the Center Union Party, led by his father. After the national victory of the Center Union in 1964, he was appointed to the post of minister to the prime minister and later deputy minister of coordination. These activities were cut off by the military coup of April 21, 1967. As was expected, Papandreou was arrested by the colonels who headed the new regime. His release the following year was partly the result of a campaign mounted by many of his colleagues, fellow scholars, and political friends outside Greece.

After his release he first went to Sweden where he became professor of economics at Stockholm University (1968-1969) and from there to Canada where he taught at York University in Toronto. During one of his first appearances on American television, Papandreou said that his release was a major mistake of the colonels and that some day he was going to return to active politics in Greece. Indeed, during the colonels' regime he led an active anti-junta movement in Europe and the United States known as PAK (Panhellenic Liberation Movement) that was decidedly anti-colonel and critical of any nation which helped the colonels stay in power. PAK remained active until July 1974, when the dictatorship fell.

From Opposition Leader to Prime Minister

Papandreou returned to Greece in September 1974 and organized the Panhellenic Socialist Movement (PASOK), of which he became chairman. In the next election, held in November 1974, PASOK obtained 15 seats in Parliament, winning 13.5 percent of the vote. That was only the beginning. Capitalizing on his experiences outside Greece, Papandreou organized PASOK as a socialistic political party, the first in Greece's history. The result was impressive. By the following elections (November 1977) PASOK doubled its vote percentage and became the main opposition party in Parliament with 93 seats. As leader of the opposition, Papandreou began a barrage of criticism of the New Democracy Party by insisting that a more fundamental change in Greece's domestic and foreign policy was needed. Indeed in the elections of October 18, 1981, Papandreou campaigned with the slogan *Allaghi* (change), which led to PASOK's triumph with 48 percent of the vote and 173 seats in Parliament. In the PASOK-dominated government sworn in on October 21, 1981, Andreas Papandreou became prime minister, assuming as well the portfolio of the ministry of defense.

Papandreou's victory was received as a breath of fresh air, and the confidence in his leadership was not different from that inspired by John F. Kennedy in the United States 20 years earlier. With his American wife Margaret Chadd and their four children, Papandreou proceeded to leave his mark on the Greek political scene. The emphasis was decidedly socialistic, although many foreign observers wondered whether Greek socialism was going to follow a Western European model—mainly, honoring civil liberties and democratic processes as guaranteed by the constitution of 1974—or a third world model of socialism which could move the country in the direction of a single party state. Partly because of the interest of Papandreou's wife Margaret, PASOK actively championed women's rights, and on several issues PASOK policy widened the separation between church and state. Understandably, the Papandreou experiment faced formidable difficulties, the most serious being inflation, continuous devaluation of the drachma, and hesitation of foreign investors to take their chances with a country in "socialist transition."

The domestic policy was tied to Greece's foreign policy, especially its anti-NATO or anti-American stance automatically associated with Papandreou's general policy. Many called him "NATO's bad boy," who was going to get rid of the American bases or at least have them renegotiated with terms more advantageous to Greece. Part of the change that Papandreou sought from the beginning was a change in the attitude of the great powers, especially the United States, who seemed to take the Greeks for granted. It was his way of searching for national dignity.

Papandreou's troubles with the Western alliance stemmed from Greece's troubles with Turkey over the Cyprus issue and with the economic and military aid extended to both Greece and Turkey by the United States. These tensions had their impact on the Greek economy and politics and account partly for the loss of some of PASOK's

power in the June 2, 1985 elections and in the municipal elections the following year. Papandreou then became more conciliatory toward the West, even toning-down his rhetoric. In fact, his moderate policies left some socialists a bit disillusioned, whereas his former critics began to appreciate his stabilizing role positioned between East and West and his attempts to attract foreign investors to Greece.

One of the distinctive features of Papandreou's foreign policy was his emphasis on détente, peace, and international cooperation. He advocated nuclear free zones in the Balkans and in northern Europe, as well as a nuclear free corridor in central Europe. But probably his most important move was with the "Initiative of the Six"—Greece, India, Argentina, Mexico, Tanzania, and Sweden—which urged the leaders of the superpowers to put an immediate halt to all nuclear weapon tests. The "Initiative of the Six" won the international peace prize of the Beyond War Foundation. On a personal level, Papandreou received honorary doctor degrees from York University (Canada), Humbold University (Berlin), and Cracow University (Poland).

In 1988 Papandreou underwent successful open heart surgery in London. He began campaigning for his third term as prime minister with his young mistress, Diamitra Liania. He divorced his wife Margaret and declared Diamitra as the new first lady of Greece. Shortly thereafter, Papandreou was accused of helping to embezzle hundreds of millions of dollars by ordering state corporations to transfer their holdings to the Bank of Crete, where the interest was allegedly used to benefit the Socialist party. The combination of the bank corruption scandal, his public extramarital affair, and Greece's economic downturn caused Papandreou to lose favor with his citizens; he lost the election to the New Democratics.

In 1992 Papandreou was cleared of all connections to the Crete Bank financial scandal, whereupon he called for immediate general elections with the charge that the New Democratics' 1990 victory was achieved as the result of false accusations. Papandreou returned to power as prime minister in 1993 with the promise to bring stability and economic development to Greece.

In January 1996, after being hospitalized for two months for heart and lung problems, Papandreou resigned from office stating that the country could not be "incapacitated" by his illness. He ordered the Socialist party to immediately proceed to elect a new prime minister. He was succeeded by Costas Simitis, former industry minister. Papandreou died on June 23, 1996 of heart complications at his home in Greece. Papandreou was survived by his wife Diamitra, and his four children.

Further Reading

There is no biography or monographic study of this charismatic and controversial figure. Much information about his ideas and political activities may be gathered from Papandreou's own book *Democracy at Gunpoint* (1970), which is largely autobiographical. Also useful for the 1950s and 1960s is Keith Legg, *Politics in Modern Greece* (1969) and for the later period Richard Clogg, editor, *Greece in the 1980s* (1983). Two more recent studies are Roy C. Macridis, *Greek Politics at a Crossroads—What Kind of Socialism* (1984) and Zafiris

Tzannatos, editor, *Socialism in Greece* (1986). Finally, the following studies shed considerable light on Greece and Papandreou: Guillermo O'Donnell, Philippe G. Schmitter, and Laurence Whitehead, editors, *Transitions from Authoritarian Rule. Southern Europe* (1986); Jed C. Snyder, *Defending the Fringe. NATO, the Mediterranean, and the Persian Gulf* (1987); Frances Nicholson and Roger East, *From Six to Twelve: the Enlargement of the European Communities* (1987); and Richard Pomfret, *Mediterranean Policy of the European Community. A Study of Discrimination of Trade* (1986). Also see the Websites http://www.gaepis.org/bnews/reuters1.html and http://www.cnn.com/WORLD/9606/22/papandreou/. □

Louis-Joseph Papineau

Louis-Joseph Papineau (1786-1871) was a French-Canadian radical political leader. He played a major role in the events leading to the Rebellion of 1837 in Lower Canada, although he took no part in the rebellion itself.

Louis-Joseph Papineau was born on Oct. 7, 1786, in Montreal. He was educated at the Seminary of Quebec and then read law. In 1809 he was elected to the Legislative Assembly of Lower Canada for the country of Kent; in 1814 he won the right to represent the Riding of Montreal West in the Assembly. He was appointed Speaker of the Assembly in 1815 and occupied that important office almost continuously until 1837.

Papineau quickly became the recognized leader of the *patriotes,* the French-Canadian reformers, and his political strength was such that in 1820 the governor, Lord Dalhousie, sought to gain his support by offering Papineau a seat on the Executive Council. Papineau accepted and then resigned almost immediately when he found that he could not influence policy. He came increasingly to dislike the control that the British government exercised over the political life of the colony.

Papineau continued to agitate during the 1830s for various reform measures, including Assembly control of crown revenues and an elective legislative council. From 1835 to 1837 he managed to block many bills in the Assembly having to do with the granting of money to the executive. In March 1837 the British government ordered the governor, Lord Gosford, to pay the expenses of government from crown funds. Papineau was incensed.

On Oct. 23, 1837, a meeting of *patriotes* was held at St. Charles, during the course of which armed rebellion was advocated. Warrants were issued for the arrest of Papineau and others on charges of high treason. Papineau fled into the United States and watched the progress of the rebellion from that sanctuary.

In 1839 Papineau went to Paris and remained there until the general amnesty of 1847 allowed him to return. He was elected to the Legislative Assembly of the United Province of Canada in 1848 and remained a member until 1854, when he retired to private life. But other politicians, notably Louis-Hippolyte Lafontaine, had superseded him during his enforced absence, and Papineau never regained his ascendancy in the political life of the colony. He died on Sept. 23, 1871.

Further Reading

A good biography of Papineau is Alfred D. DeCelles, *Papineau; Cartier* (1904), in "The Makers of Modern Canada Series." It was slightly revised and appeared at the end of volume 5 of "The Makers of Modern Canada Series" anniversary edition in 1926. A more recent short study is Fernand Ouellet, *Louis-Joseph Papineau: A Divided Soul* (1960; trans. 1961). See also the interesting studies of Papineau in Mason Wade, *The French Canadians, 1760-1967* (1955; 2 vols., rev. ed. 1968), and Jacques Monet, *The Last Cannon Shot: A Study of French-Canadian Nationalism, 1837-1850* (1969). □

Philippus Aureolus Paracelsus

The Swiss doctor and alchemist Philippus Aureolus Paracelsus (1493-1541) is noted for opposing Galen's medical theories and for founding medical chemistry.

The real name of Philippus Aureolus Paracelsus was Theophrastus Bombastus von Hohenheim. He was born in Einsiedeln. His father instructed him in Latin, botany, chemistry, and the history of religion. When Theophrastus was 9, his father was appointed town physician at Villach, and the boy attended the mining school there. For his secondary education he went to Basel. Through visits to Italy he learned of classical medical theory; after studies in the faculty of arts at the University of Vienna, he went back to Italy, receiving his doctorate in medicine from the University of Ferrara in 1515. During this Ferrara period he took the name Paracelsus.

Paracelsus resumed his study of metals briefly at Schwatz in the Tirol and then began a series of travels that lasted, almost without exception, to the end of his life. He served as an army physician in Denmark from 1518 to 1521, and the following year he joined the Venetian military forces. By 1526 Paracelsus had settled at Tübingen and gathered around him a small group of students. Later that year he was on the road again, this time to Strassburg, where he bought his citizenship and apparently intended to settle down.

During all these travels, Paracelsus was spreading the anti-Aristotelian position that the four elements (earth, air, fire, and water) were composed of primary principles: a fire-producing principle (sulfur), a principle of liquidity (mercury), and a principle of solidity (salt). From a medical viewpoint, salt was thought to be a cleanser, sulfur a consuming agent, and mercury a transporter of the product of consumption. Shaping the normal healthy organism is a

principle called an archeus. When an imbalance occurs among the three principles in man, there is disease, and the office of the doctor is to help the archeus by supplying the right medicines. Advocating the treatment of like by like, Paracelsus therapy is thus homeopathic in theory. During his travels he acquired a reputation as a healer; all his practical success would support his theory of the three principles.

In 1526 Paracelsus was summoned to Basel to treat a patient, and he remained on as town physician, a post that included a lectureship at the university and supervision of the apothecaries. His lectures drew large audiences, but his teaching and style were unpopular with the authorities. He openly challenged the traditional books on medicine and the teaching of medicine by textual analysis; he preferred to lecture in German rather than Latin; he refused to prescribe the medicines of the local apothecaries; and, though sympathetic with some of the ideas of the Reformation, he was a Roman Catholic. In 1528 Paracelsus had to flee to escape arrest and imprisonment.

Shortly before the flight from Basel, Paracelsus completed the most important of his earlier works, *Nine Books of Archidoxus,* a reference manual on secret remedies. Between 1530 and 1534 he wrote his bestknown works, the *Paragranum* and the *Paramirum,* both dealing with cosmology. He returned to medical writing with the *Books of the Greater Surgery* in editions of 1536 and 1537; this was his only work that was a publishing success. The *Astronomia magna,* done between 1537 and 1539, shows his most mature thinking about nature and man.

Paracelsus claimed that the pillars of his outlook on the world were philosophy, astronomy, alchemy, and virtue. It might be convenient to sample this outlook by emphasizing only alchemy here. For Paracelsus, alchemy was not only an earthly science but a spiritual one, requiring moral virtue on the part of the knower. At his highest, such a knower was not a theoretician but an activist; Paracelsus emphasized wisdom as practical rather than contemplative.

Paracelsus believed that to every evil there was a counteracting good and to every disease, a cure. He valued alchemy not because it might turn baser metals into gold, but because it might discover the means of restoring youth and prolonging life. He was looking for something like an elixir. Yet alchemy was not restricted to the chemist; it was at work in the whole of nature. Relating his natural philosophy to his religious beliefs, he pointed out that Christ came not as a scholar or a philosopher but as a healer. Many of Christ's miracles were healings of the sick. Most importantly, he healed the wounds of sin. Alchemy thus provided Paracelsus with a natural philosophy and a view of Christianity.

Paracelsus underscored the relation between the macrocosm and the microcosm as an argument for going to nature to understand man. According to his macrocosm-microcosm theory, "Everything that astronomical theory has profoundly fathomed by studying the planetary objects and the stars . . . can also be applied to the firmament of the body." The physician is the god of the microcosm. Such was the cosmology which Paracelsus espoused.

During the post-Basel period and especially after 1531, Paracelsus appears to have undergone a spiritual conversion which prompted him to renounce material possessions. In 1534 he came as a beggar and tramp, to use his own words, to Innsbruck, Vipiteno, and Merano. The plague was raging in these cities, and he ministered to the victims. In this new spirit that animated him, Paracelsus was especially attentive to the poor and the needy. He tended to a more mystical view of man and especially of the physician. He had long stressed a so-called light of nature, which was human reason. He thought that such a light was a radiation of the Holy Spirit.

In 1540 Paracelsus arrived in Salzburg a sick man, and he died there on Sept. 24, 1541.

Further Reading

Many of Paracelsus' own writings are gathered in Jolande Jacobi, ed., *Paracelsus: Selected Writings,* translated by Norbert N. Guterman (2d ed. 1958). Biographies of his life and work include Anna M. Stoddart, *The Life of Paracelsus* (1911); John Maxson Stillman, *Theophrastus Bombastus von Hohenheim Called Paracelsus* (1920); John Hargrave, *The Life and Soul of Paracelsus* (1951); Henry M. Pachter, *Paracelsus: Magic into Science* (1951), and Sidney Rosen, *Doctor Paracelsus* (1959). □

Arvi Parbo

Australian business executive, Arvi Parbo (born 1926) was a postwar immigrant who progressed through the ranks of a mining company to become its chief executive. He was concurrently chairman of three of Australia's largest companies. Arvi was made a Knight Bachelor for services to industry in 1978.

Arvi Parbo was born near Tallinn, Estonia, in February 1926. Along with thousands of his countrymen, he fled from his homeland ahead of the Russian occupation in 1944, ending up in a refugee camp in Germany. In 1946 he began to study mining engineering at the Clausthal Mining Academy, but through his vacation work in local mines he realized that the opportunities for mining engineers in Germany were limited. Rather than change careers, Parbo decided in 1948 that he would emigrate to Australia because, in addition to having a mining industry, it was offering relatively speedy immigration to wartime refugees.

Education in Australia

Parbo arrived in Australia in November 1949. He began working in a quarry near Adelaide, but quickly arranged employment in a factory nearer to the University of Adelaide where in 1951 he began part-time study toward a Bachelor of Engineering degree. His studies in Germany gained him exemption from some of the courses which other students were required to complete. Unlike the other students, however, Parbo had to master the language of his new country while studying and working. In 1953 he married Saima Soots, a fellow Estonian whom he had met in Germany. The first of their three children was born while Parbo was studying. Although a scholarship allowed him to eventually become a full-time, Parbo had to work part-time to supplement his scholarship. He completed his studies in March 1956, graduating with first class honors.

Shortly after graduating, Parbo joined Western Mining Corporation, a small but dynamic gold-mining company. His first position was underground surveyor at Bullfinch, which was Western Mining's operating base in the Yilgarn region of Western Australia. In 1958 he was appointed underground manager of a new mine in the Yilgarn region.

The Manager

In 1960 Parbo was appointed technical assistant to Western Mining's managing director under the company's policy of giving men who showed "particular promise" a year's experience in general management at the head office. Parbo had been with the company for only four years when he was singled out as showing particular promise, and he remained at the head office for four years rather than the usual one year. His time there proved to be a critical period in which the diversification strategy Western Mining had initiated in the early 1950s began to bear fruit.

After establishing the viability of a bauxite deposit in the Darling Ranges of Western Australia, Western Mining began to investigate the possibility of establishing an integrated bauxite mining and processing operation with the Aluminum Company of America (ALCOA). Parbo worked with the ALCOA representatives on a feasibility study of the project, and he accompanied Western Mining's managing director when he went to the United States to negotiate with ALCOA. As a result of these negotiations, ALCOA of Australia was formed to establish an integrated bauxite mining and processing operation. Western Mining took a 20 percent (subsequently increased to 44 percent) shareholding in ALCOA of Australia.

Parbo was transferred back to Western Australia as deputy general superintendent in 1964. Two years later the company discovered nickel at Kambalda in that state. By drawing on the expertise of Parbo and other personnel based in Western Australia, Western Mining established a fully operational nickel mine and primary processing plant within 18 months of discovering the deposit. The speedy development of the deposit allowed the company to capitalize on the strong demand for nickel in the late 1960s.

The Chief Executive

The day after the Kambalda mine was commissioned, Parbo was transferred back to Melbourne to become general manager. The next step was chief executive, although the chairman and board of Western Mining may have planned a longer apprenticeship for Parbo than fate provided. In 1971 the company's managing director retired due to ill health and Parbo was appointed managing director at the age of 45. In 1974 the chairman retired and Parbo became both chairman and managing director of Western Mining. Three years later he also became chairman of ALCOA of Australia. In 1986 he relinquished the position of managing director of Western Mining but remained chairman of the company and chairman of ALCOA of Australia.

Western Mining was an extremely successful company. Despite the exhaustion of some of its gold mines and the erratic fortunes of gold mining, it grew to become the second largest of the specialized mining companies in Australia. It is difficult to identify the role Parbo played in this growth, but the best starting point is to identify the reasons for the company's success. The main reasons are good management of its operations and aggressive and wide-ranging exploration for new mineral deposits, coupled with judicious purchases of other mining companies. Good operational management clearly reflects the quality of the management team rather than the quality of the chief executive, although a corporate structure that had clear lines of responsibility and accountability was also important. By 1974 Parbo concluded that the company's diversification program had begun to blur the lines of responsibility. To rectify the problem, Western Mining adopted a multi-divisional organizational structure. As Parbo explained at the time, the new structure allowed the nickel, gold, fuel and energy, and exploration divisions to operate as separate businesses, each with its own manager who had responsibility for the performance of the division.

In the area of corporate strategy, Parbo modestly pointed out that Sir Lindesay Clark initiated the aggressive exploration policy which proved so important to the company. Yet Parbo ensured that the policy was sustained even when times were tough. Nickel took over from gold as the company's major mineral by the early 1970s, yet the nickel market became oversupplied by 1971. In 1974 the company's problems were compounded by an international recession which affected the market for all its minerals. Western Mining's exploration activities employed 330 people at the time, and the company could have offered some comfort to shareholders by cutting back on exploration. However, as Parbo said in November 1974, "When you are exploring today you are thinking about conditions in 10 years' time" (*National Times,* November 11, 1974). The company's continued search for new mineral deposits throughout the recession yielded a handsome return with the discovery of the large copper, gold, and uranium deposit at Olympic Dam in South Australia, as well as smaller deposits elsewhere. Development of the Olympic Dam deposit began in 1983 with Western Mining as a 51 percent shareholder in the venture.

By the mid-1990s, under Parbo's direction, Western Mining was setting new records in the production of nickel, aluminum, copper, and gold.

Honors

Perhaps the best indicator of Parbo's contribution to Western Mining is the respect he gained from his peers. He held numerous official positions in engineering, mining, and trade associations and was president of the Australasian Institute of Mining and Metallurgy. With a background in

mining engineering, this may not be surprising. However, Parbo was also acknowledged by the broader business world. He was elected the inaugural president of the Business Council of Australia, an organization formed in 1983 to represent the interests of Australia's larger companies. He was also awarded the Ian Storey Medal by the Australian Institute of Management in 1984 and the Melbourne University Graduate School of Management Award in 1985. Perhaps the greatest accolade came in 1989 when Parbo was appointed chairman of Australia's largest company, the diversified mining and steel-making group, BHP.

Parbo also won numerous honors outside his field, including five honorary Doctor of Science degrees, a place on the Board of Advisors for the Constitutional Centenary Foundation, membership on the Advisory Council for the Tasman Institute Ltd. and on the Future Needs Reference Group. He became president of the Academy of Technological Sciences and Engineering, a Fellow of The Royal Society of Victoria, co-chair of the Korea Market Session of the National Trade and Investment Outlook Conference of 1996, ex-officio member of the Prime Minister's Science and Engineering Council, and a participant in the Constitutional Conference of 1991, among other honors.

Further Reading

G. Lindesay Clark's *Built on Gold: Recollections of Western Mining* (1983) provides some information about Sir Arvi Parbo's early career. *The New Boy Network* by Ruth Ostrow (1987) includes an entry on Parbo. Aside from these two references, the major source of information is newspaper and journal articles. The best of these include: "Why BHP Went for Arvi Parbo," *Business Review Weekly* (November 18, 1988); "From Quarryface to Boardroom: a Matter of Learning the Tune," the *Australian* (June 29, 1985); "Digging to the Top of the Pile," the *Age* (August 21, 1982); and "Profile of a Winning Minerals Explorer," the *National Times* (May 27, 1978).

Information may also be obtained through Internet sites maintained by Western Mining, the Constitutional Centenary Foundation, the Tasman Group, the Academy of Technological Sciences and Engineering, and the Prime Minister's Science and Engineering Council. □

Ambroise Paré

The French military surgeon Ambroise Paré (1510-1590) restored and reformed the surgical art through his practice, writings, and personal leadership to earn the sobriquet "father of modern surgery."

Ambroise Paré was born in Bourg-Hersent (now absorbed into Laval). His father seems to have been barber-surgeon to the Comte de Laval. His elder brother and his brother-in-law were also barber-surgeons, under whom he may have served his apprenticeship. From 1532 to 1537 Paré served under the surgeons of the Hôtel-Dieu in Paris as a clinical assistant studying anatomy and surgery. This experience, unusual for the times, Paré acknowledged was of the greatest importance to his future career.

Unable to pay for licensure, Paré joined his patron, René de Montejan, a colonel general of infantry, as military surgeon in the French expedition of 1537 to Turin. In his first campaign he realized that, on the basis of the poisonous nature of gunpowder, the accepted method of cauterizing gunshot wounds with boiling oil was destructive, and he therefore substituted more humane treatment.

On the death of Montejan in 1539, Paré returned to Paris now able to pay his fees to be accepted into the Company of Barber-Surgeons. A few months later he married Jeanne Mazelin, daughter of a wine merchant, by whom he had three children.

In Paris, Paré visited the celebrated physician Jacques du Bois (Sylvius), who encouraged him to write on his experiences with gunshot wounds. However, the outbreak of war with Spain saw Paré accompanying the Vicomte de Rohan on campaigns before Perpignan, in the Hainaut, and before Landrecies. This delayed the completion of his first book, *The Method of Curing Wounds Made by Arquebus and Other Firearms* (1545). Written in the vernacular instead of Latin, the book had a practicality and sound common sense that made it instantly popular and its author famous. Thereafter books on his experiences appeared in almost every decade of his long life. His *Anatomy,* based on Vesalius, contained his important contribution to midwifery, reintroducing podalic version. His texts on surgery reintroduced the ligature in amputation. These many writings were gathered together in his *Works* (1575), which disseminated his teachings throughout the world.

Paré served in many campaigns, and beginning with Henry II, was surgeon to no less than four successive kings of France. With Vesalius, Daza Chaçon, and Jean Chapelain, he attended at the tragic death of Henry II, killed in a joust with the Comte Montgomery which eventually split France in civil war. Paré cited the case to establish the fact that the brain can be injured without fracture of the skull. His last piece of writing, *The Apology and Voyages,* is a supreme literary achievement and unique historical document in which he defends his methods. Paré was the emancipator of surgery, whose modesty and humanitarianism is remembered by his aphorism, ''Je le pensay, et Dieu le guarit'' (I dressed it, and God healed it).

Further Reading

The Apologie and Treatise of Ambroise Paré, edited by Geoffrey Keynes (1952), contains the *Voyages* and other important excerpts. Two excellent but rare biographies of Paré are Stephen Paget and Francis Packard, *Ambroise Paré and His Times, 1510-1590* (1897), and *Life and Times of Ambroise Paré, 1510-1590,* edited and translated by Francis Packard (1921). A recent study is Wallace Hamby, *Ambroise Paré: Surgeon of the Renaissance* (1967). A superb bibliography containing several important essays is Janet Doe, *A Bibliography of the Works of Ambroise Paré* (1937). □

Vilfredo Pareto

The Italian sociologist, political theorist, and economist Vilfredo Pareto (1848-1923) is chiefly known for his influential theory of ruling elites and for his equally influential theory that political behavior is essentially irrational.

Vilfredo Pareto was born in Paris on July 15, 1848. His father, an aristocratic Genoese, had gone into political exile in France about 1835 because he supported the Mazzinian republican movement. He returned to Piedmont in 1855, where he worked as a civil engineer for the government. Vilfredo followed his father's profession after graduating from the Polytechnic Institute at Turin in 1869. He worked as director of the Rome Railway Company until 1874, when he secured an appointment as managing director of an iron-producing company with offices in Florence.

In 1889 Pareto married a Russian girl, Dina Bakunin, resigned his post with the iron company for a consultancy, and for the next 3 years wrote and spoke against the protectionist policy of the Italian government domestically and its military policies abroad. His reputation as a rebellious activist led to an intimate acquaintance with the economist Maffeo Pantaleoni. This association led to Pareto's interest in pure economics, a field in which he quickly became proficient and well known. His reputation gained him an appointment in 1893 to the prestigious post of professor of political economy at Lausanne University.

In 1894 Pareto published his first noted work, *Cours d'économie politique,* which evoked a great deal of commentary from other economists. Two years later he inherited a small fortune from an uncle, a windfall which caused him to think of retiring to pursue research. At this point he began to develop the theories for which he is most famous, elitism and irrationalism in politics.

In his own earlier political career Pareto had been an ardent activist in behalf of democracy and free trade, as had been his father before him. The reasons for the marked change in his political outlook have been much disputed, ranging from the Neo-Freudian analytical account, to the interpretation which stresses certain developments in his own career, to the explanation which maintains that, quite simply, he changed because of the results of his own vast studies. By the time his next book, *The Manual of Political Economy,* was published in 1906, his ideas on elites and irrationalism were already well developed. The following year he resigned from his chair of political economy at Lausanne to devote all his energies to researching his theories.

Pareto retired to his villa at Celigny, where he lived a solitary existence except for his 18 Angora cats (the villa was named "Villa Angora") and his friend Jane Régis, a woman 30 years younger than he who had joined his household in 1901, when his wife left him. In 1907 he began writing his most famous and quite influential work, *The Treatise on*

Sociology; he completed it in 1912 and published it in 1916. (The work was published in English translation as *The Mind and Society* in 1935 in a four-volume edition.) In 1923 he secured a divorce from his wife and married Jane Régis. Later the same year he died.

Pareto's theory of elitism is sometimes simplistically explained on the basis of his aristocratic heritage. However, as recent scholarship has shown, throughout his life and in his published works he often expressed extreme distaste with the titled Italian aristocracy, just as he was anti-socialist, anti-government-interventionist, anti-colonialist, anti-militarist, anti-racialist, and "anti-anti-Semitic." Attracted to fascism when it first came to power in Italy, he later opposed it. He is perhaps best described as an iconoclastic individualist.

The Mind and Society is at one and the same time a debunking of Marxism and of the bourgeois state. Pareto's method of investigation is inductive or positivistic, contemptuously rejecting natural law, metaphysics, and deductive reasoning. On the basis of very extensive historical and empirical studies, Pareto maintained that in reality and inevitably the true form of government in any state is never a monarchy, hereditary aristocracy, or democracy but that always all social organizations, including states, are governed by a ruling elite. This ruling elite, which has greater vitality and usefulness than other elites, dominates them until it in turn is overturned by a more powerful elite— Pareto's theory of "the circulation of elites." Political behavior itself, both of the masses and of the elites, is basically emotional and nonrational. The function of reason is to justify past behavior or to show the way to future goals, which are determined not by reason but by emotional wants.

Further Reading

Elitism is today, in one variety or another, the leading approach to the analysis of empirical political behavior by political scientists. Consequently, the literature on the subject, and on Pareto, is enormous. A good general introduction is James Burnham, *The Machiavellians: Defenders of Freedom* (1943). Pareto's name is almost always coupled with Gaetano Mosca's. For an approach which stresses the difference, even antagonism, between the two, see the introduction to James H. Meisel, ed., *Pareto and Mosca* (1965); the first nine essays in this work discuss various aspects of Pareto's life and work. See also George C. Homans and Charles P. Curtis, *An Introduction to Pareto* (1934), and Franz Borkenau, *Pareto* (1936).

Additional Sources

Powers, Charles H., *Vilfredo Pareto,* Newbury Park, Calif.: Sage Publications, 1987.
Vilfredo Pareto, (1848-1923), Aldershot, Hants, England; Brookfield, Vt., USA: E. Elgar Pub., 1992. □

Jacques Parizeau

In 1994 voters in the Canadian province of Quebec elected the Parti Québecois to a majority of seats in

the National Assembly. The victory put PQ president Jacques Parizeau (born 1930) in the post of premier.

On September 12, 1994, voters in the Canadian province of Quebec elected the Parti Québecois (PQ) to 77 of 125 seats comprising the National Assembly, that province's legislature. The victory put PQ president Jacques Parizeau, a longtime advocate of independence for the largely French-speaking province, in the post of premier. Jacques Parizeau had repeatedly asserted that a vote for the PQ was a vote for independence. His promise at the time of his election: putting a referendum on secession before the voters of Quebec within a year. Although, the election results were seen more as a reflection of Quebec's anger at the ruling Liberal Party, which had ruled the province for nine years, rather than a vote for Quebec's secession; a referendum vote did take place on October 30, 1995. The results yielded a nearly even split between the Yes and No sides with a strong majority of Quebec's non-francophone population voting "No" to secession. Parizeau announced his intention to resign his position the next day.

The Parti Québecois was founded in 1968 by René Lévesque, a former Liberal Party minister, who, along with a growing number of French-speaking Québecois, as the inhabitants of the province are known, had come to believe that the province must secede from the Canadian federation. Quebec is the largest in area of Canada's ten provinces and territories. Its population of just over seven million makes it the second most populous after Ontario.

More than 80 percent of Québecois speak French as their first language and many of these feel isolated and oppressed in a North America dominated by English-speaking people. They believe that the only way to maintain their cultural identity is to separate from Canada and form their own country. For nearly two decades, Parizeau has been in the vanguard of those seeking secession.

The forces aligned against secession, however, are formidable and consist of a reported 60 percent of the population of Quebec, a vast majority of Canadians as a whole, and major powers in the media. One month before the election, *Business Week* quoted John McCallum, chief economist at the Royal Bank of Canada, as saying that international markets "are taking a dim view of Canada" in light of growing separatist support. Brian I. Neysmith, president of the Canadian Bond Rating Service, said in the same publication, "The markets will react very negatively if the PQ wins a large majority. International investors will decide that Canada is not the safe haven it used to be." The weekly Canadian news magazine *Maclean's* was very blunt in its pre-election appraisal of Parizeau and his separatist rhetoric. In a scathing article titled "A Legend In His Own Mind" a writer for the source remarked, "The delusion in Canada resides mainly in the brain of Jacques Parizeau. He has become a victim of his own propaganda. He actually believes it, a man walking around in a vacuum of his own creation." And: "Jacques Parizeau is operating in a dreamland. As most longtime bureaucrats do. If he wins, as probable, his election, he is going to have to contend with real people. They are called Canadians. Our only wish is good luck." Still, the new premier called a referendum and, when it was rejected, predicted that the issue would be revisited in the future.

Parizeau was born on August 9, 1930, into a wealthy, well-connected family. His great-grandfather made the family fortune in lumber late in the 19th century and served for a while in the provincial legislature. Parizeau's grandfather had been a distinguished surgeon and the dean of the medical faculty at the University of Montreal. His father was a professor of history at the University of Montreal's business school, the École des Hautes Études Commerciales (HEC), and was cofounder of a brokerage and insurance firm that became one of the most prosperous in Quebec and greatly expanded the Parizeau wealth. In the 1970s the firm was reorganized under a holding company named Sordacan. Today, Sordacan is the 17th-largest insurance broker in the world and is run by Jacques's younger brother Robert. Interestingly, Jacques himself was given no shares in the family company, a mysterious edict directed by his father for reasons unknown. His mother was active in the women's rights movement of the 1930s, fighting for suffrage and more humane working conditions for women. During World War II she received the Order of the British Empire (OBE) for her relief work at home.

Parizeau was educated at exclusive private schools and the Collége Stanislas in suburban Montreal. From there he enrolled in the HEC where he studied economics and distinguished himself as an excellent student. He then went to Paris and to the London School of Economics (LSE), where he earned a Ph.D. under the tutelage of the Nobel laureate James Edward Meade. While in England, Parizeau developed a strong British accent and a lordly manner that have earned him a measure of scorn. As *Maclean's* stated, "[He] is a delightful man to view. Highly educated with an Oxford accent and a vocabulary that would put most Canadians to shame, he has the certainty of an economist—an economist once having been defined as someone who is good at numbers but doesn't have the personality to be an accountant." Even publications not so overtly hostile to the premier have commented on this quality of seemingly aloof erudition, and it has been reported that his political handlers have tried for years to get him to appear more approachable. The *New York Times* reported, "Only after giving himself up to image builders in the seven-week election campaign just ended did he discard his three-piece Saville Row pinstripes for sports jackets and learn to trim often ponderous, professorial speeches into sound bites."

After graduating from the LSE, Parizeau returned to Canada and took a position as a lecturer in economics at the HEC. In the late 1950s, Parizeau began working in government, while retaining his chair at the HEC. (He gave it up only in 1989.) His first position was as a researcher for the Bank of Canada, the federal, government-owned bank comparable to the American Federal Reserve. From this post, Parizeau became involved in economic planning on the national and then provincial level. In 1961 he became an economic adviser to Quebec's provincial government, then headed by Liberal premier Jean Lesage. Here, Parizeau played a substantial role in the so-called Quiet Revolution, a series of sweeping economic reforms that brought wide socialist reform to the province. In 1966 the Liberals were ousted by the Union Nationale, but Parizeau was retained by the new government as a consultant to the Council of Ministers.

Parizeau joined the Parti Québecois in 1969 and began working in earnest for separation. In 1970 he became chairman of the party's national executive council. Four years later the PQ adopted a platform that called for a referendum on separation within a year of winning a majority. In 1976 the PQ was swept into office, largely as a result of the call for a referendum. The first PQ government was headed by René Lévesque with Parizeau serving as finance minister and president of the Treasury Board. During this administration, Parizeau is credited with instituting the Quebec Stock Savings Plan, which provided tax incentives to investors in small, Quebec-based businesses. He is blamed, on the other hand, for the ill-advised decision to nationalize the asbestos industry just before the industry collapsed due to reports of links between asbestos and cancer. He also oversaw a 500 percent increase in the budget deficit and a 600 percent increase in the provincial debt. The promised vote on secession took place in 1980, four years after the PQ won election. As in the debate which took place over a decade later, emotions ran high prior to the vote and both sides campaigned fiercely. The vote was 60 to 40 percent against secession.

In 1984 Lévesque announced his intention to drop secession from the PQ platform in favor of negotiations with the federal government in the Canadian capital of Ottawa on other options. Parizeau and several other die-hard separatists resigned. In 1985, amid deepening economic troubles in the province and a void in PQ leadership as Lévesque grew gravely ill, the Liberals were voted back into office. Two years later, as the PQ continued to flounder, Parizeau announced his intention to seek the party's leadership. He was alone among contenders for the post to advocate a total separation from Canada. In 1988 he was elected party leader.

Prior to the 1989 provincial elections Parizeau again asserted that in the event of a PQ victory, he would hold a referendum on secession. In an interview with *Maclean's* he pleaded his case that the time was right and tried to counter arguments that secession would be economically devastating: "[Businesses] know that sovereignty is not a handicap to growth. The Canada-United States Free Trade Agreement has changed their perspective considerably. Having access to the large American market leaves the mind far more serene to discuss sovereignty for Quebec." Despite Parizeau's predictions, the party lost the elections. Parizeau, however, was elected to his old seat in the National Assembly and continued his campaign for independence. His new target for attack was the Meech Lake accord, an agreement reached between Quebec and the federal government that granted Quebec constitutional recognition as a "distinct society." Parizeau objected to the accord as a trick by Ottawa to defuse nationalist support for independence by granting token recognition. The accord had to be approved by all the Canadian provinces by June 22, 1990, and when that deadline passed with two provinces having refused to approve it, many Québecois felt shunned by the majority English-speaking Canadians and support for independence skyrocketed. Polls showed 60 percent of Québecois favoring the establishment of an independent Quebec—the highest numbers ever reported.

On July 24, 1994, Liberal party premier Daniel Johnson called for provincial elections to be held on September 12. Parizeau immediately went on the offensive, calling for a referendum on sovereignty. One of the principal issues regarding separation was the cost to Quebec, and this became a major theme of the campaign as it was waged through the summer. Many economists had figured the cost as enormous—far too burdensome to justify. Parizeau countered that secession would save $3 billion (Canadian dollars) just in eliminating federal duplication and waste, and that the money saved could then be spent on job creation and other measures to bolster Quebec's anemic economy. Johnson, as quoted in the *New Republic,* countered, "There are contradictions, paradoxes, make-believe appeals to people's gullibility.... These people will say anything to get elected." Eric Kierans, a longtime Canadian cabinet minister, told *Maclean's,* "There was a time when Parizeau had a sound grasp of economics, then his politics clouded his vision. Now, he's someone with no sympathy at all for Canada."

Other sticking points for separatists were the amount of Canada's national debt the new country would assume, the drawing of boundaries, and Quebec's status vis-à-vis the

North American Free Trade Agreement (NAFTA). Parizeau assumed that Quebec would immediately be granted signatory status in NAFTA, but the New Republic reported that "the Clinton administration responded that the province's place in NAFTA . . . was not assured." A further impediment to the realization of Parizeau's dream was the Cree Indians, who inhabit vast areas in the north of the province. They claim title to huge amounts of land and were not at all calmed by Quebec's claims to respect their rights of self-determination. There were also sizable enclaves of English-speaking citizens of Quebec who intimated that their vote would be to remain associated with Canada.

Parizeau was unmoved by all the logistical, economic, and legal obstacles so many insisted would confound any realistic expectations of separation. For him it was a matter of cultural survival, and he felt that the sooner a referendum was held, the better. The New York Times quoted him as telling reporters after the 1994 election in which he was elected premier of Quebec, "We have lost a great deal of time in Quebec, for many years, in these never-ending debates. There has been a price to pay for this uncertainty. Let's decide." While the resulting October 1995 referendum was defeated, a majority of French-speaking citizens of Quebec did indicate by their vote that they desired more power for their province. According to Barry Came, Maclean's, Parizeau forecasted a new push for independence, saying "Don't forget that three-fifths of us voted Yes. It wasn't quite enough, but very soon it will be enough. Our country is within our grasp." Parizeau believes that getting Montreal's sputtering economy back on track is a way to convince Quebeckers to vote for idependence.

Parizeau announced his resignation on October 31, 1995; but, he faced leaving his office on the coattails of scandal. According to Maclean's, "At issue are 25 research contracts worth $2.7 million that were handed out . . . by [Richard] Le Hir's [former minister of restructuring] now-dismantled . . . department for work on 44 studies examining various aspects of Quebec sovereignty with a view to providing the PQ government with ammunition in the referendum battle." Additionally, in September 1995 Quebec's Liberal Opposition charged that some of the contracts had been awarded "without tender to companies linked to senior employees working for Le Hir's department." Parizeau referred the matter to Guy Breton, Quebec's Auditor General, who confirmed the illegalities in a report issued on December 5, 1995. Breton also cited Pierre Campeau, deputy minister in the restructuring department, and Claude Lafrance, a consultant. He disclosed that other officials in Parizeau's government were aware of the potential scandal. Yet, they reacted by either firing or forcing the whistle-blowers to resign.

Although Parizeau responded quickly to the report by initiating several actions including increasing the scope of contracts to be examined further by Breton, Liberals allegedly uncovered another contract which involved Parizeau, himself. This contract awarded $90,000 to Yvon Martineau, later appointed president of Hydro Quebec, for three-months work as a juridical counsellor for referendum planning. Breton's final report, originally due in January, was released on March 14, 1996, after Lucien Bouchard, leader of the Bloc Quebecois, succeeded Parizeau and was sworn in as premier on January 29, 1996. In the report, Breton reiterated that contracts involving millions of dollars were issued in violation of conflict-of-interest laws.

According to Elizabeth Thompson, a reporter for the Montreal Gazette, "While auditor-general Guy Breton was reluctant to blame anyone, he said Parizeau, Le Hir and former secretary-general Louis Bernard were responsible for overseeing what went on. In practice, however, Breton said he found no evidence that they were involved in wrong-doing or were aware of what was going on under their noses." The reaction of those named in the report was to point blame away from themselves. It had been hoped that Parizeau's departure from office would defuse the scandal. According to Maclean's, "there [were] many in the PQ who [were] breathing a sigh of relief, hoping that when Parizeau [went], he [would] take l'affaire Le Hir with him." But with the Surete du Quebec's economic-crimes squad conducting an investigation, it appears l'affaire Le Hir will outlive Parizeau's political career.

Further Reading

Business Week, August 8, 1994; November 7, 1994.
Christian Science Monitor, May 30, 1996.
Detroit Free Press, September 13, 1994; September 19, 1994.
Facts on File, February 1, 1996, pp. 56-57.
Maclean's, September 25, 1989; August 15, 1994; September 12, 1994; November 6, 1995, p. 18; December 25, 1995, p. 38.
Montreal Gazette, January 9, 1996, p. A8; March 14, 1996, p. A11.
New Republic, September 19, 1994; September 26, 1994.
New York Times, September 14, 1994; September 15, 1994. □

Chung Hee Park

Chung Hee Park (1917-1979) was a soldier, revolutionary leader, and president of South Korea from 1963 to 1979. He led the military coup of May 16, 1961, which toppled the Korean Second Republic and President Syngman Rhee.

Pak Chông-hŭi (who Westernized his name to Chung Hee Park) was born into a poor farming family in a tiny village named Sangmo-ri in Kyôngsang-pukdo, a southeastern province of Korea, on Sept. 30, 1917. The youngest among five sons and two daughters of Pak (Park) Sông-bin, he was shorter and slighter than the other children. Though a loner, he excelled in his work and was recommended by the grammar school to enter a normal school in Taegu, the provincial capital. Normal schools gave inexpensive, terminal, vocational training to bright but poor students, most of whom were satisfied to build a career as grammar school teachers.

Park taught at the grammar school of Mungyng, a small town in Kyngsang-pukdo. After two years of teaching in a sleepy provincial town, he entered the military academy of

Manchukuo, the puppet state of militarist Japan, in 1940. Training at the academy was a path for some ambitious young Koreans to become members of the officer corps of the imperial Japanese army. Upon graduation from the military academy in Tokyo in 1944, Park was assigned to the Japanese army in Manchuria (the Kwantung army) as a second lieutenant until the Japanese surrender on September 2, 1945.

Army Career

When Park was discharged from the defeated army, he returned to his home village and spent a year of quiet desperation. It was predictable that he would join the newly organized South Korean constabulary, as did many of his contemporaries with similar military backgrounds. When he entered the Korean Military Academy in September 1946, he resumed the military career that he had started earlier. Upon graduation in December of the same year, he had earned the rank of captain. South Korea's constitution was adopted on July 17, 1948, making it an independent nation separated from the communist-controlled north.

Park was forced out of the army in 1948, over charges that he had collaborated with communists. He was recalled when North Korea invaded the south in June of 1950. Park's career was marked by a steady rise through the ranks of the new army that was rapidly expanding—particularly during the Korean War.

By 1953, the last year of the Korean War, Park had advanced to the rank of brigadier general; he was 36, a

relatively young age even in the Korean army, noted for the youth of its generals. As an artillerist, Park attended the advanced course of the U.S. Army Artillery School at Fort Sill, OK., returning to Korea for assignment as commandant of the artillery school of the Korean army. From this post he was transferred to the 5th Infantry Division as commanding general, which post he held until 1957, when he attended the Command and General Staff College of the Korean Army. Later, he was made the deputy commander of the entire Korean Second Army.

Throughout his military career Park had been known for his almost total absence from the social functions attended by most high-ranking government and military officers, their American counterparts, and American military advisers. Although many young Korean army generals conspicuously enjoyed their newly won social positions following the Korean War, Park was an exception.

Korean Politics

Politics was directly affecting the lives of many high-ranking army officers, including Park. When President Syngman Rhee's Liberal party extensively "rigged" the 1960 presidential election, numerous commanders of military units were suspected of having collaborated with the seemingly omnipotent ruling party in delivering army votes in support of Rhee. It was widely believed at about this time that the Liberal party chieftains had powerful influence over the promotions and assignments of high level military officers.

According to data revealed after 1961, a military coup d'etat was being planned in February 1960, when President Rhee and his Liberal party were preoccupied with ensuring victory at any cost in the scheduled March 15, 1960 elections. Park, then logistics base commander in Pusan, was the mastermind of the clandestine plan. Then came the student uprising of April 19, 1960, which cracked the thin veneer of order covering the nation's profound socioeconomic and political disarray. President Rhee declared martial law, but the army under the martial law commander, Lt. Gen. Song Yo-ch'an, evidently decided not to block the demonstrating students and citizenry, as some policemen attempted to do.

At the most critical juncture, when the very survival of the Rhee regime was at stake, the army command's political decision to be "neutral" in the situation was undoubtedly one of the most decisive forces which persuaded Rhee to step down. The significance of this inaction by the military in bringing about the ouster of the Rhee regime was not lost on the officer corps, and this realization was but a step removed from a conviction that an action by the military would definitely produce spectacular results.

The time shortly after the student uprising, however, was not propitious for the Korean military to take drastic political action, because the majority of the people had great expectations that political and economic conditions were going to improve rapidly under the new government of the Democrats. The military group that had planned a coup for May 1960 now decided to wait and see. The Cabinet of the Second Republic of Korea, headed by Premier Chang

Myn (John M. Chang), had been in office for less than nine months when the military officers, headed by Park, executed a carefully planned coup d'etat in the chilly pre-dawn hours of May 16, 1961.

After the Coup

The entire political structure of the Second Republic was overthrown, and the Military Revolutionary Committee, led by Park, took over all state organizations. Despite some attempts by the highest-ranking American officials to restore the constitutional government, opposition to the military dissipated by the evening of May 17. As the takeover became a firmly established fact, the Military Revolutionary Committee was renamed the Supreme Council for National Reconstruction (SCNR). It was announced on May 19 that the council, led by Park, was now the nation's "supreme governing organ," with both executive and legislative powers, plus administrative control over the judiciary. Park became the chairman of the Supreme Council on July 3.

Within two months of the coup, the political and governmental structure had undergone fundamental upheavals. The democratic polity of the Second Republic—at least in terms of theory—was now completely discredited and discarded. The representative superstructure had been decreed out of existence. A highly centralized, tightly regimented, and almost omnipotent military regime emerged under the undisputed leadership of Park. Having boosted the prestige of Park through his visit to the United States and Japan in November 1961, the military government promulgated on March 16, 1962, the sweeping Political Activities Purification Law, banning political activities by civilian politicians who were closely associated with the First and Second Republics under President Syngman Rhee and Premier Chang Myn.

When President Yun Po-sn resigned on March 22, 1962, in protest against the political "purge," Park became the acting president. While civilian politicians were stunned and paralyzed by the "purge," the Supreme Council proceeded to amend the constitution extensively. The result was a document that institutionalized a strong presidential rule with readily available emergency powers, particularly since the president controlled a majority in the National Assembly. Park resigned from active military service on August 30, 1963, and on the same day joined the Democratic Republican party. On the very next day, he accepted the presidential nomination from the party that had carefully prepared for the move under the direction of Kim Chong-p'il. The presidential election "to restore the government to civilians" was to be held on October 15. Park won, defeating Yun Po-sn, and the Third Republic of Korea was officially born on Dec. 17, 1963, with Park inaugurated as president.

Third Republic

As the political situation stabilized, the Park administration turned its attention to the economic development of South Korea. In a few years the administration was able to claim unprecedented gains in gross national product. The Park government also normalized diplomatic relations between Korea and Japan and decided on an active participation by Korean forces in the Vietnamese conflict.

President Park won his second term on May 3, 1967, by a plurality vote against his opponent, once again Yun Po-sn. In September 1969 the National Assembly, dominated by the Democratic Republican party, again amended the constitution. Park had threatened to resign as president in 1969 if the constitution was not amended to allow him to run for another term. After fierce debate in the assembly, a 1969 amendment permitted a third presidential term of four years for Park. When a referendum on the constitutional amendments was held in October 1969, voters approved the tenure amendment and in 1971 Park won his third term as president of South Korea.

Fourth Republic

Park's third term had brought him increasingly autocratic and repressive powers, which led to numerous student demonstrations. But rapid social and economic change, U.S. President Richard M. Nixon's February 1972 trip to China, and the opening of South-North dialogue led Park to strengthen the central government and his position even more. The constitution was amended by referendum in November 1972, creating the Fourth Republic.

The new constitution, called the *Yushin Honpop* (Revitalizing Reforms Constitution), was aimed at insuring political stability and creating an even stronger economy through strong presidential leadership. Park was given dictatorial powers, sparking unrest, which was violently repressed.

There were many in Korea who did not like the new constitution expressly because it gave Park dictatorial powers. Among other orders, Park issued a decree in 1975 making it illegal to criticize the government. He rigidly enforced this decree against his political enemies, insuring that his place in Korean politics was kept secure. In 1979, Kim Young Sam (future South Korea president), speaking in the U.S., called Park a dictator and said that the U.S. should encourage political reforms in Korea to insure democracy. His comments touched off more demonstrations by citizens and students in the southern towns of Pusan and Masan, forcing Park to send troops to quell the disturbances.

On October 26, 1979, Park was assassinated by the head of the Korean Central Intelligence Agency, Kim Kyu, at a private dinner. Kyu became entangled in an argument with another man at the dinner and shot him. When Park attempted to intervene, he was shot twice by Kyu, one bullet severing his spine. Park's four bodyguards were also shot and killed. How Kyu was able to kill six men—shooting Park twice—with a six-round .45 semi-automatic handgun remains a mystery. This act effectively brought an end to the *Yushin Honpop* and the Fourth Republic.

Park traveled to the U.S. several times throughout his career and met with presidents Kennedy, Johnson, Nixon, Ford, and Carter to cement good relations and create economic ties between the two governments. He also worked effectively in establishing economic ties with Japan (a former enemy) and Western European nations. Park's efforts in these areas helped to strengthen South Korea's economy, making it a powerhouse in the late 20th century.

Further Reading

There is no biography of Park in English. Booklets originally published in Korean bearing Park's name as author do not give much biographical information. There is a brief section entitled "General Park: The Man and His Ideas" in John Kie-chiang Oh, *Korea: Democracy on Trial* (1968).

There is information available on Park and South Korea's government, history and economy accessible on-line at the Republic of South Korea's Website located at korea.emb. washington.dc.us. □

Maud Wood Park

Maud Wood Park (1871–1955) was a social activist hoping to educate new voters and becoming the first president of the League of Women Voters.

Maud Wood Park became first president of the League of Women Voters , a nonpartisan organization to educate new voters following the passage of woman's suffrage in 1920. Maud Wood grew up in Boston and earned money by teaching in Chelsea High School in order to attend Radcliffe College. In 1898 she graduated summa cum laude from Radcliffe, where she was one of only two students in a class of seventy-two to favor the vote for women. While still a student, she married Charles Edward Park, a Boston architect, in 1897. The couple lived near the Boston settlement Denison House, introducing Maud Wood Park to social-reform work. Charles Park died in 1904.

Suffrage

For fifteen years Maud Wood Park was active in suffrage and civic work in Boston. She became chair of the Massachusetts Woman Suffrage Association in 1900 and executive secretary of the Boston Equal Suffrage Association for Good Government, which was devoted to combining work for suffrage with activities for civic betterment. A charismatic speaker, Park traveled widely to enlist college women in the cause of suffrage. In 1916 her friend Carrie Chapman Catt, president of the National American Woman's Suffrage Association (NAWSA), persuaded Park to join the NAWSA's Congressional Committee and to go to Washington to lobby directly for the federal suffrage amendment. Thus Park led the "front-door lobby" to win suffrage.

League of Women Voters

Park agreed to serve as first president of the League of Women Voters (LWV), the organization that succeeded the NAWSA. She said that the league's purpose should be to "promote reforms in which women will naturally take an interest in a greater degree than men—protection for working women, children, public health questions, and the care of dependent and delinquent classes." Under Park's leadership the LWV adopted a thirty-eight-point program of legislative measures. Though women's organizations divided in the 1920s, Park helped form the Women's Joint Congressio-

nal Committee (WJCC) in 1920, with representatives from nine other women's organizations, and then became its head. The WJCC succeeded in winning two important pieces of legislation: the Sheppard-Towner Maternity and Infancy Protection Act of 1921 and the 1922 Cable Act, which granted independent citizenship to married women. The league also served to pressure the Women's Bureau to end child labor and promote social legislation on behalf of women. Because of serious illness, Park resigned from the presidency of the league in 1924, but she continued for the rest of her life to lecture and work on behalf of women.

Further Reading

Eleanor Flexner, *Century of Struggle: The Woman's Rights Movement in the United States* (Cambridge: Harvard University Press, 1959). □

Robert E. Park

Robert E. Park (1864-1944) was a pioneer American sociologist who specialized in the dynamics of urban life, race relations, and crowd behavior and was largely responsible for standardizing the field of sociology as practiced in the United States.

Robert Ezra Park was born on February 14, 1864, near the town of Shickshinny, in Luzerne County, Pennsylvania. After the Civil War his father, a veteran of the war, took the family to live in Red Wing, Minnesota, where Park was to spend the first 18 years of his life. There he got to know Norwegian immigrants struggling to build a new life in a new land, and he shared in their adventures. He even briefly encountered Jesse James, who asked him directions to the nearest blacksmith shop while fleeing from a bank robbery (1876).

When Park graduated from high school in 1882, his father decided that Robert was "not the studious type" and that no further education was necessary. Robert ran away from home, worked on a railroad gang during the summer, earned $50, and enrolled at the University of Minnesota as a freshman in engineering. Although he had problems studying he passed his freshman courses, and his father relented and offered to finance further studies. Robert entered the University of Michigan, abandoned his interest in engineering, and majored in philosophy. He took philosophy courses with John Dewey, of whom Park said that studying with him was "an adventure that was taking us beyond the limits of safe and certified knowledge into the realm of the problematical and unknown." Park graduated in 1887 with a BA degree and a Phi Beta Kappa key.

Additional Education Leads to Sociology

Returning to Red Wing briefly, and inspired by Dewey and by a course in Goethe's *Faust* to seek adventure in the world, Park became a newspaper reporter, first in Minneapolis, then in Detroit (where he was city editor of two papers),

Denver, New York, and Chicago. He spent 11 years learning the reporter's craft and in the process "developed an interest in sociological subjects, based on observations of urban life.

Spurred on by his father, by his marriage (1894) to the artist Clara Cahill, and by Dewey, he decided to return to university life because he "was interested in communication and collective behavior and wanted to know what the universities had to say about it." He received a Master's degree in philosophy from Harvard University (1899) and moved his family to Berlin. He enrolled at the Friedrich-Wilhelm University, where he expanded his interests in the newspaper to the broader concerns of human social life, particularly in its unplanned aspects, such as crowds and public gatherings, crazes and mobs. At the university he was exposed to the writing and lectures of the sociologist Georg Simmel; indeed, the course that he took from Simmel was the only course in sociology that Park ever had in his entire life. He received his Ph.D. in philosophy from the University of Heidelberg in 1903, having written a thesis titled "Crowds and Publics: A Methodological and Sociological Investigation," regarded today as a classic study of both collective phenomena and social change.

Park returned to Harvard in 1903 and spent a year as assistant in philosophy while he completed his thesis. In 1904 he became secretary of the Congo Reform Association, a group organized in England and dedicated to publicizing atrocities perpetrated against Blacks in what was then the Congo Free State. The organization hoped to bring pressure for reform on King Leopold II of Belgium, who was solely responsible for administration of the area. "To fight such iniquity as this [Park wrote] is a great privilege." He wrote a series of articles for the muckraking periodical *Everybody's Magazine,* which generated considerable public outcry leading eventually (1908) to the formal annexation of the Congo by Belgium and the substitution of parliamentary control for personal rule. With this the Congo Reform Association ceased to function.

In 1905, while working with the association, Park felt himself to be "sick and tired of the academic world" and "wanted to get back into the world of men." Introduced to the noted African American teacher and reformer Booker T. Washington, Park was invited to become a publicist for Washington's Tuskegee Institute in Alabama. Sensing that this might be an opportunity both to help the cause of African Americans and to learn about them and about the South, and in the process "get back into the world," Park accepted the offer. Together they toured Europe (1910) comparing and contrasting the plight of Southern African Americans and European laborers and peasants. In that year, too, he helped organize the National Urban League. Park served Washington as confidant, as well as serving as director of public relations of the institute. He assisted Washington in preparation of the latter's *The Man Farthest Down* (1912) and appears as one of its authors. In 1912 Park organized an International Conference on the Negro at Tuskegee.

University of Chicago Tenure

As the conference opened, Park had decided to leave Tuskegee in order to spend more time with his family. Attending the conference was the sociologist W. I. Thomas who, after a lengthy correspondence, invited Park to join him on the faculty of the Department of Sociology at the University of Chicago, then one of a few departments of sociology in the United States. Park came to Chicago in 1913 and remained there until 1936, well past his formal retirement in 1933. He served as president of the American Sociological Society in 1925. He was a visiting professor at the University of Hawaii from 1931 to 1933; travelled extensively in China, India, South Africa, the Pacific, and Brazil; and in 1936 joined the faculty of Fisk University, Nashville, Tennessee, and taught intermittently as a visiting professor. He died in Nashville a week short of his 80th birthday, on February 7, 1944.

During his tenure in the Chicago department, both in his writing and in teaching a generation of students who for the most part themselves became influential sociologists, Park virtually single-handedly shepherded sociology from the ranks of a movement to better the world to the status of a science of social life. First, with his younger colleague Ernest W. Burgess, he tried to define sociology in a way that was more than simply arm-chair theorizing about society and its problems. Their *Introduction to the Science of Sociology* (1921, 1924) presents sociology as both "a point of view and a method for investigating the processes by which individuals are inducted into and induced to cooperate in some sort of permanent corporate existence [called] society." Therefore, second, Park tried to make sociology a research-oriented field of study by suggesting a strategy for social research and a laboratory—the city—in which this research could be carried out (see his 1915 article "The City: Suggestions for the Investigation of Human Behavior in the Urban Environment"). He coined the term "human ecology" to suggest that one dimension of sociological study. Finally, he argued that the problems of society could not be understood, let alone ameliorated, without a thoroughly documented awareness of the varieties of social processes that give rise to such problems.

Throughout his work one finds a continuing concern with social transformation and change that characterized his doctoral thesis. Additionally, the notion persists that the sociologist is very much like the reporter. But the sociologist's depiction of "the Big News" differs from the reporter's story in that the sociologist has a set of analytical categories in which to place that story, to establish relations between events over the longer term, and to predict as accurately as evidence might permit on the basis of what has happened in the past what might well happen in the future. His approach to sociology as the outcome of human communication raised the Department of Sociology at Chicago to a pre-eminent level, and his views still are influential.

Everett C. Hughes, one of Park's distinguished students, said of his mentor:

Park's genius was to arouse a student's interest in a small project and develop it into a large one, stated in universal terms. . . . He was a tireless teacher. He insisted that data gathered for research should not be used for social casework or individual therapy. He tried to understand and guide his students in their efforts to learn and communicate clearly what they were learning. . . . [His] teaching always gave the sense of something in the making; he said in a handwritten note, 'Science is not knowledge. It is the pursuit of knowledge.'

Further Reading

One can best learn of Park as person and sociologist by reading his own work. In addition to his doctoral dissertation, which has been translated into English (1972), Park was the author, co-author, or editor of six books: *The Man Farthest Down: A Record of Observation and Study in Europe,* with Booker T. Washington (1912, reprinted 1983), demonstrates Park's commitment to civil rights at a time when such commitment among whites was rare; *Introduction to the Science of Sociology,* with Ernest W. Burgess (1921, 1924, reprinted 1969, 1981), is perhaps the classic statement of sociology as "the American science"; *Old World Traits Transplanted,* with W. I. Thomas and Herbert A. Miller (1921, reprinted 1969); *The Immigrant Press and Its Control* (1921, reprinted 1970); *The City,* editor, with Ernest W. Burgess and Roderick D. Mc-Kenzie (1925, reprinted 1967), which constitutes the first major thrust of American sociology toward the use of the urban environment as a sociological laboratory; and *An Outline of the Principles of Sociology,* editor (1939), a simple but solid introduction to what sociology is all about.

Park's collected papers were edited in three volumes by Everett C. Hughes, Charles S. Johnson, Jitsuichi Masuoka, Robert Redfield, and Louis Wirth (1950-1955). They deal, in turn, with Park's approach to race and culture, to human communities, and to human behavior as reflected in collective behavior, news, and public opinion. The first volume of the three contains "An Autobiographical Note," which Park dictated to his secretary when at Fisk University and which was found among his papers after his death. An earlier "Life History" was published in the *American Journal of Sociology* in September 1973. Works about Park include Fred F. Matthews, *Quest for An American Sociology: Robert E. Park and the Chicago School* (1977); one of Park's many students, Winifred Raushenbush, *Robert E. Park: Biography of a Sociologist* (1979); and Everett C. Hughes, also a student of Park, "Robert E. Park," in *The Sociological Eye,* edited by Hughes (1971).

Additional Sources

Lal, Barbara Ballis, *The romance of culture in an urban civilization: Robert E. Park on race and ethnic relations in cities,* London; New York: Routledge, 1990.

Raushenbush, Winifred, *Robert E. Park: biography of a sociologist,* Durham, N.C.: Duke University Press, 1979. □

William Hallock Park

The American physician and public health official William Hallock Park (1863-1939) was the first to **systematically apply bacteriology to the diagnosis, prevention, and treatment of the common infectious diseases.**

Williiam Hallock Park was born on Dec. 13, 1863, in New York City. He entered the College of the City of New York in 1878. Graduating in 1883, he entered the New York College of Physicians and Surgeons and received his medical degree in 1886. After serving at Roosevelt Hospital for a few years, he went to Europe in 1889 to study otolaryngology. On his return to the United States he practiced in this field during the next 2 years at Bellevue Hospital, Vanderbilt Clinic of the College of Physicians and Surgeons, Roosevelt Hospital, and the Manhattan Eye and Ear Hospital. While engaged in this work, Park was also developing an interest in the new science of bacteriology, which gradually became of principal importance to him.

In 1893 Park was appointed bacteriological diagnostician and inspector of diphtheria with the New York City Department of Health. Within a few years he was assistant director of the research laboratory and by 1904, director.

The first and greatest achievement of Park and his associates concerned diphtheria; they devised routine methods of diagnosis for the disease. In 1894, when diphtheria antitoxin was discovered in Europe, Park and his staff were the first in the world to devote their energies to its large-scale preparation.

In 1898 Park was appointed adjunct professor of bacteriology and hygiene and a director of the Carnegie Laboratory of the newly merged Medical College of New York and the Bellevue Hospital Medical School. He was made full professor of bacteriology and head of a new department of bacteriology in 1900. In 1914 he was offered the deanship but declined because of conflict with his work with the city. In 1899 he coauthored *Bacteriology in Medicine and Surgery: A Practical Manual for Physicians, Health Officers and Students.*

Early in the 20th century Park turned his attentions to the problems of milk sanitation, and his paper "The Great Bacterial Contamination of the Milk of Cities" (1901) is considered a landmark in the fight for clean milk.

A significant factor in Park's success was his ability to staff his laboratory with outstanding people and to guide their work in the most fruitful directions. His associates made outstanding contributions to the study of tuberculosis, smallpox, poliomyelitis, influenza, and measles. Park died on April 6, 1939.

Further Reading

The only biography of Park is Wade W. Oliver, *The Man Who Lived for Tomorrow: A Biography of William Hallock Park, M.D.* (1941), a detailed study of Park's associates as well. See also Paul De Kruif, *Microbe Hunters* (1926). □

larly as a result of physical and mental illness. On March 4, 1955, he made his final public appearance; he died 8 days later.

Parker's earliest records reveal that he was already developing the more complex harmonic approach that was characteristic of his mature work. This style is notable for a then unheard-of variety of rhythmic accentuation, harmonic complexity allied to an acute melodic sensitivity, solo lines that employ a wider range of intervals than had previously been the norm, and a disregard for the four- and eight-bar divisions of the standard jazz repertoire. This approach and his strident, even harsh, tone made it difficult for the casual listener to follow the logic of his choruses. Also, with major changes taking place in the rhythm section, it was not altogether surprising that his music sometimes met with opposition or downright incomprehension. Another facet of Parker's playing was its extraordinary technical facility, enabling him to express his ideas with the greatest clarity even at the most rapid tempos.

Parker composed a number of tunes that became jazz standards, though these were usually casually assembled items based on chord sequences of popular tunes. In terms of melodic skill, his recordings of ballads such as "Embraceable You" and "How Deep Is the Ocean" are even more revealing than his interpretations of the bebop repertoire. He spawned dozens of imitators, but his own achievements were unique.

Charles Christopher Parker Jr.

Charles Christopher Parker, Jr. (1920-1955), American musician, was one of the most widely influential soloists in jazz history.

Charlie Parker, widely known as Yardbird or Bird, was born in Kansas City, Kans., on Aug. 29, 1920. His mother bought him an alto saxophone in 1931, and in the following years he played with several prominent local big bands. In 1941 he became a member of Jay McShann's band, with which he made his first commercial recordings.

At this time Parker met Dizzy Gillespie, widely accepted as the cofounder with Parker of the jazz style that became known as bop or bebop. In 1945 they recorded the definitive titles in the new idiom. Although younger musicians quickly realized his genius, Parker met with considerable hostility from musicians of earlier stylistic persuasions. In 1946, as a result, he suffered a mental breakdown and was committed for 6 months to a sanitarium. Upon his release he formed his own quintet and worked with this format for several years, mainly in the New York City area. He also toured with Norman Granz's "Jazz at the Philharmonic" and made trips to Paris in 1949 and Scandinavia in 1950. From his teen-age years Parker had been a narcotics addict, and in the last 5 years of his life he worked irregu-

Further Reading

Robert George Reisner, *Bird: The Legend of Charlie Parker* (1962), contains a great deal of material on Parker by his fellow musicians and friends, some of it more colorful than enlightening. A critical study that offers many valuable insights into Parker's music is Max Harrison, *Charlie Parker* (1960). See also Marvin Barrett, *The Jazz Age* (1959), and Albert McCarthy, *Jazz on Record: A Critical Guide to the First Fifty Years, 1917-1967* (1968). □

Dorothy Rothschild Parker

Dorothy Rothschild Parker (1893-1967), American humorist, was known for her biting prose and verse satires. Numerous critics expressed admiration for her unique talent.

Born in New Jersey to Scottish-Jewish parents, Dorothy Parker attended Miss Dana's School there and finished her education at the Blessed Sacrament Convent in New York City. During 1916-1917 she was on the editorial staff at *Vogue,* and from 1917 to 1920 she was an editor and drama critic for *Vanity Fair.* Fired from the last position for her caustic, devastating reviews of several important plays, she began her popular column, "Constant Reader," in the *New Yorker,* where she continued her witty attacks on the contemporary literary scene.

After collaborating with Elmer Rice on an unsuccessful play, *Close Harmony* (1924), Parker left the New *Yorker* as her first collection of verse, *Enough Rope,* became an instant best seller. She devoted herself to writing short fiction and verse, and her story "Big Blonde" won the O. Henry Prize in 1929. A second volume of poems, *Sunset Gun* (1928), was followed by her first collection of short stories, *Lament for the Living* (1930). Displaying a fine perception of human nature as well as a general cynicism regarding life, Parker had already become famous for her mordant quips, such as: "Guns aren't lawful;/ Nooses give;/ Gas smells awful;/ You might as well live."

In the early 1930s Dorothy Parker moved to Hollywood to write movies, meanwhile continuing her literary career. Her major output during this period included a collection of verse, *Death and Taxes* (1931); a volume of short stories, *After Such Pleasures* (1932); *Collected Stories* (1942); and *Collected Poetry* (1944). The last two surveys of Parker's literary talent are characterized by their sardonic, elegantly dry commentaries on the fickle quality of fortune. "She is not Emily Brontë or Jane Austen," noted Edmund Wilson, "but she has been at some pains to write well and she has put into what she has written a state of mind, an era, and a few moments of human experience that nobody else has conveyed."

Parker's intense involvement with political and social issues, which brought her before the House UnAmerican Activities Committee in 1951, limited her literary efforts in later life. However, she did find time to teach at the University of California. In a final gesture she bequeathed almost her entire estate to Martin Luther King, Jr., and the National Association for the Advancement of Colored People.

Further Reading

John Keats, *You Might as Well Live: The Life and Times of Dorothy Parker* (1970), the only full-length study, lacks depth. The most understanding biographical reminiscence is in Anita Loos's autobiography, *A Girl like I* (1966). Lillian Hellman, *An Unfinished Woman: A Memoir* (1969), has a moving chapter on Dorothy Parker. The finest critical studies are Somerset Maugham's introduction to *Dorothy Parker* (1944), a collection of poems and stories, and Edmund Wilson's essay on her in *A Literary Chronicle, 1920-1950* (1956). □

Ely Samuel Parker

Ely S. Parker (1828-1895) was the first Native American commissioner of Indian affairs. During the Civil War, Parker, a close friend and colleague of General Ulysses S. Grant, served the Union cause and penned the final copy of the Confederate army's surrender terms at the Appomattox Courthouse in 1865.

Ely Samuel Parker (Ha-sa-no-an-da) was born in 1828 at Indian Falls on the Tonawanda Indian Reservation, near Akron, New York, the second of six children of a distinguished Seneca family. His mother was Elizabeth Johnson (Ga-ont-gwut-ywus, c. 1786-1862), a Seneca Indian and member of the wolf clan. His maternal grandfather, Jimmy Johnson (So-So-Ha'-Wa), was a grandson of the Seneca prophet Handsome Lake, one of the major "speakers" and authorities of the Longhouse Religion (Gai-wiio) of the Iroquois. Ely Parker's father, Seneca Chief William Parker (Jo-no-es-do-wa, c. 1793-1864), was a veteran of the War of 1812 and a grandson of Disappearing Smoke (also known as Old King) a prominent figure in the early history of the Seneca.

Parker was also a collateral relative of many major figures in the history of the Iroquois including the tribal leader Cornplanter, Governor Blacksnake, and the great orator Red Jacket. This familial background was a factor which influenced his later role in service to his people. Chief William Parker owned a large farm on the reservation and became a converted member of the newly formed missionary Baptist church. Ely reputedly received his first name from Ely Stone, one of the local founders of the mission. Supposedly the Parker surname derived from a Congregational missionary friend of Chief William Parker, Reverend Samuel Parker (1779-1866), son of a Revolutionary War veteran, who briefly served in western New York until 1812 when he become prominent in missionary activities in the West. According to Arthur C. Parker in a biography, William Parker, his two brothers, and Elizabeth Johnson, Ely's mother, had migrated to Tonawanda from the Allegany Reservation at the same time that Handsome Lake was driven from Allegany to Tonawanda.

Ely Parker received his preliminary formal education at the Baptist boarding school which was associated with the mission church on the Tonawanda Reservation. Leaving the mission school at ten years of age, Parker had only a rudimentary knowledge of English, being able to understand but not speak the language. He was taken to Canada for several years where he was taught to hunt and fish, returning to the Tonawanda Reservation at the age of twelve resolved to learn English and to further his formal education. He eventually was assigned the job of interpreter for the school and the church.

Becomes Intermediary with Government Delegations

Recognizing Parker's abilities in his early teens, the Seneca chiefs designated him to assist the numerous Seneca tribal delegations to Albany and Washington, D.C. He served in the vital role of translator and intermediary, accompanying his father and other Seneca chiefs on official trips. It was during one of these trips to Washington that Ely was to attend a dinner in the White House at the invitation of President James K. Polk. The experience of direct involvement in Seneca and Iroquois political and diplomatic affairs was to provide Parker with a valuable and practical educational foundation and stand him in good stead later in life.

Later, he attended Yates Academy from 1843 to 1845 and Cayuga Academy from the fall of 1845 to 1846, where he received the typical classical education of the time, leaving school at the age of eighteen. Lewis Henry Morgan (1818-1881), who had previously attended Cayuga Academy in Aurora, New York, assisted Parker in being admitted to the institution. Parker ultimately left Cayuga Academy to, once again, accompany another Seneca delegation to Washington. Parker's early role during this period was critical in the fight by the Tonawanda Seneca to regain the title to their reservation which had been taken from them in the Buffalo Creek Treaty of 1832, which should have been null and void since the Tonawanda Seneca chiefs had not signed or participated in the treaty. The Tonawanda Reservation had not been restored to the Seneca in the so-called "Compromise" Treaty of Buffalo Creek of 1842 and occupied the diplomatic and legal attention of the Tonawanda Seneca for many years. A portion of their former reservation was finally purchased in 1857, following a treaty of that year.

Parker met Morgan during one of his visits to Albany in 1844, in the company of his maternal grandfather Sachem Jimmy Johnson and Chief John Blacksmith. This meeting with the Seneca delegation provided the initial opportunity for Morgan to begin the collection of data on the Seneca, with Parker serving as interpreter. Their friendship was to last for the rest of their lives. Parker became the major informant for the continuing anthropological data that provided the ethnographic basis of Morgan's famous *League of the Ho-de-no-sau-nee, or Iroquois* (1851), considered to be the first and one of the finest ethnographies of an American Indian group. Morgan acknowledged his great debt to the young Parker and his collaboration by dedicating this major scientific publication to him when Parker was still a teenager.

Parker's value to the Seneca was formally recognized by his tribespeople and further enhanced in 1852 when he was designated to fill the vacant Seneca chief's wolf clan title of Do-ne-ho-ga-wa (Keeper of the Western Door), one of the major titles in the Iroquois Confederacy. This title had previously been held by the venerable Chief John Blacksmith who had died in 1851. At that time Parker received the Red Jacket medal that had been given to Red Jacket by President George Washington in 1792 and inherited by Jimmy Johnson, Parker's grandfather. Parker retained his title and the medal for the remainder of his life.

Becomes an Engineer

Beginning in 1847, Ely Parker continued his education with the thought that he would become a lawyer by "reading of the law" in the offices of Angel and Rice in Ellicottville, New York, north of the Allegany Reservation. This firm had represented the Seneca Indians in several cases, and Parker had been previously acquainted with W. P. Angel when he had served as sub-agent from 1846 to 1848 for the New York Indian Agency. The house that Parker occupied during his stay in Ellicottville remains. Parker, however, was denied admittance to the bar in the State of New York on the basis of his race, in that Indians were not citizens of the United States, an event that did not occur until 1924.

Parker turned his attention to the field of civil engineering, attending Rensselaer Polytechnic Institute. In this field he quickly became a recognized success, obtaining a number of important positions, beginning with work on the Genesee Valley Canal in 1849, and later with the Erie Canal. After a political difference of opinion, Parker left the Canal Office in Rochester in June, 1855. He moved on to engineering positions in Norfolk, Detroit, and finally, in 1857, he accepted the position of superintendent of construction for a number of government projects in Galena, Illinois, where he resided for a number of years. It was here that Parker initially became acquainted with a store clerk and army veteran, Ulysses S. Grant. They established a lifelong friendship.

Begins Military Career during Civil War

With the outbreak of the Civil War, Parker tried to obtain a release from his engineering responsibilities at Galena but did not receive one. The decision resulted in his resignation in 1862. Parker then returned to the Tonawanda Reservation to request and gain his father's approval to go to war. Once again, his race proved to be an obstacle to obtaining a army commission from either the governor of New York or from the Secretary of War. In fact, Secretary William H. Seward informed Parker that the rebellion would be suppressed by the whites, without the aid of Indians. Eventually, Parker was commissioned in the early summer of 1863 as captain of engineers and was briefly assigned to General J. E. Smith as division engineer of the 7th Division, XVII Corps. Later that year, on September 18th, Parker became Grant's staff officer at Vicksburg. A year later, on August 30, 1864, Parker was advanced to lieutenant-colonel and became Grant's military secretary. It was Parker who made draft corrections in the terms of surrender at Appomattox Court House, April 9, 1865, and penned the final official copies that ended the Civil War. Parker later reported that General Robert E. Lee was momentarily taken aback on seeing Parker in such a prominent position at the surrender. Apparently initially believing Parker to be a black man, Lee finally shook hands with Parker and said, "I am glad to see one real American here." Parker replied, "We are all Americans."

At the conclusion of the Civil War, Parker continued as Grant's military secretary. He was also commissioned a brigadier-general of volunteers as of the date of surrender at Appomattox. In addition, two years later, on March 2, 1867, Parker's gallant and meritorious service was recognized through his appointment as first and second lieutenant in the cavalry of the Regular Army, and brevet appointments as captain, major, lieutenant-colonel, colonel, and brigadier-general, also in the Regular Army.

On Christmas Day, 1867, with Ulysses S. Grant as best man, Parker married Miss Minnie Orton Sackett (1850-1932) of Washington, D.C., the stepdaughter of a soldier who had died in the war. In 1878, Ely and Minnie had a daughter, Maud Theresa Parker (d. 1956), from whom Ely Parker's descendants are derived.

Enters into Troubled Political Career

Following the election to the presidency, Grant appointed Parker as Commissioner of Indian Affairs, on April 13, 1869, the first American Indian to hold the office. Parker resigned from the army on April 26th. Although a strong advocate for assimilation of the American Indian and supporter of Grant's Peace Policy, directed to the improvement of the American Indian, Parker also sought major reform and restructuring of the Bureau of Indian Affairs, an unpopular policy in some political quarters. In addition, his humanitarian and just treatment of the hostile western Indians created many influential political enemies in Washington. Especially troublesome was the relationship with the Sioux and the implementation of the provisions of the Fort Laramie Treaty which had bee signed in 1868, ending Red Cloud's War of 1866-1868.

Finally, accused of defrauding the government, a committee of the House of Representatives tried Parker in February, 1871. The charges against Parker involved the assignment of contracts at the Spotted Tail Agency (formerly the Whetstone Agency) on the White River. He was completely exonerated of any misconduct, but nevertheless resigned from government service in July feeling that the office of commissioner had been greatly reduced in authority and effectiveness.

Parker entered the stock market on Wall Street and made a fortune which he eventually lost in settling a defaulted bond of his business partner. Other attempts as business opportunities also proved unsuccessful. Later, Parker served with the New York City Police Department. Ely Samuel Parker died on August 31, 1895, at his home in Fairfield, Connecticut, where he was initially buried. In 1897, his remains were reinterred with those of Red Jacket and his ancestors in Forest Lawn Cemetery, Buffalo, New York.

Further Reading

Armstrong, William H., *Warrior in Two Camps: Ely S. Parker, Union General and Seneca Chief,* Syracuse University Press, 1978.

Morgan, Lewis Henry, *League of the Ho-de-no-sau-nee, or Iroquois,* Sage and Company, 1851; reprinted, Corinth Books, 1962, 1990.

Olson, James C., *Red Cloud and the Sioux Problem,* University of Nebraska Press, 1965.

Parker, Arthur C., *The Life of General Ely S. Parker: Last Grand Sachem of the Iroquois and General Grant's Military Secretary,* Buffalo Historical Society Publication, 1919.

Tooker, Elisabeth, "Ely S. Parker, Seneca, ca. 1828-1895," in *American Indian Intellectuals: 1976 Proceedings of the American Ethnological Society,* West Publishing Co., 1978, pp. 14-29.

Waltmann, Henry G., "Ely Samuel Parker, 1869-71," in *The Commissioners of Indian Affairs: 1824-1977,* edited by Robert M. Kvasnicka and Herman J. Viola, Lincoln, University of Nebraska Press, 1979, pp. 123-131.

Yeuell, Donovan, "Ely Samuel Parker," *Dictionary of American Biography,* edited by Dumas Malone, Charles Scribner's Sons, 1934, pp. 219-220. □

Horatio William Parker

Horatio William Parker (1863-1919) was one of the most respected American composers of the late 19th century and professor of music at Yale University.

life and work is contained in Gilbert Chase, *America's Music, from the Pilgrims to the Present* (1955; 2d ed. 1966).

Horatio Parker was born on Sept. 15, 1863, in Auburndale, Mass. At 14 he began taking piano lessons from his mother and soon wrote a collection of songs for children. At 16 he became organist of a church at Dedham and began to compose hymns and anthems.

In 1882 Parker went to Europe to study at the Royal School of Music in Munich. While abroad he married fellow music student Anna Plossl, a Munich banker's daughter. Upon returning to America, Parker settled in New York, teaching at the Cathedral School in Garden City. He taught at the National Conservatory of Music in New York City at the time Antonin Dvořák was its director and in 1893 became choirmaster and organist at Trinity Church in Boston. The following year Parker was appointed head of the Music Department of Yale University, a position he held until his death. While at Yale, he organized the New Haven Symphony Orchestra.

Although Parker attempted a number of symphonic and instrumental pieces, his choral music was his finest work. His most lasting composition, the oratorio *Hora Novissima* (1891-1892), was written during a time when he was grieving over the loss of a sister. Here the composer reveals his ability at massed choral effects, as well as his skill for developing hymnlike themes. The music is masculine and vital, if at times overly calculated. He received the National Conservatory Award in 1892 for his cantata *The Dream King and His Love.*

Parker's first opera, *Mona,* won a $10,000 prize offered by the directors of the Metropolitan Opera House for the best American opera. It was premiered on March 14, 1912, but was dropped from the Metropolitan repertoire after four performances. His second opera, *Fairyland,* was also awarded a $10,000 prize, this time by the National Federation of Music Clubs; the work was performed six times in 1915 during the federation's biennial in Los Angeles.

Parker served as editor in chief for a series of graded songbooks for children and remained actively interested in music education in the public schools. He received a doctor of music degree from Cambridge University in 1902, by which time his choral works were enjoying considerable success in England. He commanded greater social standing than most American musicians of his day, although his strong-willed, individualistic personality made him a figure of controversy among students and colleagues. He died at Cedarhurst, N.Y., on Dec. 18, 1919.

Further Reading

An interesting, personalized account of Parker is George W. Chadwick's *Horatio Parker* (1921). Isabel Parker Semler, *Horatio Parker* (1942), is based primarily on the composer's papers and family letters. The best brief discussion of Parker's

Additional Sources

Kearns, William, *Horatio Parker, 1863-1919: his life, music, and ideas,* Metuchen, N.J.: Scarecrow Press, 1990.

Semler, Isabel Parker, *Horatio Parker: a memoir for his grandchildren,* New York: AMS Press, 1975. ☐

Quanah Parker

Quanah Parker (died 1911) was a leader of the Comanche people during the difficult transition period from free-ranging life on the southern plains to the settled ways of reservation life. He became an influential negotiator with government agents, a prosperous cattle-rancher, a vocal advocate of formal education for Native children, and a devout member of the Peyote Cult.

Quanah Parker was born to Peta Nocona, a Quahadi (Kwahado, Quahada) Comanche war leader, and Cynthia Ann Parker, a white woman who had been captured by the Comanche and raised as an Indian. Cynthia's family, the Parkers, were influential people in prestatehood Texas, so the raid on Ft. Parker on May

19, 1836, is considered a major event in Texas history. Several family members died in the raid, but nine-year-old Cynthia was one of those taken alive. She and her brother were adopted by the Natives, but her brother apparently died soon after. Cynthia was renamed Preloch and was brought up in a traditional Quahadi village.

In her middle teens, Cynthia married Peta Nocona. About 1852 (some sources say as early as 1845), Quanah was born to them as their band camped at Cedar Lake, Texas. Approximately three years later, Quanah's sister Topsannah ["Prairie Flower"] was born. Their childhood coincided with major changes in Comanche life, as American settlement increased and free range for Indians and buffalo decreased. Cynthia's family kept up the search for her throughout the years. Finally, in 1861, Texas Rangers recaptured Cynthia and brought her and Topsannah back to her relatives. Although she knew about her early years, Cynthia had become completely Comanche, and she mourned for her Indian family and friends. It is believed that Prairie Flower died in the mid-1860s, and Cynthia followed her to the grave in 1870.

Back amid the Quahadi, Quanah was trying to adjust to the loss of his beloved mother and sister. The death of Peta Nocona in 1866 or 1867 was a further blow to the young man. For all intents and purposes now an orphan, Quanah found himself at the mercy of the charity of other relatives, while becoming the object of taunts from other Quahadi for his mixed ancestry. He must have been a striking figure among his people, taller and thinner than other Comanches, with a lighter complexion and grey eyes. Still, he felt himself

to be unquestioningly Comanche in his beliefs and way of life.

The Move to Indian Territory

In 1867, the Treaty of Medicine Lodge was signed, which called for the settlement of the Comanche, Cheyenne, Riowa, Kiowa-Apache, and Arapaho onto reservations in Indian Territory (later the state of Oklahoma). Most of the Comanche bands accepted the treaty, but the Quahadi would resist settlement the longest, refusing to recognize the document. Seven years of periodic raiding and open hostility towards white settlers and frontier towns ensued, with retaliation against the Comanche for these incidents. The final insult in the minds of the Quahadi was the increasing presence of buffalo hunters, professionals hired to hunt the huge animals for the eastern market and to undercut the basis of Plains Indian life, forcing them onto reservations to avoid starvation. In June of 1875, a group of 700 allied tribes' warriors attacked a group of buffalo hunters at a fortification called Adobe Walls, in the Texas Panhandle. Three days of bitter fighting led to an eventual turning back of the Indian raiding force, and the beginning of two years of relentless pursuit of the Quahadi by General Ranald Mackenzie. Until recently, published accounts of Quanah Parker's life reported that he led the Indians against Adobe Walls, became the war chief of the Quahadi during Mackenzie's pursuit, and reluctantly surrendered to reservation life as the last fierce war leader of the free Comanche. Recent works show that Quanah was too young to have been a war chief, but report that he did fight at Adobe Walls.

The Quahadi surrendered to reservation settlement in 1875. The person who was most likely their leader at that time was Eschiti ["Coyote Droppings"], who had been the leader who incited the raid on Adobe Walls. A medicine man as well as a civil leader, Eschiti would see his influence decrease as Quanah Parker's increased with the favor of the Indian Agent. Early on, the agent had courted Parker's good graces, believing that, as a mixed-blood, Parker could be more easily converted to white ways and could then influence his people to change also. However, the agent had not taken into account that Parker's mixed ancestry was the reason many staunchly traditional Comanche refused to accept his leadership. That he was being "created" as an Indian leader by white officials caused further conflict.

A Chief Emerges

These first years of settled life took quite a toll on the Quahadi: Not only was their old way of life dying, many Indian people sickened and died as well. Perhaps this alarmingly high death rate also accounted for a lack of rivals to contest Quanah Parker's rising power. In fact, his most potent competitor, Mowaway, who had been a war chief, chose to rescind his position in 1878, virtually clearing the way for Quanah to become the "principal chief" of the Comanche around Ft. Sill.

Quanah Parker then moved quickly from the status of a "ration chief" (one who is recognized as the leader of a small band of reservation-dwellers who count collectively as one unit for the purpose of handing out rations) to a member of the Comanche Council. Throughout the late 1870s, the council functioned mainly to agree to whatever the Indian Agent decided. The single major disagreement between the agency and the council in this period arose over the Indian Department's decision to consolidate the Wichita, Kiowa, Kiowa-Apache, and Comanche agencies and to move the headquarters from Ft. Sill to the Washita River. This change would place the source of rations some sixty miles distant from the Comanche settlements. With rations being handed out three times per week, most Comanche would be constantly in transit to or from the headquarters. Parker joined in with other, more traditional leaders in opposing this move. The growing anti-Quanah faction regarded this as one of his last "loyal" acts. Already, Parker's accommodation of whites was earning him enemies.

Heading into the 1880s, Texas cattlemen were regularly driving cattle across Comanche lands on the way to railheads at Dodge City and Abilene, Kansas. The sparingly grazed grasslands were lush and provided a last chance for cattle barons to fatten their stock before sale. At first, the Comanche ignored this trespassing, as the cattlemen also ignored the occasional poaching of a cow by the Indians. Eventually though, the ranchers in the areas adjoining Comanche land intentionally ranged their herds on Comanche grasslands. In 1881, the Comanche Council formally protested the actions. Sensing that Quanah Parker was a man who could see both sides of the issue, the cattlemen agreed to put him (and Eschiti) on their payroll to ride with white "cattle police" keeping an eye on property lines. Later, Permansu (also known as "Comanche Jack") would join them.

Being on the cattlemen's payroll provided Quanah Parker with money, "surplus" cattle, and influence among the cattle barons. He started his own herd with gift cattle and a blooded bull, courtesy of the king of the cattle barons, Charlie Goodnight. Parker started his own ranch, where he would eventually build his famous residence, the Star House. More a mansion than a house, it was two-storied with a double porch, its metal roof was decorated with prominent white stars, and the interior was richly appointed in the manner of wealthy non-Indians of the day. Some of Quanah's detractors said he had built the Star House to lord over the more traditional leaders of the Comanche; others said he needed the room for his seven wives and seven children.

The Indian Agency was appalled that Quanah, a strong believer in formal education for his people and their participation in the developing money economy of Indian Territory, was an equally strong believer in polygamy and the Peyote Cult. It is not certain when Quanah was introduced to the peyote rite (originally a religion of the native peoples of northern Mexican deserts), but he was well respected in the Comanche branch of the faith, becoming a "road man" (a ritual leader). When the Ghost Dance swept the Plains tribes, and people from the Lakota to the Paiute were dancing themselves into trances, trying to make the buffalo return, Parker rejected the movement. He remained true to his peyotism, but would accept the inclusion of elements of Christianity, some said in honor of his mother.

"Progressive" in Two Worlds

In 1884, Quanah Parker made his first of 20 trips to Washington, D.C. This one dealt with changes in the lease arrangements the Comanche had been able to work out with the cattle ranchers. The Comanche were profitably leasing grasslands they were not using themselves, and they resented the property changes that would come with allotment in severalty, the process of dividing tribally held land into individually owned plots. Despite several trips, Quanah was unable to stave off the allotment under the terms of the Jerome Commission, but he did improve the deal for his people.

The ever-present anti-Quanah Parker faction on the reservation criticized Quanah for trying to arrange a larger allotment for himself and a higher price per acre payment for the sale of surplus land. However, he was still a very influential leader. In the 1890s, the Indian Agent was issuing official "chief certificates," a sort of identification, and Quanah was able to convince the agency that he should be issued the certificate for the principal chieftainship. This done, Eschiti was finally completely deposed, and Parker went so far as to have letterhead printed with his name and the emblazoned title of principal chief. The action further impressed white men, but further embittered the more traditional Comanche.

Starting in 1886, Quanah Parker had been a judge of the Court of Indian Affairs, but lost his position as the tribe made the final move towards allotment near the end of the century. The breakup of communally held lands and the resulting breakdown of age-old tribal traditions greatly angered many Comanche and they saw Quanah as the source of their problems. They saw that Quanah courted a public image as a "progressive" Indian in the eyes of white America, becoming something of a national celebrity. Visitors to the Star House would include Theodore Roosevelt and British Ambassador Lord Bryce. In fact, Quanah would be one of the four Indian chiefs to ride in President Theodore Roosevelt's inaugural parade.

The Circle Is Completed

In the first decade of the 20th century, Quanah Parker's influence began to wane. On a personal level, two of his wives left him, angered over what they saw as a self-important pursuit of plural wives. Tonarcy was considered his principal wife, but among his others were Topay, Chony, Mahcheettowooky, and Aerwuthtakum. Since most of his wives were widows when he married them, Parker saw this arrangement as a way to take care of women who would otherwise have had to rely on relatives for their survival, due to their young ages. In the sphere of tribal politics, Quanah was also losing ground. Allotment had reduced his land base and therefore his personal fortune, and he would eventually resort to taking a paid position with the Indian Service as an "assistant farmer."

By the beginning of 1911, Quanah Parker was in obvious poor health. He had rheumatism and his heart was weakening. In February, after a long and tiring train ride, he took to his bed, suffering from heart trouble. On February 25th, 1911, Quanah Parker died at the Star House, Tonarcy at his side. Despite criticism during his life from traditional Comanche, Quanah Parker was so revered that the procession to his resting place was said to be over a mile long. After a Christian service in a local church, Quanah was buried next to his mother's and sister's reinterred remains in Cache County, Oklahoma. Four years later, graverobbers broke into his grave, taking the jewelry with which he had been buried. The Parkers ritually cleaned and then reburied him. Quanah Parker, Cynthia Ann, and Topsannah were all moved to Ft. Sill Military Cemetery in 1957. The life of Quanah Parker is today seen as the extraordinary story of a person successfully living in two worlds, two minds, two eras.

Further Reading

Andrews, Ralph W., *Indian Leaders Who Helped Shape America, 1600-1900,* Seattle, Superior Publishers, 1971.

Dockstader, Frederick J., *Great North American Indians,* New York, Van Nostrand Reinhold, 1977.

Edmunds, R. David, *American Indian Leaders: Studies in Diversity,* Lincoln, University of Nebraska, 1980.

Hagan, William T., *Quanah Parker, Comanche Chief,* Norman, University of Oklahoma, 1993. □

Theodore Parker

Theodore Parker (1810-1860), American clergyman and militant, was a leading advocate of transcendentalism and a vocal abolitionist.

Theodore Parker was born in Lexington, Mass., on Aug. 24, 1810. His schooling was scanty, but he eagerly educated himself. By the time he was 17 he knew enough to teach school, and for the next 4 years he worked in local elementary schools. In 1830 he passed the entrance examinations for Harvard, but he did not have enough money to enroll as a resident student and so he continued with his teaching. In 1832 he opened his own school in Watertown, Mass. He also studied for the course examinations which Harvard allowed him to take.

Having accumulated a modest amount of money, Parker enrolled in the Harvard Divinity School in 1834. Although he later called it an "embalming" institution, he reveled in his studies. He learned no less than 20 languages there. The faculty was already discarding some of the doctrines hallowed in New England theology, but Parker found himself discarding still more. By graduation day he even had some doubts about the miracles described in the Bible and the virgin birth of Christ.

Though several congregations were attracted to this strenuous scholar, he accepted a call in 1837 to an unpretentious parish in a suburb of Boston, West Roxbury. He promptly married Lydia Cabot, and 3 months later was ordained a Unitarian minister. He soon plunged into the religious controversies boiling up in the Boston area. He was increasingly sympathetic to the leaders of the transcendental movement, especially Ralph Waldo Emerson. Emerson had come to believe in a personal religion that dispensed with creeds, rituals, and church polity and substituted the relation of the individual soul to the oversoul. Parker issued a pamphlet supporting him.

Parker's most striking formulation came in a sermon he delivered in 1841, "The Transient and Permanent in Christianity." His theme was Emersonian: the permanent is the direct worship of God by the individual; the transient is the ritualistic and the priestly. His position aroused the antagonism of his fellow ministers, and they closed their pulpits to him. In 1843 the Boston Association of Ministers asked him to resign; he declined and went to Europe for a year. While traveling he met a number of theological liberals, especially in Germany, whose thought was often as advanced as his and far beyond that of his Boston colleagues.

On Parker's return he discovered that no congregation in the Boston area was willing to hear him. However, he had ardent supporters, and they formed their own congregation. It became the Twenty-eighth Congregational Society of Boston.

Parker put the welfare of his new congregation first, but he also worked hard for social and political causes. In lectures and sermons, in word and deed, he fought for the amelioration of poverty, improvement of public education, prison reform, and temperance. The deepening struggle over slavery aroused his greatest efforts as well as the fiercest public opposition to them. His *A Letter to the People of the United States Touching the Matter of Slavery* appeared in 1848. He took an active part in attempts to rescue fugitive slaves from the Massachusetts authorities. He aided John Brown of Kansas and encouraged the antislavery efforts of such political leaders as Senator Charles Sumner.

After a strenuous lecture tour in 1857, Parker took sick. In the next 2 years his condition grew worse, and in desperation he decided to travel. He died in Florence, Italy, on May 10, 1860.

Further Reading

The best biography of Parker is Henry Steele Commager, *Theodore Parker* (1936; with a new introduction, 1960). Parker is discussed in William R. Hutchison, *The Transcendentalist Ministers: Church Reform in the New England Renaissance* (1959), and Lawrence Lader, *The Bold Brahmins: New England's War against Slavery, 1831-1863* (1961). □

Sir Henry Parkes

The Australian statesman Sir Henry Parkes (1815-1896) was a champion of Australian federation, and his eloquent appeals to colonial leaders to forget their differences were a potent influence in bringing success to the federal movement.

The son of a tenant farmer, Henry Parkes was born in Warwickshire, England, on May 27, 1815. He had only sketchy schooling and began working at the age of 8. As a young man, he joined the Birmingham Political Union (a Chartist-inspired group) and began to read widely. Parkes reached Sydney in 1839 as an assisted immigrant. He worked as a farmhand before setting up a small business. His interest in politics was rekindled through contact with local Chartists, and in 1850 he established the *Empire* as the workingman's voice at a time when self-government was being granted New South Wales. Leading the attack on sections of the Constitution Bill that were considered to support landholding privileges, Parkes campaigned for a parliamentary seat and was elected.

Because of poor management the *Empire* failed, and in 1858 Parkes suffered insolvency, leading to his temporary political eclipse. He went to London to promote Australian immigration in 1861, returning to Sydney to reenter Parliament in 1863. He became colonial secretary in 1866 and carried the Public Schools Act, providing unified administration under an Education Council. Embroiled in sectarian issues, he had few supporters when he again faced financial difficulties (this time as a merchant) in 1870.

Chief Ministries

His insolvency cleared, Parkes was reelected in 1871 and became the acknowledged leader of the democratic group. A free trader, he virtually eliminated customs duties during his first term as premier of New South Wales (1872-

1875). After clashes with the Legislative Council over electoral reform, his ministry became ineffectual. His second ministry (1877) lasted 5 months.

Parkes was knighted in 1877 and late in 1878 joined erstwhile opponents to form a third ministry. The Public Instruction Act of 1880 was a landmark; it provided for free, secular, and compulsory education and ended subsidies for church schools. An electoral law widened the franchise.

With his ministry's defeat in 1883, Parkes eased away from the political round but did not hold to his stated intention to retire. In 1887 he led a vigorous free-trade campaign; his fourth ministry slashed recently increased import duties and imposed a stiff poll tax on Chinese. Parkes was again premier in 1889-1891, following a brief ouster, but his drive for social reform had faded.

Call for Australian Federation

By now an ardent advocate of federal union, Parkes called for a national Parliament to set policies on defense, immigration, and customs duties. A meeting of premiers in 1890 resulted in a constitutional convention under his presidency which in 1891 drafted a Constitution Bill; but although his forceful oratory and commanding personality won many adherents to the federal cause, Parkes failed to carry the measure in his own Parliament.

In October 1891 Parkes resigned the premiership when the newly formed Labour party withdrew support, and he was not elected at the poll of 1895. He died on April 27, 1896.

Further Reading

Parkes's speeches before the national Australasian Conventions of 1890 and 1891 are recorded in the convention records. Biographies are C. E. Lyne, *Life of Sir Henry Parkes* (1897), and Thomas Bavin, *Sir Henry Parkes: His Life and Work* (1941). Parkes's role as a colonial leader is dealt with in P. Loveday and A. W. Martin, *Parliament Factions and Parties: The First Thirty Years of Responsible Government in New South Wales, 1856-1889* (1966). Aspects of his work related to the federal movement are discussed in John Quick and Robert R. Garran, *Annotated Constitution of the Australian Commonwealth* (1901), and in Sir George Houston Reid, *My Reminiscences* (1917).

Additional Sources

Martin, A. W. (Allan William), *Henry Parkes: a biography*, Carlton, Vic.: Melbourne University Press, 1980.
Travers, Robert, *The grand old man of Australian politics: the life and times of Sir Henry Parkes*, Kenthurst, NSW: Kangaroo Press, 1992. □

Francis Parkman

Francis Parkman (1823-1893), American historian, brilliantly narrated the Anglo-French conflict for control of North America in a great multivolume work.

Francis Parkman was born to wealth in Boston, Mass., on Sept. 16, 1823. As an undergraduate at Harvard, he had the advantage of study with the historian Jared Sparks, who gave Parkman his first reading list on the "Old French War." Through letters of introduction to other scholars, Sparks eased the young man's path.

While still a sophomore (he graduated in 1844), Parkman planned a history of the "Old French War" which would end with England's conquest of Canada. An older contemporary historian, George Bancroft, who had gone over some of the ground later traversed by Parkman, provided a framework for his more gifted successor. James Fenimore Cooper's "Leather-Stocking Tales" and Sir Walter Scott's "Waverley Novels" were spurs to Parkman's ambition to write a great history on a North American theme. An accolade from qualified judges would still the doubts of his father and win the applause of Englishmen who derided American cultural achievements.

Firsthand Research

For Parkman, books, teachers, and archives were not enough. His untiring zeal for perfection demanded onsite inspection of the contested region in America. In the summer of 1845, on a trip westward, he gathered information from old settlers, talked with Indians, and studied the topography of the region near Detroit. The next year Parkman went farther west to see Indians in their native state, unchanged by contact with white civilization. This, he said, was a necessary part of training for his lifework. His experiences in the wilderness gave Parkman color and texture for

much of his subsequent writing. The immediate result was his classic, *The Oregon Trail* (1849).

Parkman's health, never robust, worsened after his trip westward. Partial blindness and severe headaches almost made an invalid of him. To aid his writing he used a frame constructed like a gridiron, and with it he composed *The Conspiracy of Pontiac* (1851). At first he could manage only six lines a day. With improved health he worked faster. Aid was offered by Catherine S. Bigelow, whom he married in 1850 and who acted as his amanuensis. Parkman was forever battling illness, terming it the "Enemy." He was a sociable man, his friends Boston's intellectual élite, his correspondents widely dispersed scholars. Despite chronic illness he conveyed the impression of a strong, big-boned Yankee.

His Great Work

Parkman hoped to start work on the beginnings of the Anglo-French struggle immediately after *Pontiac*. But ill health delayed *The Pioneers of France in the New World* until 1865. He had, however, already written large parts of other volumes in his projected series. *The Jesuits in North America* (1867) paid tribute to the courage and martyrdom of the Catholic missionaries. In *La Salle and the Discovery of the Great West* (1869; revised 1879) the French explorer is the heroic figure, caught in tragic circumstances yet facing frightening odds with immense courage.

The theme of *The Old Regime in Canada* (1874) was France's attempt to tighten its hold on its American colony and its eventual failure. Parkman, like other historians of the romantic school, was less interested in the slow process of establishing a civilization than in its unusual, colorful incidents. In this volume, however, he came close to later social historians with such chapters as "Marriage and Population" and "Trade and Industry," which were skillfully interwoven with his narrative.

Count Frontenac and New France under Louis XIV (1877) celebrated the greatest man ever to represent his country in the New World. Parkman's masterpiece, *Montcalm and Wolfe* (1884), was acclaimed the finest in the series. With this judgment the author himself agreed. He was unsure of how to fill the chronological gap between *Frontenac* and *Montcalm and Wolfe*, but he managed to do so with *A Half Century of Conflict* (1892). The absence of a central character around whom to spin his narrative deprived this final volume in the series of the dramatic interest that enlivened its predecessors.

Parkman's rapport with his aristocratic heroes, cast in a medieval mold, stemmed from his own political beliefs. He preferred a conservative republic, with restricted suffrage, where, he said, "intelligence and character and not numbers hold the reins of power." The pageantry of war fascinated him; the military instincts, he thought, were always "strongest in the strongest and richest nature."

Scholarly Opinion

In his own time Parkman was criticized for unsympathetic treatment of Indians and for alleged bias against Catholicism. Historians have charged him with neglect of social forces which they felt were as important as dominant leaders in directing the course of history. He also failed to consider the role of sea power in the conflict between England and France. However, unstinted admiration is given to his brilliant artistry in maintaining the pace of his narrative.

Though details of Parkman's great work have been altered by later writers, the main structure still stands. What historian Henry Adams wrote to Parkman when *Montcalm and Wolfe* was published has remained the verdict of admiring readers: With your previous books, said Adams, it "puts you in the front rank of living English historians." Parkman died in Jamaica Plain, Mass., on Nov. 8, 1893.

Further Reading

Letters of Francis Parkman, edited by Wilbur R. Jacobs (2 vols., 1960), which has a good short biography, is particularly revealing of Parkman's thoughts. *Representative Selections,* edited by Wilbur L. Schramm (1938), excellent on Parkman's milieu, politics, and theory of historical writing, contains selections from his writings. Biographies are Charles Haight Farnham, *Life of Parkman* (1900); Henry Dwight Sedgwick, *Francis Parkman* (1904); and Mason Wade, *Francis Parkman: Heroic Historian* (1942).

The quality of Parkman's work is examined in Otis A. Pease, *Parkman's History* (1953); David Levin, *History as Romantic Art* (1959); and Howard Doughty, *Francis Parkman* (1962). A chapter on Parkman by Joe Patterson Smith is in *American Historiography,* edited by William T. Hutchinson (1937), and in Michael Kraus, *The Writing of American History* (1953). Parkman is discussed in a study of the revolution in ideals and outlooks brought about by the Civil War: George M. Fredrickson, *The Inner Civil War: Northern Intellectuals and the Crisis of the Union* (1965).

Additional Sources

Doughty, Howard, *Francis Parkman,* Cambridge, Mass.: Harvard University Press, 1983, 1982.

Jacobs, Wilbur R., *Francis Parkman, historian as hero: the formative years,* Austin: University of Texas Press, 1991. □

Rosa Lee McCauley Parks

On December 1, 1955, Rosa Lee Parks (née McCauley; born 1913) refused to relinquish her seat to a white passenger on a racially segregated Montgomery, Alabama bus. She was arrested and fined but her action led to a successful boycott of the Montgomery buses by African American riders.

Born Rosa McCauley in Tuskegee, Alabama, on February 4, 1913, the young girl did not seem destined for fame. Her mother was a teacher and her father, a carpenter. When she was still young she moved with her mother and brother to Pine Level, Alabama, to live with her grandparents. A hard-working family, they were able to provide her with the necessities of life but few luxuries while attempting to shield her from the harsh realities of racial

segregation. Rosa attended the Montgomery Industrial School for Girls, graduated from the all-African American Booker T. Washington High School in 1928, and attended Alabama State College in Montgomery for a short time.

She married Raymond Parks, a barber, in 1932. Both Rosa and her husband were active in various civil rights causes, such as voter registration. Parks worked with the National Association for the Advancement of Colored People (NAACP) Youth Council and in 1943 was elected to serve as the secretary of the Montgomery branch. This group worked to dismantle the barriers of racial segregation in education and public accommodations but made little progress during the 1940s and early 1950s. In the summer of 1955 white friends paid Parks' expenses for a two-week interracial seminar at Tennessee's Highlander Folk School, a program designed to help people to train for civil rights activism.

Parks worked at various jobs over the years—as a housekeeper, an insurance saleswoman, and a seamstress. In 1955, while working at Montgomery Fair department store as a tailor's assistant, she discovered her name in the headlines. On the fateful night of December 1st, she was very tired as she headed for her bus, but had no plans for initiating a protest. According to the segregation laws in Montgomery, white passengers were given the front seats on the bus. Even if no white riders boarded, African Americans were not allowed to sit in those seats. If white passengers filled their allotted seats, African American riders—who had to pay the same amount of bus fare—had to give their seats to the whites. All of the bus drivers were instructed to

have African Americans who disobeyed the rules removed from the bus, arrested, and fined. Some of the bus drivers demanded that African Americans pay their fares up front, get off the bus, and reenter through the back doors so that they would not pass by the seats of white patrons.

On December 1, 1955, Parks, who had taken a seat directly behind the white section, was asked to yield her seat to white passengers. Parks recognized the driver as one who had evicted her from a bus 12 years before when she refused to reenter through the back door after paying her fare. The bus driver threatened to have her arrested but she remained where she was. He then stopped the bus, brought in some policemen, and had Parks taken to police head-quarters.

Certainly her case was not a unique; African Americans had been arrested for disobeying the segregation laws many times before. However, in 1954 the Supreme Court had rendered an important decision in *Brown vs. Board of Education,* which held that educational segregation was inherently illegal. The decision encouraged African Americans to fight more boldly for the end of racial segregation in every area of American life. Thus, NAACP officials and Montgomery church leaders decided that Parks' arrest could provide the necessary impetus for a successful bus boycott. They asked Montgomery's African American riders—who comprised over 70 percent of the bus company's business—to stop riding the buses until the company was willing to revise its policies toward African American riders and hire African American bus drivers.

Meeting at Dexter Avenue Baptist Church, the ministers and their congregations formed the Montgomery Improvement Association and elected the young Reverend Martin Luther King, Jr. as president. The boycott was extremely successful, lasting over 380 days. When the case was taken to the Supreme Court, the Justices declared that segregation of the Montgomery buses was illegal and officially desegregated them on December 20, 1956.

Parks and some of her family members, fired by their employers or continually harassed by angry whites, decided in 1957 to move to Detroit, Michigan. There they had a great deal of difficulty finding jobs, but Parks was finally employed by John Conyers, an African American member of the U.S. House of Representatives. She served as his receptionist and then staff assistant for 25 years while continuing her work with the NAACP and the Southern Christian Leadership Conference (SCLC) and serving as a deaconess at the Saint Matthew African Methodist Episcopal Church.

Parks received numerous awards, including an honorary degree from Shaw College in Detroit, the 1979 NAACP Spingarn Medal, and an annual Freedom Award presented in her honor by the SCLC. In 1980 she was awarded the Martin Luther King Jr. Nonviolent Peace Prize and in 1984 the Eleanor Roosevelt Women of Courage Award. In 1988 she founded the Rosa and Raymond Parks Institute for Self-Development, to train African American youth for leadership roles, and began serving as the institute's president. In 1989 her accomplishments were honored at the John F. Kennedy Center for the Performing Arts in Washington,

D.C. Parks was in demand as a public speaker and traveled extensively to discuss her role in the civil rights movement.

In September 1994 Parks was beaten and robbed in her Detroit home. She fully recovered from this incident and remained active in African American issues. In October 1995 she participated in the Million Man March in Washington D.C., giving an inspirational speech.

Fellow civil rights leaders, friends, and family of Parks, expressed concern about her demanding schedule and finances in September 1997. They were unable to get answers from Parks' attorney, Gregory Reed, and personal assistant, Elaine Steele, who together had formed The Parks Legacy, a corporation that controlled the public property rights to Parks' image. According to court records, the "selling" of Parks included fees for autographs and pictures of the civil rights legend, her appearance in a rock video, and her image on a phone-calling card. An article in the *Detroit News* noted, "Civil rights leaders and marketing experts fear the products cheapen Parks' image and legacy as the mother of the civil rights movement."

Further Reading

Virtually no history of the modern civil rights movement in the United States fails to mention the role of Rosa Parks. She tells her own story in *The Autobiography of Rosa Parks* (1990). Others relate her history in a book entitled *Don't Ride the Bus on Monday* by Louise Meriwether (1973) and in two children's books, one by Eloise Greenfield, *Rosa Parks* (1973) and another by Kai Friese, *Rosa Parks* (1990). Among several interesting works specifically relating to the boycott is Jo Ann Robinson's *The Montgomery Bus Boycott and the Women Who Started It* (1987). Also see the *Detroit News* (August 29, 1997, and September 28, 1997). ☐

Parmenides

The Greek philosopher Parmenides (active 475 B.C.) asserted that true being and knowledge, discovered by the intellect, must be distinguished from appearance and opinion, based on the senses. He held that there is an eternal One, which is timeless, motionless, and changeless.

P armenides was born in Elea in southern Italy in the late 6th century B.C. Socrates, in Plato's *Thaetetus,* tells how as a young man he met Parmenides and Zeno on their visit to Athens about 450. Little else is recorded about the details of Parmenides's life. He wrote a didactic poem in hexameters, the meter of the Homeric epics and of the oracular responses at Delphi, in which he described a divine revelation. Fragments of the poem remain and provide a fair idea of what he attempted to prove, although even when the entire poem was extant there were problems of interpretation.

The poem consists of a prologue and discussions of the Way of Truth and the Way of Opinion. In the allegorical prologue, the narrator is carried on a chariot to the realm of

Light by the daughters of the Sun. There he is met by an unidentified goddess whose revelations make up the rest of the work. The Way of Truth is the way of the intellect; it discovers True Being, which is unitary, timeless, motionless, and changeless although spatially limited. Its opposite, Non-Being, cannot be intellectually known and is therefore to be denied as a concept. The contradictory Heraclitean notion of Simultaneous Being and Non-Being is also denied.

The Way of Opinion, which is the usual path of mortals, deals with the evident diversity of nature and the world perceived through the senses. The validity of sense data and of the objects perceived through the senses is denied. Parmenides insists on not confusing the physical objects with those of the intellect, although in the light of this disclaimer his elaborate explanations of various physical phenomena are somewhat puzzling. These explanations, whether they represent a summary of popular beliefs, Pythagorean thought, or Parmenides's own attempts to explain the world in the most plausible way through the use of the (necessarily false) senses, contain a few shrewd observations in an astronomical scheme that is impossible to reconstruct. Underlying all physical reality are the external opposites, Fire and Darkness. A mixture of the two governs the makeup of all organic life.

Parmenides's importance lies in his insistence on the separation of the intellect and the senses. His allegorical discussion of the paths of thought represents the earliest attempt to deal with the problems of philosophical method.

Further Reading

The extant fragments of Parmenides's poem are collected in Hermann Diels, ed., *Die Fragmente der Vorsokratiker* (1957), translated by Kathleen Freeman in *Ancilla to the Pre-Socratic Philosophers* (1948) and discussed by her in *The Pre-Socratic Philosophers* (1946; 3d ed. 1953). Excellent discussions and commentaries on Parmenides are in G. S. Kirk and J. E. Raven, *The Presocratic Philosophers* (1962), and W. K. C. Guthrie, *A History of Greek Philosophy* (3 vols., 1962-1969). General discussions of Pre-Socratic philosophy as part of the development of Greek thought may be found in the standard histories of Greek literature, of which a noteworthy example is Albin Lesky, *A History of Greek Literature* (trans. 1966). □

Parmigianino

The Italian painter Parmigianino (1503-1540) was a pioneer of the mannerist style, within which his work shows an essentially decorative emphasis and accomplished smoothness.

The real name of Parmigianino a nickname meaning "little man from Parma," was Francesco Mazzola. He was born on Jan. 11, 1503, in Parma. After his father, a painter, died in 1505, Parmigianino was brought up by two painter uncles. His own first works show an easy assimilation of the most sophisticated local styles, first Francesco Francia's and then Correggio's.

At the age of 19 Parmigianino was commissioned to execute frescoes for the Parma Cathedral; he painted a series of saints that rival Correggio's in their sinuous grace and gentle shadows. Soon thereafter Parmigianino extended these qualities into a personal idiom in the frescoes of the story of Diana and Acteon for a castle at Fontanellato; the figures are built up by a sketchy, pasty brushstroke that suggests an environment of fresh air but also confirms the elegant artificiality basic to mannerism, the frank embrace of the fact that painting differs in its essentials from nature.

Visually, mannerism is the intentional distortion of the proportions of the human figure and of spatial relationships. Good art for the early Renaissance was the successful imitation of nature, and this goal seemed to be achieved by High Renaissance artists. Their successors, such as Correggio, were thus able to learn it as apprentices and concern themselves rather with harmonious variations on ideal natural beauty. By the same token, the next generation could easily learn variants on ideal beauty which were already abstracted from their origins in nature and so could concern themselves with artifice and stylized distortion, as Parmigianino did.

In 1524 Parmigianino went to Rome, taking as a sample work his *Self-portrait in a Convex Mirror,* a distortion of his own appearance meant to amuse and attract praise for its technical virtuosity. In Rome he developed an elegant style of painting Madonnas, with a harder and smoother surface.

Parmigianino fled the sack of Rome in 1527 and went to Bologna. In his *Allegorical Portrait of Charles V* (1529-1530), executed in Bologna, where Charles V was crowned in 1530, he produced a pioneer formulation of the absolutist state portrait. Beginning in 1531, back in Parma, Parmigianino painted his most classic statements: the almost perversely erotic *Cupid Sharpening His Bow,* with Cupid seen from the rear but turning with a smile, and the *Madonna of the Long Neck* (1534), both paintings unified by a crisp twining line. His great church commission for S. Maria della Steccata in Parma, begun (1531) with six decorative female figures, was neglected when he developed a passion for alchemy. Threatened with a lawsuit for breach of contract in 1539, he fled to Casalmaggiore, where he died on Aug. 24, 1540.

Parmigianino was an accomplished draftsman. He was also the first Italian painter to be an etcher.

Further Reading

Sydney J. Freedberg, *Parmigianino: His Works in Painting* (1950), is a sound although needlessly elaborate visual analysis. A. E. Popham, *The Drawings of Parmigianino* (1953), contains an excellent summary text. □

Charles Stewart Parnell

The Irish nationalist leader Charles Stewart Parnell (1846-1891) made home rule for Ireland a major factor in Irish nationalism and British politics.

Charles Parnell's County Wicklow, Anglo-Irish, Protestant-gentry family had earned a patriotic reputation in Ireland by opposing the Act of Union with Britain and by supporting Catholic emancipation. His American mother was a passionate Anglophobe. Although Parnell was educated in England, used English speech patterns, and possessed the aloof manner associated with the English establishment, he inherited his family's devotion to Irish interests.

His Obstructionist Tactics

In 1875 Parnell entered the House of Commons, lending his Protestant-gentry respectability to home rule. Two years later he joined Joseph Biggar in systematic obstruction of British legislation. Described by Parnell as an active parliamentary policy, obstruction was a reaction to British indifference to Irish problems, to the cautious and conciliatory parliamentary tactics and leadership of Isaac Butt—father of home rule and chairman of the Irish party—and to the growing cynicism of Irish opinion toward nationalist politics.

Butt joined outraged British politicians and journalists in denouncing the "barbarian" tactics of Parnell and Biggar, claiming they had damaged home rule by alienating British opinion. Parnell insisted that the achievement of home rule depended on the determination of Irish nationalist members of Parliament to demonstrate that the union could be as unpleasant for the British as it was for the Irish.

Avoiding a direct challenge to Butt's control over the moribund Irish party or the impoverished Home Rule League, Parnell awaited the next general election. He used obstruction to attract notice and favor, courting Irish opinion at home and in the ghettos of Britain and the United States. In 1879 Parnell accepted the presidency of the National Land League, a New Departure instrument designed by Irish-Americans to bring republicans into contact with the Irish peasant masses. Financed by Irish-American dollars, the Land League demanded the end of landlordism, but it was prepared to accept agrarian reform along the way.

Leader of the Irish Party

The results of the general elections of 1880 gave Parnell the votes to command the Irish party. William Gladstone, the prime minister, responded to the near-revolutionary Land League agitation with a mixed coercion-conciliation policy. The 1881 Land Act gave Irish tenant farmers secure tenures at fair rents, freeing them from serfdom. But Parnell rejected the act as inadequate, and the government imprisoned him for encouraging agrarian disturbances. He was released in 1882 after promising to accept government improvements in the Land Act in exchange for Irish party support of future Liberal efforts to solve the Irish question. The truce was known as the Kilmainham Treaty.

After 1882 Parnell concentrated on building an effective Irish party to promote home rule. Instead of reviving the outlawed Land League, he used Irish-American money to pay the expenses of talented and sincere nationalists prepared to stand for Parliament. Parnell's genius, Irish-American dollars, and the Reform Bill of 1884 gave the Irish party more than 80 members in the House of Commons.

Irish-Liberal Alliance

With an effective party behind him, Parnell in 1885 played balance-of-power politics in the House of Commons, forcing both Liberals and Conservatives to bid for Irish votes. Gladstone made the highest offer: home rule. The Irish then turned the Conservatives out of office and installed the Liberals. In 1886 Gladstone introduced a home-rule bill which was defeated by defections in Liberal ranks. The Irish-Liberal alliance lasted for 30 years, limiting the freedom of the Irish party and pushing British anti-Irish, no-popery, imperialistic opinion in a conservative direction. Home rule became the most emotional issue in British politics.

At the beginning of December 1889, Parnell was the unchallenged master of Irish nationalism. He dominated Irish opinion, bringing extremist types into the mainstream of constitutional nationalism. He commanded Irish-American financial resources, and he had captured the Liberal party for home rule. But that month the tides of Parnell's fortune began to recede when Capt. William O'Shea submitted a petition suing his wife, Katherine, for divorce, naming Parnell as correspondent.

Downfall and Death

Irish nationalists assumed that Parnell would emerge from the courtroom an honorable man. Parnell, however, anxious to marry Katherine O'Shea who had been his mistress since 1880, decided not to contest William O'Shea's charges, and his image was tarnished by the captain's testimony. Although the Irish party reelected Parnell its chairman in November 1890—just after the divorce—British Nonconformists demanded that Gladstone separate the Liberals from a public sinner. Gladstone insisted that the Irish party drop Parnell as its leader. On Dec. 6, 1890, after days of bitter debate, a majority of home-rule members of Parliament decided that the fate of Irish freedom was more important than the position of one man. Parnell, a supreme egotist, refused to accept the realities of the Liberal alliance. He appealed to the Irish people in three by-election contests. Opposed by the Catholic hierarchy and clergy, Parnell lost the by-elections and his health in the process. He died of rheumatic fever at Brighton on Oct. 6, 1891.

Parnell bequeathed a shattered parliamentary party, a bitter and divided nationalist opinion, and the myth of a martyred messiah. He became a symbol of resistance to British dictation, clericalism, and inhibiting Victorian and Irish Catholic moralities.

Further Reading

Still the best biography of Parnell is Richard Barry O'Brien, *The Life of Charles Stewart Parnell* (2 vols., 1898; repr. 1968). Briefer is Jules Abels, *The Parnell Tragedy* (1966). See also St. John Ervine, *Parnell* (1925), and William O'Brien, *The Parnell of Real Life* (1926).

Lawrence J. McCaffrey, *Irish Federalism in the 1870's: A Study in Conservative Nationalism* (1962), discusses the beginning of Parnell's political career and his contest with Butt. Parnell's leadership of the Irish party and the forces of nationalism in the 1890s is brilliantly analyzed in Conor Cruise O'Brien, *Parnell and His Party, 1880-1890* (1957). Francis Stewart L. Lyons, *The Fall of Parnell, 1890-91* (1960), is a detailed, objective, and very well-written analysis of the factors and motives that destroyed Parnell's leadership and split Irish nationalism. Thomas N. Brown's excellent *Irish-American Nationalism* (1966) discusses the relationship between Parnell, Irish-American nationalism, and home rule. Herbert Howarth, *The Irish Writers' Literature and Nationalism, 1880-1940* (1958), contains an interesting interpretation of the impact of the Parnell myth on Irish writing.

Additional Sources

Bew, Paul, *Charles Stewart Parnell,* Dublin: Gill and Macmillan, 1991.
Byrne, Edward, *Parnell: a memoir,* Dublin: Lilliput, 1991.
Foster, R. F. (Robert Fitzroy), *Charles Stewart Parnell: the man and his family,* Hassocks Eng.: Harvester Press; Atlantic Highlands, N.J.: Humanities Press, 1976.
Kee, Robert, *The laurel and the ivy: the story of Charles Stewart Parnell and Irish nationalism,* London: Hamish Hamilton; New York, N.Y., USA: PenguinBooks, 1993.
Kissane, Noel, *Parnell: a documentary history,* Dublin: National Library of Ireland, 1991.
Lyons, F. S. L. (Francis Stewart Leland), *Charles Stewart Parnell,* New York: Oxford University Press, 1977.
Parnell in perspective, London; New York: Routledge, 1991. □

Vernon Louis Parrington

The American historian Vernon Louis Parrington (1871-1929) is known for his three-volume intellectual history of America, *Main Currents in American Thought*.

Born at Aurora, Ill., on Aug. 3, 1871, Vernon Parrington was of Scotch and Irish descent. His father was a school principal in New York and Illinois, served in the Union Army, and became a judge of probate in Kansas. While growing up near Pumpkin Ridge, Kans., Vernon early became acquainted with the sources of agrarian discontent, and he later recalled his bitter feelings at seeing a year's corn crop used for fuel. Searching for answers, he found inspiration in the writings of William Morris, who "laid bare the evils of industrialism . . . and convinced me . . . that the businessman's society, symbolized by the cash register and existing solely for profit, must be destroyed to make way for another and better ideal."

After 2 years at the College of Emporia, a Presbyterian institution, Parrington entered Harvard as a junior and graduated in 1893. His Harvard experience was not happy, and he afterward referred acidly to his eastern alma mater. Returning to the College of Emporia, he taught English and French while obtaining his master of arts degree. He also ran unsuccessfully for the school board on a "Citizen's" ticket. In 1897 he was appointed instructor in English and modern languages at the University of Oklahoma, where he stayed for 11 years. Meanwhile he married Julia Rochester Williams in 1901 (they had two daughters and a son), did research in London and Paris (1903-1904), wrote some poetry, and took an interest in archeology. Fired from his job in 1908 because of a "political cyclone," Parrington accepted an assistant professorship at the University of Washington in Seattle.

There Parrington formed a close friendship with J. Allen Smith, a political scientist whose book *The Spirit of American Government* (1907) claimed to expose the antagonism between the Declaration of Independence, with its romantic egalitarian spirit, and the Constitution, a "reactionary document" drafted by representatives of "wealth and culture" to prevent effective popular rule. Smith saw a strong Federal government as the weapon of the propertied classes, and he opposed any extension or centralization of national power. His ideas profoundly affected Parrington, who later dedicated his book to Smith. Until 1927 Parrington wrote little: a chapter in the *Cambridge History of American Literature,* a few encyclopedia articles, an anthology, and some reviews. In 1927 the first two volumes of his *Main Currents in American Thought,* entitled *The Colonial Mind* and *The Romantic Revolution in America,* were published and received the Pulitzer Prize for history. The third volume, *The Beginnings of Critical Realism in America,* was incomplete when Parrington died on June 16, 1929, but was afterward published together with the earlier volumes in a one-volume edition.

Meaning of *Main Currents*

Though Parrington used the subtitle "An Interpretation of American Literature from the Beginnings to 1920," he denied writing "a history of American literature." His true subject was the history of American liberalism, seen as a long struggle between freedom and individualism on the one hand and privilege and authoritarianism on the other. The roots of the struggle were always in economic relations, and literary productions were strategic elements in the fight. For Parrington, writers embodied or exemplified some interest of an age, and each was considered in relation to his battle position. Mark Twain was a great frontier republican; Walt Whitman, a great democrat; and William Cullen Bryant, a fighter for free labor. Parrington deliberately slighted the "narrowly belletristic." He had little understanding or appreciation for writers who would not or could not carry a spear in the war.

As Parrington unfolded the story, from the days of the Pilgrims to his own time "idealists" had contended with "realists," humanitarians with crass materialists, agrarians with capitalists, Jeffersonians with Hamiltonians, and decentralizers with centralizers who sought to control the power of the state in order to dominate and exploit the majority. In generation after generation, between these opposing hosts, mighty battles had been fought, and historic defeats had been imposed on the democratic forces. The Constitution itself was an early monument to a victory of financiers and capitalists over agrarians, who held to the romantic idealism of the Declaration of Independence. A half century afterward, the democratic army of Jacksonian Democracy had gone down before the cunning Whig propaganda of business and industrial interests. Once again, in 1896, the old Jeffersonian cause, led now by William Jennings Bryan, had failed to throw off the yoke of eastern capital. Thereafter the trend in government was toward increasing centralization with consequent loss of individual freedom. The future looked bleak, as a new cynicism was corroding the Jeffersonian faith in human nature and education.

Scholarly Opinion

During the 1930s *Main Currents* had enormous prestige in the academic world. The liberals embraced it as the "usable new history" that James Harvey Robinson and Charles A. Beard had been calling for, and to them it was a "realistic" guidebook to the American past. In 1952 over 100 American historians rated *Main Currents* the most important work published in the field during the period 1920-1935. Yet its influence was relatively short-lived. Parrington's judgments were in many instances revealed to be simply mistaken, and his conflict thesis began to be recognized as artificial and overly simplistic. Especially in the 1950s, with the rise of a "consensus history" that stressed elements of basic agreement in the American tradition, *Main Currents* lost scholarly respect. Even with a renewed emphasis upon the place of social struggle in American history, it is unlikely that Parrington's interpretation will ever again appear plausible. But if its Jeffersonian partisanship is out of fashion, *Main Currents* continues to be read

for the distinction of its literary style, perhaps the most brilliant since Francis Parkman's. Many of Parrington's individual portraits remain unsurpassed, and his description of the post-Civil War national orgy of venality and vulgarity as the "Great Barbecue" has become classic.

Further Reading

The most extensive study of Parrington, together with an excellent annotated bibliography, is in Richard Hofstadter, *The Progressive Historians* (1968). Parrington is examined in the context of American historiography in Robert Allen Skotheim, *American Intellectual Histories and Historians* (1966). Important analyses are in Alfred Kazin, *On Native Ground* (1942; abridged with a new postscript, 1956), and Lionel Trilling, *The Liberal Imagination* (1950).

Additional Sources

Hall, H. Lark, *V.L. Parrington: through the avenue of art*, Kent, Ohio: Kent State University Press, 1994.

Hofstadter, Richard, *The progressive historians—Turner, Beard, Parrington*, Chicago: University of Chicago Press, 1979, 1968. □

Sir Charles Algernon Parsons

Sir Charles Algernon Parsons (1854-1931) was a British engineer who perfected the steam turbine that bears his name.

Charles Parsons was born on June 13, 1854, in London. His father, William Parsons, 3d Earl of Rosse, was a distinguished astronomer and sometime president of the Royal Society. Charles and his brothers were tutored by eminent scholars working in his father's observatory at Birr Castle, Parsonstown (now called Birr), in King's County, Ireland (Offalay, Eire). He attended Trinity College, Dublin (1871-1873), and Cambridge University (1873-1877), where he distinguished himself in mathematics. He then worked at the Armstrong engineering works located at Newcastle-upon-Tyne (1877-1881).

In 1884 Parsons joined a Gateshead partnership and entered the new field of electrical engineering. The production of cheap electricity in quantity demanded prime movers with outputs and efficiencies high above those of reciprocating engines. Thus Parsons developed the steam turbine, a machine with a long conceptual but no practical history. Stream freely expanding from high to low pressures acquires velocity and may form a jet which can impinge on a turbine wheel and yield useful work. But to get the most out of a high-pressure jet, a singlestage turbine would have to rotate at speeds above the capacities of materials then available. By setting a series of turbine wheels on one shaft and limiting the pressure drop between adjacent wheels, Parsons was able to reduce shaft and peripheral speeds to acceptable limits. By allowing steam to expand across the turbine blades, he was able to improve performance further;

Frank Parsons

Frank Parsons (1854-1908) was an American educator and reformer whose grasp of problems of public ownership and municipal affairs made him influential among reformers and administrators.

Frank Parsons was born on Nov. 14, 1854, in Mount Holly, N.J., of Scotch-Irish and English parents. A brilliant student, he entered Cornell University at the age of 15, graduating first in his class 3 years later with a degree in civil engineering. After working with a railroad that went bankrupt, he taught school at Southbridge, Mass. He decided that he needed a law degree and completed 3 years of study in a year, passing the bar examination in 1881. The effort damaged his health; he spent 3 years in New Mexico for renewal.

Persons entered law practice in Boston but found it unsatisfying. He joined a publisher, for whom he prepared legal textbooks. While formulating a social philosophy which would result in a spectacular outpouring of writings and social efforts, he developed habits of reading and social contacts that affected his later career. Thus his lectures on English literature, given over several years at Boston's Young Men's Christian Association, became his successful *The World's Best Books* (1889). In 1892 he assumed a lectureship at Boston University, which he held until 1905.

In *Our Country's Need* (1894) Parsons formulated his views of "mutualism," which attempted to reconcile individual liberty and socialism. Influenced by England's Herbert Spencer and by America's Edward Bellamy and "Christian socialism," Parsons sought to devise ways of controlling such basic institutions as the telegraph and the railroad, while honoring private industry and individual initiative. He combined radicalism and conservatism. *Rational Money* (1898), *The Telegraph Monopoly* (1899), *The City for the People* (1899), and *Direct Legislation* (1900) established him as an earnest and competent social critic.

From 1897 to 1899, while maintaining his Boston connections, Parsons was also a professor at Kansas State Agricultural College, radicalized by the Populist party's success in that state. When a change in administration cost him and his associates their positions, they founded Ruskin College of Social Science at Trenton, Mo., with Parsons as a dean and professor. After this idealistic venture failed, Parsons returned to Boston. He became deeply involved in numerous reform causes and traveled across country and to Europe. He advised the progressive owner of Filene's Department Store in Boston on adding cooperative features to his personnel policies, and he was involved in building the Civic Service Home, a settlement aiding immigrant groups. In 1905 he helped organize the Breadwinner's Institute, which offered education and a diploma to the poor.

Parsons' *The Story of New Zealand* (1904), *The Trusts, the Railroads, and the People* (1906), *The Heart of the Railroad Problem* (1906), and his constant flow of articles made him an outstanding academic voice for progressivism, but

and by introducing the steam between a pair of coupled but opposed turbine sets, he avoided thrusts on the end bearings. He patented these and other innovations in 1884.

Electric generators then worked at about 1,500 revolutions per minute (rpm), while Parsons' turbine worked at 18,000 rpm. Undaunted, he designed and built a generator suitable for direct coupling. Thus, the turboalternator was born, and by 1889 several hundred were in use, mostly for ship lighting. That year Parsons set up his own works in Newcastle, concentrating at first on large turboalternators for urban electricity supplies.

In 1894 Parsons turned to the marine applications of the steam turbine and built the *Turbinia,* 100 feet long and displacing 44 tons. After many experiments with screw designs, it reached speeds of 34 knots in 1897. Despite initial apathy, the turbine became standard in British warships from 1905. For fast liners the turbine soon proved its economy; and with Parsons' development of suitable gear trains, the reciprocating engine was displaced from many slower ships. He was knighted in 1911, and he died on Feb. 11, 1931, in Kingston, Jamaica.

Further Reading

A biography of Parsons is Rollo Appleyard, *Charles Parsons: His Life and Work* (1933). A booklet by Robert Hodson Parsons, *The Steam Turbine and Other Inventions of Sir Charles Parsons* (1942; rev. ed. 1946), is useful. The historical scene and background are set out in Henry Winram Dickinson, *A Short History of the Steam Engine* (1938; 2d ed. 1963). □

contributed to the debilitation which caused his death on Sept. 26, 1908. Published posthumously were his *Choosing a Vocation* (1909), a pioneer work in the vocational field, and *Legal Doctrine and Social Progress* (1911).

Further Reading

Howard V. Davis, *Frank Parsons* (1969), emphasizes Parsons' role as the founder of vocational guidance. Arthur Mann, *Yankee Reformers in the Urban Age* (1954), devotes a chapter to him. □

Talcott Parsons

American sociologist, Talcott Parsons (1902-1979), analyzed the socialization process to show the relationship between personality and social structure. His work led to the development of a pioneering social theory.

Talcott Parsons was born on Dec. 13, 1902, in Colorado Springs, Colorado. He graduated from Amherst College in 1924, where he majored in biology, but decided to do graduate work in economics. In 1924-25 he attended the London School of Economics. He took his doctorate at Heidelberg University in Germany in 1927. While at Heidelberg, he translated Max Weber's *The Protestant Ethic and the Spirit of Capitalism,* which exercised a great influence upon young American sociologists.

Parsons was an instructor in the department of economics at Harvard University from 1927 to 1931. During this period he studied the works of Alfred Marshall, the great classical theorist and codiscoverer of the principle of marginal utility; Émile Durkheim, the French sociologist; and Vilfredo Pareto, the Italian sociologist. Parsons' *The Structure of Social Action* (1937) fuses the theories of Durkheim, Pareto, and Weber into a single new body of theory and shows their relationship to Marshall's type of economic theory. Parsons became a full professor of sociology at Harvard in 1944. He held that position until his retirement in 1973.

The pioneering social theory developed by Parsons is abstract and complex. As a frame of reference for his system, he adopted the social action theory and stressed the structural-functional approach as the only way for sociology to achieve systematic theory. He stated that personality formation develops out of action organized around individuals, while action organized around relations of actors leads to a social system which consists of a network of roles. A third system which is indispensable to the personality system and the social system is the cultural system, which constitutes the standards and channels for guiding action. These three systems interpenetrate one another, and Parsons focused on the analysis of the socialization process to show the relationship between personality and the social structure.

The areas in which Parsons made contributions included the classification of the role of theory in research; the analysis of institutions; the outline of systematic theory in sociology; the voluntaristic theory of action; the analysis of specific structure and roles, kinship, occupations, and professions; and the analysis of certain modern problems of aggression, fascism, and anti-Semitism. He also made significant scholarly and practical contributions in his writings on the academic profession and on racial and intercultural relations. He was elected president of the American Sociological Association in 1949 and served as secretary from 1960 to 1965.

Parsons died of a stroke on May 8, 1979, while giving a series of lectures in Munich, Germany. The obituary in the *New York Times* the next day described Parsons as "A towering figure in the social sciences," who was responsible for "the education of three generations of sociologists."

Further Reading

Parsons' work is examined in M. Black, ed., *The Social Theories of Talcott Parsons: A Critical Examination* (1961); William C. Mitchell, *Sociological Analysis and Politics: The Theories of Talcott Parsons* (1967); Peter Hamilton, ed., *Readings from Talcott Parsons* (1985); and Roland Robertson and Bryan S. Turner, ed., *Talcott Parsons: Theorist of Modernity* (1991). There is also a brief discussion of Parsons' importance in Manuel Conrad Elmer, *Contemporary Social Thought: Contributors and Trends* (1956). □

Blaise Pascal

The French scientist and philosopher Blaise Pascal (1623-1662) was a precocious and influential mathematical writer, a master of the French language, and a great religious philosopher.

Blaise Pascal was born at Clermont-Ferrand on June 19, 1623. He was the son of Étienne Pascal, king's counselor and later president of the Court of Aids at Clermont. Blaise's mother died in 1626, and he was left with his two sisters, Gilberte and Jacqueline. In 1631 the family moved to Paris.

Young Geometer

When Pascal was 12, he began attending meetings of a mathematical academy. His father taught him languages, especially Latin and Greek, but not mathematics. This ban on mathematics merely served to whet the boy's curiosity. He experimented with geometrical figures, inventing his own names for standard geometrical terms.

In 1640 the Pascal family moved to Rouen. There, still taught mainly by his father, Blaise worked with such intensity that his health deteriorated. Nevertheless, he had arrived at one of the most beautiful theorems in geometry. Sometimes called by him his "mystic hexagram," it is a theorem concerned with the collinearity of intersections of lines. It does not concern metrical properties of figures but is, in fact, at the very foundation of an important, and at the time almost entirely undeveloped, branch of mathemat-

of the famous *Provincial Letters*. Their framework is that of a correspondence between a Parisian and a friend in the provinces from Jan. 13, 1656, to March 24, 1657. They were circulated in the thousands through Paris under a pseudonym (Louis de Montalte), and the Jesuits tried to discover the author, whose wit, reason, eloquence, and humor made the order a laughingstock.

The *Pensées*

Knowledge of Pascal's personal life is slight after his entry to Port Royal. His sister Gilberte tells of his asceticism, of his dislike of seeing her caress her children, and of his apparent revulsion from talk of feminine beauty. He suffered increasingly after 1658 from head pains, and he died on Aug. 19, 1662.

At his death Pascal left an unfinished theological work, the *Pensées,* an apology for Christianity, in effect, which was published 8 years later by the Port Royal community in a thoroughly garbled and incoherent form. A reasonably authentic version first appeared in 1844. It deals with the great problems of Christian thought, faith versus reason, free will, and preknowledge. Pascal explains the contradictions and problems of the moral life in terms of the doctrine of the Fall and makes faith and revelation alone sufficient for their mutual justification.

The *Pensées,* unlike the *Provincial Letters,* were not worked over and over by their author, and in style they would not, perhaps, mark him out as a great literary figure. The *Letters,* however, give Pascal a place in literary history as the first of several great French writers practicing the polite irony to which the language lends itself. The *Pensées* could almost have been written by another man, for in them reason is ostensibly made to take second place to religion. But they are both, in their different ways, among the great books in the history of religious thought.

Later Mathematical and Scientific Work

Pascal's writings on hydrostatics, relating his experiments with the barometer to his theoretical ideas on the equilibrium of fluids, were not published until a year after his death. His *Treatise on the Equilibrium of Liquids* extends Simon Stevin's analysis of the hydrostatic paradox and enunciates what may be called the final law of hydrostatics: in a fluid at rest the pressure is transmitted equally in all directions (Pascal's principle). Pascal is important as having forged links between the theories of liquids and gases, and between the dynamics of rigid bodies and hydrodynamics.

Pascal's principal contribution to mathematics after his entry to Port Royal related to problems associated with the cycloid—a curve, with the area of which the best mathematicians of the day were occupied. He published many of his theorems without proof, as a challenge to other mathematicians. Solutions were found by John Wallis, Christopher Wren, Christian Huygens, and others. Pascal published his own solutions under the assumed name of Amos Dettonville (an anagram of Louis de Montalte), and contemporary mathematicians often referred to him by this name.

The mathematical theory of probability made its first great step forward when a correspondence between Pascal

ics—projective geometry. Pascal then set to work on a book, *Essay on Conics,* finished in 1640, in which the mystic hexagram was given central importance. It contained several hundred propositions on conic sections, bringing in the work of Apollonius and his successors, and was remarkable not only because of the writer's age (16) but also because of its treatment of tangency, among other things.

Jansenists and Port Royal

In 1646 Pascal's father had an accident and was confined to his house. He was visited by some neighbors who were Jansenists, a group formed by Cornelis Jansen, a Dutch-born professor of theology at Louvain. Their beliefs were contrary to the teachings of the Jesuits. The Pascals came under the influence of the Jansenists, with resultant fierce opposition to, and from, the Jesuits. Jacqueline wished to join the Jansenist convent at Port Royal. Étienne Pascal disliked the idea and took the family away to Paris, but after his death in 1651 Jacqueline joined Port Royal. Pascal still enjoyed a more worldly life, having a number of aristocratic friends and a little more money to spend from his patrimony. In 1654, however, he was completely converted to Jansenism, and he commenced an austere life at Port Royal.

Provincial Letters

In 1655 Antoine Arnauld, a prolific writer in defense of Jansen, was formally condemned by the Sorbonne for heretical teaching, and Pascal took up his defense in the first part and Pierre de Fermat revealed that both had come to similar conclusions independently. Pascal planned a treatise on the subject, but again only a fragment survived, to be published after his death. He never wrote at great length on mathematics, but the many short pieces which survive are almost always concise and incisive.

Further Reading

An excellent biography of Pascal is Jean Mesnard, *Pascal: His Life and Works* (1951; trans. 1952). Other studies of his life and work include Morris Bishop, *Pascal: The Life of Genius* (1936); Frank Thomas Herbert Fletcher, *Pascal and the Mystical Tradition* (1954); and Ernest Mortimer, *Blaise Pascal: The Life and Work of a Realist* (1959). Jack Howard Broome, *Pascal* (1966), is a lucid and practical introduction to Pascal's life and thought aimed at the beginner. It is a mark of Pascal's importance that most histories of this period of mathematics, science, or religion deal with his work at some length. □

Boris Leonidovich Pasternak

The Russian poet, novelist, and translator Boris Leonidovich Pasternak (1890-1960) was the foremost writer of the Soviet period. He constantly endeavored to shape the means of artistic expression to the ends of his integrity and concern for mankind.

B oris Pasternak was born on Feb. 10, 1890, in Moscow. His parents and their friends provided an artistic, musical, and literary environment that nurtured Pasternak's creative aspirations. His father, Leonid O. Pasternak, was a prominent painter of the naturalist school, and his mother, Rosa F. Kaufman, was an accomplished concert pianist. Music was Pasternak's first inclination. Under the tutelage of Aleksandr Scriabin, he began to study musical composition at the age of 13. Pasternak soon abandoned music for philosophy. In 1909 he enrolled as a student at the philosophy faculty of Moscow University. Inspired by the thinking of the German philosopher Hermann Cohen of Marburg University, Pasternak traveled to Marburg in 1912 for the summer semester. He extended his travels to Italy before returning to Moscow, where he completed his studies in 1913.

Early Works

Pasternak's experience at Marburg turned him toward poetry, but it would always be a poetry endowed with the inquisitive spirit of philosophy. His first two books of poetry, *A Twin in the Clouds* (1914) and *Over the Barriers* (1917), partake of the mixed atmosphere of romanticism and experiment then current in the futurist movement. Pasternak's acquaintance with the leading futurist poet, Vladimir Mayakovsky, proved formative. In his next book of lyrics, *My Sister, My Life* (1922), Pasternak attained complete independence and originality.

Pasternak's early stories explore prose as an alternative form for essentially poetic themes. "The History of a Contra-octave" (1913) deals with the conflicting duties an artist owes to his art and to his family. "Apelles' Figure" (1918) shows Pasternak's versatility at its best.

The events of the 1917 Russian Revolution and the subsequent civil war (1917-1921) caused Pasternak to reexamine the substance of his art. This reexamination culminated in the novel *Doctor Zhivago* (1957). The Revolution unleashed forces of chaos long dormant in Russian civilization. Primarily in his prose, Pasternak struggled to reassert the humanism that he had known in the person of Leo Tolstoy ("The Letters from Tula," 1922) and to make a place for the individual in the mass society ("Aerial Ways," 1924).

The most significant characteristic of Pasternak's life in the 1920s is his striving to address his art to social problems. To this end, he wrote epic poems on contemporary themes. "A Lofty Malady" (1923) portrays episodes from Lenin's life; "The Year 1905" (1926) is based on the 1905 revolt; and "Lieutenant Schmidt" (1927) is based on the life of a real revolutionary. In his novel in verse, *Spektorsky* (1929), and its prose segment, *The Tale* (1929), Pasternak used events from his own life as the foundation for a narrative encompassing the years 1914 to 1924.

Role of Autobiography

Pasternak showed an unmistakable reticence about the events of his personal life. Little is known of his life in the 1920s. He married in the early 1920s and a son, Evgeny, was born. In the late 1920s his failing marriage combined with a sense of failure in his prose endeavors lead to a deep creative and psychological crisis in his life. The resolution of this crisis initiated Pasternak's later period, which saw the full development of his talent.

The crisis in Pasternak's life involved his love for Zinaida N. Neuhaus, whom he later married; his concern for his fellow poet Mayakovsky; and his growing pessimism about the future of Russian letters. Pasternak's divorce and remarriage severely strained his mental balance. At the same time, the poet Mayakovsky was undergoing a strain of another sort: he was feeling the full humiliation of the artist who has bartered his art for a political cause.

Pasternak's impressionistic, semiphilosophical autobiography *Safe Conduct* (1931) presents the problems of his crisis and proposes a solution. He resolves to put his individual creative talent in the service not of the state but of history. His book of poems *A Second Birth* (1931) concentrates on themes relating the past to the present.

Pasternak lived quietly through the 1930s in Moscow and Peredelkino, the writers' village in the suburbs of Moscow. He reassessed and redirected his artistic talent. His lifelong indifference to immediate political events probably spared him the tragic fate of many writers during Stalin's purges. During the 1930s Pasternak's resolution led him to experiments in prose (the first drafts of *Doctor Zhivago*), further poetic inspiration (*On Early Trains,* 1941), and translations.

Pasternak's translations span his career. They are expert and professional, full of the spirit and inspiration of their originals. In the 1920s Pasternak translated such diverse writers as Heinrich von Kleist and Ben Jonson. In the 1930s Pasternak translated the Georgian poets of the southern former U.S.S.R. In their mastery of German, French, and English, Pasternak's translations of the 1940s and 1950s illustrate the startling breadth of his undertaking. He translated F. von Schiller, J. W. von Goethe's *Faust,* R. M. Rilke, P. Verlaine, J. Keats, P. B. Shelley, eight of Shakespeare's plays, and several of Shakespeare's sonnets.

Pasternak's participation in World War II was minimal. He served for a time as an aerial spotter in Moscow, made one trip to the front, and was evacuated from Moscow in the face of the German invasion. He continued his translations during the war and, immediately thereafter, renewed his work on *Doctor Zhivago*.

Doctor Zhivago

The culmination of his artistic career, *Doctor Zhivago* is Pasternak's attempt to bring both prose and poetry to bear on the problems of the individual artist and his life in history. It combines an epic novel in prose of the scope of Tolstoy's *War and Peace* with a selection of poetry attributed to the hero of the novel, Yury Zhivago. The subject of the novel is an individual poet's life in conflict with his times. The novel spans the years 1902 to 1953.

In 1956 Soviet authorities refused to publish *Doctor Zhivago*. Publication of the novel in the West in 1957 led to a series of consequences unforeseen by Pasternak. He was awarded the 1958 Nobel Prize for his achievement, but critical reaction within the Soviet Union forced him to de-

cline the award. Having suffered a heart attack in 1953, Pasternak was in poor health. He lived in isolation with his family at Peredelkino. He was the focus of worldwide acclaim, yet an object of official scorn in his own country. His book of poems *When the Storm Breaks* (1959) shows not a trace of dismay in its lively pursuit of the poet's lifelong twin interests—man's life in nature and his life in history. Pasternak died on May 30, 1960.

Further Reading

The reader interested in Pasternak's life should turn to his autobiographies: "Safe Conduct" in his *Selected Writings* (trans. 1949; new ed. 1958) and *I Remember: Sketch for an Autobiography* (trans. 1959). A pictorial biography is Gerd Ruge, *Pasternak* (trans. 1959). The best comprehensive surveys of Pasternak's writings are Cecil Maurice Bowra, *The Creative Experiment* (1949), and Helen Muchnic, *From Gorky to Pasternak: Six Writers in Soviet Russia* (1961). A good treatment of the complexity of Pasternak's poetry is to be found in Dale Plank, *Pasternak's Lyric: A Study of Sound and Imagery* (1966). See also Robert Payne, *The Three Worlds of Boris Pasternak* (1961); Robert Conquest, *The Pasternak Affair: Courage of a Genius—A Documentary Report* (1962); and Donald Davie and Angela Livingstone, eds., *Pasternak* (1969).

Additional Sources

Barnes, Christopher J., *Boris Pasternak: a literary biography,* Cambridge England; New York: Cambridge University Press, 1989.

Meetings with Pasternak: a memoir, New York: Harcourt Brace Jovanovich, 1977.

Hingley, Ronald, *Pasternak: a biography,* New York: Knopf: Distributed by Random House, 1983.

Levi, Peter, *Boris Pasternak,* London: Hutchinson, 1990.

Mallac, Guy de, *Boris Pasternak, his life and art,* Norman: University of Oklahoma Press, 1981.

Pasternak, E. B., *Boris Pasternak: the tragic years, 1930-60,* London: Collins Harvill, 1990. □

Louis Pasteur

The French chemist and biologist Louis Pasteur (1822-1895) is famous for his germ theory and for the development of vaccines.

L ouis Pasteur was born on Dec. 27, 1822, in the small town of Dôle, the son of a tanner. He studied in the college of Arbois and at Besançon, where he graduated in arts in 1840. As a student preparing for the prestigious École Normale Supérieure of Paris, he did not doubt his ability. When he gained admittance by passing fourteenth on the list, he refused entry; taking the examination again, he won third place and accepted. For his doctorate his attention was directed to the then obscure science of crystallography. This was to have a decisive influence on his career.

Stereochemistry Investigations

Pasteur, under special dispensation from the minister of education, received a leave of absence from his duties as professor of physics at the lycée of Tournon to pursue research on the optical properties of crystals of the salts of tartrates and paratartrates, which had the capacity to rotate the plane of polarized light. He prepared 19 different salts, examined these under a microscope, and determined that they possessed hemihedral facets. However, the crystal faces were oriented differently; they were left-handed or right-handed, thus having the asymmetrical relationship of mirror images. Furthermore, each geometric variety of crystal rotated the light in accordance with its structure, while equal mixtures of the left- and right-handed crystals had no optical activity inasmuch as the physical effects canceled each other. Thus he demonstrated the phenomenon of optical isomers.

Pasteur was elated; he repeated his experiment under the exacting eyes of Jacques Biot, the French Academy's authority on polarized light who had brought Eilhardt Mitscherlich's work to Pasteur's attention. The confirmation was complete to the last exacting detail, and Pasteur, then 26, became famous. The French government made him a member of the Legion of Honor, and Britain's Royal Society presented him with the Copley Medal.

In 1852 Pasteur accepted the chair of chemistry at the University of Strasbourg. Here he found not only a wife but an opportunity to pursue another dimension of crystallography. It had long been known that molds grew readily in

solutions of calcium paratartrate. It occurred to him to inquire whether organisms would show a preference for one isomer or another. He soon discovered that his microorganism could completely remove only one of the crystal forms from the solution, the levorotary, or left-handed, molecule.

Studies on Fermentation

In 1854, though only 31 years old, Pasteur became professor of chemistry and dean of sciences at the new University of Lille. The course of his activities is displayed in the publications which he gave to the world in the next decades: *Studies on Wine* (1866), *Studies on Vinegar* (1868), *Studies on the Diseases of Silkworms* (1870), and *Studies on Beer* (1876).

Soon after his arrival at Lille, Pasteur was asked to devote some time to the problems of the local industries. A producer of vinegar from beet juice requested Pasteur's help in determining why the product sometimes spoiled. Pasteur collected samples of the fermenting juices and examined them microscopically. He noticed that the juices contained yeast. He also noted that the contaminant, amyl alcohol, was an optically active compound, and hence to Pasteur evidence that it was produced by a living organism ("living contagion").

Pasteur was quick to generalize his findings and thus to advance a biological interpretation of the processes of fermentation. In a series of dramatic but exquisitely planned experiments, he demonstrated that physical screening or thermal methods destroyed all microorganisms and that when no contamination by living contagion took place, the processes of fermentation or putrefaction did not take place either. "Pasteurization" was thus a technique which could not only preserve wine, beer, and milk but could also prevent or drastically reduce infection in the surgeon's operating room.

Another by-product of Pasteur's work on fermentation was his elucidation of the fact that certain families of microbes require oxygen whereas others do not. Yeast, he showed, was a facultative anaerobe; when oxygen was not present, as in the vats of beer or wine manufacturers, it would derive its energy from the sugar, converting it to alcohol; under more favorable conditions (for the yeast) where oxygen was available, alcohol did not accumulate, and the process continued to the complete conversion of sugar to carbon dioxide and water. This insight divided the scientific community, and it was only in 1897, 2 years after the death of Pasteur, that the dispute was resolved, when a cell-free extract of yeast proved capable of fermenting a sugar solution. Thus it turned out that the living organism synthesized an enzyme which carried out the conversion.

Silkworms and Microbial Disease Theory

In 1865 Pasteur was called upon to assist another ailing industry of France—silk manufacture—which was being ruined by an epidemic among silkworms. He took his microscope to the south of France and in an improvised laboratory set to work. Four months later he had isolated the pathogens causing the disease, and after 3 years of intensive work he suggested the methods of bringing it under control.

Pasteur's scientific triumphs coincided with personal and national tragedy. In 1865 his father died; his two daughters were lost to typhoid fever in 1866. Over-worked and grief-stricken, Pasteur suffered a cerebral hemorrhage in 1868 which left part of his left arm and leg permanently paralyzed. Nonetheless, he pressed on, hardly with interruptions, on his study of silkworm diseases, already sensing that these investigations were but his apprenticeship for the control of the diseases of higher animals, including humans.

The Franco-Prussian War, with its trains of wounded, stimulated Pasteur to press his microbial theory of disease and infection on the military medical corps, winning grudging agreement to the sterilization of instruments and the steaming of bandages. The results were spectacular, and in 1873 Pasteur was made a member of the French Academy of Medicine—a remarkable accomplishment for a man without a formal medical degree.

Pasteur was now prepared to move from the most primitive manifestations of life, crystals and the simpler forms of life in the microbial world, to the diseases of the higher animals. The opportunity arose through a particularly devastating outbreak of anthrax, a killer plague of cattle and sheep in 1876/1877. The anthrax bacillus had already been identified by Robert Koch, and Pasteur now set about proving that the agent of disease was precisely the living organism and not a related toxin. He diluted a solution originally containing a source of infection of anthrax by a factor of 1 part in 100^{100}. Even at this enormous dilution, the residual fluid carried death, thus proving that it was the constantly multiplying organism that was the source of the disease.

In 1881 Pasteur had convincing evidence that gentle heating of anthrax bacilli could so attenuate the virulence of the organism that it could be used to inoculate animals and thus immunize them. In a dramatic demonstration of this procedure, carried out with the whole of France as witness, Pasteur inoculated one group of sheep with the vaccine and left another untreated. Upon injection of both groups with the bacillus, the untreated died; the others lived, and thus a scourge that had crippling economic effects was brought under control.

Pasteur's ultimate triumph came with the conquest of rabies, the disease of animals, particularly dogs, which gives rise to the dreaded hydrophobia of humans. The problem here was that the causative agent was a virus, hence an entity not capable of growth in the scientists' broth which nurtured bacteria. Pasteur worked for 5 years in an effort to isolate and culture the pathogen. Finally, in 1884, in collaboration with other investigators, he perfected a method of cultivating the virus in the tissues of rabbits. The virus could then be attenuated by exposing the incubation material to sterile air over a drying agent at room temperature. A vaccine could then be prepared for injection. The success of this method was greeted with jubilation all over the world. Animals could now be saved, but the question arose as to the effect of the treatment on human beings. In 1885 a 9-year-old boy, Joseph Meister, was brought to Pasteur. He was suffering from 14 bites from a rabid dog. With the agreement of the child's physician, Pasteur began his treatment with the vaccine. The injections continued over a 12-day period, and the child recovered.

Honors from the World

In 1888 a grateful France founded the Pasteur Institute, which was destined to become one of the most productive centers of biological study in the world. In the closing paragraphs of his inaugural oration, Pasteur said: "Two opposing laws seem to me now to be in contest. The one, a law of blood and death opening out each day new modes of destruction, forces nations always to be ready for the battle. The other, a law of peace, work and health, whose only aim is to deliver man from the calamities which beset him. The one seeks violent conquests, the other, the relief of mankind. The one places a single life above all victories, the other sacrifices hundreds of thousands of lives to the ambition of a single individual. The law of which we are the instruments strives even through the carnage to cure the wounds due to the law of war. Treatment by our antiseptic methods may preserve the lives of thousands of soldiers. Which of these two laws will prevail, God only knows. But of this we may be sure, science, in obeying the law of humanity, will always labor to enlarge the frontiers of life."

Pasteur's seventieth birthday was the occasion of a national holiday. At the celebration held at the Sorbonne, Pasteur was too weak to speak to the delegates who had gathered from all over the world. His address, read by his son, concluded: "Gentlemen, you bring me the greatest happiness that can be experienced by a man whose invincible belief is that science and peace will triumph over ignorance and war. . . . Have faith that in the long run . . . the future will belong not to the conquerors but to the saviors of mankind."

On Sept. 28, 1895, honored by the world but unspoiled and overflowing with affection, Pasteur died near Saint-Cloud. His last words were: "One must work; one must work. I have done what I could." He was buried in a crypt in the Pasteur Institute. There is a strange postscript to this story. In 1940 the conquering Germans came again to Paris. A German officer demanded to see the tomb of Pasteur, but the old French guard refused to open the gate. When the German insisted, the Frenchman killed himself. His name was Joseph Meister, the boy Pasteur had saved from hydrophobia so long ago.

Further Reading

The definitive biographies of Pasteur are René Dubos, *Louis Pasteur, Free Lance of Science* (1950), and Pierre Vallery-Radot, *Louis Pasteur: A Great Life in Brief* (trans. 1958). See also Jacques Nicolle, *Louis Pasteur, a Master of Scientific Enquiry* (1961). For the technical achievement in microbiology see Henry James Parish, *A History of Immunization* (1965). □

Kenneth Patchen

Kenneth Patchen (1911-1972) was a major American experimental poet and novelist influenced by Dadaism and Surrealism.

Kenneth Patchen's father was a steel worker in Youngstown and, later, in Warren, Ohio. As a young man Patchen followed his father's example and worked briefly in the mills, but, having decided to be a writer, he attended college, then travelled around the country, and, while supporting himself with odd jobs, spent what time he could developing his abilities with language. In 1934 he married Miriam Oikemus, to whom he would dedicate all of his nearly four dozen books, and two years later he published his first volume of poetry, *Before the Brave.*

Before the Brave showed Patchen's strong leftist political sensibility, formed in part by his youth in the steel towns and in part by his travels around the country during the Depression. Critics initially labelled him one of the leftist writers of the decade, but if he was a political poet (and in fact his intense political convictions remained with him throughout his life), he was a writer more strongly affected by the Dadaist and Surrealist movements. His response to these movements, however, was restrained. Patchen was no one's disciple, but the Dadaist and Surrealist influence can be felt in the free, whimsical associations characteristic of

his work and in his determined lack of concern for traditional forms of literature.

Although Patchen liked to deny this influence, it can be seen clearly in, for example, the very title *Aflame and Afun of Walking Faces,* his series of prose pieces that retain the external characteristics of traditional fables but which revel in freewheeling Dadaist absurdities. In traditional fables, marvelous things happen—animals talk, snow falls in July, etc.—but these are justified by various conventions; the story, for example, may be an allegory, and the talking animals are supposed to be representations of human types, or the absurdities may be justified as ways of entertaining the reader while he is (although perhaps unaware of this) being taught a moral truth. But Patchen dispenses with the justifications and lets the fable take its own direction, no matter how absurd (and usually, at the same time, hilarious) that may be. The result is wonderful Dadaist nonsense.

Patchen shared with the Dadaists and Surrealists a dislike for the traditional moral and aesthetic objectives of literature. He did not make his work conform to preconceived literary patterns or expectations but was concerned rather with the way language can create or reflect subtle moods and emotional states, and his work was extremely experimental in seeking that end.

His political convictions, as noted earlier, remained with him, and *The Journal of Albion Moonlight* (1941), the prose work for which he is best known, has in its anti-war or pacifist emphasis a political dimension, but the real achievement here, as in all Patchen's major work, rests in the evocation of feeling and mood. *The Journal of Albion Moonlight* presents and sustains, like the work of Franz Kafka (to which it is clearly indebted), the sense of loss, fear, despondency, paranoia, and general emotional suffering. In other words, the book evokes, as no other book of its time did so well, the moods and emotions many Americans must have felt when they found themselves in the summer of 1940, when the book was written, on the brink of another military cataclysm.

Four years later Patchen published *Memoirs of a Shy Pornographer* (1945), a novel which evokes an entirely different set of emotions and moods. On the one hand, it satirizes popular culture—particularly the characters, plots, and language of popular movies, radio dramas, and novels—but Patchen's main achievement lies in sustaining a level of high burlesque, the hilarity of movies like screwball comedies (which, since very little is sacred in this book, he also satirizes). He followed *Memoirs of a Shy Pornographer* with *Sleepers Awake* (1946), a Dadaist collage of non sequiturs and startling associations, mixed together with experiments using different type faces. He had varied the use of type faces in some of his earlier work but never as exuberantly and creatively as in *Sleepers Awake.*

The range of Patchen's abilities can be clearly sensed in his poetry, which ranges from political polemic to love poems (Patchen was one of the great love poets of the century), occasional metaphysical complexities, and extravagant comedy. His poetry is marked by delightful verbal surprises and sudden twists of language. It assumes an extraordinary range of poetic forms, from prose poems to exquisitely-constructed songs.

Both the poetry and the prose are characterized by a sense of innocence, wonder, joy, and, above all, delight in playing with language. From time to time Patchen was deeply sentimental and melodramatic, yet what continues to astonish readers is that he succeeded in attempting such a vast range of fictional and poetic possibilities.

Patchen also wrote plays and essays, and he invented what he called "Picture Poems." In these, illustrations and language are brought together in a new format. They are not intended as comments on each other but as inseparably unified aspects of works of art. The "Picture Poems" involve the total fusion of two art forms. Patchen also attempted a fusion of music and literature in a highly regarded series of poetry readings he gave with jazz accompaniment in the late 1950s.

A reader encountering Patchen's work without any knowledge of his background might assume that he lived a robustly healthy life, but in fact nothing could be further from the truth. Patchen suffered from periods of great depression and from an acute spinal problem that kept him semi-paralyzed and in agony during much of the last 30 years of his life. His work involved the victory of his artistic imagination over extraordinary odds. The vast range of Patchen's achievement is all the more astonishing when one realizes the formidable physical and psychological barriers that he overcame in order to make it possible.

Further Reading

Essential books for a study of Patchen include *Kenneth Patchen* (1978) by Larry R. Smith; *Kenneth Patchen and American Mysticism* (1984) by Raymond Nelson; and *Kenneth Patchen: A Collection of Essays* (1977), edited by Richard G. Morgan, which collects important essays by, among others, William Carlos Williams, Babette Deutsch, Kenneth Rexroth, John Ciardi, Henry Miller, Jonathan Williams, and David Gascoyne. Reminiscences together with celebrations of Patchen's achievement can be found in Alan Clodd's *Tribute to Kenneth Patchen* (1977). □

Vallabhbhai Patel

The Indian political leader Vallabhbhai Patel (1875-1950) helped to organize the Indian nationalist movement and after independence in 1947 succeeded in integrating several hundred princely states into the Republic of India.

Vallabhbhai Patel was born on Oct. 31, 1875, in Gujarat, western India, into the traditionally agriculturalist Lewa Patidar caste. Both Patel and his older brother Vithalbhai learned English, traveled to Britain, and were called to the bar. On returning to India, Patel developed a lucrative practice in Ahmadabad and began to participate in civic and political affairs.

In 1917 Patel came under the influence of Mohandas Gandhi and was an important organizer of several *Satyagraha,* or militant nonviolent campaigns, to secure justice for the peasants of Gujarat. These included the Kheda Satyagraha of 1917-1918 and the famous Bardoli Satyagraha of 1927-1928, during which he received the title of Sardar, or leader. Between 1917 and 1928 he also served in the Ahmadabad municipality.

With the fame he gained in the Bardoli Satyagraha and in the Ahmadabad municipality, Patel emerged as an important figure among the Gandhian leadership of the Indian National Congress at the end of the 1920s. He served for many years on the working committee of the Congress, was Congress president in 1931, helped organize noncooperation efforts, and was a member of the parliamentary board of the Congress. The British-run government of India imprisoned Patel numerous times during the 1930s and World War II.

From 1945 Patel was virtual co-leader of the Congress with Jawaharlal Nehru. They accepted plans for the partition of India even over the objections of Gandhi. Patel was a minister of the interim government and, following independence and the partitioning of the subcontinent into India and Pakistan, became deputy prime minister in 1947. He was also minister for states and, with the assistance of V. P. Menon, carried through the extraordinary feat of persuading several hundred semi-independent princely states to join the Indian union. This effort was crucial to the national integration of India and was the most important accomplishment of Patel's career.

Throughout his political career, Patel concentrated on party organization, often displaying strength and decisiveness. By background and inclination he was a staunch Hindu and tended to be a conservative in politics. He identified with the Indian business community and generally opposed Nehru's socialism. Patel was distrustful of the Indian Moslems but was pressed to a moderate position on communal affairs by Nehru. Patel had a severe heart attack in 1948, some months after Gandhi's assassination. Although he continued his work for 2 years, he never fully recovered.

Further Reading

A standard work on Patel is Narhari D. Parikh, *Sardar Vallabhbhai Patel* (2 vols., 1953-1956), a lengthy and sympathetic account written by a close associate of Patel. A more critical assessment is contained in Michael Brecher, *Nehru: A Political Biography* (1959), a well-written account of Patel's Congress rival. Additional detailed information about Patel can be found in Vapal P. Menon, *The Story of the Integration of the Indian States* (1956) and *The Transfer of Power in India* (1957).

Additional Sources

Ahluwalia, B. K., *Sardar Patel: a life,* New Delhi, Sagar Publications 1974.

Chopra, Pran Nath, *The sardar of India: biography of Vallabhbhai Patel,* New Delhi: Allied Publishers, 1995.

Gandhi, Rajmohan, *Patel, a life,* Ahmedabad: Navajivan Pub. House, 1990.

Krishna, B., *Sardar Vallabhbhai Patel, India's iron man,* New Delhi: Indus, 1995.

Murthi, R. K., *Sardar Patel: the man and his contemporaries,* New Delhi: Sterling Publishers, 1976.

Panjabi, Kewalram Lalchand, *The indomitable Sardar,* Bombay: Bharatiya Vidya Bhavan, 1977.

Patel, I. J., *Sardar Vallabhbhai Patel,* New Delhi: Publications Division, Ministry of Information and Broadcasting, Govt. of India, 1985.

Prabhakar, Vishnu, *Sardar Vallabhbhai Patel,* New Delhi: National Book Trust, India, 1977, 1976.

Shankardass, Rani Dhavan, *Vallabhbhai Patel, power and organization in Indian politics,* New Delhi: Orient Longman, 1988. □

Walter Horatio Pater

The English author Walter Horatio Pater (1839-1894) was the most influential figure in the Esthetic movement of the late 19th century. His writings reveal a mind of sensibility and discrimination, embodying its judgments in carefully wrought prose.

By the 1860s and 1870s the younger generation of British intellectuals was beginning to react against the excessive weight of moral criteria prevalent in critical judgments on the fine arts. Walter Pater led the way in this reaction by stressing the diversity of artistic experience and the need for flexibility in judgments. He directed critical attention to discrimination of the special and essential character of each work of art or artistic personality and to precise analysis of the effect each produces upon the individual. In effect, he developed refinement of critical response into a philosophy of life.

Pater was born at Shadwell, East London, on Aug. 4, 1839. His father, a surgeon of Dutch descent, died when Walter was a child, and the boy was brought up chiefly by an aunt. He attended King's School, Canterbury, and then entered Queen's College, Oxford, in 1858. In his youth he was devout, but at the university he became more questioning about Christian beliefs. His interest in literature was already quite pronounced. After taking his degree (1862), he settled in Oxford and in 1864 gained a fellowship at Brasenose College.

Pater now began to write for the reviews. His intense reading in English authors was evident in a piece on Coleridge published in the *Westminster Review* of 1866. It was the basis of a later, fuller essay on Coleridge and drew an important distinction between the relativity of modern thought and the absolutism of the past. Pater was coming within the influence of the "art for art's sake" movement, under the leadership of Algernon Charles Swinburne and such French writers as Théophile Gautier. They claimed for art the specialized techniques of analysis and criteria of value that pertained to scientific investigation.

The Renaissance

Pater's reverence for the revived classical humanism of the Italian Renaissance was evident in a series of essays on Leonardo da Vinci, Botticelli, and Pico della Mirandola and on Michelangelo's poetry that he published in the *Fortnightly Review* (1869-1871). These, together with a few others, a preface, and a conclusion, formed the basis of the collection *Studies in the History of the Renaissance* (1873). This book, by far the most influential of all Pater's writings, is well known for its rhetorical set pieces, such as the celebrated meditation on Leonardo's *Mona Lisa*. However, it is packed with subtle discriminations and esthetic speculations. The famous conclusion, with its assertion that "not the fruit of experience, but experience itself, is the end" of life, and its exhortation "to burn always with this hard gemlike flame," became the rallying cry of a generation of esthetes. Some tended to overlook the context of intense intellectual concentration and esthetic analysis in which Pater's words found their meaning and application, and they responded to his call as an invitation to active paganism. Similar misunderstanding also gave rise to hostility and satire, as in W. H. Mallock's *The New Republic* (1877), in which Pater was lampooned. Somewhat embarrassed, Pater withdrew the conclusion from the second edition (1877), replacing it in the third (1888) when he could direct his readers to a fuller treatment of his thought in *Marius the Epicurean*.

Career at Oxford

Pater now became the leader of a cult of disciples at Oxford, but fears about the decadent tendencies of his writings prevented his advance in the university. His own habits, however, remained ascetic. He was always by nature shy; his temperament was doubtless in a part a response to his ugliness. His rooms at Brasenose remained the center of his work for most of his life, though for a time he also kept an address in Kensington or outside the college in Oxford.

The most sustained exposition of Pater's point of view is contained in his philosophical novel *Marius the Epicurean* (1885), which traces the spiritual evolution of a young Roman in the time of the Antonines as he comes under the influence, successively, of Cyrenaic philosophy, the stoicism of Marcus Aurelius, and the ardor and courage of the early Christian community. In spite of its many passages of great beauty, the novel is fatiguing as a whole. However, it does absolve Pater from the charge of advocating a narrowly conceived pleasure as the goal of life.

Late Works

Pater continued to write articles for periodicals, largely on Greek and English literature, philosophy, and the fine arts. A group of philosophic character sketches were collected in 1887 as *Imaginary Portraits*. Some of his most discriminating literary criticism was contained in the volume *Appreciations* (1889). This collection was introduced by his famous article "Style," which had appeared the preceding year in the *Fortnightly Review*. The volume concluded with a postscript on the meaning of the terms "classical" and "romantic" which offered his well-known

definition of the romantic character in art as the "addition of strangeness to beauty." His volume *Plato and Platonism* appeared in 1893.

After several bouts of illness, Pater suffered a heart attack and died suddenly on July 30, 1894. His former pupil C. L. Shadwell posthumously edited several volumes of his work: *Greek Studies* (1895), *Miscellaneous Studies* (1895), and *Gaston Latour* (1896), an unfinished novel.

Further Reading

The standard biography of Pater is Thomas Wright, *The Life of Walter Pater* (2 vols., 1907; repr. 1969). Another general introduction to his life and work and is Arthur Christopher Benson, *Walter Pater* (1906; repr. 1968). For studies of Pater's thought and criticism see Ruth C. Child, *The Aesthetic of Walter pater* (1940); Graham Hough, *The Last Romantics* (1949); and the relevant chapters in René Wellek, *A History of Modern Criticism, 1750-1950,* vol. 4: *The Later Nineteenth Century* (1965). See also Arthur Symons, *A Study of Walter Pater* (1932). Recommitted for background on the Esthetic movement are William Gaunt, *The Aesthetic Adventure* (1945), and Jerome Buckley, *The Victorian Temper* (1951).

Additional Sources

Donoghue, Denis, *Walter Pater: lover of strange souls,* New York: Knopf: Distributed by Random House, 1995.

Levey, Michael, *The case of Walter Pater,* London: Thames and Hudson, 1978.

Monsman, Gerald Cornelius, *Walter Pater's art of autobiography,* New Haven: Yale University Press, 1980.

Walter Pater, a life remembered, Calgary, Alta, Canada: University of Calgary Press, 1987. ☐

Andrew Barton Paterson

Andrew Barton Paterson (1864-1941) was an Australian folk poet popularly known as "Banjo" Paterson from his pen name, "The Banjo." His swinging rhythms captured the atmosphere of the land, life, and humor of Australia's people.

The son of a grazier, Andrew Paterson was born at Narrambla near Orange, New South Wales, on Feb. 17, 1864. While attending Sydney Grammar School he lived with his grandmother, a writer of verse and a member of Sydney's literary set. The lad spent school vacations on his father's property in the Yass district; here he absorbed the frontiersman's lore and developed a love of the outdoors. At 16 he entered Sydney University; when he graduated, he practiced law in Sydney.

Adopting the name "The Banjo" from a racehorse, Paterson began contributing narrative-type verse to the *Bulletin* of Sydney, then establishing itself among men living secluded lives in the hinterland. He became a leading exponent of the "bush ballad," writing about horsemen, drovers, shearers, and other outdoorsmen, with an emphasis on action and comradeship.

''Clancy of the Overflow''—a rollicking verse with ''the true jingle of the snaffle and spur''—appeared in 1889; it was among Paterson's most durable verses. A book of ballads, *The Man from Snowy River and Other Verses* (1895), achieved immediate success. While on a visit to Winton in western Queensland, in 1895 Paterson wrote the ballad ''Waltzing Matilda'' to an old English marching tune; it was to move through the status of a national folk song to become Australia's unofficial national anthem.

Although his output was uneven in quality and generally inferior to the best of Henry Lawson, Paterson evoked the feeling of the campfire and the open land and established himself as the most popular of the Australian balladists. In practically all his writing he emphasized adventure and good fellowship, and he colored his verse with humor and irony. His characters possess vitality and an optimistic approach. Lawson was among those who considered that Paterson's ballads gave a wholly idealized picture of bush life; certainly Paterson's view was colored by association with men of wealth, and although he was not oblivious to social tensions and the hard life of the underdog, he showed the compassion of a considerate observer rather than the deep social involvement of Lawson.

In 1899 Paterson left law practice for journalism. He published a collection of verse (1902), a novel, *An Outback Marriage* (1904), and a collection of traditional ballads, *Old Bush Songs* (1904). In 1908 he decided to return to the rural scene; he bought a grazing property and lived the outdoor life, writing intermittently.

Enlisting for war service in 1915, Paterson was abroad until 1919, when he returned to Sydney. He wrote *Saltbush Bill, J.P., and Other Verses* (1917) and *Collected Verses* (1921); the latter enjoyed wide popularity. He died at Sydney on Feb. 5, 1941.

Further Reading

An appreciation of Paterson's work is given in Archie J. Coombes, *Some Australian Poets* (1938). Edmund M. Miller, *Australian Literature,* edited, with a historical outline and descriptive commentaries, by Frederick T. Macartney (1938; rev. ed. 1956), contains a concise biography of Paterson which quotes characteristic verses. An appraisal of the various aspects of Paterson's talent and an assessment of the significance of his ballads in the national literary movement can be found in Henry Mackenzie Green, *Australian Literature, 1900-1950,* vol. 1 (1963).

Additional Sources

Roderick, Colin Arthur, *Banjo Paterson: poet by accident,* North Sydney: Allen & Unwin, 1993.

Semmler, Clement, *The Banjo of the bush: the life and times of A.B. ''Banjo'' Paterson,* St. Lucia, Qld., Australia: University of Queensland Press; Lawrence, Mass.: Distributed in the USA and Canada by Technical Impex Corp., 1984, 1974. □

William Paterson

William Paterson (1745-1806) was a leading advocate of the interests of the small states at the American Constitutional Convention of 1787. As a justice of the U.S. Supreme Court, he sought to strengthen the Federal government.

Brought by his parents from County Antrim, Ireland, to New Jersey at the age of 2, William Paterson grew up in Princeton, where his father kept a store. He entered the new College of New Jersey (Princeton University), receiving a bachelor of arts degree in 1763 and a master of arts in 1766. He earned a reputation as a classical scholar, orator, and village gallant. In 1764 he began studying law, was admitted to the bar in 1768, and for 8 years had a moderately successful country practice.

The American Revolution provided Paterson virtually full-time public employment. A member of various New Jersey Revolutionary conventions, he helped draft the state's first constitution in 1776. Briefly a state legislator and militia officer, Paterson spent most of the war as attorney general, attending sessions of criminal court all over the state. When he returned to private practice in 1783, he had become one of the half-dozen leading public figures in New Jersey.

Paterson's best-known public service came during the Constitutional Convention of 1787, where he upheld the right of the states to equal representation in the Federal

legislature. He proposed many measures to strengthen the general government, including the power to lay and collect taxes, establishment of executive and judicial branches, and the making of acts and treaties "supreme law." But in heated debate in June 1787, Paterson eloquently and defiantly led the small states in resisting those who held that representation according to population was the only just basis. The result was the famous "Great Compromise," giving the states equality in the Senate.

Paterson served briefly in the U.S. Senate and was governor of New Jersey before George Washington appointed him to the U.S. Supreme Court in 1793. He was an able, energetic judge, upholding Federal power. He further displayed his legal learning in making a digest, *Laws of the State of New Jersey* (1800), and in devising rules for common law and chancery courts there.

Further Reading

Paterson's speeches are in Max Farrand, ed., *The Records of the Federal Convention of 1787* (4 vols., 1937), and his court decisions are in the appropriate volumes of *United States Reports*. The best sketches of Paterson's life are Gertrude S. Wood, *William Paterson of New Jersey, 1745-1806* (1933), and Julian P. Boyd, "William Paterson," in Willard Thorp, ed., *The Lives of Eighteen from Princeton* (1946). W. J. Mills, ed., *Glimpses of Colonial Society and the Life of Princeton College, 1766-1773, by One of the Class of 1763* (1903), depicts Paterson's early life from his own letters and literary productions.

Additional Sources

O'Connor, John E., *William Paterson, lawyer and statesman, 1745-1806,* New Brunswick, N.J.: Rutgers University Press, 1979. □

Simón Iturri Patiño

Simón Iturri Patiño (1862-1947) was a Bolivian industrialist and entrepreneur. He controlled the richest tin mines in the world.

Simón Iturri Patiño was born in the provincial capital of Cochabamba in June 1862. His background and youth are largely unknown and surrounded by secrecy. He was born into a very humble family of mixed Spanish and Indian blood and in his youth worked in a rural general store and later as a conductor of mule trains in the Bolivian mountains.

About 1900 Patiño received the deed for a small tin mine in return for a modest personal loan he made to a miner. That mine turned out to be fabulously rich, and with profits from it Patiño bought more and more mining property, culminating in his purchase of the giant Catavi mine, largest and richest in the world.

Patiño revealed his true financial genius by his brilliant investments. He used much of his tin profits to buy control of tin smelters in England and new tin mines in Malaya. He also purchased ships and railroads to transport his tin from the mine to the consumer. By 1925 he had significant interests in, if not control of, every stage in the mining, refining, and finishing of tin, which, because of the popularity of the tin can, was constantly increasing in value. It is estimated that by 1925 Patiño owned properties valued at more than $500 million and enjoyed a personal annual income greater than the Bolivian national budget.

After 1920 Patiño traveled widely, rarely returning to his native country. He was diplomatic envoy of Bolivia to Spain (1920-1926) and to France (1926-1941). He received these positons because of his immense wealth, and he used them for their privileges of tax exemption and diplomatic immunity.

From 1920 to his death Patiño exercised a powerful influence on the successive governments of Bolivia. By controlling as much as 60 percent of his country's exports, he helped shape its foreign policy as well. For many years his contributions financed the dominant Liberal party, which had a modern Bolivia as its goal. When that support ended, the party was seriously undermined.

Patiño, though himself a man of very humble origins, had little social conscience and cared little for the welfare of his workers, who suffered from very poor pay and terrible working conditions. In 1943 troops massacred protesting miners at his Catavi mine, a clear sign that the government would protect the Patiño interests at any cost.

Patiño died in Buenos Aires on April 20, 1947. His mines continued in the family until 1952, when President Victor Paz nationalized them.

Further Reading

The only genuine biography of Patiño is in Spanish. Information on the Patiño economic empire can be found in Harold Osborne, *Bolivia: A Land Divided* (1954; 3d ed. 1964).

Additional Sources

Geddes, Charles F., *Patiño, the tin king,* London, R. Hale 1972. □

Alan Stewart Paton

Alan Stewart Paton (1903-1988) was a South African writer and liberal leader. His novel *Cry, The Beloved Country* won him world acclaim for the insights it gave on South Africa's race problem.

Alan Stewart Paton was born in Pietermaritzburg in the Natal Province, a former British colony that is now part of the Republic of South Africa, on January 11, 1903. From 1919 to 1922 he attended the University of Natal, from which he graduated with degrees in science and education. At this time Paton began writing poetry and dramas. In 1925 he became the assistant master at the Ixopo High School and, in 1928, joined the staff of Pietermaritzburg College. He was appointed principal of the Diepkloof Reformatory in 1935 and retired from government service in 1948. Thereafter, Paton devoted his life to writing, lecturing on the race question, and organizing the Liberal Party of South Africa.

Paton the Activist

The Diepkloof Reformatory, just outside Johannesburg, had been administered as a prison for delinquent youths from the slums rather than an institution for their rehabilitation. Paton insisted that this defeated the purpose of the reformatory. He introduced reforms which enabled some of the young to regain their self-respect. His granting of weekend leave was considered revolutionary. To the surprise of some of his colleagues, most of the boys returned at the end of their leave.

Paton began writing *Cry, The Beloved Country* in 1947 while touring American and European prisons and reformatories. In 1948 *Cry, The Beloved Country* was published, becoming an immediate success. At the same time, the predominantly Afrikaner Nationalist party was returned to power on the apartheid slogan that white's must remain master of South Africa. To Paton and those who shared his views, it was not enough for white liberals to preach race conciliation; they had to involve themselves actively in opposition to apartheid. Early in the 1950s he took part in the formation of the Liberal Association, which later became the Liberal Party of South Africa (SALP). He was

elected its president in 1953 and remained in this position until the government enacted a law making the party illegal.

The SALP welcomed South Africans of all races in its ranks and sought to establish an open society in which merit would fix the position of the individual in the life of the nation. It advocated nonviolence and set out to collaborate with the black Africans' political organizations. Like most leaders of the SALP, Paton was criticized bitterly in the Afrikaans press for identifying himself with black Africans. The underlying fear was that he and his colleagues were creating potentially dangerous polarizations in the white community.

The party, however, gained a substantial following among both blacks and whites. In 1960 the government decided to take action against it. Peter Brown and Elliot Mngadi, national chairman and Natal secretary respectively of the SALP, were banned. Some of the party's leaders fled the country, while others like Hyacinth Bhengu and Jordan K. Ngubane, were arrested and tried on conspiracy charges. Paton was spared the arrests and the bannings. The government did, however, seize his passport upon his return from New York after having accepted the Freedom House Award honoring his opposition to racism. After a little less than ten years the government returned Paton's passport. That made it possible for him to undertake a world tour (1971) during the course of which he was showered with honors in America and Europe.

Paton the Writer

As a writer, Paton was a subject of controversy in his country. *Cry, The Beloved Country* made a tremendous impression outside South Africa and among the English-speaking in the republic. The nationalist-minded Afrikaners dismissed it, as a piece of liberalistic sentimentality. It caused only a minor stir in the black African community, where Paton was criticized for using stereotypes in depicting his black African characters. He was accused of approaching the black Africans from white perspectives which projected them either as the victims of violent and uncontrolled passions or as simple, credulous people who bore themselves with the humility of tamed savages in the presence of the white man.

The years after 1948 were to see a long list of publications from Paton's pen. In 1953 he published *Too Late, the Phalarope.* This was followed by *Land and the People of South Africa* (1955), *South Africa in Transition* (1956), *Hope for South Africa* (1958), *Tales from a Troubled Land* (1960), *Debbie Go Home* (1961), *Hofmeyr* (1965), *South African Tragedy* (1965), *Instrument of Thy Peace* (1967), *The Long View* (1968), *For You Departed* (1969), *Creative Suffering: The Ripple of Hope* (1970), *Knocking on the Door: Alan Paton/Shorter Writings* (1975), and *Towards the Mountain: An Autobiography* (1988). In addition to these, Paton wrote a musical, *Mkhumbane,* for which Todd Matshikiza, the exiled African composer, wrote the music. Paton also wrote the play, *Sponono,* in 1965.

Among the more significant awards Paton received were doctorates in literature from Kenyon College (1962), Natal University (1968), and Harvard University (1971); the London *Sunday Times* Special Award for Literature (1949); a doctorate in literature and the humanities from Yale University (1954); the Freedom House Award (1960); and an award from the Free Academy of Art, Hamburg, Germany (1961).

Paton died of throat cancer on April 12, 1988 at his home outside Durban shortly after completing *Journey Continued: An Autobiography.* He was mourned as one of South Africa's leading figures in the anti-apartheid movement. Shortly after his death, his widow, Anne (Hopkins) Paton released a large portion of the contents of Paton's study for the establishment of The Alan Paton Centre on the Pietermaritzburg campus of the University of Natal. The university set aside space for this permanent memorial to Paton for future generations of writers and activists.

In 1996 American actor James Earl Jones and Irish actor Richard Harris starred in a film version of *Cry, The Beloved Country* and received critical acclaim for their portrayal of Paton's characters.

Further Reading

A perceptive study of Paton is Edward Callan *Alan Paton* (1968). Some biographical information on Paton can also be found in the *Washington Post* (June 6, 1991) and the *San Francisco Chronicle* (March 19, 1989). Information on *Cry, The Beloved Country* as a film can be found in the *New York Times* (December 19, 1994). A brief biography of Paton appears in the A&E Television Network's on-line biography Website located at www.biography.com. □

St. Patrick

St. Patrick (died ca. 460) was a British missionary bishop to Ireland, possibly the first to evangelize that country. He is the patron saint of Ireland.

Although Patrick was the subject of a number of ancient biographies, none of them dates from earlier than the last half of the 7th century. A great deal of legendary information, often contradictory, gathered around his name. Of the various works ascribed to Patrick, the authorship of only two is certain, the *Confession,* written in his later years, and the *Letter to the Soldiers of Coroticus,* written at some point during his career as bishop. These two works provide the only certain knowledge of Patrick's life.

Patrick was born in a village that he identified as Bannavem Taberniae, probably near the sea in southwestern Britain. Evidence does not allow a more exact date for his birth than sometime between 388 and 408. His father, Calpornius, was both a deacon and a civic official; his grandfather, Pontius, was a priest. Patrick's family seems to have been one of some social standing, but, in spite of the clergy in it, he did not grow up in a particularly religious or intellectual environment.

At the age of 16 Patrick was abducted by Irish pirates and taken to Ireland, where he tended sheep and prayed for 6 years. In his words, "The love of God and His fear came to me more and more, and my faith was strengthened." In this religious fervor a voice came to Patrick, promising him a return to his own country.

Patrick was given passage on a ship by its sailors. The details of his voyage home are unclear; some believe that Patrick returned from Ireland to Britain by way of Gaul. This seems unlikely. Again, little is known of this period in his life. It may be that he resumed his education, although he was never learned. Indeed, he wrote at the beginning of the *Confession,* "I blush and fear exceedingly to reveal my lack of education; for I am unable to tell my story to those versed in the art of concise writing."

Elected a bishop, Patrick was sent by the Church in Britain to evangelize Ireland. His friends tried to dissuade him from "throwing himself into danger among enemies who have no knowledge of God." But Patrick believed that he had a divine call. One purpose of the *Confession* is to set forth his confidence in that calling and to witness the divine help that enabled him to fulfill it.

As a missionary bishop in Ireland, Patrick was a typical 5th-century bishop. He recorded that he baptized many thousands of people. He celebrated the Eucharist, instituted nuns and monks, and ordained clergy. No record shows that he consecrated other bishops or indeed that other bishops existed in Ireland.

The *Letter to the Soldiers of Coroticus* gives the details of one event in his career. In reprisal for an Irish raid on the southwestern coast of Britain, Coroticus attacked the Irish coast, indiscriminately slaughtering its inhabitants. The *Letter* reports that one band of Coroticus's soldiers killed a group of newly baptized persons and took more captive. Patrick excommunicated Coroticus and called upon him to repent his crime and to free his prisoners.

Criticism of Patrick's work came to him from Britain; his seniors, he records, "brought up sins against my laborious episcopate." The basis for such charges is unknown; they did include his betrayal by a friend to whom Patrick had much earlier confessed a sin that he had committed at the age of 13. The *Confession* appears to be in part Patrick's defense of and justification of his episcopate to his superiors in Britain.

Although Patrick probably made his headquarters at Armagh, as a missionary he traveled around the island a great deal. It is not certain where he died; local traditions give various locations. It is also impossible to date his death more precisely than approximately 460. Patrick himself wrote a suitable epitaph in his *Letter:* "I, Patrick, a sinner, unlearned, resident in Ireland, declare myself to be a bishop."

Further Reading

Two compilations of St. Patrick's writings are *St. Patrick: His Writings and Life,* translated by Newport J. D. White (1920), and *The Works of St. Patrick,* translated and annotated by Ludwig Bieler (1953). The best and most recent study of

Patrick is Richard P. C. Hanson, *Saint Patrick: His Origins and Career* (1968), a careful analysis of all the sources, which presents convincing arguments for accepting only the *Confession* and *Letter* as factual. John B. Bury, *The Life of St. Patrick and His Place in History* (1905), is a reconstruction of events based upon the ancient chronicles and legends. Thomas F. O'Rahilly, *The Two Patricks* (1942), asserts that another bishop sent to Ireland was called Patrick. See also Paul Gallico, *The Steadfast Man: A Biography of St. Patrick* (1958). □

Jennie R. Patrick

Jennie R. Patrick (born 1949) is the first African American woman to earn a doctorate degree in chemical engineering. A successful chemical engineer, manager, and educator who has applied her skills at a number of different companies and universities, she has also been honored with the Outstanding Women in Science and Engineering Award in 1980, and by CIBA-GEIGY Corp. in its Exceptional Black Scientist poster series in 1983.

Jennie R. Patrick was born January 1, 1949, in Gadsden, Alabama, one of five children of James and Elizabeth Patrick, working-class parents who emphasized knowledge as an escape from poverty. Patrick was both nurtured and challenged in a segregated elementary school and junior high, but in high school she was one of the first participants in a controversial and sometimes explosive program of racial integration, where she successfully overcame violence and unsupportive white teachers to graduate with an A-minus average in 1969.

Patrick was accepted at several prestigious universities, but chose to begin her pursuit of engineering at Tuskegee Institute, which she attended until 1970 when the chemical engineering program was eliminated. She then transferred to the University of California at Berkeley to finish her degree, receiving her B.S. in 1973 and meanwhile working as an assistant engineer for the Dow Chemical Company in 1972 and for the Stauffer Chemical Company in 1973. She continued her education at the Massachusetts Institute of Technology (MIT), receiving a Gilliland Fellowship in 1973, a DuPont Fellowship in 1974, and a Graduate Student Assistant Service award in 1977. She was also awarded a fellowship in 1975 from the American Association of University Women, and a National Fellowship Foundation Scholarship in 1976.

Her research at MIT involved the concept of superheating, where a liquid is raised above its boiling temperature but does not become a vapor. She investigated the temperature to which pure liquids and mixtures of two liquids could be superheated. Patrick finished her research and completed her doctorate in 1979. While pursuing her graduate studies, Patrick worked as an engineer with Chevron Research in 1974 and with Arthur D. Little in 1975.

After completing her doctorate, Patrick joined the Research and Development Center at General Electric (GE) in Schenectady, New York, where she held the position of research engineer. Her work there involved research on energy-efficient processes for chemical separation and purification, particularly the use of supercritical extraction. In supercritical processes, the temperature and pressure are varied so that a substance is not a liquid or a gas, but a fluid. Unique properties make these fluids useful in both separations and purification processes. She has published several papers on this work, and has received patents for some of her advancements.

Patrick remained at GE until 1983, when she accepted a position at Philip Morris as a project manager in charge of the development of a program to improve several of the company's products. Patrick transferred to the Rhom and Haas Company in 1985, as manager of fundamental chemical engineering research. In this position she interacted with all aspects of the chemical business, from engineering to marketing to manufacturing. By being exposed to the overall business she was able to direct development of new research technology within her division and promote its implementation throughout the company. In 1990, Patrick became assistant to the executive vice president of Southern Company Services, a position that emphasized her management skills in both the business and technical aspects of the company. Having earlier held adjunct professorships at Rensselaer Polytechnic Institute from 1982 to 1985 and the Georgia Institute of Technology from 1983 to 1987, Patrick decided to make teaching a bigger part of the her life. In January 1993, she left Southern Company Services and returned to Tuskegee University, as the 3M Eminent Scholar and Professor of Chemical Engineering. In addition to her teaching duties, Patrick is developing research projects in material sciences, is actively involved in leadership roles at Tuskegee, and remains firmly committed to helping minority students find success, particularly in the fields of science and engineering.

Further Reading

Outstanding Young Women of America, Junior Chamber of Commerce, 1979, p. 981.

Sammons, V. O., editor, *Blacks in Science and Medicine,* Hemisphere Publishing Co., 1990, p. 185.

Bradby, Marie, "Professional Profile: Dr. Jennie R. Patrick," in *US Black Engineer,* fall, 1988, pp. 30–33.

"Engineering Their Way to the Top," in *Ebony,* December 1984, pp. 33–36.

Kazi-Ferrouillet, Kuumba, "Jennie R. Patrick: Engineer Extraordinaire," in *NSBE Journal,* February, 1986, pp. 32–35. □

Ruth Patrick

Ruth Patrick (born 1907) has pioneered techniques for studying the biodiversity of freshwater ecosystems over a career that spans sixty years. Her studies of microscopic species of algae, called diatoms, in rivers around the world have provided methods for monitoring water pollution and understanding its effects.

Federal programs to monitor the status of freshwater rely on Ruth Patrick's method of growing diatoms on glass slides. Her studies of the impact of trace elements and heavy metals on freshwater ecosystems have demonstrated how to maintain a desired balance of different forms of algae. For example, she showed that addition of small amounts of manganese prevents the overgrowth of blue-green algae and permits diatoms to proliferate.

Patrick received the prestigious Tyler Ecology Award in 1975, and serves on numerous governmental advisory committees. She advanced the field of limnology, the study of freshwater biology, and in the late 1940s established the Department of Limnology at the Academy of Natural Sciences in Philadelphia. She remained its director for more than four decades. Headquarters for her research are in Philadelphia, with a field site in West Chester, Pennsylvania. An estuary field site at Benedict, Maryland, on the Patuxent River near Chesapeake Bay, serves for studies of pollution caused by power plants.

Patrick was born in Topeka, Kansas, on November 26, 1907. Her undergraduate education was completed at Coker College, where she received a B.S. degree in 1929. She obtained both her M.S. degree in 1931 and her Ph.D. in botany in 1934 from the University of Virginia. The roots of Patrick's long and influential career in limnology can be

traced to the encouragement of her father, Frank Patrick. He gave his daughter a microscope when she was seven years old and told her, "Don't cook, don't sew; you can hire people to do that. Read and improve your mind." Patrick's doctoral thesis, which she wrote at the University of Virginia in Charlottesville, was on diatoms, whose utility derives from their preference for different water chemistries. The species of diatoms found in a particular body of water says a lot about the character of the water.

When Patrick joined the Academy of Natural Sciences in 1933, it was as a volunteer in microscopy to work with one of the best collections of diatoms in the world; she was told at the time that women scientists were not paid. For income she taught at the Pennsylvania School of Horticulture and made chick embryo slides at Temple University. In 1937 persistence paid off, and she was appointed curator of the Leidy Microscopical Society with the Academy of Natural Sciences, a post she held until 1947. She also became associate curator of the academy's microscopy department in 1937, and continued in that capacity until 1947, when she accepted the position of curator and chairman of the limnology department at the academy. Continuing as curator, in 1973 she was offered the Francis Boyer Research Chair at the academy.

In the late 1940s Patrick gave a paper at a scientific meeting on the diatoms of the Poconos. In the audience was William B. Hart, an oil company executive, who was so impressed with the possibilities of diatoms for monitoring pollution that he provided funds to support Patrick's research. Freed from financial constraints, Patrick undertook a comprehensive survey of the severely polluted Conestoga Creek, near Lancaster, Pennsylvania. It was the first study of its kind, and launched Patrick's career. She matched types and numbers of diatoms in the water to the type and extent of pollution, an extremely efficient procedure now used universally.

By her own account Patrick has waded into 850 different rivers around the globe in the course of her research. She participated in the American Philosophical Society's limnological expedition to Mexico in 1947 and led the Catherwood Foundation's expedition to Peru and Brazil in 1955. Patrick was an advisor to several presidential administrations and has given testimony at many hearings on environmental problems and before congressional committees on the subject of environmental legislation. She was an active participant in drafting the federal Clean Water Act.

In 1987 Patrick coauthored a book, *Groundwater Contamination in the United States,* which provides an overview of groundwater as a natural resource, and a state-by-state description of policies designed to manage growing problems of contamination and depletion. Another of her concerns is global warming, the rise in the earth's temperature attributed to the buildup of carbon dioxide and other pollutants in the atmosphere. In an interview reported in the *Philadelphia Inquirer* in 1989, Patrick said, "We're going to have to stop burning gasoline. And we're going to have to conserve more energy, develop ways to create electricity from the sun and plants, and make nuclear power both safe and acceptable."

Patrick has received many awards in addition to the Tyler prize, including the Gimbel Philadelphia Award for 1969, the Pennsylvania Award for Excellence in Science and Technology in 1970, the Eminent Ecologist Award of the Ecological Society of America in 1972, the Governor's Medal for Excellence in Science and Technology in 1988, and the National Medal of Science in 1996. She holds many honorary degrees from United States colleges and universities. Patrick has authored over 130 papers, and continues to influence thinking on limnology and ecosystems. Her contributions to both science and public policy have been vast.

Further Reading

Detjen, Jim, "In Tiny Plants, She Discerns Nature's Warning on Pollution," in *Philadelphia Inquirer,* February 19, 1989.
Washington Post, July 27, 1997, p. D1.
The Wonderful World of Dr. Ruth Patrick, unpublished paper by Geraldine J. Gates, Wharton School, University of Pennsylvania, February 16, 1987. □

Simon Nelson Patten

The American economist Simon Nelson Patten (1852-1922) predicted that with modern technology and proper social planning the United States and Europe could move from an economy of scarcity to one of abundance.

Simon Patten was born on May 1, 1852, in Sandwich, Ill. There he imbibed a profound belief in the Protestant ethic and the efficacy of achieving social reform through such established and conservative institutions as the Republican party and the Presbyterian Church. He attended the University of Halle (1876-1879), where he came under the influence of the Younger Historical school, a group of economists who believed that scholars should use their expertise to help solve modern social problems. His German experience reinforced his belief in social reform and planned change, but within an American context—that is, change and reform through voluntary action with minimal governmental control.

After several years of apprenticeship teaching in primary and secondary schools, Patten in 1887 was appointed professor of economics at the Wharton School of the University of Pennsylvania. He held this important post until 1917, when his vigorous antiwar views got him into trouble and he was forced into premature retirement.

Patten was a forceful teacher and a prolific writer. Over the years he published 22 books and several hundred articles, both scholarly and popular. Not a truly cogent or profound or systematic thinker, Patten was constitutionally unable to synthesize his ideas into a magnum opus. *The New Basis of Civilization* (1907), an outgrowth of lectures he delivered in 1905 at the New York School of Social Work, was his most important work. It ran through eight editions between 1907 and 1923. Yet it revealed only a few elements of his theories.

Basically, Patten appeared to be working toward a theory of social behavior for mankind that would fuse the principles of the New Testament with the technology of a modern industrial society. He believed that with the new technology the earth's resources were adequate to provide an economy of abundance for the Western world; that is, there was enough wealth available so that everyone could achieve a proper diet, good basic housing and clothing, and an education that would meet the job requirements of industry. What was lacking was group social action to achieve these desired goals. Such a cultural lag could be overcome by reform, but for Patten these reforms could not go much beyond those advocated by Progressive politicians of the Robert La Follette type. Consequently, the United States still had not achieved Patten's economy of abundance when he died on July 24, 1922, at Browns Mills, N.J.

Further Reading

The standard biography of Patten is Daniel M. Fox, *The Discovery of Abundance: Simon N. Patten and the Transformation of Social Theory* (1967), which provides a good discussion of Patten's career and a sound analysis of his basic ideas. □

Frederick Douglas Patterson

Frederick Douglas Patterson (1901–1988) was president of Tuskegee Normal and Industrial Institute and creator of the United Negro College Fund.

I n 1935 Frederick Douglas Patterson became president of Tuskegee Normal and Industrial Institute, one of the foremost African American institutions of higher education in the country. His stated purpose at the time of his inauguration was not only to increase the vocational training of his students but also to raise them to higher levels of academic competency and thus make them more qualified wage earners. He is also remembered for his creation in 1943 of the United Negro College Fund, an organization dedicated to raising and distributing scholarships to deserving minority students.

School Lunches

After adding courses on the principles of nutrition and dietetics to the curriculum of Tuskegee, Patterson oversaw the adoption and growth of the federally sponsored school-lunch program. He felt that this program must be expanded because academic achievement rested on a strong nutritional base, which many underprivileged children lacked. He firmly believed that for Tuskegee to thrive, the school had to reach its potential students before they fell victim to poverty.

The Carver Foundation

In the early 1940s Patterson's administration also established the George Washington Carver Foundation, which provided grants and monies to qualified students. Begun in 1940 by Carver himself, the foundation nearly doubled its assets in six years, rising from thirty-three thousand dollars to sixty thousand dollars. The fund expanded its base by undertaking research from commercial firms, and by 1947 eleven students working under grants were researching in paper, ink, foods, and animal nutrition.

Creation of the United Negro College Fund

In 1943 Patterson called a meeting of the heads of all of the major predominantly black institutions of higher education to plan a joint fund-raising venture. The result was the organization of the United Negro College Fund, of which he was elected president. Originally twenty-seven institutions joined the organization, which was incorporated in New York. By 1945 the group had grown to thirty-two members, and by 1947 the organization was raising more than a million dollars annually.

National Committees

As a member of President Harry S Truman's Commission on Higher Education, Patterson helped file a 1947 report calling for the reorganization of higher education in the United States. The commission listed as its main priority doubling the number of students attending college. It also called for more types of scholarships, fellowships, and grants and called for the end of segregation—not because of ethical questions but because of the duplication of separate but comparable black and white programs. The commission also called for free education for all through the junior college level and a lowering of tuition and fees at colleges, graduate schools, and professional schools. Most of these suggestions were not enacted.

Construction

In 1946 Patterson's plan to improve the housing of farmers earning substandard incomes was reported and discussed in *The New York Times* . He felt that these lower-class tenants could create building blocks and erect fireproof structures inexpensively. This report attracted several potential investors, models were built on the Tuskegee campus, and the students constructed a four-room house for a neighboring farmer. As in other ventures, Patterson was in housing a man of vision and versatility.

Further Reading

Frederick D. Patterson, *Chronicles of Faith: The Autobiography of Frederick D. Patterson* (Tuscaloosa: University of Alabama Press, 1991). ☐

George Smith Patton Jr.

The American Army officer George Smith Patton, Ir. (1885-1945), was one of the outstanding tactical commanders of World War II. His campaigns in Sicily, France, and Germany were distinguished by boldness and an imaginative use of armor.

George Patton was born on Nov. 11, 1885, in San Gabriel, Calif. His family was one of the wealthiest in the state. After attending private schools, he went to the U.S. Military Academy, graduating in 1909 and joining the cavalry. He loved horses and was one of the Army's best polo players. He was an eccentric, both at the academy and later in the Army, noted for speaking his mind and for his steady stream of curse words.

Despite his mannerisms—which most of his contemporaries found offensive—Patton was hardworking, intelligent, and courageous. He moved ahead rapidly in the Army. He was the first officer detailed to the Tank Corps in World War I, and he led tanks in action. In 1921 Patton returned to the cavalry. He went back to the armored branch in 1940 and quickly rose to division command.

During World War II, in November 1942, Patton led the American forces landing at Casablanca, Morocco. His first real opportunity to shine came in July 1943, when he led the U.S. 7th Army in the invasion of Sicily. He soon became famous for his daring assaults, rapid marches, and use of armor. He also, however, slapped a hospitalized enlisted man suffering from shell shock (Patton accused him of cowardice). His immediate superior, Gen. Dwight Eisen-

hower, refused to bow to popular pressure and dismiss Patton but did order him to stay quietly in his headquarters in occupied Sicily.

In spring 1944 Eisenhower brought Patton to England and gave him command of the U.S. 3d Army, which had the task of driving the Germans out of north-central France after the Allies broke out of the Normandy beachhead. Patton activitated the 3d Army early in August 1944 and started it across France, pausing only when his tanks ran out of fuel. By then (late September) he had cleared most of France of the enemy.

Patton's flamboyant character, his caustic remarks to his troops, the pearl-handled pistols he wore on his hips, and most of all his performance combined to make him a national hero. He enjoyed this role, which made it difficult for him to accept Eisenhower's decision to give priority in scarce supplies to the forces of British general Bernard Montgomery. In March 1945 Patton regained the headlines, as he drove the 3rd Army over the Rhine River before Montgomery could get his troops across. Patton then drove through Germany and by the end of the war had his troops in Austria.

Placed in charge of the occupation forces in Bavaria, Patton was soon in trouble. His use of former Nazi officials to help administer the area ran counter to official American policy and made him a target for liberal criticism. He made matters worse when he argued the point to the press. Eisenhower removed him from command. Patton died on Dec. 21, 1945, as a result of an automobile accident in Germany.

Further Reading

Patton's family gathered his diary and other notes and published them as *War as I Knew It* (1947). Probably the most objective biography of the controversial Patton is the study by Ladislas Farago, *Patton: Ordeal and Triumph* (1963), which makes judicious use of the Army's official histories of World War II. Robert S. Allen, *Lucky Forward: The History of Patton's Third U.S. Army* (1947), is a highly laudatory account. Patton's nephew, Fred Ayer, Jr., wrote *Before the Colors Fade: Portrait of a Soldier, George S. Patton, Jr.* (1964), a sympathetic view by one closely associated with Patton. See also Harry Hodges Semmes, *Portrait of Patton* (1955), and Charles R. Codman, *Drive* (1957). ☐

St. Paul

St. Paul (died c. 66 A.D.), the first systematic theologian and writer of the Christian Church, has been the most influential teacher in the history of Christianity. He was the Christian Church's apostle to the Gentiles.

Paul, whose original name was Saul or Sh'aul, was born in the town of Tarsus, Cilicia (in modern southeastern Turkey), of Jewish parents belonging to the tribe of Benjamin. Both his parents were Roman citizens. It is safe to assume that Paul's earliest language was Koine Greek, the household language of all educated Roman citizens throughout the empire. Paul was sent at an early age to Jerusalem to attend Bible school. Studying with a famous rabbi, Gamaliel, he learned to write in both Greek and Hebrew and became thoroughly versed in the law. It seems certain that Paul studied in Jerusalem during the three years of Jesus' public life and that he was present at the time that Jesus was crucified by the Romans. He may even have seen and heard Jesus preach. He certainly must have heard of Jesus and his movement among the people.

Paul's Times

Paul lived in the closing days of the Second Jewish Commonwealth. When he was young and studying rabbinic theology, Palestine already lay under complete Roman domination. The Jewish people no longer exercised any real national sovereignty. The traditional boundaries of Israel, as known from the previous Hasmonaean and Salamonic kingdoms, had been severely reduced. Rome preferred to govern its captive peoples by dividing them into manageable provinces. By the time Paul had converted to Christianity and was launched on his extensive missionary journeys, affairs in Palestine had taken a turn for the worse. The calm and relative stability that had lasted during the reign of King Agrippa I, was severely shaken after his death. A new spirit of nationalism and revolt against the foreign invader rose among the leading Jewish class, the Pharisees. Throughout Palestine the younger generation of Pharisees molded the spirit of the people in such a way that the Jewish

revolt of 66 A.D. and the consequent destruction of Jerusalem in 70 A.D. became inevitable.

Paul derived from his early education a thorough knowledge of both the oral and the written Jewish law. He also learned of the traditional rabbinic method of scriptural interpretation and commentary. Paul was thus heir to the long, rich, and varied tradition of Pharisaism as it culminated in the latter days of the Second Temple. Apparently, Paul had gained an outstanding reputation as a young rabbinic student because he was authorized by the Jewish authorities to seek out and prosecute members of a new sect who proclaimed that Jesus of Nazareth was the Messiah and that the Kingdom of God was at hand. Paul apparently made several trips throughout Palestine in search of Christians. On one such trip from Jerusalem to Damascus, about the year 34 A.D., Paul was completely changed.

Paul's Conversion

Four accounts of Paul's conversion exist (Acts 9:3-19; 22:6-21; 26:12-18; and Galatians 1:12-16). According to the essential spirit of these sources, Paul underwent a supernatural experience in which he came to believe that Jesus was actually the Messiah of Israel and that God had called Paul to preach the message of Jesus to all men. The story adds that he was blinded and forced to fast for three days until a Christian named Ananais laid hands on him and restored his sight, after which he was baptized. The usual date assigned to this event is between 34 and 36 A.D.

Paul spent the next three years of his life in Damascus with the Christians. He then returned to Jerusalem and was accepted by Peter and the other Christians. Paul then went to his home city of Tarsus and spent about six years preaching in parts of Syria and Cilicia. After a final year spent at Antioch, he and Barnabas were commissioned by the Christian authorities to go to the surrounding nations and preach the Christian message.

Missionary Journeys

During the next 15 years Paul undertook three extensive journeys in the eastern Mediterranean region. At the time Paul undertook his travels, that part of the world was protected by the Pax Romana. Paul had no difficulty in traveling or in communicating. Throughout the eastern Mediterranean a network of well-guarded and well-preserved roads, serviced by Roman garrisons, connected fortified and prosperous towns. A common language, Koine Greek, was spoken throughout the eastern Mediterranean and was used for all communications. Correspondence by mail was a daily and ordinary method of communication. Furthermore, sea lanes for commerce and for passenger traffic were open between Palestine, Turkey, Greece, Italy, North Africa, and the main Greek islands.

Throughout the eastern Mediterranean, scattered but well-organized communities of Jews existed in all the principal localities. Between these Jewish communities and the central authority in Jerusalem, constant communication was maintained. The communities of Jews living outside Palestine depended upon the Palestinian authorities for the fixing of the Jewish calendar, the regulation of the Jewish year, the offering of sacrifices in the Temple, and the general authentication of doctrines, scrolls, and teachers.

Until the latter period of his life, Paul moved through these Jewish communities as a Jew. This fact has often been obscured by the later opposition between Paul and the Jews and between Christianity and Judaism. Only toward the end of his life was Paul not welcome in the synagogues of the Jewish communities. Christians in general were refused entry into synagogues only in the last 20 years of the first century.

Paul's first journey, which began about 45 A.D., took him through Cyprus and southeastern Turkey; he then returned to Antioch by the same path. On his second journey, Paul went overland through Turkey and then to mainland Greece, passing through Athens and returning to Palestine in the same year through Rhodes. He landed at Tyre on the shores of Palestine about 52 A.D. During this second journey Paul wrote his two Letters to the Thessalonians. On his third journey, Paul departed from Antioch, again traveled across Turkey, visited Ephesus and Chios, and then proceeded through Macedonia to visit mainland Greece again. He returned home by sea from the southwest coast of Turkey to the Palestinian port of Tyre. During this third journey, Paul composed his Letter to the Galatians, his two Letters to the Corinthians, and his Letter to the Romans.

Between the beginning of his missionary journeys and his death, Paul wrote a number of letters that later became part of the Christian New Testament. Before his death he composed a total of 13 letters. A 14th letter, the Letter to the Hebrews, traditionally bearing Paul's name, is now generally considered to have been written by a disciple of Paul's.

Paul's teaching rested on three main principles: Jesus was the Son of God and the Messiah foretold by the prophets of Israel; by his death, Jesus had atoned for all men's sins and opened heaven for humanity; the Mosaic Law had, by the fact of Jesus' salvation, been abrogated and replaced by the Law of Jesus. There was, therefore, no longer any distinction between Jew and Gentile. Paul frequently used texts from the Bible to prove his points, interpreting them according to the rabbinic method of exegesis that he had learned in Jerusalem.

Attitude toward the Law and the Jews

Two outstanding traits of Paul's writings concern the Jewish law and the Jewish people as the chosen ones of God. His attitude on both points requires explanation. In regard to the law, Paul believed that since Christ had come the law had not been merely changed and ennobled but that it had been abrogated. Later anti-Semitism fed on Paul's terminology and concepts in describing the Jewish law, oral and written, as merely an exercise in legalities. No trace of this negative attitude exists in Paul's writings. A persuasion is posited that all the nobility of the law and all the salvation promised to the law had been transferred to the new law of Jesus. Paul separated world history into two distinct parts: the time prior to the coming of Jesus, when the law was God's manifest way of leading men to salvation; and the time after the death of Jesus, when belief in and love of Jesus was the sole means of salvation.

In his later days, Paul probably eliminated any necessity of observing the law. In order to understand his attitude, it is well to remember that the Council of Jerusalem (ca. 49 A.D.) had liberated all Jewish converts to Christianity from any obligation of observing the Jewish law. As Paul progressed in his teachings, he came up against sterner and sterner opposition from the Jewish authorities. Doubtless, this opposition hardened Paul in his opinion that the Jewish law served only to blind the Jews and possibly the Gentiles to the truth of Jesus.

A constant doubt, however, remained in Paul's mind concerning his attitude to the Jews as the chosen people. In his Letter to the Romans, Paul declared that the Jews were and would remain the chosen people of God. He asserted this, as he remarked, because God's decisions are immutable. On the other hand, as a Christian believer, he maintained that Christians occupied a special place in God's favor since they had become the carriers of the salvation of Jesus, which had become predominant in God's scheme for man. In order to escape this difficulty, Paul resorted to the subterfuge of declaring that the Jews remained the chosen people but that a veil of ignorance had been drawn over their eyes. He declared that this veil would be lifted only on the last day, when the world came to an end and Jesus returned to judge all men.

Teaching Methods

Paul's teaching methods never altered throughout his missionary journeys. In every town he visited, he went to the local synagogue or meeting place of the Jewish community and preached first to the Jews. He then preached to the local Gentiles. However, as his name became known and as his preaching expanded, Paul encountered greater and greater opposition from the Jewish communities. His preaching then became directed more and more toward the Gentiles. From both Jews and Gentiles, Paul suffered severe physical and social hardships: being whipped, stoned, imprisoned, treated with indignity, and banished on several occasions. He developed from the beginning of his apostolate a rather acid critique of his former coreligionists, maintaining that in following the law of Moses and in refusing to believe in Jesus they were declining to follow their destiny as the chosen people of God. Thus, opposition to Paul mounted in the Jewish communities that were outside Palestine, and the message filtered back to Jerusalem that Paul posed a threat to Judaism in the Diaspora.

Final Journey

Back in Jerusalem after his third missionary journey, Paul proposed a trip to Rome and Spain. During his stay he was recognized by certain Asian Jews, who immediately attacked him as a renegade and troublemaker for the Jewish communities. In the ensuing melee, Paul was saved by the Roman civil authorities who intervened. Paul was arrested as the cause of the disturbance. As a Roman citizen, he was saved from assassination and then transferred to Roman coastal headquarters, Caesarea, where he was tried by the Roman procurator, Felix.

To escape being sent back for trial in Jerusalem, where he would have received certain death, Paul used his right as a Roman citizen to be transferred to Rome for trial by Caesar. He arrived in Rome after a sea voyage in the spring of 60 A.D. During the years of his captivity in Rome, he composed his Letters to the Colossians, to the Ephesians, to the Philippians, to Philemon, to Timothy, and to Titus. Little is known of his subsequent life except that he possibly paid a visit to Spain before his death. He was martyred, according to all accounts, sometime in 66 or 67 A.D. in Rome.

Paul's Influence

Paul's influence as a theologian and thinker throughout the later development of Christianity has been incalculable and all-embracing. He was the first Christian thinker to structure the message of Jesus and his immediate followers into definite doctrines. Paul took the basic facts of Jesus' life and his main formulation of doctrine and molded them into the simple terms of a Semite and Judaic thinker. Using his Hellenistic background and systematic training, Paul translated both facts and doctrine into a broad theological synthesis characterized by a universalism of salvation, an intricate theory of grace, and a central function of Jesus as man and as God. St. Augustine drew on Paul's doctrines to organize his own thought and thus molded all subsequent Roman Catholic theological development and formulation until the 20th century.

It was on Paul too that such medieval theologians as St. Albertus Magnus, St. Anselm, and St. Thomas Aquinas drew to substantiate and to authenticate their speculations. Paul's writings also provided the 16th-century reformers with their basic ideas. These religious thinkers preferred to return to Paul's text rather than to adhere to the metaphysical speculations that had developed in Christianity throughout 1,500 years.

Further Reading

The literature on St. Paul is vast. Among studies by Roman Catholic authors are Robert Sencourt, *Saint Paul: Envoy of Grace* (1948), and Amédée Brunot, *Saint Paul and His Message* (trans. 1959). Protestant viewpoints on Paul are given in William M. Ramsay, *St. Paul the Traveller and the Roman Citizen* (1895); Martin Dibelius, *Paul* (trans. 1953); William Barclay, *The Mind of St. Paul* (1958); and Walter Schmithals, *The Office of Apostle in the Early Church* (1969). Joseph Klausner, *From Jesus to Paul* (trans. 1943), examines Paul's role in early Christianity from the viewpoint of a Jewish scholar. William D. Davies, *Paul and Rabbinic Judaism: Some Rabbinic Elements in Pauline Theology* (1948), discusses the influence of Judaism on Paul's teachings. John Knox, *Chapters in a Life of Paul* (1950), offers a chronology of Paul's life and an interpretation of his role in the formation of Christianity. Other studies of Paul's life and teachings include Charles H. Dodd, *The Meaning of Paul for Today* (1920); Alan H. McNeile, *St. Paul: His Life, Letters, and Christian Doctrine* (1920); Wilfred L. Knox, *St. Paul and the Church of Jerusalem* (1925); and Johannes Weiss, *The History of Primitive Christianity* (1937). □

Paul I

The Russian czar Paul I (1754-1801), the son and successor of Catherine the Great, reigned from 1796 until his assassination in 1801. Noted for his tyranny, he reversed many of his mother's policies.

Born on Sept. 20, 1754, Paul I was the son of Emperor Peter III and Catherine the Great. Empress Elizabeth brought Paul up under her personal supervision, and his schooling was under the direction of Nikita Ivanovich Panin, who later became Catherine's chief diplomatic adviser. Under the guidance of a carefully selected group of teachers, Paul studied geography, history, and mathematics. He learned to speak Russian, French, and German fluently. At the age of 19 Paul married Wilhemina, daughter of the landgrave of Hesse, but this marriage was brief and unhappy. His wife died in childbirth in April 1776. In September of that year Paul married Sophie Dorothy, Princess of Württemberg, who took the name of Fedorovna. Between 1777 and 1798 Fedorovna bore four sons and six daughters.

Catherine disliked Paul intensely and on several occasions attempted to change the law of succession to his disadvantage. In 1783 she gave him an estate near St. Petersburg. Paul spent the next 13 years in semiretirement at Gatchina, living the life of a country squire and garrison commander. He made rare appearances at the royal court and opposed both his mother's domestic and foreign policies.

Despite Catherine the Great's attempts to make Paul's son Alexander her successor, Paul ascended the Russian throne following his mother's death in 1796. One of his first legislative measures was the abolition of the arbitrary power of the czar to nominate his successor, a power that had contributed to political instability in 18th-century Russia. A law promulgated on the day of Paul's coronation made the crown hereditary in the house of Romanov and defined the order of succession based on primogeniture.

Paul as emperor repealed many of the nobles' privileges, restricted the duties and powers of the imperial guards, and tried to place restrictions on the exploitation of the serfs by the upper classes. Paul encouraged trade and industry, and he also attempted to modernize the armed forces. His conduct, however, was on occasion erratic and tyrannical, such as in his prohibition of foreign travel, Western music and books, and various types of dress.

In foreign policy, Paul joined in 1798 the second coalition against France, but Russia withdrew a year later. In order to discourage English interference with neutral shipping, Paul formed an armed neutrality league with Denmark, Sweden, and Prussia.

Paul's unpredictable—possibly mentally ill—behavior led to a conspiracy to force his abdication. His son Alexander assented to the coup d'etat of March 11, 1801. However, when Paul refused to abdicate, the conspirators strangled him.

Further Reading

The most authoritative study of the reign of Paul I is in Russian. Martha Edith Almedingen, *So Dark a Stream: A Study of the Emperor Paul I of Russia, 1754-1801* (1959), is a popularly written biography. There is a good section on Paul in Alexander A. Kornilov, *Modern Russian History* (3 vols., 1912-1914; trans., 2 vols., 1916-1917), and in Ronald Hingley, *The Tsars: Russian Autocrats, 1533-1917* (1968). Hans Rogger, *National Consciousness in 18th Century Russia* (1960), traces the emergence of a sense of national identity among the cosmopolitan elite.

Additional Sources

McGrew, Roderick E. (Roderick Erle), *Paul I of Russia, 1754-1801,* Oxford: Clarendon Press; New York: Oxford University Press, 1992.

Paul I, a reassessment of his life and reign, Pittsburgh: University Center for International Studies, University of Pittsburgh, 1979. □

Paul III

Paul III (1468-1549) was pope from 1534 to 1549. He was a man of keen intelligence, intense energy, and dogged tenacity. His pontificate was somewhat equivocal, stamped at once with a lingering Renaissance mentality and the strong new impulse toward religious renewal.

Alessandro Farnese, who became Paul III, was born on Feb. 29, 1468, in Canino into one of the more powerful Renaissance families of northern Italy. After his education in Rome and in Florence at the court of Lorenzo de' Medici, he entered the service of the Church. Created a cardinal in 1493 by Pope Alexander VI, he continued his warm friendships with artists, scholars, and humanists. He was ordained in 1519. In the conclaves of 1521 and 1523 he was almost elected to the papacy. This office he received on Oct. 13, 1534.

During his 15 years as pope, Paul III created a new atmosphere about the papacy. He raised to the College of Cardinals most exemplary men, such as Marcello Cervini (who became Marcellus II), Reginald Pole, Giampietro Carafa (later Paul IV), and Gasparo Contarini. In 1526 Paul inaugurated the incisive review of the central problem of reform in the Church known as the *Consilium de emandanda ecclesia*. In 1542 he founded the Congregation of the Roman Inquisition, or the Holy Office, as the final court of appeal in trials of heresy. He encouraged many new religious communities and gave papal approbation of the Society of Jesus (Jesuits) in 1540 and of the Ursulines in 1544.

Paul's greatest encouragement to the Catholic reform was the opening of an ecumenical council which he tried to inaugurate as early as 1537 at Mantua. Because of immense difficulties, arising in large measure from the international rivalry between the Holy Roman emperor Charles V and the

Paul IV

Paul IV (1476-1559) was pope from 1555 to 1559. He was one of the most energetic of the reforming popes of the 16th century. Known for his harsh and imperialistic manner, he broke many of the papal ties with the secular elements of the Renaissance.

Giampietro Carafa, who became Paul IV, was born into the Neapolitan aristocracy at Capriglio a Scala on June 28, 1476. In the household of his uncle, Cardinal Oliviero Carafa, he received a superb training in Latin, Greek, and Hebrew. With his learning he combined a simple manner of life and a burning ambition for reform in the Church. Soon after his ordination as priest he was made, in 1505, the bishop of Chieti. In 1518 he became the archbishop of Brindisi. In 1524 he joined Cajetan in founding an apostolic-orientated group of priests known as the Theatines. In 1536 Pope Paul III created him a cardinal and in 1549 archbishop of Naples. On May 23, 1555, he was elected pope and took the name Paul IV.

Paul used his new powers extensively and severely to achieve reform in the Church. He sentenced to the galleys monks whom the police found absent from their monasteries. He drove bishops from Rome back to their sees. In 1559 he issued the first Index of Forbidden Books under the supervision of the Congregation of the Inquisition. Adamant in regard to the purity of the faith, he suspected two excellent cardinals, Giovanni Morone and Reginald Pole, of softness toward heresy, imprisoned Morone, and tried to have Pole return from England. In contrast to his predecessors, he declined to use the major instrument for reform, the Council of Trent, and left it suspended during his pontificate.

Paul marred his religious ambitions by nepotism and nationalism. Blind to the serious defects of his unprincipled nephew, Cardinal Carlo Carafa, he entrusted him with extensive administrative power in ecclesiastical business. Only toward the end of his pontificate did he become aware of his nephew's evil conduct and exile him. As a Neapolitan, he had a deep resentment of the Spanish control of southern Italy. This feeling led him into the ill-advised war with Philip II in November 1556. The war ended with a Spanish victory and the Peace of Cave on Sept. 12, 1557. Paul also had strained relations with the Austrian Hapsburgs, threatening to depose Charles V and refusing to recognize Ferdinand I, partly because of imperial acquiescence to the Religious Peace of Augsburg (1555) and partly because Ferdinand accepted the office of emperor without the Pope's approval.

Although Paul was himself an excellent classicist, he was not a patron of the arts. When he died on Aug. 18, 1559, the Roman populace, which intensely disliked his stern policies, rioted and destroyed his statues and the buildings of the Inquisition.

French king Francis I, he succeeded only in December 1545 in getting the council under way at Trent. Further difficulties followed, and Paul transferred the council to Bologna in February 1548 and finally suspended it in September 1549.

Retaining his early enthusiasm for art and scholarship, Paul was ambitious to give Rome the primacy in these fields. He restored the Roman University, which had been utterly destroyed in the sack of Rome (1527), and energetically tried to staff it with outstanding scholars. He arranged for new catalogs in the Vatican Library and for the preservation of damaged manuscripts. He commissioned Michelangelo to paint the *Last Judgment* in the Sistine Chapel and to reconstruct St. Peter's and the Capitol.

Paul marred his reign by the concern, so typical of the Renaissance, for the advancement of his family. He installed Pierluigi Farnese, one of the four natural children he had fathered before he became pope, as the Duke of Parma and Piacenza. After Paul became pope, he made two of his grandsons cardinals. Paul died on Nov. 10, 1549.

Further Reading

A good modern comprehensive study of Paul III is in Ludwig Pastor, *History of the Popes,* vols. 11 and 12, translated by Ralph F. Kerr (1912), which contains a full bibliography and list of sources. For background consult Alan P. Dolan, *Catholicism: An Historical Survey* (1968), and Karl H. Dannenfeldt, *The Church of the Renaissance and Reformation* (1970). □

Further Reading

A good comprehensive study of Paul IV is Ludwig Pastor, *History of the Popes,* vol. 14, translated by Ralph F. Kerr (1924), which includes a full bibliography and list of sources. □

Paul VI

Paul VI (1897-1978) became pope of the Roman Catholic Church in 1963. He reigned during a period of great change and ferment in the Church following the Second Vatican Council.

The future pope was born Giovanni Battista Montini at Concesio (Lombardy), Italy, on September 26, 1897. His father was Giorgio Montini, a well-to-do landowner, editor of the daily *Il Cittadino di Brescia,* and representative for Brescia in the Italian Chamber of Deputies. He was a vigorous defender of Catholic ideals against the anticlericalism of the day. Giovanni's mother, Giuditta Alghisi Montini, was a member of the lesser nobility and a leader among the Catholic women of Brescia. There were two other sons, Ludovico (born 1896) and Francesco (born 1899).

Giovanni Montini received his primary and secondary education at Brescia's Arici Institute under the direction of the Jesuits. By temperament he was rather shy and retiring,

intelligent and ascetic; physically he was somewhat frail. He was accepted at the diocesan seminary but permitted to live at home. Montini was ordained to the priesthood on May 29, 1920. During the following summer he served as a parish curate, but that fall he was sent to Rome for graduate studies at the Gregorian University. He then entered the papal school for foreign-service training. On the completion of his studies he was sent to Warsaw as a minor official at the nunciature but, for reasons of health, was recalled to Rome later in the year and assigned duties in the Vatican Secretariat of State. This was to be his place of work, in positions of ever-increasing importance and responsibility, for the next 31 years.

Early Career

During his early years in Rome, Montini served as assistant chaplain to Catholic students at the University of Rome and, in 1925, was named national moderator of the Federazione Universitaria Cattolica Italiana (FUCI). His intellectual interests and knowledge of modern philosophy and literature admirably equipped him to work with college students. After the Fascist suppression of all Catholic youth organizations in 1931, he helped found the Movimento Laureati Cattolici to continue this apostolate among university graduates.

These activities, however, were extracurricular as far as Montini's Vatican responsibilities were concerned. In October 1924 he was made an assistant secretary in the office of the Secretariat of State; the following April he was promoted to the rank of *minutante* (secretary, with clearance to work

on confidential papers). These duties were relatively routine, but in February 1930, when Cardinal Eugenio Pacelli became papal secretary of state, Montini's life changed abruptly. From the beginning Pacelli singled him out for special training; and when, in 1933, a young American priest in the Secretariat, Monsignor Spellman (later Cardinal Spellman, Archbishop of New York), was returned to his own country as auxiliary bishop of Boston, Pacelli filled the vacancy by naming Montini to his own personal staff.

In February 1939 Pius XI died, and on March 2 Pacelli was elected pope on the first ballot of the conclave, taking the name Pius XII. The new pontiff retained Montini in his regular duties under the secretary of state, and in 1944 he became undersecretary for ordinary affairs, dealing with the Church's internal administration.

World War II was a period of intense diplomatic as well as humanitarian activity for the Vatican—activity rendered exceptionally difficult by the fact that the Holy See was completely hemmed in by one of the belligerent powers.

Montini directed the Vatican's extensive war relief services. He did much to rescue and hide political refugees, especially Jews, and prevent their falling into the hands of the German and Italian forces. Toward the war's end he acted as liaison between the Vatican and the Americans sent to Italy to establish the War Relief Services, and he engaged the Secretariat of State in intensive efforts to resettle displaced persons.

After the war Montini continued his regular duties at the Vatican, being named prosecretary of state in 1953. On him fell the chief responsibility for organizing the Holy Year in 1950 and the Marian Year in 1954.

Archbishop of Milan

In November 1954 Montini was appointed archbishop of Milan and was soon deeply involved in the active pastoral ministry. He mingled with workers in Milan streets—often being greeted by jeers—toured factories, went down into mines, and visited communist districts. He engaged in dialogue with the communists, acknowledging the legitimacy of many of their complaints about labor conditions, but insisting that a solution to these problems could be found in proper implementation of the Church's traditional social teachings.

During his 8 years in Milan, Montini blessed or consecrated 72 churches and left another 19 under construction at his departure. He made the staggering total of 694 visitations to parishes of the diocese and regularly addressed pastoral letters to both clergy and laity. He established an Office of Charity to provide free medical and legal advice for the poor and devoted special attention to the problems arising from constant and increasing immigration into the area. In education, he established schools for the social formation of laity and clergy and founded, at the University of the Sacred Heart, the Overseas College for Catholic students from underdeveloped countries. In December 1958 Pius's successor, John XXIII, elevated Montini to cardinal.

John XXIII died on June 3, 1963. On June 19 Cardinal Montini entered the Sistine Chapel with 79 other cardinals (the largest conclave in history); two days later he was elected pope, taking the name Paul VI. He was crowned on June 30 in an outdoor ceremony held in St. Peter's Square.

Second Vatican Council

The Second Vatican Council, which John XXIII had opened on Oct. 11, 1962, had ushered in an era of profound and sometimes disconcerting change for the Catholic Church. By Church law an ecumenical council ceases immediately upon the death of the pope who convoked it, and its continuation rests solely upon the wishes and judgment of his successor. As if to remove all doubts instantly and fully, Pope Paul announced that the council would go on, and just five days later (June 27) he convoked the second session for September 29.

During the next three years Pope Paul's vital interest in and cooperation with the work of the council were marked in virtually all that he said and did. He relaxed secrecy requirements and set up a press committee to make the council's work continuously known to news media. An additional number of non-Catholic observers were invited, and some laymen admitted as auditors; in 1964, just before the third session, some women were invited to attend. One of his chief concerns was to assure that the council fathers could work in an atmosphere of freedom, and many of the procedures instituted were designed with this in mind.

As the council developed, a major issue for debate was "collegiality," or the shared authority of the bishops with the Roman pontiff. Pope Paul showed his belief in and full accord with this concept in a number of ways. He agreed to establish the Synod of Bishops, a representative body of bishops selected from all over the world to advise and assist the pope in governing the Church.

After four sessions and the publication of 16 vital documents (four constitutions, nine decrees, and three declarations), the council came to its solemn close on December 8, 1965. In the months and years that followed, Pope Paul worked tirelessly to implement its pronouncements. The first Synod of Bishops, held in Rome from September 29 to October 29, 1967, was attended by some 200 bishops from all parts of the world. Other notable actions were: the reform of the Curia; the revision of the Code of Canon Law; the renewal of the sacred liturgy, with emphasis on the use of the vernacular together with the preservation of Latin; the liberalization of the rules governing mixed marriages; the creation of the Council of the Laity to promote the lay apostolate; and the formation of the Pontifical Commission for Justice and Peace. Despite reform and implementation, Pope Paul repeatedly cautioned that renewal must proceed deliberately and without sacrificing any of the Church's sacred deposit of faith. He issued admonitions against unfounded theological speculations, unauthorized experimentation in the liturgy, and any attempts to weaken the authority of the Roman pontiff and the hierarchy.

Pope Paul and Ecumenism

From the beginning of his pontificate Paul VI showed an especial concern for the relations of the Catholic Church with other religious bodies and for eventual Christian unity. During Vatican II he extended special courtesy and consideration to non-Catholic observers. His ecumenical concern was particularly notable in the case of the Orthodox Church. During his 1964 trip to the Holy Land he had two cordial conversations with Patriarch Athenagoras I of Constantinople, and at the solemn closing of the Second Vatican Council there took place the historic occasion when he and the Patriarch removed and consigned "to oblivion" the mutual excommunications which in 1054 had resulted in the Great Schism between the Eastern and Western Churches.

Pope Paul's relations with Protestantism were also cordial. In 1965 the World Council of Churches proposed the creation of a mixed commission to explore the possibilities of dialogue between the council and the Catholic Church, and he promptly sent Cardinal Bea to Geneva to accept the proposal. In March 1966 he welcomed to the Vatican the Most Reverend Arthur M. Ramsey, Archbishop of Canterbury, and discussed relations between Catholicism and the Anglican Church. In 1968 Pope Paul sent greetings to the Tenth Lambeth Conference of Anglican Bishops and to the Fourth General Assembly of the World Council of Churches. Both of these meetings were attended by Catholic observers. On his June 1969 trip to Geneva he was warmly received at the headquarters of the World Council of Churches. In these ecumenical endeavors, however, the Pope frequently cautioned against any attempt to modify or gloss over essential Catholic teachings. He insisted that unity cannot be brought about at the expense of doctrine.

Encyclicals and Travels

Characteristic of the pontificate of Paul VI were his encyclicals. Besides two brief ones urging devotion and prayer to the Blessed Virgin Mary, there were (through September 1969) five major encyclicals. *Ecclesiam suam* (August 6, 1964; On the Church) dealt with the awareness that the Church has of its nature and on the fact that this awareness must be constantly increased and deepened. This can be done only by constant internal renewal. The Church must engage in dialogue not only among its own members but with all men, including those whose views and beliefs are opposed to its own. *Mysterium fidei* (September 3, 1965; The Mystery of Faith) restated the Church's traditional teaching on the Eucharist, especially the doctrine of the Real Presence and of transubstantiation, or the change effected by the words of consecration in the Mass. *Populorum progressio* (March 6, 1967; On the Development of Peoples) was one of Pope Paul's most important pronouncements, an encyclical in the tradition of Leo XIII's *Rerum novarum,* Pius XI's *Quadragesimo anno,* and John XXIII's *Mater et Magistra* and *Pacem in terris.* It extended and deepened, in the light of modern conditions, the social teachings of his predecessors. *Sacerdotalis caelibatus* (June 24, 1967; On Priestly Celibacy) was a response to widespread urgings for some relaxation of the Latin Church's traditional rule of celibacy

for the priesthood and religious. The Pope, admitting that celibacy was difficult, nevertheless upheld it by appeals to Scripture and tradition and declined to modify the law in any way. *Humanae vitae* (July 25, 1968; On Human Life) was one of the best-known and most widely discussed papal documents in history. It upheld the Church's traditional teaching on contraception—a teaching already stated with clarity by Pius XI and Pius XII.

A unique feature of Pope Paul's reign, breaking with long-standing tradition, was his travels to so many parts of the world. These journeys—to the Holy Land, to India, to the UN headquarters in New York, and to Portugal, Turkey, Colombia, Switzerland, and Uganda—seemed not only to indicate his eagerness for personal knowledge of and contact with all parts of the Universal Church over which he presided, but also a desire to relate the Church to the modern world and to contribute to a solution for the world's problems.

World Peace

The greatest of these problems was, of course, that of lasting peace. Pope Paul's pontificate took place in a time of ever-increasing international tension and dangers. No pope ever worked harder to achieve world peace. It was the subject of many written documents and a constantly recurring theme of his discourses. Much effort turned on the war in Vietnam. He repeatedly addressed letters to the heads of the warring nations and met with such world figures as U.S. president Lyndon B. Johnson and UN secretary general U Thant to discuss means of ending the war. Simultaneously he sought to bring peace to other parts of the world: in the Middle East, in the Dominican Republic, in the Congo, and in Nigeria. He continued the policy initiated by John XXIII of entering when possible into negotiations with communist nations. Both Soviet president Nikolai Podgorny and foreign minister Andrei Gromyko met with Pope Paul. At various times agreements were reached with Hungary, Czechoslovakia, and Yugoslavia that resulted in a lifting of some of the restrictions on religious activities in those countries and in the Holy See's being permitted to name bishops to vacant dioceses.

Pope Paul died of a heart attack on August 6, 1978, at Castel Gandolfo and was succeeded by John Paul I.

Further Reading

The Pope Speaks: Dialogues of Paul VI with Jean Guitton (trans. 1968) provides informal and delightful insights into the Pope's thoughts on many subjects. Guitton, a French lay theologian and a close personal friend of the Pontiff, compiled these dialogues from actual conversations with him and published them with Pope Paul's permission. A number of biographies and studies of Paul VI appeared after his accession to the pontificate. All have their merits, but soon became dated. The best and most readable are John G. Clancy, *Apostle for Our Time: Pope Paul VI* (1963), and William E. Barrett, *Shepherd of Mankind* (1964). Xavier Rynne (pseudonym), *Vatican Council II* (1968), offers a vivid if occasionally sensational day-by-day account of the four years of Vatican II; the portion "The Second Session" contains a good biographical sketch of Pope Paul. His obituary was found in the Catholic Encyclopedia. □

Wolfgang Ernst Pauli

The Austrian theoretical physicist Wolfgang Ernst Pauli (1900-1958) was awarded the Nobel Prize in Physics for his discovery of the exclusion principle, known as the Pauli principle.

Wolfgang Pauli the son of Wolfgang Joseph Pauli, a professor in the University of Vienna, was born in that city on April 25, 1900. Brilliant at school, he studied theoretical physics in the University of Munich under Arnold Sommerfeld (1918-1921) and graduated as a Doctor of Philosophy. Sommerfeld asked him to write the article on relativity for the *Encyclopedia of Mathematical Sciences.* The article, over 200 pages long, was published in 1921; it was translated into English and Italian in 1958 and is still definitive.

Pauli was an assistant to Max Born at Göttingen (1921-1922) and to Niels Bohr at Copenhagen (1922-1923). He then spent 5 years as a lecturer in the University of Hamburg, and in 1928 he became professor of physics in the Federal Institute of Technology at Zurich.

In 1921 the generally accepted theory of the atom was that advanced by Bohr in 1913. In the case of the hydrogen atom with its single electron, the state of the atom was defined by a single quantum number representing the energy in the possible circular orbits of the electron. By postulating an additional set of quantum numbers Sommerfeld later extended Bohr's theory to cover the elliptical orbits in complex atoms, and a third set was later postulated to explain the atom in a magnetic field. The Bohr-Sommerfeld theory explained the hydrogen atom satisfactorily; but in the case of complex atoms it did not explain the doublet nature of the series of the alkali spectra, nor did it explain the anomalous Zeeman effect which Pauli had tried to elucidate while he was at Copenhagen.

In 1924-1925 Pauli published his theoretical solution of the anomalous Zeeman effect. To explain it, others had suggested that the third, or magnetic, quantum number should be regarded as having a half-integer value. But Pauli postulated a fourth quantum number, a fourth degree of freedom. This he regarded as having one of two values only—a property he later defined as "two-valuedness not describable classically." He then defined his "principle," which is now usually stated as follows: no two electrons in the same atom can have all four quantum numbers equal. Recognized from the time of its publication as important, it was not at once called the exclusion, or Pauli, principle. In 1925 G. E. Uhlenbeck and S. A. Goudsmit introduced the hypothesis of electron spin, with possible quantum numbers of either $+ \frac{1}{2}$ or $- \frac{1}{2}$. About this time the new mechanics, as exemplified by Werner Heisenberg's matrix mechanics and Erwin Schrödinger's wave equation, was making headway, but these methods did not easily explain the problem of the hydrogen atom because it involved the inverse-square law in the attractive force. In 1926 Pauli solved this problem brilliantly by identifying his hypothetical fourth degree of freedom with Uhlenbeck and Goudsmit's "spin,"

and since then this degree has been called the spin quantum.

Between 1928 and 1930 Pauli first attempted—partly in collaboration with Heisenberg—to apply the quantum principle to the interaction of radiation and matter. These three papers constituted the first steps in quantum field theory. In the early 1930s, to explain the phenomenon of beta decay of nuclei, by which an unpredictable amount of energy appeared to be lost, Pauli postulated the existence of a neutral particle of low mass but with spin $\frac{1}{2}$. For this particle Enrico Fermi later coined the name "neutrino."

Pauli was visiting professor at the University of Michigan (1931, 1941) and at the Institute for Advanced Study, Princeton (1935-1936, 1940-1945). He received many honors, including the Nobel Prize for Physics in 1945. In 1953 he was elected a Foreign Member of the Royal Society. He died in Zurich on Dec. 15, 1958.

Further Reading

There is a biography of Pauli in *Nobel Lectures, Physics, 1942-1962* (1964), which also includes his Nobel Lecture. For his work see N. H. de V. Heathcote, *Nobel Prize Winners, Physics, 1901-1950* (1953); B. Hoffmann, *The Strange Story of the Quantum* (2d ed. 1959); and A. d'Abro, *The Rise of the New Physics,* vol. 2 (1951). □

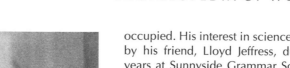

Linus Carl Pauling

The American chemist, Linus Carl Pauling (1901-1994), was twice the recipient of a Nobel Prize. He clarifies much that was obscure in the determination of the exact tri-dimensional shapes of molecules, revealed the nature of the chemical bond, helped to create the field of molecular biology, proposed the concept and coined the term "molecular disease;" founded the science of ortho-molecular medicine, and was an activist for peace.

Linus Carl Pauling was born in Portland, Oregon, on February 28, 1901. He was the first of three children born to Herman Henry William Pauling and Lucy Isabelle "Belle" (Darling) Pauling. His father was a druggist who struggled to make a living for his family. With his business failing, Herman Pauling moved the family to Oswego, seven miles south of Portland, in 1903. But, he was no more successful in Oswego and moved the family to Salem in 1904, to Condon (in northern Oregon) in 1905, and back to Portland in 1909. In 1910 his father died of a perforated ulcer, leaving his mother to care for the three young Pauling children.

As a child, Pauling read continuously and, at one point, his father wrote to the local newspaper asking for readers to suggest additional books that would keep his young son

occupied. His interest in science was apparently stimulated by his friend, Lloyd Jeffress, during his grammar school years at Sunnyside Grammar School. Jeffress kept a small chemistry laboratory in a corner of his bedroom where he performed simple experiments. Pauling was intrigued by these experiments and decided to become a chemical engineer.

During his high school years, Pauling continued to pursue his interest in chemistry. He was able to obtain much of the equipment and materials he needed for his experiments from the abandoned Oregon Iron and Steel Company in Oswego. His grandfather was a night watchman at a nearby plant and Pauling was able to "borrow" the items he needed for his own chemical studies. Pauling would have graduated from Portland's Washington High School in 1917 except for an unexpected turn of events. He had failed to take the necessary courses in American History required for graduation and, therefore, did not receive his diploma. The school corrected this error 45 years later when it awarded Pauling his high school diploma—after he had been awarded two Nobel Prizes.

In the fall of 1917 Pauling entered Oregon Agricultural College (OAC), now Oregon State University, in Corvallis. He was eager to pursue his study of chemical-engineering and signed up for a full load of classes. But finances soon presented a serious problem. His mother was unable to pay family bills at home and, as a result, Pauling regularly worked 40 or more hours a week in addition to studying and attending classes. By the end of his sophomore year, he could not afford to stay in school and decided to take a year off and help his mother by working in Portland. At the last minute, OAC offered him a job teaching quantitative analysis, a course he had completed as a student just a few months earlier. The $100-a-month job allowed him to return to OAC and continue his education.

During his junior and senior years, Pauling learned about the work of Gilbert Newton Lewis and Irving Langmuir on the electronic structure of atoms and the way atoms combine with each other to form molecules. He became interested in how the physical and chemical properties of substances are related to the structure of the atoms and molecules of which they are composed and decided to make this topic the focus of his own research.

During his senior year, he met Ava Helen Miller while teaching chemistry in a home-economics class. They were married June 17, 1923, and later had four children: Linus Jr., born in 1925; Peter Jeffress, born in 1931; Linda Helen, born in 1932; and Edward Crellin, born in 1937.

Pauling received his bachelor's degree from OAC on June 5, 1922 and began attending the California Institute of Technology (Cal Tech) in Pasadena the following fall. He received his doctorate *summa cum laude* in chemistry (with minors in physics and mathematics) on June 12, 1925. During his graduate studies, he was assigned to work with Roscoe Gilley Dickinson on the X-ray analysis of crystal structures. His first paper, published in the *Journal of the American Chemical Society* (JACS) in 1923, was a direct result of this work. Pauling's entire scientific life is connected with Cal Tech and he would publish six more papers on the structure of other minerals before graduation.

After graduation, Pauling decided to travel to Europe and study in the new field of quantum mechanics with Arnold Sommerfeld in Munich, Niels Bohr in Copenhagen, and Erwin Schrodinger in Zurich. The science of quantum mechanics was less than a decade old and based on the revolutionary concept that particles can sometimes have wave-like properties, and waves can sometimes best be described as if they consisted of mass-less particles. He had been introduced to quantum mechanics while at OAC and was eager to see how this new way of looking at matter and energy could be applied to his own area of interest. After two years in Europe, he and Ava left Zurich and returned to Cal Tech.

Pauling was appointed to Cal Tech's faculty of theoretical chemistry in the fall of 1927 as an assistant professor and would stay on there until his leave as a full professor of chemistry in 1963. In addition, from 1937 to 1958, he headed the Gates and Crellin Chemical Laboratories.

The central theme of Pauling's work was always the understanding of the properties of chemical substances in relation to their structure. He began by determining the crystal structure of various inorganic compounds and complexes with a view to deriving from these the principles governing the structure of molecules. He went on to the prediction of the chemical and physical properties of atoms and ions based upon theoretical considerations. In 1928 Pauling introduced rules relating to the stability of complex ionic crystals which greatly facilitated structural studies.

Pauling spent the summer of 1930 traveling around Europe visiting the laboratories of Laurence Bragg in Manchester, Herman Ludwigshafen and Sommerfeld in Munich. In Ludwigshafen, Pauling learned about the use of electron diffraction techniques to analyze crystalline materials. Over the next 25 years, Pauling and his colleagues would use this technique to determine the molecular structure of more than 225 substances.

Using what he had learned over the summer, Pauling and R.B. Corey began studying the structure of amino acids and small peptides. They postulated that polypeptide chains, especially those derived from fibrous proteins, form spirals of a particular configuration—this was the alpha helix. On April 6, 1931, Pauling published the first major paper on this topic ("The Nature of the Chemical Bond") and was awarded the American Chemical Society's Langmuir Prize for "the most noteworthy work in pure science done by a man 30 years of age or less."

This was a bold proposal for the newly appointed full professor to make. But it has been repeatedly confirmed since, and is now known to apply also to significant portions of the polypeptide chains in the so-called "globular proteins." Pauling would write six more papers on the same topic, continually refining his work.

In some ways, the 1930s mark the pinnacle of Pauling's career as a chemist. During that decade he was able to apply the principles of quantum mechanics to solve a number of important problems in chemical theory.

In 1939 Pauling published his book *The Nature of the Chemical Bond and the Structure of Molecules and Crystals*. This book has been considered by many as one of the most important works in the history of chemistry. The ideas presented in the book and related papers are the primary basis upon which Pauling was awarded the Nobel Prize for Chemistry in 1954.

In the mid-1930s Pauling was looking for new fields to explore and soon found his interest turning to the structure of biological molecules. This was a surprising choice for Pauling, because earlier in his career he had mentioned that he wasn't interested in studying biological molecules. The interest of the newly-formed department of biology at Cal Tech in hemoglobin was derived from the discovery by Pauling and C.D. Coryell in 1936 of a change in the magnetic properties of hemoglobin upon oxygenation. These studies, although they dealt mainly with heme structure, led to an interest in the globin portion of the molecule. This finally culminated in the 1949 proposal that humans may manufacture more than one kind of adult hemoglobin. Sickle-cell anemia was shown to be due to the presence of a type of hemoglobin which tends to aggregate and crystallize under conditions of reduced oxygen, with distortion and malfunctioning of the red blood cell. This was the first documented instance of a "molecular" disorder, a discovery of major import to medicine, biochemistry, genetics, and anthropology.

The 1940s were a decade of significant change in Pauling's life. He had never been especially political and, in fact, had only voted in one presidential election prior to World War II. But in this decade he quickly began to immerse himself in political issues. One important factor in this change was the influence of his wife, who had long been active in a number of social and political causes. Another factor was probably the war itself. As a result of his own wartime research on explosives as a principal investigator for the Office of Scientific Research and the National Defense Research Commission, Pauling became more concerned about the potential destructiveness of future wars. As a result, he decided while on a 1947 trip to Europe that he would raise the issue of world peace in every speech he made in the future, no matter what the topic.

From that point on, Pauling's interests turned from scientific to political topics. He devoted more time to speaking out on political issues, and the majority of his published papers dealt with political, rather than scientific, topics. In 1957, with the help of his wife and many others, he organized a petition calling for an end to nuclear bomb testing. In January of the following year, he presented this petition at the United Nations with over 11,000 signatures from scientists all over the world. In 1958 he published his views on the military threat facing the world in his book *No More War!*

His views annoyed many in the scientific and political communities and he was often punished for these views. In 1952 the U.S. State Department denied him a passport to attend an important scientific convention in England because his anti-communist statements were not "strong enough." Only after his fourth try did he succeed in receiving a "limited passport." In 1960 he was called before the Internal Security Committee of the U.S. Senate to explain his antiwar activities. But neither popular nor professional disapproval could keep Pauling from protesting, writing, speaking, and organizing conferences against the world's continuing militarism. In recognition of these efforts, Pauling was awarded the 1963 Nobel Prize for Peace.

In 1966 Pauling again found a new field to explore: the possible therapeutic effects of vitamin C. Pauling was introduced to the potential value of vitamin C in preventing colds by biochemist Irwin Stone. He soon became intensely interested in the topic and summarized his views in the 1970 book *Vitamin C and The Common Cold.*

In 1974 Pauling testified before the U.S. Senate Subcommittee on Health on food supplement legislation. He advocated controls over vitamins but did not want to classify them as drugs. In 1986 he published *How To Live Longer and Feel Better,* and in 1990, along with Daisaku Ikeda Seimei, he published *In Quest of the Century of Life —Science and Peace and Health.*

Pauling's views on vitamin C have received relatively modest support in the scientific community. Many colleagues tend to feel that the evidence supporting the therapeutic effects of vitamin C is weak or nonexistent, though research on the topic continues. Other scientists are more convinced by Pauling's argument. He is regarded by some as the founder of the science of ortho-molecular medicine, a field based on the concept that substances normally present in the body (such as vitamin C) can be used to prevent disease and illness.

Pauling's long association with Cal Tech ended in 1963, at least partly because of his active work in the peace movement. He "retired" to become a research professor in the physical and biological sciences at the Center for the Study of Democratic Institutions in Santa Barbara, California. He went on to teach chemistry at the University of California in San Diego and Stanford University in Palo Alto. In 1972 he founded, along with Arthur B. Robinson and Keene Dimick, the Institute of Orthomolecular Medicine as a non-profit California organization to engage in scientific research. Later, it was re-named the Linus Pauling Institute of Science and Medicine.

Pauling received many awards during his successful career. He was a member of the National Academy of Sciences and of the Royal Society, from which he received the Davy Medal in 1947; the American College of Physicians presented him with its Phillips Memorial Award in 1956; and in the same year he received the Avogadro Medal from the Italian Academy of Sciences.

On August 19, 1994 Pauling died of cancer at his ranch outside Big Sur, California. After his death, research continued on every aspect of his earlier discoveries, especially his theory on vitamin C and its effects on disease and the human body. His career exemplified the highly productive results that clear theory along with daring experimental approaches and a courageous imagination can bring.

Further Reading

Short biographies of Pauling are in Eduard Farber, *Nobel Prize Winners in Chemistry, 1901-1961* (rev. ed. 1963), and Nobel Foundation, *Chemistry: Including Presentation Speeches and Laureates's Biographies* (1964). A personal reminiscence of Pauling and his scientific work is in James Dewey Watson, *The Double Helix: A Personal Account of the Discovery of the Structure of DNA* (1968). Pauling's efforts for peace and disarmament are recounted in detail in Mortimer Lipsky, *Quest for Peace: The Story of the Nobel Award* (1966).

Other biographies of Pauling appear in Anthony Serafini *Linus Pauling: A Man and His Science* (1989) and Ted George Goertzel *Linus Pauling: A Life In Science and Politics* (1995). Probably the best source for information on Pauling is maintained by the Oregon State University Library with its *Ava Helen and Linus Pauling Papers,* which were donated in 1986 by Pauling himself and are available on-line at www.orst.edu. □

Luciano Pavarotti

Probably the most popular tenor since Caruso, Luciano Pavarotti (born 1935) combined accuracy of pitch and quality of sound production with a natural musicality. His favorite roles were Rodolfo in Puccini's *La Bohème,* Nemorino in Donizetti's *L'Elisir d'Amore,* and Riccardo in Verdi's *Un Ballo Maschera.*

L uciano Pavarotti was born on the outskirts of Modena in north-central Italy on October 12, 1935. Although he spoke fondly of his childhood, the family had little money; its four members were crowded into a two-room apartment. His father was a baker who, according to Pavarotti, had a fine tenor voice but rejected the possibility of a singing career because of nervousness. His mother worked in a cigar factory. World War II forced the family out of the city in 1943. For the following year they rented a single room from a farmer in the neighboring countryside, where young Pavarotti developed an interest in farming.

Pavarotti's earliest musical influences were his father's recordings, most of them featuring the popular tenors of the day—Gigli, Martinelli, Schipa, and Caruso. At around the age of nine he began singing with his father in a small local church choir. Also in his youth he had a few voice lessons with a Professor Dondi and his wife, but he ascribed little significance to them.

After what appears to have been a normal childhood with a typical interest in sports—in Pavarotti's case soccer above all—he graduated from the Schola Magistrale and faced the dilemma of a career choice. He was interested in pursuing a career as a professional soccer player, but his mother convinced him to train as a teacher. He subsequently taught in an elementary school for two years but finally allowed his interest in music to win out. Recognizing the risk involved, his father gave his consent only reluctantly, the agreement being that Pavarotti would be given

free room and board until age 30, after which time, if he had not succeeded, he would earn a living by any means that he could.

Pavarotti began serious study in 1954 at the age of 19 with Arrigo Pola, a respected teacher and professional tenor in Modena who, aware of the family's indigence, offered to teach without remuneration. Not until commencing study with Pola was Pavarotti aware that he had perfect pitch. At about this time Pavarotti met Adua Veroni, whom he married in 1961. When Pola moved to Japan two and a half years later, Pavarotti became a student of Ettore Campogalliani, who was also teaching the now well-known soprano, Pavarotti's childhood friend Mirella Freni. During his years of study Pavarotti held part-time jobs in order to help sustain himself—first as an elementary school teacher and then, when he failed at that, as an insurance salesman.

The first six years of study resulted in nothing more tangible than a few recitals, all in small towns and all without pay. When a nodule developed on his vocal chords causing a "disastrous" concert in Ferrara, he decided to give up singing. Pavarotti attributed his immediate improvement to the psychological release connected with this decision. Whatever the reason, the nodule not only disappeared but, as he related in his autobiography, "Everything I had learned came together with my natural voice to make the sound I had been struggling so hard to achieve."

A measure of success occurred when he won the Achille Peri Competition in 1961, for which the first prize was the role of Rodolfo in a production of Puccini's La Bohème

to be given in Reggio Emilia on April 28 of that year. Although his debut was a success, a certain amount of maneuvering was necessary to secure his next few contracts. A well-known agent, Alesandro Ziliani, had been in the audience and, after hearing Pavarotti, offered to represent him. When La Bohème was to be produced in Lucca, Ziliani insisted that Pavarotti be included in a package deal that would also provide the services of a well-known singer requested by the management. Later Ziliani recommended him to conductor Tullio Serafin, who engaged him in the role of the Duke of Mantua in Verdi's Rigoletto.

Pavarotti's Covent Garden debut in the fall of 1963 also resulted from something less than a direct invitation. Giuseppe di Stefano had been scheduled for a series of performances as Rodolfo, but the management was aware that he frequently canceled on short notice. They therefore needed someone whose quality matched the rest of the production, yet who would learn the role without any assurance that he would get to sing it. Pavarotti agreed. When di Stefano canceled after one and a half performances, Pavarotti stepped in for the remainder of the series with great success.

His debut at La Scala in 1965, again as Rodolfo, came at the suggestion of Herbert von Karajan, who had been conducting La Bohème there for two years and had, as Pavarotti said, "run out of tenors." He was somewhat resentful that the invitation did not come from La Scala management. Also in 1965 Pavarotti made his American debut in Miami as Edgardo in Donizetti's Lucia di Lammermoor. Illness troubled him during his New York debut at the Metropolitan Opera in November 1968 and compelled him to cancel after the second act of the second performance.

Nineteenth-century Italian opera comprised most of Pavarotti's repertoire, particularly Puccini, Verdi, and Donizetti, who he found the most comfortable to sing. He treated his voice cautiously, reserving heavier roles until later years. Still his rendering of Cavaradossi in Puccini's Tosca was criticized, both for the light quality of his voice and for his misinterpretation of the role. He sang few song recitals, as he regarded them as more strenuous than opera. Very few opera singers are convincing actors and Pavarotti is not among them. He improved considerably over the years, however, and by the mid-1980s he spent nearly as much time on his acting as on his singing. Although by that time he felt that he had covered the range of roles possible for him, he had not exhausted everything inside that range. Among the roles he hoped to add were Don Jose in Bizet's Carmen and the title role in Massenet's Werther. In 1972 he starred in a commercial film, Yes, Giorgio. His solo album of Neapolitan songs, "O Sole Mio," outsold any other record by a classical singer.

Throughout the 1980s Pavarotti strengthened his status as one of the opera world's leading figures. Televised performances of Pavarotti in many of his greatest and favorite roles not only helped him maintain his status, but to broaden his appeal. He was able to reach millions of viewers each time one of his opera performances and solo concerts was seen. He also began to show increasing flexibility as a recording artist. He recorded classical operas, songs by Henry Mancini and Italian folk songs, thus becoming the world's third highest top selling musician, right behind Madonna and Elton John. By the time he proposed and staged the first "Three Tenors" concert at the Baths of Caracalla in Rome, Pavarotti was unabashedly thrilled with his immense popularity. "I want to be famous everywhere" he told *Newsweek* and he continually showed his appreciation to the fans that made him. "I tell you, the time spent signing autographs is never enough" he continued in the same interview.

He received his share of criticism and rejection as well. He was barred from contracts with the Lyric Opera of Chicago 1989 because he canceled performances excessively due to bad health. He was sued by the BBC in 1992 for selling the network a lip-synched concert. He was booed at La Scala during a performance of Don Carlo. He finally canceled tours and took several months off to rest.

Pavarotti returned to the stage with concerts before 500,000 people in Central Park. Critics accused him of blatant commercialism, but the crowds loved the performances. He learned a new role, Andrea Chenier, for a 1996 Metropolitan Opera broadcast. Pavarotti was praised for both his diligence, his survival, and the fact that he undertook a new role at the age of 61. In 1997 the three tenors—Placido Domingo, Jose Carreras and Pavarotti—toured to mixed reviews but delighted audiences who seemed unwilling to let Pavarotti even think of retiring.

Further Reading

Pavarotti's popularity was such that he was in the media constantly. Unfortunately, the information ranged widely in its credibility. Recommended are articles by R. Jacobson appearing in *Opera News* (March 14, 1981 and February 14, 1979). A short and fairly objective profile by Giorgio Gualerzi appeared in the British publication *Opera* (February 1981). An autobiography, *Pavarotti: My Own Story,* with William Wright (1981) is comprised of articles by Pavarotti and by those around him, including his wife, his accompanist, and his manager. While the book contains information, and even wit and charm, one must do a lot of sifting to find it. The discography and list of first performances appearing as appendices are helpful. Critic Alan Blythe regards his Rodolfo in *La Bohème* conducted by Karajan (London) and his Arturo in Bellini's *I Puritani* conducted by Bonynge (London) to be among his finest recordings. □

Cesare Pavese

Cesare Pavese (1908-1950), novelist, poet, and critic, ranks as perhaps the most important Italian novelist of the 20th century. His work fuses considerations of poetic and epic representation, the theme of solitude, and the concept of myth.

Cesare Pavese was born on Sept. 9, 1908, at Santo Stefano Belbo in the Piedmont, the son of a lower-middle-class family of rural background. Although his family lived in Turin, Pavese never severed his childhood ties with the countryside. He lived with his parents and, after their death, with his sister's family until the end of his life.

After graduating from the University of Turin in 1930 with a thesis on Walt Whitman, Pavese began translating American novels and worked for the publishing house of Einaudi. In 1935 Pavese was arrested with members of the anti-Fascist group Giustizia e Libertà and was expelled from the Fascist party, to which he had belonged since 1932. He was exiled for 3 years to southern Italy, where he began to write his first short novels. Pavese returned to Turin in 1936, having been pardoned, and he continued his translations and began to work full time for Einaudi in 1938. He did not participate in the war or in the Resistance, and he became a member of the Communist party in 1945. He spent most of the last 2 war years as "a recluse among the hills" with his sister's family, with whom he returned to Turin in April 1945. On June 24, 1950, Pavese was awarded the coveted Strega Prize, and on August 27, having for years courted the idea of suicide, he died by his own hand in the Hotel Roma in Turin.

Preoccupations and Themes

Pavese was without doubt the most universally cultured Italian writer of his generation. Shy, introspective, and suffering from numerous neuroses, he counted among the great experiences of his life his encounter with American literature and with myth, the latter becoming increasingly dominant in his work. Thus the idea of the return to the past that the artist must accomplish and the treasury of memory both play an important part in his literary approach, for which he believed he had found the answer in myth. A central theme of his work is, furthermore, the question of solitude in all its aspects.

The publication dates of Pavese's works often did not coincide with their times of composition; nor did the manner of publication—many of his short novels were published collectively—necessarily indicate an internal schema. His works may be seen in the Goethean sense as "fragments of a great confession," there being no necessity or possibility of discerning a progressive development because all his writings, in the manner of a free fugue, circle around the same themes; it was Pavese's conviction that "every authentic writer is splendidly monotonous inasmuch as there prevails in his pages a recurrent mark, a formal law of fantasy that transforms the most diverse material into figures and situations which are almost always the same."

His Poetry

Pavese began his career with poetry. It was his aim to write objective expository verse of narrative character: *poesia-racconto.* He tended later toward *immagine-racconto,* "image-recital," convincing himself in the end of the "exigency of a poetry not reducible to a mere recital." Thus, in his own words, the antilyric verse of *Lavorare stanca* (1936) was "an objective development of soberly expounded cases." In a style that moves between interior monologue and *discours indirect libre* and in a language close to dialect or, at least, to the spoken idiom, he recounted the adventure of an adolescent proud of his country origins whose experience of the city in the end conveys only a sense of tragic solitude. Late in life Pavese returned to confessional poetry with the nine poems of *La terra e la morte* (1947; written 1945) and *Verrà la morte e avrà i tuoi occhi* (1951; written 1950).

First Novels

Pavese's first published novel, *Paesi tuoi* (1941), represents, with Elio Vittorini's *Conversazione in Sicilia* (1941), a point of departure for Italian neorealism. Its programmatic flouting of conventions in all possible aspects—in language, style, and theme—and its almost documentary nature set a pattern for that whole movement. The novel was based on the antinomical character of country life and city life; yet the former was not at all idealized but shown in its bare, raw, and wretched existence with its story of incestuous passion. Nevertheless, there was an underlying nostalgic feeling for the earth, for the primeval, a mythical yearning for a return to the fountains, to the springtide of life, that underlies all of Pavese's writing.

La spiaggia (1942) is a variation of Pavese's theme of the eternal return, coveted forever as it is frustrated. It is a story of flight and evasion with its protagonist couple in vain attempting to return to the lost paradise of their youth. *Il carcere* (1949; written 1938-1939), according to its author "a tale about country and sex," is the story of Pavese's own exile, the experience of solitude and isolation. A thematic connection links *Il compagno* (1947; written 1946) and *La casa in collina* (1949; written 1947-1948). Although the political engagement in these two stories is stressed more than the myth, it becomes evident that the search for myth in the end implies a flight from historical presence and responsibility. Thus the solitary hero of the latter story, autobiographically close to his author, eventually evades responsibility with his final flight into myth, into the hills of his origin.

Later Works

The three stories published together in 1949—*La bella estate* (written 1940), *Il diavolo sulle colline* (written 1948), and *Tra donne sole* (written 1949)—center on man's encounter with the city. As fascinating as the city might have seemed initially, it leads to complete disillusionment and isolation, entailing the impossibility of a return to the paradise of yore. This disillusionment is the experience of the women protagonists of *La bella estate* and *Tra donne sole*, as well as that of the couple in the symbolically charged *Il diavolo sulle colline*. *La luna e i falò* (1950; written 1949) represents a sum total of Pavesian symbolism and the thematic myth of the eternal return. It is to the hills of Santo Stefano Belbo, the hills of his childhood, that the protagonist, symbolically called Anguilla, returns, only to leave them again in search of his true self.

Feria d'agosto (1946) is a collection of prose poems and theoretical notes on the subjects of myth and childhood. *I dialoghi con Leucò* (1947)—in the guise of a conversation between mortals and Olympians—presents the result of Pavese's inquiries into the problems and implica-

tions of myth along the lines of Viconian philosophy and Jungian thought. *La letteratura americana e altri saggi* (1951) contains Pavese's critical writings on American literature, a considerable amount of which he translated. *Il mestiere de vivere*, his diary for the years 1935-1950 (published posthumously in 1952), ranks as one of the outstanding documents of its time. Of an uncompromising frankness as well as an unusual degree of introspection, it contains lucid observations on Pavese's personality and literary theory and astute reflections on a culture whose most sensitive representative he was. Also posthumously published were the short-story collection *Notte di festa* (1953; written 1936-1938) and the novel *Fuoco grande* (1959; written with Bianca Garufi in 1946).

Further Reading

Major studies of Pavese are in Italian. Two good studies in English of Pavese's work are Gian Paolo Biasin, *The Smile of the Gods: A Thematic Study of Cesare Pavese's Works* (1968), and Donald W. Heiney, *Three Italian Novelists: Moravia, Pavese, Vittorini* (1968). Recommended for general historical background is Sergio Pacifici, *A Guide to Contemporary Italian Literature: From Futurism to Neorealism* (1962).

Additional Sources

Lajolo, Davide, *An absurd vice: a biography of Cesare Pavese,* New York: New Directions, 1983.
Lajolo, Davide, *Pavese*, Milano: Rizzoli, 1984. □

Ivan Petrovich Pavlov

The Russian physiologist Ivan Petrovich Pavlov (1849-1936) pioneered in the study of circulation, digestion, and conditioned reflexes. He believed that he clearly established the physiological nature of psychological phenomena.

Ivan Pavlov was born in Ryazan on Sept. 26, 1849, the son of a poor parish priest, from whom Pavlov acquired a lifelong love for physical labor and for learning. At the age of 9 or 10, Pavlov suffered from a fall which affected his general health and delayed his formal education. When he was 11, he entered the second grade of the church school at Ryazan. In 1864 he went to the Theological Seminary of Ryazan, studying religion, classical languages, and philosophy and developing an interest in science.

Making of a Physiologist

In 1870 Pavlov gained admission to the University of St. Petersburg (Leningrad), electing animal physiology as his major field and chemistry as his minor. There he studied inorganic chemistry under Dmitrii Mendeleev and organic chemistry under Aleksandr Butlerov, but the deepest impression was made by the lectures and the skilled experimental techniques of Ilya Tsion. It was in Tsion's laboratory that Pavlov was exposed to scientific investigations, resulting in his paper "On the Nerves Controlling the Pancreatic Gland."

After graduating, Pavlov entered the third course of the Medico-Chirurgical Academy (renamed in 1881 the Military Medical Academy), working as a laboratory assistant (1876-1878). In 1877 he published his first work, *Experimental Data Concerning the Accommodating Mechanism of the Blood Vessels,* dealing with the reflex regulation of the circulation of blood. Two years later he completed his course at the academy, and on the basis of a competitive examination he was awarded a scholarship for postgraduate study at the academy.

Pavlov spent the next decade in Sergei Botkins laboratory at the academy. In 1883 Pavlov completed his thesis, *The Centrifugal Nerves of the Heart,* and received the degree of doctor of medicine. The following year he was appointed lecturer in physiology at the academy, won the Wylie fellowship, and then spent the next 2 years in Germany. During the 1880s Pavlov perfected his experimental techniques which made possible his later important discoveries.

In 1881 Pavlov married Serafima Karchevskaia, a woman with profound spiritual feeling, a deep love for literature, and strong affection for her husband. In 1890 he was appointed to the vacant chair of pharmacology at the academy, and a year later he assumed the directorship of the department of physiology of the Institute of Experimental Medicine. Five years later he accepted the chair of physiology at the academy, which he held until 1925. For the next

45 years Pavlov pursued his studies on the digestive glands and conditioned reflexes.

Scientific Contributions

During the first phase of his scientific activity (1874-1888), Pavlov developed operative-surgical techniques that enabled him to perform experiments on unanesthetized animals without inflicting much pain. He studied the circulatory system, particularly the oscillation of blood pressure under various controlled conditions and the regulation of cardiac activity. He noted that the blood pressure of his dogs hardly varied despite the feeding of dry food or excessive amounts of meat broth. In his examination of cardiac activity he was able to observe the special nerve fibers that controlled the rhythm and the strength of the heartbeat. His theory was that the heart is regulated by four specific nerve fibers; it is now generally accepted that the vagus and sympathetic nerves produce the effects on the heart that Pavlov noticed.

In the course of his second phase of scientific work (1888-1902), Pavlov concentrated on the nerves directing the digestive glands and the functions of the alimentary canal under normal conditions. He discovered the secretory nerves of the pancreas in 1888 and the following year the nerves controlling the secretory activity of the gastric glands. Pavlov and his pupils also produced a considerable amount of accurate data on the workings of the gastrointestinal tract, which served as a basis for Pavlov's *Lectures on the Work of the Principal Digestive Glands* (published in Russia in 1897). For this work Pavlov received in 1904 the Nobel Prize in physiology or medicine.

The final phase of Pavlov's scientific career (1902-1936) was primarily concerned with ascertaining the functions of the cerebral cortex by means of conditioned reflexes. Prior to 1900, Pavlov observed that his dogs would secrete saliva and gastric juices before the meat was actually given to them. The sight, odor, or even the footsteps of the attendant were sufficient to trigger the flow of saliva. Pavlov realized that the dogs were responding to activity associated with their feeding, and in 1901 he termed such a response a "conditioned reflex," which was acquired, or learned, as opposed to the unconditioned, or inherited, reflex. He faced a dilemma: could he embark on the study of conditioned reflexes by applying physiological methods to what was generally viewed as psychic phenomena? He opted to follow Ivan Sechenov, who considered that, in theory, psychic phenomena are essentially reflexes and therefore subject to physiological analysis.

The important lectures, papers, and speeches of Pavlov dealing with conditioned reflexes and the cerebral cortex are presented in *Twenty Years of Objective Study of the Higher Nervous Activity* (*Behavior*) *of Animals: Conditioned Reflexes* (1923) and *Lectures on the Work of the Cerebral Hemispheres* (1927). He not only concerned himself with the formation of conditioned responses but noted that they were subject to various kinds of manipulation. He discovered that conditioned responses can be extinguished—at least temporarily—if not reinforced; that one conditioned stimulus can replace another and yet produce identical conditioned responses; and that there are several orders of conditioning. In time Pavlov developed a purely physiological theory of cortical excitation and inhibition which considered, among other things, the process of sleep identical with internal inhibition. However magnificent his experiments were in revealing the responses of animals to conditioning stimuli, he encountered difficulty in experimentally proving his assertion that conditioned responses are due to temporary neuronal connections in the cortex.

In 1918 Pavlov had an opportunity to study several cases of mental illness and thought that a physiological approach to psychiatric phenomena might prove useful. He noted that he could induce "experimental neuroses" in animals by overstraining the excitatory process or the inhibitory process, or by quickly alternating excitation and inhibition. Pavlov then drew an analogy between the functional disorders in animals with those observed in humans. In examining the catatonic manifestations of schizophrenia, he characterized this psychopathological state as actually being "chronic hypnosis"—chiefly as a consequence of weak cortical cells—which functions as a protective mechanism, preserving the nerve cells from further weakening or destruction.

In Pavlov's last scientific article, "The Conditioned Reflex" (1934), written for the *Great Medical Encyclopedia,* he discussed his theory of the two signaling systems which differentiated the animal nervous system from that of man. The first signaling system, possessed both by humans and animals, receives stimulations and impressions of the external world through sense organs. The second signaling system in man deals with the signals of the first system, involving words, thoughts, abstractions, and generalizations. Conditioned reflexes play a significant role in both signal systems. Pavlov declared that "the conditioned reflex has become the central phenomenon in physiology"; he saw in the conditioned reflex the principal mechanism of adaptation to the environment by the living organism.

Philosophy and Outlook

Pavlov's endeavor to give the conditioned reflex widest application in animal and human behavior tended to color his philosophical view of psychology. Although he did not go so far as to deny psychology the right to exist, in his own work and in his demands upon his collaborators he insisted that the language of physiology be employed exclusively to describe psychic activity. Ultimately he envisioned a time when psychology would be completely subsumed into physiology. Respecting the Cartesian duality of mind and matter, Pavlov saw no need for it inasmuch as he believed all mental processes can be explained physiologically.

Politically, most of his life Pavlov was opposed to the extremist positions of the right and left. He did not welcome the Russian February Revolution of 1917 with any enthusiasm. As for the Bolshevik program for creating a Communist society, Pavlov publically stated, "If that which the Bolsheviks are doing with Russia is an experiment, for such an experiment I should regret giving even a frog." Despite his early hostility to the Communist regime, in 1921 a decree of the Soviet of People's Commissars, signed by Lenin himself,

assured Pavlov of continuing support for his scientific work and special privileges. Undoubtedly, Soviet authorities viewed Pavlov's approach to psychology as confirmation of Marxist materialism as well as a method of restructuring society. By 1935 Pavlov became reconciled to the Soviet Communist system, declaring that the "government, too, is an experimenter but in an immeasurably higher category."

Pavlov became seriously ill in 1935 but recovered sufficiently to participate at the Fifteenth International Physiological Congress, and later he attended the Neurological Congress at London. On Feb. 27, 1936, he died.

Further Reading

Still the finest biographical study of Pavlov is the one produced by his senior surviving student, Boris P. Babkin, *Pavlov: A Biography* (1949). Also useful are Ezras A. Asratian, *I. P. Pavlov: His Life and Work* (1953), and Harry K. Wells, *Ivan P. Pavlov: Toward a Scientific Psychology and Psychiatry* (1956). For the influence of Pavlov on Soviet psychology see Raymond A. Bauer, *The New Man in Soviet Psychology* (1952), and *A Handbook of Contemporary Soviet Psychology,* edited by Michael Cole and Irving Maltzman (1969). An early history of Russian physiology is in Alexander S. Vucinich, *Science in Russian Culture: A History to 1860* (1963). □

Anna Pavlova

Anna Pavlova (1881-1931) was in her time—and is perhaps even now—the most famous dancer in the world. From her early classical training at St. Petersburg's Imperial Ballet School, Pavlova carried on incessant, globe-covering tours, everywhere making new audiences for the ballet.

Anna Pavlova, whose exact origins are as unfixable as the startling images she created on stage, was born on January 31, 1881, in St. Petersburg. She was the daughter of a washerwoman, and reputedly her father was reserve soldier Matvey Pavlov, whom Pavlova never knew. The implication exists, however, of illegitimate and well-born Jewish parentage.

According to Pavlova, she cared to be nothing but a dancer from the age of eight, when she attended a performance of *The Sleeping Beauty* at the Maryinsky Theatre. Two years later she was accepted as a student at St. Petersburg's Imperial Ballet School. This extraordinary training-ground for classical dancers offered its students lifelong material protection; the Czar himself was its direct and highly visible benefactor. In return, the school demanded a fervent and almost monastic physical dedication.

The young Pavlova, considered frail—she was often characterized as too thin later in her career—and not conventionally beautiful, was nevertheless exceptionally supple, with beautifully arched insteps. Her talents impressed ballet master Marius Petipa, who was to become her most revered mentor. Pavlova's work with Petipa, as well as such other legendary Maryinsky teachers and choreographers as

Christian Johanssen, Pavel Gerdt, and Enrico Cecchetti, provided a classical foundation, steeped in directly-inherited ballet tradition, that was to serve as her never-to-be-forgotten physical and artistic heritage.

Pavlova made her company debut at the Maryinsky on September 19, 1899. Competition from her contemporaries and near-contemporaries was marked, yet Anna Pavlova soon claimed as her own a loyal sector of Maryinsky balletomanes, who recognized in the young dancer an extraordinarily poetic and expressive quality.

Pavlova's first tour in what was to become a lifetime of innumerable performances for strange audiences (it is estimated that Anna Pavlova travelled over 400,000 miles in the pre-air-travel age and was seen by millions) was to Moscow in 1907. In February 1910, Pavlova, partnered by the brawny Moscow dancer Mikhail Mordkin, made her first appearance in America, at the Metropolitan Opera House. This tour was like countless others to come, in that most of the audiences had never before seen classical ballet in other than highly degenerate form. This was true even in cities such as Boston and Baltimore. There was simply no critical vocabulary for what it was that Pavlova did—all agreed exquisitely—on stage; writers were reduced to calling Pavlova's faultless pirouettes "twirls" and the ballets themselves "ocular operas."

Although these early tours were undertaken with the Czar's consent, Pavlova's final trip to Russia occurred in the summer of 1914. She was travelling through Germany en route to London when Germany declared itself at war with her homeland on August 2, 1914. Pavlova was briefly detained; more crucially, her protection from and obligations to the Czar and his Maryinsky Theatre were practically, if not emotionally, at an end.

From this point until her death, Pavlova continued to make grueling, globe-covering tours, always with her own company—international in make-up, volatile, and variable in dance talent—to support. The early war years found her back in America; 1917 took her to South America; 1919 to Bahia and Salvador. A 1920-1921 tour to America represented Pavlova's fifth major tour of the United States in a decade, and in 1923 the company travelled under the aegis of impresario Sol Hurok to Japan, China, India, Burma, and Egypt. South Africa, Australia, and New Zealand were given a glimpse of Pavlova in 1926, and 1927-1928 were dedicated to a British and continental tour.

Although Pavlova's repertoire grew and was influenced by exposure to foreign cultures and by the often shocking innovations in classical technique and choreography being brought to the dance by Isadora Duncan and Diaghilev's Ballets Russes, she remained by temperament and financial imperative a more conservative classicist. She kept several of the great ballet classics, such as *Giselle* and *The Sleeping Beauty,* in the company's repertoire; her own popular signature pieces were the *Bacchanale,* a duet attributed to Pavlova's former fellow-student Mikhail Fokine, and her eerily beautiful *The Swan.*

It was Pavlova's ability to accept her role as emissary for her art, often with good humor and always with a kind of missionary zeal and self-discipline, that brought vast audiences to her and eventually to the ballet itself. She was willing to let her art find its own level of appreciation, whether in the most discriminating theaters of Europe or, when the economic stresses of maintaining an ungainly touring company dictated, in London's music halls or even New York's gigantic home to vaudeville, the Hippodrome.

Pavlova's rare private days were spent at Ivy House in Hampstead, London, where she kept a menagerie of exotic birds and animals—including a pair of pet swans that were undoubtedly a source of imagery for Pavlova's famous on-stage version. Her companion, manager, and perhaps husband (Pavlova was contradictory concerning the exact nature of their relationship) was Victor Dandré, a fellow exile from St. Petersburg.

Pavlova died of pleurisy in The Hague on January 22, 1931. She had performed incessantly until her death; her final words were to ask for her Swan costume to be prepared and, finally, "Play that last measure softly."

Further Reading

Anna Pavlova: Her Life and Art (1982) by Keith Money is the most comprehensive and perhaps the most accurate biography of the dancer. John and Roberta Lazzarini's *Pavlova* (1980) gives a fine account of Pavlova's repertoire. Two books by Pavlova's associates are Victor Dandré's sometimes misleading but essential *Anna Pavlova* (1932) and Algeranoff's (born Algernon Harcourt Essex) *My Years With Pavlova* (1957), based on his diaries kept from 1921 to 1930, the years he was a member of Pavlova's company.

Additional Sources

Fonteyn, Margot, Dame, *Pavlova: portrait of a dancer,* New York, N.Y., U.S.A.: Viking, 1984.

Pavlova, a biography, New York: Da Capo Press, 1979, 1956.

Lazzarini, John, *Pavlova: repertoire of a legend,* New York: Schirmer Books; London: Collier Macmillan, 1980.

Money, Keith, *Anna Pavlova, her life and art,* New York: Knopf: Distributed by Random House, 1982.

Anna Pavlova, New York: Dover Publications, 1974. □

John Howard Payne

John Howard Payne (1791-1852) was America's first international actor-dramatist. Though he was a prolific playwright, he is best remembered for his song "Home, Sweet Home."

John Howard Payne was born in New York City on June 9, 1791. Against his family's wishes he early took to the theater. He edited his own newspaper, the *Thespian Mirror,* "to promote the interests of American drama," when he was 14. The following year his first play was produced. He made his debut as an actor in 1809 as young Norvall in *Douglas* by John Home and was an immediate sensation. By 1813, however, Payne's popularity had waned and he left for England.

This sensitive, unstable, charming man spent the next 20 years in Europe. Though Payne first acted and later wrote prolifically for the theater, he was constantly chased by creditors and became famous without becoming prosperous. His plays were sold outright to managers so that he gained no sustained income, and the lack of a copyright law at this time permitted them to be pirated.

All of Payne's important works are adaptations or translations. *Brutus* (1818), his most popular production, was adapted from five other dramas. Yet his work was dramatically superior to his sources and became a vehicle for numerous tragedians over the next 70 years. He was deeply influenced by the French drama. The best of his adaptations from the French, *Thérèse* (1821), a melodrama, earned enough to release him from debtors' prison, to which he had been sent after an unsuccessful attempt at managing Sadler's Wells Theatre in 1820.

Clari (1823) was popular in its own right, and one of its songs, "Home, Sweet Home," with Payne's lyrics and a Sicilian melody, outlasted the play. Payne received no financial reward from its subsequent popularity, for he had sold the play. With his friend Washington Irving, whose collaboration remained anonymous, he wrote *Charles the Second* (1824), a bright and clever comedy.

In 1832 Payne returned, discouraged, to his own country. He had written or adapted over 60 plays, yet he was still in debt and had no permanent place in London's theater, where, he insisted, "much prejudice had been excited against me . . . for having so strongly asserted my American principles." But he found himself a celebrity at home and was feted in various cities. Benefit performances of his plays raised nearly $10,000—most of it taken immediately by creditors.

Payne wrote no more plays. In 1842 he was appointed American consul at Tunis. He died there on April 9, 1852.

Further Reading

The standard biography of Payne is Gabriel Harrison, *John Howard Payne: His Life and Writings* (rev. ed. 1885). It is complete and sound in its evaluation. Rosa P. Chiles, *John Howard Payne* (1930), is a good modern appreciation. Arthur H. Quinn, *A History of the American Drama: From the Beginning to the Civil War* (1923), contains an excellent chapter, "John Howard Payne and the Foreign Plays." □

Cecilia Payne-Gaposchkin

Cecilia Payne-Gaposchkin (1900-1979) was a pioneer in the field of astronomy and one of the most eminent female astronomers of the twentieth century. She was the first to apply the laws of atomic physics to the study of the temperature and density of stellar bodies and to conclude that hydrogen and helium, the two lightest elements, were also the two most common elements in the universe.

Cecilia Payne-Gaposchkin's revelation that hydrogen, the simplest of the known elements, was the most abundant substance in the universe has since become the basis for analysis of the cosmos. Yet she is not officially credited with the discovery, made when she was a 25-year-old doctoral candidate at Harvard, because her conservative male superiors convinced her to retract her findings on stellar hydrogen and publish a far less definitive statement. While she is perhaps best known for her later work in identifying and measuring variable stars with her husband, Sergei I. Gaposchkin, Payne-Gaposchkin helped forge a path for other women in the sciences through her staunch fight against sexual discrimination at Harvard College Observatory, where she eventually became the first woman appointed to full professor and the first woman named chairman of a department that was not specifically designated for a woman.

Cecilia Helena Payne was born on May 10, 1900, in Wendover, England, the eldest of three children born to Edward John and Emma Leonora Helena (Pertz) Payne of Coblenz, Prussia. Her father, a London barrister, died when she was four years old. Her mother, a painter and musician, introduced her to the classics, of which she remained fond throughout her life. Payne-Gaposchkin recalled that Homer's *Odyssey* was the first book her mother read to her as a child. She knew Latin by the time she was 12 years old, became fluent in French and German, and showed an early interest in botany and algebra. As a schoolgirl in London she was influenced by the works of Isaac Newton, Thomas Huxley, and Emmanuel Swedenborg.

In 1919 she won a scholarship to Newnham College at Cambridge University, where she studied botany, chemistry, and physics. During her studies there, she became fascinated with astronomy after attending a lecture on Albert Einstein's theory of relativity given by Sir Arthur Eddington, the university's foremost astronomer. Upon completion of her studies in 1923 (at that time women were not granted degrees at Cambridge), Payne-Gaposchkin sought and obtained a Pickering Fellowship (an award for female students) from Harvard to study under Harlow Shapley, the newly appointed director of the Harvard Observatory. Thus, Payne-Gaposchkin embarked for the United States, hoping to find better opportunities as a woman in astronomy. Harvard Observatory in Boston, Massachusetts, became her home for the rest of her career—a "stony-hearted stepmother," she was said to have called it.

Payne-Gaposchkin's career at Harvard began in 1925, when she was given an ambiguous staff position at the Harvard Observatory. By that time she had already published six papers on her research in the field of stellar atmospheres. That same year, she was awarded the first-ever Ph.D. in astronomy at Radcliffe. Her doctoral dissertation, *Stellar Atmospheres,* was published as Monograph No. 1 of the Harvard Observatory. A pioneering work in the field, it was the first paper written on the subject and was the first research to apply Indian physicist Meghnad Saha's recent theory of ionization (the process by which particles become electrically charged by gaining or losing electrons) to the science of measuring the temperature and chemical density of stars. However, she was discouraged in her views and was convinced to alter them by Henry Norris Russell, a renowned astronomer at Princeton who several years later reached her same conclusions and published them, thereby receiving credit for their origin. Despite this, Payne-Gaposchkin's research remains highly regarded today; Otto Struve, a notable astronomer of the period, was quoted in *Mercury* magazine as saying that *Stellar Atmospheres* was "undoubtedly the most brilliant Ph.D. thesis ever written in astronomy."

In 1926 when she was 26 years old, she became the youngest scientist to be listed in *American Men of Science.* But her position at Harvard Observatory remained unacknowledged and unofficial. It was not until 1938 that her work as a lecturer and researcher was recognized and she was granted the title of astronomer, which she later requested to be changed to Phillips Astronomer. From 1925 until 1938 she was considered a technical assistant to Shapley, and none of the courses she taught were listed in the Harvard catalogue until 1945. Finally, in 1956 when her colleague Donald Menzel replaced Shapley as director of the Harvard Observatory, Payne-Gaposchkin was "promoted" to professor, given an appropriate salary, and named chairman of the Department of Astronomy—the first woman to hold a position at Harvard University that was not expressly designated for a woman.

Payne-Gaposchkin's years at Harvard remained productive despite her scant recognition. She was a tireless researcher with a prodigious memory and an encyclopedic knowledge of science. She devoted a large part of her research to the study of stellar magnitudes and distances. Following her 1934 marriage to Gaposchkin, a Russian emigre astronomer, the couple pioneered research into variable stars (stars whose luminosity fluctuates), including research on the structure of the Milky Way and the nearby galaxies known as the Magellanic Clouds. Through their studies they made over two million magnitude estimates of the variable stars in the Magellanic Clouds.

From the 1920s until Payne-Gaposchkin's death on December 7, 1979, she published over 150 papers and several monographs, including "The Stars of High Luminosity" (1930), a virtual encyclopedia of astrophysics, and *Variable Stars* (1938), a standard reference book of astronomy written with her husband. She also published four books in the 1950s on the subject of stars and stellar evolution. Moreover, though she retired from her academic post at Harvard in 1966, becoming Emeritus Professor of Harvard University the following year, she continued to write and conduct research until her death. Her autobiography, writings collected after her death by her daughter, Katherine Haramundanis, was entitled *Cecilia Payne-Gaposchkin: An Autobiography and Other Recollections* and was published in 1984.

Payne-Gaposchkin was elected to the Royal Astronomical Society while she was a student at Cambridge in 1923, and the following year she was granted membership in the American Astronomical Society. She became a citizen of the United States in 1931. She and her husband had three children: Edward, born in 1935, Katherine, born in 1937, and Peter, born in 1940—a noted programmer analyst and physicist in his own right. In 1934 Payne-Gaposchkin received the Annie J. Cannon Prize for significant contributions to astronomy from the American Astronomical Society. In 1936 she was elected to membership in the American Philosophical Society. Among her honorary degrees and medals, awarded in recognition of her contributions to science, are honorary doctorates of science from Wilson College (1942), Smith College (1943), Western College (1951), Colby College (1958), and Women's Medical College of Philadelphia (1961), as well as an honorary master of arts and doctorate of science from Cambridge University, England (1952). She won the Award of Merit from Radcliffe College in 1952, the Rittenhouse Medal of the Franklin Institute in 1961, and was the first woman to receive the Henry Norris Russell Prize of the American Astronomical Society in 1976. In 1977 the minor planet 1974 CA was named Payne-Gaposchkin in her honor.

Payne-Gaposchkin is remembered as a woman of boundless enthusiasm who refused to give up her career at a time when married women with children were expected to do so; she once shocked her superiors by giving a lecture when she was five months pregnant. Jesse Greenstein, astronomer at the California Institute of Technology and friend of Payne-Gaposchkin, recalled in *The Sciences* magazine that "she was charming and humorous," a person given to quoting Shakespeare, T.S. Eliot, and Gilbert and Sullivan. Her daughter remembers her in the autobiography *Cecilia Payne-Gaposchkin* as a "world traveler, . . . an inspired seamstress, an inventive knitter and a voracious reader." Quoted in *Sky and Telescope,* Payne-Gaposchkin revealed that nothing compares to "the emotional thrill of being the first person in the history of the world to see something or to understand something."

Further Reading

Abir-Am, P. and D. Outram, editors, *Uneasy Careers and Intimate Lives: Women in Science 1789–1979,* Rutgers University Press, 1987.

Kass-Simon, G. and Patricia Farnes, editors, *Women of Science: Righting the Record,* Indiana University Press, 1990.

Bartusiak, Marcia, "The Stuff of Stars," in *The Sciences,* September/October, 1993, pp. 34–39.

Dobson, Andrea K. and Katherine Bracher, "A Historical Introduction to Women in Astronomy," in *Mercury,* January/February 1992, pp. 4–15.

Lankford, John, "Explicating an Autobiography," in *Isis,* March 1985, pp. 80–83.

Lankford, John and Ricky L. Slavings, "Gender and Science: Women in American Astronomy, 1859–1940," in *Physics Today,* March 1990, pp. 58–65.

Smith, E., "Cecilia Payne-Gaposchkin," in *Physics Today,* June 1980, pp. 64–66.

Whitney, C., "Cecilia Payne-Gaposchkin: An Astronomer's Astronomer," in *Sky and Telescope,* March 1980, page 212–214. □

Octavio Paz (dancing with woman)

Octavio Paz

The Mexican diplomat, playwright, and essayist, Octavio Paz (born 1914) was internationally regarded as one of the principal poets of the twentieth century. His work was formally recognized in 1990 when he was awarded the Nobel Prize in literature, the first Mexican to be so honored.

"Poetry," wrote Octavio Paz in *El arco y la lira* (*The Bow and the Lyre*), "is knowledge, salvation, power, abandonment. An operation capable of changing the world, poetic activity is revolutionary by nature; a spiritual exercise, it is a means of interior liberation." According to Paz, poetry is a form of transcendence, removing the self from history and offering in its place a vision of pure or essential being and time. Poetry is sacred, providing salvation in a secular world.

Paz was born March 31, 1914, to a distinguished Mexican family. His father, a lawyer from a mixed Spanish and Indian background, participated in the Mexican Revolution and was politically prominent. The family lost much of its wealth, however. While Paz was growing up they could not maintain the grand house near Mexico City in which they lived. The elegant furnishings, Paz once said, had to be moved to different parts of the house as various rooms became uninhabitable. For a while he occupied a room with one of its walls gone and only screens to keep out the weather. The surrealist character of his early work may owe something to that curious world he knew as a boy.

Although reared as a Roman Catholic, he broke from the Church when he was still young. His poetry may perhaps be understood in part as an effort to find a substitute for it. He published his first book in 1933 when he was 19. Four years later he went to Spain and participated in the civil war there. In Paris and then back in Mexico he met various members of the surrealist movement. Returning to Europe once again, he met André Breton, and his association with surrealism deepened. Paz was soon recognized as a major surrealist poet. *¿Aguila o sol?* (1950) collects some of his strongest work from that period.

Surrealism may have appealed to Paz partly because of its effort to locate a reality greater than that immediate to the senses. Oriental philosophy promised a similar release from the material world. Paz not only became a profound student of Eastern culture, but lived for a while in Japan. Between 1962 and 1968 he served as the Mexican ambassador to India. He resigned in 1968 as a protest against the massacre of student demonstrators by the Mexican government.

The Eastern vision of a non-dualistic, non-Cartesian universe is central to Paz's work. For the Hindu, as he told Rita Guibert in an interview, the real is outside time and history. So is it in his poetry, too. Eastern philosophy, like surrealism, probably did not so much influence Paz as provide correspondences or parallels to central ambitions in his poetry. It is Mexico which seems to be the great abiding fact in his work. In a sense, Paz's poetry begins with the recognition that isolation and solitude are inevitable for everyone, and that they are especially characteristic of Mexican life. The individual is divided not only from the world but also from his or her true self. "We are condemned to live alone," he wrote in *El larerinto de la soledad* (*The Labyrinth of Solitude*). "Self-discovery is above all the realization that we are alone: it is the opening of an impalpable, transparent wall—that of our consciousness—between the world and ourselves."

Solitude can be transcended both in the creation of poems and in the re-creation which occurs whenever they are understood. The function of the poem then is essentially ritualistic. It exorcises the anxieties and fears that rise from the inevitable alienation of modern life and, through rhythmic configuration and image, initiates the reader into an awareness beyond time. In part the poem derives its power from eros as in the world of medieval troubadours for whom transfiguration was possible through love and sexuality.

In addition to his poetry, Paz was a major critic of his country's social and political life. In a succession of books beginning with *El larerinto de la soledad,* he saw the Mexican dilemma as arising in part from the fact that its culture has roots in both Spanish colonial and native Indian traditions. One tradition buttresses the other in maintaining a hierarchical and in some ways conservative society, vastly different from the world to the north. The United States seems either to have no origins or to have origins that are

fundamentally European, but Mexican culture derives from Spain and the Counter-Reformation on the one hand and distinctly non-European cultures and values on the other. The United States and Mexico share the same continent, but their cultures and values are hugely different.

Paz was very interested in the world to his north. He lived at various times in the United States and taught at Harvard and the University of Texas. His only play is an adaptation of Nathaniel Hawthorne's "Rappaccini's Daughter," and his poems include meditations on John Cage and Joseph Cornell, those masters of silence and stillness. Perhaps the American poet who most shares his epic and transcendent poetics is Walt Whitman.

Paz also published books on Marcel Duchamp and Claude Lévi-Strauss. He wrote on politics, religion, anthropology, archaeology, and poetics. He edited various anthologies and translated from Japanese, Portuguese, English, French, Swedish, and other languages. He also worked on joint projects with various artists and edited a series of literary magazines. He taught at various universities, including Cambridge.

Paz distinguished himself as a diplomat, critic, editor, translator, playwright, and essayist, but it was as a poet that he was internationally known. His poetic theories are widely respected, and his poetry is considered among the best any poet of his generation has yet published. This was confirmed by the Swedish Academy of Letters, which awarded Paz the 1990 Nobel Prize in literature, citing his work's "sensuous intelligence and humanistic integrity." The Academy also quoted one of his love poems:

Woman
fountain in the night.
I am bound to her quiet flowing

Since winning the Nobel Prize, Paz has continued to write. In 1994 he produced *The Double Flame: Love and Eroticism,* an exploration of the current state of love in Western cultures. Two other prose pieces from 1994 include *Essays on Mexican Art* and *My Life with the Wave.*

Further Reading

A great poet often attracts prominent poets as translators, and much of Paz's work is available in excellent English versions. Muriel Rukeyser was among his first translators, and her version of "Sun Stone" is itself a major poem. All of his poetry from 1957 to 1987 has been translated by Eliot Weinberger, and individual poems have been translated by Elizabeth Bishop, Paul Blackburn, Denise Levertov, Mark Strand, Charles Tomlinson, and William Carlos Williams, among others. The two major collections in English are *Early Poems: 1935-1955* (1973) and *The Collected Poems of Octavio Paz: 1957-1987* (1987), edited by Eliot Weinberger. The essential prose works include *The Labyrinth of Solitude,* translated by Lysander Kemp (1961), and *The Bow and the Lyre,* translated by Ruth L. C. Simms (1973). Paz generated a formidable amount of commentary in English as well as Spanish. See especially *The Perpetual Present: The Poetry and Prose of Octavio Paz,* edited by Ivar Ivask (1973) and *Toward Octavio Paz: A Reading of His Major Poems, 1957-1976* by John M. Fein (1986). □

Victor Paz Estenssoro

Victor Paz Estenssoro (born 1907) was a reformer, political thinker, and president of Bolivia. He instituted a series of widespread reforms that revolutionized Bolivian society.

Victor Paz was born to a middle-class family of mixed Spanish and Indian blood in the small and isolated northeast town of Tarija in 1907. He received his education at the University Mayor de San Andrés in La Paz and later studied economics in Germany. Paz worked in the government as a senior finance official from 1932 to 1933. During the Chaco War with Paraguay (1932-1935), he fought in the infantry, rose to the rank of captain, and was decorated for heroism.

After the war Paz filled a succession of government posts that brought him increasingly into the world of Bolivian politics. He became the deputy for his home in Tarija from 1938 to 1939. He taught economic history at La Paz University from 1939 to 1941. In 1940 he was promoted to the post of national deputy for Tarija, a post he would hold until 1943.

As part of the general intellectual and social unrest sweeping the country after the Chaco War, Paz helped to found the National Revolutionary Movement (MNR), a radical political party, in 1942.

The MNR reflected a need to change Bolivian society and institute reform on all levels. Its most active segments, liberal intellectuals and restive army officers, began plotting immediately. Some of their pronouncements began to sound similar to the fascist doctrines then current in the political world.

In 1943 Paz and the MNR aided an army coup which ousted president Enrique Peñaranda. The new president, Major Gualberto Villaroel, drew heavily upon the leadership of the MNR for his cabinet, appointing Paz minister of finance. The United States, likening the MNR to fascism, refused to recognize the new government. Soon the MNR leaders had been weeded out of the government by Villaroel, who wanted to disassociate himself from them. In 1946 Paz gave up his post at the ministry of finance and fled to Buenos Aires.

In Exile

In his Argentine exile, Paz studied the techniques and rhetoric of dictator, Juan Perón, a man who relied heavily upon the intense nationalism of the common people to keep himself in power. He was in Argentina when Villaroel's regime was brought down in a violent revolution. The President was shot and then hung from a lamp post in front of the presidential palace.

From Buenos Aires, with the protection of Perón, Paz began planning a comeback. With other MNR leaders in Bolivia and Argentina, he planned the abortive 1949 coup. Despite its failure, Paz and the MNR gained increased pop-

ularity among Bolivians who were becoming disillusioned with their traditional political leaders.

In 1951 the rightist regime in power, feeling falsely secure, issued a call for open elections. Despite government pressure and a very restricted franchise, which prohibited the illiterate majority from voting, the government candidate placed a poor second to Paz. Since he had not won a clear majority, however, the government threw the election into the very conservative Congress for a predictable anti-Paz decision. But before the Congress could vote, the military intervened, taking over the nation and banning the MNR as a subversive party.

Rebellion and Reform

The people of Bolivia reacted swiftly; the miners rose against the government in the mountains, and in La Paz the urban proletariat erupted in bloody street fighting. When the smoke cleared, it was apparent that, for the first time in history, the Bolivian people had become involved.

Paz returned from exile in May 1952 and was duly installed as president. Hernán Siles Zuazo became his vice president, and Juan Lechín, radical chief of the armed miners, was appointed secretary of labor. The MNR government lived up to its promises of reform at once. The great tin mines were nationalized, the army was weakened and counter-balanced by a workers' militia, and a sweeping land reform program was promulgated. Great landed estates were divided among the landless peasantry. The Quechua and Aymara Indians were returned their original lands and these all but forgotten people were integrated into Bolivia's political and economic systems. With the economic support of the United States, which saw in Paz and the MNR as a viable alternative to communism, a development plan was launched in 1954. The government was able to resist and repress a conservative reaction.

By the time Paz left the presidency in 1956, to become ambassador to England, Bolivia had been transformed. The election itself, which gave power to Siles Zuazo, saw all Bolivians over the age of 21 eligible to vote for the first time in history. Paz was back in Bolivia for the 1960 elections, which he easily won. In 1961 he announced an ambitious ten-year plan for Bolivia. Predicated on large amounts of US aid, the plan aimed at developing the forgotten eastern region of Bolivia—the Beni and Santa Cruz lowlands. The same year a new constitution was passed which allowed Paz to be continually reelected (unusual in Latin America).

It soon became clear that Paz was championing himself more than the MNR as a movement, and the party began to become seriously fragmented. By 1963 he had chosen the moderate General Rène Barrientos Ortuño of the air force, as his running mate for the coming elections. 1964 saw rising opposition among conservatives to Paz's continuing rule within the MNR and to the MNR itself. Unrest was becoming endemic by the time Paz and Barrientos won the October elections. On November 4 Vice-President Barrientos, acting "to save the nation," launched a coup which threw Paz out of power. In the name of order, Barrientos and the military ruled until his election in 1966. Paz, the self-proclaimed "indispensable man," settled into exile first in England as a professor of economics at London University, and then in Lima, Peru as a lecturer in economics at the National English University.

Returning from exile, he was again elected president in 1985, and was successful in implementing more economic reforms. These "shock therapy" programs reversed a hyperinflationary process that had seen Bolivia's annual rate of inflation rise to 24,000 percent. Paz's reforms reduced this to a respectable ten to twenty percent and made the Bolivian economy one of the most respected in South America. Paz's economic reforms were used as a blueprint for many countries in Eastern European. During his second period in office Paz assisted the US in its drug enforcement efforts. He attempted to solve the ever-persistent problems of high infant mortality and illiteracy.

Paz left office at the conclusion of his term in 1989 and was replaced by Jaime Paz Zamora in Bolivia's third successive democratic presidential election. Zamora was elected by the Bolivian Congress after the MNR candidate, Gonzalo Sanchez de Lazado failed to win a majority. This peaceful transition of power was a testament to Paz's legacy as a dominant figure in Bolivian politics and history.

Further Reading

Perhaps the best work on Paz and his political life is Robert J. Alexander, *The Bolivian National Revolution* (1958). Also informative is Alberto Ostria Gutierrez, *The Tragedy of Bolivia: A People Crucified* (1958). For a more detailed discussion of the 1966 Bolivian coup, consult William Handforth Brill

Military Intervention in Bolivia: The Overthrow of Paz Estenssoro and the MNR (1967). For a more general treatment see Harold Osborne, *Bolivia: A Land Divided* (1954; 3d ed. 1964). There is a brief biography of Paz located at the A&E Entertainment Networks Website at www.biography.com. There is also some more general history on Paz and the Bolivian nation and government maintained at Roberto Ortiz de Zarate's Political Datasets at www.ehu.es and a site maintained by Bolivian CAFÉ at jaguar.pg.cc.md.us. □

Péter Pázmány

The Hungarian prelate Péter Pázmány (1570-1637), one of the great figures of the Counter Reformation, restored Roman Catholicism to Hungary. A superb stylist, he has been hailed as the father of modern Hungarian prose.

Péter Pázmány was born into a noble Protestant family at Nagyvárad on Oct. 4, 1570. Guided by his Roman Catholic stepmother, he became a convert at the age of 13. Pázmány attended the Jesuit college at Kolozsvár, entering the Jesuit novitiate at Cracow in 1587. He studied philosophy in Vienna and theology in Rome under Gabriel Vásquez and Robert Bellarmine. In 1598 Pázmány became professor of philosophy at the University of Graz. In 1601 he began a 2-year visit to Hungary, where he initiated his brilliant literary career with his *Answer to Stephen Magyary*, the first Catholic controversial work in the Hungarian language. Between 1603 and 1607 Pázmány again taught at Graz. There, continuing to write in Hungarian, he became known for the vigor and lucidity of his prose. In 1607, at the invitation of the archbishop of Esztergom and primate of Hungary, Ferenc Forgács, Pázmány returned to Hungary.

Pázmány then began a long period dedicated to reclaiming Catholic losses in Hungary. At first he concentrated on the Protestant aristocracy, traveling from castle to castle, debating and exhorting key families to return to the Roman Catholic Church. More than 30 of these families did so. In 1613 Pázmány produced the greatest of his controversial writings, *A Guide to Divine Truth,* a work that he modeled on the *Controversies* of Robert Bellarmine.

In 1616 Pázmány reached a major turning point in his life. In October 1615 Archbishop Forgács had died. The Emperor wanted Pázmány to succeed as primate of Hungary. Since the Jesuit Constitutions forbade the acceptance of positions of honor, Pope Paul V transferred Pázmány from the Society of Jesus to the Order of Somaschi, and in 1616 Pázmány was consecrated archbishop of Esztergom. As a promoter of ecclesiastical reform, he founded the Pázmáneum at the University of Vienna for the training of Hungarian priests, supported the Collegium Germanicum-Hungaricum in Rome, held frequent synods, carried out the decrees of the Council of Trent, introduced the Roman Missal and Breviary throughout Hungary, supported Jesuit schools, and founded the University of Nagyszombat (now

the University of Budapest), which he entrusted to the Jesuits. In 1629 Pázmány was made a cardinal.

Despite his esteem for the Hapsburgs, Pázmány fought against Austrian encroachments on Hungarian identity. He failed in an important diplomatic venture in Rome. During the Thirty Years War Pázmány unsuccessfully urged Pope Urban VIII to condemn the Franco-Swedish alliance and to join a league of Catholic princes against Gustavus ll and the German Protestants. A disappointed man, Pázmány severely criticized the Pope and the Roman Curia. In 1635 he published his last great literary work, *Sermons for Sundays and Holydays*. Pázmány died at Pozsony on March 19, 1637.

Further Reading

Imre Lukinich, *A History of Hungary in Biographical Sketches* (trans. 1937), has a study of Pázmány. Pázmány's career is discussed briefly in Denis Sinor, *History of Hungary* (1959), and Carlile Aylmer Macartney, *Hungary: A Short History* (1962). □

Jaime Paz Zamora

Jaime Paz Zamora (born 1939) moved from being an extreme leftist revolutionary to become a middle-of-the-road president of Bolivia. His party, the Move-

ment of the Revolutionary Left, also evolved over a period of 20 years.

Jaime Paz Zamora was born on April 15, 1939, in the city of Cochabamba. His father was a general in the Bolivian army. Victor Paz Estenssoro, an influential Bolivian politician, was his uncle. Paz Zamora attended the Jesuit high school in Sucre and studied for the priesthood at a seminary in Cordoba, Argentina. He abandoned that career shortly before being ordained. Later, he studied social sciences at the Catholic University of Louvain, Belgium.

Academics

Upon returning to Bolivia in the mid 1960s, Paz Zamora taught sociology and international relations at San Andrés University in La Paz. He joined the Christian Democratic Party, but gradually adopted more radical politics. In 1970 some members of his Revolutionary Christian Democratic Party (PDC-R) participated in a brief and ill-fated guerrilla action in which Paz Zamora's brother died.

Movement of the Revolutionary Left

Paz Zamora was among the founders of MIR (Movement of the Revolutionary Left) in 1971. This party drew its support from a broad spectrum of organizations and ideological currents. Adopting an extremely radical posture to the left of orthodox communist parties, MIR called for Bolivia's "national liberation" from imperialism through the cre-

ation of a "social revolutionary block" of peasants, workers, and middle-class groups. It represented a revival of revolutionary nationalism. From the beginning, the party showed internal cleavages. During the authoritarian regime of General Hugo Banzer (1971-1978), MIR and other leftist organizations were outlawed and its leaders persecuted. Paz Zamora spent most of these years either in exile or underground in Bolivia, coordinating MIR's resistance campaign against the Banzer regime. For these activities he was imprisoned in 1974.

Between 1978 and 1982, when Bolivia plunged into political and economic chaos, Paz Zamora emerged as a prominent figure in national politics. He led MIR into a moderate left-of-center alliance, the Democratic and Popular Union (UDP). This group achieved a growing plurality of votes in two national elections in 1979 and 1980, but was denied power. In both elections Paz Zamora stood as candidate for the vice-presidency beside the UDP's presidential candidate, Hernan Siles Suazo, leader of the left wing of the National Revolutionary Movement. During the 1980 electoral campaign Paz Zamora narrowly escaped death when the small plane carrying him and four other UDP leaders to campaign crashed immediately after taking off from La Paz airport. The remaining passengers and crew were killed.

In January 1981, during the brutal and corrupt Garcia Meza military regime, security forces tortured and killed eight MIR leaders in La Paz. In October 1982, however, the military was forced to hand over power to the recognized winners of the June 1980 elections and Paz Zamora became Bolivian vice-president in the UDP administration headed by Siles Suazo. MIR had taken increasingly moderate political stances since the late 1970s, becoming the Bolivian affiliate of the Socialist International.

Only three months after assuming office, in January 1983, the MIR cabinet ministers collectively resigned from the increasingly unstable Siles Suazo administration because of disagreements over economic policies. Paz Zamora stayed on as vice-president until December of 1984 when he resigned in order to run for president in the June 1985 elections. At this point the old cleavages within MIR came to the surface and the party broke into three different movements. Paz Zamora became undisputed leader of the trunk MIR, now a social-democratic, populist party devoid of any Marxist leanings.

From Vice-President to President

In the June 1985 elections Paz Zamora came in third with ten percent of the vote. Two months later his uncle, Victor Paz Estenssoro, candidate of the MNR, once again became president. He immediately embarked upon a rigorous economic austerity program which succeeded in bringing down inflation and reducing the foreign debt at a high cost to miners, industrial workers, and the urban poor. Paz Zamora and MIR pursued a moderate congressional opposition to his uncle's administration, which depended on support from the major right-wing party. MIR became the second strongest party in the municipal elections of December 1987.

In the elections of May 1989, Paz Zamora, as presidential candidate of MIR, came in third with nearly 20 percent of the votes. During the campaign no major ideological differences emerged between Paz Zamora and his two major conservative competitors. Calling for the creation of a "new majority," he sought to portray a young, dynamic image, often compared to the Kennedy mystique. He received the backing of Hugo Banzer's Democratic National Action Party (AND) for the congressional run-off elections, virtually assuring his victory. Paz Zamora took office as Bolivia's president on August 6, 1989, heading a formal MIR-AND coalition. As late as the mid 1980s a coalition with Banzer would have been unthinkable. But by 1989 Paz Zamora and his party had followed the conservatives in abandoning many of the state-interventionist policies in place since the 1952 MNR-led revolution.

The Paz Zamora Administration

During his first year in office, Paz Zamora continued liberal economic policies designed by Harvard economist Jeffrey Sacks. Hoping to create the "institutional and juridical framework of the new Bolivian state," Paz Zamora and his team sought to reduce the foreign debt, attract investment in mining and industry, and privatize government-held businesses, including the national airline and railroad companies. A new foreign investment law passed in September 1990 lifted curbs on capital transfers. A bill liberalizing foreign investments in joint mining ventures was pending in Congress in late 1990. Paz Zamora was walking a tightrope between demands by his conservative coalition partner for faster economic liberalization and protests by the unions, small retail merchants, and peasants about a "sell-out" of Bolivia. In several instances he had to slow down or retrench in the face of adamant popular protests. Paz Zamora also took up a favorite theme of Bolivian nationalism—access to the Pacific Ocean. In bilateral negotiations in December of 1989 he achieved approval from Peru's president, Alan Garcia, for a Bolivian corridor to the sea in Chilean (formerly Peruvian) territory. This concession was immediately rejected by Santiago.

Paz Zamora found himself caught between interest in receiving economic assistance from the United States and his reluctance to allow the U.S. military to form an alliance with Bolivian forces to fight drug production. His government was pushing hard to receive more funds from the U.S. for coca crop substitution, but resisted pressures to involve the army in drug eradication programs. Arguing that military intervention would be ineffective and would risk undermining fragile civilian control of the Bolivian military, Paz Zamora dragged his feet until economic threats forced him to allow U.S. Special Forces to train Bolivian army personnel. The concession was unpopular at home and fueled anti-American feelings. Armed forces officials eventually called for the expulsion of U.S. drug agents.

Paz Zamora passed the presidential baton to the MNR's Sanchez de Lozada in 1993. Lozada had defeated the AND/MIR coalition's candidate by a 34 percent to 20 percent margin in an election deemed fair by observers. In 1997

General Hugo Banzer was returned to power. Paz Zamora placed in third, winning 17 percent of the vote.

Further Reading

No biography of Paz Zamora exists in English. The best, although opinionated, political history of contemporary Bolivia is James Dunkerley's *Rebellion in the Veins; Political Struggle in Bolivia, 1952-1982* (1984). Solid structural analyses are offered by Jerry Ladman, editor, *Modern-Day Bolivia, Legacy of the Revolution and Prospects for the Future* (1982) and James M. Malloy and Eduardo Gamarra, *Revolution and Reaction: Bolivia 1964-1985* (1988). The best overall history in English is still Herbert S. Klein, *Bolivia, The Evolution of a Multi-Ethnic Society* (1982).

Accounts of Paz Zamora's years as president, including discussion of his resistance to the involvement of the United States military in fighting drug production, can be found on the Internet in background notes prepared by the National Trade Data Bank of the U.S. Department of Commerce and posted in April 1997, in a Lindesmith Center's drug policy briefing paper entitled ''A Fundamentally Flawed Strategy: the U.S. 'War on Drugs' in Bolivia,'' (September 18, 1991) and in a paper written by USAF Major Antonio L. Pala entitled ''The Increased Role of Latin American Armed Forces in UN Peacekeeping: Opportunities and Challenges.'' □

Elizabeth Palmer Peabody

Elizabeth Palmer Peabody (1804-1894), an American educator, author, and prominent member of the New England intellectual community, promoted the new kindergarten movement in the United States.

Elizabeth Peabody was born in Billerica, Mass., on May 16, 1804. Her sister Mary married educator Horace Mann, and her sister Sophia married author Nathaniel Hawthorne. Elizabeth's early education was at her mother's schools in Salem and Lancaster, Mass., where, although still a child, she did much of the instruction. This experience nourished her sense of mission and reform.

Beginning in 1820, Peabody made a number of unsuccessful attempts to establish her own schools, meanwhile serving as unpaid secretary to William Ellery Channing, the Unitarian leader. Her *Reminiscences of William Ellery Channing, D.D.* (1880) discloses the extensive influence of Channing on her career and educational thought. In 1834 she became Bronson Alcott's assistant in the famous Temple School in Boston, described in her *Record of a School* (1835). When it closed, she opened a bookstore and publishing business which provided an outlet for the early efforts of Hawthorne and Margaret Fuller. The store endured for 10 years, becoming a transcendentalist salon. In addition, in 1842-1843 she published the *Dial,* a journal of transcendentalist opinion.

Peabody returned to her first interest, education, in 1845. Although teaching, she found time to write grammar and history texts and, in 1849, to establish a short-lived literary journal, *Aesthetic Papers.* She also toured to promote the study of history and wrote the *Chronological History of the United States* (1865).

Increasingly Peabody's attention turned to the education of the very young, and from 1860 to 1880 she devoted herself to organizing kindergartens along lines established by the German educator Friedrich Froebel. Her purpose was to develop children ''morally and spiritually as well as intellectually'' and ''to awaken the feelings of harmony, beauty, and conscience'' in the pupils. Her efforts resulted in a publicly supported kindergarten in Boston in 1860, the first in the country. But uncertainty about the institutions's effectiveness led her to make a pilgrimage to Germany in 1867 to observe Froebel's disciples. After returning she furthered the cause through public lectures and, from 1873 to 1875, as publisher of the *Kindergarten Messenger.*

Peabody's remaining years were absorbed in championing Native American education, lecturing in Alcott's Concord School of Philosophy, and writing. Despite failing vision she finished *Last Evening with Allston* (1886), a tribute to the Boston painter and poet Washington Allston, and a collection of her earlier essays. She died on Jan. 3, 1894.

Further Reading

Ruth M. Baylor, *Elizabeth Palmer Peabody: Kindergarten Pioneer* (1965), is a thoroughly documented study with an excellent bibliography. Louise H. Tharp, *The Peabody Sisters of Salem* (1950), is a more popular treatment and, although sometimes impressionistic, is well written. See also the essay on Miss Peabody in Gladys Brooks, *Three Wise Virgins* (1957).

Additional Sources

Tharp, Louise Hall, *The Peabody sisters of Salem,* Boston: Little, Brown, 1988. ☐

George Peabody

George Peabody (1795-1869), American merchant, financier, and philanthropist, amassed a fortune during his business career. He began as a merchant and ended as a banker and dealer in American securities in England.

B orn on Feb. 18, 1795, in Danvers, Mass., George Peabody had a limited education before being apprenticed to a grocer at the age of 11. He subsequently was involved in other mercantile establishments, served briefly in the War of 1812, and became a partner of Elisha Riggs in a wholesale dry-goods establishment in Georgetown, D.C., in 1812. The partners opened branches in Baltimore, New York, and Philadelphia, and Peabody went to London in 1827. When Riggs retired 2 years later, Peabody became the senior partner. He settled permanently in England in 1837.

Peabody arrived on London's financial scene with some appreciation of the need for foreign capital in America and the opportunities which awaited those involved in such capital movements. In 1835 he arranged for a substantial loan for Maryland in London. A year later he was one of the incorporators and the president of the Eastern Railroad—one of the first successful railroads in New England. His firm, George Peabody and Company, specialized in foreign exchange and American securities. In 1843 he ended his mercantile pursuits, and over the next 20 years he accumulated the bulk of his $12 million fortune acting as an international banker and offering diversified services to British and American clients. He also acted as an unofficial ambassador to England, strengthening Anglo-American ties whenever possible.

Operating at a time when American demand for foreign capital was almost insatiable, Peabody showed a sensitivity to current conditions that enabled his firm to sidestep the effects of the Panic of 1837, which destroyed some of his competitors. During the years that followed, while American securities were declining and American credit was under severe attack, he bought substantial amounts of depressed securities and influenced American businesses and states and other political entities to honor their obligations to foreign bondholders. The consequence was great personal advantage to Peabody and Company as well as considerable benefit to the political entities involved when normal economic conditions were restored. The firm adopted similar tactics during the Panic of 1857. Once again, Peabody and Company assisted by massive credits extended to American entities by British banks, and the company profited greatly because its confidence in the long-range prospects of the American economy had led it to purchase great amounts of depressed American securities.

While engaged in international banking and acting as the chief institution funneling British capital into the United States, Peabody personally began the systematic program of donations which made him the world's first great philanthropist. The bulk of his fortune went to various scientific and educational institutions and to programs supporting the poor of England and the United States.

Further Reading

Accounts of Peabody are Philip Whitwell Wilson, *George Peabody, Esq.: An Interpretation* (1926), Edwin Palmer Hoyt, *The Peabody Influence: How a Great New England Family Helped To Build America* (1968), and Franklin Parker, *George Peabody: A Biography* (1971). An early brief view is Jabez Lamar Monroe Curry, *A Brief Sketch of George Peabody* (1898; repr. 1969). For useful background see Lewis Corey, *The House of Morgan* (1930).

Additional Sources

Hidy, Muriel E., *George Peabody, merchant and financier: 1829-1854,* New York: Arno Press, 1978 i.e. 1979.
Parker, Franklin, *George Peabody, a biography,* Nashville: Vanderbilt University Press, 1995. ☐

Thomas Love Peacock

The work of the English novelist and satirist Thomas Love Peacock (1785-1866) is distinguished by its incisive penetration of the intellectual tendencies of his time. He ranks high as a comic novelist of ideas.

Thomas Love Peacock, the son of a London merchant, was educated for a business career and not for a life of artistic pursuits. Finding work in an office uncongenial, he was able to leave his job and to live for a while on his inherited income. During these years he began to write poetry, and he became a close friend of Percy Bysshe Shelley. After the poet's death, Peacock became his literary executor and edited a volume of memorials. Peacock married Jane Gryffydh, a lady mentioned in glowing terms in Shelley's poem "Letter to Maria Gisborne."

In this period Peacock also began to write the satirical novels on which his reputation rests. The first group includes *Headlong Hall* (1815), *Melincourt* (1817), and *Nightmare Abbey* (1818). His pattern in these works was to dispense with all but the most mechanical plotting and to devote his attention to extended conversations between the inhabitants and guests at characteristic English country houses. *Headlong Hall* includes Mr. Foster, an optimist; Mr. Escot, a pessimist; Mr. Jenkinson, an advocate of the status quo; and Dr. Gaster, a minister more distinguished by his worldliness than by his piety. *Melincourt* has a more inte-

grated plot, centering on the wooing of a wealthy heiress. Its main interest lies, however, in its satirical portraits of William Wordsworth, Samuel Taylor Coleridge, Robert Southey, Thomas Malthus, and Lord Monboddo. *Nightmare Abbey* continues the satire of poets and philosophers of the day, including Coleridge, Lord Byron, and Shelley.

In 1819 Peacock joined the East India Company and became a competent and successful executive of colonial affairs. He continued his imaginative writing. In addition to poetry, he published two romance-novels dealing with fairy-tale plots and characters. *Maid Marian* (1822) is set in medieval England and concerns the legendary exploits of Robin Hood's band. *The Misfortunes of Elphin* (1829) is a parody of the Arthurian legend in which King Arthur, Queen Guinevere, and the Welsh bard Taliesin figure.

After these forays into the romance-novel, Peacock returned to his true métier with another satirical novel, *Crotchet Castle* (1831). Leading intellectual figures of the day satirized in this work include Coleridge, the rigorous school of Scottish economic thinkers, and those who joined in the period's growing tendency to glorify the Middle Ages. Perhaps the most remarkable achievement of Peacock's career was, however, his production of another novel of the same type almost 30 years afterward. *Gryll Grange* (1860) shows the marks of age in its tendency to ramble from scholarly to domestic subjects and in its avoidance of personal satire of leading intellectual figures. *Gryll Grange* was Peacock's last novel. He was one of the most incisive commentators on the cultural life of England in the first half of the 19th century.

Further Reading

The most readable biography of Peacock is Carl Van Doren, *The Life of Thomas Love Peacock* (1911; repr. 1966). The best critical studies are Howard Mills, *Peacock: His Circle and His Age* (1968), and Carl Dawson, *His Fine Wit* (1970).

Additional Sources

Freeman, A. Martin (Alexander Martin), *Thomas Love Peacock: a critical study,* Philadelphia: R. West, 1977. ☐

Charles Willson Peale

Charles Willson Peale (1741-1827), American painter and scientist, was a solid and sometimes strikingly original painter, as well as an inventor and a museum founder.

Charles Willson Peale was born in Queen Annes Country, MD, on April 15, 1741. His father was an adventurer from Rutlandshire, England, who emigrated to Maryland after he had been caught embezzling. In Maryland he took a position as a schoolmaster and married. He died, leaving no inheritance, when Charles was 9, and the boy and his mother were forced to fend for themselves. At the age of 13 Charles was apprenticed to a saddler;

shortly afterward he learned watchmaking. By the time he was 21 and married, he had added clock-making and upholstering to his repertoire and had taught himself painting after having been inspired by an amateur artist.

Successful Portraitist

Peale received some instruction from the Maryland artist John Hessalius. In 1766 wealthy citizens of Maryland raised £83 to send him to London to further his training in art, studying with Benjamin West. He remained until 1769. While there he painted an elaborately symbolical portrait, *Pitt as a Roman Senator.* On his return Peale settled in Annapolis. In 1772 he painted the first portrait ever done of George Washington. The exuberance of the Peale family and their warmth toward one another is recorded in the *Peale Family* (1773), which includes the artist, his wife, mother, brothers, sister, his old nurse, and an unidentified baby. Peale had such great success as a Portraitist just prior to the Revolution that he was able to move his business to Philadelphia. His portraiture combines a freshness and affability with a certain naive stiffness.

Peale served with distinction in the Revolution. As a first lieutenant in the militia, he crossed the Delaware with Washington and spent the dreadful winter at Valley Forge, where he did miniatures of some 40 officers. He gained the intimate friendship of Washington, Benjamin Franklin, and Thomas Jefferson.

In 1781 Peale added an exhibition gallery to his Philadelphia studio, where he housed 44 of his portraits of outstanding American leaders. His wife died in the 1790s as a result of her eleventh pregnancy, and Peale soon remarried. In all, he fathered 17 sons and daughters, who were named after famous painters chosen from the pages of a dictionary of painters.

Peale liked to present a tour de force in some paintings. The *Staircase Group* (1795) shows his sons Titian Ramsay and Raphaelle, life-size, climbing a narrow stairway. The painting was exhibited in a doorframe as a trompe l'oeil, and the shadows the figures cast and an accurately painted card on a step added to the effect. On one occasion, Peale's desire for novelty took a macabre turn. In *Rachel Weeping* (1772) he shows his first wife weeping over her dead child prominently laid out in the foreground. In the portrait of his brother James (1822) the sitter is shown in a novel way: he is seated at his desk at night, his face illuminated by a lamp.

Scientific Interests

Throughout his lifetime Peale maintained an enduring and active interest in many branches of science. He did silhouettes with the physiognotrace, a machine used to record profiles. He patented a fireplace, porcelain false teeth, and a new kind of wooden bridge; perfected the polygraph, a kind of portable writing desk which could make several copies of a manuscript at once; invented a rude motion picture technique; and wrote papers on engineering, hygiene, and other subjects.

In 1786 Peale established the first scientific museum in America. It contained living species of snakes, turtles, toads, and fish as well as stuffed birds and animals. The crowning touch was an entire mastodon skeleton, which he helped excavate on a farm in upstate New York in 1801. He depicted this event in an extraordinary painting, *The Exhuming of the Mastodon* (1806-1808). It contains 75 figures and shows the great wheel used to lift the water from the marl pit where the bones were embedded, the plank room, and the army tent where the excavators slept. It is loosely classified as one of the first American genre pieces. In the painting *The Artist in His Museum* (1822) Peale shows himself lifting a curtain to reveal the contents of his museum.

Peale fought to have his museum established as a state institution, and in 1802 it was transferred to the upper floor of the State House (the present Independence Hall). He established the Columbianum in 1795, America's first public exhibition of both modern paintings and the Old Masters. Out of this he organized the Pennsylvania Academy of the Fine Arts, which received its charter in 1806 and which stands today as the oldest art school in America. He died in Philadelphia on Feb. 22, 1827.

Further Reading

Charles Coleman Sellers, *Charles Willson Peale* (2 vols., 1947; 1 vol., rev. ed. 1969), is an extremely lively and well-documented account, with ample quotations from Peale's elaborate "Letterbooks." Peale is discussed in Charles H. Elam, comp., *The Peale Family: Three Generations of American Artists* (1967). For general background see Oliver W. Larkin, *Art and Life in America* (1949; rev. ed. 1960).

Additional Sources

Peale, Charles Willson, *Charles Willson Peale and his world,* New York: H.N. Abrams, 1983.

Sellers, Charles Coleman, *Mr. Peale's Museum: Charles Willson Peale and the first popular museum of natural science and art,* New York: Norton, 1980. □

Norman Vincent Peale

Norman Vincent Peale (1898-1993) was a religious leader who developed a blend of psychotherapy and religion based on the idea that nearly all basic problems are personal. He spread this message through his radio and television programs and through his popular book *The Power of Positive Thinking* and other writings.

Norman Vincent Peale was born in the small Ohio town of Bowersville on May 31, 1898, son of the local Methodist minister. The family moved frequently, in the Methodist itinerant tradition. They were not wealthy, and young Peale earned money delivering papers, working in a grocery store, and selling pots and pans door-to-door.

Graduating in 1920 from Ohio Wesleyan, a Methodist-founded college, Peale worked as a reporter on two newspapers, the Findlay (Ohio) *Morning Republican* and the Detroit *Journal,* for about a year before deciding that his life work lay elsewhere. Ordained to the Methodist ministry in 1922, he took a master's degree and an S.T.B. (Bachelor of Sacred Theology), both in 1924, from the theological school at Boston University. Faculty members at BU were religious liberals, many interested in the relationship between psychology and religion—a life-long concern of Peale's.

After serving from 1922 to 1924 as pastor in Berkeley, Rhode Island and then from 1924 to 1927 in Brooklyn, New York, Peale crowned his Methodist career with an appointment to University Methodist Church in Syracuse, New York. He married Loretta Ruth Stafford, herself an active church worker, in 1930.

In 1932 Peale changed his denomination from Methodist to Dutch Reformed, when he moved to the 300-year-old Marble Collegiate Church in New York City. This church traced its parish life back to Dutch New Amsterdam and was to be Peale's home church for the next half-century.

Peale and Smiley Blanton, a psychoanalyst, established a religio-psychiatric outpatient clinic next door to the church. The two men wrote books together, notably *Faith Is the Answer: A Psychiatrist and a Pastor Discuss Your Problems* (1940). In 1951 this blend of psychotherapy and religion grew into the American Foundation of Religion and Psychiatry, with Peale serving as president and Blanton as executive director.

Peale started a radio program, "The Art of Living," in 1935. Under sponsorship of the National Council of Churches he moved into television when the new medium arrived. In the meantime he had begun to edit the magazine *Guideposts* and to write books: *The Art of Living* (1937), *A Guide to Confident Living* (1948), and most notably, *The Power of Positive Thinking* (1952).

Peale's books enjoyed only a modest circulation until the great religion boom after World War II, a movement of which Peale was both a maker and a beneficiary. By the early 1950s the publishing climate for books like Peale's was highly favorable. *Publisher's Weekly* noted (January 23, 1954) that "the theme of religion dominates the non-fiction best-sellers in 1953," including such gems as *The Power of Prayer on Plants* and *Pray Your Weight Away.* The most successful such book, *The Power of Positive Thinking,* was on the *New York Times* best-seller list for three years and was translated into 33 languages.

If Peale had his ardent admirers, he had also his vocal detractors. He was accused of watering down the traditional doctrines of Christianity, of stressing materialistic rewards, and of counseling people to accept social conditions rather than reform them. Also, his best-known book was replete with "two 15-minute formulas," "a three-point program," "seven simple steps," "eight practical formulas," and "ten simple rules." Some readers found his message too easy to be plausible.

Asked to compare Peale with St. Paul, the two-time presidential candidate Adlai Stevenson of Illinois quipped that he found Paul appealing and Peale appalling. That remark perhaps reflected political bias. Boston University's liberalism may have loosened Peale's theology, but it did not seem to influence his politics. For a time Peale was chairman of the ultraconservative Committee for Constitutional Government, which lobbied vigorously against New Deal measures. In 1960 Peale, as spokesman for 150 Protestant clergymen, opposed the election of John Kennedy as president. "Faced with the election of a Catholic," Peale declared, "our culture is at stake." The uproar resulting from that pronouncement caused the pastor to back off from further formal partisan commitments, possibly to avoid offending part of the mass audience for his primary religio-psychological message. He was, however, politically and personally close to President Nixon's family. In 1968 he officiated at the wedding of Julie Nixon and David Eisenhower. He continued calling at the White House throughout the Watergate crisis, saying "Christ didn't shy away from people in trouble." It has been argued that even his "positive thinking" message was by implication politically conservative: "The underlying assumption of Peale's teaching was that nearly all basic problems were personal."

In 1984 Peale was awarded the Presidential Medal of Freedom by Ronald Reagan. In that same year, after 52 years at the pulpit, Peale retired from preaching at Marble Collegiate Church. For the next seven years he spoke to an average of 100 groups a year (a live audience numbered in the millions) and made frequent television and radio appearances. During this time he also produced more than a dozen books.

Peale died at his home in Pawling, New York on December 24, 1993, at the age of 95. He was survived by his wife Ruth and their three children.

Further Reading

Autobiographical anecdotes and fragments are scattered throughout Peale's books, especially his later ones. Arthur Gordon wrote a biography, *Norman Vincent Peale: Minister to Millions* (1958), a book sufficiently romanticizing its subject that it was readily transformed into a Hollywood movie, *One Man's Way* (1963); the book was revised and retitled *One Man's Way* in 1972. Douglas T. Miller described the context of Peale's literary success in the article "Popular Religion of the 1950s: Norman Vincent Peale and Billy Graham," in *Journal of Popular Culture* (Summer 1975). Donald Meyer has placed Peale in his longer-range historical context in *The Positive Thinkers: A Study of the American Quest for Health, Wealth and Personal Power from Mary Baker Eddy to Norman Vincent Peale* (1965). See also George, Carol V.R., *God's Salesman: Norman Vincent Peale and The Power of Positive Thinking* (1993). □

Rembrandt Peale

The American painter Rembrandt Peale (1778-1860) was a competent, if uneven, portraitist. His earlier portraits are fresher and more expressive than his later ones.

R embrandt Peale was born in Bucks County, Pa., on Feb. 22, 1778. He studied first with his father, the renowned painter, Charles Willson Peale, and then with Benjamin West in England in 1801. He returned to the United States in 1804 and set up a studio in Philadelphia. An important work of this period is the graceful, richly handled portrait of Thomas Jefferson (1805) at the age of 62.

Peale made two trips to France, in 1808 and 1809-1810, carrying letters from Jefferson, an intimate of his father. Peale came to know the painters Jacques Louis David and François Gérard, the sculptor Antonio Canova, and the American émigré painter John Vanderlyn. In Paris, Peale painted portraits of famous men for his father's museum. His work was sometimes marred by a hard linear quality, as he tried to rival the smooth, silky quality of David, but sometimes it had a beautiful mellow tone.

Peale was instrumental in founding the Pennsylvania Academy of the Fine Arts with his father, whom he succeeded as director in 1810. Dominating the academy's show of 1812 was his first historical painting, *The Roman Daughter*. The subject was daring: an imprisoned father kept alive by milk from his daughter's breast. He executed several "porthole" paintings of George Washington, the best known being the one he executed in 1822.

In 1825 Peale was elected president of the American Academy of the Fine Arts. Later he established a museum and picture gallery in Baltimore, Md. For several years, in mid-career, he taught art in Philadelphia public schools. In 1853 his instruction book, *Graphics: The Art of Accurate*

Delineation, was published. He died in Philadelphia on Oct. 3, 1860.

Peale's most ambitious painting was *The Court of Death* (1820), a huge canvas containing 23 allegorical figures. Based on ''Death,'' a poem by Beilby Porteus, it depicted Faith, Hope, Virtue, and Pleasure, who had been posed for by his daughters, and Old Age, modeled on his father. Death was a hooded figure at whose feet a young man had been struck down. The dramatic contrast of lights and darks was typical of the romantic period in art, especially in Europe, but the allegorical mode was part of the sentiment of the republican era in America. The work was sent on tour as a ''great moral painting.''

Further Reading

A short sketch of Peale's life is in Municipal Museum of Baltimore, *An Exhibition of Paintings by Rembrandt Peale* (1937). There is information on him in Charles Coleman Sellers, *Charles Willson Peale* (2 vols., 1947; 1 vol., rev. ed. 1969), and Charles H. Elam, comp., *The Peale Family: Three Generations of American Artists* (1967). For a good discussion of Peale and the general historical background see Oliver W. Larkin, *Art and Life in America* (1949; rev. ed. 1960).

Additional Sources

Miller, Lillian B., *In pursuit of fame: Rembrandt Peale, 1778-1860,* Washington, D.C.: National Portrait Gallery; Seattle: University of Washington Press, 1992. □

rule. His forceful speeches and writings helped to build support for the separatist cause, while his key position in the Volunteer militia enabled him to coordinate its activities with those of the IRB.

When plans for a countrywide insurrection were frustrated by last-minute errors, Pearse and his fellow conspirators resolved to proceed with an armed rising in Dublin. They knew they had no chance of military success, but they believed their example would rouse the Irish people from political apathy and inspire them to fight for national freedom. On Easter Monday, April 24, 1916, the rebels occupied buildings in the center of Dublin and proclaimed the Irish Republic. Pearse served as supreme commander of the 1,600 insurgents and signed the surrender order on April 29, when further resistance to British attacks appeared futile. The rebel leaders were quickly tried and condemned to death by military courtsmartial. Pearse was executed on May 3, 1916.

Pearse was an impassioned idealist who dedicated himself completely to the cause of Irish nationalism. The executed leaders of 1916 became popular martyrs for the cause of Irish liberty, and the Easter Rising opened a struggle with Britain that won independence for most of Ireland in 1921. Although Pearse did not realize his dream of a united and Gaelic Ireland, he remains for many of his countrymen the heroic incarnation of the Irish revolutionary ideal; it seems that this was the role in which Pearse desired to be cast.

Patrick Henry Pearse

The Irish poet, educator, and revolutionary nationalist Patrick Henry Pearse (1879-1916) was a leader of the Easter Rising of 1916 against the British.

Patrick H. Pearse was born in Dublin on Nov. 10, 1879, the son of an English father and an Irish mother. In his youth he was a fervent supporter of the Irish language revival movement, and he developed a mystical devotion to the ideals of Ireland's ancient Gaelic civilization. After graduating from the Royal University in 1901, he practiced law briefly but soon turned his talents to education. In 1908 he founded St. Enda's College, an experimental secondary school for boys.

Pearse became increasingly active in politics during the home rule controversy of 1912-1914. He gained a reputation as an orator and moved steadily toward an extreme nationalist position. In November 1913 he helped to form the Irish Volunteers, a nationalist militia, and he probably joined the secret Irish Republican Brotherhood (IRB) soon afterward.

When the Volunteer movement split in September 1914 over the question of its policy on World War I, Pearse became director of organization for the militant minority that opposed support of Britain against Germany. Thereafter, he rose rapidly in the councils of the IRB, playing an important part in its plans for an insurrection against British

Further Reading

Pearse's works are gathered in *Collected Works of Patrick H. Pearse: Plays, Stories, Poems* (1917) and *Collected Works of Patrick H. Pearse: Political Writings and Speeches* (1922). The only full-length biography of Pearse is Louis N. Le Roux, *Patrick H. Pearse,* translated by Desmond Ryan (1932), which should be supplemented by Ryan's own vivid recollections of Pearse in *Remembering Sion: A Chronicle of Storm and Quiet* (1934).

Additional Sources

Carty, Xavier, *In bloody protest: the tragedy of Patrick Pearse,* Dublin: Able Press, 1978.

Edwards, Ruth Dudley, *Patrick Pearse: the triumph of failure,* New York: Taplinger Pub. Co., 1978, 1977.

Moran, Sean Farrell, *Patrick Pearse and the politics of redemption: the mind of the Easter Rising, 1916,* Washington, D.C.: Catholic University of America Press, 1994.

Murphy, Brian P., *Patrick Pearse and the lost republican ideal,* Dublin: James Duffy, 1991. □

Lester Bowles Pearson

Lester Bowles Pearson (1897-1972) was a distinguished Canadian diplomat and recipient of the Nobel Peace Prize. Later he became leader of the Liberal party and prime minister of Canada.

Lester Bowles Pearson was born in Toronto, Ontario, on April 23, 1897. His education at the University of Toronto was interrupted by World War I, during which he served overseas in Egypt, Greece, and Great Britain. Pearson afterward returned to the university, graduating in 1919. He then went to Oxford, receiving a second bachelor's degree and a master's degree. From 1924 to 1928 he taught history at the University of Toronto. In 1929 he left academia to enter the Department of External Affairs in Ottawa.

Pearson's diplomatic career kept him in Ottawa until 1935, when he was sent to London as first secretary to the Canadian High Commission, a post he held until 1941. He returned to Ottawa as assistant undersecretary of state for external affairs, and in 1942 went to Washington as the Canadian representative. In 1945 he was the senior adviser to the Canadian delegation at the San Francisco Conference. The next year he became the senior civil servant in the Department of External Affairs.

In Active Politics

Pearson's career changed direction in 1948, when he entered active politics as a member of the Liberal party and as secretary of state for external affairs. He was successful in winning election to Parliament, a feat that he was to repeat in every general election he contested. As Canada's foreign minister, Pearson had a brilliant career. He was a founder of the North Atlantic Treaty Organization and the author of NATO's so-called Canadian article (Article 2), calling for economic and social cooperation between the treaty signatories. In 1951-1952 he was chairman of the North Atlantic Council, and in 1952 he was elected president of the United Nations General Assembly for a 1-year term.

The culmination of Pearson's career came during the Suez crisis of October-November 1956. There had been no word of the impending Anglo-French assault, but with news of the attack Pearson flew to the United Nations at New York. There, hysteria was in the air, and it seemed inevitable that Britain and France would be roundly condemned for their sins. Pearson was angry, too, but realized that it would be dangerous for the Western position generally if Canada's allies suffered from a blanket condemnation.

As a result, Pearson ventured a calming suggestion: ''We need action . . . not only to end the fighting but to make the peace. . . . I therefore would have liked to see a provision . . . authorizing the Secretary-General to begin to make arrangements for a United Nations force large enough to keep these borders at peace while a political settlement is being worked out.'' Canada, he added, would be glad to contribute to such a force.

Pearson's inspired suggestion was seized upon as a way out of the difficult situation. Within 24 hours, a force was organized on paper, and the immediate crisis was on the way to resolution. For his efforts in helping to create the UN Emergency Force, Pearson was awarded the Nobel Peace Prize in 1957.

Prime Minister

Largely on the strength of his international reputation, Pearson was chosen to become the leader of the Liberal party in 1958. The party was in opposition, disorganized and demoralized, a situation that was to become worse in the short run. In the election of 1958 Pearson led the Liberals to a crushing defeat, and the party was reduced to 48 of 265 seats in the Commons. Reorganization began soon, and by 1962 the Liberals were on their way back. In the election of that year the party won 98 seats, and after John Diefenbaker's government was defeated in the House of Commons in 1963, Pearson led the Liberals to a narrow victory in that year's general election.

Pearson's government was almost immediately in trouble, a condition that persisted for the next five years. The first budget was almost completely withdrawn after fierce attacks; there were serious scandals involving ministers and people in the Prime Minister's office; and the province of Quebec was increasingly restive in confederation. Above all was the extraordinary bitterness between Pearson and the leader of the opposition, Diefenbaker—a bitterness that dominated the political scene and almost discredited Parliament.

But Pearson's administration was not unmarked with success. The Prime Minister listened sympathetically to Quebec and developed a formula of "cooperative federalism" to deal with its demands. The Royal Commission on Bilingualism and Biculturalism was also created. The government strengthened social welfare legislation and introduced socialized medicine. A distinctive Canadian flag was designed and approved. And relations with the United States, although sometimes difficult with Lyndon Johnson, continued to remain close.

In 1965 Pearson called an election in an effort to improve his government's minority position in the House of Commons. But the electorate was apparently unimpressed with the Pearson record and returned yet another minority government. After two more years in office, Pearson announced his decision to retire in late 1967. He stepped down as prime minister in April 1968. His retirement was not to be leisurely, however, for he was quickly drafted to head the World Bank Commission on International Aid and Development. In this capacity he traveled 75,000 miles and visited 76 world leaders. Pearson also joined the faculty of Carleton University in Ottawa to lecture on international affairs. He soon accepted an appointment as chancellor of the university.

Pearson suffered from cancer of the liver and died at his home near Ottawa on December 27, 1972. He was remembered in the *New York Times* as being "boyish, diffident, disarming, a statesman, and an unhappy warrior in politics."

Further Reading

There are no scholarly studies of Pearson. The best sources are John Robinson Beal, *Pearson of Canada* (1964), and Peter Newman, *The Distemper of Our Times: Canadian Politics in Transition, 1963-1968* (1968). Also useful is Terence Robertson, *Crisis: The Inside Story of the Suez Conspiracy* (1965).

Biographical information and a study of Pearson's policies as prime minister can be found in two works by Peter Stursberg, *Lester Pearson and the American Dilemma* (1980) and *Lester Pearson and the Dream of Unity* (1978). Pearson's obituary appears in the *New York Times* (December 28, 1972). □

Robert Edwin Peary

The American explorer Robert Edwin Peary (1856-1920) is famous for his discovery of the North Pole; he was one of the last and greatest of the dog team-and-sledge polar explorers.

Robert Peary was born in Cresson, Pa., on May 6, 1856, but he lived in Maine after the death of his father in 1859. Entering Bowdoin College in 1873, Peary studied civil engineering. An outstanding student of strong, independent judgment, he graduated in 1877.

After working as a county surveyor in Maine and a draftsman in Washington, D.C., Peary passed the civil engineering examinations of the U.S. Navy and was commissioned in 1881. In 1884-1885 he worked on the ship canal survey in Nicaragua, but while there his interest was attracted to the Arctic. He made a brief reconnaissance trip to the Disko Bay area of Greenland in 1886, but his professional duties returned him to Nicaragua for 2 more years. Then, from 1888 to 1891, while engaged in naval engineering along the Eastern seaboard, he prepared for more Arctic work.

In June 1891 Peary, his young wife, and five others, including Matthew Henson, Peary's assistant in all his subsequent Arctic expeditions, and Frederick A. Cook, the party's surgeon and ethnologist, left New York for Greenland. Before returning home in 1892, Peary made a 1,300-mile trek to northeastern Greenland, discovering new land and indicating the insularity of Greenland. Popularly acclaimed for these achievements, Peary was able to organize and finance another Greenland expedition, which began in 1893 and lasted until 1895. This time he attempted additional explorations, but severe weather and illness prevented success. He returned home with two of the three huge meteorites he had discovered (the third was recovered after trips in 1896 and 1897) and with revised plans on polar travel.

Peary's next Arctic journey, from 1898 until 1902, represented his first serious effort to reach the North Pole. He labored and suffered mightily in organizing and conducting this expedition, but he failed to get close to his objective. A major reason for this was the fact that he had eight toes amputated in 1899, although he continued in the field and reached 84°17′N in 1902 before being forced back.

Now realizing the need to reach higher latitudes by ship before embarking with sledges, Peary raised sufficient money to have a ship, the *Roosevelt*, constructed, and he set out in July 1905 on his seventh expedition. Reaching the

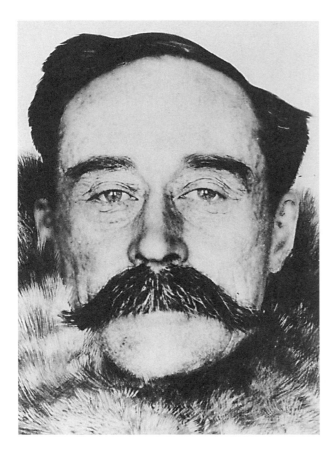

north coast of Grant Land and wintering there, Peary and his support party set out with sledges in March 1906. After several weeks of arduous travel over broken ice, the party, weak and exhausted, reached 87°16′N but was forced to turn back with its goal less than 175 miles away.

In July 1908 Peary embarked on what he knew would be his last polar attempt. Accompanied by able assistants and well-equipped, well-trained Eskimos, Peary led a party of 24 men, 19 sledges, and 133 dogs northward from Cape Columbia. His plan called for various support parties to break the trail and carry additional supplies for the main party of six, which alone would cover the last few miles to the pole. On April 1, near the 88th parallel, the final support party turned back, and Peary, Henson, and four Eskimos went on, reaching 90°N on April 6, 1909.

Peary returned to announce his discovery, only to learn that 5 days previously Cook had proclaimed a 1908 visit to the pole. Peary, always austere and direct in manner, minced no words in challenging the authenticity of Cook's claims. In the bitter controversy that followed, the general public often sided with Cook, whose unheralded expedition had dramatic appeal over the carefully planned and officially sponsored labors of Peary. In succeeding years, however, Peary's claims were validated and recognized by Congress and the major geographic societies of the world, whereas Cook's claims, always dubious, did not receive official sanction and suffered from the exposure of additional Cook frauds.

Peary spent his final years as a champion of aviation and the need for greater military preparedness. He died in Washington, D.C., on Feb. 20, 1920.

Further Reading

Peary's own books are *Northward over the "Great Ice"* (1898); *Nearest the Pole* (1907); *The North Pole* (1910); and *Secrets of Polar Travel* (1917). The best biographies of Peary are William Herbert Hobbs, *Peary* (1936), and John Edward Weems, *Peary: The Explorer and the Man* (1967). See also Donald B. MacMillan, *How Peary Reached the Pole: The Personal Story of His Assistant* (1934). The considerable literature on the Peary-Cook controversy is capably reviewed in John Edward Weems, *Race to the Pole* (1960). □

Hermann Max Pechstein

Hermann Max Pechstein (1881-1955) was a German painter and graphic artist and, as a member of the artist group "Die Brücke" (The Bridge), was one of the early Expressionists.

Born on December 31, 1881, in Eckersbach (a suburb of Zwickau in Saxony, Germany), Pechstein went through the required schooling and in 1896 began a four year apprenticeship with a decoration (house) painter. Having passed his examination, he began his studies at the School for Applied Arts in Dresden. After two years he entered the Academy of Fine Arts, where only one year later he became a "master-student" of Professor Otto Gussmann, who also assisted him in obtaining his first commissions. Wall paintings and designs for stained-glass windows and mosaics were successfully completed even before he graduated in 1906 with the Saxon State Prize.

In the year of his graduation he painted a number of ceilings and an altarpiece for the Third German Crafts Exhibit in Dresden. (Later, another painter had to paint a thin coat of white over Pechstein's ceiling because the colors were considered too bright!) During this exhibit he met Erich Heckel, one of the founders of the famous artist group "Die Brücke" (The Bridge), in 1905. Heckel introduced him to members Ernst Ludwig Kirchner and Karl Schmidt-Rottluff, who welcomed him as a friend. Shortly thereafter Pechstein made his first trip to Italy, where works of the Etruscans and the early Renaissance artists impressed him most. On his return he stayed for some months in Paris, where he looked at the new art and met, among others, Kees van Dongen, who introduced him to the other members of the Fauve group which had formed around Henri Matisse.

In 1908 Pechstein settled permanently in Berlin, which promised greater opportunities and more commissions than the staid Dresden. By this time he had perfected his graphic techniques (he made over 800 graphic works, with lithographs the most numerous, followed by approximately 270 woodcuts) and had begun to make sculptures of figures and heads, following the example of his artist friends. During this period he was the most popular of the Expressionists and was considered the leader of the Brücke group. In 1911 his Brücke friends also moved to Berlin, and he opened with Kirchner a short-lived art school, called MUIM Institut (*Moderner Unterricht in Malerei,* or modern instruction in painting). When Pechstein's paintings were rejected by the jury of the Berlin *Sezession* exhibition organization, he and a number of the other rejected artists decided to form a *Neue Sezession* (new secession), which had its first exhibit at the Galerie Macht. At this time Pechstein also made contact with Kandinsky, Marc, and Macke of the Munich Blue Rider group. While the largest part of the public and many of the critics still opposed the new style of abbreviation of forms and freedom of colors, others began to realize and recognize the talents and abilities of these young painters. When Pechstein exhibited again with the old *Sezession,* the Brücke members dismissed him from their group.

Pechstein managed to obtain a number of commissions, and after a successful retrospective exhibit of his works at the Gurlitt gallery he received financial assistance from the gallery owner to travel to the Palau Islands in the Pacific (which at that time were still in German possession). Most of Pechstein's main motifs had always been figures in nature, the human form in natural surroundings. He hoped to find that simplicity of natural life which he had tried to imagine earlier in his works on the islands. This attraction of a "primitive" life had already led to the discovery of the expressive powers of Oceanic and African art (in the ethnographic museums) not only by the young Expressionists but also in France (Picasso's attraction to these arts is the best known). However, Pechstein's stay in the Palau Islands was shortened by the outbreak of World War I and Pechstein's subsequent internment by the Japanese. He finally made his way back—in part as a coal stoker on a steamer—through Manila, San Francisco, and New York. On his return to Germany he was immediately drafted and served in the war until 1917.

A period of outstanding creativity began. Painting his experiences in the Pacific based on his sketches, he made a number of woodcuts which were issued in portfolios. He also illustrated books and designed stained-glass windows and mosaics. Shortly after the end of the war he became active, together with a number of other Expressionist artists, in trying to assist the public acceptance of the new German Republic and at the same time assuring that the arts could truly participate in the creation of a new society. He became the co-founder of the *Arbeitsrat für Kunst* (Workers' Council for the Arts) and of the *Novembergruppe,* the two most active artist organizations. They set examples for the artists in other cities in Germany. When the hopes for a new society began to fade, Pechstein's intensity and spontaneity began to wane.

He spent most of his summers either on the shores of the Baltic Sea or in small villages in the province of Pommerania, painting and designing windows—in 1926 he created a series of windows for the International Labor Office in Geneva—but for a time abandoning his graphic arts. He received many commendations and prizes, among them ones from the Carnegie Institute in Pittsburgh, Pennsylvania,

and from several states in Germany. He was appointed professor at the Prussian Academy and had great success as a teacher. When the Nazis took over power in 1933 he encountered difficulties, and in 1937 his art was declared "degenerate." He was prohibited to paint, dismissed from the Prussian Academy, and had to witness the removal of 326 of his works from the collections of German museums. He stayed most of the time in Pommerania until 1944, when he was drafted for a short time to perform forced labor. After a short internment by the Russians, he returned to Berlin. His apartment and his studio had been destroyed and many of his works lost. He was appointed professor at the Academy of Fine Arts and concentrated on his teaching duties until his death on June 19, 1955.

Pechstein's career as an artist falls into three periods. The first creative phase was closely tied to his friendship with the Brücke group and lasted until 1912. The second phase began with his return from the Palau Islands and lasted until 1924. During this period his colors became softer and his compositions more balanced. Prevented from working between 1933 and 1945, he began to paint again after the war—mostly watercolors. Today most of the larger museums own some of his works, his graphic works being highly treasured.

Further Reading

Pechstein wrote his memoirs (edited by L. Reidemeister; Wiesbaden, 1960). Excerpts from his diaries from the Palau Islands were edited by H.-G. Sellenthin (Feldafing, 1956). The first monograph on Pechstein was published in 1916 by Walter Heymann (Munich, Piper) and the first partial oeuvre catalogue of his graphic works was compiled by Paul Fechter (Berlin, 1921). In 1950 and in 1981 two films on Pechstein and his works were made in Germany. Exhibition catalogues provide valuable comments and introduction to biography and works. Pechstein's first exhibit in the United States was at the gallery Karl Lilienfeld (1935, New York); later exhibits were held at the gallery Van Diemen-Lilienfeld, New York, and at the gallery Dalzall-Hatfield, Los Angeles, and in New York by Helen Serger/La Boetie. The standard texts on Expressionism in general are Bernard S. Myers, *The German Expressionists, a Generation in Revolt* (New York, n.d.) and Peter Selz, *German Expressionist Painting* (1974). A small paperback by John Willett (1978) is a general introduction to this period. □

Robert Newton Peck

Robert Peck (born 1928) won critical and popular acclaim for his first novel, *A Day No Pigs Would Die* (1973). Critics lauded its unsentimental rendering of farm life and the often brutal realities of the natural world, and the book is now a frequently studied text in junior high school classrooms.

eck was born in rural Vermont to Shaker farmers whose hard yet rewarding lives inspired much of his fiction. He commented: "*A Day No Pigs Would Die* was influenced by my father, an illiterate farmer and pig-slaughterer whose earthy wisdom continues to contribute to my understanding of the natural order and the old Shaker beliefs deeply rooted in the land and its harvest." The first of his family to learn to read and write, Peck was profoundly influenced by his grade school teacher and later based the character Miss Kelly in the Soup series of novels on her. As a young man he found employment as a lumberjack, hog butcher, and paper-mill worker. He joined the United States Army infantry during World War II, serving for two years in Italy, Germany, and France. After the war he received his bachelor's degree from Rollins College and studied law at Cornell University. He later became an advertising executive, writing jingles for television commercials, but abandoned this career following the successful publication of *A Day No Pigs Would Die* in 1973. He now divides his time between Vermont and Florida, where he is the director of Rollins College Writers Conference.

Told in a spare yet vivid style, *A Day No Pigs Would Die* revolves around thirteen-year-old Rob Peck and his relationship with his austere father, a farmer and hog butcher. Rob, in return for helping a neighbor's cow give birth, receives a sow that soon becomes his beloved pet. The pig proves barren, however, and Rob must help his father slaughter it, knowing that their meager income prohibits the luxury of a useless animal. Through this experience, he comes to understand the meaning of love and the necessity of death. He is also able to face the loss of his father, who, though silent on the subject, has been slowly dying. The reaction of reviewer Christopher Lehmann-Haupt to *A Day No Pigs Would Die* echoed the estimation of many critics: "[This novel] is a stunning little dramatization of the brutality of life on a Vermont farm, of the necessary cruelty of nature, and of one family's attempt to transcend the hardness of life by accepting it. And while . . . there is no rhetoric about love—in fact nobody in *A Day No Pigs Would Die* ever mentions the word love, or any other emotion for that matter—love nevertheless suffuses every page."

In the Soup series of novels, Peck embellishes upon his childhood adventures with Soup, his mischievous best friend whose practical jokes often result in mayhem at such small-town functions as parades and school plays. Among the best known of these books are *Soup* (1974), *Soup and Me* (1975), *Soup for President* (1978), and *Soup's Drum* (1980). Most critics have found that while the plots of the books have grown increasingly repetitive, the stories' slapstick humor ensures their continuing appeal for young readers. A similar estimation has been accorded to Peck's series of novels revolving around the character Trig, a preteen tomboy living in 1930s Vermont whose antics often arouse the displeasure of her elders. *Trig* (1977), *Trig Sees Red* (1978), *Trig Goes Ape* (1980), and *Trig or Treat* (1982) have also been faulted for what many reviewers regarded as Peck's superficial treatment of female characters, a criticism leveled against much of his fiction.

Other novels by Peck evince his interest in colonial America and the Revolutionary War. Such novels as *Fawn* (1975), *Rabbits and Redcoats* (1976), *The King's Iron* (1977), and *Eagle Fur* (1978) feature adolescents who come of age amidst historical events such as the capture of Fort Ticonderoga by Ethan Allen and Benedict Arnold. Critics have praised the sense of place, strong characterizations, and powerful scenes of these books, yet find them marred by what they perceive as Peck's puerile treatment of violence and sexual relationships. The uneven quality of these novels typifies Peck's work following *A Day No Pigs Would Die.* However, most critics concur with the estimation of Anne Scott MacLeod that "those who admired *Pigs* have often been disappointed by Peck's work since that strong beginning. Nevertheless, we look with interest at each new title by this erratic author, hoping that he will sometime match the achievement of that first powerful, moving story."

Further Reading

Authors and Artists for Young Adults, Volume 3, Gale, 1990.
Contemporary Literary Criticism, Volume 17, Gale, 1981.
Peck, Robert Newton, *Fiction Is Folks,* Writer's Digest Books, 1983.
Something about the Author Autobiography Series, Volume 1, Gale, 1986, pp. 235-247.
Twentieth-Century Children's Writers, 3rd edition, St. James Press, 1989.
Twentieth-Century Young Adult Writers, St. James Press, 1994.
Horn Book, August, 1973; October, 1973; April, 1976; December, 1976. □

Pedrarias

The Spanish conqueror Pedrarias (ca. 1440-1531), or Pedro Arias de Avila in full, has a reputation as a bloodthirsty tyrant. His positive achievements, however, included the founding of Panama City and Nicaragua.

Pedrarias was born in Segovia and in early life won distinction as a soldier in Africa. He married the aristocratic Isabel de Bobadilla y de Peñalosa, whose intelligence and influence furthered his advancement. In 1513 King Ferdinand appointed Pedrarias governor of the Isthmus of Darién to supersede Vasco Núñez de Balboa, who had governed there unofficially since 1511.

Already an elderly man, Pedrarias sailed to the Isthmus in the spring of 1514, accompanied by his wife and bearing the title Captain General and Governor of Castilla de Oro, which meant he was to govern the mainland west of the Gulf of Urabá. He took 2,000 armed men, for the King hoped Pedrarias would add substantially to the meager Spanish mainland conquests made thus far.

Reaching the town of Antígua del Darién on June 29, 1514, Pedrarias began a legal prosecution of Balboa, whom he regarded as a dangerous rival and who indeed had the support of nearly all the original settlers. The *residencia,* or judicial hearing, on Balboa's conduct progressed to a point and then was indefinitely postponed. The rivals patched up their quarrel, and there was even a betrothal of Balboa to Pedrarias's daughter in Spain. Yet the two men remained opponents, for Balboa intended to launch ships on the Pacific and sail southward to Inca Peru, while Pedrarias awaited a chance to rid himself of a competitor and seize the ships. When Balboa's sailing time approached, Pedrarias arrested him and transferred him to the settlement of Acla, where the interrupted *residencia* was resumed. In January 1519 Balboa and four of his principal comrades died on the scaffold at Acla.

Pedrarias, now without a rival in the Isthmus, ordered or permitted exploring expeditions to go southward and northwestward. Pascual de Andagoya moved toward Peru, and after his return the work was taken up by Francisco Pizarro and Diego de Almagro. Andrés Niño and Gil González, acting independently of Pedrarias, explored the Pacific coasts of Costa Rica and Nicarao (Nicaragua) and discovered Fonseca Gulf. Pedrarias, meanwhile, had founded Panama City in 1519 and moved his headquarters to the Pacific side. A new governor, Lope de Sosa, reached Darién in 1520 to relieve Pedrarias and conduct his *residencia,* which promised to go badly for the old governor. Luckily for Pedrarias, Sosa took sick and died in his cabin before debarking. Though a subordinate then went through the forms of a hearing, no one dared come forward to voice a complaint.

Pedrarias now transferred to Nicaragua, with which his remaining years were chiefly occupied. He returned briefly to the Isthmus in 1527 for a *residencia* before another

governor, Pedro de los Ríos, but as he had taken to Nicaragua most of those likely to voice grievances, he had little difficulty clearing himself. In the meantime he had trouble with subordinates in Nicaragua, one of whom, Gil González, he beheaded.

Pedrarias died on May 30, 1531, in the town of León, which he had founded. He had had the satisfaction of triumphing over all his foes and rivals and of putting many of them to death.

Further Reading

The best biography of Pedrarias is Pablo Álvarez Rubiano, *Pedrarias Dávila* (1944), a straightforward account that neither condemns nor exonerates him. A contemporary of Pedrarias, Peter Martyr of Angleria, discusses Pedrarias's feud with Balboa in *De orbe novo,* translated and edited by Francis Augustus MacNutt (1912). Charles L. G. Anderson, *Life and Letters of Vasco Núñez de Balboa* (1941), and Kathleen Romoli, *Balboa of Darién, Discoverer of the Pacific* (1953), include accounts of Pedrarias. □

Pedro I

Pedro I (1798-1834) was a Portuguese king and emperor of Brazil. As prince regent of Brazil, he declared the independence of Brazil and then became emperor.

Pedro was born on Oct. 12, 1798, at the Queluz Palace in Lisbon, the son of the prince regent of Portugal (later João VI) and his wife, Carlota Joaquina, the daughter of the Spanish Bourbon king Charles IV. In 1807 the royal family fled to Brazil to escape Napoleon's invading armies. Pedro adapted well to the Brazilian milieu. He was an excellent horseman, enjoyed the military life, and could compete with common soldiers and officers equally. Also, he early demonstrated musical talents and later composed some music of creditable amateur quality. He was considered to be handsome, and women found him attractive.

In 1817 Pedro married Carolina Josefa Leopoldina, the daughter of Francis I of Austria. Her intelligence, consideration, and personality quickly earned her the respect and admiration of the Portuguese and Brazilians, as well as of her husband, but she was unable to distract him from his amorous affairs.

In 1816 Pedro's father became João VI, King of Portugal and Brazil, which had been elevated from the status of a colony to a kingdom in 1815. In 1821 João VI was forced to return to Portugal and leave Pedro as the prince regent. Recognizing the independence sentiments in Brazil, and observing what was occurring in the Spanish colonies of the New world, the King advised his son to declare Brazil independent and take the throne for himself rather than allow an adventurer to take over the country. On Sept. 7, 1822, supported by Brazilians who feared that the Portuguese would reduce the country to colonial status again,

and following the advice of his wife and his chief counselor, José Bonifácio de Andrada e Silva, Pedro declared the independence of Brazil and established the Empire of Brazil with himself as emperor.

In 1823 Pedro I called a constituent assembly to formulate a constitution but dissolved the body later that year. He promulgated a constitution on March 24, 1824, which remained Brazil's charter until 1889. The period was disturbed by dissension between native-born Brazilians and those born in Portugal. Pedro I was Portuguese and thus suspect to Brazilians, especially after he signed a treaty of peace with Portugal which left unresolved some basic issues concerning future relations between the two countries. When João VI died in 1826, Pedro I inherited the Portuguese crown, but the ruling of both countries by the Emperor was unacceptable to the Brazilians. Pedro I abdicated the Portuguese throne in favor of his daughter Maria da Glória, who was betrothed to her uncle Miguel.

Although he accepted constitutional monarchy, Pedro I was an absolutist in his approach to government. With difficulty he accepted advice from the legislative branch of the government, and his attitudes led to conflict with liberal Brazilians.

Pedro's long-standing affair with Domitilia de Castro, upon whom he bestowed the title of Marquêsa de Santos, was a cause of much criticism and provoked opposition. The Empress, Leopoldina, had widespread public support when the Emperor moved his mistress into the palace. Leopoldina died in 1827, and Pedro I continued his relationship with the Marquêsa de Santos until 1829, when he married Amélia Augusta Eugénia Napoleona, daughter of Eugene of Litchenberg.

In April 1831 Pedro I unexpectedly abdicated in favor of his 5-year-old son, who became Pedro II. Returning to Portugal, Pedro took up the cause of his daughter Maria da Glória, whose position as Maria II of Portugal was being challenged by her uncle Miguel. Dom Pedro directed the political and military campaign which defeated his brother and, acting as regent, had his daughter declared of age, although she was less than 18 years old. A few days later, on Sept. 24, 1834, he died in the Queluz Palace.

Further Reading

A study of Pedro I is Sergio Corrêa da Costa, *Every Inch a King: A Biography of Dom Pedro I, First Emperor of Brazil* (trans. 1950). Additional material is in Clarence Henry Haring, *Empire in Brazil: A New World Experiment with Democracy* (1958).

Additional Sources

Macaulay, Neill, *Dom Pedro: the struggle for liberty in Brazil and Portugal, 1798-1834,* Durham, N.C.: Duke University Press, 1986. □

Pedro II

Pedro II (1825-1891) was the second emperor of Brazil. His wise rule brought internal peace and progress to Brazil while most of his Latin American neighbors were absorbed in disastrous civil strife.

On Dec. 2, 1825, Pedro was born in the imperial residence at São Christovão. When his father, Pedro I, abdicated in 1831, young Pedro literally became the ward of the nation. His education, so rigidly structured that almost all of his waking time was spent in study, prepared him well for his future duties.

Until Pedro reached the age of 18, Brazil was to be ruled by a regency, but during a 9-year interregnum the empire almost disintegrated. Recognizing the regency's utter failure, liberals forced a declaration of Pedro's majority on July 23, 1840. In 1843 he married Princess Thereza Christina of Naples. By 1850 order was restored, and the monarchy entered an era of internal stability. At first glance, Pedro II's government resembled the British parliamentary system, but in reality the Emperor was the master of state. His judicious exercise of the *poder moderador* (moderating power) created a political balance which ensured domestic peace during most of his 49-year reign.

For over 2 decades Pedro had to contend with British economic and political preeminence-an inheritance from the old Portuguese Empire. He encountered a major crisis after the British Parliament passed the Aberdeen Act in 1845, as British ships arbitrarily entered Brazilian ports and cut out vessels engaging in the African slave trade. In De-

cember 1862 Britain temporarily blockaded Rio after a series of altercations between British seamen and Brazilian officials.

Pedro II's intervention in faction-torn Uruguay involved Brazil in a war with Argentina's Juan Manuel de Rosas in 1851-1852. Chaotic conditions persisted in Uruguay into the 1860s, and in September 1864, as a result of attacks on Brazilian nationals, Pedro sent in imperial troops. Capitalizing on the situation, Paraguayan dictator Francisco Solano López attacked the Mato Grosso region in December. Brazil joined Argentina and Uruguay in the War of the Triple Alliance in May 1865 but bore the brunt of the battle as Pedro refused compromise or mediation until López was eliminated. The 5-year conflict was expensive for Brazil: it drained the treasury, cost 50,000 lives, and postponed many urgent domestic reforms. After the war a conjunction of several factors served to destroy the Braganza dynasty. Although Pedro was still overwhelmingly popular, the monarchy was not. He encouraged the Republican party, founded in 1870, and republican ideas circulated widely in a press whose freedom he carefully guarded.

In the 1870s Brazil experienced its first serious church-state conflict. The bishops of Olinda and Pará, contrary to the orders of Pedro, a former Masonic grand master, continued to censure *irmandades* (lay brotherhoods) in their districts which refused to abjure Freemasonry. When the bishops persisted in defying civil authority, they were arrested and sentenced to 4 years at hard labor in early 1874. Pedro eased the situation in September 1875 by granting an amnesty but had already lost the support of the clergy.

The slavery issue also weakened the Emperor's position. Although he was an ardent abolitionist, he temporized on emancipation as he realized that the slave-owning *fazendeiros* were his strongest support. But the proclamation of total, uncompensated abolition in March 1888 alienated the planters.

The major factor in the downfall of the monarchy, however, was the rise of militarism. After the Paraguayan War, the army, inspired by positivism, developed an arrogant disregard for civilian leadership. A serious illness in 1887 greatly impaired Pedro's physical and mental ability, and his inaction during the army coup on Nov. 15, 1889, doomed the empire. On November 16 the republic was proclaimed, and on the next day the royal family was exiled. Pedro died in Paris on Dec. 5, 1891.

Further Reading

The best book on Pedro II is Mary Wilhemine Williams, *Dom Pedro the Magnanimous: Second Emperor of Brazil* (1937). The open admiration for her subject does nothing to diminish the quality of Dr. Williams's standard work. See also Clarence Henry Haring, *Emire in Brazil: A New World Experiment with Monarchy* (1958). □

Sir Robert Peel

The English statesman Sir Robert Peel (1788-1850) served as prime minister during 1834-1835 and 1841-1846. He played an important role in modernizing the British government's social and economic policies and sponsored the repeal of the Corn Laws in 1846.

Sir Robert Peel was in the great tradition of 19th-century administrative reformers. Though not a doctrinaire, he drew on the most advanced thinking of his day in his reform of British criminal law, the prisons, the police, and fiscal and economic policies. By making government a positive instrument in social reform and by his pragmatic approach to social and political problems, Peel also made an important contribution to shaping the philosophy of the modern Conservative party. Despite the fact that his repeal of the Corn Laws broke his party, Peelite traditions lingered on. Peelites such as William Gladstone also carried these traditions into the Liberal party.

Robert Peel was born on Feb. 5, 1788, at Chamber Hall, Bury, Lancashire, close to the cotton mills that had made his father's immense fortune. The elder Peel had become one of the greatest manufacturers in England. He was not, however, content with business success. In 1790 he bought a great agricultural estate in Staffordshire, and in the same year he entered Parliament for the neighboring borough of Tamworth, where he had also acquired property and parliamentary influence. The younger Peel was brought up as a country gentleman. In 1800 his father was made a baronet, the title his son later inherited.

Sir Robert intended his son for the governing class, and he gave him an aristocratic education at Harrow and at Christ Church, Oxford. At both institutions the younger Peel distinguished himself as a scholar. Oxford was only commencing to offer the opportunity for a rigorous education, and Peel chose the harder path. He was the first scholar in the history of the university to graduate with first-class honors both in the classics and in mathematics.

Early Political Career

In 1809, the year after his graduation from Oxford, Peel's father bought him entry into Parliament for the borough of Cashel in Ireland. His maiden speech in the House of Commons was generally acclaimed. The next year, at the age of 22, Peel joined the government as undersecretary for war and the colonies.

Peel's chief at the War Office was Lord Liverpool, and when Liverpool became prime minister in 1812, he offered his young subordinate the critical post of chief secretary for Ireland. Though the office did not carry a Cabinet seat, it was one of the most challenging the government had to offer. After the English union with Ireland in 1801, the chief secretary had become not only a key figure in the administration of Ireland but also the representative of the Irish government in the British Parliament. The social and religious conflicts that rent Ireland throughout the 19th century made it almost impossible to govern. Peel achieved the impossible. As chief secretary for 6 years, until 1818, he established a reputation for a happy mixture of firmness and compassion. Among other reforms, Peel pioneered in the establishment of a permanent Irish police force and laid the foundations for famine relief.

After his retirement from the chief secretaryship, Peel stayed out of office for 4 years. He remained, however, one of the government's most distinguished supporters on the back benches. In 1817 Oxford had conferred on him its highest honor by electing him to one of the university's two parliamentary seats. In 1819 Peel chaired the committee of the House of Commons that made the crucial recommendation that Britain return to the gold standard, and the statute that accomplished this was commonly known as "Peel's Act." It was also during this period that Peel made a singularly happy marriage with society belle Julia Floyd.

Home Secretary

In 1821 Peel was recalled to high office as home secretary in Lord Liverpool's government. He remained in that office, with one brief interlude in 1827-1828, until 1830. In large part because of him, this period is known as the "age of liberal Toryism." Benthamite and evangelical reformers had long argued against Britain's legal and penal system which attempted little more than frightening citizens not to commit crimes. Peel went a long way toward meeting their demands by establishing a system aimed at preventing crimes and at reforming criminals rather than simply punishing them. Savage death penalties for minor crimes were largely abolished, and the criminal laws were made simpler and more humane. Prisons were also reformed and brought under the supervision of the central government. And, in the Metropolitan Police Act of 1829, Peel laid the foundations of a modern professional police force. This act established the London police force, whose members were called, after him, "Peelers" or "Bobbies."

Catholic Emancipation

Though Peel helped to introduce liberal elements into Toryism, he was also long associated with the illiberal opposition to full civil and political rights for Roman Catholics. There were few Catholics in England; but they were in the overwhelming majority in Ireland, and the Catholic question became closely tied with the Irish question. Those who favored Catholic emancipation became known as "Catholics." The people who opposed were known as "Protestants." Peel, a fervent Anglican, became the leading "Protestant" spokesman. He argued that emancipation would exacerbate the already bitter feelings between Roman Catholics and Protestants in Ireland and that it would weaken the established Anglican Church in both countries. It was largely for his stand on this topic that Peel refused to join the government of the "Catholic" Tory George Canning in 1827. In 1829, however, as home secretary and leader of the House of Commons in the government of the Duke of Wellington, Peel played a leading role in carrying Catholic emancipation. The reason for his reversal was simple. In 1828 the Irish had demonstrated their ability to return Roman Catholic members to a House of Commons in which they could not legally sit. Wellington argued that to enforce the law would mean civil war. Peel agreed with him. The specter of civil war overcame their scruples. They felt that it was their duty to King and to country to avert that disaster by carrying emancipation. By so doing they splintered the Tory party. Peel particularly was denounced as a turncoat, and strongly "Protestant" Oxford humiliated him by defeating him for reelection.

Peel's First Ministry

Peel was deeply wounded. About this time he began commonly to be described as cold and haughty. However, his reputation among his close friends was very different. Strikingly tall and handsome, with curly red hair, he was a plesant and jovial companion. In his immediate circle, he was much loved. He had always been sensitive and shy with strangers, and his experiences in 1829 only increased these tendencies; Peel retreated behind a cold and reserved exterior.

Attacked by some of its own former supporters and under pressure from the advocates of parliamentary reform, the government of Wellington and Peel staggered to its dissolution late in 1830. Its place was taken by the Whig administration of Lord Grey of Reform Bill fame. Peel led the battle against the bill in the Commons, but it became law in 1832. For a brief period in 1834-1835 the King quarreled with his Whig ministers and called on Peel to head a Tory government. But the King could no longer appoint whom he wished to office, and Peel's government was soon defeated by a hostile majority in the Commons and by the electorate in 1835. Peel's first government is notable mainly in that it allowed him to redefine Tory goals, particularly in the Tamworth Manifesto, which he issued to his constituents on the eve of the general election. On behalf of what he now called the Conservative party, Peel accepted the Reform Act and its implications and pledged constructive reforms that would strengthen the basic institutions of the country. And though he was in opposition, Peel came to play a dominating role in the years after 1835 as Whig support in Parliament and in the country steadily diminished. The government of Lord Melbourne came to exist largely on Peel's sufferance. Hence the great reforms of the period, particularly municipal and Church reforms, bore Peel's imprint and filled in the outlines of the Tamworth Manifesto.

The Great Years

Peel might easily have come to power in 1839 had not his coldness offended the young Queen Victoria. By 1841, however, the Whig government had reached the end of the road, and the Queen was forced to accept Peel as her prime minister. The greatest achievement of Peel's ministry was to establish the principle of free trade. The best economic thought of the day favored it, and the academics were backed by the vociferous demands of the industrial middle classes. Peel favored it because he thought it was in the best interests of the country. He felt that free trade would bring prosperity to manufacturers and increased employment to the working classes, and that it would lower the cost of living. Gradually from 1842 onward trade was freed, and by 1845 the only outstanding anomaly in the system was the protection of agriculture afforded by the Corn Laws. These laws were ardently supported by Tory squires, who com-

posed a large section of Peel's support in Parliament. Peel was therefore not anxious to press this issue, but he was ready to do so if the Corn Laws caused real suffering. In the autumn of 1845 the Irish potato crop rotted in the ground. There was not enough grain in the British Isles to fill the need. The alternatives were quite simply repeal of the Corn Laws or starvation. Peel would have preferred the Whigs to carry repeal, but they would not. He therefore did it himself in 1846. Once more he was denounced as a traitor, and the party broke apart. Again Peel had done his duty to Queen and to country, knowing full well that in so doing he was probably ending his brilliant political career.

This time it was the end. For 4 years after 1846 Peel remained active and influential as the leader of a loyal Peelite remnant of his party. But on July 2, 1850, he died following a riding accident, and his great career was ended.

Further Reading

Norman Gash is engaged on a modern biography of Peel, only the first volume of which has been completed: *Mr. Secretary Peel: The Life of Sir Robert Peel to 1830* (1961), a superb study. An excellent assessment of Peel's whole career as a statesman is in Asa Briggs, *The Age of Improvement* (1959).

Additional Sources

Evans, Eric J., *Sir Robert Peel: statesmanship, power, and party,* London; New York: Routledge, 1991.
Gash, Norman, *Peel,* London; New York: Longman, 1976.
Gash, Norman, *Sir Robert Peel: the life of Sir Robert Peel after 1830,* London; New York: Longman, 1986.
Read, Donald, *Peel and the Victorians,* Oxford, UK; New York, NY, USA: B. Blackwell, 1987. □

Charles Pierre Péguy

The French poet and author Charles Pierre Péguy (1873-1914) was a fervent Roman Catholic, patriot, and social reformer. Through his writings and actions he influenced many Frenchmen who went to war in 1914.

Born into a working-class family in Orléans on Aug. 7, 1873, Charles Péguy was able, thanks to scholarships, to attend Lakanal, the celebrated lycée outside Paris, and the École Normale Supérieure in Paris, another celebrated academic institution. At the École Normale he studied under Henri Bergson, whose antirationalistic philosophy did much to confirm Péguy's mystic bent. Although Péguy wished to become a teacher, he failed the *agrégation* examination and then became a writer. His first work, *Jeanne d'Arc, Domrémy, les Batailles,* written in collaboration with Marcel Baudouin, revealed Péguy's socialist orientation and his Christian inspiration, both of which grew deeper. *Jeanne d'Arc* is a "drama dedicated to all who will have died fighting against universal evil, to all who will have died to found the universal socialist Republic." It appeared in 1897. Three years later Péguy founded the periodical *Cahiers de la quinzaine* as a means of communicating his ideas directly. He then concentrated his energies on polemical writing until, a few years before his death, he began working on the great liturgical poems for which he is now famous.

Political Writings

Péguy's ideological views are strong and stern; yet, at least when observed from a distance and en bloc, they appear more than a little contradictory. Péguy was a militant defender of Capt. Alfred Dreyfus but not an enemy of the army; he could not accept all the teachings of the Church, yet he was profoundly Christian; he was a Socialist and at the same time a severe critic of the Socialist party. Some of the contradictions, however, disappear when his thought is placed in its historical context and its fluctuations and evolution are traced. When a student at Lakanal, Péguy moved toward socialism in proportion as he moved away from the Church. Then, when a student at the École Normale, although his fervor for socialism had in no way abated, he moved closer to the Church. By a curious but not illogical itinerary, Péguy went from a defense of social causes like Dreyfusism to a defense of army and nation, whose honor he vindicated by refusing all conformism and whitewash. From the nation he moved to a defense of the Church—Joan of Arc is a double heroine. Yet not until 1908 did Péguy declare openly that he had found his faith again. And still there were reserves and recantations; his Christianity was never quite orthodox, just as his socialism was always highly individualistic. From 1900 Péguy declared his objections to the Socialist party openly. He deplored socialism's identification with materialism and atheism as well as its tacit approval of conformism and collectivism. When the Tangier incident brought home to him the danger that threatened France, socialism with its internationalism and pacifism finally had nothing more to say to Péguy. For the rest of his life he campaigned for Church and country.

A close look at Péguy's ideas in historical context and chronology reveals most clearly that in every instance his stand was dictated by a passion for truth and justice. And this passion gave his thought its basic coherence. It was in the name of truth and justice that he published his *Cahiers* and, in its pages, did not hesitate to attack any institution—the Church, the university, the Socialist party—that he found guilty of betraying its mission or, as he said, of sacrificing a *mystique* to a *politique*. In the name of truth and justice he invited contributions from thinkers of diverse tendencies. Although its circulation was never very large, the *Cahiers de la quinzaine* thus exercised a significant force in the spiritual and intellectual life of pre-World War I France.

Péguy's Poetry

Péguy's conversion in 1908 gave impetus to his creative work. He revised his *Jeanne d'Arc* and composed the extraordinarily long lyrical meditations that he called *mystères* and *tapisseries*. In *Jeanne* he had mingled prose and verse. For the *mystères* he used free verse with blanks and full stops, which created a very personal rhythm pat-

tern. *Le Porche du mystère de la deuxième virtu* (1911) is one of the most famous. For subsequent works Péguy preferred a more orthodox line. The 8,000 verses of *Eve* (1913), completed a few months before his death, were written in unbroken Alexandrines. But Péguy's phrasing was still the solemn and repetitious sort associated with a litany. Each strophe repeats the preceding one with only minor variation to indicate the slow but sure progress of the poem. Their rhythm has reminded critics of a soldiers's step or of the plodding footfall of a peasant. In structure Péguy's poems constitute vast accumulations of pious rhapsody and reflexion, a verbal cathedral, as it were, raised to the glory of God. Péguy's poetry stands somewhat outside the French traditions, far removed from symbolist or modernist trends.

Charles Péguy enlisted on the first day of World War I and shortly afterward was killed leading his men in a charge in the Battle of the Marne on Sept. 5, 1914.

Further Reading

Julien Green and Ann Green published two volumes of translations of Péguy's works, *Basic Verities: Prose and Poetry* (1943) and *Men and Saints: Prose and Poetry* (1944). There are two additional volumes published by Julien Green, *God Speaks: Religious Poetry* (1945) and *The Mystery of the Charity of Joan of Arc* (1950). Pansy Pakenham translated *The Mystery of the Holy Innocents, and Other Poems* (1956). Majorie Villiers, *Charles Péguy: A Study in Integrity* (1966), is the first full-length biography of Péguy in English. Two valuable introductions to Péguy are Alexander Dru, *Péguy* (1956), which provides a chronological survey of the events of his life, and Nelly Jussem-Wilson, *Charles Péguy* (1965), which includes useful appendixes. A critical study is Yvonne Servais, *Charles Péguy: The Pursuit of Salvation* (1953). Hans A. Schmitt, *Charles Péguy: The Decline of an Idealist* (1967), is a moral study.

Additional Sources

St. Aubyn, Frederic C. (Frederic Chase), *Charles Péguy,* Boston: Twayne Publishers, 1977. □

I. M. Pei

Chinese-American architect, I. M. Pei (born 1917), directed for nearly 40 years one of the most successful architectural practices in the United States. Known for his dramatic use of concrete and glass, Pei counted among his most famous buildings the East Wing of the National Gallery of Art in Washington, D.C. the John Hancock Tower in Boston, and the Rock and Roll Hall of Fame Museum in Cleveland, Ohio.

Ieoh Ming Pei was born in Canton, China, on April 26, 1917. His early childhood was spent in Canton and Hong Kong, where his father worked as director of the Bank of China. In the late 1920s the Pei family moved to

Shanghai, where I. M. attended St. Johns Middle School. His father, who had many British banking connections, encouraged his son to attend college in England, but I. M. decided to emigrate to the United States in order to study architecture at the University of Pennsylvania. Upon his arrival in 1935, however, he found that the University of Pennsylvania's curriculum, with its heavy emphasis on fine draftsmanship, was not well suited to his interest in structural engineering. He enrolled instead in the Massachusetts Institute of Technology.

While at M.I.T. Pei considered pursuing a degree in engineering, but was convinced by Dean William Emerson to stick with architecture. Pei graduated with a bachelor's degree in architecture in 1940, winning the American Institute of Architects Gold Medal and the Alpha Rho Chi (the fraternity of architects). He was immediately offered the prestigious Perkins Traveling Fellowship. Pei considered going to Europe or returning to China, but with both regions engulfed in war, he decided to remain in Boston and work as a research assistant at the Bemis Foundation (1940-1941).

From Professor to Architect

With America's entry into World War II, Pei obtained a position at the Boston engineering firm of Stone and Webster, where he designed structures for national defense projects (1941-1942). In this capacity he had the opportunity to work extensively with concrete, a material that he was later to use successfully in his own work.

In 1942 Pei married Eileen Loo, a Chinese student recently graduated from Wellesley College. After the wedding Pei left his job at Stone and Webster and moved to Cambridge, Massachusetts, where Eileen enrolled in Harvard's Graduate School of Landscape Architecture. Through her, Pei was introduced to the Harvard Graduate School of Design, which had recently come under the direction of Walter Gropius and Marcel Breuer. Excited by the chance to work with these two leading exponents of the modern International Style, Pei enrolled in the summer of 1942. Here, in the company of such figures as Philip Johnson, Pei was introduced to the work of Europe's most progressive architects. He absorbed their ideas about designing unornamented buildings in abstract shapes—buildings that frankly exposed their systems of support and materials of construction.

Pei's work at Harvard was interrupted in early 1943 when he was called to serve on the National Defense Research Committee in Princeton, New Jersey. He maintained his contacts in Cambridge, however, and between 1943 and 1945 formed informal partnerships with two other students of Gropius, E. H. Duhart and Frederick Roth. With these men, Pei designed several low-cost modernistic houses that were intended to be built of prefabricated plywood panels and "plug-in" room modules. Several of these designs were awarded recognition in *Arts and Architecture* magazine and thus served to give Pei his first national exposure.

Although he continued to work for the National Defense Research Committee until 1945, Pei returned to Harvard in 1944. The following year he obtained a lectureship on the faculty of the Graduate School of Design. In 1946, having obtained his master's degree in architecture, Pei was appointed assistant professor. While teaching, he worked in the Boston office of architect, Hugh Stubbins (1946-1948).

Pei's career as a Harvard professor ended in 1948 when, at the age of 31, he was hired to direct the architectural division of Webb and Knapp, a huge New York contracting firm owned by the real estate tycoon William Zeckendorf. A bold developer with tremendous capital, Zeckendorf specialized in buying run-down urban lots and building modern high rise apartments and offices. As architect of Webb and Knapp, Pei oversaw the design of some of the most extensive urban development schemes of the postwar era, including the Mile High Center in Denver and Hyde Park Redevelopment in Chicago (both 1954-1959). These projects gave Pei the opportunity to work on a large scale and with big budgets. Moreover, he learned how to negotiate compromises with community, business, and government agencies. In his words, he learned to consider "the big picture."

His Own Architectural Firm

By mutual agreement, Pei and his staff of some 70 designers split from Webb and Knapp in 1955 to become I. M. Pei & Associates, an independent firm, but one which still initially relied on Zeckendorf as its chief client. It was for Zeckendorf, in fact, that Pei and his partners designed some of their most ambitious works—Place Ville Marie, the commercial center of Montreal (1956-1965); Kips Bay

Plaza, the Manhattan apartment complex (1959-1963); and Society Hill, a large housing development in Philadelphia (1964).

In terms of style, Pei's work at this time was strongly influenced by Mies van der Rohe. Certainly the apartment towers at Kips Bay and Society Hill owe much to Mies' earlier slab-like skyscrapers sheathed in glass grids. But unlike Mies, who supported his towers with frames of steel, Pei experimented with towers of pre-cast concrete window frames laid on one another like blocks. This system proved to be quick to construct and required no added fireproof lining or exterior sheathing, making it relatively inexpensive. The concrete frames also had the aesthetic advantage of looking "muscular" and permanent. Soon Pei acquired a reputation as a pragmatic, cost-conscious architect who understood the needs of developers and had the ability to produce solid-looking no-nonsense buildings.

During the 1960s Pei continued to build Miesian "skin-and-bones" office and apartment towers (the Canadian Imperial Bank of Commerce in Toronto and 88 Pine Street in New York, were both completed in 1972), but he also began to get commissions for other types of buildings that allowed him more artistic expression. Among the first of these was the National Center for Atmospheric Research in Boulder, Colorado (1961-1967). For this project Pei borrowed ideas from the work of Le Corbusier and Louis Kahn to create a monumental structure of exposed concrete. Distinguished by a series of unusual hooded towers, and photogenically situated against the backdrop of the Rocky Mountains, the NCAR complex helped to establish Pei as a designer of serious artistic intent. Film enthusiasts remember this building as the setting for the Woody Allen film, *Sleeper.* In 1964 his stature increased when he was chosen to design the John F. Kennedy Library, although the building's dedication would be 15 years later, due to rigorous work and study.

Pei's reputation as artist-architect was further enhanced with his design for the Everson Museum of Art at Syracuse University in New York (1962-1968). Again Pei turned to reinforced concrete, this time molded into four monolithic gallery blocks, boldly cantilevered and arranged in a pinwheel manner around a large interior court. The design met with considerable acclaim, and Pei was soon asked to design one art museum after another: the Des Moines Art Center in Iowa (1968); the Mellon Art Center in Wallingford, Connecticut (1972); the University of Indiana Art Museum in Bloomington (1980); the west wing of the Museum of Fine Arts in Boston (1981); and the Portland Museum of Art in Maine (1983).

Triangles and Curtains of Glass

Of his many museums, Pei became best known for the East Wing of the National Gallery in Washington, D.C. (1968-1978). Located on a prominent but oddly shaped site, Pei cleverly divided the plan into two triangular sections—one containing a series of intimate gallery spaces and the other housing administrative and research areas. He connected these sections with a dramatic sky-lit central court, bridged at various levels by free-floating passageways. Technological innovation is evident on the exterior, where

space-age neoprene gaskets have been inserted between the blocks of marble to prevent cracks from developing in the walls. The overall design so impressed noted critic Ada Louise Huxtable that she declared in 1974, "I. M. Pei . . . may very likely be America's best architect."

Unlike so many other students of Gropius and the International Style, Pei showed concern that his buildings were "contextual," that they fit into their pre-existing architectural environments. The East Wing, for instance, was carefully related in height to the older main block of the National Gallery, and it was sheathed in similarly colored marble. For the apartments he built in Philadelphia during the 1950s Pei used brick, the city's traditional building material. And for his projects in China, such as the Luce Chapel at Taunghai University in Taiwan (1964) and the Fragrant Hill Hotel near Beijing (1983), he incorporated architectural forms and details indigenous to the Orient.

Although his reputation was slightly tarnished in the mid-1970s when plates of glass mysteriously fell out of his John Hancock Tower in Boston (1973), Pei was still considered a master of curtain glass construction in the 1980s. He demonstrated this again in the glass-sheathed Allied Bank Tower in Dallas (1985) and later worked on a well-publicized glass pyramid built in the courtyard of the Louvre Museum in Paris (1987). But his magnificent work in glass would not stop there. In September of 1995, The Rock and Roll Hall of Fame Museum was dedicated in Cleveland, Ohio. In an interview with *Technology Review,* Pei explained the concept. "These are the things I tried to imbue in the building's design—a sense of tremendous youthful energy, rebellion, flailing about. Part of the museum is a glass tent leaning on a column in the back. All the other forms—wings—burst out of the tent. Their thrusting out has to do with the rebellion. This, for me, is an expression of the musical form of rock and roll."

A man of gracious character and tact, Pei managed to preserve lasting associations with the other members of his firm, thereby fostering one of the most stable, quality-conscious practices in the country. Moreover, he maintained the trust and patronage of countless corporations, real estate developers, and art museums. Among his numerous awards he placed personal significance on receiving the Medal of Liberty from President Ronald Reagan at the Statue of Liberty. To him, it was a symbol of acceptance and respect from the American people.

When not designing buildings, Pei enjoyed gardening around his home in Katonah, New York. He had four children, two of whom worked as architects in his busy office on Madison Avenue.

Further Reading

There is still no monograph on Pei. The best single presentation of his work remains Peter Blake and others, "I. M. Pei and Partners," *Architecture Plus* 1 (February and March 1973). For biographical information and a fine appraisal of his buildings see Paul Goldberger, "The Winning Ways of I. M. Pei," *New York Times Magazine* (May 20, 1979). Also helpful are a number of recorded interviews; the two best are Andrea O. Dean, "Conversations: I. M. Pei," *Journal of the American Institute of Architects* (June 1979) and Barbaralee Diamonstein, "I. M. Pei: 'The Modern Movement Is Now Wide Open'," *Art News 77* (Summer 1978). See also Paul Heyer, *Architects on Architecture* (1966).

A chronological list of Pei's major works appears in the *Macmillan Encyclopedia of Architects* (1983). Articles on individual buildings can be found in either the *Art Index* or the *Avery Index to Architectural Periodicals.* Ada Louise Huxtable offers a critic's view of some of Pei's buildings in her book *Kicked a Building Lately?* (1976). Pei himself wrote very little, but see two articles by him: "Standardized Propaganda Units for the Chinese Government," *Task* 1 (1942), and "The Sowing and Reaping of Shape," *Christian Science Monitor* (March 16, 1978). ☐

Charles Sanders Peirce

Charles Sanders Peirce (1839-1914) was one of America's most important philosophers. Many of his writings were not published until after his death, but he made important contributions in both philosophy and science. His work in logic helped establish the philosophical school of thought known as pragmatism.

Charles Sanders Peirce was born on September 10, 1839, to Benjamin Peirce and Sarah (Mills) Peirce. His father was a professor at Harvard University and a leading mathematician of his day, and his mother was the daughter of Elijah Mills, U.S. senator from Massachusetts. Peirce grew up in the academic environment of Harvard at a time when science was challenging traditional religious views. He attended local private schools and then Cambridge High School, but his father closely supervised his education, exercising him in games of concentration and complicated mathematical analyses. Peirce was later to comment that his father's educational influence on him was the most important one.

Peirce entered Harvard in 1855 and graduated in 1859, one of the youngest members of the class. His interests pointed in the direction of philosophy, but at the urging of his father he entered scientific work. In 1861 he secured a position with the United States Coast Survey, for which he conducted scientific statistical research, a position he held until 1887. He also continued his formal education. In 1863 Harvard awarded him the B.Sc. in chemistry, *summa cum laude.* Over the following years his work in science was of such note that in 1877 he was elected a fellow in the American Academy of Arts and Sciences and was made a member of the National Academy of Science. Peirce's interest in philosophy continued, however. From 1864 to 1871 he gave occasional lectures in logic and the philosophy of science at Harvard and was a member of a select intellectual circle that included such luminaries as Ralph Waldo Emerson and John Fiske.

Scholar and Author

Because of circumstances and temperament, Peirce did not make teaching his career. His most significant academic post was as a lecturer in logic at the Johns Hopkins University from 1879 to 1884. He also lectured occasionally at the Lowell Institute and at Bryn Mawr College. He was an inspiring teacher for advanced students, but his insistence on logical precision and his use of a highly technical vocabulary did not appeal to most students. He once described himself as vain and ill-tempered; certainly he was a proud person, conscious of his intellectual power, and often insensitive to the feelings of others. Peirce's temperament apparently affected his first marriage, to Harriet Melusina Fay in 1862, which ended in divorce in 1883. However, his second marriage, to Juliet Frossy, lasted until his death.

A creative and productive scholar, Peirce worked long hours and wrote voluminously. Yet his philosophical work remained obscure until 1898, when William James recognized him as one of the originators of philosophical pragmatism. This reputation grew out of several articles Peirce published in *Popular Science Monthly,* particularly "How To Make Our Ideas Clear" (1878). In this piece he quarrelled with the accepted view in logic, dating back to Rene Descartes, that a clear idea is defined as "one which is so apprehended that it will be recognized wherever it is met with, and so that no other will be mistaken for it." Peirce labeled this "a prodigious force of clearness of intellect as is seldom met with in this world" and held that it was really based on the subjectivism of familiarity and not on the merits of logic itself. Descartes' use of methodical doubt, set forth in the *cogito* ("I think; therefore, I am"), was intended to permit at least some skepticism and to reject the practice of appealing to authority for the source of truth; instead, it transformed the traditional appeal to authority into an appeal to subjective introspection.

Rather than seeking the foundation of logic in subjective introspection, Peirce maintained, it is necessary to look to experience in the objective world. The action of thought is excited or motivated by the irritation of doubt, and this activity ceases when a belief is attained. In other words, Peirce held, the production of belief is the sole function of thought. But we also want beliefs that are sound, and hence we need a conception of logical thought process which will lead to clear ideas upon which sound beliefs may follow. The essence of belief is the establishment of sound habits of conduct in the world of people, events, things, and ideas. For Peirce, it was inconceivable that we should have an idea in our minds which relates to anything but conceivable sensible effects. As he put it, "Consider what effects, that might conceivably have practical bearings, we conceive the objects of our conception to have. Then, our conception of these effects is the whole of our conception of the object." In other words, "Our idea of anything *is* our idea of its sensible effects. . . ." Many people took this to be a skeptical and materialistic principle, but Peirce pointed out that it was only an application of the principle of logic recommended by Jesus: "'Ye may know them by their fruits. . . .'" Peirce was pleased with James's recognition of his work, but he came to disagree with the latter's rendition of the principle as "Truth is what works." This interpretation led Peirce, in 1905, to devise another name for his own views, and he settled on the term "pragmaticism," allowing that it was "ugly enough to be safe from kidnappers."

Scientist and Philosopher

During his work with the United States Coast Survey, Peirce conducted astronomical research at the Harvard Observatory which resulted in the only complete book he published during his lifetime, *Photometric Researches* (1878). In 1884, while teaching at Johns Hopkins, he also published *Studies in Logic,* a collection of essays by himself and some of his students. He did, however, publish a number of articles in journals such as *The Monist, North American Review, The Nation, Journal of Speculative Thought, Hibbert Journal,* and *Popular Science Monthly.* He was a significant contributor to such standard reference works as *Century Dictionary* (1889-1891) and *Dictionary of Philosophy and Psychology* (1901-1905).

In his later years Peirce's philosophical reputation and fortune, never very extensive, suffered decline. When he retired from the Coast Survey in 1887, he and his wife Juliet moved to the countryside near Milford, Pennsylvania. Gradually indebtedness, advancing age, and ill health took their toll. He approached the end of his life in poverty and without the recognition his work deserved. He finally succumbed to cancer on April 20, 1914.

The greater part of his work was not published until after his death when his papers were purchased by Harvard University. Much of this collection was disorganized, with many parts undated and with important manuscripts in several drafts. Nevertheless, significant portions have been published and have afforded scholars easier access. *The Collected Works of Charles Sanders Peirce,* volumes 1 to 6 (1931-1935) and volumes 7 and 8 (1966), made most of his major writings available. More recently, *Writings of Charles Sanders Peirce: A Chronological Edition,* volume 1 (1982), helped show the evolution of his thought in the early years. Future volumes are expected.

Along with these publications has come a better appreciation of Peirce's many contributions. Not only did he provide valuable work in logic, but in several other fields of philosophy as well. He grew to intellectual maturity during the time when Darwin's theory of natural selection created significant changes in people's outlooks. Although Peirce was well grounded in science, Darwinian naturalism was not a major part of his philosophical outlook. Instead, his thrust was toward the Kantian philosophical tradition of seeking the philosophical foundations of science in metaphysics or first philosophy. Peirce developed an evolutionary cosmology, but it was based on objective idealism rather than naturalism, which helps account for his attempt to separate himself from James and other pragmatists. These undercurrents in Peirce's thought led him to explore a wide range of philosophical interests, including the history of philosophy, the theory of signs, phenomenology, and perception—explorations which are now being more thoroughly studied by contemporary scholars.

Further Reading

Biographical material on Charles Sanders Peirce, written by Paul Weiss, may be found in the *Dictionary of American Biography,* volume XIV (1934). The same material is reprinted in *Perspectives on Peirce* (1965), which also contains critical essays on Peirce's philosophical contributions. More recent is the biographical sketch of Peirce's early life by Max H. Fisch, "Introduction," *Writings of Charles Sanders Peirce,* volume I (1982). The most complete edition of Peirce's writings is *The Collected Papers of Charles Sanders Peirce,* volumes I-VIII (1931-1935, 1966). Selected papers may be found in *Essays in the Philosophy of Science* (1967). A helpful analysis of the overall philosophy is Christopher Hooking, *Peirce* (1985), which also contains a biographical sketch in the introduction. A briefer treatment is Peter Turley, *Peirce's Cosmology* (1977). □

Floriano Peixoto

Floriano Peixoto (1839-1895) was the second president of Brazil. His ruthless leadership as the "Iron Marshall" in the face of widespread armed rebellion is given credit for holding Brazil together in the early republican period.

loriano Peixoto was born into a planter-class family of small landholdings in Maceió, Alagoas, on April 30, 1839. While still a youth, he enlisted in the army as a common soldier. In 1861 he entered the military school in Rio to study military engineering. Leaving the school in 1865 to fight in the Paraguayan War, he earned successive promotions to lieutenant colonel.

After the war Peixoto returned to Rio, finished his engineering course, and held a series of minor commissions. By 1883 he had risen to the rank of brigadier general, and the following year he became president and military commander of the province of Mato Grosso.

When the monarchy fell in November 1889, Peixoto was simultaneously serving as field marshal, adjutant general, and senator from Alagoas. Feigning loyalty to the empire, he joined the rebelling army and led the coup when illness incapacitated Marshal Manoel Deodoro da Fonseca.

In May 1890 Peixoto became minister of war in Deodoro's provisional government. On Feb. 24, 1891, the Constituent Assembly elected Deodoro Brazil's first president and Peixoto the vice president. Peixoto soon aligned with the Congress, with whom Deodoro was constantly fighting, and his home became a meeting place for enemies of the President. Deodoro's limited political ability and continuous altercations with the Congress led to his resignation on Nov. 24, 1891. The following day Peixoto became Brazil's second president.

Peixoto's disregard for the Congress, refusal to call new elections, purge of state presidents, and harsh dictorship aroused immediate opposition. In January 1892 short-lived military uprisings aggravated the political turmoil, while inflation and decreasing agricultural production compounded the general confusion.

Although Peixoto quickly and ruthlessly crushed all opposition, the most serious threats to his position came from the province of Rio Grande do Sul and the navy. In Rio Grande insurgents bearing the standards of federalism and positivism launched an attack from Uruguay on Feb. 9, 1893.

On Sept. 6, 1893, Adm. Custódio José de Mello led a naval revolt in Guanabara Bay. Mello controlled the sea but failed to get any land support and made no attempt to join with the rebels in Rio Grande. The army remained loyal to Peixoto and securely fortified Rio. The two forces reached an impasse, and the navy finally surrendered on April 16, 1894. Mello and the naval leaders, plus many defeated Rio Grande federalists, fled to Buenos Aires. The flight of these two groups terminated the pronouncements, but Peixoto followed his victories with summary executions, bloody reprisals, and firm dictatorship.

As the end of Peixoto's term approached, many feared that he would lead a coup and continue his regime. Lack of adequate support, and perhaps more significant, increasingly poor health, forced him to accept a new election. On Nov. 15, 1894, Prudente de Morais Barros took office, and a short time later Peixoto fell gravely ill. He died in Barra Mansa, Rio de Janeiro, on June 29, 1895.

Further Reading

There is no recent study of Floriano Peixoto, but he is treated in some detail in José Maria Bello, *A History of Modern Brazil, 1889-1964* (1954; trans. 1966), and in Charles Willis Simmons, *Marshal Deodoro and the Fall of Dom Pedro II* (1966). □

Pelagius

The British theologian Pelagius (died ca. 430) held that the human will is free to do either good or evil and taught that divine grace only facilitates what the will can do itself. Pelagianism was condemned by the Church.

oon after 400 Pelagius appeared in Rome. Widespread evidence indicates that he came originally from the British Isles. Whatever his origin, when Pelagius arrived in Rome, he was a layman. Perhaps it was his style of life or the nature of his moral teachings that caused others to refer to him as a monk, but he belonged to no monastic order or community. Even Augustine, who became Pelagius's severest critic, both referred to him as a monk and praised the upstanding character of his life.

While in Rome, Pelagius first heard of Augustine through his reading of a prayer from Augustine's *Confessions:* "Give what Thou commandest and command that Thou wilt." To Pelagius, the philosophy expressed in this prayer sounded like the total abandonment of human responsibility and a denial of the ethical dimensions of the Christian faith. If all moral action, thought Pelagius, depends solely on God—both the commanding as well as the ability to obey—God is either an arbitrary tyrant or else man is a creature deprived of free will. Pelagius conducted his teaching along these lines while he was in Rome, and it was to this teaching that an able lawyer, Caelestius, responded, leaving his profession of advocacy and becoming Pelagius's disciple, companion, and the popularizer of his views.

Travel to Africa

In 409 Alaric the Goth threatened Rome with his barbarian armies. Before he sacked Rome in 410, Pelagius and Caelestius had left Italy, staying in Sicily for a while and then sailing to North Africa. Their ship landed at Hippo, the see city of Augustine. Pelagius hoped to meet Augustine, but unfortunately he was away on business. Their arch-rivalry might have turned into a friendship had these two theologians ever met. Leaving Hippo, Pelagius and his lawyer friend moved to Carthage, where soon their views found loyal adherents as well as bitter opponents. But it was not until 411, after Pelagius had departed for the East leaving Caelestius behind, that the Pelagian controversy broke out and Augustine was enlisted as its chief theological prosecutor.

Caelestius was charged first and subsequently given a hearing at a Carthaginian synod under Bishop Aurelius. The heretical doctrine he was alleged to hold was that Adam, even before the Fall, was mortal and would have died even if he had not sinned. This doctrine, in the mind of the Africans, implied that Caelestius believed neither in original sin nor in the necessity of infant baptism. He was said, further, to have taught that man's sin is his own and not inherited from Adam. Against these and other charges Caelestius defended himself but to no avail; the synod excommunicated him, and he left North Africa.

But Caelestius's Pelagian views continued to spread, and soon Augustine was preaching and writing with intense fervor against this new heresy, arguing that the whole lump of humanity is infected with sin and that only the grace administered in baptism can wash away the guilty stain. In spite of these admonitions from the Doctor of Grace, the controversy continued, and it was not long before the articulate bishop of Eclanum, Julian, stepped in to argue the Pelagian cause, forcing Augustine, by the clarity of his logic, into positions regarding the doctrines of grace and predestination that have been burdensome to Western Christendom ever since.

Theological Controversy

The major events connected with the outbreak in North Africa of Pelagianism all occurred after Pelagius's departure. Leaving Africa, Pelagius went to Palestine. He found in John, the bishop of Jerusalem, one who not only sympathized with his views but who became a political ally as well. His chief enemy was Jerome, the scholarly ascetic who had left Rome to establish a monastery in Bethlehem and who, by disposition, was critical of Pelagius and his views. This disposition was not alleviated when Pelagius openly attacked Jerome's asceticism, especially his views on marriage. Soon after Pelagius's arrival in Palestine, Orosius, a zealous defender of the faith from Spain, arrived in Bethlehem to confer with Jerome. He brought with him news of Augustine's anti-Pelagian views and of the Carthaginian condemnation of Caelestius and Pelagianism. Orosius's news caused such a furor that John called a diocesan synod to examine the issues, allowing each side to present its case. However, in spite of Orosius's accusations, John was unmoved by the Western arguments and was in no way willing to accept the ecclesiastical authority of Augustine. "I am Augustine here!" he said. So the zealous Orosius lost the debate, and Pelagius's position seemed secure—at least in the East.

The turning point came, however, when the Augustinians presented a brief to Rome, requesting judgment on the validity of the condemnation of Pelagianism, in 411. Pope Innocent I expressed his sympathy with the North Africans and with Orosius and stated his views in a letter of excommunication of Pelagius, which reached Jerusalem in the winter of 417. Pelagius's cause was further harmed when news reached Innocent that Jerome's monastery had been sacked by an angry mob; it was unjustly assumed that Pelagius had participated in the violence. The letter of excommunication was followed by another sent directly to the bishop of Jerusalem decrying both the attack on the monastery and the fact that John was harboring a heretic in his midst.

Pelagius's fortunes seemed definitely on the wane. One glimmer of hope, however, occurred when the news of Innocent's death in March 417 arrived in Palestine. Perhaps his successor, Zosimus, might be more sympathetic to Pelagius's views. Therefore, Caelestius presented himself to Zosimus and argued his case. The Pope was impressed and for some time contemplated lifting the excommunication against them and pronouncing both Caelestius and Pelagius orthodox. But persuasive letters from North African bishops, as well as from Jerome, convinced him to rescind his tentative pronouncement in favor of Pelagianism. When Praylius, John's successor in Jerusalem, joined in Zosimus's final condemnation, Pelagius was beaten. Weary of the conflict, he left Palestine. History does not record where he went or what happened to him thereafter.

The theological question to which Pelagius addressed himself had to do with man's created capacity for good. Was it possible to lead a sinless life? Augustine answered No (with the exception of the Virgin Mary, whose sinlessness Augustine *did* assert); for Augustine divine grace must precede every virtuous act. Pelagius said that it was *possible* for man not to sin, but Augustine asserted that it was not possible for man not to sin. The caricature of Pelagianism found in many orthodox textbooks and devotional manuals is hardly one that Pelagius would recognize. He never, for instance, denied the need for grace or for infant baptism; he never accepted the position that man can, by his own moral efforts, achieve his salvation. On basic doctrinal issues, Pelagius was certainly orthodox; and on matters of Christian morality his chief concern was to foster among Christian people a right regard for the ethical responsibilities he saw as inherent in the Gospel message.

Further Reading

The few surviving works of Pelagius cannot be found in English translation except where they are quoted by an author, such as Augustine, whose works have been translated. Two modern studies of Pelagius and Pelagianism in English deserve special notice: John Ferguson, *Pelagius: A Historical and Theological Study* (1956), and Robert F. Evans, *Pelagius: Inquiries and Reappraisals* (1968). A good introductory survey of the course of the Pelagian controversy and of the issues involved can be found in Gerald Bonner, *Augustine of Hippo: Life and Controversies* (1963).

Additional Sources

Rees, B. R. (Brinley Roderick), *Pelagius, a reluctant heretic,* Woodbridge, Suffolk; Wolfeboro, N.H.: Boydell Press, 1988. □

Pele

Pele (born 1940), called "the Black Pearl," was the greatest soccer player in the history of the game. With a career total of 1,280 games, he may have been the world's most popular athlete.

Edson Arantes Do Nascimento Pele, who took the name Pele, was born October 23, 1940, in Tres Coracoes, Brazil, the son of a soccer player. His father's coaching paid off, for when he was 11 he played for his first soccer team, that of the town of Bauru, Brazil. He moved up in competition with outstanding play, and when he was 15 he was playing for the team from the village of Santos. He soon received broader exposure when he was loaned to the Vasco da Gama team in Rio di Janeiro.

In 1958 he went to Stockholm, Sweden to compete in the World Cup championship. His play there helped his country win its first title. He returned to Santos, and his team went on to win six Brazilian titles. In 1962 he again played on the World Cup team, but an injury forced him to sit out the contest.

Soccer is a low scoring game, but on November 19, 1969, before a crowd of 100,000 in Rio di Janeiro, Pele scored his 1,000th goal. He was not only a high scorer, but a master of ball handling as well. It seemed that the ball was somehow attached to his feet as he moved down the field.

In 1970 Pele again played for Brazil's World Cup team, and in Mexico City they beat Italy for the championship. It was Pele's play, both in scoring and in setting up other goals, that won them the title. When he announced that he would retire from international competition after a game to be played July 18, 1971, plans were made to televise the event throughout the world. He had scored a total of 1,086 goals. After his retirement he continued to play until he was signed to play for the New York Cosmos of the North American Soccer League for a reported three-year, $7 million contract. A year later New York was at the top of their division, and in 1977 the Cosmos won the league championship. Pele retired for good after that victory, but continued to be active in sports circles, becoming a commentator and promoter of soccer in the United States. When the World Cup came to Detroit in 1994, Pele was there, capturing the hearts of millions of fans around the world. Later that spring, he married his second wife, Assiria Seixas Lemos. In May of 1997, he was elected Minister of Sports in his home country of Brazil.

Further Reading

Two books—Joe Marcus' *The World of Pele* (1976) and *Pele's New World* (1977) by Peter Bodo and David Hirshey—provide excellent reading, as well as illustrations. The best book on Pele is by Pele himself—*My Life and the Beautiful Game* (1977). □

Cesar Pelli

Acclaimed by the American Institute of Architects (AIA) in 1991 as one of the ten most influential living American architects, Cesar Pelli (born 1926) has designed some of the most remarkable buildings— ranging from high-rise office towers to private homes—in the late 20th century.

Chief among Pelli's award-winning achievements are the San Bernardino City Hall in San Bernardino, California; the Pacific Design Center Phases I and II in Los Angeles, California; the United States Embassy in Tokyo, Japan; and the World Financial Center and Winter Garden at Battery Park, New York, which has been hailed as one of the ten best works of American architecture designed since 1980.

Though Pelli trained as a modern architect in the 1950s and was influenced by Eero Saarinen, he remains unclassifiable. His structures have been praised by Douglas Davis in a 1986 *Newsweek* article as "lyrical, technically sophisticated buildings that are neither 'modern' nor 'postmodern.' Each attempts to please on many levels at once, captivating clients and public but frustrating critics."

Pelli was born on October 12, 1926, in Tucumán, Argentina. He studied architecture at the University of Tucumán, earning his Bachelor's of Architecture in 1949. After graduating, Pelli married fellow student Diana Balmori, who has become an accomplished landscape and urban designer and who founded the firm Balmori Associates. For the next two years Pelli served as director of design at OFEMPE, a government organization sponsoring and building subsidized housing in Tucumán. In 1952, an Institute of International Education scholarship led Pelli to the University of Illinois School of Architecture in Champagne-Urbana, where he earned a Master's degree in Architecture in 1954.

Influenced by Saarinen

For the next ten years, Pelli worked as a designer with the firm of Eero Saarinen & Associates in Bloomfield Hills, Michigan, and Hamden, Connecticut. With Saarinen, whom Pelli credits as one of his greatest influences along with Le Corbusier, he served as project designer for the TWA Terminal Building at JFK Airport, New York, and the Morse and Stiles Colleges at Yale University. Though he had briefly returned to Argentina to teach architectural design at his alma mater, Universidad Nacional de Tucumán in 1960, Pelli became a U.S. citizen in 1964.

The same year, Pelli took the position of director and vice president of design with Daniel, Mann, Johnson, & Mendenhall (DMJM) in Los Angeles. In 1968, he served as partner for design at Gruen Associates in Los Angeles and for two of his eight years with Gruen, Pelli was a visiting professor at the University of California. During this period, Pelli designed several award-winning projects, including the San Bernardino City Hall, the Commons of Columbus in Indiana, the Pacific Design Center, and the U.S. Embassy in Tokyo.

Founds Own Architectural Firm

In 1977 Pelli moved to Connecticut to become the Dean of the School of Architecture at Yale University. That same year, he founded Cesar Pelli & Associates in New Haven with his wife Diana and Fred W. Clarke. Since the firm's inception, Pelli has designed each of its projects, although he actively solicits input from the more than 60 architects and designers who are employed in his studio. In 1984, he resigned his post at Yale, devoting full attention to his firm, but continues to lecture on architecture.

One of the jewels in Pelli's crown of large-scale design is the World Financial Center and Winter Garden at Battery Park City in Manhattan. Begun in 1991, this project features 4 office towers ranging in height from 34 to 51 stories, the Winter Garden, and a 3.5 acre landscaped public plaza. Other gems in Pelli's portfolio include the expansion and renovation of the Museum of Modern Art in New York City; the North Carolina Blumenthal Performing Arts Center in Charlotte; the Arnoff Center for the Arts in Cincinnati; the Francis Lehman Loeb Art Center at Vassar College; Herring Hall at Rice University; and the Boyer Center for Molecular Medicine at Yale University. Commenting on Pelli's design of Carnegie Hall Tower, Douglas Davis has pointed out in *Newsweek,* that ''[despite] the vast discrepancy in their sizes, the new skyscraper and the earthbound . . . hall seem of a piece. Over and again, Pelli's buildings defer—despite their ingenuity—to their sites and to their context. His architecture is unfailingly humane and courtly.''

This observation corresponds with Pelli's own philosophy, which he articulated in the August 1988 issue of *Architectural Digest:* ''We should not judge a building by how beautiful it is in isolation, but instead by how much better or worse that particular place . . . has become by its addition. If the city has not gained by the addition, we should seriously question the design and the building itself, no matter how beautiful and theoretically correct it may be.'' Other noteworthy buildings designed by Cesar Pelli & Associates include the Norwest Center, Minneapolis, Minnesota; Nations Bank Corporate Center and Founders Hall in Charlotte; the Mathematics Building and Lecture Hall at the Institute for Advanced Study in Princeton; North Terminal at Washington National Airport; and the Physics and Astronomy Building at University of Washington/Seattle.

Selected to Design Malaysian Twin Towers

In 1994 construction began on twin office towers in Kuala Lumpur, Malaysia, completed in 1996. Cesar Pelli & Associates served as design consultant to the architect-of-record, Kuala Lumpur City Centre (KLCC) Berhad Architectural Division, as well as a host of other U.S., Canadian, and Malaysian firms on an architectural project which ultimately surpassed the Sears Tower in Chicago as the world's tallest building. The office towers are the first phase of a multi-billion dollar development project situated on a 97-acre site in Kuala Lumpur City Centre. Petronas, Malaysia's national oil and gas company that owns 51 percent of KLCC, occupies the towers.

In his distinguished career as an architect, Pelli has been the recipient of numerous awards from such institutions as the American Academy of Arts and Letters, the American Institute of Architects, the National Academy of Design, and the International Academy of Architecture. He has been awarded the 1995 AIA Gold Medal and the Charles Bulfinch Award; in addition, he is the only architect to have received a Connecticut State Arts Award and is among one of the few American architects to receive First Class licensure in Japan. Several honorary degrees have been bestowed upon Pelli, including any honorary doctorate from the Pratt Institute in New York City.

Perhaps Pelli's greatest reward, however, is to explore one of his completed structures; as he stated in his 1988 *Architectural Digest* essay, ''[there] is nothing quite so pleasurable for me as to visit my buildings when they're finished and occupied. It is like being part of a miracle taking place. Months and even years of caring and dreaming become a reality.''

Further Reading

Contemporary Architects, 3rd edition, edited by Muriel Emanuel, New York, St. James Press, 1994, pp. 738-41.
The Encyclopedia of American Architecture, 2nd edition, edited by Robert T. Packard, New York, McGraw-Hill, 1995, pp. 475-79.
Architectural Digest, August 1988, pp. 29-32, 36; July 1990, pp. 124-27, 178; August 1991, pp. 178-79.
Architectural Record, August 1991, pp. 100-07.
Civil Engineering, July 1994, pp. 63-65.
Newsweek, August 4, 1986, p. 61.
Additional information for this profile was obtained from biographical materials acquired from Cesar Pelli & Associates Inc. Architects, 1995. □

Leonard Peltier

American Indian rights activist Leonard Peltier (born 1944) was convicted in the shooting deaths of two Federal Bureau of Investigation (FBI) agents at Pine Ridge Indian Reservation in South Dakota.

Driving at top speed and unannounced into a remote community at the Pine Ridge Indian reservation in South Dakota was an imprudent decision for two FBI agents to make on June 26, 1975. Yet that's exactly what agents Jack Coler and Ronald Williams did that day, in pursuit of an Indian youth on a minor theft complaint. It was almost predictable that gunfire would result: The reservation—desperately poor, and home to 10,000 Lakota Sioux—was a cauldron of violence and fear. The legendary 71-day siege at Wounded Knee had happened there just two years before. By 1975, American Indian Movement (AIM) members camped out at the Jumping Bull community were engaged in a full-blown war between full-blood and mixed-blood residents of Pine Ridge.

"Traditionals" trying to return the tribe to its original culture were battling "progressives." Mixed bloods, with apparent support from the FBI and Bureau of Indian Affairs (BIA) police, were fighting to maintain power. And mixed blood tribal council president Richard Wilson was allegedly using a private army, his so-called GOON (Guardians of the Oglala Nation) squad, to commit violence to hold onto his

power over BIA funds and negotiations for uranium mining contracts. Over 60 unsolved murders between May of 1973 and June of 1975, including those of women and children, gave this period the name "the reign of terror." It also gave Pine Ridge the highest per capita murder rate in the United States—and the highest ratio of FBI agents to citizens.

Amidst this frightening environment agents Coler and Williams met their deaths, close-up and execution-style. Also shot to death, with a bullet through his forehead, was young tribal member Joseph Stuntz. Exactly who provoked the shootout is still unknown. But the violence that day created one of the best known political prisoners of our time: Leonard Peltier, incarcerated for two life terms at Leavenworth Federal Penitentiary in Kansas. Peltier says he didn't kill Coler and Williams and has support in his campaign for clemency—or, at the least, a new trial—from the likes of Amnesty International, 50 Congressional representatives, filmmakers Michael Apted and Robert Redford, and over a hundred support groups worldwide—even the Eighth Circuit Court of Appeals judge who—on legal technicalities—rejected Peltier's case.

On June 26, 1994, a crowd estimated at 3,000 demonstrated peacefully in Washington, D.C., for Peltier's freedom. A month later, a 3,800-mile Walk for Justice culminating in the capital featured meetings with sympathetic senators. Petitions for clemency with more than half a million signatures had already been delivered to the White House in December of 1993—though Peltier's parole board had told him he must serve an additional 15 years to be reconsidered for release. The board cited "the nature of [Peltier's] offense" as the reason for its severity. But just what, exactly, Peltier's offense was unclear.

Peltier, an Indian of Chippewa, Cree, Lakota, and French descent, was born on September 12, 1944, in Grand Forks, North Dakota. The son of Leo and Alvina Peltier, he was raised by paternal grandparents Alex and Mary Peltier, who took him briefly to Butte, Montana, where his grandfather worked in logging and the copper mines. The family relocated again to Turtle Mountain reservation in North Dakota, where Peltier lived until he was nine. He was then sent to Wahpeton Indian School about 150 miles away, and experienced the typical brutal education Indian children endured in those days—separated from their culture, forced to speak English and to live in the white man's world.

Peltier stayed at the school through the ninth grade. Later in life he would pick up his education again, completing his general equivalency degree. As a young man in his twenties, Peltier worked as a welder, construction laborer, and at an auto shop he co-owned in Seattle. The partners used the upstairs room as a halfway house for other Indians coming out of prison or in need of alcohol counseling. Their generosity eventually led to financial ruin. During these years he married twice and fathered seven children; he also cared for two more children who were adopted.

Peltier has said he was politicized by the 1958 takeover of the BIA building at Turtle Mountain. He was not present at Wounded Knee but was at a similar takeover at Fort Lawton. Early on, he joined the American Indian Movement, journeying to Pine Ridge Reservation to help out in response to the tensions there between traditionals, mixed bloods, and federal authorities. As part of that action, Peltier was one of the AIM members who moved onto the property of an elderly couple, the Jumping Bulls, and set up what they called a "spiritual camp," though their obvious purpose was to protect traditionals from tribal president Wilson's men. The group, which former FBI chief Clarence Kelly would later describe in court as nonviolent, advocated sobriety and performed community improvement tasks.

The morning of June 26, 1975, the then-30-year-old Peltier has said, was warm and beautiful. In a statement released by his defense committee, Peltier says he remembers lying in his tent, enjoying the weather and listening to women laughing and gossiping outside as they prepared breakfast. When he heard gunfire, he at first he dismissed it as practice shooting in the woods. Then he heard screams. He says he grabbed his shirt and rifle and started running for the houses nearby where he feared the Jumping Bulls might be trapped.

The two FBI agents meanwhile had driven down a dirt road into the compound in separate cars in pursuit of young Jimmy Eagle, who was accused of stealing a pair of cowboy boots. Eagle, the agents radioed, was driving a red pickup truck. But soon their routine messages turned panicky. "If you don't get here quick, we're gonna be dead," the agents radioed in to the FBI in Rapid City. A third agent, Gary Adams, who was in the area, immediately sped to the site.

Gunfire erupted. AIM members Bob Robideau and Norman Brown, who were at the compound, said that the agents fired first and that they fired back. Others joined in. Coler was hit first in the arm. The FBI says that Coler and Williams, who only had .38s, were trying to get their rifles from the trunk. Robideau later said the AIM members didn't know the men were agents. Williams, who put up his hand as if to ward off an attack, was shot through his hand into his head at close range. Coler was also shot through the head. And Stuntz was killed in the crossfire as well—though his death was never investigated.

Adams, who at first reported he saw a red pickup exiting the compound at 12:18 p.m., arrived shortly thereafter and reported heavy gunfire. He was soon joined by 350 U.S. marshals, FBI agents, and BIA police, who began a massive manhunt.

Charged in the agents' deaths were Robideau, Darrelle Butler, Jimmy Eagle, and Peltier. But at first these men attempted to evade the law: together with the other armed AIM members, they fled to higher ground, where, they later said, they prayed for the safe journey of the three victims' spirits to the next world. For awhile they hid out at the home of an old man named Crow Dog. Within days, Butler and Robideau had been arrested; Peltier made it over the border to Canada.

There, on February 2, 1976, he too was arrested. But negotiations for his extradition were delayed, so the judge, Edward McManus, decided to go ahead with the trial of Robideau and Butler (charges against Eagle had been dismissed) in Cedar Rapids, Iowa, that June. Many sources describe what followed as a miscarriage of justice.

The government had the task of proving that the defendants aided and abetted the killings, which by law made them as guilty as the person who fired the fatal shots. But the defendants argued that they fired in defense, and blasted the prosecution's weak circumstantial evidence. The star witness, a man named James Harper, who claimed he'd heard Butler boasting of the crime in jail, was also discredited: His landlady came forward to call him a low-life and a liar. When the jury's verdict came back "not guilty," the Indian community celebrated joyously.

AIM supporters assumed they now had nothing to worry about with Peltier; his extradition was arranged in December of 1976. But there was an undercurrent to events. The prime evidence the government had to support its extradition case was a trio of affidavits from an Indian woman named Myrtle Poor Bear, who was widely believed to be mentally unstable. The affidavits were suspiciously inconsistent: In the first one she said she wasn't even at Jumping Bull compound; in the second she said she was there with Peltier and was his girlfriend; in the third she supplied even more "details." Poor Bear today says the affidavits were a sham. In the documentary *Incident At Oglala*, the overweight, gap-toothed woman says agents threatened to take away her daughter and told her, "We'll put you through a meat grinder." Added Poor Bear in the film: "I didn't even know Leonard; I didn't know what Leonard looked like til I met him in the courtroom."

Peltier's 1977 trial was moved to Fargo, North Dakota. The jury was all white; and the first judge, at Cedar Rapids, was replaced by Judge Paul Benson, who had been reversed by the Eighth Circuit Appeals Court for making anti-Indian statements during at least one of his previous trials. In fact, Benson repeatedly ruled against the defense during Peltier's trial.

This time government prosecutors also adopted a more aggressive strategy, apparently reasoning that the jury needed to be reminded that the agents were shot at point-blank range; bloody crime scene photos were repeatedly displayed. Witness Mike Anderson testified that he saw Peltier's vehicle pursued into the compound, that Peltier got out and shot the agents. Prosecutors also showed jurors a .223 shell casing they said had been found in Coler's car trunk; it came from an AR-15 traced to Peltier. Jurors were convinced: Peltier was convicted and sentenced to two consecutive life terms.

A long series of unsuccessful appeals followed. Oral arguments before the Eighth Circuit Appeals Court in 1985 were not successful; the court did not believe that the legal test for reversal had been met. But the court did conclude a year later that the FBI's suppression of information "cast a strong doubt on the government's case."

One source of doubt was the government's claims about the shell casing. The defense sought a retrial on the grounds that documents obtained from FBI files under the Freedom of Information Act included, among other suppressed evidence, an October 2, 1975, teletype from an FBI ballistics expert stating that the gun alleged to have been Peltier's contained a "different firing pin" than that used in the killings. The report was based on tests carried out on bullet casings found at the murder scene. At a district court hearing in 1984 ballistics expert Evan Hodge testified that the teletype referred to *other* casings found at the scene. But the defense submitted additional evidence showing that Peltier's alleged gun had been eliminated as the murder weapon.

Another source of doubt was the red pickup truck supposedly driven into the compound, with agents Coler and Williams in pursuit. On the witness stand, Agent Gary Adams reneged his original description of events, saying he'd seen a *red and white* pickup truck leaving the scene at 1:26 p.m. (not a *red pickup* at 12:18 p.m., as he'd originally testified). Defense lawyers said this allowed the government to pin the FBI killings on Peltier, who owned a red and white suburban *van,* present at the encampment.

Perhaps the strongest inconsistency came from the government's own admission: prosecutor Lynn Crooks told the appeals court that although the government tried Peltier for first degree murder, naming him as "the man who came down and killed those agents in cold blood," it did not really know this to be true. Crooks defended this statement at a 1991 court hearing, pointing out how aiders and abettors are punishable to the same degree as principals. *After the trial* and *after Peltier's conviction,* the government seemed to be changing its theory to make Peltier an aider and abettor rather than the premeditated murderer it had originally called him. Said Crooks in court: "My personal perspective is that [Peltier] went down and blew those agents' heads off. All evidence pointed to that. But we didn't prove it."

Adding to the murkiness of the case was a 1990 interview with a witness referred to as "Mr. X," conducted by journalist Peter Matthiessen (author of *In the Spirit of Crazy Horse,* a 1983 book about the Peltier case that was barred from publication for eight years by unsuccessful libel suits brought by an FBI agent and the governor of South Dakota). Mr. X told Matthiessen it was *he* who had fired the fatal shots, though he would not come forward, believing that he had acted in self-defense.

Along with the heavy media coverage of the July, 1991 hearing, other events coalesced that year: Appeals Judge Gerald Heaney, who'd written the Eighth Circuit Opinion, appeared on the CBS show *West 57th,* calling the Peltier case "the toughest decision I ever had to make in 22 years on the bench." Heaney also wrote an extraordinary letter to Hawaii senator Daniel Inouye, chairman of the Senate Committee on Indian Affairs, noting the "possibility that the jury would have acquitted Leonard Peltier had the records and data improperly withheld been available to him in order to better exploit and reinforce the inconsistences casting strong doubts upon the government's case."

Inouye made an overture to then-President George Bush for a commutation. Fifty Congressmen signed a "friend of the court" brief on Peltier's behalf. And Amnesty International, year after year, has kept Peltier on its political prisoners list, citing not just the AIM leader's case but "FBI misconduct" in the trials of other AIM members. Others have collected evidence of government collusion in the ambush murder of Oglala Sioux civil rights leader Pedro Bissonnette, the execution of AIM member Anna Mae Pictou Aquash, and numerous assassination attempts against AIM leader Russell Means.

During a parole hearing in December, 1995, prosecuter Lynn Crooks admitted again that no evidence exists against Peltier, further stating the the government never really accused him of murder and that if Peltier were retried, the government could not reconvict. Nevertheless, the Parole Board decided against granting parole because Peltier continues to maintain his innocence and because he was the only one convicted. Although this reasoning sounds ridiculous, it has thus far held up, and a petition for executive clemency remains unanswered three years after being filed with the Department of Justice.

Peltier, meanwhile, remains in prison, and continues his appeal. He has become an accomplished artist of Native American themes; his paintings, which sell for as much as $6,000, bring money in for his defense committee. Peltier also is engaged to defense team member Lisa Faruolo. He has said through Faruolo that if released he will continue to work for economic investment and social services on the reservation. "Right now, I'm being stored like a piece of meat," Peltier said in the *Incident at Oglala* documentary. But, he added, "I've got my dignity and self-respect, and I'm going to keep that, even if I die here."

Further Reading

Peter Matthiessen, *In the Spirit of Crazy Horse,* Viking, 1983, reissued, 1991.

Christian Science Monitor, February 3, 1994.

Esquire, January 1992.

The Leonard Peltier Story, "http://www.inicom.net/peltier/ story.html," Cowpath Productions, July 22, 1997.

Nation, May 13, 1991; July 18, 1994.

Washington Post, June 27, 1994.

Additional information was obtained from the Amnesty International *Annual Report,* 1988, 1990, 1992, 1993, and 1994; *Incident at Oglala,* a 1992 documentary; and a personal interview with Lisa Faruolo, October 9, 1994. □

Krzysztof Penderecki

Krzysztof Penderecki (born 1933) was the best known of a group of vigorous and adventuresome Polish composers who emerged in the 1950s.

Krzysztof Penderecki was born in Debica, Krakow district, a Polish provincial town, on November 23, 1933 and started his musical studies as a child. During the German occupation of Poland in World War II he experienced some of the Nazi atrocities against Poland's Jewish population. "The problem of that great apocalypse (Auschwitz), that great war crime, has undoubtedly been in my subconscious mind since the war, when as a child, I saw the destruction of the ghetto in my small native town of Debica," he said.

Penderecki was educated in Krakow where he took courses at the Jagallonian University. He also attended the State Higher School of Music in Krakow from 1955 to 1958. The following year he gained prominence when three compositions he had submitted to a competition organized by the Polish Composer's Union won the first three prizes. These compositions—*Strophen* for orchestra, *Emanations* for two string groups, and *Psalms of David* for a cappella choir—show that he was familiar with the music of Anton Webern, Béla Bartók, and Igor Stravinsky.

Penderecki stayed on at the State Higher School of Music after graduation as a lecturer in composition from 1958 to 1966 and remained from 1972 to 1987, as rector, after it had become the Academy of Music. He was also a professor from 1972 at the Academy of Music.

Penderecki also took the position of visiting teacher at Yale University (from 1972) and at Essen Folkwang Hochschule fur Musik (1966 to 1968) as a professor of composition.

In 1965 he married Elzbieta Solecka and they would later have two children, a son and daughter.

In his *Threnody for the Victims of Hiroshima* (1961) Penderecki achieved a highly original style. Written for 52 strings, it sounds like electronic music. Most of the pages of the score consist of diagrams with symbols he invented to convey his wishes. The opening page, for instance, calls for the strings, divided into 10 groups, to play "the highest note possible." The entrances are staggered, played fortissimo, and held for 15 seconds. The whistling sound is shrill and

frightening, like the approach of an airplane. In the course of the piece the players are directed to raise or lower written notes by a quarter or three-quarters of a tone, to play between the bridge and tailpiece, to tap the body of the instrument with fingers and bows, and to play with a wide variety of timbral effects. There are frequent huge clusters of massed half steps and glissandos of such clusters, producing a sound that resembles jet engines warming up. There is no meter. At the bottom of each page there is a wide line with a designation in seconds indicating how long the section should be played. The conductor indicates the beginnings of new time blocks, but there are no beats or subdivisions of them.

Other instrumental pieces by Penderecki that exploit new and expressive instrumental sounds are *Anaklasis* (1960), *Polymorphia* (1961), *De Natura Sonoris* (1966), and *Capriccio* for violin and orchestra (1968). He also made important contributions to choral literature in works that call for vocal sounds as novel as the sounds he drew from the orchestra. His major choral works are *Stabat Mater* (1963) for three a cappella choirs, *St. Luke Passion* (1966), *Dies Irae* (1967) dedicated to the memory of the victims of Auschwitz, *Slavic Mass* (1969), *Kosmogonia* (1970), *Ecloga VIII* (1972), *Magnificat* (1974), *De Profundis* (1977), *Te Deum* (1979), *Lacrimosa* (1980), *Agnus Dei* (1981), and *Polnisches Requiem* (1984). Other Penderecki works include *Praeludium* (1971), *Partita* (1971), *Symphony No. 1* (1973), *The Dream of Jacob* (1974), *Symphony No. 2* (1980), *Viola Concerto No. 2* (1982), *Passacaglia* (1988), and the opera *The Black Mask* (1986).

The *Passion* follows the baroque pattern and has a narrator and a baritone personifying Christ. The chorus acts both as commentator and participant when it sings the part of the crowd. Penderecki makes great use of a twelve-tone row that consists largely of seconds and thirds, including the familiar B-A-C-H motive (B-flat, A, C, B). Both orchestra and choir use clusters and glissandos, and the choir hisses, shouts, laughs, whispers, and chants. The *St. Luke Passion* brings together a wide variety of styles; it is a successful amalgamation of tonal resources from the Gregorian chant to the latest experimental sound.

Unlike some of the so-called avant-garde composers, Penderecki did not believe that the fundamental nature of music had changed. He said: "The general principle at the root of a work's musical style, the logic or economy of development, and the integrity of a musical experience embodied in the notes the composer is setting down on paper never changes. The idea of good music means today exactly what it meant always. Music should speak for itself, going straight to the heart and mind of the listener."

Penderecki's works are continually performed throughout the world and he holds teaching or advisory positions at universities around Europe and the world. He is considered by many as one of the most original composers in the world and has been honored with memberships in the Royal Academy of Music in London (1975), the Royal Academy of Music in Stockholm (1975), and the Akademie der Kunste in Germany (1975). He has been honored by nations around the world with the Herder Prize of Germany (1977), the

Grand Medal of Paris (1982), the Sibelius Prize of Finland (1983), the Premio Lorenzo il Magnifico of Italy (1985), the Wolf Prize (1987), Academia de Bellas Artes, Granada (1989), and the Das Grosse Verdienstkreuz des Verdienstordens (1990).

In 1997 Penderecki joined many other composers and performers for a birthday concert in honor of Russian composer Mstislav "Slava" Rostopovich at the Theatres des Champs-Elysees in Paris. His work compared favorably to that of other modern composers—like Vladimir Spivakov, Van Cliburn, Semyon Bychkov, and Seiji Ozawa—and was a testament to the originality and power of his music.

Further Reading

There is an extensive biography and listing of Penderecki's works in Brian Morton and Pamela Collins *Contemporary Composers* (1992). More general information on Penderecki is contained in Stefan Jarocinski *Polish Music* (1965), Ludwik Erhardt *Contemporary Music in Poland* (trans.1966), and Peter S. Hansen *An Introduction to Twentieth Century Music* (3d ed. 1971). Information on the Rostopovich birthday concert featuring Penderecki can be found in the *New York Times* (March 29, 1997). □

Edmund Pendleton

The American political leader Edmund Pendleton (1721-1803) became a liberal among the Virginia gentry, of which he was a part.

Edmund Pendleton was born into the Virginia colony's elite on Sept. 9, 1721. However, his father's early death and the subsequent loss of the family's property left Pendleton to shift for himself. His upper-class origins eventually served him well, but his early years were ones of struggle. His education came through apprenticeship to a county clerk, and his law degree was similarly gained. Only in 1752, on his election to the House of Burgesses, did his pedigree become significant. Thereafter, as he recouped his family's lost wealth, he took his place among Virginia's gentlemen.

As the Colonies' rupture with England widened, Pendleton emerged as a staunch opponent of the mother country. This role had carried him to the forefront of Virginia politics by the outbreak of the Revolution. He was designated a member of the Virginia Committee of Correspondence in 1773 and of the Continental Congress a year later, and he rose to the presidencies of both the Virginia Revolutionary Convention and the Committee of Safety in 1775. The last-mentioned post effectively placed Pendleton at the head of the Revolutionary government in the Old Dominion.

After a period of retirement from politics, Pendleton was elected president of the Virginia convention of 1788, called to ratify the Federal Constitution. His key efforts in the debates of that body, and his friendship with George Washington, should have caused this now eminent lawyer to gravitate toward the Federalist party. However, his early struggles and his admiration for Thomas Jefferson and James Madison were changing his political philosophy. A newly cultivated democratic bent led the Virginia aristocrat to espouse the equality of all men under law and the avoidance of government by the upper classes only; once Pendleton embraced these liberal views, his political course was set.

After declining George Washington's offer of a U.S. district judgeship in 1789, Pendleton went to work for the Jeffersonian Republican party. He was president of the Virginia Court of Appeals from 1779 until his death. In 1793 he led a public meeting in Virginia devoted to criticizing Federalist foreign policy. In 1799 Jefferson and John Taylor persuaded Pendleton to write a pamphlet which was of considerable importance in the Republican campaign of 1800. The aged Pendleton, however, was far too feeble to partake of the victory he had helped forge, and he died on Oct. 26, 1803.

Further Reading

The preeminent work on Pendleton is David J. Mays, *Edmund Pendleton, 1721-1803: A Biography* (2 vols., 1952). An older study is Robert L. Hilldrup, *The Life and Times of Edmund Pendleton* (1939). For an appraisal of Pendleton in the context of his times see Noble E. Cunningham, *The Jeffersonian Republicans: The Formation of Party Organization, 1789-1801* (1957).

Additional Sources

Mays, David John, *Edmund Pendleton, 1721-1803: a biography*, Richmond: Virginia State Library, 1980, 1984. ☐

George Hunt Pendleton

George Hunt Pendleton (1825-1889), American politician and a leader of the Democratic party, sponsored the first civil service reform law in 1883.

George Pendleton was born in Cincinnati, Ohio, on July 29, 1825. He graduated from Cincinnati College in 1841 and, in 1844, traveled extensively in Europe and the Near East. He married into an aristocratic Southern family, studied law, and was admitted to the Ohio bar in 1847.

After 3 years in the Ohio Senate, Pendleton was elected to the U.S. House of Representatives in 1856. He succeeded Stephen Douglas as a leader of Midwestern Democrats when Douglas died. At the time of the Civil War, southern Ohio was a center of antiwar sentiment in the Union, and Pendleton became the head of a group of Democrats who opposed President Abraham Lincoln's policies at every turn.

After the war Pendleton became a harsh critic of Republican Reconstruction measures, but he increasingly emphasized currency questions in his political deliverances. The "Ohio Idea," which Pendleton traded on as his own, called for the redemption of the government's war bonds in paper money rather than gold, thereby establishing "greenbacks" as the permanent legal tender. Sentiment in favor of the "Idea" was high, and Pendleton remained in the public spotlight. But conservative financiers were still framing Federal fiscal policy, and deflation held the day.

After he was defeated by Rutherford B. Hayes for governor in 1869, Pendleton became president of the Kentucky Central Railroad, a position he held for 10 years. In 1878, however, he was elected to the Senate for a single term. At this time, all government appointments—down to clerkships—were at the disposition of the party in power. Despite reformers' disgust with the spoils system, it was impossible to put together a majority in favor of civil service reform until, in 1881, President James Garfield was assassinated by a mentally ill office seeker. The public furor could not be ignored. In 1883, Pendleton introduced an act establishing the Civil Service Commission, and it was passed by huge congressional majorities. By the end of the century the spoils system in politics was fairly well ended. The Pendleton Act earned Pendleton an immortality that his otherwise lackluster career would not have.

In 1884 Pendleton was defeated for renomination. In compensation for his long party services, President Grover Cleveland named him minister to Germany, where he served until his death. A dashing political leader, Pendleton was known as "Gentleman George" and is perhaps more charitably remembered for his fashionable haberdashery in an age of drab clothing than for any significant contributions to American political life.

Further Reading

Except for virtually worthless campaign tracts, there is no biography of Pendleton. Howard Wayne Morgan, *From Hayes to McKinley* (1969), provides a conveniently secured backdrop of Pendleton's political world; and Matthew Josephson, *The Politicos, 1865-1896* (1938), includes a sympathetic but brief account. ☐

Wilder Graves Penfield

The American-born Canadian neurosurgeon, Wilder Graves Penfield (1891-1976), founded and was the first director of the Montreal Neurological Institute. He diagnosed the cause of epilepsy and perfected a surgical cure.

Wilder Graves Penfield was born in Spokane, Washington, on January 26, 1891. He was one of three children born to Charles Samuel and Jean (Jefferson) Penfield. His father was a physician and died when Penfield was very young. To support herself and her family, Penfield's mother became a writer and Bible teacher. Penfield spent his early years at the Galahad School in Hudson, Wisconsin, where his mother worked as a housekeeper.

Upon graduation in 1909, Penfield was accepted at Princeton University. He was active in extra-curricular activities and became president of his class. He was so good at football, that upon graduation in 1913, he was hired as a coach. After graduation from Princeton with a degree in literature, Penfield held a Rhodes scholarship and a Beit Memorial Research fellowship at Oxford University, where he studied with Sir William Osler and Sir Charles Scott Sherrington. He married Helen Katherine Kermott in 1917 and eventually raised four children. Penfield received his medical degree from Johns Hopkins University in Baltimore in 1918. He worked in Sherrington's research laboratory at Oxford from 1919 to 1921.

Penfield returned to the US in 1918 to receive training in general surgery and neurosurgery in New York City. In 1924 he founded the Laboratory of Neurocytology at Presbyterian Hospital, Columbia University, and worked there as associate attending surgeon from 1921 to 1928. In 1928 he was appointed neurosurgeon to the Royal Victoria Hospital and the Montreal General Hospital. It was here that he perfected his surgical operation for severe epilepsy. He had learned, perfected, and adapted the many techniques used in this operation from visits to Europe he had made while at Montreal.

The results of one of these operations in 1931 gave Penfield the idea to write a general textbook regarding

neurosurgery. Instead of writing it all himself, he decided to ask other specialists in this field to contribute to the book. The resulting book, *Cytology and Cellular Pathology of the Nervous System* (1932), turned into a three volume discussion of neurology. The collaboration that had produced the book gave Penfield the idea to create an institute furthered by the same cooperative techniques. He established the Montreal Neurological Institute on this idea and became its first director in 1934, holding this post until 1960. He was a professor of neurology and neurosurgery at McGill University from 1933 to 1954.

Penfield became a naturalized Canadian citizen in 1934 and served as a colonel in the Royal Canadian Army Medical Corps from 1945 to 1946. He headed many wartime projects including investigating motion sickness, decompression sickness, and air transportation of persons with head injuries. Penfield's wartime experiences supplied two books; *Manual of Military Neurosurgery* (1941) and *Epilepsy and Cerebral Localization* (1941).

After the war he continued his studies on epilepsy by undertaking a study of the removal of brain scars resulting from birth injuries. He was a fellow of the Royal Society of London and of the Royal Society of Canada and received the Order of Merit from Queen Elizabeth (1953). He also received numerous scientific awards and lectureships. He helped found the Vanier Institute of the Family and served as its first president (1965-1968).

After his retirement from the Montreal Neurological Institute in 1960, Penfield set out on what he called his "second career" of writing and lecturing around the world. Not one to take to retirement easily, Penfield said " . . . rest is not what the brain needs. Rest destroys the brain." He traveled abroad many times during this period and even lectured in China and Russia.

Penfield published *The Difficult Art of Giving, The Epic of Alan Gregg* (1967), a biography of the Rockefeller Foundation and the director who had approved the $1.2 million grant for the founding of the Montreal Neurological Institute, during this period. *Second Thoughts; Science, the Arts and the Spirit* (1970) and *The Mystery of the Mind: A Critical Study of Conscience and the Human Brain* (1975) were also published as he lectured around the world. Penfield finished his final work, the autobiographical *No Man Alone: A Surgeons Story,* just three weeks before his death from abdominal cancer in Montreal's Royal Victoria Hospital on April 5, 1976. This work was published posthumously in 1977 and was a fitting tribute to a man who was remembered by his friends and colleagues as one who always thought of his discoveries as just "exciting beginnings."

Medical Research

Penfield chose epilepsy as his special interest and approached the study of brain function through an intensive study of people suffering from this condition. In choosing this approach, he was influenced by Sherrington and by John Hughlings Jackson, a British neurologist who viewed epilepsy as "an experiment of nature," which may reveal the functional organization of the human brain. To this study Penfield brought the modern techniques of neurosurgery—which allow the surgeon to study the exposed brain of the conscious patient under local anesthesia—while using electrical methods for stimulating and recording from the cortex and from deeper structures. The patient is able to cooperate fully in describing the results of cortical stimulation. By this surgical method it is possible in some patients to localize and remove a brain lesion responsible for epileptic attacks. Penfield used this approach primarily for the treatment of focal epilepsy. His pioneer work yielded impressive results, and his techniques for the surgical treatment of epilepsy became standard procedure in neurosurgery.

Writings and Theories

Penfield's *The Cerebral Cortex of Man* (1950) summarizes the results of mapping the principal motor and sensory areas of the cortex, including the delineation of a new "supplementary motor area" and a "second sensory area." The results of temporal lobe stimulation are described in *Epilepsy and the Functional Anatomy of the Human Brain* (1954), and his remarkable observations on temporal lobe epilepsy are also recorded there. Penfield also defined four areas of the cortex concerned with human speech function and described them in *Speech and Brain-Mechanisms.*

Penfield was convinced that the brain of man—including all cortical areas—is controlled and "organized" through a group of subcortical centers. These centers lie within the upper brainstem and include the thalamus. For this functionally important area he coined the term "centrencephalon," and his view may be described as a "centrencephalic" theory of cerebral organization. In his view consciousness, self-awareness, depends upon the integrating action of this subcortical system, which in some way, as yet unknown, unites the brain into a single functioning organ. There is much evidence for such a theory, and Penfield developed it in his Sherrington Lectures, *The Excitable Cortex in Conscious Man* (1958).

Further Reading

The best biographical information on Penfield is his own *No Man Alone: A Surgeon's Story* (1977). There is an autobiographical sketch by Penfield in *McGraw-Hill Modern Men of Science* (1966). Also helpful are John F. Fulton and Leonard G. Wilson, eds., *Selected Readings in the History of Physiology* (1930; 2d ed. 1966), Ragnar Granit, *Charles Scott Sherrington: An Appraisal* (1967) and *Current Biography* (1968). A short obituary of Penfield appears in *Current Biography* (1976). A much longer obituary appears in the *New York Times* (April 6, 1976). □

William Penn

William Penn (1644-1718) founded Pennsylvania and played a leading role in the history of New Jersey and Delaware.

The heritage of William Penn was his part in the growth of the Society of Friends (Quakers) and role in the settlement of North America. Penn's influence with the British royal family and his pamphlets on behalf of religious toleration were important factors in the consolidation of the Quaker movement. He gave witness in America to the liberal faith and social conscience he had propounded in England in a career committed to religious and political values that have become inseparable from the American way of life.

William Penn was born in London on Oct. 14, 1644, the son of Adm. William Penn and Margaret Jasper. Adm. Penn served in the parliamentary navy during the Puritan Revolution. Although rewarded by Cromwell and given estates in Ireland, he fell into disfavor and took part in the restoration of Charles II. An intimate of the Duke of York, Adm. Penn was knighted by Charles II. With so influential a father, there seemed little doubt that William's prospects were attractive.

Early Manhood

Nothing better demonstrates how young Penn represented his period than his early religious enthusiasm. At the age of 13 he was profoundly moved by the Quaker Thomas Loe. Afterward, at Oxford, he came under Puritan influences. When he refused to conform to Anglican practices, the university expelled him in 1662.

At his father's request Penn attended the Inns of Court, gaining knowledge of the law. A portrait of this time shows

him dressed in armor, with handsome, strong features, and the air of confidence of a fledgling aristocrat.

Quaker Advocate

Appearances, in Penn's case, were deceiving. While supervising his father's Irish estates, Penn was drawn into the Quaker fold. His conversion was inspired by the simple piety of the Quakers and the need to provide relief for victims of persecution. At the age of 22, much to his father's distress, Penn became a Quaker advocate. His marriage in 1672 to Gulielma Maria Springett, of a wellknown Quaker family, completed his religious commitment.

Penn's prominence and political connections were important resources for the persecuted Quakers. A major theme of his voluminous writings was the inhumanity and futility of persecution. One remarkable achievement during this period was Penn's handling of the "Bushell Case." Penn managed to persuade a jury not to subject a Quaker to imprisonment only for his faith. When the magistrate demanded that the jury change its verdict, Penn maintained successfully that a jury must not be coerced by the bench. This landmark case established the freedom of English juries.

Colonial Proprietor

Religious persecution and colonization went hand in hand as the Quakers looked to America for a haven. Various problems invited Penn's association with the Quaker interests in New Jersey. Apart from his influence in England, Penn was active in mediating quarrels among the trustees. Doubtless, too, Penn contributed to the "Concessions and Agreements" (1677) offered to settlers, although he was not its principal author. This document gave the settlers virtual control over this colony through an elected assembly. It also offered a forthright guarantee of personal liberties, especially religious toleration and trial by jury, which the Quakers could not obtain in England.

The manifest liabilities of New Jersey formed a prelude to the founding of Pennsylvania. Of major importance, however, was Penn's Quaker faith and unyielding devotion to religious and political freedom; this underlaid his conception of Pennsylvania as a "Holy Experiment." In addition, Penn thought the colony could become a profitable enterprise to be inherited by his family.

Penn's proprietary charter contained many elements of previous grants. Penn and his heirs were given control over the land and extensive powers of government. The document reflected the period in which it was written: in keeping with new imperial regulations, Penn was made personally responsible for the enforcement of the Navigation Acts and had to keep an agent in London; he was required to send laws to England for royal approval.

In several ways Pennsylvania was the most successful English colony. Penn's initial treaties with the Indians, signed in 1683 and 1684, were based on an acceptance of Indian equality and resulted in an unprecedented era of peace. Penn also wrote promotional tracts for Pennsylvania and arranged circulation of these materials abroad. The response was one of the largest and most varied ethnic migrations in the history of colonization. Moreover, Pennsylvania's economic beginnings were usually successful. A fertile country, the commercial advantages of Philadelphia, and substantial investments by Quaker merchants produced rapid economic growth.

Despite this success Pennsylvania was not without problems. An immediate concern was its borders, especially those with Maryland. Because of anomalies in Penn's charter, an area along the southern border, including Philadelphia, was claimed by Lord Baltimore. This problem was only partly ameliorated when Penn secured control over what later became Delaware from the Duke of York. Just as troublesome were political controversies within the colony. Although Penn's liberal spirit was evident in the political life of Pennsylvania, and he believed that the people should be offered self-government and that the rights of every citizen should be guaranteed, he did not think the colonists should have full power. In order to provide a balance in government, and partly to protect his own rights, he sought a key role in running the colony. What Penn envisaged in his famous "Frame of Government" (1682) was a system in which he would offer leadership and the elected assembly would follow his pattern.

Almost from the start there were challenges to Penn's conception. Controversies developed among the respective branches of government, with the representatives trying to restrict the authority of the proprietor and the council. Disputes centered on taxation, land policy, Penn's appointments, and defense. "For the love of God, me, and the poor country," Penn wrote to the colonists, "be not so governmentish, so noisy, and open in your dissafection." Other difficulties included Penn's identification with James II, which brought him imprisonment and a temporary loss of the proprietorship in 1692-1694. No less burdensome was his indebtedness. Penn's liabilities in the founding of Pennsylvania led to his imprisonment for debt, a humiliating blow.

Final Years

After the Glorious Revolution in England, Penn and his family went to live in Pennsylvania. Arriving in 1699, he reestablished friendly contacts with the Indians and worked hard to heal a religious schism among the Quakers. He also labored to suppress piracy and tried to secure expenditures for colonial self-defense, demanded by the Crown but resisted by pacifist Quakers.

Penn's major achievement was the new charter of 1701. Under its terms the council was eliminated, and Pennsylvania became the only colony governed by a unicameral legislature of elected representatives. This system, which lasted until 1776, permitted the Delaware settlers to have their own legislature. Penn was obliged to return to England late in 1701 to fight a proposal in Parliament which would have abrogated all proprietary grants. He never saw Pennsylvania again.

Penn's last years were filled with disappointment. His heir, William, Jr., was a special tribulation because of his dissolute life-style. After the death of his first wife in 1694, Penn married Hannah Callowhill in 1696. Perplexed by debts, colonial disaffection, and the general antipathy of the King's ministers toward private colonies, Penn almost completed the sale of Pennsylvania to the Crown in 1712 before he suffered his first disabling stroke. He died at Ruscombe, Berkshire, on July 30, 1718.

Further Reading

Though many books treat Penn, a fully satisfactory biography has yet to be written. An enjoyable account, emphasizing Penn's personal life and character, is Catherine O. Peare, *William Penn* (1957). Of value on Penn's political and religious ideals are Edward C. Beatty, *William Penn as a Social Philosopher* (1939), and Mary M. Dunn, *William Penn: Politics and Conscience* (1967).

Works dealing with selected subjects include Edwin B. Bronner, *William Penn's "Holy Experiment": The Founding of Pennsylvania, 1681-1701* (1962); Joseph E. Illick, *William Penn the Politician* (1965); and Gary B. Nash, *Quakers and Politics: Pennsylvania, 1681-1726* (1968). A superior general account of the founding of Pennsylvania and other colonies is Charles M. Andrews, *The Colonial Period of American History* (4 vols., 1934-1938). The most recent synthesis is in Wesley F. Craven, *The Colonies in Transition, 1660-1713* (1968). □

J. C. Penney

Chain store executive, pioneer in profit sharing, and philanthropist, J(ames) C(ash) Penney (1875-1971) built a corporate empire following business precepts based on the Golden Rule.

The seventh of 12 children, only six of whom grew to maturity, J. C. Penney was born on September 16, 1875, on his father's farm near Hamilton, Missouri. His father, the Reverend James Cash Penney, Sr., served as an unpaid preacher for a fundamentalist sect known as Primitive Baptists and farmed to earn a living. His mother, Mary Frances Paxton Penney, was a Kentuckian. Life was joyless and difficult for the family, and at the age of eight young Penney was told that he had to buy his own clothes. This was not primarily because of necessity, but rather to teach him the value of money and self-reliance. To earn money he purchased a pig, fattened it, and sold it for a profit, then bought others. Later his father ordered him to sell his pigs before they were ready for a top price because they were objectionable to the neighbors, so he turned to growing and selling watermelons.

Penney graduated from Hamilton High School in 1893 but did not have the money for higher education. With the aid of his father he secured a position as a clerk in a local dry goods and clothing store. Starting on February 4, 1895, he was paid $25 a month. Never athletic or physically robust, a little more than two years after he started working his health began to fail. On the advice of his physician he left in 1897 for Colorado to regain his health. He worked briefly at two stores and then bought a butcher shop but went bankrupt rather than donate whiskey to the cook of a local hotel in order to obtain business.

A promising new opportunity came when Penney was employed by a Longmont, Colorado, merchant, T. M. Callahan, to work in Callahan's first store in his small Golden Rule Mercantile Company chain. In March 1899 Callahan sent the young man to work at his Evanston, Wyoming, store at a salary of $50 a month. Soon thereafter, on August 24, 1899, he married Berta A. Hess who would bear two sons, Roswell Kemper and James Cash, Jr. Three years later, Penney was sent to the town of Kemmerer, Wyoming, to open a new Golden Rule Store there. The store was capitalized at $6,000, of which one-third was Penney's, making him a junior partner. The chance to share in ownership increased his ambition, excited his imagination, and gave him the idea of someday having a chain of stores of his own based on the same principle of partner-owners who shared in the profits. He lived frugally in an attic room over the store at first. He opened the store at 7:00 a.m., closed at 9:00 or 10:00 p.m., and worked half a day on Sunday.

In 1903 he acquired one-third interest in another Golden Rule store, and a year later he supervised a third store in which he was sold a one-third interest. In 1907 Penney bought the other two-thirds interest in these three Golden Rule stores. He found, selected, and trained men, convinced that store managers had the duty to share their experience with their promising salesmen. He delegated responsibility, put his faith in his people, and eventually made them partners when new stores were opened. Individual store managers shared one-third of the profits, a motivating factor for success in business according to Penney. By 1909 he gave up personal management of the Kemmerer store and moved to Salt Lake City to establish a headquarters for all his stores.

In January 1913 Penney's chain was incorporated and the name was changed to J. C. Penney Company. The headquarters for the 48-store chain moved to New York City in 1914. Penney continued the expansion and in 1924 opened the 500th store in his hometown of Hamilton, Missouri. The company continued to operate as a partnership until 1927, when there were over 1,000 stores, necessitating full incorporation. Managers had from 1907 been given stock in the chain, the amount determined by the profits of their individual stores. In 1927 they exchanged this stock for stock in the company as a whole.

Penney was president of the company until 1917, chairman of the board of directors from 1917 to 1946, and honorary chairman of the board from 1946 to 1958. By the time of his death on February 12, 1971, he had created a vast corporate empire. There were 1,660 stores with annual sales of over $4 billion, making J. C. Penney second only to Sears, Roebuck and Co. in nonfood retailers in the country. All 50,000 employees, or "associates" as Penney called them, shared in the profits.

Penney liked being called "The Man with a Thousand Partners," a phrase he used in the title of an autobiography. He claimed that "the ethical means by which my business associates and I have made money is more important than the fact that we have achieved business success."

After leaving the presidency of the company in 1917, Penney spent more time on his outside interests. One was cattle breeding. He ran a 705-acre farm in New York state from 1922 to 1953 raising purebred Guernsey dairy cattle. He operated another farm in New York state and eight or nine farms in Missouri. Penney was also involved with many charitable and religious endeavors and was a prodigious speaker. He was active in the Young Men's Christian Association, Boy Scouts, National 4-H Club, Allied Youth Inc., and Laymen's Movement for a Christian World. He founded a home for retired religious workers in Florida in memory of his parents. Although he had only a limited education, he was the recipient of 17 honorary degrees and many other honors, awards, and citations.

During his 95 years, Penney was married three times and had five children and nine grandchildren. His first wife died in 1910, and in 1919 he married Mary Hortense Kimball. She died in 1923 after bearing a son, Kimball. Three years later, in 1926, he married Caroline B. Autenrieth, who bore two daughters, Mary Frances and Carol.

Penney's rise to fame and fortune was not an unmarred success story. A major financial disaster struck in the 1929 stock market crash. Penney lost $40 million when several banks from which he had borrowed foreclosed on loans secured by his personal holdings of stock. He let his servants go and wound up weakened in spirit and health and facing a $7 million debt at the age of 56. But Penney was able to start over again with borrowed money and soon regained control of his "empire." In his later years he reflected: "I believe in adherence to the Golden Rule, faith in God and the country. If I were a young man again, those would be my cardinal principles."

Further Reading

Penney was the author of several books about his life, including *J. C. Penney: The Man With a Thousand Partners* (1931), *Fifty Years With The Golden Rule* (1950), *Lines of a Layman* (1956), and *View from the Ninth Decade* (1960). Biographies include *J. C. Penney, Merchant Prince* by Beatrice Plumb (1963) and Norman Beasley's *Main Street Merchant* (1948). *Webster's American Biographies* (1974) also includes information on Penney. Articles appear in *TIME* (June 20, 1949), *FORTUNE* (September 1950), *LIFE* (May 14, 1951, and October 3, 1955), *Newsweek* (September 19, 1960), and the *Rotarian* (May 1953). His obituary appeared in the *New York Times* on February 13, 1971.

Additional Sources

Curry, Mary E. (Mary Elizabeth), *Creating an American institution: the merchandising genius of J.C. Penney,* New York: Garland Pub., 1993. □

Boies Penrose

Boies Penrose (1860-1921) was a conservative U.S. senator and also led the Republican state political machine in Pennsylvania.

Boies Penrose was born in Philadelphia on Nov. 1, 1860, of a distinguished family with a tradition of public service. Consistent with his family's social position, he attended Harvard, graduating second in the class of 1881. His commencement oration, on Martin Van Buren as a political leader, foreshadowed his career choice. Although he returned to Philadelphia after graduation and entered law practice, his life interest was politics and government rather than the legal profession. Even as a practicing lawyer, he collaborated on a scholarly study, *The City Government of Philadelphia* (1887).

During the 1880s Penrose showed some affinity for an independent, reform approach to politics, but he soon decided that his ambition for political office would be advanced more readily through the Republican state organization. He became the protégé and lieutenant of the machine's leader, Matthew Quay, and was elected to the state legislature of 1885 and the senate from 1886 to 1897, serving as president pro tem of the latter body after 1890. With Quay's backing, he was elected to the U.S. Senate in 1897.

In both state and national politics, Penrose took a conservative line. In the Senate, where he served from 1897 until his death, he was a mainstay of the Old Guard resistance to progressivism, following the lead of Nelson W. Aldrich, whom he succeeded as chairman of the influential Senate Finance Committee in 1911. His legislative efforts were mainly on behalf of higher tariff rates. On the state level, Penrose became the leader of the Pennsylvania Republican organization upon Quay's death in 1903. An opponent of most reform ideas (except for the direct primary), Penrose represented Pennsylvania on the Republican Na-

tional Committee from 1904 until 1912. He was temporarily displaced, but when the Progressives' power weakened, Penrose regained control of the state party and dominated it from 1916 until he died in Washington, D.C., on Dec. 31, 1921.

Although known as a party boss, Penrose avoided the graft that marred the records of many such men of his time. He was at his best working behind the scenes through committees and private conferences, but he was a forceful and intelligent speaker who could command public support and was twice elected senator by popular vote. Quick-witted, cynical, and aloof, he devoted himself to leading the Republican state organization and defending corporate interests, thus leaving behind a record of successful pursuit of power but virtually no legacy of idealism or statesmanship.

Further Reading

There is no modern scholarly biography of Penrose. Regrettably, both Walter Davenport, *Power and Glory: The Life of Boies Penrose* (1931), and Robert Douglas Bowden, *Boies Penrose: Symbol of an Era* (1937), are superficial appraisals of Penrose's career. □

Roger Penrose

The British mathematician and physicist, Sir Roger Penrose (born 1931), made striking and original con-

tributions to the study of geometry, relativity, quantum mechanics, and the human mind.

Roger Penrose was born in Colchester, England, on August 8, 1931. His father was the geneticist Lionel Penrose, an expert on mental defects, whose interest in geometry was communicated to his son. The Penrose family was illustrious in British intellectual life in the 20th century. Jonathan Penrose won the British chess championship ten times in the 1950s and 1960s. It is not surprising that the intellectual life of the Penrose household was lively.

Penrose received his undergraduate degree from University College, London, and then proceeded to Cambridge for his doctorate. While an undergraduate he discovered a theorem concerning conic sections from which some of the basic theorems of projective geometry follow as special cases. As part of his work for his doctorate he rediscovered some important results in the theory of matrices. From 1964 to 1966 he was a reader in applied mathematics at Birkbeck College at the University of London, advancing to full professor in 1966.

The study of mathematics in Britain has always included a large amount of applied mathematics and even physics, so it is not unexpected that much of Penrose's best-known work looks more like physics than pure mathematics. He and Stephen Hawking studied black holes in collaboration and the two of them identified the basic characteristics of black holes, which result from the collapse of large stars. The mass becomes so concentrated that even photons (light particles) are unable to escape. As a result, even if it is possible to recognize the existence of a black hole from its effects on nearby objects, it would be impossible to observe the interior of the black hole itself.

Starting from his interest in the question of whether space and time are smooth or divided into discrete units, Penrose investigated many aspects of quantum mechanics. While he was at Cambridge, Penrose tried to build mathematical models for quantum mechanics using the basic elements of real numbers. One of the long-standing problems of 20th-century physics has been to combine the apparently conflicting fields of relativity and quantum mechanics. Penrose attempted to find a resolution via twistor geometry, which is based on complex numbers. This ambitious project remains far from completion, but the study of twistors has become an industry within physics in its own right.

Penrose collaborated with his father on the creation of a visual illusion that was incorporated into lithographs by the Dutch artist M. C. Escher, whose work included many mathematical elements. Also within the area of geometry, Penrose made a striking contribution to the study of tilings. A tiling is a method of covering the entire plane with polygons, for example squares or equilateral triangles. Tilings using those figures are called periodic because the pattern repeats regularly in moving about the plane. The question was whether it would be possible to tile (cover) the plane with a nonrepeating pattern.

Before Penrose made his contribution, others had already shown that it was possible to tile the plane in a nonperiodic fashion. The first solution used an immense number of different tiles, and the best solution known in 1974 still used six tiles of different shapes. In that year Penrose found a nonperiodic tiling using only two different shapes. Although this geometric contribution seems far removed from his studies of astrophysics and quantum mechanics, it also reflects the width of his scientific background.

In 1966 Penrose received the Adams Prize from Cambridge University and in 1971 the Dannie Heineman Prize for Physics from the American Physical Society. The next year he was elected to the Royal Society and in 1973 he succeeded to the prestigious Rouse Ball Chair of Mathematics at Oxford University. He shared two awards with his collaborator Stephen Hawking; the 1975 Royal Astronomical Society's Eddington Medal and the 1988 Wolf Prize for physics. Penrose held visiting positions at many leading universities in the United States including Cornell, Texas, California, and Princeton.

Penrose became known to the general public thanks to the best-selling book *The Emperor's New Mind,* which appeared on both sides of the Atlantic in 1989. Hawking had written a book to similar acclaim a couple of years before but had not tried to include any equations other than Einstein's $e = mc^2$. Penrose's book includes that equation and hundreds of others as it ranges over computers, minds, and the laws of physics, to mention just the subjects explicitly named in the subtitle. *The Emperor's New Mind* may have been the best book about modern science yet written. Within 18 months it had run through numerous printings.

During a historic lecture series at the Isaac Newton Institute for Mathematical Sciences at Cambridge University in 1994, Penrose and Hawking recreated the famous Bohr-Einstein debate. In public lectures Penrose and Hawking presented their distinctive views on the universe, its evolution and impact on quantum theory. The same year, Penrose was knighted for his numerous contributions to science. *Shadows of the Mind* (1994) once again demonstrated the ability of Penrose to communicate complex theoretical physics to a general audience.

What distinguished Roger Penrose among the physicists and mathematicians of his time was the breadth and depth in his work. Some of the essays that he wrote illustrate the attention that he gave to his intellectual ancestors, such as Sir Isaac Newton. His influence on his students was profound.

Further Reading

There is an article on Penrose in the McGraw-Hill set on *Modern Scientists and Engineers* (1980). A more personal glimpse is available in Martin Gardner's introduction to Penrose's *The Emperor's New Mind* (1989). A good discussion of tilings and Penrose's work is in B. Grunbaum and G. Shephard's book *Tilings and Patterns* (1986). Articles on Penrose can be found in the popular science journals *Scientific American* and *Science*. An account of the 1994 Penrose-Hawking debate is presented in *The Nature of Space and Time* (1996). □

Claude Denson Pepper

Attorney, state representative, U.S. senator, and U.S. representative, Claude Denson Pepper (1900-1989) worked tirelessly as the champion of the working class, the poor, and the elderly.

Claude Denson Pepper was born September 8, 1900, on a farm near Dudleyville, Alabama. He spent his youth working at home and attending public school, then went off to the University of Alabama at Tuscaloosa, graduating in 1921. His early years were marked by ambition and desire—he carved "Claude Pepper, United States Senator" on a tree at the age of ten. Pepper worked his way through college hauling coal and ashes before sunrise at a power plant. This did not interfere with his enterprises at the university, however. He was a member of the track squad, the debate team, and Phi Beta Kappa. After college he was admitted to Harvard Law School (he was a classmate of Supreme Court Justice Felix Frankfurter), from which he graduated in 1924. After graduation he taught at the law school of the University of Arkansas for a year (one of his students, J. William Fulbright, later became a colleague in the U.S. Senate).

Pepper established a law practice in Perry, Florida, and was elected in 1928 to the Florida Democratic Executive Committee and then to the Florida House of Representatives. He was defeated in his reelection bid two years later, however. Pepper resumed his law practice in 1931, but returned to electoral politics in 1934, attempting to unseat U.S. Senator Park Trammell. Even though he had little statewide recognition, he forced a run-off in the Democratic primary and lost the election by a mere 4,050 votes. Fate bespoke Pepper when both U.S. senators died within months of each other in 1936. Pepper filed for the seat previously held by Duncan Fletcher, and because of his showing in 1934, won the election without opposition.

Pepper was reelected in 1938 and again in 1944, but was defeated by George Smathers in 1950. Pepper was an avid "New Dealer" and supporter of President Franklin D. Roosevelt. He advocated the views of labor, fought for minimum wages, urged the adoption of a national health insurance, and supported Social Security—positions which he maintained 40 years later as a member of the House of Representatives. Pepper's allegiance to liberal causes never weakened, and the elements of his 1950 electoral defeat were evident early in his career. Because he was an interventionist, he unpopularly advocated early entry into World War II (and was hung in effigy for running against the isolationist fervor of the times). Following the war he met with Joseph Stalin and advocated a softer approach in dealing with Russia. His attitude toward Russia, coupled with his positions favoring labor, opposing business, and favoring integration of the races, left him too vulnerable in the conservative backlash following World War II. A strong opposition group led by Edward Ball, a DuPont executive, accumulated a huge campaign war chest and plotted six years for his election defeat.

Ironically, it was someone whom Pepper had helped several times in his political career, George Smathers, who dealt Pepper his defeat in the 1950 Senate race. Smathers turned his back on his old patron and waged a well-orchestrated and well-financed campaign that utilized the fear of communism evident in the days of Joseph McCarthy (The "Red Pepper" tag was used). The tactics and strategies employed by the Smathers campaign led to the election being called one of the dirtiest campaigns in the history of politics in the United States. After that devastating defeat Pepper resumed the practice of law. He attempted to run for the Senate again in 1958, but lost soundly in the primary.

He remained at his law practice until 1962 when he was elected to the U.S. House of Representatives (from a newly created liberal district in Miami). Pepper was reelected to each succeeding Congress into the mid-1980s. His first committee assignment in the House of Representatives was to the banking and currency committee. Within two years Pepper was appointed to the prestigious rules committee. In addition, he served as chairman of the select committee on crime in the late 1960s, and during the late 1970s and early 1980s he was chairman of the select committee on aging. Within this latter capacity he assumed a role as advocate for the elderly and gained national prominence in working to protect the interests of America's senior citizens. He was instrumental in getting the Social Security program through its financial crisis in the early 1980s, saving the program from bankruptcy and fighting to prevent cuts in benefits. In 1983 he was appointed chairman of the rules committee.

Pepper served in office until his death in Washington, D.C., on May 30, 1989. Following a memorial service, his remains were lain in state at the Rotunda of the United States Capitol, considered the most suitable place for the nation to pay final tribute to one of its most eminent citizens.

Further Reading

Robert Sherrill, in *Gothic Politics in the Deep South* (1968), devotes a chapter to the Pepper-Smathers election of 1950. Pepper appeared on the cover of *Time* magazine twice—once during his reelection campaign of 1938, when the race was covered as a referendum on Franklin Roosevelt's New Deal policies, and once as advocate of the elderly in 1983. He was the subject of numerous articles in the *Wall Street Journal, Harpers,* and the *New Republic,* among others. □

Sir William Pepperell

Sir William Pepperell (1696-1759) was an American colonial merchant and soldier who commanded the land forces which captured the French fortress of Louisbourg.

The son of a prosperous merchant, William Pepperell was born on June 27, 1696, at Kittery Point, Maine (then part of Massachusetts). He was taken into his father's firm, known as the William Pepperells, which dealt in lumber, fish, and shipbuilding. European products were imported for sale. Profits were invested in land, and by 1724 young William owned almost the entire townships of Sacco and Scarboro. Business often took him to Boston, where on March 16, 1724, he married Mary Hirt.

Pepperell was made a militia colonel in 1726, in command of all Maine militia. That same year he was elected to the Massachusetts General Court as a representative from Kittery, and the following year he became an assistant, or member of the council, a position he held until his death. For 18 years he served as president of the council. Although he had no legal training, Pepperell was appointed chief justice of Massachusetts in 1730. At his father's death in 1734 he inherited the bulk of his estate and in 1744 made his son Andrew a partner in the firm.

In 1745, when war broke out between England and France (the North American conflict is called King George's War), Pepperell was sent with 3,000 or 4,000 men to attack Ft. Louisbourg in Canada. On April 30, 1745, he joined the British fleet there. Displaying little military skill, Pepperell besieged the fort in almost comic-opera fashion, but the corrupt and inefficient French surrendered June 17. Pepperell's greatest forte was his popularity with the troops and his ability to get along with the naval officers. In 1746 he was created a baronet, the first native American ever so honored. In 1749 he was received by the King.

Because of extensive landholdings, Pepperell wound up his mercantile affairs. In 1753 he was on a commission to negotiate a treaty with the Maine Indians. At the outbreak of the French and Indian War, the Crown ordered him to raise

1,000 men. Created a major general in 1755, Pepperell commanded the eastern frontier. In 1756, as president of the council, he acted as governor of Massachusetts. On Feb. 20, 1759, he was commissioned lieutenant colonel in the regular army, but because of failing health he took no further role in the war. He died that year on July 6.

Further Reading

Charles Henry Lincoln edited *The Journal of Sir William Pepperell Kept during the Expedition against Louisbourg* (1910). The standard biography is Usher Parsons, *Life of Sir William Pepperell, Bart.* (1856). See also John Francis Sprague, *Three Men from Maine: Sir William Pepperell, Sir William Phips, James Sullivan* (1924). A later study is Byron Fairchild, *Messrs. William Pepperell: Merchants at Piscataqua Bay* (1954). □

Samuel Pepys

The English diarist and public official Samuel Pepys (1633-1703) kept a diary that provides a graphic account of English social life and conditions during the early period of the Restoration.

Samuel Pepys was born on Feb. 23, 1633, in London. His father was a tailor. Pepys was sent to school first at Huntingdon and later to St. Paul's in London. In June 1650 he entered Trinity College, Cambridge, but he trans-

ferred to Magdalene College the following October and graduated in 1653.

In 1655 Pepys married Elizabeth St. Michel, the young daughter of a Huguenot exile. The couple was apparently supported at first by Pepys's cousin Sir Edward Montagu, later the Earl of Sandwich, whose service Pepys entered. In 1660 Pepys accompanied Montagu as secretary on the voyage that returned Charles II to England. That same year Pepys was appointed clerk of the acts at the Navy Office. This appointment was significant because Pepys was to serve the navy in some capacity for the greater part of his life, working to improve its efficiency and to ensure its integrity.

In 1662 Pepys was appointed one of the commissioners for Tangier, which was then occupied by the English; 3 years later he was named treasurer. When the Dutch War broke out in 1665, he was appointed surveyor general of the Victualing Office in addition to his regular duties for the navy, and he remained at his post throughout the Great Plague of 1665 although most inhabitants left London. Pepys saved the Navy Office from the Great Fire of 1666 by having the buildings around it destroyed. When the Dutch War ended in 1668, the Duke of York entrusted Pepys with the task of acquitting the navy of mismanagement.

Pepys's appearance before Parliament evidently whetted his own aspirations for a seat. He was elected to Parliament in 1673 and again in 1679. In 1673 the King transferred Pepys from the Navy Office to the secretaryship of the Admiralty. At the time of the Popish Plot in 1678,

Whig opponents of the Duke of York accused Pepys of giving naval secrets to the French. Pepys resigned his office and was imprisoned in the Tower in 1679, but the charges against him were unfounded, and Pepys was vindicated and freed in 1680.

Pepys's wife had died in 1669. His principal companions since then had been such men of taste and knowledge as John Evelyn, Christopher Wren, and John Dryden. In 1684 Pepys was elected president of the Royal Society. That same year he was also restored to the secretaryship of the Admiralty, retaining the post until the Glorious Revolution of 1688.

After Pepys retired from public life in 1689, he led a relatively quiet life. He published his *Memoirs . . . of the Royal Navy* in 1690. He corresponded with friends and acted as consultant to the navy. He died on May 26, 1703.

Pepys is remembered today for the diary he kept for 9 1/2 years in the 1660s. In his diary, written in cipher, Pepys recorded both the significant and trivial events of his public and private worlds. Together with his impressions of his own domestic situation, he recorded his thoughts about Charles II, the Great Plague of 1665, the Great Fire of 1666, the Restoration theater, the King's mistresses, the Dutch War, and the Duke of York. Failing eyesight caused him to discontinue the diary while still a young man, but its intimate record of his daily life and of the early Restoration remains both interesting and historically valuable.

Pepys's diary was not transcribed and published until 1825. The first virtually complete edition was issued between 1893 and 1899, edited by H. B. Wheatley.

Further Reading

The definitive study of Pepys is Cecil Emden, *Pepys Himself* (1963). Earlier biographies include Arthur Ponsonby, *Samuel Pepys* (1928), and Arthur Bryant, *Samuel Pepys* (3 vols., 1933-1939). Marjorie Hope Nicolson, *Pepys' Diary and the New Science* (1965), offers some discussion of the place of Pepys and the Royal Society in the history of ideas. The definitive edition of Pepys's diary is *The Diary of Samuel Pepys* (11 vols., 1970-83, new ed. 1996) edited by Robert Latham and William Matthews.

Additional Sources

Bradford, Gamaliel, *Samuel Pepys,* New York: Haskell House, 1975.

Kirk, Clara Marburg, *Mr. Pepys and Mr. Evelyn,* Folcroft, Pa.: Folcroft Library Editions, 1974.

Lubbock, Percy, *Samuel Pepy,* Folcroft, Pa. Folcroft Library Editions, 1974; Norwood, Pa.: Norwood Editions, 1977.

Meynell, Esther, *Samuel Pepys: administrator, observer, gossip,* New York: Haskell House, 1976.

Ollard, Richard Lawrence, *Pepys: a biography,* Oxford Oxfordshire; New York: Oxford University Press, 1984.

Tanner, J. R. (Joseph Robson), *Samuel Pepys and the Royal Navy,* Philadelphia: R. West, 1977.

Taylor, Ivan E. (Ivan Earle), *Samuel Pepys,* Boston: Twayne Publishers, 1989.

Wheatley, Henry Benjamin, *Samuel Pepys and the world he lived in,* New York: Haskell House Publishers, 1975. □

Petrus Peregrinus

Petrus Peregrinus (active 1261-1269) was a French scholastic and scientist whose famous letter on magnetism is one of the monuments of experimental research in the Middle Ages.

Only the scantiest details are known about the life of Petrus Peregrinus, also known as Pierre de Maricourt. He very probably studied at the University of Paris. He wrote a treatise on the astrolabe, *Nova compositio astrolabii particularis,* after 1261.

In 1269, when he wrote the letter which won him lasting renown, Peregrinus was in the French army of the crusaders who were attacking Lucera, a city in southern Italy. Like Archimedes in ancient Syracuse, Peregrinus was engaged in military engineering, such as the making of machines to sling stones and fireballs against Lucera.

While working on such military problems, Peregrinus was led to wonder about the possibility of keeping a machine in perpetual motion. He worked on this question by diagraming a wheel that would be turned perpetually by a magnet. To explain his novel theories to a friend at home, Peregrinus wrote the *Epistola and Sigerum de Foucaucourt miletum de magnete* in August 1269, outlining his observations and theories on magnetism. Because the recipient, addressed as "the dearest of friends," was not a learned man, Peregrinus had to instruct him in fundamentals. Anticipating what was to be the standardized science of only a much later period, these fundamentals were not only right for the most part but were also influential on other writers. Peregrinus is thus transitional between medieval and modern science.

Among the more important observations and theories of Peregrinus concerning the magnet were the identification of the polarity, north and south, in a magnet and the generalization that like poles repel and unlike poles attract; the recognition that any portion of a magnet is a magnet (a remote anticipation of the modern molecular theory of magnetism); the discovery that stronger magnets can neutralize weaker ones; the construction of a magnetized needle pivoted in a circle (an anticipation of the compass, which was to be developed 50 years later); and the use of a magnet to drive a wheel, thus adumbrating the magnetic motor. Though seeing magnetism everywhere on the globe, Peregrinus did not draw the conclusion that the earth was magnetic. He held that from the north and south poles of the heavens "the poles of lodestone derive their virtue."

Further Reading

The Letter of Petrus Peregrinus on the Magnet, A.D. 1269 was translated by Brother Arnold (1904). For a discussion of Peregrinus see Sir Thomas Clifford Allbutt, *The Rise of the Experimental Method in Oxford* (1902). See also Alistair Cameron Crombie, *Robert Grosseteste and the Origins of Experimental Science, 1100-1700* (1953), and his *Medieval and Early Modern Science,* vol 1: *Science in the Middle Ages: V-XIII Centuries* (1959). □

S. J. Perelman

S. J. Perelman (1904-1979) was probably the funniest American writer of the 20th century. He was a master of word-play and a cultural parodist without equal.

S. J. Perelman was once described in these graphic terms:

> Under a forehead roughly comparable to that of the Javanese or the Piltdown man are visible a pair of tiny pig eyes, lit up alternately by greed and concupiscence. His nose, broken in childhood by a self-inflicted blow with a hockey stick, has a prehensile tip, ever quick to smell out an insult; at the least suspicion of an affront, Perelman, who has the pride of a Spanish grandee, has been known to whip out his sword-cane and hide in the nearest closet. He has a good figure, if not a spectacular one; above the hips, a barrel chest and a barrel belly form a single plastic unit which bobbles uncertainly on a pair of skinny shanks. . . . A monstrous indolence, cheek by jowl with the kind of irascibility displayed by a Vermont postmaster while sorting the morning mail, is perhaps his chief characteristic.

That fanciful profile is from an introduction to *The Best of S. J. Perelman* and is signed, quite suspiciously, by one Sidney Namlerep ("Perelman" spelled backwards), who could write no more reverently about himself than about anyone or anything else. The real Sidney Jerome Perelman was born Jewish in Brooklyn on February 1, 1904, and grew up in Providence, Rhode Island. His father worked, though not steadily, as machinist, dry-goods merchant, and poultry farmer. Perelman's earliest cultural influences were pop novels and movies, which were to provide much of the grist for his satiric mill.

Cartoonist, Satirist, Parodist

Perelman's first ambition was to be a cartoonist, and his earliest work was published in a number of college humor magazines, including the one at his own school, Brown University, which he left in 1924 three credits shy of a degree (trigonometry having thrice thwarted him). He became, in 1926, a regular cartoon contributor to *Judge*, a top humor magazine of the 1920s and 1930s. One of his more widely reprinted cartoons shows a man confronting a doctor and confessing, "I've got Bright's disease, and he has mine." In another, a woman in a soap commercial enters an apartment and says, "Don't mind us, Verna, we just dropped in to sneer at your towels." The big problem Perelman had as a cartoonist was that his verbal sense was more insistent than his visual, so that the captions kept getting longer and eventually replaced the cartoons entirely.

While at Brown University Perelman had become good friends with a kindred eccentric, novelist Nathanael West. In 1929 Perelman married West's sister, Laura, with whom he later collaborated on a number of plays and screenplays; their marriage also produced two children, a son and a daughter.

Perelman's first book, *Dawn Ginsbergh's Revenge* (1929), typifies his vernacular style, an unlikely but hilarious blend of strait-laced mandarin and wiseguy showbiz. Hollywood was sufficiently impressed by the book to hire him as a script-and-gag-writer, and he distinguished himself in the early 1930s with his screenplays for two Marx Brothers films, "Monkey Business" and "Horse Feathers," in which his classic insane lines found the perfect foil in the zany persona of Groucho.

Perelman's apprentice work (1926-1931) at *Judge*, some of it reissued posthumously in *That Old Gang of Mine: The Early and Essential S. J. Perelman* (1984); his essays for *The New Yorker*, beginning in the early 1930s; his screenwriting (he won a Best Screenplay Oscar in 1956 for "Around the World in Eighty Days"); and his comic writing for the stage, including a play written with Ogden Nash, the 1943 hit musical "One Touch of Venus," are all of a piece. They exhibit equally Perelman's zany irreverence and his verbal dexterity, and the target is always the same—pretence in all of its forms. Nor did he spare himself; he appears as a figure of frustration or cowardice in many of his pieces, either fuming over "assemble it yourself" instructions for mail-order items or dealing ineffectually with recalcitrant lackeys or cunning yokels.

Always an Irreverent Approach

Perelman was more of a parodist than a satirist—that is, he most often ridiculed other cultural forms. Typically he would seize upon an advertisement or a trivial newspaper or magazine item wherein he detected some absurdity which he would then amplify in a cliché-ridden form. For example, in "Beat Me, Post-Impressionist Daddy" (the title itself a parody of a pop tune, "Beat Me, Daddy, Eight to the Bar") Perelman's imagination was caught by the ad campaign for the movie version of "The Moon and Sixpence," based on Somerset Maugham's fictionalized treatment of the life of Gauguin; the poster, quoting from the movie and adding its own commentary, proclaims, "Women are strange little beasts! You can treat them like dogs (*he did!*)—beat them 'til your arm aches (*he did*) . . . and still they love you (*they did*)." Pondering this dubious philosophy, Perelman proceeded to invent a series of letters between Gauguin and a Parisian friend in which the Tahitian-based painter complains, "My arms are so tired from flailing these cows that I can hardly mix my pigments."

In another piece, entitled "Button, Button, Who's Got the Blend," Hostess Cup Cakes' boasts of a "secret chocolate blend" set off a Perelman playlet involving the secret formula's theft from the company safe and featured a cast of stock theatrical types: the noble hero who falsely confesses in order to shield someone; the real culprit, who is the hero's girlfriend's ne'er-do-well brother; the shrewd police inspector who guesses the truth; and so forth. A new method for dispersing stampeding buffalos, suggested by a correspondent to a British sporting magazine, gave rise to "Buffalos of the World, Unite!," a hilariously wayward response by Perelman in which he assumed a stiff-backed, ultra-suspicious persona who opposed this newfangled challenge to a hallowed tradition: "I hold no buff for the briefalo—I beg pardon, I should have said 'I hold no brief for the buffalo,' but I am too choked with rage about this matter to be very coherent."

Sometimes Perelman needed no immediate stimulus for his parodies. "Scenario," for example, without preliminary comment launches forth on a patchwork excursion of clichés torn from a thousand war, crime, love, and adventure movies and pulp fiction stories: "There was a silken insolence in his smile. . . . No quarter, eh? Me, whose ancestors scuttled stately India merchantmen. . . . Me, whose ancestors rode with Yancey, Jeb Stuart, and Joe Johnston through the dusty bottoms of the Chickamauga? Oceans of love, but not one cent for tribute. Make a heel out of a guy whose grandsire, Olaf Hasholem, swapped powder and ball with the murderous Sioux through the wheels of a Conestoga wagon. . . ."

Perelman's comic essays give the impression that he was addicted to slick magazines, trashy fiction, commercial theater, journalism, movies, and advertising (he never troubled himself with television), but he was also in fact a serious reader, and some of his literary parodies are classic. Spoofing Clifford Odets' romantic Marxism, "Waiting for Santy" casts a capitalist Santa Claus as wage-enslaver of a reindeer proletariat (Panken, Briskin, Rivkin, Ranken, and Ruskin). "A Farewell to Omsk" (the title of which wings another literary bird) humorously captures the gloomy intensity of Dostoevsky: "An overpowering desire to throw himself at her feet and kiss the hem of her garment filled his being." "Farewell, My Lovely Appetizer" is an impeccable take-off on the hard-boiled detective fiction of Raymond Chandler: "I kicked open the bottom drawer of her desk, let two inches of rye trickle down my craw, kissed Birdie on her lush, red mouth, and set fire to a cigarette."

Perelman's collections are largely gleaned from his work at *The New Yorker*; they include *Acres and Pains* (1947), *Westward Ha!; or, Around the World in Eighty Clichés* (1948), *The Ill-Tempered Clavichord* (1952), *The Road to Miltown; or, Under the Spreading Atrophy* (1957), *The Most of S. J. Perelman* (1958), *Chicken Inspector No. 23* (1966), and *Baby, It's Cold Inside* (1970), which introduced the raffish Irish poet Shameless McGonigle. But the best of Perelman, culled largely from *Crazy Like a Fox* (1944), is to be found, quite aptly, in *The Best of S. J. Perelman* (1947).

John Updike has said that Perelman was not a satirist who "made you dislike anything [but] a celebrant of his own past and of the books he had read, of the weeds on his Pennsylvania estate, and above all of the language itself." Not much rancor, but tons of iconoclasm, and no patience at all for Will Rogers' democratic boast about never having met a man he didn't like (which Perelman dismissed as dangerous claptrap).

Perelman had lived for 40 years on farm land in Bucks County, Pennsylvania, but when his wife died in 1970 he sold the property and, ever the Anglophile, moved to London. The migration was not a success: his first year there his overcoat was stolen in a restaurant; worse, Perelman's desire for English stability was thwarted by changes in the cultural landscape; finally, he missed the stimulus of his native culture. He returned to the United States in 1972 and took up an uneasy residence in New York City, which he had always detested. In 1978, a year before his death, Perelman was interviewed by public television and provocatively observed that of the various peoples that he had encountered in his many travels, only two lacked a sense of humor—the Germans and the French. He died of natural causes on October 17, 1979, in his Gramercy Park Hotel apartment in New York City.

Further Reading

Though his writing gives no evidence of it, Perelman's family life was unhappy, as Douglas Fowler's biography, *S. J. Perelman* (1983), reveals. A new biography by Dorothy Herrmann, *S. J. Perelman: A Life* (1986), contains a great many more revelations. A collection of Perelman's letters, edited by Prudence Crowther, *Don't Tread on Me* (1987), is probably the humorist's last word. □

Shimon Peres

Shimon Peres (born 1923) served as Israel's prime minister from 1984 through 1986 and again in 1995, following the assassination of Yitzhak Rabin. He was awarded the Nobel Peace Prize for his role in negotiations with the Palestinians, along with Yitzhak Rabin and Yasser Arafat.

Shimon Peres was born to Yitzhak and Sara Persky in 1923 in Volozhin, Poland. In 1931 Yitzhak Persky emigrated to Palestine, with his family following two years later. In Palestine, the family changed their name legally to Peres. Peres began his studies at Tel-Aviv's Balfour School and continued at the Ben-Shemen agricultural school and youth village. Joining the clandestine Jewish self-defense organization the Haganah in 1941, Peres helped found Kibbutz Alumot in the lower Galilee where he met his future wife, Sonya Gelman. They married in 1945 and had three children.

Peres became actively involved in politics as a young member of Mapai, the dominant labor party. He served as secretary-general of Hanoar Haoved, the Histradrut labor federation's youth movement, and was a delegate in 1946 to the 22nd World Zionist Congress. He was also a position commander of Hagganah, and dedicated to fulfilling the organizations goals. It was during this period that Peres first came to the attention of David Ben-Gurion, leader of the campaign for Jewish statehood in Palestine. A strong relationship developed in which Peres earned the trust of the future first prime minister and, in return, showed steadfast loyalty in the many struggles of that period.

Under Ben-Gurion's patronage Peres came to assume increasingly more responsible positions after Israel became an independent nation in 1948. In the war for independence (1948-1949) he was assigned to the newly-formed ministry of defense and remained there until 1959. During that decade Peres served as chief of the naval department in 1948, was sent to the United States in 1950 on an arms-procurement mission (as well as to complete his education), and in the years 1952-1959 filled the top administrative post of director-general of the ministry.

Peres is remembered for having played a key role in Israeli national security. First, he was instrumental in establishing the indigenous Israeli defense industries. Second, at a time when Israel found itself isolated diplomatically in the face of mounting Arab threats and militarization, Peres encouraged collaboration with France. His secret contacts in Paris resulted in a flow of sophisticated weapons and military technologies from France, enabling Israel to conduct the successful Sinai campaign in 1956.

Peres simultaneously rose in the Mapai Party's ranks as one of the "young guard," which included such other distinguished figures as Moshe Dayan, Abba Eban, and Yigal Allon. But while respected for his managerial skills, Peres also earned the enmity of party stalwarts who regarded him as more of a technocrat. Peres was often allowed to exercise authority beyond his job description that earned him both the criticism and envy of other ministers. He earned a reputation as a shrewd effective negotiator, who often succeeded by bypassing diplomatic channels and establishing his own relationships. Nevertheless, he earned a high place on the party's list of candidates and was first elected to the Knesset (Israel's parliament) in 1959. He then served as deputy defense minister. Leaving Mapai, he helped form the breakaway Rafi Party and was returned to the Knesset in 1965. Three years later he helped negotiate a formal reconciliation with Mapai, resulting in the Labour/Alignment. Returned to the Knesset in 1969, Peres served as minister of immigrant absorption and minister-without-portfolio until August 1970, when he was given the post of minister for transport and communication. In the aftermath of the Yom Kippur War (1973) Peres briefly served as minister of information as part of a cabinet reshuffle.

When Golda Meir stepped aside as leader of the Alignment in 1974, a fiercely-contested succession struggle found Peres losing to Yitzhak Rabin by a narrow margin, 298 votes to 254. The Knesset endorsed the Rabin government in June, with Peres as minister of defense. Despite a strained personal and working relationship, Peres was actively involved in the separation of forces agreements with Syria and Egypt during the "shuttle diplomacy" of U.S. Secretary of State Henry Kissinger. He also administered the West Bank territories and restored the Israel Defense Forces to a peak of efficiency after the 1973 fighting.

The 1977 national elections witnessed a major reversal in Israeli politics, with the opposition Likud Party swept into office and Labour now out of power for the first time in 29 years. Peres, replacing Rabin as party chief, demonstrated admirable dedication in rebuilding the Alignment's political fortunes. A tireless campaigner, widely-read, and an experienced parliamentarian, Peres was a sharp critic of Begin government policies. He was especially critical of the aims and conduct of Operation "Peace for Galilee," the invasion of Lebanon launched in June 1982.

In the 1984 elections the Israeli electorate failed to issue a clear mandate to either of the two major blocs: Likud or the Alignment. In the resultant deadlock it became necessary to seek some form of collaboration. These efforts led to formation of the National Unity Government. It was agreed that Peres would serve as prime minister for the first two years of the four-year term, after which he shifted position, serving as foreign minister and vice premier under Yitzhak Shamir.

During his term as prime minister Peres concentrated on a number of immediate priorities which centered on disengagement from Lebanon, checking the rampant inflation and restoring economic growth, streamlining the work of the prime minister's office and of the unwieldy 25-member cabinet, and deepening the 1979 peace treaty with Egypt while seeking resolution of the Arab-Israel conflict through his "Jordanian option." He also strengthened ties with the United States while improving the Israeli image and international position. During this time Peres became known for his efforts to work out a peaceful solution to the Palestinian problem on the West Bank.

In 1992 Peres lost party leadership to Rabin, but was appointed foreign minister in the new Labor cabinet. As foreign minister, he used his considerable negotiating skills to bring about the prospect of peace between the Israelis and Palestinians. Often criticized for his desire to grant the Palestinians more autonomy, Peres' maintained that negotiation was the only way to settle the centuries-long conflict. In 1994 the Nobel Peace Prize was awarded to Peres, Rabin, and Yassar Arafat in recognition of their role in forging the Palestinian autonomy agreements.

On November 4, 1995, this promise of peace was dealt a devastating blow when Rabin was assassinated by a right wing Israeli student. Peres assumed the role of prime minister, vowing to continue the peace negotiations. In February 1996 he called for new elections, hoping that they would renew his mandate for peace. It appeared that he would win the election, when a Palestinian suicide bomber killed 24 Israelis. The mood of the public changed and Likud's candidate, Benjamin Netanyahu, became the new prime minister.

In May 1997 Peres, afraid that he would lose his re-election bid to be Labor party leader, proposed creating the new post of Party President. He then served an ultimatum that if the party would not throw support for the post, he would not run for it. The party postponed any discussion and thereby informed Peres that his days as Labor party leader were numbered. He retired from his position.

Further Reading

Additional information on Peres can be found in Matti Golan, *Shimon Peres: A Biography* (1982) and in Peres' own book *David's Sling* (1982). See also Bernard Reich, *Israel: Land of Tradition and Conflict* (1985). *Political Leaders of the Contemporary Middle East and North Africa: A Biographical Dictionary* (1990); the *Electronic Telegraph* (February 26, 1996, March 6, 1996, February 20, 1996, February 12, 1996, November 22, 1995, November 6, 1995). □

Isaac Loeb Peretz

The Jewish poet, novelist, and playwright Isaac Loeb Peretz (1851-1915) was the leader of Yiddishism, a cultural movement dedicated to making Yiddish the national language of Jewish people throughout the world.

Isaac Peretz was born in Zamość, Poland. Early Hasidic influences were counteracted by the progressive atmosphere in his native town. Peretz's first linguistic affiliation was with Hebrew, and although he later became the leader of Yiddishism, his devotion to Hebrew remained unchanged.

At the age of 3 Peretz studied the Bible in Hebrew, and at the age of 6 he studied the Talmud. In his youth he read widely in Polish literature. At an early age Peretz married the daughter of a man who dabbled in Hebrew poetry, and he settled in a little town where he became a partner in a brewery business. Peretz subsequently divorced his wife and spent the years 1876-1877 in Warsaw, where he made his living as a Hebrew teacher. At that time he began his literary activities. His first poem, written in Hebrew, was published in *Hashahar* in 1877.

Peretz then returned to Zamość, where he married again and intended to found a Hebrew school. However, he entered a partnership in a flour-milling business. Soon afterward a new Russian legal code was adopted, and Peretz decided to become a lawyer. He passed the district court law examinations, and for the next 10 years Peretz practiced law successfully. During these years he wrote Hebrew and Yiddish poems, but he did not publish them. By this time Peretz was also interested in Jewish social problems. Because of the interest he took in the poor, Peretz was later considered a Socialist, and this may have been the reason why his license to practice law was revoked. In 1886 Peretz returned to Warsaw. There he worked as a lawyer, but later he undertook a tour through certain parts of Russia and Poland in order to gather statistics for an economic survey. This tour also gave Peretz material on and insight into Jewish life for his stories and poems, as exemplified in his *Pictures from a Journey through the Country.* In 1887 the poem "Monish," which marked Peretz's future importance to Yiddish literature, appeared in Sholem Aleichem's *Die Yiddishe Folksbibliotek (The Jewish Popular Library)*. Later, as editor of the annual *Yiddishe Bibliotek,* Peretz published articles on chemistry, physics, economy, and other subjects. His poems "Melodies of the Time" and "The Little Town" greatly impressed critics and readers alike.

At that time Peretz also expressed in his larger literary works his profound appreciation of Hasidic life. In 1889 an informer reported to the authorities that he was a revolutionary, and Peretz was deprived of his license to practice law. With the support of his friends he soon obtained a post as secretary of the Jewish Community of Warsaw and remained its employee in increasingly important capacities until his death.

In 1890 Peretz's first book—a collection of stories—was published under the title *Familiar Pictures*. With the help of other men of letters he began editing *The Jewish Library*—a series of publications dealing with literature and social problems. These publications became the focal and rallying point of burgeoning Yiddish literature and literary talent. Peretz was not permitted to publish a Yiddish daily; but he published occasional "Holiday Pages," which greatly contributed to the promotion of Yiddish literature. In 1894 he published an impressive book of Hebrew love poems and short stories. In his drama *Die goldene Kait (The Golden Chain)* and in such other Hasidic treatments as *By Night at the Old Market* Peretz expressed appreciation of the Jewish spiritual tradition. He spoke the language of the common man and expressed the pain, idealism, and messianic hope that lodged in Jewish hearts.

In 1899 Peretz was arrested as a Socialist and spent 2 months in prison. In his enthusiasm for the labor movement he belittled the Lovers of Zion and the Zionist movement, although he clearly stated that in principle he was no opponent of these national movements.

Peretz's many hardships affected his health, and on April 3, 1915, he suddenly succumbed to a heart attack.

Further Reading

An anthology in English of Peretz's work is *In This World and the Next: Selected Writings,* translated by Moshe Spiegel (1958). Maurice Samuel, *Prince of the Ghetto* (1948), is a biographical account. Peretz is discussed in Charles A. Madison, *Yiddish Literature: Its Scope and Major Writers* (1968). □

Carlos Andrés Pérez

Carlos Andrés Pérez (born 1922) served as president of Venezuela and oversaw the nationalization of his country's oil industry. In May 1993 he was impeached on allegations of embezzlement and misuse of public funds. After more than two years of house arrest, Pérez was released in September 1996.

Carlos Andrés Pérez, the son of Antonio and Julia Pérez, was born in 1922 in the Andean town of Rubio in the western state of Táchira, Venezuela. His father, a member of the rural middle class, owned both a pharmacy and a small coffee hacienda. Even as a youth Pérez was devoted to politics. He headed student organizations and in 1935 joined in political demonstrations in Rubio which followed the death of Venezuela's long-time dictator, Juan Vicente Gómez (1909-1935). In 1939 his family moved to Caracas, where he completed his secondary education at the Liceo Andrés Bello. He then studied law at the Universidad Central de Venezuela.

In Caracas Pérez met the man who would become his political mentor, Rómulo Betancourt. He joined Betancourt's Acción Democrática (Democratic Action Party) and worked as a youth leader and organizer for the party.

Acción Democrática's goal was to bring both democracy and social reform to Venezuela. In 1945 a coalition of Acción Democrática activists and junior military officers overthrew the government of General Isaías Medina Angarita. Betancourt headed the revolutionary junta and chose Pérez as his personal secretary. But Acción Democrática rule lasted only three years. In late 1948 military officers overthrew the government. Ten years of military dictatorship, principally under Colonel Marcos Pérez Jiménez, followed.

Between 1948 and 1958 Pérez spent time both in Venezuelan prisons and in exile in various Latin American countries. He and other Acción Democrática leaders returned to Venezuela in 1958 following the overthrow of Pérez Jiménez. With the election of Betancourt as president in late 1958, Venezuela was set on the course of political democracy. For the next 15 years Pérez served in a variety of governmental, legislative, and party posts. Most notably, he directed the Ministry of Interior between 1962 and 1963, using that office to suppress left-wing radicals who challenged the Betancourt government.

With crucial support from Betancourt, Pérez secured his party's nomination for president in 1973. An outgoing, energetic man, he conducted a vigorous campaign. Drawing on campaign tactics popular in the United States, Pérez, known popularly as "Cap," brought his "democracy with energy" theme to the people by walking more than 3,000 miles during his campaign. His efforts won him 49 percent of the vote, a broad mandate in a multicandidate election.

President Carlos Andrés Pérez assumed office in 1974 in what seemed a fortuitous time for Venezuela. The nation was a leading producer of oil, and the price had increased from $2 a barrel in 1970 to $14 in 1974, in the aftermath of the Arab oil embargo of 1973 and the global energy shortage. Venezuela presumably would now have the income to diversify its economy, create a modern industrial state, and uplift the conditions of the poor. President Pérez immediately announced that Venezuela would use its new power to nationalize the oil industry. Venezuela paid the American and British-Dutch oil companies, which had operated in Venezuela since the 1920s, approximately $1 billion for their properties, and on January 1, 1976, took control of the industry.

Pérez also moved aggressively on other fronts. With overwhelming majorities in Congress, he ruled by decree and launched a series of ambitious industrial development plans. Major projects included a petrochemicals complex, an integrated steel industry, shipworks, and a subway system for Caracas. In addition, Pérez boldly pushed Venezuela into the forefront of international politics, as he lectured the industrial nations on their duty to aid the poor nations of the world.

Pérez probably pushed Venezuela too fast and too far. Oil revenues were not inexhaustible; Venezuela incurred massive international debts for financing development projects. The country was also short of managerial talent. Reports of gross administrative inefficiency, waste, and even corruption rocked the Pérez government. Moreover, these long-term development projects did not address the pressing concerns of Venezuela's poor. By the end of his term, Pérez was highly unpopular. Even his erstwhile ally, Rómulo Betancourt, denounced him. His party lost the presidency in the 1978 election. Yet his successor, the Christian Democrat Luis Herrera Campíns (1979-1984), proved even less successful at managing Venezuela's oil bonanza.

In 1988 Pérez again campaigned for presidential election and won by a wide margin against Eduardo Fernández. He began his second term in office on February 2, 1989 and celebrated with a lavish inaugural party. This term, however, proved to be more tumultuous than the previous one. In 1992 he managed to suppress two attempted military coups. The first uprising was by the army, occurring in February of that year; the second was by the Air Force in November. The brutal coup attempts stalled economic programs and rocked Venezuela's political structures. Then, in May 1993 Pérez was impeached for allegations of misuse of public funds and embezzlement. Pérez and two aides were accused of having diverted public funds to pay for his 1988 election campaign and the ensuing extravagant inaugural celebration. He was also accused of improperly spending 250 million bolivars (US $17 million) of national security money on a 1990 foreign policy initiative, by sending Venezuelan police to provide personal protection for Nicaraguan president, Violeta Chamorro. Pérez was subsequently expelled from Acción Democrática. In May 1994, too old to be imprisoned, he was placed under house arrest to await the outcome of his trial.

In May 1996 the Venezuelan Supreme Court found Pérez guilty of misusing public funds, but acquitted him of the more serious embezzlement charge. He was sentenced to two years and four months of house arrest. Taking into account the time served after his impeachment in 1993, Pérez was released on September 19, 1996. He was stripped of his title as honorary senator, a position given to all former presidents. Although the Venezuelan constitution prohibits those sentenced to less than three years from being barred from office, Pérez missed the cutoff by eight months. A newly freed man, and still supported by grassroots Acción Democrática members, Pérez proclaimed that he intended to run for Venezuela's senate in 1998 in his home state of Táchira and restore his reputation.

Further Reading

There is no complete biography of Pérez in English. For background and information see David Eugene Blank, *Venezuela: Politics in a Petroleum Republic* (1984) and Judith Ewell, *Venezuela: A Century of Change* (1984). For Venezuela's relations with the foreign oil industry see Stephen G. Rabe, *The Road to OPEC: United States Relations with Venezuela, 1919-1976* (1982). □

Javier Pérez de Cuéllar

Peruvian foreign service officer and world statesman, Javier Pérez de Cuéllar (born 1920), reached the pinnacle of a long diplomatic career with his installation in January 1982 as secretary general of the United Nations. The fifth man to hold that post, he was the first Latin American and the second non-European to lead the world body. Pérez de Cuéllar served two terms as secretary general until 1992.

A man of aristocratic lineage, Javier Pérez de Cuéllar was born in Lima, Peru, on January 19, 1920. His businessman father died when Pérez de Cuéllar was four years old. He received his primary and secondary education in private schools and enrolled in the law program at Lima's Catholic University. To support his studies the young man became a clerk in the Ministry of Foreign Affairs. In 1944, after obtaining his law degree, he entered Peru's highly-regarded diplomatic corps, later quipping that it allowed him to discover the world "at someone else's expense."

Initially posted as first secretary in Peru's Paris embassy, Pérez de Cuéllar became a member of his country's delegation to the first session of the United Nation's General Assembly in 1946. Later he served as first secretary to Peru's diplomatic missions in Great Britain, Bolivia, and Brazil. In 1961 he returned home to fill a series of administrative posts within the foreign ministry and to teach at the Diplomatic Academy of Peru. He also authored two texts on international law and diplomacy. Following a two-year assignment as ambassador to Switzerland, Pérez de Cuéllar was named

secretary general of the Ministry of Foreign Relations. When Peru established formal ties with the Soviet Union in 1969, the veteran diplomat became Lima's first ambassador to Moscow. Two years later Pérez de Cuéllar led Peru's permanent delegation to the United Nations, a post he retained until 1975. He served as president of the U.N. Security Council in 1974.

A consummate diplomat, Pérez de Cuéllar was noted for his quiet, self-effacing personality, his Old-World charm and gentility, and his skill in working effectively with discordant factions. The tall, distinguished-looking man seemed to have been born in a conservative, pin-striped suit—the uniform of his profession. He spoke English and French in addition to his native Spanish. The twice-married grandfather wrote poetry and was a devotee of Hispanic literature, especially the classics.

Appreciating the Peruvian's talents, U.N. Secretary General Kurt Waldheim dispatched him to Cyprus in 1975 to defuse the explosive dispute between the Greek and Turkish elements. Although he did not resolve the deeply-rooted problems on that troubled island, Pérez de Cuéllar persuaded the two sides to begin negotiations. Again in 1981 Waldheim called him away from the Peruvian embassy in Caracas, Venezuela, to serve as the Secretary General's personal representative in calming a crisis between Pakistan and Afghanistan. In October of that year, Lima named him ambassador to Brazil. In a patently political effort to embarrass the president, however, the Peruvian Congress blocked the confirmation of Pérez de Cuéllar and several other ambassadorial nominees. Peru's most distinguished and visible diplomat resigned from the foreign service in protest. His vindication came quickly.

In the closing weeks of 1981, as Waldheim's term drew to a close, politicking began for the election of a new secretary general for the United Nations. The procedure involved nomination by the 15-member Security Council, each of whose five permanent representatives (the U.S., Soviet Union, Britain, France, and China) had an absolute veto. Formal election of the nominee by the General Assembly had, in the past, been automatic. Austrian Kurt Waldheim, standing for a third term, had the unenthusiastic support of the Western powers and the Soviet Union. The Chinese, however, insisted that a new leader be chosen from the less-developed countries of the Third World and endorsed the popular Tanzanian foreign minister, Salim Ahmed Salim.

Waldheim and Salim ultimately withdrew from the deadlocked contest, and nine new candidates entered the fray. Among this group Javier Pérez de Cuéllar alone proved acceptable to the superpowers. The Western nations had no serious objections to him. He had won the respect of the Soviets during his ambassadorship in Moscow. Pérez de Cuéllar benefited from Peru's 20-year ''independent'' foreign policy and its more recent leadership role among the less-developed nations. The secret balloting produced ten positive and one negative vote for the Peruvian diplomat; the Soviet Union and three other members of the Security Council abstained. On December 15, the General Assembly approved the new secretary general by acclamation, and Javier Pérez de Cuéllar was ceremoniously installed for a five-year term on the first day of 1982.

Some observers doubted that the gentle Peruvian had the hard ''cutting edge'' they believed necessary for leadership of the world organization. Others, however, deemed him the right man for that critical moment. The long-time rivalry between East and West, the more recent tensions between North and South (the developed and less-developed countries), and myriad regional conflicts threatened the survival of the U.N. Its inability to bring peace to the Middle East, Central America, and other troubled regions suggested that the organization had failed to achieve its primary objective. As many new Third World nations swelled the body to 160 members, the increasingly radical complexion of the United Nations soured the U.S. and its Western allies. The failure to agree upon a declaration of past accomplishments and future objectives during the October 1985 40th anniversary celebration seemed indicative of the body's factional paralysis.

Pragmatic and independent as secretary general, Pérez de Cuéllar carefully protected his necessary role as ''honest broker.'' He had not campaigned for his post and declared his intention not to seek reelection. Pérez de Cuéllar admitted that the U.N. had serious defects and labored with limited success to reform and revitalize the organization. He placed special emphasis on enhancing the independence, efficiency, and morale of U.N. employees and on depoliticizing its subsidiary agencies to regain broad support for their work. He asserted that the U.N. was ''the most authentic expression of the international community in all its diversity'' and asked member states to ponder what advantages might be gained from its destruction.

With the perspective of a Third World man, Pérez de Cuéllar frequently pointed to the organization's successes in promoting economic development, health, and education. Reflecting his Western cultural heritage, the Secretary General urged member states to strengthen the rule of law in an increasingly anarchic world and to ''restore civility to international life.'' And as the elected representative of five billion people, he often spoke as an international every-man, voicing concern about world hunger and disease, abuses of human rights, the ''scourge of war,'' and the ultimate ''threat of nuclear catastrophe.''

Toward the end of his first term, the five permanent members of the Security Council asked Pérez de Cuéllar to accept a second five-year appointment. His acceptance indicated good recovery from a quadruple heart-bypass operation in mid-1986.

Pérez de Cuéllar's tenure as secretary-general was marked by significant change—primarily the collapse of the Soviet Union and the end of the Cold War. The U.N. evolved from an international organization stymied by bipolarity into an institution sought for peacekeeping assistance around the globe. Although he was powerless in resolving conflicts in the Falkland Islands, Lebanon, and the Persian Gulf, Pérez de Cuéllar was praised for his role as a mediator and ''honest broker'' in global diplomacy. He was succeeded on January 2, 1992 by Egyptian diplomat Boutros Boutros-Ghali.

Pérez de Cuéllar was decorated by 25 countries. In October 1987 he was awarded the Prince of Asturias Prize for the promotion of Ibero-American co-operation. In January 1989 he received the Olof Palme Prize for International Understanding and Common Security by the Olof Palme Memorial Fund. In February 1989 he was awarded the Jawaharlal Nehru Award for International Understanding. In addition to his awards, Pérez de Cuéllar has received honorary doctorate degrees from several universities around the world.

Further Reading

A book-length biography of Pérez de Cuéllar has yet to appear. However, a column devoted to the Secretary General's activities and statements (entitled ''The 38th Floor'') is published in each issue of the *UN Chronicle*. Works treating the United Nations during the Pérez de Cuéllar era include Toby T. Gati, editor, *The US, the UN, and the Management of Global Change* (1983); Peter R. Baehr, *The United Nations: Reality and Ideal* (1984); and Raymond Carroll, *The Future of the UN* (1985), a book written for young adults. □

Adolfo Pérez Esquivel

Adolfo Pérez Esquivel (born 1931), distinguished as an Argentine artist, became a human rights activist based on Christian pacifism and was awarded the Nobel Peace Prize in 1980.

Adolfo Pérez Esquivel was born in Argentina on November 26, 1931, the son of Spanish immigrants. His mother died when he was a young boy and his father, a coffee salesman, was often away on business. Pérez Esquivel was essentially raised by the nuns and priests who ran the Roman Catholic schools he attended. He has remained a devout Catholic. His pacifistic views are based on his commitment to the message of the Gospels and on his reading of Catholic thinkers such as St. Augustine, a 4th century philosopher, and Thomas Merton, a 20th century American monk. "I believe that one has to listen to the silence of God, what He is asking from each one of us. It's necessary to make a choice. My mission is to carry the message of the Gospel and to live it profoundly with my brothers," he told *America.* Interested in art, he graduated from the National School of Fine Arts in Buenos Aires in 1956. In the same year he married Amanda Pérez, a pianist and composer who gave up her career after the couple's three sons were born. Initially uninvolved politically, he became known as a sculptor and art professor. Two themes inspired his art: Indian cultures and motherhood. These preoccupations anticipated his later activism after two developments in the 1960s and 1970s altered his noncontroversial existence.

Became Involved with Social Justice Programs

One development was the Argentine military's repeated intervention in politics. From the mid-1970s the generals were increasingly committed to extreme repres-

sion, which resulted in the "Dirty War" in which thousands of Argentine citizens "disappeared." According to *Newsday* retired Lt. Commander Adolfo Scilingo was the first Argentine official to admit that more than two thousand political prisoners were stripped, drugged, and thrown into the sea from aircraft under the 1976-83 military dictatorship.

The second development to raise Pérez Esquivel's consciousness was the dedication of a small group of people to peace and human rights, foreshadowing an eventual wave of demands for democracy in the 1980s. The Fellowship of Reconciliation, an interfaith pacifist organization with origins dating to World War I, sent Austrians Jean Goss and Hildegard Goss-Meier to Latin America in 1962 to identify both Catholic and Protestant clergy who might support a nonviolent movement for justice based on Christian principles. Their travels resulted in international pacifist meetings which led to the formation of Service for Peace and Justice. The newly founded group established a small secretariat to coordinate a network of local nonviolent action groups in several countries, including Argentina.

Back home by the early 1970s, Pérez Esquivel had organized a crafts cooperative for a poor urban neighborhood and engaged in a hunger strike to protest escalating violence by both guerrillas and the police. In 1973 he founded *Paz y Justicia,* a monthly periodical. During the following year Pérez Esquivel began a campaign for solidarity with Indians in Ecuador. It was in Ecuador that he had a religious experience in the form of a dream in which he saw the crucified Christ in an Indian poncho. This inspired his book, *Christ in a Poncho,* which was published in English in 1983.

Wider travel and confrontation with authorities followed in the next three years. He supported the Agrarian Leagues of Paraguay against persecution and was arrested in Brazil, where he supported workers' complaints. Back in Argentina he founded the Ecumenical Movement for Human Rights, which assisted families of the people who "disappeared," and he created the Permanent Assembly for Human Rights, which monitored government policy. In 1976 he visited Ecuador again, but was arrested. He then traveled in the United States and Europe. When he sought to renew his passport in April 1977, the Argentine authorities imprisoned him for over a year without any charge and tortured him with cattle prods, electric shocks, and ice cold showers. "During the 32 days I spent in the torture center there were times when the morning light shone on the walls and I could see writings there: names of loved ones, essays, insults, the names of favorite soccer teams. But what impressed me most and something I'll never forget, was a big message written in blood: 'God does not kill.' the life and death, anguish and hope of the people were in that cell," Pérez Esquivel told the *Washington Post* in 1984. He added that in moments of hardship he looks for signs. "I am a man of hope," he said.

Won Nobel Prize

International pressure secured his release from jail, which was followed by house arrest for several months.

Confinement brought recognition: Pax Christi, the Catholic pacifist organization, awarded him the Pope John XXIII Prize; Amnesty International, which worked for the release of political prisoners, adopted him as a prisoner of conscience. In Northern Ireland, Mairead Corrigan and Betty Williams nominated him for the Nobel Peace Prize. Corrigan and Williams had won the 1976 Nobel Peace Prize for their grassroots effort to bring peace to their beleaguered province.

In October 1980 came the announcement that the little known Pérez Esquivel had been selected over many other nominees for the prize. According to *Newsweek* the Nobel committee said of Pérez Esquivel: "He is among those Argentines who have shone a light in the darkness. He champions a solution that dispenses with the use of violence. The views he represents carry a vital message to many other countries, not least in Latin America." Argentine media reportage was restrained but, ironically, Argentine law required the government to pay him a lifetime pension. On December 10, Pérez Esquivel accepted the prize in Oslo "in the name of the poorest and smallest of my brothers and sisters." Before 1980 only six Nobel laureates had been Latin American. The Nobel Committee's selection of Pérez Esquivel in 1980 was one important factor in the restoration of civilian rule in Argentina in 1983.

Continued to Work for Peace and Justice

In the 1980s and 1990s, Pérez Esquivel's pacifist activism took new forms. At home he championed the Mothers of the Plaza, a group who silently protested the "disappearance" of family members. He joined other Nobel laureates who journeyed to Nicaragua in 1984 to deliver humanitarian aid, and to Asia in 1993 to support Burmese democracy advocate Aung San Suu Kyi. In June 1995, along with five other Nobel Peace Prize winners, he wrote to Chinese premier, Li Peng asking for the release of jailed dissident Wei Jingsheng, an advocate of democracy in China.

Pérez Esquivel offered three nonviolent steps to redress injustice: (1) call a specific injustice to the attention of appropriate authorities; (2) if that step fails, appeal to public opinion through such acts as prayer and fasting; (3) if that fails, engage in civil disobedience. He strongly believed that political stability is impossible in Latin America without social justice and the elimination of poverty. In a 1991 article in *Le Monde diplomatique,* reprinted in *World Press Review* he lashed out at the budget reducing measures imposed on Latin American countries by the World Bank and the International Monetary Fund which resulted in decreased expenditure on health, education, and other antipoverty programs—"It is a policy which has caused the gulf between rich and poor nations to go on widening. A time bomb has begun ticking, and no number of promises or soothing words will defuse it. The governments of the world must come to their senses and construct the new economic order—they must rediscover the virtues of sharing."

Further Reading

To understand better the context of Pérez Esquivel's work, refer to a standard history of his native land such as *Argentina* (1987) by David Rock; for sources of his inspiration see *Twentieth-Century Pacifism* (1970) by Peter Brock and selected entries from Harold Josephson (ed.), *Biographical Dictionary of Modern Peace Leaders* (1985) and an entry in *Nobel Prize Winners,* Tyler Wasson (ed.). Pérez Esquivel's own book, *Christ in a Poncho,* was first published in French in 1981; it recounts stories of pacifist resistance by disadvantaged Latin American groups he supported. For additional glimpses of his philosophy read his op ed piece in the *New York Times* (March 30, 1985) and the interview in *America* (December 27, 1980). In 1992 Temple University Press released a translation of Service for Peace and Justice's report on human rights violations in Uruguay, 1972-1985. *Paz y Justicia* carried a biography of Pérez Esquivel in the October-December 1980 issue. See also *Time* (October 27, 1980); *World Press Review* (March 1991). □

Marcos Pérez Jiménez

Marcos Pérez Jiménez (born 1914) was a Venezuelan military officer who helped overthrow a constitutional government in 1948 and then ruled as a dictator during the 1950s. He fled his country after a coup in 1958, was charged with political crimes, and remained in exile.

Marcos Pérez Jiménez was from the Venezuelan state of Táchira, born in the town of Michelena in 1914. His father was a farmer and his mother a schoolteacher. After being educated in his home town and Colombia, Pérez Jiménez entered the Military Academy of Venezuela. An outstanding student, he graduated at the top of his class in 1934 and then studied at military colleges in Peru. There he met other Latin American officers who believed that the military must play a leading role in the lives of Latin American nations and promote technological progress.

Pérez Jiménez rose to national prominence on October 18, 1945, when he participated, with other junior officers and civilian politicians, in the overthrow of the government of General Isaías Medina Angarita. Pérez Jiménez had helped organize a secret military lodge, the Patriotic Military Union, whose members believed that the civilian and military leaders of Venezuela were incompetent and dishonest. The young officers were joined in their conspiracy by the Democratic Action (Acción Democrática) Party. These idealistic young Venezuelans, led by Rómulo Betancourt, wanted a democratic and socially progressive Venezuela.

In the new government, which was first headed by Betancourt and then by Rómulo Gallegos, Pérez Jiménez served as chief of staff of the armed forces. But military officers chafed under civilian rule, concluding that elected politicians could never give Venezuela the nationalism, patriotism, and progress it needed. Led by Lt. Col. Carlos Delgado Chalbaud and Pérez Jiménez, the military overthrew the democratically elected Gallegos government on November 24, 1948.

Delgado Chalbaud assumed control of Venezuela, with Pérez Jiménez acting as second-in-command. But in 1950 Delgado Chalbaud was assassinated. While it has never been determined who ordered the assassination, Pérez Jiménez was the most obvious beneficiary of his superior's death. Pérez Jiménez initially ruled through a figurehead. After staging a fraudulent election, he declared himself president in December 1952.

Pérez Jiménez was a vigorous and energetic dictator. He relied on his skills as an organizer and planner to fulfill his goals. His motto was the "New National Ideal," a philosophy that put a higher premium on national unity and material and technological progress than on political freedom and intellectual and moral improvement. He believed that the armed forces—disciplined, trained, and ostensibly non-partisan—could best carry out this mission.

In practice, the New National Ideal consisted mainly of lavish public works projects for Caracas, the capital city. The construction of new hotels, office buildings, apartments, and super-highways transformed Caracas into a glittering, modern city. In addition to public construction, Pérez Jiménez concentrated his energies and the nation's money on the armed forces, the mainstay of his regime. Soldiers lived like aristocrats with impressive barracks and social clubs and the latest in military hardware.

Along with revivifying Caracas and bestowing favors on the military, Pérez Jiménez brutally suppressed political and civil liberties with the aid of his efficient secret police. Leaders of the outlawed Acción Democrática Party were tortured and murdered. Social programs such as land reform that Acción Democrática had instituted between 1945 and 1948 were overturned.

In foreign policy Pérez Jiménez took an anti-communist stance and closely aligned his country with the United States. He also attracted U.S. investment and awarded generous contracts to American oil companies. The United States, under President Dwight Eisenhower, thanked the unsavory dictator by awarding him a Legion of Merit medal, the nation's highest award for foreign personages.

Venezuelans eventually came to abhor the dictatorship. Protests mounted over the political repression and wasteful spending on the military. Many suspected that Pérez Jiménez and his henchmen had stolen public funds. After a series of mass uprisings, Pérez Jiménez fled in late January 1958, first to the Dominican Republic and later to Miami, Florida. In December 1958 Venezuelans elected Rómulo Betancourt, who had returned from exile, as president. Since then Venezuela has maintained a political democracy.

In 1959 the Betancourt government asked the U.S. to extradite Pérez Jiménez on the grounds that he was responsible for political crimes, murder, and embezzlement. After lengthy court hearings, the U.S. agreed in 1963 to deport the former dictator if the charges were limited to financial mis-

conduct. Venezuela then initiated legal proceedings against Pérez Jiménez, which lasted five years. In August 1968 Venezuelan judges ruled that Pérez Jiménez had personally enriched himself while in office and gave him a four-year prison sentence. Since he had been in jail during his trial for more than four years, the court permitted Pérez Jiménez to leave immediately for exile in Spain.

After 1968 Pérez Jiménez attempted to influence Venezuelan political life. Politicians loyal to him attracted a small amount of electoral support. In 1972 he briefly returned to Venezuela and registered to run for president. The Venezuelan legislature responded by enacting a constitutional amendment barring ex-presidents convicted of crimes from serving again. Officials also suggested that Pérez Jiménez might be tried for other crimes if he returned to Venezuela. In effect, Pérez Jiménez was condemned to perpetual exile. He returned to Spain and was politically inactive thereafter.

In light of Venezuela's widespread poverty, unemployment, and corruption, some citizens preferred the efficiency of dictatorial rule and credited the Pérez Jiménez government for controlling street crime and using the country's oil wealth to build skyscrapers, bridges, and South America's finest highway system.

Further Reading

There is no complete biography of Pérez Jiménez in English. For information and background, see Winfield J. Burggraaff, *The Venezuelan Armed Forces in Politics, 1935-1959* (1972) and Judith Ewell, *The Indictment of a Dictator: The Extradition and Trial of Marcos Pérez Jiménez* (1981). A useful history of Venezuela is John Lombardi's *Venezuela: The Search for Order, the Dream of Progress* (1982). For U.S. relations with Venezuela see Stephen G. Rabe, *The Road to OPEC: United States Relations with Venezuela, 1919-1976* (1982). □

Giovanni Battista Pergolesi

The Italian composer Giovanni Battista Pergolesi (1710-1736) excelled in comic opera, and his works in this genre had a profound influence on the course of operatic history.

Born in the small town of Iesi near Ancona on Jan. 4, 1710, Giovanni Battista Pergolesi received instruction on the violin from the Marchese Gabriele Ripanti and other musical training from the two priests who directed the cathedral choir and gave public instruction in music. His obvious talent led to his enrollment in the famous Conservatorio dei Poveri di Gesù Cristo in Naples, under the patronage of the Marchese Cardolo Maria Pianetti of Iesi. Pergolesi's studies there probably began in 1726, and one of his teachers was the composer Francesco Durante.

Pergolesi's career as a professional composer was launched with the opera *Salustia* at the Teatro San Bartolomeo in Naples in 1732. His first truly successful works were written later that year: *Lo frate 'nnammorato* was an *opera buffa* written in the local dialect; and a Mass commissioned by the city after a series of earthquakes won public praise from the composer Leonardo Leo. A series of dramatic and sacred works followed, including an apparently minor one, the intermezzo *La serva padrona*, performed between the acts of his *opera seria Il prigionier superbo* in 1733.

Pergolesi was made deputy to the official *maestro di cappella* of the city of Naples, was twice summoned to Rome to direct performances of operatic and sacred works, and was for a time in the service of the Prince of Stigliano and the Duke of Maddaloni. His health failing, he went to the Capuchin monastery in Pozzuoli, completing there his Stabat Mater shortly before his death on March 16, 1736, at the age of 26.

At the time of his death Pergolesi appeared to have been a talented composer of largely local fame, but circumstances thrust him into the small group of people whose posthumous fame was greater than that achieved during their lifetime. Opera needed new directions. *La serva padrona* was revived in Parma in 1738, then done in Bologna, Graz, Venice, and Dresden, and soon in all parts of Europe. The freshness of its character delineation and music attracted those who were weary of the stilted conventions of *opera seria*. Parisians who were disillusioned with traditional French opera—among them the writers Friedrich Melchior Grimm, Jean Jacques Rousseau, and Denis Diderot—rallied behind the work and made it an issue in the War of the Buffoons. This modest work received some 200 performances in the city in the 1750s.

With the fame of *La serva padrona* came success also for other of Pergolesi's compositions that might otherwise have remained neglected. His best pieces are characterized by freshness and liveliness and a fluid handling of solo voices. A large number of sacred, secular, and instrumental works published after his death and attributed to him are undoubtedly spurious.

Further Reading

The standard work on Pergolesi is in Italian. The best source in English is F. Walker's article in *Grove's Dictionary of Music and Musicians,* vol. 6 (5th ed. 1954); Walker did not merely condense other writings on Pergolesi but did considerable original research. For general background see Donald Jay Grout, *A Short History of Opera* (2 vols., 1947; 2d ed. 1965).

Additional Sources

Pergolesi, Napoli: S. Civita, 1986. □

Pericles

Pericles (ca. 495-429 B.C.) was the leading statesman of Athens for an unprecedented period and brought it to the height of its political power and its artistic achievement. The years from 446 to 429 have been called the Periclean Age.

Pericles was the son of Xanthippus, a distinguished statesman and general of aristocratic family (probably the Bouzygae), and Agariste, a niece of the famous statesman Cleisthenes, the leader of a powerful clan, the Alcmeonidae. He inherited great wealth; indeed, as a young man, he financed the costly production of Aeschylus's play *The Persae* in 472. Pericles received the best education available, studying music under Damon and mathematics under Zeno of Elea, a pioneer in theoretical physics.

Eminently fitted for a public career, Pericles chose to follow the example of Cleisthenes and advocate a more advanced democracy.

Champion of Radical Democracy

Pericles became prominent first in the law courts, where he prosecuted the leading statesmen and finally Cimon, the leading conservative power. In the Assembly, Pericles advocated hostility toward Sparta and radical constitutional reform at home. He worked in close association with Ephialtes, an older and more established leader of democratic views. They were both elected generals for a year sometime before 462, and in 462-461, when Cimon was the most influential of the generals in office, they made a concerted attack upon him.

A crucial decision on foreign policy was in the making—whether to prosecute the war against Persia as the

Legislator of Domestic Affairs

The political career of Pericles after the ostracism of Cimon divides into two parts. The first ended in 443, when he secured the ostracism of his leading opponent, Thucydides. Pericles also passed further legislation against the Areopagus, introduced pay for political services, and in 451 restricted Athenian citizenship to children of Athenian parentage on both sides. He was entrusted with special financial responsibilities as commissioner for the building of the Long Walls, linking Athens to the Piraeus, and as commissioner for the building of the Parthenon and the Propylaea on the Acropolis from 447 onward. It is not known how far he was involved in the implementation of the war on two fronts—against Sparta in Greece and against Persia in Egypt, which resulted in a stalemate on land in 457 and a heavy defeat in Egypt in 454.

Pericles played a leading part in the critical years following 454. His founding of Athenian colonies on the territories of Athens's "allies" was a key factor in converting a coalition into an Athenian empire. He certainly approved of Athens's appropriating the allied moneys, and he advocated their use for domestic purposes. He proposed the recall of Cimon, which resulted in victories over Persia and a truce with Sparta. Pericles's own operations as a military commander in western waters in 455 and 454 were successful.

Between 448 and 446 Pericles is associated with the renewal of hostilities with Sparta. He began with a diplomatic offensive, offering to all Greek states the freedom of the seas and the celebration of the end of the Persian Wars—an event marking the conclusion of the Peace of Callias with Persia early in 448. When diplomacy failed, Pericles commanded an expedition to Delphi which reversed Sparta's policy there and made the renewal of hostilities almost inevitable. In 447-446 the storm broke: Athens's power in Boeotia collapsed; Euboea revolted; Megara broke free from Athenian occupation; and Sparta, at the head of its Peloponnesian coalition, invaded Attica.

In command of an Athenian army Pericles crossed to Euboea and then rushed back to face the enemy in Attica. To everyone's amazement the Spartan king withdrew his army. The miracle was never explained, although Pericles was said by some to have bribed the king. In any case Pericles hurried back to Euboea and stamped out the revolt. Peace was obtained in 446. Athens had lost most of its gains, but its empire was recognized. Pericles's general policy was finally approved by the ostracism of Thucydides in 443.

Periclean Democracy

In the second part of Pericles's political career, from 443 to 429, he was the leading personality in Athens. His foreign policy was to suppress any revolt in the Athenian empire and to resist Sparta. When Samos revolted in collusion with Persia, Pericles acted boldly and successfully as commander of the Athenian forces, and the punishment of Samos was a warning to others. He paraded the naval power of Athens with an expedition in the Black Sea (ca. 437), and he advised Athens to make alliances with Corcyra (Corfu), a leading naval power in the west, in 433. This

leader of a coalition of maritime states and as the nominal partner of an inactive Sparta, or to attack Sparta, exploit the coalition for that purpose, and make war with Persia a secondary matter. The issue in home policy was between the status quo, with the Areopagus Council acting as a brake on democratic radicalism, and an unimpeded implementation of majority decisions in the Assembly.

The two issues were inextricably linked not only by past history but also by ideological and material considerations. These issues were to face Athens throughout the life of Pericles, but the fateful step was taken in 462-461, at a time when Persia was on the defensive and Sparta was crippled by the effects of earthquakes, followed by internal dissension.

Sparta's appeals to Athens, its ally, for help against the uprising were granted on the advice of Cimon and against the advice of Ephialtes. While Cimon and the army were serving in Laconia in 462, Ephialtes and Pericles carried out their radical democratic reforms, stripping the Areopagus Council of all constitutional powers and making the authority of the Assembly and the Heliaea (people's courts) absolute.

Meanwhile, in Laconia, Sparta dismissed the Athenian army under Cimon's command. This insulting treatment enraged Athens. In spring 461 Cimon was ostracized, and Athens made alliances with Sparta's enemies, Argos and Thessaly. At this time Ephialtes was assassinated, and Pericles, in his early 30s, became the undisputed leader of the radical democrats.

alliance was within the letter of the treaty of peace with Sparta, signed in 446-445, but contrary to its spirit.

Diplomatic and military incidents followed which resulted in war with Sparta and its allies in 431. Pericles's strategy was an offensive by sea, avoidance of battle on land, and control of the empire. Its adoption led to the concentration of the Athenians inside the walls of Athens. There plague struck down a third of Athens's armed forces, two sons of Pericles among them. The people turned against him for the first time. He was fined but reelected general for 429, the year of his death. He had been unhappily married and lived with a leading courtesan, Aspasia. He was buried near the Academy.

His Legacy

The form of democracy which Pericles developed in Athens used majority rule more fully than any constitution since then. Yet Pericles dominated the people; in conditions of complete political equality and freedom, he imposed his will and maintained his policy. To admirers of democracy he is almost without a peer. The society which he led was imbued with his ideas—an overmastering love of Athens, a passionate belief in freedom for Athenians, and a faith in the ability of man.

Pericles's trust in the intellect was shared by Athens's leading thinkers. His love of Athens found expression in the conception and the details of the Parthenon and the Propylaea. He was a frank imperialist, enlightened perhaps, but severe. He courted war, when he thought war would win advantages for Athens. As a strategist, he is certainly not above criticism, and in the long run his policies brought not victory but a disaster which shattered the power and degraded the democracy of Athens.

Further Reading

Ancient sources on Pericles are Thucydides and Plutarch. A good account of Pericles's life and work is by Edward Mewburn Walker and Frank Ezra Adcock in *The Cambridge Ancient History,* vol. 5 (1927). Studies of Pericles and his time include Evelyn Abbott, *Pericles and the Golden Age of Athens* (1897); Compton Mackenzie, *Pericles* (1937); Andrew R. Burn, *Pericles and Athens* (1949); Victor Ehrenberg, *Pericles and Sophocles* (1954); C. A. Robinson, ed., *The Spring of Civilization: Periclean Athens* (1955); and Henry Dickinson Westlake, *Individuals in Thucydides* (1968). □

Frances Perkins

Frances Perkins (1882-1965), American social worker, U.S. secretary of labor, and civil service commissioner, was the first woman to serve in a presidential Cabinet.

Frances Perkins was born in Boston, Mass., on April 10, 1882, and grew up in Worcester, the daughter of a manufacturer. At the age of 16 she entered Mount Holyoke College. Following her graduation in 1902, she spent 2 years in Worcester as a social worker for the Episcopal Church. She then taught school near Chicago before working at Hull House. After studying at the University of Pennsylvania's Wharton School of Finance, she took a master's degree at Columbia University in 1910.

Perkins next became executive secretary of the Consumers' League of New York, which investigated industrial conditions and lobbied for ameliorative legislation. In 1913 she married Paul Caldwell Wilson, a financial statistician, and they had one daughter.

Between 1919 and 1929 Miss Perkins was industrial commissioner for the state of New York. She helped get further reductions of the work week for women, the publication of monthly figures on unemployment within the state, and other reforms. She was also active in immigrant education programs and won the confidence of both trade unionists and middle-class reformers. In 1929 newly elected governor Franklin D. Roosevelt made her labor commissioner of New York. Four years later she followed Roosevelt (now president) to Washington as secretary of labor, the first woman to hold a Cabinet appointment.

Although opposed by both business groups and the leadership of the American Federation of Labor (AFL) because of her sex and her liberal social and economic views, Perkins did a reasonably good job. Her department improved the operation of the Children's Bureau, began issuing regular unemployment figures, and contributed significantly to the standardization of state labor laws and the formulation of the Social Security Act. The Labor De-

partment proved ineffectual in dealing with the industrial disturbances of the 1930s and with the strife between the AFL and the emergent Congress of Industrial Organizations (CIO).

Despite persistent, often harsh, criticism, Perkins stayed in office, resigning only after Roosevelt's death in 1945. Soon after, however, President Harry Truman appointed her to the U.S. Civil Service Commission. She served quietly and rather obscurely until she resigned in 1953. For the next 12 years Perkins lectured at Cornell University and other institutions. She died in New York City on May 14, 1965.

Further Reading

Autobiographical information on Perkins is in her *The Roosevelt I Knew* (1946). The most scholarly account of her career as secretary of labor is in Arthur M. Schlesinger, Jr., *The Age of Roosevelt* (3 vols., 1957-1960). □

William Maxwell Evarts Perkins

Recognized as the greatest American editor of fiction, William Maxwell Evarts Perkins (1884-1947) was legendary in his lifetime for discovering and developing brilliant authors.

Maxwell Perkins was born on September 20, 1884, in New York City; grew up in Plainfield, New Jersey; attended St. Paul's Academy in Concord, New Hampshire; and graduated from Harvard College in 1907. Although an economics major in college, Perkins had the good sense to also study under Charles Townsend Copeland, a famous teacher of literature who helped prepare Perkins for his calling.

After working as a reporter for *The New York Times*, Perkins joined the venerable publishing house of Charles Scribner's Sons in 1910. That same year he married Louise Saunders, also of Plainfield, who would bear him five daughters. At the time he joined it, Scribner's was known for publishing eminently respectable authors such as John Galsworthy, Henry James, and Edith Wharton. However, much as he admired these older giants, Perkins wished to bring Scribner's into the 20th century by publishing younger writers. Unlike most editors, he actively sought out promising new artists and made his first big find in 1919 when he signed F. Scott Fitzgerald. This was no easy task, for no one at Scribner's except Perkins had liked *The Romantic Egotist,* the working title of Fitzgerald's first novel, and it was rejected. Even so, Perkins worked with Fitzgerald to drastically revise the manuscript and then lobbied it through the house until he wore down his colleagues' resistance.

The publication of *This Side of Paradise* (1920) marked the arrival of a new literary generation that would always be associated with Perkins. Fitzgerald's profligacy and alcohol-

ism put great strain on his relationship with Perkins. Nonetheless, Perkins remained his friend as well as his editor to the end of Fitzgerald's too-short life, advancing him money, making personal loans, and encouraging the unstable genius in every way. Perkins rendered yeoman service as an editor too, particularly in helping Fitzgerald with *The Great Gatsby* (1925), his masterpiece, which benefitted substantially from Perkins' criticism.

It was through Fitzgerald that Perkins met Ernest Hemingway, publishing his first novel, *The Sun Also Rises,* in 1926. A daring book for the times, Perkins had to fight for it over objections to Hemingway's profanity raised by traditionalists in the firm. The commercial success of Hemingway's next novel, *A Farewell to Arms* (1929), which rose to number one on the best-seller list, put an end to questions about Perkins' editorial judgment.

The greatest professional challenge Perkins ever faced was posed by Thomas Wolfe, whose talent was matched only by his lack of artistic self-discipline. Unlike most writers, who are often blocked, words poured out of Wolfe like a mighty Niagara. A blessing in some ways, this was a curse too, as Wolfe's affection for each and every one of his sentences was boundless. After a tremendous struggle, Perkins induced Wolfe to cut 90,000 words from his first novel, *Look Homeward Angel* (1929). His next, *Of Time and the River* (1935), was the result of a two-year battle during which Wolfe kept writing more and more pages in the face of an ultimately victorious effort by Perkins to hold the line on size. Grateful to Perkins at first for discovering him and helping him realize his potential, Wolfe later came to resent the popular perception that he owed his success to his editor. This was true in part, for without Perkins' firm hand it is unlikely that Wolfe could have been published. Wolfe left Scribner's after provoking numerous fights with Perkins to justify his departure. This ingratitude hurt Perkins, but did not keep him from serving selflessly as Wolfe's literary executor after his untimely death in 1938.

Although his reputation as an editor is most closely linked to these three, Perkins worked with many other writers. He was the first to publish J.P. Marquand and Erskine Caldwell. His advice was responsible for the enormous success of Marjorie Kinnan Rawlings, whose The Yearling (1938) grew out of suggestions made by Perkins. It became a runaway best-seller and won the Pulitzer Prize. Alan Paton's Cry the Beloved Country (1946) was another highly successful Perkins book. His last discovery was James Jones, who approached Perkins in 1945. Perkins persuaded Jones to abandon the novel he was working on at that time and launched him on what would become From Here to Eternity (1951). By this time Perkins' health was failing and he did not live to see its success, nor that of Hemingway's The Old Man and the Sea (1952), which was dedicated to his memory. Perkins died on June 17, 1947 in Stamford, Connecticut.

Perkins was noted for his courtesy and thoughtfulness, which, though justly admired, are not what made him great. Among his gifts, two in particular stand out. He recognized good writing wherever he found it and nursed along writers as few editors did. That Ring Lardner has a reputation today, for example, is owing to the fact that Perkins saw him as more than a syndicated humorist. Perkins believed in Lardner more than the writer did in himself, and despite the failure of several earlier collections he coaxed Lardner into letting him assemble another under the title How To Write Short Stories (1924). The book sold well and, thanks to excellent reviews, established Lardner as a literary figure.

Apart from his roles as coach, friend, and promoter, Perkins was unusual among editors for the close and detailed attention he gave to books, and for what the novelist Vance Bourjaily, another of his discoveries, called his "infallible sense of structure." Although he never pretended to be an artist himself, Perkins could often see where an author ought to go more clearly than the writer did. That was true even of Fitzgerald, whose craftsmanship was exemplary. For this, and for his nurturing of talent, American literature is much in his debt.

Further Reading

There is only one biography of Perkins, the excellent A. Scott Berg, Max Perkins: Editor of Genius (1978). Perkins' editorial papers are in the Charles Scribner's Sons collection at Princeton University. Perkins became known to the general public in his lifetime as a result of a profile by Malcolm Cowley, "Unshaken Friend," New Yorker (April 1 and 8, 1944). ☐

George Perle

The American musician, George Perle (born 1915), was active in nearly all aspects of the field. Best known as a composer, he developed a convincing language that he called "twelve-tone tonality." He also wrote numerous articles and books and remained active as a teacher and pianist into the 1980s.

George Perle was born in Bayonne, New Jersey, on May 6, 1915. His parents had emigrated to the U.S. from Russia shortly before his birth. He spent most of his boyhood on farms in Wisconsin and Indiana. While still a high school student Perle began his formal training by taking piano and harmony lessons at the Chicago College of Music. He continued in Chicago at DePaul University from 1935 to 1938, studying composition with Wesley La Violette.

Discovery of the music of Schoenberg awakened him to new possibilities of sound organization, but it was Berg's Lyric Suite that, "like a revelation in the literal biblical sense," affected him most profoundly. In the late 1930s he became director of the New Music Group of Chicago and, with composers Robert Erickson and Ben Weber, introduced many works, including several by Schoenberg, Berg, and Webern. Upon studying the serial works of these masters Perle felt let down by what he believed to be a lack of control over the harmonic dimension. He then began formulating the means of harmonic organization that would eventually appear in his book Twelve-Tone Tonality (1977).

Perle studied composition with Ernst Krenek from 1939 to 1941 and received an M.A. degree from the American Conservatory of Music in Chicago in 1942. Perhaps his best known compositions from this period are the two Rilke Songs for soprano and piano (1941), composed according to his twelve-tone tonal method.

After serving in the U.S. Army from 1943 to 1946, Perle accepted his first teaching post at the College of the City of New York in 1948. Positions at the University of Louisville (1949-1957) and at the University of California at Davis (1957-1961) followed. During this time Perle also studied with Curt Sachs and Gustave Reese at New York University, where he received his doctorate in musicology in 1956. In 1961 he accepted a post as assistant professor at Queens College of the City University of New York, where he became a full professor from 1966 into the mid-1980s. He also held visiting professorships at Juilliard, the University of Southern California, Yale University, the Berkshire Music Center at Tanglewood, the State University of New York at Buffalo, Columbia, and the University of Pennsylvania.

One of three principles of organization distinguishes most of Perle's mature compositions since the late 1930s. Regardless of the principle, Perle's works tend to be fairly bright sounding, rhythmically complex, virtuosic, and tone-centered. The latter term refers to modern music that emphasizes one or more tones or chords, and yet does so without the triadic hierarchies producing the "gravitational pull" of the tonal music of the 18th and 19th centuries. A few compositions, however, such as the *Variations on a Welsh Melody* (1952) for band, are tonal.

Perhaps taking a hint from Schoenberg's pre-serial, atonal works, Perle composed works that he described as "freely or intuitively conceived in a twelve-tone idiom that combines various serial procedures with melodically generated tone-centers, intervallic cells, symmetrical formations, etc." These works are most frequently scored for solo instruments and include music written up until the mid-1960s. Prominent are the following: *Sonata for Solo Viola* (1942); *Three Sonatas for Solo Clarinet* (1943); *Hebrew Melodies for Solo Cello* (1947); *Quintet for Strings* (1958); *Sonata I for Solo Violin; Wind Quintet* (1959); and *Sonata II* (1963); *Monody for Flute* (1960); *Monody II for Double Bass* (1962); *Three Inventions for Bassoon* (1962); *Short Sonata for Piano* (1964); *Solo Partita for Violin and Viola* (1965); and *Wind Quintet III* (1967).

These smaller-scale and often monophonic compositions gave Perle an opportunity to develop some of the subtle rhythmic techniques that characterize his music. He wrote, "A rhythmic . . . ideal toward which I progress . . . was that of a beat variable in duration but at the same time as tangible and coherent as the beat in classical music, and of an integration between the larger rhythmic dimensions and the minimal metric units." A technique of "metric modulation" usually ascribed to Elliott Carter, but perhaps independently invented by Perle, furnished a means for controlling a variable duration of the beat in these works and, indeed, throughout his entire output. Metric modulation is accomplished by introducing a cross-rhythm (e.g., duplets or triplets) within an established pulse rate and then basing a new pulse rate on the altered note value.

Contrary to general belief, relatively few of Perle's compositions adhere strictly to the serial method formulated by Schoenberg, the third string quartet (1947) being a notable exception. In later serial works Perle utilized extensions of the method developed by Milton Babbitt. The *Three Inventions for Piano* (1957), for example, are organized on the principle of "combinatoriality," whereby the operations of transposition and inversion on the first half of the row (called a hexachord) produce a new hexachord containing the six pitches (or preferably "pitch classes") not included in the first. The total of the two hexachords then includes all the notes of the chromatic scale.

Many of Perle's works after 1939, and perhaps all of them since 1968, are based on a twelve-tone method of his own devising, unique in that the row exists purely as precompositional matter designed primarily to control the vertical or harmonic aspect of the music. The row is constructed in such a way that, along with its inversion, the adjacencies of any particular note (axis-tone) in both forms will produce a four-note chord of the same intervallic structure. Adjacencies further removed from the axis-tone provide additional harmonic material, all of which can be emphasized by orchestral coloring and instrumental doublings. Prominent among compositions employing this twelve-tone tonality (or twelve-tone modality, as it is some-

times called) are the *Rilke Songs* (1941); *Rhapsody for Orchestra* (1953); the *Fifth String Quartet* (1960); *Three Movements for Orchestra* (1960); *Toccata for Piano* (1969); the *Seventh String Quartet* (1973); *Songs of Praise and Lamentation* (1974) for mixed chorus a cappella; *13 Emily Dickenson Songs* (1978) for soprano and piano; *A Short Symphony* (1980); and *Ballade for Piano* (1982); the Wind Quarter Number 4 composed in 1984 and the winner of the 1986 Pulitzer Prize *Sonata à cinque* (1986), String Quarter No. 8. dating from 1989 and titled *Windows of Order* and *Sinfonietta II*.

In addition to his wide renown as a composer, Perle was a distinguished musical scholar and theorist. *Serial Composition and Atonality* (rev. ed. 1977) is a standard text on the music of Schoenberg, Berg, and Webern, and *Twelve-Tone Tonality* (1977) has become an important contribution to post-Schoenbergian twelve-tone theory. *The Operas of Alban Berg. Vol. I: Wozzeck* and *Vol. II: Lulu* (1980, 1985) establish him as one of the world's foremost Berg authorities. The latter book contains his rather sensational discovery of Berg's secret love affair, encoded in the notation and text of the opera. Perle was also a co-founder and former director of the International Alban Berg Society. He received numerous honors throughout his career, including Guggenheim fellowships (1966, 1974), membership in the American Academy and National Institute of Arts and Letters (1978), three Deems Taylor awards for various writings including his book on *Wozzeck,* the Kinkeldey award of the American Musicological Society, the Pulitzer Prize for Music (1986), and commissions from the Fromm Foundation, Koussevitzky Foundation, MacArthur Foundation, and National Endowment for the Arts, among others.

Perle was honored in 1991 as he and his pianist wife, Shirley Rhoads, wound up their three-year residency in San Francisco, where Perle had officiated as an unusually popular composer-in-residence with the San Francisco Symphony. In appreciation of his residency, the orchestra honored him by proclaiming a George Perle Week in February of 1991. The honorary week followed shortly after Richard Goode had played the world premiere of Perle's Piano Concerto and it embraced the first performance of Perle's *Sinfonietta II* along with a varied program of four chamber works.

Further Reading

Surprisingly little has been written about Perle, and much of this appears in lesser-known journals. Exceptions are the *Musical Quarterly* (1975), which contains a thorough description of *Songs of Praise and Lamentation,* and *Perspectives of New Music* (1982-1983), which discusses his tone-centered music. Thorough and fairly accurate biographical coverage appears in David Ewen's *American Composers: A Biographical Dictionary* (1982). See also the article by Tim Page in honor of Perle's 70th birthday in the *New York Times* (May 5, 1985). □

Eva Duarte de Perón

Eva Duarte de Perón (1919-1952) was the second wife and political partner of President Juan Perón of Argentina. A formidable political figure in her own right, she was known for her campaign for female suffrage, her role with organized labor, and her organization of a vast social welfare program which benefited and gained the support of the lower classes.

The youngest of five children, María Eva Duarte was born on May 7, 1919, in the little village of Los Toldos in Buenos Aires province. Following the death of her father, the family moved to the larger nearby town of Junín, where her mother ran a boarding house. At the age of 16, Evita, as she was often affectionately called, left school and went to Buenos Aires with the dream of becoming an actress. Lacking any theatrical training, she obtained a few bit parts in motion pictures and on the radio, until she was finally employed on a regular basis with one of the larger radio stations in Buenos Aires.

In November 1943 she met Colonel Juan Perón, who had just assumed the post of secretary of labor and social welfare in the military government which had come to power the previous June. Eva developed an intimate relationship with the widowed Perón, who was beginning to

organize the Argentine workers in support of his own bid for the presidency. Becoming Perón's loyal political confidante and partner, she rendered him valuable assistance in gaining support among the masses. In October 1945, following Perón's arrest and imprisonment by a group of military men opposed to his political ascendancy, she helped to organize a mass demonstration which led to his release. A few days later, on October 21, 1945, Eva and Juan Perón were married.

Now politically stronger than ever, Perón became the government candidate in the presidential election set for February 1946. In an action unprecedented for Argentine women, Señora de Perón participated actively in the ensuing campaign, directing her appeal to the less privileged groups of Argentine society, whom she labeled *los descamisados* ("the shirtless ones").

Following Perón's election, Eva began to play an increasingly important role in the political affairs of the nation. During the early months of the Perón administration she launched an active campaign for national woman suffrage, which had been promised in Perón's electoral platform. Due largely to her efforts, suffrage for women was enacted in 1947, and in 1951 women voted for the first time in a national election.

Eva also assumed the task of consolidating the support of the working classes and controlling organized labor. Taking over a suite of offices in the Secretariate of Labor, Perón's former center of power, she used her influence to seat and unseat ministers of labor and top officials of the General Confederation of Labor, the chief labor organization in Argentina. For all practical purposes she became the secretary of labor, supporting workers' claims for higher wages and sponsoring a host of social welfare measures.

Because of her own lower-class background, Eva readily identified with the working classes and was fervently committed to improving their lot. She devoted several hours every day to audiences with the poor and visits to hospitals, orphanages, and factories. She also supervised the newly created Ministry of Health, which built many new hospitals and established a remarkably successful program to eradicate such diseases as tuberculosis, malaria, and leprosy.

A large part of her work with the poor was carried out by the María Eva Duarte de Perón Welfare Foundation established in June 1947. Financed by contributions, often forcefully exacted, from trade unions, businesses, and industrial firms, it grew into an enormous semi-official welfare agency which distributed food, clothing, medicine, and money to needy people throughout Argentina, and even upon occasion to those suffering from disasters in other Latin American countries.

Enjoying great popularity among the *descamisados*, Eva Perón aided significantly in making the masses feel indebted to the Perón regime. On the other hand, her program of social welfare and her campaign for female suffrage aroused considerable opposition among the *gente bien* (social elite), to whom Eva was unacceptable because of her own humble background and earlier activities. Eva was driven by the desire to master those members of the oligarchy that had rejected her and she could be ruthless and vindictive with her enemies.

In June 1951 it was announced that Eva would be the vice-presidential candidate on the re-election ticket with Perón in the upcoming national election. Eva's candidacy was strongly supported by the General Confederation of Labor. But opposition within the military and her own failing health caused her to decline the nomination. Already suffering from cancer, Eva died on July 26, 1952, at the age of 32.

After Eva's death, which produced an almost unprecedented display of public grief, Perón's political fortunes began to deteriorate, and he was finally overthrown by a military coup in September 1955.

Eva Perón remains a controversial figure in Argentine history. Diminutive, attractive, and highly vivacious, both her friends and her enemies agreed that she was a woman of great personal charm. Her supporters have elevated her to popular sainthood as the patroness of the lower-classes, and the sympathetic portrayal of her in the 1997 film *Evita*, starring American actress Madonna, reintroduced Eva to the American public. By the oligarchy and a large part of the officer corps of the military, however, she is greatly detested. There is still considerable difference of opinion regarding her true role in the Perón regime and her ultimate place in Argentine history.

Further Reading

A useful autobiographical account of Eva Perón is provided in her *My Mission in Life* (1953). One of the most valuable studies of her career is Nicholas Fraser and Marysa Navarro, *Eva Perón* (1980). Two other important works are Julie Taylor, *Eva Perón: The Myth of a Woman* (1979), and John Barnes, *Evita, First Lady: A Biography of Eva Perón* (1978). Maria Flores, *The Woman with the Whip* (1952) is also useful. Richard Bourne, *Political Leaders of Latin America* (1967) provides a balanced sketch of Eva's role in the Perón regime. For background on the Perón era see Robert J. Alexander, *Juan Domingo Perón: A History* (1979) and Joseph A. Page, *Perón: A Biography* (1983). A 1986 book, *Perón and the Enigma of Argentina* by Robert D. Crassweller, drew mixed reviews. □

Isabel Martinez de Perón

Isabel Martinez de Perón (born 1931) became the first female president in Latin America when she assumed the Argentine presidency upon the death of her husband, Juan Perón. Her term in office was characterized by political violence and economic instability until she was finally overthrown by the military.

Isabel Perón was born María Estela Martinez Cartas on February 4, 1931, in La Rioja, a provincial capital in the impoverished mountainous region of northwestern Argentina. Her father, a local bank manager, died when she was still a young child. By the time of her father's death, the family had moved to Buenos Aires, where she studied piano, dance, and French, although she was not able to finish her formal education.

After leaving school she became a dancer, performing in folk music groups, night clubs, and finally the ballet corps of two leading theaters in Buenos Aires. She acquired the name Isabel on her confirmation in the Catholic Church and later adopted it as her professional name when she began her dancing career.

In 1956, while on tour with a dance troupe through Latin America, she met Juan Perón, who had recently been ousted from the Argentine presidency after roughly ten years in power. Giving up her career as a dancer, she became Perón's personal secretary and accompanied him into exile in Madrid, where the two were married in 1961.

Juan Perón in Exile

Although Juan Perón was not allowed to return to Argentina, he retained control of the Peronist movement. It remained a strong political force in the country despite being suppressed under the provisional military government of General Pedro Aramburu. With a return to civilian rule following the election of Arturo Frondizi in 1958, the Peronists were again permitted to participate in politics, and they showed surprising strength in the 1962 election. The military intervened, however, to annul the results and depose Frondizi.

During the new military regime of President José María Guido a conflict over control of the government took place

between two factions within the military: the Reds, who favored a hard line against the Peronists, and the Blues, who favored a more moderate constitutional line. The Blues gained ascendancy, and in July 1963 new elections were held in which Arturo Illia won the presidency. Illia took a conciliatory approach toward the Peronists, permitting them to put up candidates in the congressional elections scheduled for March 1965.

It was during this period that Isabel Perón received her political baptism, travelling to Argentina as Perón's emissary to promote those candidates endorsed by him and to try to build support among the new generation of Peronist leaders who favored Peronism without Perón.

The Peronists not only made significant gains in the congressional elections, but won two important by-elections in April and May of the following year, which foreshadowed a possible Peronist victory in the crucial presidential election in 1969. In June, alarmed by the success of the Peronists, the military ousted President Illia and installed General Juan Carlos Onganía as president.

Rejecting the transitional role of the prior military regimes, the Onganía government suppressed not only Peronism, but all conventional political activity and announced its intention to remain in power for an indefinite period of time. By 1969, however, Argentina's growing economic distress had contributed to the outbreak of political violence, which culminated in the kidnaping and murder of former president Aramburu, by a group of left-wing Peronists called the Montoneros. Increasing concern among top military leaders about the ability of Onganía to control the growing wave of guerrilla attacks led to his replacement by General Roberto Levinston. Political unrest continued to grow, however, and in March 1971 General Alejandro Lanusse, who was known to favor a return to democracy, assumed the presidency.

Upon taking office Lanusse proclaimed his intention to hold democratic elections and permitted the reestablishment of political parties, including the Peronists. Lanusse's decision to open negotiations with the now aged Juan Perón and to end his 16 years of exile occasioned Isabel Perón's next mission to Argentina. She remained there from December 1971 to March 1972, engaging in talks with the Lanusse government and attempting without success to unify the Peronist movement, which by now had become deeply divided between militant right-wing and left-wing factions. Although Perón was prohibited from running for the presidency in the elections scheduled for March 1973, his own hand-picked candidate, Héctor Cámpora, won the election, polling almost 50 percent of the vote. In a well-orchestrated plan to bring Juan Perón back to power, Cámpora resigned from office, setting the stage for new elections in which Juan Perón automatically became the leading candidate.

Return to Argentina and Victory

At the insistence of Juan Perón, his wife was named his vice-presidential running-mate. Despite strong opposition to her candidacy, she played a significant role in the new presidential race, campaigning vigorously in behalf of Juan

Perón who, because of his health, made few personal appearances.

On September 23, 1973, the team of Juan and Isabel Perón won a landslide victory. A month after taking office, Juan Perón suffered a mild heart attack, and Isabel began to take over many of his duties as head of state. With the death of her husband on July 1, 1974, Isabel Perón officially assumed the presidency, becoming the first woman in Latin American history to hold the office. She inherited a number of intractable political and economic difficulties: a badly divided Peronist movement, a growing wave of terrorism, and a rapidly worsening economic situation.

The deep divisions within the Peronist movement emerged full blown after she took power. Her policy of favoring the right-wing Peronists over the left-wing groups served to exacerbate the struggle between the two factions and contributed to the increase in political violence and terrorist activity. In addition to the bombings, kidnappings, and killings by left-wing urban guerrillas, a right-wing death squad, the Argentine Anti-Communist Alliance (AAA) began a campaign to eradicate leftist terrorists, including members of Peronist groups. With the country on the verge of total anarchy, Isabel Perón declared a state of siege in November 1974, but the terrorist conflict continued unabated.

On the economic front, she was confronted with soaring inflation, mounting foreign debts, and growing unemployment. Her efforts to restrict wages and introduce other austerity measures to combat inflation, which had climbed to well over 300 percent by mid-1975, met with stiff resistance from the leaders of the labor unions, who called a series of costly and destructive strikes that increased political unrest.

The Fall of Isabel Perón

Within the government Isabel Perón was hampered by repeated cabinet crises. A serious political liability was her minister of social welfare and personal secretary, José López Rega, an old-line Peronist and the guiding force behind her conservative policies. Revelations concerning his illicit financial activities and his involvement with the operations of the AAA led to his resignation and flight into exile, much to the discredit of the president.

Facing severe criticism from all sides for her inability to control the violence or stabilize the economy, Isabel Perón took a leave of absence in September and October 1975, ostensibly to recover from exhaustion. Adding to her difficulties were charges by the opposition that she had misappropriated governmental funds.

In December a group of dissident Air Force officers staged an abortive coup. The more moderate military officers, led by General Jorge Rafaél Videla, urged that she resign. Perón insisted that she would serve out the remainder of her term, scheduled to end in May 1977. As the political and economic situation continued to deteriorate, she sought to counter the demands for her resignation by finally offering to hold new elections before her term expired. But the offer came too late, and on March 24, 1976, she was deposed in a bloodless coup. After seizing power and placing her under house arrest, a three-man military junta named General Videla president of a new military regime.

Isabel Perón remained in protective custody for five years. In 1981 she was convicted of corruption, but released and allowed to go into exile. She remained in Spain until pardoned by the Argentine government in 1983.

After two years of exile, Isabel Perón was invited to return by President Raúl Alfonsín, who won Argentina's 1983 election, ending a fifty-three year succession of the brutal military regimes marked by the reign of General Videla. Alfonsín reportedly cultivated his relationship with Perón in an attempt to improve his standing with the Peronist party. She also appeared to be in better standing in her former country, as the Senate passed a bill restoring her extensive real estate holdings and her reputation.

Issues began to surface which called into question Isabel Perón s knowledge of Argentina's "dirty war" practices after the military overthrew her in 1976. Argentinians representing victims of the former dictatorship gathered outside a National Court hearing held in Madrid in February 1997. Perón was questioned on her knowledge of the campaign of torture, kidnappings and murder under the military dictatorship between 1976 and 1983. As stated in *El Universal,* a Mexican newspaper, Perón denied learning of the human rights abuses during the "dirty war," despite the claims of those who hold her responsible for the beginning of the repression in 1976 and consider her to be an accomplice in those crimes. Perón may be called again to give testimony along with relatives of victims and diplomats.

Further Reading

There is no adequate study of Isabel Perón in either English or Spanish. Guido Di Tella, *Argentina under Perón, 1973-1976: The Nation's Experience with a Labor-Based Government* (1983) deals with Perón's second presidency and Isabel's period in power after his death. Also of value, especially for activities of the revolutionary left during this period, is Donald C. Hodges, *Argentina, 1943-1976: The National Revolution and Resistance* (1976). □

Juan Domingo Perón

Juan Domingo Perón (1895-1974) was one of modern Argentina's most important political figures. Although his government was removed from power in a military/civilian uprising, he continued to wield enormous influence on national affairs for many years and was eventually returned to the nation's highest office.

Juan Domingo Perón was born in Lobos in the province of Buenos Aires on October 8, 1895. There is no evidence that his parents were married at the time of his birth. In a status-conscience country, the fact of his illegitimate birth may have been, in later life, a source of resentment. In 1899 his father, Mario Thomás Perón, left the

family to search for better economic opportunities in Patagonia. Once settled on a ranch near Rio Gallegos, the family was reunited. It was here that Perón came to appreciate the "terrible differences" between the middle-class existence of his own family and those of the ranch hands (*peones*), who slept "in the shed, without sheets, with only one or two blankets, sometimes even without a bed."

There were a lack of schools in southern Patagonia, so in 1904 Perón's parents sent him and his brother to elementary school in Buenos Aires, the capital city. Far from his family and home, Perón learned to live by his wits.

By the age of 15, Perón participated in sports while barely making passing grades in academics. It was at this age that he decided against a university education in medicine and passed the entrance exam for the Colegio Militar, the Argentine military academy. It was in the closeness of the military barracks that Perón found the camaraderie that he had not had a chance to enjoy as a child.

He entered the army upon graduation in 1913 as a second lieutenant in the infantry, but his career was not outstanding. He was a champion fencer, had a good reputation as an instructor in various military schools, and had experience abroad as military attaché in Chile. He was promoted to the more respected rank of lieutenant in 1915, but it was not until 1919 that he showed signs as a leader and teacher.

It was in that same year, when Perón was 24-years-old, that Eva (or Evita) Duarte was born near the village of Los Toldos in Buenos Aires province. Eva's unwed mother, Juana Ibarguren, was assisted in the birth by an Indian midwife. The baby was denied the surname of her father, a respected landowner. Eva was also plagued by the stigma of her illegitimate birth. In 1931 her family moved to the small town of Junin. Three years later they moved to Buenos Aires.

The hard working and charismatic Perón was promoted to captain in 1924 and in 1926 was assigned to the Escuela de Guerra (Superior War College) where he trained intensely for three years. In 1929 he married his girlfriend of three years, Aurelia Tizón.

Argentina suffered a coup in September of 1930 brought on by the spreading world depression. Perón was a minor participant in the coup, but it taught him a valuable lesson. He felt that the massive mobilization of civilians in favor of the coup had helped the military victory. This was a lesson he would use to his advantage in the future.

In 1931 Perón was assigned to teach at the Superior War College where he spent five years teaching, writing several books, and developing talents critical to his later political career.

Perón's wife died in 1938 from uterine cancer and he was extremely distraught. He was sent to Italy for 22 months, where he witnessed both the fascism of Benito Mussolini and the Nazism of Adolph Hitler. Some historians state that Perón's "fascist" inclinations can be traced to this period.

Perón returned to Buenos Aires and was assigned to mountain troops in the province of Mendoza. In 1942 he was promoted to the rank of a full colonel. Perón found the

Argentine military to be divided and ill at ease. They were split between those who sympathized with the Axis powers, those who favored the Allied powers, and those who wanted to remain neutral during World War II. There were also worries concerning the United States sale of military hardware to Brazil, threatening to tip the balance of power in southern Latin America.

His career took an upswing after the military coup d'etat of June 4, 1943. The coup, which put General Pedro Pablo Ramirez in the presidency, was highly unpopular among the civilian population. As a result, Perón and other younger officers realized that the soldiers had to rally civilian support if they were to remain in power. After some hesitation, they turned to the organized labor movement for such support. Perón became secretary of labor and between 1943 and 1945 built up a wide constituency among the country's urban and rural working classes. He did so by supporting strongly those unions which would cooperate with him and by enacting by decree a large body of labor and social legislation.

It was in the Ramirez administration that Perón met Eva in January of 1944. It was as secretary of labor that she first gained his attention. She soon became his mistress, but Perón did not keep the 24-year-old hidden away. Instead he treated her as if she were his wife. The relationship produced volumes of gossip, but Perón did not seem to mind.

As a result of supporting the unions, the working classes, and his affair with Eva, Perón became very popular. When he was overthrown by rival military men on October 17, 1945, he was not concerned and married Eva four days later. He was returned to power largely by the influence of his labor supporters. Thereafter, he became a presidential candidate in the elections of February 1946, which he won by a 54 percent majority.

Perón remained president for more than nine years. During this time he continued to picture himself as the paladin of the workers and of the country's lower classes in general, while bringing the labor movement under iron government control. During much of the period, he followed a very nationalistic economic policy, nationalizing the railroads and some public utilities. He used the new Industrial Bank, as well as tariff protection, to sponsor industrialization. He also tried to expand Argentine international influence, not only in Latin America and the Western Hemisphere, but also is Europe and the Middle East. His intellectual advisors developed and propagated a supposed philosophy of *justicialismo,* which he pictured as being something between capitalism and communism.

During his years in power, Perón continually increased pressure on the opposition: seizing or closing its press, gerrymandering districts to reduce its representation in Congress, and persecuting its leaders by placing them in jail or forcing them into exile. In 1954 he sought to reduce the power of the Roman Catholic Church which, until a few years before, had been one of his important supporters.

At the same time, Perón took steps toward setting up a cooperative state. He sought to force virtually all interest groups into government-dominated organizations of workers, entrepreneurs, professionals, and students. In two prov-

inces which adopted new constitutions, citizens were given direct representation in the legislatures.

The death of Eva from cancer in 1952 dealt a crushing blow to Perón. She was accorded cult status. There were even attempts to have her canonized as "Santa Evita."

In September 1955 Perón was overthrown by a military-civilian uprising. He went into exile, first in Paraguay and subsequently Venezuela, Panama, and the Dominican Republic, finally settling in Spain. He still maintained direct contact with his supporters, who represented about 25 percent of the electorate and continued to dominate the labor movement.

The new government tried to make the citizens forget Juan Perón. But giving in to public pressure, *Perónists* were gradually tolerated and eventually allowed to run for elected office.

In the election of 1973, labor, youth, and those disenchanted with military rule voted for the *Perónist* ticket. That ticket won a victory, but the *Perónist* president, Hector Cámpora, proved to be a disaster. He resigned later that year, setting the stage for the return to power of Perón.

A new election was held in September of 1973 and Perón won, but he was plagued by age, illness, and fatigue. The country drifted as inflation increased and the economy went out of control. Perón died of a heart attack on July 1, 1974, passing control of the nation to his vice president and third wife, the politically inexperienced Maria Estela ("Isabel") Martinez de Perón. She ruled Argentina another year and a half, but the country was quickly coming apart. She was removed from power by a military coup in July of 1976.

The memory and popularity of the Peróns, (especially Eva), remained long after their deaths. In the presidential election of 1989, a *Perónist* candidate, Carlos Saul Menem, won. In January of 1997, Eva's life story was told in *Evita,* a motion picture featuring an international cast portraying the life of Eva and Juan Perón. *Evita* featured American actress, Madonna as Eva Perón and British actor, Jonathan Pryce as Juan Perón.

Further Reading

A good deal has been written about Perón and his regime. Two general studies are Robert J. Alexander *The Perón Era* (1951) and George I. Blanksten *Perón's Argentina* (1953). Also very useful is Arthur P. Whitaker *The United States and Argentina* (1954). Whitaker's *Argentine Upheaval: Perón's Fall and the New Regime* (1956) is a good description of the circumstances leading up to and surrounding Perón's overthrow. James Bruce *Those Perplexing Argentines* (1953), written by a former U.S. ambassador, contains insights into the early years of the Perón regime. A fine study of Perón's relations with labor during and after his period in power is Samuel L. Baily *Labor, Nationalism and Politics in Argentina* (1967). Joseph R. Barager, ed., *Why Perón Came To Power: The Background to Perónism in Argentina* (1967), provides interpretive essays by American and Argentine historians and statesmen. Much has been written posthumously on Perón. Biographical information can be gleaned from Joseph A. Page *Perón, A Biography* (1983); Frederick C. Turner and José; Enrique Miguens *Juan Perón and the Reshaping of Argentina* (1983);

and Joel Horowitz *Argentine Unions: the State and the Rise of Perón, 1930-1945* (1990). A brief biography of Perón appears on-line at the A&E Network Biography site located at www.biography.com. □

Henry Ross Perot

Businessman and activist, Henry Ross Perot (born 1930) founded the successful data processing company, Electronic Data Systems (EDS). He entered politics in 1992 as the Independent Party candidate for U.S. president.

R oss Perot was born in Texarkana, Texas, on June 27, 1930. His father was a cotton broker and horse dealer. The young Perot was much impressed by his father's negotiating skills and by his mother's discipline and religious principles. Perot grew up in Texarkana and spent one year at the local junior college. He then attended the U.S. Naval Academy, graduating in 1953, the president of his class. After graduation, he spent four years at sea.

At the Naval Academy Perot had received a basic education in engineering. He had no special training in electronics or computing. However, his personal qualities impressed an IBM representative who visited him on the aircraft carrier to which Perot was assigned. When Perot left the Navy, he was hired by IBM to sell computers in Dallas. He was most successful. At the same time Perot became convinced that a business could make money by leasing unused computer time to clients who needed it. IBM wasn't interested in the concept, so in 1962 Perot started his own business, Electronic Data Systems. His first client, Collins Radio in Iowa, flew tapes and personnel to Dallas to have programs run on a computer at an insurance company there.

In the years that followed, EDS expanded. Operating under contract, EDS personnel ran entire data processing departments for insurance companies, banks, and state and national governments. In the mid 1960s the U.S. Congress passed national health insurance programs for the poor and elderly. These programs, Medicaid and Medicare, were administered by individual states. EDS expanded its programs for processing medical insurance claims from private companies to state offices. This business accounted for about a quarter of EDS income by 1968 and proved highly profitable. At the end of the 1960s EDS went public. Perot sold a small fraction of his shares in the business for $5 million.

In the following decades Perot became known for his international and philanthropic concerns. During the Vietnam War, reportedly in response to a request from government officials, he tried to improve the treatment of American prisoners of war in North Vietnam. In December of 1969 Perot attempted to send two planeloads of food, gifts, and medical supplies to the prisoners. The Vietnamese refused to accept delivery of the goods, but the publicity

surrounding the episode may have led to improved conditions in the prison camps. In 1973, after the return of the prisoners, Perot financed a weekend party for those who had been held at the Son Tay camp, as well as for a team of Green Berets who had tried unsuccessfully to rescue them in late 1970. Perot also sought out veterans for staff positions at EDS. The firm set strict standards of dress and conduct for its employees. It also required trainees to sign a contract stating that if they left the company to work for a competitor within three years of their hiring, they would reimburse EDS $12,000 for their training.

In the early 1970s EDS attempted to improve data processing on Wall Street by purchasing a subsidiary of a stock brokerage firm. Unfortunately, the firm was in serious financial difficulties. Perot himself invested some $97 million in this firm and in another brokerage firm, before deciding to dissolve both businesses in 1974. He lost some $60 million in the process.

In the late 1970s EDS expanded to international operations. Its first overseas contract was with a Saudi Arabian university. Then, in 1976, the firm was hired to manage data processing for the social security system of the Shah of Iran. Two years later Iranian officials concluded that EDS had been paying too much money to its Iranian advisers. Iran stopped payment on its contract, and EDS notified the government that it was suspending operations. Two leading EDS officers were arrested and imprisoned. Perot set out to win their release, even paying a quiet visit to Iran himself. An EDS rescue team was formed and trained, but did not penetrate the prison where the men were held. Reportedly at the urging of an Iranian employee of EDS, an Iranian mob broke into the prison and released all the prisoners. The EDS officials escaped and, with the rescue team, fled the country on foot. Perot encouraged the British journalist and novelist Ken Follett to write a sympathetic account of the episode.

As EDS grew, it was ever on the lookout for new markets. At the same time auto manufacturer General Motors sought to diversify its holdings. Investment bankers at the Wall Street firm of Salomon Brothers suggested EDS as one of several possible acquisitions. Roger Smith, the chairman of GM, greatly admired entrepreneurs like Perot and hoped that EDS might be able to unify data processing in his company's diverse operations. Smith did not consult his own data processing staff about the proposed merger. He also apparently was unconcerned by EDS's lack of experience in the use of computers in design and manufacturing.

After lengthy negotiations, GM purchased EDS in June 1984. Owners of EDS stock had a choice of receiving payment entirely in cash or partly in cash and partly in a new issue of GM stock, designated GME. Dividends from this stock were tied directly to the performance of EDS. EDS executives expected to receive bonuses in shares of stock when their performance merited it. For the 45 percent of EDS stock that Perot owned, he received nearly $1 billion in cash and 5.5 million shares of the new stock. He also remained head of EDS and was elected to the board of directors of GM.

EDS set out to take over all data processing operations at GM. It encountered resistance from both executives and those at other levels and did not feel it received sufficient backing from Roger Smith. Perot also discovered that he did not, in fact, control the award of bonuses to EDS personnel. Moreover, GM auditors expected to review the books at EDS, just as they did at other parts of GM. Perot first broke openly with Smith in the fall of 1985 over the question of whether GM should purchase Hughes Aircraft. Perot objected and was ignored. Tensions between EDS and GM were exacerbated by the poor performance of GM vehicles in the marketplace and by Perot's criticisms of GM's way of doing business. In the fall of 1986 GM voted to buy out Perot's GME shares, ending his connection with EDS. Perot agreed and promised not to open a new profit-making data processing business for three years. By 1989 GM and Perot were in court over the question of whether Perot had held to this agreement in forming a new company, Perot Systems.

Perot was noted for his campaign to improve the school systems of the state of Texas and his contributions to various schools and educational institutions. He married Margot Birmingham in 1956. They had four children.

Perot's career took a definitive turn in 1992 when he spearheaded a campaign to have himself elected president of the U.S. under the Independent Party. Critics were amazed that this virtual, political unknown commanded 18 percent of the popular vote. Perot ran again in 1996, receiving a less impressive 8 percent of the vote. However, his presence is still felt in the realm of politics. Perot remains both a politician and a businessman. It is estimated that his net worth is over $3 billion.

Further Reading

For more information on two of H. Ross Perot's greatest adventures/misadventures see Ken Follett, *On Wings of Eagles* (1983) and Doron P. Levin, *Irreconcilable Differences: Ross Perot versus General Motors* (1989). A look at the man himself, especially his relationship with General Motors' Roger Smith, is Todd Mason, *Perot: An Unauthorized Biography* (1990). Perot is also listed in *Forbes* "400 Richest People in America 1997" (July 1997). □

Pérotin

Pérotin (active ca. 1185-1205), of the Notre Dame school in Paris, was the central figure in polyphonic art music during his time and the century thereafter. He was the first to write three-and four-part compositions and invented numerous musical techniques.

Of the life of Pérotin or Perotinus, absolutely nothing is known. For some time it was believed that a number of documents, dating from 1208 to 1238, referred to the composer, but this has recently been shown not to be the case. All we know is his name, the titles of some of his works, and his achievements, which are mentioned in two treatises: one by an eminent philosopher and music theorist, John of Garland, an Englishman who taught at the University of Paris during the second quarter of the 13th century; and the other by an anonymous English student, actually his voluminous class notes taken during the 1270s in Paris. The student informs us that Pérotin "edited" the *Magnus liber organi* (Great Book of Organa) of his predecessor at the Cathedral of Notre Dame in Paris, Léonin, by shortening the long sections of these compositions in which a free-flowing melody was laid over a slow-moving *cantus firmus*, that is, a series of notes taken from preexisting music—here from Gregorian chants of the Mass or the daily prayer hours. On the other hand, Pérotin added many sections, or clausulae, in discant style, where both voices were regulated by rhythmic patterns in strict meter. Of this style, the anonymous writer tells us, Pérotin was the greatest master (*optimus discantor*). Over 500 such discant clausulae are extant, some short ones undoubtedly the work of Léonin and of Pérotin's disciples, but the bulk probably Pérotin's own works.

These clausulae were not only sung at services, within the organa, but apparently also enjoyed as instrumental and vocal chamber music. Poets soon discovered that this metric music could well serve poetic texts, and they invented poems to go with the upper part, while leaving the *cantus firmus,* to be played by an instrument. The text (*mot* in French) gave the name motet to the new songlike species, which was at first based on Pérotinian discant clausulae but soon became independent of them. The motet was the central type of 13th-century art music. It first carried Latin texts connected with the feasts to which the clausulae belonged, presumably in the last decade of the 12th-century, but soon after the turn of the century it began also to employ French secular texts, many of them including quotations from contemporary *trouvère* poems and romances.

Pérotin's name is not directly connected with the motet, but the anonymous English student lists several of his works in other categories. Pérotin, he informs us, was the first to compose organa in three voice parts, some 30 of which are preserved. He also wrote two long four-part organa (ca. 1198-1200) whose fame spread throughout the Continent: *Viderunt omnes* for Christmas and *Sederunt* for the Mass of St. Stephen's Day, the day after Christmas. These works show great ingeniousness and many technical innovations, such as imitation, use of melodic and rhythmic motives and their variation for unifying a larger work, phrase repetition for the creation of structure, and rhythmic patterning of a Gregorian chant to serve as the basis of his clausulae. As in the organum, Pérotin also advanced to three-and four-part writing in his conductus, strophic Latin songs whose texts were sung simultaneously in all voices but could also be sung by a single person with instruments playing the other parts.

During Pérotin's time Paris became the center of Western culture. The Cathedral of Notre Dame neared completion and with it the Gothic style of architecture its zenith. The various philosophical schools that had grown up around it during the 12th century gave birth to the first general university outside Moorish Spain, where Aristotelian science stimulated a great intellectual debate. Pérotin's music was carried from this center to all the Western countries, where it was sung and imitated well into the 14th century.

Further Reading

Some of the music of Pérotin is available in modern transcription in various publications and also on records. The best account of his achievements is in Donald Jay Grout, *A History of Western Music* (1960). □

Claude Perrault

Claude Perrault (1613-1688), French scientist, architect, and engineer, designed the east front of the Louvre in Paris, the finest example of the classicistic phase of the French baroque style.

Claude Perrault was born on Sept. 25, 1613, in Paris. He was trained as a doctor and was a respected member of the Académie des Sciences. He was also a serious student of architecture and archeology, and the influential position of his younger brother Charles, intermediary of Louis XIV's prime minister, Jean Baptiste Colbert, in the newly founded academies of science, architecture, sculpture, and painting gave Claude access to the inner circle of artists and architects.

The celebrated Italian architect Gian Lorenzo Bernini had been invited to Paris by Louis XIV in 1665 to furnish designs for the east front of the Louvre, but his excessively

Italian baroque designs were inappropriate for the essentially French medieval and French-adapted Renaissance palace, and he departed after a few months. In the spring of 1667 Colbert appointed Louis Le Vau and Charles Le Brun, first architect and first painter respectively to the king, and Perrault to produce in collaboration an appropriate design. Louis XIV selected one of the two suggested projects. Though Perrault was recognized by contemporaries as the designer of the east front, known as the Colonnade, there is still controversy as to whether the preponderant hand was that of Perrault or of Le Vau. Nevertheless, it was Perrault who furnished the solutions to the many problems inherent in the Colonnade project. Roman archeology, of which he had a profound knowledge, was vitally animated and adjusted, in accordance with his theory, to suit the site and the King's requirements of grandeur. The Colonnade was executed largely between April 1667 and 1670.

Other works by Perrault are the Observatoire (1668-1672) in Paris and the château of Sceaux (1673-1674; destroyed), built for Colbert. Perrault designed the triumphal arch of the Porte Saint-Antoine in Paris, selected in competition over designs of Le Vau and Le Brun (begun in 1669 but never completed). Perrault's designs for the reconstruction of the church of Ste-Geneviève in Paris, the present Panthéon (ca. 1675), were discovered recently.

In his *Treatise of the Five Orders* (1676) Perrault attacked the theories of proportion of antiquity. By drawing lucid distinctions between things of absolute and relative beauty, he shook to the foundations the authority of classical antiquity and opened the way for modern values. The

Colonnade showed his aversion to both the frozen formulas of the academic tradition and the emotional excesses of the Italian baroque and demonstrated that architectural proportions truly concordant with French taste could be elastic and subjective. He also published an exhaustively annotated edition of the classical Roman architect Vitruvius (1673; 2d ed. 1684). He died in Paris on Oct. 9, 1688.

Further Reading

Little of consequence, either general or specific, has been written about Perrault. The best primary source in English is John James's translation of Perrault's *Treatise of the Five Orders of Columns in Architecture* (1708). For background information see Reginald Blomfield, *A History of French Architecture, 1661-1774* (2 vols., 1921), and Anthony Blunt, *Art and Architecture in France, 1500-1700* (1953).

Additional Sources

Perrault, Charles, *Charles Perrault: memoirs of my life,* Columbia: University of Missouri Press, 1989. □

Auguste Perret

Auguste Perret (1874-1954), a French architect and building contractor, was one of the first to use concrete as an architecturally significant material, and his works had an important influence upon the International Style of the 1920s in Europe.

Auguste Perret the son of a building contractor, was born at Ixelles near Brussels on Feb. 12, 1874. His early theoretical training came from reading the works of Eugène Emmanuel Viollet-le-Duc, who advocated the reintegration of architectural form and techniques of construction, which had gone separate ways in the 19th century. Perret studied at the École des Beaux-Arts (1891-1895) in Paris in the studio of Julien Guadet, from whom he learned traditional classical composition and theory. Perret left without a degree and joined his father's firm. This, at the death of the elder Perret in 1905, became Perret Frères, including as principals Auguste and his brother Gustave. Perret Freres both designed its own buildings and executed the designs of others in reinforced concrete.

Reinforced concrete combines the monolithic compressive strength of concrete with the tensile strength of steel rods. Its use in building began in the late 19th century. Perret raised the material to architectural distinction in such buildings as the three upon which his reputation principally rests: an apartment building at 25b Rue Franklin (1903) and a garage at 51 Rue de Ponthieu (1905), both in Paris, and the Church of Notre Dame (1922) at Le Raincy near Paris.

At the Rue Franklin apartment the reinforced-concrete frame is for the first time clearly expressed, if not exposed, on the exterior. The frame is covered with smooth ceramic tiles, whereas the nonstructural wall panels are covered with tiles bearing a foliate pattern. The structural frame, in addition, creates point supports that eliminate stationary, load-bearing partitions within the apartments, and this results in potentially flexible, open plans.

The facade of the garage is an exposed reinforced-concrete frame filled in with glass and arranged according to classical rules rather than by inner structural logic. Its stark rectangularity and openness made it a favorite of the next generation of architects.

The church at Le Raincy is perhaps Perret's most impressive design. Nave and side aisles of nearly identical height are separated by tall, very slender reinforced-concrete columns sustaining overhead thin concrete vaults. The exterior walls surrounding this light, open hall are mere screens of precast, concrete latticework filled with colored glass that changes from yellow at the entrance to purple behind the altar. Such works helped to establish concrete as an acceptable architectural material in the 20th century, even if they did little to further the technology of reinforced-concrete construction.

Perret continued to be active to the end of his life, rebuilding, for example, the destroyed centers of Le Havre and Amiens after World War II. He died in Paris on Feb. 25, 1954.

Further Reading

The basic work on Perret is Peter Collins, *Concrete: The Vision of a New Architecture* (1959), the last half of which is devoted to "The Contribution of Auguste Perret." A slightly different interpretation of his work is in Reyner Banham, *Theory and Design in the First Machine Age* (1960). Bernard Champigneulle, *Perret* (1959), in French, is an indispensable reference work because of its many good photographs and drawings of Perret's work. Henry-Russell Hitchcock, *Architecture: Nineteenth and Twentieth Centuries* (1958; 2d ed. 1963), contains a chapter on Perret's work. □

Jean Baptiste Perrin

French physicist Jean Baptiste Perrin (1870-1942) helped to prove that atoms and molecules exist, an achievement that earned him the 1926 Nobel Prize in physics.

Jean Baptiste Perrin was born in Lille, France, on September 30, 1870, and raised, along with two sisters, by his widowed mother. His father, an army officer, died of wounds he received during the Franco-Prussian War. The young Perrin attended local schools and graduated from the Lycée Janson-de-Sailly in Paris. After serving a year of compulsory military service, he entered the Ecole Normale Supérieure in 1891, where his interest in physics flowered and he made his first major discovery.

Between 1894 and 1897 Perrin was an assistant in physics at the Ecole Normale, during which time he studied cathode rays and X rays, the basis of his doctoral dissertation. At this time, scientists disagreed over the nature of cathode rays emitted by the negative electrode (cathode) in a vacuum tube during an electric discharge. Physicists disagreed among themselves over whether cathode rays were particles—a logical assumption, since they carried a charge—or whether they took the form of waves.

In 1895 Perrin settled the debate simply and decisively using a cathode-ray discharge tube attached to a larger, empty vessel. When the discharge tube generated cathode rays, the rays passed through a narrow opening into the vessel, and produced fluorescence on the opposite wall. Nearby, an electrometer, which measures voltage, detected a small negative charge. But when Perrin deflected the cathode rays with a magnetic field so they fell on the nearby electrometer, the electrometer recorded a much larger negative charge. This demonstration was enough to prove conclusively that cathode rays carried negative charges and were particles, rather than waves. This work laid the basis of later work by physicist J. J. Thomson, who used Perrin's apparatus to characterize the negatively charged particles, called electrons, which were later theorized to be parts of atoms.

In 1897 Perrin married Henriette Duportal, with whom he had a son and a daughter. He received his doctorate the same year, and began teaching a new course in physical chemistry at the University of Paris (the Sorbonne). He was given a chair in physical chemistry in 1910 and remained at the school until 1940. During his early years at the University of Paris, Perrin continued his study of the atomic theory, which held that elements are made up of particles called atoms, and that chemical compounds are made up of mole-

cules, larger particles consisting of two or more atoms. Although the atomic theory was widely accepted by scientists by the end of the nineteenth century, some physicists insisted that atoms and molecules did not actually exist as physical entities, but rather represented mathematical concepts useful for calculating the results of chemical reactions. To them, matter was continuous, not made up of discrete particles. Thus, at the dawn of the twentieth century, proving that matter was discontinuous (atomic in nature) was one of the great challenges left in physics. Perrin stood on the side of the "atomists," who believed that these tiny entities existed. In 1901 he even ventured (with no proof) that atoms resembled miniature solar systems. His interest in atomic theory led him to study a variety of related topics, such as osmosis, ion transport, and crystallization. However, it was colloids that led him to study Brownian motion, the basis of his Nobel Prize-winning discovery of the atomic nature of matter.

In 1827 the English botanist Robert Brown reported that pollen grains suspended in water were in violent and irregular motion, a phenomenon at first ascribed to differences in temperature within the fluid. Before the end of the century, however, scientists generally accepted the notion that the motion might be caused by bombardment of the pollen grains by molecules of the liquid—an apparent triumph for atomic theory. Yet some scientists remained skeptical.

In 1905 Albert Einstein calculated the mathematical basis of Brownian motion, basing his work on the assumption that the motion was due to the action of water molecules bombarding the grains. But Einstein's work, though elegant, lacked laboratory experiments needed to demonstrate the reality of his conclusions. It fell to Perrin to bolster Einstein's calculations with observations. From 1908 to 1913, Perrin, at first unaware of Einstein's published paper on the subject, devoted himself to the extremely tedious but necessary experiments—experiments now considered classics of their kind. He hypothesized that if Brownian movement did result from molecular collisions, the average movements of particles in suspension were related to their size, density, and the conditions of the fluid (e.g., pressure and density), in accordance with the gas laws. Perrin began by assuming that both pollen grains and the molecules of the liquid in which they were suspended behave like gas molecules, despite the much greater size of the grains.

According to Einstein's equations governing Brownian motion, the way the particles maintained their position in suspension against the force of gravity depended partly on the size of the water molecules. In 1908 Perrin began his painstaking observations of suspensions to determine the approximate size of the water molecules by observing suspensions of particles. He spent several months isolating nearly uniform, 0.1-gram pieces of gamboge—tiny, dense extracts of gum resin, which he suspended in liquid. According to Einstein's molecular theory, not all particles will sink to the bottom of a suspension. The upward momentum that some particles achieve by being bombarded by molecules of the fluid will oppose the downward force of gravity. At equilibrium, the point at which the reactions balance each other out, the concentrations of particles at different heights will remain unchanged.

Perrin devised an ingenious system to make thousands of observations of just such a system. He counted gamboge particles at various depths in a single drop of liquid only one twelve-hundredth of a millimeter deep. The particle concentration decreased exponentially with height in such close agreement with the mathematical predictions of Einstein's theory that his observations helped to prove that molecules existed.

In essence, his system behaved like the Earth's atmosphere, which becomes increasingly rarified with height, until, at the top of a very tall mountain, people may find it difficult to breathe. Furthermore, it was already known that a change in altitude of five kilometers is required to halve the concentration of oxygen molecules in the atmosphere, and that the oxygen atom has a mass of sixteen. Based on his knowledge of the gas laws, Perrin realized that if, in his tiny system, the height required to halve the concentration of particles was a billion times less than the height it took to halve the concentration of oxygen in the atmosphere, he could, by simple proportion, calculate the mass of a gamboge particle relative to the oxygen molecule.

Einstein had linked to Brownian motion the concept of Avogadro's number, the number of molecules in any gas at normal temperature and pressure, now known to be 6.023×10^{23}. According to Avogadro's hypothesis, equal volumes of all gases at the same temperature and pressure contain equal numbers of molecules. Furthermore, the total mass of a specific volume of gas is equal to the mass of all the individual molecules multiplied by the total number of these individual molecules. So a gram-molecule of all gases at the same temperature and pressure should contain the same number of molecules. (A gram-molecule, or mole, is a quantity whose mass in grams equals the molecular weight of the substance; for example, one gram-molecule of oxygen equals sixteen grams of oxygen.) Only if this were true would the concept that each individual molecule contributes a minute bit of pressure to the overall pressure hold true, and individual entities called molecules could be said to exist.

Perrin calculated the gram-molecular weight of the 0.1-gram particles in the equilibrium system and therefore knew the number of grams in a gram-molecule of the particles. Then he divided the gram-molecular weight by the mass in grams of a single particle. The result, 6.8×10^{23}, was extremely close to Avogadro's number. Thus, Perrin had demonstrated that uniform particles in suspension behave like gas molecules, and calculations based on their mass can even be used to calculate Avogadro's number. This demonstrated that Brownian motion is indeed due to bombardment of particles by molecules, and came as close as was possible at the time to detecting atoms without actually seeing them. "In brief," Perrin said during his Nobel Prize acceptance speech, "if molecules and atoms do exist, their relative weights are known to us, and their absolute weights would be known as soon as Avogadro's number is known."

Perrin's work ranged farther afield than equilibrium distribution of particles and Avogadro's number, however.

As an officer in the engineering corps of the French army during World War I, he contributed his expertise to the development of acoustic detection of submarines. His commitment to science, however, did not inhibit his social graces. He was a popular figure who took a genuine interest in young people, and held weekly parties for discussion groups in his laboratory. Following the war, Perrin's reputation continued to grow. In 1925, he became one of the first scientists to use an electric generator capable of producing a continuous current of 500,000 volts. At the time, he predicted that someday much larger machines of this type would let physicists bombard atoms, and thus make important discoveries about the structure of these particles.

In 1929 after being appointed director of the newly founded Rothschild Institute for Research in Biophysics, he was invited to the United States as a distinguished guest at the opening of Princeton University's new chemical laboratory. In 1936 Perrin replaced Nobel laureate Irene Joliot-Curie as French undersecretary of state for scientific research in the government of Premier Léon Blum. The following year, as president of the French Academy of Science, he assumed the chair of the scientific section of an exhibit in the Grand Palais at the 1937 Paris exposition. The project enabled him to help the average person, including children, to appreciate the wonders of science, from astronomy to zoology.

His flourishing reputation was further enhanced in 1938 when he informed the French Academy of Science, of which he had been a member since 1923, and was then president, that his collaborators had discovered the ninety-third chemical element, neptunium, a substance heavier than uranium. Four years earlier, Enrico Fermi (who was awarded the 1938 Nobel Prize in physics and directed the first controlled nuclear chain reaction) had artificially created Neptunium, a so-called transuranium element, by bombarding uranium (element 92) with neutrons. Perrin's announcement that Neptunium existed in nature excited speculation among physicists that there also might exist even more undiscovered elements, which turned out to be the case.

His blossoming career did not shield the French physicist from concerns over what he considered to be a steady encroachment by totalitarian governments around the world on the freedom of science to express itself. A socialist and outspoken opponent of fascism, Perrin expressed his concerns during a speech delivered at the Royal Opera House in London before the International Peace Conference, reported in the *New York Times.* He asserted that world science stands or falls with democracy, and decried the fact that scientists seemed unable to understand "how financiers and capitalists as a whole cannot see that it is to their interest not to support those powers which, if they are successful, will ruin them." Perrin also criticized what he called "an irrational world that made it difficult to extend higher education or grant more aid to science but relatively easy to raise money for costly armaments." He voiced concern over what he believed was the coming war—World War II—which he feared would cost millions of lives, as well as threaten "the democracy that is the spirit of science.'' Perrin also warned that the victory of totalitarianism would mean ''perhaps a thousand years of ruthless subjugation and standardization of thought, which will destroy the freedom of scientific research and theorizing.''

Perrin's fears were realized in September of 1939, when France joined Great Britain in entering World War II against Germany following that country's invasion of Poland. By the end of September, the French government appointed Perrin president of a committee for scientific research to help the war effort. The situation became particularly grim in the summer of 1940, when German troops swept into Paris. Perrin fled the city and took up residence in Lyon as a refugee. In December 1941 he moved to the United States, where he lived with his son, Francis Perrin, a visiting professor of physics and mathematics at Columbia University. While in the United States, Perrin sought American support for the French war effort and helped to establish the French University of New York.

Perrin spoke out against the German occupation and French collaboration with the enemy. He was particularly disturbed when the Germans began operating an armaments industry in the suburbs of Paris using forced labor. Following Allied aerial bombardment of the factories, the *New York Times* reported that Perrin defended the action as ''one of the sad necessities'' of the war. Speaking before five hundred guests at the first dinner of the French American Club in New York City, in March 1942, Perrin asked, ''Who does not understand that it was imperative to put an end to this?'' A few weeks later, Perrin took ill, and ten days later he died at the age of seventy-one at Mount Sinai Hospital in New York.

Three years after the defeat of Germany and the end of the war, diplomats and scientists in New York paid homage to Jean Perrin at ceremonies held at the Universal Funeral Chapel. Afterwards, Perrin's ashes were placed aboard the training cruiser Jean d'Arc at Montreal, on which they were transported to France for burial at the Pantheon, a magnificent former eighteenth-century church converted to civic use. Among his many honors in addition to the Nobel Prize, Perrin received the Joule Prize of the Royal Society of London in 1896 and the La Caze Prize of the French Academy of Sciences in 1914. In addition, he held honorary degrees from the universities of Brussels, Liège, Ghent, Calcutta, and Manchester and from New York, Princeton, and Oxford universities. Perrin was also a member of the Royal Society of London and scientific academies in Italy, Czechoslovakia, Belgium, Sweden, Romania, and China.

Further Reading

New York Times, March 27, 1938, p. 7; August 3, 1938, p. 21; March 10, 1942, p. 7; April 18, 1942, p. 15. □

Harold Robert Perry

Harold Perry (1916-1991) was the first African American bishop in the Roman Catholic church's modern age.

Harold Perry's elevation to the position of bishop in 1966 was a signal that the hierarchy inside the Vatican—essentially the spiritual and authoritarian fathers of the world's millions of Catholics—were sympathetic to the civil rights struggles of African Americans both inside and outside of the faith. Perry's achievement was also a timely marker of Catholicism's efforts at liberalizing some facets of the church.

Had French Catholic Upbringing

Perry was born in Lake Charles, Louisiana, in 1916, the oldest of six children. His father was a rice mill worker, and the Perry children grew up Catholic and French-speaking in the bilingual Creole region. They also learned tolerance of others at the knees of their parents, as Perry recalled in an interview with *Ebony*'s Era Bell Thompson. ''They taught us not to resent white people. . . . 'Be sure,' they would caution, 'that there is no prejudice on your part.''' Perry knew from an early age that he wished to enter the priesthood, and entered a Society of Divine Word Seminary in Bay St. Louis, Mississippi, at age 13. The Divine Word flock had been founded in 1875 in Holland and trained Catholic

priests in several countries. Two of Perry's brothers followed him into the seminary, but later went on to medical school instead.

Perry was ordained into the Roman Catholic priesthood in 1944, and joined only 25 other African American men to have done so in the country at the time. Over the next few years he served as a parish priest in religious communities across Louisiana, Mississippi, and Arkansas. In 1952 his superiors assigned him to found a parish in Broussard, Louisiana, where a large number of African-American Catholics lived. During this era, the city and surrounding areas that made up the Archdiocese of New Orleans were home to the largest contingent of Roman Catholics in the United States, but out of nearly 45 million Catholics nationwide, only 700,000 were of African American descent. At the time, a contingent of New Orleans' white Catholics were gaining notoriety for their reluctance to integrate. When an African American priest was assigned to one Louisiana church in 1955, some of its members refused to attend services. Segregation of New Orleans' parochial schools was another issue: when the Archbishop forced them to integrate in 1962, an opposition movement grew until three well-known and especially vehement white protesters were excommunicated.

Became Active in Civil Rights

After setting up the parish in Broussard, Perry was appointed rector at his alma mater, the Bay St. Louis seminary. It was there he became more active in the civil rights movement, although he refused to participate in the more confrontational methods of protest. He joined the board of the National Catholic Council for Interracial Justice when it was founded in 1960, and President John F. Kennedy invited him to a special White House conference on civil rights issues in 1963 along with 250 prominent religious leaders. That same year, Perry also became the first African American cleric to deliver the opening convocation of the U.S. Congress. Such work on behalf of improved relations between blacks and whites in America came to the attention of Pope Paul VI. The pope was particularly interested in making a show of support toward improved racial relations after the Watts riots in Los Angeles during the summer of 1965.

Met the Pope

In September of 1965, Perry journeyed to Rome for the consecration (the rite that takes place when a priest becomes a bishop) of another black priest, Carlos Lewis of Panama. Upon his arrival, he was informed that the Vatican's appointment bureau wished to meet with him, and there he learned that the pope was about to name him auxiliary bishop to the Archbishop of New Orleans, Philip Hannan. Shortly thereafter, Perry met with the pope for the first time on what was also the priest's 49th birthday. His appointment was announced to the press with much fanfare, and civic and religious leaders of all races and faiths sent their congratulations, including President Lyndon Johnson. The president of the New Orleans Interdenominational Ministerial Alliance told *America* magazine that Perry's ele-

vation to bishop "places the Archdiocese of New Orleans in the 21st century," evidence that "the ground before Christ's cross is level and that all are equally redeemed."

Despite the accolades, however, Perry's consecration as bishop and his return home to the deep south was tarnished by some detractors. A few white Catholics in New Orleans protested outside his official reception, and one of those excommunicated earlier for objecting to the parochial schools' integration told *Time* magazine that Perry's elevation to auxiliary bishop was "another reason why God will destroy the Vatican." Perry recognized the significance of his achievement in an era when African Americans were finding their voices in an attempt to rectify a long history of institutional mistreatment and social prejudice, but declared to *Ebony'* s Thompson, "My appointment is a religious one, not a civil rights appointment. My religious work comes first.... I feel that the greatest contribution I can make to raise the dignity of my people, is being a good religious bishop and fulfilling my office to the utmost of my ability."

Within a few years, however, Perry was using his position to speak out on behalf of civil rights issues a bit more assertively. In the fall of 1968, he told an interviewer in New Zealand that African Americans "have made all the gains we can from a liberal approach; the methods used in the future must be radical." Perry also stated that until the United States began spending more federal funds to combat racism, "we can see little hope for any appreciable change in the near future." Perry remained auxiliary bishop of New Orleans until his death in 1991.

Further Reading

America, October 16, 1965, p. 425; November 16, 1968, p. 461.
"New Orleans Priest is First U.S. Negro to Be Named Catholic Bishop in 90 Years," in *Ebony,* February 1966, p. 62.
Jet, August 5, 1991, p. 9-10; July 18, 1994, p. 27.
"Historic Bishops," in *Time,* October 8, 1965, p. 70. □

Matthew Calbraith Perry

The American naval officer Matthew Calbraith Perry (1794-1858) is best known for the treaty he negotiated with Japan, which first opened that country to the Western world.

Matthew C. Perry was born on April 10, 1794, in Newport, R.I. After being educated in local schools, he entered the navy as a midshipman in 1809. His first duty was aboard a vessel commanded by his elder brother, Oliver Hazard Perry. He next served aboard a powerful 44-gun frigate, taking part in encounters with two British ships and in a commerce-raiding expedition in northern European waters. In 1813 he was transferred to the frigate *United States,* which was marooned in New London,

Conn., then under blockade by the British navy. He took advantage of the period of inactivity by journeying to New York, where he courted and married Jane Slidell in 1814.

Years of Varied Activity

For the next 17 years Perry was engaged in duties at sea of the widest variety: fighting Algerian pirates in the Mediterranean; carrying American Negroes to Liberia, where a colony of repatriated slaves was being established; transporting (in the schooner *Shark,* his first command) the American commissioner to the new colony; and hunting down slave traders and pirates. In 1830 he was given command of the sloop *Concord* and charged with carrying to Russia the new American minister, John Randolph. There Perry was received by the Czar, who offered him the rank of flag officer if he would join the Russian navy. That offer, in the words of Perry's biographer, he "politely but firmly declined."

In 1833 Perry began a decade of shore duty in the New York Navy Yard as second officer, later becoming commander. During those years he made significant contributions to the technological and educational development of the Navy. In 1833 he led in establishing the Naval Lyceum at the yard, which included a museum, reading room, and lectures "to promote the diffusion of useful knowledge" among the officers. He also helped found the *Naval Magazine.* Some years later he was a member of a board of examiners that prepared the first course for the soon to be established Naval Academy at Annapolis.

If he deserved the title "chief educator of the navy," Perry also earned the appelation "father of the steam navy," for it was he who pushed the replacement of sail by steam in the propulsion of war vessels, who helped design both hulls and engine of the new steamships, and who was given command of the first of the Navy's steam warships, *Fulton II.* It was in that ship that he set up the first naval school of gun practice.

In 1843 Perry took command of the Africa Squadron, newly organized to hunt for slave traders. Three years later, in the war with Mexico, Perry played an important role, leading an expedition in the capture of several coastal cities (using sailors as infantry) and, as commander of the Gulf Squadron, supporting Gen. Winfield Scott's storming of Veracruz. When the war ended in 1848, Perry was put on special duty in New York supervising the construction of ocean mail steamships. Then came the capstone of his career: the mission to Japan.

Opening Japan

Americans had been trading with China since 1844, so a way station in the Japanese islands for purchasing coal and supplies now became imperative. Protection for American seamen engaged in whaling in the northern Pacific Ocean was also needed. Perry carried a letter to the Japanese emperor from the American president requesting a treaty covering those matters as well as the right of Americans to trade in Japanese ports.

Perry set out from Norfolk, Va., on Nov. 24, 1852, with four ships and arrived at Edo (modern Tokyo) on July 2, 1853. He demanded of the Japanese officers who came out to meet his vessel the right to take the President's letter to the Emperor, but he was told he must go to Nagasaki, the only place open to foreigners. Perry refused, and when the Japanese saw his decks cleared for action, they relented. So Perry went onshore and, in an elaborate ceremony, delivered the letter to two princes representing the Emperor and promised to return in 12 months for the answer.

Rumors of French and Russian naval activity in Japanese waters brought Perry back in February 1854 (he had gone only to Hong Kong). This time, his reception was friendly (chiefly because he had seven well-armed ships in his squadron), and the Emperor appointed five commissioners to treat with him. At Yokohama the representatives of the two nations began negotiations and, on March 31, 1854, concluded a treaty which opened two ports, Hakodate and Shimoda, for trade and supplies and guaranteed fair treatment for shipwrecked American sailors.

His mission completed, Perry returned to New York in January 1855, a hero receiving "warm congratulations" from the secretary of the Navy, $20,000 from Congress, gifts from several cities, and acclaim on all sides. The parties and receptions over, Perry turned his attention to preparing the report of his expedition, which he completed in late December 1857. He died on March 4, 1858.

Further Reading

Samuel Eliot Morison, *"Old Bruin": Commodore Matthew C. Perry, 1794-1858* (1967), is the best biography. Arthur

Walworth, *Black Ships off Japan: The Story of Commodore Perry's Expedition* (1946; rev. ed. 1966), is excellent on the Japanese phase. □

Oliver Hazard Perry

Oliver Hazard Perry (1785-1819) was the American naval officer in command during the Sept. 10, 1813, victory on Lake Erie, one of the great American naval triumphs of the War of 1812.

O liver Hazard Perry was born in South Kingston, R.I., on Aug. 20, 1785. He received his elementary education there. In 1799 he served as midshipman with his father, Capt. Christopher Raymond Perry, in the West Indies during the quasi-war with France. He also served in the Mediterranean during the Tripolitan War, performing creditably.

Perry was in command of a flotilla at Newport, Va., when war broke out in 1812, but he was given command of American naval forces on Lake Erie in March 1813. Perry built a small fleet under conditions of extreme difficulty. By August he had 10 ships, the brigs *Lawrence* and *Niagara* being the largest. Perry could not get his largest ships across the Erie bar in the presence of the enemy fleet led by Comm. Robert H. Barclay until the latter relaxed his blockade for unknown reasons.

Barclay finished a large new ship, the *Detroit.* Desperately short of supplies, he challenged the Americans. The fleets met on Sept. 10, 1813. The Americans had superior firepower, but there was little difference in manpower. At 10 A.M. the *Lawrence* was cleared for action and hoisted its battleflag, "Don't give up the ship." Action lasted from 11:45 A.M. until 3:00 P.M. After all the *Lawrence* 's guns were disabled, Perry rowed to the *Niagara.* Fifteen minutes after the *Niagara* moved into the heavy action, the British fleet surrendered. American casualties numbered 27 killed and 96 wounded, and British losses were 41 killed, 94 wounded. Perry dashed off his famous dispatch following the victory, "We have met the enemy and they are ours."

The victory was of major significance, for America now controlled Lake Erie until the war ended. Also, Gen. William Henry Harrison was enabled to capture much of Upper Canada, and the American peace negotiators were able to assert American claims to the Northwest.

Perry was promoted to captain in September 1813 and shortly thereafter received the thanks of Congress. Following the war he served in the Mediterranean. He died of yellow fever on Aug. 23, 1819, after completing a diplomatic mission to Venezuela and Buenos Aires. His body was interred at Port of Spain, Trinidad.

Further Reading

Charles J. Dutton, *Oliver Hazard Perry* (1935), is an adequate biography, but minor factual errors abound. The best discussions of the Battle of Lake Erie in terms of strategy and signifi-

cance can be found in Alfred Thayer Mahan, *Sea Power in Its Relation to the War of 1812* (2 vols., 1905). Also useful is Olin H. Lyman, *Commodore Oliver Hazard Perry and the War on the Lakes* (1905), and Harry L. Coles, *The War of 1812* (1965).

Additional Sources

Dillon, Richard, *We have met the enemy: Oliver Hazard Perry, wilderness commodore,* New York: McGraw-Hill, 1978. □

Ralph Barton Perry

The American philosopher Ralph Barton Perry (1876-1957) was a leader of the New Realist movement and the originator of the interest theory of value.

R alph Barton Perry was born on July 3, 1876, in Poultney, Vt. He received his bachelor of arts degree from Princeton University in 1896 and his master of arts and doctor of philosophy degrees from Harvard University in 1897 and 1899. After teaching at Williams and Smith colleges, he joined the faculty of Harvard in 1902.

In 1910 Perry joined in the publication of "The Program and First Platform of Six Realists" in the *Journal of Philosophy.* The New Realist movement, which flourished during the first 2 decades of the 20th century, opposed idealism. New Realism claimed that the world is not dependent on the mind and that the knowledge relation is accidental or external to the object known.

Perry contributed to the cooperative volume *New Realism* (1912). In *Present Philosophical Tendencies* (1912) Perry maintained that the cardinal principle of New Realism is "the independence of the immanent," meaning that the same object which is immanent in the mind when known is also independent of the mind.

During World War I Perry served in the U.S. Army as a major. He was also secretary of the War Department Committee on Education and Special Training. From this experience came *The Plattsburg Movement* (1921). In 1919 Perry returned to Harvard. He was elected president of the Eastern Division of the American Philosophical Association in 1920.

Perry's *General Theory of Value* (1926) contended that interest is "the original source and constant feature of all value" and defined interest as that which belongs to the motor-affective life of instinct, desire, and feeling. Recognizing that interests conflict, he was concerned with the problem of comparative value. Morality, he held, originates with the conflict of interests, and moral value consists in the most inclusive integration of interests—"harmonious happiness."

In 1930 Perry was appointed Edgar Pierce professor of philosophy at Harvard. He won a Pulitzer Prize for his two-volume biography, *The Thought and Character of William James* (1935). In 1936 he became chevalier of the Legion of Honor (France). He also received many honorary degrees.

Perry retired from Harvard in 1946 and was Gifford lecturer at Glasgow University until 1948. His lectures were published in *Realms of Value* (1954), a critique of human civilization in the light of the interest theory of value. On Jan. 22, 1957, he died in a hospital near Boston.

Further Reading

The best treatments of Perry's thought are in the following: W. H. Werkmeister, *A History of Philosophical Ideas in America* (1949); Joseph L. Blau, *Men and Movements in American Philosophy* (1952); Lars Boman, *Criticism and Construction in the Philosophy of the American New Realism* (1955); and Andrew J. Reck, *Recent American Philosophy* (1964). □

William James Perry

William James Perry (born 1927) became President Clinton's second secretary of defense after the resignation of Les Aspin. A Washington insider, Perry was the second technocrat to hold this significant government position.

William James Perry was born October 11, 1927, in Vandergrift, Pennsylvania, the son of a grocer, Edward Martin Perry, and Mabelle Estelle (Dunlop) Perry. He excelled in mathematics and music, playing piano in a swing band.

Perry entered the U.S. Army in 1946 and served as a surveyor in the Corps of Engineers in Japan and Okinawa for a year. On December 29, 1947, he married Leonilla Mary Green, with whom he had five children: David Carter, William Wick, Rebecca Lynn, Robin Lee, and Mark Lloyd. Despite family responsibilities, Leonilla Perry eventually became a certified public accountant, formerly associated with the firm of Hemming and Morse in San Mateo, while Perry became a mathematician. He graduated with a B.A. (1949) and M.A. (1950), both in mathematics, from Stanford University.

Perry taught at the University of Idaho for the 1950-51 academic year and worked as a research engineer at Boeing in 1951. The fall of that year he entered Penn State University to study for a doctorate. He taught as an instructor there from 1951 to 1954. At the same time, he served as a mathematician at HRB-Singer in State College, Pennsylvania. In 1954 he became director of GTE Sylvania's defense laboratory in Mountain View, California—a post he held for ten years. In 1957 Penn State awarded him a Ph.D. in mathematics.

Perry had become a reserve officer in the army and continued to go on training tours, one of which resulted in a hearing loss because of artillery fire. His expertise in electromagnetic systems and partial differential equations, combined with his knowledge of military systems, led to further advancement. In 1964 Perry became president of ESL, Inc., a firm specializing in military electronics in Sunnyvale, California. From 1966 on, he also served as a technical consul-

tant at the Department of Defense and as a mathematics instructor at the University of Santa Clara.

Perry moved to Washington, D.C., to work full time in 1977 when he became undersecretary for research and development in the Carter administration, under the direction of Secretary of Defense Harold Brown. Perry's record in that position has been a topic of considerable debate. A believer in using high-tech weapons to counter the Soviet Union's numerical advantage in both manpower and conventional weapons, Perry pushed the Pentagon and Congress to develop advanced weapons systems such as laser-guided bombs, cruise missiles, the F-117 Stealth fighter, and the Apache helicopter. He was also identified with such questionable programs as the MX missile, the Maverick missile, the F-18, the Divad gun, and the B-2 Stealth bomber, the most expensive aircraft in aviation history. Scheduled to cost $200 million each in the late 1970s, the first B-2 entered the Air Force inventory at a cost of $2.2 billion in 1994. He caused critics to believe he was not concerned with costs when he blocked Secretary Brown's attempt to monitor procurement by creating an Office of Testing and Evaluation.

Although not a public figure, Perry became a Washington insider. He was a trusted adviser to former Senator Sam Nunn of Georgia and an admirer of Al Gore of Tennessee. He also worked with such Republican defense experts as Brent Skowcroft, with whom he chaired the Aspen Strategy Group. When Perry left Washington in 1981 he had gained a solid reputation in the Capitol as well as a Distinguished Public Service Medal from the Department of Defense

(1980) and a Distinguished Service Medal from the National Aeronautics and Space Administration (NASA), (1981).

Relocating in San Francisco, Perry became president of the investment banking firm Hambrecht and Quist, a post he held until 1985. He then became head of Technical Strategies and Alliances, a defense-related industry in Menlo Park, California. He left that firm in 1989 to become a professor of mathematics and co-director of the Center for International Security and Arms Control at Stanford University.

In 1993 he returned to Washington to serve as deputy secretary for defense in Bill Clinton's administration—a post he made clear he did not intend to serve in President Clinton's second term. His announced goal was to reduce procurement costs by relying more heavily on off-the-shelf commercial products while still contracting for such specialty weapons as nuclear submarines, fighter planes, and tanks. When Les Aspin resigned from the Defense Department in December 1993 and Bobby Ray Inman withdrew his name from consideration the following month, Perry agreed to serve, although he told friends of his reluctance to fight the kind of battles he had seen Aspin and Brown experience. Easily approved on February 3, 1994, Perry was the first technocrat to become secretary of defense since Harold Brown. He faced many problems, not the least of which was how to reduce the defense budget while still maintaining adequate armed forces. Following the chaotic tenure of Aspin, a *New York Times* report asserted in 1996, that Perry quickly restored order, discipline, and morale— three qualities crucial to military effectiveness. Despite his soft-spoken nature, Perry emerged as an articulate and candid spokesman for the Administration's policies. His record was tarnished however, by the June 1996 terrorist bombing in Saudi Arabia killing 19 American servicemen. Perry and his top aides were criticized for failing to put a premium on security at American installations in the Middle East.

Despite criticisms, Perry has received numerous awards, including the Presidential Medal of Freedom (1997); the Department of Defense Distinguished Service Medal (1980 and 1981); and Outstanding Civilian Service Medals from the Army (1962 and 1997); the Air Force (1997); the Navy (1997); the Defense Intelligence Agency (1977 and 1997); NASA (1981); and the Coast Guard (1997). He received the American Electronic Association's Medal of Achievement (1980); the Eisenhower Medal (1996); the Forrestal Medal (1994); and the Henry Stimson Medal (1994). The National Academy of Engineering selected him for the Arthur Bueche Medal (1996). He has been honored with awards from enlisted personnel of the Army, Navy, and the Air Force. Perry has received decorations from the governments of Germany, France, Korea, Albania, Poland and Hungary.

Perry is the Michael and Barbara Berberian Professor at Stanford University, with a joint appointment in the Department of Engineering and the Institute for International Studies.

Further Reading

Additional information on Perry can be found in *American Men and Women of Science;* P. Glastris, "The Powers That Shouldn't Be: Five Washington Insiders the Next Democratic President Shouldn't Hire," *Washington Monthly* (October 1987); R.W. Apple, Jr., "Leading Contender Is Said To Decline Top Defense Post," the *New York Times* (January 24, 1994); Eric Schmitt, "A Wide-Ranging Insider: William James Perry," the *New York Times* (January 25, 1994); and Douglas Jehl, "Pentagon Deputy Is Clinton's Choice for Defense Chief," the *New York Times* (January 25, 1994). For Perry's ideas on defense and how to pay the price, see his "Defense Investment Strategy," *Foreign Affairs* (Spring 1989), and "Desert Storm and Deterrence," *Foreign Affairs* (Fall 1991). □

Saint-John Perse

The French poet and diplomat, Saint-John Perse (1887-1975) ranks among the greatest French poets of the 20th century. His work is epic in nature, characterized by a cosmic vision and a lofty rhetoric. He won the Nobel Prize for literature in 1960.

Saint-John Perse was born Alexis Saint-Léger Léger on a family-owned island near Guadeloupe in the West Indies on May 31, 1887. At the age of 11 he went to the southern French city of Pau, where he attended school. He then studied at the University of Bordeaux and subsequently traveled extensively before establishing himself in Paris to prepare for the Foreign Service exams. He was accepted by the French Foreign Service in 1914 and spent the years from 1916 to 1921 in China. During the 1920s and 1930s he was again in Paris, rising in the service to the rank of secretary general. His brilliant diplomatic career ended in 1940, however, because he opposed appeasement of the Nazis. After the defeat of the French armies, he left France for England and Canada, and then the United States where he obtained a consultantship in French poetry at the Library of Congress. He remained in the U.S. until 1959. His eventual return to France, after so many years, became almost an apotheosis. Not only were all his political rights, honors, and privileges reinstated, but he was also acclaimed on all sides for his poetry.

The diplomat and the poet in Perse always remained apart. Unlike Paul Claudel, he refused to pursue a career on two fronts or to let his diplomatic career show through his literary works. His pseudonym, the source of which he never revealed, allowed him to establish and maintain individual identities as a diplomat and a poet.

Perse's first work, *Éloges* (*Praises*), was published in 1911, before he entered the Foreign Service. It is a collection of youthful poems praising life and depicting the marvels of a tropical island. Portions of the collection had been appearing since 1909 in the *Nouvelle revue française. Amitié du Prince* (1921) took its inspiration from ancient sacerdotal sources.

Anabase (*Anabasis*), written in China and published in 1924, is the saga of a great conqueror who founds a city, crosses a desert, and takes to the high seas. *Exil* (*Exile*) appeared in 1944, after Perse had been relieved of his duties and deprived of French citizenship. Its main theme is man in exile, and it speaks for all the solitary of the earth, beginning with the poet. Here, for the first time, Perse took up the problem of the creative artist vis-à-vis society, himself, and his work. It led him into an expression of solidarity with his fellowmen and into a recognition of exile and instability as conditions of life. The preoccupations of the poems published in the early 1940s—*Exil* was followed by *Rains* and *Snows*—crystallized in *Vents* (*Winds*), a work of about 2,500 lines that traces the genesis of the universe from its beginnings. The wind represents many things during the course of this epic, but basically it suggests everlasting change and movement. The sea, which was the subject of Perse's great work of the 1950s, *Amers* (1957; *Seamarks*), stands for vastness, limitless space. Together with its opposite, narrowness, it constitutes a polarity that, as a sort of life principle, inspires the poetic imagination. Again, in *Chroniques* (1960), nature was evoked but specifically as background for a recapitulation of human history.

Perse's enormous poetic frescoes demonstrated an epic gift uncommon today. He used a verse form of multiple cadences similar to the "verset" invented by Paul Claudel, and his tendency toward periphrase and allegory and his majestic images all suggested Claudel.

Perse died on September 20, 1975, at his villa in Giens, on the French Riviera. His substantial appeal to poets, including T.S. Eliot, and the wealth of praise accorded his work stand in sharp contrast to his creative output. "Mr. Perse's productivity was minuscule," wrote the *New York Times,* "he published only seven volumes, all genuinely slender."

Further Reading

A general comprehensive study in English is Arthur Knodel, *Saint-John Perse: A Study of His Poetry* (1966). A very useful introduction, it offers a full discussion of each one of the poet's works. Other sources of information about Perse include the *New York Times.* □

John Joseph Pershing

John Joseph Pershing (1860-1948) was commander in chief of the American Expeditionary Force in Europe during World War I.

John J. Pershing was born at Laclede, Mo., on Dec. 13, 1860. He graduated from West Point in 1886 with an outstanding record. Assigned to the cavalry, he campaigned against the Apache Indians in the Southwest. From 1891 to 1895 he was a military instructor at the University of Nebraska, where he earned a law degree in 1893. During the Spanish-American War he served with great distinction in the campaign around Santiago, Cuba. In 1899 Pershing went to the Philippines. He served in Mindanao for 4 years during the Philippine insurrection, and his help in suppressing the Moro revolt earned the praise of President Theodore Roosevelt. The President then recommended his promotion to brigadier general despite his low seniority; the appointment, delayed for 3 years, was finally confirmed in 1906.

Meanwhile, Pershing gained valuable experience as military attaché in Tokyo and as an observer of the Russo-Japanese War (1904-1905). In 1906 he returned to the Philippines, holding important commands there until 1914, when he assumed command at the Presidio in California. In 1915, while he was away on special assignment, his wife and three daughters perished in a tragic fire; only his son survived.

Pershing's next assignment, intensely difficult and frustrating, made the general an important public figure: he commanded the "punitive expedition" sent into Mexico during 1916 to chastise the Mexican bandit Pancho Villa. Despite his failure to capture Villa, Pershing gained considerable public commendation for his careful adherence to instructions and his dedication to duty. The expedition was withdrawn early in 1917, just prior to the American entry into World War I. Pershing was now a thoroughly experienced troop commander, although he had never held an important staff position in the War Department. A reserved and hard-bitten soldier, known as "Black Jack" to his troops, he gained their respect if not their affection.

Service during World War I

In May 1917 President Woodrow Wilson and Secretary of War Newton Baker chose Pershing to command the American Expeditionary Force going to Europe in support of the Allies. Arriving in France during June, Pershing immediately began planning the organization and employment of a large American army. Pershing decided to create an independent American force commanded by its own officers with its own support echelons in a distinct sector in France. In choosing this course, he challenged various European leaders who favored "amalgamating" American troops by small units into European armies as replacements.

For over a year, despite ever-growing military crises in France, Pershing single-mindedly pursued his idea of an independent American army and in this process gained the support of the War Department and President Wilson, overcoming efforts by Allied leaders to force various forms of amalgamation. Pershing argued that national pride dictated the formation of an independent force. He also claimed that the United States could make its most effective contribution to victory by following his course.

Western Strategy

Pershing also committed himself to the "Western strategy"—the view that the Western coalition should concentrate most of its military power in France against the principal enemy, Germany, rather than expend energy in secondary theaters such as Mesopotamia or Macedonia against lesser foes such as Turkey or Bulgaria. Pershing looked with jaundiced eye upon diversionary projects in Russia and elsewhere because such endeavors seemed certain to vitiate the effort in France, where he believed the war would be won or lost.

Pershing's plan required a huge program of mobilization and training for American troops in the United States. Several million men would have to be transported to France where, after additional training, they would be maneuvered as a separate force under his command. One drawback was the limited supply of shipping, a consequence of the need to supply the Allies in the face of Germany's great undersea campaign against noncombatant vessels. In late 1917 the British and French sought to trade shipping for amalgamation, but Pershing successfully resisted, even after Germany's great "end-the-war" offensive in March 1918. The Allies helped provide shipping sufficient to transport over 2,500,000 American troops to France. Still, Pershing's force had to depend heavily on European arms and equipment.

Although some American units participated in battles under French or British command during the summer of 1918, it proved impossible to employ the American army as an independent unit until September, when it attacked and reduced the great German salient at Saint-Mihiel. Pershing wished to attack ahead from that position, but French marshal Ferdinand Foch, who had become generalissimo, persuaded him to shift his forces northward into the Meuse-Argonne sector in order to participate in the final assault against the crumbling German army.

For some 47 days, beginning on Sept. 26, 1918, Pershing sustained the offensive in exceedingly difficult terrain. Eventually the battle was won, but heavy casualties, problems of command, and logistical difficulties lent some substance to earlier European doubts about the Americans' ability to develop optimal combat efficiency in a relatively short time. The bravery and determination of the American "doughboys" ultimately compensated for lack of experience and proper organization. When Germany sought peace in October, Pershing advocated unconditional surrender, but President Wilson overruled him and supported an early armistice. The sudden end of hostilities on November 11 deprived Pershing of the opportunity to prove the full mettle of the American army and to vindicate his policies in battle.

Last Years

In 1919 Pershing returned to a hero's welcome and to the rank of general of the armies, the highest title ever accorded except to George Washington. In 1921 he became chief of staff and presided over important reforms in the War Department. He left active service in 1924 but continued to perform important duties, first as chairman of the commission to South America to administer the Tacna-Arica plebiscite (1925) and then as chairman of the American Battle Monuments Commission that cared for military cemeteries in France. In 1931 he published a two-volume work entitled *My Experiences in the World War,* which earned a Pulitzer Prize (1932). He died in Washington, D.C., on July 15, 1948, one of the most honored soldiers in American history.

Further Reading

Biographies of Pershing include Richard O'Connor, *Black Jack Pershing* (1961), Harold McCracken, *Pershing* (1931), and Frederick Palmer, *John J. Pershing* (1948). See also Army Times, ed., *The Yanks Are Coming* (1960). □

16th Earl of Perth

The English statesman James Eric Drummond, 16th Earl of Perth (1876-1951), was the first secretary general of the League of Nations.

Eric Drummond, Earl of Perth, was born on Aug. 17, 1876. He was educated at Eton and began his Foreign Office career in 1900. He advanced slowly but in 1906 became private secretary to Lord Edmond Fitzmaurice, the parliamentary undersecretary. Perth held this post until 1910 except for a short interval in 1908. In 1908 and again in 1910-1911, he was précis writer for Sir Edward Grey, the foreign secretary.

Perth's work with Grey was the beginning of a period extending to 1919 in which he developed close friendships with his chiefs. From 1912 to 1915 he was private secretary to Herbert Asquith, the prime minister, and then to the succession of foreign secretaries from 1915 to 1919, Grey, Arthur Balfour, and George Curzon. His ability was so highly regarded that when a candidate was needed for the position of secretary general of the League of Nations, Balfour nominated Perth.

Accepted by Georges Clemenceau of France and Woodrow Wilson of the United States, Perth became permanent head of the League. During his 14-years tenure, he set up the secretariat to provide a body of expert opinion on technical matters and to permit the delegates to concentrate on settling controversial issues. Perth was particularly active in the continuing disarmament question and in the negotiations for the admission of Germany to the League of Nations.

Perth left the League in 1933 and was appointed British ambassador to Mussolini's Italy. At Rome he attempted to represent British policy and report the Italian government's intentions in a full and fair way. He did not see all the dangers of fascism, but he was skeptical of Italy's motives. Perth did not foresee the close alliance between Germany and Italy, and he shared some of the responsibility for Britain's policy of appeasement. In his favor, Perth was always loyal to the Foreign Office; he did not support attempts by Prime Minister Neville Chamberlain to use irregular diplomatic channels in dealing with Mussolini. He also had a part in influencing Italy to remain neutral during the early months of World War II.

It was while Perth was in Rome, that he inherited the title of his half brother, and from Aug. 20, 1937, he was known as Lord Perth. He retired from the diplomatic service in May 1939. Later he served in the British war effort as chief adviser on foreign publicity in the Ministry of Information

(1939-1940). After the war, as deputy leader of the Liberal party in the House of Lords, he spoke frequently in defense of the diplomatic corps.

Perth was married and had one son and three daughters. He died on Dec. 15, 1951.

Further Reading

Perth's League of Nations career is discussed in Francis P. Walters, *A History of the League of Nations* (2 vols., 1952). His more controversial role of ambassador in Rome is the subject of Felix Gilbert's "Two Ambassadors: Perth and Henderson" in Gordon A. Craig and Felix Gilbert, eds., *The Diplomats* (1953), and in Count Galeazzo Ciano, *The Ciano Diaries, 1939-1943* (1946) and *Hidden Diary, 1937-1938* (trans. 1953).

Additional Sources

Barros, James, *Office without power: Secretary-General Sir Eric Drummond, 1919-1933,* Oxford: Clarendon Press; New York: Oxford University Press, 1979. □

Perugino

Perugino (ca. 1450-1523) was a leading central Italian painter whose art anticipated that of the High Renaissance.

Pietro Vannucci, called Perugino was born in Città della Pieve near Perugia. According to Giorgio Vasari, Perugino, after being introduced to the artist's craft in his native town, went to Florence, where he studied with Andrea del Verrocchio. Perugino's presence in Florence in 1472 is documented. He traveled fairly extensively between Florence, Umbria, and Rome during the 1470s. In October 1481 he was one of the artists commissioned to execute frescoes for the newly completed Sistine Chapel in Rome.

Perugino worked in Rome and Perugia until 1486, when he moved to Florence, where he remained more or less continually until 1496. In 1491 he served on a commission to choose a model for the facade of the Cathedral in Florence. In 1496 or 1497 he moved to Perugia, though he continued to have interests in Florence. For example, in 1503 he was a member of a committee of Florentines empowered to choose the location for Michelangelo's *David.* Perugino continued to fulfill commissions in widely diverse locales such as Mantua and Rome, but he concentrated most of his artistic activities during the early 1500s in Umbria. He died of the plague in February or March 1523 in Fontignano.

Perugino's earliest works are lost. Two panels, a *Miracle of St. Bernardino* (1473) and an *Adoration of the Magi* (ca. 1475), are the earliest of the generally accepted examples of his art. The first painting is especially fine in its symmetry, uncrowded groups of figures, and pearly Umbrian landscape. The frescoes in the Sistine Chapel (1481-1482) are the most important of Perugino's early works. In *Christ Giving the Keys to St. Peter* Perugino arranged a frieze of figures across the foreground. In the background is an ideal architectural setting with a vast, open square and a symmetrical domed building flanked with two antique triumphal arches. In composition and clarity this design foreshadowed the balanced designs so common among the High Renaissance masters of the early 16th century.

Perugino painted a number of pictures during his Florentine period (1486-1496) in which figures and architecture are interrelated. Among them, the *Vision of St. Bernard* (1491-1494) and the *Madonna Enthroned* (1493) are noteworthy. His masterpiece of this period is the *Crucifixion* fresco (ca. 1495) in the convent of S. Maria Maddalena dei Pazzi, Florence. The clarity, symmetry, and balance of the composition are accented by the limited number of figures, the distant landscape, and the real and painted architecture. The sentimental expression is somewhat mitigated by the austerity of the fresco.

The frescoes (1497-1500) in the Sala dell'Udienza of the Collegio del Cambio, Perugia, are among Perugino's major accomplishments. They combine an elaborate Neoplatonic allegory with real and painted architecture to produce a remarkably unified system of decoration. One of the frescoes has a fine bust-length self-portrait. Perugino's art during the 1500s was criticized by his contemporaries. For instance, Isabella d'Este condemned his painting *Combat of Love and Chastity* (1505), which she had commissioned.

Perugino was one of the key transitional artists between the art of the 15th century and the High Renaissance. His compositions, with their emphasis on balance and clarity, and his treatment of almost infinite space anticipated the achievements of the great masters of High Renaissance classicism.

Further Reading

The standard work on Perugino is in Italian. The chapter on him in Raimond van Marle, *The Development of the Italian Schools of Painting,* vol. 14: *The Renaissance Painters of Umbria* (1933), is useful. ☐

Max Perutz

Max Perutz (born 1914) pioneered the use of X-ray crystallography to determine the atomic structure of proteins by combining two lines of scientific investigation—the physiology of hemoglobin and the physics of X-ray crystallography. His efforts resulted in his sharing the 1962 Nobel Prize in chemistry with his colleague, biochemist John Cowdery Kendrew.

Perutz's work in deciphering the diffraction patterns of protein crystals opened the door for molecular biologists to study the structure and function of enzymes—specific proteins that are the catalysts for biochemical reactions in cells. Known for his impeccable laboratory skills, Perutz produced the best early pictures of protein crystals and used this ability to determine the structure of hemoglobin and the molecular mechanism by which it transports oxygen from the lungs to tissue. A passionate mountaineer and skier, Perutz also applied his expertise in X-ray crystallography to the study of glacier structure and flow.

Perutz was born in Vienna, Austria, on May 19, 1914. His parents were Hugo Perutz, a textile manufacturer, and Adele Goldschmidt Perutz. In 1932, Perutz entered the University of Vienna, where he studied organic chemistry. However, he found the university's adherence to classical organic chemistry outdated and backward. By 1926 scientists had determined that enzymes were proteins and had begun to focus on the catalytic effects of enzymes on the chemistry of cells, but Perutz's professors paid scant attention to this new realm of research. In 1934, while searching for a subject for his dissertation, Perutz attended a lecture on organic compounds, including vitamins, under investigation at Cambridge University in England. Anxious to continue his studies in an environment more attuned to recent advances in biochemical research, Perutz decided he wanted to study at Cambridge. His wish to leave Austria and study elsewhere was relatively unique in that day and age, when graduate students seldom had the financial means to study abroad. But Hugo Perutz's textile business provided his son with the initial funds he would need to survive in England on a meager student stipend.

In 1936, Perutz landed a position as research student in the Cambridge laboratory of Desmond Bernal, who was pioneering the use of X-ray crystallography in the field of biology. Perutz, however, was disappointed again when he was assigned to research minerals while Bernal closely guarded his crystallography work, discussing it only with a few colleagues and never with students. Despite Perutz's disenchantment with his research assignments and the old, ill-lit, and dingy laboratories he worked in, he received excellent training in the promising field of X-ray crystallography, albeit in the classical mode of mineral crystallography. "Within a few weeks of arriving," Perutz states in Horace Freeland Judson's *Eighth Day of Creation: Makers of the Revolution in Biology,* "I realized that Cambridge was where I wanted to spend the rest of my life."

During his summer vacation in Vienna in 1937, Perutz met with Felix Haurowitz, a protein specialist married to Perutz's cousin, to seek advice on the future direction of his studies. Haurowitz, who had been studying hemoglobin since the 1920s, convinced Perutz that this was an important protein whose structure needed to be solved because of the integral role it played in physiology. In addition to making blood red, hemoglobin red corpuscles greatly increase the amount of oxygen that blood can transport through the body. Hemoglobin also transports carbon dioxide back to the lungs for disposal.

Although new to the physical chemistry and crystallography of hemoglobin, Perutz returned to Cambridge and soon obtained crystals of horse hemoglobin from Gilbert Adair, a leading authority on hemoglobin. Since the main goal of X-ray crystallography at that time was to determine the structure of any protein, regardless of its relative importance in biological activity, Perutz also began to study crystals of the digestive enzyme chymotrypsin. But chymotrypsin crystals proved to be unsuitable for study by X-ray, and Perutz turned his full attention to hemoglobin, which has large crystal structures uniquely suited to X-ray crystallography. At that time, microscopic protein crystal structures were "grown" primarily through placing the proteins in a solution which was then evaporated or cooled below the saturation point. The crystal structures, in effect, are repetitive groups of cells that fit together to fill each space, with the cells representing characteristic groups of the molecules and atoms of the compound crystallized.

In the early 1930s, crystallography had been successfully used only in determining the structures of simple crystals of metals, minerals, and salts. However, proteins such as hemoglobin are thousands of times more complex in atomic structure. Physicists William Bragg and Lawrence Bragg, the only father and son to share a Nobel Prize, were pioneers of X-ray crystallography. Focusing on minerals, the Braggs found that as X-rays pass through crystals, they are buffeted by atoms and emerge as groups of weaker beams which, when photographed, produce a discernible pattern of spots. The Braggs discovered that these spots were a manifestation of Fourier synthesis, a method developed in the nineteenth century by French physicist Jean Baptiste Fourier to represent regular signals as a series of sine waves. These waves reflect the distribution of atoms in the crystal.

The Braggs successfully determined the amplitude of the waves but were unable to determine their phases, which would provide more detailed information about crystal structure. Although amplitude was sufficient to guide scientists through a series of trial and error experiments for studying simple crystals, proteins were much too complex to be studied with such a haphazard and time consuming approach.

Initial attempts at applying X-ray crystallography to the study of proteins failed, and scientists soon began to wonder whether proteins in fact produce X-ray diffraction patterns. However, in 1934, Desmond Bernal and chemist Dorothy Crowfoot Hodgkin at the Cavendish laboratory in Cambridge discovered that by keeping protein crystals wet, specifically with the liquid from which they precipitated, they could be made to give sharply defined X-ray diffraction patterns. Still, it would take twenty-three years before scientists could construct the first model of a protein molecule.

Perutz and his family, like many other Europeans in the 1930s, tended to underestimate the seriousness of the growing Nazi regime in Germany. While Perutz himself was safe in England as Germany began to invade its neighboring countries, his parents fled from Vienna to Prague in 1938. That same summer, they again fled to Switzerland from Czechoslovakia, which would soon face the onslaught of the approaching German army. Perutz was shaken by his new classification as a refugee and the clear indication by some people that he might not be welcome in England any longer. He also realized that his father's financial support would certainly dwindle and die out.

As a result, in order to vacation in Switzerland in the summer of 1938, Perutz sought a travel grant to apply his expertise in crystallography to the study of glacier structures and flow. His research on glaciers involved crystallographic studies of snow transforming into ice, and he eventually became the first to measure the velocity distributions of a glacier, proving that glaciers flow faster at the surface and slower at the glacier's bed.

Finally, in 1940, the same year Perutz received his Ph.D., his work was put to an abrupt halt by the German invasions of Holland and Belgium. Growing increasingly wary of foreigners, the British government arrested all "enemy" aliens, including Perutz. "It was a very nice, very sunny day—a nasty day to be arrested," Perutz recalls in *The Eighth Day of Creation.* Transported from camp to camp, Perutz ended up near Quebec, Canada, where many other scientists and intellectuals were imprisoned, including physicists Herman Bondi and Tom Gold. Always active, Perutz began a camp university, employing the resident academicians to teach courses in their specialties. It didn't take the British government long, however, to realize that they were wasting valuable intellectual resources and, by 1941, Perutz followed many of his colleagues back to his home in England and resumed his work with crystals.

Perutz, however, wanted to contribute to the war effort. After repeated requests, he was assigned to work on the mysterious and improbable task of developing an aircraft carrier made of ice. The goal of this project was to tow the carrier to the middle of the Atlantic Ocean, where it would serve as a stopping post for aircrafts flying from the United States to Great Britain. Although supported both by then British Prime Minister Winston Churchill and the chief of the British Royal Navy, Lord Louis Mountbatten, the ill-fated project was terminated upon the discovery that the amount of steel needed to construct and support the ice carrier would cost more than constructing it entirely of steel.

Perutz married Gisela Clara Peiser on March 28, 1942; the couple later had a son, Robin, and a daughter, Vivian. After the war, in 1945, Perutz was finally able to devote himself entirely to pondering the smeared spots that appeared on the X-ray film of hemoglobin crystals. He returned to Cambridge, and was soon joined by John Kendrew, then a doctoral student, who began to study myoglobin, an enzyme which stores oxygen in muscles. In 1946 Perutz and Kendrew founded the Medical Research Council Unit for Molecular Biology, and Perutz became its director. Many advances in molecular biology would take place there, including the discovery of the structure of deoxyribonucleic acid (DNA).

Over the next years, Perutz refined the X-ray crystallography technology and, in 1953, finally solved the difficult phase dilemma with a method known as isomorphous replacement. By adding atoms of mercury—which, like any heavy metal, is an excellent X-ray reflector—to each individual protein molecule, Perutz was able to change the light diffraction pattern. By comparing hemoglobin proteins with mercury attached at different places to hemoglobin without mercury, he found that he had reference points to measure phases of other hemoglobin spots. Although this discovery still required long and assiduous mathematical calculations, the development of computers hastened the process tremendously.

By 1957, Kendrew had delineated the first protein structure through crystallography, again working with myoglobin. Perutz followed two years later with a model of hemoglobin. Continuing to work on the model, Perutz and Hilary Muirhead showed that hemoglobin's reaction with oxygen involves a structural change among four subunits of the hemoglobin molecule. Specifically, the four polypeptide chains that form a tetrahedral structure of hemoglobin are rearranged in oxygenated hemoglobin. In addition to its importance to later research on the molecular mechanisms of respiratory transport by hemoglobin, this discovery led scientists to begin research on the structural changes enzymes may undergo in their interactions with various biological processes. In 1962, Perutz and Kendrew were awarded the Nobel Prize in chemistry for their codiscoveries in X-ray crystallography and the structures of hemoglobin and myoglobin, respectively. The same year, Perutz left his post as director of the Unit for Molecular Biology and became chair of its laboratory.

The work of Perutz and Kendrew was the basis for growing understanding over the following decades of the mechanism of action of enzymes and other proteins. Specifically, Perutz's discovery of hemoglobin's structure led to a better understanding of hemoglobin's vital attribute of absorbing oxygen where it is plentiful and releasing it where it is scarce. Perutz also conducted research on hemoglobin from the blood of people with sickle-cell anemia and found that a change in the molecule's shape initiates the distortion of venous red cells into a sickle shape that reduces the cells' oxygen-carrying capacity.

In *The Eighth Day of Creation,* Judson remarks that Perutz was known to have a "glass thumb" for the difficult task of growing good crystals, and it was widely acknowledged that for many years Perutz produced the best images of crystal structures. In the book, published in 1979, Perutz's long-time colleague Kendrew remarks that little changed over the years, explaining, "If I had come into the lab thirty years ago, on a Saturday evening, Max would have been in a white coat mounting a crystal—just the same." Although Perutz retired in 1979, he continued to work as a professor for the MRC Lab of Molecular Biology at Cambridge and also served as a patron for the Cambridge University Scientific Society.

Further Reading

Cambridge University Scientific Society, 1997, "http://cygnus.csi.cam.ac.uk/CambUniv/Societies/cuss/patrons/patrons.htm," July 22, 1997.

Judson, Horace Freeland, *The Eighth Day of Creation: Makers of the Revolution in Biology,* Simon & Schuster, 1979.

"X-rays Mark the Spots," in *The Economist,* November 21, 1992, pp. 100–101. □

Rose Pesotta

Rose Pesotta (1896–1965) was one of only a few women labor activists who fought diligently to improve the standards of American sweat shops, especially for women, by organizing unions.

The Great Depression had a tremendous impact on workers in the United States. While all suffered from the devastating loss of jobs and economic deterioration, women especially were adversely affected. By 1933 almost two million women were unemployed. Married women were discriminated against more than married or single men and single women. Wages for women plummeted, and some women did not even make five dollars for a week's work. Workplace conditions worsened as the Depression increased. In the garment industry, where many women were employed, work standards deteriorated and the sweatshops were revived.

Outsider

Franklin D. Roosevelt took immediate steps to rectify the economic problems facing the country after he was elected president. The pro-labor stance taken by the administration helped unions gain tremendous power in the 1930s. One of the most powerful was the International Ladies Garment Workers Union (ILGWU), led by David Dubinsky, aided by a young anarchist named Rose Pesotta who was often sent to the fiercest antiunion factories to organize workers. As the only paid woman organizer in a male-dominated union, Pesotta had to fight to get her voice heard within the union. Her anarchism and commitment to women made her an outsider and were issues that she had to deal with throughout her career.

Militant

Pesotta was one of the militant female labor organizers working for the ILGWU, a group that included Fannia Cohn, Pauline Newman, and Rose Schneiderman. Each of these early female leaders faced difficult decisions regarding working within the union because of the discrimination they saw in the union hierarchy and in the shops. These women, however, realized that without a union the conditions would be much worse. Pesotta chose to work within the ILGWU and challenged the positions taken by the male leaders. Questioning the authority of the men in the union led Pesotta to be labeled as a troublemaker. Although the women mentioned were able to achieve positions of power, women were still largely absent from union leadership. It was socially unacceptable for women to aspire to these positions.

Vice President

Pesotta used early successes in unionizing on the West Coast, particularly in Los Angeles and San Francisco, as a catapult into the upper echelons of ILGWU leadership. Pesotta was nominated and elected a vice president of the union in 1934, even though she did not agree to be a candidate. She could not logically justify a position on the executive board with her anarchist background. Pesotta seemed to enjoy the honor for her accomplishments and remained a vice president for the next ten years. Dubinsky, like Pesotta, was fiercely anticommunist and an advocate of social reform; thus, he took her under his wing.

Success

Pesotta found success almost everywhere she went, and after the ILGWU pledged itself to the fledgling Congress for Industrial Organizations (CIO) the union began to lend her out to other organizing drives. Pesotta was the only "woman organizer" helping at the United Auto Workers strike in Flint, Michigan, and at the Akron rubber workers strike in the late 1930s. It was Pesotta's job to raise the morale of the strikers by working with the wives, daughters, and sisters. She often spoke at meetings of the strikers and led them in union songs. She also filmed the strikes with her movie camera, and the workers were eager to pose for her, thus increasing her familiarity with the strikers. Pesotta played an important role in the Flint sit-down strike. She was involved in the negotiations and diligently supported the strikers. During this strike thugs attacked and beat her, causing a lifelong hearing impairment. When the strike was finally settled, Pesotta was one of the CIO and UAW leaders who led the workers out.

Difficulty

Pesotta was an anarchist in philosophy but a pragmatist in action. She made the choice to be practical based on her experiences as a union organizer. She came under fire from fellow anarchists for being too willing to compromise and for her position as a bureaucrat. Pesotta also increasingly ran into difficulties with Dubinsky. She criticized him for ruling the ILGWU as a dictatorship and for the sexism she so plainly saw within the union. Publicly she was loyal to Dubinsky, but privately she began to view him as a sellout and lost all respect for him. Their differences grew so great that Dubinsky sent Pesotta to Los Angeles in 1940, a form of banishment to which she vigorously objected.

Return to the Factory

After a difficult time organizing in Los Angeles, marked by internal fighting with local male ILGWU leaders, Pesotta surprised everyone by returning to the sewing machine at a dress factory in New York City. In fact, Pesotta had been devastated by her experiences in Los Angeles. She was not allowed to manage the locals she had organized on the West Coast and felt abandoned by Dubinsky and the other members of the executive board. For the next few years Pesotta searched for purpose in her life after the many years of organizing. Sometimes she lost jobs in the dress industry because of her previous years of agitation.

Legacy

Pesotta was marginalized and isolated from the ILGWU because she was an outspoken woman trying to make changes in a male-dominated hierarchy. Her anarchism further threatened those in power. In many cases

women had subservient and powerless roles in the 1930s. Pesotta dared to step out of the role society gave her. She is one of the few women who made it past the bastions of male power in the 1930s and tried to instill her own brand of feminism into the labor movement.

Further Reading

Elaine Leeder, *The Gentle General: Rose Pesotta, Anarchist and Labor Organizer* (Albany: State University of New York Press, 1933). □

Johann Heinrich Pestalozzi

The Swiss educator Johann Heinrich Pestalozzi (1746-1827) envisioned a science of education based on the psychology of child development. He laid the foundation of the modern primary school.

Johann Pestalozzi was born in Zurich on Jan. 12, 1746. His father died shortly afterward, and Pestalozzi was raised in poverty. This early experience with the life of degradation of the poor developed in him an acute sense of justice and a determination to help the underprivileged. He chose to enter the ministry, but his studies in theology at the University of Zurich were without distinction. He tried law and politics, but his humanitarianism was mistaken for radicalism and he became very unpopular even with those he sought most to help. In 1769 he settled on his farm, "Neuhof," at Birr, Switzerland, where he planned to fight poverty by developing improved methods of agriculture.

At Neuhof, Pestalozzi realized that schoolteaching was his true vocation and that as a schoolmaster he could fulfill his desire to improve society by helping the individual to help himself. In 1775 he turned his farm into an orphanage and began to test his ideas on child rearing. In 1780 he wrote *The Hours of a Hermit,* a series of generally sad maxims reflecting his view of man's somber plight in the world and the failure of his own attempts at reform at Neuhof. He first experienced success with *Leonard and Gertrude* (1783), which was widely acclaimed and read as a novel and not, as it was intended to be, as an exposition of his pedagogical ideas.

His newfound fame brought Pestalozzi to Stanz, where he took over an orphanage in 1798, and then to Burgdorf, where he ran a boarding school for boys from 1800 to 1804. In 1801 he published *How Gertrude Teaches Her Children,* a sequel to his earlier novel and an expansion of his educational thought. But it was at Yverdun, where he was the director for the next 20 years of a boarding school for boys of many nationalities, that Pestalozzian principles of education were applied and observed by world leaders.

According to Pestalozzi, "the full and fruitful development" of the child according to his own nature is the goal of education. The school and teachers provide only the environment and guidance, respectively, most appropriate to free expression that allows the natural powers of the child to

develop. Instruction should be adapted to each individual according to his particular changing, unfolding nature. Rather than from books, the child should learn by observing objects of the real world. Sense perceptions are of supreme importance in the development of the child's mind. Pestalozzi described such a detailed methodology both for child development and for the study of the child that a definite system of teacher training evolved also.

Honors flowed in; Yverdun became a showplace. These were two causes of the ultimate collapse of the school. Pestalozzi's fame brought out some of his more disagreeable characteristics, and the original atmosphere of fellowship disappeared in the influx of visitors to the school. The school closed amid disputes and lawsuits; Pestalozzi died an embittered man on Feb. 17, 1827, in Brugg. But his ideas were used in establishing national school systems during the 19th century, and his influence among educators continues to be great to this day.

Further Reading

The best books on Pestalozzi are in German. In English the two works of J. A. Green, *The Educational Ideas of Pestalozzi* (1907) and *Life and Work of Pestalozzi* (1913), are still useful. Gerald L. Gutek, *Pestalozzi and Education* (1968), explores Pestalozzi's contributions to contemporary educational theory and practice.

Additional Sources

Downs, Robert Bingham, *Heinrich Pestalozzi, father of modern pedagogy*, Boston, Twayne Publishers 1975. □

Henri Philippe Pétain

The French general and statesman Henri Philippe Pétain (1856-1951), a military hero in World War I, headed the collaborationist Vichy regime during World War II. Officially considered a traitor, he is admired by many of his countrymen as a supreme patriot.

Philippe Pétain was born to peasant parents on April 24, 1856, at Cauchy-à-la-Tour. After a private boarding-school education, he entered Saint-Cyr in 1876 and graduated 2 years later. An advocate of defensive rather than offensive strategies, he became an instructor at the École de Guerre in 1888. Nearly 60 years old and without active-duty experience in 1914, Petain had had a far from brilliant career. World War I changed that radically.

Hero of Verdun

Promoted to brigadier general on Aug. 31, 1914, Pétain distinguished himself at the Battle of the Marne (1914) and in June 1915 was named a full general and given command of the 11th Army. When the Germans decided in 1916 to end the war with a massive concentrated attack on the French line at Verdun, Pétain was ordered to stop the offensive at all costs. Promising that "they shall not pass," he held Verdun but at the enormous cost of 350,000 men. Subsequently a great popular hero, he became chief of the general staff in April 1917, and a month later he succeeded Gen. Robert Nivelle as commander in chief.

Pétain assumed his command over a French army near disintegration. Years of indecisive war had sapped morale, and mutinies were endemic. Combining harsh disciplinary measures with humane redress of grievances, he very quickly reestablished order. Without these reforms the French army would not have withstood the final German offensives of 1918.

Between the World Wars

Named marshal of France on Nov. 21, 1918, Pétain emerged from the war second only to Ferdinand Foch in prestige. It was only natural that Pétain was regarded as a high military authority, but the consequences later proved catastrophic. Vice president of the Supreme War Council after 1920 and inspector general of the army after 1922, Pétain used his influence to orient French military planning along defensive lines. He favored the construction of heavily armed fortifications along the Franco-German frontier. Against the protests of such young rebels as Charles De Gaulle, who urged a strategy of mobile mechanized warfare, Pétain's influence was decisive, and the Maginot Line was constructed on the Franco-German border. French government and military leaders were determined to prepare France for any future war.

Retiring from the army in 1931, Pétain entered politics in 1934 as minister of war in the short-lived authoritarian government of Gaston Doumergue. Increasingly contemp-

chical and authoritarian regime under the formula of his so-called National Revolution. Little more than empty rhetoric ("Work-Family-Fatherland") and the cult of Pétain, his Vichy regime was a scarcely disguised client state of Nazi Germany.

Of necessity, Pétain's central principle in foreign policy was collaboration with the Third Reich. Above all, he wanted to keep France out of the war and to keep Germany as faithful to the armistice terms as possible. Opposed, however, to the all-out collaboration urged by Laval, Pétain replaced him with Adm. Jean Darlan in 1941. Under pressure from Berlin, Laval returned to office in April 1942.

The crisis of the Vichy regime occurred in November 1942 following the Allied landings in North Africa and the German occupation of Vichy France. Urged to flee, Pétain refused, believing that it was his duty to share the fate of his countrymen. He still refused even after ultracollaborationists were imposed upon him by the Germans, and thus he implicated himself in their treason. Arrested by the retreating Nazis on Aug. 20, 1944, and sent to Germany, Pétain voluntarily returned to France in April 1945. Immediately arrested and brought to trial by the provisional government of his onetime protégé Charles De Gaulle, Pétain was convicted of treason, militarily degraded, and sentenced to death. His sentence was commuted to life imprisonment by De Gaulle, and Pétain died 6 years later, on July 23, 1951, on the Île d'Yeu.

Estimates of Pétain's Career

Pétain remains an acutely controversial figure in recent French history. He is the object of an as yet unsuccessful effort at rehabilitation, his right-wing admirers depicting him as the "crucified savior of France" and claiming that his self-sacrifice after 1940 "will one day count more for his glory than the victory of Verdun." Not only did Pétain save France from the fate of Poland, they insist, but by playing a double game he tricked Adolf Hitler into staying out of North Africa, which made possible the eventual Allied victory in 1945. Preposterous as these claims are, the impression they give of Pétain is only slightly more misleading than that given by official Resistance historiography, which unfailingly portrays him as an arch-villain and as a criminal traitor to France.

Further Reading

A well-researched and interesting work on Pétain is Richard Griffiths, *Pétain: A Biography of Marshal Philippe Pétain of Vichy* (1972). For the period before 1940 the major work is Stephen Ryan, *Pétain the Soldier* (1969). For the Vichy period there is an enormous partisan literature whose purpose is either to condemn or exonerate Pétain. An example of the first is Robert Aron, *The Vichy Regime, 1940-1944* (1955; trans. 1958); and of the second, Sisley Huddleston, *Pétain: Patriot or Traitor?* (1951). Recommended for general background are Denis W. Brogan, *The Development of Modern France, 1870-1939* (1940; rev. ed., 2 vols., 1966), and Paul Marie de La Gorce, *The French Army: A Military-Political History* (trans. 1963).

tuous of parliamentary politics and such Socialist experiments as the Popular Front, and a known partisan of dictatorial regimes, Pétain provided a figure in the late 1930s around which right-wing opponents of the Third Republic could rally.

Vichy Regime

Ambassador to Spain at the outbreak of World War II, Pétain was recalled and appointed vice-premier in May 1940 by Premier Paul Reynaud in an attempt to bolster his foundering government. With the fall of France imminent, Reynaud resigned on June 16, 1940, and President Albert Lebrun asked the 84-year-old Pétain to form a new government whose first task would be to negotiate an armistice with the Germans. No one seemed to care that the rapid collapse of the French army in 1940 had been largely due to the outdated principles on which Pétain had organized it and to its lack of mechanized equipment, whose supply he had opposed.

On June 22 Pétain concluded an armistice with the Nazis that divided France into two zones: the north and the Atlantic coastline under German military occupation, and the rest of France under the direct administration of Pétain's government. Militarily, France retained control of its fleet, but its army was drastically reduced to 100,000 men.

Meeting in national assembly at Vichy on July 10, 1940, a rump parliament voted full constituent powers to Pétain. The next day he was named chief of state, and with Pierre Laval he then began the task of constructing a hierar-

Additional Sources

Lottman, Herbert R., *Pétain, hero or traitor: the untold story*, New York: W. Morrow, 1985.

Smith, Gene, *The ends of greatness: Haig, Pétain, Rathenau, and Eden: victims of history*, New York: Crown Publishers, 1990. □

St. Peter

St. Peter (died ca. 65) is traditionally considered to be the head of Jesus' 12 Apostles and the first bishop of Rome.

Peter's original name was Simon, Peter being a name given him by Jesus. At the time of Jesus' public life, Peter was a grown man. This would place his birth sometime around the end of the 1st century B.C. Of his early life we know little except that he came from the village of Bethsaida in Galilee and that his father was a fisherman. By the time he met and joined Jesus, he was already married (Mark 1:30); he lacked any formal education (Acts 4:13) and worked the fishing nets with his father and his brother Andrew at the lakeside town of Capernaum. Andrew also joined the group of Jesus' disciples on the same day.

His Times

As far as can be judged, Peter was a member of the ordinary people of Palestine, who were normally considered by educated Jewish classes to belong to *Am harez,* the people of the land. This term was used in a derogatory fashion to describe those who were ignorant of the niceties and deeper values of Judaism and the Jewish way of life. In addition, Peter was a Galilean and therefore shared the spirit of independence and opposition to Jerusalem which was traditional in that northern province.

Recent researches into the daily life of the ordinary people in Palestine paint a fairly clear picture of Peter's social conditions: extreme poverty, a very fideistic approach to religion, a reliance on superstition, and an extreme dependence on the vagaries of natural elements. Furthermore, in the northern parts of Palestine, removed from proximate influence of Jerusalem, more revolutionary ideas easily took hold. Unrefined and undeveloped ideas about the Messiah and about the salvation of Israel easily took the form of political movements, extremist organizations, and a readiness to disassociate oneself from the authoritarian structure of southern Judaism.

The general atmosphere in Palestine when Peter reached his adult life in the mid-20s of the 1st century A.D. was one of tension over the universal presence of the Roman conqueror and foreboding born of a strictly religious persuasion that the arrival of the Jewish Messiah was imminent as the only possible solution for Israel's difficulties. Indeed, we find more than once in the Gospels that the followers of Jesus, headed by Peter, attempted to force Jesus to accept the role of king. Even after the resurrection of Jesus, Peter and the others asked him when and how he would restore the kingdom of Israel. It is certain that Peter's attachment to Jesus, at least in the beginning, was largely based on the persuasion that Jesus would indeed restore the kingdom of Israel and that Peter and the other Apostles would be leaders in the new era.

Association with Jesus

Peter and Andrew were among the first to be chosen by Jesus to be his close followers. Thereafter Peter accompanied Jesus everywhere. Jesus gave Peter the added name of Cephas, an Aramaic appellation meaning "rock." This was translated into Greek as *Petros* (from the Greek *petra,* "rock") and became the Latin *Petrus* and the English Peter. The Gospels differ as to when Jesus conferred this name on him.

Throughout the public life of Jesus, Peter is represented in the Gospels as the spokesman and the principal member of Jesus' followers. He is the first named in all the lists given of these followers and was present with a privileged few at special occasions: when Jesus brought the daughter of Jairus back to life; when Jesus had a special communication with Moses and Elias on Mt. Tabor; and in the Garden of Gethsemane on the night before Jesus died. Peter was the first of the Apostles to see Jesus after his resurrection from the dead.

Jesus, according to the Gospel, gave Peter special assignments, such as paying the tribute or tax to the authorities on behalf of Jesus and his group. Jesus also said that he would build his new organization on Peter's leadership

(Matthew 16:17-19) and entrusted his followers and believers to him (John 21:15-19). Many commentators have thrown doubt on the texts which ascribe this special role to Peter, but it is certain that the Gospels thus present Peter as the chosen leader.

The same character is assigned to Peter in the Acts of the Apostles and in the few references which we find in Paul's letters. Paul went to Jerusalem to see Peter and be approved by him. About 14 years later, it appears that Peter headed the Christian evangelization of the Jews, in distinction to Paul, who preached to the Gentiles, and to James, who was bishop of Jerusalem.

In the early days after the death of Jesus, Peter is presented in the Acts again as the leader of Jesus' followers. The Jewish Sanhedrin treated him as the leader, and he preached the first mass appeal to the Jerusalemites about Jesus. He also directed the economic life of the Christian community and decided who would be admitted to it. About 49, when the Christians faced their first major decision—whether to admit non-Jews to their group—it was Peter who received guidance from God and made a positive decision accepted by all the other followers of Jesus present. That there was a difference of opinion concerning doctrinal matters between himself and Paul is beyond doubt. Paul, besides, reproached Peter for a certain insincerity and even manifested independence from Peter.

We are told of various missionary trips which Peter undertook in order to preach about Jesus. He was finally imprisoned by Herod and released miraculously by an angel. He then "departed and went to another place" (Acts 12:17). After 49, we have no direct record in the Acts about Peter, and we have to rely on external testimony.

Roman Sojourn

From all we can learn and surmise, it does appear that Peter occupied a position of importance in Rome and was martyred there under the rule of Nero (37-68). The earliest testimony comes from a letter of Clement written about the year 96 in Rome. A letter of Ignatius of Antioch (died ca. 110) also implies Peter's presence and authority in Rome, as does the saying of Gaius, a Roman cleric (ca. 200). Gaius speaks of the Vatican shrine and the "founders" of this church. Finally, all the early lists of the bishops of Rome start with Peter's name as the first bishop.

Excavations at the Vatican have yielded no cogent and conclusive evidence either of Peter's presence in Rome or of his burial beneath the Vatican. They have, however, uncovered an ancient shrine which dates from approximately 160. Collateral evidence suggests that it was the burial site of some venerated figure, and Roman Catholic tradition identifies that figure with Peter. There is no direct testimony in the New Testament that Peter's position as leader of the Apostles was meant to be passed on to his successors, the bishops of Rome, as the primacy of the popes over all of Christianity. This is a separate question and depends on subsequent Church development and evolution of its beliefs.

Tradition designates Peter as author of two letters which carry his name, although doubt has been thrown on Peter's authorship of at least the second. Various apocryphal documents which certainly date from the 2d century are ascribed to Peter. There is also the fragmentary Acts of Peter, which purports to relate how Peter ended his life as a martyr.

It appears from the first of the two letters ascribed to Peter that his outlook as a Jew and a Semite was never influenced by Greek or other non-Jewish thought. He reflects the mentality of a 1st-century Jew who believes that Jesus came as the Messiah of Israel and as the fulfillment of all Israel's promises and expectations. Some of Peter's statements would not now be acceptable to orthodox Christian thought. From what we know of Peter and his life, he seems to have made the transition from Palestine to Rome as from one Jewish community to another Jewish community, never fundamentally changing his instincts as a Jewish believer, except insofar as he totally accepted Jesus as the Messiah of Israel.

Further Reading

For accounts of Peter's life and work see William T. Walsh, *St. Peter, the Apostle* (1948), and Oscar Cullmann, *Peter: Disciple, Apostle, Martyr: A Historical and Theological Study* (trans. 1953). See also Jocelyn Toynbee and John Ward-Perkins, *The Shrine of St. Peter and the Vatican Excavations* (1956), and Engelbert Kirschbaum, *The Tombs of St. Peter and St. Paul* (trans. 1959).

Additional Sources

Barrett, Ethel, *Peter, the story of a deserter who became a forceful leader,* Ventura, CA: Regal Books, 1982.

Dyet, James T., *Peter, apostle of contrasts,* Denver, Colo.: Accent Books, 1982.

Grant, Michael, *Saint Peter: a biography,* New York: Scribner, 1995. □

Peter I

Peter I (1672-1725), called Peter the Great, was czar of Russia from 1682 to 1725. His reign was marked by a program of extensive reform known as Westernization and by the establishment of Russia as a major European power.

Contemporaries abroad tended to admire Peter I for his reforms and to fear him because of his country's growing power, but his reforms were generally unpopular with his subjects, not only because they entailed higher taxes and harder work for almost everyone but also because they disturbed ancient religious and cultural traditions. After his death, Russians soon came to realize that Peter had been the country's greatest ruler and that his reign had indeed been a high point in their history. That evaluation is still generally accepted by historians.

Peter was born in Moscow on May 30, 1672, the only son of Czar Alexis and his second wife, Natalia Naryshkin. The 13 children of Alexis' previous marriage included 3 who became prominent during Peter's youth: able and ambitious Sophia, half-blind and half-witted Ivan, and amiable Feodor, who succeeded Alexis in 1676.

Peter's formal education, entrusted to private tutors, began when he was 7 but was interrupted 3 years later, when Czar Feodor died without having named an heir. Sophia and a small group of supporters favored the frail Ivan, her 15-year-old brother, to succeed Feodor. Another group favored the robust and intelligent Peter and at once proclaimed him czar, planning that his mother serve as regent. That arrangement was quickly upset, however, when Sophia received the help of the Moscow troops and compelled the installation of Ivan as "First Czar," Peter as "Second Czar," and herself as regent.

Formative Years

During the next 7 years little was required of Peter except that he take part in formal ceremonies. Fascinated by military activities, he spent much time at games involving arms practice and battle maneuvers, at first with young friends and later with two regiments of soldiers that he was permitted to recruit and train. His curiosity and abundant energy led him also to the study and practice of the skills involved in navigation and such crafts as carpentry, stone-cutting, and printing. In the course of these pursuits, he came into contact with a number of foreign residents and gained from them knowledge of the world outside Russia.

Disturbed by the trend of his development, Peter's mother mistakenly decided that she could change it by arranging for his marriage; at her direction, he was married

to Eudoxia Lopukhin in January 1689. Still, he showed no inclination to forgo his first interests or his unconventional activities.

Political opposition to Sophia's regency came to a head during Peter's 17th year, and, impressed by the assurance of strong support if he would assert himself, Peter declared her office vacant and sent her away to a convent. That done, he returned to his habitual pursuits and continued to neglect personal responsibilities, even after Eudoxia had borne him a son, Alexis, in 1690. By that time he was a striking figure, impressive as a potential ruler but with scant interest in the duties involved.

It was not until 1695, when he had his first taste of actual fighting, against the Turkish forces at Azov, that Peter began to give serious thought to the problems he faced as czar. The death of "First Czar" Ivan during the following year finally brought him close to the full import of his position.

First Steps

Having been impressed at Azov by his country's lack of adequate fighting ships, Peter began with characteristic zeal to plan for an efficient navy. He sent groups of young men to western European countries to study navigation and ship-building; then, in 1697, he himself followed—an unprecedented step for a Russian czar—to acquire firsthand information and to hire shipwrights for service in Russia. He visited Holland, England, Germany, and Austria. In those countries he was impressed not only by their technological superiority over Russia but also by what seemed to him a superior style of life. When he returned to Russia in 1698, he was ready to make many changes.

One of Peter's first acts was to order that men shave off their beards, and when he met stubborn resistance, he modified his order only to the extent of imposing a tax on those who chose to keep their beards. He also shattered tradition by requiring that the old Russian calendar (which reckoned time from the creation of the world) be abandoned in favor of the Julian calendar used in the West. At the same time, he was dealing with two other matters, a revolt among the Moscow troops and the annoying presence of his unwanted wife, Eudoxia; he speedily quelled the revolt with savage executions and terminated his marriage by forcing Eudoxia into a convent.

Great Northern War

The handling of some of his problems, Peter soon learned, required more than his usual imperious tactics. During his European tour, he had obtained assurances of Western cooperation in forcing Sweden to cede the territory that Russia needed as an outlet to the Baltic Sea. He began the undertaking by a declaration of war on Sweden in 1700.

Peter led his forces in their first major encounter with the Swedes at Narva in November 1700 and was severely defeated by inferior numbers. Resorting to the means he had used with the navy—remodeling by Western patterns—he began at once to whip into shape a better organized, equipped, and trained army. In 1703 he led it to a redeeming victory and took from Sweden the mouth of the

Neva River. He designated the site for a city to be named St. Petersburg and to become the imperial capital. A year later he captured Narva.

Taking advantage of a few years of respite while the Swedes were engaged with other enemies, Peter worked purposefully to strengthen Russian arms and to keep under control the domestic discontent that was breaking into open revolt in many areas, particularly along the Don and the Volga rivers. He was obliged to return to the war in mid-1709, however, to meet a Swedish invasion led by Charles XII. The opposing forces met at Poltava, where the Russians won a decisive victory. The battle did not end the war, but it marked a turning point and vindicated Peter's belief in his methods. Moreover, it had a profound psychological effect on the western European states, who now saw Russia as a formidable power.

Twelve years of indecisive hostilities followed the Poltava victory. In 1711 Peter had to divert some of his troops to the south, where the Turks, encouraged by Sweden, had attacked Russia. After a year of unsuccessful fighting, he had to cede the port of Azov, Russia's only point of access to the Black Sea. Meanwhile, intermittent fighting kept the main war going, and it was not until 1718 that Sweden reluctantly agreed to a consideration of peace terms. By the resulting Treaty of Nystad, signed in September 1721, Sweden ceded Ingria, Estonia, Livonia, and a portion of Karelia, thus giving Russia a firm foothold on the Gulf of Finland and the Baltic Sea. Since Peter had already established Russian influence in Courland, his country was now a major Baltic power, having been provided with ''a window to Europe'' by the new acquisitions. In recognition of what he had achieved, the Russian Senate, a body created by Peter, conferred upon him the titles of ''the Great'' and ''Emperor.''

Personal Problems

After he freed himself of Eudoxia, Peter became attracted to Catherine Skavrenska, a Lithuanian girl of humble origin, and married her secretly, delaying until 1712 the public recognition of her as his consort. When Catherine bore a son, the Czar had him christened Peter Petrovich and anticipated his succession to the throne. Alexis, the son by his first marriage, had become a lazy, weak-willed, and hostile young man who resisted being molded to his father's standards. In the belief that Alexis was actually plotting against the throne, Peter ordered that he be taken to prison; and there, after being questioned under torture, Alexis died. Yet the Czar's problem was not solved: in 1719 Peter Petrovich died, leaving him no son as successor. Alexis had left a son, Peter Alekseyevich; but the Czar chose to bypass him and to decree, in 1722, that thereafter each ruler of Russia was free to name his heir. It is probable that Peter intended to name his wife, Catherine, as his heir, but he continued to postpone the formality.

Domestic Reforms

Although Peter carried out many reforms in his early years as czar, his major work as a reformer was done in the last decade of his reign. His goal was to create a powerful and prosperous state, efficiently and honestly administered, to which every subject could contribute. To achieve that goal, he refashioned many existing institutions and initiated new policies, generally guided by what he had learned of western Europe. He reorganized the country's entire administrative structure and promulgated the Table of Ranks, classifying civil service, military, and naval positions and providing for advancement on the basis of merit from lower to higher positions. He encouraged industry and commerce, spurred the development of science, and laid the foundations of the Academy of Sciences, which was established soon after his death. He instituted Russia's secular schools, eliminated the obsolete characters from the Russian alphabet, and established the country's first newspaper.

Even the Church felt the force of Peter's great energy. Although a religious man, he had no respect for the privileges accorded to the Church, was critical of many of its policies, and resented its resistance to his reforms. When Patriarch Adrian, head of the Russian Orthodox Church, died in 1700, Peter did not permit the vacancy to be filled. Finally, in 1721, he abolished the post of patriarch, substituting for it the Holy Synod, a board of prelates who were to direct the affairs of the Church under the supervision of a layman appointed by the czar.

Apparently, Peter found his greatest satisfaction in the development of St. Petersburg. He intended that this modern city become the center of the new Russia as Moscow had been the center of the old. He declared it to be the country's new capital and gradually transferred to it the central administrative offices. Built in Western style rather than the traditional Russian, it provided a visible symbol of his reforms.

Last Years

After the war with Sweden, Peter began to think seriously of his country's interests in Asia. At his direction, Russian forces conquered Kamchatka on the Pacific, and a Russian expedition explored the area now known as the Bering Strait. With prospects of more immediate value, he successfully pursued a war against Persia to strengthen Russia's position on the Caspian.

The treaty ending the war with Persia had yet to be ratified in 1724, when Peter's health began to fail rapidly. Characteristically, he continued to drive himself to the very limit of his strength, still postponing the designation of an heir. He died on Jan. 28, 1725, in the city that he had founded.

Further Reading

A study of Peter I is L. Jay Oliva, *Russia in the Era of Peter the Great* (1969). Ian Grey, *Peter the Great* (1960), is a comprehensive biography based on recent scholarship. A superb account of Peter's reign is Vasilii O. Klyuchevsky, *Peter the Great,* translated by Liliana Archibald (1958). Benedict Humphrey Sumner provides a brief, lucid survey of Peter's place in Russian history in *Peter the Great and the Emergence of Russia* (1950). Sumner also wrote the more specialized *Peter the Great and the Ottoman Empire* (1949).
Eugene Schuyler, *Peter the Great* (2 vols., 1884), is the most detailed biography available in English; it is somewhat dated

but quite useful. Marc Raeff, ed., *Peter the Great: Reformer or Revolutionary?* (1963), is a collection of differing views about Peter by his contemporaries and later observers. Raeff's *Origins of the Russian Intelligentsia: The Eighteenth-century Nobility* (1966) details the profound changes that Peter made in Russian society. The myth created around the image of Peter is discussed in Michael Cherniavsky, *Tsar and People: Studies in Russian Myths* (1961). Peter's life was fictionalized in Alexei Tolstoy, *Peter the Great* (trans. 1936). ☐

Peter I

Peter I (1844-1921) was king of Serbia from 1903 to 1918 and of the Serbs, Croats, and Slovenes from 1918 to 1921. He introduced constitutional monarchy to Serbia and was the first post-World War I monarch of the unified Yugoslav state.

Peter was born in Belgrade on July 11, 1844. His father was Prince Alexander Karageorgevic. After his older brother died, Peter became heir to the Serbian principality, which his father had ruled since 1842. However, in 1858, while Peter was abroad in Switzerland, his father was forced to abdicate in favor of the rival Obrenovic family. The young prince then began a long period of exile abroad in the service of other states.

After completing his studies in France, Peter entered the French officer corps in 1867. He fought in the Franco-Prussian War of 1871. Returning to southern Europe, in 1875 he joined the Herzegovinian revolt against Turkey, which soon spread to the South Slav territories still under direct Turkish control. Austrian intervention in 1876, however, forced Peter to leave the area.

In 1883 Peter married Zorka, daughter of Prince Nicholas of Montenegro, in which state he also became an honorary senator. After his wife's death in 1890 he returned to Switzerland.

In 1903 King Alexander of Serbia was assassinated, and Peter returned to his homeland as constitutional monarch. Peter I was crowned in Belgrade on Sept. 21, 1904. The aging Peter pursued liberal policies, but by the time Serbia was engulfed by World War I, he had already appointed his heir, Alexander, as regent.

Peter's vitality returned when war broke out. Although he was forced to retreat across Albania late in 1915, the King became the focus of national resistance. At the war's end Peter returned to his capital; there he was proclaimed king of a new South Slav state on Dec. 1, 1918.

Unfortunately, the new state over which Peter I ruled was large enough to threaten Italian interests. The last years of his reign were marked by a contest with Italy over the town of Fiume. Negotiations between the two countries saw the Yugoslavs forced to grant Fiume status as a free port. When Peter died near Belgrade on Aug. 16, 1921, the issue was still feeding fuel to the fires of Italian nationalism.

Further Reading

The historical background to Peter's reign may be studied in David Thomson, *Europe since Napoleon* (rev. ed. 1966). A. J. P. Taylor, *The struggle for Mastery in Europe, 1848-1918* (1954), establishes the diplomatic framework. Special aspects are treated in Wayne S. Vucinich, *Serbia between East and West: The Events of 1903-1908* (1954). An account of the Serbian campaigns of 1914-1915 is given by John C. Adams in *Flight in Winter* (1942). ☐

Peter III

Peter III (ca. 1239-1285) was king of Aragon and count of Barcelona from 1276 to 1285 and king of Sicily from 1282 to 1285. He was one of medieval Spain's greatest rulers.

The son of King James I of Aragon and Violante (Yolanda) of Hungary, Peter (or Pedro) III inherited the crown of Aragon in 1276, after his father's extensive conquests had increased both Aragonese power and prestige. In 1262 Peter had married Constance, daughter of Manfred of Sicily and granddaughter of the emperor Frederick II, and had inherited in 1266 the Hohenstaufen family claim to the kingdom of Sicily. Aragon's geographical and economic orientation toward the Mediterranean, Aragonese claims on the kingdom of Sicily, and Peter's great personal abilities made him the first monarch in the Spanish peninsula to participate actively and successfully in the wider affairs of Europe and the Mediterranean.

At the beginning of his reign Peter committed his resources to the construction of a large fleet and the assemblage of a formidable military force. His first target for expansion was the kingdom of Tunis, in whose internal affairs the kings of Aragon had long had an interest. He concerned himself for 6 years with the exploitation of political rivalries among the Moslem rulers of North Africa, but his interest in Aragonese expansion into the Mediterranean did not end there. The crisis in Sicilian politics that occurred between 1266 and 1282 offered him an opportunity to intervene. In 1266 Charles of Anjou, the brother of King Louis IX of France, had defeated the last of the Hohenstaufen rulers of Sicily and, with papal support, had been named king of Sicily. Charles's rule had been harsh; his ambitions had extended to the control of the papacy and the conquest of the Byzantine Empire; and his French nobles and military garrisons had outraged the people of Sicily. In 1282 the population of the island rose up and massacred the French garrisons (the "Sicilian Vespers"), and after a brief period of independence they offered the crown of the kingdom to Peter III because he was the husband of Constance, the last member of the Hohenstaufen family.

Peter's reign in Sicily was challenged by Charles of Anjou, the papacy, and Charles's nephew King Philip III of France. The power of the Aragonese and Sicilian fleets, under the command of the brilliant admiral Roger of Loria, maintained the integrity of the island and confined Charles's forces to the mainland portion of the kingdom in southern Italy. Upon Charles's death in 1285, Philip III invaded Aragon, stirring up a revolt against Peter by Aragonese who resented their King's overseas preoccupations. Philip also played upon the resentment felt toward Peter by his brother King James I of Majorca. Philip, however, died later in 1285, and Peter drove the French from Aragon shortly before he died on Nov. 11, 1285.

In addition to his considerable achievements in North Africa and Sicily, which laid the base for later Aragonese expansion into the eastern Mediterranean, Peter faced the difficulties of a divided kingdom and the wide resentment against his overseas enterprises. In 1283 the nobles and cities of Aragon demanded that he recognize their liberties and cease his demands for unusual fiscal grants. Peter responded with the famous General Privilege, sometimes called the "Magna Carta of Aragon," a gesture that conciliated his subjects and restored his prestige. His career thus represented both the extension of Aragonese influence in the Mediterranean world and the peaceable definition of the terms according to which king and subjects recognized the limits of their powers in Aragon.

Further Reading

There is no biography of Peter III in English. Excellent accounts of his reign are in Roger Bigelow Merriman, *The Rise of the Spanish Empire in the Old World and the New*, vol. 1 (1918), and Sir Stephen Runciman, *The Sicilian Vespers* (1960). A

good example of Peter's subsequent popularity may be seen in the 14th-century work by Ramón Muntaner, *The Chronicle of Muntaner* (trans., 2 vols., 1920-1921). □

Carl Peters

The German explorer, adventurer, and colonizer Carl Peters (1856-1918) was primarily responsible for putting a vast area of East Africa under German domination.

Carl Peters was born in Neuhaus near the mouth of the Elbe River. As a schoolboy, he exhibited a streak of romanticism; he dreamed of far-off lands and of the ways in which to achieve personal glory by emulating David Livingstone, Sir Richard Burton, Heinrich Barth, and other explorers of Africa.

In 1883 Peters returned home after a long visit to Britain, during which he had become infected with the fever of imperialism. He contemplated colonial adventure with new enthusiasm, spoke and wrote of the importance of colonial acquisition to the health of the new Germany, and in 1884 finally managed to persuade a number of older men of influence to join him in founding the Gesellschaft für Deutsche Kolonisation (German Colonization Society).

The society was consciously intended to propel Germany into imperial conflicts with Britain and France. Peters and his friends considered a colony in Latin America or in the Pacific. But their attentions soon turned to Africa. In particular they planned to occupy St. Lucia Bay in northern Natal, South Africa. Preparations went forward, only to be suspended when the extent of British and Zulu opposition was appreciated. Peters then turned to eastern Africa—to the mainland opposite Zanzibar, where German merchants had long been active. Here there were no other immediate European rivals, and Africans were not known to be hostile.

Peters planned a daring enterprise. Backed by the society, Peters, Count Joachim Pfeil, Karl Jühlke, and August Otto secretly traveled from Hamburg to Aden, where they took deck-class accommodations for the voyage to Zanzibar. Still incognito, they arrived there only to find a cable from Otto von Bismarck, the imperial chancellor, warning them that Germany could not support their scheme.

Founding of German East Africa

Undaunted, Peters and his companions quickly crossed to the African mainland and followed the valley of the Wami River toward modern Kilosa. In return for trinkets and spirits, African chiefs and headmen unwittingly, even frivolously, signed away their lands. By December 1884 Peters had obtained 124 treaties giving him exclusive sovereignty over about 2,500 square miles of what became eastern Tanganyika.

Peters returned home with his treaties toward the close of the West African Conference at Berlin, where European

Die Gründung von Deutsch-Ost-Afrika (1906; The Founding of German East Africa).

Further Reading

The standard biography of Peters is in German. For an understanding of his activities in East Africa, an essential work in English is Reginald Coupland, *The Exploitation of East Africa, 1856-1890* (1939). □

Edith R. Peterson

A medical researcher specializing in cell cultures, Edith R. Peterson (1914-1992) was the first scientist to grow myelin, the outer covering of nerve cells, in a test tube. Her discovery aided research into multiple sclerosis, muscular dystrophy, and other diseases of the nervous system.

Peterson was born Edith Elizabeth Runne on June 24, 1914, in Brooklyn, New York, to Hermann and Else Helmke Runne. Peterson's father, co-owner of a restaurant and catering establishment, died suddenly in 1920, shortly before he was to take a trip to Germany to join his wife and two daughters, who were visiting relatives. After staying in Germany for the next six years, the family returned to the United States, where Peterson's mother obtained employment designing custom dresses. In 1937 Peterson received a B.S. degree from Barnard College; two years later she earned a master's degree in zoology from Columbia University. In September of 1941 she married Charles Peterson, a commercial artist. The couple had a son, Wesley, in 1952 and a daughter, Rhonda Lea, in 1954.

In the early 1940s Peterson went to work in the laboratory of Margaret Murray at Columbia University. While working there, she was able to grow functional nerve cells using cultures containing chicken embryos. She utilized organotype culture which, unlike other methods of growing cells, involves having cells simulate the actual structure and functions of the organs from which they have been taken. Peterson succeeded in growing the actual nerve cells, brain, and spinal cord of chickens. In doing so she was also able to grow myelin, the insulating sheath surrounding nerve cells—the first time this had been done. This discovery aided research on multiple sclerosis, a disease that involves the degeneration of the myelin in the brain and spinal cord.

In 1966 Peterson left Columbia to work with Dr. Murray Bornstein at the Albert Einstein College of Medicine of Yeshiva University in the Bronx, New York. There she concentrated her studies on muscular dystrophy, a wasting disease affecting skeletal muscles. In addition to her research, she taught her techniques for organotype culture to students from the United States, Asia, and Europe.

Peterson retired in 1990 following a stroke that hindered her ability to use her right hand. Shortly afterward, she and her husband moved to Middletown, New York. Peterson died of a stroke on August 15, 1992.

territorial claims to Africa were being arbitrated and apportioned. Bismarck at first refused to accept them, but after Peters threatened to assign his newly acquired territories to King Leopold II of Belgium, Bismarck agreed to issue an imperial charter by which Germany claimed and "protected" all of the lands which lay roughly between Lake Tanganyika and the dominions of the sultan of Zanzibar. On behalf of the society and Germany Peters had gained control of a large region for which, admittedly, he and his successors would have to fight on numerous occasions against Africans.

Peters served as director of German East Africa until 1888, during which time he developed a reputation for brutality in his dealings with Africans. In the next year he returned to Africa in order to try to prevent what was to become Uganda and Kenya from falling into British hands. Successfully racing a British expedition to the capital of the Ganda king Mwanga, he obtained a critical agreement giving Germany substantial rights over the peoples around Lake Victoria. The omnibus Anglo-German territorial settlement of 1890 erased these hard-won advantages, however, and Uganda and Kenya were placed within the British sphere of influence.

Peters returned once again to Germany, where he busied himself with propaganda in favor of colonies and with the preparation of several books: *New Light on Dark Africa* (1891); *Das Deutsche-Ostafrikanische Schutzgebiet* (1895; The German East African Protectorate); *Die Deutsche-Ostafrikanische Kolonie* (1899; The German East African Colony); *The Eldorado of the Ancients* (1902); and

Further Reading

Edelson, Edward, *The Nervous System,* Chelsea House, 1991.
Rosner, Louis, and Shelley Ross, *Multiple Sclerosis,* Prentice-Hall, 1987.
"Edith Peterson, 78; Studied Cell Cultures," in *New York Times,* (obituary). □

John Frederick Peto

The American painter John Frederick Peto (1854-1907) developed a personal manner of painting trompe l'oeil still life.

John Frederick Peto was born on May 21, 1854, of an old Philadelphia family. His father, a gilder and picture framer, later sold fire-fighting equipment. Peto studied at the Pennsylvania Academy of Arts, but William Harnett's work was the overwhelming influence on his career. Peto seems to have known him before Harnett went to Europe in 1880 and acknowledged him as his model. He would never have painted the way he did without Harnett, for Peto was a born follower, a born disciple, but with genuine talent of his own.

From 1875 to 1889 Peto worked as a painter in Philadelphia, but he evidently was not very successful, and few pictures from this period can be identified. His career as an artist was frustrating. Occasionally he exhibited at the Pennsylvania Academy, but he was not very involved in the city's artistic life. He was not a forceful personality. In 1887 he married Christine Pearl Smith of Ohio. According to their daughter, he went west to paint a picture for the Stag Saloon in Cincinnati. This was the great era of the saloon in American painting, and the Stag Saloon had a gallery of pictures. This commission was probably the high point in Peto's artistic career.

In 1889 Peto moved to Island Heights on the New Jersey shore. He had acquired a reputation as a cornet player and could make a living there playing at the community's camp meetings. He lived out his life at this forgotten village on the shore, selling pictures to summer visitors and forgotten by the artistic world. He died there on Nov. 23, 1907.

At their best Peto's paintings fully deserve the Harnett signature which was forged on many of his paintings, and sometimes they have a radiance and luminosity of their own. Peto painted different kinds of still life: piles of books, writing tables, money. His specialty, particularly during the Philadelphia years, was "rack" pictures. These paintings, usually sold to business offices, show nets of tape which were used as office mail holders, with old envelopes held by the narrow bands; the handwriting is twice as legible as in life. On the painted wall, next to the rack, he displayed tiny newspaper clippings, old bits of string, perhaps a notebook trapped in the tape, sometimes an old card with torn edges, even a clay pipe. These paintings have a unique sheen and poetry.

It is remarkable that Peto maintained his professional standards as well as he did under trying circumstances. It is understandable that some of his later work is careless.

Further Reading

The authoritative account of Peto is in Alfred Frankenstein's fascinating *After the Hunt: William Harnett and Other American Still Life Painters* (1953). Frankenstein not only gives a full account of Peto's life but he also succeeds in disentangling his work from Harnett's, with which it had for so long been confused. □

Petrarch

The Italian poet Petrarch (1304-1374), or Francesco Petrarca, is best known for the lyric poetry of his *Canzoniere* and is considered one of the greatest love poets of world literature. A scholar of classical antiquity, he was the founder of humanism.

Petrarch has been called the first modern man. He observed the external world and analyzed his own interior life with a new awareness of values. Painfully conscious of human transience, he felt it his mission to bridge the ages and to save the classical authors from the ravages of time for posterity. He also longed for fame and for permanence in the future. Petrarch attained a vast direct knowledge of classical texts, subjecting them to critical evaluation and prizing them as an expression of the living human spirit. His attitude provided the first great stimulus to the cultural movement that culminated in the Renaissance.

Petrarch's life was marked by restlessness, yet one of its constant motives was his devotion to cherished friends. Equally constant was an unresolved interior conflict between the attractions of earthly life, particularly love and glory, and his aspirations toward higher religious goals.

Early Years and Education

Petrarch was born on July 20, 1304, in Arezzo, where his family was living in political exile. His parents were the Florentine notary Ser Petracco and Eletta Canigiani. His childhood was spent at Incisa and Pisa until 1312, when his family moved to Avignon, then the papal residence. A housing shortage there obliged Petrarch, his younger brother Gherardo, and their mother to settle in nearby Carpentras, where he began to study grammar and rhetoric. Beginning in 1316, Petrarch pursued legal studies at the University of Montpellier. But already he preferred classical poets to the study of law. During one surprise visit Petrarch's father discovered some hidden books and began to burn them; however, moved by his son's pleading, he spared Cicero's *Rhetoric* and a copy of Virgil from the fire. About this time Petrarch's mother died.

In 1320 Petrarch and Gherardo went to Bologna to attend the law schools. They remained in Bologna—with two interruptions caused by student riots—until their fa-

ther's death in 1326. Free to pursue his own interests, Petrarch then abandoned law and participated in the fashionable social life of Avignon.

Laura and the *Canzoniere*

On April 6, 1327, in the church of St. Clare, Petrarch saw and fell in love with the young woman whom he called Laura. She did not return his love. The true identity of Laura is not known; there is, however, no doubt regarding her reality or the intensity of the poet's passion, which endured after her death as a melancholy longing. Petrarch composed and revised the love lyrics inspired by Laura until his very last years. The *Canzoniere,* or *Rerum vulgarum fragmenta,* contains 366 poems (mostly sonnets, with a few canzoni and compositions in other meters) and is divided into two sections: the first is devoted to Laura in life (1-263) and the second to Laura in death (264-366). Petrarch became a model for Italian poets. The influence of his art and introspective sensibility was felt for more than 3 centuries in all European literatures.

When the income of Petrarch's family was depleted, he took the four Minor Orders required for an ecclesiastical career, and in the fall of 1330 he entered the service of Cardinal Giovanni Colonna. In 1333, motivated by intellectual curiosity, Petrarch traveled to Paris, Flanders (where he discovered two of Cicero's unknown orations), and Germany. Upon returning to Avignon, he met the Augustinian scholar Dionigi di Borgo San Sepolcro, who directed him toward a greater awareness of the importance of Christian patristic literature. Until the end of his life, Petrarch carried

with him a tiny copy of St. Augustine's *Confessions,* a gift from Dionigi. In 1336 Petrarch climbed Mt. Ventoux in Provence; on the summit, opening the *Confessions* at random, he read that men admire mountains and rivers and seas and stars, yet neglect themselves. He described this experience in spiritual terms in a letter that he wrote to Dionigi (*Familiares* IV, 1).

Major Works in Latin

Petrarch's reputation as a man of letters and the canonries to which he was appointed at various times assured him the ease and freedom necessary for his studies and writing. He participated during this period in the polemic concerning the papal residence, expressing in two *Epistolae metricae* his conviction that the papacy must return to Rome. Early in 1337 Petrarch visited Rome for the first time. The ancient ruins of the city deepened his admiration for the classical age. In the summer he returned to Avignon, where his son, Giovanni, had been born, and then went to live at Vaucluse (Fontaine-de-Vaucluse) near the source of the Sorgue River. There he led a life of solitude and simplicity, and he also conceived his major Latin works. In 1338 Petrarch began his *De viris illustribus,* and about that time he also started his Latin epic on Scipio Africanus, the *Africa.* In Vaucluse, Petrarch probably also worked on his *Triumphus Cupidinis,* a poetic ''procession,'' written in Italian, in which Cupid leads his captive lovers. In 1340 Petrarch received invitations simultaneously from Paris and Rome to be crowned as poet. He chose Rome. His coronation on April 8, 1341, was a personal victory and a triumph for art and knowledge as well.

Middle Years

On returning from Rome, Petrarch stopped at Parma. There, on the wooded plateau of Selvapiana, he continued his *Africa* with renewed inspiration. In April 1343, shortly after Petrarch had returned to Avignon, Gherardo became a Carthusian monk. That same year Petrarch's daughter, Francesca, was born. Gherardo's decision to become a monk deeply moved Petrarch, leading him to reexamine his own spiritual state. Though his Christian faith was unquestionably sincere, he felt incapable of his brother's renunciation. His inner conflict inspired the *Secretum* a dialogue in three books between St. Augustine and Petrarch. In it Petrarch expressed his awareness of his failure to realize his religious ideal and his inability to renounce the temporal values that motivated his life. That year Petrarch also began a treatise on the cardinal virtues, *Rerum memorandarum libri.*

In the fall of 1343 Petrarch went to Naples on a diplomatic mission for Cardinal Colonna. He recorded his travel impressions in several letters (*Familiares* V, 3, 6). Upon his return he stopped at Parma, hoping to settle at Selvapiana. But a siege of Parma by Milanese and Mantuan troops forced him to flee to Verona in February 1345. There, in the cathedral library, he discovered the first 16 books of Cicero's letters to Atticus and his letters to Quintus and Brutus. Petrarch personally transcribed them, and these letters of

Cicero stimulated Petrarch to plan a formal collection of his own letters.

From 1345 to 1347 Petrarch lived at Vaucluse and undertook his *De vita solitaria* and the *Bucolicum carmen* the latter a collection of 12 Latin eclogues. Early in 1347 a visit to Gherardo's monastery inspired Petrarch to write his *De otio religioso*. In May of that year an event occurred in Rome that aroused his greatest enthusiasm. Cola di Rienzi, who shared Petrarch's fervent desire for the rebirth of Rome, gained control of the Roman government through a successful revolution. Petrarch encouraged Cola with his pen, exhorting him to persevere in his task of restoring Rome to its universal political and cultural missions. Petrarch then started out for Rome. But Cola's dictatorial acts soon brought down upon himself the hostility of the Pope and the antagonism of the Roman nobles. News of Cola's downfall, before the year was over, prompted Petrarch to write his famous letter of reproach (*Familiares* VII, 7), which tells of his bitter disillusionment.

The Black Death and Milanese Period

Rather than proceed to Rome, Petrarch remained in Parma, where in May 1348 news of Laura's death reached him. The Black Death deprived Petrarch of several of his close friends that year, among them Cardinal Colonna. His grief is reflected in the poems he then wrote to Laura and in his letters of this period, one of the most desolate letters being addressed to himself (*Ad se ipsum*). Three eclogues and the *Triumphus mortis* (following the *Triumph of Love* and the *Triumph of Chastity*) were also inspired by the pestilence.

Because of the losses Petrarch had suffered, a period of his life seemed to have ended. In 1350 he began to make the formal collection of his Latin prose letters called *Familiares*. Since 1350 was a Year of Jubilee, Petrarch also made a pilgrimage to Rome. On his way he stopped in Florence, where he made new friends, among whom was Giovanni Boccaccio. After a brief stay in Rome, Petrarch returned northward and arrived in Parma in January 1351. In the meantime, Pope Clement VI was soliciting Petrarch's return to Avignon, and Florence sent Boccaccio with a letter of invitation promising Petrarch a professorship at the university and the restitution of his father's property. Petrarch chose Provence, where he hoped to complete some of his major works. He arrived in Vaucluse in June 1351, accompanied by his son. In Avignon that August he refused a papal secretaryship and a bishopric offered to him. Petrarch was impatient to leave the papal "Babylon" and wrote a series of violent letters against the Curia (*Epistolae sine nomine*).

In the spring of 1352, Petrarch returned to Vaucluse, resolved to leave Provence. The following spring, after visiting Gherardo, he crossed the Alps and greeted Italy (*Epistolae metricae* III, 24). For 8 years he stayed in Milan under the patronage of Giovanni Visconti and later Galeazzo II Visconti, enjoying seclusion and freedom for study while using his pen to urge peace among Italian cities and states. He worked on the *Canzoniere,* took up old works (*De viris illustribus*), and began the treatise *De remediis utriusque fortunae*. Petrarch was also entrusted with diplomatic missions that brought him into direct relationship with heads of state, including the emperor Charles IV.

Padua, Venice, and Arquà

In June 1361 Petrarch went to Padua because the plague (which took the life of his son and the lives of several friends) had broken out in Milan. In Padua he terminated the *Familiares* and initiated a new collection, *Seniles*. In the fall of 1362 Petrarch settled in Venice, where he had been given a house in exchange for the bequest of his library to the city. From Venice he made numerous trips until his definitive return to Padua in 1368. During this period a controversy with several Averroists gave rise to an *Invective* on his own ignorance.

Petrarch's Paduan patron, Francesco da Carrara, gave him some land at Arquà in the Euganean Hills near Padua. There Petrarch built a house to which he retired in 1370. He received friends, studied, and wrote, and there his daughter, Francesca, now married, joined him with her family. Despite poor health, Petrarch attempted a trip to Rome in 1370, but he had to turn back at Ferrara. Except for a few brief absences, Petrarch spent his last years at Arquà, working on the *Seniles* and on the *Canzoniere,* for the latter of which he wrote a concluding canzone to the Virgin Mary. The *Posteritati,* a biographical letter intended to terminate the *Seniles,* remained incomplete at Petrarch's death. He revised his four *Triumphs* (of Love, Chastity, Death, and Fame), adding two more (of Time and of Eternity). Petrarch died on the night of July 18/19, 1374, and he was ceremonially buried beside the church of Arquà.

Further Reading

The major critical biography of Petrarch is Ernest H. Wilkins, *Life of Petrarch* (1961). A more entertaining work is Morris Bishop, *Petrarch and His World* (1963). A standard study of Petrarch's poetry is Ernest H. Wilkins, *The Making of the "Canzoniere" and Other Petrarchan Studies* (1951). Petrarch's correspondence can be studied in James H. Robinson and Henry W. Rolfe, *Petrarch: The First Modern Scholar and Man of Letters* (1898; rev. ed. 1914); Ernest H. Wilkins, *Petrach's Correspondence* (1960); and Morris Bishop, *Letters* (1966). □

Sir William Matthew Flinders Petrie

Sir William Matthew Flinders Petrie (1853-1942) was an English archeologist who revolutionized excavation methods, thus laying the basis for modern archeological techniques.

Flinders Petrie was born on June 3, 1853, at Charlton near Greenwich. He was educated at home because of his ill health. At the age of 22, he published his *Inductive Metrology,* a study of ancient weights and measures. He also studied British archeological sites, including Stonehenge, from 1875 to 1880. From 1880 onward, he plunged into an active career of surveys and excavations in Egypt and Palestine interspersed with lectures in London and the publication of a prodigious output of 40 large volumes furnished with numerous plates, a series of popular books, and his autobiography.

Petrie began his excavations at the Giza pyramids in Egypt (1880). From 1881 to 1896 his archeological work was done on behalf of the Egypt Exploration Fund. He next excavated the Temple of Tanis (1884), the city of Naucratis (1885), the town of Daphnae and its environs (1886), the sites of Hawara, Illahun, and Ghurab in the Faiyûm, Egypt (1888-1890), and the temple and pyramids of Maydum (1891). In 1892 he was appointed Edwards professor of Egyptology at University College, London, a post he held until 1933. He then excavated the town of Coptos (Qift; 1895), discovering also the painted pavement of Tell el Amarna, the predynastic site of Nakada (1895), and the temples at Thebes (1897). In 1894 he founded the Egyptian Research Account as his own fund-raising and publishing venture.

Petrie spent 6 years (1898-1904) excavating the necropolis of Abydos, uncovering the royal cenotaphs of predynastic times. He excavated at Dandarah, Memphis, and again in the Faiyûm. Here he found a magnificent collection of Twelfth-Dynasty jewelry. He excavated in Palestine from 1922 to 1938.

Before Petrie, archeologists merely extracted from excavation sites any objects they considered to be works of art. But they did not follow the stratification of a site in relation to established chronologies. Petrie and his students and followers introduced systematic examination of any object found in a site. Second, he excavated so as to uncover and leave intact the different layers of the site and their relative position within it. Third, he developed what is known today as sequence dating, a system of chronology based on close study of the stylistic and technical development which every object found on a site exhibited. It was thus in his work as an excavator that Petrie made his biggest contribution. His views on epigraphy and the origin of the alphabet roused strong opposition. He was knighted in 1923 and died on July 23, 1942, at Jerusalem.

Petrie's best-known works are *A History of Egypt,* 6 vols. (1894-1925); *The Royal Tombs of Abydos I and II* (1900-1902); *Abydos I-III* (1902-1904); *Researches in Sinai* (1906); *The Formation of the Alphabet* (1912); *Tombs of the Courtiers* (1925); and *Seventy Years in Archaeology* (1931).

Further Reading

Petrie's work is discussed in Charles M. Daugerty, *The Great Archaeologists* (1962).

Additional Sources

Drower, Margaret S., *Flinders Petrie: a life in archaeology,* Madison, Wis.: University of Wisconsin Press, 1995. □

Petronius Arbiter

The Roman voluptuary Petronius Arbiter (died ca. 66) is the ascribed author of the *Satyricon,* a fragmentary picaresque novel generally considered one of the most brilliant productions of Latin literature.

The "Arbiter" of the ascribed author's name is clearly intended to imply an identification with the Petronius who is called *elegantiae arbiter,* or judge of elegance, by Tacitus, and whose death by suicide in 66 is described by Tacitus in a famous passage. The author's identity has been vigorously disputed by those who feel that the novel should rather be ascribed, on the basis of style, customs described, and other internal evidence, to the 2d or 3d century, but the majority of scholars are willing to accept the former identification as probable.

His Life

Petronius had proved his ability as proconsul (governor) of Bithynia and later as consul under Nero. Modern scholarship has thus identified him with Titus Petronius Niger and showed that his first name was incorrectly reported (as Gaius) by Tacitus and correctly by Pliny the Elder and Plutarch. He then, according to Tacitus, by the assumption or imitation of vice and by his authority in matters of taste and style, became such an influential favorite of Nero that the Emperor would not approve of anything as elegant or artistic without Petronius's approval. This influence aroused the jealousy of Nero's powerful and sinister favorite, Tigellinus, who bribed a slave to implicate Petronius with Scaevinus, the major figure in the recently discovered conspiracy of Piso.

Nero's court was in Campania, and Petronius hurried to him to defend himself, but at Cumae he found that his case was hopeless and decided to commit suicide. The end was worthy of the man: he refused to indulge himself in sentimentality or a fashionable and ostentatious show of consoling himself with philosophy, such as had marked the end of Seneca. He had his veins cut, and alternately closed and reopened, while he played at composing verses with his friends, rewarded or punished his slaves, ate a good dinner, and took a nap, so that, as Tacitus says, his death, even though forced on him, would seem as though it had come by chance.

At the end Petronius refused to declare his loyalty to Nero, as was customary (largely in order to prevent the confiscation of the estate), but wounded the Emperor's vanity by composing and sending to him a detailed and categorical account of Nero's debaucheries and experiments in vice, and he broke his signet ring in order to prevent it from being used to forge documents which would endanger others.

The *Satyricon*

The similarity of the character of Petronius as described by Tacitus to that which one can ascribe to the author of the *Satyricon* is perhaps the best argument for their identity. The *Satyricon* is witty, elegant, and sophisticated: the author clearly had wide experience of literature, good society, and men of all ranks and conditions, as well as a freedom from moral and sentimental restraints and inhibitions and a taste for the licentious which resembles that of Petronius.

The plan of the work, in a mixture of prose and verse known as Menippean satire, is apparently based, somewhat loosely, on a parody of the *Odyssey:* just as Odysseus suffers from the wrath of Poseidon, so Encolpius, the hero, suffers from the wrath of Priapus, the phallic god, who afflicts him with impotence, and he wanders around, through a series of low and scandalous adventures, in search of a cure with his companions, the scoundrelly boy Giton, with whom he is in love, and the equally disreputable Ascyltus.

The fragments we have seem to come from the fifteenth and sixteenth books and represent part of a series of excerpts made in late antiquity or the early Middle Ages. The only long passage preserved is the "Dinner of Trimalchio," which was discovered at Trogir in Dalmatia about 1650. It shows the dinner party of a vulgar parvenu freedman in a small Italian town, attended by the three protagonists and an assortment of lowborn but successful men, and is delightful not only for its picture of vulgar ostentation and ignorant aping of good society but also for its keen psychology, with the refined but decadent and worthless protagonists played off against the boorish but vital and human local citizens. It is also the best representation of common, ordinary Latin speech (Vulgar Latin) preserved from antiquity.

In addition, a series of elegant short poems have been preserved under the name of Petronius. There are, however, grave differences in style among them, and there is no agreement as to which, if any, are actually by him. There have been numerous forgeries of fragments of Petronius, some of which have been used by unwary editors and translators.

Further Reading

A major study of the *Satyricon* is H. D. Rankin, *Petronius the Artist: Essays on the Satyricon and Its Author* (1970). See also John P. Sullivan, *The Satyricon of Petronius: A Literary Study* (1968); Gilbert Bagnani, *Arbiter of Elegance: A Study of the Life and Works of C. Petronius* (1954); and John Wight Duff, *A Literary History of Rome in the Silver Age from Tiberius to Hadrian* (1927; 3d ed. by A. M. Duff, 1964) and *Roman Satire* (1936). The introduction and notes to William Arrowsmith's translation (1959), although elementary, are interesting and generally accurate. □

Antoine Pevsner

The Russian constructivist sculptor and painter Antoine Pevsner (1886-1962) was one of the founders of the ultramodern abstract school in Moscow in the 1920s. His art is severely geometrical, elegant, intellectual, and uncompromising.

Antoine Pevsner was born on Jan. 18, 1886, in Orel, the son of a copper refinery executive. He and his two brothers, Alexei and Naum, were interested in science and specialized in engineering in school. Antoine and Naum (who took the surname Gabo) then turned to art. Pevsner studied at the Academy of Fine Arts in Kiev (1908-1910) and in St. Petersburg (1911). In Moscow he saw the collections of impressionist, Fauve, and cubist art which belonged to Ivan Morosov and Sergei Stchoukine (Shchukin).

In 1912 Pevsner went to Paris, where he saw the cubist art of Pablo Picasso, Georges Braque, and Alexander Archipenko. Pevsner began to paint in 1913. With the outbreak of World War I he joined Gabo in Norway. In 1917 they moved to Moscow, where Pevsner became a member of the faculty at the progressive Fine Arts and Technical School. The presence of Kasimir Malevich and Vladimir Tatlin on the faculty brought Pevsner into contact with suprematism.

Pevsner and Gabo were swept up in the cause of avant-garde art and supported the Revolution as a force for the liberation and promotion of advanced social and artistic programs. They became disenchanted once it was required that art lose its autonomy and be used as a tool to propagate political philosophy. They thought that the constructivists led by Tatlin had become doctrinaire, and so they detached themselves from their former colleagues more and more. They published their position in the 1920 Realistic Manifesto. They stated that there was a need for new art forms and that dynamic rhythms must assume dominance over mass to emphasize space-time relationships and express the modern spirit. Once the Communist government had withdrawn its support and begun to suppress all free artistic expression as "formalism," artists had the choice of either conforming to official policy or leaving. Pevsner and Gabo left.

Pevsner went to Berlin, where he turned to sculpture and made his first construction. Finding this new experience congenial, he concentrated on sculpture thereafter. In 1924 he settled in Paris. Characteristic of his work at this time are *Portrait of Marcel Duchamp* (1926) and *Torso* (1924-1926). He began to use plastics and brass sheeting, which he cut and fixed to a surface to form the effect of a high relief. Light and shadow play an important role in these works. In 1927 he and Gabo collaborated on sets for Sergei Diaghilev's ballet *La Chatte*.

Pevsner became a French citizen in 1930. The next year he became a founding member of the Abstraction-Création group. He supported a similar group, Réalités Nouvelles, 14 years later. Pevsner's sculpture developed gradually and showed no sharp turns in conception. In the mid and late 1930s he used ribbing on sheet metal to emphasize linear movement, as in *Construction for an Airport* (1937). In it, parabolically turned planes appear as if activated by some centrifugal force which suggests consumption of space. Later, Pevsner had his works cast in bronze; this gave them a rich consistency unlike that of welded constructions.

In 1948 Pevsner and Gabo had a comprehensive retrospective exhibition at the Museum of Modern Art in New York City. Pevsner produced two works on a monumental scale: *Dynamic Projection in the 30th Degree* (1950-1951) for University City in Caracas, Venezuela, and *Developable Column of Victory* (*Flight of the Bird,* 1955) for the General Motors Technical Center in Warren, Mich. He died in Paris on April 12, 1962.

Further Reading

Recommended are Alexei Pevsner, *A Biographical Sketch of My Brothers: Naum Gabo and Antoine Pevsner* (trans. 1964), and the catalog of the Museum of Modern Art 1948 exhibition, *Naum Gabo, Antoine Pevsner,* with an introduction by Herbert Read and brief texts by Ruth Olson and Abraham Chanin.

□

Luang Phibun Songkhram

Luang Phibun Songkhram (1897-1964) was a military officer and prime minister of Thailand. An ardent proponent of Thai nationalism, he was the dominant figure in the first decades of constitutional government.

B orn in a farming village near Bangkok on July 14, 1897, Phibun Songkhram was originally named Plaek. He attended Buddhist monastery schools and entered the royal military academy in Bangkok in 1909. Completing his studies in 1914, he went into the artillery corps. In 1924 he was sent to France for advanced military studies and met there Thai students who were to be prominent in the politics of the 1930s, especially Pridi Phanomyong and Khuang Aphaiwong. Returning to Bangkok in 1927, he served in the directorate of operations and the general staff of the army, rising to the rank of major, and in 1928 was given the title by which he was known thereafter, "Luang" Phibun Songkhram, which he later took as his family name.

Phibun was one of the organizers of the Revolution of June 24, 1932, which ended the absolute monarchy, and served in the first governments of the new regime. He joined with Phraya Phahon in 1933 to overthrow civilian government and establish the dominant role of the army in national politics. He won prominence in suppressing the rebellion of Prince Boworadet later that year.

In 1934 Phibun became minister of defense and greatly strengthened the army. He established paramilitary youth organizations on the then popular fascist model and publicly expressed ultranationalist and irredentist views. Surviving three assassination attempts, he succeeded Phahon as prime minister in December 1938 and retained for himself the portfolios of interior and defense.

After the fall of France, Phibun provoked war with French Indochina in 1940-1941 to regain territories lost earlier. When Japanese troops invaded Thailand on Dec. 8, 1941, Phibun immediately allied Thailand with Japan, a move made easier by close prewar relations, and spared the country Japanese occupation while regaining temporarily much of the territory lost to Britain and France in the 19th century.

When the war turned against Japan in 1944, Phibun was ousted, and civilian government under Pridi's leadership was restored. Pridi's ties with the Allies ensured Thailand exemption from treatment as a defeated enemy at the end of the war. Economic dislocation and official corruption increased public impatience with civilian government in 1946-1947, and the suspicious death of King Ananda (1946) gave the military an opportunity to revive its claim to rule. An army coup d'etat in 1947 was followed by Phibun's return as prime minister the following year.

Phibun's second term as prime minister was clouded by rivalries among his military supporters and by increasing public dissatisfaction with corruption and economic stagnation. His attempt to rally popular support through open elections in 1957 backfired when, in spite of flagrant electoral corruption, Phibun's party barely won a majority of the legislative seats. A military coup by Gen. Sarit Thanarat, with strong public support, followed in September 1957, and Phibun retired to exile in Japan, where he died on June 11, 1964.

Phibun's most important legacy to Thailand was his promotion of Thai values and nationalism, a source of considerable national strength, together with his reaffirmation of the values of modernization. His strong championing of the role of the military in national politics, however, established a political imbalance not easily corrected.

Further Reading

There is no biography of Phibun in any Western language. His career can be followed in David A. Wilson, *Politics in Thailand* (1962), and Frank C. Darling, *Thailand and the United States* (1965). □

Phidias

The Greek sculptor Phidias (active ca. 475-425 B.C.), the dominant artistic figure of the 5th century, was best known for two chryselephantine cult statues, the "Athena Parthenos" in the Parthenon, Athens, and the "Zeus" in the Temple of Zeus, Olympia. He also supervised the construction and sculptural adornment of the Parthenon.

Literary sources for the life and career of Phidias, while often anecdotal in nature, are unusually abundant; among the most important are Plutarch, in *Life of Perikles,* and Pausanias, the latter with eyewitness descriptions of the colossal chryselephantine (gold and ivory) cult statues. Pliny the Elder, in *Natural History,* alludes to the 83d Olympiad (448-444 B.C.) as the time of Phidias's greatest activity. While his major commissions were done at Athens and Olympia, he also executed statuary at Delphi, Plataea, Thebes, and Pallene in Achaea. Phidias was unusually versatile, being renowned as a sculptor not only in bronze but also in marble and in the difficult technique of fashioning and assembling gold, ivory, and wooden components into chryselephantine statues. He is said to have originally been a painter. It is around his involvement with the Parthenon project, however, that any reconstruction of his career must be built.

Phidias's early works, that is, those done before about 450 B.C., all mentioned by Pausanias, include a gold-and-ivory image of Athena at Pallene, Achaea; the *Apollo Parnopios* on the Acropolis, Athens, commemorating Athens's salvation from a horde of locusts (thought by some scholars to be the Kassel *Apollo* type); and the bronze dedicatory group erected by Athens at the beginning of the Sacred Way at Delphi from one-tenth of the spoils of the Battle of Marathon. The motley lineup of figures in the Marathon group included gods (Apollo, Athena), the eponymous heroes of the Athenian tribes (Erechtheus, Kekrops, and so on), mythical Athenian kings (Theseus, Kodros), and the contemporary military hero Miltiades. The arrangement, to which Hellenistic rulers (Antigonos, Demetrios, Ptolemy) were added later, was probably side by side on a long rectangular base, similar to the monument of the eponymous heroes on the west side of the Athenian Agora.

Three Athena Statues

Three other important single statues loom large in any discussion of Phidias's style and career. The first of these, the *Athena Areia* dedicated in the sanctuary of Athena at Plataea, is said to have been over life-size and of a compos-

Phidias (sculpting)

ite technique in which the drapery was gold-covered while the flesh parts (head, arms) were carved in marble. This technique, an elaboration of that known as "akrolithic," in which the extremities are carved in stone and attached to a wooden core, is closely akin to the chryselephantine technique. The *Athena Areia,* paid for again from spoils of the Persian Wars, may have been a pan-Hellenic dedication, perhaps erected after the Peace of Kallias (449 B.C.). Pausanias connected it with the spoils of the Battle of Marathon, while Plutarch (*Life of Aristides*) preferred the Battle of Plataea (479 B.C.).

The *Athena Promachos,* a colossal standing bronze statue of Athena armed, was erected about 450 B.C. on the Acropolis, almost certainly north of the site of the Parthenon. While there are dim reflections of it on Athenian coins of the 2d century A.D. as an imposing element in the appearance of the Acropolis, no undisputed copies have yet come to light. The height of the *Athena Promachos* has been estimated as up to 25 feet, making Pausanias's comment that sailors could see sunlight reflected from her helmet and spear tip as they rounded Cape Sounion not impossible. The coins show Athena holding a Nike in her right hand; she may have balanced a shield or spear with her left. The overall composition may not have differed greatly from that of the *Athena Parthenos.*

Phidias perfected a different, peaceful interpretation of the patron goddess of Athens in the *Athena Lemnia,* dedicated on the Acropolis, also about 450 B.C., by cleruchs—Athenian citizens who garrisoned a military colony on the island of Lemnos (Pausanias). The beauty and delicate proportions of this statue are praised by ancient authors, especially Lucian (*Imagines*). On the basis of A. Furtwängler's reconstruction (1893), combining a body in Dresden and a head in Bologna, generally favored by scholars, the goddess appears unarmed, looking downward at her helmet, which she holds in her right hand. In this original, unconventional work, we see Phidias's ennobling, yet humanizing vision of the Olympian gods taking shape.

Attributed Works and Parthenon Activity

Among numerous other statues ascribed by classical authors to Phidias, much scholarly argument has ensued over identification of the *Amazon* submitted by Phidias to the famous competition at the Artemision of Ephesus, which received second place to Polykleitos's entry (Pliny, *Natural History*). Many scholars have favored identification of this work with the Mattei *Amazon* (Vatican Museums, Rome). Other even more controversial sculptures include an *Aphrodite Ourania* in Elis, Greece (Pausanias), in which the goddess rested her left foot on a tortoise, and an Aphrodite seen by Pliny (*Natural History*) in the Portico of Octavia in Rome, thought by some scholars to have been a seated statue; these attributions, however, remain hypothetical.

Although Plutarch states that Phidias was in charge of the entire Parthenon project, exactly how he was able to organize and supervise the complex staff of designers, sculptors, and masons required for the construction and execution of the building and its sculptures is still not understood. While scholars have been unable to point definitively to any single figure or feature in the sculptural ensemble as being by Phidias, B. Schweitzer (1940) has proposed that the underlying scheme was Phidias's and that he may well have participated in the carving of individual metopes, figures in the frieze, and three-dimensional statues in the pedimental groups.

The *Athena Parthenos*

Phidias's most justly famed creations were his two colossal gold-and-ivory cult statues. The *Athena Parthenos,* probably over 35 feet in height, is known through brief literary descriptions in Pliny (*Natural History*) and Pausanias and from copies and representations in various media. The picture that emerges is a standing, fully armed, and elaborately dressed Athena, holding a small statue of Nike in her outstretched right hand and cradling her spear with her left. Her shield rested against her right leg; nearby was a coiled serpent. Her helmet, sandals, and shield were richly decorated; the base of the statue depicted the birth of Pandora watched by 20 gods. The technique of construction, while not known for certain, probably included face, arms, and other skin areas pieced together in ivory, while the drapery, of very thin gold, was applied in detachable sections over a shaped wooden interior. The core probably contained an armature of beams. The projecting right arm may have been supported by a column, as is the case in the Varvakeion statuette. Both the *Athena Parthenos* and the *Zeus* had a

reservoir under the base for liquid, which helped to keep the statue from drying out and cracking.

The two best copies of the *Athena Parthenos,* the Varvakeion and Lenormant statuettes, both marble miniatures of Roman date (National Museum, Athens), are invaluable for providing a general idea of the statue's proportions and appearance. Two other small replicas, from Patras, Greece, and Bitolj, Yugoslavia, have been identified. Among other sculptural copies and adaptations, the over life-size version from the Library of the Sanctuary of Athena in Pergamon (Staatliche Museen, Berlin) is very important. A detailed reproduction of the head exists on a gem signed by the Roman gem cutter Aspasios (Museo Nazionale Romano, Rome). In addition, the battle of Greeks and Amazons represented on the shield is known, at least in its main outlines, through a number of copies, the most important of which include the unfinished shield on the Lenormant statuette, the "Strangford Shield" (British Museum, London), and individual pairs of fighters on large neo-Attic reliefs (Museum, Piraeus). The combatants, arranged in pairs, swirl around a large central Gorgon head. The compositions of the battle of gods and giants, on the concave side of the shield, and the birth of Pandora on the base have still not been identified with certainty.

The *Zeus*

The other gold-and-ivory colossus, the seated cult statue in the Temple of Zeus at Olympia, received extravagant praise from writers in antiquity (Pausanias; Dio Chrysostomos, *Orationes;* Strabo, *Geography;* Pliny, *Natural History;* and Quintilian, *Institutio oratoria*). Phidias depicted Zeus seated upon an elaborately decorated throne adorned with gold, ivory, ebony, and semiprecious stones. He constructed the statue in a workshop just west of the Temple of Zeus which had measurements identical to those of the cella. Strabo's remark that if the god had arisen he would have unroofed the temple suggests, however, that Phidias did not adequately plan the statue for its restricted spatial setting.

Excavations of the workshop have uncovered much debris, including terra-cotta forms used to fashion sections of the exterior gold plating of the drapery, scraps of worked ivory, tools, and fragments of molded glass and worked obsidian from the inlaid ornamentation of the statue. When the information is published, it will be invaluable for interpreting and dating the statue, as well as for our knowledge of the chryselephantine technique.

According to Pausanias, Zeus, like the *Athena Parthenos,* held a Nike in his right hand; his left hand held a scepter. Every part of the god's costume and throne was covered with ornamentation; the slaughter of the Niobids, on the sides of the seat, and the birth of Aphrodite, on the base, are only two of the elaborate compositions mentioned. Surprisingly few copies of the *Zeus* have been identified; the entire composition is preserved on Hadrianic bronze coins from Elis, several gems of Roman date, and a small silver statuette (Museum of Fine Arts, Boston). The head also appears on Roman bronze coins from Elis.

The date of the *Zeus* has been much debated; some scholars believe that it was finished about 448 B.C., before Phidias went to Athens to assume command of the work on the Parthenon, while others, on the basis of indications about Phidias's trial for impiety at Athens, advocate a date after 432 B.C. The later date is now supported by the style of the pottery found with the workshop debris at Olympia, which belongs to the last quarter of the 5th century. Among this pottery is a small black-glaze mug with ''I belong to Phidias'' scratched in Greek on the bottom.

Phidias was a master of many media and techniques and unsurpassed at innovation. His conceptual genius translated the new interpretations of the gods that were emerging in contemporary Athenian literature into tangible, visible images. Given free rein by powerful patrons for the most grandiose commissions in the history of Greek art, Phidias responded with the creation of the high classical style in sculpture. With the exception of Michelangelo in the 16th century, perhaps no other Western sculptor has been more influential upon subsequent generations. In the light of what we now know of Phidias's style, the judgment of ancient critics, who considered him to have been the greatest Greek sculptor, seems eminently justified.

Further Reading

For a discussion of the ancient sources on Phidias see Jerome J. Pollitt, *The Art of Greece, 1400-31* B.C. (1965). The article ''Phidias'' by Giovanni Becatti in the *Encyclopedia of World Art,* vol. 11 (1966), has a bibliography of the earlier scholarly literature. Phidias is also discussed in G. M. A. Richter, *The Sculpture and Sculptors of the Greeks* (4th ed. 1970). □

Philip

Philip (died 1676), Native American chief, led his Wampanoag tribe and their allies in a losing fight against the encroachments of New England colonists.

Philip was born probably at the tribal village of the Wampanoag Indians at Mount Hope, R.I. His father, Massassoit, sachem (chief) of the tribe, took his two sons to the Plymouth settlement and asked that they be given English names; the elder son was renamed Alexander, and the other was called Philip.

Alexander became sachem of the Wampanoag upon the father's death. In 1661, however, Alexander was arrested by the Plymouth Bay colonists; on the way to Plymouth he sickened and died suddenly, causing the Native Americans to believe that he had been poisoned. The next year Philip became sachem.

As sachem, Philip renewed his father's treaty with the colonists and lived peacefully with them for 9 years. But gradually Philip became hostile to the whites because their increasing numbers resulted in scarcity of game, failure of the Native Americans' fisheries, and encroachment on Na-

tive American lands. Purchasing English goods or guns with land, the Native Americans were gradually being forced into marginal swamplands.

Philip's arrogance contributed to the growing tensions. He declared himself the equal of his ''brother,'' Charles II. He also began plotting against the settlers. In 1671 he was summoned to Taunton, Mass., and confronted with evidence of his plotting, but he was released after signing a statement of submission, paying a fine, and surrendering part of his tribe's firearms.

The open break between the two races came in 1675. Philip's former secretary, Sassamon, was murdered by the Wampanoag, who believed that Sassamon had betrayed Native American secrets to the settlers. Three Wampanoag braves were executed for this crime. Philip reacted by sending his tribe's women and children to live with the Narragansett Indians and by making an alliance with the Nipmuck. On June 24, 1675, their attack on a colonial village triggered King Philip's War.

The fighting spread to Plymouth and Massachusetts Bay colonies, west to the Connecticut River, and north to Vermont. The Native Americans killed men, women, and children in these raids. The United Colonies of New England sent a combined army to try for a decisive battle, but Philip preferred stealth, ambush, and surprise raids in which he generally displayed wily and effective leadership. However, he was unsuccessful in persuading the Mohegan and Mohawk Indians to join him.

The colonists tried a new strategy. On Dec. 19, 1675, Governor Josiah Winslow and 1,000 troops attacked the Narragansett village, killed 1,600 Native Americans, and captured the Wampanoag women and children, selling many of them into slavery in the West Indies and South America. They also destroyed Native American crops, offered amnesty to deserters, and advertised a reward for any Native American killed in battle.

Philip saw his army melt away. With a few faithful followers he was pursued from place to place; meanwhile, his wife and son were captured and sold into slavery. In the swamps near Mount Hope he was shot on Aug. 12, 1676, by a Native American serving the colonials. Philip's body was beheaded and drawn and quartered, and his head was exhibited at Plymouth for 20 years.

Philip's war saw 12 colonial towns destroyed, thousands of deaths, and colonial debts of £100,000. His victories were largely the result of colonial inefficiency, but the war was the result of increasing pressure for land from the growing number of British colonists in America.

Further Reading

Accounts of Philip are in George Madison Bodge, *Soldiers in King Philip's War* (1892; 3d ed. 1906); G. W. Ellis and J. E. Morris, *King Philip's War* (1906); James Truslow Adams, *The Founding of New England* (1921); and Douglas Edward Leach, *Flintlock and Tomahawk: New England in King Philip's War* (1958).

Additional Sources

Apes, William, *Eulogy on King Philip, as pronounced at the Odeon in Federal Street, Boston,* Brookfield, Mass.: L.A. Dexter, 1985. □

Philip II

Philip II (1165-1223), sometimes called Philip Augustus, ruled France from 1180 to 1223. He made the Crown more powerful than any feudal lord, more than tripled the royal domain, and turned the balance of power between France and England in favor of France.

Born in Paris on Aug. 21, 1165, Philip became the seventh Capetian king of France in 1180, when his father, Louis VII, died. As he grew to manhood, he became distrustful, cynical, and crafty, but physically sickly and tense. He had a practical intelligence but was not particularly interested in study.

Wars with England

Philip inherited from his father the difficult problem of trying to defend the small royal domain centering on Paris and Orléans against the much more extensive holdings of Henry II of England. By inheritance, marriage, and war, Henry had acquired lands extending from Normandy on the English Channel through Maine, Anjou, and Aquitaine to the Pyrenees. Although young Philip faced seemingly hopeless odds, he exploited the jealousy of Henry's sons, and when Henry invested his favored youngest son, John, with all the King's Continental holdings except Normandy, John's older brother Richard became an ally of Philip and fought his aging father. In 1189 Henry was forced to recognize Richard as heir to all his lands and Philip as his feudal lord for his lands in France. Shortly afterward, Henry II died.

The power struggle had been interrupted by the preparations for the Third Crusade following the fall of Jerusalem in 1187. Now Philip reluctantly joined Frederick I (Frederick Barbarossa) and Richard I, who had become king of England on the death of Henry II. Philip and Richard went to the East together but soon began to quarrel. When the Anglo-French forces recaptured Acre, Philip felt that he had done enough crusading and returned to France to take advantage of Richard's absence in the East.

Richard, unable to capture Jerusalem from Saladin, returned home through Austria but was taken prisoner there and held for ransom. He did not reach the West until May 1194, and in his absence Philip had joined forces with John to recover Normandy. The ensuing warfare between Philip and Richard ended when Richard was killed (1199) in a minor skirmish in central France and John became king of England.

Philip now became John's enemy and used feudal law to dispossess him of his Continental holdings. In 1202 he summoned John to his court to answer a charge made

against him, but John refused to come, and Philip therefore declared John's holdings in France forfeit, occupying Normandy and all English lands north of the Loire River. With the occupation of Normandy, the Capetians now had access to the English Channel and deprived John of easy access to his Continental fiefs.

Relationship with the Pope

Although preoccupied with defending his kingdom against England, Philip was not unmindful of the opportunities for acquisitions in southern France. In 1207 Pope Innocent III invited Philip to lead a crusade there against the spread of heresy, but Philip declined to take part unless the Pope made John stop fighting in Poitou—something Innocent III could not do. A decade later Philip was still avoiding direct participation in the crusade, but he did permit his son, Louis of France, to lead a French army into Toulouse.

In January 1213, John was excommunicated and deposed for his spoliation of the Church. His troubles with his own English barons encouraged Pope Innocent III to urge Philip to invade England, seize John, and put Louis of France, now married to a niece of John's, on the English throne. But when John turned over England to the Pope and received it back as a papal fief, Innocent ordered Philip to give up the invasion.

John, restored to power with papal protection, then organized an Anglo-Flemish-German coalition to recover his French fiefs. In 1214 Philip met the challenge by sending his son Louis of France as leader of a French army against John, who had led an attack from southwestern France. But John fled rather than fight. Meanwhile, Philip led another French army northeastward from Paris to meet John's ally, Otto IV of Germany, who was about to invade France with an army of English, German, and Flemish knights. Philip crushed this army at Bouvines on July 27, 1214. The students in Paris celebrated the French victory for 7 days and 7 nights.

Bouvines was one of the decisive battles of European history because it led to the ruin of John, upset the balance of power in Europe in favor of France for over a century, and marked the end of the German Empire as the dominant political power in the Christian West. After Bouvines, John returned to England, where he died in 1216. Philip was able to live out his life in peace, certain of Capetian ascendancy.

Internal Reforms

While Philip was enlarging his kingdom, he was also developing and instituting a plan of civil service whereby men were given high office on the basis of competence rather than hereditary right. To assure obedience in the outlying provinces, where distance encouraged independence, Philip instituted salaried bailiffs responsible for the administrative, military, and judicial supervision of the areas assigned to them.

Philip encouraged the growth of town governments by selling charters and privileges to them, and thus he won the support of town bourgeoisie against the restless nobility. Most of the towns granted new charters were on the frontiers of the royal domain. For Philip they were defensive posts

with military obligations. Incomes from this source, from the fees levied on foreign merchants and fairs for protection, and from the profits of justice gave the King the money needed to finance a professional army and government bureaucracy. By the time Philip died, he had become the richest and most powerful lord in the realm.

Philip loved Paris, which during his reign became the religious, political, and academic capital of France. It was Philip who gave the first charter to the University of Paris. Written after a town-and-gown riot, it recognized the right of students to enjoy clerical status and autonomy. Philip also built a wall around Paris for its defense and, in 1186, ordered the streets paved with stone to overcome the air pollution and stench caused by garbage and other household waste thrown into the streets and the effluvia of the pigs and other animals that roamed about.

Ill since September 1222, Philip died at Mantes on July 14, 1223, while on his way to Paris. He left France prosperous and at peace, and the strongest power in western Europe. He was called Augustus by his biographer, Rigord, who compared him to the Roman caesars because he had enlarged the realm and increased its income.

Further Reading

The most thorough study of Philip II is in German. In English, Philip is discussed in more general works on his time: Achille Luchaive, *Social France at the Time of Philip Augustus* (1912); Charles Petit-Dutaillis, *The Feudal Monarchy in France and England from the Tenth to the Thirteenth Century* (1936); Robert Fawtier, *The Capetian Kings of France: Monarchy and Nation, 987-1328* (1962); and Kenneth Setton, *A History of the Crusades* (2 vols., 1962), which includes a discussion of the Third Crusade. □

Philip II

Philip II (382-336 B.C.) was a king of Macedon, a conqueror, and a leader of the Corinthian League. He suppressed his feudal barons, forged a professional army infused with a national spirit, and developed novel military tactics.

Philip II was born in Macedon to King Amyntas II of the royal house of Argeadae and his Illyrian wife, Eurydice. Philip cherished his Greek heritage. Some Greeks, especially the hostile Athenian Demosthenes, disclaimed his and the Macedonians' claim to membership in the Greek race and labeled Philip a barbarian or non-Greek. This left him with a marked inferiority complex. Culturally the Macedonians were less advanced than their southern Greek neighbors, had remained rural rather than urban, and retained a strongly Indo-European feudal and tribal sociopolitical structure. As king, Philip would actively work to import Greek culture to Macedon and to increase trade and urbanization.

As a youth of 15, Philip was sent as a hostage to Thebes, where he lived for 3 years. The military and political ideas acquired there greatly influenced him. He became king in 359 B.C., after his older brother Perdikkas was killed in battle fighting the Illyrians. As regent for Perdikkas's young son Amyntas, Philip jealously guarded the throne against three pretenders whom foreign powers supported. Only 24 years old, Philip acted with skill and energy, defeating the hostile powers and winning the army's support.

Philip ruled his feudal nobles as chieftain, or "first among equals," in a highly aristocratic structure. His power, given to him by the chief nobles, included supreme generalship of the aristocratic cavalry and infantry forces, supreme judge as leader, or father, of the tribes, and chief priest. By acclamation, the assembly of the army, which possessed the right and duty, confirmed Philip's privileges.

Forging a Professional Army

Philip extended his dominance over the northern Macedonian tribes and their petty chieftains and thereby established the foundations of Macedonian greatness in the north. The landed nobility, or select "Companions," were bound to serve him in a feudal manner as cavalry. Philip was perhaps the first to organize the free peasantry and shepherds into a regular infantry, to incorporate them into military territorial divisions, and to raise their political status, allowing them to participate in the assembly of the army and to obtain its privileges. This strengthened his royal position and diminished the power of the aristocracy.

Philip contracted an alliance with Neoptolemos, king of the Illyrian Molossians, and married his daughter Olympias in 357 B.C. The proud, impulsive, and independent queen bore him Alexander (later, Alexander the Great) in 356 B.C. and a daughter, Cleopatra, the next year.

Building an Empire

In 357 B.C. Philip seized Thracian Amphipolis and the silver and gold mines of Mt. Pangeios, which produced 1,000 talents annually. The mines were the foundation of his power. His new silver and gold coins quickly structured Aegean commerce. Athens retaliated by claiming protection over Amphipolis and waged 11 years of intermittent warfare. Following the Sacred War over Delphi, which erupted in 356 B.C., Philip became involved in southern Thessaly. In 348 B.C. he destroyed Chalcidian Olynthos.

By 340 B.C. Philip held the territory from the Hellespont to Thermopylae. He had also pressed eastward toward the Bosporus and employed, for the first time in Greece, the Syracusan siege machines against Perinthos and Byzantion. Southern Greece feared Philip's empire, but many hailed him as the only man capable of ending their petty, parochial interstate wars. In his *Philip* (346 B.C.), the Athenian Isocrates urged Philip to unite Greece in a military federation and bring peace and concord to the Greeks by waging war against the Persian Empire.

A minor disruption, again centered at Delphi, brought Philip southward as arbiter, but hostile Thebes and Athens gathered forces against him at Boeotian Chaeronea in the summer of 338 B.C.. He defeated the Greeks, and the following winter a meeting of all the Greek states except Sparta was held at Corinth. There Philip constructed a league of states. He was automatically elected commander in chief of the self-governing military allies.

In 337 B.C. Philip prepared Macedon and the league to invade Persia. By early 336 B.C. his general, Parmenion, crossed the Hellespont, but at home jealous noblemen and Philip's wife plotted his assassination. At the festive wedding of his daughter, Cleopatra, to King Alexander of Epirus, Philip was stabbed to death.

Further Reading

Biographies of Philip's son, Alexander the Great, usually devote the first chapter to Philip and Macedon. A thorough and scholarly work is Ulrich Wilcken, *Alexander the Great* (1931; trans. 1932), and interesting and insightful is the study by Andrew Robert Burn, *Alexander the Great and the Hellenistic Empire* (1947; 2d rev. ed. 1964). Richard Haywood, *Ancient Greece and the Near East* (1964), contains an excellent description of the rise of Macedon and of Philip's Greek world. See also *The Cambridge Ancient History*, vol. 6: *Macedon, 401-301* B.C. (1927), edited by J. B. Bury, S. A. Cook, and F. E. Adcock.

Additional Sources

Cawkwell, George, *Philip of Macedon,* London; Boston: Faber & Faber, 1978.
Ellis, John R., *Philip II and Macedonian imperialism,* London: Thames and Hudson, 1976.

Hammond, N. G. L., *Philip of Macedon,* Baltimore: Johns Hopkins University Press, 1994.
Philip II of Macedon: a life from the ancient sources, Westport, Conn.: Praeger, 1992.
Philip of Macedon, Athens: Ekdotike Athenon, 1980. ☐

Philip II

Philip II (1527-1598) was king of Spain from 1556 to 1598. During his reign the Spanish Empire was severely challenged and its economic, social, and political institutions strained almost to the breaking point.

The son of Emperor Charles V, Philip II inherited the larger portion of his father's dominions: Spain, the Low Countries (basically the Netherlands and Belgium of today), Franche-Comté, Sicily and southern Italy, the duchy of Milan, and Spain's colonies in the New World, including Mexico and much of South America. But the inheritance inevitably included the host of problems which his father had left unsolved or which were incapable of being solved. The other part of Charles's dominions, the Holy Roman Empire, was bequeathed to his brother Ferdinand, Philip's uncle.

Philip was born in Valladolid on May 21, 1527, at the outset of the religious and political wars that divided Europe and drained the resources of every major European country. France, the principal opponent of Emperor Charles's ambition, was likewise the chief rival of Philip's Spain. When he acceded to the throne in 1556, the two countries were still at war; peace was concluded at Cateau-Cambrésis in 1559, largely because both states were financially exhausted.

The need to find money and enforce order in his territories led to Philip's clash with his Dutch subjects, a clash that produced the first war for national independence in modern European history and eventually drew Philip into the ill-fated Armada expedition. Spain's resources, including its commercial and military lifeline to northern and southern Italy, were meanwhile threatened in the Mediterranean by the Turkish fleet and the incursions of pirates, largely operating out of North African ports.

On the one side combating rebellious Protestant subjects and on the other confronting the advance of Islam, Philip II has often been depicted as the secular arm of the Catholic Church, a religious zealot who sought to erase heresy and infidelity through military conquest. This, however, is a simplification and is misleading. He was indeed a devout Catholic and vitally concerned with the suppression of "heresy" in all the territory over which he ruled. But his policies and choices must also be viewed in the light of what he considered to be Spanish national interests.

Early Life

Philip's first marriage (1543) was to his cousin Maria of Portugal, who lived but 2 years, leaving a son, Don Carlos.

To consolidate his empire and afford protection for his holdings in the Low Countries, Charles then married Philip to Mary Tudor of England, the Catholic queen of a basically Protestant country. Philip's stay in England was not a happy one, and Mary died in 1558 to be succeeded by her half sister, Elizabeth. His ties with England broken, Philip returned to Spain via Flanders in 1559. In that year the peace treaty with France was signed. The temporary harmony between the two powers was symbolized by Philip's marriage with Elizabeth of Valois, the daughter of the king of France, who proved to be his favorite wife.

Philip had succeeded his father as king of Spain in 1556. Unlike Charles V, Philip was to be a "national" monarch instead of a ruler who traveled from one kingdom to another. Though he was to travel widely throughout the Iberian Peninsula, he would never leave it again.

Personally, Philip was fair, spoke softly, and had an icy self-mastery; in the words of one of his ministers, he had a smile that cut like a sword. He immersed himself in an ocean of paperwork, studying dispatches and documents and adding marginal comments on them while scores of other documents and dispatches piled up on tables and in anterooms.

With the problems of communication in Philip's far-flung empire, once a decision was made it could not be undone. As king, he preferred to reserve all final decisions to himself; he mistrusted powerful and independent personalities and rarely reposed much confidence in aides. This personal stamp of authority during Philip's reign was in sharp contrast to the era of minister-favorites in 17th-century Spain. His private life included a delight in art, in the cultivation of flowers, in religious reading (his reign coincided with the great age of Spanish mysticism), and above all in the conception and building of the Escorial, the royal palace outside Madrid whose completion was perhaps the greatest joy of his life.

A combination palace, monastery, and mausoleum, the Escorial was Philip's preferred place for working. In a complex that included a place for his own tomb, naturally the thought of his successor concerned Philip greatly. His son Don Carlos was abnormal, mentally and physically, and on no account fit to become a responsible ruler. Philip was aware that contacts had been made between his son and political enemies. He had Don Carlos arrested, and what followed is one of the great historical enigmas: Don Carlos died on July 25, 1568, under mysterious circumstances that have never been explained satisfactorily. Did Philip have his son executed or did he die of natural causes? There is no persuasive proof on one side or the other. This incident was one of the most publicized in Philip's reign and one which naturally served to blacken his reputation. In any event, his fourth marriage, to Anne of Austria, produced five children, one of whom survived to succeed as Philip III.

Relations with Rome

During the Council of Trent (1545-1563) there was usually strong doctrinal accord between the papacy and Spanish bishops. The major difference lay in varying interpretations of the rights of Spanish bishops and their king vis-à-vis the Holy See. The King had almost total control over the Spanish Catholic Church, and although Spanish arms could advance Catholic interests, if Philip's Spain were to become supreme in Europe the Pope risked being reduced to a chaplain. One momentous occasion when they worked together came in the joint venture of Spain, the Vatican, and Venice against the Turkish navy. At Lepanto, in 1571, the Catholic forces devastated the enemy fleet. It was the most signal victory of Philip's career. Yet, although the Turks soon rebounded, Philip was never again to ally himself so strongly with Rome. The relations between Spain and the Vatican illustrate how senseless it is to speak of the "monolithic nature" of Catholicism in this era.

Dutch Revolt

In an attempt to shore up his depleted treasury and instill more centralization into his dominions, Philip disregarded the prerogatives and local traditions in the Low Countries, the most prosperous of the territories under his rule. In the 1560s he sought to exact more taxes, to impose more bishops, and to reshuffle the administration, thus provoking an increasingly militant opposition.

Protestant attacks upon Catholic churches, coupled with increasing resistance from the predominantly Catholic population, were followed by a severe response from Spain. A Spanish army moved against the rebels, executed several of their leaders, and opened the way to a broader war which lasted throughout Philip's reign. It was truly a war for national independence, with brutality and heroism on both

sides and a growing identification of Protestantism (especially Calvinism) with opposition to Spain's political, religious, and economic policies. The rebels, entrenched in the north, declared themselves independent under the name of the United Provinces. The southern part (roughly the area comprising Belgium) remained under Spanish control.

Since the Dutch were subsidized by the English, and since Spanish supply ships could not safely move through the English Channel, Philip concluded that a conquest of England was necessary for the pacification of the Netherlands. But at the same time that the Dutch were in revolt, there were repeated clashes between the French royal armies and French Calvinists. The ups and downs of the warfare in France and in the Netherlands were viewed as barometers of the fortunes of European Protestantism versus Catholicism. After Philip's death, a truce with the Dutch was arranged in 1609. Though war was to break out again, the independence of the United Provinces was recognized in 1648.

The Armada

The need to cut off English subsidies and control the English Channel so as to throttle the Dutch revolt led Philip to undertake the Armada, the most famous event of his reign. The plan was for a huge fleet to rendezvous with Spanish troops in the Netherlands and then proceed to the military conquest of England, serving Philip's military and political ends and immeasurably injuring the Protestant cause. The skill of the English navy and adverse weather conditions led to a total fiasco. Though most of his ships eventually returned home to port and though Philip still dreamed of a future campaign, the expense of the expedition and the psychological shock of failure resulted in the "invincible" Armada's becoming the symbol of Philip's failure to achieve a Spanish predominance in Europe.

French Relations

As Philip sought to put down the rebellion in the Netherlands, he fomented dissension in France. French Protestants were sometimes subsidized by Spanish agents to ensure confusion in the enemy camp. Philip tried (unsuccessfully) to install his own candidate on the French throne, and Spanish troops became embroiled in the French wars. The struggle with France drew Spanish strength away from the Netherlands and so eased the pressure on the Dutch rebels. Peace was reached at the Treaty of Vervins in 1598, several months before Philip's death.

Domestic Affairs

The complexity and extent of these foreign ventures had, of course, a tremendous impact on the economy and life of Spain. There was a constant need for money and in a country where only careers in the Church and the army carried prestige and where commerce and manual labor in general were frowned upon, the already-staggering economy was crippled by a series of disasters. The costly adventures abroad were punctuated by abrasive relations between Philip and his Spanish domains over taxation and jurisdiction; a diminishing flow of silver from the American mines; a decreasing market for Spanish goods; a severe inflation; several declarations of government bankruptcy; and an agricultural crisis that sent thousands into the cities and left vast areas uncultivated. All these, together with plagues and the defeat of the Armada, were crushing blows—economically, socially, and psychologically.

Any one of these myriad problems and crises would have taxed the ingenuity of a government. Taken together and exacerbated by the strain of incessant warfare, they shook Spain to its roots. The union of Portugal to Spain in 1580 may have given Philip satisfaction but hardly lightened his burdens. He worked methodically, even fatalistically, puzzled by the workings of a God who would permit such calamities to occur. Spain had already entered into a period of sharp decline at his death on Sept. 13, 1598, at El Escorial.

Further Reading

Although it does not emphasize social and economic issues as much as contemporary studies do, Roger Bigelow Merriman, *The Rise of the Spanish Empire in the Old World and in the New*, vol. 4 (1934), remains a superb study of Philip II and his reign based on extensive archival research. A good introduction to the Spain of Philip II, with special emphasis on social and economic forces, is John H. Elliott, *Imperial Spain, 1469-1716* (1963); it has a fine bibliography. Also excellent are John Lynch, *Spain under the Habsburgs,* vol. 1 (1964), and H.G. Koenigsberger, *The Habsburgs and Europe, 1516-1660* (1971). A lively narrative enriched by verbal portraits of important figures of the time is Edward Grierson, *The Fatal Inheritance: Philip II and the Spanish Netherlands* (1969). The Armada expedition is brilliantly recounted by Garrett Mattingly in *The Armada* (1959), one of the finest and most interesting products of modern historical scholarship. Recommended for general historical background are Pieter Geyl, *The Revolt of the Netherlands, 1555-1609* (1932; 2d ed. 1958), and John H. Elliott, *Europe Divided, 1559-1598* (1969). ☐

Philip III

Philip III (1578-1621) was king of Spain from 1598 to 1621. He was dominated by minister-favorites, and his personal impress on events was slight.

On April 4, 1578, Philip III was born in Madrid, the son of King Philip II, whom he succeeded in 1598, when he was 20 years old. From the outset of his reign he virtually gave over the government to Francisco de Lerma, his favorite, who was the true ruler of Spain for the next 2 decades. Philip's inheritance included the crises and dilemmas that had wracked Spain during the previous half century. During the first 2 years of his reign, the country was ravaged by a plague that probably wiped out the 15-percent increase in the Spanish population in the 16th century. Although projects of a reforming nature, including plans to restructure the tax system, were submitted to the King and his ministers, regional traditionalism and vested interests blocked change.

In 1607 the Crown was forced to repudiate its debts. The drain of funds caused by the Dutch War and the futility of pursuing the struggle in the Netherlands led to a 12-year truce in 1609. In effect, it indicated Spain's failure to subdue its rebellious subjects in the Netherlands. To camouflage this failure, news of the truce was accompanied by a popular measure, the expulsion of the Moriscos (Moors converted to Christianity). They were looked upon with suspicion as potential allies of Spain's enemies and with resentment as hardworking people who saved most of their money. Stringent measures against them had been taken earlier under Philip II. Now about 275,000 Moriscos were expelled; most went to North Africa. Spain suffered economic loss, especially in Aragon and Valencia, though not as much as following the expulsion of the Jews in 1492.

The time limit on the truce with the Dutch symbolized the expectancy throughout Europe that war would again break out, and not only in the Netherlands. Spain entered the Thirty Years War, which began in Bohemia in 1618, but its early successes were short-lived, and Spain's participation in the war contributed still more to its overall decline.

Lerma was overthrown in 1618 and succeeded by the Duke of Uceda. Meanwhile, Philip engaged in devotional exercises or whiled away his time hunting, enjoying the theater, and hosting lavish banquets, his role seemingly reduced to providing an heir to the throne. His marriage to Margaret of Austria produced eight children, one of whom succeeded him as Philip IV upon his death on March 31, 1621. His daughter Anne of Austria became the consort of Louis XIII of France.

Further Reading

A good introduction to the problems of Philip's reign, especially the social and economic issues, is John H. Elliott, *Imperial Spain, 1469-1716* (1963). R. Trevor Davies, *The Golden Century of Spain, 1501-1621* (1937; rev. ed. 1954), is a useful survey of the reign and includes a discussion of the literature and art of the period.

Additional Sources

Dennis, Amarie, *Philip III: the shadow of a king,* Madrid, Spain: A.W. Dennis, 1985. □

Philip IV

Philip IV (1268-1314), called Philip the Fair, ruled France from 1285 to 1314. His reign was one of the most momentous in medieval history because Philip successfully challenged the traditional power of the papacy in France, thereby strengthening the monarchy.

Son of King Philip III and Joan of Navarre, Philip IV was tall, handsome, and fair, but his character remains enigmatic. His power was great as a result of the Crown's acquisition of numerous fiefs in recent decades, but long and expensive wars with England caused a severe financial crisis. This crisis prompted the King to raise money through rigorous collection of incomes due, forced loans, high taxes, and debasement of the coinage. The Jews were expelled from France in 1306 and the "Lombards" (Italian bankers) in 1311. The property of each group was confiscated. Philip also seized the wealth of the Knights Templar after pressuring the weak Pope Clement V into suppressing them.

Philip introduced various governmental reforms, including the Chamber of Accounts to supervise finances. The Parlement of Paris, a judicial body, was made more specialized. A new institution, the States General, which included clergy, nobles, and commoners, was first called in 1302 in order to win support for royal policy against the papacy.

Continuing financial crises led to a conflict with Pope Boniface VIII over the right of the King to tax the French clergy without papal consent. The Pope finally conceded the point when threatened by the loss of his revenues from France.

In 1301 Philip's conflict with the papacy was revived by the arrest of Bishop Bernard Saisset of Pamiers. The bishop's trial in the royal court led to Boniface's demand that he be released and his convocation of all French bishops to Rome in November 1302. In reply Philip called the first States General, which met at Notre Dame in Paris in April 1302. At this meeting he launched a vicious attack against the Pope and against papal right to intervene in French affairs. The papal council in Rome resulted in the papal bull *Unam sanctam,* which reaffirmed papal authority over temporal affairs and the papal right to correct a king's morally wrong public acts. Philip's reply was evasive. He had already sent Guillaume de Nogaret to seize the Pope preparatory to having him tried and deposed by a council. Boniface was seized and mistreated at Anagni in September 1303. Liberated by the townspeople, the aged pope died 3 weeks later of the effects of the ordeal.

Philip summoned the States General twice more—in 1308 and 1314—chiefly in order to gain support for his wars against the Flemish. He died on Nov. 29, 1314.

Further Reading

The conflict with the papacy that occurred during Philip's reign has been the subject of numerous studies, such as that of Philip Hughes, *A History of the Church,* vol. 3 (1949). Charles T. Wood, *Philip the Fair and Boniface VIII* (1967), gives excerpts from various works which show the state of the problem at the time. For an overall view of Philip's reign see "France: The Last Capetians" in *The Cambridge Medieval History,* vol. 7 (1932).

Additional Sources

Strayer, Joseph Reese, *The reign of Philip the Fair,* Princeton, N.J.: Princeton University Press, 1980.

Wood, Charles T., comp., *Philip the Fair and Boniface VIII: state vs. papacy,* Huntington, N.Y.: R. E. Krieger Pub. Co., 1976, 1971. □

Philip IV

Philip IV (1605-1665) was king of Spain from 1621 to 1665. During his reign Spain was engaged in foreign wars and torn by internal revolt.

Born on April 8, 1605, Philip IV succeeded his father, Philip III, in 1621. He was more intelligent than his father but like him allowed his government to be run by minister-favorites. Philip's principal minister, Gaspar de Guzmán, Count of Olivares, dominated his councils and was the effective ruler of Spain for more than 20 years. In 1627 the ruinous expenses of Spain's involvement in the Thirty Years War forced the government to declare itself bankrupt; the war effort continued, however, and the Mantuan campaign (1628-1631) led to an open conflict with France, which became intensified in 1635.

Spanish troops at first came close to Paris, but the situation rapidly deteriorated. Olivares's desperate attempts to raise funds for the prosecution of the war provoked dissent and rebellion, and in 1640 Catalonia went into open revolt, murdered the king's agent there, and welcomed French aid in its struggle against the government of Castile. Soon afterward, Portugal rebelled and declared itself independent from Spain. Olivares's counterpart in France, Cardinal Richelieu, supplied money to both Catalonia and Portugal as French troops occupied Catalonia.

In January 1643, after visiting the war front in Aragon, Philip dismissed Olivares and declared that he would rule without a favorite. However, he soon employed one in the person of Don Luis de Haro, a nephew of Olivares. On May 19, 1643, the Spanish infantry was vanquished by the French at Rocroi. Since the beginning of the 16th century, the Spanish infantry had been regarded as the best in Europe; its defeat symbolized the downfall of Spain as a military power.

A dreary succession of setbacks marked the second half of Philip's reign. Another bankruptcy was declared in 1647, and in the same year unsuccessful revolts against Spanish rule erupted in Sicily and Naples. These events convinced Richelieu and his successor, Cardinal Mazarin, that, by pursuing an all-out war against Spain, France could gain considerable land and power in the European theater. Thus the war between the two countries continued after the Peace of Westphalia (by which Spain officially recognized the independence of the United Provinces) had concluded the Thirty Years War in 1648. Although civil war in France (the Fronde) gave the Spanish some slight respite, it could not stave off the inevitable. For although Catalonia was won back in 1652, bankruptcy was again declared in 1653.

The union of Cromwell's England with France in the war against Spain proved to be the coup de grace. Spain lost both Dunkerque and Jamaica to the English. In the Peace of the Pyrenees, concluded with France in 1659, Spain gave up Artois and territories in the Spanish Netherlands, together with Rosellón and part of Cerdaña. As part of the "peace package," a marriage was arranged between Philip IV's daughter, Maria Theresa, and the young Louis XIV. The waiver of the Infanta's inheritance rights to Spanish territory was contingent on the payment of a dowry of 500,000 escudos, which the French as well as the Spanish knew could never be paid. After Philip's death this clause was used as a pretext for the seizure of still more Spanish territory in the Low Countries during the War of Devolution.

Philip IV died on Sept. 17, 1665, just before Portugal's independence was recognized. In the course of his reign he had married twice. His first wife, Elizabeth of Bourbon, died in 1644; their only child died 2 years later. His second wife, Maria Anna of Austria, gave birth to one son who survived, the hapless Charles II, who was destined to be the last Hapsburg monarch of Spain.

Further Reading

There is no suitable study of Philip IV in English. The best book on the earlier half of his reign is John H. Elliott, *The Revolt of the Catalans: A Study in the Decline of Spain, 1598-1640* (1963), in which he brilliantly fulfills the promise of the subtitle. Elliott's other book, *Imperial Spain, 1469-1716* (1963), is an excellent overview of the period with a choice bibliography. Recommended for general historical background are C. V. Wedgwood, *The Thirty Years War* (1938), and Carl J. Friedrich, *The Age of the Baroque, 1610-1660* (1952). □

Philip V

Philip V (1683-1746), first Bourbon king of Spain, reigned from 1700 to 1746. During this period Spain began to recover from the long decline it had experienced during the 17th century and to regain a voice in the affairs of Europe.

The grandson of Louis XIV of France and his wife Maria Theresa, daughter of Philip IV of Spain, Philip V was born in Versailles on Dec. 19, 1683. In November 1700 the last Hapsburg king of Spain, Charles II, died after naming Philip his heir to Spain, the Spanish Indies, the Spanish Low Countries, and Naples and Sicily. At Versailles, Philip was proclaimed king of Spain by his grandfather, and on Jan. 28, 1701, he entered Spain. He was never again to set foot on French soil.

War of the Spanish Succession

Philip entered Madrid in April 1701. In May 1702 England, Austria, and the United Provinces, fearing the possible union of Spain and France, simultaneously declared war on them. Meanwhile, Archduke Charles, the great-grandson of Philip III of Spain and brother of the Austrian emperor, declared himself the rightful king of Spain, launching the War of the Spanish Succession.

The first hostilities took place in Italy, where Philip went to protect his threatened possessions. While he was

there, the British took Gibraltar; Portugal declared war against him; and Catalonia, Valencia, and Aragon rose on behalf of the Archduke Charles. Castile, Navarre, and the Basque provinces, however, remained loyal to Philip. He returned to Spain and in 1707 forced the enemy to evacuate Madrid, meanwhile bringing Valencia and Aragon under his control. In 1710 a Franco-Castilian army decisively defeated the Anglo-Austrian-Catalan army, and in 1714 Philip forced Barcelona to surrender, bringing the war to an end.

By this time the major European powers had signed a series of treaties collectively known as the Peace of Utrecht (1713-1715). Philip was recognized as the legitimate king of Spain; in return he gave up all claims to the throne of France and surrendered the Spanish Low Countries, Naples, and Sicily to the Austrians, and Gibraltar to the British.

Internal Reforms

Now that the war was over and his claims to Spain and the Spanish Empire secured, Philip turned to the task of strengthening the monarchy and introducing the reforms necessary for the economic recovery of the kingdom. With the assistance of able ministers such as the Frenchman Jean Orry and the Spaniards Melchor de Macanaz and José Patiño, Philip accomplished much. Orry gradually remodeled the royal household along French lines and began the gargantuan task of financial reform. Meanwhile, Patiño was building up the country's navy and introducing much-needed reforms into the armed forces. Roads were built and canals repaired; foreign craftsmen and technicians were brought to Spain. On the eve of his death Philip V could boast of an army that had vindicated the national honor in the field of battle, a marine force that had once more awakened the attention of Europe, and many establishments that signaled the revival of industry, trade, and the arts.

Marriages and the Line of Descent

Like his grandfather, Philip possessed the Bourbon sexual appetite, but he also had a high moral sense that prevented him from having sexual relations with anyone except his legitimate wife. Thus the young king was heavily influenced by his first wife, Maria Luisa of Savoy, who had married him, when she was 13, in the spring of 1701. Maria Luisa in turn was controlled by the cunning 60-year-old Princess des Ursins, whom Louis XIV had planted in the Spanish court to represent the interests of France.

Maria Luisa died on Feb. 14, 1714. She and Philip had had four sons, of whom two would live to succeed him as kings of Spain. On Sept. 16, 1714, Philip was married by proxy to the 21-year-old Elizabeth Farnese of Parma. She arrived in Spain in December 1714 and, as one of her first official acts, dismissed the imperious Princess des Ursins.

Elizabeth soon exercised much power over her husband. She often went hunting with him and was enchanted by the palace he had built at La Granja. This little model of Versailles was to become their favorite residence. Elizabeth and Philip had several sons and daughters. Since none of them seemed to have a chance of inheriting the throne of Spain, Elizabeth set out to look for other thrones in Italy. In this she was assisted by the powerful Giulio Alberoni, whose consuming goal was to drive the Austrians out of Italy. They were eminently successful; by 1735 Elizabeth's eldest son, Charles, was king of Naples and Sicily; another son was Duke of Parma; and a third son was cardinal archbishop of Toledo and primate of Spain.

In early 1724 Philip abdicated in favor of his son Luis. It was believed at the time that Philip had taken this step in order to be free to claim the French throne should Louis XV die without a son. A few months after this abdication, however, Luis died of smallpox and Philip returned to the throne. The years passed, and Philip became the victim of acute melancholia. In the 1740s he became increasingly ill and bedridden, and on July 9, 1746, he died of apoplexy. He was succeeded by Ferdinand VI, the only surviving son of his first marriage.

Further Reading

There is no biography of Philip V available in English, and those available in Spanish are few and unsatisfactory. A very useful account of Philip and his reign, however, can be found in Charles Petrie, *The Spanish Royal House* (1958). Also recommended are Edward Armstrong, *Elisabeth Farnese* (1892), and Simon Harcourt Smith, *Alberoni* (1944). ☐

Philip VI

Philip VI (1293-1350) was king of France from 1328 to 1350. His reign began with a crisis in the succession to the crown and culminated in the rupture between the kings of France and England which precipitated the Hundred Years War.

The son of Charles of Valois and the grandson of Philip III of France, Philip VI was born without any prospect of becoming king of France. He had been Count of Maine and, as of 1326, Count of Anjou and Valois. Like other contemporaries, he had been a knightly adventurer and had participated in the Italian wars of the Lombard cities against the Visconti family of Milan.

Succession Crisis

Upon the death of the last direct Capetian king, Charles IV, in 1328, Philip was named regent of France, for Charles's widow, Joan of Evreux, had been pregnant at his death. On April 1, 1328, Joan gave birth to a daughter, but an assembly of nobles passed over the daughter's claim in favor of that of Philip. On May 29, 1328, Philip VI was crowned king of France.

Each of the kings of France from Hugh Capet to Philip IV had produced a male child who succeeded his father as king. Thereafter, although there was never a law of direct male succession, it was traditional to pass over a deceased king's daughters for his brother. Although succession only through male descent was counter to the law that governed the inheritance of private estates in France, Philip V and Charles IV claimed that the crown of France descended by a higher law, one that excluded female succession. When Charles died in 1328, therefore, France faced a crisis of succession to the royal throne for which it had never had to prepare itself: there were a number of different claimants to the throne, several of them women and several whose claims derived through women. In addition, there were complicating political factors, all of which played a part in the final outcome.

There were two claimants whose claims did not depend upon female succession. Edward III of England claimed the throne through his mother, daughter of Philip IV, on the basis of her being able to transmit to a male child the claim which she could not make as a woman herself. Philip VI based his claim to the throne on complete male descent, as the son of the son of Philip III; on expediency—he had been regent successfully for 2 months and was well liked by the nobility; and on the prestige of the Valois house.

King of France

The personality of Philip VI is difficult to assess. He has been criticized both as being (like his son and successor, John II) an irresponsible chivalric knight who found a throne by accident and as being a calculating ruler who promoted lowborn unruly officials over the heads of the French nobility. He was interested in questions of theology and soon received the nickname of "the Very Devout Christian." He continued the tradition, begun in the reign of his grandfather, Philip III, of royal patronage of the arts and book collecting. He was certainly ceremonial, both in battle, which was unwise, and in the life of the court, which may have enhanced his royal prestige. In general, he appears to have been unable to use his resources wisely or effectively and never to have acquired control over the army, a defect which was sharply revealed by the English victories in the last decade of his reign. Not raised and educated for the throne, Philip VI was faced with too many severe crises in too short a period of time, crises with which he was temperamentally, financially, and politically unable to deal.

Gascony, Scotland, and England

King Edward III of England was not only a rival claimant of the throne of France but also Philip's vassal for the duchy of Gascony, a maritime strip of wealthy territories on the southwestern coast of France; and as Edward's overlord, Philip VI claimed certain rights of homage and certain rights of judicial intervention in Gascony. France, too, had long supported anti-English candidates to the throne of Scotland. On the other hand, the wealthy population of Flanders, whose count was also a vassal of Philip's, had stronger financial ties with England. From Edward's extremely reluctant homage to Philip in 1331 to the outbreak of war in 1339, relations between the two kings centered upon this complex of interests and alliances.

French intervention in the duchy of Gascony was followed by English support for Edward Balliol as king of Scotland, with Philip supporting the claim of David II. Edward, fearing a French invasion of Scotland, began in 1337 to form a series of alliances with France's northern and western neighbors and to foment rebellion in Flanders. Philip replied by declaring Gascony confiscated by the French crown, and Edward countered by reviving his claim to the throne of France and by launching his first Continental campaign in 1339.

Hundred Years War

On one level, the war began as a dispute between a lord and his vassal, but the intensity of the campaigns, the economic and political pressures, and France's fatal military weakness soon carried it beyond the level of a feudal conflict almost to the extent of a war between nations. Neither side possessed sufficient resources to gain complete victory.

Although English armies were smaller than those of the French, their superior organization and tactics made them militarily superior, and Philip's inability to reform French military organization and technique cost him dearly, as it would his successors. England fomented revolts in Flanders (1337) and Brittany (1341), destroyed the French fleet at Sluis (1340), and finally opened a campaign on several fronts, particularly in Gascony and Normandy, culminating in the shattering defeat of Philip's army at Crécy in 1346. Edward was not able financially to follow up his victory, nor was Philip sufficiently energetic or confident to attack the English again. But in 1347 Edward captured Calais, forcing Philip to beg the States General for more money.

The following year, 1348, witnessed yet a further disaster in the arrival of the Black Death, which ravaged Europe and wreaked havoc with the social and economic order of France. The length of the war, the final defeats at Crécy and Calais, the reluctance of his subjects to finance the war

adequately, and the plague tormented the final years of Philip's reign. He died on Aug. 22, 1350.

Further Reading

There is no biography of Philip VI in English. Good recent surveys of his reign are Kenneth Fowler, *The Age of Plantagenet and Valois* (1967), and, in somewhat greater detail, Edouard Perroy, *The Hundred Years War* (1945; trans. 1951). A near-contemporary account of the origins of the war is that of Jean Froissart, *The Chronicles of England, France, and Spain* (many eds.). □

Philip the Good

Philip the Good (1396-1467) was Duke of Burgundy from 1419 to 1467. His brilliant and sumptuous court was the most celebrated in Europe, and Burgundian power and cultural life flowered under his patronage.

Born at Dijon on July 31, 1396, Philip the Good was the son of Duke John the Fearless and Margaret of Bavaria. At first created Count of Charolais—the traditional title of the heir apparent of Burgundy—he became the third Valois Duke of Burgundy upon the assassination of his father in 1419.

Contemporary portraits and descriptions depict Philip as tall, with broad shoulders and keen eyes. He was brave, intelligent, and fond of the ostentation that characterized the life of the high aristocracy of the 15th century. "His appearance alone proclaimed him Emperor, and his natural graces made him worthy of a Crown," a contemporary wrote at a point in Philip's career when he may have been thinking of acquiring both an empire and a crown. Philip's rule coincided with the great flowering of Burgundian art, music, and literature, of which he was the most spectacular patron, and his reign is recorded in several lively contemporary chronicles, some expressly commissioned by Philip.

Early 15th-century Burgundy was a collection of territories assembled by Philip's predecessors, Philip the Bold and John the Fearless, based upon the duchy of Burgundy in southeastern France. The first two Valois dukes had added to this core, however, and constructed a series of territories to the north and west of France, and Philip the Good completed the process of acquisition by gaining Alsace, Holland, Hainaut, Friesland, and Brabant. The Duke of Burgundy was thus the most powerful subject of the king of France, and Philip's influence was of the greatest importance in determining the outcome of the Hundred Years War between France and England.

At the time of his accession, Philip's personal and political sympathies lay with the English, as had his father's, and they were intensified by his (and others') suspicions that Charles VI's son (later, Charles VII) had had a hand in the assassination of John the Fearless. After signing the Treaty of Troyes in 1420, Philip entered Paris in triumph with Henry

V of England, witnessed Charles VI's designation of Henry as his legal successor to the throne of France, and completed the formal condemnation of those guilty of his father's murder.

Upon the sudden deaths of both Henry V and Charles VI in 1422, Philip stood aside, and the Duke of Bedford was named regent for the young Henry VI, now ruler of both England and France. In 1423 the alliance between England and Burgundy was cemented by Bedford's marriage to Philip's sister Anne. For the next decade Philip concentrated upon the policy of acquiring lands to round out his extensive holdings in the north of France. The great French successes under Joan of Arc in 1429-1430 may have begun to turn Philip toward an alliance with Charles VII of France. Between 1431 and 1435 Philip was undecided, finally settling his differences with the king of France in the Treaty of Arras in 1435, although he lent the King little real support. From 1435 on, Philip turned his attention to the Low Countries, remaining apart from the French offensive of 1450-1453, which drove the English out of France.

Philip's interests, however, were not confined to the Low Countries and the Anglo-French conflict. He had been born a few months before his father had led the disastrous Crusade of Nicopolis in 1396, and the memory of his father's endeavor coupled with the fall of Constantinople to the Ottoman Turks in 1453 spurred Philip to take the crusaders' vow himself. At a famous banquet held at Lille in 1454, he took the "Vow of the Pheasant," an elaborate crusading pledge that he never fulfilled.

Never entirely welcome or entirely trusted in France, Philip offered asylum to the Dauphin Louis (later Louis XI) from 1456 until the death of Charles VII in 1461. In that year he entered Paris in triumph with Louis XI. Trusted no more by his former protoégé than by Charles VII, Philip soon returned to Burgundy, and his domains fell into the hands of the Croy family.

At the height of his power, Philip was the most influential man in Europe. His control extended into France, the Low Countries, Germany, and Italy. He was regarded as the most noble prince of his day, and he may have considered accepting from the Emperor a royal crown, which would thus have turned Burgundy into a kingdom. Philip died at Bruges on June 15, 1467, leaving his son Charles the Bold to inherit the Great Duchy of the West.

Further Reading

The standard work is now Richard Vaughan, *Philip the Good* (1970), a clearly written and scholarly study; it is the third volume of a projected four-volume study of the rise and fall of Valois Burgundy. Philip's reign is well treated in Joseph Calmette, *The Golden Age of Burgundy* (1963). A picture of the rich court life of Burgundy is drawn in Otto Cartellieri, *The Court of Burgundy* (1926; trans. 1929); and the range of Burgundian culture is described in the brilliant work of J. H. Huizinga, *The Waning of the Middle Ages* (1924). □

Arthur Phillip

Arthur Phillip (1738-1814) was an English naval officer and the first governor of New South Wales. His views of predominantly free settlers foreshadowed the sentiments of the later emancipists.

Arthur Phillip was born on Oct. 11, 1738, in London and attended the Greenwich school for seamen's sons before serving an apprenticeship in the merchant navy. During the Seven Years War (1756-1763) he transferred to the Royal Navy and rose to the rank of lieutenant. Subsequently he retired on half pay, becoming a farmer in Hampshire. In 1774 the Admiralty allowed Phillip to serve as a captain in the Portuguese navy, and he later rejoined the Royal Navy during the American War of Independence. At 48 Capt. Phillip was offered a position as governor of a penal colony about to be established at Botany Bay, Australia.

The 11 ships of the 1st Fleet reached Botany Bay in January 1788 after a voyage of 8 months. As the site for a permanent settlement Phillip chose Sydney Cove inside a great natural harbor a few miles north of Botany Bay. Three-quarters of the 1,030 persons who disembarked there were convicts, the remainder marines and officials.

For 5 years Phillip, with unflinching optimism, struggled to create a viable colony with unsuitable human material. Convicts, mostly lower-class criminals from Britain's burgeoning towns, were granted small farms on the expiry of their sentences, but this did not transform them into an

industrious peasantry. The marines, who initially received no land, were dissatisfied because they could not advance their personal fortunes in such a remote outpost. Only 13 free settlers of the kind that Phillip wanted in order to create a thriving colony arrived during his term as governor.

Starvation was a constant threat. The 1st Fleet carried sufficient provisions for only 2 years; the 2d Fleet did not reach Sydney until June 1790, and the 3d Fleet in July 1791. Until supplies arrived, the inhabitants were allocated rations insufficient for a day's hard work, and stocks of clothing were exhausted. Parramatta, a township 15 miles upstream, became the center for colonial agriculture because of its fertile soil. Although convict labor was employed on government farms, the lack of draft animals and implements, and the problems associated with a new environment, impeded agricultural progress.

When Phillip returned to England in December 1792 owing to illness, the small settlement of 3,000 people could not produce its food requirements. But the New South Wales Corps, which replaced the disgruntled marines in 1791, was fostering trade with merchants from India and the United States, and the arrival of more ships ensured the colony's physical survival. Because of its cost to the British taxpayer, however, the settlement's long-term future remained in doubt.

Although Phillip's vision of a colony with predominantly free settlers was not immediately realized, he did succeed in piloting the settlement through its early years of deprivation, and before he left, the outlines of a solution to

the colony's economic problem were discernible. But the extensive powers vested in the governor encouraged autocratic rule and led to future conflicts.

After returning to England, Phillip resumed his naval career and became a rear admiral in 1798. In 1805 he retired to Bath, where he died on Aug. 31, 1814, shortly after becoming an admiral of the blue.

Further Reading

Two major biographies of Phillip are George Mackaness, *Admiral Arthur Phillip, Founder of New South Wales, 1738-1814* (1937), a long, detailed, and generally sympathetic account; and a more penetrating study of the settlement's early years by M. Barnard Eldershaw, *Phillip of Australia: An Account of the Settlement at Sydney Cove 1788-1792* (1938).

Additional Sources

Frost, Alan, *Arthur Phillip, 1738-1814: his voyaging,* Melbourne; New York: Oxford University Press, 1987.
Hawkesbury River history: governor Phillip, exploration, and early settlement, Wisemans Ferry, N.S.W.: Dharug and Lower Hawkesbury Historical Society; Sydney South, N.S.W.: Distributed by Hawkesbury River Enteprises, 1990. □

David Graham Phillips

The interests of David Graham Phillips (1867-1911), American journalist and novelist, ranged from the plight of women to corruption in Congress.

David Graham Phillips was born on Oct. 31, 1867, in Madison, Ind. During his happy and comfortable childhood he developed especially close ties to his older sister Carolyn. After high school Phillips entered Asbury (DePauw) University, where he roomed with the future U.S. senator Albert J. Beveridge, a man whom Phillips considered a symbol of the success that can come from hard work. When Beveridge graduated, Phillips went to Princeton, where he received a degree in 1887.

After college Phillips began working on the staff of the *Cincinnati Times-Star.* He wrote for a succession of newspapers, culminating his newspaper career as editorial writer for the *New York World.* His first novel, *The Great God Success* (1901), published under the pseudonym John Graham, won acclaim from popular critics and encouraged him to leave the *World* in 1902 to devote himself to "serious" writing. From then on he worked long hours on a regular daily schedule, writing 22 more novels, a play, and a series of essays.

Many of Phillips's novels employ journalistic techniques to examine the "hidden" story behind a dramatic situation, but this often results in pasteboard characterizations. He was interested in a variety of social problems. In *The Second Generation* (1907) he contrasts the evils of inherited wealth with the virtues of the working class. *The Plum Tree* (1905), *Light Fingered Gentry* (1907), and *The Conflict* (1911) consider the corruption of power and money that accompanied the rise of American democracy. He dealt with the social and economic situation of women in *Old Wives for New* (1908), *The Hungry Heart* (1909), *The Price She Paid* (1912), and his best-known novel, *Susan Lenox* (1917), the story of the rise to success of an illegitimate country girl turned prostitute.

Phillips's essays exposing corruption and greed in Congress, "The Treason of the Senate" (1906), appeared in *Cosmopolitan* and immediately brought reactions from men in power. His work was called sensational and distorted, and he acquired the title of muckraker. But he had little taste for bucking public opinion and so returned to fiction.

On Jan. 23, 1911, Phillips was shot by a mentally ill violinist who believed that Phillips's novel *The Fashionable Adventures of Joshua Craig* (1909) had libelously portrayed his family. Phillips died the next day. His sister Carolyn, with whom he had lived for years, prepared his last works for posthumous publication.

Further Reading

Abe C. Ravitz, *David Graham Phillips* (1966), is biographical and evaluative. Kenneth S. Lynn's excellent *The Dream of Success: A Study of the Modern American Imagination* (1955) contains a chapter on Phillips. Isaac F. Marcosson, *David Graham Phillips and His Times* (1932), remains useful for its account of Phillips's journalistic work. Louis Filler, *Crusaders for American Liberalism* (1939), describes the whole muckraking movement.

Additional Sources

Filler, Louis, *Voice of the democracy: a critical biography of David Graham Phillips, journalist, novelist, progressive,* University Park: Pennsylvania State University Press, 1978. □

Wendell Phillips

Wendell Phillips (1811-1884), American abolitionist and social reformer, became the antislavery movement's most powerful orator and, after the Civil War, the chief proponent of full civil rights for freed slaves.

Wendell Phillips was born on Nov. 29, 1811, into a wealthy, aristocratic Boston family. Gifted, handsome, and brilliant, he excelled in his studies at Harvard, where he graduated in 1831, and in the study of law, which he undertook with the great Joseph Story. Phillips was admitted to the bar in 1834 and opened an office in Boston. In 1835, from his office window, he saw William Lloyd Garrison being dragged through the street by a mob, an event that changed his attitude toward slavery. Phillips's meeting with Ann Terry Greene, an active worker in the Boston Female Antislavery Society, increased his interest in the abolition movement. They were married on Oct. 12, 1837. He wrote later that "my wife made an out-and-out abolitionist of me, and always preceded me in the adoption of various causes I have advocated."

Phillips enlisted in the cause at a meeting on Dec. 8, 1837, to protest the death of antislavery editor Elijah Lovejoy in Illinois. After the attorney general of Massachusetts condoned the Illinois mob, Phillips sprang to the platform: his eloquent defense of Lovejoy catapulted him into the ranks of abolitionist leaders. Breaking with his family and friends and relinquishing his law practice, he joined Garrison and became, next to Garrison, New England's best-known abolitionist. The true reformer, Phillips said, must be prepared to sacrifice everything for his cause; he is "careless of numbers, disregards popularity, and deals only with ideas, consciences, and common sense." Like Garrison, Phillips attacked what he believed to be the "proslavery" Constitution, rejected political action, and ultimately demanded the division of the Union if slavery was not immediately abolished. A persuasive and elegant speaker, he could be so denunciatory that he was several times nearly mobbed.

During the early Civil War, Phillips censured Abraham Lincoln's reluctance to free the slaves, calling him "a first-rate second-rate man" whose "milk-livered administration" conducted the war "with the purpose of saving slavery." He welcomed the Emancipation Proclamation but violently opposed Lincoln's reelection in 1864, and in 1865 he resisted Garrison's attempts to terminate the American Antislavery Society. Phillips maintained that the African Americans' freedom would not be achieved until they possessed the ballot and full civil and social rights. Garrison lost, and Phillips remained president of the society until 1870.

Phillips's other causes included prohibition, women's rights, prison reform, greenbacks, an 8-hour day, and Labor unions. He helped organize the Labor Reform Convention and the Prohibition party in Massachusetts, and both nominated him for governor in 1870. A revolutionary idealist, he envisioned an American society "with no rich men and no poor men in it, all mingling in the same society . . . all opportunities equal, nobody so proud as to stand aloof, nobody so humble as to be shut out." His political involvement, however, and his increasing radicalism, which led him to advocate "the overthrow of the whole profit-making system . . . , the abolition of the privileged classes . . . , and the present system of finance," alienated some of his friends and reduced his effectiveness as a reform leader.

Phillips remained popular on the lyceum circuit, speaking sometimes 60 times a year and earning up to $15,000 annually. He died on Feb. 7, 1884.

Further Reading

Three excellent biographies of Phillips are Ralph Korngold, *Two Friends of Man: The Story of William Lloyd Garrison and Wendell Phillips, and Their Relationship with Abraham Lincoln* (1950); Oscar Sherwin, *Prophet of Liberty: The Life and Times of Wendell Phillips* (1958); and Irving H. Bartlett, *Wendell Phillips: Brahmin Radical* (1961).

Additional Sources

Bartlett, Irving H., *Wendell and Ann Phillips: the community of reform, 1840-1880,* New York: Norton, 1979.
Sherwin, Oscar, *Prophet of liberty: the life and times of Wendell Phillips,* Westport, Conn.: Greenwood Press, 1975, 1958.
Stewart, James Brewer, *Wendell Phillips, liberty's hero,* Baton Rouge: Louisiana State University Press, 1986. □

Philo Judaeus

Philo Judaeus (ca. 20 B.C.-ca. A.D. 45) was a Hellenistic Jewish philosopher. An important example of philosophical syncretism, he was a Diaspora Jew prepared to concede a good deal to Hellenism in his interpretation of the Scriptures.

Philo Judaeus was born in Alexandria, but the exact date of his birth is unknown. The only public event in his life occurred when he led a delegation of Alexandrian Jews to the emperor Caligula in A.D. 40 to protest the recent ill treatment of Jews by Greeks in their city. His account of the proceedings survives in the treatise entitled *Legatio ad Gaium.*

This remarkable document almost certainly tells less than the whole story about why friction arose between Jews and Greeks in Alexandria. But it provides an interesting portrait of the emperor Caligula and his attitude toward the problem of Jews and emperor worship. Whether through boredom at the length of the delegation's pleas or through genuine conviction, he observed of the Jews' refusal to worship him as a god, "I think that these people are not so much criminals as lunatics in not believing that I have been given a divine nature." The delegation, which had been understandably alarmed when Caligula brought up the question of emperor worship in his opening remarks, was heartily relieved when his concluding statement suggested merely pity and condescension rather than ill will.

Treatises and Essays

Philo's major writings, however, consist largely of moral treatises and philosophico-theological essays on topics of scriptural interest. As a religious believer, he was convinced that the truth of things was to be found ultimately in the teachings of Moses; as a philosopher, he felt a need to express this truth in terms that were intelligible to a world imbued with the ideas of Greek philosophy. His works consequently suggest frequent tension between an attempt to interpret the Scriptures in the light of Greek philosophy and an attempt to criticize Greek philosophy in the light of scriptural truth.

The latter is particularly clear in Philo's doctrine of God. For Philo the believer, God is the only reality that is eternal; He is also totally "other" and unknowable. His providence is "individual," manifesting itself in direct intervention in the universe, with suspension, if need be, of laws of nature for the benefit of meritorious individuals. Of His own goodwill, He endows the human soul with immortality. These views were strongly contrasted by Philo with Greek views, such as those found in Plato's *Phaedo* and *Timaeus,* in which both matter and the Ideas are said to be coeternal with God; Providence is said to be manifested in the basic laws of nature, and the human soul is said to be of its very nature immortal.

Philosophical Eclecticism

"Nonnegotiable dogma aside, however, Philo was more than willing to use the thought forms of Greek philosophy on those many matters on which honest disagreement among believers seemed to him allowable. The Greek philosophy in question is an amalgam drawn from many sources. His stress on the symbolic importance of certain numbers (4, 6, 7, 10, for example) suggests contemporary neo-Pythagorean influence. The views that causality is fourfold, that virtue lies in a mean, that God is to be seen as the prime mover of the universe, show the clear influence of Aristotle.

The spirit of Plato emerges clearly in Philo's general acceptance of notions such as the theory of Ideas, and the belief that the body is a tomb or prison, that life for man should be a process of purification from the material, that cosmic matter preceded the formation of the cosmos, and that the existence of God can be inferred from the structure and operations of the universe. The influence of stoicism emerges in his doctrines of man's "unqualified" free will, of the need to live in accord with nature, of the need to live free from passion, and of the "indifference" of what is beyond one's power.

In his interpretation of Scripture, Philo seems to have adhered to its "spiritual" rather than to its literal truth. Thus the literal idea of a 6-day creation is rejected, and the story of Adam's rib is written off as mythical. Less acceptable to modern taste, perhaps, was his pervasive use of allegorical interpretation.

Doctrine of the Logos

Among non-Jews Philo was probably best known for his doctrine of the Logos, which was widely thought to have influenced (whether directly or indirectly is not known) the author of the Fourth Gospel. This doctrine seems to have been born of Philo's attempt to reconcile both his belief in a uniquely transcendent, eternal creator and his general acceptance of the Platonic theory of Ideas. He rejects the Ideas as eternal, transcendent entities. Rather, they are temporal and part of God's creation. Their exemplars, however, do exist eternally—as thoughts in the mind of God. The home of the Ideas he called the Logos, or Reason, and this Logos, like the Ideas, was said to exist both transcendentally, as an eternal exemplar in the mind of God, and temporally, as part of God's creation. With this doctrine Philo attempted to bridge the gap between a God who is totally "other" and the material universe; the Logos, being (unlike God) *both* transcendental *and* temporal, was the all-important intermediary linking man and the universe to their creator.

Further Reading

A Greek text and translation of Philo's complete works is in the Loeb Classical Library edition, *Philo* (10 vols., 1929-1962), of F. H. Colson and G. H. Whitaker. A useful shorter work is *Philo's Philosophical Writings* (1946), selections edited by Hans Lewy. Harry A. Wolfson, *Philo* (2 vols., 1947; rev. ed. 1948), is the major English-language work on the philosopher. For a sympathetic general introduction in English see Erwin R. Goodenough, *An Introduction to Philo Judaeus* (1940; rev. ed. 1963). □

Sir William Phips

Sir William Phips (c. 1650-1695) was an American shipbuilder and soldier and became the first royal governor of the British colony of Massachusetts.

Born of humble parents on the colonial Maine frontier of Massachusetts on Feb. 2, 1650/1651, William Phips was early apprenticed to a ship's carpenter in Boston and afterward followed that trade there. Following his marriage to Mary Hull, he became a shipbuilder, and at one time he captained a vessel. In 1683 the British king Charles II provided him with H.M.S. Rose to make an expedition to recover gold from sunken Spanish galleons off the Bahama Islands. The first attempt was unsuccessful, but in a second venture off Hispaniola, which was backed by the Duke of Albemarle, Phips recovered treasure valued at £300,000. For this he was knighted in 1687. As an additional reward, James II appointed Phips provost marshal general of the Dominion of New England under Edmund Andros.

Phips was received coldly in this new position, and he returned to England to complain. There he allied himself with Increase Mather in seeking governmental change and the restoration of the old charter rule in Massachusetts. From this time on he was a political ally of Increase Mather and his son Cotton, who hoped Phips would unite the various factions and help return Massachusetts to the conditions existing before the charter had been revoked in 1684.

In 1690, because of the influence of the Mathers, Phips was chosen to command the Massachusetts troops against the French at Port Royal, Nova Scotia. Here he won a decisive victory. A similar expedition by the northern colonies against Canada failed miserably. During his absence Phips was elected magistrate. Sailing to England to seek funds for another attack on Canada, he was delayed until the new charter was granted to Massachusetts. Again, because of the influence of the Mathers, Phips was appointed the first royal governor of Massachusetts. He took over his duties in May 1692, and it was his decision that brought the witchcraft trials in Salem to an end.

The people of Massachusetts expected Phips to return the colony to the conditions existing before 1684. But his violent temper and continual references to his humble beginnings marked his administration and were partly responsible for disputes over military, religious, economic, social, and political affairs. Charged with maladministration, he returned to England to answer the charges. His death in London on Feb. 18, 1695, probably saved him from the humiliation of a recall.

Further Reading

Cotton Mather's biography, edited by Mark Van Doren, *The Life of Sir William Phips* (1929), is unreliable and is Mather's apology for his part in having Phips appointed governor. A more recent study is Harold W. Felton, *William Phips and the Treasure Ship* (1965). Other works on Phips include H.O. Thayer, *Sir William Phips* (1927); Cyrus H. Karraker, *The Hispaniola Treasure* (1934); and Alice Lounsberry, *Sir William Phips* (1941). □

Photius

The Byzantine scholar and writer Photius (ca. 820-891) was patriarch of Constantinople and leader of the Orthodox Byzantine Renaissance.

Photius was trained from his early years to be a philosopher and scholar. He taught at the Imperial Academy at Constantinople. He became known to the imperial court when his brother Sergius married the sister of Empress Theodora. Appointments followed. He was put in charge of the Chancellery and became a member of the Senate. While he was absent on a diplomatic mission to the Arabian caliph in 855, there was a palace revolt. Empress Theodora was deposed by her brother Bardas. Photius was recalled, ordained priest and bishop within 6 days, and then appointed patriarch to replace Ignatius, who had been forced to resign by the new regent, Bardas.

Pope Nicholas I confirmed all these actions except the nomination of Photius, in spite of the fact that all the bishops of the Church acknowledged Photius as patriarch. Photius was excommunicated by Nicholas, and he responded by summoning a synod in 867 and proposing to condemn all papal interference in the Eastern Church. The new emperor, Michael III, a supporter of Photius, requested Louis II of France to depose Pope Nicholas. Michael, however, was assassinated by Basil I, his coemperor. The latter became emperor and reinstated Patriarch Ignatius in November 867. Furthermore, a council called for the occasion and sitting from 867 to 870 condemned and excommunicated Photius, who then went into exile.

But the new emperor found that Photius remained the choice of the vast majority of the clergy, and eventually he was recalled from exile, reconciled with Patriarch Ignatius, and succeeded the latter when he died in 877. Photius's troubles, however, were not over. Emperor Leo VI, probably under strong pressure from the Pope and also because of palace intrigues, forced Photius to resign in 886. He retired to a monastery and died there in the spring of 891.

Photius is an important figure both in the history of relations between Eastern Orthodoxy and the Roman Catholic Church and in the literature and learning of Eastern Christianity. He was a forewarning to Rome and the papacy of the coming schism between Western and Eastern Chris-

tianity. Between the 9th and the 11th centuries, when the final schism took place, Photius was one of those whose views helped to fashion the antipapal view which finally triumphed. Photius, in fact, labored against any final ecclesiastical rupture, and he died in communion with Rome. As a churchman, he was responsible for the spread of Byzantine religion to Bulgaria, Russia, and Moravia. As a scholar, he has left some works of immense value: his *Biblioteca,* a bibliography of 280 works with his comments; his *Lexicon;* and his *Amphilochia,* which is a catechetical question-and-answer discussion of religion. His *Mystagogia* is a theological work concerning the Trinity. There are numerous letters, sermons, homilies, and treatises of his extant.

Further Reading

The most complete studies of Photius in English are Francis Dvorniks, *The Photian Schism, History and Legend* (1948) and *The Patriarch Photius in the Light of Recent Research* (1958). For extensive background on the Byzantine Empire during the time of Photius see George Ostrogorski, *History of the Byzantine State* (1940; trans. 1954; rev. ed. 1969), and Romilly Jenkins, *Byzantium: The Imperial Centuries A.D. 610-1071* (1967). □

Duncan Phyfe

Duncan Phyfe (1768-1854), Scottish-born American cabinetmaker, was one of the best-known and finest furniture makers in the United States.

Duncan Phyfe was born at Loch Fannich. He probably served an apprenticeship as a cabinetmaker. The Phyfe family emigrated to Albany, N.Y., in 1783 or 1784, where the father opened a cabinetmaking shop. Duncan soon went to New York City; he is listed in the New York Directory for 1792. He eventually settled on Partition (later Fulton) Street, buying additional property as his business expanded. His high-quality furniture was very much in demand in New York and Philadelphia. It is also believed that he had agents in the South.

Phyfe carried on the business under his own name until, in 1837, it was changed to Duncan Phyfe and Son. Ten years later, because he had amassed a great fortune, he decided to discontinue the business and sold the entire stock on hand at auction. Upon retirement he lived in the house on Fulton Street until his death in 1854.

European furniture pattern books were available to both Phyfe and his patrons at the outset of his career. His early work shows a fondness for the designs of Thomas Sheraton. Next he came under the influence of the French Directoire style and, a bit later, the Empire style, two influences which have come to be considered the most characteristic of his work. In the period between 1837 and 1847, the Phyfe firm produced heavy plain furniture which in no way had the style or quality of his earlier works.

Reddish mahogany from Cuba and Santo Domingo was greatly favored by Phyfe at the beginning of his career.

He paid as much as $1,000 for a single log and personally supervised the cutting of the veneers. Much of Phyfe's fame as a cabinetmaker was based on his artistic use of veneers. His other chief decorative devices were turning, reeding, and carving. After 1830 much of the furniture was made of rosewood. Phyfe summed up the quality of the late work with the phrase "butcher furniture." His furniture was expensive in its day; bills dated 1816 indicate that a "piece" table cost $265 and a sofa $122.

In addition to developing an individual style and producing high-quality workmanship, Phyfe introduced the factory method into American cabinetmaking. From the apprenticeship system, with no division of labor, he evolved a system where individual craftsmen performed specific duties. All of the work was executed, however, under Phyfe's supervision, and his personal genius was largely responsible for the excellence of his furniture.

Further Reading

The best work on Phyfe is Nancy McClelland, *Duncan Phyfe and the English Regency, 1795-1830* (1939). A biography and analysis of his furniture are in Charles O. Cornelius, *Furniture Masterpieces of Duncan Phyfe* (1922). A sketch of Phyfe's life and work is in Ethel Hall Bjerkoe, *The Cabinetmakers of America* (1957). □

Edith Piaf

Edith Giovanna Gassion, known as Edith Piaf (1915-1963), was a French music hall/cabaret singer whose specialty was the love ballad.

Edith Gassion was born in Belleville, a congested working-class neighborhood of Paris, on December 19, 1915. Her mother, Anetta Maillard (Gassion), was a café singer who went by the name Line Marsa. Of Algerian circus descent, she was a habitual drifter. Edith's father, Louis Alphonse Gassion, was from Normandy, a slim, five-foot-tall circus acrobat who worked in the Paris streets when he was not on tour in provincial France. He had three theatrical sisters, one of whom, Edith's Tante (Aunt) Zaza, performed in tightrope acts.

Louis was also a drifter, but he loved Edith and took care of her, in his own way, when he could. In contrast, Edith's mother casually abandoned the girl in infancy. This child, Edith Piaf, was to become an enormously popular singer of international fame, noted for her generosity. Later she looked after her father financially, but she could never bring herself to forgive her mother.

Edith was reared initially by her maternal grandmother, Ména (Emma Said ben Mohamed), who had managed a circus performing-flea show. Tante Zaza rescued lice-infested Edith from Ména's filthy hovel in Paris. Zaza took the child (aged about seven) to the care of her paternal grandmother, a cook in a local brothel (a *maison close*) in Bernay, a village in Normandy.

An incident of "blindness" in Piaf's early childhood was apparently conjunctivitis; her "miraculous" cure at the shrine of St. Teresa at Lisieux was probably after the disease had vanished. The prayers of the young ladies of the Bernay brothel may have had nothing to do with the cure, but Piaf said: "Miracle or not, I am forever grateful."

Early in the 1920s (about 1923) Edith Gassion left Bernay and went on a life of circus travels in Belgium and northern France, living in a caravan with her father and his various *amours,* who acted as mothers. Acrobatics had not interested Edith, but she sang. As the decade closed, Louis managed to acquire a 22-year-old common-law wife, Yéyette. In March 1931 Yéyette had a child, Denise, in Belleville, Paris, where all three of them had gone to live. Edith resolved to leave. She met Simone Berteaut, who was a companion throughout many adventures and was an "evil presence" sometimes. In the early 1930s they went around together in the economically depressed city, working at odd jobs and begging. Edith frequently sang as a *chanteur des rues* (streetsinger). The French urban working class was fairly small, compared with Britain, Germany, or the United States; there was not much for penniless French women to do–dressmaking, hairdressing . . . or prostitution.

The Naming of Edith Piaf

In 1931 Edith fell in love with Louis Dupont, an errand boy whom she called "P'tit Louis." They lived in a room at the Hotel de l'Avenir, rue Orfila. In February 1933 Edith, who was barely 18, gave birth to a daughter, Marcelle. Soon after, she left P'tit Louis for a soldier of the French Foreign Legion. She sang at small bars and clubs in Montmartre and Pigalle (the famed entertainment district), meeting the *demi-monde* of Paris and all sorts of people– talented crossdressers, lesbians and homosexuals, musicians, theatrical agents, poets, and composers. Singing at a *bal musette* in Pigalle early in 1935, she heard from P'tit Louis that her daughter had meningitis; Marcelle died in eight days later. To pay funeral costs, Edith, it was said, had to prostitute herself.

In October 1935 Edith met Louis Leplée, a former Montmartre drag artist who had opened a sophisticated dinner club, Gerny's, in the smarter Champs-Elysees area. Leplée heard Edith singing the popular song *Comme un moineau* ("like a sparrow") in the street. Leplée called her "La Môme Piaf" ("The Kid Sparrow"). Ten new songs were selected for her by Leplée; he made her wear a simple black skirt and pullover and no makeup, as he had first seen her singing in the streets. Amid long applause, Maurice Chevalier said "She has got what it takes!" The singer Edith Piaf was born.

Six months later local gangsters murdered Leplée. Piaf then met Raymond Asso, a writer who made her a "star" and went to live with Asso at the Hôtel Piccadilly in Pigalle. Piaf called him "mon poète." Asso trained her in everything–vocal instruction, gestures, how to spell and write, what she should read, even eating manners and hygiene. Piaf said "He taught me what a song really is." As a result, at the age of 20 she made her début at a large Paris vaudeville theater and was a hit.

Later other composers and writers amplified Piaf's repertoire with typical Piaf "blues" ballads. On stage Piaf had superb technical skills. Her songs had dramatic fire, tragedy, and anguish. She had much the same build as her father— two inches under five feet tall and some 90 pounds in weight. But she possessed the voice to bewitch audiences— throaty, throbbing yet tender. ("Who is that plain little woman, with a voice too big for her body?" asked Mistinguett, herself an aging star, slightly jealous.) Tossed auburn hair, big eyes, pale, mournful face, Piaf seemed a waif, a castaway on the stage of life, troubled by everything that she witnessed. There was a special Piaf stance, arms-outstretched, fingers turned inwards, calculated to have and hold the listener in a minor state of doomed love, nostalgia, and regret.

In March 1937 Raymond Asso managed to obtain for Piaf a contract at the Théâtre de l'ABC, complete with her little black dress and starched white collar. She was a complete success, with songs created by Asso. The next year, 1938, was a good year for Piaf's career. Asso installed her in the Hôtel Alcina on the Avenue Junot with a Chinese cook and a secretary. But Piaf and Asso were quarreling, Simone Berteaut was back, and Piaf was sleeping with other men. In September 1939 World War II broke out in Europe and Asso was called into the French Army. Piaf met another lover, actor Paul Meurisse.

Piaf had first sung on radio in 1936 and had a first hit record in 1937, *Mon Légionnaire* (words by Asso/music by Monnot), with a bugle-call flourish. She herself wrote some thirty songs and performed about two hundred others in her life. *La vie en rose* was famous all over the world. Jean Cocteau wrote a play for her, *Le Bel Indifférent,* which was staged in Paris in 1940 at Les Bouffes-Parisiens theater. Among films was *Montmartre-sur-Seine* (1941), made during World War II. During the war Piaf remained mainly in Paris, miserably, along with Jean Cocteau.

Becomes an International Star

In the postwar period of European reconstruction and economic boom after 1945, Piaf became an international star, with ten tours to the United States. She made her first trip to New York in October 1947, accompanied by a male nonet, Les Compagnons de la Chanson; they made a light-hearted film together, *Neuf Garcons—Un Coeur* (1947). The nine young Frenchmen were an example of Piaf's professional generosity—she always sought new talent, both as entertainers and/or as lovers. Eddie Constantine, Charles Aznavour, and Yves Montand are some singers she coached. Piaf said "You have to send the elevator back down, so that others may get to the top." Even though her standard fee (in the 1950s) was $1,000 a night, her finances were always a problem. She gave as much as she took.

Piaf was much in love with the world middleweight boxing champion Marcel Cerdan for two years; he was killed in an air crash in 1949. She was awaiting his plane in New York. Piaf had a bent toward mysticism all along, and Cerdan's death led her to talk to him on the "other side."

Nevertheless, she married Jacques Pills (a singer) in 1952 and divorced him in 1957. At the end of her life (1962) she married a 27-year-old singer, Théo Sarapo.

Her death on October 11, 1963 at the age of 47 was due to a liver ailment and internal hemorrhage caused by a life of drink, drug dependency, accidents, and wear-and-tear. Jean Cocteau died seven hours after hearing of his friend's death, at age 74. *Non, je ne regrette rien* ("No, I do not regret anything"), her song of 1960, was a fitting tribute.

A year earlier at a comeback at Paris' Olympia Music Hall, Piaf had tottered on stage, barely able to walk, her hands twisted by arthritis; but she sold a million copies, in France alone, of a recording of that event–*Live at the Olympia*. Piaf was buried in the famous Père Lachaise Cemetery, along with Colette, Sarah Bernhardt, Oscar Wilde, Chopin, and Balzac. Over 100,000 people came to see her bier at her Paris flat, and 40,000 went to the cemetery.

Piaf was the darling of the French people. She sang almost totally in the French language, very often in Parisian slang, in a voice that was somewhat metallic, loud, and direct. Her gestures were in pantomime, echoing the sufferings of daily existence, working-class scenes of factories, chimney blocks, and mean streets, trains slowly speeding up out of Paris railroad stations taking their passengers away from true love. "I have given my tears, paid so many tears for the right love," she said.

Noel Coward, the English satirist and playwright, wrote in his 1956 diary "Piaf in her dusty black dress is still singing sad songs about bereft tarts longing for their lovers to come back . . . but I do wish she would pop in a couple of cheerful songs just for the hell of it." Like Billie Holiday, Judy Garland, Janis Joplin, and numerous other singers, Piaf was bent on self-destruction. She needed suffering. At the end of her life she faced death with equanimity. Piaf said in *Ma Vie*:

Peut m'arriver n'importe quoi
J'm'en fous pas mal . . .
J'etais heureuse, et prête.
(No matter what happens
I couldn't care less . . .
I am happy, and ready)

Further Reading

Piaf's two autobiographies are full of feeling but sometimes factually inaccurate—*Au Bal de la Chance* (Paris, 1958), translated as *The Wheel of Fortune,* preface by Jean Cocteau (London, 1965); and, published after her death, *Ma Vie* ("My Life," Paris, 1964). Biographies are uneven. *Piaf* (1969, 1972) by Simone Berteaut, who pretended to be Piaf's half-sister, was a compilation of half-truths. Euloge Boissonade, *Piaf et Cerdan* (Paris, 1983), tells of the ill-fated love story. Denise Gassion, *Piaf, Ma Soeur* (translated as *Piaf, My Sister,* Paris, 1977), is not as accurate as Margaret Crosland, *Piaf* (London, 1985). Obituaries include *New Statesman* (October 18, 1963), London *Times* (October 12, 1963), and the *New York Times* (October 12 and October 15, 1963).

Additional Sources

Bret, David, *The Piaf legend,* New York: Parkwest, Robson Books, 1989.

Crosland, Margaret, *Piaf,* New York, N.Y.: Fromm International Pub. Corp., 1987, 1985.

Lange, Monique, *Piaf,* New York: Seaver Books, 1981.

Piaf, Edith, *My life,* London; Chester Springs, PA.: Peter Owen, 1990. □

Jean Piaget

The Swiss psychologist and educator Jean Piaget (1896-1980) is famous for his learning theories based on identifiable stages in the development of children's intelligence.

Jean Piaget was born on August 9, 1896, in Neuchâtel, Switzerland, the son of a historian. When he was 11, his notes on a rare part-albino sparrow were published, the first of hundreds of articles and over 50 books. His help in classifying Neuchâtel's natural-history museum collection stimulated his study of mollusks (shellfish). One article, written when he was 15, led to a job offer at Geneva's natural-history museum; he declined in order to continue his education. At Neuchâtel University he finished natural-science studies in 1916 and earned the doctoral degree for research on mollusks in 1918.

Piaget's godfather introduced him to philosophy. Biology (life) was thus merged with epistemology (knowledge), both basic to his later learning theories. Work in two psychological laboratories in Zurich introduced him to psychoanalysis. In Paris at the Sorbonne he studied abnormal psychology, logic, and epistemology, and in 1920 with Théodore Simon in the Binet Laboratory he developed standardized reasoning tests. Piaget thought that these quantitative tests were too rigid and saw that children's incorrect answers better revealed their qualitative thinking at various stages of development. This led to the question that he would spend the rest of his life studying: How do children learn?

After 1921 Piaget was successively director of research, assistant director, and co-director at the Jean Jacques Rousseau Institute, later part of Geneva University, where he was professor of the history of scientific thought (1929-1939). He also taught at universities in Paris, Lausanne, and Neuchâtel; was chairman of the International Bureau of Education; and was a Swiss delegate to UNESCO (United Nations Economic and Scientific Committee). In 1955 he founded the Center for Genetic Epistemology in Geneva with funds from the Rockefeller Foundation and in 1956 he founded and became director of the Institute for Educational Science in Geneva.

In studying children, particularly his own, Piaget found four stages of mental growth. These are a sensory-motor stage, from birth to age 2, when mental structures concentrate on concrete objects; a pre-operational stage, from age 2 to 7, when they learn symbols in language, fantasy, play, and dreams; a concrete operational stage, from age 7 to 11, when they master classification, relationships, numbers, and ways of reasoning about them; and a formal operational

but these refinements did not alter his basic beliefs or theories.

Piaget received honorary degrees from Oxford and Harvard universities and made many impressive guest appearances at conferences concerning childhood development and learning. He remained an elusive figure, though, preferring to avoid the spotlight. A quieter life allowed him to further develop his theories.

Piaget kept himself to a strict personal schedule that filled his entire day. He awoke every morning at four and wrote at least four publishable pages before teaching classes or attending meetings. After lunch he would take walks and ponder on his interests. "I always like to think on a problem before reading about it," he said. He read extensively in the evening before retiring to bed. Every summer he vacationed in the Alpine Mountains of Europe and wrote extensively.

Piaget died on September 17, 1980 in Geneva, Switzerland and was remembered by the *New York Times* as the man whose theories were "as liberating and revolutionary as Sigmund Freud's earlier insights into the stages of human emotional life. Many have hailed him as one of the country's most creative scientific thinkers."

Further Reading

A synthesis of Piaget's work is in Jean Piaget and Bärbel Inhelder, *The Psychology of the Child* (1969); Hans G. Furth, *Piaget and Knowledge: Theoretical Foundations* (1969), contains a brief autobiographical statement by Piaget. *Studies in Cognitive Development: Essays in Honor of Jean Piaget,* edited by David Elkind and John H. Flavell (1969), has an excellent opening chapter by J. McV. Hunt on the impact of Piaget's work. Piaget's obituary in the *New York Times* (September 17, 1980) also provides some biographical information.

The literature on Piaget's work is large. Among the studies are Joseph M. Hunt, *Intelligence and Experience* (1961); John H. Flavell, *The Developmental Psychology of Jean Piaget* (1963); Molly Brearley and Elizabeth Hitchfield, *A Guide to Reading Piaget* (1966); Herbert Ginsburg and Sylvia Opper, *Piaget's Theory of Intellectual Development: An Introduction* (1969); Henry William Maier, *Three Theories of Child Development: The Contributions of Erik H. Erikson, Jean Piaget, and Robert R. Sears, and Their Applications* (1969); Ruth M. Beard, *An Outline of Piaget's Developmental Psychology for Students and Teachers* (1969); and David Elkind, *Children and Adolescents: Interpretive Essays on Jean Piaget* (1970). A less complicated explanation of Piaget's theories appears in Nathan Isaacs' *A Brief Introduction to Piaget* (1988). A bibliography of Piaget's extensive works appears in Judith A. McLaughlin *Bibliography of the Works of Jean Piaget in the Social Sciences* (1988). □

stage, from age 11, when they begin to master independent thought and other people's thinking.

Piaget believed that children's concepts through at least the first three stages differ from those of adults and are based on actively exploring the environment rather than on language understanding. During these stages children learn naturally without punishment or reward. Piaget saw nature (heredity) and nurture (environment) as related and reciprocal, with neither absolute. He found children's notions about nature neither inherited nor learned but *constructs* of their mental structures and experiences. Mental growth takes place by *integration,* or learning higher ideas by assimilating lower-level ideas, and by *substitution,* or replacing initial explanations of an occurrence or idea with a more reasonable explanation. Children learn in stages in an upward spiral of understanding, with the same problems attacked and resolved more completely at each higher level.

Harvard psychologist Jerome Bruner and others introduced Piaget's ideas to the United States circa 1956, after which the translations of his books into English began. The post-Sputnik (1957) goal of American education, to teach children how to think, evoked further interest in Piaget's ideas. His definable stages of when children's concepts change and mature, derived from experiments with children, are currently favored over the hitherto dominant stimulus-response theory of behaviorist psychologists, who have studied animal learning.

Piaget's theories developed over years as refinements and further explanations and experiments were performed,

King Piankhi

The Nubian king Piankhi (reigned ca. 741-ca. 712 B.C.) began the conquest of Lower Egypt which resulted in the establishment of the Twenty-fifth, or "Ethiopian," Dynasty of pharaohs. This was one of the few times in African history when a state from

the interior of the continent played a role in the politics of the Mediterranean.

Piankhi was the hereditary ruler of the kingdom of Cush on the Upper Nile in what is now the northern Sudan. About 741 B.C. he succeeded his father, Kashta, who seems to have founded this Nubian Kingdom. By this time Lower Egypt had been in full decline for almost half a millennium. The Egyptian state was torn by internal power struggles among petty rulers, so the situation was ripe for a strong invader to take over. Piankhi moved steadily down the Nile, conquering towns one by one. By 721 B.C. he was in possession of Heracleopolis, and finally he captured Heliopolis in the Delta.

At this point Piankhi regarded the conquest of Egypt as complete, and he returned home to his Cushite capital in Napata after placing the Egyptian rulers in tributary status. He was received in Napata with much acclaim for having humiliated the former Egyptian overlords of Nubia, but the tributary states which he left soon fell under the sway of a local ruler named Tefnakht, who reasserted Egyptian independence.

A great deal is known about the details of Piankhi's campaign because he built a huge stele in Amon with a lengthy inscription. This account is regarded as unusually rational and lively by modern Egyptologists.

Just like the Nubian rulers who followed him, Piankhi was culturally very conservative, and he sought to strengthen some of the institutions which were undergoing decline in Egypt. In the brief time he was in Lower Egypt, he oversaw the restoration of some crumbling temples. Upon his return to Cush he introduced the Egyptian custom of building pyramids for royal mausoleums, and he had a great pyramid built for himself in Kuru, south of Napata on the Nile. He rebuilt the temple at Jebel Barkal and also built a number of other temples in the Egyptian style.

Curiously, all the Egyptian sources dwell on Piankhi's love of fast horses. He instituted the practice of decorating teams of horses to pull royal chariots, and the remains of a team of horses were found in his tomb at Kuru.

Further Reading

There is no biography of Piankhi, but considerable detail on his conquest of Egypt is in the translation of his inscription at Amon in E.A. Wallis Budge, *Books on Egypt and Chaldaea: Egyptian Literature*, vol. 2: *Annals of Nubian Kings* (1912). An excellent, brief discussion of the relationship between ancient Egypt and the Sudan by A. Arkell is in Roland Oliver, *The Dawn of African History* (1961). Arkell's *A History of the Sudan* (1961) is also very useful. Considerable attention is given to Piankhi and the ''Ethiopian'' pharaohs in James Henry Breasted's classic *A History of Egypt* (1905; 2d ed. 1909). □

Renzo Piano

The Italian architect, lecturer, and designer Renzo Piano (born 1937) is best known for his work with Richard Rogers on the Centre Pompidou in Paris (1971-1977). He gained an international reputation from projects executed in Italy, France, England, the United States, Germany, Senegal, and Japan.

Renzo Piano was born in Genoa, Italy, on September 14, 1937. He entered the Polytechnic of Milan in 1959 to study architecture and from 1962 to 1964 worked under the guidance of Franco Albini. In 1964 he received his diploma and subsequently worked with his father, a building contractor, in Genoa. It was on building sites that the young architect acquired the rudiments of his experimental and craftsmanlike philosophy. Between the years 1965 and 1970 Piano worked with Louis Kahn in Philadelphia and with Z.S. Makowsky in London studying stressed-skin space grids and three-dimensional structures in tension.

Two of his earliest architectural products were a woodworking shop and a factory for sulphur extraction. The woodworking shop in Genoa (1965) was based on a simple steel lozenge structural element and was conceived as an open-ended structure—what Piano calls ''a work in progress.'' The factory for sulphur extraction at Pomezia, Italy (1966), was made of detachable elements so that the structure could be disassembled and reassembled to move along the path of the mining operations.

His collaboration with Richard Rogers began in 1971 when, together with the engineering firm of Ove Arup and Partners, they won the international competition for the design of the Centre National d'Art et Culture Georges Pompidou, more familiarly known as the Beaubourg. It was roundly criticized for its high-tech appearance. However, Piano did not see it as an industrial building, but as a prototype based on fine craftsmanship. In order to leave the interior spaces clear, the mechanical services and plant were placed on the exterior of the building. New developments in information systems and communications could be accommodated in these flexible spaces. The functions of the Beaubourg are multiple and varied: a public library, a museum of modern art, services of documentation and research, a cinema, a theater, and a place for travelling exhibitions and music.

Even more demanding of Piano and Rogers' talents was the building done for the Institut de Recherche et Coordination Acoustique/Musique (IRCAM) in the center of Paris (1973-1977). To provide improved acoustics, they designed an underground structure whose roof forms a plaza at street level. New spatial formulations were needed to accommodate studios, workshops, and the experimental concert hall with variable acoustics. At IRCAM scientists and musicians work as equals exploring uncharted waters in an effort to abolish the boundary line that separates science and art.

In 1977 Piano formed an association with Peter Rice, the structural engineer for Beaubourg's superstructure. The two men were asked to solve an ever-broadening base of design problems. One area of design to which Piano and Rice applied their skills was a modular system of office furnishing which integrated the functions of lighting, climate-control, and communications in Milan, Italy (1977). In 1978 Fiat called upon them to invent the car of the 1990s—to transform the image of the automobile. When a multi-disciplinary team arrived at a prototype capable of change but not manifesting any design innovations, Fiat suspended the experiment.

In a completely different vein, Piano and Rice set up a one week neighborhood workshop in Otranto, Italy (1979), under the sponsorship of the United Nations Economic and Scientific Committee (UNESCO) as an experiment in urban reconstruction. A mobile workshop was erected in the Otranto square to serve the purposes of restoration, documentation, and retraining. Work was carried out with the help of local skilled labor and craftsmen. People were allowed to remain in their homes with a minimum of disturbance of their daily lives. It was planned that continued maintenance of the historic town center would become a source of employment for local people in hopes of reviving their dormant craft skills.

Piano and Rice joined with the Arvedi steel and piping factory in Cremona, Italy (1980), to develop a new system of construction, the Arvedi Space Frame system. This system was used for the spectacular entrance to the Cremona Trade Fair, where the combination vertical platform and canopy served as a spatial backdrop for and graphic symbol of the fair. It was scheduled to be used on a grand scale flanking the Seine river at the Parisian Universal Exhibition in 1989.

In the mid-1980s Piano was associated with Richard Fitzgerald in Houston, Texas. This was the result of work on the museum for the Menil Collection of Symbolist and African Art, opened in 1987. Whereas Piano had wanted to demystify culture with the design for the Beaubourg, here he saw the need to establish a cultural landmark where none had existed. Light played the crucial role in the design of the Houston museum. A complex study of the behavior of light in a variety of conditions was carried out and resulted in the use of a basic structural element, "the leaf," to form the roof.

In the mid-1990s, his projects ranged from the giant $2 billion Kansai airport in Japan to the Potsdamer Platz in the heart of Berlin, to a small arts center on the pacific island of New Caledonia. In Turin, his firm was rehabilitating the marvelous 1925 Lingotto Fiat factory, which consists of a structure a third of a mile long, with an auto test track on the roof. Outside of the Menil Collection in Houston, his work was little known in the United States until an exhibition opened at the Architectural League in New York, which ran in January of 1983, then traveled to the Menil Collection through the end of March.

Though Piano collaborated with different architects, he saw success as the result of team-work. His "studio" revolved around several operative bases. The oldest was located in Paris in the historic center of Le Marais where architects from nine different countries worked together. In Genoa there was a planning workshop where architects, structural engineers, economists, and other specialists provided a multi-disciplinary approach to solving problems. The London office of engineers, Ove Arup and Partners, carried out much of the scientific research, and the London computer was used for all the work. The office in Houston was specific to the work done there. Telephone cables and computers provided lines of communication between the various teams.

Piano drew on technological know-how, but tried to go beyond the clash between creativity and science. He believed in craftsmanship and the latest technology. According to Piano, the architect should understand his materials and use them to the best of their conditions. Through systematic research, she or he should control technology. Piano wanted his work to be studied for its methodology rather than for its architectural forms. With each design he started at the beginning and arrived at a solution specific to it. Because each design was separate, there was no consistent artistic development, in the traditional sense, in Piano's work.

Many people associate Piano with the boisterous design of the Centre de Georges Pompidou. Admittedly it was not been easy for him to shake that stigma. Following the construction of the Centre, Piano was labeled "high tech"—something he insisted didn't fit him, "it implies that you aren't thinking in a poetic way" and that is contrary to his nature. Piano claimed to be a humanist techie—while embracing the spirit of modernism, he held dear the spirit of his Renaissance forebears. Technology, for Piano, is a means as well as an end, but never something visually specific, technology is not alien to nature but part of nature.

Further Reading

Articles on Piano may be found in many international architectural magazines, such as *Domus, Casabella,* and the *Architectural Review.* Piano is listed in *Contemporary Architects,* edited by Muriel Emanuel (1980), and the exhibition catalogue *Renzo Piano/Pezzo per Pezzo,* edited by Gianpiero Donin (1982), contains an English translation of the Italian text. The most comprehensive and richly illustrated study of Piano and his projects and his buildings is Massimo Dini's *Renzo Piano* (1984). Piano, Rogers, and others authored *The Building of Beaubourg* (1978). □

Francis Picabia

Francis Picabia (1879-1953) was a French artist, writer, and bon vivant who contributed to various art movements in the 20th century and became best known as a leader of Dada in Paris.

Francis Picabia viewed his art as an intimate extension of his life. It was a means to express his likes and dislikes, his thoughts and feelings—often without bothering to distinguish between those which were serious or trivial, public or private. That attitude made for enormous variety in the styles and quality of his work, and he insisted on such freedom of expression even when it meant that most of the public might not like or understand what he was doing.

Picabia was born in Paris on or about January 22, 1879. His mother was French and his father was a Spaniard living in Paris. Both parents came from wealthy, distinguished families, and Francis—their only child—was thoroughly spoiled, especially after his mother died when he was seven. He entered the School of Decorative Arts in 1895 and later studied with several teachers, including Félix Cormon. In 1902 he met the sons of the aged impressionist painter Camille Pissarro, who introduced him to their father. Picabia became an Impressionist and travelled extensively to record scenes of France in the relatively objective manner of that style.

Impressionism to Abstraction

By 1908 Picabia had become dissatisfied with Impressionism. He began to paint in more subjective and abstracted styles, particularly the styles of Fauvism and Cubism. He was encouraged by Gabrielle Buffet, a music student whom he married in 1909. They talked about developing "pure painting"—an art which did not imitate nature but could express profound meanings through form and color alone. They compared "pure painting" to music which did not imitate the sounds of nature but which stirred the souls of listeners by harmony and rhythm. At this time Picabia became an active member of the avant-garde in French art. He helped to finance and organize the important

exhibition of the Section d'Or in 1912. The poet and art critic Guillaume Apollinaire named him as one of the artists creating "pure painting" or Orphism.

In 1913 Picabia and his wife visited New York to see the famous Armory Show which introduced modern European art to America. They became friends of the American photographer Alfred Stieglitz, who organized an exhibition of Picabia's work at his gallery, called 291. Two of Picabia's most renowned paintings, *Udnie* (1913) and *Edtaonisl* (1913), were huge, abstract compositions based on experiences during that trip to New York.

Machine Style to Dada

When World War I began in Europe, Picabia was drafted into the army. In 1915 he was sent on a supply mission to the Caribbean, but when his ship reached New York he neglected that mission in order to work again with Alfred Stieglitz. It was an important period during which Picabia began to write poetry and to develop a radically new style of painting based on curious machines. Most of the machines were symbolic of man and human activities, because Picabia believed that machines had become the touchstone of the modern world and that man had made machines in his own image. Many of the paintings also incorporated unusual titles and seemingly nonsensical inscriptions. Picabia was influenced in this new style by his French friend Marcel Duchamp, who also settled in New York in 1915.

Late in 1915 Picabia resumed his military mission. For two years he moved around from the Caribbean to Barcelona, Spain, to New York again. In late 1917 he left America permanently for Europe.

In 1919 Picabia met the Dadaists in Zürich who had been attracted by his unusual machine paintings and volumes of poetry bearing such titles as *Platonic False Teeth* and *Poems and Drawings of the Daughter Born without a Mother*. The leader of Zürich Dada, Tristan Tzara, moved to Paris in January 1920. A Dada movement began immediately under the leadership of Tzara, Picabia, and André Breton. Parisians were outraged by their deliberately offensive publications, exhibitions, and public activities. Picabia's painting, poetry, and magazine entitled *391* were considered anti-art and anti-literature. By mid-1921, the Dadaists in Paris were quarreling among themselves, and Picabia left the movement. A Dadaist irreverence continued to flavor his work, including his collaboration with René Clair in 1924 on the film *Entr'acte*. That film became the intermission for Picabia's ballet, *Relâche,* produced in 1924 by the Swedish Ballet with music by Erik Satie.

Years in the South of France

In 1924 Picabia and his new wife, Germaine Everling, moved to Mougins on the French Riviera. There he lived the life of a playboy until the outbreak of World War II. He extended his reputation for numerous girl friends and fast automobiles. During the early 1930s, he began living on his yacht with Olga Mohler, who became his last wife in 1940.

Picabia continued to work prodigiously as a painter. From about 1924 to 1928 he produced collages and distorted figurative paintings later called "the Monsters." His next paintings, from 1928 into the early 1930s, were called "transparencies." They were characterized by multiple layers of transparent images—many drawn from sources in ancient and Renaissance art—which created poetic, dream-like effects. Later in the 1930s Picabia produced a variety of simplified figurative studies, superimposed images, and abstract compositions.

During World War II Picabia's life style became more modest. Most of his paintings presented sentimental subjects—nudes, toreadors, flower girls—derived from popular reproductions in postcards and cheap magazines.

After the war, in 1945, Picabia and Olga returned to Paris. His work flourished in a new round of abstract art. Many old friendships were renewed, and he published several volumes of poetry. He died in Paris on November 30, 1953.

Further Reading

Picabia's writings are available in French in *Francis Picabia. Ecrits* (2 vols., 1975 and 1978). Picabia's magazine, *391,* has been reproduced in a study by Michel Sanouillet (1960). The most extensive study of Picabia is William Camfield, *Francis Picabia* (1979). An abbreviated study by Camfield is the exhibition catalogue of the Solomon R. Guggenheim Museum, *Francis Picabia* (1970). Picabia's role in Orphism has been explored by Virginia Spate in *Orphism* (1979).

Additional Sources

Picabia, New York: Rizzoli, 1985. □

Pablo Picasso

The Spanish painter, sculptor, and graphic artist Pablo Picasso (1881-1973) was one of the most prodigious and revolutionarys artists in the history of Western painting. As the central figure in developing cubism, he established the basis for abstract art.

Pablo Picasso was born Pablo Blasco on Oct. 25, 1881, in Malaga, Spain, where his father, José Ruiz Blasco, was a professor in the School of Arts and Crafts. Pablo's mother was Maria Picasso and the artist used her surname from about 1901 on. In 1891 the family moved to La Coruña, where, at the age of 14, Picasso began studying at the School of Fine Art. Under the academic instruction of his father, he developed his artistic talent at an extraordinary rate.

When the family moved to Barcelona in 1896, Picasso easily gained entrance to the School of Fine Arts. A year later he was admitted as an advanced student at the Royal Academy of San Fernando in Madrid; he demonstrated his remarkable ability by completing in one day an entrance examination for which an entire month was permitted.

But Picasso found the atmosphere at the academy stifling, and he soon returned to Barcelona, where he began to study historical and contemporary art on his own. At that time Barcelona was the most vital cultural center in Spain, and Picasso quickly joined the group of poets, painters, and writers who gathered at the famous café Quatre Gats.

In 1900 Picasso made his first visit to Paris, staying for three months. In 1901 he made a second trip to Paris, and Ambroise Vollard gave him his first one-man exhibition. Although the show was not financially successful, it did arouse the interest of the writer Max Jacob, who subsequently became one of Picasso's closest friends and supporters. For the next three years Picasso stayed alternately in Paris and Barcelona.

First Works

At the turn of the century Paris was the center of the international art world. In painting it had spawned such masters as Georges Seurat, Claude Monet, Paul Cézanne, Vincent Van Gogh, and Henri de Toulouse-Lautrec. Each of these artists practiced advanced, radical styles. In spite of obvious stylistic differences, their common denominator lay in testing the limits of traditional representation. While their works retained certain links with the visible world, they exhibited a decided tendency toward flatness and abstraction. In effect, they implied that painting need not be predicated upon the values of Renaissance illusionism.

Picasso emerged within this complicated and uncertain artistic situation in 1904 when he set up a permanent studio

in an old building called the Bateau Lavoir. There he produced some of his most revolutionary works, and the studio soon became a gathering place for the city's vanguard artists, writers, and patrons. This group included the painter Juan Gris, the writer Guillaume Apollinaire, and the American collectors Leo and Gertrude Stein.

Picasso's early work reveals a creative pattern which persisted throughout his long career. Between 1900 and 1906 he worked through nearly every major style of contemporary painting, from impressionism to Art Nouveau. In doing so, his own work changed with unprecedented quickness, revealing a spectrum of feelings that would seem to lie beyond the limits of one human being. In itself this accomplishment was a mark of Picasso's genius.

The *Moulin de la Galette* (1900), the first painting Picasso executed in Paris, presents a scene of urban café society. With its acrid colors and sharp, angular figures, the work exudes a sinister, discomforting aura. The rawness of its sensibility, although not its superficial style, is characteristic of many of his earliest works.

Blue and Pink Periods

The years between 1901 and 1904 were known as Picasso's Blue Period, during which nearly all of his works were executed in somber shades of blue and contained lean, dejected, and introspective figures. The pervasive tone of the pictures is one of depression; their color is symbolic of the artist's personal hardship during the first years of the century—years when he occasionally burned his own

drawings to keep warm—and also of the suffering which he witnessed in his society. Two outstanding examples of this period are the *Old Guitarist* (1903) and *Life* (1903).

In the second half of 1904 Picasso's style exhibited a new direction. For about a year he worked on a series of pictures featuring harlequins, acrobats, and other circus performers. The most celebrated example is the *Family of Saltimbanques* (1905). Feeling, as well as subject matter, has shifted here. The brooding depression of the Blue Period has given way to a quiet and unoppressive melancholy, and the color has become more natural, delicate, and tender in its range, with a prevalence of reddish and pink tones. Thus this period was called his Pink Period.

In terms of space, Picasso's work between 1900 and 1905 was generally flat, emphasizing the two-dimensional character of the painting surface. Late in 1905, however, he became increasingly interested in pictorial volume. This interest seems to have been stimulated by the late paintings of Cézanne, ten of which were shown in the 1905 Salon d'Automne. In Picasso's *Boy Leading a Horse* (1905) and *Woman with Loaves* (1906) the figures are vigorously modeled, giving a strong impression of their weight and three-dimensionality. The same interest pervades the famous *Portrait of Gertrude Stein* (1906), particularly in the massive body of the figure. But the face of the sitter reveals still another new interest: its mask-like abstraction was inspired by Iberian sculpture, an exhibition of which Picasso had seen at the Louvre in the spring of 1906. This influence reached its fullest expression a year later in one of the most revolutionary pictures of Picasso's entire career, *Les Demoiselles d'Avignon* (1907).

Picasso and Cubism

Les Demoiselles d'Avignon is generally regarded as the first cubist painting. Under the influence of Cézanne, Iberian sculpture, and African sculpture (which Picasso first saw in Paris in 1907) the artist launched a pictorial style more radical than anything he had produced up to that date. The human figures and their surrounding space are reduced to a series of broad, intersecting planes which align themselves with the picture surface and imply a multiple, dissected view of the visible world. The faces of the figures are seen simultaneously from frontal and profile positions, and their bodies are likewise forced to submit to Picasso's new and radically abstract pictorial language.

Paradoxically, *Les Demoiselles d'Avignon* was not exhibited in public until 1937. Very possibly the picture was as problematic for Picasso as it was for his circle of friends and fellow artists, who were shocked when they viewed it in his Bateau Lavoir studio. Even Georges Braque, who by 1908 had become Picasso's closest colleague in the cubist enterprise, at first said that "to paint in such a way was as bad as drinking petrol in the hope of spitting fire." Nevertheless, Picasso relentlessly pursued the implications of his own revolutionary invention. Between 1907 and 1911 he continued to dissect the visible world into increasingly small facets of monochromatic planes of space. In doing so, his works became more and more abstract; that is, representation gradually vanished from the painting medium, which correspondingly became an end in itself—for the first time in the history of Western art.

The evolution of this process is evident in all of Picasso's work between 1907 and 1911. Some of the most outstanding pictorial examples of the development are *Fruit Dish* (1909), *Portrait of Ambroise Vollard* (1910), and *Ma Jolie* (also known as *Woman with a Guitar,* 1911-1912).

Cubist Collages

About 1911 Picasso and Braque began to introduce letters and scraps of newspapers into their cubist paintings, thus giving birth to an entirely new medium, the cubist collage. Picasso's first, and probably his most celebrated, collage is *Still Life with Chair Caning* (1911-1912). The oval composition combines a cubist analysis of a lemon and a wineglass, letters from the world of literature, and a piece of oilcloth that imitates a section of chair caning; finally, it is framed with a piece of actual rope. As Alfred Barr wrote (1946): "Here then, in one picture, Picasso juggles reality and abstraction in two media and at four different levels or ratios. If we stop to think which is the most 'real' we find ourselves moving from esthetic to metaphysical speculation. For here what seems most real is most false and what seems remote from everyday reality is perhaps the most real since it is least an imitation."

Synthetic Cubist Phase

After his experiments in the new medium of collage, Picasso returned more intensively to painting. His work between 1912 and 1921 is generally regarded as the synthetic phase of the cubist development. The masterpiece of this style is the *Three Musicians* (1921). In this painting Picasso used the flat planes of his earlier style in order to reconstruct an impression of the visible world. The planes themselves had become broader and more simplified, and they exploited color to a far greater extent than did the work of 1907-1911. In its richness of feeling and balance of formal elements, the *Three Musicians* represents a classical expression of cubism.

Additional Achievements

The invention of cubism represents Picasso's most important achievement in the history of 20th-century art. Nevertheless, his activities as an artist were not limited to this alone. As early as the first decade of the century, he involved himself with both sculpture and printmaking, two media which he continued to practice throughout his long career and to which he made numerous important contributions. Moreover, he periodically worked in ceramics and in the environment of the theater: in 1917 he designed sets for the Eric Satie and Jean Cocteau ballet *Parade;* in 1920 he sketched a theater interior for Igor Stravinsky's *Pulcinella;* and in 1924 he designed a curtain for the performance of *Le Train Bleu* by Jean Cocteau and Darius Milhaud. In short, the range of his activities exceeded that of any artist who worked in the modern period.

In painting, even the development of cubism fails to define Picasso's genius. About 1915, and again in the early 1920s, he turned away from abstraction and produced drawings and paintings in a realistic and serenely beautiful classical idiom. One of the most famous of these works is the *Woman in White* (1923). Painted just two years after the *Three Musicians,* the quiet and unobtrusive elegance of this masterpiece testifies to the ease with which Picasso could express himself in pictorial languages that seem at first glance to be mutually exclusive.

By the late 1920s and the early 1930s surrealism had in many ways eclipsed cubism as the vanguard style of European painting. Launched by André Breton in Paris in 1924, the movement was not one to which Picasso was ever an "official" contributor in terms of group exhibitions or the signing of manifestos. But his work during these years reveals many attitudes in sympathy with the surrealist sensibility. For instance, in his famous *Girl before a Mirror* (1932), he employed the colorful planes of synthetic cubism to explore the relationship between a young woman's image and self-image as she regards herself before a conventional looking glass. As the configurations shift between the figure and the mirror image, they reveal the complexity of emotional and psychological energies that prevail on the darker side of human experience.

Guernica

Another of Picasso's most celebrated paintings of the 1930s is *Guernica* (1937). Barr described the situation within which it was conceived: "On April 28, 1937, the Basque town of Guernica was reported destroyed by German bombing planes flying for General Franco. Picasso, already an active partisan of the Spanish Republic, went into action almost immediately. He had been commissioned in January to paint a mural for the Spanish Government Building at the Paris World's Fair; but he did not begin to work until May 1st, just two days after the news of the catastrophe." The artist's deep feelings about the work, and about the massacre which inspired it, are reflected in the fact that he completed the work, that is more than 25 feet wide and 11 feet high, within six or seven weeks.

Guernica is an extraordinary monument within the history of modern art. Executed entirely in black, white, and gray, it projects an image of pain, suffering, and brutality that has few parallels among advanced paintings of the 20th century. No artist except Picasso was able to apply convincingly the pictorial language of cubism to a subject that springs directly from social and political awareness. That he could so overtly challenge the abstractionist trend that he personally began is but another mark of his uniqueness.

After World War II Picasso was established as one of the Old Masters of modern art. But his work never paused. In the 1950s and 1960s he devoted his energies to other Old Masters, producing paintings based on the masterpieces of Nicolas Poussin and Diego Velázquez. To many critics and historians these recent works are not as ambitious as Picasso's earlier productions.

Picasso Politics

Picasso also came out publicly after the war as a communist. When he was asked why he was a communist in 1947, he stated that "When I was a boy in Spain, I was very poor and aware of how poor people had to live. I learned that the communists were for the poor people. That was enough to know. So I became for the communists."

Sometimes the communist cause was not as keen on Picasso as Picasso was about being a communist. A 1953 portrait he painted of Joseph Stalin, the then recently deceased Soviet leader, caused a clamor in the Party's leadership. The Soviet government banished his works from their nation after having them locked in the basement of the Hermitage Museum in St. Petersburg. Picasso appeared amused at this and continued on unaffected.

Although Picasso had been in exile from his native Spain since the 1939 victory of Generalissimo Francisco Franco, he gave 800 to 900 of his earliest works to the city and people of Barcelona. For his part, Franco's feelings about Picasso were reciprocated. In 1963, Picasso's friend Jaime Sabartés had given 400 of his Picasso works to Barcelona. To display these works, the Palacio Aguilar was renamed the Picasso Museum and the works were moved inside. But because of Franco's dislike for Picasso, Picasso's name never appeared on the museum.

Picasso was married twice, first to dancer Olga Khoklova and then to Jacqueline Roque. He had four children, one from his marriage to Khoklova and three by mistresses. Picasso kept busy all of his life and was planning an exhibit of 201 of his works at the Avignon Arts Festival in France when he died.

Picasso died at his 35-room hilltop villa of Notre Dame de Vie in Mougins, France on April 8, 1973. He was remembered as an artist that, throughout his life, shifted unpredictably from one pictorial mode to another. He exhibited a remarkable genius for sculpture, graphics, and ceramics, as well as painting. The sheer range of his achievement, not to mention its quality and influence, made him one of the most celebrated artists of the modern period.

Further Reading

Because of his long life and unceasing production, Picasso has inspired numerous books. The classic monograph, which no one interested in the master can afford to overlook, is Alfred H. Barr, Jr., *Picasso: Fifty Years of His Art* (1946). Picasso's early years are discussed in Gertrude Stein, *Picasso* (1938); Anthony Blunt and Phoebe Pool, *Picasso: The Formative Years* (1962); Fernande Olivier, *Picasso and His Friends* (1965); and Pierre Daix and others, *Picasso: The Blue and Rose Periods* translated by Phoebe Pool (1967). The later years of Picasso are documented in Roberto Otero *Forever Picasso: An Intimate Look At His Last Years* (1974). For an overall view see Roland Penrose, *Portrait of Picasso* (1957) and *Picasso: His Life and Work* (1958). A thoughtful interpretation of the master's themes and major styles is given in Wilhelm Boeck and Jaimé Sabartes, *Picasso* (1955). Picasso's obituary can be found in the *New York Times* (April 8, 1973).
The most complete catalog of Picasso's work, C. Zervos, *Pablo Picasso: Oeuvres* (21 vols., 1942-1969), is in French. Specialized studies include Los Angeles County Museum of Art, *Picasso: Sixty Years of Graphic Works* (1967), and Roland Penrose, *The Sculpture of Picasso* (1967). For broad surveys of cubism see Robert Rosenblum, *Cubism and Twentieth-Century Art* (1960; rev. ed. 1966), and Edward F. Fry, *Cubism* (1966). □

Paloma Picasso

As the daughter of one of the twentieth century's most influential artists, Paloma Picasso (born 1949) hesitated to enter the world of design. She did not want to be compared to her father, nor did she relish the unavoidable notoriety his name would provide. Once she began to show the jewelry she created for Zolotas of Greece in 1971, however, critics were genuinely impressed.

The success of the pieces Picasso produced for Tiffany & Company encouraged Picasso to design and market items ranging from fashion accessories to china. These items, including eyewear, cosmetics, and leather goods, may be identified by their bold shapes and brilliant colors, and are sold and appreciated throughout the world. Picasso's face is just as easily recognized. Posing in glossy magazine advertisements with her perfume, Paloma Picasso, the designer is, according to *Hispanic,* "her own best model." While Pablo Picasso transformed aesthetic standards in the fine arts, his trend-setting daughter has independently introduced fresh perspectives in fashion design.

Born April 19, 1949, Paloma Picasso has always been surrounded by art and artists. Pablo Picasso, the Spanish painter who was instrumental in the development of cubism, and Françoise Gilot, the French painter, named their daughter after the "paloma," or dove, that Picasso had created for the posters announcing an International Peace Conference in Paris, France.

As a teenager developing her own tastes and styles, Paloma Picasso was reluctant to pursue artistic goals. "In the beginning, I tried not to think that I would have to do anything artistic," she related in *Hispanic.* "From the time I was fourteen, I stopped drawing completely. . . . I thought, 'I don't want to become a painter like my father,' but I didn't know what else I wanted to become." Picasso's urge to create soon surpassed her hesitation; she began to study jewelry design and fabrication while still in her teens.

Personal and Business Partnership with Lopez-Cambil

After the elder Picasso died, Paloma Picasso lost interest in designing. "I had given up designing when my father died in 1973," she recounted to the *New York Times.* "I didn't feel like doing anything. I just looked at all the paintings, and there was the sense of being overwhelmed." Picasso's father had left no will, and his illegitimate children, Paloma, her brother Claude, and her half-sister Maya, brought suit for their share of the estate, which was valued at $250 million. When Paloma Picasso finally won her share of the inheritance, which was estimated to be close to $90 million, she chose some of her father's works. As the French government had also received a huge sum and a collection of works as taxes from the estate, Picasso consented to assist it in the creation of the Musée Picasso in Paris.

Although Picasso had temporarily given up designing, she began another artistic endeavor. She starred in a motion picture that won the Prix de l'Age d'Or, 1974's *Immoral Tales* (*Contes Immorreaux*). Directed by Walerian Borowczyk, the movie was praised by critics, and Picasso's performance as a Hungarian countess with eccentric sexual desires was met with enthusiasm. The *New York Times* reported, "Paloma Picasso, the late Pablo's daughter . . . has a magnificent figure and a face as beautiful as her father's drawings from his classical period." While Picasso has not since pursued acting, she has often expressed her hope to portray the designer Coco Chanel in a motion picture.

Picasso met the Argentine playwright and director Rafael Lopez-Cambil (known by his pen name, Rafael Lopez-Sanchez) after her father's death. When she began to work again, it was for Lopez-Cambil; Picasso designed the sets for some of his productions. The relationship between Picasso and Lopez-Cambil became personal, and the couple married in 1978.

The wedding was an event. Wearing a red, black, and white Yves St. Laurent original for the ceremony, and a heart-shaped, red, Karl Lagerfeld gown for the disco reception, Picasso once again excited the fashion world. The *New York Times* stated that during these years, Paloma Picasso had become "something of a muse to Paris couturiers," and especially to the designers of her wedding gowns. The petite woman had once again impressed the design world.

Association with Tiffany & Company

In 1980, John Loring, senior vice-president of Tiffany & Company, asked Picasso to create jewelry for the company. "When Tiffany's asked me about doing jewelry, I was thrilled," Picasso told the *New York Times*. She had always wanted to design for an American store. "I went into all the great jewelry shops of Paris. They are so grand, the salespeople seem to look down on you. As a customer you feel threatened. Tiffany is a great place because all kinds of people come in, just like Woolworth's." The company was equally enthusiastic about Picasso, whose pieces are priced from just over $100 to $500,000. Loring spoke of her in *Hispanic*, "Paloma has taken the gaudiness out of jewelry but kept the glitter," and Henry B. Platt, Tiffany's president, proudly exclaimed in *Newsweek* that "for the first time, people can hold a Picasso in their hands and try it on."

Brilliant gems framed in blocks of gold, large stones or metal pendants on simple cords, and gold or silver "hugs and kisses" ("X's" and "O's") are characteristic of Picasso's work. Unusual combinations of pearls, vibrant semi-precious stones, and metals are also prominent. Although her creations portend a new aesthetic for jewelry, Picasso, commented *Newsweek*, "rejects fine-art pretensions." The designer told the magazine, "This [jewelry] is something people can wear, rather than hanging it on the wall or putting it on the table. I like things to be used." In the *New York Times*, Picasso remarked that while "jewelry should be jewelry, something that you wear," it "is more permanent, less superficial than fashion." Picasso continues to design fabulous jewelry for Tiffany & Company. Her tenth anniversary collection, which was presented in 1990, was described in *Mirabella* magazine as "having the raw power of just-cut stones and just-mined minerals. Her gems are deep pools of color hung on thick veins of gold."

Collaborated with Husband on Fragrance Development

In 1984 the plan to reinforce the Paloma Picasso image began with her fragrance, "Paloma Picasso." It seemed natural for her and her husband to come up with Paloma's own designer scent; Picasso's grandfather, Emile Gilot, was a chemist and perfume manufacturer.

With his experience in the theater, Lopez-Cambil carefully developed the fragrance project. He came up with a particular image for Picasso, which culminated in one of the most well known advertisements in the world, photographed by Richard Avedon, whereby Paloma Picasso the person was inextricably linked to Paloma Picasso the brand. As a couple and a team, this particular partnership had the advantage of a brilliant artistic director and a gifted designer.

Picasso, who habitually clothed herself in red, black, and gold, stated in *Vogue* that the perfume resembles herself: "What you see is what you get. I wanted my fragrance to be like that too." She made a similar remark in the *New York Post* when she announced that her perfume, which is priced at over $150.00 an ounce, is a "fragrance for a strong woman like myself." Picasso extended her fragrance collection and produced her signature lipstick, Mon Rouge, which escalated to her hallmark color, also know as Paloma Red.

Expanded Picasso Image

The continual success of Paloma and Rafael's ventures encouraged them to broaden their creative horizons even further. In 1987 Rafael expanded the Paloma Picasso image by creating a New York City-based company, Lopez-Cambil Ltd., to produce and distribute Paloma Picasso accessories—handbags, belts, umbrellas, and small leather goods—to be imported from Italy. This collection, labeled as Couture accessories, gained international notoriety for its flawless quality and impeccable design, which fueled the creation of their relatively less-expensive line, entitled "By Paloma Picasso." Both casual and elegant, this collection allows Picasso to reach a larger audience, with a comprehensive range of contemporary, affordable accessories, which constitutes a fast-growing part of the company.

In 1992 the men's fragrance Minotaure was launched with great success. Picasso designed the bottle and packaging, while Lopez-Cambil developed the concept, the name, and the cologne's first advertising campaign.

In addition to Paloma Picasso boutiques in Japan and Hong Kong, Picasso's accessories are available throughout the United States, Europe, and the Far East. Paloma Picasso creations in Europe also include cosmetics and fragrances for L'Oreal in France, sunglasses and optical frames for a German company, hosiery for Grupo Synkro in Mexico, and bed ensembles, towels, bathrobes, and dressing gowns for KBC in Germany. As in the United States, home design has become a new era of creation for Paloma Picasso, with collections of bone china, crystal, silver, and tiles for Villeroy & Boch and fabrics and wall coverings for Motif.

Further Reading

Harper's Bazaar, December 1989, pp. 144-50; January 1991, pp. 123-26.
Hispanic, October 1988, p. 36; December 1988, pp. 28-33; May 1991, pp. 20-26.
House and Garden, November 1990, pp. 236-76.
House Beautiful, February 1989, pp. 103-104.
Mirabella, November 1990; December 1990.
Newsmakers, Volume 1, Detroit, Gale Research, 1991, pp. 89-92.
Newsweek, October 20, 1980, p. 69.
New York Post, March 26, 1984.
New York Times, March 11, 1976; June 9, 1980, p. B16; April 22, 1990, p. S38.
New York Times Magazine, April 22, 1990, p. 38.
Vogue, April 1981, pp. 229-31; December 1985, pp. 318-31; January 1990, pp. 190-97.
Working Woman, October 1990, pp. 140-45.
Additional information for this profile was provided by a Lopez-Cambil Ltd. biography of Paloma Picasso, 1995. □

Auguste Piccard

The Swiss scientist Auguste Piccard (1884-1962) is famed for his explorations of the stratosphere and the ocean depths.

Born into an academic family in Basel on Jan. 28, 1884, Auguste Piccard was educated there and at the Zurich Polytechnic. From 1907 he taught in Zurich, was early interested in aviation, and studied the behavior of balloons. In 1922 he went to Brussels University as professor of physics, where he remained until 1954 (except during the war years, which he spent in Switzerland). He wished to investigate the physics of the stratosphere, a region which was beyond the range of sensitive automatic instruments until the advent of electronics and continuous radio monitoring from the ground. Supported by the Belgian Fonds National de la Recherche Scientifique, in 1930 Piccard designed a hydrogen balloon supporting an airtight cabin to carry an observer into the stratosphere. With this balloon (named *FNRS*) in 1931-1932 he reached record heights of over 50,000 feet. Thus was a new era of scientific exploration opened. Lack of funds prevented his participation in further flights.

In 1937 Piccard turned to deep-sea exploration and developed the bathyscaphe, the underwater analog of his stratosphere balloon. Aided again by the Belgian foundation, work began but was interrupted by war. Thus the first

bathyscaphe, *FNRS 2,* was not completed until 1948. It consisted of a strong spherical cast-steel capsule with Plexiglas windows supported by a lightly constructed float filled with petroleum. As in an air balloon, vertical movement was controlled by the release of ballast or supporting fluid. In the bathyscaphe iron-shot ballast was retained by energized electromagnets and released by interrupting the current. Dives off Dakar in 1948 proved the utility of the system.

In 1950 the vessel was transferred to the French navy and a new bathyscaphe, *FNRS 3,* was constructed. Initially under the direction of Piccard, it utilized the pressure capsule and much essential equipment from the *FNRS 2.* But difficulties with the French and contacts made in Italy by Piccard's son, Jacques, led to their building a third bathyscaphe, the *Trieste,* with Swiss and Italian funds in 1952-1953. Essentially similar to the *FNRS* vessels, the new bathyscaphe had many improvements, including a forged-steel capsule. A successful dive of more than 10,000 feet was completed off Capri in 1953. Shortage of funds hampered research until 1957, when support was received from the U.S. Navy. After evaluation the *Trieste* was purchased and shipped to San Diego. In 1960, with a strengthened observation capsule and increased buoyancy, the bathyscaphe dived 35,800 feet to the bottom of the Challenger Deep in the Mariana Trench off Guam, the world's deepest known hole.

From 1954 Piccard led an active retirement in Lausanne, where he died on March 24, 1962. Most of the *Trieste's* work after 1953 was directed by Jacques Piccard.

Further Reading

Auguste Piccard, *In Balloon and Bathyscaphe* (1956), and Jacques Piccard and Robert S. Dietz, *Seven Miles Down* (1962), provide informative, if popularized, accounts of the Piccards' work. G. Houot and P. Willm, *Two Thousand Fathoms Down* (1955), gives an illuminating but chauvinistic account of the *FNRS 3.* □

Edward Charles Pickering

The American astronomer Edward Charles Pickering (1846-1919) was a pioneer in the fields of stellar spectroscopy and photometry.

Edward Pickering was born on July 19, 1846, in Boston, Mass., of a distinguished New England family. After studying at Boston Latin School, he attended Lawrence Scientific School, graduating *summa cum laude* in 1865. He taught mathematics at that institution for a year and then moved to Massachusetts Institute of Technology, becoming Thayer professor of physics in 1868. He married Elizabeth Wardsworth Sparks in 1874.

In 1876 Pickering accepted the directorship of the Harvard Observatory, an appointment that both surprised and angered many, for he had no experience as an observational astronomer. The choice of a physicist, however, placed Harvard in the leadership of the trend, growing since the midcentury, toward a "new astronomy" which used the methods of the physicist to seek a knowledge of stellar structure and its evolution. The day of the observer, who noted the positions of heavenly bodies, was virtually over, and Pickering's appointment to such an important post may well have symbolized the victory of the new astronomy over the old.

The most important achievement of Pickering's directorate was in stellar photometry, a field barely explored with large instruments at the time. When he began the work, even the magnitudes of the stars were not fixed on any generally accepted scale. Pickering established a widely accepted scale and employed instruments, at least one— the meridian photometer—of his own invention, to achieve unprecedented accuracy in determining the magnitudes of 80,000 stars.

Pickering's second work, begun in 1885, was the compilation of a "photographic library," as he called it, giving a complete photographic chart of the stellar universe down to the eleventh magnitude on some 300,000 glass plates. From such plates the past record of the stars may be studied; Pickering, for example, was able to plot the path of Eros in the sky from photographs taken 4 years before this asteroid was discovered.

Pickering was also a leader in stellar spectroscopy, laying the foundation for the method of spectral classification now universally accepted and obtaining the material for the *Draper Catalogue,* containing 200,000 stars. He twice received the Gold Medal of the Royal Astronomical Society, was a member of the National Academy of Sciences, and was a founder in 1898 of the American Astronomical Society, of which he was later president. By the time of his death, on Feb. 3, 1919, he was generally recognized as one of the two or three outstanding astronomical researchers in America.

Further Reading

The only source of biographical data on Pickering is Solon I. Bailey, *The History and Work of Harvard Observatory, 1839-1927* (1931). Bailey's memoir of Pickering, with a bibliography of Pickering's writings, is in National Academy of Sciences, *Biographical Memoirs,* vol. 15 (1934). □

Timothy Pickering

Timothy Pickering (1745-1829) was an American Revolutionary soldier before becoming secretary of war and then secretary of state under President Washington.

Timothy Pickering was born in Salem, Mass., on July 17, 1745, the son of Timothy and Mary Wingate Pickering. He graduated from Harvard College in 1763, studied law in Salem while serving as a clerk in Essex County, and was admitted to the bar in 1768. He became register of deeds in 1774. In 1766 he was commissioned a lieutenant in the county militia. He was a colonel by 1775 and was appointed by George Washington as adjutant general of the U.S. Army in 1777, becoming quartermaster general in 1780.

After the Revolution, Pickering became a merchant in Philadelphia. He moved in 1787 to western Pennsylvania, where he was elected to represent Luzerne County in the state convention that ratified the Federal Constitution. Appointed as postmaster general by President Washington in 1791, he served for over 3 years before becoming secretary of war in January 1795. Washington made him secretary of state late in 1795, and he continued in that post when John Adams became president.

An ardent Federalist and a bitter critic of the French Revolution, Pickering became a leading advocate of the quasi-war with France that followed the "XYZ affair" in 1798. Fearful of "French influence" in American politics, he viewed the Jeffersonian Republicans as subversives, and he supervised the enforcement of the Sedition Law against Jeffersonian critics of the Adams administration. Always more loyal to Alexander Hamilton than to Adams, however, Pickering broke with the President when Adams insisted on negotiating a settlement with France. Adams finally dismissed him from the Cabinet on May 10, 1800.

After a brief return to western Pennsylvania, Pickering moved to Massachusetts, where he became U.S. senator in 1803. A virulent opponent of presidents Thomas Jefferson and James Madison, he urged the establishment of a northern confederacy in 1804, arguing that peaceful secession was the only way to protect New England's commercial interests. Defeated for the Senate in 1811, he served on the Executive Council of Massachusetts in 1812-1813 before winning election to Congress, where he again became Madison's leading opponent from 1813 to 1817. A controversialist to the end, he wrote a polemical pamphlet criticizing John Adams in 1824. Pickering died in Salem on Jan. 29, 1829.

Further Reading

The biography of Pickering by Octavius Pickering and C. W. Upham, *The Life of Timothy Pickering* (4 vols., 1867-1873), is uncritical. Specialized studies include Hervey P. Prentiss, *Timothy Pickering as the Leader of New England Federalism, 1800-1815* (1934), and Gerald H. Clarfield, *Timothy Pickering and American Diplomacy, 1795-1800* (1969).

Additional Sources

Clarfield, Gerard H., *Timothy Pickering and the American Republic,* Pittsburgh, PA.: University of Pittsburgh Press, 1980.
□

Conte Giovanni Pico della Mirandola

The Italian philosopher and humanist Conte Giovanni Pico della Mirandola (1463-1494) was a brilliant exemplar of the Renaissance ideal of man.

The youngest son of a princely Lombard house, Giovanni Pico della Mirandola received a Church benefice when he was 10 years old. However, Pico quickly surpassed the routine expectation of a career in Church or state. At the University of Padua from 1480 to 1482, when the city and its university enjoyed the liberal patronage of Venice, welcomed Eastern scholars, and offered one of Europe's richest civic cultures, he studied Aristotelianism and Hebrew and Arabic religion, philosophy, and science. By 1487 his travels and education, broadened to include Florence and Paris, had steeped Pico in a unique variety of languages and traditions. Committed to no exclusive source of wisdom and disappointed by the philosophic weakness of the Italian humanists' study of classical culture, he sought a core of truth common to this vast knowledge.

The young man's first and most famous venture was a challenge to Europe's scholars for public disputation at Rome in 1487. Pico prepared to defend 900 *conclusiones*— 402 drawn from other philosophers (most heavily from scholastic, Platonic, and Arabic thinkers) and 498 his own. However, a papal commission, suspicious of such diversity, condemned 13 of Pico's theses. The assembly was canceled, and he fled to Paris, suffering brief imprisonment before settling in Florence late in 1487. His writings for the disputation were banned until 1493.

unfinished attack on astrology, rejected occult thought which subordinated human will to deterministic forces.

Further Reading

Many works are collected and translated by Paul Miller and others in Pico's *On the Dignity of Man; On Being and the One; Heptaplus* (1965). For samples of the extensive scholarly disputes about Pico see Avery Dulles, *Princeps Concordiae: Pico della Mirandola and the Scholastic Tradition* (1941), which has a critical bibliography; Eugenio Garin, *Italian Humanism: Philosophy and Civic Life in the Renaissance* (1952; trans. 1965); Ernst Cassirer, *The Individual and the Cosmos in Renaissance Philosophy* (1963); and Paul Oskar Kresteller's three works: *Renaissance Thought: The Classic, Scholastic and Humanistic Strains* (1955; rev. ed. 1961), *Eight Philosophers of the Italian Renaissance* (1964), and his edition of *Renaissance Essays* (1968), which contains an essay by Cassirer on Pico. □

Franklin Pierce

The administration of Franklin Pierce (1804-1869), fourteenth president of the United States, was marred by the bitter quarrel resulting from the passage of the 1854 Kansas-Nebraska Act.

Franklin Pierce was born in Hillsborough County, N.H., on Nov. 23, 1804, the son of a Revolutionary general and governor of New Hampshire. Pierce graduated from Bowdoin College and studied law under Levi Woodbury, who was secretary of the Treasury under Andrew Jackson and Martin Van Buren. Following his father, Pierce joined the Democratic party, supporting Jackson for election in 1828. Pierce served in the New Hampshire Legislature (1828-1832) and in the U.S. House of Representatives (1832-1842). Pierce declined President James Polk's offer of the position of attorney general, instead accepting appointment as U.S. attorney for New Hampshire. During the Mexican War, Pierce served as a brigadier general under Winfield Scott.

Because he was relatively unknown and had not antagonized voters, Pierce received the Democratic nomination for president in 1852. Though he was elected over Scott, the Whig candidate, his overall majority was only 50,000 out of over 3 million votes cast.

As president, Pierce was mainly concerned with promoting national unity by including all Democratic factions in the Cabinet and by strictly adhering to the Compromise of 1850. Pierce hated change and relied on tradition to steer the government. However, his hopes for unity were destroyed by the passage of the Kansas-Nebraska Act, which repealed the Missouri Compromise of 1820. Enactment of this law led to a revolt by antislavery Democrats and to the creation of the Republican party, replacing the Whig party in the North. Pierce's vigorous enforcement of the Fugitive Slave Act alienated the same elements.

At Florence, Pico joined Lorenzo de' Medici's Platonic Academy in its effort to formulate a doctrine of the soul that would reconcile Platonic and Christian beliefs. Pico's ambition, which many critics attribute to youthful confusion, can be measured by his plan to harmonize Plato and Aristotle and to link their philosophies with revelations proclaimed by the major religions. Preparatory treatises included the *Heptaplus* of 1489, a commentary on Genesis stressing its correspondence with sacred Jewish texts, and the work *De ente et uno* of 1492, on the nature of God and creation.

Pico gradually renounced Medicean splendor, embraced the piety of the reforming friar Girolamo Savonarola, and began writing in defense of the Church. Pico's philanthropy kept pace with his purchase of manuscripts, as he built one of Europe's great private scholarly collections. He died of fever on Nov. 17, 1494, as French soldiers occupied Florence.

Described as being "of feature and shape seemly and beauteous," Pico combined physique, intellect, and spirituality in a way that captivated both the lovers of *virtù* and Christian reformers. In his *De hominis dignitate,* written to introduce his abortive Roman congress, Pico had God endow Adam with "what abode, what form, and what functions thou thyself shalt desire . . . so that with freedom of choice and with honor, thou mayest fashion thyself." This early tract asserted the philosophy that Pico's later and more complex works stressed: the active intellect can discern right from wrong, truth from illusion, and is free to guide the soul, indeed to bind all men, to union with a common creator. Pico's late work *Disputationes in astrologiam,* an

Kansas created other major problems. Pierce's inept gubernatorial appointee in Kansas was unable to prevent either the election frauds committed by the Missourians who crossed the border or the violence that erupted between pro- and antislavery settlers. By 1856 complete chaos existed in Kansas; two governments were established, and Pierce was helpless to control the situation.

In foreign policy, Pierce and his secretary of state, William L. Marcy, generally followed expansionistic policies. They tried to purchase Cuba and officially recognized the regime set up by the American adventurer William Walker in Nicaragua. Pierce also tried to increase American prestige by mediating the Crimean War between England and Russia.

Because of Northern opposition to Pierce, James Buchanan defeated him at the Democratic convention in 1856. He retired to New Hampshire and was accused of being a Southern sympathizer during the Civil War. He died in Concord on Oct. 8, 1869.

Further Reading

The only biography of Pierce is Roy Nichols, *Franklin Pierce: Young Hickory of the Granite Hills* (1931; 2d rev. ed. 1958), a sympathetic portrait. Material on his administration and the politics of the era is in Ivor D. Spencer, *The Victor and the Spoils: A Life of William Marcy* (1958), and Philip S. Klein, *President James Buchanan: A Biography* (1962). □

Piero della Francesca

Piero della Francesca (ca. 1415-1492), painter, mathematician, and theorist, was one of the most influential Italian artists of the early Renaissance.

Piero della Francesca was the son of Benedetto dei Franceschi, a shoemaker and tanner in Borgo San Sepolcro near Arezzo. Piero was called "della Francesca," according to Giorgio Vasari, because he was raised by his mother, who had been widowed before his birth.

Piero was mentioned in a document of Sept. 7, 1439, as "being with" Domenico Veneziano when Domenico was painting in S. Egidio and S. Maria Nuova, Florence. During the 1440s Piero was in San Sepolcro and Ferrara. In 1451 he executed a frescoed portrait of Sigismondo Malatesta in the Tempio Malatestiano, Rimini. On April 12, 1459, he was paid for work (lost) done in the Vatican, Rome. He decorated the choir of S. Francesco, Arezzo, between 1452 and 1466. From 1467 until his death he remained in San Sepolcro except for brief periods in Bastia (1468), Urbino (1469), and Rimini (1482). He served on the town council of San Sepolcro and was a member of the Company of St. Bartholomew. His will is dated July 5, 1487. Vasari relates that the artist was blind and had to be led about by a boy during his last years. Piero died on Oct. 12, 1492.

The *Baptism of Christ* is a good introduction to Piero's style. Within an arched frame the baptism is taking place in a landscape strikingly similar to the countryside around San Sepolcro. The static, dour figures arranged in regular geometric patterns across the panel's surface are lit by the limpid, luminous Umbrian light. To the left, a trio of angels restricts the view into the distance; to the right, space opens up to reveal a disrobing figure and, further back, a group of bearded patriarchs before a distant landscape. In this picture Piero showed a concern for rational, measurable space, luminosity, and pearly colors. No documents are associated with this picture. Some scholars consider it Piero's earliest work, about 1440-1445; others date it in the early 1450s.

The legend of the True Cross in the choir of S. Francesco, Arezzo, is Piero's most extensive fresco cycle. The scenes are filled with impassive, static figures that impart a soothing quietness to the various episodes. Even in the battle scenes there is a sense of order and quiet rather than confusion and noise. His interest in clearly articulated, rational space can be seen in the *Meeting of Solomon with the Queen of Sheba;* his interest in the effects of light in the *Dream of Constantine,* the first realistic nocturnal scene in Italian art. These murals were painted between 1452, the date of the death of Bicci di Lorenzo, the artist first commissioned to paint them, and Dec. 20, 1466, when a document referred to them as complete.

Other noteworthy works from Piero's mature period are the *Flagellation,* a panel; the *Madonna del Parto,* a fresco in the cemetery chapel at Monterchi; and the *Resurrection,* a detached fresco. In the *Resurrection* the life-size Risen

Christ steps wearily from his sarcophagus while looking directly out at the beholder. Piero depicts him as a manly figure with the awesome vigor of a Byzantine Pantocrator. Behind Christ a mauve Umbrian landscape is lit by the moist, pearly light of dawn, and in the foreground four soldiers are sleeping.

Piero was aware of Flemish painting, as can be seen in his *Nativity*. He probably knew the art of Rogier van der Weyden and may have met him, for Rogier was in Ferrara the same time (ca. 1450) as Piero. He would certainly have known Justus of Ghent, who served the court at Urbino. The Flemish qualities in Piero's work include his use of the oil paint technique and some iconographic types, such as the Madonna del Parto and the Madonna of Humility in the *Nativity*.

In 1465 Piero executed a diptych portrait of Federigo da Montefeltro, the Duke of Urbino, and his wife. The artist's major work for Federigo was the altarpiece, *Madonna with Saints and Donor,* which dates in the late 1470s.

Piero wrote three treatises. *De prospectiva pingendi,* written before 1482, deals with linear perspective and is still the definitive work on the subject. The other treatises are concerned with painting and business mathematics.

Further Reading

All modern scholarship concerning Piero della Francesca derives from the pioneering work of Roberto Longhi. Longhi's works, which date from 1914 to 1942, are in Italian, but the fruits of his discoveries have been incorporated in English-language works. Kenneth Clark's readable monograph is *Piero della Francesca* (1951; 2d ed. 1969). Also useful is Piero Bianconi, *All the Paintings of Piero della Francesca* (trans. 1962). Bernard Berenson wrote interesting essays on Piero in his *Central Italian Painters of the Renaissance* (1897; 2d rev. ed. 1909) and *Piero della Francesca; or, The Ineloquent in Art* (1954). □

Arthur Cecil Pigou

The English economist Arthur Cecil Pigou (1877-1959) is best known for his basic contributions to the theory of welfare economics and for his defense of neoclassic economics against the attacks of the Keynesian school.

Son of an army officer, A.C. Pigou was born on Nov. 18, 1877. Educated at Harrow and King's College, Cambridge, he compiled a brilliant record that included numerous prizes. He was made a fellow of King's College in 1902 and, in 1908, succeeded Alfred Marshall in the chair of political economy.

Like Marshall, Pigou felt that the study of economics could be justified only as a means of improving human society. Building upon the base of Marshallian economics, he set out modifying, expanding, and adapting the apparatus so that it could be directly applied to the exploration of ways and means by which social intervention would yield benefits in terms of economic welfare.

Wealth and Welfare (1912) contains, in embryonic form, the central core of Pigou's contribution to economic theory. Beginning from the proposition that economic welfare depends upon the size, the manner of distribution, and the variability of the national dividend, Pigou carefully analyzed the competitive economic system to find how it falls short of the ideal and the means by which the ideal can be achieved. The central concept of his analysis was the distinction between private and social net product—private product being the product that accrues to the individual making a decision concerning production, and social net product being the net product that accrues to society as a result of the decision. In a competitive economy, decisions are made in such a way as to maximize private net product but not necessarily social net product. Appropriate taxes and subsidies could, however, make private and social net products equal, thus leading each individual to behave in a way that maximizes social welfare.

In 1933 Pigou published *The Theory of Unemployment,* a book that was held in great esteem by orthodox economists. As such, it became a prime target for attack by John Maynard Keynes in his *General Theory of Employment Interest and Money* (1936). Pigou answered with several books and articles in which he attempted to reformulate his position in the light of Keynes's criticisms. In the end, his most lasting contribution was to point out that, as long as wage and price flexibility exists, the value of assets, the prices of which are fixed in money terms, will rise as wages and prices fall, reducing the propensity to save and, consequently, increasing the propensity to consume. It follows from the "Pigou effect" that Keynes's "under-employment equilibrium" is not a true equilibrium but a state of disequilibrium occasioned by inflexible wages and prices.

Pigou died on March 7, 1959, at the age of 81.

Further Reading

No biography or complete bibliography of Pigou's work has been published. The King's College Library catalog lists almost 30 books and over 100 pamphlets and articles. For background see Philip Charles Newman, *The Development of Economic Thought* (1952); Edmund Whittaker, *Schools and Streams of Economic Thought* (1960); and Ben B. Seligman, *Main Currents in Modern Economics: Economic Thought since 1870* (1962). □

Zebulon Pike

The career of Zebulon Pike (1779-1813), American soldier and explorer, was dominated by ambiguously motivated explorations of the American West. During one of these he unsuccessfully tried to climb the Colorado mountain named for him, Pike's Peak.

Zebulon Pike was the son of a U.S. Army major of the same name. Zebulon was born on Jan. 5, 1779, in Lamberton (now Trenton), N.J. He entered his father's company as a cadet and was commissioned a first lieutenant when he was 20 years old. He served on the frontier with the Army but made no particular mark until Gen. James Wilkinson chose him to lead an expedition to find the source of the Mississippi River.

Pike left St. Louis, Mo., on Aug. 9, 1805, in a keelboat. He got 100 miles above the Falls of St. Anthony in Minnesota before winter closed in on his 20-man party. He took a few men onward, hauling supplies on sleds, and decided that Lake Leech was the source of the mighty Mississippi. He was wrong; Lake Itasca is the actual source. Wilkinson may not have cared where the true source lay. There were rumors that Wilkinson was using Pike to test British reaction to American invasion of the fur-trapping country. Even more likely was the story that the expedition was a dry run to test Pike for a venture closer to Wilkinson's heart.

Returning to St. Louis, Pike was sent out again on this pet expedition of the wily Wilkinson. Ostensibly, Pike was to explore the headwaters of the Arkansas and Red rivers and to "approximate" the settlements of New Mexico. Perhaps no one will ever know exactly what was in Wilkinson's mind, but the American general, who was a paid secret agent of Spain, was not above double-crossing the Spanish. If Pike had questions, he was too good and obedient an officer to balk at the orders of his general. He set out on April 30, 1806, mindful of Wilkinson's impossible admonition not to give alarm or offense to the Spaniards. He knew that

relations between the United States and Spain on their common frontier had never been good, but especially so since the expedition of Meriwether Lewis and William Clark in 1804-1806.

While Pike was making his preparations in St. Louis, Spanish spies in the United States were rushing word of the proposed march to Chihuahua, Mexico, where Don Nemesio Salcedo y Salcedo maintained his headquarters as commander in chief of the northern provinces of New Spain. The general ordered a force of cavalry under Lt. Don Facundo Melgares to move north out of Santa Fe, pick up Native American allies, and stop Pike.

Pike moved from the Pawnee Indian villages on the Republican River to the area of modern Pueblo, Col., and tried—unsuccessfully—to climb Pike's Peak. He then explored South Park and the head of the Arkansas River in the Rocky Mountains before turning southward in search of the source of the Red River, as ordered. Crossing the Sangre de Cristo Mountains, Pike halted on the Conejos fork of the Rio Grande and built a fort of cottonwood logs. This was intended as a defense against Native Americans, not Spaniards, according to Pike. Melgares did not find Pike in the great open spaces of the High Plains, but another Spanish detachment did. They came up to Pike's stockade and invited him to visit Santa Fe with them. Pike told them that he thought he was on the Red River, not the Rio Grande, but accepted the "invitation" and went to Santa Fe; here Melgares took over, escorting him to Chihuahua.

If he was indeed a prisoner, Pike was treated very well by the Spaniards. However, they confiscated most of his papers. (He managed to conceal some notes in his men's rifle barrels.) Finally, after a year's absence, he was returned to the United States at Natchitoches, La., by a Spanish escort.

Pike's name was now linked with Wilkinson's, and the young explorer had to protest his innocence directly to Secretary of War Henry Dearborn. The latter absolved him of all complicity in any plot against Spaniards or anyone else. Though the information that Pike brought back on the western plains region and the Rocky Mountains was useful, it pales when contrasted with the rich and detailed journals of Lewis and Clark.

Resuming his military career, Pike became a major in 1808 and a colonel in 1812. After the outbreak of the War of 1812 he was promoted to brigadier general (1813) and took command of the troops attacking York (now Toronto), Canada. In the assault he personally led his men to victory. Rifle fire and shore batteries were keeping off the landing of the American troops at York when he personally took command, telling one of his aides: "By God, I can't stand here any longer. Come on, jump into my boat." He then led the assault on the heavily defended town. The British withdrew but they deliberately exploded their powder magazine. Forty of their own men were killed in the blast along with 52 Americans. Another 180 U.S. soldiers lay wounded, among them Gen. Zebulon Pike. He was in terrible pain from a piece of stone which had broken his spine. Moved to a boat and then to the flagship *Madison,* he lived long enough, in agony, to hear the cheers of his victorious men and to have a

captured British flag placed under his head as a pillow. He died on April 27, 1813.

Pike's *An Account of Expeditions to the Sources of the Mississippi . . .* (1810), though clumsily put together for the press, managed to capture the imagination of a large segment of the American public which was curious about the West. Later editions proved to be more dependable and less chaotic. It is as difficult to judge Pike the writer as Pike the explorer, for he apparently was intent on putting things in the best light. Thus his account is not as honest a work as Lewis and Clark's journals. Still, Pike was a dedicated American soldier and a patriot.

Further Reading

Pike's career has attracted the attention of many historians of the West, and there is no shortage of books and articles about his expeditions. The most scholarly biography is W. Eugene Hollon, *The Lost Pathfinder: Zebulon Montgomery Pike* (1949). Less scholarly is John Upton Terrell, *Zebulon Pike* (1968). An excellent edition of Pike's travel accounts is Donald Jackson, ed., *The Journals of Zebulon M. Pike, with Letters and Related Documents* (1966). □

Charles Alfred Pillsbury

Charles Alfred Pillsbury (1842-1899), American businessman, built the largest flour-milling company in the world in the late 19th century.

Charles A. Pillsbury was born to a farming family in New Hampshire. After graduating from Dartmouth College in 1864, he spent several years in Montreal engaged in various business ventures. In 1869 he settled in Minneapolis and purchased an interest in a flour mill at the suggestion of his uncle John S. Pillsbury, a leading citizen of the town. In 1870 Charles Pillsbury, his uncle, and father formed a family partnership which became the nucleus of the Pillsbury milling empire.

During the 1870s the Pillsbury interests expanded rapidly. By 1880 the family partnership had acquired four other mills, and in 1881 they built the largest single flour mill in the world. Although Charles Pillsbury initially devoted his efforts to mill management, he later traveled widely in Europe, becoming familiar with market conditions and investigating new milling techniques. He imported the roller process into the United States from Hungary and also was one of the first mill operators to install the middlings purifier. These two innovations permitted the production of fine flour from the hard spring wheat of the region, giving further impetus to the growth of Minneapolis as a flour-milling center.

Disaster struck in 1881, when three mills burned, but the Pillsburys rebuilt the mills, and by 1889 the three main units had a capacity of over 10,000 barrels of flour per day. During the 1880s wheat and flour prices sank to depressed levels, and competition became severe. Because of this and because of their desire to gain a foothold in the British

market and utilize the worldwide British marketing facilities, the Pillsburys in 1899 merged with competing mills under the aegis of a British syndicate and became the Pillsbury-Washburn Company Ltd., the largest flour-milling organization in the world.

The Pillsburys retained a large stock interest in the combine, and Charles Pillsbury was made managing director. In this capacity he became an innovator in marketing as well as technology. Bypassing the commission merchants who traditionally sold flour-mill output, he established a national, and eventually an international, marketing organization that made the trade name "Pillsbury's Best" known throughout the world.

A simple, direct, unaffected man of great energy, Pillsbury was highly revered not only in the milling trade but among farmers, whose interests he constantly defended.

Further Reading

There is no biography of Pillsbury. Perhaps the best sketch of his life and career is in Return I. Holcombe and William H. Bingham, eds., *History and Biography of Minneapolis and Hennepin Country, Minnesota* (1914). The volume by David D. Pilsbury and Emily A. Getchell, *The Pillsbury Family* (1898), also contains a sketch of Charles Pillsbury. The history of the Pillsbury Company is treated in a somewhat romanticized fashion by Philip W. Pillsbury, *The Pioneering Pillsburys* (1950). A more objective account is contained in Charles Byron Kuhlmann, *The Development of the Flour-milling Industry in the United States* (1929). □

Germain Pilon

Germain Pilon (ca. 1535-1590) was the leading French sculptor of his time. Trained in the Italianate mode of Fontainebleau, he developed an independent style that combined realism and emotional intensity.

Germain Pilon, the son of a mason, was born in Paris. He may have been a pupil of the sculptor Pierre Bontemps. The Italian painter and designer Francesco Primaticcio constituted a more important influence on Pilon's early work. In 1560 Pilon worked for Primaticcio on the monument for the heart of Henry II (now in the Louvre, Paris). The Three Graces that support the urn transcend the formal elegance of design and cool, graceful figures of the Fontainebleau school in their beautifully manipulated draperies and intelligent, piquant faces. By 1561 Pilon was active at Fontainebleau, where he carved four wooden statues of classical figures for the Queen's garden.

Between 1563 and 1570, under Primaticcio's initial direction, Pilon executed the monumental tomb of Henry II and Catherine de Médicis in the Valois chapel at Saint–Denis. This tomb is at once grander and more somber in its elaborate sculptural program than the monument for Henry II's heart. Above the tomb of Henry II and Catherine are the kneeling bronze figures of the King and Queen garbed in all the regal splendor of their robes of state; they are in dramatic contrast to the recumbent marble figures of the sovereigns poignantly shown as nearly naked corpses below. The lower part of the tomb has four standing bronze figures of Virtues and a series of bas-reliefs in marble and bronze.

In 1570 Pilon was named sculptor to the king, Charles IX. No large-scale work survives from the 1570s, when Pilon was chiefly active making a distinguished series of portrait busts and medals of royal and noble personages. One of his strongest characterizations, the bronze bust of Jean de Morvilliers, foreshadows the incisive portrait of Chancellor René de Birague a decade later. This later portrait belonged to one of the two major projects that engaged Pilon in the 1580s: the continued work for the Valois chapel in Saint-Denis and tombs for the Birague family chapel in Ste-Catherine du Val-des-Ecoliers, Paris.

The sculpture that remains from Pilon's work for the Valois chapel shows an astonishing range, from the almost Spanish emotionalism of the *St. Francis* (now in the church of SS. Jean et François, Paris), to the Michelangelesque breadth of the *Risen Christ* (in the church of SS. Paul et Louis, Paris), to the formal grace of the marble *Sorrowing Madonna* (in the Louvre). The painted terra-cotta model for this Madonna is more personal and expressive, recalling the austere dignity of the Virgin of the famous Avignon *Pietà*.

Pilon's tombs for the Birague family were largely destroyed in the French Revolution, but the portions that remain (now in the Louvre) show his full powers as a sculptor in their assured characterizations of the praying chancellor and the more delicate interpretation of his wife, Valentine

Balbiani. The jewellike precision of her costume and the gaiety of the supporting angels make all the more haunting the ravaged features of her cadaver carved in low relief at the base of the tomb. The bronze relief of the *Deposition* was also executed for the Birague chapel.

Pilon died in Paris on Feb. 3, 1590. He left no followers capable of carrying forward his expressive late style, but his carefully wrought earlier portraits continued to serve as models for later generations of sculptors.

Further Reading

The most important sources on Pilon are in French. Anthony Blunt, *Art and Architecture in France, 1500-1700* (1954; 2d ed. 1970), includes an appreciative and thoughtful account of Pilon and his contemporaries. □

Joseph Pilsudski

The Polish general and statesman Joseph Pilsudski (1867-1935) played a large role in the reestablishment of an independent Polish state and became its first president in 1918.

Joseph Pilsudski was born on Dec. 5, 1867, at Zulow in the Vilna district of Russian Poland, the second son of a family of the lower gentry. The harsh treatment of the Poles under Russian rule and the anti-Russian feeling pervading his environment inspired him with a hatred of Russia and a desire to liberate his country from foreign domination.

Suspended from medical school at Kharkov in 1886, Pilsudski returned to Vilna and was exiled for 5 years to Siberia in 1887 for allegedly conspiring to assassinate Czar Alexander III. Pilsudski returned home in 1892, joined the Polish Socialist party, and became its leader in 1894. He soon became editor of its clandestine newspaper, *Robotnik* (The Worker), but his press was discovered in Lódz, and he and his wife were arrested in 1900. Pilsudski escaped, however, in May 1901, and he settled in Cracow in Austrian Galicia.

Needing foreign aid for Poland's liberation, Pilsudski went to Japan in 1904 during the Russo-Japanese War, but he met resistance there from Roman Dmowski, who had convinced the Japanese that Pilsudski's projects were not feasible. To assist the spread of the revolutionary movement in Russia, Pilsudski entered Russian Poland at the end of 1904, but after the failure of the revolution in 1905 his Polish Socialist party split; Pilsudski's faction insisted on the party's primary goal of creating an independent Poland, whereas the left faction wished this goal to be deemphasized. In Austrian Poland, Pilsudski began to form a secret force in 1908 that would become a Polish national army. By 1910 Pilsudski was receiving assistance from Austrian military forces.

In World War I Pilsudski commanded the 1st Brigade of the Polish Legion against the Russians under Austro-Hungarian command. In order to free their soldiers for duty on

the Western front, the Central Powers proclaimed the independence of Poland on Nov. 5, 1916, and Pilsudski was appointed chief of the military section of the Polish State Council; but when the Central Powers refused to accept the polish army as an organ of a Polish state, Pilsudski was defiant and was arrested by the Germans in July 1917, and jailed in Magdeburg.

Released in the fall of 1918, Pilsudski returned to Warsaw in November 1918, where he was proclaimed head of state and commander in chief of the Polish armed forces. Agreeing with the Polish National Committee, which was supported by the Western powers, he named Dmowski, right-wing leader, as first Polish deputy to the Paris Peace Conference. Poland's first Parliament in 1919 confirmed Pilsudski as chief of state, with Ignace Jan Paderewski as prime minister. Almost immediately, Pilsudski needed to defend Polish territory against attack by the Red Army, and initially he was successful in occupying much territory that had belonged to historical Poland but that had long been under Russian rule. He favored a federal organization of the new state to include these territories, whereas Dmowski favored their outright annexation to the Polish state. A Soviet counteroffensive reached the environs of Warsaw, but Pilsudski, created marshal of Poland on March 19, 1920, repelled it with the assistance of French general Maxime Weygand, ending the Soviet threat by August 1920.

The new constitution of March 1921, which limited executive powers considerably, caused Pilsudski's retirement from the presidency, although he continued as army chief of staff; he resigned this post also on May 29, 1923,

when a conservative government took power. Disillusioned with the workings of the parliamentary system, Pilsudski marched with troops on Warsaw on May 12, 1926, and though elected president by the National Assembly on May 31, 1926, he refused the position and served as minister of defense until his death.

From late 1926 to 1928, and again in 1930, Pilsudski served as Polish prime minister, ruling dictatorially and arresting members of the Sejm who opposed his rule. He was the real ruler of Poland, choosing the holders of important offices. His associates August Zaleski and Józef Beck held the foreign office during the period, concluding a nonaggression treaty with the Soviet Union in July 1932 and another with Germany in January 1934, although Pilsudski himself had wanted to oppose Adolf Hitler's entry to power with force. On May 12, 1935, Pilsudski died and was buried in Wawel Cathedral in Cracow. His collected works were published at Warsaw from 1930 to 1936 with selections appearing in English in 1931.

Further Reading

Pilsudski wrote *Joseph Pilsudski: The Memories of a Polish Revolutionary and Soldier* (trans. 1931), which deals with his personal experiences prior to 1923. Alexandra Pilsudski, his wife, wrote *Memoirs of Madame Pilsudski* (1940). The best biography in English is still William Fiddian Reddaway, *Marshall Pilsudski* (1939). The definitive account of Pilsudski's seizure of power is Joseph Rothschild, *Pilsudski's Coup d'Etat* (1966). See also M. K. Dziewanowsk, *Joseph Pilsudski: A European Federalist, 1918-1922* (1969).

Additional Sources

Garlicki, Andrzej, *Joseph Pilsudski: 1867-1935,* London: Scolar Press; Brookfield, VT: Ashgate Publishing, 1995.
Pilsudski, a life for Poland, New York: Hippocrene Books, 1982. □

Pinckney Benton Stewart Pinchback

Pinckney Benton Stewart Pinchback (1837-1921) was the first African American to become governor of a state.

Although he was not elected by popular vote, P. B. S. Pinchback advanced to the governor's office in Louisiana when political turmoil reached a crisis point. For much of his life Pinchback found himself in unique circumstances because he was of mixed heritage. On one hand, he was able to achieve some of the education, business opportunities, and material comforts normally available only to whites of the day. However, he was also the victim of discrimination as well. When asked once of which heritage he drew upon as a source of pride, Pinchback replied, "I don't think the question is a legitimate one, as I have no control over the matter. A man's pride I regard as born of his associations, and mine is, perhaps, no exception to the rule."

Pinchback was born in May of 1837 in Macon, Georgia, to a slave and her former master who were by then living together as husband and wife. At the time the family was on its way to begin a new life in Mississippi, where the senior Pinchback had purchased a new, much larger plantation. As a youngster, Pinchback lived in relatively affluent surroundings, and his parents even sent him north to Cincinnati to attend high school. In 1848 his father died, and to add to the grief of his wife and five children, the paternal relatives were vengeful. They disinherited Pinchback's mother and her children. To evade the possibility that the northern Pinchbacks would legally appropriate the children as slave property, Pinchback's mother fled with all five to Cincinnati. P. B. S. Pinchback worked for many years on the boats that plied the Ohio and Mississippi Rivers. Some were notorious dens of gambling, and it was on such a vessel that Pinchback encountered a posse of white gamblers who took him on as their personal assistant. He soon became an experienced swindler himself in three-card monte and chuck-a-luck, but to avoid great repercussions, his victims were only his fellow African American coworkers on the boat.

Fought in Civil War

In 1860, when Pinchback was 23, he married Nina Hawthorne, a 16-year-old from Memphis. When the Civil War broke out the following year, Pinchback hoped to fight

on the side of the Union troops against the South. The main issue in the conflict between North and South was slavery, and Pinchback's heritage gave him an insight into the status of both blacks and whites in the country. In 1862 he furtively made his way into New Orleans, which was then under occupation by Northern troops. There he raised several companies of the Corps d'Afrique, part of the Louisiana National Guard, and was the military body's only officer of African American descent.

In 1863, passed over twice for promotion and tired of the prejudice he encountered at every turn, Pinchback resigned from the Guard. When the war ended and the slaves were emancipated, he and his wife moved to Alabama, eager to test out their new freedom as full citizens. However, racial tensions in their new surroundings were reaching shocking levels of viciousness. Occupying Union forces shared equally prejudiced views as those of their former Confederate enemies, and would sometimes don the Confederate uniform at night and terrorize the newly freed African Americans. The movements of African Americans were also restricted by the so-called "black codes" across the South, and it became obvious that white Southern politicians were going to do everything possible to prevent them from gaining any political power. Pinchback's political career was born out of this hostile climate. He began speaking out at public meetings and soon became a well-known orator who urged the former slaves to organize politically.

Pinchback eventually returned to New Orleans with his family. Now a committed Republican—the party of Abraham Lincoln originally established to oppose slavery—he was elected a delegate to the Republican State Convention and even spoke before the assembly. His orations helped win him election to the party's Central Executive Committee. During the Constitutional Convention of 1867-68, Pinchback accepted the candidacy for a state senator on the Republican ticket. He campaigned vigorously for both himself as well as his close political ally, Henry Clay Warmoth, another radical Republican and Pinchback's mentor. When Pinchback narrowly lost his bid for the state senate seat, he charged voting fraud. The newly convened legislature agreed and allowed him to take his oath of office.

Joined State Senate

Pinchback joined a Louisiana senate that held 42 representatives of African American descent—half of the chamber—and 7 of 36 seats in the senate, and his battles against the state's racist Democrats brought him enemies. Walking down the street in New Orleans in September of 1868, an attempt was made on his life, but Pinchback fired back in time. The more conservative Democrat newspapers vilified him as unfit to hold public office. As James Haskins noted in *Pinckney Benton Stewart Pinchback*, "a turning point came for Pinchback at this time; he would continue to work for his people and for himself, but he would no longer trust *any* whites, and he would take anything he could get from them." Pinchback was not the only one. By 1871 nearly the entire state legislature had degenerated into political corruption; abuse of power and misuse of public funds became synonymous with the Reconstruction era.

In 1871, Warmoth's lieutenant governor, an African American physician named Oscar Dunn, died suddenly of pneumonia. In a bid to thwart Democratic control of the state, Pinchback's name was put forth by the Warmoth faction as Dunn's replacement, and the senate elected him by a narrow margin in December of that year. The lieutenant governorship also brought with it the post of president pro tempore of the state senate. At the time of Pinchback's ascension to Louisiana's second-highest political office, the political climate in the state was fractious and violent. A second legislature had convened, called the Customshouse senate, and both political bodies were vying for legal control of the state, asserting that they represented the electorate. Mostly Democrats, this group had long tried to impeach Warmoth, but had backed off when Pinchback replaced Dunn as lieutenant governor.

Became First African American Governor

Pinchback continued in his role as lieutenant governor for the rest of 1872, but by the fall of that year many Republicans in the state had turned on Warmoth and wished to unseat him. Election results once again came into dispute, and Warmoth enacted a special extended legislative session to settle the problem. Through complicated political maneuverings—and with the help of Pinchback— a House majority ejected Warmoth from his governor's post on November 21; Pinchback took the oath of office a short time later. The state's Democrats were naturally enraged to have a man of African American descent in the governor's chair, but the state's Supreme Court upheld the legality of Pinchback's ascension.

Formal impeachment proceedings against Warmoth were underway, while Pinchback went about fulfilling his duties as acting governor. Pinchback became the recipient of vicious hate mail from across the country as well as more local threats on his own life. A hundred years later, Pinchback was still the only African American to have achieved such a position of political power, although he had not been elected by popular vote. When final tallies came in and were accepted for the November, 1872 election, Republican William Kellogg was declared governor and was sworn in on January 13, 1873, ending Pinchback's brief but historical executive stint.

In that same election Pinchback had run for a U.S. Senate seat, and in January of 1873 he became a congressman. It was a public office he had long coveted, and with it he achieved another pioneering accomplishment as the state's first African American representative to Washington. His victory, however, was short-lived, as opposing factions in the state unseated him by charging election fraud and naming a white candidate instead. It was the beginning of a reversal of the political gains African Americans had achieved since the war's end.

In 1885, nearing 50 years old, Pinchback took up the study of law at Straight University and was a member of its first graduating class. In the early 1890s Pinchback and his family moved to New York City, where he served as a U.S. marshal, but later they settled in Washington, D.C. Sadly, the achievements he had worked toward—mainly the polit-

ical enfranchisement of African Americans—were by then legally and illegally reversed. With the reassertion of state legislative control by Southern Democrats and the 1896 U.S. Supreme Court ruling *Plessy vs. Ferguson* permitting "separate but equal" public facilities, white power was again firmly entrenched in the South. The number of registered black voters in Louisiana was one indication: it fell from 130,000 in 1896 to 1,300 in just eight years.

Pinchback died in December of 1921 and was buried in the Metairie Ridge cemetery of New Orleans. In an eightieth birthday party a few years earlier, the poet Bruce Grit had celebrated Pinchback's Reconstruction era achievements, when he and other African Americans obtained a fair measure of political power. "The equality we seek is not to come to us by gift, but by struggle, not physical but intellectual," declared Grit. "In this struggle we should be as wise as serpents, and harmless as doves. The civic and political experiences of Governor Pinchback should serve as a guide to our young men in the future and help them to break down the barriers which were set up by designing white men of his own political faith. . . . He is one among the last of the old guard and he has fought a good fight."

Further Reading

Sobel, Robert, and John Raimo, editors, *Biographical Directory of the Governors of the United States, 1789-1978,* Meckler Books, 1978, p. 572.

Haskins, James, *Pinckney Benton Stewart Pinchback,* Macmillan, 1973. □

Gifford Pinchot

Gifford Pinchot (1865-1946), American conservationist and public official, was chiefly responsible for introducing scientific forestry to the United States.

Gifford Pinchot was born in Simsbury, Conn., on Aug. 11, 1865, the scion of an old Huguenot family of moderate wealth and high public spirit. He graduated from Phillips Exeter Academy and Yale University and studied forestry in Europe on his own. After successfully instituting the first systematic forest program in the United States on the Vanderbilt estate in North Carolina, he served in 1896 on the National Forest Commission. Two years later he became head of the Division of Forestry in the Department of Agriculture.

Pinchot's influence increased enormously during the presidency of Theodore Roosevelt. He was influential in Roosevelt's decision to transfer millions of acres of forest lands to the reserves. He devised a system for controlled use of waterpower sites, and, above all others, he shared responsibility with Roosevelt for the notable advances in forestry and conservation between 1901 and 1909.

Unlike some ultraconservationists, Pinchot distinguished between the utilization and the exploitation of natural resources. Controlled use was the key to his philosophy. To this end he opened forests to selective cutting and leased the grasslands within them for grazing. He also converted some of the country's greatest lumber interests to the selective-cutting principle of "perpetuation of forests through use."

A driving, zealous man, Pinchot made many enemies and was attacked fiercely by western interests and anti-intellectuals in Congress. Yet he won the steadfast devotion of his subordinates. After Roosevelt left office, Pinchot fumed over the apparent slowdown in conservation under President William Howard Taft. Finally he charged Taft's secretary of the interior, Richard A. Ballinger, with a "giveaway" of valuable lands in Alaska. The charge was an exaggeration, and Taft subsequently dismissed Pinchot from the government. The publicity given the incident, however, made Taft more sensitive to conservation during the remainder of his administration.

Pinchot ran unsuccessfully for the U.S. Senate on the Pennsylvania Progressive party ticket in 1914. He later returned to the Republican party and served two terms as governor of Pennsylvania (1923-1927 and 1931-1935). Both terms were marked by controversy and highlighted by enactment of considerable Progressive legislation. In 1914 he had married Cornelia Bryce, by whom he had one son. Pinchot died on Oct. 4, 1946.

Further Reading

Pinchot's autobiography, *Breaking New Ground* (1947), is partisan but of surpassing importance. Martin Nelson McGeary, *Gifford Pinchot, Forester-Politician* (1960), is a full, scholarly, and appreciative biography. Its account of the Ballinger affair was updated by James L. Penick, Jr., *Progressive Politics and Conservation: The Ballinger-Pinchot Affair* (1968). Samuel P. Hays, *Conservation and the Gospel of Efficiency* (1959), the most exhaustive study of the early conservation movement, is harsher in some of its judgments on Pinchot than the evidence warrants.

Additional Sources

Anderson, Peter, *Gifford Pinchot: American forester,* New York: Watts, 1995.
Pinchot, Gifford, *Breaking new ground,* Washington, D.C.: Island Press, 1987, 1974. □

Charles Pinckney

Charles Pinckney (1757-1824), American politician and diplomat, was a leading figure in South Carolina politics during the early years of the republic.

Charles Pinckney was born on Oct. 26, 1757, into a wealthy South Carolina family. Little is known of his early life except that he served in the militia during the Revolution and was captured at the fall of Charleston in 1780. After his release Pinckney took up the practice of law and won a seat in the South Carolina Legislature.

As a defender of Southern interests, Pinckney served in the Continental Congress from 1784 to 1787. His brilliant attack on a proposed treaty with Spain that would have surrendered American navigation rights on the Mississippi convinced Congress to pigeonhole the scheme. He was the youngest delegate to the Federal Constitutional Convention, where he made important contributions to the committee deliberations that became part of the ratified Constitution. After the convention he published a pamphlet purportedly describing his personal contributions, and in 1819 he made statements which aroused a controversy settled only by scholarly analysis almost a century later. It was clear that Pinckney had considerably overstated his case yet deserved credit for his perspicacious outline of the national government.

In 1788 Pinckney married Mary E. Laurens, and they had three children before her death in 1794. Pinckney plunged into local politics and served at both the 1788 and 1790 state constitutional conventions. He was thrice chosen governor (in 1789, 1791, and 1796) and on Dec. 6, 1798, was in the unique position of being an outgoing governor, congressman-elect, and senator-designate. Pinckney deserted the Federalist party to follow Thomas Jefferson and was instrumental in carrying South Carolina for Jefferson in the 1800 presidential election. Jefferson returned the favor by appointing Pinckney minister to Spain. In the Spanish mission Pinckney hoped to settle numerous boundary and commercial disputes that kept relations between the two powers strained. The Louisiana Purchase changed the

nature of Pinckney's problem, and he left Spain in 1805 with little accomplished.

Pinckney returned to the South Carolina Legislature and was elected governor a fourth time in 1806. After one term, where he pushed for election reforms that favored the growing backcountry populace (such as universal suffrage for white males), Pinckney served two terms in the state legislature. In 1818 he was elected to the U.S. Congress. After serving one term, he returned to Charleston, practiced law, and dabbled in farming until his death on Oct. 29, 1824.

Further Reading

The only separate study of Pinckney is Andrew Jackson Bethea, *The Contribution of Charles Pinckney to the Formation of the American Union* (1937). Pinckney's later career is recounted in David Duncan Wallace, *The History of South Carolina* (4 vols., 1934; 1 vol., abr., 1951). □

Charles Cotesworth Pinckney

Charles Cotesworth Pinckney (1745-1825), American statesman, was a patriot leader and an emissary to France. He was twice the Federalist nominee for president.

Charles Cotesworth Pinckney was born on Feb. 14, 1745, in Charleston, S.C. He was taken to England in 1753 and educated at Westminster School and Oxford. Destined for a legal career, he attended Middle Temple (1764-1769) and was admitted to practice. Despite his English residence, Pinckney regarded America as home, and he returned full of patriotic ardor. He served as attorney general for three South Carolina districts. His marriage to Sally Middleton strengthened his ties with the colony's leading families.

Following the rupture with England, Pinckney was active on his colony's Committee of Intelligence. He became a militia captain and was chairman of the committee that drafted South Carolina's 1776 constitution. In July 1777 he tried to join George Washington's northern command, but no battlefield opportunities came his way, and Pinckney soon returned to South Carolina. When the British finally attacked Charleston, his bad advice led to a disastrous American defeat in May 1780 during which Pinckney himself was captured.

After the war Pinckney veered toward a nationalistic course in his support of enlarged powers for the Continental Congress. He resumed his lucrative law practice, but his personal life was saddened in 1784 by his wife's death, which left him with three young daughters. Chosen as a delegate to the Federal Convention in 1787, Pinckney supported a stronger central government and was an adamant

defender of slavery. He signed the Constitution and worked successfully for its ratification in his home state.

Pinckney turned down an offer to become secretary of war in 1794 and later also rejected the secretary of state post. However, in 1796 he was persuaded to become the American minister in Paris, taking on the job of appeasing the French government's anger over Jay's Treaty. Pinckney's mission of reconciliation was early discredited by scheming French diplomats, and he was expelled in 1797. Later, under the new president, John Adams, Pinckney, John Marshall, and Elbridge Gerry were appointed special envoys to heal the Franco-American breach. The ensuing discussions, with demands for bribes and Pinckney's famous "No, no, not a sixpence" in reply, were a diplomatic fiasco exposed to the world in the "XYZ" correspondence.

Steadily, Pinckney's political stance became more Federalist; in 1800 he was advanced as the party's vice-presidential candidate. He was the Federalist candidate for president in 1804 and 1808. Three successive defeats in elections ended his national ambitions. Thereafter, he devoted his energies to South Carolina's affairs, particularly education and philanthropy. He died on Aug. 16, 1825. In his eulogy the "not a sixpence" remark became "Millions for defense, not a cent for tribute"—one of the great slogans of American history.

Further Reading

The only complete biography of Pinckney is Marvin R. Zahniser, *Charles Cotesworth Pinckney: Founding Father* (1967). Pinckney's papers in the Library of Congress have not been published, but letters to him from Washington and Hamilton can be found in John C. Fitzpatrick, *The Writings of George Washington* (39 vols., 1931-1944), and Harold C. Syrett and Jacob E. Cooke, *Papers of Alexander Hamilton* (15 vols., 1961-1969). The edited papers of John Adams, Rufus King, and other contemporaries should also be consulted. □

Gregory Goodwin Pincus

Gregory Goodwin Pincus's (1903-1967) research in endocrinology resulted in pathbreaking work on hormones and animal physiology. However, he is best known for developing the oral contraceptive pill.

As his friend and colleague Hudson Hoagland remarked in *Perspectives in Biology and Medicine:* "[Pincus'] highly important development of a pill . . . to control human fertility in a world rushing on to pathological overpopulation is an example of practical humanism at its very best." In addition, Gregory Goodwin Pincus also participated in the founding of the Worcester Foundation for Experimental Biology and the annual Laurentian Hormone Conference.

Pincus was born in Woodbine, New Jersey, on April 9, 1903, the eldest son of Joseph and Elizabeth Lipman Pincus.

His father, a graduate of Storrs Agricultural College in Connecticut, was a teacher and the editor of a farm journal. His mother's family came from Latvia and settled in New Jersey. Pincus' uncle on his mother's side, Jacob Goodale Lipman, was dean of the New Jersey State College of Agriculture at Rutgers University, director of the New Jersey State Agricultural Experiment Station, and the founding editor of *Soil Science* magazine.

After attending a public grade school in New York City, Pincus became an honor student at Morris High School where he was president of the debating and literary societies. As an undergraduate at Cornell University, he founded and edited the *Cornell Literary Review*. After receiving his B.S. degree in 1924, he was accepted into graduate school at Harvard. He concentrated on genetics under W. E. Castle but also did work on physiology with animal physiologist W. J. Crozier. Pincus credited the two scientists with influencing him to eventually study reproductive physiology. He received both his Master of Science and Doctor of Science degrees in 1927 at the age of twenty-four. Pincus married Elizabeth Notkin on December 2, 1924, the same year he completed his undergraduate degree. They had three children—Alexis, John, and Laura Jane.

In 1927 Pincus won a three-year fellowship from the National Research Council. During this time, he travelled to Cambridge University in England where he worked with F.H.A. Marshall and John Hammond, who were pioneers in reproductive biology. He also studied at the Kaiser Wilhelm Institute with the geneticist Richard Goldschmidt. He returned to Harvard in 1930, first as an instructor in biology and then as assistant professor.

Much of the research Pincus did during the early part of his career concentrated on the inheritance of physiological traits. Later research focused on reproductive physiology, particularly sex hormones and gonadotrophic hormones (those which stimulate the reproductive glands). Other research interests included geotropism, the inheritance of diabetes, relationships between hormones and stress, and endocrine function in patients with mental disorders. He also contributed to the development of the first successful extensive partial pancreatectomy in rats.

The development of the oral contraceptive pill began in the early 1930s with Pincus' work on ovarian hormones. He published many studies of living ova (eggs) and their fertilization. While still at Harvard he perfected some of the earliest methods of transplanting animal eggs from one female to another who would carry them to term. He also developed techniques to produce multiple ovulation in laboratory animals. As a consequence of this work, he learned that some phases of development of an animal's ovum were regulated by particular ovarian hormones. Next, he analyzed the effects of ovarian hormones on the function of the uterus, the travel of the egg, and the maintenance of the blastocyst (the first embryonic stage) and later the embryo itself. By 1939 he had published the results of his research on breeding rabbits without males by artificially activating the eggs in the females. This manipulation was called "Pincogenesis," and it was widely reported in the press, but it was not able to be widely replicated by other researchers.

After returning from a year at Cambridge University in 1938, Pincus became a visiting professor of experimental zoology at Clark University in Worcester, Massachusetts, where he stayed until 1945. It was at Clark that Pincus began to work with Hoagland, though they had known each other as graduate students. Together they began to research the relationship between stress and hormones for the United States Navy and Air Force. Specifically, they examined the relationship between steroid excretion, adrenal cortex function, and the stress of flying. While at Clark University, Pincus was named a Guggenheim fellow and elected to the American Academy of Arts and Sciences.

In the spring of 1943, the first conference on hormones sponsored by the American Association for the Advancement of Science was held near Baltimore. Since the conference was held at a private club, African American scientist Percy Julian was excluded. Pincus protested to the management, and Julian was eventually allowed to join the conference. Although not an organizer the first year, Pincus was involved in reshaping the conference the following year, along with biochemist Samuel Gurin and physiological chemist Robert W. Bates. They held the conference in the Laurentian mountains of Quebec, Canada, and from then on the conference was known as the Laurentian Conference, and Pincus was its permanent chairperson. In addition to his administrative duties, he edited the twenty-three volumes of *Recent Progress in Hormone Research,* a compendium of papers presented at the annual conferences.

With Hoagland, Pincus also co-founded the Worcester Foundation for Experimental Biology (WFEB) in 1944. Hoagland served as executive director of the WFEB; Pincus served as director of laboratories for twelve years and then as research director. The WFEB served as a research center on steroid hormones and provided training for young biochemists in the methods of steroid biochemistry. From 1946 to 1950 Pincus was on the faculty of Tufts Medical School in Medford, Massachusetts, and then from 1950 until his death he was research professor in biology at Boston University Graduate School. Many of his doctoral students at these universities completed research at the WFEB.

Pincus had been conducting research on sterility and hormones since the 1930s, but it was not until the 1950s that he applied his theoretical knowledge to the idea of creating a solution to the problem of overpopulation. In 1951 he was exposed to the work of Margaret Sanger, who had described the inadequacy of existing birth control methods and the looming problem of overpopulation, particularly in underdeveloped areas. By 1953, Pincus was working with Min-Chueh Chang at the WFEB, studying the effects of steroids on the fertility of laboratory animals.

Science had made it possible to produce steroid hormones in bulk, and Chang discovered a group of compounds called progestins which worked as ovulation inhibitors. Pincus took these findings to the G. D. Searle Company, where he had been a consultant, and shifted his emphasis to human beings instead of laboratory animals. Pincus also brought human reproduction specialists John Rock and Celso Garcia into the project. They conducted clinical tests of the contraceptive pill in Brookline, Massachusetts, to confirm the laboratory data. Pincus then travelled to Haiti and Puerto Rico, where he oversaw large-scale clinical field trials.

Oscar Hechter, who met Pincus in 1944 while at the WFEB, wrote in *Perspectives in Biology and Medicine* that "Gregory Pincus belongs to history because he was a man of action who showed the world that the population crisis is not an 'impossible' problem. He and his associates demonstrated that there is *a* way to control birth rates on a large scale, suitable alike for developed and underdeveloped societies. The antifertility steroids which came to be known as the 'Pill' were shown to be effective, simple, contraceptive agents, relatively safe, and eminently practical to employ on a large scale." Pincus spent much of the last fifteen years of his life travelling to explain the results of research. This is reflected in his membership in biological and endocrinological societies in Portugal, France, Great Britain, Chile, Haiti, and Mexico. His work on oral contraceptives was also recognized by awards such as the Albert D. Lasker Award in Planned Parenthood in 1960 and the Cameron Prize in Practical Therapeutics from the University of Edinburgh in 1966. He was elected to the National Academy of Sciences in 1965.

Pincus died before the issue of *Perspectives in Biology and Medicine* commemorating his sixty-fifth birthday was published. Although ill for the last three years of his life, he had continued to work and travel. He died in Boston on August 22, 1967, of myeloid metaplasia, a bone-marrow disease which some speculate was caused by his work with organic solvents.

Further Reading

Dictionary of Scientific Biography, Volume 10, Scribner, 1970, pp. 610–611.

Ingle, Dwight J., "Gregory Goodwin Pincus," in *Biographical Memoirs,* Volume 42, Columbia University Press, 1971, pp. 228–270.

Hechter, Oscar, "Homage to Gregory Pincus," in *Perspectives in Biology and Medicine,* spring, 1968, pp. 358–370.

Hoagland, Hudson, "Creativity—Genetic and Psychosocial," in *Perspectives in Biology and Medicine,* spring, 1968, pp. 339–349. □

Pindar

Pindar (522-438 B.C.), the greatest Greek lyric poet, brought choral poetry to perfection. Unlike the personal lyrics of his predecessors, his works were meant to be recited by choruses of young men and women and accompanied by music.

Pindar was born at Cynoscephalae, near Thebes, in Boeotia of a very prominent aristocratic family, the Aegeidae, who traced their genealogy back to Aegeus and even to Cadmus of Thebes with connections in Sparta, Thera, and Cyrene. He was the son of Daiphantus and Cleodice. His family seems to have had considerable interest in music, especially in flute-playing, which became important at Delphi in the worship of Apollo and was perfected and highly regarded at Thebes. Having received his elementary education under Scopelinus in Thebes, he was sent to Athens, where he was educated under Apollodorus, Agathocles, and Lasus of Hermione, a competitor of Simonides. It was Lasus who is reputed to have written the first treatise on music, brought to the voice a harmonized flute accompaniment, and perfected the dithyramb.

Returning to Thebes, Pindar competed in poetry contests with Myrtis and Corinna, the latter winning over him and advising him, because of his penchant for including an overwhelming amount of mythological allusions, "to sow with the hand, not with the whole sack." At 20, he composed his first ode, *Pythian Ode X.* His earliest preserved *Olympian Ode* was composed in 484. Pindar traveled extensively throughout the Greek world and achieved a Panhellenic reputation and numerous commissions. For Hiero I, the tyrant of Syracuse, he wrote encomia, as well as for Alexander I of Macedon, Archelaus of Cyrene, Theron of Agrigentum, the Thessalian Aleuadae, and the Alcmeonid Megacles. In Hiero, Pindar thought he saw a champion of civilized Hellenism against the forces of barbarism. He visited Sicily and was familiar with other Sicilians, notably the tyrant of Acragas, Theron, and his nephew, Thrasyboulus.

Mention should also be made of Pindar's relation with the island of Aegina. Eleven of his odes were written for Aeginetan victors. This is remarkable since it constitutes

nearly one-fourth of his total output. Aegina (whose founding nymph, Aegina, was reputed to be a sister of Thebe) was subjected to Athenian imperial aggression during the Peloponnesian War, and Pindar in *Pythian Ode VIII* may be cloaking a criticism of this policy. He did not tire of praising the Aeacidae, Peleus and Telamon, and their offspring, Achilles and Ajax.

Thebes's unfortunate capitulation to the Persians during the Persian Wars (480-479 B.C.) and cooperation with the invading enemy left Pindar a distressed member of a disgraced and defeated state. Though apparently sympathetic to Athens, he was in no position to sing Athens's praises too loudly, even after Thebes became a subject ally of Athens about 457.

Pindar may have visited the games. At Delphi, he was particularly honored. Even his descendants are reported to have been given special recognition because of their progenitor. He was married to Timoxena and had one son, Daiphantus, and two daughters, Protomache and Eumetis.

Works and Thought

Not all of Pindar's works have been preserved. He composed hymns, paeans, prosodia (processionals), dithyrambs, parthenia (maiden songs), hyporchemata (dance songs), encomia, dirges, and epinikia (victory odes in honor of athletic heroes). Forty-four of the victory odes celebrate winners of Olympian, Pythian, Nemean, and Isthmian games, which were religious as well as athletic occasions. These odes are brilliant in form but difficult and complex. Richmond Lattimore (1947) observes, "Competition [in the games] symbolized an idea of nobility which meant much to Pindar; and in the exaltation of victory he seems sometimes to see a kind of transfiguration, briefly making radiant a world which most of the time seemed, to him as to his contemporaries, dark and brutal."

An epinikion was sung by a chorus of men or boys at a private occasion for the winner, his family, and friends—any of these people having commissioned it. Apparently, contracts were made specifying fees, details about the winner and his family to be included, and mythical allusions to be interwoven in the commemorative ode. The victor, the event, and the festival had to be indicated, and the poet had to laud the winner for his excellence, as well as offer felicitations to his family and state. Pindar does all this skillfully. He weaves the facts into the ode gradually and highlights not the victor but the festival, the aristocratic descent of the victor, a mythological event suggested by the life of the victor, or a myth connected with the holy occasion, the victor, or the victor's native place. This "myth" constitutes the heart of the ode. The technical structure is *prooimion* (prelude), arche (beginning), *katatrope* (first transition), *omphalos* (center), *metakatatrope* (second transition), *exodion* (conclusion), and *sphragis* (seal). The transitions are important and often quite abrupt. There are three stanzas: strophe, antistrophe, and epode.

Pindar was aristocratic in temper, Panhellenic in spirit, and proud of his noble background. Profoundly religious and moral, he "corrected" myths to ensure religious orthodoxy. He saw properly used wealth as an honor to this world, but he also spoke of the next world. He believed in the righteousness of the gods, in the supremacy of Zeus, and in the majesty and justice of Apollo, and it is of Apollo that he saw himself the servant.

Pindar reflects an oligarchic society that was threatened by the rise of democratic Athens. John H. Finley, Jr. (1947), states: "Victory to Pindar is itself only a figure for this state of being, which is a mark of the divine in the world. Hence victory and poetry, different as they are, are equally dependent upon the gods, whose hand is increasingly seen in the late poems in friendship and inner harmony also." Pindar is a poet of light, which he sees most closely associated with the gods. Finely points out that Pindar tries "to grasp the bright chain that binds men to gods or, better, the radiance that descends from gods to men, touching events with the divine completeness."

So great a reputation did Pindar achieve that it is reported that when Alexander the Great devastated Thebes, only Pindar's house was left untouched.

Further Reading

An excellent collection of Pindar's work is Selected Odes, translated with interpretative essays by Carl A.P. Ruck and William H. Matheson (1968); each ode is introduced with an essay setting forth the occasion, structure, and theme of the poem. Other collections include Thomas D. Seymour, *Selected Odes of Pindar* (1882), and Richmond Lattimore, *The Odes of Pindar* (1947). Among the critical studies are John H. Finley, Jr., *Pindar and Aeschylus* (1947), a sensitive exposition of Pindar's use of myth and image; C. M. Bowra, *Pindar* (1965), intended as a critical introduction but filled with undiscussed and often unfamiliar allusions; and Mary A. Grant, *Folktale and Hero-tale Motifs in the Odes of Pindar* (1967). ☐

Philippe Pinel

The French physician Philippe Pinel (1745-1826) was the major figure in early efforts to provide humane care and treatment for the mentally ill.

Philippe Pinel was born on April 20, 1745, in the hamlet of Roques. At 17 he entered the Collège d'Esquille in Toulouse to prepare for the priesthood, but he soon decided to study medicine. He received his doctorate in 1773 and continued his medical education at the University of Montpellier, France's leading medical school. In 1778 he settled in Paris, where he devoted himself to general studies in science while tutoring in mathematics. Pinel's work on clinical medicine, *Nosographie philosophique* (1789), was a standard textbook for 2 decades, and several 19th-century schools of thought on clinical medicine trace their origin to it.

Pinel's interests in the mentally ill gradually developed, and in 1793, through the aid of friends in the Revolutionary government of France, he was appointed physician-in-chief at l'Hospice de Bicêtre, a large mental institution in Paris. There he encountered the characteristic cruel treatment of mental patients, as they were beaten, locked in dirty cells, and generally made to suffer in the hands of ignorant keepers. Perhaps worst of all, they were commonly restrained with chains. Pinel immediately insisted that the restraints be removed, and, in spite of warnings that unchained patients would become violent, he unchained 49 inmates on May 24, 1793. All responded favorably.

In 1795 Pinel assumed the responsibility for the mental patients at l'Hôpital de la Salpêtrière, where he continued his policy of nonrestraint and brought about many significant and far-reaching reforms in the care and treatment of mental patients. Humane treatment under the watchful eye of trained and compassionate personnel in the institution made possible the recovery of many otherwise doomed patients. Pinel also introduced the practice of keeping case histories, which proved a valuable source of information in later efforts to understand insanity. The new concepts of the care of the mentally ill were published in Pinel's *Traité médico-philosophique sur l'aliénation mentale* (1801; *Treatise on Insanity,* 1806).

Pinel was professor of hygiene and pathology at the University of Paris from 1794 until 1822, when he was removed by the government because of his past association with persons involved in the Revolution and because he had served as a consulting physician to Napoleon I for a few years after 1805. However, at the time of his death, on Oct. 25, 1826, Pinel was still active at Salpêtrière.

Further Reading

The best source of information on Pinel's ideas and methods is his *Treatise on Insanity,* translated by David Daniel Davis (1806; repr. 1962). A good recent study of Pinel, especially for the relation he felt to the medical ideas of Greek antiquity, is Walter Riese, *The Legacy of Philippe Pinel* (1969). □

Allan Pinkerton

Allan Pinkerton (1819-1884) was the father of many American police detection techniques and founder of America's most famous detective agency.

Allan Pinkerton was born in Glasgow on Aug. 25, 1819, the son of a police sergeant who was later wounded during the Chartist riots. Pinkerton himself became a Chartist and, fearing for his safety after participating in the turmoil, emigrated to the United States in 1842. He settled in a Scottish community at Dundee, Ill. He became an outspoken abolitionist, allegedly serving as the local conductor on the Underground Railroad.

While working as a cooper in Dundee, Pinkerton was instrumental in capturing a group of counterfeiters. After several private commissions in detective work, he was named deputy sheriff of Kane County in 1846. In 1850 he became the first detective on the reorganized police department of Chicago. He simultaneously organized a private agency, leaving public service soon afterward.

Pinkerton's agency, unlike the typical agency of the day, was run with strict propriety. He would not, for example, undertake investigations of the morals of a woman, the stock-in-trade of most private detectives, except in connection with some other crime. Nor did he set his fees according to how much money he regained in a theft case, a practice which frequently tied detectives to the underworld. Pinkerton's operatives received uniform fees, set in advance, plus expenses. Pinkerton quickly developed a national reputation as a result of work for the U.S. Post Office, the Chicago and Northwestern Railroad, and the Illinois Central Railroad (through which he developed a valuable friendship with its president, George McClellan).

In 1861 Pinkerton was investigating alleged Confederate sabotage of a railroad in Maryland when he claimed to have unearthed a scheme to assassinate the president-elect, Abraham Lincoln, then on his way to his inauguration. Pinkerton convinced Lincoln to revise his plans for entering Washington, D.C., and he supervised Lincoln's secret journey. Pinkerton later discussed the organization of a national secret service with the President but, when nothing developed, joined his old client, now Gen. McClellan, as head of intelligence in the Army's Ohio Department. When McClellan left the Army in 1862, Pinkerton resigned his post and spent the rest of the war investigating cotton speculation frauds in the Mississippi Valley.

Following the war, Pinkerton turned active direction of his flourishing agency over to his two sons, although he

continued to take an interest in agency affairs and kept control of central policy. He supervised the agency's growth in its chief fields of endeavor: the pursuit and capture of train robbers like the James gang; the supplying of a private corps of armed guards to industries and special events such as county fairs; and the breaking of labor unions. He became a vociferous enemy of labor unions.

Pinkerton had a penchant for self-celebration, writing some 20 books about his and his detectives' exploits. He died on July 1, 1884.

Further Reading

Pinkerton's own books tell little about him or about his detective agency. Scarcely more credible is James D. Horan and Howard Swiggett, *The Pinkerton Story* (1951), an idolatrous study approved by the Pinkerton agency. Morris Friedman, *The Pinkerton Labor Spy* (1907), hostile toward the Pinkertons, is dated.

Additional Sources

Pinkerton, Allan, *The expressman and the detective,* New York: Arno Press, 1976 c1874. □

Augusto Pinochet Ugarte

Augusto Pinochet Ugarte (born 1915) led the military movement of 1973 that toppled the elected Chilean government. An army general, he proceeded

to govern in an authoritarian manner while attempting to rebuild the economy and permanently alter Chile's political system.

Augusto Pinochet Ugarte was born in the Chilean port city of Valparaiso on November 15, 1915. From his early years he aspired to a military career. Because of his small stature Pinochet was rejected twice by the National Military Academy before he matriculated at the Escuela Militar's four year officer training course in Santiago. He graduated in 1936 and was promoted to second lieutenant in 1938. He married Maria Lucia Hiriart and had three daughters and two sons.

During his early professional career Pinochet distinguished himself as a specialist in military geography and geopolitics. His 1968 book *Geopolitica* (*Geopolitics*) went through several editions. He also stood out as a student in the Infantry School, in the War Academy (staff school), and in other advanced courses. He held several staff and command posts during these years, posts which provided him with numerous contacts with other officers in the army, air force, navy, and carabineros (national police). Pinochet served on the Chilean military mission in Washington, D.C. in 1956. He taught at the Military School, at the War Academy, and at Ecuador's national war college in the 1950s and 1960s. It was during these early military years that he developed the ideals that guided his military career: patriotism, public service and respect for authority.

Early in his career, Pinochet was not interested in the political debates that dominated civilian society. A cousin said "his ideological orientation was an enigma. If he had any, he had not demonstrated publicly." By 1970, the year Salvador Allende Gossens was elected to the presidency, Pinochet had been promoted to division general—the highest rank in the Chilean army. In 1971 he became commandant of the Santiago garrison, one of the most sensitive and influential army assignments owing to the size of the garrison and to its location in the capital city. By this time Pinochet was firmly convinced that political demagoguery and Marxism were disruptive, hypocritical, and incompatible with, in his words, "the moral principles that should uphold society. . . ." He traced his hostility to Marxism to events of the late 1930s, when Marxists participated vociferously in government, and to the Cold War years when the Chilean Communist Party was briefly outlawed. He also became skeptical of the ability of Chile's democratic system to withstand Marxism.

The 1970 presidential election confirmed his deep suspicions, for it gave power to the Marxist Allende despite the fact that he was a minority candidate. As garrison commandant Pinochet was an eyewitness to the social, economic, and political turbulence accompanying the Allende administration's efforts to turn Chile toward socialism through the control of national institutions. Outwardly he seemed to remain loyal to the legitimately elected government. When the army commander-in-chief, General Carlos Prats Gonzalez, became interior minister during a serious trucking strike of late 1972, Pinochet became acting commander-in-chief. He held this position again on the eve of the September 11, 1973 putsch.

On that day the armed forces seized power. Allende was killed in the presidential palace. Pinochet claimed that Allende committed suicide. That was refuted by Allende's widow and others who claim that Allende was murdered by Pinochet's troops. Pinochet became president of the Junta of Government, a body composed of military commanders-in-chief. A year later he became president of the Republic of Chile. His term of office was formally extended later through the adoption of a constitution giving him an eight-year term (1981-1989). Allende's loyalists tried to maintain resistance, but it proved costly. Over 1500 lives were lost by the end of the day. Fearful of internal resistance, the junta declared itself in a state of internal war. The U.S. CIA was instrumental in providing the junta with The White Book, a manual for executing a successful coup and caused hundreds to be beaten and tortured by the army and police.

From late 1973 until late 1976 the country was in an economic depression, the aftermath of Allende's policies and the economic pressures that had been applied by both foreigners and Chileans between 1970 and 1973. This was also a period of harsh authoritarian rule. Inflation was gradually reduced in the mid-1970s, and by 1978 Chileans, especially those of the middle and upper sectors, were talking of an "economic miracle" based on free enterprise, foreign loans, and "denationalization" of the economy. Pinochet's popularity peaked in 1978 when a plebiscite confirmed his leadership and policies—although a growing opposition denied the validity of the vote. In the early 1980s Chile suffered from the world recession, and the government resorted to stricter controls of the press, the exile of some dissidents, curfews, and repression characteristic of the early years of Pinochet's rule. At the same time he oversaw a shift in economic policy that revived the role of the state, which he and his supporters had blamed for Chile's misfortunes prior to 1973.

The supporters of Pinochet liked his role as Chile's strongman, the one figure capable of controlling the armed forces and the symbol of anti-Marxism. But he also became the figure toward whom a growing opposition (church leaders, labor, politicians, human rights advocates, leftists) directed its energies. The United States and other foreign governments were cautious in relations with his government. Through this period he maintained his resolute anti-Communism and showed an uncanny ability to survive politically in a country marked by unsolved economic and social problems. Pinochet was able to do this because of his own abilities, but also because of the strength of discipline in the military, the inability of opposition leaders to agree on policy, and the fear of many Chileans that alternatives would be worse than his authoritarianism.

These factors became subjects for increasing debate within the government, throughout Chile, and in the world press in 1983 when opposition leaders organized mass demonstrations against the regime's economic, political, and social programs. Beginning in May of that year miners, students, workers, and dissident political leaders took to the streets to register their discontent. Pinochet used armed force to quell the demonstrations, then began talks aimed at political compromise. When talks stalled he again used strong-arm tactics, claiming as usual that politicians and Marxists were to blame for Chile's problems.

In 1986 Pinochet survived an attempted assassination with only minor injuries. But the international outcry against his alleged violations of human rights continued to grow louder. The new constitution that had been seven years in the making was ratified by plebiscite in 1980. Even though it was approved, the election was declared a fraud. The constitution called for Pinochet to serve another eight years. This time actually permitted the opposition party to mount a successful campaign to remove him from office. The U.S. Congress financed $2 million worth of media consultants, poll judges and a parallel vote count to ensure a somewhat fair election. On October 5, 1989, 55% of the Chilean people voted to remove Pinochet from office. He was able to retain power until free elections installed a new president, Patricio Alwyn on March 5, 1990. Although he abdicated his title as president, Pinochet remained on as commander in chief of the army. After stepping down as president, Pinochet devoted himself to modernizing and computerizing his beloved army. Even at 80, he still saw himself as a force within Chilean society, very much in charge of the armed forces until his constitutionally forced retirement in March 1998.

Further Reading

Pinochet's own version of his role in government can be found in his *The Crucial Day* (1982). Frederick M. Nunn's *The Military in Chilean History* (1976) provides information on the military and political background to Pinochet's rise to power. Critical of the military and Pinochet, and sympathetic to his predecessor, are Robinson Rojas Sandford, *The Murder of Allende and the End of the Chilean Way to Socialism* (1975), and Ian Roxborough, Phil O'Brien, and Jackie Roddick, *Chile: The State and Revolution* (1977). Robert Moss' *Chile's Marxist Experiment* (1973) is favorable to Pinochet. *Pinochet: the Politics of Power* 1988 and *A Nation of Enemies: Chile under Pinochet* assess the situation since the coup. □

Harold Pinter

The English playwright Harold Pinter (born 1930) ranks among the foremost postwar British dramatists. A master of menace, he invested his plays with an atmosphere of fear, horror, and mystery.

Harold Pinter was born on Oct. 10, 1930, the only son of a Jewish tailor, in Hackney, East London. He won a scholarship to the local school, Hackney Downs Grammar School. In 1948 he entered the Royal Academy of Dramatic Arts and then joined a repertory company as an actor and toured England and Ireland. After marrying actress Vivien Merchant in 1956, he began writing plays, giving up the poetry, short stories, monologues, and an autobiographical novel, *The Dwarfs,* that he would eventually publish in 1990.

In 1957 Pinter completed two one-act plays, *The Room* and *The Dumb Waiter,* as well as the full-length play *The Birthday Party.* The relationship of villain and victim emerges gradually in all three of these plays. In *The Dumb Waiter* two hired gunmen experience strange terrors while receiving orders delivered via a dumbwaiter shaft until one performs the assigned task by killing the other. In *The Birthday Party* impulse and instinct war with repression on many levels as Stanley fences with his companions—motherly Meg; luscious Lulu; apathetic Petey; and his tormentors, the irresistible instruments of conformity, Goldberg and McCann.

Pinter adapted his radio play *A Slight Ache* (1959), about a wife who exchanges a stranger for her husband, from his short story "The Examination" and later made it into a stage play. He next wrote two revue sketches, *Pieces of Eight* and *One to Another.* Another radio play, *A Night Out* (1960), followed.

Pinter's first West End success was *The Caretaker* in 1960 (adapted for film in 1962). In it, a devious old tramp is befriended and sheltered in his cluttered room by the kindly Aston until his calculating brother ousts the would-be caretaker. *Night School* appeared on radio the same year, depicting two aunts mothering Walter as he pursues a tart who has rented his room while he has been in prison.

The Dwarfs, derived from Pinter's novel, also first appeared on radio in 1960. It presents a pair of threatening figures cruelly descending upon the hapless Len with his disintegrating fantasies about ghoulish dwarfs. Pinter later adapted two television plays for the stage: *The Collection* (1961), which expresses a husband's fears of his wife's infidelity with one of a pair of men in an adjoining apartment; and *The Lover* (1963), in which a jaded married couple seek sexual stimulus in role playing. The British Broadcasting Corporation (BBC) broadcast his short story "The Tea Party" in 1964 and televised it throughout Europe the following year.

In Pinter's full-length play *The Homecoming* (1965) the theme of sexual cruelty reappears. A professor teaching in an American university returns to his father's home in London on summer vacation with his wife. She stays on as the whore-mistress for his father and brothers, and he agrees to return to the United States alone.

BBC television produced Pinter's *The Basement* (originally a film script entitled *The Compartment*) in 1967. The following year he wrote three one-act plays: *Landscape,* an exchange of reminiscences in non-connecting monologues between two old people; *Silence,* which mixed a three-person monologue and dialogue in a kind of dramatic poem; and the funny sketch *Night.* His full-length drama *Old Times* (1971) has no plot; it is a play about the past. The three characters spend an evening reminiscing about events that may or may not have occurred.

In 1973 Pinter was made the Associate Director of the National Theatre, a post he would hold until 1983. Pinter's first marriage dissolved in 1980. In the same year he married Lady Antonia Fraser.

Pinter's early plays were labeled "comedies of menace" and occur in confining room sanctuaries, in which men, beset by robotizing social forces, surrender the remnants of their individuality. In his later plays he is especially concerned with what he regards as the nearly impossible task of verifying appearances. He creates images of the human condition that are despairing yet also comic in his deft handling of dialogue that attacks, evades communication, and shields privacy with debasing non sequiturs, pat clichés, repetitions, contradictions, and apt bad syntax. Pinter thinks of speech as "a constant stratagem to cover nakedness." This period of his life became one of his most prolific. He contributed many works, some of which are: *No Man's Land* (1975), *Betrayal* (1978), *Poems And Prose 1949-1977* (1978), *I Know The Place* (1979), *Family Voices* (1981), *Other Places* (1982), *One For The Road* (1984), *Mountain Language* (1988), *The Heat Of The Day* (1989), *Party Time* (1991), *Moonlight* (1993), *99 Poems In Translation* (1995), and *Ashes To Ashes* (1995).

Further Reading

The most thorough critical study of Pinter is Arnold P. Hinchliffe *Harold Pinter* (1967). Other studies are Walter Kerr *Harold Pinter* (1967); Ronald Hayman *Harold Pinter* (1968) in the "Contemporary Playwrights" series; Lois G. Gordon *Stratagems to Uncover Nakedness* (1969); James R. Hollis *Harold Pinter: The Poetics of Silence* (1970); and Victor L. Cahn *Gender and Power in the Plays of Harold Pinter* (1993). Recommended for general background are Martin Esslin *The Theatre of the Absurd* (1961); John Russell Taylor *The Angry Theatre* (1962; 2d rev. ed. 1969); Ruby Cohn *Currents in Comtemporary Drama* (1969); and Mel Gussow *Conversations with Pinter* (1994). Pinter is also listed in the 1997 edition of *Who's Who*. ☐

Isaac Pinto

Isaac Pinto (1720-1791), Jewish merchant and scholar, supported the American patriots during the Revolutionary period.

Isaac Pinto, born probably in Portugal, was of Sephardic Jewish ancestry. His tombstone establishes his birthdate as June 12, 1720. The family came to America, possibly via Jamaica, sometime before 1740. Pinto was named on the roll of New York City's early synagogue Shearith Israel for 1740-1741, but he entered the import-export business, traveled widely, and apparently had varying places of residence. He lived for a time in Norwalk, Conn., and was perhaps the Isaac Pinto who signed a Stratford, Conn., petition in 1748. He was certainly a wholesale wine merchant in Charleston, S.C. (1760-1762), but New York City was his primary abode. In 1764 he signed a petition against a colonial legislative act requiring new buildings in lower Manhattan to be of brick or stone; 4 years later the *New York Journal* carried his advertisement for selling "Choice South Carolina Pink Root."

Pinto was an excellent Hebraist and an expert in the laws of Jewish ritual slaughtering. He probably translated *The Form of Prayer . . . for a General Thanksgiving . . . for the Reduction of Canada* (1760). His *Evening Service of Roshashanah . . .* (1761, published anonymously) and *Prayers for Shabbath, Rosh-Hashanah and Kippur* (1766, published under his name) were the first Jewish prayer books published in America. Even then, many Jews in America were unfamiliar with Hebrew, and Pinto issued his volumes without a Hebrew text for "improvement . . . in the Devotion" of his coreligionists. Pursuing his scholarly interests, he corresponded in 1773 with Rabbi Isaac Karigal of Palestine (visiting Newport, R.I.) and later with President Ezra Stiles of Yale College (who referred to him in 1790 as "a learned Jew at New York").

Many of Pinto's activities can be deduced only on the basis of scanty evidence, but he unquestionably espoused the colonial cause against England. In 1770 he favored continuation of the Nonimportation Resolutions of 1765, and he wrote numerous pro-American articles (presumably as "A.B." and "Philatheles") for the *New York Journal*. Some authorities also credit him with the series in biblical style, "The Chapters of Isaac the Scribe," that appeared in this newspaper during the autumn of 1772.

When the New York Jewish community reorganized itself in 1784, Pinto was asked to be clerk of the congregation, but he apparently felt he was too old to accept the office. He never married. Near the end of his life he taught Spanish in New York City, where he died on Jan. 17, 1791. His obituary in the *New York Journal* noted his ability as a linguist, historian, and philosopher and referred to his staunch support of American liberties.

Further Reading

Detailed information on Pinto is nearly nonexistent. The best account, although brief and incomplete, is in David de Sola Pool, *Portraits Etched in Stone* (1952). The most authoritative study on Colonial Jewry is Jacob R. Marcus, *The Colonial American Jew, 1492-1776* (1970). ☐

Horace Pippin

Horace Pippin (1888-1946) was one of America's principal African American artists and among the foremost primitive painters of the 20th century.

Horace Pippin was born in West Chester, Pa. According to his own account, he began to make pictures at the age of 7. In 1895 he went with his mother to Goshen, N.Y., where he attended school. At 14 he was employed doing odd jobs on a farm; a year later he began unloading coal for a living. In 1912 he took a job in a storage warehouse. He enlisted in the Army in 1917 and was sent to France, where he was badly wounded. He was honorably discharged from the infantry in 1919 and married the following year.

In the 1920s Pippin revived his interest in art. In 1930 he painted his first oil, *End of the War: Starting Home*, a World War I scene. Christian Brinton discovered Pippin's work in 1937 and arranged for a one-man exhibition at the West Chester Community Center. In 1940 Pippin attended classes at the Barnes Foundation in Merion, Pa., the only formal art education he received. That year Albert C. Barnes wrote the introduction to the catalog of the Pippin show held in Philadelphia.

In his portrait of Paul B. Dague, the deputy sheriff of West Chester County (1936), Pippin scrupulously included various insignia—buttons, a medal, seal, and gavel—all indicative of the sitter's position of authority. Pippin sometimes borrowed from other sources, such as calendar illustrations. His *Woman at Samaria* (1940) was mostly modeled on an old book engraving, but the blood-red sky may have been inspired by his own memory of a sunset. In the 1940s he became freer and more inventive in his use of colors, as in the portrait of Christian Brinton (1940), where a rich color pattern is used for the necktie and the handkerchief folded in the jacket pocket.

Three canvases (1942) commemorate the saga of the antislavery activist John Brown: the *Trial of John Brown,*

Horace Pippin (right)

John Brown Reading His Bible, and *John Brown Going to His Hanging.* In 1943 Pippin painted a grim *Crucifixion.* But many of his works have a poetic, intimate quality, such as *Saying Prayers* (1943), in which two children, about to go to bed, kneel beside their mother. Here, as in much of Pippin's work, there is an instinctive feeling for design; the door, window, large stove, and leaning umbrella are powerful forms, geometrically reduced.

Very little of Pippin's work has to do with social protest or with historical events. He loved to paint the simple things he knew best—interior scenes showing the tenderness of members of a family toward one another, still lifes, and people working together on a farm.

Further Reading

Selden Rodman, *Horace Pippin: A Negro Painter in America* (1947), is a well-documented, sympathetic introductory essay with 50 plates, most of them in black and white. □

Luigi Pirandello

The works of the Italian playwright, novelist, and critic Luigi Pirandello (1867-1936) generally portray Italian middle-class society. Combining relativistic thinking with a specific Pirandellian brand of humor, he probed the conflict between essence and appearance.

With Henrik Ibsen and August Strindberg, Luigi Pirandello revolutionized modern drama in all its aspects, from staging to the form of the play. His own specific contribution to the modern theater should be seen in the fact that he imposed upon the art form of theater itself the principles of analytic decomposition which Ibsen was still content to apply to human psychology.

Pirandello was born on June 28, 1867, in Girgenti (now Agrigento), Sicily, the son of a prosperous sulfur mine owner. He received his first schooling in Girgenti, and his formative years were spent at the universities of Palermo, Rome, and Bonn, where he obtained his doctorate in 1891 with a thesis on his native dialect. Upon his return to Italy he entered literary life and wrote his first novel in an artists' colony on Monte Cavo near Rome. In 1894 Pirandello married the daughter of a business associate of his father's, and the couple moved to Rome, where their three children were born. After some years Pirandello accepted a position as professor of Italian at Rome's R. Istituto di Magistero Femminile and in 1908 obtained the chair of Italian language and stylistics at the same institution.

Through a flooding of his father's mine in 1903, Pirandello lost his patrimony as well as his wife's substantial dowry, which had been invested in his father's business. Upon learning of the disaster, his wife suffered a shock and developed a paranoid condition which progressively worsened. She remained with the family, but as the scenes of jealousy became more trying, she was admitted to a nursing

home in 1919 and remained there until her death in 1959. There is no doubt that Pirandello's peculiar approach to the problems of essence and appearance was conditioned by this firsthand experience: he once said that a madwoman had led his hand for 15 long years. Throughout this time Pirandello continued his writing, scarcely noted by the rank and file of Italy's critics, and only the clamorous success of *Sei personaggi in cerca d'autore* (1921; *Six Characters in Search of an Author*) brought him national recognition and international fame.

In 1924, at a critical time for the regime following the Matteotti murder in June, Pirandello joined the Fascist party, and in September of the same year he founded, with state support, the Teatro d'Arte di Roma, of which he became director. From this time dates his friendship with Marta Abba, the leading actress of the troupe and his second muse. Mainly staging plays of Pirandello, the troupe went on several foreign tours, to England, France, and Germany (1925), to Vienna, Prague, and Budapest (1926), and to South America (1928). This venture proved too costly in the end, and the Teatro d'Arte was dissolved in 1928. Beginning with this year Pirandello took up frequent and extensive residences abroad, especially in Paris and Berlin.

In 1929 Pirandello was elected a member of the newly founded Accademia d'Italia, and in 1934 he was awarded the Nobel Prize for literature. He was a tall man with a pointed beard and piercing eyes. Pirandello died on Dec. 10, 1936, in his Roman apartment, which subsequently was declared a national monument and houses the Centro di Studi Pirandelliani. Pirandello's ashes were transferred to

his birthplace, where they now rest in a huge rock under a solitary pine tree, a setting he had imagined for his birth in his unfinished *Informazioni sul mio involontario soggiorno sulla terra.*

Career as a Playwright

Analytical in nature and for the most part lacking in action, Pirandello's plays are dialectical disquisitions on essence and appearance, illusion and reality, the problem of personal identity, the impossibility of objective truth and of communication. His dramatic production (some 43 plays in all) is thus an illustration of his relativistic and pessimistic tenets and philosophical beliefs. As he conceived of his probe into these aspects mainly as a process of unmasking, he published his collected plays under the title *Maschere nude* (*Naked Masks*).

Sei personaggi in cerca d'autore (1921), the first play of a trilogy, is an inquiry into the esthetic problems involved in translating the "ideal reality" of the six characters into the casual reality of the stage, represented by the actors and its transitory contingencies of time. The action is continually interrupted by comments paralleling it, the characters themselves are drawn as types, and the stage directions even recommend that they wear masks. Their story is only incidental to the more important aspect of the play, the clash and exchange between the two worlds of art and life.

In the second play, *Ciascuno a suo modo* (1924; *Each in His Own Way*), this analytical preoccupation comes out even more clearly in that the dialectical approach is carried to the point where action and ensuing reflection on it are already sharply defined in the outer form of the play: after each of the two acts there follow *intermezzi corali,* in which the preceding action is discussed. In the last play of the trilogy, *Questa sera si recita a soggetto* (1930; *Tonight We Improvise*), we see the consequences of this approach; it no longer makes any pretense at taking seriously the play within the play: the director, Dr. Hinkfuss, has his actors improvise on a scenario, a short story by Pirandello.

Many of Pirandello's one-act plays, such as *Il berretto a sonagli* (1918), *Liolà* (1917), *La giara* (short story 1909; play 1917), *La patente* (short story 1911; play 1918), and *Lumie di Sicilia* (short story 1900; play 1911) draw thematically on his Sicilian environment and belong to his regional-naturalistic production; some of them were originally even written in Sicilian dialect.

The great bulk of Pirandello's later production, however, is concerned with the concept of the mask in its different aspects: for Pirandello, the fiction, the mask alone, either self-imposed or, as in most cases, forced on by society, makes life possible. If this mask is ever torn off, willingly or by force, man is no longer able to live, to function in a society based upon the law of common fictions: either he returns to wearing his mask, to "living" the life of the dead, or he becomes "crazy," "insane" as far as society is concerned. By refusing to wear the mask, Pirandello's characters in the eyes of this world choose death. Thus they may die the symbolical death of insanity, or they may choose to take their own lives in earnest and throw away with their lives the mask and imposed form, as does Ersilia Drei of

Vestire gli ignudi (1923; *Naked*). They even may, willingly, choose a mask as a token of their freedom, as does the protagonist of *Enrico IV* (1922; *Henry IV*), one of Pirandello's strongest plays. He chooses to wear the mask of insanity in full consciousness, a decision he has sealed with a murder; and, ironically, society—the world of the masks—cannot hold him responsible because he has taken refuge behind a mask and beaten society at its own game.

Other plays center more directly on Pirandello's relativistic convictions concerning reality and illusion. Thus *Così è (se vi pare)* (1918; *Right You Are If You Think You Are*) explores the dual aspect of truth. His later plays, such as *Diana e la Tuda* (1927), *Trovarsi* (1932), *Quando si è qualcuno* (1933), are too-rigid exemplifications of the "life versus form" formula the Italian critic Adriano Tilgher had coined for Pirandello's production at the time. Of the trilogy on "modern myths" which Pirandello had envisaged, he completed only the first two plays. *La nuova colonia* (1928) portrays the rather pessimistic chances he gives society for a decent communal life, whereas *Lazzaro* (1929), his "religious myth," voices his pantheistic religious convictions. The last of these plays, the "myth of art," *I giganti della montagna* (1938; *The Mountain Giants*), remained unfinished.

The Novels

Whereas Pirandello's importance as an innovator in the field of drama is undisputed, in general his novels do not depart from the conventional form of the genre. Thus his first novel, *L'esclusa* (1901; *The Outcast*), and the short novel *Il turno* (1902) are written in the realist tradition.

With *Il fu Mattia Pascal* (1904; *The Late Mattia Pascal*), a novel that clearly carries the imprint of Pirandello's characteristic later approach, he first asserted himself on the international scene. Its theme is intrinsically connected with Pirandello's concept of the mask and the antinomy between reality and illusion. The hero, Mattia Pascal, flees what are to him unbearable situations—"masks" he is forced to wear—only to realize that these flights were in vain, for he does not have the courage to cope with the ensuing consequences.

Giustino Roncella nato Boggiòlo, first published under the title *Suo marito* (1911), treats an important aspect of Pirandello's concept of artistic creation: the antinomy between life and art. *I vecchi e i giovani* (1913; *The Young and the Old*) is a historical novel that covers the events in Italy between 1892 and 1894. The following novel, *Si gira* (1915), published later as *Quaderni di Serafino Gubbio operatore* (1932), again focuses on the problematic relationship between life and art, which is seen here through the world of cinematographic art. Pirandello's last novel, *Uno, nessuno e centomila* (1925-1926; *One, None, and a Hundred Thousand*), is a series of disconnected observations on the motif of the plurality of personality.

Short Stories and Criticism

As he intended to write one short story per day of the year, Pirandello published his stories with the collective title *Novelle per un anno*. The definitive edition, however, con-

tains only about 232 stories (1922-1937). It may well be that Pirandello's short stories will remain the most durable part of his work. They contain a host of motifs and often develop themes and plots taken up in full in later novels or plays. Thus the story *Quand'ero matto . . .* (1902) anticipates *Uno, nessuno e centomila,* and *Colloqui coi personaggi I, II* (1915) and *La tragedia di un personaggio* (1911) contain the nucleus of *Sei personaggi in cerca d'autore. Il pipistrello* (1919) exemplifies art-life antinomy in a casuistical manner; the problem of the mask and man's flight from it is the concern of stories such as *Il treno ha fischiato* (1914), *La maschera dimenticata* (1918), and *La carriola* (1917).

Many of Pirandello's essays explore problems of artistic creation such as *Illustratori, attori e traduttori* (1908). *Arte e scienza* (1908) discusses esthetic theory and contains also a categorical rejection of Benedetto Croce's esthetics. Pirandello's major essay *L'umorismo* (1908) establishes his own concept of humor.

Further Reading

The most recent and concise study of Pirandello in English is Oscar Büdel, *Pirandello* (1966; 2d ed. 1969). Important previous English studies are Walter Starkie, *Luigi Pirandello* (1926; 3d rev. ed. 1965), and Domenico Vittorini, *The Drama of Luigi Pirandello* (1935). Recommended for general historical background are Eric Bentley, *The Playwright as Thinker* (1946), and Lander McClintock, *The Age of Pirandello* (1951).

Additional Sources

Giudice, Gaspare, *Pirandello: a biography,* London; New York: Oxford University Press, 1975. □

Giovanni Battista Piranesi

Giovanni Battista Piranesi (1720-1778), Italian engraver and architect, is best known for his etchings of ancient and baroque Rome and grandiose architectural constructions of his own imagination.

Giovanni Battista Piranesi was born on Oct. 4, 1720, at Mojano di Mestre near Venice, the son of a stonemason. His early training in Venice under his uncle, Matteo Lucchesi, an architectural engineer, gave Piranesi a grasp of the means of masonry construction—scaffolding, winches, hawsers, pulleys, and chains—that stayed with him the rest of his life. His understanding of the vocabulary of classicism came largely from Andrea Palladio's book on architecture; his knowledge of architectural renderings he drew in part from Ferdinando Bibiena's book on civil architecture (1711); and his manner of placing buildings on a diagonal, sharply foreshortened, probably came from contemporary Venetian stage design.

In 1740 Piranesi went to Rome as a draftsman on the staff of the Venetian ambassador, Marco Foscarini. In Rome he learned to etch from Giuseppe Vasi. Trained as an architect but unable to find commissions, Piranesi published in 1743 a book of prints of imaginary buildings of enormous scale, inspired by the architecture of imperial Rome. The project was a financial failure.

By 1744 Piranesi was back in Venice, probably working in the studio of Giovanni Battista Tiepolo. From this period date Piranesi's etchings called grotesques: rococo shapes interlaced with fragments of ancient ruins. He returned to Rome in 1745, this time to stay. He took a consignment of prints (not his own) with him to sell as a publisher's agent and thus was able to get a financial foothold.

In 1745 Piranesi's first real success came with his *Carceri d'invenzione,* or *Imaginary Prisons,* 16 large plates that are often considered his masterpieces. "Only a stage-struck engineer," wrote Hyatt Mayor (1952), "could have conjured up these endless aisles, these beams draped with tons of chain, these gangplanks teetering from arch to arch, these piers that stand like beacons for exploring loftiness and light. . . . Piranesi rendered such more-than-Roman immensities like a true Venetian by letting his etching needle scribble and zigzag until it sketched areas of shade as translucent as a Guardi wash." Later, when he reworked the copperplates, he made the shapes sharper and darker, creating new drama but destroying the translucency of the light.

Piranesi's next enterprise was to record the ruins of ancient Rome. It was to be the biggest project of his life. In 1756, after more intensive archeological studies than any known previously, studies that were much implemented by his knowledge of civil engineering, Piranesi published his *Roman Antiquities,* four huge volumes containing over 200 folio plates. It won him immediate and widespread fame. He was made an honorary member of the Society of Antiquaries in London in 1757. In Rome the painters welcomed him into the Academy of St. Luke in 1761.

The only architectural work Piranesi executed was for Cardinal Giovanni Battista Rezzonico, Grand Prior of the Knights of Malta. He completely remodeled the church that belongs to that order, St. Maria del Priorato (1764-1766). The decorative program he devised for the church is outstanding in its originality. Classical motifs, combined in unclassical ways, are commingled with banners, shields, warship prows, arrows, and musical instruments in such a way as to produce an extraordinarily rich mélange of crisp, angular, two-dimensional patterns carried out in stucco reliefs.

The system of ornamentation that Piranesi invented for the church he elaborated and disseminated through a new set of engravings that he published under the title *Diverse Manners of Ornamenting . . . Houses* (1769). It became, a generation later, the basis for the style known today as Empire. At a much earlier date it was introduced into England by Piranesi's friend Robert Adam.

Throughout most of his adult life Piranesi made etchings of views of the city; not only its antiquities, such as the Pantheon, but also its contemporary masterpieces such as the Capitoline and Piazza Navona. The scenes are animated with tiny, frail, fluttering figures.

On Nov. 9, 1778, while making drawings of the newly discovered temples at Paestum, Piranesi died. Long before then his prints of his adopted city had caught the imagination of much of Europe. In 1771 Horace Walpole urged his fellow Englishmen to "study the sublime dreams of Piranesi, who seems to have conceived visions of Rome beyond what it boasted even in the meridian of its splendour. Savage as Salvator Rosa, fierce as Michelangelo, and exuberant as Rubens, he has imagined scenes that would startle geometry, and exhaust the Indies to realize."

Further Reading

The standard work in English on Piranesi is still Arthur M. Hind, *Giovanni Battista Piranesi* (1922). The best modern study in English is A. Hyatt Mayor, *Giovanni Battista Piranesi* (1952). Also useful is Hylton Thomas, *The Drawings of Giovanni Battista Piranesi* (1954). □

Jean Henri Otto Lucien Marie Pirenne

The writings of the Belgian historian Jean Henri Otto Lucien Marie Pirenne (1862-1935) renewed 20th-century ideas about the origins of European cities. His teaching created a major school of Belgian medievalists.

Henri Pirenne was born at Verviers on Dec. 23, 1862. At the University of Liège he studied history with Godefroid Kurth and Paul Fredericq. He received his doctorate in philosophy in 1883 and won a scholarship that allowed him to study in Berlin and Paris. In 1885 he organized the teaching of paleography and diplomatics at the University of Liège, and in 1886 he was named professor at the University of Ghent, where he remained for 40 years.

During World War I Pirenne was imprisoned for resisting the German occupation. Moved from prison camp to prison camp, he learned Russian in one, taught Belgian history to the Belgian prisoners in a second, and without the aid of books or notes wrote a *History of Europe* (1936) in a third. "He was a teacher without peer," a student later wrote, "exciting his young students with his forceful and colorful rhetoric and by the originality of his ideas." From his seminar at Ghent there issued a large number of eminent Belgian and American medievalists.

In 1893 Pirenne published an article on the origins of medieval towns. Worked out in later articles and in two books, *Belgian Democracy: Its Early History* (1910) and *Medieval Cities* (1925), his thesis came to dominate studies of medieval urban institutions. Some historians argued that medieval town constitutions originated in ecclesiastical immunities, others that towns were outgrowths of medieval servile communities, and still others that they descended from primitive free communities. Pirenne maintained that the early medieval town was only a fortress, economically dependent on the countryside. With the economic revival of the 10th and 11th centuries, however, old cities were reborn and new towns created in the form of trading settlements near the older fortresses. These created their own law and a new status of personal freedom. Though Pirenne's argument was largely intuitive, the validity of his thesis for northern European towns was demonstrated by the research his views inspired.

In 1922 Pirenne published another provocative article, "Mohammed and Charlemagne," in which he argued that the break between antiquity and the Middle Ages came with the closing of the Mediterranean by the Moslem conquest of Africa and Spain. Worked out in a book by the same title (1937), the thesis inspired other historians to turn their attention to the economic history of the early Middle Ages, and it still remains the starting point for discussions of the societies of Merovingian and Carolingian Europe. Pirenne also wrote a *History of Belgium* (7 vols., 1900-1932). He died at Ukkel on Oct. 24, 1935.

Further Reading

A memoir and an evaluation of Pirenne's work by Charles Verlinden appear in Joseph T. Lambie, ed., *Architects and Craftsmen in History* (1956). A study of Pirenne by James L. Cate is in Samuel William Halperin, ed., *Some 20th-Century Historians: Essays on Eminent Europeans* (1961). Alfred F. Havighurst, ed., *The Pirenne Thesis: Analysis, Criticism, and Revision* (1958; 2d ed. 1969), contains Pirenne's major statements on Mohammed and Charlemagne and a selection of the critical literature this work evoked.

Additional Sources

Lyon, Bryce Dale, *Henri Pirenne: a biographical and intellectual study,* Ghent: E. Story-Scientia, 1974. □

Pisanello

Pisanello (ca. 1395-1455), painter and medalist, was a leading master of the International Gothic style of painting in Italy and created the first example of the Renaissance medal.

Probably born in Pisa, Antonio Pisano, called Pisanello was raised in Verona by his mother, Isabetta, a native of that city, after the death of his father, Pucio di Giovanni, a Pisan. Nothing is known of Pisanello's early years. He may have been a pupil of Stefano da Verona, whose influence is seen in Pisanello's early *Madonna of the Quails* (ca. 1415).

Between 1419 and 1422 Pisanello was in Venice collaborating with Gentile da Fabriano on the frescoes for the Great Council Hall of the Ducal Palace (repainted 1479). From 1422 to 1426 Pisanello was in Mantua and Verona. The frescoed *Annunciation* above the Brenzoni tomb in the church of St. Fermo, Verona, is signed and dated (1424-1426). He journeyed to Rome after the death of Gentile da Fabriano in 1428 to complete Gentile's frescoes (destroyed) in St. John Lateran. He remained there until July 1432, when he was granted a safe-conduct to leave the city by Pope Eugenius IV.

From 1432 to 1439 Pisanello moved back and forth between Verona and Ferrara. Most of his extant paintings date from this period, including the frescoed *Legend of St. George* on the entrance arch of the Pellegrini Chapel in St. Anastasia, Verona; the *Vision of St. Eustace;* the *Portrait of a Ferrarese Princess,* sometimes called *Ginevra d'Este;* the *Portrait of Lionello d'Este;* the *Madonna in Glory with Saints Anthony Abbot and George;* and the *Portrait of the Emperor Sigismund.* In these works Pisanello blended decorativeness with carefully observed naturalistic detail. His interest in naturalistic detail and in subtly stylized courtly figures can better be seen in the numerous extant drawings by him and his school, including those in the famous Codex Vallardi.

The Byzantine emperor John VII Palaeologus attended the Church council which convened in Ferrara in 1438. Pisanello's earliest extant medal with a portrait of the Emperor was cast in 1439. His medals were cast rather than struck, a method which permitted much greater subtlety of modeling. A fine portraitist, he took great pains with the reverses as well, showing a special fondness for animal figures. His medals are among his finest works, displaying a breadth of modeling and conception most unusual for the time.

In 1439 Verona, then under Venetian protection, was sacked by the army of the Duke of Mantua, a supporter of Milan in its war with Venice. After Venice recovered Verona, Pisanello, who was a member of the court of

Mantua at the time, was accused of offenses against Venice. He was condemned to prison but was allowed to leave Venice in 1442, when his mother died in Verona.

In 1443 Pisanello cast a medal to commemorate the wedding of Lionello d'Este and Maria of Aragon in Ferrara. In 1445 he made a medal for Sigismondo Pandolfo Malatesta of Rimini. In 1448 he was in Naples, where he was a member of the court of King Alfonso III of Aragon. His medal of the King dates from 1449. After 1450, documentary references to Pisanello disappear. He died in October 1455, according to a letter written by Carlo de' Medici.

Further Reading

A work on Pisanello in English in Enio Sindona, *Pisanello* (1961). G. F. Hill, *Pisanello* (1905), remains a useful but somewhat out-of-date monograph. See also Jakob Rosenberg, *Great Draughtsmen from Pisanello to Picasso* (1959). □

Giovanni Pisano

The late Gothic art of the Italian sculptor Giovanni Pisano (ca. 1250-1314) set the stage for the development of the Renaissance style.

The son of the sculptor Nicola Pisano, Giovanni Pisano was listed as an assistant to his father in the contract of Sept. 29, 1265, for the pulpit in the Siena Cathedral. The terms of his employment indicate that he must have been a youthful apprentice; hence it is assumed that he was born about 1250. Giovanni carved the holy-water font in St. Giovanni Fuorcivitas, Pistoia, in the early 1270s and collaborated with his father on the Fontana Maggiore, Perugia, which was completed in 1278. Between 1278 and 1284 Giovanni executed a group of half-length figures including a prophet, St. Mark, and the Madonna (now in the Civic Museum, Pisa).

From 1284 to 1294 Giovanni worked on the Siena Cathedral, executing a number of life-sized statues of kings, prophets, and sibyls for the facade and flank. These statues, originally placed on the level above the portals, are among his most dynamic and lively works. They are covered with heaps of deeply folded drapery that assumes an animation of its own. The generally twisting postures of the figures and the strong outward glances of their eyes create a sense of movement and vibrancy. They are, in Pietro Toesca's words, "Gothic and Michelangelesque at the same time."

Giovanni worked in Pisa from about 1295 to 1300. From this period date three standing Madonnas preserved in Pisa: one in St. Maria della Spina; one in the Cathedral Museum; and an exquisite ivory statuette in the Cathedral Treasury, which strongly suggests that Giovanni had direct contact with French Gothic sculpture either through a visit to France or through exposure to French art brought to Italy.

Giovanni's marble pulpit for St. Andrea in Pistoia, completed in 1301, is in his finest Gothic style. Like Nicola Pisano's Pisa Baptistery pulpit, Giovanni's pulpit in Pistoia is

hexagonal, but he introduced Gothic achitectural elements, such as the ogive arch, whereas Nicola had used Romanesque elements. The style of the narrative reliefs is, likewise, strikingly different. Instead of concentrating attention on the figures, Giovanni emphasized the abstract movement of light and shade across the surface. The carving is deeply cut, in places undercut, to emphasize the rhythmic movements of the figures and the backgrounds. The poses and gestures of individual figures tend to be made part of an overall rhythmic design, always graceful, always elegant. Where an episode lends itself to a dramatic depiction, as in the Massacre of the Innocents, Giovanni yields to a frank emotional display.

In 1302 Giovanni was commissioned to make a marble pulpit for the Cathedral in Pisa. It is markedly different from his and his father's other pulpits. Polygonal, with curving rather than flat sides, the architectural portions are elaborate and sculpturesque. The various parts of the pulpit are uneven in execution, which suggests the presence of numerous assistants. Work on this pulpit continued until 1310, during which time Giovanni carved two standing Madonnas: the altar Madonna for the Arena Chapel in Padua, before 1305, and the so-called Madonna della Cintola for the Cathedral in Prato, after 1305. Both Madonnas are works of great charm and are considered autograph works. The Madonna della Cintola, a less than half life-size marble statue, twists to look at the Child. Her figure is covered with drapery arranged in deep folds that fall in regular curves around her hips and down her legs. The Child, whose face is on the same level as the Madonna's, looks outward toward the faithful and raises a chubby hand in benediction.

In 1313 Giovanni was called to Genoa to execute the tomb of Margaret of Luxemburg, fragments of which are now in the Palazzo Bianco, Genoa. The last documentary reference to Giovanni is dated 1314, when he was in Siena.

Further Reading

Two studies of Giovanni Pisano are Adolfo Venturi, *Giovanni Pisano: His Life and Work* (1928), and Michael Ayrton, *Giovanni Pisano: Sculptor,* with an introduction by Henry Moore (1970). An important background study with information on Giovanni is John Pope-Hennessy, *Introduction to Italian Sculpture,* vol. 1: *Italian Gothic Sculpture* (1955). □

Nicola Pisano

The Italian sculptor Nicola Pisano (ca. 1220-1278) liberated sculpture from the hieratic Byzantine manner. His art marked the beginning of the Italian Gothic style.

The birthplace of Nicola Pisano has been the subject of speculation among scholars. His name would seem to indicate that he was a Pisan, but two documents relating to the marble pulpit of the Cathedral in Siena (1265-1268) that he executed refer to him as Nicola d'Apulia (Nicholas of Apulia, in southern Italy) rather than the more common Nicola Pisano. The significance of his birthplace derives from the remarkably classical quality of his earliest extant work, the marble pulpit in the Baptistery of Pisa, signed and dated 1260. Emperor Frederick II, whose court was near Naples, was an admirer of ancient Roman civilization. He encouraged artists to work in the more realistic style of Roman antiquity rather than the more abstract contemporary Romanesque and Byzantine styles. If Nicola had been a native of Apulia and trained in the sculptural workshops of the Emperor, the classical character of the Pisa Baptistery pulpit would be easier to explain. No definitive solution to this problem is possible, however, with the evidence presently available.

The pulpit for the Baptistery in Pisa is adorned with narrative reliefs depicting the Life and Passion of Christ on five of its six sides. Nicola reduced to a minimum the number of figures telling the story so that they dominate the rectangular field. Among them are a number of direct quotations from antique works brought to Pisa by its fleet. The style of the reliefs is remarkably classical and depends on a few monumental figures moving in a stately way across the foreground. Nothing else carved by Nicola bears such a strong resemblance to the antique.

A contract dated Sept. 29, 1265, commissioned Nicola to build a similar marble pulpit for the Cathedral in Siena. The pulpit, which was completed by 1268, varied somewhat in format and style from the Pisan one. He expanded the format by making the pulpit octagonal, and he made the narrative easier to read by substituting statuettes for the clustered columns used to divide the reliefs in the earlier work. In style they reveal a concern for the surface play of highlights and shadows, achieved by deeper cutting and undercutting, and for a growing elegance and grace among the figures, similar to that of Gothic sculpture.

The Gothicism of the Siena Cathedral pulpit continued in Nicola's great secular monument, the Fontana Maggiore in Perugia. This was a joint undertaking of Nicola and his son, Giovanni Pisano. Probably begun in 1277, the fountain was finished in 1278. It consists of two superimposed polygonal stone basins topped with a circular bronze basin carried by three caryatid figures. The lower basin is decorated with reliefs; the upper basin is decorated with statuettes affixed to the angles. In the portions usually attributed to Nicola, the style represents a resolution between the earlier classicizing tendencies and the later Gothicizing tendencies of his art. The work of Giovanni, on the other hand, was wholeheartedly in the new style, that is, the Gothic.

Further Reading

George H. and Elsie R. Crichton, *Nicolo Pisano and the Revival of Sculpture in Italy* (1938), is a sound monograph. See also Georg Swarzenski, *Nicolo Pisano* (1926). Up-to-date information can be found in John Pope-Hennessy, *An Introduction to Italian Sculpture,* vol. 1: *Italian Gothic Sculpture* (1955). □

Camille Pissaro

The French painter Camille Pissarro (1830-1903) was one of the original impressionists. Although his work is generally less innovative than that of his major contemporaries, it is no less important in reflecting the new style.

Camille Pissarro was born in St. Thomas, Virgin Islands, on July 10, 1830. His father, a Portuguese Jew, ran a general store. Although Pissarro attended school in Paris and demonstrated an exceptional talent for drawing, he returned to St. Thomas in 1847 to work in the family business. During the ensuing years his interest in art persisted, and in 1855 his parents finally yielded to his ambition to become a painter.

Pissarro reached Paris in time to see the important World's Fair of 1855. He was particularly impressed by the landscapes of Camille Corot and other members of the Barbizon group, who had taken the first steps toward working directly from nature, and by the ambitious and forthright realism of Gustave Courbet, although his own work increasingly gravitated toward landscape rather than figurative subjects.

During the next 10 years Pissarro received some academic training at the École des Beaux-Arts, but he spent most of his time at the Académie Suisse, where free classes were offered. This was an important gathering place for those artists whose ambitions and sensibilities lay outside the teaching of the official schools, for it offered greater opportunity to discuss and develop personal ideas about painting and art in general. In this setting Pissarro became friends with Claude Monet, Pierre Auguste Renoir, Alfred Sisley, and Paul Cézanne, who were seeking alternatives to the established methods of painting. Pissarro's works at this time were occasionally, though by no means consistently, accepted at the annual Salons. More importantly, however, he received critical backing and encouragement from Émile Zola.

During the Franco-Prussian War in 1870-1871 Pissarro and Monet went to London, where they were impressed by the landscape paintings of John Constable and J.M.W. Turner. By this time Pissarro and Monet had begun to work directly from nature and to develop the unique style that would later be called impressionism. In their pursuit of this new and revolutionary direction, the lessons of the earlier English landscapists provided crucial and much-needed support, particularly in terms of the loose handling of paint, the abstractness, and the strong response to nature which characterized their own paintings. When Pissarro returned to his home at Louveciennes near Paris, he found that the Prussians had destroyed nearly all of his paintings.

By the early 1870s the work of Pissarro and his colleagues had been rejected by the Salon on repeated occasions. In 1874 they held their own exhibition, a show of "independent" artists. This was the first impressionist exhibition (the term "impressionist," originally used derisively, was actually coined by a newspaper critic). There were seven similar exhibitions until 1886, and Pissarro was the only artist who participated in all eight. This fact is important because it reveals something about Pissarro's relation to impressionism generally: he was the patriarch and teacher of the movement, constantly advising younger artists, introducing them to one another, and encouraging them to join the revolutionary trend that he helped to originate.

In 1892 there was a large retrospective of Pissarro's work, and he finally gained the international recognition he deserved. Characteristic paintings are *Path through the Fields* (1879), *Landscape, Eragny* (1895), and *Place du Théâtre Français* (1898). He died in Paris on Nov. 12, 1903.

Further Reading

Pissarro is the subject of critical analysis in these works by John Rewald: *Camille Pissarro* (1963), a monograph on the artist; *C. Pissarro* (1965), an exhibition catalog; and *The History of Impressionism* (1961), in which Pissarro's role in the development of impressionism is well documented.

Additional Sources

Adler, Kathleen, *Camille Pissarro: a biography,* New York: St. Martin's Press, 1978, 1977.
Cogniat, Raymond, *Pissarro,* New York: Crown Publishers, 1988, 1981.
Lloyd, Christopher, *Camille Pissarro,* Geneva: Skira; New York: Rizzoli, 1981.
Pissarro, Camille, *Camille Pissarro,* New York: H.N. Abrams, 1989.
Pissarro, Camille, *Pissarro,* New York: Crown Publishers, 1975.

Shikes, Ralph E., *Pissarro, his life and work*, New York: Horizon Press, 1980. ☐

Walter Piston

Walter Piston (1894-1976), American composer, wrote traditionalist music of great technical skill which was neoclassic in its orientation. He was highly influential as an educator.

Walter Piston was born on Jan. 20, 1894, in Rockland, Maine. His grandparents had settled there after their arrival from Italy, and soon after dropped the final "e" from their original name of Pistone. At the age of ten young Piston moved to Boston with his family and, after graduating from high school, studied painting at the Massachusetts Normal School, where he graduated in 1916. Music was a secondary interest to Piston until World War I. During the war he served in a service band and taught himself how to play most of the wind instruments. "They were just lying around and no one minded if you picked them up and found out what they could do," he said about this time in his life.

Returning to the United States in 1919, he entered Harvard University and began to study music seriously. He graduated in 1924 with the highest honor of *summa cum laude* and went to Paris, where he studied with Paul Dukas and Nadia Boulanger.

In 1926 Piston returned to the United States and joined the Harvard University faculty. From 1944 on he was professor of music; he was the first occupant of the Naumberg chair, a position of great distinction. He retired from Harvard in 1960.

The performance of his *Symphonic Piece* in 1928 by the Boston Symphony began Piston's long association with that orchestra. *The Incredible Flutist,* first performed in 1938 with dancers, proved a major success. Subsequent performances and a recording of the suite derived from the ballet score secured a national reputation for Piston. Thereafter there were many commissions and honors. He had received a Guggenheim fellowship in 1935. He was elected to the Institute of Arts and Letters in 1938 and the American Academy of Arts and Science in 1940. Piston was awarded the Pulitzer Prize for the Third Symphony in 1948 and for the Seventh Symphony in 1961. He received the New York Music Critics Circle Award in 1945 for the Second Symphony and again, in 1959, for the Viola Concerto. His Sixth Symphony, was included in the programs of the Boston Symphony, when, in 1956, it became the first American orchestra to tour the Soviet Union.

Piston's eminence as a music educator was enhanced by the publication of his books, *Principles of Harmonic Analysis* (1933), *Harmony* (1941), *Counterpoint* (1947), and *Orchestration* (1955). These works combine traditional viewpoints with individual concepts. Through their popularity as texts in American conservatories and universities,

his influence as a teacher was more extensive than as a composer.

Piston wrote music of originality and vitality. His neoclassic attitude is reflected by a concentration on large abstract orchestral and chamber works. He was interested primarily in formal concepts and leaned upon classical models. His work can be quite complex, rhythmically and tonally, and it expresses a high degree of balance and uniform excellence. Above all, he was highly skilled in the disciplined control of his material and in his knowledge of the orchestra. His craftsmanship reveals a polish and elegance that reflect the highest traditional values.

Piston died on November 12, 1976 at his home in Belmont, Massachusetts and was remembered by the *New York Times* music critic as a man "who has thoroughly mastered the ground principles of his art; who knows what he wants to do and how to do it; whose basis is a thorough command of counterpoint and form, on which is superimposed brilliant treatment of the orchestra."

Further Reading

A number of Piston's compositions are described in David Ewen, *The World of Twentieth-century Music* (1968). For an interesting view see Wilfred Mellers, *Music in a New Found Land: Themes and Developments in the History of American Music* (1965). See also the discussions of Piston in Aaron Copland, *The New Music, 1900-1960* (1941; rev. ed. 1968), and Joseph Machlis, *Introduction to Contemporary Music* (1961). A study of Piston's music and a biography of the composer are published in Howard Pollack *Walter Piston* (1982). Piston's obituary appears in the November 13, 1976 edition of the *New York Times.* □

William Pitt the Elder

The British statesman William Pitt the Elder, 1st Earl of Chatham (1708-1778), was one of the most striking political figures of the 18th century. Known as the Great Commoner, he served as war minister under George II and led Britain to victory over the French.

Willliam Pitt was born on Nov. 15, 1708, the son of a Cornish member of Parliament. Educated at Eton and at Oxford, in 1735 he entered Parliament. Pitt immediately showed himself to be a violent opponent of Sir Robert Walpole. His opposition to Hanoverian policy also lost him the favor of George II, a factor which prevented his obtaining office after Walpole's fall in 1742. In 1746 Pitt was appointed paymaster general, but this office carried little political influence.

Intensely ambitious, conscious of his power in the Commons, and impatient in his secondary role, Pitt aimed at supreme power. In September 1755 he gained admission to the Cabinet and dominated the great debate (November 13-14) on the war with France. His speech on this occasion, wrote Horace Walpole, "like a torrent long obstructed, burst forth with more commanding impetuosity." Dismissed because of his opposition, Pitt set out to rouse popular enthusiasm for the war, pressing for increases in the army and navy, for more troops to be sent to America, and for the establishment of a national militia. In December 1756 Pitt became secretary of state under the nominal leadership of the Duke of Devonshire; this ministry was replaced in July 1757 by a coalition between Pitt and Lord Newcastle. They worked well together and were responsible for England's victories in the Seven Years War.

His Character

Probably the most marked trait in Pitt's character was his aloofness. He was a solitary man who, according to his nephew, "lived and died without a friend." Politically his isolation meant that he was not a party man and worked badly in a team. In the Commons his aggression and commanding presence compelled attention. A contemporary wrote, "He was tall in his person with the eye of a hawk, a little head, thin face, long aquiline nose, and perfectly erect." Pitt also had great courage—a rare quality in 18th-century statesmen. He was not afraid to assume responsibility for war with the French, provided he was given full powers. "I know that I can save this country and that no one else can," he said in 1756. His greatness as a war minister was that he invigorated the nation and imbued it with his own confidence and resolution.

But as George II grew older, Pitt's position became less secure. His alliance with Lord Bute and the Prince of Wales failed when Pitt adopted the policy of a Continental war. George III, who became king in 1760, opposed Pitt but could not begin his reign by dismissing the minister who had led Britain to victory. Instead, he tried to separate Newcastle from Pitt and, with Newcastle's compliance, secured Bute's admittance to office as secretary of state. In September 1761 Pitt, now isolated in the Cabinet, resigned over the conduct of the war. He hoped, he said, "never to be a public man again." Yet he remained the key figure in the Commons, and much of the confusion in politics during the next 5 years resulted from his unpredictable conduct.

Later Career

Between 1762 and 1764 Pitt, who was ill with gout, attended Parliament infrequently, leaving the opposition disjointed and leaderless. He declined to take office on the dismissal of the Grenvilles in 1765 and again in January 1766, when he was also asked for his opinion "on the present state of America." Pitt delivered his views on America during a debate on January 14: "It is my opinion that this kingdom has no right to lay a tax upon the colonies. At the same time I assert the authority of this kingdom over the colonies to be sovereign and supreme in every circumstance of government and legislation whatsoever." Pitt considered this distinction between taxation and legislation essential to freedom. But he apparently never realized that to allow the American colonies the power of taxation inevitably meant allowing them separate sovereignty.

On the collapse of the Rockingham administration in July 1766, Pitt was at last given the opportunity to form an independent administration. He set out "to dissolve all factions and to see the best of all parties in Administration," but he succeeded only in ranging all the political groups against him. His health prevented him from assuming regularly the leadership of the Commons, and his acceptance of the earldom of Chatham in August 1766 showed a fatal misunderstanding of the source of his political strength. Deprived by his aloofness and arrogance of loyal and reliable colleagues, he had to fall back on lazy and inexperienced ministers. When, early in 1767, illness prevented Chatham from attending the Cabinet and Parliament, he had no reliable deputy to weld his diversified Cabinet into a team. Finally, in the spring of 1767, he succumbed to an attack of manic depression, and for over 2 years he played virtually no part in politics.

The last 10 years of Chatham's life were anticlimactic. He returned to politics in 1769, but he had few followers and was as difficult to work with as ever. In 1771, no longer a political force, he practically ceased to attend Parliament. The outbreak of the American war reawakened something of his old vigor, and he fought to preserve the colonies for Britain. While speaking in Parliament on this subject, he fell ill and died a month later on May 11, 1778. He was buried in Westminster Abbey.

Further Reading

The major modern biography of Chatham is a three-volume work by O. A. Sherrard, *Lord Chatham: A War Minister in the Making* (1952), *Lord Chatham: Pitt and the Seven Years' War* (1955), and *Lord Chatham and America* (1958). A detailed single-volume biography is provided by Brian Tunstall, *William Pitt, Earl of Chatham* (1938). J. H. Plumb, *Chatham* (1953), is shorter and most interesting. On Chatham's unsuccessful administration, John Brooke, *The Chatham Administration, 1766-1768* (1956), is essential.

Additional Sources

Ayling, Stanley Edward, *The elder Pitt, Earl of Chatham,* London: Collins, 1976.
Black, Jeremy, *Pitt the Elder,* Cambridge England; New York: Cambridge University Press, 1992.
Brown, Peter Douglas, *William Pitt Earl of Chatham, the great commoner,* London: Allen & Unwin, 1978.
Peters, Marie, *Pitt and popularity: the patriot minister and London opinion during the Seven Years War,* Oxford: Clarendon Press; New York: Oxford University Press, 1980.
Robertson, Charles Grant, Sir, *Chatham and the British Empire,* Westport, Conn.: Greenwood Press, 1984.
Sherrard, Owen Aubrey, *Lord Chatham: a war minister in the making,* Westport, Conn.: Greenwood Press, 1975.
Sherrard, Owen Aubrey, *Lord Chatham: Pitt and the Seven Years' War,* Westport, Conn.: Greenwood Press, 1975. □

William Pitt the Younger

The English statesman William Pitt the Younger (1759-1806) introduced important financial and administrative reforms, girded England for war against Revolutionary and Napoleonic France, and attempted to solve the perennial Irish problem.

The second son of William Pitt, 1st Earl of Chatham, the younger William Pitt was born on May 28, 1759, at the family estate of Hayes, near Bromley, Kent. It was a year of triumph for his father, and for England, which was victorious on land and on sea against the French. Thus his birth appeared auspicious—and Pitt fully lived up to the expectations that he excited in family and acquaintances. His accomplishments at least equaled those of his illustrious father.

Pitt's Personality

Although in early childhood Pitt suffered from frail health, almost from the beginning he showed great intellectual promise and an interest in politics. Pitt later outgrew his physical frailty, but he always retained the sense of personal destiny that his abilities and interests early inspired and that his family encouraged. As a youth, Pitt was painfully shy; in adulthood he did not lose this quality, but he hid it behind a facade of cold aloofness. Those who did not know him well assumed that his coldness revealed his true nature, and his reputation has survived as a man utterly lacking in human sympathy and feeling. That picture is a false one, however, for in his personal relationships with friends and family he showed himself warm, amiable, and witty.

His Political Stance

Politically, Pitt was a pragmatist. He believed in reform for the sake of honest, humane, and efficient administration rather than for the sake of any abstract theory. For him politics was the art of the possible, and he believed that it was better to do the best one could in any given situation than surrender office (and thus lose the chance of serving one's country) because of an insistence on the impossible. Although he was scrupulously honest regarding his own conduct and financial dealings (he rejected an offer of £100,000 because he feared it might prejudice his political independence), and although he was contemptuous of those who sold their votes and influence for money or advancement, on more than one occasion he resorted to the then current methods of jobbery and bribery in order to win support on important issues. Pitt's political convictions were rooted in the 18th-century English constitution: he always upheld the right of the monarch to choose his ministers and to participate in government, and at the same time he always maintained the privileges of Parliament in the legislative process and in the governing of the country. Pitt foresaw the eventual supremacy of the House of Commons over both Lords and King, but he did not do anything to bring about that situation. Pitt sometimes displayed a deep, almost uncanny, insight, but in only one respect might he be deemed a visionary: he had an abiding faith in the greatness that Britain could achieve.

Early Career

In 1781 Pitt became a Member of Parliament from a pocket borough. His eloquence in debate soon distinguished him, and he was favorably compared with his late father. Ambitious, self-confident, and eager both to show his abilities and to serve his country, he did not leap at his first opportunities, which were minor offices. He chose instead to preserve his political independence and to wait for more responsible positions. His chance came in July 1782, when he accepted the office of Chancellor of the Exchequer in Lord Shelburne's ministry. During his chancellorship Britain signed preliminary peace treaties with the United States, France, Spain, and Holland. Parliamentary opposition to these treaties caused Shelburne to resign his office in February 1783. A month later Pitt also resigned.

Pitt became head of the ministry on Dec. 19, 1783, when he took office as First Lord of the Treasury and Chancellor of the Exchequer. He was then only 24 years old, and he lacked a majority in the House of Commons, which greeted the announcement of his appointment with laughter. His first task was to win the confidence of the Commons. He already possessed the support of the King and the House of Lords. Pitt's eloquence and steadiness of purpose favorably impressed the Commons, and these qualities together with the skillful politicking of John Robinson gained Pitt an overwhelming victory at the polls in 1784. With the support of a majority in Commons, Pitt then embarked on the important business of leading Britain into a period of hitherto unparalleled prosperity and strength. In this endeavor he was not, as Lord North had been, the compliant tool of the King. For his part, George III refrained from interference,

seemingly happy to have found at last a strong minister whom he could trust.

Pitt made his greatest achievements between 1784, when he won a parliamentary majority, and 1789, when the outbreak of the French Revolution brought new problems that eventually led to war. In the realm of finances, Pitt's contemporaries accounted him little less than a wizard, and his accomplishments in this area seem to justify their esteem. Through various reforms and through reducing wherever possible corrupt and inefficient practices, he achieved a surplus in the national budget. His greatest financial success was his establishment in 1786 of the sinking fund to pay off the national debt. In the field of colonial administration Pitt brought about reforms in the governing of both India and Canada.

Not all of Pitt's efforts met with success. Several of his attempts at very necessary reforms encountered so great a weight of parliamentary or monarchical opposition that, recognizing the impossibility of pushing them through, he abandoned them. Others of Pitt's legislative failures—his unsuccessful attempts at parliamentary reform, the abolition of the slave trade, and the reform of the Poor Law, and the failure of much of his Irish policy—were owing to the temper of his times.

Pitt's Later Career

After the outbreak of the French Revolution in 1789, Pitt strove at first to maintain a British attitude of neutrality, but the revolutionary excesses of behavior and of thought could not remain forever isolated in France. France declared war on England in 1793, and this crisis was accompanied by a republican scare that led, among other coercive measures, to the suspension of the Habeas Corpus Act in 1794. Many Whigs joined the government in this vote, only a few diehards remaining with Charles James Fox in opposition. The remainder of Pitt's career grew increasingly worrisome and was chiefly occupied with winning the war against France.

One important concern apart from the French war, however, was the Irish problem. Pitt decided that parliamentary union of Ireland with England and Catholic emancipation (so that Roman Catholics could hold office) must be accomplished. He achieved the legislative union in 1800 with the aid of a massive program of outright bribery. But his plan for Catholic emancipation met with the King's adamant refusal. Pitt regarded it as so important that he would not remain in office in view of George III's objections. He accordingly resigned in March 1801.

His Last Years

For some time Pitt supported the ministry of his successor, but he eventually lost confidence in Henry Addington's ability. Pitt was recalled to office in May 1804 and helped to rededicate England to the struggle against Napoleon Bonaparte. But his long years of wartime service had undermined his health, and the news of the defeat of England's allies at the Battle of Austerlitz shattered Pitt completely. His health declined rapidly, and he died on Jan. 23, 1806.

Pitt left tremendous debts (the financial wizard had paid no attention to his personal accounts) but no children to pay them. He had never married. His devotion was solely lavished upon his country. His last words were of England: "Oh, my country! How I leave my country!"

Further Reading

The biography of Pitt by John Ehrman, *The Younger Pitt* (1969), is an outstanding work of scholarship which deals exhaustively with Pitt's early years, to 1789. A brief but thoughtful biography is John W. Derry, *William Pitt* (1962). Important older works include P. H. Stanhope, 5th Earl Stanhope, *Life of the Right Honourable William Pitt* (4 vols., 1861-1862), and Lord Rosebery, *Pitt* (1891). Studies of aspects of Pitt's career include the works of J. Holland Rose, *William Pitt and National Revival* (1911) and *William Pitt and the Great War* (1911), and D. G. Barnes, *George III and William Pitt, 1783-1806* (1939). Two useful books for background reading are Asa Briggs, *The Age of Improvement* (1959), and J. Steven Watson, *The Reign of George III* (1960).

Additional Sources

Jarrett, Derek, *Pitt the younger,* New York: Scribner, 1974.
Reilly, Robin, *William Pitt the Younger,* New York: Putnam, 1979, 1978. □

Pius II

Pius II (1405-1464) was pope from 1458 to 1464. He is remarkable for the contrast between his early life as a writer and poet of the Renaissance and his later life as a conservative pope.

Pius II was born Enea Silvio de' Piccolomini (often in Latin, Aeneas Sylvius) at Corsigniano, Italy. He did not take Holy Orders until the age of 41, having spent most of his life enjoying a worldly existence as a writer of profane literature and as secretary to many prominent men. Piccolomini spent many years at the Council of Basel and helped elect the antipope Felix V. In 1442 he met Emperor Frederick III, who created him poet laureate and made him his private secretary. In 1445 Piccolomini was converted from the disorderly life he had been leading and made his peace with the orthodox ranks of the Church. Pope Nicholas V made him bishop of Trieste in 1447 and of Siena in 1449, and he became a cardinal in 1456. On Aug. 19, 1458, he was elected pope, taking the name Pius II in honor of the "pius Aeneas" of the Roman poet Virgil.

Pius II's character now changed rather dramatically. His supporters had expected him to be a patron of the arts, but he chose instead to be a medieval pope, completely out of step with his times. Throughout his pontificate his main concern was to organize a crusade against the Turks, who had captured Constantinople, ending the Byzantine Empire, in 1453. This preoccupation made him neglect more practical matters, notably the settlement of the Hussite problem, which quarrel he continued with the Bohemians led by George of Podebrad, and French aggression in Italy. For-

merly a skilled diplomat, Pius II handled these problems badly. His papal conservatism is shown by his bull *Execrabilis* (1460), which declared heretical the idea that a general council of the Church is superior to the pope. With this bull he helped to kill the conciliar movement, which had attempted urgent reforms in the Church.

In June 1464 Pius II took the cross and set out on a crusade against the Turks. He had almost no support, and he probably hoped that other princes would be shamed into following him. Pius II became ill and died at Ancona on Aug. 15, 1464. Although his writings lack depth of conviction, he had considerable charm both as an artist and as a person; and this charm may have accounted for his rise to prominence. Deep conviction came to him only after he had assumed the responsibilities of the papacy, and although his pontificate may be justly criticized as an anachronism, his thwarted crusade of 1464 testifies to his courage and to his devotion to duty. He had changed from a lighthearted young man to a dedicated religious leader, but unfortunately his conception of papal duty belonged to a vanished era.

Further Reading

Pius II's own writings are important documents of the early Renaissance, as well as enjoyable reading. An abridged translation of his *Commentaries* by Leona C. Gabel and F. A. Cragg was published under the title *Pius II: Memoirs of a Renaissance Pope* (1960). The standard biography of him is Catherine M. Ady, *Pius II: The Humanist Pope* (1913). □

Pius IV

Pius IV (1499-1565), by backing the Council of Trent in its last and extremely tense period, emerged as one of the great popes of the Catholic Reformation. By his temperate and tractable approach, he broke with the severe regime of his predecessor, Paul IV.

Giovanni Angelo de' Medici, who became Pius IV, was born into the lesser nobility of Milan on March 31, 1499. His family was not related to the famous Medici of Florence. He received his early education at Pavia, and in 1525 he earned a doctorate in canon and civil law at the University of Bologna. The next year Medici began his service in the Church as a protonotary apostolic. Under Pope Paul III he gained a breadth of experience in administration within the papal states and in diplomacy on missions to Hungary and Transylvania. At the age of 46 Medici was ordained a priest. The same year, 1545, Paul III appointed him archbishop of Ragusa in Sicily and 4 years later raised him to the cardinalate. In 1556 Pope Paul IV assigned him to the archdiocese of Foligno. On Dec. 25, 1559, Medici was elected pope and took the name Pius IV.

Pius IV faced a serious challenge to his diplomatic finesse in the problem of the Council of Trent, which had been suspended since 1552. In 1562 the council was reassembled by his mandate. With astute diplomacy he guided the council's third period, the most stormy and difficult of all, to a successful conclusion on Dec. 4, 1563. During the remainder of his pontificate Pius IV implemented the Tridentine Decrees. In this task, as well as in the application of the Index and in supervising the work of the Inquisition, his sense of moderation and flexibility came to the fore. His sense of statesmanship and his smooth efficiency in administration also greatly aided him. One of Pius IV's chief aides was his nephew, Charles Borromeo, who served in the post of papal private secretary and whom Pius IV created a cardinal and archbishop of Milan in 1560.

Pius IV supported humanistic and artistic ventures in Rome in many ways. He encouraged Giovanni Pierluigi da Palestrina; he appointed to the cardinalate such eminent humanists as Girolamo Seripando, Stanislaus Hosius, and Guglielmo Sirleto; and he remained a loyal supporter of Michelangelo and heartened him in his work on the dome of the Basilica of St. Peter's. Various edifices and improvements in Rome bear his name: the Porta Pia on the Via Nomentana, the Borgo Pio, and the Villa Pia. Pius IV died in Rome on Dec. 9, 1565.

Further Reading

Even though research calls for some modifications, the best modern comprehensive study of Pius IV is in Ludwig Pastor, *History of the Popes, from the Close of the Middle Ages,* vols. 15 and 16, translated by Ralph F. Kerr (1928), which contains a full bibliography and list of sources. For background consult Alexander Clarence Flick, *The Decline of the Medieval Church,* vol. 2 (1930), and Karl H. Dannenfeldt, *The Church of the Renaissance and Reformation* (1970). □

Pius V

Pius V (1504-1572) was pope from 1566 to 1572. An austere man, he put the decrees of the Council of Trent into effect and thus occupies a central position in the Catholic Reformation.

Antonio Ghislieri, who became Pius V, was born on Jan. 17, 1504, at Bosco Marengo near Alessandria in northern Italy. He was from a poor family. At 14 years of age Ghislieri entered the Order of Preachers and took the name Michele. He received his higher education as a friar at Bologna. In 1528 he was ordained at Genoa.

For more than 20 years Ghislieri gained a wide breadth of experience as professor of theology, superior in his order, and member of the Inquisition in Pavia, Como, and Bergamo. His dedication to the work of the Inquisition brought him to the attention of officials in Rome, including Giampietro Carafa, the future Pope Paul IV. In 1551 Pope Julius III appointed Ghislieri commissary general of the Roman Inquisition. Under Paul IV, Ghislieri was given greater responsibilities: in 1556 the bishopric of Sutri and Nepi, in 1557 the cardinalate, and in 1558 the post of grand inquisitor of the Roman Church. Pope Pius IV assigned him to the see of Mondovi in 1560. On Jan. 7, 1566, Ghislieri was elected pope and took the name Pius V.

Pius V had a twofold preoccupation: the preservation of the purity of the faith and the advancement of Church

History of the Popes, from the Close of the Middle Ages, vols. 17 and 18, translated by Ralph F. Kerr (1929), with a full bibliography and list of sources. For background consult John P. Dolan, *Catholicism: An Historical Survey* (1968), and Karl H. Dannenfeldt, *The Church of the Renaissance and Reformation* (1970).

Additional Sources

Anderson, Robin, *St. Pius V, a brief account of his life, times, virtues & miracles,* Rockford, Ill.: Tan Books and Publishers, 1978. ☐

Pius VI

Pius VI (1717-1799), who was pope from 1775 to 1799, reigned during one of the most critical periods in the history of the Church. He combated, with little success, the anticlericalism of the Enlightenment and the French Revolution.

Pius VI was born Gianangelo Braschi at Cesena, Italy, on Dec. 25, 1717. He took a degree in law and then became secretary to Cardinal Antonio Ruffo, in whose service he remained until 1753. Braschi gained the attention of Pope Benedict XIV through some clever diplomacy and was appointed canon of St. Peter's, Rome, and private secretary to the Pope. He was made bishop in 1758 and treasurer of the apostolic chamber in 1766. The title of cardinal was bestowed upon him on April 26, 1773.

The death of Clement XIV late in 1774 occasioned bitter controversy over the selection of a new pope. After a conclave of 4 months' duration, Braschi was chosen with the understanding that he would continue the anti-jesuit policies of his predecessor, who had dissolved the Society of Jesus in 1773. Immediately upon becoming pope, Pius VI had to face two problems of great magnitude. Internally, the Church, secular and regular, stood in need of great reform. From without, meanwhile, it was being battered by the rationalist exponents of the Enlightenment in all the major countries of Europe.

Among the Church's attackers were several crowned heads, traditionally supporters of the Church but now operating under the influence of the principles of enlightened despotism. Emperor Joseph II of Austria seized Church properties in 1782 with the intention of using the income from them to make priests salaried officials of the state. He followed the confiscations with restrictions upon the number of festivals and observances permitted to the Church. Pius VI went personally to Austria and objected, but his objections were ineffectual.

Shortly after the French Revolution broke out in 1789, the new French government confiscated the property of the Church, an obvious and enormous source of wealth. The Civil Constitution of the Clergy, promulgated in 1790, made French priests paid employees of the state. Pius VI temporized and attempted to bring about some improvement in

---

reform. He used the Inquisition, although more moderately than Paul IV; severely punished bishops who remained absent from their sees; examined the spiritual tenor of religious orders; implemented the decrees of the Council of Trent; and simplified to the point of austerity the style of life of the papal household. In 1566 Pius V issued the Roman Catechism.

Pius V influenced the liturgical life of the Church in a monumental way. In 1568 he issued the *Breviarium Romanum* and in 1570 the *Missale Romanum,* thereby removing the multiplicity of forms in the breviary and in the Mass and creating, with minor exceptions, a liturgical uniformity throughout the Church. In 1567 he made the greatest theologian of his order, St. Thomas Aquinas, a Doctor of the Church.

In his foreign policies Pius V experienced both failure and success. Misjudging the situation in England, he seriously blundered in 1570, when he announced that English Catholics no longer owed allegiance to Queen Elizabeth. His action worsened the situation of England's persecuted Catholics. Against the Turks he was successful. He built up the Holy League and on Oct. 7, 1571, a fleet of Spanish, Venetian, and papal ships defeated the Turkish fleet at Lepanto in the Gulf of Corinth. Pius V died on May 1, 1572. He was canonized in 1712 by the Church.

Further Reading

The best modern comprehensive study of Pius V, though recent research calls for some modifications, is in Ludwig Pastor,

the relations between the Church and the French government; however, when an oath of loyalty to the new French constitution was demanded of the clergy, the Pope formally denounced the Civil Constitution and the entire Revolutionary movement on March 10, 1791.

The French Church remained in confusion, and Pius VI allied himself with the enemies of France. Napoleon's forces invaded and occupied the papal territories in 1796, and on Feb. 15, 1798, occupied Rome. Pius VI was taken prisoner and, while still in captivity, died broken and abject in Valence on Aug. 29, 1799.

Further Reading

The most satisfactory treatment in English is in Ludwig Pastor, *The History of the Popes, from the Close of the Middle Ages,* vols. 39 and 40 (trans. 1952-1953). For the tensions between Pius and Joseph II see also M. C. Goodwin, *The Papal Conflict with Josephinism* (1938). □

Pius VII

Pius VII (1740-1823), who was pope from 1800 to 1823, began his reign with some sympathy for the liberal goals of the French Revolution, but under Napoleon he withdrew to a conservatism more consistent with the traditions of his Church.

orced into an ambiguous relationship with the French Empire and later with the restored Bourbon monarchy, Pius VII expended most of his energies combating the Gallican separatism of the state-dominated French clergy by emphasizing papal supremacy throughout the entire Church and by striving for a revival of Ultramontanism.

Pius VII was born Luigi Barnabà Chiaramonti at Cesena, Italy, on Aug. 14, 1740. At the age of 18 he entered the Benedictine monastery of S. Maria in his native city. He later became a teacher within the Benedictine order and was assigned to teach at the Benedictine colleges of Parma and Rome. Chiaramonti was made bishop of Tivoli in 1782 and bishop of Imola in 1785. In the latter year he also received the cardinal's hat.

The conclave that elected Chiaramonti to the papal chair was forced to gather at Venice because of the seizure of Rome by French forces in the final months of his predecessor's reign. Pius VI had died in French captivity, and the resulting paralysis of the machinery of the Church evidenced itself in a consistory that took 7 months to elect a pope. Cardinal Chiaramonti became Pope Pius VII on March 14, 1800.

Concordat of 1801

Pius VII's first task as supreme pontiff was to establish a modus vivendi with Napoleon I. Negotiations produced the Concordat of 1801, which removed the confusion that had plagued the French clergy since the promulgation of the Civil Constitution in 1790. The concordat stated that Roman

Catholicism was the religion of most Frenchmen, implying thereby that other religions would be tolerated. It further provided that the French clergy would be paid by the state, thereby tacitly closing the door to any hope that the property confiscated from the Church during the Revolution would be returned. In the following year the French government added to these provisions the so-called Organic Articles, which withdrew all papal jurisdiction from France except that specifically authorized by the government.

Pius protested but could do nothing. Napoleon was the master of Europe, and the papacy was prostrate, its power to influence European affairs at its lowest ebb in centuries. Napoleon's last decade witnessed the relations between himself and the Pope degenerate badly. In 1804 Pius VII suffered the humiliation of being virtually forced to crown Napoleon emperor of the French. Rome was once again occupied by French soldiers in 1808, and in 1809 Napoleon formally annexed the papal territories to France. When Pius excommunicated the Emperor and his army, he was imprisoned by Napoleon. Until the invasion of France by the Allies in 1814, Pius VII was forced to do Napoleon's bidding, and it was only Napoleon's ultimate defeat that restored to Pius his personal liberty and some hope for the future of the papacy.

Congress of Vienna

Pius's imprisonment, however, had a bright side for the Pope. It gave him a special aura of martyrdom, so that when he arrived back in Rome in May 1814, he was greeted most warmly. His absence had made Italian hearts grow fonder. The Congress of Vienna, meanwhile, in its construction of a post-Napoleonic Europe, made some encouraging decisions for the papacy. The Papal States were returned to the Pope, and changes in diocesan boundaries were made to correspond with new territorial settlements. A series of concordats, with legitimate monarchs and not with revolutionaries, followed. Pius VII was glad to return to the papacy's habitual policy of seeking to live in harmony with kings. The Society of Jesus was restored, and on the surface the Church seemed to be moving once again toward the power and prestige it had possessed during the last years of the *ancien régime*. However, Pius was forced to accept the bitter fact that the Church of the Metternich era would be far less influential than the Church of prerevolutionary days. Louis XVIII resisted any resumption of papal jurisdiction in France, and the Austrian government, although well disposed toward the papacy, would not repudiate the reforms made under Joseph II, which, prior to the French Revolution, had reduced ecclesiastical privileges.

Nevertheless, Pius found the reactionary atmosphere prevalent throughout Europe satisfying. He clearly resisted all further social change. In Italy the social legislation introduced in the Napoleonic era was repealed. Pius seconded this repudiation of social reform and proceeded in the manner of his fellow monarchs in the Papal States. He condemned the Carbonari, an underground liberal society, in 1821. Meanwhile, Pius VII conducted negotiations with France for modifications of the Concordat of 1801. His repeated efforts in this direction, however, proved unsuc-cessful. The French government, with its traditional determination to control the clergy within its borders, was unwilling to yield to Rome the jurisdiction it had so recently wrested from it.

Pius VII believed that the Church, in order to retain its integrity and in order not to descend to the level of a series of weak national churches, had to reassert itself. He believed that the papacy needed to strengthen itself and to maintain at least some measure of authority over the clergy of the countries of Europe. This large task was undertaken by the Pope, although he knew that he could not complete it. He died on Aug. 20, 1823.

Further Reading

Books on Pius VII in English are few. The best are two extensive works by Edward E. Y. Hales, *Revolution and Papacy 1769-1846* (1960) and *The Emperor and the Pope* (1961). The latter is a specific study of relations between Napoleon and Pius.

Additional Sources

Hales, Edward Elton Young, *The Emperor and the Pope: the story of Napoleon and Pius VII,* New York: Octagon Books, 1978, 1961.

O'Dwyer, Margaret M., *The papacy in the age of Napoleon and the Restoration: Pius VII, 1800-1823,* Lanham, MD: University Press of America, 1985. □

Pius IX

Pius IX (1792-1878) was pope from 1846 to 1878. He began his reign devoted to liberal ideals but, embittered by the anticlericalism of Italian liberals and by the assault on papal territories by the new kingdom of Italy, became an important foe of progress and change.

Pius IX was born Giovanni Maria Mastai-Ferretti on May 13, 1792, at Senigallia, Italy. He became archbishop of Spoleto in 1827 and bishop of Imola in 1832. He was already recognized as a liberal when he was created a cardinal in 1840. On the death of Gregory XVI a conclave divided between progressive and conservative prelates chose, on June 16, 1846, Mastai-Ferretti as pope in preference to the reactionary Luigi Lambruschini.

The new pope began his pontificate—the longest in history—by initiating badly needed reforms. Improvements in financial administration and in the treatment of criminals in the Papal States were followed by an easing of the censorship. The political innovations of 1847 decreed that only the secretary of state had to be a priest and that the council of advisers to the pope and his ministers would be elected officials. A municipal government was established for Rome, part of which was made up of elected representatives. While presiding over these specific liberal changes in his own territories, Pius IX lent encouragement to Italian nationalism.

But that he was always a reformer and never a revolutionary Pius IX quickly proved after the revolutions of 1848. His enforced departure from Rome to Gaeta and the establishment of a Roman Republic cooled his ardor for Italian nationalism. Devoted first and always to the welfare of the Church, he had been willing to support the introduction into it of democratic elements, but he would never agree to the loss of the Pope's temporal power.

When the movement for Italian unity broke out into war in 1859, Pius IV attempted to remain neutral, but he could not keep the papal territories from being dismembered. His refusal to yield any part of these dominions in negotiations with the victorious Piedmontese caused him to lose them all. On Sept. 18, 1860, the Papal States were overrun, and only the presence of French troops protected Rome. The liberal kingdom of Italy was established, and to his dying breath Pius IX remained its bitterest enemy.

As long as the French garrisoned Rome, Pius IX was able to hold his capital, and from it he fired all the spiritual weapons in his arsenal. The famous *Syllabus of Errors* of 1864, a list of erroneous modernistic statements, specifically repudiated the notion that the Pope would ever ally himself with progress or modern civilization. The Vatican Council on July 18, 1870, made the ancient doctrine of papal infallibility into a dogma of the Church. Pius IX had made it his unremitting task to reimpose on the faithful the Ultramontane authority of the medieval Church.

The French withdrew their troops from Rome in 1870 upon the outbreak of the Franco-Prussian War. Italian sol-

diers took the city on September 20 of that year, and in October a plebiscite was held in which an overwhelming majority voted to make Rome a part of the Italian kingdom. Pius IX spent the rest of his life in the Vatican. He refused to negotiate with the new kingdom, whose Parliament unilaterally declared that the Pope still retained his sovereignty and absolute control over the Vatican. He could conduct diplomatic relations with other states and was compensated for the loss of his territories. These arrangements did not placate him, and he died unreconciled on Feb. 7, 1878.

Further Reading

The best study in English of Pius IX is the biography by Edward E. Y. Hales, *Pio Nono* (1954). See also Hales's *The Catholic Church in the Modern World* (1958). For a valuable and thorough treatment of the dogma of papal infallibility consult Edward Cuthbert Butler, *The Vatican Council* (2 vols., 1930).

Additional Sources

Coppa, Frank J., *Pope Pius IX, crusader in a secular age,* Boston: Twayne Publishers, 1979. □

Pius X

Pius X (1835-1914) was pope from 1903 to 1914. He is best remembered for his liturgical and canonical reforms rather than for any contribution to world peace or Church unity.

Giuseppe Melchiorre Sarto, who became Pius X, was born at Riese, Trieste Province, Italy, on June 2, 1835. His parents were poor. He was trained for the priesthood at Padua and became a parish priest in Venice, where he stayed until 1875, when he became canon at Treviso Cathedral and superior of Treviso Seminary. Becoming bishop of Mantua in 1884, he was made a cardinal by Leo XIII in 1893. Three days later Leo made him patriarch of Venice. He was elected pope on Aug. 4, 1903.

In his policies Pius X reverted to the main lines of Pius IX, forgoing the social reforms and political intent which had characterized Leo's pontificate. Pius X set out to develop the spiritual qualities of priests and people and to ensure that modern scientific theories and methodology made no inroads into the faith of his Church. Here he showed a complete and dogmatic intransigence. He seized the occasion for action when a group of Catholic Bible scholars applied the latest scientific data to the Bible and produced certain conclusions. Pius X took action chiefly in the form of an encyclical letter, *Pascendi,* and in a decree, *Lamentabili* (both issued in September 1907).

In the letter Pius X attacked what has been called modernism, condemning 65 propositions which according to Pius undermined the traditional dogma of Christianity. Modernism, in essence, tended to renounce certain traditional dogmas for the sake of accommodating certain modern scientific theories. It represented a "modernizing"

attempt, and hence its name. The letter of Pius had untold effects on both the faith of individuals and the intellectual life of the Church as well as on the whole approach of the Church to modern man. Many left the Church or were excommunicated. Research and intellectual inquiry were stifled for well over 40 years until the reign of Pius XII.

The attitude of Pius X made the Church unattractive to many outside it, and it cut off Church institutions from any active participation in the intellectual life of biblical scholars. Pius imposed the annual renewal of an oath by all Roman Catholic seminary professors and academicians that they reject the 65 propositions, or formulations, of modernism, thus effectively hampering the inner development of Roman Catholic philosophy and theology. Pius X backed up this decree and letter by relegating a whole series of books to the Index of Forbidden Books and by imposing a rigorous control over the Pontifical Biblical Commission, so that all professors and students of Bible matters were under surveillance and control.

Pius X instituted a reaction against the Christian Democrats, the Catholic party in Italy. He objected to any Catholic in Italy or elsewhere conducting a social or political life independently of the Church hierarchy. He condemned popular Catholic parties in Italy and France, including Charles Maurras's Action Française. In this matter Pius carried Leo XIII's political paternalism to an extreme and rejected democratic ideals. In pursuance of this policy a break with the French government was inevitable because of the secularizing philosophy of that government and the law of 1905 separating Church and state in France. Tension

between Russia and the Vatican grew over Poland. Pius had uneasy relations with Germany, Austria, and the United States for the same reasons.

As a Church reformer, Pius X was more successful. He reformed the teaching of catechism and the education and preaching of priests. He promoted reverence for the Eucharist and various other liturgical reforms. He initiated a rewriting of the Church Code of Canon Law, and he modernized the Curia, or central administration of the Roman Church.

Perhaps one of Pius's greatest achievements was the improved condition of Vatican relations with the Italian state. Pius ceased labeling the state as a usurper of papal possessions, and by abstention from polemics he reached a modus vivendi with the state in which neither side admitted wrong or accused the other of doing wrong. A more realistic view of the facts came to be held on both sides. The fear of socialism also seemed to draw liberals and conservatives together on the political scene, and gradually Italian Catholics were allowed to participate in political life. Pius laid down seven conditions under which a Catholic might vote for political candidates. These were summarized in the socalled Gentilioni Pact of 1913. Pius X's moral attitude was again clearly manifested in his refusal to approve of the Austrian and German cause at the outbreak of World War I and in his denunciation of all recourse to violence as a means of settling disputes. Pius, who died on Aug. 20, 1914, was declared a saint by Pius XII in 1954.

Further Reading

Biographical works on Pius X include Katherine Burton, *The Great Mantle* (1950); M.G. Dal-Gal, *Pius X: Life Story of the Beatus* (1954); Francis A. Forbes, *Pope St. Pius X* (1954); and V.A. Yzermans, *All Things in Christ* (1954). For background see A.R. Vidler, *The Modernist Movement in the Roman Church* (1934).

Additional Sources

Diethelm, Walter, *Saint Pius X: the farm boy who became Pope*, San Francisco: Ignatius Press, 1994.
O'Brien, Felicity, *St Pius X*, London: Catholic Truth Society, 1976. □

Pius XI

Pius XI (1857-1939) was pope from 1922 to 1939. During his reign the Lateran Treaty between the Vatican and Italy was signed.

Ambrogio Damiano Achille Ratti, who became Pius XI, was born at Desio near Milan, Italy, on May 31, 1857. Ordained a priest in 1879, and having already acquired a name as a brilliant scholar, he devoted most of the subsequent 43 years to work as a Church librarian. He was known as a Latin paleographer and developed new library classification systems. Already known to Benedict XV as a man of exceptional qualities, he was selected by Benedict for diplomatic service and sent as apostolic visitor in 1918 to Poland. The following year he became apostolic nuncio in Poland. He returned to Italy in 1921 and became cardinal archbishop of Milan. He was elected pope on Feb. 6, 1922.

The first crisis facing Pius XI concerned the newly born Fascist movement led by Benito Mussolini. At the heart of Vatican policy as formed by the preceding three popes, there lay a fundamental principle of Church political policy and, in addition, an urgent desire to solve the "Roman question." The principle dictated that the Church should always have and seek the protection of a secular arm to protect it from attack, to grant it special immunity and privileges, and to channel its teachings. The Roman question concerned the status of the Vatican as a temporal power. When the Italian nationalist movement of 1870 deprived the papacy of its territorial possessions, the succeeding popes refused to acquiesce in the act. They refused to leave the Vatican even for short visits.

Pius XI, in the tradition of latter-day popes, saw in the new Fascist state the secular arm which the Church always sought. He supported the Fascist regime with certain qualifications, and in 1929 the government of Mussolini signed the Lateran Treaty with the Vatican. According to this, the Vatican recognized the kingdom of Italy and, in return, was recognized as a fully sovereign state. As such, the Vatican was granted a small but clearly indicated portion of Rome (the Vatican State) together with other holdings throughout the city and elsewhere in Italy. A financial indemnification was made by the Fascist regime to the Vatican in return for the Vatican's definitive renunciation of all claims to the former Papal States. Most importantly, the neutrality of the Vatican was guaranteed for all future military conflicts. A concordat was also signed, between the regime and the Vatican, which regulated the position of the Church in Italy. It provided for Church marriages, compulsory religious instruction in schools, and the exclusive position of Catholicism as the state religion of Italy.

Pius XI was also successful with the Mexican government in negotiating a peace between Church and state. But his concordat with Hitler's Germany was quickly violated. Pius denounced the violation in his encyclical letter *Mit brennender Sorge* (1937). In pursuance of Vatican policy and with an innate fear of Soviet Marxism, Pius sided with Franco's cause during the Spanish Civil War. It was a policy which Pius XII, his successor, was to pursue with unfavorable results during World War II. When Mussolini's government introduced anti-Semitic legislation in 1938, Pius denounced it together with all prevalent racial theories. Pius set out from the beginning of his reign to establish the Church on the international scene by increasing the number of diplomatic missions abroad, thus taking advantage of the desire of many governments for collaboration with the Vatican as a moral force in international politics.

In the field of missionary activity, particularly in Africa and Asia, Pius XI set out to rid Roman Catholic missions of their very close identification with various imperial and nationalistic powers. He encouraged plans for developing an indigenous clergy to replace the foreign missionaries.

Within the Church, Pius gave his sanction to the building of Catholic Action groups in order to provide the hierarchies with an indirect say in political matters. On the fortieth anniversary of Leo XIII's *Rerum novarum,* Pius XI issued his own letter on social affairs, *Quadragesimo anno* (May 15, 1931). He elaborated on Leo's teachings concerning social reform and the economic structure of human society in relation to religious belief and practice. Toward non-Catholic Christianity, Pius had a negative attitude and issued his *Mortalium animos* (1928), in which he imposed a stern attitude toward non-Catholics and the nascent ecumenical movement among Protestants. The closing years of Pius XI's reign were marked by a close association with the Western democracies, as these nations and the Vatican found that they were both threatened by the totalitarian regimes and ideologies of Hitler, Mussolini, and the Soviet Union. In the last months of his life, Pius XI saw the gathering clouds of World War II. Although he used every resource of the Vatican, he was unable to prevent the final union of wills between Hitler and Mussolini. He died on Feb. 10, 1939.

Further Reading

Pius XI's writings were translated and edited by Edward Bulloch as *Essays in History Written between the Years 1890-1912* (1934). Biographies of Pius XI include Philip Hughes, *Pope Pius the Eleventh* (1937), and Zsolt Aradi, *Pius XI: The Pope and the Man* (1958). Pius XI is also discussed in Carlo Falconi, *The Popes in the Twentieth Century* (1967; trans. 1968).

Additional Sources

Anderson, Robin, *Between two wars: the story of Pope Pius XI (Achille Ratti, 1922-1939)*, Chicago: Franciscan Herald Press, 1977. ☐

Pius XII

Pius XII (1876-1958), pope from 1939 to 1958, guided the Roman Catholic Church through the difficult years of World War II and the postwar period, when much of the eastern Catholic Church was heavily persecuted by Soviet communism.

Pius XII was born Eugenio Maria Giuseppe Pacelli in Rome on March 2, 1876. Because of poor health he was allowed to study for the priesthood at his home. Ordained a priest in 1899, he took up work in the Vatican Secretariat of State in 1901, working there until 1917. In that year he became archbishop of Sardis and was sent to Munich as apostolic nuncio to Bavaria. In 1918 he became nuncio in Berlin to the new Weimar Republic. During his German years Pacelli acquired a love of the German people and a knowledge of German affairs. He was a close observer and on a few occasions an eyewitness of Bolshevik riots in Germany, which developed a strong fear in him that Soviet Marxism was the prime enemy of Christendom. This fear, together with his love of Germany, influenced his judgments during World War II. Pius XI recalled Pacelli to Rome in 1929 and named him a cardinal. In 1930 he became secretary of state, remaining at this post until his election as pope on March 2, 1939.

Pius XII's main determination, upon the outbreak of World War II in September 1939, was to preserve cordial relations with all belligerents. He had concluded from his years in Germany that the Vatican should engage in the role of international peacemaker. He therefore refused, in spite of Anglo-American pressures, clearly to declare against the Axis Powers or publicly to describe the German invasion of Soviet Russia as a crusade against communism, as the Axis Powers wished him to do. His attempted neutrality in word and action led Pius XII into an extreme form of abstention from all effective moral protest in the war. He consequently did not intervene to denounce or to halt the Nazi campaign against the Jews or the genocidal acts of the Hitler regime.

This lack of action brought much public criticism of Pius after the war. The Pope, it was argued, had a moral obligation to speak out specifically against all and every kind of injustice. In his defense, it has been alleged—accurately—that any such denunciation might have brought the full wrath of Hitler upon the Church in all the occupied countries as well as in Germany. Privately, Pius organized shelters and other places of refuge for Jews. He also organized the highly effective Work of St. Raphael, which aided in locating and resettling war refugees. The Vatican itself and many Vatican buildings were used, with Pius's tacit approval, for sheltering war refugees, downed pilots, and Allied military personnel.

Toward the end of the war, when Communist partisans appeared in northern Italy, Pius XII communicated his fears to President Franklin Roosevelt of the United States, and in postwar Italy Pius organized Catholic Action groups, which played a great part in bringing the Christian Democrats to power in 1948, thus keeping Italy within the western orbit. Pius continued to battle against Italian communism to the end of his life, issuing a formal excommunication decree against all Catholics who joined the Communist party. At the end of Pius XII's reign, the status of the Church was high on the international scene; his popularity had waned among the intellectuals of the Church; and Pius had placed the Vatican in intransigent positions regarding both non-Catholics and non-Christians.

Role in the Church

Within the Roman Church, Pius XII exercised an authoritarian influence on all developments. In spite of his dogmatic intransigence regarding the ecumenical movement and his refusal to meet with leaders of Eastern Orthodox churches, many of Pius's provisions and reforms laid the ground for the more radical reforms achieved by the Second Vatican Council (called by his successor, John XXIII) and for the participation of Roman Catholics in the ecumenical movement. Pius introduced evening Mass, relaxed the laws on fasting, encouraged the indigenous hierarchies of Africa and Asia, permitted the use of the vernacular in certain Church ceremonies, and reformed the ancient liturgy of the Easter celebration. In doctrine and in theology, Pius was extremely conservative and fomented in the Roman government of the Church a repressive and reactionary spirit. The various offices and ministries of the Vatican, under his rule, exercised great control over the teachings and writings of Roman Catholic scholars and thinkers. This state of affairs provoked the counterreactions characteristic of John XXIII's reign and facilitated the work of the Second Vatican Ecumenical Council.

Pius ruled autocratically, imposed his views, and expected exact obedience from all. But not all of his directives concerning the teaching of the Church on dogmatic matters were repressive in their final effect. His *Divino afflante Spiritu* (1943) gave fresh life to Roman Catholic biblical studies by admitting that the Bible as a book had been influenced in its literary forms by the cultures in which its various parts had been composed. His *Humani generis* (1950), although repressive in many ways, did not completely block all scientific inquiry into the natural truths underlying the facts of religion and religious territory.

Pius XII was the first pope to make use of the radio on an extensive scale. Indeed, he took every suitable occasion to address both Catholics and non-Catholics on a variety of subjects. During his pontificate the prestige of the Church rose enormously, and his presence in Rome attracted more pilgrims and visitors from varying faiths and countries than ever before in the history of the Vatican. Pius XII died at Castel Gandolfo, the summer residence of the popes, on Oct. 9, 1958.

Further Reading

For Pius XII's own writings see Sister M. Claudia Carlen, *Guide to the Documents of Pius XII, 1939-49* (1951). A biography of him is Oscar Halecki, *Eugenio Pacelli, Pope of Peace* (1951; rev. ed. 1954). Pius is discussed in John P. McKnight, *The Papacy: A New Appraisal* (1953). The controversial question of Pius XII's role immediately preceding and during World War II is the subject of Carlo Falconi, *The Silence of Pius XII,* translated by Bernard Wall (1970). Pius is also examined in Falconi's earlier and somewhat controversial work, *The Popes in the Twentieth Century* (1967; trans. 1968). □

Francisco Pizarro

The Spanish conquistador Francisco Pizarro (ca. 1474-1541) was the obscure adventurer and ruffian who discovered and overthrew the Inca empire of Peru. Assassin of the Inca Atahualpa, Pizarro was assassinated in turn by his own countrymen.

Francisco Pizarro was born at Trujillo in Estremadura. The illegitimate son of a poor *hidalgo* (small landholder of the petty nobility), he never learned to read and may have earned his keep herding his father's swine. This allegation is often cited by Pizarro's detractors in terms of a comparison with Herná Cortés the better-born

conqueror of Mexico. But the destruction wreaked by Cortés upon Aztec civilization was no less far-reaching than Pizarro's impact upon the society of Peru.

Pizarro left Spain for the New World in the wake of the early discoveries. He joined Alonso de Ojeda on the latter's disastrous expedition to Colombia and subsequently accompanied Vasco Núñez de Balboa on his march to the South Sea (Pacific Ocean). It was Pizarro who later arrested the condemned Balboa on orders from the great explorer's rival, Pedrarias de Ávila. He then settled down as an *encomendero* (lord of Indian serfs) in Panama.

Yet Pizarro remained a conquistador without a conquest. Emboldened by tales of fabulous kingdoms to the south, he went into partnership with another adventurer, Diego de Almagro, and a priest, Luque. This combination financed and led several voyages of reconnaissance. Pizarro then journeyed to Spain, where the Emperor commissioned him to undertake the southern conquest and to establish a province of New Castile. So empowered, he returned to the New World, accompanied by his half brothers Gonzalo, Hernando, and Juan Pizarro, his cousin Pedro Pizarro, and Martin de Alcántara. At the end of 1530 Pizarro set sail with 180 men for Peru.

Conquest of Peru

Pizarro arrived at a time most favorable for his designs. Atahualpa, brother of the Inca Huáscar, had usurped the throne and moved the seat of government from the traditional Andean stronghold of Cuzco to Cajamarca in the

north. It was on the northern coast, at Tumbes, that Pizarro's forces landed; and after consolidating his position, the conqueror marched on the new capital in 1532. Tricked into capture under cover of false negotiations, Atahualpa sought to buy his freedom with his gold. The loot delivered, the monarch was slain. Meanwhile, reinforced by troops under Almagro, the Spanish had captured and sacked Cuzco itself. In 1535 Pizarro founded his own capital of Lima near the coast, thus originating the troublesome later-day distinction between the Indian society of the mountains and the Hispanicized civilization of the seaboard.

The Spanish conquest has shed some of its glamour in the light of modern research. Peruvians under Manco Capac, successor to the deposed Huáscar, held out against the Spanish for 40 years more; Indian revolts recurred for another 200. The question persists: why was this great civilization mortally wounded, if not instantly overthrown, by the Estremaduran adventurer? The immediate answer lies in the outbreak of civil war within the Peruvian ruling class, a division which gave Pizarro his opportunity. Atahualpa's rivals rejoiced in his downfall, just as enemies of the Aztecs had at first welcomed and abetted the invasion of Cortés. Yet the explanation for the Spanish success must be sought deeper in the structure of society, where it can be grasped in the relation between the social divisions within these native American empires and the level of technology.

Like the leaders of the splendid civilizations of the ancient Near East, the priestly and military ruling classes of the Incas and Aztecs employed the surplus appropriated from producers to subsidize irrigation and flood-control projects, to build large cities and road networks, and to underwrite the production of craftsmen-artists. But unlike the agrarian producers of those earlier civilizations, the peasants lacked suitable draft animals, wheeled vehicles, and plows. Under these conditions the productivity of labor was extremely low, and it required a stern labor discipline, upheld by a powerful religiopolitical orthodoxy, to extract a level of surplus product sufficient to the requirements of the ruling classes. Divided among themselves, such rulers were further weakened by the hostility of subject peoples and the passivity of agrarian producers. Faced with a determined neofeudal enemy skilled in the art of conquest from the center outward, they were less able to mobilize resistance, and to sustain it, than the primitive peoples of the north, the far south, and the east. In the final analysis, writes a historian of European expansion, J. H. Parry, these civilizations' "combination of wealth and technical weakness was their undoing."

His Death

Cortés had been able to overcome immediate challenges from Spanish competitors; Pizarro was not so fortunate. Tensions between original invaders and latecomers divided the conquistadors into two parties, respectively led by Pizarro and his sometime associate Almagro. The situation was only briefly eased by an Almagro expedition to Chile. Upon his return he seized Cuzco and confronted the Pizarros in the Las Salinas War. Captured by Hernando Pizarro in 1538, Almagro was executed; but his shade

haunted Francisco until his own murder in Lima (June 26, 1541) by members of the defeated faction. Civil war persisted until 1548, when the Spanish government finally asserted its authority over the new colony. Of the band of marauding brothers, only Hernando survived the Pizarro "victory" over the Incan empire.

Further Reading

William H. Prescott, *History of the Conquest of Peru* (1847; and many subsequent editions), is the classic treatment of Pizarro and his victims. The story was retold in John Hemming's excellent *The Conquest of the Incas* (1970). John Alden Mason, *The Ancient Civilization of Peru* (1957; rev. ed. 1964), is a useful introduction to the pre-Columbian societies of the region. John Horace Parry, *The Spanish Seaborne Empire* (1966), is the best single-volume treatment of its subject. □

Solomon Tshekisho Plaatje

Solomon Tshekisho Plaatje (1878-1932) was a South African writer whose historical novel *Mhudi* depicts the attempts of an African tribe and a group of Boers to attain their freedom.

Sol T. Plaatje was born into a family of Tswana origin in Southern Transvaal (South Africa). He was educated at a Lutheran mission school. Because of his uncommon knowledge of several European and African languages, he served as interpreter in several South African courts. When the Anglo-Boer War broke out in 1899, he enlisted in the British army. After the war he became a frequent contributor to English newspapers in Cape Town and Kimberley. In 1901 he founded the first Tswana newspaper, the *Kimberley Korante oa Bechoana,* which he edited until 1908.

When the South African Natives National Congress was founded in 1912 in the hope of defending the rights of the black population, which were threatened by the racialist policy of the Afrikaners, Plaatje was elected its first secretary general. And when the Botha government introduced the Native Land Bill, which aimed at depriving the blacks of much of their landed property, Plaatje traveled through the Orange Free State, gathering evidence about the hardships suffered by the Africans. In 1914 he was a member of the Congress delegation which vainly sought protection from the London government.

While the deputation returned to Africa empty-handed, Plaatje stayed in Britain, where he worked as a journalist. He published *Native Life in South Africa* (1915), *Sechuana Proverbs and Their English Equivalents* (1916), and, with the help of Daniel Jones, a *Sechuana Phonetic Reader* (1916). Presumably also at that time he started writing *Mhudi,* the first novel composed in English by a black South African.

After the war Plaatje attended the Pan-African Congress organized in Paris by W. E. B. Du Bois and subsequently made a lecture tour in Canada and the United States. Back in South Africa in the early 1920s, Plaatje withdrew from

Additional Sources

Willan, Brian, *Sol Plaatje: a biography,* Johannesburg: Ravan, 1984.

Willan, Brian, *Sol Plaatje, South African nationalist, 1876-1932,* Berkeley: University of California Press, 1984. □

Max Karl Ernst Ludwig Planck

The German physicist Max Karl Ernst Ludwig Planck (1858-1947) discovered the quantum of action which provided the key concept for the development of quantum theory.

Max Planck was born on April 23, 1858, in Kiel. The son of a distinguished jurist and professor of law, he inherited and sustained the family tradition of idealism, trustworthiness, conservatism, and devotion to church and state. Planck studied at the University of Munich (1875-1877) and the University of Berlin (1877-1878). At Berlin he took courses from Hermann von Helmholz and Gustav Kirchhoff.

Returning to Munich, Planck completed his thesis for his doctorate in 1879. It was on the second law of thermodynamics, Planck's favorite theme throughout his long and productive life. However, his keen insight into the second law of thermodynamics gained him no professional recognition whatsoever. Displaying his characteristically indomitable will, Planck refused to become discouraged and to allow his researches to be interrupted.

In 1880 Planck completed his *Habilitationsschrift,* which enabled him to become a privatdozent (lecturer) at the University of Munich. In that tenuous position he waited in vain for years to receive an offer of a professorship, longing to be independent professionally, as well as from his parents, with whom he was still living. He submitted a paper, "The Nature of Energy," In 1885 for a prize to be awarded by the University of Göttingen in 1887. He received the second prize (the first prize was not awarded), and in 1889, after the death of Kirchhoff, he became associate professor at Berlin. Three years later he was promoted to full professor. He remained in Berlin for the rest of his life.

Planck's early years at Berlin were also the years during which his scientific horizons expanded enormously. There was at the time great interest in physical chemistry, and he contributed to this field, first, by introducing key concepts such as thermodynamic potentials, and, second, by applying these concepts to specific problems. Many of his early researches are in his famous *Lectures on Thermodynamics* (1897), in which he also introduced many of our modern definitions, symbols, and examples.

active politics, as did several other African leaders, driven to despair by their sense of importance; yet he continued to help his people as a journalist, a social worker, and an educator. In 1916 he had contributed an essay to Sir Israel Gollancz's *Book of Homage to Shakespeare.* Later, Plaatje translated two of Shakespeare's plays into Tswana: *The Comedy of Errors* (1930) and *Julius Caesar* (1937).

In 1930 *Mhudi,* which had been rejected by several publishers, was printed in Lovedale. It is a historical novel of remarkable objectivity and serenity which deals simultaneously with the fratricidal fighting among Bantutribes in the 1830s and with the Great Trek of the Boers fleeing northward to shed British supremacy in the same period. That Plaatje named his book after the heroine of the story suggests that part of his concern was to counteract current European misconceptions about the Africans' alleged contempt for and ill treatment of women. But his basic purpose was to point out, in a skillful, unobtrusive way, the similarity in situation and aspiration between the Barolong tribe, who were trying to free themselves from the yoke of the Amandebele, and the white Boers, who were bent on evading British rule. Plaatje died on June 19, 1932.

Further Reading

For general literary background see R. H. W. Shepherd, *Bantu Literature and Life* (Lovedale, South Africa, 1955); Claude Wauthier, *The Literature and Thought of Modern Africa: A Survey* (1964; trans. 1966); and Janheinz Jahn, *Neo-African Literature: A History of Black Writing* (1966; trans. 1968).

Blackbody Radiation and Quantum of Action

In 1897 Planck returned to the second law of thermodynamics. What attracted his attention were the experiments being carried out at the National Physical Laboratory in Berlin-Charlottenburg on so-called blackbody radiation, the radiation emitted by a "perfect emitter," that is, a body that reemits all of the radiation incident on it. Of particular interest was the spectral energy distribution—the amount of energy emitted at each radiant frequency—of blackbody radiation. Planck sought to relate this radiation to the second law of thermodynamics. In 1900 he obtained a new radiation formula by interpolation between two experimentally determined spectral limits, the high-frequency limit consistent with Wien's law and the low-frequency limit consistent with the data of Planck's colleagues Rubens and Kulbaum. Planck's law had been discovered.

Planck's law was no more than a "lucky intuition," as Planck called it. This was terribly unsatisfactory, and therefore he immediately began "the task of investing it with a true physical meaning." "After a few weeks of the most strenuous work of my life," he recalled, "the darkness lifted and an unexpected vista began to appear." Two crucial insights were involved. The first involved a profound break in Planck's conception of the second law of thermodynamics. In all of his earlier researches, he had regarded the second law as "absolute" as the first—both were laws that admitted of no exceptions. Now he found himself driven inexorably to the conviction that Ludwig Boltzmann, not he,

had been correct in arguing that the second law is an irreducibly statistical law: the entropy is directly related to the probability that a given microscopic (atomic) state will occur.

Planck's second insight involved a sharp break with all earlier physical theory. He found that to theoretically derive his interpolated blackbody radiation law, it was necessary to assume, contrary to all earlier assumptions, that the energy stored in the blackbody oscillators is not indefinitely divisible but is actually built up out of an infinite number of "bits," or quanta of energy. He concluded that the energy of each quantum is a multiple of the quantum energy hf, where f is the frequency of the oscillator and h is now universally known as "Planck's constant" or "Planck's quantum of action."

Other Scientific Work

When Planck in 1900 made the discovery that immortalized his name and won for him the Nobel Prize in 1919 and numerous other honors, he was 42 years old. In subsequent years he continued to work at a steady pace and contribute to topics of current interest. In addition to the work already discussed, he studied the statistical aspects of white light, dispersion, and the optical properties of metals; probed various topics in statistical mechanics and kinetic theory; and applied quantum theory to systems of many degrees of freedom, to molecular rotational spectra, and to chemical bonding.

Planck was one of the first to champion Albert Einstein's 1905 special theory of relativity. Planck's deep interest in relativity, and his general admiration and appreciation of Einstein's revolutionary insights, made it natural that he should try to persuade Einstein to join the Berlin faculty. He succeeded in bringing Einstein to Berlin in 1914.

Last Decades

As permanent secretary (1912-1938) of the mathematics-physics section of the Prussian Academy of Science and as president (1920-1937) of the Kaiser Wilhelm Gesellschaft (now called the Max Planck Gesellschaft), Planck saw many of his esteemed Jewish colleagues, including Einstein, persecuted. As James Franck, who resigned his Göttingen professorship in protest against Hitler's policies, recalled, "Planck hated Hitler's laws, but they were the Law and therefore must be obeyed as long as they were in force." Planck at one point tried personally to convince Hitler of the damage he was doing German science, but his words had no effect. Planck's Berlin villa was destroyed by bombs. His son Erwin was involved in the July 1944 attempt on Hitler's life and in 1945 died at the hands of the Gestapo. Planck died in Göttingen on Oct. 4, 1947.

Further Reading

Planck described his life and work at some length in his *Scientific Autobiography and Other Papers,* translated by Frank Gaynor (1949), and more briefly in *The Philosophy of Physics,* translated by W.H. Johnston (1936), and *A Survey of Physical Theory,* translated by R. Jones and D.H. Williams (1960). Planck's work is discussed in Philipp Frank, *Einstein: His Life and Times,* translated by George Rosen (1947; 2d rev. ed. 1957), and Max Jammer, *The Conceptual Development of Quantum Mechanics* (1966). For a serious appraisal of Planck's work the reader should also consult the writings in professional journals, especially those of Martin J. Klein of Yale University, as well as the obituary notices by Max Born in the Royal Society of London, *Obituary Notices of Fellows of the Royal Society,* vol. 6 (1948-1949). □

Sylvia Plath

Sylvia Plath (1932-1963), poet and novelist, explored her obsessions with death, self, and nature in works that expressed her ambivalent attitudes toward the universe.

S ylvia Plath was born in Boston's Memorial Hospital on October 27, 1932, to Aurelia and Otto Plath. Otto, who was a biology professor and a well-respected authority on entomology at Boston University, would later figure as a major image of persecution in his daughter's best known poems—"Daddy," "The Colossus," and "Lady Lazarus." His sudden death, eight years after Sylvia's birth, plunged the sensitive child into an abyss of grief, guilt, and angry despair which would haunt her for life and provide her poetry with the central motifs and tragic dimensions that characterize it.

Although she promised never to speak to God again after the death of her father, Plath, on the surface at least, gave the appearance of being a socially well-adjusted child who excelled in every undertaking, dazzling her teachers in the Winthrop public school system and earning straight A's for her superior academic skills and writing abilities. She was just eight and a half when her first poem was published in the Boston Sunday *Herald.*

Plath lived in Winthrop with her mother and younger brother, Warren, until 1942, when Aurelia Plath purchased a house in Wellesley. These early years in Winthrop provided the poet with her powerful awareness of the beauty and terror of nature and instilled in her an abiding love and fear of the ocean, which she envisioned as female:

> Like a deep woman, it hid a good deal;
> it had many faces, many delicate terrible veils.
> . . . if it could court, it could also kill.

Thus, even then, Plath was expressing her antithetical attitudes toward existence, embracing life and rejecting it simultaneously.

Wellesley, likewise, influenced Plath's life and values. It was a middle-class, highly respectable, educational community whose attitudes were at first accepted wholeheartedly by the young idealistic girl who was beginning to have her poems and stories published in *Seventeen* magazine. Her first story, "And Summer Will Not Come Again," appeared in August 1950.

In September 1950 Plath entered Smith College in Northhampton on a scholarship. There she once again excelled academically and socially. Dubbed the golden girl by teachers and peers, she planned diligently for her writing career. She filled notebooks with stories, villanelles, sonnets, and rondels, shaping her poems with studious precision and winning many awards.

In August 1952 she won *Mademoiselle's* fiction contest, earning her a guest editorship at the magazine for June 1953. Her experiences in New York City were demoralizing and later became the basis for her novel *The Bell Jar* (1963). Upon her return home Plath, depressed and in conflict with her hard-won image as the All-American girl, suffered a serious mental breakdown, attempted suicide, and was given shock treatments. In February 1953 she had recovered enough to return to Smith. She was graduated *summa cum laude* and won a Fulbright fellowship to Cambridge, where she met her future husband, the poet Ted Hughes. They were married June 16, 1956, in London.

After earning her graduate degree Plath returned to America to accept a teaching position at Smith for the academic term 1957-1958. She quit after a year to devote full time to her writing. For a while she attended Robert Lowell's poetry seminar, where she met Anne Sexton. Sexton's and Lowell's influences were decisive for her poetic development. Both poets opened up for her very private and taboo subjects and introduced her to new kinds of emotional and psychological depths.

Plath and her husband were invited as writers-in-residence to Yaddo, in Saratoga Springs, where they lived and worked for two months. It was here that Plath completed many of the poems collected in *The Colossus,* her first volume, published in 1960, the year her first child—Frieda—was born. Another child, Nicholas, was born two years later.

The Colossus was praised by critics for its "fine craft," "fastidious vocabulary," "potent symbolism," and "brooding sense of danger and lurking horror" at man's place in the universe. But it was criticized for its absence of a personal voice, "its elaborate checks and courtesies," and its "maddening docility and deflections."

Not until "Three Women: A Monologue for Three Voices" (1962)—a radio play which was considered by some critics to be her transitional, formative work—would she begin to free her style and write more spontaneous, less narrative, less expository poetry. "Three Women" foreshadows some of Plath's later poetry in that its structure is dramatic and expressive of those highly personal themes that mark her work.

As it developed, her poetry became more autobiographical and private in imagery. Almost all the poems in *Ariel* (1965), considered her finest work and written during the last few months of her life, are personal testimonies to her angers, insecurities, fears, and overwhelming sense of loneliness and death. At last she had found the voice that had for so long eluded her.

> Peel off the napkin
> O my enemy.
> Do I terrify?

Not surprisingly, that voice offended many people for its unflinching directness and use of startling metaphors. In "Lady Lazarus" her father, "Herr Doktor," is compared to a Nazi scientist: "Herr Enemy." In "Daddy" dead Otto becomes a "fascist, a brute chuffing me off like a Jew/A Jew to Dachau, Auschwitz, Belsen."

Violent and frighteningly vivid in its depiction of suicide, death, mutilation, and brutality, *Ariel* shocked critics and induced in its creator a powerful new sense of self. In his introduction to *Ariel,* Robert Lowell described that new self as "something imaginary, newly, wildly and subtly created . . . hardly a person . . . but one of those superreal, hynotic, great classical heroines. . . ."

In later poetry published posthumously in *Crossing The Water* (1971) and *Winter Trees* (1971) this new self was able to voice its long-suppressed rage over "years of doubleness, smiles, and compromise."

Ironically, although Plath is often regarded by critics as the poet of death, her final poems, which deal with self and how self goes about creating and transcending itself in an irrational, destructive, materialistic world, clearly express her yearning for faith in the healing self-transforming powers of art.

> Miracles occur,
> If you care to call those spasmodic
> Tricks of radiance miracles. The wait's begun

> again,
> The long wait for the angel
> For that rare, random descent.

Despite this sense of possible redemption, Plath could not escape the tragedy that invaded and overwhelmed her personal life. By February 1963 her marriage had ended; she was ill and living on the edge of another breakdown while caring for two small children in a cramped flat in London ravaged by the coldest winter in decades. On Monday, February 11, she killed herself. The last gesture she made was to leave her children two mugs of milk and a plate of buttered bread.

Further Reading

A good biography of Plath is Edward Butscher's *Sylvia Plath: Method and Madness* (1976). Other books of interest are *Letters Home* by Sylvia Plath, edited by Aurelia Plath (1975); *The Journals of Sylvia Plath* (1982); *Sylvia Plath: The Poetry of Initiation* by Jon Rosenblatt (1979); *Plath's Incarnations* by Lynda Bundtzen (1983); *A Closer Look at Ariel: A Memory of Sylvia Plath* by Nancy Hunter Steiner (1973); *Sylvia Plath and Ted Hughes* by Margaret Dickie Uroff (1980); *Sylvia Plath* by Caroline King Barnard (1978); *Plath: Poetry and Existence* by David Holbrook (1976); and *The Art of Plath: A Symposium,* edited by Charles Newman (1970). □

Plato

The Greek philosopher Plato (428-347 B.C.) founded the Academy, one of the great philosophical schools of antiquity. His thought had enormous impact on the development of Western philosophy.

Plato was born in Athens, the son of Ariston and Perictione, both of Athenian aristocratic ancestry. He lived his whole life in Athens although he traveled to Sicily and southern Italy on several occasions, and one story says he traveled to Egypt. Little is known of his early years, but he was given the finest education Athens had to offer the scions of its noble families, and he devoted his considerable talents to politics and the writing of tragedy and other forms of poetry. His acquaintance with Socrates altered the course of his life. The compelling power which Socrates's methods and arguments had over the minds of the youth of Athens gripped Plato as firmly as it did so many others, and he became a close associate of Socrates.

The end of the Peloponnesian War (404 B.C.) left Plato in an irreconcilable position. His uncle, Critias, was the leader of the Thirty Tyrants who were installed in power by the victorious Spartans. One means of perpetuating themselves in power was to implicate as many Athenians as possible in their atrocious acts. Thus Socrates, as we learn in Plato's *Apology,* was ordered to arrest a man and bring him to Athens from Salamis for execution. When the great teacher refused, his life was in jeopardy, and he was probably saved only by the overthrow of the Thirty and the reestablishment of the democracy.

Plato was repelled by the aims and methods of the Thirty and welcomed the restoration of the democracy, but his mistrust of the whimsical *demos* was deepened some 4 years later when Socrates was tried on trumped up charges and sentenced to death. Plato was present at the trial, as we learn in the *Apology,* but was not present when the hemlock was administered to his master, although he describes the scene in vivid and touching detail in the *Phaedo.* He then turned in disgust from contemporary Athenian politics and never took an active part in government, although through friends he did try to influence the course of political life in the Sicilian city of Syracuse.

Plato and several of his friends withdrew from Athens for a short time after Socrates's death and remained with Euclides in Megara. His productive years were punctuated by three voyages to Sicily, and his literary output, all of which has survived, may conveniently be discussed within the framework of those voyages.

The first trip, to southern Italy and Syracuse, took place in 388-387 B.C., when Plato made the acquaintance of Archytas of Tarentum, the Pythagorean, and Dion of Syracuse and his infamous brother-in-law, Dionysius I, ruler of that city. Dionysius was then at the height of his power and prestige in Sicily for having freed the Greeks there from the threat of Carthaginian overlordship. Plato became better friends with Dion, however, and Dionysius's rather callous treatment of his Athenian guest may be ascribed to the jealously which that close friendship aroused. On Plato's return journey to Athens, Dionysius's crew deposited him on the island of Aegina, which at that time was engaged in a

minor war with Athens, and Plato might have been sold as a prisoner of war had he not been ransomed by Anniceris of Cyrene, one of his many admirers.

His Dialogues

On his return to Athens, Plato began to teach in the Gymnasium Academe and soon afterward acquired property nearby and founded his famous Academy, which survived until the philosophical schools were closed by the Christian emperor Justinian in the early 6th century A.D. At the center of the Academy stood a shrine to the Muses, and at least one modern scholar suggests that the Academy may have been a type of religious brotherhood. Plato had begun to write the dialogues, which came to be the hallmark of his philosophical exposition, some years before the founding of the Academy. To this early period, before the first trip to Sicily, belong the *Laches, Charmides, Euthyphro, Lysis, Protagoras, Hippias Minor, Ion, Hippias Major, Apology, Crito,* and *Gorgias.* Socrates is the main character in these dialogues, and various abstractions are discussed and defined. The *Laches* deals with courage, *Charmides* with *sophrosyne* (common sense), *Euthyphro* with piety, *Lysis* with friendship, *Protagoras* with the teaching of *arete* (virtue), and so on. The *Apology* and *Crito* stand somewhat apart from the other works of this group in that they deal with historical events, Socrates's trial and the period between his conviction and execution. The unifying element in all of these works is the figure of Socrates and his rather negative function in revealing the fallacies in the conventional treatment of the topics discussed.

Plato's own great contributions begin to appear in the second group of writings, which date from the period between his first and second voyages to Sicily. To this second group belong the *Meno, Cratylus, Euthydemus, Menexenus, Symposium, Phaedo, Republic, Phaedrus, Parmenides,* and *Theaetetus.* Development of ideas in the earlier dialogues is discernible in these works. The *Meno* carries on the question of the teachability of virtue first dealt with in *Protagoras* and introduces the doctrine of *anamnesis* (recollection), which plays an important role in Plato's view of the human's ability to learn the truth. Since the soul is immortal and has at an earlier stage contemplated the Forms, or Ideas, which are the eternal and changeless truths of the universe, humans do not learn, but remember.

The impetus for learning or remembering the truth is revealed in the *Symposium,* where the ascent from corporeal reality to eternal and incorporeal truth is described. The scene is a dinner party at the house of the tragic poet Agathon, and each guest contributes a short speech on the god Eros. Socrates, however, cuts through the Sophistic arguments of his friends and praises Eros not as a separate and independent god but as an intermediary between gods and men. It is Eros who causes men to seek beauty, although for a time the unenlightened lover may think that what he is really seeking is the corporeal body of his beloved. Ultimately, however, one progresses from love of the body to love of the beauty which the body represents, and so forth, until one realizes that the ultimate goal sought is contemplation of beauty itself and of the Forms. The Forms are the true reality and impart their essence in some way to ephemeral, corporeal objects, and man may come to know this true reality through rigorous discipline of mind and body, and Plato went so far as to draw up a rough outline for a utopian state in his *Republic*.

The *Republic*

Socrates is again the main character in the *Republic*, although this work is less a dialogue than a long discussion by Socrates of justice and what it means to the individual and the city-state. The great utopian state is described only as an analogue to the soul in order to understand better how the soul might achieve the kind of balance and harmony necessary for the rational element to control it. Just as there are three elements to the soul, the rational, the less rational, and the impulsive irrational, so there are three classes in the state, the rulers, the guardians, and the workers. The rulers are not a hereditary clan or self-perpetuating upper class but are made up of those who have emerged from the population as a whole as the most gifted intellectually. The guardians serve society by keeping order and by handling the practical matters of government, including fighting wars, while the workers perform the labor necessary to keep the whole running smoothly. Thus the most rational elements of the city-state guide it and see that all in it are given an education commensurate with their abilities.

The wisdom, courage, and moderation cultivated by the rulers, guardians, and workers ideally produce the justice in society which those virtues produce in the individual soul when they are cultivated by the three elements of that soul. Only when the three work in harmony, with intelligence clearly in control, does the individual or state achieve the happiness and fulfillment of which it is capable. The *Republic* ends with the great myth of Er, in which the wanderings of the soul through births and rebirths are recounted. One may be freed from the cycle after a time through lives of greater and greater spiritual and intellectual purity.

Plato's second trip to Syracuse took place in 367 B.C. after the death of Dionysius I, but his and Dion's efforts to influence the development of Dionysius II along the lines laid down in the *Republic* for the philosopher-king did not succeed, and he returned to Athens.

Last Works

Plato's final group of works, written after 367, consists of the *Sophist*, the *Statesman*, *Philebus*, *Timaeus*, *Critias*, and the *Laws*. The *Sophist*, takes up the metaphysical question of being and not-being, while the *Statesman* concludes that the best type of city-state would be the one in which the expert is given absolute authority with no hindrance to his rule from laws or constitution. The *Timaeus* discusses the rationality inherent in the universe which confirms Plato's scheme, while the *Laws*, Plato's last work, once again takes up the question of the best framework in which society might function for the betterment of its citizens. Here great stress is laid on an almost mystical approach to the great truth of the rational universe.

Plato's third and final voyage to Syracuse was made some time before 357 B.C., and he was no more successful in his attempts to influence the young Dionysius than he had been earlier. Dion fared no better and was exiled by the young tyrant, and Plato was held in semicaptivity before being released. Plato's *Seventh Letter*, the only one in the collection of 13 considered accurate, perhaps even from the hand of Plato himself, recounts his role in the events surrounding the death of Dion, who in 357 B.C. entered Syracuse and overthrew Dionysius. It is of more interest, however, for Plato's statement that the deepest truths may not be communicated.

Plato died in 347 B.C., the founder of an important philosophical school, which existed for almost 1,000 years, and the most brilliant of Socrates's many pupils and followers. His system attracted many followers in the centuries after his death and resurfaced as Neoplatonism, the great rival of early Christianity.

Further Reading

A readable translation of the Platonic corpus may be found in the edition by Benjamin Jowett, *The Dialogues of Plato* (1953), which contains analyses. Special treatments may be found in J. Burnett, *Greek Philosophy* (1914); A.E. Taylor, *Plato: The Man and His Work* (1927); and Paul Shorey, *What Plato Said* (1933). □

Thomas Collier Platt

Thomas Collier Platt (1833-1910), U.S. Senator and Republican party leader in New York State, personified machine politics of the late 19th century.

Thomas Platt was born on July 15, 1833, in Owego, N.Y., the son of a lawyer. Thomas entered Yale in 1849, but illness forced him to withdraw. He married in 1852 and during the next decade established a drugstore (which quickly became a center for county political activity), speculated in timber lands, and became president of a local bank.

Platt held local offices during the 1860s, but his political career began in earnest when, in 1870, he organized the "southern tier" of upstate New York for U.S. senator Roscoe Conkling, then the state's political captain. From 1874 to 1878 Platt served in the U.S. House of Representatives, and in 1881 he was elected to the Senate. A dispute over patronage with the forces of President James Garfield culminated a few months later in the joint resignation of Platt and Conkling from the Senate. However, Platt remained powerful in state politics.

After 1879 Platt headed the United States Express Company, which handled the business of the Erie Railroad; in this strategic position he dispensed favors to rural editors, politicians, and legislators along the Erie line. He pioneered a patronage technique whereby powerful corporations, anxious for protection and privilege, contributed directly to party coffers. He oiled the wheels of this "business govern-

Additional Sources

Platt, Thomas Collier, *The autobiography of Thomas Collier Platt,* New York, Arno Press, 1974, c1910. □

Plautus

Plautus (ca. 254-ca. 184 B.C.) was a Roman writer. His theatrical genius, vitality, farcical humor, and control of the Latin language rank him as Rome's greatest comic playwright.

D uring the 3d century B.C., Roman writers began to imitate the forms and contents of Greek literature. Unlike the early poets, Plautus confined himself to one area: translation and adaptation of Greek New Comedy (ca. 336-ca. 250 B.C.).

Knowledge of the life of Plautus, whose full name was Titus Maccius Plautus, is scant. Random remarks by later Roman writers and others furnish the questionable details. From Cicero the date of Plautus's birth can be placed about 254 B.C. and his death about 184 B.C. Festus, scholar of the 2d century A.D., gives Plautus's birthplace as the small town of Sarsina in Umbria, Italy. From Aulus Gellius, a grammarian from the 2d century, comes the traditional and fascinating, if brief, account of Plautus's life in Rome.

Plautus earned money by working in the theater but promptly lost it in trade. He returned to Rome penniless and for a time supported himself by working as a laborer in a flour mill. During this period he wrote three plays (not extant). Scholars who accept this romantic career suggest that it may have been reported in Plautine prologues now lost.

That Plautus earned money by theatrical work is generally accepted and may mean that he was a stagehand, carpenter, playwright, or actor. His mastery of stagecraft and comic effect suggests long experience as an actor prior to writing plays. Most intriguing is precisely how Plautus, an Umbrian from rural Sarsina, managed to acquire both a knowledge of Greek and the superb control of Latin displayed in his dramas.

His Works

The total of Plautus's plays is probably close to 50. Twenty plays are extant more or less in their entirety: *Amphitruo* (Amphitryon), *Asinaria* (The Comedy of Asses), *Aulularia* (The Pot of Gold), *Bacchides* (The Two Bacchides), *Captivi* (The Captives), *Casina* (Casina), *Cistellaria* (The Casket), *Curculio* (Curculio), *Epidicus* (Epidicus), *Menaechmi* (The Twin Menaechmi), *Mercator* (The Merchant), *Miles Gloriosus* (The Braggart Warrior), *Mostellaria* (The Haunted House), *Persa* (The Girl from Persia), *Poenulus* (The Carthaginian), *Pseudolus* (Pseudolus), *Rudens* (The Rope), *Stichus* (Stichus), *Trinummus* (The Three Penny Day), and *Truculentus* (Truculentus). Fewer

ment" by seeking advice from many quarters. His flexibility earned him the title "Easy Boss," but he demanded absolute loyalty once decisions were made.

Platt served in the U.S. Senate from 1897 to 1909; his record was undistinguished. In 1898, beset by pressures from reformers, he helped elect Theodore Roosevelt governor of New York. The two worked in uneasy harmony, making appointments, reforming the civil service, and launching various conservation measures. However, Roosevelt was too independent for Platt, and in 1900 he supported Benjamin B. Odell, an organization man, for governor and tried to shelve Roosevelt by arranging to nominate him as vice president. The plan failed doubly when President William McKinley's assassination made Roosevelt president, and Odell displayed an unsuspected progressivism.

Platt died in New York City on March 6, 1910. Although he never practiced the grosser forms of political corruption, his death spurred widespread attack on the machine politics with which he was popularly associated.

Further Reading

The Autobiography of Thomas Collier Platt (1910), compiled and edited by L. J. Lang, combines fact, fiction, and narrative; despite inaccuracies, it illuminates his methods and motives. A careful study of Platt's political techniques is Harold F. Gosnell, *Boss Platt and His New York Machine* (1924). DeAlva S. Alexander, *Four Famous New Yorkers* (1923), relates Platt's career to New York politics. G. Wallace Chessman, *Governor Theodore Roosevelt* (1965), examines Platt's relation with Roosevelt between 1898 and 1900.

nected with the plot and violation of dramatic illusion are clear evidence of Plautus's concern for entertaining his audience with a good laugh even at the expense of careful workmanship and finish.

Themes display considerable variety. There are plays of subdued comedy (*Captivi*), sentimental comedy (*Cistellaria*), romance (*Rudens*), mythological travesty (*Amphitruo*), and coarse farce (*Asinaria*). Mistaken identity and deception, either individually or jointly, give rise to the misunderstandings and complications on which the plays turn. Plautus appears to rely on earlier native Italian farces for the devices of trickery and impersonation.

Plautus's Characterization

Roman comedy for the most part paid careful attention to delineation of character but within a framework of types in which subtlety, complexity, and individuality were severely restricted. The Plautine cast of characters often includes the traditional figures: the young man (*adulescens*) hopelessly in love but lacking the courage and resourcefulness to achieve his desires; the aged parent (*senex*) who must be deceived and won over; the slave (*servus*) whose cunning and bustling create humor and intrigue; the young girl (*virgo*) of acknowledged free birth or to be rescued from shame; the courtesan (*meretrix*) who may be mercenary or noble; the hungry but shrewd parasite (*parasitus*); the despised slave dealer (*leno*); and the soldier (*miles*) whose boasting is equaled only by his stupidity.

But Plautus's originality and desire to entertain his audience have particularized many stock characters by exaggerated and imaginative portrayal. Characters especially suited to farce (Euclio and Pyrgopolynices) are among Plautus's most memorable creations of imagination and fantasy.

Command of Language and His Influence

Plautus captures the language of ordinary life, and to it he contributes novelty, vitality, and spontaneity. At a time when the Latin language was still quite fluid in inflection, syntax, and vocabulary, Plautine selection, combination, and invention set a high standard. Dialogue is rapid, racy, and filled with assonance, alliteration, and picturesque expressions. The vocabulary exploits and augments the available supply of terms of affection and abuse. Often tautology catches the carelessness or garrulity of ordinary speech. Plautus has no rival in ability to coin comic terms and names, for instance, *Bumbomachides Clutomestoridysarchides,* ''Battlebomski Mighty-adviser-of-wretched-strategy.''

The plays of Plautus enjoyed immediate success during his lifetime and were restaged and read by Romans after his death. The Middle Ages found his language difficult and his morality objectionable. During and after the Renaissance in Italy and other European countries, Plautine comedies were staged, translated, and imitated in vernacular compositions. Lodovico Ariosto (1474-1533), called the true founder of the modern European stage, reproduced in an Italian setting, in his *La cassaria* and *I suppositi,* the form and spirit of Plautine models.

than 100 lines survive from the *Vidularia* (The Traveling Bag).

All the plays are based on Greek originals, especially those by the 3d- and 2d-century B.C. comic playwrights Menander, Diphilus, and Philemon. Dates for the production of only two plays are known: *Stichus* (200 B.C.) and the *Pseudolus* (191 B.C.). Approximate dates for some plays are derived from reference to contemporary persons and events, amount of sung verses, and various criteria of style and technique. Modern chronological studies suggest the following relative datings—early period: *Asinaria, Mercator, Miles Gloriosus* (ca. 205 B.C.), *Cistellaria* (before 201 B.C.); middle period: *Stichus* (200 B.C.), *Aulularia, Curculio;* late period: *Pseudolus* (191 B.C.), *Bacchides, Casina* (185/184 B.C.).

Plautus's Style

The middle of the 1st century B.C. witnessed a revival of interest in Plautus and the restaging of many of his plays with consequent altering of original prologues. Some plays have no prologue; others have deferred prologues; and still others have authentic prologues or prologues based on those composed by Plautus. Often the prologue furnishes the audience with details necessary to understanding the opening of a complicated plot, or it may even explain in advance the outcome of the play with a consequent loss of suspense and surprise but a gain of irony. As a rule, the Plautine play presents one plot with one problem and one set of characters; these simple plots of Plautus allow comic digression and repetition. Humorous passages loosely con-

William Shakespeare's *Comedy of Errors* (1592) reflects the *Menaechmi* and the *Amphitruo;* and Ben Jonson's *The Case is Altered* (1597) blends the *Aulularia* and the *Captivi.* The esteem Plautus enjoyed among 16th-century dramatists is clear when Shakespeare has Polonius in *Hamlet* say, "Seneca cannot be too heavy nor Plautus too light."

Further Reading

Paul Nixon, *Plautus* (5 vols., 1916-1938), provides both text and translation of Plautus's works; translations are also given in G. E. Duckworth, *The Complete Roman Drama* (2 vols., 1942). For excellent treatment of almost every aspect of Plautus see Duckworth's *The Nature of Roman Comedy* (1952). Critical studies are Gilbert Norwood, *Plautus and Terence* (1932), and Erich Segal, *Roman Laughter: The Comedy of Plautus* (1968). The Greek sources of Plautus's work are considered in Philippe E. Legrand, *The New Greek Comedy* (1917). Margaret Bieber, *The History of the Greek and Roman Theatre* (1939; 2d ed. 1961), includes discussion and illustrations of archeological remains. See also W. Beare, *The Roman Stage* (1950; 3d ed. 1965). □

Galo Plaza Lasso

The Ecuadorian statesman Galo Plaza Lasso (1906-1987) was his country's most modern-minded president, and he distinguished himself in the service of international organizations.

Galo Plaza Lasso was born on February 17, 1906, in New York, when his father, Gen. Leonidas Plaza Gutiérrez, a former president of Ecuador, was on his way to serve as Ecuadorian minister in Washington. Within a few years the family returned to Ecuador, where the elder Plaza came to occupy the presidency a second time (1912-1916). After completing his primary and secondary education in Quito, young Plaza went back to the United States and attended the universities of California (Berkeley) and of Maryland and Georgetown University.

Back in Ecuador in 1932, Plaza introduced modern techniques in the administration of the family estate, particularly in dairy farming, and his improvements were widely imitated. Soon he entered politics, helped by a personal background that included his father's role as standard-bearer of the Liberal-Radical party, the family connections of his mother, Doña Avelina Lasso, and a modern outlook which he had acquired during his residence in the United States; all of this combined with a personal charm and unassuming behavior.

In 1937 Plaza was elected councilman of Quito and mayor in 1938. In December of that year President Mosquera appointed him minister of national defense, a post he retained through 1939. In July 1944 President José Maria Velasco sent him to Washington as ambassador. As such, he was a member of the Ecuadorian delegation at the Chapultepec and San Francisco conferences, both in 1945. The following year he returned to Ecuador to organize the

National Democratic Civic movement, a moderate democratic coalition. Elected senator in 1947, he won the presidential election of 1948.

The Presidential Years

Plaza's presidential term was marked by internal tranquillity. During his campaign he had proclaimed his dedication to effective democracy, and the nation saw in him the man who would bring its political and material regeneration. Plaza kept his promise, even though there were some who took undue advantage of the democratic tolerance of his administration. On the other hand, favorable international conditions and the well-conceived policies of the government brought prosperity to the country. Exports increased, and in general the economic life of the country was stimulated.

At the end of his term, Plaza could look back on 4 years of a highly successful administration. There were no precedents in Ecuador for such a combination of prosperity, stability, and effective democracy. In addition, Plaza's administration initiated a 12-year period marked by these characteristics. In 1952 he transmitted his presidential powers to his legally elected successor, Velasco—the first time in 28 years that a constitutional president was able to complete his full term.

The International Arena

In 1958 Plaza presided over the meetings of the Special Committee of the Economic Commission for Latin America

(CEPAL), which laid the foundations for the Latin American common market. In the same year he headed the successful mission of United Nations observers sent to Lebanon; and in 1960 he presided over the committee charged by the United Nations to deal with the evacuation of Belgian military bases in the Congo.

In the 1960 presidential elections of Ecuador, Plaza was the candidate of the Liberal-Radical party. He was opposed by the Conservative candidate, who had the backing of the outgoing administration, and by charismatic former president Velasco. The latter won. However, the party that had nominated Plaza was a weak electoral force, having been discredited in the past, and 1960 was throughout Latin America a year marked by a high tide of anti-United States feelings, a factor which helped Velasco against Plaza.

From May 1964 to the end of 1965 Plaza served as the personal representative of the secretary general of the United Nations and as mediator in Cyprus, a mission which turned out to be surprisingly successful in the face of extremely serious difficulties.

On February 13, 1968, Plaza was elected secretary general of the Organization of American States (OAS). Thereafter Plaza was able to reorganize the secretariat of the organization so as to render it more efficient, and he gave the OAS the dynamic and straightforward leadership which it had been sadly lacking. After leaving the OAS in 1975, Plaza went back to Ecuador as an elder statesman, helping to mediate his country's internal struggles. He was also active in the Inter-American Dialogue. Plaza died of a heart attack on January 28, 1987 in Ecuador.

Further Reading

Plaza's political career is discussed in George I. Blanksten, *Ecuador: Constitutions and Caudillos* (1951), and Edwin E. Erickson and others, *Area Handbook for Ecuador* (1966).

Additional Sources

(Tenenbaum, Barbara, ed.) *Encyclopedia of Latin American History and Culture,* Simon & Schuster Macmillan, 1996.
The New York Times Biographical Service, January 28, 1987. □

Georgi Valentinovich Plekhanov

The Russian revolutionist and social philosopher Georgi Valentinovich Plekhanov (1856-1918) is considered the founder of Russian Marxism.

Georgi Plekhanov was born on Nov. 29, 1856, to a petty gentry family with a tradition of military service. In 1873 he entered the Konstantinovskoe Military School in St. Petersburg. Because of an unresolved conflict between loyalty to the czar and to the people, he left school after one semester.

Plekhanov entered the Russian revolutionary movement at a time when its efforts to establish a new order based on the peasant commune were at a low ebb. Rejected by the peasants and repressed by the police, the socialist revolutionaries established a conspiratorial and centralized revolutionary organization, Land and Liberty. When the organization divided over the question of whether to continue socialist agitation or to begin political struggle by means of terror, Plekhanov rejected the use of terror and formed the Black Redistribution. To escape arrest he fled to Europe in 1880.

In Geneva, Plekhanov continued his study of Marxism, and in 1883 he founded the first Russian Marxist revolutionary organization, the Group for the Emancipation of Labor. His *Socialism and Political Struggle* (1883) and *Our Differences* (1885) are his major theoretical contributions to Russian Marxism. Plekhanov criticized his former comrades for failing to recognize the decline of the peasant commune and the growth of Russian capitalism with a proletariat and bourgeoisie, which made possible the strategy of a two-stage revolution: first, the proletariat with the bourgeoisie against the czarist autocracy to achieve the bourgeois revolution; second, the proletariat against the bourgeoisie to achieve the socialist revolution.

Socialist revolutionaries in Russia condemned Plekhanov's transition from populism to Marxism as heresy. His influence in Russia was minimal until the 1890s, when unrest produced by serious famine and rapid industrialization turned many socialists to Marxism. His Marxist view of history, *The Development of the Monistic View of History* (1894), published under the pseudonym Beltov, pointed ultimately to victory for the revolutionaries and helped to spur the formation of Marxist groups within Russia and to secure him an international reputation among European Social Democrats. In *Essays on the History of Materialism* (1896) Plekhanov invented the term ''dialectical materialism'' to describe Karl Marx's use of G. W. F. Hegel's dialectic on a materialistic basis.

V. I. Lenin, who at this time entered the Russian Social Democratic movement, soon went beyond Plekhanov's ideas and advocated a Marxist party in which the leaders formed a disciplined and conspiratorial group. The question of organization divided the Second Congress of the Russian Social Democrats in 1903. At first Plekhanov supported Lenin and the Bolshevik faction, but he soon feared that Lenin had confused a dictatorship *of* the proletariat with a dictatorship *over* the proletariat. His attempt to take an independent stand between the Bolsheviks and the Mensheviks was weakened by the Russian Revolution of 1905, which tested his theory of the two-stage revolution and found it inadequate. It proved that the more militant the proletariat became, the more the bourgeoisie sided *with* rather than *against* the czarist autocracy.

In 1909 Plekhanov began *The History of Russian Social Thought,* his attempt to relate social thought to the prevailing mode of production. He applied the same methodology to art and literature and produced the first substantial Marxist literary criticism in his *Letters without Address,* which he had begun in 1899.

Following the collapse of the Russian monarchy in February 1917, Plekhanov insisted that Russia was only in the bourgeois stage of revolution and that it must remain in the war against Germany. This stance alienated him form the militant revolutionaries who favored the popular demand for peace and land. After the Bolsheviks seized power in October, Plekhanov found himself isolated and ill. He died on May 30, 1918.

Further Reading

The only complete study of Plekhanov and his times in a Western language is Samuel Baron, *Plekhanov: The Father of Russian Marxism* (1963). It is both a perceptive study of Plekhanov's life and writings and a profound analysis of the relationship of Russian Marxism to Russian populism, social democracy, and bolshevism. Another excellent guide to Plekhanov's relationship to the Russian revolutionary movement is in Leopold H. Haimson, *The Russian Marxists and the Origins of Bolshevism* (1955).

Additional Sources

Baron, Samuel H., *Plekhanov in Russian history and Soviet historiography,* Pittsburgh: University of Pittsburgh Press, 1995.
□

Plenty Coups

Plenty Coups (ca. 1848-1932) was one of the first of the Crow to settle down and begin farming after reservation settlement.

Plenty Coups was the last of the traditional Crow chiefs and led the tribe in its transition from the "buffalo days" to reservation life. He served with the U.S. Army at the Battle of the Rosebud in 1876. However, Plenty Coups is best remembered for his leadership of the tribe after reservation settlement. He was among the first of the Crows to settle down, begin farming, open a store and build a two story log home. He often negotiated for his people with U.S. representatives, both in Washington and on the reservation, in the many attempts to reduce or open Crow lands to further white settlement between 1880 to 1920. After 1904, he was effectively recognized as the single most important Native American tribal leader both by the federal government and his own people. He represented all American Indians at the burial of the Unknown Soldier in Washington in 1921. He died in 1932, still fighting for the rights of his people at the end of his life.

The last of the traditional Crow chiefs was born not far from present day Billings, Montana around 1848. His name was given to him by his grandfather, from a dream that the boy would count many coups (a war deed), live to an old age, and become a chief. At some point in his life, he was also given the name Bull That Goes Into (or Against) the Wind. He was a member of the Sore Lips clan of the Mountain Crow, one of the three divisions of the tribe. His father Medicine Bird died when Plenty Coups was young.

His mother was named Otter Woman and he had a sister named Goes Well. Plenty Coups was first married at the age of 24 to Knows Her Mother. His last two wives were Kills Together and Strikes the Iron. Though he married about 12 different times, he had only two children, both of whom died young. Plenty Coups adopted and raised some poor children, but he told Frank Bird Linderman in his biography *American* that he considered all the Crows as his children.

The Crow were often at odds with their neighbors the Lakota Sioux, and Plenty Coups was no exception. At the age of nine, he lost a brother who was killed by the Lakota. Grant Bulltail, whose grandfather was raised by Plenty Coups, explained that in all two brothers and the parents of Plenty Coups were killed by the Lakota. According to Linderman. after his brother was killed Plenty Coups went on a fast, as he did on several occasions throughout his life, in hopes of receiving a vision which would give him power and direction. In his greatest vision, he saw the buffalo disappear and spotted buffalo, or cattle, appear in their place. A forest was destroyed by a storm, except for a single tree. This tree held the lodge of the Chickadee, who survived the storm because he was a sharp listener who learned from others and knew where to pitch his lodge.

The dream was interpreted to mean that the cattle which replaced the buffalo represented the whites taking over Crow country. The tree which survived was the Crows, who would survive the coming of the white man because, like the Chickadee, they listened and learned from the experiences of other tribes and placed themselves (pitched their lodges) in the right place. This powerful vision guided Plenty Coups throughout his life. It told him to adapt to and cooperate with the whites so the Crows would survive and prosper. It guided him as leader of the tribe through the difficult times ahead.

War Deeds and Chieftainship

With the aid of his powerful visions and medicines (objects with spiritual power), Plenty Coups became a feared warrior. He joined the Fox warrior society early in his career. Tribal historian Joseph Medicine Crow explained that Plenty Coups was particularly noted for horse capturing, one of the four war deeds required to become a Crow chief. The four deeds were: the capturing of a horse picketed in front of an enemy lodge (tipi), the leadership of a successful war party, capturing a weapon from an enemy in combat, and striking the first coup (hitting an enemy with the hand or an object) in a battle. Plenty Coups was able to achieve each of these deeds many times over. He became a chief by the age of 25 or 26, and, by the age of 30, had completed each of the deeds four times. In 1876, he fought alongside General George Crook and Chief Washakie of the Shoshones against the Lakota and Cheyenne in the Battle of the Rosebud. Eight days later, other Crows served as scouts for George Armstrong Custer at the Battle of the Little Big Horn.

Reservation Life and Rise to Tribal Leadership

Though Plenty Coups earned a strong reputation as a war chief, he did not become a peacetime leader of his people until he became a reservation chief. He began to rise in importance in the mid to late 1870s or early 1880s. As noted by Frederick Krieg in "Chief Plenty Coups: The Final Dignity," the government recognized him as head chief by 1890. However, it may not have been until after the death of Chief Pretty Eagle in 1904 that his people gave him the same honor. Plenty Coups demonstrated his power in 1908, when the tribe abandoned an internal factional struggle and united behind him to fight the first of the bills which proposed to open the reservation to white settlement. From that time on, he played the leading role in the political struggles over this issue, which eventually resulted in the Crow Act of 1920.

Plenty Coups' strong dedication to his people was evident. He advocated a policy of cooperation with and adaptation to the whites. However, he also expressed resentment toward the white man. He told Frank Linderman in *Plenty Coups* that "[w]e made up our minds to be friendly . . . but we found this difficult, because the white men too often promised to do one thing and then, when they acted at all, did another. They spoke very loudly when they said their laws were made for everybody; but we soon learned that although they expected us to keep them, they thought nothing of breaking them themselves . . . we know that with all his wonderful powers, the white man . . . is smart, but not wise, and fools only himself." In 1914, artist Joe Scheurle accompanied Plenty Coups on a tour of a Chicago zoo. As quoted in C. Adrian Heidenreich's article "The Crow Indian Delegation to Washington, D.C., in 1880," Scheurle wrote that "the superintendent of the zoo brought out a trained chimpanzee which immediately began searching Plenty Coups' pockets. When asked how he liked the animal, Plenty Coups replied, 'No! No like him, much like white people.'" Toward the end of his life, having witnessed about 50 years of the new reservation life with its changes, Plenty Coups told Glendolin Wagner in the book *Blankets and Moccasins* that "nothing the white man has given can make up for the happy life when vast plains were unfenced."

Plenty Coups preferred the old lifestyle of the "buffalo days" to the new ways. Even in his adaptation to the new lifestyle forced on the Crows, he tried to retain many of the tribal traditions. Plenty Coups became a Catholic in 1917, when he was baptized at St. Xavier, Montana, yet he also continued to practice traditional Crow religion. On one occasion, as Norman Wiltsey noted in his article "Plenty Coups: Statesman Chief of the Crows," Plenty Coups once scolded his men by telling them to work in the new way, but also to continue to fast and sweat in the traditional way. He said, "I am ashamed of you, self-pity has stolen your courage, robbed you of your spirit and self-respect; stop mourning the old days—they are gone with the buffalo. Go to your sweat lodges and cleanse your bodies so you may be fit to pray to Ab-badt-dabt-deah ["Akbaatatdía", God] for forgiveness. Then clean out your dirty lodges and go to work!"

Although Plenty Coups supported many of the tribe's traditional ways, he also fought to preserve his people's control over Crow land, resources, and lives. In these battles, Plenty Coups proved himself a strong leader. Krieg describes an 1890 meeting in which Plenty Coups stated, "I would like to see all of [the Crows] supplied with wagons, plows, mowing machines, and such farming implements as they may need. . . . I want the men who have cattle here on the Crow lands . . . to make them work and teach them the white man's ways so that they may learn. . . . we want to cut our own hay; we want the white man to buy hay from us; we don't want to beg and buy our hay from them. This is our land and not white men's . . . if they won't employ Crows to work, put them off entirely." In 1893, while negotiating with the Chicago, Burlington, and Quincy Railroad over the construction of a railroad in the Little Big Horn valley, Plenty Coups demanded that Indians be hired by the railroad company. On another occasion, he asked that the tribal herd be distributed among the Crows and that the Crows be consulted in management of tribal affairs.

Plenty Coups also realized early that good education was necessary for the tribe to prosper. As cited in Norman Wiltsey's book *Brave Warriors,* he told the Crows that "education is your most powerful weapon. With education you are the white man's equal; without education you are his victim." Yet, he did not see education as a way for the Crows to blend into white society while forgetting their own people. As he told Glendolin Wagner for *Blankets and Moccasins,* he wished them "to go to school and become well educated . . . then . . . to come back home on the reservation and work their land." Even even with a partial adoption of white ways, Plenty Coups encouraged a strong loyalty to the tribe and tribal self sufficiency.

It is easy to say that Plenty Coups was an assimilationist, eager to cooperate with the whites at the expense of his own people. However, the circumstances and historical context suggest that the Crows were threatened with not just cultural, but actual physical, extinction. In addition, though Plenty Coups was friendly to whites, it was not any great love for whites or admiration of their ways that guided his actions, but what was best for the Crows. Just as the military alliance with the United States in the 1860s and 1870s was the best policy at that time for the tribe—to preserve Crow lands and lives—so too did the adoption of the new ways enable the people to survive a new threat—starvation and the taking of the remainder of Crow lands by the government and white farmers and cattlemen.

Plenty Coups demonstrated his leadership during the difficult period of adjustment to reservation life in three ways: in his advice to the people, in his own life, and in his political leadership and statesmanship. He urged the people to get a good education and to farm their land, as well as to continue to practice their traditional Crow religion. Plenty Coups put his beliefs into practice in his own life. He was one of the earliest and most successful farmers on the reservation. He had established a garden by 1882. After he settled in what is now Pryor, Montana in the mid 1880s, he often exhibited at agricultural fairs the largest potatoes in Yellowstone County. Eventually, he developed a farm where he also raised apples, grain, wheat, hay, and oats. Plenty Coups also lived in a log house, eventually building the only two story log house among the Crows. This building and his barn can still be seen today in Pryor.

Plenty Coups in Politics

Few other old Crow chiefs had accomplished more war deeds than Plenty Coups, but none could match him as a political leader and statesman around and after the turn of the century. An impressive, dignified speaker, he showed his negotiating skill in dealing with ranchers, railroad companies, and often with the U.S. government. He met with Indian agents, tribal attorneys, and congressmen over such issues as irrigation projects, grazing leases, and land cessions. At times, he requested that the government provide farm equipment and training, improved schooling, and that it lease out tribal lands for oil and gas mining with the revenues going to tribal members. He often called meetings with tribal members over these same issues. Officials of railroad companies also found that he was a tough bargainer, yet fair.

While Plenty Coups may have been cooperative with the whites regarding such issues as farming and education, land was quite a different matter. Between 1880 and 1921, he traveled to Washington, D.C., at least ten times to fight proposed land concessions by the Crows. The heaviest period of travel took place in the ten years between 1908 and 1918. During this time, the Montana congressional delegation made its strongest effort to open the reservation to general homesteading. The Crows recognized these proposals as threats to the well-being of the tribe, and the people ended their factionalism and united behind Plenty Coups to defeat the measures. Although other leaders played roles in uniting the Crows, it was Plenty Coups who was the guiding figure, especially in the Congressional hearings in Washington D.C.

Still, Plenty Coups and the other older chiefs were aided in their victory by young Crows and mixed bloods, the first generation to be educated in the white man's schools. Young men such as Robert Yellowtail were especially valuable as interpreters, and their schooling also served as their training ground for future tribal leadership. The victory over the general opening of the reservation served as the ultimate proof of the wisdom of Plenty Coups' vision. The chief's advice that education is "your most powerful weapon" with which "you are the white man's equal" was correct. Yet, true to the spirit of the old ways of the warrior, after Senator Thomas J. Walsh withdrew his bill at a Senate hearing in 1917, Plenty Coups approached the senator and reached out toward him with his cane, symbolically striking a coup.

Plenty Coups in Retirement

The defeat of the general opening of the reservation ended Plenty Coups' heavy involvement in tribal affairs. Although he no longer wielded political power, he still occupied the role of an elder statesman for Native Americans. In 1921, the War Department chose him to represent all Indian tribes at the Burial of the Unknown Soldier of World War I in Arlington National Cemetery near Washington,

D.C. On November 11, 1921, in the presence of the President and high ranking men from the victorious Allied nations, Plenty Coups placed a wreath of flowers, his war bonnet, and his coup stick at the tomb. The war bonnet can still be seen today at the cemetery. Though informed that only the President was to speak, Plenty Coups did make a speech which was actually a prayer. It was the last speech made before the coffin was lowered.

On March 4, 1928, Plenty Coups executed a deed of trust that set apart 40 acres of his land in Pryor to be used as a park and recreation ground for both Crows and whites. Plenty Coups had been inspired by a visit to Mt. Vernon with the 1880 delegation and wished to create a similar memorial. The deed also arranged for a museum to be set up in one room of his two story house. According to Wiltsey's article, Plenty Coups stated that the park was to be a memorial not to him, but to the Crow nation, and that it should be "a reminder to Indians and white people alike that the two races should live and work together harmoniously." Since 1962, the house and grounds have been administered as a state park. The museum was transferred from a room in the old house to a new museum building in 1973.

In the last years of his life, Plenty Coups took on the role of the official greeter of important visitors to Crow country. In addition to General James Harbord, who had ceremoniously accepted the 40 acres on the part of the government, and World War I supreme Allied commander Marshall Ferdinand Foch of France, Vice President Charles Curtis, who was part Kansa Indian, visited in 1928. Even in his last months of life, Plenty Coups was thinking of the good and future of his people. On November 7, 1931, the old chief made one of his last official statements. He wanted the Pryor and Big Horn Mountains on the reservation reserved from allotment, the trust period for allotments extended for 26 years, and the money from the Crow Land Claim given to the children of the tribe. He passed away a few months later on March 4, 1932.

Further Reading

Curtis, Edward S., *The North American Indian,* Volume 4: *The Apsaroke, or Crows; The Hidatsa,* Johnson Reprint Corporation, 1980.

Hoxie, Frederick E., "Building A Future On the Past: Crow Indian Leadership in an Era of Division and Reunion," in *Indian Leadership,* edited by Walter Williams, Sunflower University Press, 1984.

Hoxie, Frederick E., *Parading through History: The Making of the Crow Nation, 1805-1935,* Oxford University Press, 1995.

Linderman, Frank Bird, *American: The Life Story of a Great Indian, Plenty-coups, Chief of the Crows,* John Day, 1930; published as *Plenty-Coups, Chief of the Crows,* University of Nebraska Press, 1962.

Medicine Crow, Joseph, *From the Heart of the Crow Country: The Crow Indians' Own Stories,* Orion Books, 1992.

Wagner, Glendolin Damon, and William A. Allen, *Blankets and Moccasins: Plenty Coups and His People, the Crows,* Caxton Printers, 1933; reprinted, University of Nebraska Press, 1987.

Wiltsey, Norman B., *Brave Warriors,* Caxton Printers, 1964.

Yellowtail, Robert Summers, *Robert Summers Yellowtail, Sr., at Crow Fair, 1972,* Wowapi, 1973.

Ewers, John C., "A Crow Chief's Tribute to the Unknown Soldier," *American West,* 8:6, November 1971; 30-35.

Heidenreich, C. Adrian, "The Crow Indian Delegation to Washington, D.C., in 1880," *Montana, the Magazine of Western History,* 31:2, spring 1981; 54-67.

Krieg, Frederick C., "Chief Plenty Coups, the Final Dignity," *Montana, the Magazine of Western History,* 16:4, October 1966; 28-39.

Wiltsey, Norman B., "Plenty Coups: Statesman Chief of the Crows," *Montana, the Magazine of Western History,* 13:4, September 1963; 28-39.

Bradley, Charles Crane, "After the Buffalo Days: Documents on the Crow Indians from the 1880s to the 1920s" (master's thesis), Montana State University, 1970.

Bulltail, Grant, interview with Timothy Bernardis conducted March 15, 1985.

Lowie, Robert H., "Notes on Crow Chiefs," in Robert Harry Lowie Papers, Bancroft Library, University of California, Berkeley.

Medicine Crow, Joseph, personal communication to Timothy Bernardis, May 15, 1985.

Plenty Coups Papers, held at Plenty Coups Museum, Pryor, Montana. Wildschut, William, unpublished manuscript on the life of Plenty Coups based on interviews conducted with Plenty Coups, held in the Archives of the National Museum of the American Indian, Heye Foundation, New York, New York. Yellowtail, Robert Summers, class lecture for "Crow History—Post-Settlement" (tape-recording), May 15, 1984, held at Little Big Horn College Archives, Crow Agency, Montana. Yellowtail, Robert Summers, "Notes on Crow Chiefs," held in Little Big Horn College Archives, Crow Agency, Montana. ☐

Pliny the Elder

Pliny the Elder (23-79) was a Roman encyclopedist. His greatest and only surviving work, the *Natural History,* has been called one of the most influential books ever written in Latin.

Pliny whose full name was Gaius Plinius Secundus, was born at Comum in the region north of the Po River and was educated in Rome. After the military career normal for his social rank, during which he served as a cavalry officer in Germany (47-57), he practiced law. During Nero's reign (54-68), Pliny found it prudent to concentrate on literature. He performed official tasks in various provinces for the emperor Vespasian (69-79), whom he knew well.

Pliny's true occupations, however, which he practiced constantly, were reading and writing. He had a voracious hunger for knowledge of all kinds and was diligent in collecting it. Some of his 102 volumes, which were described by his nephew, Pliny the Younger, were *On the Use of the Javelin in the Cavalry;* a biography in 2 books of his friend Pomponius Secundus; *On the German Wars,* a complete history in 20 books of all Roman wars with Germans up to his own times; *The Student,* in 3 books, on the education from childhood of an orator; *Doubtful Speech,* 8 books on grammar; and a continuation in 31 books of the history by Aufidius Bassus.

Natural History

Book 1 of the *Natural History* contains a long preface to the emperor Titus, in whose reign the work was completed, and a table of contents for the remaining books together with the authors consulted. Books 2-6 describe the universe and the surface of the earth; book 7 treats man; books 8-11 treat animals; books 12-19, plants; books 20-27, the use of plants in medicines; books 28-32 deal with medicines derived from animals; and books 33-37, with minerals and their use in the arts.

Pliny's work is by no means scientific in the modern sense. It contains many errors, some the result of his mistranslating Greek, most due to the haste with which he worked and his uncritical acceptance of his sources. Nevertheless, it remains the chief source of information on topics ranging from lost works of art to popular magic and includes much on history, literature, and Roman ritual and customs.

Pliny was admiral of the fleet at Misenum in 79, when the great eruption of Vesuvius occurred on August 24. According to his nephew, Pliny the Younger, his scientific curiosity impelled him to approach the volcano more closely in order to inspect its smoke cloud. He was informed that a lady of his acquaintance, whose house was at the base of the volcano, was in danger and unable to escape by land. He rescued his friend by ship and, noting that many others were in a like situation, ordered the ships of the fleet to be used to evacuate them from the danger area. He continued on to Stabiae (4 miles north of Pompeii), from which all the occupants were fleeing, continually describing each new phase of the eruption and ordering that a slave note down his observations exactly as he made them. When the earthquakes and fire grew more intense, he was unable to escape. His body was discovered 2 days later on the beach at Stabiae, where he had died, apparently of asphyxiation.

Further Reading

Pliny's *Natural History,* with Latin text and English translations by H. Rackham and others, is in the Loeb Classical Library (10 vols., 1938-1963). Pliny is examined in detail in H. N. Wethered, *The Mind of the Ancient World: A Consideration of Pliny's Natural History* (1937), and is discussed in H. J. Rose, *A Handbook of Latin Literature* (1936; 3d ed. 1966). There is a brief biography in George Schwartz and Phillip W. Bishop, eds., *Moments of Discovery: The Origins of Science* (1958). Pliny's contribution is covered in Charles Singer and others, eds., *A History of Technology,* vol. 2 (1956). □

Pliny the Younger

Pliny the Younger (ca. 61-ca. 113) was a Roman author and administrator. He left a collection of letters which offers intimate glimpses into public and private life during the Roman Empire.

Born of the wealthy Caecilius family at Comum in northern Italy, Pliny the Younger, as he was later known, was probably given his early education by tutors at home and then sent to Rome to study. He inherited the full estate of his uncle Pliny the Elder at his death in 79 and at this time changed his name to Gaius Plinius Caecilius Secundus.

Pliny began his career as a lawyer at the age of 18 and enjoyed success at the bar. In his 20s he entered the magistracy of Rome and held various posts over a period of about 30 years, including a seat on the court which heard inheritance cases, the presidency of the board in charge of the banks of the Tiber and the sewers of Rome, positions in the military and senatorial treasuries, and the consulship. In 110 Trajan sent him on a special mission to investigate corruption in Bithynia. He died there about 2 years later.

Pliny's letters are preserved in 10 books. The first 9 contain 247 personal letters, and the tenth is his official correspondence with Trajan from Bithynia. Also preserved is his *Panegyricus,* a speech praising Trajan. The letters of books 1-9, selected, rewritten, and arranged with care by their author, were published in his lifetime. The letters of book 10 were published posthumously.

The topics of the letters are quite diverse, although each has a single subject and is written with skill, the style being historical, poetical, or oratorical to suit the theme. Some are to young men whose careers Pliny wished to further. Many are on moral, philosophical, political, or literary subjects. Many have to do with business and litigation. Others are descriptive. One considers the existence of ghosts—and contains a fascinating ghost story. Yet another tells of his third wife's touching devotion.

The letters are the best source available for the political and social history of Rome for the period they cover. In addition, there emerges from them a portrait of Pliny himself. Shrewd, magnanimous, stoical, self-satisfied, efficient, loyal, and, above all, tolerant, Pliny represents a type who at that time made workable the complex administration of the vast Roman Empire.

Further Reading

Betty Radice prepared an edition of Pliny the Younger's *Letters and Panegyricus* with Latin text and translation (2 vols., 1969); she also translated *The Letters of the Younger Pliny* (1963). See also S. E. Stout, *Scribe and Critic at Work in Pliny's Letters* (1954); Ronald Syme, *Tacitus* (2 vols., 1958); and A. N. Sherwin-White, *The Letters of Pliny* (1966). □

Maya Mikhailovna Plisetskaya

The Russian dancer Maya Mikhailovna Plisetskaya (born 1925) epitomized the best of Soviet ballet.

The career of Maya Plisetskaya, the celebrated Soviet ballerina, choreographer, teacher, and director, spans almost 50 years. Her impulsive, dynamic, and expressive dancing in the 1940s, 1950s, and 1960s epitomized the highest qualities of the Soviet ballet. Recognized as one of the world's greatest ballerinas, she endowed her roles with unique individuality, combining the pure lyrical technique of the Russian classical heritage with the fire and magic of Soviet bravura. In 1990 she still danced in roles which, though less demanding physically, enabled her to demonstrate her persuasive acting skills.

Maya Mikhailovna Plisetskaya, prima ballerina assoluta of the Bolshoi Ballet, was born on November 20, 1925, in Moscow into a Jewish theatrical dynasty. For over 70 years the Messerer family played a prominent part in the Soviet theater and films, as well as in the ballet world. Her mother, Rakhil Messerer, was a well-known silent-film actress. (Both of Maya's parents suffered during Stalin's purges in the 1930s: her mother was sent to a labor camp, and her father died.) Maya's brother, Azari, became a dancer; her Aunt Elizaveta was an actress in Moscow; and her cousin Boris was a distinguished set designer. Balletic influence came from her mother's sister and brother, Sulamith and Mikhail Messerer, both talented soloists and later distinguished teachers with the Bolshoi Ballet, who coached and encouraged the young Maya from earliest days.

As a child, Maya was always restless, constantly moving. When she was eight, her Aunt Sulamith took her to the Moscow Choreographic School, which produces most of the Bolshoi dancers. She requested that they admit Maya a year earlier than the usual entrance age because of the child's obvious talent and also because "at home, she just can't help dancing." Maya was accepted and began the hard and dedicated life of becoming a ballet dancer. For six full days a week she took ballet lessons along with her regular school education. Gangly and thin with bright red hair, the young Maya quickly grasped the technical difficulties of classical ballet, though not always willingly. Once she was expelled for violating the disciplinary demands of the class. Unabashed, she told her teacher that she didn't care and would "go and sell apples." But in less than two weeks she was back in class again. Her teacher for six years was the legendary Yelizaveta Gerdt, whose equally famous father, Pavel, taught Anna Pavlova and Tamara Karsavina. Thus Plisetskaya is a direct link and continuation of the traditions of the Russian ballet. Gerdt called Plisetskaya her "little diamond" and lovingly polished and refined the young pupil's talent.

To be a student at the ballet school meant taking part in performances with the company at the Bolshoi Theatre. When she was 11, Plisetskaya appeared as the Bread Crumb Fairy in Asaf Messerer's production of "The Sleeping Beauty." A year later she danced the role of the cat in a children's ballet, "The Little Stork," and in her seventh year at the school, her sparkling interpretation as leading dancer in the divertissement from "Paquita" aroused much interest. In addition to her commanding presence and clear, sharp footwork, she showed a remarkable high and seemingly effortless leap, an expressive movement which was to become one of her trademarks.

Upon graduation from the school in 1943, she was accepted immediately into the Bolshoi company, not as a member of the corps de ballet but as a soloist. For the role of Masha in "The Nutcracker," Plisetskaya received the coaching of yet another legendary figure in the history of Russian ballet—Agrippina Vaganova, the director of the Leningrad ballet school whose methods of teaching were the basis at all Soviet ballet schools. Among Vaganova's pupils in Leningrad had been Galina Ulanova and Marina Semyonova. Vaganova encouraged the young ballerina to find and bring out her own individuality in each role—to make them her own.

The ensuing years saw Plisetskaya performing in all the classical roles, offering individual but convincing interpretations. She danced Raymonda, the dual role of Odette-Odile (Swan Lake), Aurora (Sleeping Beauty), Myrthe (Giselle), Kitri (Don Quixote), Tsar-Maiden (The Little Hump-backed Horse), and, of course, "The Dying Swan" which Michel Fokine created for Anna Pavlova and which later was associated as a showcase for Plisetskaya's famous plasticity—the suppleness of her back and the remarkable pliability of her arms, which ripple with grace, seemingly boneless. In contemporary Soviet works she would attack the choreography with gusto, throwing herself into the dancing and character of the role with fiery passion. Her presence dominated the stage, encompassing it with large, expansive movements, high but light jumps, spinning turns, and dynamic force. She expressed great musicality in her dancing, and her presence guaranteed excitement.

One of her most famous—and favorite—contemporary roles was Carmen, in the ballet "Carmen-Suite" by Cuban choreographer Alberto Alonso. The ballet gave full rein to her dramatic and artistic talent. She portrayed the young girl as a passionate, tempestuous, and sensual character. Bizet's famous score was arranged by Rodion Shchedrin, Plisetskaya's husband. The French choreographers Roland Petit and Maurice Bejart created "La Rose Malade" and "Isadora," respectively, for her.

Another facet of Plisetskaya's talent was her choreography. Her ballets "Anna Karenina," "The Seagull," and "Lady with a Lapdog" are all based on Russian literature with music especially composed by Shchedrin and created as vehicles for her own star quality. She focused the spot light on the drama and psychological aspects of the stories rather than concentrating solely on the dancing. Plisetskaya won the top civilian award, the Lenin Prize, in 1964 and the French Pavlova Prize in 1962. She taught master classes in many cities, including New York, and was the artistic director of The National Ballet of Spain beginning of 1988.

After her departure from the Bolshoi Ballet, Plisetskaya continued to astound audiences world wide. She was accorded one of the highest tributes that a dancer could receive, an international ballet competition was named for her in 1994. Unlike similar competitions, participants in the "Maya" competition were allowed freedom in their choice of dance, with only one or two compulsory selections. The Second "Maya" International Ballet Competition ended in mild controversy when all the top honors went to Russian dancers. When most prima ballerinas would have long retired, Plisetskaya continued to perform on stage. In 1996, at age seventy, she received rave reviews for her remarkable performance of her signature "The Dying Swan" at New York City Hall. Her ability to work was phenomenal, and her talent remarkable. Plisetskaya was the "prima ballerina assoluta."

Further Reading

Further information on Maya Plisetskaya and her work can be found in *Maya Plisetskaya. Essays on her work by Voznesensky, Vavra, Gayevsky, Komissarzhevsky, Lvov-Anokhin, Tyurin, Shuvalov* (Moscow: 1976; in English) and in *Maya Plisetskaya* by Natalia Roslavleva (Moscow: 1956; in English). *Era of Russian Ballet* by Natalia Roslavleva (London: 1966) contains references to Plisetskaya's contribution to Russian ballet, as does *The Russian Ballet: Past and Present* by Alexander Demidov (London; in English). *Russian Ballet on Tour*, photographs by Alexander Orloff, text by Margaret Willis (1989), has a section devoted to Plisetskaya. Reviews and articles can be routinely found in the *St. Petersburg Press.* □

Plotinus

The Greek philosopher Plotinus (205-270) was the founder of the Neoplatonic school of philosophy, which became the most formidable rival of Christianity in the declining years of the ancient world.

Plotinus was born perhaps in the Egyptian town of Lyco, or Lycopolis. He turned to philosophy at the age of 28 and studied for 11 years with the eminent philosopher Ammonius Saccas at Alexandria.

In 243, desiring to learn about Eastern philosophy, Plotinus joined the expedition led by the Roman emperor Gordian III against the Persians. However, Gordian was murdered, and Plotinus was forced to flee to Antioch and then Rome.

Upon his arrival in Rome, Plotinus began to take students, and his influence in the city soon became great among both professional philosophers and other intellectuals. The emperor Gallienus held Plotinus in such high esteem that he considered founding a philosophers' city in Campania on the ruined site of an early Pythagorean settlement. Plotinus's habits of life were austere. He ate and slept only as much as necessary, and he never married. When he fell ill late in life, he left Rome and retired to Campania, where he died.

Plotinus did not begin to write until he was 50 years old. His work, the *Enneads,* was arranged and published some 30 years after his death by his most famous pupil, Porphyry. It consists of six groups of nine essays and deals with the whole range of ancient philosophical thought with the exception of political theory. Ennead 1 deals with ethics and esthetics; Enneads 2 and 3 deal with physics and cosmology; Ennead 4 treats psychology; and Enneads 5 and 6 deal with metaphysics, logic, and epistemology. The style of these essays is highly personal—sometimes brilliant, sometimes concise to the point of obscurity—but at all times fascinating and indicative of Plotinus's keen and sensitive mind.

His Philosophical System

At the heart of Plotinus's religiophilosophical system is a supreme divinity which is infinite, unitary, and good. It is the ultimate but not the direct cause of all that is, although it is under no compulsion or necessity to produce anything outside itself. Indeed, it is so perfect that it lacks nothing. It simply *is.* Between this supreme existent and the known world is the supersensual world, made up of three types of being.

The first, produced by an overflow or radiation of the perfect One, is the World-Mind, which is conscious of multiplicity but holds all together in eternal contemplation. It is equivalent to Aristotle's Unmoved Mover and the realm of Plato's Ideas, or Forms. It is also the organizational principle of the universe.

Next comes the World-Soul, produced by the World-Mind and less unitary in that it is further removed from the One and perceives things sequentially. It is therefore the cause of time and space, although it is superior to them since it is eternal.

Finally, there is Nature, the furthest removed from the One and the least creative of the three supersensual beings. Nature corresponds to the Stoic immanent World-Soul. The physical world is a projection of its dreamlike consciousness.

According to Plotinus, man's role in this universe is a unique one. Unlike other animal and plant life, he has within himself the possibility of using his intellect to aspire to unity with the supersensual world. Indeed, through strict discipline, it is even possible to achieve union with the One, but such occurrences are rare. Plotinus claimed to have reached that height of ecstasy himself four times.

The three types of supersensual beings correspond to three types of thought which men may engage in. The lowest, corresponding to the dreamlike consciousness of Nature, is unclear and undisciplined thought. The next, corresponding to the thought of the World-Soul, is discursive thought. The third, corresponding to the unitary thought of the World-Mind, is apprehension of the whole in a single experience of the mind.

Ecstasy of Oneness

The ecstasy which Plotinus claimed to have experienced was one step further. It was a complete union with God, the infinite, unitary, and beneficent One. This experience was impossible to describe. Since God is completely self-sufficient and has no need to be conscious of anything, so the man who reaches the height of ecstatic union with Him finds himself in a state of totally indescribable self-sufficiency and oneness. It is an experience equivalent to the mystical union with God described by Christian mystics.

Plotinus's teachings attracted many followers. The most noteworthy were Porphyry and Iamblichus, who carried on his teachings with slightly different emphasis. Neoplatonism, through the development of the many schools it spawned, came to embrace a great number of mystical and superstitious beliefs from the East. It proved to be a resilient and attractive rival to Christianity, and even after Justinian closed the philosophical schools in 529, Neoplatonism remained influential in the development of thought during the Middle Ages and the Renaissance.

Further Reading

Original texts and readable translations of the works of Plotinus are provided in A. H. Armstrong, *Plotinus* (1966). An excellent commentary is Émile Bréhier, *The Philosophy of Plotinus,* translated by Joseph Thomas (1958). See also W. R. Inge, *The Philosophy of Plotinus* (2 vols., 1928). Originally written in the late 19th century, Eduard Zeller's *Outlines of the History of Greek Philosophy,* 13th ed. revised by Wilhelm Nestle and translated by L.R. Palmer (1957), is still useful although slightly dated. Discussions of Neoplatonism in the context of the history of Greek literature can be found in standard works on that subject, notably Albin Lesky, *A History of Greek Literature* (1966). See also Thomas Whittaker, *The Neo-Platonists* (1928).

Additional Sources

Davison, William Theophilus, *Mystics and poets,* Folcroft, Pa.: Folcroft Library Editions, 1977.
Plotinus, *The essence of Plotinus: extracts from the six Enneads and Porphyry's Life of Plotinus, based on the translation by Stephen Mackenna: with an appendix giving some of the most important Platonic and Aristotelian sources on which Plotinus drew, and an annotated bibliography,* Westport, Conn.: Greenwood Press, 1976, 1934. □

Plutarch

The Greek biographer, historian, essayist, and moralist Plutarch (ca. 46-ca. 120) has been described as one of the most influential writers who ever lived.

Paradoxically, Plutarch the man who was the biographer of many others, had no biographer except for a scant notice in Suidas. What we know of his life is reconstructed from casual references in his own works. Plutarch was apparently born of a wealthy family in Chaeronia in Boeotia, had two brothers, Timon and Lamprias, and a grandfather named Lamprias. His parents' names are uncertain. Some say his father's name was Autobulus, some say Nicarchus, and we do know of a great-grandfather named Nicarchus. Plutarch is believed to have had a liberal education at Athens, where he studied physics, rhetoric, mathematics, medicine, natural science, philosophy, Greek, and Latin literature in 66. Ammonius of Lamptrae, a Plato scholar with religious and Neoplatonic interests, may have been his tutor. To complete his education, Plutarch traveled extensively in Greece and Asia Minor and visited Alexandria, Egypt.

Plutarch married Timoxena, daughter of Alexion (ca. 68), who bore him four sons, Soclarus, Chairon, Autobulus, and Plutarchus, and one daughter, Timoxena. Only Autobulus and Plutarchus survived Plutarch. All evidence indicates a happy marriage and a close family. Other relatives by marriage mentioned as members of the family in the *Moralia* are Craton, Firmus, and Patrocleas.

Plutarch taught in Chaeronia and represented his people before the Roman governor and in Rome. In Rome he made important contacts and lectured on philosophy and ethics in various parts of Italy. He spent much time in Italy between 75 and 90; he apparently never mastered the Latin language, though he gained the friendship of notable Romans. The latter half of his life, Plutarch enjoyed the intellectual benefits of the Pax Romana, mostly in Chaeronia. He held many civic positions, both high and low; the most notable one—that of head priest of Delphi—he held with distinction for 20 years and elevated to an importance it had not had in his time. During the latter part of his life he is thought to have written most of the *Lives* and some portions of the *Moralia.*

His Works

Plutarch is perhaps best known for the *Moralia* and the *Lives,* works which have much in common and have had enormous influence on later writers and the literatures of Europe and even America. He was very much concerned with men's moral conduct and individual moral guidance in an age when men were losing their faith in religion and philosophy. The *Moralia,* written as dialogues, letters, and lectures, is really a collection of 83 treatises on diverse subjects such as vegetarianism; superstition; Epicurean, Stoic, and Academic philosophy; dietetics; divine justice; prophecy; demonology; conjugal relations; family life; mysticism; and helpful precepts.

that made Plutarch available to North and through North to the English-speaking world.

Further Reading

The Loeb Classical Library's *Plutarch's Lives,* translated by Bernadotte Perrin (11 vols., 1914-1926), is indispensable, as is the Loeb's *Plutarch's Moralia,* translated by Frank Cole Babbitt and others (15 vols., 1927-1969). An exhaustive and still essential study is Bishop Richard C. Trench, *Plutarch: His Life, His Lives and His Morals* (1873), which remained the primary study until Reginald Haynes Barrow, *Plutarch and His Times* (1967). C. J. Gianakaris, *Plutarch* (1970), is a convenient synthesis and appraisal which contains an extensive bibliography. A work on Plutarch's moral interests is George D. Hadzsits, *Prolegomena to a Study of the Ethical Ideal of Plutarch and of the Greeks of the First Century A.D.* (1906); and on religion, John Oakesmith, *The Religion of Plutarch* (1902).

Special studies provide powerful evidence of Plutarch's widespread influence: Frederick Morgan Padelford, trans. and ed., *Essays on the Study and Use of Poetry by Plutarch and Basil the Great* (1902); Roy Caston Flickinger, *Plutarch as a Source of Information on the Greek Theater* (1904); Charles Frederick Tucker Brooke, ed., *Shakespeare's Plutarch* (2 vols., 1909); Roger Miller Jones, *The Platonism of Plutarch* (1916); Edmund Grindlay Berry, *Emerson's Plutarch* (1961); and Terence John Bew Spencer, ed., *Shakespeare's Plutarch* (1964). Recommended surveys of classical historiography which include discussions of Plutarch are Michael Grant, *The Ancient Historians* (1970), and Stephen Usher, *The Historians of Greece and Rome* (1970). □

The *Lives* (often called *Parallel Lives*) are biographies of soldiers and statesmen of repute, generally presented in pairs of lives, first a Greek, then a Roman, followed by a comparison. Twenty-three of these have survived and four single lives; that is, four comparisons are lacking. There is no detailed chronology, but the *Lives* were probably published between 105 and 115. Plutarch utilizes Greek sources primarily and is interested in providing pleasure and guidance for moral and political behavior. Plutarch's language is generally lucid and crisp.

Plutarch was not a profound philosopher but a popularizer in the best and most enduring sense of the word. He did not establish a philosophic system but was eclectic in his use of various systems. He warmly admired Plato and knew Pythagoras and other Greek philosophers. He severely criticized Epicureanism and stoicism but used these systems as it suited him. One critic finds him a humanist par excellence; others see him inclined toward mysticism and monotheism. He was an author of uncommon common sense who influenced Sir Philip Sidney, Edmund Spenser, Ben Jonson, William Shakespeare, John Dryden, John Milton, Robert Herrick, George Chapman, Jonathan Swift, Walter Savage Landor, William Wordsworth, Robert Browning, Mary Shelley, and H.G. Wells in England; Ralph Waldo Emerson and Herman Melville in the United States; J.W. von Goethe and Friedrich von Schiller in Germany; and French drama of the late 16th and the entire 17th century. Sir Thomas North's English translation of the *Lives* (1579) provided Shakespeare with the sources for three plays, and it was the translation (1559) by Frenchman Jacques Myot

Konstantin Petrovich Pobedonostsev

The Russian statesman and jurist Konstantin Petrovich Pobedonostsev (1827-1907), as director general of the Holy Synod, became a champion of czarist autocracy, orthodoxy, and Russian nationalism.

Konstantin Pobedonostsev was born on May 21, 1827, in Moscow. His father, Peter V. Pobedonostsev, a professor at the University of Moscow, educated Konstantin at home until he enrolled at the St. Petersburg School of Jurisprudence in 1841. From his father, he learned to read Old Church Slavonic, French, Latin, and German. He also studied the Bible, the writings of the Russian Orthodox Church Fathers, Greek and Roman classics, Russian history, and Russian literature. He graduated from the School of Jurisprudence with a wide knowledge of Western judicial institutions, laws, and literatures.

Pobedonostsev first won acclaim as a historian of Russian judicial institutions and as a specialist in Russian civil law. In 1846 Pobedonostsev was assigned to the eighth department of the Senate in Moscow. In 1853 he became secretary of the seventh department. In 1859 he was named lecturer in Russian civil law at Moscow University.

In 1861 Pobedonostsev was appointed tutor in Russian history and law to the heir to the throne, the future Alexander III, and was named executive secretary of the Senate. He moved to St. Petersburg into a life of great influence in the central governmental bureaucracy and the court. He employed his tutorial position to mold the views of the imperial heir. Pobedonostsev emphasized the ties between Russian Orthodoxy and Russian national history. By the late 1870s his influence on Alexander had become overwhelming.

In 1872 Pobedonostsev became a member of the State Council, a body that advised the Czar concerning projected laws. Most of the significant legislation and decrees of the 19th century received their final review and drafting in this Council. Pobedonostsev's main responsibility as a Council member was civil and ecclesiastical matters. His work in the Council contributed to his appointment in 1880 as director general of the Holy Synod of the Russian Orthodox Church. For the remainder of his life he was a member of both the Council and the Senate. His service in the highest organs of the czarist government naturally gave him power in shaping Russia's domestic policies.

Pobedonostsev's reputation in Russian history rests largely upon his accomplishments as director general of the Holy Synod. For 25 years his influence on the religious and political life of Russia was enormous as a result of his official positions and his relations with the czars, their wives, the imperial family, and the court.

In 1881 Pobedonostsev advised Alexander III concerning the selection of his ministers, most of whom were named upon his recommendation. The Czar consented to Pobedonostsev's policy of the Russification of minority groups, particularly Jews and dissenters. As director general, Pobedonostsev attempted to restrict the number and the rights of other religious groups in Russia. Under his influence Alexander III opposed any limitation of his autocratic powers, tightened censorship, tried to suppress all opposition opinion, and persecuted religious nonconformists.

Pobedonostsev also tutored the future Nicholas II and was one of his most influential advisers until the Revolution of 1905. In his writing Pobedonostsev strongly attacked Western rationalism and liberalism. He died in St. Petersburg on March 23, 1907.

Further Reading

Pobedonostsev's *Reflections of a Russian Statesman* (1896; trans. 1898) constitutes a strong and earnest criticism of many of the views of liberals both in Russia and in Europe and helps to explain the reaction of the imperial government to all signs of public expression of liberal hopes. A reprint (1965) has a useful foreword by Murray Polner. The only biography in English is Robert F. Byrnes's solid work, *Pobedonostsev: His Life and Thought* (1968). See also the article on Pobedonostsev in Arthur E. Adams, ed., *Imperial Russia after 1861: Peaceful Modernization or Revolution?* (1965). □

Pocahontas protecting John Smith (bent over rock)

Pocahontas

Pocahontas (ca. 1595-1617) was the daughter of a Native American chief in Virginia at the time of its colonization by the British. Her marriage to an English settler brought 8 years of peace between the Indians and the British.

The real name of Pocahontas was Matoaka. As a child, she was called Pocahontas, meaning "playful one," and the name stuck. Her father was Powhatan, chief of a confederation of Algonquian tribes that bore his name.

In 1607 English colonists sent by the Virginia Company founded Jamestown. Pocahontas often played at the fort. In 1608, according to a story of debated authenticity, she saved the life of Capt. John Smith, who had been captured by Powhatan's warriors and was to be clubbed to death. The salvation of John Smith was the salvation of Jamestown colony.

Relations between the Native Americans and the colonists were not smooth in Virginia, however. In 1613, while Pocahontas was visiting the village of the Potomac Indians, Capt. Samuel Argall of the vessel *Treasurer* took her prisoner as security for Englishmen in Indian hands and for tools and supplies which the Indians had stolen. She was taken to

Jamestown as a hostage. There she was treated with courtesy by the governor, Sir Thomas Dale, who was touched by her gentility and intelligence. After instruction in the Christian religion, she was baptized and took the name Rebecca.

John Rolfe, a gentleman at Jamestown, fell in love with her and asked Dale for permission to marry her. Dale readily agreed in order to win the friendship of the Indians, although Pocahontas may have been married earlier to a chief named Kocoum. Powhatan also consented, and the marriage took place in Jamestown in June 1614 in the Anglican church. Both Native Americans and Englishmen apparently considered this a bond between them, and it brought 8 years of peaceful relations in Virginia.

In 1616 the Virginia Company wished Pocahontas to visit England, thinking that it would aid the company in securing investments from British financiers. Rolfe, Pocahontas, her brother-in-law Tomocomo, and several Indian girls sailed to England. Pocahontas was received as a princess, entertained by the bishop of London, and presented to King James I and Queen Anne. Early in 1617 Pocahontas and her party prepared to return to Virginia, but at Gravesend she developed a case of smallpox and died. She was buried in the chancel of Gravesend Church. Her only child, Thomas Rolfe, was educated in England, and he returned to Virginia to leave many descendants bearing the name Rolfe.

Further Reading

The best biography of Pocahontas is by Grace Steele Woodward, *Pocahontas* (1969). Other interesting works are John G. Fletcher, *John Smith—Also Pocahontas* (1928) and W. M. Murray, *Pocahontas and Pushmataha* (1931). Philip L. Barbour's *Pocahontas and Her World* (1970) is essentially a history of the early years of Virginia and written from the Indian point of view. ☐

Po Chü-i

Po Chü-i (772-846) was a Chinese poet best known for his ballads and satirical poems. He held the view that good poetry should be readily understood by the common people and exemplified it in poems noted for simple diction, natural style, and social content.

On Feb. 28, 772, Po Chü-i was born in Hsin-cheng, Honan, to a family of poets and minor officials. In his childhood he stayed with his mother and other members of the family while his father went south to take up prefectural positions in the Yangtze region. When military governors of the northern provinces rebelled against the government in 782, the family moved southward to Fu-li (northern Anhwei) and later to Chü-chou (western Chekiang) to be near Po's father, who held successive official appointments in these districts.

In his early youth Po Chü-i prepared himself for the civil service examination but was delayed in taking it by his father's death in 794. In 800 he went to Ch'ang-an, the capital, where he soon obtained the *chinshih* degree. Three years later, after having passed the Board of Civil Service examination, he was appointed collator at the Imperial Secretariat, to work with books and documents in the archives.

Civil Service Career

Po Chü-i made friends with the young literary set in the capital. Many of them, including Yüan Chen and Liu Yü-hsi, remained his lifelong poetic companions, and several rose to prominence as prime ministers. In 806, after passing the palace examination, he became magistrate of Chou-chih in the metropolitan area. In his official role as tax collector, he personally witnessed the sad plight of the people. Upon returning to the court the following year, he was appointed member of the Han-lin Academy (807), to draft imperial edicts, and junior reminder (808) in the State Chancellery, to advise the Emperor on his remissions. In 811 he was intendant in the Census and Revenue Bureau of the metropolitan area when his mother died.

Earlier (804) Po Chü-i had moved the members of his family to their ancestral site at Hsia-kuei near Ch'ang-an and had married (807) the daughter of the influential Yang family, by whom he had a daughter the next year. After his mother's death, he retired to Hsia-kuei for mourning. About the same time, he lost his daughter. His health deteriorated because of these afflictions, and he was often sick. It was not until 814 that he regained his health and went back to the capital, where he was given a position as junior counselor in the Eastern Palace, that is, to the crown prince.

Major Poetry

During these years in the capital, Po Chü-i wrote some of his most celebrated poems, such as the *Ballad of Everlasting Sorrow, Songs of the Land of Ch'in* (the Ch'ang-an district), and the *New Music Bureau Poems*. The last two groups of poems, totaling 60 pieces, are imitation folk songs in which he attacked militarism, the draft, heavy taxation, court extravagance, official abuses, and oppression. One of the poet's barbs was directed at the powerful eunuchs, who not only preyed upon the people but seized power in the government.

In 815 Po Chü-i himself fell victim to the eunuchs' political machinations, was banished from the capital, and was sent as a subprefect to Chiang-chou (modern Chiuchiang in Kiangsi). The job involving little official duty, he spent his time in visiting scenic spots and writing poems, including the famous *Ballad of the Lute*. While in Chiang-chou, he made the first collection of his poetry, which numbered some 800 pieces at that time. He also expounded his literary credo in a letter to Yüan Chen: "Literature should be written to serve one's own generation, and poems and songs to influence public affairs."

In 818 Po was appointed governor of Chung-chou in Szechwan, even farther away from the center of T'ang culture. While there, he compiled a group of poems, *Bamboo Sprig Songs*, describing local customs. In the winter of 820 he returned to the capital for a minor position in the Board of Punishments. The end of his political exile, however, brought no joy to the poet, who found himself a reluctant eyewitness to further political intrigues and corruptions.

Po Chü-i spent the happiest years of his official career in Hangchow and Soochow (Wuhsien), where he was governor respectively in 822-824 and 825-826. Unlike Chungchou, these were populous and beautiful cities. While in Hangchow, he built an embankment around the West Lake that was known henceforth as the Po Embankment. After returning to Ch'ang-an from these provincial posts, he held two of the highest government positions in his life, superintendent of the Imperial Secretariat (827) and vice president of the Board of Punishments (828). But by that time he was weary of officialdom and ready for retirement.

His Retirement

Earlier, in 825, during the interval between his two governorships, he had purchased a house in Loyang, which he made his home when he left Ch'ang-an in 829 to take up a sinecure appointment as the "guest of the crown prince." Except for a 2-year period (831-833) as mayor of metropolitan Honan (Loyang), Po had no active official duty and led a carefree, leisurely, and peaceful life, disturbed only by the death of his family members and friends. He took philosophically these losses as well as his lonely old age. He continued to write poems—a total of 3,500 by the time he made the final collection of his poetic works in 839. The last years of his life were uneventful. He died in September 846, at the advanced age of 74.

Po Chü-i's poetic fame was already widespread during his lifetime. He was not only one of the most productive of the T'ang poets, but also the most fortunate in that a large bulk of his writings has survived. They give a clear picture of the poet's life, his personality and temperament, his likes and dislikes. They also reveal his social and political views, the events of his time, and his relationships with friends— many of them influential scholar-officials who guided the destiny of the nation in the early 9th century. Several hundred of his poems are immensely popular and will remain a lasting monument to his achievement. By stressing the utilitarian and moral concept of literature in the Confucian tradition, he brought to Chinese poetry a new direction, a sense of moral integrity, and a serious concern for the social problems of the period.

Further Reading

The best-known English translator of Po Chü-i is Arthur Waley, who has done a large number of Po's poems. Waley's *Life and Times of Po Chü-i* (1949) is a critical study with new translations of 100 poems; his *Chinese Poems* (1948) is recommended for wider familiarity with Chinese poetry. See also Eugene Feifel, *Po Chü-i as a Censor* (1961), and Howard S. Levy, *Translations from Po Chü-i's Collected Works,* vol. 1: *The Old Style Poems* and vol. 2: *The Regulated Poems* (1971). ☐

Edgar Allan Poe

Unquestionably one of America's major writers, Edgar Allan Poe (1809-1849) was far ahead of his time in his vision of a special area of human experience—the "inner world" of dream, hallucination, and imagination. He wrote fiction, poetry, and criticism and was a magazine editor.

Edgar Allan Poe was best known to his own generation as an editor and critic; his poems and short stories commanded only a small audience. But to some extent in his poems, and to an impressive degree in his tales, he pioneered in opening up areas of human experience for artistic treatment at which his contemporaries only hinted. His vision asserts that reality for the human being is essentially subterranean, contradictory to surface reality, and profoundly irrational in character. Two generations later he was hailed by the symbolist movement as the prophet of the modern sensibility.

Poe was born in Boston on Jan. 19, 1809, the son of professional actors. By the time he was 3, Edgar, his older brother, and younger sister had lost their mother to consumption and their father through desertion. The children were split up, going to various families to live. Edgar went to the charitable Richmond, Virginia, home of John and Frances Allan, whose name Poe was to take later as his own middle name.

A New Family

The Allans were wealthy then and were to become more so later, and though they never adopted Poe, for many years it appeared that he was to be their heir. They treated him like an adopted son, saw to his education in private academies, and took him to England for a 5-year stay; and at least Mrs. Allan bestowed considerable affection upon him.

As Edgar entered adolescence, however, bad feelings developed between him and John Allan. Allan disapproved of his ward's literary inclinations, thought him surly and ungrateful, and gradually seems to have decided that Poe was not to be his heir after all. When, in 1826, Poe entered the newly opened University of Virginia, Allan's allowance was so meager that Poe turned to gambling to supplement his income. In 8 months he lost $2,000. Allan's refusal to help him led to total estrangement, and in March 1827 Poe stormed out on his own.

Poe managed to get to Boston, where he signed up for a 5-year enlistment in the U.S. Army. In 1827, as well, he had his *Tamerlane and Other Poems* published at his own expense, but the book failed to attract notice. By January 1829, serving under the name of Edgar A. Perry, Poe rose to the highest noncommissioned rank in the Army, sergeant major. He was reluctant to serve out the full enlistment, however, and he arranged to be discharged from the Army on the understanding that he would seek an appointment at West Point. He thought that such a move might cause a reconciliation with his guardian. That same year *Al Araaf, Tamerlane and Minor Poems* was published in Baltimore and received a highly favorable notice from the novelist and critic John Neal. Armed with these new credentials, Poe visited Allan in Richmond, but another violent quarrel forced him to leave in May 1830.

The West Point appointment came through the next month, but, since Poe no longer had any use for it, he did not last long as a cadet. Lacking Allan's permission to resign, Poe sought and received a dismissal for "gross neglect of duty" and "disobedience of orders." His guardian, long widowed, had taken a young wife who might well give him an heir, and Poe realized that his hopes of a legacy were without foundation.

Marriage and the Search for a Place

During his early years of exile Poe had lived in Baltimore for a while with his aunt Maria Clemm and her 7-year-old daughter, Virginia. He returned to his aunt's home in 1831, publishing *Poems by Edgar Allan Poe* and beginning to place short stories in magazines. In 1833 he received a prize for "MS. Found in a Bottle," and John Pendleton Kennedy got him a job on the *Southern Literary Messenger*. In 1836 Poe married his cousin Virginia—now 13 years old—and moved to Richmond with his bride and mother-in-law. Excessive drinking lost him his job in 1837, but he had produced prolifically for the journal. He had contributed his *Politian*, as well as 83 reviews, 6 poems, 4 essays, and 3 short stories. He had also quintupled the magazine's circulation. Rejection in the face of such accomplishment was extremely distressing to him, and his state of mind from

then on, as one biographer put it, "was never very far from panic."

The panic accelerated after 1837. Poe moved with Virginia and her mother to New York, where he did hack work and managed to publish *The Narrative of Arthur Gordon Pym* (1838). Then they moved to Philadelphia, where Poe served as coeditor of *Burton's Gentleman's Magazine.* In 2 years he boosted its circulation from 5,000 to 20,000 and contributed some of his best fiction to its pages, including "The Fall of the House of Usher." In 1840, furthermore, he published *Tales of the Grotesque and Arabesque.* But there was trouble at *Burton's,* and in 1841 Poe left for the literary editorship of *Graham's Magazine.*

It was becoming clear that 2 years was about as long as Poe could hold a job, and his stay at *Graham's* confirmed this principle. Though he contributed skillfully wrought fiction and unquestionably developed as a critic, his endless literary feuding, his alcoholism, and his inability to get along very well with people caused him to leave after 1842.

Illness and Crisis

The Murders in the Rue Morgue and *The Man That Was Used Up* emerged in 1843, and a Philadelphia newspaper offered a $100 prize for his "The Gold Bug," but Poe was now facing a kind of psychological adversity against which he was virtually helpless. His wife, who had been an absolutely crucial source of comfort and support to him, began showing signs of the consumption that would eventually kill her. When his burden became too great, he tried to relieve it with alcohol, which made him ill.

After great struggle Poe got a job on the *New York Mirror* in 1844. He lasted, characteristically, into 1845, switching then to the editorship of the *Broadway Journal.* Although he was now deep in public literary feuds, things seemed to be breaking in his favor. The 1844 publication of the poem "The Raven" finally brought him some fame, and in 1845 the publication of two volumes, *The Raven and Other Poems* and *Tales,* both containing some of his best work, did in fact move him into fashionable literary society. But his wife's health continued to deteriorate, and he was not earning enough money to support her and Clemm.

Poe's next job was with *Godey's Lady's Book,* but he was unable to sustain steady employment, and amid the din of plagiarism charges and libel suits, his fortunes sank to the point that he and his family almost starved in their Fordham cottage in the winter of 1846. Then, on Jan. 30, 1847, Virginia Poe died.

The wonder is not that Poe began totally to disintegrate but that he nevertheless continued to produce work of very high caliber. In 1848 he published the brilliantly ambitious *Eureka,* and he was even to make a final, heart-wrenching attempt at rehabilitation. He returned to Richmond in 1849, there to court a now-widowed friend of his youth, Mrs. Shelton. They were to be married, and Poe left for New York at the end of September to bring Clemm back for the wedding. On the way he stopped off in Baltimore. Nobody knows exactly what happened, and there is no real proof that he was picked up by a gang who used him to "repeat" votes, but he was found on October 3 in a stupor near a saloon that had been used as a polling place. He died in a hospital 4 days later.

World of His Work

It is not hard to see the connection between the nightmare of Poe's life and his work. Behind a screen of sometimes substantial, sometimes flimsy "reality," his fictional work resembles the dreams of a distressed individual who keeps coming back, night after night, to the same pattern of dream. At times he traces out the pattern lightly, at other times in a "thoughtful" mood, but often the tone is terror. He finds himself descending, into a cellar, a wine vault, a whirlpool, always falling. The women he meets either change form into someone else or are whisked away completely. And at last he drops off, into a pit or a river or a walled-up tomb.

Poe's critics interpret this pattern to represent the search of the individual for himself by going deep into himself and his ultimate arrival at the unplumbed mystery of his inner self. This search has come, of course, to characterize much of 20th-century art, and it is the distinguished accomplishment of Poe as an artist that his work looks forward with such startling precision to the work of the century that followed.

Further Reading

Arthur H. Quinn, *Edgar Allan Poe: A Critical Biography* (1941), is extremely reliable. Two very readable treatments are Hervey Allen, *Israfel: The Life and Times of Edgar Allan Poe* (1934), and William R. Bittner, *Poe: A Biography* (1962). A thorough study is Edward C. Wagenknecht, *Edgar Allan Poe: The Man behind the Legend* (1963). Two critical studies which supplement each other are Patrick F. Quinn, *The French Face of Edgar Allan Poe* (1957), which concentrates on the fiction, and Edward H. Davidson, *Poe: A Critical Study* (1957), which emphasizes the poetry. See also Killis Campbell, *The Mind of Poe* (1933); Haldeen Braddy, *Glorious Incense: The Fulfillment of Edgar Allan Poe* (1953); and Harry Levin, *The Power of Blackness* (1958). Perry Miller, *The Raven and the Whale: The War of Words and Wits in the Era of Poe and Melville* (1956), and Sidney P. Moss, *Poe's Literary Battles: The Critic in the Context of His Literary Milieu* (1963), discuss Poe in the context of his times. For a full list of Poe's works see Robert E. Spiller and others, eds., *Literary History of the United States,* vol. 3 (1948; 3d rev. ed. 1963). □

Jules Henri Poincaré

The French mathematician Jules Henri Poincaré (1854-1912) initiated modern combinatorial topology and made lasting contributions to mathematical analysis, celestial mechanics, and the philosophy of science.

Henri Poincaré was born at Nancy on April 29, 1854. His father was a physician. Henri attended elementary school and the lycée in Nancy and entered the École Polytechnique in Paris at the age of 18.

There he demonstrated his brilliance in mathematics and also his phenomenal memory. Although his eyesight was poor, he never took notes in class, and after reading a book he could recall the page on which any statement occurred.

Strangely enough, at this time Poincaré seems not to have fathomed his own mathematical power, for in 1875 he entered the School of Mines with the intention of becoming an engineer. But 3 years later he qualified as a mining engineer and earned his doctorate of mathematical sciences with a thesis based on a difficult problem in differential equations. On the strength of this and other papers, he was appointed professor of mathematical analysis at Caen in 1879. Two years later he obtained a position at the University of Paris, and in 1886 he was made a professor there.

Poincaré's scientific output was prodigious and amazingly comprehensive. The generality and originality of his methods enabled him to master and then break new ground in mathematical physics, celestial mechanics, and nearly every branch of pure mathematics. It was Poincaré's style to emphasize qualitative solutions rather than quantitative recipes. He published several papers on the behavior of solutions and on the properties of integral curves. In 1895 he published *Leçons sur le calcul des probabilités* (Lessons on the Calculus of Probabilities). He was led to the study of the behavior of divergent and convergent series through his work in celestial mechanics. This led to further investigations of quadratic forms, integral invariants, and double intervals of periodic orbits. He also was actively involved in work on electromagnetic theory.

In 1906 Poincaré published a more general work, *La Science et l'hypothèse* (Science and Hypothesis), propounding a relativistic philosophy. In philosophy he advocated a variety of pragmatism which he called "conventionalism." "One does not ask," he said, "whether a scientific theory is true, but only whether it is convenient." He thought that mathematical logic was barren, and when he heard that antinomies had crept into the logistic system of Bertrand Russell and Alfred North Whitehead he could barely conceal his glee. "Logistic is no longer barren," he wrote, "it engenders antinomies."

Poincaré was elected to the Academy of Sciences in 1887, and he became president of that body in 1906. Two years later he was elected to the literary section of the French Institute, in recognition of his popular works on the philosophy and methods of science, which were widely read in France and translated into six languages. He was appointed a member of the Académie Française in 1909 and elected a foreign member of the Royal Society in 1894. Poincaré died in Paris on July 17, 1912.

Further Reading

Poincaré's views on the philosophy of science are best gained from his own works, especially his *Science and Method*, translated by Francis Maitland (1915). The best biography of Poincaré in English is in Eric T. Bell, *Men of Mathematics* (1937). See also volume 2 of Ganesh Prasad, *Some Great Mathematicians of the Nineteenth Century: Their Lives and Their Works* (2 vols., 1933-1934), and Tobias Dantzig, *Henri Poincaré: Critic of Crisis* (1954).

Additional Sources

Folina, Janet, *Poincaré and the philosophy of mathematics,* New York: St. Martin's Press, 1992. □

Raymond Poincaré

The French statesman Raymond Poincaré (1860-1934) served as president of France during World War I and four times as its premier.

French politics from 1912 to 1929 was largely dominated by the figures of Raymond Poincaré and Georges Clemenceau. As premier, and then as president before World War I, Poincaré pursued a nationalistic policy that contributed toward world tension. During World War I he entrusted the premiership to Clemenceau. Returning to active politics in 1922, Poincaré, as premier, followed an intransigent policy toward Germany, occupying the Ruhr in order to ensure German payment of reparations, an action that contributed to economic collapse in Germany. He also dealt effectively with French financial crises in 1924 and 1926.

Education and Early Career

Poincaré was born at Bar-le-Duc in Lorraine on Aug. 20, 1860. The son of a meteorologist and civil servant, he was educated at the lycées of Bar-le-Duc and Louis le Grand in Paris, and he studied law at the Sorbonne. Poincaré then practiced law in Paris, contributed to political journals, and served in the Department of Agriculture.

In 1887 Poincaré was elected deputy for the Meuse. At that time Louis Madelin described him as "short, slender, rather pale, with crewcut hair, and his serious face framed by a young beard." Later observers were impressed by his unemotional and distant manner.

Poincaré became a member of the Budget Commissions of 1890-1891 and 1892, and he served during 1893 and 1894 in the Cabinets of Charles Dupuy, first as minister of education and then as minister of finance. Next he became minister of public instruction in the Ribot Cabinet. In 1895 he was chosen vice president of the Chamber of Deputies, and Poincaré retained this position until 1897. In 1899 President Émile Loubet asked him to form a Cabinet, but he was unsuccessful because he would not accept a Socialist minister in his coalition.

From this time until 1912, Poincaré refused to join any government except for a brief period between March and October 1906, when he was minister of finance in the Sarrien Cabinet. He emphasized his withdrawal from an active role by accepting a seat in the Senate. During this period Poincaré devoted himself to his law practice, and he became one of the wealthiest and most successful lawyers in France. In 1909 his literary efforts won him election to the French Academy.

Political Ideas

Poincaré's political ideas remained relatively constant throughout his career. He was conservative in his basic outlook, and as the balance of power in the legislature shifted to the left, he found himself and the moderates, whom he represented, moving to the right. He was fundamentally anticlerical, believing that the Church should remain in its own sphere and play no part in education or politics. He was a dedicated republican and a patriot of the Lorraine variety whose sentiments had been molded by the German seizure of most of Lorraine in 1870.

First Premiership

In the reaction after the crisis at Agadir, Morocco, in January 1912, Poincaré formed a "national ministry." He emphasized the need for a strong, authoritative government, and his program called for electoral reform at home and maintenance of France's alliances and friendships abroad. Poincaré expressed his desire for peace, but he also stressed military preparedness.

Concerned to maintain France's security and prestige, Poincaré supported Russia's policy during the First Balkan War, and later he again assured the Russians that they could depend upon France. Poincaré also obtained a reorganization and strengthening of the French navy. His government entered into a naval agreement with Great Britain that resulted in France's concentrating its fleet in the Mediterranean. Poincaré also reestablished friendly relations with Italy after a naval incident in January 1912. By the end of 1912 Poincaré was widely acknowledged as France's strongest statesman.

Poincaré's Presidency

In December 1912 Poincaré announced his intention to run for the presidency of the republic, although open candidacies were not customary. Poincaré's campaign marked the climax of the strong presidency agitation that had been growing for some time. He openly advocated a fuller use of the president's constitutional powers, and he doubtless expected to revitalize the weak office of the presidency. On Jan. 17, 1913, he was elected the ninth president of the French Republic by the National Assembly.

His strong nationalist beliefs led Poincaré to support the bill raising the term of military service from 2 to 3 years. He was, to a large extent, responsible for its passage, and he maintained it despite opposition, which continued to grow. This active role in policy formulation made him a party president, and it produced frequent attacks upon him by the left Radical-Socialist elements.

In foreign affairs Poincaré followed the program he had inaugurated as premier, supporting Théophile Delcassé as ambassador to Russia and attempting to preserve peace by ensuring that the Entente powers pursued a strong and united policy. He made state visits to England in June 1913 and to Russia in July 1914, and he was returning to France by way of the Scandinavian capitals when Austria delivered its ultimatum to Serbia on July 23, 1914. Hastening to Paris,

he urged Russia to delay mobilization, and he presided over the foreign-policy decisions of the Cabinet.

During the war Poincaré worked tirelessly to maintain morale. He urged Frenchmen to perform heroically and visited training camps, hospitals, and front lines. In November 1917 in a decision proving his statesmanship and self-sacrifice, Poincaré called upon his traditional political foe, Clemenceau, to form a Cabinet. During the peace negotiations, Poincaré found himself again in opposition to Clemenceau. Poincaré supported Marshal Ferdinand Foch in his campaign for a separate Rhineland, and he disputed Clemenceau's policy, urging a firm stand and heavy reparations. These attempts to influence policy were generally unsuccessful, and Poincaré completed his term of office in January 1920. He had been France's strongest president, but he had made no basic alteration in the office.

Second Premiership

Reelected as senator from the Meuse, Poincaré accepted the premiership in January 1922, and he retained this post, together with the Ministry of Foreign Affairs, until June 1, 1924. The chief problem at this time was reparations. Poincaré insisted that Germany fulfill its obligations. Unable to reach agreement on policy with the British in Interallied conferences held in London and Paris, Poincaré's government decided to act alone. When Germany defaulted on fuel deliveries in January 1923, French and Belgian troops occupied the Ruhr. The Germans adopted a policy of passive resistance for some months, and the German mark collapsed completely. The cost of occupation was undermining the French economy as well, and Poincaré agreed to an Anglo-American proposal to review the reparations issue. The result was the Dawes Plan, accepted in April 1924, which stabilized the mark, provided foreign loans for Germany, and reduced reparations payments.

The international exchange situation produced a financial crisis in France during the first quarter of 1924. Poincaré's adroit moves on the money market, and a 20 percent increase in indirect taxes in order to pay for the Ruhr occupation, saved the situation, but the taxes were unpopular. Attacks by the Radicals and Socialists won a substantial victory for the Cartel of the Left in the general elections of May 11, 1924, and when the new Chamber assembled, Poincaré resigned. During the next 2 years, though he retained his Senate seat, Poincaré was relatively inactive in politics.

Third Premiership

The economic policies of the Cartel proved unsatisfactory, and in the midst of a serious financial crisis, President Gaston Doumergue recalled Poincaré to head a National Union government. Public confidence was restored, and the franc immediately rose from 50 to 40 per American dollar. The legislature granted Poincaré decree powers to meet crises. He introduced new taxes, mostly indirect; he reduced government expenses; he created, through constitutional amendment, an inviolate fund to meet bond payments; and he increased interest rates. The result was a budgetary surplus and an exchange rate of 25 francs per dollar. The elections of April 1928 brought victory for the National Union, which had supported Poincaré, and, shortly after, he officially devalued the franc, establishing it at one-fifth its prewar value.

Fourth Premiership

The Radical-Socialists withdrew their support and obliged Poincaré to resign on Nov. 7, 1928, but he formed a new ministry on November 12 and retained his post until July 1929, when ill health forced him to retire. He refused a fifth offer of the premiership in 1930. Meanwhile, he had published his memoirs in 10 volumes, entitled *Au service de la France* (*In the Service of France*), describing the events of 1911-1920 and his role in them. Poincaré died in Paris on Oct. 15, 1934.

Further Reading

Poincaré's memoirs have been translated as *The Memoirs of Raymond Poincaré* (4 vols., 1926-1930). The chief biographical work in English is Sisley Huddleston, *Poincaré: A Biographical Portrait* (1924), a postwar study that is necessarily incomplete. Poincaré's role as president is well analyzed by Gordon Wright, *Raymond Poincaré and the French Presidency* (1942).

Additional Sources

Poincaré, Raymond, *The memoirs of Raymond Poincaré,* New York: AMS Press, 1975. □

Born in 1924 in Miami, Florida, but raised in the Bahamas, Poitier experienced severe poverty as a boy. His father, a tomato farmer, "was the poorest man in the village," the actor recalled in an interview with Frank Spotnitz for *American Film.* "My father was never a man of self-pity," he continued, adding that the elder Poitier "had a wonderful sense of himself. Every time I took a part, from the first part, from the first day, I always said to myself, 'This must reflect well on his name.'" The family moved from the tiny village of Cat Island to Nassau, the Bahamian capital, when Poitier was 11 years old, and it was there that he first experienced the magic of cinema.

After watching rapt as a western drama transpired on the screen, Poitier recollected gleefully to Chris Dafoe of the *Los Angeles Times,* he ran to the back of the theater to watch the cowboys and their horses come out. After watching the feature a second time, he again went out to wait for the figures from the screen to emerge. "And when I told my friends what had happened, they laughed and they laughed and they said to me, 'Everything you saw was on film.' And they explained to me what film was. And I said, 'Go on.'"

Thrown Out of First Audition

Poitier made his way to New York at age 16, serving for a short time in the Army. He has often told the story of his earliest foray into acting, elaborating on different strands of the tale from one recitation to the next. He was a teenager, working as a dishwasher in a New York restaurant. "I didn't study in high school," he told *American Film's* Spotnitz. "I never got that far. I had no intentions of becoming an actor."

Sidney Poitier

Actor Sidney Poitier's (born 1924) presence in film during the 1950s and 1960s opened up the possibility for bigger and better roles for black performers.

At a 1992 banquet sponsored by the august American Film Institute (AFI), a bevy of actors, filmmakers, and others gathered to pay tribute to Sidney Poitier. Superstar Denzel Washington called the veteran actor and director "a source of pride for many African Americans," the *Los Angeles Times* reported, while acting luminary James Earl Jones ventured that his colleague had "played a great role in the life of our country." Poitier himself was typically humble in the face of such praise, but he has acknowledged that his presence on film screens in the 1950s and 1960s did much to open up larger and more nuanced roles for black performers. "I was selected almost by history itself," he averred to Susan Ellicott of the London *Times.*

After gracing dozens of films with his dignified, passionately intelligent presence, Poitier began to focus increasingly on directing; a constant in his life, however, has been his work on behalf of charitable causes. And he has continued to voice the need for film projects that, as he expressed it to *Los Angeles Times* writer Charles Champlin, "have a commonality with the universal human condition."

Seeing an ad for actors in the *Amsterdam News,* a Harlem-based newspaper, he went to an audition at the American Negro Theater. "I walked in and there was a man there—big strapping guy. He gave me a script."

The man was Frederick O'Neal, a cofounder of the theater; impatient with young Poitier's Caribbean accent and shaky reading skills, O'Neal lost his temper: "He came up on the stage, furious, and grabbed me by the scruff of my pants and my collar and marched me toward the door," the actor remembered to *Los Angeles Times* writer Champlin. "Just before he threw me out he said, 'Stop wasting people's time! Why don't you get yourself a job as a dishwasher.'" Stunned that O'Neal could perceive his lowly status, Poitier knew he had to prove his antagonist wrong. "I have, and had, a terrible fierce pride," Poitier told the audience at the American Film Institute fête, as reported by *Daily Variety.* "I determined right then I was going to be an actor."

Poitier continued in his dishwashing job; in his spare time he listened assiduously to radio broadcasts, he noted to Champlin, "trying to lighten the broad A that characterizes West Indian speech patterns." He had some help in one aspect of his informal education, however: *Daily Variety* quoted his speech at the AFI banquet, in which he thanked "an elderly Jewish waiter in New York who took the time to teach a young black dishwasher how to read, persisting over many months." Ultimately, Poitier returned to the American Negro Theater, persuading its directors to hire him as a janitor in exchange for acting lessons.

Poitier understudied for actor-singer Harry Belafonte in a play called *Days of Our Youth,* and an appearance one night led to a small role in a production of the Greek comedy *Lysistrata.* Poitier, uncontrollably nervous on the latter play's opening night, delivered the wrong lines and ran off the stage; yet his brief appearance so delighted critics, most of whom otherwise hated the production, that he ended up getting more work. "I set out after that to dimensionalize my understanding of my craft," he told Champlin.

Poitier made his film debut in the 1950 feature *No Way Out,* portraying a doctor tormented by the racist brother of a man whose life he could not save. Director Joseph Mankiewicz had identified Poitier's potential, and the film bore out the filmmaker's instincts. Poitier worked steadily throughout the 1950s, notably in the South African tale *Cry, the Beloved Country,* the classroom drama *The Blackboard Jungle,* and the taut *The Defiant Ones,* in which Poitier and Tony Curtis played prison escapees manacled together; their mutual struggle helps them look past racism and learn to respect each other. Poitier also appeared in the film version of George Gershwin's modern opera *Porgy and Bess.*

First Black Actor to Win Academy Award

It was in the 1960s, however—with the civil rights movement spearheaded by Dr. Martin Luther King, Jr., and others gathering momentum—that Poitier began to make his biggest mark on American popular culture. After appearing in the film adaptation of Lorraine Hansberry's play *A Raisin in the Sun,* in a role he'd developed on the stage, he took the part of an American serviceman in Germany in the 1963 production *Lilies of the Field.* This role earned him a best actor statuette at the Academy Awards, making him the first black actor to earn this honor.

"Most of my career unfolded in the 1960s, which was one of the periods in American history with certain attitudes toward minorities that stayed in vogue," Poitier reflected to Ellicott of the London *Times.* "I didn't understand the elements swirling around. I was a young actor with some talent, an enormous curiosity, a certain kind of appeal. You wrap all that together and you have a potent mix."

The mix was more potent than might have been anticipated, in fact; by 1967 Poitier was helping to break down filmic barriers that hitherto had seemed impenetrable. In *To Sir, With Love* Poitier played a charismatic schoolteacher, while *In the Heat of the Night* saw him portray Virgil Tibbs, a black detective from the North who helps solve a murder in a sleepy southern town and wins the grudging respect of the racist police chief there. Responding to the derisive labels flung at him, Poitier's character glowers, "They call me *Mister* Tibbs." The film's volatile mixture of suspense and racial politics eventually spawned two sequels starring Poitier and a television series (Poitier did not appear in the small screen version).

Even more stunning, Poitier wooed a white woman in the comedy *Guess Who's Coming to Dinner;* his fiancée's parents were played by screen legends Spencer Tracy and Katherine Hepburn. The film was considered a watershed because it was Hollywood's first interracial love story that did not end tragically. Poitier's compelling presence—articulate, compassionate, soft-spoken, yet demanding respect from even the most hostile—helped make this possible. Reflecting on the anti-racist agenda of filmmakers during this period, Poitier remarked to Ellicott, "I suited their need. I was clearly intelligent. I was a pretty good actor. I believed in brotherhood, in a free society. I hated racism, segregation. And I was a symbol against those things."

Key Activist for Civil Rights

Of course, Poitier was more than a symbol. At the AFI banquet, reported David J. Fox in the *Los Angeles Times,* James Earl Jones praised his friend's work on behalf of the civil right struggle, declaring, "He marched on Montgomery [Alabama] and Memphis [Tennessee] with Dr. Martin Luther King, Jr., who said of Sidney: 'He's a man who never lost his concern for the least of God's children.'" Indeed, Rosa Parks, who in 1955 touched off a crucial battle for desegregation simply by refusing to sit in the "negro" section of a Montgomery bus, attended the tribute and lauded Poitier as "a great actor and role model."

In 1972 Poitier took a co-starring role with Belafonte in the revisionist western *Buck and the Preacher* for Columbia Pictures. After a falling out with the director of the picture, Poitier took over; though he and Belafonte urged Columbia to hire another director, a studio representative saw footage Poitier had shot and encouraged him to finish the film himself. "And that's how I became a director," he told *Los Angeles Times* contributor Champlin.

Poitier is best known for helming comedic features co-starring his friend comedian Bill Cosby; in addition to the trilogy of caper comedies of the 1970s—*Uptown Saturday Night, Let's Do It Again,* and *A Piece of the Action*—they collaborated on the ill-fated 1990 fantasy-comedy *Ghost Dad,* which was poorly received by both critics and moviegoers. Poitier also directed the hit 1980 comedy *Stir Crazy,* which starred Richard Pryor and Gene Wilder, as well as several other features.

Poitier took only a handful of film roles in the 1980s, but in 1991 he played Supreme Court justice Thurgood Marshall in the television film *Separate but Equal.* James Earl Jones described the performance as "a landmark actor portraying a landmark figure, in one of the landmark moments of our history." And in 1992 he returned to the big screen for the espionage comedy-drama *Sneakers,* which co-starred Robert Redford, River Phoenix, and Dan Aykroyd. "It was a wonderful, breezy opportunity to play nothing heavy," he noted to Bary Koltnow of the *Orange County Register.* "It was simple, and I didn't have to carry the weight. I haven't done that in a while, and it was refreshing."

That year also saw the gala AFI tribute to Poitier, during which the actor welcomed young filmmakers into the fold and enjoined them to "be true to yourselves and be useful to the journey," reported *Daily Variety.* "I fully expected to be wise by now," Poitier noted in his speech, "but I've come to this place in my life armed only with the knowledge of how little I know. I enter my golden years with nothing profound to say and no advice to leave, but I thank you for paying me this great honor while I still have hair, and my stomach still has not obscured my view of my shoetops."

Poitier observed to Champlin that during this "golden age" the demands of art had taken a back seat to domestic concerns to a large degree. "It's very important, but it's not the nerve center," he insisted. "There is the family, and there is music and there is literature" as well as political issues. Poitier noted that he and his wife, actress Joanna Shimkus, travel a great deal since they reside in California and have children in New York, and, as the actor put it, "I live in the world."

Poitier returned to the small screen for 1995's western drama *Children of the Dust.* As a presence, reported Chris Dafoe of the *Los Angeles Times,* "it's apparent that he's viewed with respect, even awe, by virtually everyone on the set." Costar Michael Moriarty observed that Poitier lived up to his legendary status: "You see a face that you've grown up with and admired, someone who was an icon of America, a symbol of strength and persistence and grace. And then you find out that in the everyday, workaday work of doing movies, he is everything he symbolizes on screen."

Poitier continued to star in television movies with 1996's *To Sir With Love II* (directed by Peter Bogdanovich) and the 1997 Showtime docudrama *Mandela and de Klerk.* The latter tells the story of Nelson Mandela's last years in prison to his election as leader of South Africa. Both received mixed reviews.

For Poitier, the challenge of doing meaningful work involves transcending the racial and social barriers he helped tumble with his early film appearances. He has insisted that large budgets are not necessary to make a mark and that violence too often seems the only way to resolve conflicts on the screen. "We suffer pain, we hang tight to hope, we nurture expectations, we are plagued occasionally by fears, we are haunted by defeats and unrealized hopes," he said of humans in general in his interview with Champlin, adding that "when you make drama of that condition, it's almost as if words are not necessary. It has its own language—spoken everywhere, understood everywhere."

Further Reading

American Film, September 1991, pp. 18-21, 49.
Daily Variety, March 16, 1992, p. 18.
Los Angeles Times, March 8, 1992 (Calendar), p. 8; March 14, 1992, pp. F1, F4; February 26, 1995 (Television Times), pp. 5-6.
New York Times, April 6, 1996, p. A20; February 15, 1997, p. A15.
Orange County Register, September 11, 1992, p. P6.
Times (London), November 8, 1992. □

John Charles Polanyi

John Charles Polanyi (born 1929) was a Canadian scientist whose work with chemical reactions led to the construction of a "chemical laser" and to a share of the 1986 Nobel Prize in Chemistry.

John Polanyi was descended from a gifted Hungarian family. His grandfather, Mihaly Pollacsek, was a successful railway builder, and his grandmother was active in the intellectual life of Budapest. From a line of assimilated Jews, Mihaly gave the family its Hungarian name, Polanyi. Among their remarkable children, Laura was an intellectual whose ideas of "rural sociology" influenced Tito. One son, Adolph, became an engineer and moved to Brazil. Another, Karl (1886-1964), was one of the century's influential critics of market capitalism. John's father, Michael, was an accomplished chemist and philosopher. When Hitler came to power, Michael moved his family from Berlin, where John was born (January 23, 1929), to England. He joined the faculty of Manchester University, where as a professor of chemistry he did pioneering work on the mechanisms of elemental reactions. He spent his later years writing books of philosophy.

During World War II Polanyi was sent to safety in Toronto, along with other children who were "adopted" by faculty of the University of Toronto. He entered Manchester University in 1946 and received his Ph.D. in chemistry in 1952 on the basis of his work measuring the strengths of chemical bonds in compounds that have been subjected to very high temperatures. That same year he accepted a postdoctoral fellowship at the National Research Council of Canada (NRC) in Ottawa, where he worked with E.W.R. Steacie and spent a few months in the laboratory of future

Nobel laureate Gerhard Herzberg. Polanyi had already directed his work to the study of the motions of newly-born reaction products and to the telltale imprints of the forces that created them. After two years at Princeton University, he returned to Canada in 1956 as a lecturer in chemistry at the University of Toronto, where he served as a university professor after 1974.

In 1958 Polanyi and his graduate student assistant, Kenneth Cashion, published their first findings on infrared chemiluminescence (the emission of light by an atom or molecule that is in an excited state). By introducing newly-formed atomic hydrogen into a stream of chlorine gas at low temperatures, they found that instead of losing their energy in collisions, the newly-formed hydrogen chloride molecules discharged it in a cascade of infrared photons. In one of those coincidences of discovery that mark the history of science, Arthur Schawlow (a graduate of the University of Toronto) and Charles H. Townes almost concurrently developed the principle of the laser, for which they shared a Nobel Prize in 1964. Polanyi was quick to realize that his findings could have important practical implications for the construction of a powerful "chemical laser." In 1964, J.V.V. Kasper and G.C. Pimentel were able to construct such a laser based on chemical reactions. Since then these "vibrational" lasers have made enormous contributions to science, medicine, and industry. Beyond this considerable practical benefit, Polanyi's discoveries provided a new way of investigating the very nature of chemical reactions themselves.

Polanyi's contributions to science were recognized on a global scale in 1986 when he shared the Nobel Prize in Chemistry with Dudley Herschenbach and Yuan T. Lee for developing "a new field of research in chemistry . . . in which the extremely weak infrared emission from a newly-formed molecule is measured." His later work focused on the use of spectroscopy (the science that deals with the analysis of the light spectrum) to gain an insight into what he called the "molecular dance" in chemical reactions, the process by which chemicals change partners.

Polanyi was an articulate and urbane man whose interest and influence ranged far beyond his contributions to chemical science. He was a vocal critic of short-sighted government science policies that look skeptically on the value of "pure" research because it may not have immediate practical or economic benefit. His own work is a testament to the value of fundamental research, not only in the practical development of the laser but in its contribution to a deeper human understanding of nature. He asked potential sponsors if they could have foreseen that his obscure work on "infrared luminescence" would lead to the development of lasers.

Polanyi was active in the peace and disarmament movements as founding chair of the Canadian Pugwash Group and as a speaker and prolific author. In 1996 he forcefully argued that war-torn Bosnia would only have a future if western peace keepers remained. He also spoke widely on the nature of science and its relation to creativity, art, and as a force for positive change in society. In a 1994 speech at University of California at Berkeley, he emphasized the responsibility scientists have to forging peace and solving world problems: "Science is an enterprise that can only flourish if it puts the truth ahead of nationality, ethnicity, class and color." He received numerous honors in addition to the Nobel Prize, including Canada's highest civilian honor, Companion of the Order of Canada (1979). He was co-winner of the Wolf Prize in 1982, received the Izaak Walton Killam Memorial Prize (1988), the Royal Medal of the Royal Society of London (1989), the Bakerian Prize (1994) and more than two dozen honorary doctorates from universities in six countries. In the 1990s Polanyi, still a professor of physical, polymers and materials chemistry at University of Toronto, continued his research on the photochemistry of absorbed molecules.

Further Reading

There is no book on John Polanyi, though Tyler Wasson, ed., *Nobel Prize Winners* (1987) and Laylin K. James, ed., *Nobel Laureates in Chemistry 1901-1992* (1993) contain good information on the scientific discoveries and can be used to trace other developments of the laser. *Science* (November 7, 1986), *New Scientist* (October 23, 1986), and *Scientific American* (December 1986) describe the scientific discoveries. *Maclean's* (October 27, 1986) and *Saturday Night* (February 1987) also contain information on Polanyi. Peter Drucker's *Adventures of a Bystander* deals with the Polanyi family. Polanyi himself published over 180 papers in scientific journals and produced a film, "Concepts in Reaction Dynamics" (1970). Internet sources for information about Polanyi include the University of Toronto chemistry department Web site (www.chem.utoronto.ca), the GSC Society Web site (www.science.ca/css/gcs/scientists/Polanyi/polanyi.html); the Web site for the "Nobels for the Future" conference in Milan, 1993 (www.smau.it/nobel/nobel94/homes94.titm), and the Berkeley chemistry department Web site, (www.cchem.berkeley.edu/Publications/Newsletter/Volume2/Polanyi_Story.html.) ☐

Further Reading

No complete biography or bibliography of Polanyi's work has been published. An analysis of Polanyi's economics is in the introduction to George Dalton, ed., *Primitive, Archaic and Modern Economies: Essays of Karl Polanyi* (1968). ☐

Karl Polanyi

Karl Polanyi (1886-1964) was a Hungarian economic historian. His view of laissez-faire capitalism as a fleeting episode in history and of a new world economy as having evolved from it led to better understanding of nonmarket economies.

Born in Vienna on Oct. 25, 1886, Karl Polanyi was the son of a prosperous entrepreneur. The family fortune suffered reverses, however, and while attending the University of Budapest, he had to serve as a tutor to support his family. His problems were intensified by radical political activities which led to his banishment. He completed his education and received his degree in law at Kolozsvár in July 1909 and was called to the bar in 1912.

Polanyi was general secretary of the Radical Citizens party of Hungary for a short time and served in the army during World War I. The close of the war found him gravely ill, and he was taken to Vienna to convalesce. There he met and, in 1923, married Ilona Duczynska. From 1924 to 1933 he wrote on world affairs for two periodicals. With the rise of fascism, Polanyi emigrated to England. He lectured and conducted tutorial classes for the Workers Educational Association and the extramural programs of Oxford University and the University of London (1937-1940). He also made tours in the United States, lecturing on international affairs. He was resident scholar at Bennington College, Vt. (1940-1943), and during this period wrote *The Great Transformation* (1944).

Polanyi was a visiting professor at Columbia University (1947-1958). Even after his retirement, his productive work continued. Out of the Interdisciplinary Project on Economic Aspects of Institutional Growth, which was the joint responsibility of Polanyi and Conrad M. Arensberg, came *Trade and Market in the Early Empires,* a book that greatly influenced the course of economic anthropology as well as economic history. Polanyi founded the journal *Co-Existence* as a means of stimulating objective and scientific discussion of the problems of peaceful coexistence. The first issue was published shortly after his death on April 23, 1964.

Perhaps the central motif of Polanyi's thought is that although 19th-century laissez-faire capitalism was a brief and unique episode in man's history, orthodox economics proceeds upon the assumption that the relation between the economy and society that prevailed in that period still prevails. Existing categories and modes of analysis being inappropriate, he set out to develop new and broader ones. His work along these lines has been of lasting value, particularly to the understanding of nonmarket economies.

Michael Polanyi

Michael Polanyi (1891-1976), a medical doctor, physical chemist, social thinker, and philosopher, made his most important contribution in the area of humanizing scientific inquiry. He proposed a new theory of knowledge based on an appreciation of the role of the individual and the individual's and society's values in the seeking and finding of truth.

Michael Polanyi was born on March 11, 1891, in Budapest, Hungary, the fifth child of Michael Pollacsek and Cecilia Wohl. His family life was marked by a rich and stimulating intellectual world that combined theoretical and practical concerns and artistic, literary, and social issues. His father was a civil engineer, and his mother was the center of a circle of poets, painters, and scholars. His two brothers and two sisters were all in their own ways distinguished. In his lifetime Michael Polanyi had four careers—medical doctor, physical chemist, social thinker, and philosopher. Leaving medicine early for the attraction of scientific research, he achieved international recognition in his other fields. His talent and breadth of knowledge made him a polymath and prepared him for the philosophical creativity that crowned his life with a vision and proposal for a new theory of knowledge—a theory intended to save advanced scientific culture from its own self-destruction by its dehumanized notion of objective detachment.

From the time of his entrance to the University of Budapest in 1908 until his death on February 22, 1976, Polanyi's life was devoted to the pursuit of scientific knowledge and to its meaning for the life of humanity. In the first part of his professional life, the advancement of scientific knowledge was his livelihood and the understanding of the implications of science for society was his avocation. In the later part of his life, the understanding of science's intellectual impact on society became his profession for the purpose of maintaining the basis of creative scientific research and for the liberation of humanity from the tyrannies based on scientism.

At the University of Budapest he was a founder in 1908 of the Galilei Circle, a progressive-minded student society devoted to discussions of science, politics, and religion. Barely 19 years old, he published his first scientific paper in 1910 and graduated as a Doctor of Medicine in 1913. His scientific interests led him to further study in chemistry at the Technische Hochschule, Karlsruhe, Germany. During this time he published several papers on the second law of thermodynamics, but the outbreak of World War I involved him as a medical officer and his scientific research was curbed until he contracted diptheria. During his convalescence he wrote a Ph.D. thesis on the adsorption of gases by solids, which not only earned him his doctorate in 1917 but also the attention of Einstein and of Fritz Haber, head of the Kaiser Wilhelm Institute of Physical Chemistry in Berlin. In 1920 he was appointed a member of the Kaiser Wilhelm Institute for Fiber Chemistry, where he developed new methods of X-ray analysis pertinent to fibrous structures, metals, and crystals. His success led to his appointment in 1923 to the Kaiser Wilhelm Institute for Physical Chemistry, where he made contributions not only in crystallography but also in reaction kinetics.

Never a one sided person, Polanyi maintained his interest in social and intellectual issues and in 1928 formed a study group on Soviet affairs with Leo Szilard, Eugene Wigner, and John Von Neumann (all became distinguished scientists). In 1933, in protest against Hitler's dismissal of Jewish professors, he resigned his position at the Kaiser Wilhelm Institute. Within a few months he was invited to take the chair of physical chemistry at the University of Manchester in England, and he moved there with his wife and two sons that autumn. He had married Magda Kemeny in 1921, herself an able chemist and author of a dictionary on textile chemistry. Their two sons, George and John, became respectively an economist and a physical chemist.

During the years in Manchester he continued to be productive in research in chemical reaction rates and in transition state theory, but Polanyi's inherent concern for the relations of science and society led him into basic questions about scientific reality and the importance of human freedom. He believed from his experience in science that there was a necessary connection between the premises of a free society and the discovery of scientific truths. Around him, in the Soviet Union and in Nazi Germany, and even among some leaders in Great Britain, Polanyi saw science changing toward control by the state and losing its creative independence and search for truth.

In 1938 he joined with J. R. Baker and others in forming the Society for the Freedom of Science. Between 1935 and 1946 he visited the Soviet Union and published critiques of planned economy, did a film on economics and unemployment, and advocated reform of the patent law. These political and economic concerns were about the way a dehumanized understanding of science was supporting totalitarianism and centralized government control of science in democratic societies. Everywhere Polanyi saw a mistaken view of science as impersonal and strict detachment denying the importance of personal and shared values. In 1946 he published *Science, Faith and Society,* which set forth a new philosophy to refute scientific objectivism and to restore belief in commitment to the independence of thought guided by the principles of liberty. This paramount problem and Polanyi's grasp of it led his university in 1948 to offer him a chair in social thought in exchange for his chair in physical chemistry.

In 1951 and 1952 Polanyi gave the Gifford Lectures that became his magnum opus, *Personal Knowledge: Towards a Post-Critical Philosophy* (1958). In a comprehen-

sive treatment of human knowing he proposed overturning the last three centuries' habit of thinking that our most genuine knowledge is found by a method that separates the observer from the subject of study and proceeds by neutrally collecting data and drawing conclusions from it. Instead, Polanyi showed from the practice of science that discovery of scientific reality is guided by a passionate dedication nurtured by a conscientious community of inquirers. He upheld objective knowledge as ''personal knowledge'' because it involved human participation in strategic and significant ways. Polanyi's view meant that the most exact facts could not be separated from the values of the knower and the traditions that guided them. The foundations of a free society that saw the truth of reality as independent of people yet found by individuals seeking the truth, stating their findings, and establishing agreement by open discussion are fundamental to the pursuit of science and knowledge generally. Many modern ideologies had produced totalitarianism and nihilism by a belief in naked truth separated from moral convictions that called for respect for persons and ideals.

Polanyi's proposal gained international attention, and he lectured at many universities throughout the world. His theory meant that the truths of science, religion, and art shared a common ground. In 1958 he became senior research fellow at Merton College, Oxford University. Despite the wide recognition he attained in the intellectual world, academic philosophers sometimes ignored Polanyi as too comprehensive and not specialized enough. Polanyi refined his view into a theory called ''tacit knowing'' that showed more specifically the personal component with its faith-like structure and its decisive role in the nature of all knowing. In the United States and Great Britain societies pursuing Polanyi's thought have developed on a multi-field basis.

Further Reading

Besides the books mentioned in the article, other major works of Michael Polanyi are: *The Logic of Liberty* (1951), *The Study of Man* (1959), *The Tacit Dimension* (1966), and, with Harry Prosch, *Meaning* (1975). Works about Polanyi are: Richard Gelwick, *The Way of Discovery: An Introduction to the Thought of Michael Polanyi;* Paul Ignotus et. al, *The Logic of Personal Knowledge;* Thomas A. Langford and William Poteat, editors, *Intellect and Hope* (1968), and Harry Prosch, ''Michael Polanyi,'' *The International Encyclopedia of the Special Sciences,* vol. 18, David L. Sills, editor (1979). □

Angelo Poliziano

The Italian poet Angelo Poliziano (1454-1494), or Politian, wrote works in both Latin and Italian. Although he considered himself a humanist, he advocated free artistic creation, unencumbered by reliance on the great classical writers of antiquity.

ngelo Poliziano was born Angelo Ambrogini on July 14, 1454, at Montepulciano, Tuscany, the son of a lawyer. When he was 10, his father was murdered, and the boy was sent to live with relatives in Florence, at the Studium of which he was educated by humanists. Poliziano's dedication to Lorenzo de' Medici of a partial translation of the *Iliad* marked the beginning of a lifelong friendship with the Medici ruler, and for some time he headed Lorenzo's chancellery and was tutor to his two sons. When he lost the latter position in 1479, Poliziano abruptly left the Medici villa at Cafaggiolo in May, and after a short stay at the Medici villa in Fiesole he moved to Mantua and the patronage of Cardinal Gonzaga. The following year, however, having made his peace with Lorenzo, he returned to Florence and at the Studium obtained the chair of Greek and Latin eloquence. In 1477 Poliziano became prior of S. Paolo, and in 1486 he was named canon of the Cathedral, S. Maria del Fiore. He carried out several political missions for Lorenzo and, with Giovanni Pico della Mirandola, scouted north Italian cities for books and manuscripts for the Medici Library in 1491. The later years of Poliziano's life were spent between Fiesole, where Lorenzo had given him a villa, and Florence, where he died on Sept. 28/29, 1494.

Poliziano was a prolific writer of epigrams, both in Greek and Latin, and his partial translation of the *Iliad* (books 2-5) gained him the patronage of the Medici. His Latin odes and elegies revealed a true lyrical talent. His most important Latin writings, however, include the *Praelectiones* (or *Silvae*), which are introductions to classical authors treated in his courses at the Studium. The most important of them, *Nutricia* (1491), is an attempt at a history of poetry from the days of Orpheus to Poliziano's own time. In 1489 Poliziano published the *Centuria prima miscellaneorum,* consisting of textual criticism and new interpretations of doubtful passages in the classics.

Of greater interest and importance for the history of Italian literature are Poliziano's writings in the vernacular. His *Stanze per la giostra* were begun in 1475 in honor of Lorenzo's brother Giuliano. Written in ottava rima, the Stanze demonstrate Poliziano's eclectic approach to poetry, combining reminiscences of classical as well as vernacular poetry with a refined sense of style. Poliziano chose the Orpheus myth as the theme for his only drama in the vernacular and the first in Italian literature, *La favola di Orfeo.* According to its author, the play was written in 2 days in June 1480 for a celebration at the Gonzaga court in Mantua. Though the play's technique is still close to the *sacra rappresentazione,* the myth had lost its medieval Christian connotations and is transposed into the world of the pastoral.

Poliziano's poetry preferentially employed such popular poetic forms as the one-stanza rispetto and the ballata and avoided the more complex features of sonnet, sestina, and canzone. The subject of his poetry was the uncomplicated love of this world, and he often directly varied Petrarchan themes in an *imitazione al contrario.* Poliziano's activities as a translator of Greek and Roman literature were remarkable (Callimachus, Epictetus, Galen, Hippocrates, and Moschus), and his editorial attempts—such as the *Pandects*—remain respectable examples of early textual criticism.

Further Reading

Major studies of Poliziano are in Italian. A good discussion is in E. F. Jacob, ed., *Italian Renaissance Studies* (1960), and another is in Cecilia M. Ady, *Lorenzo dei Medici and Renaissance Italy* (1962). Other useful works recommended for general historical background are Jacob Burckhardt, *The Civilization of the Renaissance in Italy* (3d rev. ed., trans. 1950); Paul Oskar Kristeller, *Studies in Renaissance Thought and Letters* (1956); and André Chastel, *The Age of Humanism: Europe, 1480-1530* (trans. 1963). □

James Knox Polk

The administration of James Knox Polk (1795-1849), eleventh president of the United States, saw America at war with Mexico. As a consequence, Polk added more territory to the United States than had any other president except Thomas Jefferson.

ames K. Polk was born on Nov. 2, 1795, in Mecklenburg County, N.C. As a child, he moved to an area in Tennessee settled by his grandfather, a land speculator. After graduation from the University of North Carolina in 1818, he studied law under Congressman Felix Grundy and was admitted to the bar in 1820. Elected to the legislature in 1822, Polk became known as an opponent of the state's banks and land speculators. He supported Andrew Jackson, who was an old friend of his father, for the presidency in the election of 1824.

As a Jacksonian, Polk was elected to the U.S. House of Representatives in 1825, becoming a leader of his party. He advocated a strict states'-rights position, emphasizing the desirability of an economical government. As chairman of the powerful House Ways and Means Committee from 1833 to 1835, he supported Jackson's banking policies, including removal of the government's deposits from the Bank of the United States. As a reward for his support, Polk was elected Speaker of the House of Representatives in 1835 and served until 1839. He vastly increased the powers of the Speaker's office by assuming the burden of guiding administrative measures through Congress. He was governor of Tennessee from 1839 until 1841; he was defeated for reelection in 1841 and again in 1843.

Polk received the Democratic nomination for president in 1844; he was the compromise candidate among several contenders. The first "dark horse," he defeated the better-known Whig nominee, Henry Clay, in an extremely close election. During the campaign Polk skillfully reconciled the various Democratic factions. To attract John C. Calhoun's partisans, Polk adopted an expressionistic platform, emphasizing the incorporation of all the Oregon Territory and the annexation of Texas. Clay's last-minute endorsement of Texas annexation cost him the election, as it forced 15,000 antislavery Whigs to defect to the Liberty party.

The Presidency

Polk's cabinet, one of the most able of the antebellum period, included Secretary of State James Buchanan, Secretary of the Treasury Robert J. Walker, Secretary of the Navy George Bancroft, and Secretary of War William L. Marcy. They represented most factions of the Democratic party. Their renunciations of all presidential ambitions while in the administration, as well as Polk's decision not to run for a second term, were aimed at limiting friction within the party. This failed because of the alienation of Martin Van Buren from Polk and the commitment of antislavery Democrats to a free-soil policy in the territory acquired from Mexico after 1846.

Polk maintained a tight control over all decisions. As an administrator, he was extremely innovative. Introducing a real executive budget, he tightened up the bookkeeping operations in the various departments, which resulted in a considerable savings of money. His success as president may be determined in part by how well he achieved his goals. In his inaugural address, he set four major tasks for himself: reestablishment of the independent treasury, lowering of the tariff, settlement of the Oregon dispute with England, and acquisition of California. By his retirement in 1849 he had achieved all of these. Passage of the independent treasury completed the hard currency campaign the Democrats had begun more than a decade earlier. The basic feature of this system, in which the government received and paid its debts in specie, remained the dominant element in the American banking system until the Federal Reserve Act in 1913. Polk's commitment to a low tariff resulted in the passage of the Walker Tariff, whose rates were not substantially revised until the Civil War.

Foreign Policy

The most significant events of Polk's administration occurred in foreign policy. Since 1818 the United States and Great Britain had maintained joint occupation of the Oregon Territory. This solution no longer was workable after Polk, in his presidential campaign, laid claim to the whole region up to the southern boundary of Russian-controlled Alaska. Once he became president, he sought a more amiable solution, suggesting the extension of the 49th parallel, which already divided the United States from Canada east of the Rockies. British rejection of this position led to a minor war scare, lasting until the outbreak of the Mexican War. On the eve of that conflict, the question was settled in approximately the terms suggested by Polk.

After the annexation of Texas, which occurred as a result of a joint resolution of Congress on the last day of John Tyler's administration, Mexico broke off diplomatic relations with the United States. Polk wanted to eliminate all boundary disputes with Mexico, settle claims Americans had against the Mexican government, and acquire California. He hoped that the acquisition of California and Oregon would help to reunite the nation. Polk's emissaries failed to negotiate a treaty. When Mexico expelled John Slidell, the minister to Mexico, Polk decided upon war. He was given his opportunity when Gen. Zachary Taylor was fired upon in territory under dispute with Mexico above the Rio

Grande River. The war resolution passed the House of Representatives on May 11, 1846.

War with Mexico

Despite the outbreak of war, Polk hoped to secure California and New Mexico by diplomacy. He financed Antonio López de Santa Ana's return to Mexico after the former dictator promised to negotiate peace. However, Santa Ana took command of the army as soon as he returned home. Another plan to set up a $2 million fund to purchase peace with Mexico met with defeat in Congress.

The war was won on the battlefield, as Polk proved an exceptionally adept commander-in-chief. Taylor advanced south to the heart of Mexico, while Gen. Winfield Scott invaded Mexico through Veracruz. Polk, distrusting both men as potential Whig candidates for president, kept close control over the Army. Scott captured Mexico City in April 1848.

The final diplomatic negotiations were conducted by a State Department clerk who joined Gen. Scott in Mexico City and arranged the Treaty of Guadalupe Hidalgo. Mexico gave up California and New Mexico as well as all claims to Texas for $15 million. Thus, by the Oregon and Guadalupe Hidalgo treaties, Polk had rounded out the continental United States, except for a small piece in the Southwest, purchased from Mexico in 1853.

Polk's hope that the war and the acquisition of the West Coast would end the growing sectional agitation that was threatening to break up the Union proved forlorn. During the course of the conflict, considerable opposition to the war developed both inside and outside Congress. That most of this opposition came from the Whigs did not obscure the fact that the war had intensified sectional disharmony. This was especially evident when a group of radical Democrats led by Congressman David Wilmot introduced the Wilmot Proviso, which would have barred slavery from the territories acquired as a consequence of the war. Twice this measure passed the House of Representatives to be defeated in the Senate. But the controversy would spread during the next decade and eventually lead to the Civil War. On this issue, Polk sought a compromise that would eliminate sectional friction. Although he was a slaveholder, he attempted to revive the Missouri Compromise of 1820, whereby slaves were to be prohibited above the 36°30' parallel in the new territories. By 1848 this compromise was unacceptable to both the North and the South.

True to his commitments 4 years earlier, Polk stepped aside, supporting Lewis Cass for the presidential nomination. Zachary Taylor, the Whig candidate, defeated Cass in November. In a sense, this Democratic defeat resulted directly from Polk's administration. Van Buren broke with his party and, running as the Free Soil candidate, drew votes from Cass. The Free Soil party attracted radical Democrats and some Whigs who supported the Wilmot Proviso.

Polk had taken few vacations while in office, and when he left the presidency, his health was broken. He died in Nashville, Tenn., on June 15, 1849, just 3 months after leaving office.

Historians have generally considered Polk as one of America's "Ten Greatest Presidents." During his term he strengthened the office, achieved his legislative goals, and added a great new empire. But these goals were achieved at a great cost: the destruction of the party and the increased polarization of the sections.

Further Reading

Polk's writings are in Milo Milton Quaife, ed., *The Diary of James K. Polk during His Presidency, 1845-1849* (4 vols., 1910). The definitive biography is the first two volumes of a projected three-volume study of Polk by Charles Grier Sellers: *James K. Polk, Jacksonian, 1795-1843* (1957) and *James K. Polk, Continentalist, 1843-1846* (1966). A useful old biography with an emphasis on Polk's public life is Eugene Irving McCormac, *James K. Polk: A Political Biography* (1922; repr. 1965), which concentrates particularly on Polk's role in Tennessee politics.

Polk's presidential election is covered in Arthur M. Schlesinger, Jr., ed., *History of American Presidential Elections* (4 vols., 1971). An interesting account by a political scientist of the development of the presidency during Polk's term is Charles A. McCoy, *Polk and the Presidency* (1960). The standard account on the war with Mexico is Justin Smith, *The War with Mexico* (2 vols., 1919). Glenn W. Price, *Origins of the War with Mexico: The Polk-Stockton Intrigue* (1967), implicates Polk in Commodore Robert Stockton's attempt to launch an attack on Mexico. □

Leonidas Lafayette Polk

Leonidas Lafayette Polk (1837-1892), American agrarian crusader, editor, and orator, ranks among the foremost of the South's post-Civil War champions of the farmer.

Of sturdy yeoman stock, Leonidas L. Polk was born on April 24, 1837, in Anson County, N.C. He bypassed formal education to become a farmer like his father. During the Civil War, he served two terms in the state legislature and also saw military duty with two North Carolina regiments. He was a valued member of the state constitutional convention summoned immediately after the conflict.

Polk's heart, however, was always in farming. In 1870 he began an almost one-man crusade for the creation of a state department of agriculture. When such an agency was created 7 years later, he became its first commissioner. He held this post until 1880, when he assumed editorship of the *Raleigh News and Observer* and began an even more concerted drive to improve agricultural standards in his state.

In 1886 Polk established the *Progressive Farmer*. This newspaper became a leading organ of southern farm sentiment. At first his editorials treated the technical aspects of agriculture, but his writing quickly developed political overtones. He urged readers to organize "farmers' clubs" so as to exert greater lobbying influence on the state legislature. One direct result was the establishment in Raleigh of a

Saloutos, *Farmer Movements in the South, 1865-1933* (1960).

☐

land-grant agricultural college (now North Carolina State University).

Meanwhile, the rural-dominated National Alliance movement had rapidly spread across the nation and become the leading influence in the Democratic party of the South. When the Alliance movement reached North Carolina, Polk eagerly joined and was soon head of the state organization. In 1887 he was elected national vice president of the Alliance; 2 years later, he became its president. The Alliance reached its zenith under Polk's leadership.

The rise of the Populist party in the early 1890s seemed to Polk to offer the only hope for widespread agrarian reform. He transferred his energies to that third political party and was soon one of its key spokesmen. He was a leading candidate for first or second place on the Populist presidential ticket of 1892 but died on June 11.

Polk was a rough and forceful speaker who appealed to the masses. He never forgot—nor would he let his listeners forget—that he was a product of the land. His settling hand checked much of the turbulence within the Alliance and the Populist party.

Further Reading

The one comprehensive and reliable treatment of Polk is Stuart Noblin, *Leonidas Lafayette Polk: An Agrarian Crusader* (1949). For varying interpretations of Polk's reform measures see W. Scott Morgan, *History of the Wheel and Alliance and the Impending Revolution* (1889); Simeon A. Delap, *The Populist Party in North Carolina* (1922); and Theodore

Antonio Pollaiuolo

Antonio Pollaiuolo (ca. 1432-1498), Italian painter, sculptor, goldsmith, and engraver, was a master of anatomical rendering and excelled in action subjects, notably mythologies. This "most Florentine of artists" appealed especially to the circle of Lorenzo de' Medici.

Antonio Pollaiuolo was born in Florence. Most of the dated documents refer to his activity as a goldsmith, in which trade he began. The varied nature of his work may be observed in the following commissions: a silver cross for S. Giovanni (1457), a reliquary for the prior of S. Pancrazio (1461), a silver belt and chain for Filippo Rinuccini (1461-1462), two candelabra for S. Giovanni (1465), and the embroidery designs for two tunics, a chasuble, and a cope (1465).

In 1468 Pollaiuolo bought property near Pistoia, and his success as both artist and businessman is attested by the purchase of additional property in and near Florence in the 1480s. In 1472 he was called upon to decorate the helmet of the Duke of Urbino, and that year his name first appeared in the register of the guild of Florentine painters.

Pollaiuolo's monumental *Martyrdom of St. Sebastian* (completed 1475), his most ambitious painting, is a milestone in Renaissance art in showing muscular figures in action. Other paintings are the tiny *Apollo and Daphne,* the *Rape of Deianira,* and the elegant *Profile Portrait of a Lady.* The famous studies of concentrated muscular energy shown in the panels of *Hercules and the Hydra* and *Hercules and Antaeus* are tiny replicas of lost canvases of the Labors of Hercules painted about 1460 for the Medici palace. Pollaiuolo again used the subject of *Hercules and Antaeus* for a bronze statuette, which, like the damaged fresco painting of the frenetic *Dancing Nudes* in the Villa la Gallina near Florence, reveals his fanatical interest in the nude in action.

Pollaiuolo also executed one engraving, the famous *Battle of the Nudes* (ca. 1465). It is a masterful synthesis of his main artistic ideal: the decorative beauty, in violent posturings, of the male nude.

Pollaiuolo's most important commissions for sculpture were executed not in Florence but Rome. He was called, with his artist brother Piero, to the Vatican in 1484 to do the tombs of Sixtus IV and Innocent VIII, masterpieces of bronze casting. Though the former tomb was not finished until 1493, the artist evidently returned to Florence in 1491 to take part in a competition for the facade of the Cathedral. In 1494 he was commissioned to make a bronze bust of Condottiere Gentile Orsini. Pollaiuolo died in Rome.

Further Reading

Although old, the monograph by Maud Cruttwell, *Antonio Pollaiuolo* (1907), is still useful. Pollaiuolo's sculpture is discussed in John Pope-Hennessy, *Italian Renaissance Sculpture* (1958), and Charles Seymour, *Sculpture in Italy, 1400-1500* (1966). ☐

Albert Frederick Pollard

The English historian Albert Frederick Pollard (1869-1948) specialized in the Tudor period. He was influential in developing historical studies in British universities.

Albert Pollard was born on the Isle of Wight on Dec. 16, 1869, the son of a pharmacist. He attended Jesus College at Oxford, where he was one of the first pupils of R. L. Poole, the famous medievalist. Pollard received his degree in 1891 and won an award in scholarship in 1892 which led to his appointment as an assistant editor of the prestigious *Dictionary of National Biography* in 1893, for which he wrote approximately 500 articles. While working on the dictionary he also completed two biographical studies, *England under Protector Somerset* (1900) and *Henry VIII* (1902).

In 1903 Pollard was elected to the newly established chair of constitutional history at University College, London, which he held until 1931. At his appointment there was little interest in historical studies and few scholars in that area at University College, although the field was beginning to develop in other British universities. In his inaugural lecture Pollard set forth a program to develop historical studies, and he worked arduously on this for the next 35 years, developing curricula and requirements for degree courses.

In 1906 Pollard founded the Historical Association, which served as a link between university professors and teachers in the secondary schools, and he served as president from 1912 to 1915. In 1916 he was largely instrumental in persuading the association to acquire a foundering periodical, *History*. He edited it for the next 6 years, during which it grew immensely in circulation, quality, and influence. In 1920 he was the major force behind the founding of the university's Institute of Historical Research, which he served as director from 1920 to 1931 and as honorary director until 1939. According to one authority, Pollard was able to accomplish as much as he did for the development of historical studies because he hacked his way through the tangle of London academic politics virtually single-handedly. The institute became a national center for the research of subjects suitable for study in the libraries and archives of London, cooperating with other British universities, sponsoring conferences in conjunction with American scholars, and publishing its own *Bulletin* beginning in 1923.

Pollard was a member of a government committee on the League of Nations and served on the Committee on Parliamentary Records of 1929. He also ran unsuccessfully for Parliament twice as a Liberal candidate.

Pollard's main interest was in the Tudor period. He wrote a three-volume *Reign of Henry VII from Contemporary Sources* (1913-1914) and a life of Cardinal Wolsey (1929). He was also instrumental in promoting the modern study of parliamentary history. Generally speaking, his point of view in his many historical works has been characterized as Protestant, English, and liberal. As Pollard was not especially comfortable in handling philosophical or political ideas, his works are characterized by a preoccupation with times, places, and individual actors in history. He also often devoted an unusual amount of space to the minute analysis of words. His literary style is felicitous.

Toward the end of his life Pollard was offered a knighthood but declined it. He died on Aug. 3, 1948, at Milford-on-Sea, Hampshire.

Further Reading

Pollard's life and career are recounted in Matthew A. Fitzsimons and others, eds., *The Development of Historiography* (1954). An obituary notice by Vivian H. Galbraith is in *Proceedings of the British Academy,* vol. 25 (1949). ☐

Jackson Pollock

American painter Jackson Pollock (1912-1956) was the leading figure in abstract expressionism, a style that evolved after World War II and radicalized the history of American painting and modern art in general.

Before World War II modern painting was dominated by European developments. Although American painters were aware of them, they generally did not participate in their origin or contribute significantly to their evolution. With the advent of World War II the mainstream of modern art shifted dramatically. The numerous European artists who sought refuge in the United States exerted a profound influence on younger American painters and sculptors. From this cultural collision emerged a style whose roots lay abroad—for the most part in cubism and surrealism—but whose look and meaning were without precedent. The style became known as abstract expressionism, or "action" painting, because it frequently resulted from a direct and unpremeditated relationship between an artist and his medium.

Among American artists, Jackson Pollock was probably the single most powerful figure in giving shape to this new direction. With his example, moreover, American painting assumed a position of leadership within the international scope of modern art.

Early Work

Pollock was born on Jan. 28, 1912, in Cody, Wyo. His father was a surveyor, and Jackson spent most of his childhood in Arizona and northern California. In 1925 the family settled in southern California. Largely through the influence of his oldest brother, Jackson became interested in art. Between 1925 and 1929 he attended Manual Arts High School in Los Angeles, involved first with sculpture and later with painting.

In 1929 Pollock moved to New York City to study with Thomas Hart Benton at the Art Students League. He stayed for 2 years. Between 1931 and 1935 he made several trips to California and then decided to settle in New York. He worked on the Federal Arts Project from 1938 to 1942, and in 1940 he enjoyed his first New York exhibition—a group show which also included works by Willem de Kooning and Lee Krasner. Here Pollock met Lee Krasner, and they married in 1944.

Pollock's first one-man show took place in 1943 at the Art of This Century Gallery in New York. Owned by the celebrated collector Peggy Guggenheim, the gallery became famous during the 1940s as a showroom for unknown but gifted American artists and for the recent works of established European masters. By offering both European and American styles, the gallery played a primary role in the genesis of abstract expressionism. In 1946 Pollock and his wife moved to Easthampton, L.I., where they remained until his death.

Pollock's art during these years reveals his effort to come to grips with advanced European developments, particularly cubism and surrealism. He seems to have struggled desperately with both styles, as though they were foreign to his sensibility and could not accommodate his ambitions. An outstanding example of the struggle, *Male and Female* (1942) is dominated by two totemlike figures, symbols of man and woman, that stretch the full length of the canvas. Essentially, the figures are composed of the flat planes of synthetic cubism, with secondary planes linking them to one another and to their surrounding space. But while the figures are cubist in formal terms, their interpretation by the artist is inspired by surrealist thought. This is apparent in the mysterious symbols which are strewn across the canvas— arithmetic notations, suggestions of floating eyes, and so forth—and by the grotesque, nightmarish heads of the figures: the woman looks like a frightening cat, and the man, with gaping mouth, resembles a devouring demon. Such creatures arise from a world beyond conventional reason and visible reality.

That Pollock was struggling with his pictorial means, however, is apparent in the way *Male and Female* is painted. The paint is thickly and roughly applied. In some places the artist forced or scrubbed it onto the canvas, whereas in others he scribbled it into abstract configurations that seem determined to obscure the principal figures. As a whole the surface appears painfully executed, a torturous expression of Pollock's desire to break free from his inherited stylistic limits.

Classic Period

Between 1947 and 1950 Pollock's art matured with astonishing rapidity. He also began to receive national and international recognition. In 1948 Peggy Guggenheim included his work in an exhibition of her collection presented in Venice, Florence, Milan, Amsterdam, Brussels, and Zurich. In 1950 she organized his first European one-man exhibition, which was shown in Venice and Milan. In New York, Pollock showed twice at the Betty Parsons Gallery in 1949.

These shows clearly established Pollock as the leading figure of the new American painting. Along with the sheer quality of his work, however, his radical techniques also attracted widespread attention. About 1947 Pollock gave up conventional easel painting in favor of dripping his paint—from sticks, brushes, or syringes—onto lengths of unstretched canvas laid out on the floor of his studio. Instead of maintaining a fixed relationship to his canvas, he would work from all of its sides, frequently walking across it or through it during the creative act. This spontaneous method of working inspired the term "action" painting. Its intensely personal meaning is revealed in Pollock's statement in 1947: "When I am *in* my painting, I'm not aware of what I'm doing. It is only after a sort of 'get acquainted' period that I see what I have been about. I have no fears about making changes, destroying the image, etc. because the painting has a life of its own. I try to let it come through. It is only when I lose contact with the painting that the result is a mess. Otherwise there is pure harmony, an easy give and take, and the painting comes out well."

Although Pollock's radical techniques productively enabled his breakthrough to maturity, they also provoked considerable hostility among the general public. Not unexpectedly, *Time* led the assault, referring to the artist as "Jack the dripper." Pollock felt such hostility deeply. As Frank O'Hara wrote: " . . . Pollock was also sustaining frivolous and damaging criticism, aimed mostly at his methods, and he received them with bitterness. He was especially vulnerable because of the personal nature of his work. It is terrible to be great alone, and the public had not yet recognized with its scorn the greatness of his American contemporaries. Where Gorky had suffered from lack of attention, Pollock suffered from attention of the wrong kind."

Pollock's "drip" paintings constitute his masterpieces. Among others, these include *Full Fathom Five* (1947), *Number 1* (1948), and *Autumn Rhythm* (1950). In these he transcends the tensions and anxieties that characterize his earlier efforts. On a formal level the flat planes of cubism give way to a pictorial space generated exclusively by line. But the quality of Pollock's line is unique: as it accelerates across the surface, changing color, twisting upon itself, and generating an intricate overall web, it is experienced as a purely optical phenomenon. That is, the line is freed from all functional associations, particularly from its traditional function of describing shapes or objects. Thus, Pollock's line is felt to be exclusively pictorial—to reveal the capacity of line within the realm of painting. As O'Hara said, "There has never been enough said about Pollock's draftsmanship, that amazing ability to quicken a line by thinning it, to slow it up by flooding, to elaborate that simplest of elements, the line—to change, reinvigorate, to extend, to build up an embarrassment of riches in the mass by drawing alone."

But the "drip" paintings also embody a new relationship to surrealist thought—that is, in terms of Pollock's freewheeling method of working. Where previously he had sought to tap his unconscious self by painting images of it—mythic creatures, fantasies, and so on—the "drip" technique allowed him simply to "let go," to release spontaneously the psychic and bodily energies that surrealist theory had encouraged the artist to explore during the creative act. Thus, although the "drip" paintings do not look surrealist, their genesis owes much to that European style.

Last Years

During the 1950s Pollock exhibited regularly at the Sidney Janis Gallery in New York. But while his reputation continued to grow, he began to suffer intense self-doubt and anxiety. The most pervasive artistic problem in these years concerned figuration: Pollock seems to have wanted to accommodate human or abstract figures within the dripped webs that characterize his masterpieces of 1947-1950. His effort to do so can be seen in the black-and-white paintings of 1951-1952 and in the richly colored *Blue Poles* (1952). Many of these works have extraordinary power, but they generally lack his earlier lyrical harmony. With their crowded surfaces, they frequently appear desperate, even tragic, in the way they bare their thwarted ambitions.

Pollock never emerged from this crisis. He died in an automobile accident on Aug. 11, 1956, in Southampton, N.Y. That year a memorial exhibition at the Museum of Modern Art honored him.

Further Reading

Excellent monographs on Pollock are Frank O'Hara, *Jackson Pollock* (1959), and Bryan Robertson, *Jackson Pollock* (1960). Also useful is the New York Museum of Modern Art publication *Jackson Pollock* by Sam Hunter (1956).

Additional Sources

Cernuschi, Claude, *Jackson Pollock: meaning and significance,* New York, NY: IconEditions, 1992.

Frank, Elizabeth, *Jackson Pollock,* New York: Abbeville Press, 1983.

Friedman, B. H. (Bernard Harper), *Jackson Pollock: energy made visible,* New York: Da Capo Press, 1995.

Naifeh, Steven W., *Jackson Pollock: an American saga,* New York, NY: HarperPerennial, 1991.

Solomon, Deborah, *Jackson Pollock: a biography,* New York: Simon and Schuster, 1987.

To a violent grave: an oral biography of Jackson Pollock, New York: G.P. Putnam, 1985. □

Marco Polo

The Venetian traveler and writer Marco Polo (ca. 1254-ca. 1324) left Venice for Cathay, or China, in 1271, spent 17 years in Kublai Khan's realm, and

returned to Venice in 1295. His account of his travels is one of the most important travel documents ever written.

The scion of a noble family of Venetian merchants, Marco Polo began his long experience with Cathay through the adventures of his father, Niccolo, and his uncle, Maffeo Polo, partners in a trading operation at a time when Venice was the world leader in foreign commerce. Marco's trip to China was preceded by the prolonged odyssey of his father and uncle all the way to Peking and back. In China they were well received by the recently established Mongol prince Kublai Khan in 1266. The Polos impressed Kublai Khan with their intelligence and their familiarity with the world. For these reasons he retained their services for several years. In 1269 he sent them to Rome as his envoys with a request that the Pope send 100 Europeans to share their knowledge with him.

The Polos' mission received little attention in Rome, but in 1271 the Polo brothers, in search of further profit and adventure, set out to return to China. It was this second trip that provided the occasion for the 17-year-old Marco Polo to make his debut as a world traveler. The return to China, over land and sea, desert and mountain, took slightly more than 3 years.

Despite the failure of their mission to Rome, the Khan welcomed the Venetians back and again took them into his service. He became increasingly impressed with the

youngest Polo, who, like his father and uncle, demonstrated not only his ability in travel but also his facility for the Mongol language and for using his remarkable powers of observation.

Under the benevolence of Kublai Khan, the Polos initiated widespread trading ventures within his domain. While on these business trips around the empire Marco Polo first demonstrated his perceptiveness and his ability to relate what he saw in clear, understandable terms. His reports, which formed the basis of his famous account of his travels, contained information on local customs, business conditions, and events. It was in these reports that he displayed his talent as a detached and accurate observer. Kublai Khan read and used these reports to keep abreast of developments within his empire.

All three of the European visitors were maintained as envoys and advisers. Marco was used on several extended missions that sent him traveling over much of China and even beyond. By his own account he skirted the edge of Tibet and northern Burma. This business-diplomatic relationship between the Polos and Kublai Khan lasted more than 16 years, during which Marco served as the Khan's personal representative in the city of Yangchow.

Although the Polos enjoyed the profits of their enterprise, they began to long to return to Venice to enjoy them. They were detained primarily because of the unwillingness of Kublai Khan to release them from his service. Their chance to return to Europe came in 1292, when they were sent on a diplomatic mission, first to Persia and then to Rome. The assignment represented the Khan's way of releasing them from their obligations to him. In Persia they were to arrange a dynastic marriage between one of the Khan's regional rulers and a Mongol princess. They were detained in Persia for nearly a year when the prince died and a new marriage had to be arranged. From the Persian court, the Venetians continued their journey home, arriving in 1295, after an absence of nearly a quarter century.

Marco Polo did not return to Asia again. He entered the service of Venice in its war against the rival city-state of Genoa. In 1298 Marco served as a gentleman-commander of a galley in the Venetian navy. In September 1298 he was captured and imprisoned in Genoa. His fame as an adventurer had preceded him, and he was treated with courtesy and leniency. He was released within a year. Little is known of Marco Polo's life after his return to Venice. He apparently returned to private life and business until his death about 1324.

During his captivity in Genoa, Marco Polo dictated the story of his travels. The man he told his story to was a fellow prisoner named Rusticiano, a Pisan who wrote in the romantic style of 13th-century literature. A combination of Marco Polo's gift of observation and the literary style of Rusticiano emerged in the final version of Marco Polo's travels. The book included Marco Polo's personal recollections as well as stories related to him by others.

In his book, which was translated into most languages, Marco left a wealth of information. His cartographical information has proved remarkably accurate when tested by modern methods. His observations about customs and local characteristics have also been verified by subsequent research.

Further Reading

Ronald Catham translated *The Travels of Marco Polo* (1958). The standard biography is Henry Hersch Hart, *Venetian Adventurer: Being an Account of the Life and Times and of the Book of Messer Marco Polo* (1942), updated and reissued as *Marco Polo: Venetian Adventurer* (1967). Other works on Polo include Maurice Collis, *Marco Polo* (1960), and Hildegard Blunck, *Marco Polo: The Great Adventurer* (1966). □

Pol Pot

Pol Pot (born 1928) was a key figure in the Cambodian Communist movement, becoming premier of the government of Democratic Kampuchéa (DK) from 1976 to 1979. He directed the mass killing of intellectuals, professional people, city dwellers—perhaps one-fifth of his own people.

Pol Pot was born Saloth Sar on May 19, 1928. He was the second son of a conservative, prosperous, and influential small landowner. Pol Pot's father had social and political connections at the royal court at the Cambodian capital of Phnom Penh, some 70 miles south from Prek Sbau, the small hamlet in Kompong Thom, the province where Pol Pot was born. Visits by court officials—and, on at least one occasion, even by King Monivong himself—to Pol Pot's father's home appear to have been common. Pol Pot consistently denied that he was Saloth Sar, probably because his family and educational background clashed with Communist proletarian perceptions and because his tactical and organizational skills seemed to have flourished best in an atmosphere of extreme secrecy. Even after he had become premier of the victorious Communist Democratic Kampuchéa (DK) regime in Phnom Penh on April 5, 1976, there was widespread uncertainty about who he was.

The Education of a Radical

Pol Pot's intellectual development showed a sharp break from traditional toward radical values. He was educated in a Buddhist monastery and a private Catholic institution in Phnom Penh and then enrolled at a technical school in the provincial quiet and security of the town of Kompong Cham to learn carpentry. Despite his later claims, there is no evidence that as early as his mid-teens he joined Ho Chi Minh's Viet Minh resistance for a while. He seemed at first destined for a trade in carpentry. However, the program of French colonial policymakers to accelerate development of a more diversified "polytechnic" elite in the overseas territories enabled Pol Pot in 1949 to obtain a government scholarship to study radio and electrical technology in Paris.

In France Pol Pot joined a small circle of leftist Cambodian students—some of whom later became prominent Marxist and/or Communist Party leaders (such as Ieng Sary,

the future DK foreign minister, and Hou Yuon, an independent Marxist radical who repeatedly served in Prince Norodom Sihanouk's cabinets until his death in 1975 in the Pol Pot holocaust). Pol Pot soon became an anti-colonialist, Marxist radical. Among the European countries he visited during this period was Yugoslavia, whose determination to chart its own national Communist course of thoroughgoing reform reportedly particularly impressed him.

Upon his return to Cambodia in 1953, Pol Pot first drifted into the Viet Minh "United Khmer Issarak (Freedom) Front" of underground Cambodian Communists and radical nationalists. After 1954 the Issarak's principal above-ground organizational mainstay became the Krom Pracheachon ("Citizens Association"). The Front, along with other Cambodian political groups, opposed both the remnant of French colonial power in Cambodia and the government of Sihanouk. The latter was perceived by many Cambodians to be a French puppet. Pol Pot served for several months with Viet Minh and Issarak units, some of whom had joined in the loose leftist radical resistance groups supervised by the Krom Pracheachon. But Cambodia's 1954 achievement of independence from the French also found him increasingly involved in the organization of the Khmer People's Revolutionary Party (KPRP), the first Cambodian Communist party, founded in 1951.

In the post-independence era Pol Pot appears to have resented as much the continued heavy Communist Vietnamese influence in the KPRP and its armed units as the hothouse atmosphere of partisan political intrigues in the capital deftly manipulated by the wily Sihanouk. Pol Pot's contempt for intellectuals and politicians jockeying for favor and power was greatly increased and helped shape his own ruthless radical reforms once he assumed power. Pol Pot's mentor in these years was Tou Samouth, the onetime Unified Issarak Front's president and later the KPRP's secretary general. Like Pol Pot, Samouth was primarily interested in building the KPRP into a genuinely Cambodian, broad-based organization capable of rallying all opposition elements among peasants, urban workers, and intellectuals against the Sihanouk regime. This effort led to tensions with the Vietnamese, who continued to try to dominate the left and anti-Sihanouk Cambodian resistance.

Building a Revolutionary Party

On September 28, 1960, Pol Pot, Tou Samouth, Ieng Sary, and a handful of followers reportedly met in secret in a room of the Phnom Penh railroad station to found the "Workers Party of Kampuchea" (WPK). Samouth was named secretary general and Pol Pot became one of three Politburo members. But on February 20, 1963, at the WPK's second congress, Pol Pot succeeded Samouth as party secretary. The latter had disappeared on July 20, 1963, under mysterious circumstances and subsequently was reported to have been assassinated. Whether Pol Pot was involved in Samouth's murder remains uncertain.

For the next 13 years, as the WPK increasingly seemed to distance itself from Hanoi, Pol Pot and other top WPK cadres virtually disappeared from public notice. They set up their main party encampments in a remote forest area of

Ratanakiri province. During this period Pol Pot appears not only to have been consolidating his own leadership position in the WPK, but he also gradually and successfully contested pro-Hanoi elements in the anti-Sihanouk resistance generally. However, Pol Pot at this time carefully avoided an open breach with the Vietnamese Communists, who were consolidating their hold on the Ho Chi Minh trail and adjacent pockets of Cambodian territory. Nevertheless, a 1965 visit by Pol Pot to Hanoi designed to win acceptance as top party leader was shrouded in mutual mistrust. More successful was Pol Pot's journey and extended stay in Beijing in the same year. He remained in China for some seven months, during which time he likely received ideological and organizational schooling. Pol Pot's pro-Chinese orientation became more pronounced upon his return to Cambodia in September 1966. The WPK soon changed its name to Communist Party of Kampuchea (CPK).

CPK-instigated demonstrations against the Sihanouk regime now steadily mounted. The prince's blanket denunciation and execution of scores of what his government termed the *Khmer Rouge* ("Red Khmers") solidified the CPK-led opposition. At the same time it made that opposition appear more formidable than it actually was. In December 1969 and January 1970 Pol Pot and other CPK leaders again visited Hanoi and Beijing, evidently in preparation for a final drive against the Sihanouk regime. But the drive was preempted as on March 18, 1970, a right-wing coup in Phnom Penh overthrew Sihanouk, bringing Lon Nol to the Cambodian presidency.

Although some CPK members and other Communist Pracheachon resistance leaders—including Pol Pot's colleague the future DK President Khieu Sampan—rallied to Sihanouk's call for a united front against Lon Nol, Pol Pot himself remained aloof. After Sihanouk's fall, Hanoi had begun infiltrating some 1,000 Vietnamese-trained Cambodian Communists into Cambodia. But on orders of Pol Pot most of these were identified and quickly killed. Despite this action and clashes with Pol Pot's followers in Kompong Chom province, Hanoi avoided rupture in the interest of winning first a decisive Communist victory throughout Indochina.

In mid-September 1971 a new CPK congress reelected Pol Pot as secretary general and as commander of its "Revolutionary Army." Tensions between Hanoi and Pol Pot increased further when the CPK refused a Vietnamese request to negotiate with the Lon Nol regime and the United States as Vietnamese-U.S. discussions took place in Paris. In keeping with the Paris Accords, the Vietnamese in the early months of 1973 left some of their Cambodian encampments. But CPK "Revolutionary Army" units quickly took their place as Pol Pot further strengthened his power base. Clashes between Lon Nol's forces and Pol Pot's guerrillas, as well as new "Revolutionary Army" raids on pro-Hanoi Cambodian resistance units and on followers of Sihanouk's coalition exile government continued, however. Yet throughout 1974, in letters to Hanoi and Vietnamese party leaders and in public messages, Pol Pot affirmed his friendship and gratitude.

A Holocaust on His Own People

On April 17, 1975, Phnom Penh fell to several Communist Cambodian and Sihanoukist factions. The CPK and Pol Pot slowly managed to establish hegemony over the capital. Fighting continued between Pol Pot's "Revolutionary Army" and Vietnamese troops in disputed border territories and on islands in the Gulf of Thailand. At a meeting with Vietnamese representatives along the border in early June 1975, Pol Pot reportedly apologized for his troops' "faulty map reading." Tensions between Pol Pot and his associates and the Vietnamese did not abate, however, despite another Pol Pot visit to Hanoi in order to suggest a friendship treaty.

For nearly a year Pol Pot and other Cambodian Communists, as well as the embattled Norodom Sihanouk, struggled for power in the newly proclaimed state of "Democratic Kampuchea." Another CPK party congress in January 1976 reaffirmed Pol Pot's position as secretary general but also revealed emergent leadership rifts between Pol Pot and some outlying zone organizations of the party. Relations with Hanoi continued to worsen. On April 14, 1976, after CPK-controlled elections for a new "People's Representative Assembly" and the resignation as head of state of Sihanouk, a new DK government was proclaimed. Pol Pot, who officially had been elected to the assembly as a delegate of a "rubber workers organization," now became premier.

However, his authority still was being contested both by Hanoi-influenced party cadres and rival party zone leaders. Beginning in November 1976 Pol Pot accelerated extensive purges of rivals, including cabinet ministers and other top party leaders. This provoked repeated explosions of unrest in Kompong Thom and Oddar Meanchey.

Meanwhile, the fury of Pol Pot's social and economic reform policies carried out by the mystery-shrouded *Angka,* or "inner" party organization, eventually was to make Pol Pot's name synonymous with one of the modern world's worst holocausts. Forced evacuation, through extended death marches, of the inhabitants of major cities and resettlement and harshly exploitive labor of tens of thousands in agricultural work projects; deliberate withholding of adequate food and medical care; systematic mass killings of all "old dandruff"—i.e., suspected subversives, especially those who had white collar or intellectual occupations or political experience—all these reflected Pol Pot's brand of ideology in which Rousseauist purism and Stalinist terrorism were uniquely blended. Great emphasis was placed in Pol Pot's policies on the training of the young and on the creation of a "New Man" in Cambodia. Even after Pol Pot was driven from power, young teenagers remained among his dedicated followers in the DK's "Revolutionary Army." But the killings and deliberate neglect by the Pol Pot regime cost some 1.6 million Cambodians their lives—nearly 20 percent of the country's total population.

Regime policies prompted mounting opposition among divisional commanders and party cadres. Pol Pot's visit to China and North Korea in September and October 1977 solidified his standing among other Asian Communist leaders, even as fighting with Vietnamese border forces intensified. On December 31, 1977, all diplomatic relations with Hanoi were severed, Pol Pot charging that the Vietnamese were seeking to impose their hegemony on both Laos and Cambodia through an "Indochinese Federation."

The Fall of a Dictator

On May 26, 1978, Eastern Zone party leaders and their followers rose up in revolt against Pol Pot. But the rising failed, and thousands of cadres either were killed or, like Heng Samrin (who would succeed Pol Pot as premier), made good their escape to Vietnam. Some Eastern Zone leaders charged Pol Pot with selling Cambodia to the Chinese. Vietnamese attacks on and military penetration of DK territory became more severe and extensive during the second half of 1978. Pol Pot's premiership also became more precarious and his overtures toward the Chinese to deter Vietnamese intervention found little response. In the wake of a final Vietnamese military drive, Pol Pot and other DK leaders were forces to flee Phnom Penh on January 7, 1979. They eventually regrouped their forces and established an underground government in Western Cambodia and in the Cardamom mountain range.

On July 20, 1979, Pol Pot was condemned to death *in absentia,* on grounds of having committed genocide. The verdict was issued by a "People's Tribunal" of the new government of the "People's Republic of Kampuchea," installed with the aid of Vietnamese forces. As growing world attention focussed on the plight of wartorn Cambodia and on the bloody violence of the Pol Pot era, Pol Pot himself increasingly became a liability to his Chinese backers and the underground DK leaders. At a CPK congress on December 17, 1979, Pol Pot stepped down as DK prime minister, and the post was taken over by DK President Khieu Sampan. However, he remained as party secretary general and as head of the CPK's military commission, making him in effect the overall commander of the DK's 30,000-man guerrilla force battling the Vietnamese in Cambodia. (But throughout most of the 1980s the Vietnamese army controlled Cambodia (Kampuchea) under the presidency of Heng Samrin.)

After leaving his premiership little was known of Pol Pot's whereabouts or activities. Reportedly he repeatedly sought medical attention for a cardio-vascular condition in Beijing in the course of 1981-1983. On September 1, 1985, the DK's clandestine radio announced that Pol Pot had retired as commander of the DK's "National Army" and had been appointed to be "Director of the Higher Institute for National Defense."

Pol Pot was married to Khieu Ponnary, a former fellow student activist of his Paris days and later the CPK women's movement leader in Phnom Penh.

Captured at Last

After several years of living underground, Pol Pot was finally captured on June 18, 1997 by a rival faction of his own comrades. The Khmer Rouge had suffered from internal factionalism in recent years, and finally splintered into opposing forces, the largest of which, in the northern zone, joined with the government of Cambodia under Sihanouk and hunted down their former leader. Upon capturing him,

the guerrillas sentenced Pol Pot, leader of the modern day reign of terror, to life in prison.

Further Reading

Pol Pot kept out of the limelight even during his premiership, and no comprehensive full length biography of him as yet exists. Various stages of his life and career are dealt with in Ben Kiernan and Stephen Heder, "Why Pol Pot? Roots of the Cambodian Tragedy," *Indochina Issues* (Center for International Policy, Washington, D.C.), 52 (December 1984); Serge Thion, "Chronology of Khmer Communism, 1940-1982," in David P. Chandler and Ben Kiernan, editors, *Revolution and Its Aftermath in Kampuchea* (Yale University Southeast Asia Studies, Monograph Series, no. 25, 1983); Ben Kiernan and Chanthou Boua, editors, *Peasants and Politics in Kampuchea, 1942-1981* (1982); Michael Vickery, *Cambodia, 1975-1982* (1984); and David P. Chandler, *A History of Cambodia* (1983). For the PRK view of Pol Pot see Say Phouthong, "Fidelity to the Chosen Path," *World Marxist Review* (February 1985). The horror of the Pol Pot holocaust was reported by Elizabeth Becker in *When the War Was Over: The voices of Cambodia's revolution and its people* (1986). □

Polybios

The Greek historian Polybios (ca. 203-120 B.C.) is considered by some the greatest ancient historian after Thucydides. His view of Roman history presumed to provide the reader with historical means for individual self-improvement.

Polybios was born in Megalopolis in Arcadia, the son of Lycortas, general and statesman of the Achaean League. Through his father Polybios became involved early in the Achaean League, which he served both as ambassador to Egypt and as cavalry commander. Polybios tried to maintain the independence of the League, although in 169 B.C. he was dispatched to aid the Romans (who declined his help) in their combat against Perseus of Macedon.

Suspected by the Romans of halfhearted support of the Roman cause, Polybios, along with a thousand others, was shipped to Rome as a hostage in 166 B.C. and remained there until he obtained permission to return to his native land in 150 B.C. While in Rome, he was admitted to the most important circle of Aemilius Paulus (who had defeated Perseus of Macedonia in 168 B.C.), who appointed him tutor of his sons Fabius and Scipio the Younger. Polybios became the very close friend of Scipio, whom he accompanied to Africa in 147-146 B.C. and elsewhere upon his return from Greece.

Polybios was present at the capitulation of Carthage in 146 B.C.; and when Corinth was destroyed by the Romans in the same year, the Achaean League crushed, and Greece turned into a Roman province, it was Polybios who was entrusted with the task of reorganizing the Greeks. Apparently he did so to the satisfaction of Greeks and Romans alike, because he was honored by both. His later years were devoted to writing his *Histories*. It is reported that he died as the result of a fall from his horse while in his early 80s.

His Work

Polybios was an eyewitness to the great historical events of his day, including the war against Antiochus III of Syria (192-189 B.C.), the Third Macedonian War (171-168 B.C.), the Third Punic War (149-146 B.C.), and the defeat of Carthage and the conquest of Greece in 146 B.C. Polybios originally intended to write a universal history, with special emphasis on Rome's conquest of the then known world, which would conclude at 168 B.C. However, the sack of Corinth and destruction of Carthage were necessary additions.

Of Polybios's 40-book work only the first 5 books have survived. Because of the great mass of information which he covers (from 220 to 145 B.C.), Polybios is very generous with his explanatory notes. His first two books are large preludes to the main history, which does not begin until the third book. Polybios was influenced greatly by Thucydides and believed that a knowledge of history is an absolutely necessary guide to present action. His pragmatic view emphasizes the didactic element in history. For Polybios—no antiquarian—history was practical knowledge needed in present experience. Three essentials for the historian, according to Polybios, are geographical knowledge; a knowledge of practical politics, including the art of war; and the ability to collect, classify, and synthesize written sources.

Polybios lacked the artistic qualities of Herodotus or Thucydides, but he insisted on travel to the spots where history was made, closely examined written and oral evidence, invoked his own military experience and that of others, and utilized firsthand knowledge.

It was Polybios, a Greek, who illuminated the rise of the Roman Empire. He does not merely recount; he analyzes in terms of causal relations. In Polybios Greek and Roman historiography merge because the whole Mediterranean world was merging with Rome.

Further Reading

It is virtually impossible to find a work in English devoted to Polybios exclusively, aside from texts and commentaries. The Loeb Library translations of Polybios's *The Histories,* by W. R. Paton (6 vols., 1922-1927), are always valuable and useful. A recent translation of *The Histories* is by Mortimer Chambers, edited, abridged, and with an introduction by E. Badian (1967). Dealing with the manuscripts is John Michael Moore, *The Manuscript Tradition of Polybius* (1965). Frank William Walbank's projected three-volume work, *A Historical Commentary on Polybius* (2 vols., 1957-1967), is a scholarly, encyclopedic work that will become the standard commentary on Polybios. Walbank, in *Ancient Societies and Institutions: Studies Presented to Victor Ehrenberg on His 75th Birthday,* edited by E. Badian, deals with "The Spartan Ancestral Constitution in Polybius." Also useful is Kurt von Fritz, *The Theory of the Mixed Constitution in Antiquity: A Critical Analysis of Polybius' Political Ideas* (1954). For a discussion of Polybios and his place in ancient historiography see Stephen Usher, *The Historians of Greece and Rome* (1970). □

Polykleitos

Polykleitos (active ca. 450-420 B.C.), one of the great innovative Greek sculptors of the 5th century, stands alone in his concentration on the problems of the nude, male human body, for which he evolved a standard of proportion and representation that in one way or another influenced the subsequent development of sculpture in Western civilization.

Polykleitos, the elder of two sculptors of this name, was a master bronze caster of the Argive school. His earliest works, probably done about 450 B.C. or a little earlier, are statues of victors in athletic contests. The end of his career cannot have come long after 423, when the old temple of Hera in Argos burned and Polykleitos made a gold-and-ivory seated cult statue of Hera for the new temple.

In contrast to his contemporary Phidias, whose favorite subjects were gods and goddesses, Polykleitos portrayed mortals. He is most famous for creating an ideal nude male figure and explaining it in a book, calling both the *Canon,* that is, "rule" or "example." The *Doryphoros,* or spear bearer, a statue of a standing nude youth, has been identified as this statue, which Cicero and Pausanius plausibly attributed to Polykleitos. The original statue was in bronze; it is known from many copies, including excellent marble copies (Museo Nazionale, Naples; Uffizi, Florence). The figure is squarely built and stands in a relaxed *contrapposto* position, weight on right leg, left hand bent backward to hold a spear shaft over his shoulder. The identification most often suggested for the *Doryphoros* is Achilles. The face still preserves traces of early classical severity. Here, the human body now reacts in a relaxed, organic manner, with every part of the figure responding naturally to the principal action. The stocky torso is treated in an almost architectonic fashion, with chest and abdominal areas sharply separated from one another. That the figure was painstakingly designed cannot be denied; the system of proportions that Polykleitos embodied in his *Canon,* however, has so far eluded scholars.

The second work that can be attributed with reasonable probability to Polykleitos is a more slender and graceful athlete, the *Diadoumenos,* or youth tying a victor's fillet around his head. It is likely that this statue is considerably later than the *Doryphoros,* perhaps finished about 430 B.C. While tectonic organization, pose, and modeling all show a close relationship to the *Doryphoros,* extension of the arms horizontally away from the body at shoulder height in a more complex and active gesture points to a later, more evolved stage in Polykleitos's stylistic development. Of the numerous copies, an over-life-size marble version from Delos (National Museum, Athens) and a large terra-cotta statuette (Metropolitan Museum, New York) are outstanding. In one interpretation, the figure represents Apollo, the personification of victory; however, a specific, although unknown, human victor seems more likely.

A Herakles and a Hermes are attributed by Cicero (*Deoratore*) and Pliny (*Natural History*) to Polykleitos. The Herakles is still relatively little known; while several excellent heads have been shown with some probability to represent the Hermes, the position of the body remains unknown. Among many other athlete statues associated with Polykleitos, one may mention the *Diskophoros,* probably an early work, and the "Westmacott Athlete" and "Dresden Boy," both statues of very young athletes, done toward the end of his career.

Polykleitos's only well-known statue of a female subject is his wounded Amazon, which Pliny (*Natural History*) tells us was the winning entry in the contest at the Artemision in Ephesus. E. Berger (1966) is undecided between the "Sciarra" and the "Capitoline" types, both of which exhibit the *contrapposto* pose characteristic of works like the *Doryphoros.* Further study and discoveries will be necessary before Polykleitos's Amazon can be convincingly reconstructed. Of his other female figures, his gold-and-ivory cult statue of Hera, made for the new temple of Hera in Argos, is unique. Pausanias describes it as seated, holding a scepter in one hand, on which a cuckoo rests, and a pomegranate in the other; his observation that she wore a diadem, worked with Charites and Horai, finds partial confirmation in the decorated *polos* work on the head of Hera on late classical Argive coins. The sculpture may have been smaller than the gold-and-ivory statues of *Athena Parthenos* at Athens and *Zeus* at Olympia by Phidias.

Further Reading

For a discussion of the ancient sources on Polykleitos see Jerome J. Pollitt, *The Art of Greece, 1400-31 B.C.* (1965). Scholarly discussions of Polykleitos are found in Ernst Berger's article "Polykleitos" in the *Encyclopedia of World Art,* vol. 11 (1966); C. C. Vermeule, *Polykleitos* (1969); B. S. Ridgway, *The Severe Style in Greek Sculpture* (1970); and G. M. A. Richter, *The Sculpture and Sculptors of the Greeks* (4th ed. 1970). □

Marquês de Pombal

The Portuguese statesman Sebastião José de Carvalho e Mello, Marquês de Pombal (1699-1782), one of the most important men in the history of Portugal, became virtual dictator of his country during the reign of King Joseph I. He used his powers to introduce much-needed reforms.

The future Marquês de Pombal was born on May 13, 1699, at Soure, a small village not far from the town of Pombal, from which he later took his title. Little is known of Pombal's childhood. He derived from a rural family of the lower nobility and probably received a good education. He served in the cavalry for a while and eventually went to Lisbon, where, after working in the Academy of History, he eloped with a niece of the powerful Count of Arcoa. This marriage opened many doors for Pombal. From 1740 to 1744 he was ambassador to London, in which post he came to understand and to resent his country's economic subservience to England.

Soon after his return to Portugal in 1744, Pombal's wife died. In 1745 he was sent as his government's representative to Vienna, where he married again. Upon his return to Lisbon in 1749, Pombal was named junior minister in the government of King John V.

Not long after Pombal's appointment, John V died and was succeeded by his son, the indolent and pleasure-seeking Joseph I (reigned 1750-1777). Pombal quickly consolidated his position within the government, and by the end of 1755, after his energetic handling of the great crisis produced by the Lisbon earthquake, he was virtual dictator of Portugal, taking complete control of the machinery of government.

In his early years in power Pombal faced strong opposition both from the great noble families, which had formerly dominated the government, and from the powerful Jesuit order, whose power and influence Pombal sought to curb. On Sept. 3, 1758, an attempt was made to assassinate the King. Pombal grabbed the occasion, resolutely implicating both the high nobility and the Jesuits in the plot. In January 1759 some of the highest nobles of the land were publicly executed. Later that year the Jesuit order was expelled from Portugal forever.

Secure in power, Pombal now concentrated on his goals of strengthening the Portuguese economy and of curbing British economic preeminence in Portugal and its colo-

nies. A series of administrative reforms brought Portugal and Brazil under greater central surveillance, and a series of important economic and financial reforms followed.

Pombal reformed the University of Coimbra and set up a board of censorship to control education. He organized the state-run Company for Trade with Asia and, in 1755, the Grao-Para Company, the first of three companies intended to monopolize trade with Brazil. Pombal also reorganized the Brazilian mines, regulated the trade in tobacco and sugar, and in 1771 took over the Brazilian diamond trade for the state.

Many of Pombal's schemes were successful; others died at birth. Although he did a great deal for Portugal, he failed to put an end to its commercial subservience to England and to the generally bad economic situation in both Portugal and Brazil. The closing years of the reign of Joseph I saw no relief from financial difficulties.

King Joseph I died in January 1777. He was succeeded by his daughter Maria I and by her uncle and husband, Pedro III. They could not tolerate the dictatorial rule of Pombal. In March 1777 Pombal was dismissed, and a new ministry was chosen from the nobility. The fallen dictator first retired to his palace at Oiras. His enemies, however, had him banished to the town of Pombal. Various charges were brought against him, and he was found guilty at his trial in August 1781. However, Pombal, now ill and 82 years old, received a pardon. He died on May 8, 1782.

Further Reading

Pombal's *Memoirs* (2 vols., 1843) are important and revealing. The most useful biography of him in English is Marcus Cheke, *Dictator of Portugal: A Life of the Marquis of Pombal* (1938). A scholarly account of the political, economic, and social condition of Portugal in Pombal's lifetime is in H. V. Livermore, *A New History of Portugal* (1966).

Additional Sources

Maxwell, Kenneth, *Pombal, paradox of the Enlightenment,* Cambridge England; New York, NY: Cambridge University Press, 1995. □

Pompey

Pompey (106-48 B.C.) was a Roman general and statesman and the dominant figure in Rome between the abdication of Sulla in 79 B.C. and his own defeat by Julius Caesar at Pharsalus in 48 B.C.

Pompey or Cnaeus Pompeius Magnus, was born on Sept. 29, 106 B.C., into a family of moderate distinction at Rome. His father, Pompeius Starbo, was one of the most successful and independent Roman generals in the war against Rome's former Italian allies (90 B.C.). Pompey himself first came to public attention when he raised troops for the support of Lucius Cornelius Sulla when Sulla returned from the East to challenge the followers of

Gaius Marius. Pompey won victories for Sulla in Sicily and exacted a triumph from him.

Soon after the abdication of Sulla, Pompey showed that he did not regard himself bound by the strict provisions of the Sullan constitution. He secured from the Senate a special command against the rebel proconsul M. Aemilius Lepidus (77 B.C.), in spite of the fact that he was below the age established by the Sullan constitution for magistracies and commands. His success against Lepidus was followed by another special command against Sertorius. Sertorius, a former supporter of Marius, had fled to Spain after the defeat of the Marian faction and was waging a series of masterful guerrilla wars against Roman armies sent against him.

Pompey arrived in Spain in 76 B.C. A series of indecisive campaigns followed, with Pompey gaining slight advantages until Sertorius was murdered by one of his officers in 72 B.C. Following his victory, rather than spreading massive destruction, Pompey pursued a humane policy of granting citizenship and founding permanent settlements in Spain to ensure peace.

Consul and Reformer

After 5 years' absence, Pompey returned to Italy. He took some of the credit for the suppression of Spartacus's revolt by eliminating some elements of the gladiators' army. The result of these successes propelled Pompey together with M. Licinius Crassus, the real victor over Spartacus, into the consulship for the year 70 B.C. This again was contrary to the Sullan decrees, since Pompey had held no previous

regular political office in Rome. The two men presided over the dismantling of certain elements of Sulla's constitution.

The tribunate, which had been used by the Gracchi in the late 2nd century to push popular reform, had been stripped of almost all power by the conservative Sulla. Now Pompey and Crassus restored most of its old strength, and it became a potent instrument in the power struggles of the last years of the republic. Gaius Sempronius Gracchus had limited membership on the courts which tried Roman governors for extortion to the financial class (equestrians), and Sulla had returned control to the Senate. Now the courts were entrusted to a mixed body of senators and equestrians.

Pirate Wars and Mithridates

The next major challenge came to Pompey in 67 B.C., when he was charged with suppressing the pirates. The piratical menace had grown as the result of Rome's short-sighted suppression of the power of the Greek island of Rhodes in the 2d century B.C. Rhodes had for years kept the Mediterranean free of pirates. Now they even raided the Roman seaport of Ostia.

Pompey received a command which provided him with complete power at sea and power equal to that of any governor for 50 miles inland. Furthermore, he was granted the right to appoint 24 legates so that he could divide the Mediterranean among various subordinates and coordinate the sweeps against the pirates. The success of his planning was shown by the fact that the pirate danger was eliminated within a year. In victory, Pompey again showed a sensible humanity by settling pacified pirates in communities where they could follow peaceful activities.

This amazing triumph over the pirates led to Pompey's command against Rome's second current menace, Mithridates. This king of Pontus had been a thorn in the side of Rome for nearly 20 years. Several times he had been defeated but had always recovered. Now the Roman general Lucullus, who seemed to have finally suppressed Mithridates, was faced with an army in mutiny and political resistance at home. When Pompey received this command, which granted him almost unlimited powers in the East, in 66 B.C., Mithridates saw his days numbered and had himself killed by one of his own bodyguards. Pompey then toured the East, absorbing territories such as Syria into the empire, making treaties with many of the Asiatic princelings, founding cities, and building up vast support for himself.

The Triumvirate

However, in 62 B.C. Pompey had to return to Rome to get his agreements ratified by the Senate and rewards provided for his soldiers. He had relatively little experience in senatorial politics and discovered that the senatorial oligarchy tended to unite against powerful individuals. Pompey's political program was soon in trouble, and he had to turn to the wealthy and influential Crassus and to Julius Caesar, the consul for 59 B.C. They formed the political alliance known as the Triumvirate. Caesar used his own skill, as well as Pompey's and Crassus' resources, to pass the bills that Pompey wanted.

In spite of his difficulties with the Senate, Pompey was still the most important individual in Rome. His wealth from his Eastern connections was enormous, and he displayed it by such activities as building Rome's first stone theater. The next decade was to test all his skills. By 58 B.C. Rome was virtually ruled by political mobs like that led by P. Clodius Pulcher. Pompey was not able to control these and at one time was even forced to barricade himself in his house. Still he was the man to whom Rome turned in hours of crisis. In 57 B.C., when there was a shortage of grain, Pompey again received a special commission to deal with the crisis. In 55 B.C., after the Conference of Luca had patched up the Triumvirate, he was again consul. Following this, he received the proconsulship of the two Spains with the right to administer provinces in absentia. In 52 B.C., when after the murder of Clodius rioting engulfed Rome, he was chosen sole consul, an unprecedented step.

Meanwhile, events outside Rome were shifting the balance of power and the alliance of parties. In 59 B.C. Caesar had been a useful but not an overly powerful individual. After years of successful campaigning in Gaul, he had enormous prestige, great wealth, and a tough, loyal army. Gradually the links between him and Pompey were dissolved. The Conference of Luca had temporarily patched up their alliance. However, in 54 B.C. a major link between the two was broken when Julia, daughter of Caesar and wife of Pompey, died. She had been loved by both men and must have done much to hold them together. The sense of confrontation was increased in 53 B.C., when the third triumvir, Crassus, was killed fighting the Parthians. The fear of Caesar now drove Pompey and the Senate increasingly together.

The real crisis erupted when Caesar's command in Gaul came to an end. A faction in Rome was awaiting the day when Caesar lost his proconsular immunity and could be tried for his activities as consul and proconsul. Caesar saw this and demanded the right to stand for the consulship without leaving his province. Pompey was caught in the middle between the ambitious Caesar and an obdurate band of senators. Finally, the Senate forced the issue, and Caesar chose war.

Civil War

Pompey decided quickly that his best chance of success lay in rallying his support in the East. He abandoned Italy to Caesar and moved to Greece. Although he had the reputation of being Rome's greatest marshal, he had not been to war for over a decade, so the loyalty of old soldiers had cooled. Caesar, on the other hand, came fresh from the field of battle with a hardened army. Moreover, Caesar fought for his own interest, whereas Pompey was the general of the Senate. As such, he had to pay heed to the numerous senators who crowded his camp. In the end Caesar proved the superior strategist and tactician.

After securing his position in Italy and the West, Caesar moved against Pompey in Greece. Pompey managed to avoid being trapped at Dyrrhachium and followed Caesar's army as he retreated into Greece. The two met on the field of Pharsalus (Aug. 9, 48 B.C.), and Caesar, although outnumbered, displayed greater tactical ability, and Pompey fled in defeat. When he landed in Egypt, he was murdered at the orders of Ptolemy, the ruler of Egypt.

Further Reading

The only surviving ancient biography of Pompey is by Plutarch. For contemporary impressions of Pompey, Cicero's letters and speeches are invaluable. A study of Pompey is William Scovil Anderson, *Pompey, His Friends, and the Literature of the First Century B.C.* (1963). A briefer study of him is in Charles Oman, *Seven Roman Statesman of the Later Republic* (1934). Ronald Syme, *The Roman Revolution* (1939), places Pompey in the whole background of the fall of the republic.

Additional Sources

Greenhalgh, P. A. L., *Pompey, the republican prince,* Columbia: University of Missouri Press, 1982, 1981.

Greenhalgh, P. A. L., *Pompey, the Roman Alexander,* Columbia: University of Missouri Press, 1981, 1980.

Leach, John, *Pompey the Great,* London; Dover, N.H.: Croom Helm, 1986, 1978.

Rawson, Beryl, *The politics of friendship: Pompey and Cicero,* Sydney: Sydney University Press, 1978.

Seager, Robin, *Pompey, a political biography,* Berkeley: University of California Press, 1979. □

Georges Pompidou

Georges Pompidou (1911-1974) was the second president of the French Fifth Republic (1969-1974). He played a major role in solidifying the new system that gave France more than a generation of effective government and economic growth.

There was nothing in Pompidou's early years to suggest a career at the top of French political life. He was born on July 5, 1911, in a small town in central France. His parents were rural school teachers with strong peasant roots. Like many children of teachers, Pompidou aspired to an academic career. In 1931 he entered the prestigious Ecole normale supérieure, and by 1934 he had also passed the *aggrégation* exam (that qualifies one to teach in universities) and received a diploma from the Ecole libre des sciences politique. The small town boy, grandson of peasants, had joined the French elite.

Pompidou spent the rest of the pre-World War II years teaching, first in Marseilles and then at the noted Parisian Lycée Henri IV. He fought in an infantry regiment in World War II, and after the French defeat in 1940 Pompidou resumed his teaching duties. Quietly, Pompidou worked in the Resistance and became personal secretary to Gen. Charles de Gaulle while he was head of the provisional government between 1944 and 1946.

His relationship with General de Gaulle made it difficult for Pompidou to return to the national bureaucracy or educational system, so he took a position with the Rothschild family bank. For the entire Fourth Republic (1946-1958) and the first years of the Fifth (1958-present),

Pompidou worked at establishing his business career while discreetly maintaining ties with de Gaulle and his inner circle. He did not join de Gaulle when he returned to power in 1958, but he did serve as an informal adviser, especially in preparing the new constitution, drafting the economic recovery plan that followed, and establishing contacts with the Algerian revolutionaries.

From Businessman to Prime Minister

Georges Pompidou's formal political career started only in 1962, but it started at the top. President de Gaulle asked for and received the resignation of his first prime minister, Michel Debré. It marked the first time in French history that a president had removed a prime minister and sharpened the hostility between de Gaulle and members of Parliament, who considered it to be their responsibility to determine who served in the cabinet. That hostility mounted when de Gaulle named Pompidou to the prime ministry, since he not only was not a parliamentarian, but had never even run for elective office before. The new prime minister quickly became the main object of that hostility. When President de Gaulle proposed a referendum of questionable legality on the direct election of the president, the members of Parliament had finally had enough and passed a vote of censure (no confidence) in the Pompidou government. But instead of accepting the Pompidou government's resignation, de Gaulle dissolved the National Assembly, provoking legislative elections as well as the controversial referendum. The Gaullists won both handily, returning Pompidou and his cabinet to power with the first firm parliamentary majority in French republican history. Pompidou was to remain at the Palais Matignon until July 1968.

Those were years of tremendous accomplishment for the new republic and its prime minister. Its base of support shifted from the personal popularity of de Gaulle to a firmer foundation in mass approval of the new institutions he created. Pompidou played a critical role in that process in two respects.

First, he was the prime architect of the Gaullist political party that provided the parliamentary majority the government needed. Though the party changed its name from election to election, it quickly became a more disciplined machine than anything the French center or right had seen before. Pompidou and his collaborators began by controlling party nominations for office so that only politicians loyal to the national leadership would end up in Parliament. They also sought local notables—not the ambitious men and women of the Fourth Republic, but individuals willing to subsume their personal goals to the greater needs of the party. In particular, the Gaullists recruited candidates from the Parisian bureaucratic intellectual elite—men like Pompidou himself—who were "parachuted" into districts throughout the country.

Second, Prime Minister Pompidou played an important role in modernizing the French economy. President de Gaulle had come to power again in 1958 vowing to restore French "grandeur." For many, including Pompidou, that meant restructuring the French economy so that it could be competitive in the increasingly interdependent domestic and international markets. The Gaullists used the planning machinery they had helped establish during the liberation years in the mid-1940s. But even more they relied on the powerful but informal network of former bureaucrats who shared their image of a modern France and who dominated both Gaullist and business circles. For most of the 1960s and 1970s France had one of the most dynamic economies of the world, out performing even the West Germans.

From Prime Minister to President

Pompidou's years as prime minister were not trouble free. The government was almost too successful and generated hostility among those who felt they had lost out during the first decade of Gaullist rule. That hostility erupted in May 1968, when a minor student protest turned into a nationwide general strike that almost toppled the regime. No Gaullist leader came out of the "events of May" looking good, but none did better than Pompidou at maintaining order and trying to find a solution. To end the crisis de Gaulle once again dissolved the National Assembly, and the Gaullists once again won a landslide victory at the polls. Pompidou, however, was not named prime minister again. Instead, de Gaulle named the bland diplomat and former foreign minister Maurice Couve de Murville to head the new government, leaving Pompidou "on reserve for the Republic."

Pompidou did not have to wait long. In early 1969 de Gaulle called for a referendum to restructure the largely powerless Senate and local governments. When that referendum was defeated, de Gaulle did what he had threatened to do—he resigned.

Presidential elections were held in June, and Pompidou won an easy victory over the divided leftist and centrist opposition. As president, he continued the broad lines of Gaullist policy, but did so in a seemingly more pragmatic way. Economic growth, spurred by a variety of state policies, continued. The welfare state was expanded to provide more benefits for the working class and the poor. The Gaullist party strengthened its roots, especially in small towns where the old notables frequently still held sway. Only in foreign policy was there much change, as President Pompidou brought France closer to the United States and the North Atlantic Treaty Organization (NATO) and ended French opposition to British entry into the Common Market.

Pompidou's presidency lacked the luster and obvious success of de Gaulle's. Moreover, his accomplishments were limited by the effects of the OPEC (Organization of Petroleum-Exporting Countries) oil embargo and its implications for all Western economies and by his own increasingly crippling illness, which finally took his life on April 2, 1974. Still, Georges Pompidou will be remembered as a chief architect of the most successful republic France had known, a man who successfully presided over the transition from a charismatic leader to one who had to rely on more normal mechanisms.

Further Reading

As is the case for most French politicians, there are no biographies of Pompidou available in English. For material on his political and economic accomplishments see Jean Charlot, *The Gaullist Phenomenon* (London, 1971) and John Ardagh, *The New French Revolution* (1967), respectively. □

Pietro Pomponazzi

The Italian Aristotelian philosopher Pietro Pomponazzi (1462-1525) was associated with the rationalist and humanist currents that swept Padua, Bologna, and other northern Italian universities in the early 16th century.

The fame of Pietro Pomponazzi rests principally on the *De immortalitate animae,* published in Bologna in 1516. In this work he concluded that the immortality of the soul, a cardinal doctrine in Christianity, could not be proved by philosophical argument.

Pomponazzi was born in Mantua on Sept. 16, 1462. At the University of Padua he studied natural philosophy under Nicoletto Vernia and Pietro Trapolino, metaphysics under Francesco Securo da Nardò, and medicine under Pietro Roccabonella. After 1487, with some interruptions, he taught philosophy at Padua, where he began his commentary on Aristotle's *De anima* and had as a pupil the future cardinal and Catholic reformer Gasparo Contarini. The siege of Padua and the closing of the university in 1509 compelled Pomponazzi to move to Ferrara, where he resided for a year, finally settling in Bologna, where he remained until his death on May 18, 1525.

In his most celebrated work, the *De immortalitate animae,* Pomponazzi elaborated on Aristotle's conception of the soul as it had been interpreted and transmitted by the Alexandrians. In his concern for the new humanistic view of the worth and dignity of the individual soul, Pomponazzi came to oppose the prevailing impersonal and collectivist view of human nature held by the Averroist school. Through a series of subtle technical arguments he parted with the Averroist concept of a single, corporate, but transcendent and immortal Intellect—a concept within which there was no place for human individuality.

Pomponazzi's insistence on the soul's perishability was clearly in conflict with Catholic eschatology and moral theory—with the Church's contention that rewards and punishments for human actions are reserved for the hereafter. Pomponazzi substituted what he considered a higher ethic: the essential reward of virtue is virtue itself, and the real punishment of evil is evil itself. Pomponazzi avoided official condemnation for this view in his own lifetime, despite the great anger of Pope Leo X. However, he was compelled to make at least a partial retraction, which he did in two writings, the *Apologia* (1517) and the *Defensorium* (1519).

The rationalist and humanist bent of Pomponazzi's mind continued to exhibit itself in his later writings. In the *De incantationibus* and the *De naturalium effectuum causis* he sought natural explanations for the miracles described in the Bible. In the *De fato* he attempted to reconcile human freedom and Providence. In his efforts to separate science and philosophy from theology, Pomponazzi stands as a pioneer in the progressive secularization of thought that has characterized the modern period.

Further Reading

An English translation of the *De immortalitate animae,* with an excellent introductory essay by John Herman Randall, is in Ernst Cassirer and others, eds., *The Renaissance Philosophy of Man* (1948). The essay is reprinted, with some revisions, in Randall's *The School of Padua and the Emergence of Modern Science* (1961). The only comprehensive monograph on Pomponazzi in English is Andrew Halliday Douglas, *The Philosophy and Psychology of Pietro Pomponazzi* (1910). □

Juan Ponce de León

The Spanish conqueror and explorer Juan Ponce de León (1460-1521) conquered the island of Puerto Rico and explored the coastline of Florida, which he claimed for the Spanish crown.

Juan Ponce de León was born in San Servas. Although of noble lineage, he was penniless and like so many destitute bluebloods sought fame and fortune as a soldier. He served in the 10-year conquest of the Moslem kingdom of Granada in southern Spain. Afterward, he heard exaggerated accounts of Columbus's discovery and migrated to the island of Hispaniola (modern Dominican Republic and Haiti).

After he had put down an Indian uprising in the eastern province of the island in 1504, the Indians told Ponce de León that he would find gold on a neighboring island to the east, called Boriquien (Puerto Rico). Four years later he crossed over and conquered the island. During the conquest he shared the honors with a famous greyhound dog named Bercerillo. It was said that the Indians were more afraid of ten Spaniards with the dog than one hundred without him. Ponce de León governed Puerto Rico until the King removed him from office in 1512.

Dispossessed of his office, Ponce de León obtained a royal grant to discover and settle the island of Bimini, which was believed to lie somewhere to the northwest. An incidental objective was to locate the wondrous spring whose waters would restore youth to the aged. The myth, repeated to Ponce de León by the Indians, was of European origin. According to the legend, the spring was in the Garden of Eden, which was located somewhere in Asia—the early Spaniards believing America to be Asia.

On March 3, 1513, Ponce de León sailed from Puerto Rico and a month later anchored near the mouth of the St. Johns River on the northeast coast of Florida. Impressed with its floral beauty and having landed at Eastertide, he named

Ponce de León (right)

the land Florida, from the Spanish *Pascua florida,* "flowery Easter." While voyaging southward he encountered the strong current of the Gulf Stream as it poured through a channel. He had discovered the Bahama Channel, which later became the route of the treasure ships on their return voyage to Spain. He continued exploring the east coast and then sailed up the Gulf coast to Pensacola Bay. During his return voyage to Puerto Rico he sighted several small islands crowded with tortoises and named them the Tortugas, "tortoises."

In 1514 Ponce de León returned to Spain, where he received another grant, to colonize the "Island of Florida" at his own expense. In February 1521 the colonizing expedition landed on the Florida coast near Charlotte Harbor. The Native Americans attacked with such ferocity and persistence that the settlement was abandoned. Ponce de León, mortally wounded in battle, died a few days after having returned to Cuba. He was buried in Puerto Rico, the epitaph on his sepulcher reading, "Here rest the bones of a valiant LION [León], mightier in deeds than in name."

Further Reading

Accounts Ponce de León's life include Florian A. Mann, *The Story of Ponce de León* (1903); Frederick A. Ober, *Juan Ponce de León* (1908); and Edward W. Lawson, *The Discovery of Florida and Its Discoverer, Juan Ponce de Leon* (1946). Excellent accounts of his career are in Woodbury Lowery, *The Spanish Settlements within the Present Limits of the United States, 1513-1561* (1905); Herbert E. Bolton, *The Spanish Borderlands* (1921); and Anthony Kerrigan's translation of Andres Barcia, *Chronological History of the Continent of Florida* (1951). □

Elena Poniatowska

Elena Poniatowska (born 1933) was a feminist Mexican journalist, novelist, essayist, and short-story writer.

Elena Poniatowska was born on May 19, 1933, in Paris, France. Her father was French of Polish ancestry and her mother a Mexican who was raised in France. When she was nine Poniatowska's family moved to Mexico City. She grew up speaking French and learned English in a private British school. However, her knowledge of Spanish came from talking with the maids, so her written Spanish was largely colloquial. Poniatowska developed ties with the Mexican lower class in her youth and thus gained a sense of belonging to and an understanding of the Mexican culture. She felt and thought of herself as completely Mexican and of Spanish as her native language. Her works include characters who belong to the underprivileged classes, and she often gave voice to the powerless of her country.

She started writing as a journalist in 1954 and interviewed many famous Mexican and international writers. Many of these interviews can be found in her *Palabras Cruzadas* (1961; *Crossed Words*) and later in her *Todo*

México (1990; *All of Mexico*). Besides her famous interviews, she also wrote several novels, short stories, chronicles, plays, and poems.

Among her novels are *Hasta no verte, Jesús mío* (1969; *Until I see You, My Jesus*), which earned her the Mazatlan Prize; *Querido Diego, te abraza Quiela* (1978; *Dear Diego, love Quiela*); *La "Flor de Lis"* (1988; *The "Flower of the Lily"*); and *Tinísima* (1992; *Tinisima*). Other narratives include *Lilus Kikus* (1954; *Lilus Kikus;* later an expanded edition appeared as *Los cuentos* [*The Accounts*] *de Lilus Kikus* in 1967); *De noche vienes* (1979; *You Come at Night*); *Ay vida no me mereces* (1985; *Life, You Don't Deserve Me*); *Domingo 7* (1982; *Seventh Sunday*); *Gaby Brimmer* (1979; *Gaby Brimmer*); *Todo empezó el domingo* (1963; *Everything Started on Sunday*); and *El último guajolote* (1982; *The Last Turkey*).

Her chronicle *La noche de Tlatelolco* (1971; *Massacre in Mexico*) earned her the Javier Villarrutia Prize. She refused to accept it because she did not want to identify herself with then-President Echeverría's political establishment. Other chronicles include *Fuerte es el silencio* (1980; *Silence Is Strong*), and *Nada, nadie: las voces del temblor* (1988; *Nothing, Nobody: The Voices of the Earthquake*).

In theater, her play *Melés y Teleo* (1956; *Melés and Teleo*) uses a word game in the title, meaning "you read to me and I read to you." Finally, her poetry can be found in the Spanish publications *Rojo de vida y negro de muerte, Estaciones,* and *Abside.*

Ponistowska's skill as a novelist was her ability to combine fact with fiction. She lent her voice to the voiceless, but at the same time she took a step back and let the victims come forward to express their needs and pain, letting the Mexican people speak through her. Her settings were mostly in Mexico, and her characters were either Mexicans or people such as Angelina Beloff (*Querido Diego, te abraza Quiela*) or Tina Modotti (*Tinísima*) who lived important passages of their lives in Mexico. Many of her female characters are at the mercy of men. Their lives are ruled by a world made up of double standards. They try to do the right thing, but in the end they lose the men they loved and for whom they sacrificed. It is clear then that these women are never really appreciated.

Poniatowska had a great affinity with women and liked to write about them. But she also was interested in the poor, the weak, the street children, and the powerless. Interviewing the common people of Mexico became her trademark. After her first publication (*Lilus Kikus,* 1954), her writings became more and more political. For example, in *Querido Diego* (1978) Quiela's story is completely personal. It focuses upon her and her lover, the famous painter Diego Rivera. By comparison, in *Tinísima* (1992) Poniatowska reveals not just Modotti's emotional life but also her professional and political life as a communist.

However, Poniatowska's style often made it difficult for readers outside Mexico to appreciate her. Critics often attacked her docudrama plot twists where famous events and people coincided in remarkable meetings. For instance, *Tinísima,* published in the U.S. in 1996, received lukewarm reviews. "When history is offered in the form of fiction, caveat emptor," warned a reviewer for the *New York Times.* Explaining Poniatowska's embrace of the unique Latin-American *testimonio* form, feminist Doris Sommer wrote somewhat critically,"*Testimonio* is precisely not fiction. It is a first-person narrative in Latin America that, like other oral histories, can be elicited by sympathetic intellectuals who interview illiterate or semiliterate working people."

It has been said that Poniatowska does not offer solutions to the problems raised in her texts. This may be true, but many feel that without her chronicles, people (including many Mexicans) would still be unaware of the issues addressed. Her writings, especially her chronicles, are an excellent cultural, political, sociological, economic, and historical source of information about Mexico and its people.

Further Reading

Writings about Poniatowska have appeared mostly in Spanish. The sources listed here in chronological order are the best available in English.

Elizabeth Starcevic's chapter on Poniatowska in *Literatures in Transition: The Many Voices of the Caribbean Area: A Symposium* (1982) primarily emphasizes Poniatowska's role as the voice for the oppressed in Mexico who otherwise would not be heard. Bell Gale Chevigny discusses Poniatowska's presentation of female characters and her attention to political and social issues in an article in *Latin American Literary Review* (1985). In *Spanish American Women Writers: A Bio-Bibliographical Source Book* (1990), Beth Jörgenson provides an excellent overview of Poniatowska's major themes in her works, plus a helpful survey of the critical commentary about Poniatowska. Doris Sommer provides a feminist look at Poniatowska's work in the *Signs: The Journal of Women in Culture and Society* (Summer 1995.) An even more thorough discussion of the author's work can be found in Jörgenson's book, *The Writing of Elena Poniatowska: Engaging Dialogues* (1994). □

Pontiac

Pontiac (ca. 1720-1769), Ottawa chief and leader of the famed uprising that bears his name, was a pawn in the fight between the British and the French for supremacy in the Great Lakes region.

Pontiac was born probably on the Maumee River, of a Chippewa mother and Ottawa father. His youth is obscure, but he grew to become a sachem (chief) of the combined Ottawa, Chippewa, and Potawatomi tribes. Possibly he was present at the Chippewa defeat of Gen. Edward Braddock in 1755, when his tribes were under French influence during the French and Indian War.

In 1760, when British and American colonial troops marched to fight the French at Detroit, Pontiac met the force and learned of the British victory at Quebec. He smoked the peace pipe with the British and even helped them take Detroit, but he did not get the recognition for this that he felt he deserved. Thus in 1762, when he heard that the French were going to reinvade, he turned against the British and tried to organize a vast Indian conspiracy against them.

Pontiac rallied tribes in the vicinity of the Great Lakes to a great conference near Detroit in April 1763. Here he made a stirring speech, calling the tribes simultaneously to attack the nearest British posts. He personally led the attack on Detroit on May 7, 1763. However, his plan became known to the British, and all he could do was lay siege to the post, eventually retreating. The Conspiracy of Pontiac, as this uprising was known, did succeed in capturing 8 of the 12 posts attacked, and it inflamed the entire western frontier. And Pontiac did manage one victory, the Battle of Bloody Ridge on July 31, 1763, at which his warriors killed 60 of the 250 British troops.

Yet Pontiac's confederation quickly fell apart. In October 1763 part of the Ottawa made peace with the British, and Pontiac followed in a preliminary peace on October 31. Yet he continued to fight sporadically, not concluding a final peace with the British until July 1766.

In the spring of 1769 Pontiac visited the vicinity of St. Louis, and there on April 20 he was clubbed to death by a Peoria Indian warrior, possibly at British urging. Some contemporary accounts referred to Pontiac as a coward, and others spoke of him as only a local renegade; however, he did achieve a remarkable confederation of dissident Native American tribes, and he caught the popular imagination to become a romantic figure.

Further Reading

The standard, if somewhat romantic, account of Pontiac and his rebellion is Francis Parkman, *The History of the Conspiracy of Pontiac* (1851). More reliable is Howard H. Peckham, *Pontiac and the Indian Uprising* (1947). Milo M. Quaife edited some of the contemporary accounts in *The Siege of Detroit in 1763: The Journal of Pontiac's Conspiracy, and John Rutherfurd's Narrative of a Captivity* (1958). □

Pontormo

The Italian painter Pontormo (1494-1556) was an innovator of the mannerist style whose works influenced the subsequent development of Florentine mannerism.

Pontormo whose real name was Jacopo Carrucci, was born at Pontorme near Empoli. Apprenticed in rapid succession to several painters, including Leonardo da Vinci and Piero di Cosimo, when he was about 18 Pontormo became an assistant to Andrea del Sarto. Pontormo's first big commission, a fresco, the *Visitation* (1514), in Saints Annunziata, Florence, was part of a cycle of scenes from the life of Mary to which Andrea also contributed; it was such a success in Andrea's style that it aroused his jealousy.

The break with the classical style of the High Renaissance came about when the skill in realistic rendering had apparently reached a point in the work of Leonardo and other artists that could not be surpassed. Andrea and his contemporaries rearranged these realistic observations in handsome compositions which thus tended toward academic schemes, smooth and idealized. Andrea's pupils, in turn, formalized these patterns at one remove from nature. The mannerist artist emphasized the figure, as earlier High Renaissance painters had done, but he distorted its proportions and its relationship to space.

Pontormo's *Visitation* presents grandly robed, symmetrically grouped people in a niche, much as Andrea had done in his art, but in a series of small paintings of Joseph in Egypt (1515-1518) Pontormo scattered the figures over the picture surface, whimsically linked by impossible staircases. In the altarpiece (1518) for St. Michele Visdomini in Florence, black shadows separate the people and hide any spatial coordinates, and in the lunette fresco (1520) of the Medici villa at Poggio a Caiano, depicting the pastoral myth of Vertumnus and Pomona, the figures sit and gaze at us, making no gesture that links them in a narrative. All the figures are convincingly modeled, and his countless figure drawings are brilliant.

Of Pontormo's Passion frescoes (1523-1524) in the Certosa of Galluzzo, *Christ before Pilate* is the most famous. The figures, influenced by Albrecht Dürer, are sharply elongated, and the receding space is titled almost vertically upward. The *Deposition* altarpiece (1526) in St. Felicita in Florence is the climax of the artist's career, a mound of

rising figures in odd shades of pink and green, each crisply drawn. This painting is a masterpiece of early Florentine mannerism.

Little of Pontormo's late work has been preserved. In the 1530s he painted stylized portraits and works closely derived from Michelangelo, another phase of the use of completed art as a tool that is basic to mannerism. Pontormo's last frescoes (1546-1556; destroyed), in St. Lorenzo in Florence, executed with a new style of fluid line, were generally disliked. He died in Florence in late December 1556.

Further Reading

Frederick M. Clapp, *Jacopo Carucci da Pontormo: His Life and Work* (1916), is excellent but outdated. Janet C. Rearick, *The Drawings of Pontormo* (2 vols., 1964), is thorough and trustworthy. Pontormo is discussed in Walter Friedlaender, *Mannerism and Antimannerism in Italian Painting* (1957). □

Alexander Pope

The English poet and satirist Alexander Pope (1688-1744) was the greatest poet and verse satirist of the Augustan period. No other poet in the history of English literature has handled the heroic couplet with comparable flexibility and brilliance.

Alexander Pope inherited from John Dryden the verse from that he chose to perfect. He polished his work with meticulous care and, like all great poets, used language with genuine inventiveness. His qualities of imagination are seen in the originality with which he handled traditional forms, in his satiric vision of the contemporary world, and in his inspired use of classical models.

Pope was born on May 21, 1688, in London, where his Roman Catholic father was a linen merchant. After the Glorious Revolution of 1688 his family moved out of London and settled about 1700 at Binfield in Windsor Forest. Pope had little formal schooling, largely educating himself through extensive reading. Sir William Trumbull, a retired statesman of literary interests who lived nearby, did much to encourage the young poet. So did the dramatist and poet William Wycherley and the poet-critic William Walsh, with whom Pope became acquainted when he was about 17 and whose advice to aim at "correctness" contributed to the flawless texture and concentrated brilliance of Pope's verse.

A sweet-tempered child with a fresh, plump face, Pope contracted a tubercular infection in his later childhood and never grew taller than 4 feet 6 inches. He suffered curvature of the spine (necessitating the wearing of a stiff canvas brace) and constant headaches. His features, however, were striking, and the young Joshua Reynolds noticed in his "sharp, keen countenance . . . something grand, like Cicero's." His physical appearance, frequently ridiculed by his enemies, undoubtedly gave an edge to Pope's satire; but he was always warmhearted and generous in his affection for his many friends.

Early Poems

Precocious as a poet, Pope attracted the notice of the eminent bookseller Jacob Tonson, who solicited the publication of his *Pastorals* (1709). By this time Pope was already at work on his more ambitious *Essay on Criticism* (1711), an illuminating synthesis of critical precepts designed to expose the evils and to effect a regeneration of the contemporary literary scene.

The *Rape of the Lock* (1712, two cantos) immediately made Pope famous as a poet. The cutting off of a lock of Miss Arabella Fermor's hair by Robert, Lord Petre, had caused an estrangement between these prominent Catholic families; and Pope's friend John Caryll had suggested that he write a poem "to make a jest of it, and laugh them together again." In the poem Fermor is represented as Belinda and Lord Petre as the Baron. Adopting a mock-heroic style in the manner of Nicholas Boileau's *Le Lutrin,* Pope showed how disproportionate it was to treat the event overseriously, at the same time glancing good-humoredly at vanity and at the rococolike glitter of the *beau monde*. Rejecting Joseph Addison's advice not to enlarge his design, Pope published an extended version (1714, five cantos) containing the "machinery" of the sylphs (adopted from the Rosicrucian system) and various other epic motifs and allusions. These not only heightened the brilliance of the poem's world but also helped to place its significance and that of the "rape" in proper perspective.

Several other poems published by 1717, the date of the first collected edition of Pope's works, deserve a brief mention. "Windsor Forest" (1713), written in the tradition of Sir John Denham's "Cooper's Hill," celebrated the peace confirmed by the Treaty of Utrecht. A rich tapestry of historical and poetic allusions, it showed the Stuarts, and especially Queen Anne, in a quasi-mythical light. In 1717 appeared the sophisticated yet moving "Elegy to the Memory of an Unfortunate Lady" and "Eloisa to Abelard," an example in the Ovidian manner of the currently popular form of heroic epistle. The representation of the cloistered Eloisa's conflicting emotions toward her former lover (the scholar Peter Abelard), the denouement, and the concluding epilogue make this poem, in effect, a drama in miniature.

Translations of Homer

Pope also engaged in poetic imitations and translations. His *Messiah* (1712), published by Sir Richard Steele in the *Spectator,* was an imitation of Virgil's fourth Eclogue, based on passages from Isaiah; and his early "translations" of Chaucer included the *Temple of Fame* (1715). In later life Pope published reworkings of several of John Donne's satires. But Pope's versions of Homer were his greatest achievement as a translator.

From an early age a frequenter of Will's Coffeehouse, Pope was for a time friendly with men of both political parties. He wrote the prologue for Joseph Addison's Cato (1713), and the Whigs naturally hoped to secure his talents for their party. But growing opposition between him and Addison's followers (who met at Button's) made inevitable Pope's adherence to his other and more congenial group of literary friends—Jonathan Swift, Dr. John Arbuthnot, John Gay, and Thomas Parnell. Together they combined to form the Scriblerus Club, which aimed at a burlesque treatment of all forms of pedantry and which indirectly contributed to the creation of such works as *Gulliver's Travels* and the *Dunciad.* In 1715 Addison tried to forestall the success of Pope's translation of the *Iliad* by encouraging Thomas Tickell to publish a rival version, and this caused Pope a great deal of anxiety until the superiority of his own translation was acclaimed.

Pope undertook the translation because he needed money—the result of a sharp drop in the interest from his father's French annuities. The translation occupied him until 1720, and it was a great financial success, making Pope independent of the customary forms of literary patronage. Parnell and William Broome were among those who assisted with the notes, but the translation was entirely Pope's own. It has been highly praised by subsequent critics.

From the time his *Iliad* began to appear, Pope became the victim of numerous pamphlet attacks on his person, politics, and religion, many of them instigated by the infamous publisher Edmund Curll. In 1716 an increased land tax on Roman Catholics forced the Popes to sell their place at Binfield and to settle near the Earl of Burlington's villa at Chiswick. The next year Pope's father died, and in 1719 the poet's increased wealth enabled him to move with his mother to a semirural villa at Twickenham. There he improved house and gardens, making a special feature of the grotto, which connected house and gardens beneath the intervening road. At Twickenham, Lady Mary Wortley Montagu soon became Pope's neighbor. Several years earlier she had rivaled Martha Blount as an object of Pope's affection, but later a good deal of enmity existed between her and Pope, and she joined Lord (John) Hervey in attacking him.

During the 1720s Pope was engaged on a version of the *Odyssey* (1725-1726). Broome and Elijah Fenton were his collaborators, completing half of the translation between them. It was Pope's name, however, that sold the work, and he naturally received the lion's share of the profits (Pope earned about £9,000 from his translations of Homer). It was this translation that led to Pope's association with the young Joseph Spence, who wrote a Judicious and engaging criticism of it and who later recorded his valuable *Anecdotes* of Pope.

Editorial Work

Pope also undertook several editorial projects. Parnell's *Poems* (1721) was followed by an edition of the late Duke of Buckingham's *Works* (1723), subsequently suppressed on account of its Jacobite tendencies. The trial of his friend Francis Atterbury, Bishop of Rochester, for complicity in a Jacobite plot also caused Pope a good deal of concern. Then, in 1725, Pope's edition of William Shakespeare appeared. Pope's emendations and explanatory notes were notoriously capricious, and his edition was attacked by Lewis Theobald in *Shakespeare Restored* (1726), a work that revealed a superior knowledge of editorial technique and that gained for its author the unenviable distinction of becoming the original hero of the *Dunciad.*

The *Dunciad*

In 1726-1727 Swift was in England and a guest of Pope. Together they published three volumes of *Miscellanies* in 1727-1728, in the last of which the *Peri Bathous; or the Art of Sinking in Poetry* was included. Renewed contact with Swift must have given a great impetus to Pope's poem on "Dulness," which appeared as the three-book *Dunciad* (1728). Theobald was the prime dunce, and the next year the poem was enlarged by a ponderous apparatus (including "Notes Variorum") intended as a burlesque on the learned lumber of commentators and textual critics.

Clearly Pope used the *Dunciad* as personal satire to pay off many old scores. But it was also prompted by his distaste for that whole process by which worthless writers gained undue literary prominence. "Martinus Scriblerus" summarized the action of the poem as "the removal of the imperial seat of Dulness from the city to the polite world," and this parody of Virgil's epic was accompanied by further mock-heroic elements—the intervention of the goddess, the epic games of the second book, and the visit to the underworld and the vision of future "glories," with the former city-poet Elkanah Settle acting the part of the sybil. Indeed, despite its devastating satire, the *Dunciad* was essentially a phantasmagoric treatment of the forces of anticulture by a great comic genius.

In 1742 Pope published a fourth book to the *Dunciad* separately, and his last published work was the four-book

Dunciad (1743), which incorporated the new material and enthroned the brazen laureate Colley Cibber as prime dunce in place of Theobald. This revenge on Cibber, who had recently exposed a ridiculous escapade of the poet's youth, provided the poem with a more considerable hero. It also gained in artistic completeness, since the action of the fourth book depicted the fulfillment of Settle's prophecy.

Epistles and *An Essay on Man*

"The Epistle to Burlington" (1731), reminiscent of the *Dunciad* in its vivaciously satiric portrait of "Timon," was designed as part of a "system of ethics in the Horatian way" of which *An Essay on Man* (1733-1734) was to constitute the first book. Though this plan was never realized, the poem illustrates, along with its companion, "Epistle to Bathurst" (1733), antithetical vices in the use of riches. These two epistles were subsequently placed after those "To Cobham" (1734) and "To a Lady" (1735), which were thus intended to provide the projected *magnum opus* with an introductory section on the characters of men and women. "To Cobham" fits easily into this scheme, but "To a Lady" is rather a deliciously witty portrait gallery in Pope's best satiric manner.

"To Burlington" also compliments a nobleman friend of long standing who influenced Pope's appreciation of architecture as did Allen Bathurst his appreciation of landscape gardening. To these pursuits Pope devoted much of his time, being disposed to regard a cultivated esthetic taste as inseparable from a refined moral sense.

Pope's friendship with the former statesman Henry St. John Bolingbroke, who on his return from exile had settled a few miles from Twickenham, stimulated his interest in philosophy and led to the composition of *An Essay on Man*. Some ideas were doubtless suggested by Bolingbroke; certainly the argument advanced in Epistle 4—that terrestrial happiness is adequate to justify the ways of God to man—was consonant with his thinking. But Pope's sources were predominately commonplaces with a long history in Western thought, the most central being the doctrine of plenitude (expressed through the metaphors of a "chain" or "scale" of being) and the assertion that the discordant whole is bound harmoniously together. Even Pope's doctrine of the "ruling passion" was not original—though he gave it its most extended treatment. In essence, however, the *Essay* is not philosophy but a poet's apprehension of unity despite diversity, of an order embracing the whole multifarious creation.

The Correspondence

In 1733 Pope's mother died. The same year he engaged in a cat-and-mouse game with Curll to have his letters published in the guise of a pirated edition. Appearing in 1735, this edition allowed him to publish an authoritative edition in 1737. Such maneuvers are not easy to justify. Nor is the careful rewriting and fabrication, designed to reflect the author in the best possible light. But at least Pope's letters suggest the extent of his many friendships and something of the hospitality he enjoyed whenever he indulged his love of traveling.

Imitations of Horace

The 1730s were also the years of the *Imitations of Horace* (1733-1738), pungent and endearing by turns. How congenial to Pope were the conversational framework and Horatian independence of tone is evident from the fact that they read not like "imitations" but have the freshness of originals. Indeed, the best of them—the "Epistle to Arbuthnot" (1735) and the "Dialogues" (1738)—have no precise source. The "Epistle," with its famous portrait of Addison ("Atticus") and searing indictment of Hervey ("Sporus"), was both the satirist's *apologia pro vita sua* and his vindication of personally oriented satire. The two "Dialogues" continued this theme, introducing an additional element of political satire.

As Pope grew older, he came to rely more and more on the faithful Martha Blount, and to her he left most of his possessions. He described his life as a "long disease," and asthma increased his sufferings in his later years. At times during the last month of his life he became delirious. He died on May 30, 1744, and was buried in Twickenham Church.

Further Reading

The definitive edition of Pope's works is *The Twickenham Edition of the Poems of Alexander Pope,* edited by John Butt (10 vols., 1951-1967), a monumental and illuminating scholarly achievement. Pope's *Poetical Works,* edited by Herbert Davis (1967), presents the poems, without annotation, as in their original format.

George Sherburn, *The Early Career of Alexander Pope* (1934), is a scholarly literary biography of Pope to about 1726. A less scholarly but readable, reliable, and up-to-date biography is Peter Quennell, *Alexander Pope: The Education of Genius, 1688-1728* (1968), the first volume of a projected two-volume study. Marjorie Nicolson and G.S. Rousseau, *"This Long Disease, My Life": Alexander Pope and the Sciences* (1968), is a good treatment of Pope's illness and a history of science of the time. A short but colorful biography is Bonamy Dobrée, *Alexander Pope* (1951). See also Samuel Johnson, *The Lives of the English Poets* (3 vols., 1779-1781; several recent editions); Emily Morse Symonds, *Mr. Pope, His Life and Times* (2 vols., 1909); Edith Sitwell, Alexander Pope (1930); Norman Ault, *New Light on Pope* (1949); and William K. Wimsatt, *The Portraits of Alexander Pope* (1965).

Useful critical studies of the poetry include Geoffrey Tillotson, *On the Poetry of Pope* (1938) and *Pope and Human Nature* (1958); Aubrey L. Williams, *Pope's Dunciad* (1955); Reuben A. Brower, *Alexander Pope: The Poetry of Allusion* (1959); Thomas R. Edwards, *This Dark Estate: A Reading of Pope* (1963); and Maynard Mack, comp., *Essential Articles for the Study of Alexander Pope* (1964; rev. ed. 1968).

Recommended for general reading are James R. Sutherland, *A Preface to Eighteenth Century Poetry* (1948); Ian Jack, *Augustan Satire* (1952); and Geoffrey Tillotson, *Augustan Poetic Diction* (1964). ☐

John Russell Pope

The American architect John Russell Pope (1874-1937) was the major exemplar of the classical tradi-

tion in the United States. More than any other, he was responsible for the stylistic showcase of classical elegance demanded by the federal government and by wealthy private citizens during the first third of the 20th century. His work is mostly on the East Coast, with Washington, Baltimore, and the New York City area being major centers.

John Russell Pope was born in New York City on April 24, 1874. His father, a portrait painter of renown who had been elected to the National Academy of Design in 1857, died when Pope was only six years old. The family claimed descent from John Pope, who arrived in Massachusetts in the 1630s. His mother's family (Loomis) were also pre-Revolutionary War residents of America.

To this family background, Pope added an extraordinary talent and capacity for hard work. His family originally intended for him to study medicine, and he first attended the College of the City of New York with this in mind. After three years he enrolled at Columbia University to study architecture under William R. Ware, a major force in the training of a generation of architects. Pope excelled at his architectural studies; he served as an assistant to Ware and worked with Charles F. McKim of the distinguished firm of McKim, Meade, and White.

At graduation from Columbia in 1894 Pope won two major competitions: the university's Schermerhorn travelling fellowship for a year of study abroad and the first archi-

tecture fellowship of the American School (later Academy) in Rome. He spent the years 1895-1897 in Italy, Sicily, and Greece in serious study. Years later one commentator was to marvel at the number of measured drawings and reconstructions of ancient monuments Pope made during this time. At the conclusion of the fellowship Pope enrolled in the Ecole des Beaux Arts in Paris, completing the full course of study in less than the two years usually required. As critic Henry Russell Hitchcock wrote, "Americans, not Frenchmen, were . . . the worthiest products of the Ecole des Beaux Arts, and thus heirs of the strongest academic traditions in the world."

Launching His Career

After returning to the United States in 1900 Pope worked for three years for the architectural firm of Bruce Price before opening his own office in New York City. In the next few years he was joined by Daniel Paul Higgins and Otto R. Eggers, his life-long partners.

In 1912 Pope married Sadie G. Jones, daughter of Sarah Pembroke Jones of Wilmington, North Carolina, and Newport, Rhode Island, one of the queens of Newport society. Shortly after the death of her husband, Sarah Jones married Henry Walters of Baltimore, thus formally linking Pope to the "richest man in the South." Although the social standing of the Jones family helped to make Pope's firm visible, it was Pope's business methods and design talent that made the practice flourish and earned the numerous honors which marked his career.

Almost all of Pope's early designs were for very large houses for influential bankers, businessmen, and other prominent people. He worked successfully in the Georgian, Federal, Italian Renaissance, and 18th-century French styles. His houses have been described as setting a new standard by "achieving archaeological correctness while retaining the qualities of livability demanded" by Americans. Pope's houses, no matter what their "style," were equally elegant in design and materials. His affinity for formal design clearly shows in his Georgian and Federal houses; his Tudor houses, including his own house at Newport, were probably the most "correct" seen in the United States up to that time.

After about 1910 Pope's practice grew to include churches (he built four notable ones), one important commercial building (Union Station in Richmond, Virginia), and master plans for five colleges and universities (Hunter, Dartmouth, Johns Hopkins, Syracuse, and Yale). But it was the monumental public buildings that truly characterized Pope's work and on which his reputation rests. These buildings show his adherence to the classical tradition and demonstrate his belief that monumental architecture must have its roots in ancient Greece or Rome.

The Classical Tradition in Washington, D.C.

Beginning with the Washington [D.C.] Scottish Rite Temple (finished in 1915, based on the mausoleum at Halicarnassos), which was honored by the Architectural League as the finest building of the year, Pope's attention appears to have been captured by the development of the nation's capital. Earlier, in 1901, the U.S. Senate Park Commission (sometimes called the McMillan Commission) had restored the L'Enfant plan as the basic guideline for the development of the District. Then in 1910 the Commission of Fine Arts, under the chairmanship of D. F. Burnham, was created to oversee the architecture and planning of Washington, D.C., Pope was appointed to this commission in 1917 and served for five years. The waiting room in his office contained the framed letter from President Wilson appointing him to the commission and the letter from President Harding thanking him for his services when his term expired in 1922.

After 1922 Pope's contributions to Washington turned from words of advice into marble. Constitution Hall was completed for the Daughters of the American Revolution in 1929 (Pope took no commission for the building, seeing it as a memorial to his mother, who had been an active member of the organization) and the National City Christian Church in 1930. The American Pharmaceutical Institute (1933) was followed by the National Archives Building (1935) and the plans [unbuilt] for the Theodore Roosevelt memorial (1935). The National Gallery of Art (1939) and the Jefferson Memorial (1941) were completed by Pope's partners after his death. There were also a number of mansions designed by Pope in the city, most of which are still standing, although they are now used as embassies or by organizations rather than for private homes.

Some other buildings designed by Pope and worthy of note (it has been said that Pope designed more monumental buildings than any other architect of his generation) include: the Lincoln Memorial in Hodgenville, Kentucky (1925); the Roosevelt Memorial portion of the Museum of Natural History in New York (1936); the American Battle Monument at Montfaucon, France (1937); and the Duveen addition to the British Museum for the Elgin marbles (1937) and the Tate Gallery sculpture hall (1937), both in London.

Pope died of cancer in New York on August 27, 1937. His obituary in the *New York Times* remarked that when King George VI opened the Tate addition he "paid tribute to the genius of Mr. Pope by characterizing the building as 'the world's finest sculpture gallery.'" President Hoover had also extolled Pope's talent when he laid the cornerstone of the National Archives Building, describing the structure as "one of the most beautiful" in America. But by the time he died the "international" style had captured the leading architecture schools, and Pope's severe classicism was anathema. Published attacks on the design for the Jefferson Memorial included descriptions as "a cadaver," "a servile sham," and "decadent stylism"; whereas the more polite criticism of the National Gallery followed the British description "contemporary architecture's greatest flashback." The architect himself was sometimes derisively called "the last of the Romans." Only recently have scholars begun to re-evaluate John Russell Pope and to understand and appreciate him for what he was: a true classicist whose work is never out of style.

Further Reading

There is neither a biography of John Russell Pope nor an extensive critical study of his work. His own drawing may be seen in *Pencil Points* (December 1924); his business methods are documented in "Office Manual of John Russell Pope, Architect—Routine and Procedure," *Architectural Record* (February-March 1931). Biographical information and some evaluations of his work may be found in various publications issued at the time of his death: *American Architect and Architecture* (October 1937), *Architectural Record* (October 1937), *Architectural Forum* (October 1937), and *Journal of the Royal Institute of British Architects* (November 22, 1937). George Gurney, *Sculpture and the Federal Triangle* (1985) contains a chapter documenting Pope's involvement with the sculpture on the National Archives Building. The best short essay evaluating Pope's work is Phoebe Stanton, "A Note on John Russell Pope, Architect, 1874-1937," *Baltimore Museum of Art Annual: Studies in Honor of Gertrude Rosenthal* (1972). ☐

William James Popham

Educator William James Popham (born 1930) was a leading figure in the movement that promoted criterion-referenced measurements and was active and productive in the area of educational test development.

W. James Popham was born July 31, 1930, to William James and Anne I. Popham of Portland, Oregon. He grew up in Portland and attended the University of Portland, where he graduated *cum laude* with a Bachelor's degree in philosophy in 1953 and received his Master's degree in education a year later. After receiving his doctorate from Indiana University in 1958, Popham accepted an assistant professorship at Kansas State College in Pittsburg, Kansas. He stayed there for two years. He then accepted a position at San Francisco State College, where he taught for two years until he was appointed as an assistant professor in the Graduate School of Education at the University of California at Los Angeles (UCLA).

Popham taught at UCLA, earning associate and full professorships. In 1968 he won the UCLA Distinguished Teaching award. Upon his retirement in June, 1991, he was named professor emeritus. Popham won several teaching awards throughout his career as an educator, including a 1985 distinguished alumnus award from the Indiana University School of Education.

Popham was an active leader in regional and national organizations that promoted educational evaluation. He served on the editorial boards of several major research and evaluation journals, including *Educational Research Quarterly, Journal of Personnel Evaluation in Education,* and *Evaluation and the Health Professions.* In 1969-1970 he served as the president of the California Educational Research Association. An active member of the American Educational Research Association (AERA), he acted as chairperson for the AERA's Division B Committee on Instructional Objectives in 1968 and was vice president for AERA's Division D (Measurement and Research Methodology) from 1971 to 1972. Popham was elected president of the American Educational Research Association in 1977 and served one year in that position. From 1978 to 1981 he acted as the founding editor of *Educational Evaluation and Policy Analysis,* a quarterly journal published by AERA.

While teaching at UCLA, Popham created and served as the director of the Instructional Objectives Exchange, a clearinghouse for behavioral objectives for educators, and also worked with the Southwest Regional Laboratory for Educational Research and Development. Throughout his career he promoted the field of educational evaluation by presenting papers, creating videotapes for use in the classroom, and editing and writing books, including *Educational Evaluation,* one of the first singly-authored textbooks on that subject to be used in introductory level education classes.

In the field of educational evaluation, Popham based his work on that of B.F. Skinner, the noted behavioralist. He became involved with the programmed instruction movement, which focused on carefully sequenced learning experiences and clarified expectations for results. However, teachers using the programmed instruction method began to ask how they could evaluate when students were ready to move on with the learning sequence. These questions led to the development of more effective evaluation, which was the basis for the referenced-based movement.

Robert Glaser, in 1963, was the first to note the distinction between norm-referenced measurement and criterion-referenced measurement. The former is an evaluation of a student's performance relative to others, or the "norm," while the latter is an evaluation of a student's performance in relation to what he/she can or cannot do; that is, to determine an individual's status with respect to a defined behavioral domain. The late 1960s and early 1970s was a period of growth and optimism in the field of educational evaluation. During this time there was an increased preference for criterion-referenced measurement because it provided an "absolute" interpretation about whether a student had mastered a defined set of criteria and was more compatible with the requirements of educational evaluation.

Popham's interests and involvements mirrored this shift from programmed instruction to norm-referenced measurement and, eventually, to criterion-referenced measurement. In 1969, in his article "Implications of Criterion-Referenced Measurement" in the *Journal of Educational Measurement,* Popham stated that criterion-referenced measurement provided more suitable assessment devices than norm-referenced measurement and could be used to enhance instruction, evaluation, and decision-making by teachers. In his book *Criterion-Referenced Measurement* (1978) Popham said that "a criterion-referenced test is designed to produce a clear description of what an examinee's performance on the test actually means." The criterion-referenced measurement movement had a profound impact on the field and was the foundation for the movement toward curriculum-based assessment and measurement. Curriculum-based assessment and evaluation was considered the cutting edge in educational evaluation in the 1990s, and it

appeared to be the direction toward which the field was moving. This shift, however, could not have happened without Popham's innovative work in criterion-referenced measurement in the 1960s and 1970s. Popham believed that the role of evaluation and measurement in education would continue to grow and be "instructionally catalytic." Test material and results could be expected to increasingly influence what was taught in the classroom.

Popham's success and influence in his field was partly due to his lively, clear writing style and ability to make complex issues understandable. For example, in explaining the concept of "authentic assessment" in a 1993 article in the *Phi Delta Kappan* journal, he described a theoretical prehistoric class, "Sabertooth Tiger Hunting 101." "When prehistoric students completed a course . . . they were probably required to display their mastery by taking part in an actual tiger hunt," he wrote. "The target tiger's teeth were sufficiently sharp so that all examinees recognized that the assessment activity could induce a premature, yet thoroughly authentic, death."

After retiring from UCLA, Popham served as director of IOX Assessment Associates (formerly Instructional Objectives Exchange), a center for test development. In the 1990s, he also was active in evaluating and appraising HIV educational programs and curricula. He directed an AIDS-related technical assistance project for the U.S. Centers for Disease Control, helping teachers evaluate the effectiveness and caliber of AIDS education programs, which in a 1993 article in *Phi Beta Kappan,* Popham called "deplorable." He wrote a text-book on educational statistics with K.A. Sirotnik in an attempt to make statistics seem more like common sense to students. In 1995 he wrote *Classroom Assessment: What Teachers Need to Know,* a basic guide for classroom teachers. In 1997, he remained active as IOX director, living and working in southern California. Popham was well-liked and respected by his colleagues for his contributions to the field of educational evaluation. But above all, according to Popham himself, "Students are my main reason for staying active in the field of evaluation and measurement."

Further Reading

Brief bits of biographical information can be pieced together from the forewords and introductions of Popham's textbooks and edited collections, but no definitive collection of biographical information exists. His philosophy and beliefs about educational evaluation and assessment can be gleaned from his numerous writings. A partial listing of his textbooks and articles follows: *Classroom Assessment: What Teachers Need to Know* (1995); *Educational Evaluation* (3rd edition, 1993); *Understanding Statistics in Education,* with Kenneth A. Sirotnik (1992); and *Criterion-Referenced Measurement* (1978). See also the following articles by Popham: "Wanted: AIDS Education That Works," *Phi Beta Kappan* (March 1993); "Circumventing the High Costs of Authentic Assessment," *Phi Beta Kappan* (February 1993); "Educational Testing in America: What's Right, What's Wrong? A Criterion-Referenced Perspective," *Educational Measurement* (January 1993); "Combating AIDS on the Front Lines," *School Administrator* (August 1992); "Two-plus Decades of Educational Objectives," *International Journal of Educational Research* (January 1987); "Well-Crafted Criterion-Referenced Tests," *Educational Leadership* (February 1978); and, with T.R.

Husek, "Implications of Criterion-Referenced Measurement," *Journal of Educational Measurement* (January 1969).

□

Liubov Sergeevna Popora

Liubov Sergeevna Popova (1889-1924) was one of the preeminent artists of the Russian and Soviet avant-garde during the early 20th century.

Liubov Popova was born just outside of Moscow, near the village of Ivanovskoe, on April 24, 1889. Her family's wealth—her father was a textile merchant—and philanthropic interests ensured a thorough education in the arts and humanities, which led her, after completing gymnasium in 1906, to initially pursue a degree in literature.

Although she received instruction in painting and drawing throughout her childhood, Popova's first serious encounter with art dates from 1907-1908, when she entered the Moscow studios of Stanislov Zhukovski and Konstatin Yuon. Both artists favored a landscape tradition influenced by Impressionism, a style that in Popova's hands was rapidly modified to suit her interests in the works of Cézanne, van Gogh, and Gauguin, as well as the Neoprimitivism of Natalia Goncharova. By the end of 1908 her painting had moved well beyond naturalism to a distinct post-Impressionist treatment employing simplified forms, cloisonné, and unmodulated colors.

The next several years were marked by an ambitious travel schedule that greatly enhanced Popova's artistic development. Between the summers of 1909 and 1911 she experienced a wide diversity of art, ranging from the icons in Novgorod and Pskov to Mikhail Vrubel's symbolism in Kiev, and from the frescoes of Giotto in Italy to the Old Masters of the Hermitage in St. Petersburg. The impressions garnered during these excursions encouraged her to explore a style more independent from the direction she had taken under the guidance of Zhukovski and Yuon. In the fall of 1911, together with her friend Liudmila Prudkovskaia, she opened her own studio.

In 1912 Popova joined the collective studio organized by Vladimir Tatlin known as The Tower, where in her examinations of the human figure she confronted the synthetic conflict between direct observation and the construction of the drawing, which Picasso and Braque had resolved a few years earlier. This work, along with an introduction to European modernism through her visits to the Sergei Shchukin collection in Moscow, encouraged her to visit Paris during the winter of 1912-1913 in order to study French Cubism. There she enrolled in the "Académie La Palette," where under the instruction of Jean Metzinger and Henri Le Fauconnier she received a version of Cubism considerably modified from the purely analytical approach developed by Picasso and Braque. At the same time she became familiar with Futurism through the sculptural work of Umberto Boccioni, whose three-dimensional explorations of the relationship between the object and its surrounding space soon became central to her own painting.

When Popova returned to Russia in the fall of 1913, she was fully prepared to play a role in the uniquely Russian confluence of French Cubism and Italian Futurism. Her work over the next few years, bolstered by a second trip to Paris and Italy in 1914, focused on balancing the cubist analysis of a static object with the representation of movement and light favored by the futurists. In 1915 she showed a number of her Cubo-Futurist canvases in two important Petrograd exhibitions–"Tramway V: The First Futurist Exhibition of Paintings," which opened on March 3, 1915, and in December, "The Last Futurist Exhibition of Paintings: 0.10."

At the latter exhibition Kasimir Malevich demonstrated the path he had taken through Cubo-Futurism to abstraction with several of his Suprematist paintings. Although all the time Popova was closely allied with Tatlin's direction—several of her entries in the "0.10" exhibition were constructions similar to Tatlin's three-dimensional counter-reliefs—she was so taken by the radical departure of Malevich's non-objectivism that within a year she had fallen within the Suprematist orbit. The association resulted in a series of paintings entitled *Painterly Architectonics,* compositions of overlapping planes of color, which by 1917 had become completely nonreferential.

Like many of her colleagues, Popova was integrally involved with the cultural response to the social upheavals caused by the October Revolution of 1917. She worked on public projects, designed propaganda posters, and in 1918 joined the faculty of Svomas (Free State Art Studios, reorganized in 1920 as Vkhutemas: Higher State Art-Technical Studios), where her foundation course on color helped to form a curriculum oriented toward fusing art and industry. In March of 1918 she married the Russian art historian Boris von Eding, and in November gave birth to her son. A year later, while on a summer trip to Rostov on the Don, her husband died of typhoid fever. She nearly died of the illness herself.

In 1920 Popova became active in Inkhuk (Institute of Artistic Culture), the eventual bastion of Constructivism that oversaw the gradual rejection of aesthetic valuation in favor of art created with real materials and in real space for utilitarian purposes. Although for a time Popova attempted to reconcile her work with the three-dimensional Constructivist ideal by asserting that her paintings were essentially two-dimensional constructions, by the fall of 1921 she too had accepted the inclination within Inkhuk toward production art. In the catalogue to the exhibition "$5 \times 5 = 25$," which opened in September 1921 with the intention of being the final display of painting as an expressive medium, she described her contributions as "a series of preparatory experiments for concrete material constructions." In November of the same year she was one of 25 Inkhuk artists to sign a proclamation renouncing easel painting altogether.

Popova turned her attention toward the theater in 1922. She joined Gvytm (State Higher Theater Workshops), where she taught a course in set design and created Constructivist sets and costumes for Vsevolod Meyerkhold's productions of *The Magnanimous Cuckold* and, in 1923, *Earth in Turmoil*. At the same time she devoted herself to production work, executing designs for posters, book covers, porcelain, and, beginning in the fall of 1923, textiles and clothing. Her efforts in this direction were unfortunately short-lived. On May 25, 1924, a few days after her son, she died of scarlet fever.

Further Reading

There are two publications in English on Popova: Dmitri V. Sarabianov and Natalia L. Adaskina, *Popova,* trans. Marian Schwartz (1990), a thorough examination of her life and work; and Magdalena Dabrowski, *Liubov Popova* (1991), a catalogue that accompanied the 1991 Popova exhibition at the Museum of Modern Art in New York City. For an overview of the avant-garde in Russia and the Soviet Union, start with Camilla Gray, *The Russian Experiment in Art, 1863-1922,* revised and enlarged by Marian Burleigh-Motley (London, 1986). Other good texts include Angelica Z. Rudenstein, ed., *The George Costakis Collection: Russian Avant-Garde Art* (1981); Christina Lodder, *Russian Constructivism* (1983); *Art into Life: Russian Constructivism, 1914-1932,* exhibition catalogue (1990); and *The Great Utopia, the Russian and Soviet Avant-Garde, 1915-1932,* exhibition catalogue (1992). □

Sir Karl Raimund Popper

The Austrian philosopher Sir Karl Raimund Popper (1902-1994) offered an original analysis of scientific research that he also applied to research in history and philosophy.

Karl Popper was born in Vienna on July 28, 1902, the son of a barrister. He studied mathematics, physics, and philosophy at the University of Vienna. Though not a member of the Vienna Circle, he was in sympathy with some, if not all, of its aims. His first book, *The Logic of Scientific Discovery* (1935), was published in a series sponsored by the Circle. In 1937 Popper accepted a post in New Zealand as senior lecturer in philosophy at Canterbury University College in Christchurch.

At the end of World War II, Popper was invited to the London School of Economics as a reader, and in 1949 he was made professor of logic and scientific method. Popper then made numerous visits to the United States as visiting professor and guest lecturer. In 1950 he gave the William James Lectures at Harvard University. In 1965 Popper was knighted by Queen Elizabeth II.

Foundations of Popper's Theory

Popper's first book laid the foundations for all the rest of his work. It offered an analysis of the procedure to be used in scientific work and a criterion for the meaning of the statements produced in such work. According to Popper, the researcher should begin by proposing hypotheses. The collection of data is guided by a theoretical preconception concerning what is relevant or important. The examination of causal connections between phenomena is also guided by leading hypotheses. Such a hypothesis is scientific only if one can derive from it particular observation statements that, if falsified by the facts, would refute the hypothesis. A statement is meaningful, therefore, if and only if there is a way it can be falsified. Hence the researcher should strive to refute rather than to confirm his hypotheses. Refutation is real advancement because it clears the field of a likely hypothesis.

Understanding History and Society

Popper later applied his analysis of knowledge to theories of society and history. In *The Open Society and Its Enemies* (1945) he attacked Plato, G. W. F. Hegel, and Karl Marx as offering untenable totalitarian theories that are easily falsifiable. *The Open Society* is often considered one of Popper's most influential books of this century. It also was responsible for the prevalent use of the term "open society." Critics argue that Popper succeeded in this book and in its sequel, *The Poverty of Historicism* (1957), in formulating a deterministic theory about general laws of historical development and then refuting it. A lively controversy ensued on the issue of which philosophers, if any, held the doctrine Popper refuted. Popper found himself embroiled in a decade of polemics, particularly with partisans of Plato. Popper was thus credited with a convincing logical refutation but one misdirected in its targets.

Popper's later works *Objective Knowledge* (1972) and *The Self and Its Brain* (1977) combined his scientific theory with a theory of evolution. In the 1980s, Popper continued to lecture, focusing mainly on questions of evolution and the role of consciousness. Karl Popper died of complications from cancer, pneumonia, and kidney failure on September 17, 1994 at the age of 92.

Further Reading

A work in progress edited by Paul A. Schilpp, *The Philosophy of Karl Popper,* will contain a biographical sketch, critical essays, and Popper's replies and should become the definitive work. In the interim the best study is Mario Bunge, ed., *The Critical Approach to Science and Philosophy* (1964), a *Festschrift* for Popper's sixtieth birthday containing essays by distinguished scholars and a bibliography complete to 1964.

Additional Sources

O'Mear, Anthony, *Karl Popper,* Cambridge University Press, 1995.
Popper, Karl Raimund, *Unended Quest: An Intellectual Autobiography,* Open Court, 1978.
Honderich, Ted, ed., *Oxford Companion to Philosophy,* Oxford University Press, 1995.
The New York Times, September 18, 1994. □

Giacomo della Porta

The Italian architect Giacomo della Porta (ca. 1537-1602) was the leading Roman architect in the last quarter of the 16th century.

t was formerly thought that Giacomo della Porta was a Lombard, like many of the artists active in Rome in the 16th century, and that he was related to the sculptor Guglielmo della Porta. His earliest biographer, however, stresses that Giacomo was Roman "by birth and by skill," and this is now accepted as correct, especially as his career was crowned by his appointment as "architect to the Roman people."

Della Porta may have been apprenticed to Giacomo da Vignola, whose Roman career began about 1550, but he first emerges as a follower of Michelangelo. Della Porta designed the central window of the Palazzo dei Conservatori on the Capitol (ca. 1568) after Michelangelo's death, but it is so fantastic that it surpasses even Michelangelo's daring inventions, and for this reason it was long regarded as the work of another man, since on the whole della Porta's work is quiet, restrained, and sometimes rather dull. In any case, the mannerist extravagance of the Capitoline window soon faded.

Della Porta built a new facade for Vignola's Gesù (less elegant than Vignola's original design) and the dome of St. Peter's (1588-1590). The dome was undertaken with the best engineer-architect of the age, Domenico Fontana, and they modified Michelangelo's original design considerably. It is still not known whether they increased the height of the dome by about 27 feet because they thought that had been Michelangelo's intention or because they were forced to do so by the engineering problems they encountered. Michelangelo certainly planned a dome which was a perfect hemisphere, but he also designed one in the slightly pointed shape of the executed dome. What is certain is that they created one of the most beautiful domes ever built.

During the 1580s, della Porta built a number of churches in Rome, since this was a period of active church building, when the reforms instituted by the Council of Trent were being vigorously prosecuted. He worked on at least six churches. The two most interesting are St. Atanasio and St. Luigi dei Francesi, primarily because they derive from the model, made 60 years earlier, by Michelangelo for St. Lorenzo in Florence; they have rectangular facades instead of having the center higher than the sides. Towers were also planned, but only those of St. Atanasio were built.

Della Porta was also active as a domestic architect. His most interesting civil buildings are the great loggia at the rear of the Farnese Palace (1589) and his last work, the Villa Aldobrandini at Frascati (1598-1604). The villa has an enormous broken pediment which gives it a picturesque skyline from a distance, but it is clumsy when seen close to. In 1602 della Porta was coming back from Frascati in a coach with his patron, Cardinal Aldobrandini, when he was taken ill at the gate of Rome and died on the spot.

Della Porta's work lacks the personal and inventive genius of Michelangelo's and is less correct and studied than Vignola's, yet it constitutes an aspect of late-16th-century Roman architecture which remains to this day typical of the city and of the epoch.

Further Reading

There is no work on della Porta in English. For background material see Peter Murray, *The Architecture of the Italian Renaissance* (1963). □

Giambattista della Porta

The Renaissance scientist and dramatist Giambattista della Porta (1535-1615) is noted for his biological index of personality tendencies. He wrote 17 plays.

n the course of his writings Giambattista della Porta made misstatements about his age, presumably because he enjoyed posing as a man of mystery or perhaps because, in making himself younger than he was, he would become known as a child prodigy. In spite of his own misrepresentation, the year of his birth has been reliably established as 1535. He came from minor Neapolitan nobility.

In the spirit of the Renaissance his father's house was a kind of academy where young della Porta and his two brothers were introduced to the arts and sciences. Giambattista was tutored by an uncle. Along with the humanism of the Renaissance, his program of studies emphasized the sciences, pure and applied. In his youth he got his first taste of drama, and it is probable that some of his plays are later revisions of what he had written as a young man. From his older brother he learned astrology, and from his younger one he obtained a collection of crystals and of geological specimens.

Sometime in the 1550s, della Porta founded the Academy of the Segreti. In this group, interest was divided between genuine scientific observations and what is now recognized as magic. The *Magiae naturalis* (1558; 2d ed. 1559), destined to be one of his two most famous works in natural science, probably grew out of this first academy. It relates experiments on herbs, chemicals, and magnetism and includes opinions on the occult.

About 1580, della Porta was denounced before the Inquisition for works in magic and prophecy and was commanded to give up his practice of illicit arts. About this time also, he was befriended by the influential Cardinal Luigi d'Este, who invited him to Rome and later to Venice. During the Venetian period he worked on the parabolic mirror and on an *occhiale,* probably a magnifying glass. His work on lenses led to the false claim, which he encouraged, that he invented the telescope.

In della Porta's most renowned scientific work, *De humana physiognomia* (1586), he maintained that the physical characteristics of human beings are clues to their personalities. By viewing such physical traits as tendencies rather than as determining factors, della Porta was able to avoid fatalism and affirm individual responsibility.

In 1603 della Porta joined in an effort to keep alive a society that was later to bloom as the Academy of the Lincei and that was to claim Galileo as a member. Meanwhile, della Porta wrote works on science and mathematics and authored 17 plays, most of them comedies, which proved him to be a true Renaissance type, a humanist as well as a scientist.

Further Reading

Louise George Clubb, *Giambattista della Porta: Dramatist* (1965), deals with the literary work. For Della Porta's scientific work see George Sarton, *Six Wings: Men of Science in the Renaissance* (1957), and Lynn Thorndike, *A History of Magic and Experimental Science,* vols. 7 and 8 (1958). □

Diego José Víctor Portales Plazazuelos

The Chilean statesman Diego José Víctor Portales Plazazuelos (1793-1837) laid the foundations, after the anarchy of the postindependence years, of orderly government, respect for law, financial probity, and a strong sense of Chilean nationhood.

D iego Portales was born in Santiago of a good family. He played no part in the wars of independence against Spain but entered commerce and became drawn into politics through operating the tobacco monopoly, the proceeds from which were intended to amortize the Chilean foreign debt. Though a pragmatist rather than an orthodox party man, he championed the conservative side against the democratic liberalism which had animated the founders of independence but had led to anarchy and factionalism in political life. He was particularly opposed to the cult of the *caudillo,* or personal leader, which he strove to replace by a respect for law, constitutional processes, and the office, rather than the person, of those in power.

Portales held a succession of ministerial offices but refused to stand for the presidency himself. After withdrawing into private life for a few years to observe the effect of his reorganization of the state finances and administration, he again took over the portfolios of war and the interior in 1835 and again became the right-hand man of his friend President Joaquin Prieto. After the suppression of an attempted coup by the turbulent *caudillo* Gen. Ramón Freire, who had been exiled to Peru, Portales became convinced that Peru, which had been united in a confederation with Bolivia under the ambitious Gen. Andrés Santa Cruz and seemed to threaten Chile, must be taught a lesson. Though Chile was far inferior in population and resources, Portales prepared his country for war.

Portales did not live to see the success of Chilean arms. Though he had reorganized the army and founded a military academy to promote a spirit of professionalism and to attract the sons of good families, his authoritarian actions and caustic tongue had won him many enemies. Santa Cruz had also been stirring up the anti-Portales faction. When, on June 6, 1837, Portales went to Quillota near Valparaíso to review the troops, he was seized by a group of mutinous officers and murdered.

Though he himself fell a victim to turbulence and factionalism, Portales had succeeded in laying the foundations in Chile of honest, efficient government by civilians. Though often criticized for his high-handed ways with opponents and troublemakers, Portales was far from being a typical dictator. He hated personal display and bombast, used power for what he believed to be the indifferent to money and fame. Though admiring the pragmatic spirit of the English and believing that the Chileans, like them, should become a commercial and seafaring nation, he distrusted abstract thinking and foreign models and held that every nation must work out for itself the institutions best adapted to its own needs.

Further Reading

There is an extensive literature in Spanish on the controversial Portales. In English see the essay by Lewis W. Bealer in Alva C. Wilgus, ed., *South American Dictators during the First Century of Independence* (1937). □

Cole Albert Porter

American composer Cole Albert Porter (1891-1964) wrote songs (both words and music) for over 30 stage and film musicals. His best work set standards of sophistication and wit seldom matched in the popular musical theater.

Cole Porter was born in Peru, Ind., on June 9, 1891, the son of a pharmacist. His mother was as determined that her only son become a creative artist as his wealthy midwestern pioneer grandfather was that he enter business or farming. Kate Cole's influence proved stronger, and Porter received considerable musical training as a child. By 1901 he had composed a onesong "operetta" entitled *The Song of the Birds;* then he produced a piano piece, "The Bobolink Waltz," which his mother published in Chicago.

Porter attended Worcester Academy, where he composed the class song of 1909. At Yale (1909-1913) he wrote music and collaborated on lyrics for the scores of several amateur shows presented by his fraternity and the Yale Dramatic Association. Porter then entered Harvard Law School; almost at once, however, he changed his course of study to music. Before leaving Harvard he collaborated on a comic operetta, *See America First* (1916), which became his first show produced on Broadway. It was a complete disaster.

In 1917 Porter was in France, and for some months during 1918-1919 he served in the French Foreign Legion. After this he studied composition briefly with the composer Vincent d'Indy in Paris. Returning to New York, he contributed songs to the Broadway production *Hitchy-Koo of 1919,* his first success, and married the wealthy socialite Linda Lee.

The Porters began a lifetime of traveling on a grand scale; they became famous for their lavish parties and the circle of celebrities in which they moved. Porter contributed songs to various stage shows and films and in 1923 composed a ballet, *Within the Quota,* which was performed in Paris and New York. Songs such as "Let's Do It" (1928), "What Is This Thing Called Love" (1929), "You Do Something to Me" (1929), and "Love for Sale" (1930) established him as a creator of worldly, witty, occasionally risqué lyrics with unusual melodic lines to match.

In the 1930s and 1940s Porter provided full scores for a number of bright Broadway and Hollywood productions, among them *Anything Goes* (1934), *Jubilee* (1935), *Rosalie* (1937), *Panama Hattie* (1940), and *Kiss Me Kate* (1948). These scores and others of the period abound with his characteristic songs: "Night and Day," "I Get a Kick out of You," "You're the Top," "Anything Goes," "Begin the Beguine," "Just One of Those Things," "Don't Fence Me In," "In the Still of the Night," and "So in Love."

Serious injuries in a riding accident in 1937 plagued Porter for the remainder of his life. A series of operations led, in 1958, to the amputation of his right leg. In his last years he produced one big Broadway success (*Can-Can,* 1953). He died on Oct. 15, 1964, in Santa Monica, Calif.

Porter's songs show an elegance of expression and a cool detachment that seem to epitomize a kind of sophistication peculiar to the 1930s. He was also an authentically talented creator of original melodies. Like George Gershwin, he frequently disregarded the accepted formulas of the conventional popular song (usually a rigid 32-measure framework) and turned out pieces of charm and distinction.

Further Reading

Porter's life and career are comprehensively covered in George Eell, *The Life That Late He Led* (1967); the author's acquaintance with Porter, his access to documents, private papers, and music manuscripts, and his sympathetic yet detached approach give the book an authoritative stamp. Robert Kimball, ed., *Cole* (1971), contains a biographical essay by Brendan Gill, a good selection of Porter's lyrics, and many interesting illustrations.

Additional Sources

Citron, Stephen, *Noel and Cole: the sophisticates,* New York: Oxford University Press, 1993.

Grafton, David, *Red, hot & rich!: an oral history of Cole Porter,* New York: Stein and Day, 1987.

Howard, Jean, *Travels with Cole Porter,* New York: Abrams, 1991.

Morella, Joe, *Genius and lust: the creative and sexual lives of Noel Coward and Cole Porter,* New York: Carroll & Graf Publishers, 1995.

Schwartz, Charles, *Cole Porter: a biography,* New York: Da Capo Press, 1979, 1977. □

Katherine Anne Porter

The works of Katherine Anne Porter (1890-1980), American writer, were characterized by delicate perceptions and painstaking craftsmanship.

Katherine Anne Porter was born on May 15, 1890, in Indian Creek, Texas. She was a descendant of Jonathan Boone, brother of Daniel Boone, and a cousin of O. Henry (Sidney Porter). After the death of her mother in 1892, Porter and her four siblings went to live with their paternal grandmother. After her grandmother died in 1901, Porter was sent to several convent schools in Texas and Louisiana.

In 1906 Porter ran away from school and got married; she was divorced 3 years later. In 1911 she went to Chicago to work on a newspaper. She returned to Texas in 1914 and worked briefly as an entertainer, singing Scottish ballads.

From early childhood Porter had been writing stories, an activity she described as the unifying passion of her life, but her writing career began with hackwork, chiefly book reviews and political articles. In 1917 she joined the staff of the *Critic,* a Fort Worth weekly newspaper, and in 1918-1919 worked for the *Rocky Mountain News* in Denver. She then moved to New York, where she resumed her hackwork, which included some ghost writing. During the 1920s she traveled often to Mexico, wrote articles about the country, and studied art. She also worked on a biography of Cotton Mather (never finished) and did some book reviewing.

Porter's first volume of stories, *Flowering Judas* (1930), impressed critics with its flawless, unobtrusive style, but the book sold modestly—a fate common to most short-story collections. The title story, a masterpiece, is set in Mexico and turns brilliantly on a character contrast: Braggioni, the fat, sensual, egotistical revolutionary, and Laura, the beautiful, sensitive, sexually frigid idealist who is a mere dilettante in the revolutionary cause. Porter's use of Christian symbolism gives density to this paradoxical study of power and beauty. The title echoes what she described as the theme of her lifetime: self-betrayal in all its forms.

Flowering Judas won a Guggenheim fellowship for Porter to study abroad, and after a brief stay in Mexico she sailed in 1932 from Veracruz to Bremerhaven (which provided the setting for a novel completed 30 years later, *Ship of Fools*). A second volume of stories, *Hacienda* (1934), and a short novel, *Noon Wine* (1937), followed her marriage in 1933 to Eugene Pressly, a member of the U.S. Foreign Service in Paris. After divorcing Pressly, she married Albert Russell Erskine, Jr., whom she divorced in 1942.

Pale Horse, Pale Rider (1942) consists of three short novels, including *Noon Wine.* The title work is a bitter, tragic tale of a young woman's love for a World War I soldier who dies of influenza. It further established Porter's place in American literature: the impeccable artist of meager output. The title story of *The Leaning Tower and Other Stories* (1944), set in Berlin, deals with the menace of Nazism. *The Days Before* (1952) is a collection of essays, chiefly critical.

Porter's only novel, *Ship of Fools* (1962), was an immediate best seller but drew mixed reviews. Based on *Das Narrenschiff,* Sebastian Brant's 15th-century moral allegory, it examines the lives of an international group of voyagers; their human folly thwarts their personal lives and blinds them as well to the incipience of German fascism.

Porter became widely acknowledged outside her native Texas, where she was considered the best author who ever hailed from the state, even supplanting her cousin, the author O. Henry (*Texas Monthly,* May 1997). Among her many writing honors were a Texas Institute of Letters fiction award for *Ship of Fools,* and a Pulitzer Prize for her *Collected Stories* in 1966.

Porter's early life in Texas fostered a distaste for the lack of rights for women and social injustice had spurred her to leave, and later became entwined in her writings. The state, which still revered cowboys and the old west, for years failed to accord her status. What local critics sometimes dismissed as overly "genteel," outsiders termed "perfection of form and style" (*Texas Monthly,* May, 1997).

Porter chose the University of Maryland as site of her personal library, begun with donations of some personal papers (she had received a honorary degree from the university in 1966). In Texas, her childhood home in Kyle was turned into a museum, a smaller structure in reality than her later reminiscences.

But one of the more unusual bits of Porter memorabilia was claimed by the Southwestern Writers Collection at Southwest Texas State University in San Marcos. It was her typewritten recipe for a "genuine Mole Poblana," Mexico's "National Dish," she wrote, with chili and chocolate (*Texas Monthly,* January 1997). Apparently learned during two years living there, it was a testament to her exciting, nomadic life after her conversion to Catholicism and abandonment of an early, strict Protestant influence during childhood.

Porter died on September 18, 1980, at the age of 90, in Silver Spring, Maryland. Her ashes were buried at Indian Creek beside her mother's grave. However, her writing continued to live on. The *Letters of Katherine Anne Porter* were published a decade later.

Further Reading

There has been very little written about Porter. George Hendrick, *Katherine Anne Porter* (1965), is a competent critical biography. See also Harry John Mooney, *The Fiction and Criticism of Katherine Anne Porter* (1957). Articles of interest can be found in two issues of *Texas Monthly* (January 1997 and May 1997). Information on the Katherine Anne Porter Library at the University of Maryland can be accessed on the Internet at http://www.lib.umd.edu/UMCP/RARE/797hmpgM.html (July 29, 1997). Porter's obituary appeared in the September 19, 1980 edition of the *New York Times*. □

what impressionistic early approach in which individuals play a very small role. Soon he was working in a geometric semiabstractionist style, for example, the *Stevedores*. His attention then turned to the depiction of antinaturalistic figures in massive, statuesque proportions. Finally, he began to combine groups and individuals in a way that lends his work a spatial ambiguity or tension between foreground figures and distant groups.

In 1937 Portinari received a commission to fresco the main halls of the Ministry of Education in Rio de Janeiro. His four murals (1941) for the Hispanic Foundation in the Library of Congress, Washington, D.C., monumental and vividly colored, depict the experiences of Hispanic Americans in dominating the land and resolving intercultural conflicts. Especially striking are the frenzied pattern and grasping gestures that depict mining activity. For the church of St. Francisco at Pampulha near Belo Horizonte, he executed murals and mosaics (1942-1943) and for the United Nations Building, New York City, the murals *War* and *Peace*.

From the 1940s until his death in Rio de Janeiro, Portinari kept up an active pace, doing murals, portraits, lithographs, book illustrations, and drawings. In the *Crying Woman,* one of his late paintings, he uses somber and muted colors to convey deep emotion; the facial features are barely suggested, and the hands and forearms are greatly exaggerated, creating a powerful effect.

Cândido Portinari

The Brazilian painter Cândido Portinari (1903-1962) is best known for his murals, which fuse nativist and expressionist elements in a powerful and individual style.

Cândido Portinari was born of Italian immigrant parents in the town of Brodosque in the coffee-rich state of São Paulo. No formal education was available to the boy beyond the first years of grade school. He attributed his interest in art to the fact that at the age of 8 he began helping a house painter. He went to Rio de Janeiro when he was 15 and worked as an artists' apprentice. He was always to approach his work in a disciplined and methodical way, regarding art as a handicraft or skill that could be consciously perfected.

Portinari won admission to the National Fine Arts School and in 1928 received the coveted annual travel fellowship to Europe. The experience shook him loose from the academic style he had been taught and brought him into the so-called Brazilian modernist artistic movement.

The first canvases Portinari executed are dominated by the dark reddish brown of the soil of his native region. *Café* (1935), depicting coffee pickers at work, suggests his some-

Further Reading

Josias Leão, *Portinari: His Life and Art* (1940), includes some biographical material and has good color plates. See also the catalog by the Museum of Modern *Art, Portinari of Brazil* (1940). □

Gaspar de Portolá

The Spanish explorer and colonial governor Gaspar de Portolá (ca. 1723-ca. 1784) headed the Spanish expedition that established the first missions in Alta California.

Gaspar de Portolá was born at Balaguer in the province of Catalonia. As a young man, he joined the army and soon rose to the rank of captain of dragoons in the España Regiment. In 1767, as a reward for his services, Charles III named Portolá governor of Baja (Lower) California, and Portolá set out for Mexico to assume his new post. His first task as governor was an unpleasant one. The Spanish monarch had decreed the expulsion of the Jesuit order from Spain and its dominions, and Portolá was charged with removing the Jesuits from Baja California, an assignment he carried out with compassion and dispatch.

About this time fear of Russian intrusion from the north convinced the Spaniards of the need to expand their settlements into Alta (Upper) California. José de Gálvez, visitor general of New Spain, quickly organized a plan of occupation under the overall command of Portolá. Two ships, the *San Carlos and San Antonio,* sailed north early in 1769, while two land parties, one commanded by Rivera y Moncada and Fray Juan Crespi and the other under Portolá accompanied by Fray Junípero Serra, left a few months later. With the Rivera party ahead to open the trail, the two groups moved north. Rivera reached San Diego in May, and Portolá's party arrived in late June.

Although food was critically short and many of the men were ill, Portolá immediately set out to find the reported harbor of Monterey. Moving north from San Diego, he selected several possible mission sites, passed Monterey without recognizing the spot, and explored the region around San Francisco Bay before returning to San Diego in late January 1770. During the spring Portolá returned north and successfully located Monterey, where he and Serra established Mission San Carlos. Shortly thereafter Portolá returned to Baja California, where he remained as governor for several years.

In 1776 Portolá became governor of Puebla. Probably at this time he published his *Diario histórico,* the journal of the California expedition. Portolá served in Puebla until 1784, when he retired from active service and returned to Spain.

Further Reading

Portolá's diary of the 1769 expedition was translated by Donald E. Smith and Frederick J. Teggart as *Diary of Gaspar de Portolá during the California Expedition of 1769-1770* (1909). There has been less written about Portolá than about his more famous companion, Fray Junípero Serra. Zoeth S. Eldredge, *The March of Portolá and Discovery of the Bay of San Francisco* (1909), contains much interesting material. The best firsthand account is in Francisco Palóu, *Life of Fray Junípero Serra* (trans. 1955). See also Richard F. Pourade, *The Call to California* (1968).

Additional Sources

Boneu Companys, Fernando, *Gaspar de Portolá: explorer and founder of California,* Lerida: Instituto de Estudios Ilerdenses, 1983. □

Charles William Post

A pioneer in the manufacture and mass marketing of breakfast cereals and other consumer products, Charles William Post (1854-1914) attempted to use his wealth to affect various aspects of early 20th-century American life.

Charles William Post, who preferred to be called C.W., was born on October 26, 1854 in Springfield, Illinois, his parents having migrated there from New England. The gift for language that would make Post's advertisements famous may have been nurtured by his mother, Caroline, whose poetry was published in several magazines. A restless, peripatetic nature passed from Post's father, Charles Rollin Post, who pursued a variety of occupations as he traveled throughout the country, including time at the California gold rush as a forty-niner.

Post's formal education ended at the Illinois Industrial College (later to become the University of Illinois), where he completed only a botany course and withdrew at the age of 15. In 1876 he borrowed $500 from his mother and started a general store in Independence, Kansas. Within a year Post sold his interest in the store and returned to Springfield. There he married Ella Merriweather and engaged in the design and manufacture of agricultural implements. The failure of the manufacturing enterprise and a nervous breakdown led Post to Texas, where he developed residential real estate near Fort Worth. A second nervous breakdown in 1890 compelled Post to seek the care of a doctor, John Harvey Kellogg, who operated the Battle Creek (Michigan) Sanitarium on behalf of the Seventh Day Adventist Church. At the sanitarium Post was fed a grain-intensive vegetarian diet featuring a variety of products formulated by Kellogg himself.

Post left the sanitarium after a few months and briefly attempted to operate a competing clinic, La Vita Inn, in Battle Creek. During this time he published a book, *I Am Well!*, which promoted "mind-cure," a belief then fashionable among some American businessmen and intellectuals who denied illness as artificial and proclaimed the human mind capable of overcoming all physical disorders. La Vita Inn never attained significant success.

Early in 1895 Post began the manufacture of Postum, a grain product intended as a coffee substitute, similar to one of Kellogg's concoctions. The manufacture of Grape-Nuts, based on another Kellogg item, began the following year. Post named his new company Postum Ltd., after his original product. Postum Ltd. achieved wide-scale distribution of its products through massive spending on advertising in newspapers and magazines. Post viewed advertising as the most significant component of his business, stating that he didn't care who managed production or sales, as long as he wrote the advertising. His advertisements appealed to the health concerns of the American public, telling consumers that his products would put them on the "road to Wellville" and claiming that his breakfast items made red blood.

By the early 1900s Postum products were available nationwide and Post had become one of the top five advertisers in the country, spending over $1 million annually. His company's success made Post a millionaire. But success caused Post to grow restless, so he hired a team of professional managers to operate his company and turned his attention on other matters.

In 1902 Post proposed a type of mail currency, the "Post Check," similar to today's money order. His efforts to gain congressional support for the item met strong opposition from New York Senator Thomas C. Platt, who was the president of the U.S. Express Company, which sold its own form of postal currency. The Post Check proposal also antagonized small-town merchants who feared that the new currency would facilitate the business of large mail-order houses at their expense. Mindful that those merchants car-

ried his cereal products, Post eventually dropped his efforts on behalf of the Post Check.

Soon after, Post began to purchase what eventually became a total of more than 200,000 acres in rural west Texas. There he built an ambitious planned community, Post City. Distressed by the arid conditions in the region, Post personally oversaw a series of experiments using large quantities of explosives in an attempt to "dynamite" rain out of the sky.

Post also devoted much of his time to supporting the "open shop," joining the leaders of other small-to medium-sized business firms in attacking labor unionism. He lectured throughout the country and published full-page anti-union tirades in dozens of newspapers. Labor unions responded by organizing boycotts against Post's cereal products.

Failing health and an unhappy home life contributed to Post's death by suicide on May 9, 1914 in Santa Barbara, California. Marjorie Merriweather Post, C.W.'s only child, became Postum Ltd.'s sole owner. Under the guidance of Marjorie's second husband, the stockbroker Edward F. Hutton, Postum conducted an aggressive campaign to purchase other grocery brands, beginning with Jell-O in 1923. In 1929 Postum, which began in a barn, was transformed into the widely held General Foods Corporation.

Further Reading

C.W. Post is listed in the *National Cyclopaedia of American Biography,* the *Dictionary of American Biography,* and the *Biographical Dictionary of American Business Leaders.* Gerald H. Carson's *Cornflake Crusade* (1957) discusses the rise of the breakfast cereal industry in Battle Creek and chronicles the activities of Post, the Kelloggs, and the many others who came to Battle Creek to exploit the early 1900s' breakfast cereal fad. Nettie Leitch Major's *C.W. Post—the Hour and the Man* (1963), a biography published privately under the sponsorship of Marjorie Merriweather Post, is available in many libraries. Although this book benefits from Major's access to the Post family's papers, her treatment of Post's life also possesses the shortcomings of a commissioned work. □

Emily Price Post

For many years a leading authority on socially correct etiquette from birth to burial, Emily Price Post (1873-1960) provided solutions to social problems. With a name synonymous with proper manners, she was a successful author, daily newspaper columnist, and radio commentator.

Born into a wealthy, socialite Eastern family, the date of birth variously reported as October 3, 27, or 30, 1873, Emily Price was the only child of Bruce Price, a distinguished Baltimore architect, and Josephine Lee Price. She was educated at home and attended Miss Graham's finishing school in New York where her family had moved. She grew up in an era of footmen, servants, chaperones, and cotillions. A popular debutante, she married society banker Edwin Main Post in 1892 and had two sons, Edwin M. Jr. (1893) and Bruce Price (1895).

The Posts drifted apart, and although society frowned on divorce at that time her husband's infidelity caused the marriage to end in a divorce in 1905. She asked no alimony since there had been a small crash in the stock market in which her husband had suffered a severe financial reversal. To supplement a small income and support herself and her sons, Emily Post wrote short stories which were published in the popular fiction magazines *Ainslie's* and *Everybody's.* She also produced several novels, the first—*The Flight of a Moth*—about a young American widow attracted to an unscrupulous Russian nobleman, which was published in 1904.

As a successful writer and a woman of social position she was encouraged by an editor at Funk and Wagnalls publishers to write a book on etiquette. Emphasizing the social graces, she wrote *Etiquette—The Blue Book of Social Usage.* First published in 1922, it quickly became a best seller, going through ten revisions and 89 printings and bringing her fame and fortune.

Post's guiding precept was that good manners began with consideration for the feelings of others and included good form in speech, knowledge of proper social amenities, and charm of manner. She believed that there was a right or best way to do almost everything and that that was the way that pleased the greatest number of people and offended the fewest. Before her book had been out a month readers

deluged her with questions the book had not addressed, and these formed the basis of later revisions. Originally written for the newly rich who presumably wanted to live, entertain, and converse like the wealthy, the heroine of later editions was "Mrs. Three-In-One," a wonder woman who performed the functions of cook, waitress, and charming hostess at small, informal dinner parties without a maid. Post also started a syndicated column of questions and answers which appeared in 150 newspapers and received as many as 26,000 letters annually at her New York office in addition to those sent to newspapers in other cities. During the 1930s she had her own radio program three times weekly which continued for eight years.

Although her advice on social behavior changed over the years, her Victorian upbringing made her reluctant to part, in later editions of the book, with the chaperone. She adhered to an earlier convention that considered it improper to visit a man alone in his apartment or to go on overnight automobile trips. Her "Blue Book," which was the American standard of etiquette for decades, was reported to be second only to the Bible as the book most often not returned or stolen from libraries.

Emily Post maintained her social position, travelled extensively in Europe, and always spent the hot summer months away from New York City at a home in Tuxedo Park, New York (designed and built by her father) and later in life at Edgartown, Martha's Vineyard, in a summer home she remodelled. Besides her writings on etiquette, she wrote *The Emily Post Cook Book* (1951); *The Personality of a House* (1930), partly based on her experiences rebuilding and remodeling her summer home at Martha's Vineyard; *Children Are People* (1940), much of it derived from hours she spent with her grandson; *How To Behave Though a Debutante* (1928); and other books. In 1946 she formed the Emily Post Institute to study problems of gracious living and relinquished a great deal of her work to the staff of the institute, headed by her surviving son, Edwin.

She remained active throughout her life, awakening early, but remaining in bed to devote time to letters and the daily column. She always made her first appearance of the day at luncheon, which was served promptly at one. The arbiter of American etiquette, whose name became a household word, died in her New York apartment on September 25, 1960, at the age of 86.

Further Reading

A book about her adult life, *Truly Emily Post* (1961), is a warm and sentimental remembrance written by her son Edwin. A biography appears in *Notable American Women: The Modern Period* (1980). Among many articles, see James Cate, "Keeping Posted," *Univ. of Chicago Mag.* (May/June 1972); Hildegarde Dolson, "Ask Mrs. Post," *Reader's Digest* (April 1941); and *Newsweek* (April 25, 1955 and October 10, 1960). Her obituary appeared in the *New York Times* on September 27, 1960. □

Grigori Aleksandrovich Potemkin

The Russian administrator and field marshal Grigori Aleksandrovich Potemkin (1739-1791), a favorite of Catherine the Great, is best known for his work in the economic development of southern Russia.

Grigori Potemkin the son of a minor nobleman, was born on Sept. 13, 1739, in Chizhovo, a village of western Russia. At an early age he was taken to Moscow, where his formal education began. Intelligent and alert, he did commendably well in his preparatory studies. Later, while attending the University of Moscow, he lost all interest in scholarly pursuits and became so negligent that, in 1760, he was expelled. He left Moscow then, going to St. Petersburg to serve in the Horse Guards Regiment.

Two years later Potemkin took part in the coup that placed Catherine II (the Great) on the throne. In so doing, he gained the favorable attention of the new empress, who was inclined to be very generous to her supporters. She promoted Potemkin in rank and rewarded him with both money and land. In addition, she admitted him to her small circle of friends, where his charm and vivacity easily won him acceptance. Potemkin, both ambitious and able, took advantage of every opportunity for advancement.

As a military man, Potemkin moved ahead rapidly. By the end of the Russo-Turkish War of 1768-1774, during which he fought with distinction, he had attained the high rank of lieutenant general.

Potemkin's career then took a new turn: Catherine II began an affair with him and began to treat him with the lavishness that had marked her treatment of previous lovers. She gave him vast estates, large sums of money, and high honors. She also persuaded Joseph II of Austria to make Potemkin a prince of the Holy Roman Empire. Potemkin differed from other lovers of the Empress in having not only the inclination to assume governmental responsibilities but also the ability to carry them out successfully. Consequently, since Catherine was eager to entrust him with important tasks, he soon became one of the major forces in the empire. He became also one of the richest men in Russia; but, being profligate in his habits, he often had to appeal to the Empress for funds to meet his debts.

Although Catherine ended her affair with Potemkin in 1776, she continued to respect his capabilities and to trust his judgment (even in the selection of her lovers). He therefore retained his importance in the empire and continued to serve her—as diplomat, general, and administrator. His most important service was in the posts of governor general and military head of the region including New Russia (an expanse north of the Black Sea that Russia had taken from Turkey), Azov, and Astrakhan. Potemkin's task was to make this area militarily secure and to strengthen its economy. In order to accomplish these ends, he initiated and carried out ambitious projects for attracting settlers from Russia and abroad, building cities (including Sevastopol, Kherson, Nikolaev, and Yekaterinoslav), establishing a Russian fleet on the Black Sea, and improving the military units under his command. Meanwhile, with Catherine's approval, he conquered the Crimea and added it to the area he administered. As a reward for these achievements, he was advanced to the rank of field marshal and given the title of prince of Taurida.

The many activities connected with his work in the south did not consume all of Potemkin's energies. He made frequent trips to St. Petersburg, where he advised Catherine, served on the State Council, helped to reorganize the imperial army, and acted in diplomatic negotiations.

Nevertheless, Potemkin's chief concern remained Russia's southern affairs, and he continued to maintain a dominant place in them. He faced an important test when, in 1787, Catherine named him commander in chief of the army to oppose the Turks, who had declared war on Russia. Although an able officer and a conscientious commander, Potemkin was not a strategist, and the course of his exceptionally successful career might have been altered at this time had he not been fortunate enough to have two brilliant generals, Aleksandr Suvorov and Mikhail Kutuzov, serving under him. The war was a long and hard one. By mid-1791, however, the Turks were ready to discuss peace terms.

Potemkin was selected to negotiate with the Turkish representatives. He met them in Jassy (Iaşi) to undertake this assignment, which proved to be his last. While negotiations were still underway, he died on Oct. 5, 1791, of malaria complicated by exhaustion.

Further Reading

George Soloveytchik, *Potemkin: A Picture of Catherine's Russia* (1938), is a well-balanced biography. Another study is Jerome Dreifuss, *Catherine and Potemkin: An Imperial Romance* (1937). There is also extensive material on Potemkin in Ian Grey, *Catherine the Great: Autocrat of All Russia* (1962). □

David M. Potter

The American historian David M. Potter (1910-1971) was trained as a Civil War historian, but earned his reputation for his book *People of Plenty* (1953), which was one of the significant texts of the era. He wrote extensively on the American society, the American character, and historiography.

Following year. It was seven years, however, before he received his Ph.D. from Yale. He began his graduate study under Ulrich B. Phillips, a historian of the South, but completed work under Ralph H. Gabriel, an American intellectual historian. These two scholars influenced his choice of subjects for the rest of his life.

Potter began his teaching career as an instructor of history at the University of Mississippi in 1936. He taught there for two years before moving to Rice University. While in Texas he married his first wife, Ethelyn Henry, in 1939. He left Rice in 1942 to become master of Timothy Dwight College at Yale.

The reason for the summons to Yale was the publication of his dissertation under the title of *Lincoln and His Party in the Secession Crisis* (1942). The book achieved instant acclaim; Sir Denis Brogan characterized it as the best revised thesis since Arthur M. Schlesinger's. While at New Haven Potter divorced his wife in 1945; he remarried three years later to Mary Roberts. Potter's career continued its rapid advance in the 1940s. He became Harmsworth Professor and fellow of Queen's College, Oxford, in 1947, a singular honor for a scholar who was but 37 years old and who had written only one major book.

Not that Potter was unproductive in this period. In 1945 he edited *Trail to California: The Overland Diary of Vincent Geiger and Wakeman Bryarly,* and in 1948, along with J. H. Croushare, he edited *A Union Officer in the Reconstruction,* an account by John William De Forest. That same year he published *The Lincoln Theme and American National Historiography.* The following year he co-authored two books with T.G. Manning; they were *Nationalism and Sectionalism in America* and *Government and the American Economy.* In 1949 as well he became editor of the *Yale Review,* a post he held for two years.

In 1950 Potter became Coe Professor; in a mere eight years at Yale he had earned an endowed chair. That same year he gave the Walgreen Lectures at the University of Chicago. These lectures, published three years later as *People of Plenty: Economic Abundance and the American Character,* won Potter the reputation of being one of the best American historians of the time. The book employed insights from the social sciences, particularly anthropology, to argue that American productivity was both a cause and a result of the American character. The book expanded the Turnerian thesis and was a landmark book in American historiography.

Potter left Yale for an endowed chair at Stanford in 1961. During the 1950s and 1960s he wrote penetrating essays on American society, the American character, and historiography. These added to his fame as "one of the truly great interpreters of American history," and he became a fellow of the American Academy of Arts and Sciences as well as a member of the American Philosophical Society. He did complete two books in the 1960s: *Issues in American History: Views and Counterviews* (1966) with Curtis R. Grant and, better known, *The South and the Sectional Crisis* (1968). He also continued to give lectures, presenting the Commonwealth Fund Lecture at University College, London, in 1963 and the Walter L. Fleming Lectures at Louisiana State University in 1968.

Potter died February 18, 1971, before he could finish the many projects he had set for himself. He was unable to deliver the presidential addresses for either the Organization of American Historians or the American Historical Association. His colleagues at Stanford did complete other works. Carl Degler and Don E. Fehrenbacher edited his Fleming Lectures, which were published as *The South and the Concurrent Majority* in 1972. Fehrenbacher put a number of Potter's articles together into a book, *History and American Society* (1973). In 1976 Fehrenbacher completed *The Impending Crisis 1848-1861* (a volume in the New American Nation Series), which won a Pulitzer Prize, as well as *Freedom and Its Limitation in American Life,* a collection of essays.

Further Reading

The best evaluation of Potter's writings is by Sir Denis Brogan in Marcus Cunliffe and Robin W. Winks, editors, *Pastmasters: Some Essays on American Historians* (1969). Potter's historical ideas can also be found in an interview contained in John A. Garraty, editor, *Interpreting American History: Conversations with Historians* (1973). His work is mentioned briefly in John Higham, *History: Professional Scholarship in America* (1965). □

Dennis Potter

Dennis Potter (1935-1994) was a British essayist, playwright, screenwriter, and novelist best known as a prize-winning writer of television drama.

In the world of British popular culture, Dennis Potter was an important figure. He came to the attention of American audiences when *Pennies From Heaven,* a miniseries, was broadcast on public television stations in the late 1970s, then adapted for a Hollywood film in 1981. Though the series gathered many viewers the screenplay was nominated for an Academy Award, he first became widely known in the United States seven years later when New York's television station WNET aired his autobiographical drama *The Singing Detective.*

Potter was born May 17, 1935, in Berry Hill, Gloucestershire, the Forest of Dean, and often is the sights and sounds of this coal mining region to which he returns in his work. In *The Singing Detective,* for instance, the middle-aged protagonist must relive scenes of his childhood in the Forest of Dean in order to sort out the conflicts of his life. Potter went to Bell's Grammar School in Coleford after attending Christchurch Village School. Potter was said to be a shy child, somewhat of an introverted loner. He lived with his mother, Margeret, and siblings in the home of his paternal grandparents, but because of limited space, his mother was forced to take the children to live with her family in Hammersmith. When Potter was 14, the family moved to London, where he attended St. Clement Danes Grammar School on a scholarship.

In 1953, Potter joined the National Service at the Intelligence Corps. And remained there for two years. Later, he was sent from Sussex to Bodmin in Cornwall. He then joined the Russian Course leading to duty as a Russian Language clerk at the war office in Whitehall. When his national service ended, he won a scholarship to New College in Oxford to study Philosophy, Politics, and Economics. There, he was involved in the fortnightly Oxford Union debates, and onstage productions (Marlowe's *Dr. Faustus*) including others. He also submitted his work to the *Isis*

literary magazine and later became the editor. He resigned from the editor's seat after a misunderstanding with the owners of the magazine. Around the same time, Potter began writing for *New Statesman.*

After graduating from New College in Oxford in 1959, Potter wrote pieces for the BBC as a trainee, the *London Daily Herald* (he became its TV critic), and the *London Sun.* In 1960, the BBC produced a documentary, *Between Two Rivers,* which he wrote and narrated about the village where he was born. It was not until 1964, when he was defeated as the Labour candidate for a seat in the House of Commons, that he began to look upon writing as his vocation. By then, he was married to Margaret Morgan and had three children to support. He was also motivated by the onset of psoriatic arthropathy, a disease which causes both pain and weakness to the joints and severe scaling of the skin. About twice a year attacks were disabling enough to require hospitalizations; the rest of the time they were controlled by medication. His illness, Potter said, made him introspective, reclusive. "For me, writing is partly a cry of the soul. But at the same time, I'm bringing back the results of a journey that many people don't get a chance to make. . . ."

Potter tried his hand at movies. In 1988 he wrote the screenplay for a Nicolas Roeg film, *Track 29.* In addition to *Pennies From Heaven,* he adapted Martin Cruz Smith's *Gorky Park* for the screen. His favorite medium, however, remained television. After *Stand Up, Nigel Barton* (1965), a political satire, he produced over 30 original plays and several adaptations for British television. He also served as director when the BBC wanted to film his novel *Blackeyes* (1988). Because television uses pictures rather than words it satisfied his dream of "a common culture." "The thought of all sorts of people from all sorts of backgrounds in all sorts of circumstances seeing the same thing at the same time I find thrilling."

Potter wrote about politics, religion, popular culture, and intimate relationships, and he focused on disillusionment, infidelity, and betrayal. Some critics consider the sex scenes and language too explicit, the themes offensive and blasphemous. *Brimstone and Treacle,* his story of a brain-damaged girl raped by the devil, could not be shown by the BBC until 1987, 11 years after it was made. *Son of Man* (1969), which depicted Jesus as a common workingman, brought him four hundred pieces of hate mail a week. In addition, Potter distorted time and space, reality and fantasy, in ways no other television writer has tried. In *Pennies From Heaven* and again in *The Singing Detective* characters suddenly sing popular songs of the 1930s and 1940s which represent their fantasies or comment on the action. In *The Singing Detective,* scenes from the real world of the protagonist, hospitalized with psoriatic arthropathy, mesh with scenes from a detective novel he is writing, personal recollections, and hallucinations. The first broadcast was in 1986. After that, Potter began directing with a drama based on his novel *Blackeyes* and then a feature film *Secret Friends,* both of which were complete failures. He went back to what he knew best, the musical comedy serial *Lipstick on Your Collar.*

Potter can be looked upon as both realistic and optimistic. He liked nonnaturalistic narrative because it accurately reflects the way in which people see the world, the interpenetration of what is "out there" with their moods and memories, hopes and regrets. And he believed that as his characters came to terms with the facts of their lives through trauma and crisis, they became "sovereign human beings"; they know who they are. Despite his affinity for controversy, Potter came to be admired as an exciting and complex writer. In 1988 the *New York Times* critic Vincent Canby said of him, "He's made writing for television respectable and, possibly, an art."

February 1994, Potter was afflicted with cancer of the pancreas and liver and was given only a few months to live. Because of this, he put his energy into completing his serial *Karaoke* (1993) and the sequel *Cold Lazarus.* Both were broadcasted in 1996. In March 1994, Potter taped his last interview which aired in April. Interviewed by Melvyn Bragg, Potter talked about his life, work, ideals, and his futile future. On May 29, 1994, Potter faced the death of his wife and just a week later, his own on June 7, 1994.

Further Reading

Among the Dennis Potter works or adaptations on videotape are *Pennies From Heaven* (the 1981 film with Steve Martin), *Brimstone and Treacle* (1982), *Gorky Park* (1983), *The Singing Detective* (1986), *Track 29* (1988), and *Christabel,* his 1989 adaptation of Christabel Bielenberg's *The Past Is Myself.* These and a number of other screenplays, as well as miscellaneous nonfiction and fiction, are also available in print. Updated biographical sites can be found in the Dennis Potter Homepage online. A complete account of Potter's life and work exists in *Fight & Kick & Bite* written by W. Stephen Gilbert (1996).

The best source of biographical and critical material is periodicals, including book reviews. A summary of his life and a partial list of his works can be found in Volume 107 of *Contemporary Authors* and in *Contemporary Dramatists,* 3rd edition (1982). Two useful articles are: Alex Ward, "TV's Tormented Master" in the *New York Times Magazine* (November 14, 1988) and Graham Fuller, "Dennis Potter" in *American Film* (March 1989). □

Francis Poulenc

Francis Poulenc (1899-1963) was in many ways the most "typical" of the group of French composers known as Les Six, and he represents a trend of 20th-century music that is characteristically French.

Francis Poulenc was born in Paris to a family that was artistic, musical, and affluent. His mother was a fine pianist, and Francis began lessons at the age of 5. Later he studied with Ricardo Vines, a friend of Claude Debussy and Maurice Ravel who had played the first performances of much of their piano music. While still in his teens Poulenc met Erik Satie, who left a permanent mark on his musical ideals.

When Poulenc was 18, he wrote *Rapsodie nègre* baritone, string quartet, flute, and clarinet. Its lighthearted irreverence and music-hall atmosphere established his right to be a charter member of Les Six when the group was formed a few years later. He spent most of his life in Paris, except for concert tours that included several trips to the United States after World War II, where he accompanied baritone Pierre Bernac, who specialized in singing his songs.

Poulenc's gift was lyric; he was at his best when he was setting words to music. As the composer of over 150 songs with piano accompaniment, he is perhaps the most important songwriter of his time. He usually set the verses of poets he knew: Guillaume Apollinaire, Jean Cocteau, Paul Éluard, and Max Jacob; he performed the same service for these poets that Debussy did for the symbolists. Poulenc's early set of songs, *Cocardes* (1919), written to Cocteau's poems, suggest the Paris streets. The accompaniment, consisting of cornet, violin, bass drum, and trombone, resembles the little street bands that still play there. A later cycle, *Tel jour, tel nuit* (1937), celebrates the quiet pleasures of life with sincerity and directness.

Poulenc's two operas differ strikingly from each other. *Les Mamelles de Tirésias* (1944) is a risqué, surrealist farce; *Les Dialogues des Carmélites* (1957) is a serious and moving account of the spiritual development of a nun during the French Revolution. His religious choral works, particularly the *Litanies à la Vierge noire* (1936) and a *Stabat Mater* (1950), are frequently performed. He also wrote numerous piano solos, a sonata for two pianos, and concertos for

piano, two pianos, organ, and harpsichord. Among chamber works there are sonatas for various instruments and piano and a sextet for piano, flute, oboe, clarinet, bassoon, and horn.

Poulenc avoided large, dramatic gestures. He accepted his natural limitations and was content to write music in the spirit of the composers he most admired: Wolfgang Amadeus Mozart, Frédéric Chopin, Debussy, and Igor Stravinsky.

Further Reading

A book-length study of Poulenc is Henri Hell, *Francis Poulenc* (trans. 1959). There is a short biographical study and analysis of his work in Joseph Machlis, *Introduction to Contemporary Music* (1961).

Additional Sources

Bernac, Pierre, *Francis Poulenc: the man and his songs,* London: V. Gollancz, 1977.

Poulenc, Francis, *My friends and myself: conversations with Francis Poulenc,* London: Dobson, 1978.

Poulenc, Francis, *Selected correspondence, 1915-1963: echo and source,* London: V. Gollancz, 1991. □

Ezra Loomis Pound

Ezra Loomis Pound (1885-1972), American poet, translator, editor, critic, and esthetic propagandist whose life was surrounded by controversy, is best known for his *Cantos* (1925-1960), an epic version of the history of civilization.

Pound founded the imagist movement in American poetry and was an influential poet. He was the first to promote and publish T.S. Eliot's poetry. Recently it was discovered that Pound's suggested revisions for Eliot's *The Waste Land* (1922) were adopted in the final version of the work, revealing Pound as a sort of invisible "co-author" of one of the 20th century's most influential poems. Unfortunately, Pound's positive role as a teacher and promoter of modernist poets and poetics and as a translator of Oriental and Anglo-Saxon verse has been largely overshadowed by the spectacle of the vehemently reactionary anti-Semite and racist who actively supported the Fascists during World War II, was indicted for treason following the war, and was declared legally insane in 1945.

Ezra Loomis Pound was born on Oct. 30, 1885, in Hailey, Idaho, but spent most of his youth in Pennsylvania. In 1901 he began attending the University of Pennsylvania and then, two years later, transferred to Hamilton College in Clinton, New York, from which he graduated in 1905. He received a master of arts degree from Pennsylvania in 1906, where he taught while engaged in his studies. Among his pupils was poet William Carlos Williams. After teaching French and Spanish at Wabash College, Indiana, Pound left

for London in 1908 on a cattle boat, where he lived until 1920.

Imagist Movement

A Lume Spento (1908), Pound's first published volume, was followed in 1909 by *Personae of Ezra Pound and Exultations of Ezra Pound*. Most of his early work was late romantic in style, heavily imitative of Robert Browning, and probably influenced as well by his study of Provençal chansons. The "credo" Pound stated in 1917, calling for a new "imagist" poetry of austerity, directness, and emotional freedom, a poetry "nearer the bone," was realized in the poem *Portrait d'une femme*, published in *Ripostes* (1912), which was probably inspired by Henry James's novel *Portrait of a Lady* and which may have influenced T.S. Eliot's later poem of the same name.

Pound founded and edited the revolutionary literary magazine *Blast* in 1914 and later became the European editor of Harriet Monroe's Chicago *Poetry*, using his influence to promote and encourage Eliot. Harriet Monroe later said, "It was due more to Ezra Pound than to any other person that 'the revolution' was on."

Pound effectively preached the gospel of modernism during this period, but his own poetry for the most part did not live up to his teachings. He developed his own voice as a poet much more slowly than did Eliot, who by the time he left Harvard had already developed his mature style. Through his "creative translations" of Chinese poems in *Cathay* (1915) and his "Homage to Sextus Propertius"

(1918 and 1919) Pound's characteristic mature style gradually emerged. By the time *Hugh Selwyn Mauberley* appeared in 1920, with its echoes of Eliot's "The Love Song of J. Alfred Prufrock," Pound had achieved his artistic maturity.

In 1918 Pound began investigating the causes of World War I, the earliest evidence of his lifelong obsession with economic and political theory, to explain the failures of modern democratic society. From 1920 to 1924 Pound lived in Paris, where he was associated with Gertrude Stein and her brilliant circle of American expatriates. He dominated the avant-garde literary movements of the period. He moved to Italy in 1924, where he spent most of the rest of his life. The first of the *Cantos,* his magnum opus, appeared in 1925. In the years before World War II he published, in addition to his poetry, books on economics, art, and Oriental literature and lectured at the Bocconi University in Milan on Thomas Jefferson and Martin Van Buren.

In 1941 Pound began to broadcast propaganda from Rome attacking the American war effort. The broadcasts, which expressed his complete disillusionment with democratic culture, were largely personal diatribes on the proper nature and function of art and the artist in society—thus, his indictment for treason by the American government after the war was condemned by most artists and critics. The Italian government had faithfully observed Pound's request that he not be compelled to say anything contrary to his conscience or to his duties as an American citizen; his broadcasts were misguided attempts to "save" his homeland from what he felt was a debilitating democracy rather than calls for its destruction.

Pound was returned to the United States in 1945 under indictment for treason but never stood trial. After his lawyer successfully entered a plea of insanity, Pound was committed to St. Elizabeth's Hospital in Washington, D.C. His *Pisan Cantos* were given the Bollingen Award in 1949, largely through the influence of Eliot, who, along with William Carlos Williams and many other prominent figures in American letters, was instrumental in having Pound's indictment dismissed in 1958. That same year Pound was released from St. Elizabeth's under a storm of controversy and returned immediately to Italy.

When Pound returned to Naples he gave a fascist salute to assembled photographers and claimed he was the greatest living poet. He returned to his home in Merano and began gardening, planting grapes and, of course, writing. This period in his life was cut short by a heart attack in 1962. Afterwards he became very elusive and rarely talked to anyone. He continually worked on one singular project, trying to find a "paradise" to end his *Cantos* series. He took long walks along the streets of Venice and, as friends said, tried to come to terms with himself and his life.

There seemed to be many others as well who were trying to come to terms with Pound. The year of his death the American Academy of Arts and Sciences had turned down a request by other writers and critics to award Pound their Emerson-Thoreau Medal. By a 13 to nine vote, the Academy voted not to award Pound even though they stated that he was a great writer. They cited Pound's political views and past behavior as the reasoning behind denying him the award.

Pound died on November 1, 1972 in Venice's Civil Hospital from an intestinal blockage after falling ill at his home near St. Mark's Square.

His Writings

Pound's early imagism, a confused and ambiguous esthetic, was an attempt to make poetry scientifically respectable. Through it he hoped to be able to present in verbal images the exact equivalent of the actual object described, so that the experience of the poem would create in the reader the same sensations caused by direct experience of the object itself. Pound never acknowledged the amount of conscious and unconscious selection and control that went into the making of an imagist poem, and his own work exemplified a personalism that belied his objectivist theory. He never admitted, even to himself, that the creations of the human mind must invariably be conditioned by the process of that mind.

Perhaps the best example of Pound's imagism is "In a Station of the Metro," which has only two lines: "The apparition of these faces in the crowd; Petals on a wet, black bough." The poem is similar in format to Japanese haiku poetry, which he cited enthusiastically as authority for his later theory of the "ideogrammatic method" but which he never fully understood in its indigenous religious implications. Characteristically, Pound cited examples from the entire body of world literature in support of his various esthetic theories with little regard for their actual context or meaning; everything was shaped to fit the contours of his own mind.

"The Seafarer" (1912), one of Pound's earliest and best creative translations, brilliantly reproduces the unique consonantal "sound" of Anglo-Saxon poetry, but, characteristically, its detail and incident are considerably revised to suit his individual purposes. Many of the later *Cantos* show his command of Anglo-Saxon sonics. *Hugh Selwyn Mauberley* marked Pound's creation of the persona that would serve him throughout the *Cantos.* A debt to Walt Whitman is suggested in the very conception of the *Cantos,* a lifelong series of explorations of the self in the context of world history. But the *Cantos* fundamentally proceed through the accretion of established *literal* history, whereas Whitman's method was more organic, fashioning a personal myth which moved out to metaphorically envelop the world.

Pound's reputation as a poet ultimately must rest on the *Cantos,* which are notoriously uneven in quality. Longer than Whitman's *Song of Myself* or Herman Melville's *Clarel,* to which they might be compared, except for a few early examples they are noticeably less successful because of their obsessiveness, moral insensitivity, and unreadability. Despite Pound's claims for their scientific objectivity, the *Cantos* are in fact highly subjective and morally irresponsible. In spite of his arguments for the "ideogrammatic method," the treatment of history as self-evident "fact" in the manner of the image in an imagist poem cannot be either morally or philosophically defended. In a sense there are no real people in the *Cantos,* only stereotyped heroes and villains; it is a poem about history that fails to present humanity acting and suffering at its very center. As William Butler Yeats said of Pound's villains, he presents them as "malignants with inexplicable characteristics and motives, grotesque figures out of a child's book of beasts." Pound's best known slogan was "Make it new!" He might better have exhorted himself to "make it human."

Although the *Cantos* are part of a long American tradition of epic attempts to use history as a clue to the meaning of present experience, and despite their Emersonian emphasis on fact as the clue to form, their main thrust remains Pound's own fundamentally sentimental nostalgia for "nobler," more "heroic" past ages and his alienation from the contemporary world. His best poetry is in his creative translations, not in the major work of his career.

As early as the publication of *Mauberley* in 1920, Pound ceased developing as an artist and thinker. His final *Cantos* differ intellectually only in their degree of compressed allusion from the antidemocratic implications of his earliest fully achieved work, in which he described the modern world as "an old bitch gone in the teeth . . . a botched civilization." The immense historical erudition and intellectual idiosyncrasy of the *Cantos* make them virtually indecipherable to many readers. Indeed, the late "Rock Drill" *Cantos* are apparently intended to be unreadable, being arranged on the page as spatial sculpture rather than as understandable poetry.

Pound's influence on contemporary poets is small in comparison with that of William Carlos Williams, who more accurately exemplifies the current interest in Zen and Whitman. But those who explore the "deep image" find in Pound's work clues to a new poetics.

Further Reading

A paperback selection of Pound's poems was published in 1957. For Pound's theories see *A B C of Reading* (1934), *The Letters of Ezra Pound* (1950), and *The Literary Essays of Ezra Pound* (1954), which was edited by T. S. Eliot.

A full-length biography of Pound is Charles Norman, *Ezra Pound* (1960). For discussions of Pound's works see Peter Russell, ed., *An Examination of Ezra Pound: A Collection of Essays* (1950); the section on Pound in Babette Deutsch, *Poetry in Our Time* (1952); Harold H. Watts, *Ezra Pound and the Cantos* (1952); Lewis G. Leary, ed., *Motive and Method in the Cantos of Ezra Pound* (1954); Clark M. Emery, *Ideas into Action: A Study of Pound's Cantos* (1958); Macha L. Rosenthal, *A Primer of Ezra Pound* (1960); George S. Fraser, *Ezra Pound* (1961); George Dekker, *The Cantos of Ezra Pound: A Critical Study* (1963); L.S. Dembo, *The Confucian Odes of Ezra Pound: A Critical Appraisal* (1963); Walter E. Sutton, ed., *Ezra Pound: A Collection of Critical Essays* (1963); and the section on Pound in Hyatt H. Waggoner, *American Poets, from the Puritans to the Present* (1968). Pound's obituary can be found in the November 2, 1972 issue of the *New York Times*. □

Roscoe Pound

Roscoe Pound (1870-1964), American jurist and botanist, furthered the development of sociological jurisprudence, which significantly altered American legal thought.

Roscoe Pound was born at Lincoln, Nebr., on Oct. 27, 1870, the son of a judge. After graduating from the University of Nebraska in 1888, he earned a master of arts degree in 1889 and then attended Harvard Law School for a year. He passed the bar exam in 1890 and began practicing law, teaching at the University of Nebraska Law School, and working toward his doctorate in botany, which he earned in 1897. For several years he directed the botanical survey of Nebraska and discovered a rare lichen (later designated the "roscopoundia"). His botanical writings are still considered important.

As commissioner of appeals of the Supreme Court of Nebraska (1901-1903), Pound wrote 102 opinions that have often been cited. He was commissioner for uniform state laws for Nebraska (1904-1907) and dean of the law department at the University of Nebraska (1903-1907). He taught law at Northwestern University (1907-1909) and at the University of Chicago (1909-1910).

Pound's vast erudition included all phases of the law and jurisprudence as well as the classics and foreign languages. He often worked 16 hours a day and had a phenomenal memory and great intellectual curiosity. He became the leading exponent of sociological jurisprudence, that is, applying pragmatism to the law to make it amenable to society's needs rather than adhering to inapplicable precedents. Pound first set forth his concept of sociological jurisprudence in a 1906 address and continued to expound it for nearly a generation. At about the same time, he also began expressing his "formative era" concept, which stated that an indigenous new law for the country was evolved by American judges between 1789 and 1860.

In 1910 Pound became professor of law at Harvard. He was dean from 1916 to 1936 during what was called Harvard Law School's "golden age". He helped shape a faculty and program of legal education equipped to implement his concept of sociological jurisprudence. A large number of the law school graduates were active in formulating policies of Franklin D. Roosevelt's New Deal, and Pound supported many of its early measures. But though he had once felt that the law stifled administration, he came to feel that courts must serve as a bulwark against potential dictatorship. Similarly, he became critical of the legal realists of the 1930s, whose thinking was founded in Pound's earlier work; he felt that they placed value only on experience in setting legal standards.

In 1936 Pound resigned as dean and was assigned to one of the first Harvard "roving professorships"; for the next 11 years he taught everything from law to the classics. In 1938 he was named director of the National Conference of Judicial Councils. He received the American Bar Association's medal for "conspicuous service to the cause of American jurisprudence" in 1940. He served as adviser to the Nationalist China Ministry of Justice (1946-1949), which was reorganizing its judicial system. When he returned to the United States, he was extremely critical of America's China policy, because of its ineffective support of Chiang Kai-shek.

Pound retired from Harvard in 1947 but continued to teach at a number of law schools for several years and maintained his steady flow of publications. In all, he authored over 1,000 items, including his massive fivevolume *Jurisprudence* (1959). He died in Cambridge, Mass., on July 1, 1964.

Further Reading

Pound's own *Roscoe Pound and Criminal Justice* was edited by Sheldon Glueck in 1965. Studies of Pound include Paul Lombard Sayre, *The Life of Roscoe Pound* (1948), and Arthur Leon Harding, ed., *The Administration of Justice in Retrospect: Roscoe Pound's 1906 Address in a Half-century of Experience* (1957).

Additional Sources

Sayre, Paul Lombard, *The life of Roscoe Pound,* Littleton, Colo.: Rothman, 1981, 1948.

Wigdor, David, *Roscoe Pound; philosopher of law,* Westport, Conn., Greenwood Press 1974. □

Nicolas Poussin

Nicolas Poussin (1594-1665), one of the greatest French painters, rationally synthesized the diverse tendencies of French and Italian art. His work is a salient example of lucid control by the mind over the senses.

The art of Nicolas Poussin is a visual record of progression from the chaos of youth to self-awareness, from self-control to intellectualism, and from wisdom to harmony. In the 19th century Paul Cézanne conferred the ultimate tribute: "Every time I come away from Poussin I know better who I am."

Poussin was born in the hamlet of Villers near Les Andelys, Normandy, in June 1594. His father, who had certain claims to ancient but minor nobility, came from Soissons; he was a military man turned farmer. His mother was the widow of a lawyer, and Nicolas was destined for the law. The boy, who knew Latin from childhood, received a sound education until he was 18. His proclivity for art provoked the disapproval of his parents, and in 1612 the presence of Quentin Varin, a minor mannerist painter, in the neighborhood occasioned Poussin's flight from home.

After a brief sojourn with the painter Noël Jouvenet in Rouen, Poussin went to Paris, where the patronage of a young nobleman from Poitou enabled him to frequent the studios of the portraitist Ferdinand Elle and the mannerist

painter Georges Lallemand. About 1614 his noble friend took Poussin home to his château in Poitou, but his patron's mother did not like the alliance, and the artist departed on foot, reaching Paris exhausted and ill from malnutrition. After a year's rest with his family at Les Andelys, Poussin returned to Paris to begin a productive career.

Except for a trip to Florence about 1620-1621 and another to Lyons shortly thereafter, Poussin spent the years between about 1616 and 1624 establishing his position in Paris. He studied architecture, perspective, and anatomy; the mannerist frescoes of Francesco Primaticcio at Fontainebleau; antique sculpture; and the High Renaissance paintings of Raphael, Leonardo da Vinci, and Titian and the engravings of Giulio Romano. He frequented intellectual and artistic circles and met the Italian poet Giambattista Marino, for whom he executed a series known as the Massimi drawings. Poussin received commissions from the Jesuit Collège de Clermont in Paris and Notre Dame in Paris. When he left for Rome in 1624, he was a mature artist. On the way he stopped in Venice, where the works of Titian and Paolo Veronese profoundly influenced him.

Works, 1624-1630

Between 1624 and 1630 Poussin's life was characterized by professional vicissitudes and artistic experimentation. He vacillated, though always brilliantly, between his Paris style, based upon the study of Giulio Romano and antique sarcophagi (*Victory of Moses,* 1624-1626), the current Roman baroque style of Pietro da Cortona (*Madonna del Pilar*), the Venetian High Renaissance style of Veronese

(*Marriage of St. Catherine*) and Titian (*The Inspiration of the Poet*), and the realistic style of Caravaggio (*Massacre of the Innocents*). The conspicuous success of this period was the *Martyrdom of St. Erasmus* (1628-1629) for an altar in St. Peter's.

In spite of the patronage of the Barberini family, the confusion resulting from Poussin seeking his own style among the multiple possibilities afforded him in Rome and the fierce competition of Italian, Flemish, and French artists resulted in another illness. After being nursed back to health in the house of the French pastry cook Jacques Dughet, he married the daughter Anne Marie in 1630. Poussin decided to abandon the field of official commissions, and from then on he devoted himself exclusively to the execution of small cabinet pictures, fastidious in workmanship, for a private and cultivated clientele.

Works, 1630-1640

In the 1630s friendship with Cassiano dal Pozzo, amateur of the antique, led Poussin into a milieu of modest but genuine scholars. At this time his concern was poetical, focused upon the dramatic themes of Tasso (*Rinaldo and Armida*) and the melancholy of Ovid (*Arcadian Shepherds*). Between 1633 and 1637 his subject matter shifted to the pageantry of the Old Testament (*Adoration of the Magi*), mythology (*Bacchanals* for Cardinal Richelieu, and ancient history (*Rape of the Sabines,* two versions). During this time the coloristic fluidity of Titian, which had characterized Poussin's previous period, gave way to a statuesque plasticity of figure style, recalling Raphael's *Mass of Bolsena*. Compositions were oriented parallel to the picture plane and delineated by a controlled, linear perspective.

Between 1637 and 1640 this rational tendency increased. Poussin used various pictorial methods of painting to elicit a specific response in the educated observer, trained to understand his expressive purpose in any given work. These were the ancient Greek and Roman modes. His earlier works had been mainly in the Hypolydian mode for joyful subjects of divine glory and paradise and the Ionic mode for festive, bacchanalian subject matter. Now they became more austere, in the Dorian mode for stable, grave, and severe themes (*The Israelites Collecting Manna*); or martial, in the Phrygian mode for intense and violent themes. Poussin's fondness for the modes was motivated, according to his letter of Nov. 24, 1647, to P. F. de Chantelou, by a desire for didactic clarity in communication. For the sake of readability his compositions, from the late 1630s, were cautiously planned, the figures sculpturally modeled, the tones restricted to primary colors insistently repeated, and the psychological content underlined by emphatic, sometimes histrionic gesture and facial expression.

Return to Paris, 1640-1642

Louis XIII and Cardinal Richelieu had been urging Poussin's return to Paris since 1638, and in 1640 he did so. He was given the title of first painter to the king, a yearly pension, and lodging in a pavilion of the Tuileries Palace. His princely reception provoked the resentment of the artistic coterie. The official circle expected him to create a French "style" and be able to direct teams of artists and artisans. But Poussin was used to a contemplative atmosphere and to concentrating on a single, meticulously executed work, and the constant demand for adaptability and glib fluency in the creation of altarpieces, decorative ceilings, and designs for books, tapestries, and furniture was exhausting. Of his many Paris works the best products of that unhappy sojourn were the decorative schemes for the ceilings of the Orangerie in the Luxembourg Palace and for the Grande Galerie of the Louvre.

Mature Period, 1643-1653

In September 1642 Poussin returned to Rome, ostensibly to fetch his wife; Richelieu and Louis XIII died soon after Poussin reached Rome, enabling him to remain in his adopted country permanently. He passed the rest of his life modestly and placidly in his house in the Via Paolina, refusing countless honors, including the directorship of the Academy of St. Luke. The most important fruit of his Paris visit was a patronage truly worthy of his talents. Intellectual conservatives of the French upper bourgeoisie, like Chantelou, called forth, through their commissions, the best of the artist's talents, the embodiment of the French classical ideal.

Between 1643 and 1653 Poussin came to grips with the fundamental premise of his creative being, the triumph of human will over the passions, manifest in his works in the domination of intellect over emotion. The *Holy Family on the Steps* (1648), for example, reveals his rational procedure for achieving biblical truth. The observer is infallibly guided, through the selective simplicity and lucid formality of the essential compositional elements, to the climax of the representation, the enthronement of a nobly modest family on monumental stairs, and to the denouement, the movement of the Holy Family toward the observer.

In executing his works Poussin proceeded in the following manner. After a thorough reading of the primary sources, he made a preliminary sketch; he then constructed a small model stage upon which he could move, like chessmen, actual miniature figures made of wax. After making further drawings and altering the positions of the figures as he progressed, he made larger models. From these he painted the final scene, referring occasionally to living models to avoid sterility. Thus, by steady, almost pedestrian degrees the potentially dramatic theme was simplified to a lofty understatement. Such laborious procedures, dangerously susceptible to stereotyping by imitators, were adopted until 1690 for teaching purposes by Charles Le Brun in the Paris academic program; they also explain the objection, among even cultivated critics, to Poussin's not infrequent statuesque sterility and coloristic coldness in the works of his mature period.

Late Period, 1653-1665

In Poussin's late period he moved beyond the somewhat self-conscious and mechanical means just described. The triumph of human will over the passions, or intellect over emotion, became an ultimate statement of the reign of universal harmony over the seeming chaos of nature and human life. This final conviction is most telling in such works as *Apollo and Daphne* (1664), sometimes called his spiritual testament to the world, and *Summer* and *Autumn,* two of the cycle of the four seasons (1660-1664). Figures are set in wildly animated landscapes of fertility or desolation, forms are reduced to nearly cubistic abstraction, and action is drastically simplified. Poussin died in Rome on Nov. 19, 1665.

Further Reading

A great deal has been written about Poussin. By far the most reliable works in English are Anthony Blunt, *The Paintings of Nicolas Poussin: A Critical Catalogue* (1966) and *Nicolas Poussin* (2 vols., 1967), and Walter Friedlaender, *Nicolas Poussin: A New Approach* (1966).

Additional Sources

Blunt, Anthony, *Nicolas Poussin,* London: Pallas Athene, 1995.
Nicolas Poussin, New York: Abbeville Press, 1990. □

Terence Vincent Powderly

American labor leader Terence Vincent Powderly (1849-1924) presided over the Knights of Labor during the union's remarkable growth and rapid decline in the 1880s.

Terence V. Powderly was born in Carbondale, Pa., on Jan. 22, 1849. His parents were Irish immigrants. At 13 he began work in a railroad yard. At 17 he apprenticed himself to a machinist and began to practice the trade in 1869 in the shops of the Delaware and Western Railroad in Scranton, Pa. Interested in labor unionism, he joined the International Union of Machinists and Blacksmiths in 1871 and, in 1874, was an organizer for the Industrial Brotherhood. That year he was initiated into the Noble and Holy Order of the Knights of Labor, a small secret society centered on Philadelphia. Powderly organized the Knights' local assembly in Scranton and was elected its master workman in 1876; he was also an officer in district assembly no. 5.

In 1878, at the age of 29, Powderly was elected mayor of Scranton on the Greenback-Labor ticket. He was reelected three times. Meanwhile, in 1879, he was elected the Knights' grand master workman (general master workman after 1883). His accession marked a significant departure in Knights' policy. His predecessor, a Baptist, had been indifferent to the Catholic Church's opposition to the Knights. Powderly, although a Mason, was also a Roman Catholic and realized that the American Catholic hierarchy must be placated if the Knights were to flourish among Catholic workers. He persuaded the union to abandon its secrecy and to remove scriptural references from its ritual.

Powderly disapproved of strikes, considering them too costly for the small benefits gained. He was a humanitarian visionary, interested in the long-term goals of abolishing the wage system and instituting a cooperative society rather than in short-term gains. With his approval, various local assemblies of the Knights set up 135 producers' and consumers' cooperatives, including a coal mine.

However, as head of the union (1879-1893), Powderly had to devote much time to settling strikes the various locals became involved in. ''Just think of it!'' he wrote, ''Opposing strikes and always striking . . . battling with my pen in the leading journals and magazines of the day for the great things we are educating the people on and fighting with might and main for the little things.''

The Knights were involved in a series of dramatically successful strikes during the early 1880s. The most notable involved a strike against the railroads of financier Jay Gould. Such victories resulted in an incredible growth: in mid-1885 there were about 100,000 Knights in 1,610 local assemblies; a year later membership stood at 700,000 in almost 6,000 locals. Powderly was uncomfortable with such rapid growth, and his lack of enthusiasm in another strike against Gould (1886) contributed to the Knights' defeat and, ultimately, their decline. By 1893, when Powderly was ousted from his position, there were only 75,000 dues-paying members.

Part of Powderly's weakness as the union's leader was his interest in other than union affairs. During his first 6 years as grand master workman, he was also mayor of Scranton. He studied law, served as a county health officer, partly owned and managed a grocery store, served as vice president of the Irish Land League, tried to become the first

U.S. commissioner of labor in 1884, took great interest in political campaigns, and was an active prohibitionist. Frequently complaining about the Knights' demand upon his time, he resigned once and threatened to resign several times.

In addition, Powderly was temperamentally unsuited to the industrial turmoil of the 1880s. Disliking strikes and other conflicts, he constantly looked forward to an age of cooperation. Nor did he look the part of a labor organizer. Slender, even frail, he wore delicate spectacles and a magnificent drooping mustache and dressed impeccably. His manners were formal, even haughty. He was considered something of a snob. Ultimately these qualities neutralized his competence as an organizer and administrator, his considerable abilities as a speaker and correspondent, and his tact and diplomacy.

After retiring from leadership of the Knights, Powderly practiced law and was named commissioner general of immigration (1897). He became chief of the Division of Information in the Immigration Bureau in 1907. He died on Jan. 24, 1924.

Further Reading

The basic sources for studying Powderly are his autobiographical *Thirty Years of Labor, 1849-1924* (1889; rev. ed. 1890) and *The Path I Trod: The Autobiography of Terence V. Powderly* (1940). The most comprehensive discussion of Powderly is in Norman J. Ware, *The Labor Movement in the United States, 1860-1895* (1929). Information on Powderly can be found in any standard labor history of the period; the best is probably Foster Rhea Dulles, *Labor in America* (1949; 3d ed. 1966).

Additional Sources

Falzone, Vincent J., *Terence V. Powderly, middle class reformer*, Washington: University Press of America, 1978. □

Adam Clayton Powell Jr.

The political leader and Harlem Baptist minister Adam Clayton Powell, Jr. (1908-1972) was a pioneer in civil rights for black Americans.

Adam Clayton Powell, Jr. was born on November 29, 1908, in New Haven, Connecticut, moving with his parents at the age of six to Harlem, New York City. His father was a successful clergyman and a dabbler in real-estate. Adam was sent to Hamilton, New York, to Colgate University (1930, A.B.) and afterwards to Columbia University (Teachers College, 1932, M.A.) and studied for the ministry at Shaw University (1935, D.D.).

He was heir-apparent to his father at the Abyssinian Baptist Church in Harlem and succeeded him as pastor in 1937. Upon his return to Harlem from Colgate in 1930 he had launched a career of agitation for civil rights, jobs, and housing for African Americans. It was the era of the Depression. He led demonstrations against department stores, Bell

Telephone, Consolidated Edison, and Harlem Hospital, among others, to hire African Americans.

Elected to the city council in 1941, he continued to press for civil rights and for jobs for African Americans in public transportation and the city colleges. As editor of the militant *People's Voice* from 1942, and with a reputation gained from his church for doing something about the destitute (he directed a soup kitchen and a relief operation that fed and clothed thousands of Harlem indigents), he was a force to be reckoned with in the Depression. Leader of the largest African American church in the nation (13,000 members—a sizeable basis of support), he was ready to use his ample skill in political demagoguery and his charisma in defense of African American nationalism. At the age of 15 he had joined Marcus Garvey's African Nationalist Pioneer Movement, so he understood African American nationalism. The Emperor Haile Selassie of Ethiopia had awarded him a gold medallion for his work of relief in Harlem: he wore it everywhere. Powell's picket lines at the headquarters of the World's Fair in the Empire State Building resulted in hundreds of jobs for African Americans in 1939 and 1940.

But it was after his election to Congress that he really made his stand. He took his seat in 1945 for central Harlem. He was the first African American from an Eastern ghetto and the second African American in Congress—the first was William Dawson of Chicago. Dawson was more moderate than Powell.

As a freshman congressman Powell was appalled at being barred from public facilities in the House of Representatives: dining rooms, steam baths, showers, and barbershop. He instantly used those facilities; with political instinct, he got his staff to use them also. He engaged Southern segregationists in debate. He tried to bring about an end to segregation in the military, to get African American newsmen admitted to the Senate and House press galleries, to introduce legislation to outlaw Jim Crow in transport, and to inform Congress that the Daughters of the American Revolution were practicing discrimination.

The Southern segregationists were mainly in his own party, the Democratic Party. In 1956 Powell supported Dwight Eisenhower, a Republican seeking a second term, and did not go with Adlai E. Stevenson, the Democratic nominee. He advised Stevenson to reject Southern bigots like Long of Louisiana, Eastland of Mississippi, and Tallmadge of Georgia—all of whom were in the Democratic Party. Eisenhower won, and some Democrats were prepared to punish Powell for his defection. Some critics accused him of currying favor with the federal government over alleged tax irregularities by voting for Eisenhower. Many Democrats had switched to the Republican Party for the presidential choice, as he did, but they were not African American congressmen. Powell was his own man.

Nevertheless, Powell was a Democrat; he welcomed the advent of a new president, Democrat John F. Kennedy in 1960, and became the new chairman of the House Committee on Education and Labor. Despite a high absentee record in the House, his accomplishments as chairman were extraordinary. As Powell himself said: "You don't have to be there if you know which calls to make, which buttons to push, which favors to call in." The committee authorized more important legislation than any other: 48 major pieces of social legislation, embodying more than $14 billion. Kennedy's "New Frontier" and Lyndon Johnson's "Great Society" programs were intimately involved with this committee: education, manpower training, minimum wages, juvenile delinquency, and the war on poverty were all at stake. Presidents Kennedy and Johnson both sent Powell letters of thanks.

All the same, Powell claimed something for his African American constituents with each bill that was laid before him: this was the "Powell Amendment." It called for a stop of federal funds to any organization which practiced racial discrimination. As chairman he had great power to block Great Society legislation; he occasionally held his ground until the Powell Amendment was included in the bill.

As an African American politician and minister he was controversial; as a personality he was extravagant and irreverent. He liked the playboy image, the good life. His first wife was Isabel Washington, a Cotton Club dancer; he had to bully his father into consenting (1933). The marriage lasted ten years. "I fear I just outgrew her," he said. Wife number two was Hazel Scott, a singer and pianist; they had a good life together from 1945 to 1960, when he divorced her. His third wife was Yvette Marjorie Flores Diago, a member of an influential Puerto Rican family. His affairs were front-page news.

In March 1960 he was interviewed on a television show. He happened to call Esther James a "bag woman" during a debate on police corruption. She sued. Powell refused to make a settlement. He ignored all seven subpoenas and eight years of legal battles. He was wanted for criminal contempt of court by New York State. Finally he escaped to Bimini (Bahamas) in 1966, taking his congressional receptionist, Corinne Huff (former Miss Ohio), with him. She had been with him on a trip on the *Queen Mary* to Europe in 1962 when she was 21, together with Tamara Hall (an associate labor counsel for Education and Labor). A select committee of the House recommended public censure for Powell, a loss of seniority (his chairmanship), and the dismissal of Huff. The House voted to exclude him altogether (March 1967).

At a special election two months later Powell received a stunning victory—and he did not even campaign in Harlem. Contributions from his supporters and profits from a phonograph record ("Keep the Faith, Baby") were used to pay the damages in the James suit. In March 1968 Powell returned to Harlem triumphantly, and in January 1969 he was seated in Congress yet again, although without seniority. The Supreme Court ruled that the House acted unconstitutionally when he was unseated. Powell quipped: "From now on, America will know the Supreme Court is the place where you can get justice."

In 1970 he was defeated in the Democratic primary. He died on April 4, 1972, of prostate cancer; his ashes were scattered over Bimini. His death caused a legal squabble between his current mistress and his estranged third wife. Powell was a pioneer civil rights worker 30 years before it was fashionable; his legacy to African Americans was his "sassiness."

Further Reading

For the best reading about this subject, see Adam Clayton Powell, Jr., *Adam by Adam* (1971). Andy Jacobs' *The Powell Affair: Freedom Minus One* (1973) is the story of the vote in the House of Representatives (1967) which unseated Powell. There is an obituary in the *New York Times,* April 5, 1972, which provides additional information. □

Anthony Powell

The English novelist Anthony Dymoke Powell (born 1905), a distinguished writer of social comedy, is best known for his duodecalogy called *A Dance to the Music of Time.*

Anthony Dymoke Powell was born in Westminster, London on Dec. 21, 1905, the son of a Lieutenant Colonel in the British Army. He was educated at Eton and at Balliol College, Oxford, from which he received a bachelor of arts degree in 1926. After graduation Powell entered the publishing business in London and launched his career as a writer in 1931 with the publication of *Afternoon Men,* featuring a hero who lacks all ambition and who drifts aimlessly through bohemian circles, finding meaning nowhere. Powell's next novels—*From a View to a Death* (1933), *Agents and Patients* (1936), and *What's Become of Waring* (1939)—deal with variations on the theme of prostituted talent and the will to dominate personal relationships.

Powell married Lady Violet Pakenham in 1934, the third daughter of the Fifth Earl of Longford. In 1936 he joined Warner Brothers on a six month contract as a script writer. He soon left Warner Brothers and became a full-time writer after traveling the United States and Mexico

Sometime in the late 1930s he had the idea for a novel sequence, *A Dance to the Music of Time,* designed to illustrate the responses to change of the British upper classes. The advent of World War II, however, forced Powell to put aside all writing. From 1939 to 1941 he served in the Welsh Regiment, and from 1941 to 1945 he was a liaison officer in the intelligence Corps. Powell was decorated often and raised to the rank of major.

The first volume in Powell's series, *A Question of Upbringing,* appeared in 1951. This novel introduced many of the characters who reappeared in succeeding novels and established one of them—Nicholas Jenkins—as the narrator who is a participant in, as well as an observer and recorder of, the multiplicity of events. *A Question of Upbringing, A Buyer's Market* (1952), and *The Acceptance World* (1955) form the first trilogy in the sequence. Covering the period after World War I up to the Depression, they depict the lives of Nick and his associates as they reflect upon and attempt to understand the effect of family and schooling upon char-

acter, as they examine what the world offers in the way of work and love, and as they quit their aimless wanderings and come to realize what decisions they may be capable of making.

The second trilogy covers the period from the Depression to the beginning of World War II. *At Lady Molly's* (1957), *Casanova's Chinese Restaurant* (1960), and *The Kindly Ones* (1962) show, respectively, the complexity of deepening commitments, the struggles and the failures of marriage, and a fresh appraisal of 20 years of personal history on the eve of political chaos.

The third trilogy, which covers the years of World War II, is made up of *The Valley of Bones* (1964), *The Soldier's Art* (1966), and *The Military Philosophers* (1968). These novels follow Nick through his realization that war is hardly romantic and that a fighting unit is only as effective as the men who are in it, to his perceptions of the powerful men who have directed the war and his often melancholy musings on the state of Europe and his own life.

The fourth and final trilogy *Books do Furnish a Room* (1971), *Temporary Kings* (1973), and *Hearing Secret Harmonies* (1975) closed out the series and covers the post-World War II years with all of its changes and modern dilemmas. In 1987 the entire twelve volume set was published as *The Album of Anthony Powell's Dance To The Music of Time.*

After publishing the novella *The Fisher King* (1986). The book is about two down-on-their-luck men who meet by happenstance and strike up a friendship even though they would initially seem to have nothing in common. In 1991 *The Fisher King* was adapted as a feature film directed by Terry Gilliam (of Monty Python's Flying Circus fame) and starring actors Jeff Bridges, Robin Williams, and Mercedes Ruehl.

Powell is a reserved man and in keeping with his bashful tendencies (he was offered, and turned down, a knighthood from the Queen of England in 1973) now lives quietly with his wife in Somerset, England and still contributes pieces to publications. His most recent work, *Journals 1990-1992,* was published in 1997 and is a still further look into the man and his personal art of writing.

Further Reading

A useful overview of Powell's work can be found in Robert K. Morris *The Novels of Anthony Powell* (1968). See also the essay on Powell in Charles Shapiro *Contemporary British Novelists* (1965). Powell's memoirs up to 1992 have been published in a four volume set as *To Keep The Ball Rolling* (5th ed. 1983), from 1982 to 1986 as *Journals 1982-1986* (1995), *Journals 1987-1989* (1996), and *Journals 1990-1992* (1997). Powell and his works are discussed at length in George Lilley *Anthony Powell: A Biography* (1994), Neil Brennan *Anthony Powell* (1974), and John Russell *Anthony Powell, A Quintet, Sextet and War* (1970). A brief biography of Powell and a list of his accomplishments appears in the 1997 edition of *Who's Who*. An extensive chronology of Powell's works and life is available on-line at *Keith Marshall's Zen Mischief* Website located at www.ftech.net. □

Colin Luther Powell

American Army officer Colin Luther Powell (born 1937) served as national security adviser to President Ronald Reagan, and under President George Bush became the first African American to serve as chairman of the Joint Chiefs of Staff (1989-1993).

Colin Luther Powell was born in Harlem, New York City on April 5, 1937, the son of a shipping clerk and a seamstress, both of whom were immigrants from Jamaica. Powell spent most of his childhood in the South Bronx, then regarded as a step up from Harlem. Despite the urgings of his parents that he should "strive for a good education" in order to "make something" of his life, Powell remained an ordinary student throughout high school. At City College of New York, Powell discovered himself; his retentive mind and leadership abilities made him a conspicuous success in the Army's Reserve Officers' Training Corps (ROTC). He graduated from the program in 1958 with the rank of cadet colonel, the highest awarded, and was commissioned a second lieutenant in the U.S. Army. He was then assigned to duty in West Germany. In 1962, while stationed at Fort Devens, Massachusetts, Powell met and married Alma Vivian Johnson. The couple had three children.

Powell's next overseas assignment was in South Vietnam, where he was wounded in action. He then studied at the Command and General Staff College at Fort Leavenworth, Kansas, finishing second in a class of more than twelve hundred officers. During a second tour in Vietnam he received the Soldier's Medal for pulling several men from a burning helicopter.

The army then provided Powell the time to study for a Master's degree in business administration at George Washington University. He received the degree in 1971, after which he worked as an analyst at the Pentagon before securing what he called a "dream job": an appointment as a prestigious White House fellow in the Office of Management and Budget under the director, Caspar Weinberger, and his deputy, Frank Carlucci, two men of rising influence in Washington who perceived Powell's uncommon abilities and who would help shape his career.

A man of commanding presence at six feet one inch and 200 pounds, Powell was assigned to South Korea in 1973 to command a battalion troubled by racial animosities. "I threw the bums out of the army and put the drug users in jail," he recalled. "The rest, we ran four miles every morning, and by night they were too tired to get into trouble." Powell's prescription worked, and the tensions that had led to race riots before his arrival abated.

After additional service in Washington and an assignment as a brigade commander in the 101st Airborne Division at Fort Campbell, Kentucky, Powell returned to Washington in the late 1970s, attaining the rank of major general and holding advisory posts in the Pentagon and briefly in the Department of Energy. He next served at Fort

Carson, Colorado, and at Fort Leavenworth before becoming military assistant to Weinberger, then secretary of defense in the Reagan administration, in 1983. While Powell was assisting Weinberger, the National Security Council (NSC) began looking at the possibility of sending American missiles to Iran in the hope of expediting the release of American hostages in the Middle East and turned to Powell to provide certain information about the missiles desired by Iran. Powell complied but subsequently questioned the scheme in writing, reminding the NSC leadership that there was a legal obligation to inform Congress of the proposed arms transfer. When it was pointed out that the plan had presidential authorization, Powell did what was requested of him. The illegal missile transfer was later exposed as a key element in the controversial Iran-Contra scandal. Powell's demonstrated record of opposition to the illegality of the transfer and his excellent demeanor in testifying before congressional investigating committees served him well. In June 1986 Powell received a choice corps command in West Germany but left it after six months at President Reagan's request to become Frank Carlucci's deputy on the National Security Council. Carlucci was endeavoring to rebuild the NSC after the Iran-Contra debacle.

In 1987 Powell replaced Carlucci as national security adviser, a post he held for the duration of the Reagan administration. Arms control and attempts to topple the Sandanista government of Nicaragua ranked high on the agendas of Powell and of other key policy-makers during this period. When President-elect George Bush advised Powell that he wished to name his own national security adviser, Powell could have chosen to leave the army to earn a substantial income on the lecture circuit or perhaps in the business world. Money, however, was not sufficient inducement for Powell to retire; promoted to full (four star) general, he took over the army's Forces Command, which had responsibility for overseeing the readiness of over a million regular, reserve, and National Guard personnel based in the United States. Selected over three dozen more senior generals, Powell was nominated by President Bush in 1989 to become chairman of the Joint Chiefs of Staff (JCS), the nation's most prestigious military position. Powell was the first black officer to hold this post.

As chairman of the JCS, Powell held a key role in formulating and refining plans for the December 1989 operation that eliminated the corrupt Manuel Noriega regime in Panama. Television appearances in which Powell explained the purpose of the operation brought him to the favorable attention of the American public. "In a performance that left politicians and viewers marveling," observed a *Wall Street Journal* reporter, "he laid out the details in tough but carefully measured tones that may have done more than anything else to reassure lawmakers and the public about the predawn invasion."

Powell became similarly conspicuous during the first stages of Operation Desert Shield, the joint effort by the United States and several other nations through blockade and the mobilization of substantial forces in and near Saudi Arabia to pressure Iraqi dictator Saddam Hussein into removing his forces from neighboring Kuwait. This small, oil-rich nation had been occupied by Iraqi troops in August 1990. It soon became apparent that this operation, unlike the earlier one in Panama, would take months to decide and involved the risk of substantial casualties if and when hostilities broke out between the Iraqis and the international forces, the bulk of them American. It was thus uncertain whether Powell's largely unblemished record for excellent judgment and leadership would remain intact.

When Desert Shield turned into Desert Storm on January 16, 1991, Powell again demonstrated his successful leadership. Six weeks later the Iraqi army was crushed; the multinational forces stood completely victorious. For his part in this Persian Gulf War, General Powell, as well as field commander General H. Norman Schwarzkopf, was awarded a congressional gold medal.

When Powell was named to head the JCS, a former White House colleague remarked of his appointment: "No one ever thinks of Colin as being Black; they think of him as being good." Powell, however, never ignored his background in New York City or the prejudice he encountered in the 1960s when off base at various army posts in the South, "I've made myself very accessible to the Black press," he once told an *Ebony* reporter, "and I do that as a way of just showing people, 'Hey, look at that dude. He came out of the South Bronx. If he got out, why can't I.'" Powell believed that his position as the nation's foremost military leader and spokesman provided a unique opportunity to deliver a positive message to African American youth.

As the youngest man to serve as chairman of the Joint Chiefs, Powell would have ample opportunity to accomplish even more should he choose to remain in public service. His name had even been mentioned in connection with the vice presidency by both liberals and conservatives.

Powell remains an active figure in government. During the 1996 presidential race, it was announced that Powell would run. He declined, citing various reasons. The withdrawal was disappointing to many Americans. Powell spends his time lecturing, writing and speaking.

Further Reading

In the absence of a full biography of Colin Powell, those seeking further information can consult several articles about him, including Simeon Booker, "Colin L. Powell: Black General at the Summit of U.S. Power" in *Ebony* (July 1988); Thomas M. DeFrank, "The Ultimate No. 2' for NSC" in *Newsweek* (November 16, 1987); Carl T. Rowan, "Called to Service: The Colin Powell Story" in *Reader's Digest* (December 1989); Marshall Brown, "Powell Reaches the Pinnacle of Pentagon Power" in *Black Enterprise* (October 1989); Barrett Seaman with Dan Goodgame, "A 'Complete Soldier' Makes It" in *Time* (August 21, 1989); Lou Cannon, "Antidote Ollie North" in *Washington Post Magazine* (August 7, 1988); and Laura B. Randolph, "Gen. Colin L. Powell: The World's Most Powerful Soldier" in *Ebony* (February 1990). Information regarding Powell's political career can be read in an article by J.F.O. Mcallister entitled "The Candidate of Dreams" *Time* (March 13, 1995). □

John Wesley Powell

American geologist, anthropologist, and scientific explorer, John Wesley Powell (1834-1902) made the first dramatic descent of the Colorado River through the Grand Canyon. His life was dedicated to exploring and conserving the natural resources—scientific, scenic, economic, and human—of the American West.

John Wesley Powell was born on March 24, 1834, on a farm in western New York. During John's childhood the family migrated from Ohio to Wisconsin to Illinois, so his education was sporadic. He attended Wheaton and Oberlin colleges but obtained no degree. Powell early demonstrated interest in botany and traveled extensively, collecting specimens as part of his self-education. He joined the Illinois Society of Natural History at the age of 20 and was soon elected secretary. Prior to the Civil War, he worked as a schoolteacher and lyceum lecturer. Powell joined the Union Army and lost his right arm in the bloody Battle of Shiloh.

Released from service, Powell became professor of natural history at Illinois Wesleyan College. He transferred to the Illinois Normal University as curator of the museum, thereby gaining time and financial support for western exploration. In 1867 he conducted a party of students and amateur scientists to Colorado; he and his wife ascended Pike's Peak and explored the Grand River. The next year he

took a party of 21 men to the Rockies. In 1869 Powell and a small party descended the Colorado River through the Grand Canyon, a feat never before accomplished.

In 1871-1872 Powell voyaged down the Green and Colorado rivers a second time and for the remainder of the decade, with the financial support of Congress, explored the Colorado Plateau. His reports and lectures on natural history and the Native American tribes made him a national hero. His importance as a scientific explorer was recognized when he became director of the U.S. Geological Survey in 1880.

As a geologist, Powell provided detailed explanations of how the erosion of rivers creates gorges during periods when a rocky region is undergoing gradual elevation. His findings were published in *Explorations of the Colorado River of the West and Its Tributaries* (1875) and revised in *Canyons of the Colorado* (1895). An early conservationist, Powell was obsessed by the idea that a vast wasteland was being created in the West by farmers who, by breaking the earth's cover, were inviting erosion. He believed that water monopolists and lumbermen were excessively exploitative. Powell urged Congress to modify the land laws in the West in his *Report on the Lands of the Arid Regions of the United States.* His proposal ultimately led to the creation of the Bureau of Reclamation.

While traveling among the tribes of the High Plains, Powell took notes on their languages and customs. In 1879 he organized the Bureau of American Ethnology in the Smithsonian Institution; he directed it for 23 years. His classification of American Indian languages is still valuable. He was also responsible for the Irrigation Survey (1889), a systematic appraisal of the land and water resources of the West that became the basis for all irrigation legislation in the United States.

Perhaps Powell's greatest contribution was as an administrator who recognized that government and science should work in partnership. He urged creation of a Federal department to consolidate all government activity in the scientific field. As director of the Geological Survey, he coordinated the scientific efforts of many men and institutions. He also sponsored extensive publication programs by the Federal government, including the bulletins (begun 1883) and monographs (inaugurated 1890) of the Geological Survey. Most important was the series of atlases (from 1894).

Powell's contribution was recognized with honorary degrees from Harvard and Heidelberg universities. He died on Sept. 23, 1902, in Haven, Maine.

Further Reading

The best biography of Powell is William Culp Darrah, *Powell of the Colorado* (1951). An excellent interpretation of his career is Wallace Stegner, *Beyond the Hundredth Meridian: John Wesley Powell and the Second Opening of the West* (1954). Elmo Scott Watson tells of Powell's first western venture in *The Professor Goes West* (1954). Frederick S. Dellenbaugh, *A Canyon Voyage* (1908), is the most complete published narrative of Powell's second expedition along the Colorado River. His career within the national pattern of exploration and scientific achievement is delineated in Richard A. Bartlett, *Great Surveys of the American West* (1962), and William H. Goetzmann, *Exploration and Empire: The Explorer and the Scientist in the Winning of the American West* (1966). Young people will find a colorful account of Powell's first trip down the Colorado in Leonard Wibberly, *Wes Powell: Conqueror of the Grand Canyon* (1958).

Additional Sources

Aton, James M., *John Wesley Powell,* Boise, Idaho: Boise State University, 1994.

Stegner, Wallace Earle, *Beyond the hundredth meridian: John Wesley Powell and the second opening of the West,* Lincoln: University of Nebraska Press, 1982, 1954. □

Lewis F. Powell Jr.

Lewis F. Powell, Jr. (born 1907) was a corporate lawyer who became a U.S. Supreme Court justice. He became the intellectual leader of the Court's moderate center until his 1987 retirement.

Lewis F. Powell, Jr. was born on September 19, 1907, in Suffolk, Virginia, son of a comfortable middle-class family. Powell attended Washington & Lee College, from which he graduated in 1929, and Harvard Law School, where he studied under Felix Frankfurter, completing a

L.L.M. degree in 1932. Powell married Josephine M. Rucker on May 2, 1936, and was the father of three daughters and a son. Admitted to the Virginia bar, he entered private practice in Richmond in 1937 and became a partner in the prestigious Richmond firm of Hunton, Williams, Bay, Powell & Gibson. During World War II he served as an Air Force intelligence officer in North Africa. Returning to his Richmond practice, he gained national recognition as a corporate lawyer, subsequently serving on the board of directors of 11 major companies. A pillar of the American legal establishment, Powell served as president of the American Bar Association (1964-1965), president of the American College of Trial Lawyers (1968-1970), and president of the American Bar Foundation (1969-1971). His service as vice president of the National Legal Aid and Defender Society was instrumental in securing support of the organized bar for government-subsidized legal service for poor people.

Active in community affairs, Powell was chairman of the Richmond School Board, where during the late 1950s and 1960s he urged a moderate course in complying with *Brown* v. *Board of Education* and kept the Richmond schools open despite calls for "massive resistance" to desegregation. He led in the voluntary desegregation of Washington & Lee University. He was not, however, a leader in bringing racial equality to the South. The Fourth Circuit Court ruled in 1965 that practices of the Richmond School Board under Powell's leadership unconstitutionally perpetuated racial segregation (*Bradley* v. *School Board of Richmond*).

Appointed to the Supreme Court by Richard Nixon in 1972, Powell was viewed as cautious and pragmatic, with a skepticism for doctrinaire solutions. He was also distrustful of governmental interference in private affairs and committed to logical analysis as an aid to predictability and principled decision making. Powell quickly emerged as the intellectual leader of the Court's moderate center. He also sought to limit access to the courts by persons seeking to litigate generalized grievances. In *U.S.* v. *Richardson* (1974) he went out of his way to warn of the dangers to a democratic society of an overly activist judiciary. His personal biases also came out in business cases, where his decisions failed to strike the note of reasoned moderation that prevailed through much of the rest of his jurisprudence.

Powell was generally charry toward government regulation. On anti-trust opinions he tended to favor the business attacked. He voted against organized labor and was unenthusiastic about environmental and consumer protection, urging an extremely narrow reading of the Truth-In-Lending Act to exclude many installment transactions from its coverage (*Mourning* v. *Family Publications Service, Inc.* [1973]).

Powell's balance did show in a number of fields. In criminal law he generally ruled to increase the authority of law enforcement officials to obtain information and to decrease the zone of privacy that the individual had against government. He tended to narrow the Fifth Amendment's guarantees against self-incrimination. He refused to sustain the government's power to wiretap, however, maintaining that wiretapping was search and seizure within the meaning of the Fourth Amendment (*U.S.* v. *U.S. District Court* [1972]). On the other hand, he rejected the contention that the Fourth and Fifth amendments interlocked to provide a broad privacy area immune from governmental intrusion. Instead, he took the literal language of each amendment and read it narrowly. On the "exclusionary" rule, Powell was hostile, arguing it impeded successful law enforcement. He rejected the view that capital punishment violated the Eighth Amendment, but also the view that no constitutional constraints restricted its use. Rather, he favored a middle course, suggesting the states enact mandatory capital punishment laws (*Furman* v. *Georgia* [1972]).

In the civil liberties area, Powell was strongly separationist on matters of church and state, striking out particularly at various forms of aid to parochial schools (*Committee for Public Education and Religious Liberty* v. *Nyquist* [1973]). He supported the Court's decision in *Roe* v. *Wade* (1973) and wrote a strong opinion reasserting women's constitutional right to end their pregnancies in 1983. In *First National Bank of Boston* v. *Bellotti* (1978) he found the public's right to know more important than the state's interest in regulating corporations and wrote a seminal opinion granting First Amendment protection to corporate speech.

In the equal protection field Powell was more critical of racial discrimination in employment than he was in education, although he agreed that the 1966 Civil Rights Act reached discrimination in private schools (*Runyon* v. *McCrary* [1976]). He joined Justice William O. Douglas in denouncing the distinction between *de facto* and *de jure* segregation, calling for enforced national standards in that area. On bussing to achieve integration, he opposed large-scale, long-distance bussing requirements in metropolitan areas.

Powell's best known opinion was in *California Board of Regents* v. *Bakke* (1978), where he cast the deciding vote and wrote the authoritative individual opinion. In it he invalidated rigid racial quotas in admissions, but upheld the discretion to use race as a factor in establishing an affirmative action program. The opinion reflected Powell's judicial experience, representing a careful move between polar extremes which enabled compromise and supplied sensitive—if conservative—guidelines for future rulings.

In the preface of a 1994 biography on Justice Powell, the author mentions that shortly before Lewis Powell retired from the Supreme Court, a civil liberties leader called him ''the most powerful man in America.'' The statement, the author continues, refers to Powell's ideological center of a divided Court, and revealed the remarkable degree to which liberals had come to depend on the conservative from Virginia. President Nixon had not anticipated Powell's role as an occasional liberal when he appointed him to the Court sixteen years earlier. Unlike the other Nixon appointees, Powell proved to be highly independent, open to argument and willing to reconsider his own preconceptions.

He retired from the Supreme Court in 1987 citing age and health problems. In addition to urological problems, he suffered at night from a concerning pain in his legs. He had a blood infection in 1988 and in 1989, he contracted pneumonia while sitting on an appeals court in Florida. Powell then began to black out for no apparent reason until it was discovered that cardiac arrhythmia was to blame. A cardiac pacemaker remedied the problem, only after he suffered a fall with a resultant broken hip. His recuperation kept him sidelined until early 1991. Despite his setbacks, he continued to work, maintaining an office in the Supreme Court with a secretary, a messenger, and one clerk.

Fearing a lack of activity, he decided to chair Chief Justice Rehnquist's committee on habeas corpus in capital cases, to deliver lectures, to spend several weeks in residence at the University of Virginia and Washington and Lee, to receive various awards and honorary degrees and to sit on appeals courts in Richmond and elsewhere. He continued to do the work in which he had devoted his life.

Further Reading

Powell's career through the late 1970s is detailed well in Leon Friedman, editor, *The Justices of the United States Supreme Court: Their Lives and Major Opinions,* vol. V (1978). Useful sketches are also included in Catherine A. Barnes, *Men of the Supreme Court: Profiles of the Justices* (1978), and in the Congressional Quarterly *Guide to the U.S. Supreme Court* (1979). J. Harvie Wilkinson, *Serving Justice: A Supreme Court Clerk's View* (1974) is an interesting and sympathetic account of the author's association with the justice as well as a revealing look at the inside of the Court.

For Powell's impact on the Supreme Court and on the nation, see John C. Jefferies, Jr., *Justice Lewis F. Powell, Jr.* (1994). The book does not make an attempt to survey the nearly three thousand decisions rendered by the Supreme Court while

Powell was a member, instead it focuses on six areas of commanding interest: desegregation, abortion, Watergate, the death penalty, affirmative action, and sexual equality. □

Hiram Powers

Hiram Powers (1805-1873) was the most famous and significant of all the American neoclassic sculptors.

Hiram Powers was born on July 29, 1805, in Woodstock, Vt. The family soon moved to Cincinnati, where Powers grew up. He began his artistic career modeling wax figures for Dorfeuille's Western Museum in Cincinnati. His efforts then were noticed by the novelist Frances Trollope, who, years later, was of great assistance to him.

In 1834 Powers went to Washington, D.C., where he executed plaster portrait busts of such clients as Andrew Jackson and Daniel Webster. When Powers settled in Florence, Italy, in 1837, he made marble reproductions of these busts. He spent the rest of his life in Florence. The American sculptor Horatio Greenough, who was in Florence at that time, aided Powers socially and artistically. He also received encouragement from Bertel Thorvaldsen, then the most famous European neoclassic sculptor.

Powers continued to sculpture portraits throughout his lifetime. His patrons were visiting Americans and Europeans, some of noble heritage or of great repute. It was in the area of ideal works, however, that he made his reputation. He began creating such works as his bust *Ginevra* soon after arriving in Florence and followed this with his first full-length sculpture, *Eve Tempted*. His second full-length nude female figure, the *Greek Slave,* won him international acclaim; six full-size replicas were made. The statue became the best-known American sculpture of the 19th century because of its exhibition at the Crystal Palace in England in 1851 and the tour of several versions of the sculpture in the United States. The piece was emulated by other sculptors, both American and European.

Power's *Greek Slave* was followed by other full-length works, such as *California, America, Eve Disconsolate,* and *The Last of the Tribe,* as well as busts of these, and *Faith, Hope, Charity, Psyche, Diana,* and *Proserpine.* Over 130 replicas of *Proserpine* are known to have been made. The great disappointment of his life was the lack of serious governmental patronage; this was accorded, instead, to his contemporary Thomas Crawford. Powers did, however, furnish the U.S. Capital with sculptures of Benjamin Franklin and Thomas Jefferson.

Powers died in Florence on June 27, 1873. The entire contents of his studio, including all his plaster models, about 20 marble sculptures, and his tools, casts, and manuscripts, were later acquired by the Smithsonian Institution in Washington, D.C.

Further Reading

There is no complete study of Powers. The Smithsonian Institution, utilizing the unpublished manuscript biography of Clara Louise Dentler, planned to publish a study in 1973. Powers is discussed or referred to in general works: Lorado Taft, *The History of American Sculpture* (1903); Albert TenEyck Gardner, *Yankee Stonecutters: The First American School of Sculpture, 1800-1850* (1945); Oliver W. Larkin, *Art and Life in America* (1949; rev. ed. 1960); and Georgia S. Chamberlain, *Studies of American Painters and Sculptors of the Nineteenth Century* (1965).

Additional Sources

Reynolds, Donald M., *Hiram Powers and his ideal sculpture*, New York: Garland Pub., 1977.

Wunder, Richard P., *Hiram Powers: Vermont sculptor, 1805-1873*, Newark: University of Delaware Press; London; Cranbury, NJ: Associated University Presses, 1989-c1991. □

Powhatan

Powhatan (ca. 1550-1618) was chief of a confederation of Algonquian Indians in Virginia at the time of the British colonization of Jamestown.

Powhatan was the son of a chief reportedly driven from Florida by the Spaniards. Settling in Virginia, the chief soon conquered about five local tribes and confederated them under his leadership. Powhatan inherited this confederacy and continued to conquer other tribes so that, by the time of the colonization of Jamestown, he ruled about 30 tribes comprising some 8,000 people.

Powhatan made his headquarters at Werowocomoco, a village on the north side of the York River 15 miles from Jamestown. However, his home was at the falls of the James River (near present Richmond). This site was known as Powhata, thus the English colonists called him Powhatan.

As chief of this confederation, Powhatan was noted for ruling with rigid discipline. He was said to be very cruel to prisoners, and he always maintained a personal guard of 30 to 40 warriors. He had several wives, 20 sons, and 10 daughters, one of whom was Pocahontas.

In 1607 Powhatan was described by John Smith as a "tall, well proportioned man" with gray hair and thin beard who had an aura of sadness about him. The early colonists came to Powhatan to beg for corn, for, as the Native Americans later said, they were yet too weak to steal it. Powhatan was suspicious of the newcomers, refusing to sell them corn. He ordered ambushes of small parties of Englishmen, and several workers were murdered in the fields.

In 1608, according to a story of debated authenticity, Capt. John Smith had been captured and was about to be

Powhatan (standing, far right)

clubbed to death when he was saved by Powhatan's daughter Pocahontas. This incident did not change Powhatan's attitude toward the English. Nor did his crowning when, in 1609, acting under orders from the Virginia Company, Capt. Christopher Newport, using a gilded crown brought from England for the purpose, crowned Powhatan "Emperor of the Indies." John Smith said that Powhatan appreciated the gifts he received but could be persuaded only with difficulty to stoop to allow the crown to be put on his head.

In 1610 Smith's unsuccessful attempt to capture Powhatan triggered Indian retribution. However, in 1613 Samuel Argall captured Pocahontas and held her hostage for the good behavior of the Powhatan confederacy. An uneasy truce followed.

In 1614 John Rolfe, one of the English settlers, asked to marry Pocahontas. Governor Sir Thomas Dale agreed to the marriage, as did Powhatan, and it took place in Jamestown that June. Powhatan did not trust the colonists sufficiently to attend the wedding and sent his brother in his place.

With the marriage of Pocahontas and Rolfe, Powhatan made a formal treaty of peace with the English which he kept until his death in April 1618. He was succeeded by his second brother, Itopatin (or Opitchepan), who in a few short years would go to war with the Virginia settlers again.

Further Reading

The information about Powhatan is in Capt. John Smith, *The Generall Historie of Virginia* . . . (1624; several later editions). Also consult Frederick W. Hodge, *Handbook of American Indians North of Mexico* (2 vols., 1907-1910); Kate D. Sweetser, *Book of Indian Braves* (1913); and John R. Swanton, *The Indian Tribes of North America* (1952). □

Manuel Prado Ugarteche

The aristocratic Peruvian political leader Manuel Prado Ugarteche (1889-1967) was twice president, and although elected by conservative and centrist groups, he attempted to reduce the tensions within his nation by incorporating more popular elements.

Manuel Prado was born in Lima on April 21, 1889. His father, Gen. Mariano Ignacio Prado, was president of Peru for two short periods in the latter half of the 19th century. Manuel Prado graduated from the National School of Engineering in 1915. In 1918 he married Enriqueta Garland, and a son and daughter were born; after 40 years the marriage was annulled, amid popular outcry, and he then married Clorinda Málaga.

After getting his engineering degree, Prado became involved in the management of his family's properties, developing as his speciality the direction of the family banking interests. He also found time for other undertakings: between 1915 and 1919 he taught mathematics at San Marcos and was, in that same period, the editor of the university's *Science Review.*

Prado also initiated his political career in those years, becoming a member of the Lima Municipal Council in 1915. He then became a member of the Peruvian Congress in 1919 and, even though he had not made himself particularly notable, was forced into exile in 1921 by the dictator-president Augusto Bernardino Leguía. Prado shared that fate with most of the reformist-minded Peruvians of his day, though he himself was hardly an enthusiast for reform. He remained in exile until 1932 and did not resume his political career until 1939.

First Term

When Manuel Prado was elected president in 1939, he had apparently been chosen because of his moderation; he did, in fact, bring a considerable degree of political peace to his nation through his attempts to smooth over divisions and to reduce tensions. He had, it was rumored, reached a secret understanding with the leftwing non-Marxist APRA (Alianza Popular Revolucionaria Americana) before the election, committing himself to the legalization of the party. He did not, in fact, grant the party a legal status, but he did reduce the pressures upon it.

Although no serious attacks were made during Prado's first administration upon the fundamental problems of Peru, he became a popular president. He also managed to stay in office for his full term, something no other civilian president had done since 1914. His administration was able to capitalize upon the defeat of an Ecuadorian force in a border war in 1942, and the diplomatic settlement gave Peru title to vast areas of Amazon territories.

In 1945 Prado cooperated with a newly emerged political force, the National Democratic Front, which represented moderates, including some elements within the APRA itself. The coalition's candidate, José Luis Bustamente y Rivero, was elected as Prado's successor; but soon there was a renewal of violence at the same time that there was a virtual stalemate in government. In October 1948 the army, led by Gen. Manuel A. Odría, deposed Bustamente, outlawed the APRA once again, and established a government which lasted until 1956.

By 1956 a change seemed to be indicated: the era of prosperity under Odría had come to an end, and with it had come the collapse of the public works projects. Also at an end was the political truce that had come into existence. To ward off the threatened renewal of violence, a patchwork coalition of moderate and conservative elements persuaded Manuel Prado to accept the presidency. He took office once again in July 1956.

Second Term

Prado had received the support of the APRA, as well as that of Odría, largely because of the threat of a new reform group, the National Front of Democratic Youth, led by Fernando Belaúnde Terry.

The years of Prado's second administration were ones of crisis. The decline in Odría's last years threatened to become an economic collapse. Government revenues fell off, and, increasingly, the effects of a government-tolerated inflation were felt. Although the Prado regime had the support of a majority, including the APRA, whose adherents were named to Cabinet posts, it still had great difficulty in governing. Some of its economic problems were solved when, in 1959, Pedro Beltrán, a leading spokesman for conservative economic doctrines, was persuaded to accept the premiership and allowed to design new fiscal policies.

These policies, however, brought great unpopularity to the government since they included the elimination of subsidies on foods, gasoline, and many other necessities, as well as the adoption of various belt-tightening reductions in public expenditures. Nationalist elements were infuriated by the allegedly greater profits of foreign-owned oil companies; conservatives were embittered by the apparent dependence of the Prado government upon the APRA and the rumored "deal" that would allow the APRA to capture the coming elections. To the clamor of these two groups was added that of the reformers, represented by Belaúnde.

The election was held in early June 1962, but none of the three principal candidates (Odría, Haya de la Torre, and Belaúnde) managed to get the majority needed. When it was reported that an agreement between the followers of Odría and the APRA had been reached, elements of the army moved upon the presidential palace in the early hours of July 18 and replaced Prado with a three-man junta representing the military services. Prado was soon allowed to go into exile and remained in Paris until his death on Aug. 15, 1967.

Further Reading

There is no biography of Prado in English. For an adequate account of Peru during the years of his political prominence see Frederick B. Pike, *The Modern History of Peru* (1967). □

Michael Praetorius

The German composer and theorist Michael Praetorius (ca. 1571-1621) was a devout Lutheran who believed that music was the "handmaiden of theology." He composed a comprehensive musical repertory for the Evangelical Church.

Born in Creuzburg (Thuringia), Michael Praetorius was raised in Torgau, a small town famous for its Lutheran school. He studied at the University of Frankfurt an der Oder, and for part of the time he was organist of the university church. In 1595 he entered the service of Heinrich Julius, Duke of Brunswick, at the courts of Gröningen and Wolfenbüttel. At first installed as organist and subsequently advanced to music director (1604), Praetorius composed music for all court activities until the duke's death in 1613.

During the next 7 years Praetorius had no fixed post but was employed intermittently by several north German courts (Magdeburg, Kassel, Halle, Dresden) as musical consultant and director of musical festivities. In 1620 he was recalled to Wolfenbüttel; he died the following year.

Praetorius's voluminous output only partly reveals his overall plan for a complete corpus of secular and sacred music for all occasions. Of his secular works only one volume of dances, *Terpsichore* (volume 5 of his projected *Musa Aonia*), has come down to us. Thousands of sacred pieces are extant, most constructed on Lutheran hymn texts and tunes known as chorales. The contents of his 9-volume *Musae Sioniae* (1605-1610) range from simple *bicinia,* or two-part pieces, to enormous polychoral works for as many as 12 voices.

Baroque pieces with basso continuo, concertizing instruments, and separate choirs for soloists and chorus are first noted in Praetorius's late publications *Polyhymnia caduceatrix* (1619), *Polyhymnia exercitatrix* (1620), and *Puericinium* (1621). These mature compositions underscore his importance in transmitting Italian concerted music to Germany. Although these works are modeled on examples by Giovanni Gabrieli and Claudio Monteverdi, Praetorius, ever bound to the German chorale, rarely employed the affective style favored by the Italian innovators.

As a pendant to his music, and in part to explain its performance, Praetorius wrote a three-volume treatise, *Syntagma musicum* (1615-1620), which deals with three subjects: the history of ancient sacred and secular music, the nature and construction of musical instruments, and the performance practices of his time. Especially valuable are his definitions and explanations of early-17th-century terms

and practices. In the second volume, *De organogrpahia,* he discusses the history and construction of musical instruments. Unparalleled for its time is the appendix to this volume, the *Theatrum instrumentorum,* or pictorial atlas of instruments.

Further Reading

Praetorius's work is discussed in Manfred F. Bukofzer, *Music in the Baroque Era* (1947), and in the *New Oxford History of Music,* vol. 4 (1968). The background of the baroque musical style is treated in Paul Henry Lang, *Music in Western Civilization* (1941). □

Jakob Prandtauer

The Austrian baroque architect Jakob Prandtauer (1660-1726) is famed chiefly for his monastic and religious buildings, notably the abbey and church of Melk.

Jakob Prandtauer, born in mid-July 1660 in Stanz in the Tirol, was the son of a master mason, and he too learned the trade. He also studied sculpture and architecture, however, for by the time he was 19 he was working as a sculptor in Sankt Pölten, a city in Lower Austria not far from Vienna. By 1700 he was a master builder (*Baumeister*), working on many projects in Sankt Pölten.

From 1701 until his death Prandtauer worked for the monastery of Melk on the Danube in Lower Austria, totally rebuilding the church and all the buildings of the huge monastic complex, one of the largest of its kind. Like his great contemporaries Johann Bernhard Fischer von Erlach and Johann Lucas von Hildebrandt, Prandtauer turned to Italianate forms for his inspiration, but, as did the others, he also introduced highly personal notes into his architecture. The huge church at Melk, whose towers dominate the landscape over the Danube Valley, is embedded into the structure of the whole monastery by two wings projecting forward on either side and bound together with a curved terrace; the whole ensemble juts up out of the rock over the river. Here he created one of the most thrilling examples of baroque architecture. The stately interior, a harmony of dark-red marble and gilded ornament with golden-toned frescoes by Johann Michael Rottmayr, is reminiscent of Roman baroque examples, although Prandtauer could only have known them through engravings.

While Melk remains his most famous creation, Prandtauer also built the beautiful pilgrimage church on the Sonntagsberg (1706-1728) and the monastery at Garsten near Steyr (1703-1708), and he reconstructed the monastery of Sankt Florian near Linz, taking over the works from Carlantonio Carlone. There he built the grand staircase (1706-1714) and the great hall (Marmorsaal; 1718-1724). From 1708 on he was also in charge of works at Kremsmünster, and from 1720 at Herzogenburg, both monasteries. In every case, as was usually the practice during the period, Prandtauer not only was the architect but was actually in charge of all aspects of the construction and of the exterior and interior decoration of a project, his early training as a mason and a sculptor standing him in good stead in all these enterprises.

Prandtauer is often cited as an example of the local architect who, without training in Italy, nevertheless was able to create great buildings in the baroque style, displaying a native inventiveness and imagination which brought his work to a level of quality equal to that of Fischer von Erlach and Hildebrandt, his more formally trained contemporaries.

When Prandtauer died on Sept. 16, 1726, at Sankt Pölten, most of his projects were still unfinished. They were completed by his pupil, assistant, and cousin Joseph Mungenast, whose famous tower at Dürnstein (1721-1725) is thought to have been largely inspired by his master.

Further Reading

Information on Prandtauer can be found in John Bourke, *Baroque Churches of Central Europe* (1958; 2d ed. 1962); Nicholas Powell, *From Baroque to Rococo* (1959); and Eberhard Hempel, *Baroque Art and Architecture in Central Europe* (1965). □

Rajendra Prasad

Rajendra Prasad (1884-1963) was an Indian nationalist and first president of the Republic of India. He was an important leader of the Indian National Congress and a close coworker of Gandhi.

Rajendra Prasad was born in Saran District, Bihar State, eastern India, on Dec. 3, 1884, into the Kayastha, or scribe, caste. A devout Hindu, he received his early education in Bihar and then attended Presidency College, Calcutta. The Swadeshi movement and particularly the Dawn Society influenced him to become a nationalist. He continued his education, earned advanced degrees in law, and practiced law in Calcutta and then in Patna.

When Mohandas Gandhi arrived in Bihar in 1917 to assist the peasants in Champaran, Prasad soon joined in this activity, becoming a lifelong disciple of Gandhi. Following Gandhi's lead, Prasad joined the Indian National Congress and participated in the noncooperation campaigns of 1919 and 1921-1922. Forsaking his law practice almost entirely, he became principal of the National College in Bihar, edited nationalist papers, and mobilized peasant support for the movement. During the internal split in the Congress during the 1920s, he was a spokesman for the No-Changer group, which whole-heartedly supported Gandhi's constructive program, particularly the production of indigenous cloth (or khadi) by hand spinning.

In the 1930s Prasad, along with Vallabhbhai Patel and others, led the Gandhian Old Guard, which usually dominated the Congress organization. They opposed the Congress Socialists. Prasad was Congress president in 1934 and at Gandhi's request again served as president after the serious internal struggle of 1939. Prasad was a member of the Congress Parliamentary Board, which directed the election campaign of 1936-1937. While spending most of World War II in prison, he wrote his *Autobiography* in Hindi (trans. 1958) and a book opposing Moslem proposals for the partition of India, *India Divided* (1946).

After serving as minister for food and agriculture in the interim government, Prasad became president of the Constituent Assembly that eventually completed the constitution of the Republic of India in 1949. He was chosen interim president of his country and was elected the first president in May 1952. Five years later he was reelected for a second term. During his presidency, he toured India and many countries of Asia. In his speeches he stressed national and communal unity, the need for a national language, the scarcity of food and the ways to increase food production, and the achievements of Indian culture. He often drew upon the words and achievements of his mentor, Gandhi, and gave importance to the need for more extensive educational programs, particularly the implementation of Gandhi's basic education scheme. The difficulties of the postindependence years were eased by the close cooperation between President Prasad and Prime Minister Jawaharlal Nehru. Prasad died on Feb. 28, 1963, in Patna.

Further Reading

For more detailed information on Prasad the reader should consult Prasad's own massive *Autobiography* (1957; trans. 1958). The most useful biography is Kewal L. Panjabi, *Rajendra Prasad: First President of India* (1960).

Additional Sources

Handa, Rajendra Lal, *Rajendra Prasad: twelve years of triumph and despair,* New Delhi: Sterling Publishers, 1978.

Prasad, Rajendra, *Dr. Rajendra Prasad, correspondence and select documents,* New Delhi: Allied, 1984. □

Praxiteles

Praxiteles (active ca. 370-330 B.C.) was one of the leading Greek sculptors of the 4th century B.C. His style, refined and graceful, greatly influenced the art of his own time and the succeeding epochs.

Praxiteles was probably the son of Kephisodotos, an Athenian sculptor, since he named one of his own sons Kephisodotos, and the same name ran in families in alternate generations. Pliny the Elder, in his *Naturalis historia,* places Praxiteles in the 104th Olympiad, or 364-

361 B.C., and the base of a portrait statue from Leuktra bearing an inscription stating that Praxiteles the Athenian made it dates from about 330 B.C. These are the only definite dates we have regarding him.

At the beginning of the 4th century B.C. Athenian civilization had undergone profound changes. The disillusionment with civic values caused by the Peloponnesian War had turned artistic taste away from the idealism of Phidias's art toward a more humanized, personal view of the world and the gods. Praxiteles brought the gods down to a human level; he made them less majestic but gave them a consummate grace.

The marble *Hermes Holding the Infant Dionysos* was found in 1877 in the Heraion at Olympia, where Pausanias, who ascribes it to Praxiteles, had seen it in the 2d century A.D. Whether it is a Greek original, a Greek copy, or a good Roman copy, the statue is one of the finest ancient works preserved and shows the salient characteristics of the sculptor's style. Praxiteles softened the precisely articulated rendering of musculature of the previous century into a softer, fluid harmony of subtly modulated surfaces; and for the architectonically balanced composition of Polykleitos he substituted a languid S-curve. This curve, often called the "Praxitelean curve," is a hallmark of his sculpture.

In antiquity the most famous work by Praxiteles was the marble *Aphrodite* (*Venus*) *of Knidos.* His openly sensuous treatment of the nude female form was a new feature in

Praxiteles (on podium, center)

Greek art and created an ideal type that endured until the end of antiquity. Pliny tells us that this work made the city of Knidos famous and that it was "the finest statue not only by Praxiteles but in the whole world." Athenaios adds that Phryne, Praxiteles's mistress, was the model. There are a number of Roman copies of the statue, and it is reproduced on Roman coins from Knidos.

According to Pausanias, the base of Praxiteles's statue *Leto and Her Children* at Mantinea was decorated with a scene depicting Apollo, Marsyas, and the Muses. Three slabs from the base were found in 1877 at Mantinea: two show three Muses each, lovely draped figures, and the third depicts Marsyas playing the flute and Apollo with his Phrygian slave. The base may have been executed by one of Praxiteles's students, working from the master's designs.

The *Apollo Sauroktonos* ("lizard slayer") by Praxiteles is known from Pliny's description of it, fairly accurate Roman copies in both marble and bronze (Pliny lists it with the sculptor's bronze works), and the Roman coins from Philippopolis in Thrace and Nikopolis on the Danube. Apollo is represented as a boy leaning against a tree trunk waiting to kill a lizard with an arrow. The sinuous figure of the dreamy god perhaps illustrates better than any other work by Praxiteles how his vision of the gods differed from the emotionally neutral images of his 5th-century predecessors.

Ancient authors mention many other works by Praxiteles, and almost all have been connected with anonymous originals or copies in various museums. These include the famous *Eros,* which Pausanias says Phryne dedicated in her native city, Thespiai; a young satyr pouring wine, a bronze statue seen by Pausanias in the Street of the Tripods in Athens; the cult image of *Artemis Brauronia* on the Acropolis in Athens; and an image of Eubouleus, the swinehered of Eleusinian myth, at Eleusis.

Praxiteles's two sons, Kephisodotos and Timarchos, worked in the tradition of their father. The Praxitelean school profoundly influenced Hellenistic sculpture in its choice of themes and their formal realization. The soft fusion of planes and delicate expression of his style can be seen in particular in early Hellenistic sculpture and minor arts, for example, the Tanagra terra-cotta figurines.

Further Reading

The best work is in Italian: G. E. Rizzo, *Prassitele* (1932). Praxiteles is discussed in all general surveys of ancient Greek sculpture, among the finest of which is Gisela M. A. Richter, *The Sculpture and Sculptors of the Greeks* (4th ed. 1970). □

Raúl Prebisch

Raúl Prebisch (1901-1986) was known primarily for his work as a scholar specializing in international and development economics and for his leadership as an executive in various agencies of the United Nations. His greatest contribution to economics is known as the Prebisch thesis.

Raúl Prebisch was born on April 17, 1901, in Tucumán, Argentina. After studying economics at the University of Buenos Aires he joined the faculty of its School of Economics and was professor of political economy from 1925 to 1948. During this period he also held several important positions in the Argentine public sector. These included deputy director of the Argentine Department of Statistics (1925 to 1927), director of economic research for the National Bank of Argentina (1927 to 1930), under-secretary of finance (1930 to 1932), and first director-general of the Argentine Central Bank (1935 to 1948). In 1948 he joined the United Nations Economic Commission for Latin America (ECLA) and was appointed its executive secretary, a position he held until 1963. From 1965 to 1969 he was secretary-general of the United Nations Conference on Trade and Development (UNCTAD). After 1969 he was director-general of the United Nations Latin American Institute for Economic and Social Planning.

Prebisch achieved his greatest fame as an economist while serving with the Economic Commission for Latin America. There he began to formulate and publish his views on international trade and development, which were to have a significant impact on future Latin American policy making. Prebisch's views on international trade were a direct attack on classical-orthodox trade policy based on the theory of comparative advantage which was developed by British economist David Ricardo (1772-1823). Under comparative advantage a country was suppose to specialize in the production of those goods in which the country's efficiency was greatest. Thus, Latin America and other lesser

developed regions would specialize in the production of primary products such as foodstuffs (e.g., tropical fruits, sugar, and coffee) and raw materials (e.g., copper, tin, and bauxite), while the United States and other advanced countries would specialize in the production of manufactured goods (e.g., capital goods and machinery). Trade between nations would distribute these goods and also the benefits of international specialization and division of labor.

Prebisch challenged this view of the world and set forth what has become known as the Prebisch thesis. This theory asserts that the gains of international trade and specialization have not been equitably distributed and that the advanced, industrialized countries have reaped far greater benefits than have the lesser developed regions of the world. This was due to the fact that the relative price of manufactured exports from industrialized countries was increasing, while the relative price of primary exports from lesser developed countries was decreasing. As a result, the commodity terms of trade (a country's export prices divided by its import prices) had been moving against Latin America and other lesser developed regions for several decades.

Prebisch reached this conclusion after examining various export and import price indices for the 1876-1947 period. He explained that this secular decline in the Latin American terms of trade was due to unique demand factors and the uneven impact of technological change. Lesser developed countries exported primary products, the demand for which grows at a slow rate, while advanced countries exported manufactured goods, the demand for which grows at a rapid rate. The net results of such a relationship will be export prices of manufactured goods (Latin American imports) increasing at a more rapid rate than export prices of primary products (Latin American exports).

Prebisch also argued that technological change was more favorable to the advanced countries of the world. Primary products were sold in competitive markets so that productivity increases caused the price of raw materials and foodstuffs to decline. Industrial products, however, were produced in oligopolistic markets, typified by administered prices and price rigidity. Productivity gains in such noncompetitive markets did not result in a decline in the price of manufactured goods but were instead used to augment the incomes of capital and labor.

The Prebisch thesis had significant policy implications for Latin America. Since the price of manufactured goods was rising relative to the price of primary products, Prebisch argued that Latin America should embark upon its own process of industrialization. This process, known as import substituting industrialization, involves producing domestically manufactured goods that were previously imported. Prebisch and the Economic Commission for Latin America repeatedly stressed the need for Latin American countries to utilize industrialization as an instrument of economic growth. Latin American policy makers responded enthusiastically, and industrialization became the primary means of growth for most Latin American nations during the post World War II period.

In order to achieve industrialization Prebisch and the Economic Commission for Latin America advocated policies that were in sharp conflict with prevailing Western economic orthodoxy. They urged government to take an active role in fostering the process of industrialization. Governments were urged to implement high tariffs and restrictive import quotas in order to severely limit, and often eliminate, the importation of those manufactured goods that Latin American nations were beginning to produce themselves. Such high levels of protection would remove the threat of international competition and would provide a highly favorable environment for the profitable local production of manufactured goods.

The most critical role that the government was to perform was that of allocating foreign exchange. Large amounts of foreign exchange are required to import the machinery and capital goods necessary for the establishment of new industries. Since foreign exchange is extremely scarce in almost all lesser developed countries, Prebisch argued that the government must implement exchange controls in order to allocate foreign exchange only to those industries that it considers to be of high priority to the growth and development of the country. Thus it is by its foreign exchange policies that a government decides which industries to encourage. This decision can only be made in a rational manner if the government first engages in economic planning to determine priority sectors of the economy. This emphasis on government planning is diametrically opposed to the Western orthodox view that free market forces should determine what goods will be produced. Nevertheless, most Latin American governments have adopted policies of protection, exchange controls, economic planning, and growth strategies based upon industrialization.

Prebisch was in Santiago, Chile, advising ECLA when he died of a heart attack in 1986. He was survived by his wife Liliana and son Raul.

Many scholars believe that Raál Prebisch has had greater influence than any other single individual in focusing and shaping Latin American development policy.

Further Reading

To appreciate fully the breadth of Prebisch's work the reader should consult *Towards a Dynamic Development Policy for Latin America* (United Nations) and *Change and Development: Latin America's Great Task* (Inter-American Development Bank). Two excellent summaries of Prebisch's work are to be found in *International Economics and Development,* Luis Eugenio Di Marco (editor). See ''The Evolution of Prebisch's Economic Thought'' by Luis Eugenio Di Marco and ''The Impact of Prebisch's Ideas on Modern Economic Analysis'' by Aldo Antonio Dadone and Luis Eugenio Di Marco. The views of the Economic Commission for Latin America are summarized in *Development Problems in Latin America* (ECLA). □

Fritz Pregl

The Austrian physiologist and medical chemist Fritz Pregl (1869-1930) developed the methods of quantitative organic microanalysis.

Fritz Pregl was born on Sept. 3, 1869, in Laibach, now Ljubljana in Yugoslavia, but then a provincial capital in the Austro-Hungarian Empire. After the death of his father, a bank official, he moved in 1887 with his mother to Graz, the seat of a university. There he studied medicine and obtained his medical degree in 1894.

As a student, Pregl had been interested in physiology and upon graduation became a teaching assistant in the Physiological Institute of the university. He remained in this field as he rose on the academic ladder to attain the rank of associate professor in 1904. However, he had meanwhile also been attracted to, and become quite adept in, organic chemical laboratory research, and indeed his publications from that period reveal a strong predilection for the chemical aspects of physiology as well as for the methodological. This partial switch in his research interests became complete when, after taking a long leave of absence, he transferred his activities to the Institute of Medical Chemistry in Graz. In 1910 Pregl was called to the University of Innsbruck as full professor and head of the Institute of Medical Chemistry, only to return 3 years later in the same capacity to Graz, where he remained until his death on Dec. 13, 1930.

Pregl's great contribution to chemistry and medical science was the creation, in the years 1910-1917, of the methods of quantitative organic microanalysis. This made it possible to determine quantitatively the elements and some functional groups in organic compounds in samples weighing far less (3-5 milligrams) than was required in the procedures previously in use (100-200 milligrams).

Pregl's micromethods quickly became an invaluable tool to the organic chemist and a truly indispensable one to the biochemist. The micromethods greatly aided and accelerated the elucidation of the chemical structure of many biologically active substances of natural origin, such as hormones and vitamins, and were generally instrumental in the solution of a host of important biochemical problems. Of the many scientific honors bestowed on Pregl in recognition of this achievement, the most outstanding was the Nobel Prize for chemistry in 1923.

Pregl was an inspiring teacher who knew how to flavor his lectures with instructive experiments as well as with humor. In the 1920s chemists from all over the world flocked to his laboratory to receive instruction in microanalysis, often by him personally, in courses given practically free of charge.

Further Reading

A good profile of Pregl is in Eduard Farber, ed., *Great Chemists* (1961). There are also short biographies in Aaron J. Ihde, *The Development of Modern Chemistry* (1964), and Nobel Foundation, *Chemistry: Including Presentation Speeches and Laureates' Biographies,* vol. 2 (1966). □

Prem Tinsulanonda

Prem Tinsulanonda (born 1920), a leading military and political figure in Thailand, became prime minister of his country in 1979.

In the rapidly shifting arena of Thai military politics since 1932, the date of the end of the absolute monarchy and the introduction of representative government under a constitutional monarch, Prem Tinsulanonda gained a certain distinction. Although he was one of a large number of top generals who shifted to civilian politics, he remained as premier for a longer period than any previous premier since 1973. He did so with the clear and explicit sanction of King Bhumibol.

Like many other leading figures in Thai politics, Prem succeeded first in his military life. Born on August 26, 1920, in Songkhla, he attended the prestigious Suan Kularb High School in Bangkok and then the elite Chulachomklao Royal Military Academy. Starting as a sublieutenant in 1941, he rose gradually through the ranks until he was in 1968 commander of cavalry headquarters. He was royal aide-de-camp in 1968 (and also later in 1975). From 1973 to 1977 he was first deputy commander-in-chief and then commander-in-chief of the 2nd Army. He became commander-in-chief of the Thai armed forces in September 1978.

During the period 1977-1979 he was also deputy minister of the interior (the organization that controls the Thai police). On March 3, 1979, he was nominated to be prime minister by an overwhelming majority (399 votes of 500) of the National Assembly, and on the same day his nomination was forwarded to the royal palace for approval. He held this post into the late 1980s. He was concurrently the minister of defense, and he was the chairman of the Petroleum Authority of Thailand from 1981 to 1983.

Prem's importance lay in the stability he brought to the Thai political scene at its apex. This political longevity was threatened by an attempted military coup against his government in 1981, but the prime minister, with the strong backing of the royal family, weathered that storm. Prem's strength, in fact, was due both to the loyalty he exhibited to the monarchy and to the king's support of his position, but also to his reputation for personal integrity and his capacity to engender consensus.

In a nation that since 1932 had witnessed continued military bickering over the plums of political power, Prem had the capacity to retain support from a broad spectrum of military figures. He was not without rivals, however, and he skillfully managed the clear but unarticulated challenge to him in 1984 by Gen. Arthit Kamlang-ek over the need to devaluate the Thai currency by 17 percent, a move that was as unpopular as it was necessary.

Although the prime minister made his first official visit to the United States in October 1981 and his second in April 1984, he was no stranger to foreign travel. He attended the U.S. Army War College in 1960 and the U.S. National Defense College in 1966.

As prime minister, Prem played a positive role in the strengthening of the six country Association of Southeast Asian Nations (ASEAN) and of their cooperation. As both a general and a civilian political leader, he had to deal with the Vietnamese invasion of Cambodia and the resulting economic, social, and political issues connected with the many refugees crossing the Thai border. These were the major foreign policy and military concerns of the government. He survived coup attempts in 1981 and 1985.

After resigning as Prime Minister in 1988 Prem served as a member of the King's Privy Council and continued to have considerable influence on Thai affairs.

Further Reading

There is no English language biography of Prem. References to specific aspects of his government may be found in the standard studies on contemporary Thai politics. The Public Relations Department of the Royal Thai Government has published a booklet entitled *The Thai Prime Minister and His Task* (Bangkok, no date). □

Ranasinghe Premadasa

A long-time leader in the United National Party, Ranasinghe Premadasa (1924-1993) became the second president of Sri Lanka in 1988.

Ranasinghe Premadasa, the ninth prime minister and second president of Sri Lanka, was born on June 23, 1924, in Colombo. He came from a family of modest means. Politically a self-made man, he was the first "commoner" to be at the helm of affairs, breaking a tradition of the top leadership being in the hands of high caste landed aristocracy or those coming from affluent families.

Educated in a Christian missionary college in Colombo, Premadasa initially opted for a career as a journalist. He was a prolific writer in his mother tongue, Sinhala, including a translation of the autobiography of Jawaharlal Nehru. Keenly interested in neighborhood welfare affairs since his youth, he became increasingly involved in municipal politics, which led to his election to the Colombo Municipal Council at the early age of 26. Five years later he became Colombo's deputy mayor. Premadasa took an active part in the freedom movement during the 1930's and was imprisoned several times.

Initially Premadasa joined the Ceylon Labour Party led by A.E. Goonesinha, one of the pioneer labor leaders of the country. In 1955 he became a member of the United National Party (UNP). The UNP nominated him to contest one of the parliamentary constituencies in Colombo in March 1960 and, except for a break in the July elections of 1960, Premadasa had the rare distinction of holding the constituency for his party from 1965 into the 1990s.

Recognizing Premadasa's commitment to grassroots political institutions, Dudley Senanayake, then the prime minister of the UNP government, nominated him as the parliamentary secretary to the minister of local government

Ranasinghe Premadasa (foreground)

and to the minister of information and broadcasting in 1965. In 1968 he was elevated to be the minister of local government.

With the UNP losing the elections of 1970 and its strength being reduced from 66 in 1965 to 17 in the 1970 elections, Premadasa became the chief opposition whip and also a member of the Constituent Assembly which drafted the first post-colonial constitution for the country under which the island came to be known as Sri Lanka, discarding the colonial name given to it (Ceylon).

In the elections of 1977, however, it was the turn of the ruling Sri Lanka Freedom Party (SLFP) to lose the poll as badly or worse than the UNP had done in the 1970 elections. The UNP secured an unprecedented majority of more than four-fifths of the 168 seats in the Parliament, with the architect of this victory, J.R. Jayewardene, being elected as the prime minister. Premadasa became the deputy leader of the party as well as, once again, the minister of local government, housing and construction. He was also made chairman of the Parliamentary Select Committee, which drafted the second constitution in 1978 heralding a presidential system in place of the parliamentary system under which the country had been governed since 1948 when it attained independence.

With Jayewardene becoming the first president of the Sri Lankan Republic in 1978, Premadasa was elected as the prime minister, a position which he held for a decade. In 1988 he won the presidential election, defeating the SLFP leader, Sirimavo Bandaranaike.

On assuming office as the president, Premadasa was confronted with the formidable challenges of coping with the separatist Tamil insurgency in the north under the leadership of the Liberation Tigers of Tamil Eelam (LTTE) and the anti-systemic insurgency of the Janata Vimukti Peramuna (JVP, People's Liberation Front) in the south with its appeal addressed to Sinhalese chauvinist sentiments. While he succeeded in containing the JVP, he continued to battle with the LTTE after an infructuous bout of negotiation (for two years) with the LTTE leadership.

Despite the unsettled domestic situation in the country, Premadasa went ahead with the implementation of his schemes and programs for economic and social reconstruction. The main thrust of his approach in this respect was the launching of the village awakening movement (known in Sinhalese as *gam udawa*) as well as the *Janasaviya,* which literally means extending a "helping hand to the people."

Gam udawa envisages a civic society of self-governing village republics. *Janasaviya* aims at providing those families living under the poverty line (nearly half of the country's population) not only with a dole in the form of food stamps but also with an investment allowance. Under this scheme of poverty alleviation to be implemented in a phased manner throughout the island, the poor families would be provided with a sum of 25,000 rupees (about $6,250) over a period of two years as a modest capital requirement for the acquisition of the means of production. The object of this scheme, as stated by the president in his address to the Parliament on April 4, 1990, was "to transform a population that subsisted on food stamps into persons engaged in productive livelihood and enterprises."

Premadasa was a regional leader in the fight against terrorism and violence in South-East Asian countries. He was chairman of a regional organization devoting his energies to the development of an atmosphere of cooperation, and working for the economic uplift of poor people throughout the region. Concerned about poor pilgrims making the sacred journey to pilgrimage centers in India he was able to secure Sri Lanka donations and worked with representatives of India to inaugurate a housing project. He worked hard to promote trade, social development and improve the welfare of women and children in the region.

During the early 1990s domestic and political turbulence in Sri Lanka increased. On May 1, 1993 Premadasa died in a brutal assassination. World leaders sent their condolences, recognizing his many contributions to the people of Sri Lanka and South-East Asia. U.S. President William Clinton sent the following communique: "As Prime Minister and then as President, he worked tirelessly to promote his country's development and raise the standard of living of all Sri Lankans. His efforts made a real difference to his fellow citizens.—Hillary and I wish to extend the sympathy of the American people to the people of Sri Lanka at the loss of their leader. We send our sincere condolences to the family of President Premadasa at this tragic time."

Further Reading

There is no official biography except a slim volume entitled *A Profile of Ranasinghe Premadasa—Prime Minister of the Democratic Socialist Republic of Sri Lanka,* printed by the Sri Lankan Government Press (n.d.). Another official publication entitled *People's President: Ranasinghe Premadasa—His Vision and Mission* has, in addition to some of the major policy speeches during 1988-1989, a brief biographical sketch. A testimonial edited by Christie Cooray was *Ranasinghe Premadasa. A Felicitation Volume* (Colombo: 1985). A biographical sketch also appears in the *Ceylon Daily News, Parliament of Sri Lanka, 1977* (Colombo: 1980), which provides a who's who of the members of Sri Lankan Parliament. Though a number of his speeches are available in pamphlets, his select speeches under one cover are available only for the years 1979-1980 and 1989. The former is entitled *Time for Action,* complied by Christy Cooray (Colombo: 1980); the latter is *Selected Speeches of His Excellency R. Premadasa—President of the Democratic Socialist Republic of Sri Lanka* (Colombo: 1989). Accounts of his assassination can be found in Sri Lanka newspapers. □

Premchand

The Indian novelist and short-story writer Premchand (1880-1936) was the first major novelist in Hindi and Urdu. His writings describe in realistic detail the political and social struggles in India of the early 20th century.

P remchand, whose real name was Dhanpatrai Srivastava, was born in the small village of Lamhi a few miles from Benares. His immediate forebears were village accountants in Lamhi. His intimate acquaintance with village life began here and continued when, as a schoolteacher and subdeputy inspector of schools, he traveled extensively for 21 years through Uttar Pradesh State.

Premchand's early writing was all done in Urdu, but from 1915 he found that writing Hindi was more profitable. Hindi, using the Sanskrit-based script and borrowing heavily from Sanskrit vocabulary, was strongly promoted by the Hindu reform group called the Arya Samaj, and within a few years Hindi publications numerically outstripped those written in Urdu.

Premchand's early work in Urdu reveals the strong influence of Persian literature, particularly in the short stories. These were usually romantic love stories in which, the course of love not being smooth, various unusual devices are used to bring lovers together again. In these romantic stories and novels, however, also appear evidences of patriotic fervor and descriptions of Indian and foreign heroes who died bravely for their countries. Premchand's first collection of short stories, *Soz-e-Vatan,* brought him to the attention of the government. The British collector of Hamirpur District called them seditious and ordered that all copies be burned and that the author submit future writing for inspection. Fortunately, a few copies survived, and Premchand, in order to evade censorship, changed his name from Dhanpatrai to Premchand.

In 1920 Premchand resigned from a government high school and became a staunch supporter of Mohandas Gandhi, whose influence strongly marked Premchand's work from 1920 to 1932. With realistic settings and events, Premchand contrived idealistic endings for his stories. His characters change from pro-British to pro-Indian or from villainous landlord to Gandhi-like social servant in midstream; the frequent conversions tend to make the stories repetitious and the characters interesting only up to the point of conversion.

Premchand's last and greatest novel, *Godan,* and his most famous story, *Kafan* (The Shroud), both deal with village life. However, whatever the setting, his late work shows a new mastery. The characters appear to have taken over their own world. The claims of social, moral, and political tenets are secondary to the claims of artistry. Premchand died from a gastric ulcer. One son, Amrtrai, was a noted Hindi writer, and the other, Sripatrai, a talented painter.

Further Reading

Premchand's novel *Godan* was translated by Gordon C. Roadarmel as *Gift of a Cow* (1968). *The World of Premchand,* translated by David Rubin (1969), brings together some of the stories. A critical study of the short stories that includes a biographical introduction is Robert O. Swan, *Munshi Premchand of Lamhi Village* (1969). □

Maurice Brazil Prendergast

American painter Maurice Brazil Prendergast (1859-1924) pioneered in introducing new directions in American painting. He was the only true American postimpressionist of his generation.

M aurice Prendergast was born in St. John's, Newfoundland, on Oct. 10, 1859. When his father's grocery business failed in 1861, the family moved to Boston. He and his younger brother Charles finished their formal education by the time each was 14. Maurice worked in a dry-goods store, lettered show cards, and began sketching landscapes and cattle. In 1886, he and his brother worked their way to England on a cattle boat; they may have gone to Paris as well. Returning to Boston, they worked at routine jobs in order to save $1,000 for a return to Europe. Maurice went to Paris in 1891 and studied with Jean Paul Laurens at the Académie Julian. He made rapid progress in 3 years, working from the model rather than from casts. He was fascinated with the life and movement in the parks, boulevards, and cafés.

When he returned to America in 1894, Prendergast was an accomplished watercolorist and had assimilated qualities from Édouard Manet, James McNeill Whistler, Edgar Degas, Henri de Toulouse-Lautrec, Pierre Bonnard, and Édouard Vuillard and from Japanese prints. He was the first American artist to appreciate and understand the importance of Paul Cézanne. Until 1905 the Prendergast brothers lived together in Winchester, Mass., their principal means of support being a frame-making shop. Maurice's work was included for the first time in a public exhibition at the Pennsylvania Academy of Fine Arts in 1896; there was a one-man show in Boston the next year, and from this time until his death his paintings appeared in many exhibitions.

In 1898 Prendergast went to Venice, where he created some of his most enchanting watercolors. Arthur B. Davies invited him to join with other artists in the famous exhibition of "The Eight" in 1908, organized as a protest against the conservative tendencies of the National Academy of Design. Prendergast was in France again in 1909 and in Italy in 1911. The influence of Paul Signac is perhaps to be observed from this period.

The seven watercolors that were included in the celebrated Armory Show in 1913 revealed Prendergast as a major figure in American painting, probably the greatest of his generation. He was perhaps the first to deliberately abandon a primarily representational approach to art and to let the subject matter be dominated by purely artistic means.

Prendergast went to Europe for the last time in 1914. On his return he and his brother (also a painter) moved to New York, where Maurice spent his last decade working in a studio in Washington Square. During summers in New England, he painted in oil and watercolor brightly clad figures on beaches and in parks, often using a kind of pointillism which gives his work a tapestrylike quality, sometimes with almost expressionistic intensity, but relying even more on pure color, loosely applied in abrupt areas, to suggest form, movement, and texture. There is a combination of wistfulness and gaiety, a sense of elegance and innocence in his paintings. He characteristically introduces large numbers of figures; a sense of individuality is avoided, but there is always warmth and charm.

Prendergast was increasingly isolated in his later years because of deafness. He died in New York on Feb. 1, 1924.

Further Reading

Prendergast's *Sketches, 1899* was published in facsimile (1960). An excellent critical and biographical study, with numerous reproductions in color, is Hedley Howell Rhys, *Maurice Prendergast, 1859-1924* (1960). Margaret Breuning, *Maurice Prendergast* (1931), is a brief, useful picture book. Valuable material is in the comprehensive exhibition catalogs from retrospective shows at the Whitney Museum of American Art, New York, *Maurice Prendergast Memorial Exhibition* (1934), and the Phillips Academy, Addison Gallery, Andover, Mass., *The Prendergasts* (1938). □

William Hickling Prescott

William Hickling Prescott (1796-1859) was one of the greatest American historians. The theme that absorbed him for over 30 years was the rise and decline of the Spanish Empire.

W illiam Hickling Prescott was born in Salem, Mass., on May 4, 1796. His father, Judge William Prescott, was a prominent Federalist. William graduated from Harvard in 1814; at college he lost sight in his left eye during a dining-hall fracas. Despite this disaster and illness (which plagued him all his life), he determined to follow a literary career. He began to contribute to the *North American Review,* the leading magazine in the country, in 1821. A former schoolmate and lifelong friend, George Ticknor, urged Prescott to devote himself to Spanish studies. Thus began a career which resulted in histories that still enchant.

Other scholars had been drawn to Spain's history before Prescott entered the field in 1826, but he gave it an unmatched sheen. At Christmas, 1837, his *Ferdinand and Isabella* (3 vols.) was published; it still holds its own as the classic of this period. He then turned to Spain's conquest of Mexico. In *The Conquest of Mexico* (3 vols., 1843) he narrated the exploits of Hernán Cortés in words never surpassed. The story, thought Prescott, was "an epic in prose, a romance of chivalry." The work was his masterpiece; its material was so drenched in an air of romanticism that it seemed difficult to treat it as sober history. But he carefully sought to distinguish fact from fiction. He had many heroes and heroines but few villains. "One likes a noble character for his canvas," he said.

Prescott next published *A History of the Conquest of Peru* (2 vols., 1847). It included important material on the

civilization of the Incas. Some scholars still consider it the standard authority.

The last installment of Prescott's project was *A History of the Reign of Philip the Second* (3 vols., 1855-1858). Although he tried to be impartial, he could not overcome his bias in favor of Protestant Christianity. To him the fall of the Aztecs was unregretted, for their civilization was inferior to that of their conquerors.

Critics dislike the excessive space Prescott gave to military affairs. But he believed his function as historian was storytelling, narrating the deeds of the chevalier, the swashbuckler, the statesman. His work, based on sound scholarship and clothed in gifted language, still entrances readers more than a century after his death in Boston on Jan. 28, 1859.

Further Reading

C. Harvey Gardiner edited Prescott's histories and also materials relating to Prescott in *Literary Memoranda* (2 vols., 1961) and *Papers* (1964). Roger Wolcott, ed., *The Correspondence of William Hickling Prescott, 1833-1847* (1925), provides indispensable details. The standard biography is by Prescott's friend George Ticknor, *Life of William Hickling Prescott* (1864). A modern biography is C. Harvey Gardiner, *William Hickling Prescott: A Biography* (1969). Harry T. Peck, *William Hickling Prescott* (1905), gives important analyses of Prescott's works. William Charvat and Michael Kraus, *William Hickling Prescott* (1943), contains a biography, selections from Prescott's writings, a study of his attitudes toward history, his political ideas, and his literary style. □

Elvis Aron Presley

Elvis Aron Presley (1935-1977), the "King of Rock 'n' Roll," was the leading American singer for two decades and the most popular singer of the entire rock 'n' roll era.

Elvis Aron Presley was born in Tupelo, Mississippi, on January 8, 1935, to Gladys and Vernon Presley. His twin brother, Jesse Garon Presley, died shortly after birth. Elvis's singing ability was discovered when he was an elementary school student in Tupelo, and he participated in numerous talent contests there and in Memphis, Tennessee, where the family moved when Elvis was 13.

It was in 1953, after he graduated from L. C. Humes High School in Memphis, that Elvis, working as a truckdriver, began paying his own way into the Memphis Recording Services studio to cut his own records. Less than a year later he recorded "That's All Right Mama" for Sun Records. It became his first commercial release, selling 20,000 copies.

Elvis reached the top of the country charts with "Mystery Train" in 1955. His first number one song on the so-called "Hot 100" was "Heartbreak Hotel" (1956), which held its position for seven of the 27 weeks it was on the chart. This song also reached the top of the country charts, and it became emblematic of his ability to combine country singing with rhythm and blues, as well as with the new rage that had grown out of rhythm and blues: rock 'n' roll. The rest of the 1950s brought Elvis "living legend" status with records that included "Hound Dog" (1956), "Don't Be Cruel" (1956), "Blue Suede Shoes" (1956), "Love Me Tender" (1956), "All Shook Up" (1957), and "Jailhouse Rock" (1957). He started the 1960s in similar fashion with "It's Now or Never" (1960) and "Are You Lonesome Tonight?" (1960).

He was universally proclaimed the "King of Rock 'n' Roll" and led the new music from its beginnings in the 1950s to its heyday in the 1960s and on to its permanence in the music of the 1970s and the 1980s. His impact on American popular culture was second to none, as he seemed to affect manner of dress, hairstyles, and even behavior. John Lennon would later cite him as one of the most important influences on the Beatles. Even his gyrating hips became legendary as he continued his rock 'n' roll conquest to the extent of 136 gold records and ten platinum records. Ultimately he had the most records to make the rating charts and was the top recording artist for two straight decades, the 1950s and the 1960s.

Elvis was an instant success in television and movies as well. Millions watched his television appearances on *The Steve Allen Show, The Milton Berle Show, The Toast of the Town,* and a controversial appearance on the *The Ed Sullivan Show,* in which cameras were instructed to stay above the hips of "Elvis the Pelvis." He was an even bigger box office smash, beginning with *Love Me Tender* in 1956. Thirty-two movies later, Elvis had become the top box office

draw for two decades, grossing over $150 million. Although few of his motion pictures received critical acclaim, they showcased his music and extended his image and fame. His movies included *Jailhouse Rock* (1957), *King Creole* (1958), *G. I. Blues* (1960), *Blue Hawaii* (1961), *Girls! Girls! Girls!* (1962), *Viva Las Vegas* (1964), and *Spinout* (1966). *Wild in the Country* (1961), based on the J. R. Salamanca novel *The Lost Country,* marked his debut in a straight dramatic role.

Elvis began a well-publicized stint in the army in 1958. That year, while he was stationed in Fort Hood, Texas, his mother, to whom he was closely attached, died. The remainder of his military service was spent stationed in Germany, until his discharge in 1960. It was in Germany that he met Priscilla Beaulieu, his future wife.

Elvis's success in the entertainment industry was accompanied by numerous failures in his personal life. He arranged to have Priscilla, still a teenager, live at his new Memphis home, Graceland Mansion, while she finished high school there. He married her in 1967, and she bore him his only child, Lisa Marie Presley, in 1968. In 1973 he and Priscilla were divorced. During this time, and for his entire career, his personal manager, Col. Tom Parker, controlled his finances. As Elvis's millions grew, so too did the fiscal mismanagement of Parker, a known gambler. Parker was later prosecuted for his financial dealings, but he was acquitted. Elvis made an estimated $4.3 billion in earnings during his lifetime, but he never acquired a concept of financial responsibility. This caused frequent litigation during and after his lifetime among his management people and several record companies. Elvis had similar luck with

his friendships, and frequently surrounded himself with an entourage of thugs to shield him from an adoring public.

A weight problem became evident in the late 1960s, and in private Elvis became increasingly dependent on drugs, particularly amphetamines and sedatives. His personal doctor, George Nichopoulos, would later be prosecuted, but acquitted, for prescribing and dispensing thousands of pills and narcotics to him.

Though his weight and his drug dependency were increasing, Elvis continued a steady flow of concert performances in sold-out arenas well into the 1970s. On August 16, 1977, the day before another concert tour was about to begin, Elvis was found dead in Graceland Mansion by his fiance, Ginger Alden. The official cause of death was heart disease, although the post-mortem revelations of his drug dependency created a media event. His death caused unparalleled scenes of mourning.

Elvis continued to be celebrated as superstar and legend as much in death as he was in life. Graceland Mansion, which he had purchased in 1957 for $102,500, is the top tourist attraction in Memphis and has attracted hundreds of thousands of visitors from both America and around the world.

Further Reading

More than 200 books and countless periodical articles are available on Elvis Presley, exemplifying the intensity of his fandom. Many of the accounts are biased to an ''Elvis could do no wrong'' extreme. Other books merely capitalized on the sensationalism that surrounded his death. Paul Lichter's *The Boy Who Dared To Rock: The Definitive Elvis* (1978) is an excellent, though somewhat reverent, biography. *The Elvis Presley Scrapbook* (1977) by James Robert Parish is interesting. The best starting points for Presley facts are the references, particularly Wendy Sauers' *Elvis Presley: A Complete Reference* (1984) and *Elvis Presley: Reference Guide and Discography* (1981) by John A. Whisler. A personal account is *Elvis and Me* (1985) by his wife Priscilla Beaulieu Presley. □

Luiz Carlos Prestes

Luiz Carlos Prestes (1898–1990) was an almost mythical Brazilian guerrilla-war leader in the 1920s. He became leader of the Brazilian Communist party in the 1930s and continued in that position for almost 40 years.

L uiz Carlos Prestes first gained national prominence in 1924, when, as a young captain of engineers, he led a group of army mutineers in the state of Rio Grande do Sul against the government of President Arturo Bernardes. Hard-pressed by troops loyal to the government, Prestes led his men several hundred miles north to a juncture with another group of rebels, from the state of São Paulo, who had retreated to the area of the great Iguassú Falls on the Argentine border.

From Iguassú, the rebels began an epic march through the interior of Brazil. They fought an almost classic guerrilla war against army and state police forces in a dozen states. Prestes was chief of staff of this rebel group, which became famous as the Prestes Column.

Exile and Travels

Soon after the rebels were finally driven into Bolivia, Prestes went to Buenos Aires, where he remained for several years. Until 1930 he remained titular head of the *Tenentes,* the former military rebels, and some civilians who had joined them to form a conspiratorial political movement.

In Buenos Aires, Prestes was courted by both Stalinist and Trotskyite Communists. Although he did not immediately join either, he did assume a much more radical position than the vague social nationalism of the Prestes Column. He opposed the revolution of October 1930—led by the former governor of Rio Grande do Sul, Getulio Vargas, and supported by the great majority of the *Tenentes*—on the grounds that it was "petty bourgeois."

In 1931 Prestes went to the Soviet Union, where he was employed on various engineering projects, became a Communist, and was elected to the Executive Committee of the Communist International. Early in 1935 Prestes returned to Brazil, where he was immediately elected to the Politburo of the Communist party. He was also named honorary president of the Alianca Nacional Libertadora (ANL), a broad left-wing opposition to President Vargas. Prestes and the Communists spoke in the name of the ANL without the

authorization of its non-Communist leaders; and when the ANL was outlawed, Prestes led an attempted military insurrection in its name. When it failed, virtually all left-wing politicians were rounded up by the government. Prestes himself was captured a few weeks after the revolt, was reportedly badly tortured, and was finally sentenced to a long prison term. He remained in jail until May 1945, and his wife, a German Communist, was deported to Nazi Germany, where she died in a concentration camp.

National Politics

After Vargas had been forced to agree to end his dictatorship and had called elections for December 1945, he proclaimed a general political amnesty. It was widely rumored that before Prestes's release under this amnesty an agreement had been reached between him and Vargas. In any case, upon his release Prestes called on the Communists to support maintenance of Vargas in office until a new constitution had been written. In turn, Vargas legalized the Communist party and gave the Communists complete freedom in the labor movement.

In spite of efforts by Vargas, his supporters, and the Communists to keep him in power, he was ousted late in October 1945. In the election 6 weeks later, the Communists ran as presidential candidate Yeddo Fiuza, a former Vargas official, and presented candidates for Congress. Prestes was elected senator, and the Communists also elected 15 deputies.

Between 1945 and 1947 the Communists represented about 10 percent of the national electorate and gained extensive influence in organized labor. However, early in 1947 the Communist party was outlawed by the Supreme Electoral Tribunal, and in the following year Prestes and the Communist deputies lost their seats in Congress. Prestes went into hiding for the next 11 years.

During this period, Prestes was largely out of contact with the Communist rank and file and lower leadership. However, when a strong dissident movement against the Prestes "cult of the personality" arose in 1956, after Nikita Khrushchev's denunciation of Joseph Stalin at the Twentieth Congress of the Soviet Communist party, Prestes took the lead in purging the dissidents.

In the democratic atmosphere of the Juscelino Kubitschek administration, Prestes came out of hiding, went before a court, and purged the sedition charges pending against him. During the next 5 years, he traveled widely throughout the country in his capacity as secretary general of the Communist party. When the group who had run the party while he was in hiding tried to challenge Prestes's control, they were expelled in 1961 and established a rival pro-Chinese Communist party.

During the João Goulart administration (1961-1964), the Communists made considerable headway in organized labor and general politics. Prestes on several occasions appeared on the same platform with the President at political rallies.

However, with the overthrow of Goulart on April 1, 1964, Prestes again went into hiding, leaving behind a notebook with names and addresses of many of his associates which was captured by the police. Prestes remained secretary general of the Communist party, although his control was apparently contested by elements opposed to what they conceived to be his inept leadership. He remained the principal leader of the underground Communist party. In 1971, upon instructions from the party, Prestes moved to Moscow. He returned to Brazil in 1979, but was removed from his seat of secretary general and was eventually expelled from the party altogether. No longer a member of his party, Prestes spent his final days supporting the political ambitions of Leonel Brizola. Prestes died on March 7, 1990.

Further Reading

Useful material on Prestes's early career is in Robert M. Levine, *The Vargas Regime: The Critical Years, 1934-1938* (1970). His later career is covered in two studies by John W. F. Dulles, *Vargas of Brazil: A Political Biography* (1967) and *Unrest in Brazil: Political-Military Crises, 1955-1964* (1970). See also the excellent study by Thomas E. Skidmore, *Politics in Brazil, 1930-1964: An Experiment in Democracy* (1967).

Additional Sources

(Tenenbaum, Barbara, ed.) *Encyclopedia of Latin American History and Culture,* Simon & Schuster, 1996.

(Gorman, Robert, ed.) *Biographical Dictionary of Marxism,* Greenwood Press, 1986. □

Andries Pretorius

Andries Pretorius (1798-1853) was a South African political leader and general and till his death the most prominent and colorful Afrikaner figure.

In November 1838 the Voortrekker leader Pieter Retief and his companions were murdered at the village of the Zulu chief Dingane, and afterward the Voortrekker camp were massacred by Zulu warriors. The first efforts of both Boer and Briton to avenge these horrors met with dismal failure, leaving the Boer emigrants in a serious plight. At this stage Andries Pretorius was invited to become their leader and command a punitive expedition against Dingane.

Andries Pretorius was born on Nov. 27, 1798, at Graaff Reinet in the Cape Colony. It is unfortunate that only the scantiest details of his early life are available. He was taught by wandering teachers but in later life could express himself well in word and writing. A female admirer wrote of him as "a handsome, tall figure of between six and seven feet, upright, friendly, and captivating." The historian Theal said of him that "his knowledge and his opinions, as well as his virtues and his failings, were those of the seventeenth, not of the nineteenth century." He had his human share of temperamental imperfections and was often quick to anger, but he had no unreasoning obstinacy.

Farmer and Voortrekker Leader

Pretorius enters the historical scene in 1837 as a prosperous townsman at Graaff Reinet; he also owned farms in the district. He does not appear to have been consulted in the early projects of the border farmers, but he soon displayed a deep interest in the emigration movement. Before he finally joined the Voortrekkers in Natal, he paid a preliminary visit to the interior. He took part in the battle of Mosega, in which Mzilikazi and his Matabele (Ndebele) warriors were put to flight. Thereafter he purchased a farm near Port Natal and returned to Graaff Reinet only to sell his property. At this stage a deputation arrived from the stricken Voortrekkers in Natal and implored him to lead an expedition against Dingane. He accepted the invitation, hastened his departure, and reached the main laager in Natal on Nov. 22, 1838.

Setting out with a commando of 464 men, from the outset Pretorius insisted on the maintenance of proper discipline, which certainly had been lacking in previous cases. Though a man of decision, he never acted without calling a council of his officers.

On December 9 the Voortrekkers took the famous "Vow." It was the desire of Pretorius that the Voortrekkers make a collective promise to God that if He granted them victory they would celebrate the day of triumph, each year, as a Holy Sabbath to the glory of His name and that they would impress this duty upon their children.

Battle of Blood River

By December 15 the commando marched up the west bank of a tributary of the Buffalo named Income (Cattle River) by the Zulu but ever since known as Blood River. Under his inspired leadership his small force put to flight the vast Zulu army of more than 10,000 men in one of the most fateful battles ever fought in South Africa.

The rejoicing which greeted the commando on its return was dampened by the grim tidings that British troops had arrived at Port Natal to occupy the territory temporarily because "of the disturbed state of the native tribes" resulting from the "unwarranted occupation" of the interior by the Voortrekkers.

Republic of Natal

The Voortrekkers remained undaunted, ignored the British, and proceeded under Pretorius to establish their own republic on the land granted by Dingane. Assisted by regiments of Dingane's brother Mpande, Pretorius in 1840 succeeded in finally overthrowing Dingane. Meanwhile the British troops had also left, and the Voortrekkers had at last achieved the independence they had been looking for. Within 3 years, however, the British were back, this time to remain. Pretorius defeated them at Congella and besieged them for over a month. After their relief, an uneasy peace followed for a year, and then Britain annexed Natal.

Differences with England

Pretorius settled near Pietermaritzburg, resigned his office, and became a British subject. In 1847 he journeyed to

Grahamstown to protest before Sir Henry Pottinger, the representative of the Crown, the injustices the Natal Voortrekkers felt they had suffered. Pottinger unwisely refused to see him. This cavalier treatment infuriated Pretorius and aroused great indignation throughout South Africa.

In 1848 Sir Harry Smith, who had succeeded Pottinger, met Pretorius and a number of Voortrekkers at the foot of the Berg in Natal. The meeting was cordial, but unfortunately both men viewed the position from a totally different aspect: Smith was determined that Natal remain British, and Pretorius was adamant on the question of his people's independence. The result was that Pretorius and his followers cast off their allegiance to England.

Pretorius established himself in Rustenburg (Transvaal) and then took the bold, if unwise, step of urging burghers in Transvaal to join him in a campaign against England. Although he succeeded in evicting the British Resident from Bloemfontein, he was defeated at Boomplaats by Sir Harry Smith. He was proclaimed a rebel, and a reward of £2,000 was offered by the Cape government for his apprehension.

Sand River Convention

Meanwhile, discord ruled among the Voortrekkers in Transvaal. There were three parties, two attached to the persons of the Voortrekker leaders Pretorius and Potgieter, and that of the Volksraad, whose authority was not clearly defined. Pretorius recognized that affairs in Transvaal would never be satisfactorily settled until recognition of the independence of its people was obtained from England. At his instigation the Volksraad decided that representations should be made to the British government for peace and a permanent understanding.

In August 1851 the burghers at Winburg, who were not reconciled to life under British rule, invited Pretorius to take upon himself the government of the territory between the Orange and Vaal rivers. Being an outlaw from that territory, Pretorius could not accept the invitation, but he informed the British authorities that he had received it.

To prevent Pretorius from interfering outside Transvaal, his outlawry was reversed, and two commissioners were instructed to effect a settlement regarding the burghers beyond the Vaal. Acting without the blessing of the Volksraad, Pretorius met them and signed the Sand River Convention on Jan. 17, 1852, whereby England recognized the independence of Transvaal. It was ratified by the Volksraad after Pretorius and Potgieter had at last become reconciled.

After the bitterness of the Anglo-Boer struggles had died down, Pretorius frequently came into amicable intercourse with British officials, who invariably spoke of him in terms not merely of high respect but of warm friendliness. Perhaps the highest testimony to the regard in which he was universally held is the fact that, as he lay on his deathbed, several native chiefs who had heard of his illness and had come to pay their respects exhibited intense grief ''as they knelt successively and kissed his hand.'' He died on July 23, 1853, at Magaliesberg.

Further Reading

South African historiography lacks an objective biography of Pretorius. Gustav Preller, who had an intense admiration for Pretorius and an almost naive partisanship for the Afrikaner people, published a biography, *Andries Pretorius* (1939), but the book, meritorious for its thrilling and picturesque accounts, is far from a critical study. Recommended for general background are Sir George E. Cory, *The Rise of South Africa* (6 vols., 1910-1940); Eric Anderson Walker, *The Great Trek* (1934; 4th ed. 1960); Manfred Nathan's outstanding work, *The Voortrekkers of South Africa* (1937); and George McCall Theal, *History of South Africa,* vol. 6 (1964).

Additional Sources

Liebenberg, Barend Jacobus, *Andries Pretorius in Natal,* Pretoria: Academica, 1977. □

Abbé Prévost

The French novelist, journalist, and cleric Abbé Prévost (1697-1763) was an adventurer who lived by his intrigues and his pen. His best-known work is the novel ''Manon Lescaut.''

Antoine François Prévost d'Exiles, who is known as the Abbé Prévost, was first exposed to conventual discipline when he entered a Jesuit school at the age of 14, following his father's death. In the years that ensued, he alternated military service, love affairs, and intense literary activity with periods as first a Jesuit and then a Benedictine novice. He was ordained a Benedictine priest in 1721 and for 8 years engaged in study, teaching, and scholarly work in a variety of Benedictine communities.

Restless and unhappy, he settled for a time at St-Germain-des-Prés in Paris, where he began to write in secret the fictional compendium *Les Mémoires et aventures d'un homme de qualité qui s'est retiré du monde.* In 1728 he threw his vow of stability to the winds and fled to London. He traveled through England, eventually becoming companion and tutor to one Sir John Eyles. *Les Mémoires* was published in part in 1728. Two years later Prévost left England for Holland, and there he worked at translating works of Samuel Richardson and also published the fifth, sixth, and seventh volumes of *Les Mémoires.*

Les Mémoires is an original work written to promote broader understanding of England in France. At a time when England was regarded by Frenchmen as a bloody and barbarous nation, Prévost had learned to love that country. Unlike most previous Frenchmen who had attempted to write about England, Prévost had learned English; he had also traveled in the provinces, gathering folklore from the peasants. His book is an impassioned plea for religious tolerance. It expresses a deep admiration for the comparative ease with which the different social classes in England mingled.

Prévost recognized that the return to nature as source and subject matter of poetry was a unique phenomenon in

English literature, and he was one of the first to introduce this essential romantic theme to France. Of all the works written about England in the 18th century by foreign travelers, *Les Mémoires* is the most complete, the most unprejudiced, and the most reliable.

Once more in England, Prévost began the publication of his serial novel, *Le Philosophe anglais ou les mémoires de Cleveland* (generally known as *Cleveland*), a task that extended from 1732 to 1739. In 1733 he also began publishing the periodical *Le Pour et le contre*. Upon his return to France and his reconciliation with the Church in 1734, he published *Le Doyen de Killerine* (1735). *L'Histoire d'une grecque moderne* and *Marguerite d'Anjou*, a historical novel, were published in 1740.

After his brief exile, Prévost produced numerous translations, most notably bowdlerized versions of Richardson's novels. He also worked on anthologies of fiction and moral essays, and he served as editor for several large publishing enterprises. In 1754 he collaborated on the *Journal étranger* and was commissioned to work on the history of the Condé family.

The seventh volume of *Les Mémoires* was published separately in France 2 years after its original publication in Holland. This highly condensed novel, *L'Histoire du chevalier des Grieux et de Manon Lescaut,* has achieved, of all Prévost's works, the most lasting success. Des Grieux, its childlike hero, is unaware of life, unaware of his own desires, when suddenly he is swept away by his passion for Manon, who is all charm and sensuality. *Manon Lescaut* is

one of a handful of novels that constitute a genre uniquely French—the *roman personnel,* or personal novel. It is highly compressed, direct, sparing in style and episode; characteristically, it unfolds through a series of psychological revelations. The operas *Manon* (1884) by Jules Massenet and *Manon Lescaut* (1893) by Giacomo Puccini are based on this work.

From 1754, when Prévost was asked to write a history of the Condé family, he resided at Saint-Firmin in order to be close to the family archives in Chantilly. He died suddenly from apoplexy (or from a ruptured aorta) returning home at night through the forest of Chantilly.

Further Reading

The translation of *Manon Lescaut* by Burton Rascoe (1919) is a readable version of the novel. The Modern Library translation includes a brief introduction in English by Guy de Maupassant. The best works on Prévost are in French. A useful study in English is George R. Havens, *The Abbé Prévost and English Literature* (1921). □

Leontyne Price

Leontyne Price (born 1927) was a prima donna soprano acclaimed in most circles as one of the finest opera singers of the 20th century.

Mary Leontyne Price was born in Laurel, Mississippi, on February 10, 1927. Educated in public schools in Laurel, she then attended Central State College in Wilberforce, Ohio, where she received her Bachelor of Arts degree in 1948. Her particular interest was singing in the glee club at Central State, where she displayed an abundance of musical talent, and she decided to make a career of singing. Subsequently she entered New York's Juilliard School of Music where she studied until 1952. At the same time she took private lessons under the tutelage of Florence Page Kimball. Price was the first black singer to gain international stardom in opera, an art form previously confined to the upper-class white society. Her success signified not only a monumental stride for her own generation, but for those that came before and after her.

While still at Juilliard, Price exhibited her soprano ability at various concerts and in her appearance as Mistress Ford in Verdi's *Falstaff.* Virgil Thomson took notice of her performance and provided her with her Broadway stage debut in the Broadway revival of his *Four Saints in Three Acts.* Her ability then earned her the role of Bess in George Gershwin's *Porgy and Bess* in a touring company that met with great successes in London, Paris, Berlin, and Moscow. She also played Bess when the company appeared in the Broadway revival of *Porgy and Bess.* During the tour she married baritone William Warfield, who sang the role of Porgy. Other composers took note of Price's ability, and in 1953 she sang premieres of works of Henri Sauget, Lou Harrison, John La Montaine, and Igor Stravinsky, among others.

Price received overwhelming critical acclaim in her 1954 Town Hall concert in New York City and followed that with her first performance in grand opera, in 1955, as Floria in Puccini's *Tosca* on network television with the NBC Opera. She made her first opera stage appearance in 1957 as Madame Lidoine in Poulenc's *Dialogues of the Carmelites* with the San Francisco Opera Company. Price also toured Italy successfully that year and sang *Aida* at La Scala in Milan. She continued to sing with the San Francisco Opera, as well as with the Lyric Opera of Chicago and other major opera houses in North America.

In 1960 Price portrayed Donna Anna in *Don Giovanni* at the Salzburg Festival in Austria. On January 27, 1961, she made her debut in New York's famous Metropolitan Opera as Leonora in *Il Trovatore,* which earned a thunderous ovation and moved opera critics to regard her as one of the greats of the 20th century. She also sang the title role at the Met in *Madame Butterfly* and the role of Minnie in *La Franciulla del West (The Girl of the Golden West)*. Price appeared in 118 Metropolitan productions between 1961 and 1969. In 1965 she was awarded the Presidential Medal of Freedom by President Lyndon Johnson, who said, ''Her singing has brought light to her land.''

One of Price's greatest triumphs was her creation of the role of Cleopatra in Samuel Barber's *Antony and Cleopatra.* Its premiere opened the 1966 Metropolitan Opera season as well as the beautiful new Metropolitan Opera House in Lincoln Center. Her best and favorite performances were as Verdi heroines Elvira in *Ernani,* Leonora in *Il Trovatore,* Amelia in *The Masked Ball,* and especially as Aida.

Price made other worldwide tours that included Australia and Argentina's Teatro Colon in Buenos Aires in 1969. In the 1970s Price drastically cut the number of opera appearances, preferring to focus instead on her first love, recitals, in which she enjoyed the challenge of creating several characters on stage in succession. In 1985, Price gave her final performance at New York's Lincoln Center in the title role of Verdi's *Aida.* She was 57 years old.

Price made numerous recordings of music outside of opera because of her phenomenal voice and had honorary degrees conferred upon her from Dartmouth College, Howard University, and Fordham University, among others. Separated, and finally divorced, from Warfield, she lived in her homes in Rome and New York. Music critics universally lavished praise on her voice and her portrayals.

Further Reading

A brief biography of Leontyne Price is *Leontyne Price: Opera Superstar* (1984) by Silvia Williams. A more detailed study is Hugh Lee Lyon, *Leontyne Price: Highlights of a Prima Donna* (1973). Useful information can also be found in *Baker's Biographical Dictionary of Musicians* (1984) by Theodore Baker, *The New Grove Dictionary of American Music* (1986), and *The Biographical Dictionary of Afro-American and African Musicians* (1982) by Eileen Souther. □

Richard Price

The English Nonconformist minister and political philosopher Richard Price (1723-1791), who supported the American and French revolutions, devoted his life primarily to preaching.

Richard Price was born at Tynton, Glamorganshire, on Feb. 23, 1723. The son of a dissenting minister, he himself served as Unitarian minister to congregations in London, Stoke Newington, and Hackney for about 50 years.

Price's major work in moral philosophy is *The Review of the Principal Questions in Morals* (1758). The central issue with which this work is concerned is the question: why is an action right? Right, Price argues, is a real character of actions that is discerned by the understanding rather than by a moral sense. Right and wrong are simple ideas because they are not finally definable. Like Samuel Clarke, Price held that right and wrong are immutable. Price argues, in part, that both introspection and common sense indicate that rightness and wrongness are necessary truths known through the understanding by intuition.

Price's *Four Dissertations* (1767) included a vindication of the probability of miracles in opposition to David Hume's view of a ''complete impossibility of miracles.'' Price and Hume, evidence from letters indicates, remained good friends in spite of their differences. Price and Joseph Priestley, also good friends, although philosophical opponents, published jointly *A Free Discussion of the Doctrines of Materialism and Philosophical Necessity* (1778).

Further Reading

The most thorough analysis of Price's theories is Carl B. Cone, *Torchbearer of Freedom: The Influence of Richard Price on Eighteenth Century Thought* (1952). Also useful is Antonio S. Cua, *Reason and Virtue: A Study in the Ethic of Richard Price* (1966).

Additional Sources

Laboucheix, Henri, *Richard Price as moral philosopher and political theorist,* Oxford: Voltaire Foundation at the Taylor Institution, 1982.

Price, Richard, *The correspondence of Richard Price,* Durham, N.C.: Duke University Press; Cardiff: University of Wales Press, 1983-1994.

Thomas, David Oswald, *Richard Price, 1723-1791,* Cardiff: University of Wales Press, 1976. □

This work is a group of letters in which Priestley defends materialism and philosophical necessity, while Price attacks both of them.

An outstanding mathematician, Price was chosen a fellow of the Royal Society in 1765 for his essay resolving a difficult problem concerning probability. A few years later he applied his own solution to actuarial questions in *Observations on Reversionary Payments* (1771). In this work he laid the foundation for a modern system of life insurance and pensions.

Price's contribution to financial management was also notable. At the request of William Pitt the Younger, he formulated a program for dealing with the national debt in *An Appeal to the Public on the Subject of the National Debt* (1772). His ability in this area was so widely acknowledged by his American friends, including Benjamin Franklin, that Price was asked by the U.S. Congress to advise the new government on finance in 1778.

Price's most widely read works were those supporting the American and French revolutions. His *Observations on the Nature of Civil Liberty, the Principles of Government, and the Justice and Policy of the War with America* (1776), *Additional Observations* (1777), and *The Love of Liberty* (1789), the last sermon supporting the French Revolution, were all widely read in England, the United States, and France. Price died on April 19, 1791.

Diana García Prichard

Diana García Prichard (born 1949) is a research scientist who conducts fundamental photographic materials research for the Eastman Kodak company, and whose graduate work on the behavior of gas phases was lauded for its inventiveness and received unusual attention and recognition by the scientific community. She is also an active leader in the Hispanic community and has garnered numerous awards for her work.

Prichard was born in San Francisco, California, on October 27, 1949. Her mother, Matilde (Robleto) Dominguez García, was originally from Granada, Nicaragua. Her father, Juan García, was from Aransas Pass, Texas, and was of Mexican and Native American descent. He worked as a warehouse foreman at Ray-O-Vac. Although both of her parents received little education, they knew well the value of schooling and saw that Prichard appreciated the worth and the joys of learning. After graduating from El Camino High School in South San Francisco, Prichard entered the College of San Mateo and received her LVN degree (nursing) in 1969.

After taking some years to care for her two children, Erik and Andrea, Prichard chose a dramatic career shift and reentered academia in 1979. Interested in things scientific ever since she was young, and always intrigued and attracted by the thinking process and creativity required to do real scientific research, she enrolled at California State University at Hayward and earned her B.S. degree in chemistry/physics in 1983. She then continued her post graduate education at the University of Rochester in New York, obtaining her M.S. degree in physical chemistry in 1985. Continuing at Rochester, she entered the doctoral program and earned her Ph.D. in chemical physics in 1988.

Her graduate studies at Rochester emphasized optics, electronics, automation, vacuum technology, and signal processing with data acquisition and analysis. During this graduate work on the high resolution infrared absorption spectrum (which basically involves telling how much or what type of atoms or molecules are present), she was able to construct the first instrument ever to be able to measure van der Waals clusters. Named after Dutch Nobel prize-winning physicist, Johannes Diderick van der Waals, the van der Waals equation accounts for the non-ideal behavior of gases at the molecular level. An ideal or perfect gas is one which always obeys the known gas laws. The van der Waals equation allows scientists to predict the behavior of gases that do not strictly follow these laws by factoring in specific corrections. Van der Waals clusters are weakly bound complexes that exist in a natural state but are low in number. Prichard's work allowed other scientists to produce these rare clusters by experimental methods and thus be able to study them. Her graduate publications on this subject were themselves cited in more than one hundred subsequent publications.

Upon graduation, Prichard accepted a position with Eastman Kodak of Rochester, New York. A research scientist in the firm's PhotoScience Research Division, she conducts basic studies in silver halide materials for photographic systems. A member of Sigma Xi and Sigma Pi Sigma honor societies as well as a national board member of the Society for Hispanic Professional Engineers (SHPE) and a charter member of the Hispanic Democratic Women's Network of Washington, D.C., she also served on the Clinton/Gore Transition Cluster for Space, Science and Technology in 1992.

Prichard founded a program in Rochester called "Partnership in Education" that provides Hispanic role models in the classroom to teach science and math to limited English proficient students. She has also co-founded, within Eastman Kodak, the Hispanic Organization for Leadership and Advancement (HOLA). She is married to Mark S. Prichard, also a research scientist at Eastman Kodak. As to what she is most proud of in her career, she says that it is the fact that although her parents had little schooling, she was nevertheless able to come to love learning, obtain an advanced degree, and work in a professional field that she truly loves. □

Pridi Phanomyong

Pridi Phanomyong (1901–1983) was a civilian political leader in Thailand. He was popularly associated with opposition to military dominance and was known as a proponent of parliamentary democracy.

Pridi Phanomyong was born in Ayudhya Province, the son of a prosperous Chinese farmer and merchant by his Thai wife. From local Buddhist schools he went to Bangkok to attend secondary school and the Royal Law School, from which he graduated in 1920. Awarded a government scholarship, he studied law in Caen (1921-1924) and Paris, where he gained a doctorate in 1927. In Paris he became a leader among Thai students pressing their grievances against the Thai minister. He was also strongly influenced by French socialism.

The Rebel Inside and Out

On his return to Bangkok in 1927 Pridi was made secretary to the Department for Drafting Legislation, was given the title by which he is often known, Luang Pradit Manutham, and was assigned to teach law at Chulalongkorn University. In the general discontent with royal absolutism, exacerbated by the growing economic crisis, he was drawn into the group of officials and military officers who planned and executed the coup d'etat of June 24, 1932, which abolished the absolute monarchy and established a parliamentary regime.

The intellectual leader of the group, Pridi also took a lead in drafting the first constitutions of Thailand. His national economic policy of 1933, advocating a utopian sort of state socialism, split the government and brought about his temporary exile. He returned to serve as minister of interior (1935-1936), founded the University of Moral and Political Science (Thammasat), and, as foreign minister (1936-1938), directed the renegotiation of treaties with the Western powers. He served as minister of finance under Phibun Songkhram (1938-1941) but resigned to protest against increasing collaboration with Japan and became regent for the absent boy-king Ananda Mahidol (reigned 1935-1946).

As regent during the war, when Thailand was a nominal ally of Japan, Pridi came to direct the anti-Japanese underground Free Thai movement and was responsible for the overthrow of Phibun in 1944. Pridi's work with the Free Thai gained American support, which assisted Thailand's recovery after the war. This included establishing Thailand as an independent sovereign state. Attempting to maintain power from behind the scenes, he finally had to take leadership as prime minister in March 1946.

Resignation and Exile

Pridi's radical reputation and the economic chaos of the postwar years made his task difficult, and he did not have sufficient support to weather unsubstantiated rumors that he was responsible for the unexplained death of young King Ananda in June 1946. Pridi soon had to resign, and his power evaporated with the resurgence of military rule in 1947. He was then forced into exile. He reappeared in Communist China in 1949, associated with a Thai underground movement there, but left China to return to France in 1970. Pridi lived in Paris with his wife until he died of a heart attack on May 2, 1983.

Further Reading

Frank C. Darling, *Thailand and the United States* (1965), provides a spirited defense of Pridi. Also see (Devine, Elizabeth, ed.) *The Annual Obituary 1983,* St. James Press, 1984. □

Ivy Maude Baker Priest

A long-time activist in the Republican Party, Ivy Maude Baker Priest (1905-1975) served eight years as treasurer of the United States under President Dwight Eisenhower. She also twice won election as treasurer of California under Governor Ronald Reagan.

Ivy Maude Baker Priest was born on September 7, 1905, in Kimberly, Utah. She was the first born of the three daughters and four sons of Orange Decatur Baker and Clara Fearnley Baker. Her father was the grandson of one of the earliest Utah settlers and worked as a miner in Kimberly. Her mother was a domestic worker prior to her marriage. Orange and Clara met while on a mission to England for the Church of the Latter Day Saints.

Ivy Baker spent her school years in the Utah mining town of Birmingham, about 30 miles southwest of Salt Lake City. After her father was disabled in a mining accident, she came home from school each day to assist her mother in running a boarding house for 30 miners. She also helped her mother, who was known locally as "Mrs. Republican," by babysitting for voters on election days. In this manner Priest received her first practical political experience.

Ivy Baker graduated from Bingham Canyon High School. She had hoped to go on to college or to law school,

but her family's poverty led her to take a job selling tickets at a movie theater in order to help support the Baker household. In 1924 she married Harry Howard Hicks, a North Carolina travelling salesman. The marriage to Hicks was unsuccessful, and in 1929 the couple divorced. Baker returned to her family, now living in Salt Lake City. Here she continued to help support the Baker household, first as a long distance telephone operator and then as a department store merchandiser. After the work day ended at the department store, she made her way to a night school where she taught classes in American history.

Baker married Roy Fletcher Priest on December 7, 1935. Priest, 21 years older than Baker, was a travelling wholesale furniture salesman based in Bountiful, Utah. Moving to Bountiful, Priest was able to deepen her involvement in Utah Republican politics. She quickly proved herself to be a dynamic public speaker as well as a woman with superb organizing ability. From 1934 to 1936 she served as the president of the Utah Young Republicans. From 1936 to 1940 she was the chairwoman of the Young Republicans for 11 Western states. From 1937 to 1939 she also served as Republican committeewoman for Davis County, Utah, and as the president of the Utah Legislative Council. From 1944 to 1952 she served as the Republican national committeewoman from Utah. During these years Baker-Priest made two bids for office, both unsuccessful. The first was in 1934, when she ran for the Utah state legislature; the second, in 1950, when she ran for Congress against Reva Beck Bosone, the Democratic incumbent. Among Baker Priest's political projects during this period were her efforts to enact the first minimum wage law for Utah's working women.

The Priests had four children: Patricia Ann, Peggy Louise, Nancy Ellen, and Roy Baker Priest. Ivy Baker Priest later said that her church taught her to believe that each individual is given a particular set of talents that must be used. Her mother and husband encouraged her political activity when it was most difficult to continue, especially after the death of daughter Peggy in 1939.

Ivy Baker Priest was an early supporter of the presidential candidacy of Dwight D. Eisenhower in 1952. During Eisenhower's successful campaign she served as the assistant chairwoman of the Republican National Committee in charge of women's affairs. Her efforts for Eisenhower earned her an appointment as the 30th treasurer of the United States. She was the second woman to hold this position. Priest chose to be a politically active, visible member of the administration, averaging ten speeches a month. She was also a skilled administrator in her Treasury post, overseeing the federal government's banking facility and the issuance of much of the nation's currency. While a member of the Eisenhower administration she was also active in the American Red Cross, the International Soroptimist Club, and the Utah National Safety Council. She was chosen as one of the 20 outstanding women of the 20th century by the Women's Newspaper Editors and Publishers Association and received many honorary degrees.

Roy Priest died in 1959. Two years later Ivy Baker Priest retired from her position as treasurer and moved to California. There, on June 20, 1961, she married Sidney Williams Stevens, a Beverly Hills real estate developer. In 1966 she ran a successful campaign for treasurer of California, her first elective office. She served two four-year terms under Governor Ronald Reagan. In office, she worked to fulfill her campaign promise to invest California's revenues for high returns. She retired after two terms in office, choosing not to seek reelection because of failing health. Ivy Baker Priest died of cancer in June 1975 in Santa Monica, California.

Further Reading

Ivy Maude Baker Priest's personal papers are held by her family. They will be deposited at the University of Utah in the future and thus will be available to the public. Her autobiography, *Green Grows Ivy,* was published in 1958 and covers her life through the period when she was United States treasurer. No full biography of Priest has yet been done. Other sources do exist, however, including a news-clipping file on Priest maintained by the Utah Department of Development Services and extensive obituary notices that appeared in the Salt Lake City *Tribune* and in the *New York Times* on June 25, 1975. □

J. B. Priestley

Called by some the last "sage" of English literature, J. B. Priestley (1894-1984) had a career which spanned more than 60 years and included authoring novels, essays, plays, and screenplays.

John Boynton Priestley was born in Bradford, Yorkshire, in the North of England on September 13, 1894, the son of Jonathan Priestley, a schoolmaster. His early education was at the Bradford School, but this career was interrupted, as happened to many of his contemporaries, by service in World War I. He served with both the Duke of Wellington's and the Devon regiments from 1914 to 1919. After the war he matriculated at Trinity Hall, Cambridge, where he studied history and political science as well as English literature. Already writing and publishing as an undergraduate, he was able to pay some of his university bills by selling articles to provincial and London newspapers. In 1922 he settled in London, rapidly establishing a reputation as essayist, critic, and novelist.

From his earliest writings, Priestley may be described as a comic rationalist. The contradictions and absurdities of the human situation, he wrote, could best be borne by a stance of ironic detachment. This perspective is perhaps closest to that of Priestley's predecessor, the novelist George Meredith (1828-1909). Not surprisingly, one of the best of Priestley's early critical works is a biography of Meredith in the English Men of Letters series (*George Meredith,* 1926). Another early influence was Meredith's father-in-law, the satirist Thomas Love Peacock, subject of another fine Priestley biography in the same series in 1927.

About this time Priestley achieved great popularity himself as a novelist through two works centering on the comic interplay of people engaged in a common calling.

The Good Companions (1929) is about the joys and sorrows of the members of a repertory company in the north of England. It was a success in the United States as well as in England. The following year *Angel Pavement* appeared, whose characters worked in a small London business firm. Other notable and popular novels followed: *They Walk in the City* (1936), *The Doomsday Men* (1938), *Let the People Sing* (1939), and *Festival at Farbridge* (1951). All of these are fairly long novels, each with a lively balance between memorable, accurately-observed character and meticulously-crafted, suspenseful plot, featuring often rogueish heroes on the move—another recrudescence of the English picaresque in a tradition going back to the 1740s, beginning with Henry Fielding's *Joseph Andrews.* A strain of sentimentality is often present, but it is usually corrected by the "silvery laughter" of Priestley's comic spirit. Other novels of this author combine autobiographical detail with a social criticism less bitter than Priestley's 1930s contemporary George Orwell. Examples of this type include *English Journey* (1934), *Midnight on the Desert* (1937), and *Rain Upon Godshill* (1939).

One aspect of all of Priestley's fiction is its theatricality—from the beginning he had a fine flair for dialogue; in fact, soon after its success as a novel he adapted *The Good Companions* into a play (1931, with E. Knoblock). The next year saw the debut of Priestley as a bonafide dramatist with *Dangerous Corner;* it was a resounding success and was performed all over the world. This acclaim encouraged the author to organize his own company, for which he wrote plays of consistently high quality. Some were comedies, such as *Laburnum Grove* (1933) and *When We Are Married* (1938). As a dramatist Priestley was influenced by the theories of time and recurrence propounded by the philosopher J. W. Dunne (1875-1949), especially as developed in *Experiment with Time* and *The Serial Universe.* Dunne's concepts are dramatized in Priestley's serious "metaphysical" plays, such as *Time and the Conways* (1937), *I Have Been There Before* (1938), and *Johnson over Jordan* (1939).

After World War II, J. B. Priestley took an active role in the international cultural community. He was a United Kingdom delegate to United Nations Educational, Scientific, and Cultural Organization (UNESCO) conferences in 1946 and 1947. He was chairman of theater conferences in Paris in 1947 and in Prague the following year. In 1949 he served as president of the International Theatre Institute. Back home he was chosen chairman of the British Theatre Conference (1948) and also served as a member of the National Theatre Board (1966-1967). In 1973, then nearly 80 years of age, he served his home city of Bradford as Freeman.

To Priestley's assets of longevity and versatility we may add flexibility—his adapting of the printed word to newer media of communication during and after World War II. During the war he became even more well known than before through his talks on radio; because of his understanding of and sympathy for the average citizen he was able to make a direct personal appeal using this medium. His film credits include screenplays for *The Foreman Went to France* (1942) and *Last Holiday* (1956). Back in the world of theater, he helped the novelist Iris Murdoch translate her hit novel *A Severed Head* into a successful play (1963).

Priestley had a son and four daughters through earlier marriages; in 1953 he became part of a famous husband-wife literary team when he married the archeologist and writer Jacquetta Hawkes. She had also worked for UNESCO and in the film industry. Together they wrote the play *Dragon's Mouth* (1952) and *Journey Down a Rainbow* (1955). A stay in New Zealand enabled him to write the travel piece *A Visit to New Zealand* (1974). Priestley's autobiography, *Instead of the Trees,* appeared three years later.

Still more evidence of this writer's versatility includes the libretto for an opera, *The Olympians* (1948); *Delight,* a book of essays (1949); *The Art of the Dramatist,* criticism (1957); and *The Edwardians,* social history (1970). J. B. Priestley died quietly at his home in Stratford-on-Avon on August 14, 1984.

Further Reading

Other books by Priestley include *Ape and Angels* (1928), *The Prince of Pleasures and His Regency* (1969), and *Victoria's Heyday* (1972). His essays of five decades were collected and edited by Susan Cooper in 1969.
Two excellent assessments of Priestley's work are *J. B. Priestley* by John Braine (1978) and *J. B. Priestley, Last of the Sages* by John Atkins (1980). Perhaps Priestley will be most enduringly known for his contribution to the theater. Analysis of his contribution to this genre is made by Gareth Lloyd Evans in *J. B. Priestley: The Dramatist* (1964).

Additional Sources

Atkins, John Alfred, *J. B. Priestley: the last of the sages,* London: J. Calder; New York: Riverrun Press, 1981.
Braine, John, *J. B. Priestley,* New York: Barnes & Noble Books, 1979, 1978.
Brome, Vincent, *J.B. Priestley,* London; New York, N.Y., U.S.A.: Hamish Hamilton, 1988.
Collins, Diana, *Time and the Priestleys: the story of a friendship,* Far Thrupp, Stroud, Gloucestershire: A. Sutton, 1994.
Priestley, J. B. (John Boynton), *English journey,* Chicago: University of Chicago Press, 1984.
Priestley, J. B. (John Boynton), *Instead of the trees: a final chapter of autobiography,* New York: Stein and Day, 1977. □

Joseph Priestley

The English clergyman and chemist Joseph Priestley (1733-1804) contributed to the foundation of the chemistry of gases and discovered the role of oxygen in the animal-plant metabolic system.

Joseph Priestley was born on March 13, 1733, at Fieldhead. His mother died when he was 6, and he was reared by an aunt. Because of ill health he was unable to go to school and was educated partly by a Nonconformist minister and partly by private study. He had a gift for languages and learned about 10. He became a minister when he was 22.

Priestley moved about the country a great deal, preaching and teaching. About 1758 he began to add experiments in "natural philosophy" to his students' activities. In 1761 he moved to Warrington to teach languages in an academy established by Dissenters. There he began to take even more interest in science in general and had an opportunity to attend a few lectures in elementary chemistry.

On a trip to London in 1766 Priestley met Benjamin Franklin, who interested him in electricity. This led to fruitful experimentation—Priestley discovered the conductivity of carbon in 1766, found that an electrical charge stays on the surface of a conductor, and studied the conduction of electricity by flames—and his *History and Present State of Electricity* (1767), which at that time was definitive.

In 1767 Priestley moved to Leeds, where he lived next to a brewery. He became interested in the gases evolved during fermentation and soon discovered that carbon dioxide was being formed. He began preparing this gas at home for study and found that it could be absorbed by water. This discovery of "soda water" brought him much attention and the Royal Society's Copley Medal.

Thus stimulated, Priestley turned his attention to the preparation and study of other gases. He decided to collect them over mercury rather than water and was therefore able to prepare for the first time a variety of gases at random. His greatest discovery came in 1774, when he prepared oxygen by using a burning glass and solar heat to heat red oxide of mercury in a vacuum and collected the evolved gas over mercury. In accordance with the phlogiston doctrine, to

Further Reading

Among the biographies of Priestley are Anne Holt, *A Life of Joseph Priestley* (1931); John G. Gillam, *The Crucible: The Story of Joseph Priestley* (1954); and Frederick W. Gibbs, *Joseph Priestley: Revolutions of the Eighteenth Century* (1967). Bernard Jaffe's treatment of Priestley in his *Crucibles: The Lives and Achievement of the Great Chemists* (1930) is readable and interesting. There is also a study of Priestley in James G. Crowther, *Scientists of the Industrial Revolution* (1963).

Additional Sources

Clark, John Ruskin, *Joseph Priestley, a comet in the system: biography,* San Diego, Calif.: Torch Publications, 1990.

McLachlan, John, *Joseph Priestley, man of science, 1733-1804: an iconography of a great Yorkshireman,* Braunton, Devon: Merlin Books, 1983.

Priestley, Joseph, *Memoirs of Dr. Joseph Priestley to the year 1795, written by himself; with a continuation to the time of his decease by his son, Joseph Priestley, and observations on his writings by Thomas Cooper and William Christi,* Millwood, N.Y.: Kraus Reprint Co., 1978.

Smith, Edgar Fahs, *Priestley in America, 1794-1804,* New York: Arno Press, 1980.

Thorpe, Thomas Edward, Sir, *Joseph Priestley,* New York: AMS Press, 1976. □

which he remained loyal to his death, he called the new gas "dephlogisticated air," for he found that it greatly improved combustion. He realized that this gas must be the active component in the atmosphere and that the concept of air being a single substance was incorrect. Three years earlier he had discovered that plants had the capacity to restore to air the ability to support combustion after a candle had been burned in it. He could now identify oxygen as the agent involved in the animal-plant metabolic cycle.

Between 1772 and 1780 Priestley held the not very demanding post of librarian and companion to Lord Shelburne, and much of his best work was done through this patronage. Priestley then settled in Birmingham, where he became a member of the Lunar Club.

Priestley hated all oppression, openly supported the American and French revolutions, and denounced the slave trade and religious bigotry. As a result of his continued attacks on the government, public resentment rose against Priestley and in 1791 a mob sacked and burnt his house and laboratory. He and his family escaped to London, where he encountered harassment and snubs, and in 1794 he emigrated to the United States. He was offered various positions, including that of the presidency of the University of Pennsylvania, all of which he declined, but he did pass on much of his experimental techniques to American chemists and preached from time to time. President John Adams was among those who attended his sermons, and George Washington made him a welcome visitor to his home. Priestley died at his home in Northumberland, Pa., on Feb. 6, 1804.

Francesco Primaticcio

The Italian painter, sculptor, and architect Francesco Primaticcio (1504-1570) was instrumental in transplanting mannerist palace decoration from Italy to France and in giving French mannerist art its individual character.

Francesco Primaticcio was born in Bologna on April 30, 1504. He worked in Mantua from 1525 or 1526 until 1532 under Giulio Romano. In the Palazzo del Te, Giulio carried out one of the most elaborate programs of mannerist art in all Italy. He represented a series of mythological scenes and motifs in frescoes and stucco reliefs in a decorative style that his teacher, Raphael, had created only a few years earlier.

In 1532 Primaticcio was called to France to work on the decorations of the royal palace of Francis I at Fontainebleau. He came equipped with all the things Giulio Romano had taught him: a rich vocabulary of classical nymphs and satyrs and Roman gods and goddesses plus the fashionable new mode of paintings combined with stuccoes. Giorgio Vasari in his *Lives* (2d ed. 1568) states that "the first works of stucco done in France and the first frescoes of any account originated with Primaticcio." Together with Il Rosso, Primaticcio developed this tradition in the form that set the general direction of French palace decoration for the next 150 years.

In 1541 the King made Primaticcio one of his chamberlains. Three years later he appointed him abbot of St-Martin at Troyes, a position that carried no duties or responsibilities but an abundance of prestige and money. Meanwhile the King commissioned him to decorate one room after another at Fontainebleau with his paintings and stucco figures.

Gradually, under the influence of Parmigianino, Primaticcio's style began to change. His figures, which until now had had normal proportions, started to become fantastically elongated. Tiny heads appeared on top of long, thin, curving necks. Arms and legs tapered down to tiny hands and feet. These strange creatures lounged languidly and effortlessly in poses that were always elegant though sometimes bizarre. This figure type that Primaticcio created at Fontainebleau was endlessly repeated by French artists throughout the remainder of the 16th century and even into the 17th.

Primaticcio's works in architecture are much less well known. The most striking is the small Grotto of the Pines (ca. 1543) at Fontainebleau. Here sculptured giants appear to grow out of rough-hewn stones, and at the top of each arch the keystone seems about to slip out of place, giving the impression—quite intentionally-that the whole structure might at any moment collapse. Primaticcio designed the circular chapel for Henry II and his wife, Catherine de Médicis (ca. 1560; destroyed), at St-Denis and added a wing, the Aile de la Belle Cheminée (1568), to the palace at Fontainebleau. He died in Paris sometime between May 15 and Sept. 14, 1570.

Further Reading

The main work on Primaticcio is in French: Louis Dimier, *Le Primatice* (1928). Giorgio Vasari, *Lives of the Most Eminent Painters, Sculptors, and Architects* (many editions), contains a good although incomplete biography of Primaticcio. The best modern account is in Anthony Blunt, *Art and Architecture in France, 1500-1700* (1953). □

Miguel Primo de Rivera y Orbaneja

The Spanish general Miguel Primo de Rivera y Orbaneja (1870-1930) ruled Spain as a dictator from 1923 to 1930.

Miguel Primo de Rivera was born in Cadiz on Jan. 8, 1870, of a middle-class family that later became landowners in the Andalusian town of Jerez. He entered the General Military Academy in Toledo in 1884 and first saw service in Africa in 1893, where he won the Cross of San Fernando. Two years later he went to Cuba as an aide to Gen. Martinez de Campos. When his uncle, Gen. Fernando Primo de Rivera, was named captain general of the Philippines in 1897, Miguel went to Manila as an aide. A major in 1898, he was prevented by the collapse of Spanish military power from becoming a lieutenant general until 1919, the interim being filled with campaigns in

Morocco, a stormy military governorship of Cadiz (1915), and service as an observer at the western front during World War I.

Public notice did not come Primo's way until 1922, when, as captain general of Barcelona, he attempted to reestablish law and order at just the moment that antiwar sentiment and social unrest were pointing toward revolution. Almost by chance Primo was selected as the chief figure in the military coup d'etat that on Sept. 12, 1923, overthrew parliamentary government (possibly with the aid of King Alfonso XIII) and imposed a military dictatorship. Overnight Primo became the most important political figure in Spain.

Primo has been described as a "glorified café politician" who, though he had made no preparation for rule, nevertheless aspired to political greatness. Order was restored by suspending constitutional guarantees, dissolving the Parliament, and imposing martial law. A new party, the Patriotic Union, became Primo's political vehicle and the only legal party in the country. Aside from the King's support of it, however, it had been put together so fast that it never developed great strength. Only because Primo was able to concentrate resources and to rally the army and defeat Abd el-Krim and the Moroccans did the new regime gain some respite from political dissension. The ending of the Moroccan War in December 1925 became Primo's one solid triumph.

Internal problems, surprisingly, continued to mount. Liberals rejected Primo's local government reforms and an-

ticentralism, and radicals, despite the addition of a Socialist, Largo Caballero, to his Cabinet, did not feel that the regime was moving fast enough in making social reforms. University students and intellectuals, fearing that Primo was another Benito Mussolini, led the opposition from 1925 on, and one of Spain's most distinguished intellectuals, Miguel de Unamuno, went into exile. Primo in fact was far from being a Fascist like Mussolini; if anything he had a paternalistic view of the state that unfortunately was out of step with the growing ideological sensitivities of the Spaniards.

By 1928, as the revolt of the cadets at the Academy of Segovia showed, even the army was dissatisfied with Primo, mainly because law and order were breaking down. The next 2 years witnessed one act of rebellion after the other, but King Alfonso XIII delayed replacing Primo because the monarchy had used the regime to hide its involvement in a series of disastrous political and military setbacks just prior to the dictatorship. Finally, however, Primo had no other recourse than to resign on Jan. 28, 1930, when he left for exile in Paris. He died in Paris on March 16, 1930.

Primo's son, José Antonio, frequently defended his father during the next few years of growing political bitterness, and many aspects of his father's paternalism could be found in José Antonio Primo de Rivera's much more overtly fascist philosophy. José Antonio founded the Falange party and became the martyr of the nationalist movement.

Further Reading

Dillwyn F. Ratcliff, *Prelude to Franco: Political Aspects of the Dictatorship of General Miguel Primo de Rivera* (1957), covers Primo de Rivera's regime. Good accounts of his career are in Gerald Brenan, *The Spanish Labyrinth: An Account of the Social and Political Background of the Civil War* (1943; 2d ed. 1950), and Raymond Carr, *Spain, 1808-1939* (1966). There is also extensive material on Primo de Rivera in Charles Petrie, *King Alfonso XIII and His Age* (1963). □

V. S. Pritchett

V. S. Pritchett (1900–1997) was an English short story writer, novelist, literary critic, journalist, travel writer, biographer, and autobiographer. Though not an innovator in terms of style, he was nevertheless an interesting and highly competent writer.

V. S. Pritchett, who was born on December 16, 1900, in Ipswich, England, to Sawdon and Beatrice (Martin) Pritchett, told the story of his life in two volumes. The first of these is *A Cab at the Door: A Memoir* (the British subtitle is *Childhood and Youth, 1900-1920*), and the second is *Midnight Oil* (1971). His account of his life is humorous at times and rather detached. His father, a religious seeker, found refuge in later years in Christian Science. Micawber-like, Sawdon Pritchett was optimistic about the get-rich-quick schemes which left the family in straitened circumstances and which accounted for the title,

A Cab at the Door. The family had to move frequently, with disastrous consequences for Pritchett's formal education. The mother, Beatrice Martin, was a sometimes vain and sometimes foolish woman of a decent lower class family.

Pritchett loved literature and read Dickens and Hardy. He felt that he lacked grounding in mathematics and science. When his father, in 1915, decided that the son must learn a trade, the youth was upset at having his education interrupted. Though he didn't like his work in the leather trade, he did enjoy meeting and associating with people. At 20 he left for Paris. He continued to read not only British authors and poets but the more important modern French ones. He acquired a fluency in French of which he was very proud.

It was almost by chance that he submitted three pieces for publication in 1921. The *Christian Science Monitor* published one of these, and his career was launched. During his two-year stay in Paris he made friends with other young people, though he was rather shy and certainly innocent by today's standards. He longed for the love of a young woman and ultimately lost his innocence. Evidently there was something about this short, shy youth that brought out the maternal instinct in older women: more than once he was mothered and advised by a woman older than himself.

In 1923 he returned to London and was asked by the *Christian Science Monitor* to write a series of articles about Ireland. The extended visit to Ireland, as well as a subsequent visit to Spain, led to a series of travel books written over a span of nearly 40 years. Pritchett traveled to various

parts of Ireland to acquire first-hand material for his articles and in the process developed an admiration for the Irish, though an occasional dreariness of the landscape depressed him. When he visited Spain he was impressed with the country, and it provided him with the setting for some of his stories and furnished him with journalistic material. He published his first novel, *Clare Drummer,* in 1929 and a collection of short stories, *The Spanish Virgin and Other Stories,* in 1930. Neither book was a critical success. These were followed by another novel, *Elopement Into Exile*—or *Shirley Sanz,* to give it its British title. This book was not a critical success either.

Nothing Like Leather, which appeared in 1935, traces the material success and moral disintegration of Matthew Burkle when by dint of hard work he begins to rise in the leather tannery where he is employed. The industrial town in which the novel is set is vividly and realistically described. In 1935 *Dead Man Leading* appeared. Its setting—the jungles of Brazil—was more exotic. As in Conrad's *Heart of Darkness,* there is a symbolic journey motif, and two of the men who make the journey, Philips and Johnson, attempt to find in Wright a father figure.

After 15 years, in 1951, another novel, *Mr. Beluncle,* appeared. Like Pritchett's own father, Beluncle, the protagonist, is searching for religious fulfillment. Brendan Gill, writing in the *New Yorker,* admitted that the novel amused, yet he thought it only partially successful because he found it also "forced and cold." In *Midnight Oil* Pritchett mentions in passing that his father thought that he saw himself in the novel, and the author nowhere denies that the protagonist was based on his father, whose penchant for schemes of easy wealth has already been mentioned. It may be that the objectivity that can be achieved by the lapse of time between actual events and their recollection had not yet been reached.

Certainly Pritchett's biography of the great 19th-century novelist Honoré de Balzac deserves mention. Though Millicent Bell pointed out that in *Balzac* (1974) he broke no new ground, she found him good at "describing persons and scenes" and considered that he wrote "in a sinewy and witty style." There can be no doubt that his sympathies lie with his subject, and Balzac's lover, Madame Hanska, who might have treated the author more handsomely than she did (though she did fulfill on his deathbed her promise to marry him), comes out a decided second best.

In reviewing his *Collected Stories* (1982), Valentine Cunningham, who called Pritchett "the best living English author," commented that he was "always on the alert for the illustrative moment," that he turned "human moments into epiphanies," and that he was "celebrating the heroicism of banal life." The last comment rings true, for the lives examined are only *seemingly* banal and the deep current beneath them is all. Cunningham singled out for special praise "Many Are Disappointed"; however, another superior story, "Blind Love," which deals with a blind man and his housekeeper who hides from the world a disfiguring birthmark that the blind man cannot see, truly illustrates that a rich and turbulent life can exist beneath an outwardly placid, banal one. In 1983 *More Collected Stories* was

published. Both this collection and the earlier one go back many years. *A Man of Letters: Selected Essays* by Pritchett was published in 1986.

As a literary critic Pritchett was incisive, and in a happy choice of phrase he could lay bare for the reader an author's method of approaching his subject. In *The Myth Makers: Literary Essays* (1979) he said of Jean Genet that "he proceeds from criminal ritual to the literary without losing his innate interest in violence," and again, "Genet is the natural product of an age of violence, a cult figure for those who feel guilty because they have escaped martyrdom." In his essay on Gustave Flaubert he says of Madame Bovary of his famous novel *Madam Bovary:* "She is dignified by a real fate—not by a false word 'Fate,' one of the clichés Flaubert derided," and he described Flaubert himself as "her fellow adolescent." Of Gabriel Garcia Márquez's method in *One Hundred Years of Solitude,* he said that "Marquez seems to be sailing down the blood stream of his people," and spoke of "the slippery comedies and tragedies of daily life" as depicted in that novel.

In an essay on the British writer Henry Yorke, Pritchett called the author "sensitive to that rarity which is buried in people who outwardly might be commonplace," and he went on to say that he thought that Yorke's characters "were living in the imagination and this made him a master of comedy of what can only be called the human underground." These words aptly fit Pritchett's own method and characters.

Pritchett himself preferred his travel books, short stories, and novels to his reviews, but he was wrong to so belittle his talents as a critic, and his critical ability, if anything, grew with the passage of time. Cunningham shared Pritchett's own belief that the short stories he wrote in the 1920s were merely "apprenticeship work" and that he came into his own in the 1930s. At his very best he endowed his stories with an interest and understanding of the human condition that will be felt by readers yet unborn.

Even into his eighties, Pritchett took on an enormous workload, writing reviews nearly full time and publishing his final biography, of Chekhov, in 1988. V.S. Pritchett died in London's Whittingham Hospital on March 21, 1997, at the age of 96.

Further Reading

For additional information see "V. S. Pritchett" in *Contemporary Literary Criticism,* Vols. 1-5 (1975), and Harry Marks, "V. S. Pritchett," *Dictionary of Literary Biography,* Vol. 15, Pt. 2 (1983), to which this article is in some part indebted. Brendan Gill, "One Yes, Two Maybes," the *New Yorker* (October 13, 1951), contains a review of Pritchett's *Mr. Beluncle;* Millicent Bell, "Balzac Set Forth With Lavish 'Furnishings,'" *Sewanee Review* 50 (Summer 1974), is a sympathetic review of *Balzac;* B. L. Reid, "Putting in the Self," *Sewanee Review* 85 (Spring 1977), deals essentially with *A Cab at the Door* and *Midnight Oil* and sheds some light on Pritchett's style in autobiography; Valentine Cunningham, "Coping with Bigger Words," *Times Literary Supplement* (June 25, 1982), provides a review of Pritchett's *Collected Stories* and deals with his progress as a writer. S. S. Prawer, "The Soul of Brevity," *Times Literary Supplement* (August 17, 1984), includes a review of Pritchett's *The Other Side of the Frontier: A V. S. Pritchett*

Reader and his *Collected Stories* and is important for the comments of one first-class writer on the quality and methods of another. Additional works by Pritchett include "An Interview" conducted by Douglass A. Hughes, *Studies in Short Fiction* 13 (Fall 1976); "Henry Yorke, Henry Green," *Twentieth Century Literature* 29 (Winter 1983), which appears in an issue devoted to essays on Yorke—Pritchett evaluates the writer's work and in the process tells the reader much about his own literary values and interests. □

Proclus Diadochus

Proclus Diadochus (410-485) was a Byzantine philosopher and the last of the great Neoplatonists of antiquity. His philosophy indirectly influenced Christian thought, and he directly influenced many Renaissance thinkers.

Proclus was born in Constantinople (modern Istanbul) of Lycian parentage. He received his elementary education in Xanthus and then continued his studies in Alexandria. Among his teachers were the Sophist Leonas of Isauria and the Egyptian grammarian Orion as well as a number of Roman teachers, who taught him Latin. His basic study was rhetoric, since his intention originally was to enter the legal profession. However, on a trip to Constantinople with Leonas, Proclus appears to have been "converted" to philosophy, and on his return to Alexandria he studied Aristotle and mathematics. At the age of 19 he went to the Platonic Academy in Athens, where he studied under Plutarch of Athens, founder of the Athenian school of Neoplatonism, and Syrianus, Plutarch's immediate successor.

Syrianus greatly influenced Proclus's philosophical development, and he regarded Proclus both as his pupil and as his successor at the Academy. Under Syrianus's tutelage, Proclus read widely in Plato and Aristotle, and at 28 he had produced a number of sophisticated commentaries on different dialogues of Plato, including the monumental commentary on the *Timaeus.* When Syrianus died, the chair passed briefly to Domninus of Larissa, and it was then assumed by Proclus, who held it until his death.

According to a contemporary biographer, Proclus possessed great bodily strength and endurance and striking physical beauty. He was a practicing magician, a vegetarian, and a man of great personal asceticism. Apart from his professional teaching and writing, he must have at least occasionally spoken his mind on politics, since he left Athens at one time for a year, when political enemies were attempting to put him on trial.

In addition to his commentaries on Plato's dialogues and a commentary on Plotinus's *Enneads,* Proclus wrote important works on systematic philosophy and theology. They include the *Elements of Theology* and the *Platonic Theology,* as well as smaller treatises: *Doubts about Providence, Providence and Fate, The Continuance of Evil,* and *Conduct.* He also wrote commentaries on the Chaldean

oracles, the first book of Euclid's *Elements,* and the poets Hesiod and (possibly) Homer, several astronomical treatises, a treatise on the elements of physics, and a large number of hymns to different gods.

Further Reading

As examples of Proclus's work the reader can examine the Thomas Taylor translation of *The Commentaries of Proclus on the Timaeus of Plato* (1820) or E. R. Dodds's celebrated edition and translation of *The Elements of Theology* (1933; 2d ed. 1963). A detailed and sympathetic introduction to the life and work of Proclus is Laurence Jay Rosan, *The Philosophy of Proclus: The Final Phase of Ancient Thought* (1949). See also Thomas Whittaker, *The Neo-Platonists: A Study in the History of Hellenism* (1901; 4th ed. 1961). □

Procopius of Caesarea

The Byzantine historian Procopius of Caesarea (ca. 500-ca. 565), the last of the great classical Greek historians, was an eyewitness to, and prime reporter of, events in the reign of Emperor Justinian I.

Born in Palestinian Caesarea between 490 and 507, Procopius was thoroughly educated and probably trained in law. In 527 he was made advisor and secretary to the young general Belisarius, then imperial commander in Mesopotamia against the Persians. In this capacity Procopius accompanied Belisarius on many of his campaigns, witnessing not only the Persian hostilities but also the suppression of the Nika Riots (532), the conquest of the Vandal kingdom of North Africa (533-534), and—after a term of service in North Africa (534-536)—the first war against the Ostrogoths in Italy (535-540). Procopius was in Constantinople in 542, where he observed the beginnings of the terrible plague that struck the empire. Presumably, Procopius did not join Belisarius on his second Italian campaign. He seems to have held government posts in the capital for the remainder of his career.

Drawing upon his experiences, Procopius began during the 540s a formal history of military and political events of his day, his *History of the Wars,* written in excellent Greek. Of its eight books, the first two narrate the empire's Persian Wars, from early in the 5th century to about 550. The next two books describe the Vandalic Wars and subsequent events in North Africa to the late 540s. Three more books describe both phases of the Ostrogothic Wars, from 535 to 551. A supplementary eighth book covers events generally between 548 and 554.

Meanwhile Procopius's attitude seems to have undergone a drastic change. Apparently cool personally to Justinian and his consort Theodora, he seems at least to have shared the aspirations of their reign's early years. The subsequent disasters and disillusionments soured him—a process increased, it is thought, by his failure to obtain all the advancements he expected. Consequently, about 550, Procopius composed *The Unpublished Sections (Tà*

Empire from the Death of Theodosius I to the Death of Justinian (1923). □

Sergei Sergeevich Prokofiev

The Russian-Soviet composer Sergei Sergeevich Prokofiev (1891-1953) was a key figure in modern music. He was prolific in all genres and was a master craftsman. His works are probably the most played of 20th-century composers.

The accomplishment of Sergei Prokofiev, together with that of Dmitri Shostakovich, very nearly sums up the contribution of Soviet music in the 20th century. Although Prokofiev was a brilliant pianist and writer for piano, he sought his creative beginnings in opera. Yet very often the end product, through his lifelong habit of rewriting and recasting, was a dazzling orchestral work. His particular idiom remained distinctive although attenuated in later years under the pressure to succeed in terms not his own.

Prokofiev was born in Sontsovka (now Krasnoe) in the Ekaterinoslav Guberniya of the Ukraine, where his father managed the Sontsov family estates. Sergei's mother, a woman of considerable cultural pretension, indulged her only child's precocity. Indeed, young Prokofiev was so musically industrious that it would have been difficult to stop him. By the age of 10 he had written a number of pieces, including an opera, *Giant.* The young boy was taken to the Moscow Conservatory, and, for the next two summers, Reinhold Glière went to Sontsovka to tutor him.

At the age of 12 Prokofiev entered the St. Petersburg Conservatory. He spent the next 10 years there, and, although he later had very little good to say of the institution, its traditions, or its teachers, he received an impressive technical grounding. More important to him through the conservatory years were contacts with his fellow students Boris Asafiev and Nikolai Miaskovsky, with prominent (and rich) musical figures like Serge Koussevitsky, and with the growing body of internationally minded artists and entrepreneurs in the capital city. Prokofiev traveled to London in 1914, heard Igor Stravinsky's *Rite of Spring,* and established a liaison with the impresario Serge Diaghilev. Prokofiev was already a successful musician, published and performed, and the Diaghilev contact was the all but final stamp of Russian creative maturity in 1914.

Years Abroad

Prokofiev longed for a sustained stay and impact abroad—the Russian tradition most recently confirmed by Alexander Scriabin, Sergei Rachmaninov, and Stravinsky. But the war, Russia's faltering role therein, and the two revolutions of 1917 caused Prokofiev's Western contacts to pause. The "angels" that had financed others failed to materialize at first, and Diaghilev was not encouraging. In mid-1917 Prokofiev reached an understanding with the Chicago

anékdota), now known as the *Historia arcana,* or *Secret History.* The *Wars,* a public and semiofficial history, had been meant for circulation. In this secret memoir, not intended for publication, Procopius poured out his frustrations in terms of ridicule and abuse of Belisarius, of his wife Antonina, of Empress Theodora, and, above all, of Justinian himself. The Emperor is depicted as malicious, rapacious, a destroyer of all established order and traditions, and, in effect, an evil demon.

Though objective and skeptical about religious matters, Procopius planned an ecclesiastical history of Justinian's reign, but this work was either lost or unrealized. In the mid-550s, however, Procopius composed an account of Justinian's architectural program entitled *On the Buildings.* Organized geographically into six books, it is incomplete as planned, lacking a section on Italy.

Procopius seems to have received some higher positions at court late in life. He is last specifically heard of in 559, and the date of his death is unknown.

Further Reading

The complete works of Procopius are most readily available in the Loeb Classical Library series (7 vols., 1914-1940), with the Greek text and English translation by H. B. Dewing and G. Downey. The *Secret History* is available in paperback translation by R. Atwater (1963) and G. A. Williamson (1966). There is no comprehensive study of Procopius in English, but all major works on the age of Justinian discuss him at length. See, for example, John Bagnell Bury, *History of the Later Roman*

part of his effort was directed toward casting works for other mediums in symphonic form. Much of his work appears in the original version and in an orchestral version or versions. This includes all the ballets, parts of the Piano Sonatas, chamber works, and even his beloved opera *Flaming Angel* (as the Third Symphony).

Return to Soviet Union

In 1927 Prokofiev visited the Soviet Union and was well received. But on a second visit in 1929 the conservative Russian Association of Proletarian Musicians (RAPM) dominated the musical press and attacked the reluctant émigré. In late 1932 he was encouraged to visit again: the RAPM had been abolished, and his friends Miaskovsky, Asafiev, and Glière were enthusiastic about creative prospects in the Soviet Union. Prokofiev still hesitated, still visited, and sought and probably got assurances from high party and government sources. He finally moved to Moscow in 1936. He had done well in the West, but he was dissatisfied: as a concert pianist he had stood in Rachmaninov's shadow; and he had failed to capture that creative leadership enjoyed by Arnold Schoenberg and Stravinsky.

Through 1938 Prokofiev continued to tour the West, but the Nazi-Soviet Pact of 1939 brought on a politically anti-international period, and he never went abroad again. He was simultaneously in the throes of separation from his wife, herself an international symbol. For these reasons his autobiographical memoirs, a substantial part of which was written during the pact, are unfortunately inaccurate in discussing the West. In his memoirs he characterized his own style as shaped from four main lines of development: first, the lyric, singing line; second, the classical grounding; third, the urge to seek and innovate; and fourth, a relentless, motoric, toccatalike pulse.

Prokofiev had already begun, in his Soviet period, to write movie scores (*Lieutenant Kijé,* 1934; *Alexander Nevsky,* 1938), patriotic works (*Cantata for the Twentieth Anniversary of the October Revolution,* 1937), and works of lighter genre and direct appeal (*Peter and the Wolf,* 1936). He held at this time the notion of multiple styles for the contemporary composer. In 1939 he began another opera, *Semyon Kotko,* based on a story by Valentin Kataev. The opera dealt with Germans as enemies and was difficult to mount during first a pro-German then an anti-German period. In it Prokofiev worked out a usage for those idioms and experiments too advanced for the increasingly conservative official view of art: the depiction of inimical forces. Prokofiev's coworker, the famous director Vsevolod Meyerhold, was arrested and sent to a labor camp (where he died) for creative errors. Prokofiev seemed immune to such reprimands and punishments, which were common in the late 1930s.

industrialist Cyrus McCormick. By this time Prokofiev had composed a number of piano pieces, the *Scythian Suite* for orchestra (a recasting of a ballet, *Ala and Lolli,* commissioned but rejected by Diaghilev), the First (*Classical*) Symphony, the First Violin Concerto, and the First and Second Piano Concertos, the Third being in the works. With these behind him, McCormick's invitation in his pocket, and the consent of the new Soviet government, the composer left for the United States in 1918.

In 1921 Prokofiev's *Love for Three Oranges* was premiered in Chicago. The American years were fitful ones financially, not the least because of competition from other Russian émigrés. He began in America the opera *Flaming Angel,* which, though never performed in his lifetime, was to dominate his thinking for many years. In 1922 he moved to Ettal in the Bavarian Alps. Here he lived with his mother and with his first wife, Caroline Codina, working mostly on the *Flaming Angel* and on piano and vocal works. Eventually he settled in Paris with his family and made that the center of his activity until 1936.

The Western years were productive ones, and it is well to emphasize the point, since Soviet thinking insists that they were "unproductive years of rootless desperation." He completed (for Diaghilev) the ballets *Le Pas d'acier* (1925), *Prodigal Son* (1928), and *On the Dnieper* (1930); the operas *Love for Three Oranges* (1919) and *Flaming Angel* (1927); a number of vocal works; the Third, Fourth, and Fifth Piano Concertos; chamber works, including opus numbers 34, 35, 39, 50 and 56; and many other works. He worked constantly, often on more than one piece at a time, and no small

During World War II Prokofiev, with his second wife, Myra Mendelson, was evacuated to a series of Eastern centers. He worked on more film scores, including *Ivan the Terrible* with Sergei Eisenstein, his opera *War and Peace,* and on the Second (*Kabardinian*) String Quartet. He completed the Fifth Symphony in 1945. That year he incurred the illness, hypertension, that was finally to prove fatal, and it became clear that he was beginning to draw critical fire from official and semiofficial sources. In 1948 he was a principal target in the party and government criticism and punishment of artists. He did not live to see that criticism rescinded, as Shostakovich did. Prokofiev died on March 5, 1953.

In the works of his last 8 to 10 years Prokofiev added at least two more lines of development to those he had specified earlier. One of these was the unabashed heroic element, first used to any great extent in the Fifth Symphony. This work, with its "heroism," indicated that he had noted the combinations so successful in Shostakovich's Seventh Symphony. The other line, perhaps involuntarily developed, was that of the ingenuous—the deliberately but sincerely naive. This involved light, vulnerable, singable tunes and harmonies and showed scant trace of the caustic, irreverent treatment he often reserved for such simplicity.

In his final years Prokofiev's performances were officially limited because of his clouded political situation and were generally confined to children's concerts and children's performing groups. His last works, including the Seventh Symphony and the ballet *Stone Flower,* reflected this. He even spoke of a refreshed awareness of his own childhood. Since his death his more mature works, and especially those of his foreign period, have had increasing influence on younger composers.

Further Reading

The primary source on Prokofiev available in English is the *Autobiography, Articles, and Reminiscences* (trans. 1958), published by the Foreign Languages Publishing House. The autobiographical part was written in the late 1930s and early 1940s. The official biography is that of Israel Nestyev, published in English translation by Florence Jonas in 1960. This is an enlargement of an earlier book, and a comparison of the two is politically interesting. There are a number of biographies by Westerners, although the late ones in English— Lawrence and Elizabeth Hanson (1964), and Victor Seroff (1968)—are popular rather than accurate items. Malcolm Brown, *Symphonies of Prokofiev* (in press), should prove authoritative. No book on contemporary music is without its chapter on Prokofiev. A generous treatment is afforded in William Austin, *Music in the Twentieth Century* (1966); and a chapter with recent information appears in Stanley D. Krebs, *Soviet Composers and the Development of Soviet Music* (1970).

Additional Sources

Gutman, David, *Prokofiev,* London; New York: Omnibus Press, 1990.

Prokofiev, Sergey, *Prokofiev by Prokofiev: a composer's memoir,* Garden City, N.Y.: Doubleday, 1979.

Prokofiev, Sergey, *Soviet diary, 1927, and other writings,* Boston: Northeastern University Press, 1992.

Robinson, Harlow, *Sergei Prokofiev: a biography,* New York: Paragon House, 1988, 1987.

Sergei Prokofiev: materials, articles, interviews, Moscow: Progress Publishers, 1978.

Seroff, Victor Ilyitch, *Sergei Prokofiev: a Soviet tragedy: the case of Sergei Prokofiev, his life & work, his critics, and his executioners,* New York: Taplinger Pub. Co., 1979, 1969. □

Gabriel Prosser

Gabriel Prosser (ca. 1775-1800) was the African American slave leader of an unsuccessful revolt in Richmond, Va., during the summer of 1800.

Gabriel Prosser, the slave of Thomas H. Prosser, was about 25 years old when he came to the attention of Virginia authorities late in August 1800. Little is known of his childhood or family background. He had two brothers and a wife, Nanny, all slaves of Prosser. Gabriel Prosser learned to read and was a serious student of the Bible, where he found inspiration in the accounts of Israel's delivery from slavery. Prosser possessed shrewd judgment, and his master gave him much latitude. He was acknowledged as a leader by many slaves around Richmond.

With the help of other slaves, especially Jack Bowler and George Smith, Prosser designed a scheme for a slave revolt. They planned to seize control of Richmond by slaying all whites (except for Methodists, Quakers, and Frenchmen) and then to establish a kingdom of Virginia with Prosser as king. The recent, successful American Revolution and the revolutions in France and Haiti—with their rhetoric of freedom, equality, and brotherhood—supplied examples and inspiration for Prosser's rebellion. In the months preceding the attack Prosser skillfully recruited supporters and organized them into military units. Authorities never discovered how many slaves were involved, but there were undoubtedly several thousand, many armed with swords and pikes made from farm tools by slave blacksmiths.

The plan was to strike on the night of Aug. 30, 1800. Men inside Richmond were to set fire to certain buildings to distract whites, and Prosser's force from the country was to seize the armory and government buildings across town. With the firearms thus gained, the rebels would supposedly easily overcome the surprised whites.

On the day of the attack the plot was disclosed by two slaves who did not want their masters slain; then Virginia governor James Monroe alerted the militia. That night, as the rebels began congregating outside Richmond, the worst rainstorm in memory flooded roads, washed out bridges, and prevented Prosser's army from assembling. Prosser decided to postpone the attack until the next day, but by then the city was too well defended. The rebels, including Prosser, dispersed.

Some slaves, in order to save their own lives, testified against the ringleaders, about 35 of whom were executed. Prosser himself managed to escape by hiding aboard a riverboat on its way to Norfolk. In Norfolk, however, he was betrayed by other slaves, who claimed the large reward for his capture on September 25. Returned to Richmond, Prosser, like most of the other leaders, refused to confess to the plot or give evidence against other slaves. He was tried and found guilty on Oct. 6, 1800, and executed the next day.

Further Reading

There is no full-length biography of Gabriel. There are short biographical accounts in Herbert Aptheker, *Essays in the History of the American Negro* (1945) and in Wilhelmena S. Robinson, *Historical Negro Biographies* (1968). The best account of his rebellion is in Joseph C. Carroll, *Slave Insurrections in the United States, 1800-1865* (1938). Additional information is contained in Herbert Aptheker, *American Negro Slave Revolts* (1943; new ed. 1969), and in Robert McColley, *Slavery and Jeffersonian Virginia* (1964). Arna Bontemps, *Black Thunder* (1936), is a fictionalized treatment of Gabriel and his conspiracy. ☐

Protagoras

The Greek philosopher Protagoras (ca. 484-ca. 414 B.C.) was one of the best-known and most successful teachers of the Sophistic movement of the 5th century B.C.

Protagoras was born in Abdera, the native city of Democritus, and spent much of his life as an itinerant Sophist, traveling throughout the Greek world. He was a frequent visitor to Athens, being a friend of Pericles, and was said to have aided in framing the constitution for the colony of Thurii, which the Athenians established in southern Italy in 444/443 B.C. Plato said that Protagoras spent 40 years teaching and that he died at the age of 70. Stories about an indictment against Protagoras by the Athenians, the burning of his books, and his death at sea are probably fictitious.

Sophist Philosophy

Protagoras earned his livelihood giving lectures and instruction to individuals and groups. The system he taught had little to do with philosophy or the pursuit of an absolute truth; instead it imparted to its adherents the necessary skills and knowledge for success in life, especially in politics. These skills consisted mainly of rhetoric and dialectic and could be used for whatever ends a person desired. It was for this reason, for teaching people "to make the weaker cause the stronger," that Protagoras came under attack, indirectly by Aristophanes in *The Clouds* and directly by Plato in several of his dialogues.

Protagoras wrote on a wide variety of subjects. Fragments of some of his works survive, and the titles of others are known through later comments on them. His famous dictum "man is the measure of all things" is the opening sentence of a work variously called *Truth or Refutatory Arguments.* He also wrote *On the Gods,* a fragment of which survives. In it he says that the obscurity of the subject and the shortness of human life prevent any definite conclusions. Other works include *The Great Argument, Contradictory Arguments, On Mathematics,* and *The Art of Eristics.* The list of titles preserved in the works of the Greek biographer Diogenes Laertius may represent sections of larger works, whereas such titles as *On Ambition, On Vir-*

tues, On Human Errors, and *Trial Concerning a Fee* almost certainly represent discussions of the common themes of Sophistic speeches. The chronology of these works is unknown.

Protagoras was a perfect example of the 5th-century Sophist. Careful thinkers could, of course, easily undermine the basis of his relative theory of knowledge; but the attractiveness of his theory and the pervasive influence of his teachings were so great that no less an opponent than Plato went to great lengths to expose the fallacies and potential evil of what he represented.

Further Reading

The surviving fragments of Protagoras's works are collected in H. Diels and W. Kranz, Die *Fragmente der Vorsokratiker,* translated in Kathleen Freeman, *Ancilla to the Pre-Socratic Philosophers* (1948), and discussed in her *The Pre-Socratic Philosophers* (1946; 3d ed. 1953). An excellent discussion of the Sophists and their contributions to Greek culture is in Werner Jaeger, *Paideia: The Ideals of Greek Culture,* translated by Gilbert Highet, vol. 1 (1939; 2d ed. 1945). A brief but useful account of Protagoras's importance can be found in Albin Lesky, *A History of Greek Literature* (1966). ☐

Pierre Joseph Proudhon

The political philosopher and journalist Pierre Joseph Proudhon (1809-1864) was the greatest of the French anarchists. His insistence that a new society should be created by moral methods led to his disavowal of revolutionary violence.

Pierre Joseph Proudhon was born of a poor family in Besançon. His poverty, which persisted throughout most of his life, in no small measure explains his hatred of the existing economic order. At 19 he was apprenticed to a printer and a few years later supervised the printing of Charles Fourier's classic *Le Nouveau monde industriel et sociétaire,* which made a great impression on him. Lacking formal education, he taught himself Latin, Greek, and Hebrew, and, despite his loss of faith in religion, theology.

In 1838 Proudhon won a pension enabling him to devote himself to scholarship in Paris, and he began his prolific writing career. *Qu'est-ce que la propriété?* (What Is Property?), completed in 1840, won him notoriety because of his claim that owning property was theft. In fact, he was referring only to unjustly acquired property, rejecting communism because of its denial of human independence. He envisaged an anarchist society of largely agrarian small producers, bound together by free contracts.

A new element, however, was added to Proudhon's thought by his move to Lyons. He remained there for several years, learning about industry and becoming involved with the Mutualists, an illegal workers' association. In this kind of workers' association, properly organized for cooperative production and exchange of goods, he began to see, still

somewhat vaguely, the force for radical societal change. He insisted in *De la création de l'ordre dans l'humanité* (1843) that economic forces were the chief motivating factors of society.

In the years before the Revolution of 1848 Proudhon made the acquaintance of the leading European leftists, including Karl Marx, but refused the latter's invitation to participate in founding an international organization because he sensed Marx's intellectual authoritarianism. He also completed one of his most interesting works, *Système des contradictions économiques* (1846), in which he claimed that contradiction and conflict were the basic characteristics of society and economics. These contradictions could never be overcome, but the different forces could be balanced, as socialism, in fact, was attempting to do, so that struggle would become constructive rather than destructive. The book placed him among the leading thinkers of French socialism, important enough to merit Marx's book *The Poverty of Philosophy,* which was directed against Proudhon's ideas.

During the Revolution of 1848, Proudhon accepted the editorship of the daily *Le Représentant du Peuple,* which became one of the most popular and controversial newspapers among workers in Paris because it criticized all parties, including the new republican government. The newspaper was suppressed, but Proudhon founded a new one which became even more popular. Finally, after a series of bitter attacks against the newly elected president, Louis Napoleon, he was sent to prison, where he spent the better part of the next 3 years.

There Proudhon continued editing his newspaper and producing books. His thoughts entered a more positive stage, and he began to give a more concrete and instructive exposition of his political ideas. In *L'Idée générale de la révolution au XIX siècle* (1851) he wrote that revolution could be brought about by workers' associations which denied the rule of governments and of capitalists and which would eventually take over industry. The new society would be regulated by contracts, and mutual undertakings would be facilitated by easy credit, available on the basis of productivity. This would effectively disperse concentrated economic power and preserve economic opportunities for the petty bourgeoisie. In *La Philosophie du progrès* (1853) he rejected all order and formula in favor of progress and continual movement.

In 1857 Proudhon completed *De la justice dans la révolution et dans l'église,* in which he attacked the Catholic Church for hindering man's freedom and for perpetuating a corrupt moral order. Prosecuted for "outraging public and religious morals," he was again condemned to prison. He fled to Belgium, where he wrote *La Guerre et la paix* (1861), in which he characterized war as a consequence of capitalism. He felt that by renewing economic equilibrium there would no longer be a necessity for war and that conflict and aggression would be transformed into constructive forces. He resolved the problem of the conflict between state and individual through his concept of federalism. The basic elements of his federalism were local units of administration, small enough to be under the direct control of the people. Larger confederal groupings would act primarily as organs of coordination among local units. Ultimately, Proudhon believed that Europe would be transformed into a federation of federations.

In the last years of his life, Proudhon continued to fight the Bonapartist regime in France. He also risked unpopularity by opposing Polish and Italian nationalism because of their concern for a national central state. Nevertheless, he wielded immense influence among French workers, urging them to separate themselves from other classes and from political parties claiming to represent them. His ideas were assimilated into the French workers' movement, and the French section of the First International followed Proudhon's program in almost every detail.

Further Reading

Many of Proudhon's works are available in English translation. By far the best introduction to Proudhon is George Woodcock's excellent study, *Pierre-Joseph Proudhon: A Biography* (1956). S. Y. Lu, *The Political Theories of P. J. Proudhon* (1922), and Henri de Lubac, *The Un-Marxian Socialist* (1948), are somewhat dated treatments of specific aspects of Proudhon's thought. See also Denis William Brogan, *Proudhon* (1934). The essays on Proudhon in Roger Soltau, *French Political Thought in the 19th Century* (1931), and in G. D. H. Cole, *A History of Socialist Thought* (5 vols. in 7, 1953-1960), provide adequate introductions.

Additional Sources

Ehrenberg, John, *Proudhon and his age,* Atlantic Highlands, N.J.: Humanities Press, 1996.

Hyams, Edward, *Pierre-Joseph Proudhon: his revolutionary life, mind and works,* London: J. Murray, 1979.

Lubac, Henri de, *The un-Marxian socialist: a study of Proudhon,* New York: Octagon Books, 1978.

Rota Ghibaudi, Silvia, *Pierre-Joseph Proudhon,* Milano, Italy: F. Angeli, 1986. □

E. Annie Proulx

E. Annie Proulx (born 1935) won the 1993 PEN/ Faulkner Award for her novel *Postcards* and a Pulitzer Prize in 1994 for her next novel, *The Shipping News.*

While she was certainly not an overnight sensation, having written stories from the age of ten and published short fiction since her early 20s, E. Annie Proulx did present her own remarkable success story, one characterized by hard work and a fierce independence. The measure of her success was impressive; with her first attempt at long-form fiction, Proulx won the respected PEN/Faulkner Award and the accolades of critics and fellow authors. David Bradley, writing for the *New York Times,* dubbed *Postcards* an example of "The Great American Novel." This acclaim snowballed with the publication of *The Shipping News,* which garnered three major prizes for Proulx and brought comparisons to legendary authors William Faulkner, Theodore Dreiser, and Herman Melville. There was an overwhelmingly positive response to what Sara Rimer, writing for the *New York Times,* characterized as Proulx's "offbeat, darkly comic voice and vivid sense of place."

From Free-lance Journalist to Novelist

Proulx was transformed into a novelist after 19 years of work as a free-lance journalist. She wrote articles for magazines on a myriad of topics, of which she offered these examples to *Contemporary Authors:* "weather, apples, canoeing, mountain lions, mice, cuisine, libraries, African beadwork, cider and lettuces." Her work appeared in publications such as *Country Journal, Organic Gardening,* and *Yankee.* In the early 1980s Proulx produced a shelf full of on-assignment "how-to" books on food, gardening, and carpentering, including *Sweet & Hard Cider: Making It, Using It, and Enjoying It, The Fine Art of Salad Gardening,* and *Plan and Make Your Own Fences and Gates, Walkways, Walls and Drives.* Another journalistic venture cast Proulx as the founder and editor of a rural newspaper, the *Vershire Behind the Times,* from 1984 to 1986. The financial rewards for such work were meager; devoting time to writing short stories was a luxury—Proulx averaged two a year, nearly all of which were published.

In tiny backwoods towns in Vermont, Proulx indulged her passion for fishing, hunting, and canoeing and lived the self-made, from-scratch lifestyle suggested by her free-lance assignments. She told *Washington Post* writer David Streitfeld of her love for places "where things are still done

with a sort of awkward and almost tiresome physical input that's always so very satisfying. I can do these little chores—getting in my wood or planting in the garden—and feel quite enriched." Proulx also relishes the smallest details in her environment; she told *Time*'s John Skow of her interest in "everything . . . from tree branches and wild mushrooms to animal tracks. . . . It's excellent training for the eye. Most of us stagger around deaf and blind." This focus is something instilled in Proulx by her mother, a painter and amateur naturalist. As a child she was taught to observe the activities of ants, whom her mother would give voices, and to notice every particular, the texture of fabrics and the distinctive characteristics in a face.

An early chapter in Proulx's life could have led to a very different existence for the author. After receiving her B.A. and M.A. in history, Proulx completed doctoral orals in Renaissance economic history, the Canadian North, and China; but in 1975 she abandoned academia for fear of not finding a teaching job. As she told *Contemporary Authors,* this was jumping "from the frying pan into the fire," and left her in "brutally poor circumstances. Compensations were silence and decent fishing, both vanished now." Generally reticent about her private life, Proulx admits that she was, well, "wild" during those years. She told David Streitfeld, "I liked the rough side of things, always." The end of her academic career coincided with the end of her third marriage; as a result, Proulx raised her three sons as a single parent.

Publishes First Book

In 1983 Proulx's career as a fiction writer was boosted by a notice in *Best American Short Stories,* an honor that was repeated in 1987. Proulx published her first book, *Heart Songs and Other Stories,* in 1988. This collection introduced the reading public to Annie Proulx's gritty themes and deft, if unconventional, use of language. Against the starkly beautiful backdrop of the New England countryside and in the guise of hunting and fishing stories, Proulx depicts the struggles of men trying to cope with their emotionally and morally tangled lives. Proulx illustrates the stories with vivid verbal pictures, such as a man who eats a fish "as he would a slice of watermelon" or a woman who is as "thin as a folded dollar bill, her hand as narrow and cold as a trout."

With the addition of two new stories, a 1995 edition of *Heart Songs* was released under the same title. Kimberly G. Allen, writing for the *Library Journal,* suggested that perhaps the subject matter would not interest every reader, but concluded that "the stories flow effortlessly and the prose is elegant." In the *New York Times,* Kenneth Rosen noted that the stories are "most compelling when they're rooted in a coarse rural sexuality. At these times, their sometimes enigmatic, often lyrical images seem to complement New England's lavish but barren beauty."

When Scribner's editor Tom Jenks drew up Proulx's contract for *Heart Songs* he suggested that they include a novel in the agreement. Positive critical response to the short stories prompted her next editor, John Glusman, to reiterate the idea that she should try her hand at a novel. The resulting work, *Postcards,* proved to be a liberating experience for Proulx, who had never before considered undertaking such a task. With characteristic fervor she plunged into the assignment; it took her half an hour to form the plan for her first novel. She told the *New York Times,* "It was astonishing how easy writing a novel was compared to writing a short story. . . . I had room to expand. It was like getting into a warm bathtub. I haven't been able to write a short story since."

In many ways, *Postcards* resembles the stories found in *Heart Songs* given a larger scope. The main character is again an emotionally tortured man from New England, but Loyal Blood is cast out into a new world when he flees the family farm after accidentally killing his fiancee. Proulx plotted Blood's cross-country wanderings with her own trip across America doing research. David Bradley of the *New York Times* described the resulting book as "episodic and picaresque, a '*Huckleberry Finn*' without the laughter, '*The Grapes of Wrath,*' without the hope." Postcards Postcards is as much a novel about the land, however, as it is about a man. From a description of the Vermont farm, likening it to the opened pages of a Bible, to a Florida sky marked by "a fan of clouds like crimson knife blades," Proulx luxuriates in her freedom to sharply define the various settings in the sweeping tale.

"It was astonishing how easy writing a novel was compared to writing a short story. . . . It was like getting into a warm bathtub. I haven't been able to write a short story since."

Won Several Awards for Fiction

Postcards was undoubtedly a professional and personal success; it proved Proulx's skill and comfort working in the new form. The most tangible evidence of her achievement was receiving the 1993 PEN/Faulkner Award for fiction and its $15,000 bonus. Proulx also enjoyed the distinction of being the first woman to be so honored; the resulting *New York Times* headline read: "Shutout Ends: It's Men 12, Women 1." The accompanying article noted: "Ms. Proulx's novel was widely praised by critics for the vastness of its physical landscape and the intimacy of its language."

The very next year, Proulx capped this success by writing *The Shipping News.* This novel is a dark but comic tale set in Newfoundland, the story of a luckless newspaper reporter named Quoyle. It is packed with details of the island's landscape, weather, food, and language, all drawn in a choppy yet vibrant style. An oft-quoted passage describing the protagonist illustrates this method: "A great damp loaf of a body. At six he weighed eighty pounds. At sixteen he was buried under a casement of flesh. Head shaped like a crenshaw, no neck, reddish hair ruched back. Features as bunched as kissed fingertips." The book resulted in a steady stream of awards: first, the Heartland Prize from the *Chicago Tribune,* followed by the Irish Times International Award and the National Book Award. These honors were all topped by the 1994 Pulitzer Prize for Fiction.

In the media, the response was almost unanimously positive, even doting. An exception was a review by Verlyn Klinkenborg. Writing for the *New Republic,* she viewed these awards with a cynical eye: "*The Shipping News* is an out-and-out crowd-pleaser, a book that will certainly not diminish the commercial value of the National Book Award even as that award (and the Pulitzer Prize) increases this book's sales." Klinkenborg suspected that under the "powerfully descriptive" writing there was a dramatic and emotional vacuum. More often, however, the novel was heaped with praise; in the *Yale Review,* Walter Kendrick remarked, "*The Shipping News* reverberates with voices, each possessing a distinctive twang that Proulx exuberantly sings along with. . . . She loves dense, chewy presumably local words: stribbled, streeling, skreel, marl, scrawn, thunge, drenty, glutch. . . . People, landscape, and language fit together like rocks in an unhewn wall, forming a marvelous composite portrait of North America's last margin." In *New Statesman & Society* Roz Kaveney noted how, with the book's improbable twists of plot, "Proulx's triumph is that she makes us swallow all of this. Her work not only describes, but is imbued with, a chancy decency that looks us forthright in the eye and challenges disbelief. This is an artful novel."

The Shipping News was the result of a canoeing trip to Newfoundland, followed by careful research. After falling in love with the place, the author took at least seven trips to the island, talking to residents and absorbing the atmosphere. She pulled her characters' names from telephone directories and words from the *Dictionary of Newfoundland English.* Here the journalist and historian in Proulx surfaced, both in her interest in seemingly arcane details, and in her passion for "getting it right." She told *Time*'s John Skow, "I believe if you get the landscape right . . . the characters will step out of it, and they'll be in the right place. The story will come from the landscape."

Write about What You Don't Know

With this approach to writing fiction, Proulx breaks with the standard advice to "write what you know." Skow explained, "She says that the autobiographical content of her fiction is 'zero' and urges young novelists to ignore the customary preachment," and instead, "she says 'Write about what you'd like to know.'" In an interview for the *Rhode Islander Magazine,* Proulx elaborated, "I don't much like the kind of book that is nothing but interior self-examination. I think part of the fault lies with the bad advice writers have been getting for years. . . . Sometimes what you know is pretty boring."

In researching her next novel, Proulx became an expert on accordion music. She studied not how to play the instrument, but how to take one apart and then reconstruct it. Various magazine articles reveal that *Accordion Crimes* is about the music of immigrants and specifically about different kinds of accordion music. The author described the work in the *Rhode Islander* as "stories of immigrant lives and music on both borders—la frontera and la frontière." In this there is a hint of autobiographical interest: Proulx's father's family came to the United States from Quebec.

Reluctant Celebrity

In the wake of her fame, Proulx was hard-pressed to find the time she needed to research and write. In 1994 she managed to publish short stories in *Atlantic Monthly* and *Esquire.* On top of her schedule of book signings and readings, she was inundated with requests for interviews, many of which took place in her remote Vermont home. The resulting articles are sprinkled with her comment that the house is for sale. Proulx soon bought a second place in Newfoundland, and by the spring of 1995 had moved to Wyoming. After a visit to Arizona State University that April, the *Arizona Republic* sported the headline: "Pulitzer-winning author shuns spotlight to write" and found Proulx "prickly and bored, a master of the withering look and stony reply." The *Phoenix Gazette* offered: "Proulx . . . is not a people person. A reluctant celebrity after the publication of her second novel, she has developed a heat shield against the scorching intrusions into her private life that come with fame."

The media also revealed that Hollywood has been courting Proulx with offers to turn *The Shipping News* into a movie. The author dismissed this topic, as she has the filmmakers' offers; what interested her most was completing *Accordion Crimes,* which was released in 1996, and pressing on with other writing projects. Almost a year earlier, Proulx had told Sara Rimer of the *New York Times,* "I have at the moment three novels sitting in my head, waiting to get on paper, and I know exactly how each one is going to go." She was faced with the "Catch-22" of her celebrity status: having the financial security to become a full-time fiction writer, and yet being overwhelmed by the so-called duties of celebrity. If the past is any indication, however, the author's demand for privacy and independence will prevail and the reading public can look forward to many more novels from E. Annie Proulx.

Further Reading

Contemporary Authors, Volume 145, Gale, 1995.
Contemporary Literary Criticism, Volume 81: Yearbook 1993, Gale, 1994.
New York Times, April 21, 1993; June 23, 1994. □

Marcel Proust

The French novelist Marcel Proust (1871-1922) ranks as one of the greatest literary figures of the 20th century. He abandoned plot and traditional dramatic action for the vision of the first-person narrator confronting his world.

Marcel Proust was born to wealthy bourgeois parents on July 10, 1871, in Auteuil, a suburb of Paris. The first son of Dr. Adrien Proust and Jeanne Weil, the daughter of a wealthy Jewish financier, he was hypersensitive, nervous, and frail. When he was 9 years old, his first attack of asthma, a disease that greatly influenced his life, nearly suffocated him. In 1882 Proust enrolled in the Lycée Condorcet. Only during his last 2 years of study there did he distinguish himself as a student, attracting the interest of his philosophy professor, Marie-Alphonse Daru. After a year of military service, Proust studied law and then philosophy.

In the meantime, Proust was creating a name for himself in high society as a brilliant conversationalist with an ear for speech patterns that enabled him to mimic others with devastating ease and accuracy. His verve, dark features, pale complexion, and elegant taste fascinated the hosts of the smart Parisian set that he eagerly courted. Although he soon earned the reputation of a snob and social climber, Proust's intimate friends saw him as generous, extremely intelligent, capable of serious thinking, and as an excellent intellectual companion. But he irritated through his eagerness to please, his intensity of emotion, and his indecisiveness. Proust was not indecisive, however, about his commitment to writing.

Early Works

In 1892 and 1893 Proust contributed a number of critical notes and sketches and two short stories to the ephemeral journal *Le Banquet* and to *La Revue blanche.* He published his first work in 1896, a collection of short stories, short verse portraits of artists and musicians, and incidental pieces written during the preceding 6 years. *Les Plaisirs et les jours* (*Pleasures and Days*) received cursory notice in the press despite its preface by Anatole France. The book did little to dispel the prevalent notion of Proust as an effete dandy. His interest in analysis of rare and exquisite feelings, his preoccupation with high society, and his refined style

were all too familiar to allow his readers to see a talented and serious writer groping for eternal truths and a personal style.

In 1895, even before he published *Les Plaisirs et les jours,* Proust had made a first attempt at a major work. Unable to handle his material satisfactorily, unsure of himself, and unclear about the manner of achieving the goals he had set, Proust abandoned the work in 1899. It appeared, under the title of *Jean Santeuil,* only in 1952; from thousands of notebook pages, Bernard de Fallois had culled and organized the novel according to a sketchy plan he found among them. As a consequence the novel is uneven; many passages announce, duplicate, or are variations of passages in Proust's masterpiece, and others are incoherent or apparently irrelevant. Some, however, are beautifully lyric or analytic. *Jean Santeuil* is Proust's first attempt to come to grips with material that later yielded so much in *À la recherche du temps perdu. Jean Santeuil* is the biography of an imaginary character who struggles with himself, his family, and his environment in order to discover, justify, and affirm his artistic vocation. Through episodes and sketches Proust traced Jean Santeuil's progress toward maturity, touching upon many of the themes he later developed more fully: the impact of nature upon the sensibility; the silent work of the imagination in involuntary memory; memory bridging gaps in time; the effects of events such as the Alfred Dreyfus case upon society; the snobbery of social intercourse; the self-oriented nature of love; and the liberating power of art.

After abandoning *Jean Santeuil,* Proust returned to his studies. Although he read widely in other literatures, he was limited to translations. During 1899 he became interested in the works of John Ruskin, and after Ruskin's death (Jan. 20, 1900), Proust published an obituary of the English critic in *La Chronique des arts et de la curiosité* (Jan. 27, 1900) that established him as a Ruskin scholar. Proust's *Pélerinages ruskiniens en France* appeared in *Le Figaro* in February and was followed by several more articles on Ruskin in *Le Mercure de France* and in *La Gazette des beaux-arts.* With the help of an English-speaking friend, Marie Nordlinger, and his mother, Proust translated Ruskin's *The Bible of Amiens* (1904) and *Sesame and Lilies* (1906). Grappling with Ruskin's ideas on art and its relationship to ethics helped him clarify his own esthetic ideas and move beyond the impasse of *Jean Santeuil.*

In 1903 Proust's father died. His own health, deteriorating since 1899, suffered an even greater shock following the death of his mother in September 1905. These setbacks forced Proust into the sanatorium of Dr. Paul Sollier (in December 1905), where he entertained hopes of curing his asthma. Undoubtedly preferring his illness to any cure, Proust left, "fantastically ill," in less than 2 months. After more than 2 years of seclusion, he emerged once again into society and into print with a series of articles and pastiches published in *Le Figaro* during 1907 and 1908. From 1905 to 1908 Proust had been mysteriously working on a novel; he abandoned it, too, in favor of a new one he had begun to plan when he realized the necessity of still another dress rehearsal. He wrote pastiches of Honoré de Balzac, Gustave Flaubert, Edmond de Goncourt, Charles Sainte-Beuve, and others (February-March 1908), and this activity led Proust inadvertently to problems of literary criticism and to a clearer formulation of a literary work as an art object. By November 1908 Proust was planning his *Contre Sainte-Beuve* (published in 1954; *On Art and Literature*), a rebuttal of Sainte-Beuve, the recognized master of historical literary criticism. The true writer expresses a self, Proust felt, that is completely hidden beneath the one manifested "in our habits, in society, in our vices. If we want to try to understand that self, it is only by trying to re-create it deep in ourselves, that we can succeed." By reacting to Sainte-Beuve, Proust formulated, in terms applicable to the artist as well as to the reader, the notion that lies at the heart of *À la recherche du temps perdu,* Proust finished *Contre Sainte-Beuve* during the summer of 1909 and began almost immediately to compose his great novel.

Remembrance of Things Past

Although Proust had, by 1909, accumulated and reworked most of the material that was to become *À la recherche du temps perdu* (*Remembrance of Things Past*), he still had not fully grasped the focal point that would enable him to structure and to orchestrate his vast material. In January 1909 he had a series of experiences that bore belated fruit during the early summer of that year. The sudden conjunction of flavors in a cup of tea and toast evoked in him sensations that recalled his youth in his grandfather's garden at Auteuil. Although he had had similar experiences in the past and had considered them important, he had not realized that not only were these experiences a key element in an artist's work but also they could serve as the organizing principle of his novel. They revealed the hidden self that Proust had spoken of in *Contre Sainte-Beuve,* a present self identical to the one in various moments of past time. This process of artistic resurrection and the gradual discovery of its effectiveness, he realized, was the focal point his novel required. *À la recherche du temps perdu,* like Balzac's *La Comédie humaine,* depicts the many facets of a whole society in a specific period of history. Political events, such as the Dreyfus case; social transformations, such as the rise of the bourgeoisie and the decline of the nobility; artistic events; evaluations in music, art, and literature; and different social milieus from the working class to bohemian circles—all found their place in Proust's panorama of French life during the decades around the turn of the century. But Proust was primarily concerned with portraying not reality but its perception by his narrator, Marcel, and its capacity to provoke and reveal Marcel's permanent self, normally hidden by habit and social intercourse. From the very first words of his predominantly first-person narrative, Marcel traces his evolution through a multiplicity of recalled experiences to the final realization that these experiences, processed and stored in his memory, reflect his inner life more truly than does his outer life, that their resuscitation in their immediacy destroys spans of elapsed time, that their telling answers his long search for an artistic vocation, and that they form, in fact, the substance of his novel. A key event in the resolution of the novel is the narrator's discovery of the powers of involuntary memory.

Proust began his novel in July 1909, and he worked furiously on it until death interrupted his corrections, revisions, and additions. In 1913, after several rejections, he found in Grasset a publisher who would produce, at the author's expense, the first of three projected volumes (*Du Côté de chez Swann, Le Côté de Guermantes,* and *Le Temps retrouvé; Swann's Way, The Guermantes Way,* and *Time Regained*). After the appearance of the first volume, André Gide, who had earlier rejected Proust's manuscript on behalf of Gallimard, changed his mind and in 1916 obtained the rights to publish the subsequent volumes. Meanwhile, World War I interrupted publication but not Proust's continued expansion of his work. *À l'ombre des jeunes filles en fleur* (*Within a Budding Grove*), originally only a chapter title, appeared late in 1918 as the second volume and won the Goncourt Prize the following year. As volumes appeared, Proust continually expanded his material, inserting long sections as close to publication as the galley stage. *Le Côté de Guermantes* appeared in 1920; *Sodome et Gomorrhe* (*Cities of the Plain*), Part 1, appeared in 1921 and the two volumes of Part 2 in 1922. Feeling his end approaching, Proust finished drafting his novel and began revising and correcting proofs, expanding the text as he went along with what he called "supernourishment." Proust had completed revisions of *La Prisonnière* (*The Captive*) and had begun reworking *Albertine disparue* (*The Sweet Cheat Gone*) when, on Nov. 18, 1922, he died of bronchitis and pneumonia contracted after a series of violent asthma attacks. The final volumes of his novel appeared owing to the interest of his brother, Robert, and to the editorial supervision of Jacques Rivière: *La Prisonnière,* two volumes, 1923; *Albertine disparue,* two volumes, 1925; and *Le Temps retrouvé,* two volumes, 1927.

Further Reading

The major critical biography of Proust is George D. Painter, *Proust* (2 vols., 1959-1965). There are numerous critical studies of Proust's work in English. The most useful general introduction is Germaine Brée, *The World of Marcel Proust* (1966), which contains an extensive annotated bibliography. Other valuable studies are J. M. Cocking, *Proust* (1956); William S. Bell, *Proust's Nocturnal Muse* (1962); and Roger Shattuck, *Proust's Binoculars: A Study of Memory, Time and Recognition in "A la recherche du temps perdu"* (1963). See also the chapters on Proust in Edmund Wilson, *Axel's Castle: A Study in Imaginative Literature of 1870-1930* (1931), and Harry Levin, *The Gates of Horn: A Study of Five French Realists* (1963). For general and historical background see Alfred Cobban, *A History of Modern France* (2 vols., 1957-1961; 3d ed., 3 vols., 1966-1967), and Barbara W. Tuchman, *The Proud Tower: A Portrait of the World before the War, 1890-1914* (1966). □

William Proxmire

William Proxmire (born 1915) was a Democratic senator for Wisconsin for three decades. He was committed to careful government spending, budgetary restraint, and consumer protection.

William Proxmire was born on November 11, 1915, in Lake Forest, Illinois, a wealthy suburb of Chicago. His father was a surgeon and served as chief of staff of Lake Forest Hospital. William spent his high school years in Pottstown, Pennsylvania, at the Hill Preparatory School where he was at the head of his class academically and considered to be the "biggest grind" by his fellow students. His success there paved the way for his undergraduate years at Yale University, where, in addition to graduating with a B.A. in English in 1938, he boxed and played football.

Proxmire went on to Harvard Business School where he took his M.B.A. in 1940. Afterwards, he joined the investment firm of J. P. Morgan & Co. but left six months later to join the U.S. Army. He served in the intelligence branch of the army until the end of the war. By 1948 he had received a M.P.A. from Harvard's Graduate School of Public Administration. It was during this second tour at Harvard that Proxmire became a Democrat, much to his father's chagrin.

Although he taught for a time at Harvard and worked again for J. P. Morgan & Co. in New York, Proxmire was eager to begin a career in politics. He chose to settle in Wisconsin, taking a job as a political and labor reporter on a newspaper in the state's capital, Madison. Less than a year later Proxmire announced his candidacy for the Wisconsin State Assembly, and he won his first election that November. To win, he established a political strategy which he followed ever after: a low budget, press-the-flesh campaign

involving long hours and as much personal contact with voters as possible. As an assemblyman Proxmire started what became a life-long interest in careful spending, budgetary restraint, and consumer protection. Deciding against reelection in 1952, Proxmire ran for governor three successive times—in 1952, 1954, and 1956. He lost all three times, and it looked as if his political career had come to an end.

The death of Senator Joseph R. McCarthy in 1957, however, brought Proxmire into the special election held to fill the seat for the balance of the late senator's term. Having won the Democratic primary, Proxmire faced Walter Kohler, a man who had defeated him twice for the governorship. Although considered the underdog, Proxmire decisively defeated Kohler in the special election and then in 1958 won election to his first full term in the U.S. Senate. He served in that body for five terms, winning reelection in 1982 with 64 percent of the vote.

Proxmire's years as a senator were characterized by an independent, often idiosyncratic, stance. In his first term he quickly came up against the strong, well-organized Democratic leadership of Lyndon B. Johnson and Sam Rayburn. His attacks on these two congressional leaders as well as his opposition to major legislation proposed by President John F. Kennedy marked him early on as a legislator of independent mind. It was a role he continued to play, neither hesitating to vote against presidential appointments (in 1961 he opposed the nomination of John Connally as secretary of the navy and in 1981 he opposed the nomination of William French Smith as attorney-general) nor to stage fili-

busters in an attempt to block legislation (in 1961, a 19-hour filibuster; in 1981, a 16-hour one).

Proxmire was the ranking minority member of the Senate Appropriations Committee, and much of his influence stemmed from his concern for economy in government spending. He uncovered government waste and cost overruns in nearly all branches of government, as several of his books, including *Report from Wasteland: America's Military-Industrial Complex* (1970) and *Uncle Sam: The Last of the Bigtime Spenders* (1972), testify. To highlight government practices that were costing taxpayers millions of dollars, Proxmire established a monthly "Golden Fleece" award in 1975 for "the biggest or most ridiculous or most ironic example of government waste." The awards received a great deal of publicity, but critics thought they diverted attention from larger, more substantial issues.

The flip side of Proxmire's concern for how tax dollars were spent was his interest in consumer protection. As chairman and later ranking minority member of the Banking, Housing, and Urban Affairs Committee, Proxmire kept a close watch on the consumer credit industry and criticized the easy loan practices of the nation's banks. Proxmire sponsored the Consumer Credit Protection Act, which required lenders to inform borrowers of finance charges in writing, and the Fair Credit Reporting Act of 1970, which granted people the right to correct personal credit files maintained by credit agencies.

Proxmire's life revolved around the Senate. His energies were fully focused on business there and his colleagues attested to his grasp of the issues and the careful research he brought to his positions. He kept in close touch with his Wisconsin constituents and did not miss a rollcall between 1966 and 1985. He has been recognized as a master of campaigning and of free publicity, and, if not always the most liked, one of the most widely imitated members of the Senate. Asked to explain the intensity and energy with which he concentrated on his job, Proxmire once said, "Politics is my hobby. I eat, breathe, and sleep politics." Nevertheless, in 1987, citing his age, he announced that he would not seek reelection.

After retiring from the U.S. Senate in 1988, Proxmire continued to stir up publicity by writing a twice-weekly column for the United Feature Syndicate, focusing on national and international economic issues. At least once a month, Proxmire gives his "Golden Fleece Award" to the person or organization that is most wasteful of federal funds. Upon leaving the Senate and starting his column, Proxmire said "I started as a newspaper reporter, and after 31 years in the U.S. senate, I'm coming home to my first love at last. There's so much to complain about, apologize for, and brag about in this country. I can't wait to write about it."

Further Reading

William Proxmire has been the subject of a biography, *Proxmire* by Jay Sykes (1972), and of several magazine articles, including those in the *Atlantic* (December 1970) and the *New York Times Magazine* (April 1971 and May 1978). For more material see the yearly indexes of *Facts on File*. □

Pierre Paul Prud'hon

The work of the French painter Pierre Paul Prud'hon (1758-1823) stands between neoclassicism and romanticism. Best known for his allegorical paintings, he was also a successful portraitist.

Pierre Paul Prud'hon was born at Cluny on April 4, 1758. In 1774 he went to Dijon to study painting. He was so successful as a student that in 1780 a nobleman of the district made it possible for him to go to Paris to study at the Royal Academy. In 1784 Prud'hon won the Prix de Rome, an award given by the academy to allow promising artists to study in Italy. He was in Italy until 1788.

In 1791 Prud'hon began showing his paintings in the Paris exhibitions (Salons). During the Revolutionary turmoil of the early 1790s he retreated to Burgundy, but after 1796 he resided in Paris and by 1800 was moving in the highest circles surrounding Napoleon, the new ruler of France. Prud'hon was appointed drawing master to Empress Josephine, Napoleon's first wife, and to Empress Marie Louise, Napoleon's second wife. He also enjoyed substantial patronage from the Napoleonic government for the execution of various art projects.

During Prud'hon's career, painting in France was pervaded by a severe neoclassicism and ruled by Jacques Louis David, the painter who brought the neoclassic style to its culmination and who dominated the arts in France from about 1785 to 1815. Prud'hon was well aware of the prevailing style, and one of his best friends was Antonio Canova, the leading neoclassic sculptor of the period. However, French painting was turning away from the precise draftsmanship and sculptural solidity of neoclassicism even before 1815. Within this context of shifting styles and a transitional period, Prud'hon developed an individualistic style which stands apart from the classicism of his period; his work looks back to the soft, decorative painting of the rococo and also forward to the bravura and drama of 19th-century romanticism.

In the *Union of Love and Friendship,* an allegorical work of 1793, Prud'hon makes obvious reference to classical antiquity, but the delicacy with which the graceful nude forms are rendered, the decorative composition, and the soft atmospheric tonality are very different from David's hard classicism. By 1808, the date of *Divine Vengeance Pursuing Crime,* Prud'hon had moved decisively in the direction of early romanticism. This painting, with its swooping forms, its air of desperate drama, and its shadowy lighting, links him to the romantic style which was to replace neoclassicism about 1820 and reach its height of expression in the work of Eugène Delacroix. Prud'hon was a respected portraitist, and his most famous work in this area is *Portrait of the Empress Josephine* (1805), which shows the Empress reclining languidly in a romantic, leafy glade.

The fall of the Napoleonic regime in 1815 inevitably damaged Prud'hon's artistic career, and his later years were also marred by personal unhappiness. He died in Paris on Feb. 16, 1823.

Further Reading

There is no biography or monograph on Prud'hon in English, and reference to him must be sought in general works. Recommended surveys include Walter Friedlaender, *David to Delacroix* (trans. 1952); Fritz Novotny, *Painting and Sculpture in Europe, 1780-1880* (1960); and Jean Leymarie, *French Painting: The Nineteenth Century* (trans. 1962). An excellent analysis of the complex period in which Prud'hon began working is Robert Rosenblum, *Transformation in Late Eighteenth-Century Art* (1967). □

Nikolai Mikhailovich Przhevalsky

Nikolai Mikhailovich Przhevalsky (1839-1888) was a Russian general and traveler whose explorations were major contributions to the geography of central Asia.

Of Polish descent, Nikolai Przhevalsky was born on March 31, 1839, in Kimbory in the Smolensk district. His education was at the gymnasium in Smolensk. His military career started in 1855 with an appointment as a subaltern in an infantry regiment. In 1855 he was appointed as an officer, and in 1860 he entered the academy of the general staff. From 1864 to 1866 he taught geography at the military school in Warsaw. In 1867 he became a general officer and was assigned to Irkutsk near Lake Baikal.

Przhevalsky's first serious exploration was of the valley of the Ussuri River from its source at Lake Khanka in eastern Manchuria to its junction with the Amur River, with particular emphasis on the highlands of the Ussuri River and the foothills of the Sikhote Alin Range. The Vladivostok leg of the Trans-Siberian railway was laid out along this route.

Przhevalsky made five major expeditions. The first lasted from November 1870 to September 1873. With three men he set out from Kyakhta, south of Lake Baikal, traveled through Urga (Ulan Bator), crossed the Gobi Desert, and reached Kalgan, 100 miles northwest of Peking. On the return he explored the Ordos Plateau to the Ala Shan Range and Koko Nor and mapped parts of the upper Hwang Ho and the upper Yangtze. Finally he penetrated Tibet and reached the Drechu River.

The main objective of the second expedition (1877-1878) was to reach Lhasa through east Turkistan. Starting from Kuldja (44°N, 82°E), Przhevalsky went by way of the Tien Shan Range and Takla Makan Desert, traveling 200 miles along the foot of the Astin (Altyn) Tagh Range. He claimed to have rediscovered the great salt lake of the Chinese classical writers, Lop Nor, in the desert at 41°N, 91°E. This was one of the most interesting, yet controversial,

of all his discoveries. Von Richthofen disputed the claim on the grounds that the lake was of fresh, not salt, water and that it was too far south. Sven Hedin, in two visits to Lop Nor (1895, 1900), established that Przhevalsky's lake shifts west as a result of wind and sandstorms. Hedin also found a dried salt basin, presumably the old original Lop Nor, and a number of lakes of recent origin. Kozlov dated some of these from 1750, thus agreeing with Hedin.

The third expedition tried to reach Lhasa (1879-1880). Setting out from Lake Zaysan near the northern border of Sinkiang, Przhevalsky crossed the Dzungaria region to Hami (43°N, 93°E). Thence he went south over the Astin Tagh Range and penetrated the Tsaidam swamp and the great valley of the Kyaring Tso. Reaching Nagchu Dzong, 170 miles north of Lhasa, he was turned back by order of the Lama. He went northeast, reached the upper Hwang Ho, and crossed the Gobi Desert to Kyakhta (51°N, 47°E).

Przhevalsky's fourth journey was in the mountains between Mongolia and Tibet (1883-1885). Starting from Urga, he crossed the Gobi Desert to Koko Nor and the Tsaidam region and thence to the Astin Tagh and the Shan Kunlun. He revisited Lop Nor and confirmed his previous findings of 1878 on this interesting region. He returned to Siberia by crossing the Tien Shan to Issyk Kul, a lake on the west border of Sinkiang.

Przhevalsky's fifth and final expedition was toward Lhasa (1888), a goal he always held but never reached. On Nov. 1, 1888, Przhevalsky died at Karakol on Issyk Kul. As a monument, a large cross was set up, and as a memorial, the town of Karakol was renamed Przhevalsk.

This explorer's success depended upon small parties, moving fast. For the first expedition he chose three Cossacks. In the fourth expedition, they logged some 15,000 miles in 3 years, a tribute to their physical strength and resourcefulness in coping with severe environments, difficult terrain, and delicate relations with sometimes hostile natives.

Further Reading

Gerald Roe Crone, ed., *The Explorers: Great Adventurers Tell Their Own Stories of Discovery* (1962), has a short discussion of Przhevalsky and a selection of his writings. His career is briefly recounted in Percy Sykes, *A History of Exploration: From the Earliest Times to the Present Day* (1934; 3d ed. 1949), and Joachim G. Leithaüser, *Worlds beyond the Horizon* (trans. 1955).

Additional Sources

Rayfield, Donald, *The dream of Lhasa: the life of Nikolay Przhevalsky (1839-88) explorer of Central Asia,* Athens: Ohio University Press, 1976. □

Ptolemy I

Ptolemy I Soter (367/366-283 B.C.) was a Macedonian general under Alexander the Great, founder of

the Ptolemaic dynasty of Egypt, and biographer of Alexander.

Born in the upper Macedonian region of Eordaia to the Macedonian nobleman Lagos and Arsinoë, Ptolemy grew up in the royal court at Pella. In 343 B.C. he joined Alexander at Mieza and there studied for 3 years with Aristotle.

Ptolemy returned to Pella with Alexander by 340 B.C. and supported his younger friend's quarrel with his father, Philip, in 337 B.C. Alexander left Macedonia with his mother Olympias, Ptolemy, and his close friends for Epirus and Illyria but soon returned to Macedonia. Alexander remained estranged from Philip, who banished Ptolemy from the court because he considered him a dangerous adviser to his son.

Alexander's Adviser and General

In 336 B.C. when Philip was assassinated by a conspiracy of nobles, Ptolemy returned to the court and supported Alexander's claim to the feudal throne. Alexander, in turn, appointed him Companion, Life-guard, and Seneschal. Ptolemy accompanied Alexander on his campaigns to the Danube in 336 B.C. and to crush the Corinthian League's rebellion and to destroy perfidious Thebes in 335 B.C.

Ptolemy encouraged and aided Alexander's invasion of Asia Minor to liberate the eastern Greeks from the Persian Empire of Darius III and to invade Syria and conquer Persia.

Ptolemy fought at Issos in 333 B.C. and, riding beside Alexander, pursued Darius into the hills; he accompanied Alexander through Phoenicia and in the siege of Tyre in 332 B.C. and marched through Jerusalem to Egypt.

In Egypt, Ptolemy aided Alexander's peaceful conquest of the country and the founding of Alexandria in the western delta, and probably accompanied his king to the temple of Zeus Ammon in Siwa. Ptolemy quickly realized the immense value of Egypt, its structure as a geographical entity, and he developed keen interests in the region.

From Egypt, Ptolemy accompanied Alexander to northern Mesopotamia and the third and final major conflict with Darius's armies, at Gaugamela in 331 B.C. During the next 6 years Ptolemy campaigned with Alexander through western India and along the Indus Valley. Ptolemy recognized Alexander's claim to the Persian throne and tiara without hesitation and revealed to Alexander the instigation of Callisthenes in the conspiracy of the royal pages to assassinate him. In India, Ptolemy fought beside Alexander and in one melée saved his king's life.

At Susa in 324 B.C., when Alexander bade his Companions marry Persians, Ptolemy dutifully married Artacama, the daughter of the Persian nobleman Artabazos. But after Alexander's death Ptolemy quickly divorced her.

Ruler of Egypt

With Alexander's death in Babylon on June 13, 323 B.C., Ptolemy's political and military ambitions were freed. He momentarily recognized the faulty co-rulership of Alexander's epileptic half brother Arrhidaeios and his posthumous son Alexander and immediately claimed Egypt as his satrapy. Ptolemy strongly opposed Perdikkas, to whom Alexander gave his signet ring and the regency of the empire.

Ptolemy brought Alexander's body for burial to Memphis, though Alexander had wished to be buried at Siwa. Ptolemy built an altar there for Alexander but retained the body at Memphis until a suitable mausoleum could be built in Ptolemy's new capital, Alexandria.

Perdikkas's regency rapidly fell to violent warfare among Ptolemy, Lysimachos who held Thrace, Antigonus the "One-Eyed" in Greater Phrygia, and Seleucus who desired Syria. Until 281 B.C. the "successors" fought bitterly. In 306 B.C. Antigonus assumed the title of king and claimed all of Alexander's empire. In opposition, Ptolemy declared Egypt's independence, proclaimed himself king of Egypt, and established a dynasty which lasted until Cleopatra's suicide in 30 B.C.

After Ptolemy I divorced Artacama, he married the Macedonian noblewoman Eurydice. Unhappy with this political alliance, Ptolemy put her aside and by 317 B.C. married his widowed half sister and mistress, a niece of Eurydice, the girl Berenice (I), almost 27 years his younger. Berenice gave birth to two children, Arsinoë (II) and Ptolemy (II).

In Upper Egypt, Ptolemy I founded the city Ptolemais. As satrap of Egypt, he clashed violently with Cleomenes of Naucrates, whom Alexander in 332 B.C. had appointed financial manager of Egypt and administrative chief of the eastern delta and had entrusted with the completion of Alexandria. Cleomenes, however, had assumed the satrapship, but Alexander had pardoned him. In 321 B.C. Ptolemy charged Cleomenes with embezzlement of funds and executed him, thereby removing a political rival.

Between 306 B.C. and 286 B.C. Ptolemy concentrated on the development of his empire. He gained control of Cyrene and conquered Palestine, coastal Syria, and Cyprus. In 286 B.C. he became protector of the southern Cycladic islands and their center at Delos. Throughout his empire he established the well-constructed Ptolemaic administration: he built the legal and military organizations and the military settlements, raised mercenary armies, and conscripted native levies.

Ptolemy wrote an excellent history of Alexander and his campaigns for which he utilized Alexander's daily *Journal* and other official materials. Arrian's *Anabasis* (2d century A.D.) preserves much of Ptolemy's study.

In 285 B.C. Ptolemy abdicated in favor of his 22-year-old son, Ptolemy II. Two years later Ptolemy I died and was deified by the young king in 279 B.C. and given the title Theos Soter, "God and Savior."

Further Reading

Edwyn Bevan, *The House of Ptolemy* (1927), remains the major study of Ptolemy I and Ptolemaic Egypt. Charles Alexander Robinson, Jr., *The Ephemerides of Alexander's Expedition* (1932), discusses in detail the *Journal* used in Ptolemy's biography of Alexander. A general view of the period is in W. W. Tarn and G. T. Griffith, *Hellenistic Civilisation* (1927; 3d ed. 1963). See also J. P. Mahaffy, *The Empire of the Ptolemies* (1895). □

Ptolemy II

Ptolemy II (308-246 B.C.) was a king of Egypt, the second and greatest of the Lagid dynasty of Macedonian kings who ruled Egypt between 323 and 30 B.C. He was later known by the epithet Philadelphus, "Brother-loving," which he shared with his wife Arsinoë.

Ptolemy was born in Cos, the younger son of Ptolemy I by his favorite wife, Berenice. Small and slightly built and of delicate constitution, Ptolemy II succeeded his father, who abdicated in his favor in 285 B.C.; his elder brother, Ptolemy Ceraunus, was made king of Macedonia.

Consolidation of an Empire

Ptolemy inherited Palestine and resisted the attempts of Antiochus I, the Seleucid king of Syria, to wrest it from him. Ptolemy's ships controlled the eastern Mediterranean, and he was master of Cyprus, the Phoenician coast, and part of northern Syria, while his second marriage brought him possessions in the Aegean. A further Syrian war with Antiochus

II ended with the marriage of the Seleucid king to Ptolemy's daughter Berenice Syra. After the defeat of Pyrrhus in 275 B.C., Ptolemy concluded a treaty with Rome to which he remained faithful during the Punic Wars.

Ptolemy II was an able administrator and a farseeing statesman. At home he had two main problems: to integrate the Greeks into the essentially alien environment of the ancient land of Egypt and to increase the kingdom's productivity and prosperity. Like his father, he took pains to make himself acceptable to the Egyptian priesthood. His marriage to his sister, which scandalized the Greeks, was in the pharaonic tradition. He founded a ruler cult, deifying members of the dynasty and instituting priesthoods in their honor.

Ptolemy encouraged learning and built the great library at Alexandria, making the city a brilliant center of art and learning; the city's lighthouse, the Pharos, became known as one of the Seven Wonders of the World. In order to promote commerce, Ptolemy established a network of trading posts on the coasts of the Mediterranean, the Red Sea, and East Africa and redug the ancient canal joining the Nile to the Red Sea.

Ptolemy also undertook great schemes of land reclamation, especially in the Fayyum, where he planted Greek colonists in new towns. New methods of agriculture were introduced and the growing of vines and olives encouraged, and livestock was improved by the introduction of new breeds. Trade in many commodities became a royal monopoly, from which the Crown gained large revenues. The

luxury and profligacy of his court were unparalleled in the world of his time.

Further Reading

There is no work devoted to Ptolemy II. The best study of the age in which he lived is M. Rostovtzeff, *The Social and Economic History of the Hellenistic World* (3 vols., 1941). For Egypt under the Ptolemies see Edwyn Bevan, *The House of Ptolemy* (1927). A less detailed treatment is H. I. Bell, *Egypt from Alexander the Great to the Arab Conquest* (1948). □

Claudius Ptolemy

The Greek astronomer, astrologer, and geographer Claudius Ptolemy (ca. 100-ca. 170) established the system of mathematical astronomy that remained standard in Christian and Moslem countries until the 16th century.

Ptolemy is known to have made astronomical observations at Alexandria in Egypt between 127 and 141, and he probably lived on into the reign of Marcus Aurelius (161-180). Beyond the fact that his *On the Faculty of Judgment* indicates his adherence to Stoic doctrine, nothing more of his biography is available.

The *Almagest*

The earliest and most influential of Ptolemy's major writings is the *Almagest*. In 13 books it establishes the kinematic models (purely mathematical and nonphysical) used to explain solar, lunar, and planetary motion and determines the parameters which quantify these models and permit the computation of longitudes and latitudes; of the times, durations, and magnitudes of lunar and solar eclipses; and of the times of heliacal risings and settings. Ptolemy also provides a catalog of 1,022 fixed stars, giving for each its longitude and latitude according to an ecliptic coordinate system.

Ptolemy's is a geocentric system, though the earth is the actual center only of the sphere of the fixed stars and of the "crank mechanism" of the moon; the orbits of all the other planets are slightly eccentric. Ptolemy thus hypothesizes a mathematical system which cannot be made to agree with the rules of Aristotelian physics, which require that the center of the earth be the center of all celestial circular motions.

In solar astronomy Ptolemy accepts and confirms the eccentric model and its parameters established by Hipparchus. For the moon Ptolemy made enormous improvements in Hipparchus's model, though he was unable to surmount all the difficulties of lunar motion evident even to ancient astronomers. Ptolemy discerned two more inequalities and proposed a complicated model to account for them. The effect of the Ptolemaic lunar model is to draw the moon close enough to the earth at quadratures to produce what should be a visible increase in apparent diameter; the

increase, however, was not visible. The Ptolemaic models for the planets generally account for the two inequalities in planetary motion and are represented by combinations of circular motions: eccentrics and epicycles. Such a combination of eccentric and epicyclic models represents Ptolemy's principal original contribution in the *Almagest*.

Canobic Inscription

This brief text was inscribed on a stele erected at Canobus near Alexandria in Egypt in 146 or 147. It contains the parameters of Ptolemy's solar, lunar, and planetary models as given in the *Almagest* but modified in some instances. There is also a section on the harmony of the spheres. The epoch of the *Canobic Inscription* is the first year of Augustus, or 30 B.C.

Planetary Hypotheses

In the two books of *Planetary Hypotheses,* an important cosmological work, Ptolemy "corrects" some of the parameters of the *Almagest* and suggests an improved model to explain planetary latitude. In the section of the first book preserved only in Arabic, he proposes absolute dimensions for the celestial spheres (maximum and minimum distances of the planets, their apparent and actual diameters, and their volumes). The second book, preserved only in Arabic, describes a physical actualization of the mathematical models of the planets in the *Almagest*. Here the conflict with Aristotelian physics becomes unavoidable (Ptolemy uses Aristotelian terminology but makes no attempt to reconcile his views of the causes of the inequalities of planetary motion with Aristotle's), and it was in attempting to remove the discrepancies that the "School of Maragha" and also Ibn al-Shatir in the 13th and 14th centuries devised new planetary models that largely anticipate Copernicus's.

The *Phases*

This work originally contained two books, but only the second has survived. It is a calendar of the *parapegma* type, giving for each day of the Egyptian year the time of heliacal rising or setting of certain fixed stars. The views of Eudoxus, Hipparchus, Philip of Opus, Callippus, Euctemon, and others regarding the meteorological phenomena associated with these risings and settings are quoted. This makes the *Phases* useful to the historian of early Greek astronomy, though it is certainly the least important of Ptolemy's astronomical works.

The *Apotelesmatica*

Consisting of four books, the *Apotelesmatica* is Ptolemy's contribution to astrological theory. He attempts in the first book to place astrology on a sound scientific basis. Astrology for Ptolemy is less exact than astronomy is, as the former deals with objects influenced by many other factors besides the positions of the planets at a particular point in time, whereas the latter describes the unswerving motions of the eternal stars themselves. In the second book, general astrology affecting whole states, societies, and regions is described; this general astrology is largely derived from Mesopotamian astral omina. The final two books are devoted to genethlialogy, the science of predicting the events in the life of a native from the horoscope cast for the moment of his birth. The Apotelesmatica was long the main handbook for astrologers.

The *Geography*

In the eight books of the *Geography,* Ptolemy sets forth mathematical solutions to the problems of representing the spherical surface of the earth on a plane surface (a map), but the work is largely devoted to a list of localities with their coordinates. This list is arranged by regions, with the river and mountain systems and the ethnography of each region also usually described. He begins at the West in book 2 (his prime meridian ran through the "Fortunate Islands," apparently the Canaries) and proceeds eastward to India, the Malay Peninsula, and China in book 7.

Despite his brilliant mathematical theory of map making, Ptolemy had not the requisite material to construct the accurate picture of the world that he desired. Aside from the fact that, following Marinus in this as in much else, he underestimated the size of the earth, concluding that the distance from the Canaries to China is about 180° instead of about 130°, he was seriously hampered by the lack of all the gnomon observations that are necessary to establish the latitudes of the places he lists. For longitudes he could not utilize astronomical observations because no systematic exploitation of this method of determining longitudinal differences had been organized. He was compelled to rely on travelers' estimates of distances, which varied widely in their reliability and were most uncertain guides. His efforts, however, provided western Europe, Byzantium, and Islam with their most detailed conception of the inhabited world.

Harmonics and *Optics*

These, the last two works in the surviving corpus of Ptolemy's writings, investigate two other fields included in antiquity in the general field of mathematics. The *Harmonics* in three books became one of the standard works on the mathematical theory of music in late antiquity and throughout the Byzantine period. The *Optics* in five books discussed the geometry of vision, especially mirror reflection and refraction. The *Optics* survives only in a Latin translation prepared by Eugenius, Admiral of Sicily, toward the end of the 12th century, from an Arabic version in which the first book and the end of the fifth were lost. The doubts surrounding its authenticity as a work of Ptolemy seem to have been overcome by recent scholarship.

His Influence

Ptolemy's brilliance as a mathematician, his exactitude, and his masterful presentation seemed to his successors to have exhausted the possibilities of mathematical astronomy and geography. To a large extent they were right. Without better instrumentation only minor adjustments in the Ptolemaic parameters or models could be made. The major "improvements" in the models—those of the School of Maragha—are designed primarily to satisfy philosophy, not astronomy; the lunar theory was the only exception. Most of the deviations from Ptolemaic methods in medieval

astronomy are due to the admixture of non-Greek material and the continued use of pre-Ptolemaic elements. The *Geography* was never seriously challenged before the 15th century.

The authority of the astronomical and geographical works carries over to the astrological treatise and, to a lesser extent, to the *Harmonics* and *Optics.* The *Apotelesmatica* was always recognized as one of the works most clearly defending the scientific basis of astrology in general, and of genethlialogy in particular. But Neoplatonism as developed by the pagans of Harran provided a more extended theory of the relationship of the celestial spheres to the sublunar world, and this theory was popularized in Islam in the 9th century. The *Harmonics* ceased to be popular as Greek music ceased to follow the classical modes, and the *Optics* was rendered obsolete by Moslem scientists. Ptolemy's fame and influence, then, rest primarily on the *Almagest,* his most original work, justly subtitled *The Greatest.*

Further Reading

There is no comprehensive study of Ptolemy's life and works. Most of the scholarly discussion of Ptolemy is contained in critical editions of the Greek texts (there is still no critical edition of the *Geography*) and in numerous scholarly periodicals. One fairly complete bibliography is William H. Stahl, *Ptolemy's Geography: A Select Bibliography* (1953). For general background see H. F. Tozer, *A History of Ancient Geography* (1897; 2d ed. 1955); Percy Sykes, *A History of Exploration* (1934; 3d ed. 1950); James Oliver Thomson, *History of Ancient Geography* (1948); and C. Van Paassen, *The Classical Tradition of Geography* (1957).

Additional Sources

Newton, Robert R., *The crime of Claudius Ptolemy,* Baltimore: Johns Hopkins University Press, 1977. □

Giacomo Puccini

The Italian composer Giacomo Puccini (1858-1924) was the most successful follower of Verdi, continuing the line of Italian operatic composers into the 20th century.

B orn in Lucca on Dec. 22, 1858, into a family whose members had composed operas of local success for several generations, Giacomo Puccini learned the rudiments of music from the best local teachers, served as a church organist, and composed sacred choral works while still in his teens. A pension in 1880 from Queen Margherita made it possible for him to go to Milan for study at the conservatory. His most important teacher was the composer Amilcare Ponchielli, who encouraged him to write his first opera, *Le Villi,* in 1884. The work was entered in a competition sponsored by the Teatro Illustrato but received no recognition there; it was performed with such success at one of the smaller Milanese theaters that it was put on the stage at the famous La Scala opera house in 1885.

Edgar, done at La Scala in 1889, was a failure, but *Manon Lescaut,* performed in Turin in 1893, was favorably received and soon became a popular work throughout Italy and abroad. Puccini's first spectacular triumph came in 1896 with *La Bohème,* to a libretto by Giacosa and Illica, premiered in Turin. Its touching portrayal of episodes in the lives and loves of students in Paris and the simplicity and accessibility of the music in gay, romantic, and pathetic scenes excited and moved audiences from the first performance on, and its popularity has continued to the present day in all countries that enjoy opera.

Tosca, again to a libretto by Giacosa and Illica, which was given in Rome in 1900, was a more serious and melodramatic work, with relatively few moments of lyricism, but it was almost as successful and has also become a mainstay of the standard repertory. *Madama Butterfly,* set in Japan, was the first work in which Puccini used scales and melodies of non-Western music. It was poorly received at the first performance at La Scala in 1904 but has since become every bit as popular as *La Bohème* and probably for the same reasons: there are long passages of lush and sentimental music, tunes that are easy to remember, effective scenes of pathos, and well-calculated bits of stage business. *Madama Butterfly* was also his last completely successful work.

Welcoming the opportunity to visit America, Puccini wrote a new work for the Metropolitan Opera in New York City: *The Girl of the Golden West (La fanciulla del West).* The first performance, in 1910, was received with the expected enthusiasm, but the opera was not so well received

later and is rarely performed today. He endeavored to capture the local color of the American West; there are scenes of gambling and saloons and an attempted lynching, and some of the tunes try to sound like American songs. But in the end the music sounds just like Puccini, and not Puccini at his best.

A comic opera, *La Rondine,* given in Monte Carlo in 1917, has not held the stage. The following year Puccini wrote three one-act operas, *Il trittico,* designed to be done together as an evening's entertainment, and premiered in New York. The first, *Il tabarro,* is melodramatic, much in the style of parts of *Tosca; Suor Angelica,* set in a convent and written for women's voices, is lyric and subdued; and *Gianni Schicchi,* the most successful and often done separately, is his best comic work, rapid-paced with some fine moments of contrasting lyricism.

Death took Puccini before he could complete his last work, *Turandot.* He was nearing the end of the work when he was stricken by throat cancer and taken for an operation to Brussels, where he died on Nov. 29, 1924. The opera was completed by Alfano and first performed at La Scala, conducted by Arturo Toscanini, in 1926. It has some fine lyric moments and unusually effective dramatic ones, and in some places it makes more effective use of such pseudo-Oriental devices as pentatonic scales than did *Madama Butterfly,* but the work as a whole lacks some cohesion and has not been as perennially popular as some of his earlier operas.

Puccini's strengths are his delicate and sensitive handling of both voices and orchestra in lyric and pathetic scenes and occasionally in lively scenes as well and his ability to write melodies that audiences learn quickly and apparently never tire of hearing. His best scenes are those for one or two characters; ensemble writing in his operas rarely approaches the excitement common in the works of such predecessors as Gioacchino Rossini and Giuseppe Verdi.

Music was undergoing dramatic stylistic changes in the last decades of Puccini's life with the works of such men as Igor Stravinsky, Arnold Schoenberg, and Béla Bartók. Puccini clung to the harmonic and melodic language of the late 19th century. The problem of reconciliation between radical changes of musical language and the venerable form of opera has been a thorny one, and it should be noted that the last operas to be truly successful in terms of wide acceptance by audiences and retention in the repertory are those of Puccini and Richard Strauss, two men who remained on the periphery of the widespread innovation so characteristic of the first decades of the 20th century.

Further Reading

The Letters of Giacomo Puccini were edited by Giuseppe Adami (1928; trans. 1931). George Marek, *Puccini: A Biography* (1951), the most extensive work in English, is a subjective and romantic treatment of the composer. Puccini's operas are discussed in Max De Schauensee, *The Collector's Verdi and Puccini* (1962), and William Ashbrook, *The Operas of Puccini* (1968). For background material Donald Jay Grout, *A Short History of Opera* (1947; 2d ed. 1965), is recommended.

Additional Sources

Brown, Jonathon, *Puccini,* New York: Simon & Schuster, 1995.

Carner, Mosco, *Puccini: a critical biography,* New York: Holmes & Meier Publishers, 1977, 1974.

Greenfeld, Howard, *Puccini: a biography,* New York: Putnam, 1980.

Jackson, Stanley, *Monsieur Butterfly; the story of Giacomo Puccin,* New York, Stein and Day 1974.

Marggraf, Wolfgang, *Giacomo Puccini,* New York: Heinrichshofen: Sole selling agents, C.F. Peters, 1984.

Weaver, William, *Puccini: the man and his music,* New York: E. P. Dutton, 1977. □

Tito Puente

Tito Puente (born 1923) is widely considered to be the godfather of Latin jazz and salsa, devoting more than six decades of his life to performing Latin music and earning a reputation as a masterful percussionist. Noted for merging Latin American rhythms with contemporary jazz and big band music, Puente's prolific output encompasses over 100 albums recorded between 1949 and 1994.

Tito Puente was born in New York City's Spanish Harlem in 1923, where the hybrid of Afro-Cuban and Afro-Puerto Rican music helped create salsa music (the Spanish word for "spice" and "sauce" is salsa). By the time Puente was ten years old, he played with local Latin bands at neighborhood gatherings, society parties, and New York City hotels. Puente first performed as a young boy with a local band called Los Happy Boys, at New York City's Park Place Hotel, and by the age of 13, he was considered a child prodigy by his family, neighbors, and fellow bandmembers. As a teenager, he joined Noro Morales and the Machito Orchestra. Puente was drafted into the Navy in 1942 at the age of 19 to fight in World War II, which entailed a three-year reprieve from music.

In the late 1930s Puente had originally intended to become a professional dancer, but chose to continue performing and composing music after injuring his ankle in a bicycle accident. Puente befriended bandleader Charlie Spivak while in the Navy, and through Spivak, Puente became interested in big band composition. When Puente returned from the Navy after serving in nine battles, he received a Presidential Commendation and completed his formal musical education at the Juilliard School of Music, studying conducting, orchestration, and musical theory under the G.I. bill. He completed his studies in 1947, at the age of 24.

While at Juilliard, and for a year after he completed his studies, Puente played with Fernando Alvarez and his Copacabana Group, as well as Jose Curbelo and Pupi Campo. When Puente was 25 in 1948, he formed his own group—or conjunto—called the Piccadilly Boys, which soon became known as the Tito Puente Orchestra. He re-

corded his first hit, "Abaniquito," on the Tico Records label a year later. Later in 1949, he signed with RCA Victor records and recorded the single "Ran Kan Kan."

Puente began churning out hits in the 1950s while riding the crest of mambo's popularity, and recorded dance favorites such as "Barbarabatiri," "El Rey del Timbai," "Mambo la Roca," and "Mambo Gallego." RCA released *Cuban Carnival, Puente Goes Jazz, Dance Mania,* and *Top Percussion,* four of Puente's most popular albums in the 1950s, between 1956 and 1960. Puente established himself as the foremost mambo musician of the 1950s, and in the late 1950s, fused Cuban "cha-cha-cha" beats with big band compositions.

In the 1960s Puente began to collaborate more widely with other New York City-based musicians; he played with trombonist Buddy Morrow, Woody Herman, and Cuban musicians Celia Cruz and La Lupe. He remained flexible and open to experimentation by collaborating with others and fusing various musical styles such as mambo, jazz, salsa, and the big band sound of the 1940s. Puente epitomized the Latin-jazz crossover movement in music at the time. In 1963 on Tico Records, Puente released "Oye Como Va," which was a resounding success and is now considered a classic. Four years later in 1967 Puente performed a program of his compositions at the Metropolitan Opera at Lincoln Center.

Puente hosted his own television show called "The World of Tito Puente," broadcast on Hispanic television in 1968, and he was asked to be the Grand Marshall of New

York City's Puerto Rican Day Parade. In 1969 Mayor John Lindsay gave Puente the key to New York City as a gesture of appreciation.

Puente's music was not categorized as salsa until the 1970s, as it contained elements of big band composition and jazz as well. When Puente's classic hit "Oye Como Va" was covered by Carlos Santana in the early 1970s, a new generation was introduced to Puente's music. Santana also covered Puente's "Para Los Rumberos," which Puente recorded in 1956. Puente and Santana eventually met in 1977 in New York City's Roseland Ballroom.

In 1979 Puente toured Japan with his ensemble and discovered an enthusiastic new audience as well as the fact that he had achieved worldwide popularity. After returning from Japan, the musician and his orchestra played for U.S. President Jimmy Carter as part of the president's Hispanic Heritage Month celebration. Puente was awarded the first of four Grammy Awards in 1979 for *A Tribute To Benny More.* He also received Grammy awards for *On Broadway* in 1983, *Mambo Diablo* in 1985, and *Goza Mi Timbal* in 1989. In the course of his long career, Puente received eight Grammy Award nominations, more than any other musician in the Latin music field before 1994.

Puente recorded his last big band albums in 1980 and 1981. He toured European cities with the Latin Percussion Jazz Ensemble, and recorded albums with them as well in the 1980s. Puente continued to devote himself to composing, recording, and performing music throughout the 1980s, but his interests broadened at this time.

Puente founded the Tito Puente Scholarship Foundation to benefit musically talented children; the foundation later signed a contract with Allnet Communications to provide scholarships to music students nationwide. He appeared on The Cosby Show, and performed in a commercial for Coca-Cola with Bill Cosby. Puente also made guest appearances in the films *Radio Days* and *Armed and Dangerous.* Puente received an honorary doctorate degree from the College at Old Westbury in the 1980s and appeared at the Monterey Jazz Festival in 1984.

On August 14, 1990, Puente received a Hollywood Star in Los Angles for posterity. Puente's talent was elevated to an international audience in the mid-1980s, and he spent time in the early 1990s performing for audiences overseas. In 1991 Puente appeared—most appropriately—in the film *The Mambo Kings Play Songs of Love,* which prompted another new generation's interest in his music.

In 1991, at the age of 68, Puente released his 100th album, titled *El Numero Cien,* distributed by Sony for RMM Records. Puente released *Master Timbalero* with his Golden Latin-Jazz Allstars—comprised mainly of other band leaders—in 1994, covering classics such as "The Peanut Vendor" and "Nostalgia in Times Square," as well as the album In Session with a separate ensemble of musicians called the Latin-Jazz Allstars, is his regular touring group. Puente was awarded ASCAP's most prestigious honor—the Founders Award—in July of 1994. *Billboard*'s John Lannert wrote, "As Puente stepped up to the microphone, a segment of the audience broke into an impromptu rendition of the Puente anthem 'Oye Como Va.'"

Further Reading

Gerard, Charley, *Salsa: The Rhythm of Latin Music,* White Cliffs Media Company, 1989.
Americas, January/February 1993.
Atlanta Constitution, March 28, 1997.
Billboard, July 9, 1994.
Boston Globe, June 17, 1996.
Down Beat, June 1992; November 1993; August 1994.
Harper's Bazaar, June 1993.
Hispanic, May 1992; December 1992.
Musician, July 1994.
Newsweek, November 11, 1991; April 20, 1992.
New Yorker, March 2, 1992.
New York Times, December 19, 1996.
Rolling Stone, December 12, 1991.
Time, June 8, 1992. □

Baron Samuel von Pufendorf

The German jurist and historian Baron Samuel von Pufendorf (1632-1694) is best known for his influential writings on international and natural law. His works became standard textbooks for both juristical and historical students in the 17th and 18th centuries.

Samuel von Pufendorf was born on Jan. 8, 1632, near Chemnitz, Saxony. The son of a Lutheran minister, he began his higher education with the study of theology at the University of Leipzig. His dislike of theological studies caused him to change to legal studies, which he pursued at the University of Jena. In 1658 he traveled to Copenhagen, where he became a tutor to the children of the Swedish ambassador to Denmark. As a result of war between Denmark and Sweden, the Swedish official and his entire retinue were arrested. Pufendorf, consequently, spent 8 months in prison. He apparently used this time to reflect on his previous legal studies, for, after his release, he went to Leiden and published in 1660 a complete system of universal law in his *Elementorum jurisprudentiae universalis libri duo* (*The Two Books of the Elements of Universal Jurisprudence*). This work was dedicated to the ruler of the Palatinate, who rewarded Pufendorf by creating a new chair of political and natural law at the University of Heidelberg. While in Heidelberg, he published *De statu imperii Germanici* (*On the State of the German Empire*), a critical analysis of the organization of the Holy Roman Empire.

In 1670 Pufendorf accepted a new professorial position at the University of Lund in Sweden. There in 1672 he published his greatest work, *De jure naturae et gentium libri octo* (*The Eight Books on the Law of Nature and Nations*). A summary was published the following year, entitled *De officio hominis et civis* (*On the Duty of Man and Citizen*). In these works Pufendorf expanded upon the theories of Hugo Grotius and Thomas Hobbes. He rejected Hobbes's view of

Emelyan Ivanovich Pugachev

The Russian Cossack soldier Emelyan Ivanovich Pugachev (1742-1775) led the peasant rebellion in Russia in 1773-1775.

Emelyan Pugachev, a Don Cossack, was born in the village of Zimoveiskaya. The main course of his life was influenced initially by the fact that, as a Don Cossack, he was subject, when of age, to duty in the Russian army. In 1770, during a Russo-Turkish conflict in which he was serving, he was given a temporary leave and, at its expiration, refused to return to his regiment. Arrested, he managed to escape, thus beginning his life as a strong-willed fugitive.

In the course of his subsequent wanderings Pugachev was struck by the bitter unrest he found among the lower classes in Russia. What he saw convinced him that the time was ripe for revolt, and being a rebel by nature and having a bent toward leadership, he took upon himself the task of directing a revolt. As a basis for appeal, he decided to assume the character of Czar Peter III, having observed that many credulous people distrusted the official report that Peter had died in 1762.

With about 80 Cossacks committed to his scheme, in September 1773 Pugachev proclaimed himself Peter III and called on the oppressed to follow him in an uprising against Catherine II (the Great). He began his campaign along the Yaik (now called the Ural) River, gathering followers among disgruntled Cossacks, fugitive serfs, released convicts, religious dissenters, Bashkirs, and Tatars. Although the force he assembled was neither well trained nor well disciplined, it was large enough to defeat local military units sent against it. To widen his campaign, Pugachev undertook the capture of Orenburg (Chkalov), the major center of government strength on the Yaik River, setting up headquarters and laying siege to the city. Meanwhile, news of the revolt prompted bloody uprisings against landlords and government officials along the Volga River and in the region east of it. Thousands left their homes to join the rebel army, and they increased its numbers to about 25,000.

Late in 1773 Catherine II, judging the revolt dangerous enough to warrant her action, sent a large force to suppress it. Pugachev was compelled to end the siege of Orenburg, but he eluded capture by the government forces. Again he marshaled a sizable following and, in July 1774, was able to resume the offensive and capture the city of Kazan. At the same time, serf uprisings took place near Nizhni Novgorod (Gorki) only 275 miles east of Moscow.

Catherine, now deeply alarmed by the nearness of the revolt, sent new contingents against Pugachev. They succeeded in destroying most of his army, near Tsaritsyn (now Volgograd), but he once again evaded efforts to capture him. Still determined, Pugachev made his way to the Yaik Cossack region, hoping that Yaik and Don Cossacks would provide him with a new army. Instead of being given sup-

man in his natural state by maintaining that the state of nature was one of peace, not of war. Pufendorf developed a concept of secularized natural law, holding that natural law was concerned with man in this life and was derived from human reason.

In 1677 Pufendorf virtually gave up his preoccupation with law and turned to historical studies. In that year he became the official historian to the Swedish king. As a result, he wrote histories of the reigns of Gustavus II and Charles Gustavus. Called to the service of Elector Frederick William of Brandenburg and his successor, Elector Frederick III, Pufendorf completed a history of the former's reign, but he had barely begun one on Frederick III when he died on Oct. 26, 1694. Although his historical works were rather stilted, they were based on archival material and demonstrated a respect for truth. Pufendorf's general history of Europe, also written during this period of his life (1682), became the "first modern textbook in European history."

Further Reading

There is little biographical material on Pufendorf in English. A study of his life and ideas is Leonard Krieger, *The Politics of Discretion: Pufendorf and the Acceptance of Natural Law* (1965). See also George Louis Bissonnette, *Pufendorf and the Church Reforms of Peter the Great* (1962). General background is in Harry Elmer Barnes, *A History of Historical Writing* (1937), and Herbert Butterfield, *Man on His Past: The Study of the History of Historical Scholarship* (1960). □

port, however, he was betrayed. A group of Cossacks opposed to his aims seized him and handed him over to the authorities.

Taken in chains to Moscow, Pugachev was tried and sentenced to death. On Jan. 10, 1775, he was beheaded and quartered before a large Moscow crowd.

Further Reading

The best account, in English, concerning Pugachev is in Philip Longworth, *The Cossacks* (1970). An excellent analysis by Marc Raeff of the causes of the Pugachev revolt is in Robert Forster and Jack P. Greene, eds., *Preconditions of Revolution in Early Modern Europe* (1971). □

Augustus Welby Northmore Pugin

Augustus Welby Northmore Pugin (1812-1852) was the most influential English ecclesiastical architect of his day and the principal theoretician of the Gothic revival.

Born in London on March 1, 1812, A. W. N. Pugin was the son of, and early assistant to, Augustus Charles Pugin, the producer of pattern books of Gothic building, such as *Examples of Gothic Architecture*

(1831). The younger Pugin's conversion to Catholicism in 1834 led to a series of publications defending his chosen religion against the Established Church and advocating a correct Gothic style for its buildings. These publications had a great influence beyond the small circle of aristocratic Catholic restorationists, such as Lord Shrewsbury, who were Pugin's principal patrons.

Pugin's propaganda campaign began with the publication, at his own expense—since it was too controversial for a commercial publisher—of his intemperate *Contrasts* (1836; 2d ed. enlarged, 1841). The theme of contrast between the unity and goodness of the Middle Ages and the pluralism and degeneracy of the industrialized 19th century was common in intellectual circles of the time, but Pugin gave it architectural expression through a series of plates contrasting medieval with modern, classically inspired buildings. The final plate, in which buildings from the two periods are weighed on the scales of Truth and the modern ones "found wanting," summed up Pugin's attitude. This work established architectural criticism on an ethical basis. Only good men (that is, Christians, and more specifically, Catholics) build good buildings (that is, Gothic ones; classical buildings are pagan). John Ruskin made this a fundamental principle of architectural criticism in his popular *Seven Lamps of Architecture* (1849).

Pugin's *The True Principles of Pointed or Christian Architecture* (1841) explained the Gothic as a rational, utilitarian architectural system in stone and announced the "two great rules for design" as "1st, that there should be no features about a building which are not necessary for conve-

nience, construction, or propriety; 2nd, that all ornament should consist of enrichment of the essential construction of the building.''

In *Apology for the Revival of Christian Architecture in England* (1843) Pugin added nationalism to religion as a justification for using Gothic forms. Christian or Gothic architecture is ''the only correct expression of the faith, wants, and climate of our country . . . whilst we profess the creed of Christians, whilst we glory in being Englishmen, let us have an architecture, the arrangement and details of which alike remind us of our faith and our country.'' The classically inspired buildings of his contemporaries had no place in England because they were not Gothic and therefore neither Christian nor English.

The Present State of Ecclesiastical Architecture in England (1843), illustrating and describing Pugin's own church designs, pointed out his religious use of Gothic. His ornamental contributions in the English Perpendicular style to Charles Barry's Houses of Parliament (1836 onward) demonstrated the application of Gothic in the cause of nationalism.

Pugin's influence through these publications was farreaching, but his buildings, some 70 in all, also represent an impressive achievement. They range from small parish churches such as St. Giles's, Cheadle, Staffordshire (1841-1846), to cathedrals such as St. Chad's, Birmingham (1839-1841), and from great country houses such as Alton Towers, Staffordshire (1840-1844), the seat of Lord Shrewsbury, and Scarisbrick Hall, Lancashire (after 1837), to monastic and other institutional buildings such as St. John's Hospital, Alton, Staffordshire (1840-1842). Quality varies with the budget in these works, but all are more Victorian than Gothic, and they reflect the infant state of medieval studies of the period.

Pugin died on Sept. 14, 1852, in Ramsgate, Kent, and was buried there in the church of St. Augustine, designed and built (1846-1851) at his own expense.

Further Reading

The older biographies of Pugin by Benjamin Ferry, *Recollections of A. N. Welby Pugin* (1861), and by Michael Trappes-Lomax, *Pugin* (1933), have been superseded by Phoebe Stanton's well-illustrated *Pugin* (1970). For a brief account of Pugin's role in English Catholicism see Denis R. Gwynn, *Lord Shrewsbury, Pugin and the Catholic Revival* (1946). His buildings are discussed in the context of the architecture of his time in Henry-Russell Hitchcock, *Early Victorian Architecture in Britain* (1954). There are good chapters on Pugin's life and work in Kenneth Clark, *The Gothic Revival* (1928), and in Alexandra Clark, *Victorian Architecture,* edited by Peter Ferriday (1963).

Additional Sources

Ferrey, Benjamin, *Recollections of A. W. N. Pugin and his father Augustus Pugin,* London: Scolar Press, 1978. □

Casimir Pulaski

Casimir Pulaski (1747-1779), Polish patriot and American Revolutionary War hero, fought unsuccessfully against foreign control of his native Poland and then journeyed to America to fight in the American Revolution.

Born in Podolia, Casimir Pulaski was the eldest son of Count Joseph Pulaski. After brief service in the guard of Duke Charles of Courland (now a part of Latvia), Pulaski returned home to Poland. In 1768 he joined forces with the Confederation of Bar, a movement founded by his father, in a revolt against Russian domination of Poland. The confederation, however, proved to be too small to be victorious and was decisively defeated. Pulaski's estates having been confiscated, in 1772 at the time of the first partition of Poland he fled to Turkey. Here he remained for several years in a vain attempt to provoke the Turks into an attack on Russia. Finally, penniless and destitute, he left for Paris to seek other employment.

In the spring of 1775, as the American Revolution was beginning, the American commissioners to France gave Pulaski money to make the voyage to Boston. He arrived there armed with a letter of introduction to Gen. George Washington. Shortly after a meeting with Washington in August of that same year, Pulaski became a volunteer member of the general's staff. Distinguishing himself at the Battle of the Brandywine in September, he was consequently given command of a newly created cavalry troop in Washington's army. During the winter of 1777 he and his men served at Trenton, at Flemington, and at Valley Forge, where Pulaski shared responsibility with Gen. Anthony Wayne for the provisioning of the starving Americans. But difficulties with Wayne and some of the junior officers caused Pulaski to resign his command in March 1778.

As a result, later that same month the Continental Congress, on the advice of Washington, authorized Pulaski to raise an independent cavalry corp in the Baltimore, Md., area. Anxious for an active command, he was sent to Egg Harbor, N.J., to protect supplies there but was badly mauled by a surprise British attack on Oct. 15, 1778. He was next dispatched to defend Minisink on the Delaware River from further attacks by Native Americans. The command was too tame for Pulaski's liking, however, and 3 months later he obtained orders to join in the siege of Charleston. He reached that city on May 8 and promptly directed a headlong attack on advancing British forces. Badly defeated there, Pulaski sought vainly to redeem himself. Five months later while leading another heroic charge, this time during the siege of Savannah, he was mortally wounded. He died on board the American ship *Wasp,* probably on Oct. 11, 1779.

Further Reading

Two biographical studies in English of Pulaski are Clarence A. Manning, *Soldier of Liberty* (1945), and Wladyslaw Konopczynski, *Casimir Pulaski* (trans. 1947).

Additional Sources

Jamro, R. D., *Pulaski, a portrait of freedom,* S.l.: s.n., 1981?.

Kopczewski, Jan Stanisaw, *Casimir Pulaski,* Warsaw: Interpress, 1980.

Szymanski, Leszek, *Casimir Pulaski: a hero of the American Revolution,* New York: Hippocrene Books, 1994.

Szymanski, Leszek, *Kazimierz Pulaski in America: a monograph, 1777-1779,* San Bernardino, Calif.: Borgo Press, 1986, 1979.

□

Luigi Pulci

The Italian poet Luigi Pulci (1432-1484), an early Renaissance poet associated with the Medici family, wrote *Il Morgante maggiore,* the first literary treatment of popular Italian romances of chivalry.

Luigi Pulci was born in Florence on Aug. 15, 1432, of an impoverished noble family. When his father died in 1451, leaving a destitute widow and five children, Luigi worked for a time as clerk and bookkeeper. In 1453 Pulci married Lucrezia degli Albizzi, who bore him four sons. In 1461 he was introduced to the Medici and formed a close friendship with Lorenzo. He was devoted also to Lorenzo's mother, Lucrezia Tornabuoni, at whose request

he began the *Morgante,* probably in 1461. Pulci's collection of *Letters* reflects his warm affection for Lorenzo and Lucrezia over many years.

Lorenzo de' Medici became ruler of Florence in 1469. Soon Pulci was entrusted with various diplomatic missions. Meanwhile the Pulci family's finances had been utterly mismanaged by Luigi's brothers Luca (who died in debtors' prison in 1470) and Bernardo.

Pulci had both friends and enemies among the men of letters in the Medici household. He profoundly respected the young poet and humanist Angelo Poliziano. His most bitter adversary was Matteo Franco, with whom he exchanged a series of fiercely polemical sonnets between 1474 and 1475. The Platonist Marsilio Ficino became his opponent, perhaps because of Pulci's interest in magic and witchcraft.

The earliest edition of the *Morgante,* published in 1478, consisted of 23 cantos. It was immediately criticized by the Florentine Platonic Academy. The first complete edition, enlarged to 28 cantos and entitled *Il Morgante maggiore,* was published in Florence in 1483. Pulci adapted two 14th-century poems: *Orlando,* which narrates Roland's adventures among the pagans in the Orient, and *La Spagna,* which relates Charlemagne's war in Spain, Roland's death at Roncesvalles, and the punishment of Gano, the traitor. Pulci, however, thoroughly transformed these popular tales. Uninterested in chivalric ideals, he took his inspiration from the humble reality of bourgeois and mercantile Florence. Gano's intrigues, instead of heroism, motivate the action. The title reveals Pulci's exuberant imagination and his lightly mocking tone. Morgante, the powerful and good-natured giant, becomes the hero of the story instead of Roland. Two characters are of Pulci's invention: Margutte, the half giant, archscoundrel, and glutton whose shrewdness contrasts with Morgante's slow wit, and Astarotte, the learned devil-theologian. Pulci's language shares the picturesque efficacy of popular Florentine speech.

Toward the end of his life, Pulci's relationship with Lorenzo de' Medici may have changed, possibly because of his antagonism toward Matteo Franco. During the last 10 years of his life, Pulci had stable employment with the condottiere Roberto Sanseverino. In 1484, while traveling to Venice with Sanseverino, he became ill and died in Padua in October or November.

Further Reading

Studies of Pulci include Lewis D. Einstein, *Luigi Pulci and the Morgante Maggiore* (1902); John Raymond Shulters, *Luigi Pulci and the Animal Kingdom* (1920); and Giacomo Grillo, *Two Aspects of Chivalry: Pulci and Boiardo* (1942). □

Joseph Pulitzer

Joseph Pulitzer (1847-1911), Hungarian-born editor and publisher, was instrumental in developing yellow journalism in the United States.

Joseph Pulitzer's father was a well-to-do grain dealer. Joseph was born in Budapest in April 1847. Thin, weak-lunged, and with faulty vision, he was unable to have an army career in Europe. In 1864 he emigrated to America, enlisted in the Union cavalry, and became a mediocre soldier. The 6-foot 2-inch red-bearded youth was among the jobless at the end of the Civil War. In St. Louis, where a large German colony existed, Pulitzer worked as mule tender, waiter, roustabout, and hack driver. Finally, he gained a reporter's job on Carl Schurz's *Westliche Post*.

A short time after joining Schurz, Pulitzer was nominated for the state legislature by the Republicans. His candidacy was considered a joke because he was nominated in a Democratic district. Pulitzer, however, ran seriously and won. In the legislature he fought graft and corruption. In one wild dispute he shot an adversary in the leg. He escaped punishment with a fine which was paid by friends.

Newspaper Acquisitions

Industrious and ambitious, Pulitzer bought the *St. Louis Post* for about $3,000 in 1872. Next, he bought a German paper which had an Associated Press membership and then sold it to the owner of the *Globe* at a $20,000 profit. In 1878 Pulitzer purchased the decaying *St. Louis Dispatch* at a sheriff's sale for $2,700. He combined it with the *Post*. Aided by his brilliant editor in chief, John A. Cockerill, Pulitzer launched crusades against lotteries, gambling, and tax dodging, mounted drives for cleaning and repairing the streets, and sought to make St. Louis more civic-minded. The *Post-Dispatch* became a success.

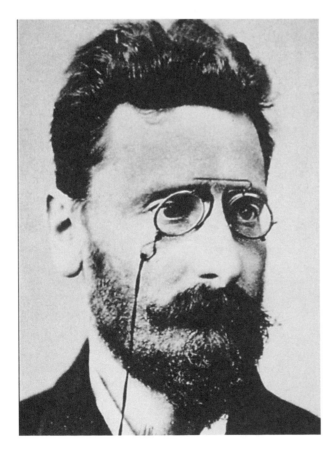

In 1883 Pulitzer, then 36, purchased the *New York World* for $346,000 from unscrupulous financier Jay Gould, who was losing $40,000 a year on the paper. Pulitzer made the down payment from *Post-Dispatch* profits and made all later payments out of profits from the *World*.

In the 1880s Pulitzer's eyes began to fail. He went blind in 1889. During his battle for supremacy with William Randolph Hearst, publisher of the *New York Journal,* Pulitzer had to rely on a battery of secretaries to be his eyes. In New York he pledged the *World* to "expose all fraud and sham, fight all public evils and abuses" and to "battle for the people with earnest sincerity." He concentrated on lively human-interest stories, scandal, and sensational material. Pulitzer's *World* was a strong supporter of the common man. It was anti-monopoly and frequently pro-union during strikes.

Pulitzer in the early part of his career opposed the large headline and art. Later, in a circulation contest between Hearst and Pulitzer in the 1890s, the two giants went to ever larger headline type and fantastic "x-marks-the-spot" art and indulged in questionable practices until Pulitzer lost stomach for such dubious work and cut back. Pulitzer defended sensationalism, however, saying that people had to know about crime in order to combat it. He once told a critic, "I want to talk to a nation, not a select committee."

Pulitzer died aboard his yacht in the harbor at Charleston, S.C., on Oct. 29, 1911. In his will he provided $2 million for the establishment of a school of journalism at Columbia University. Also, by the terms of his will, the prizes bearing his name were established in 1915.

Further Reading

Biographies of Pulitzer include Don C. Seitz, *Joseph Pulitzer: His Life and Letters* (1924); James W. Barrett, *Joseph Pulitzer and His World* (1941); and Iris Noble, *Joseph Pulitzer: Front Page Pioneer* (1947). A particularly interesting book written by one of Pulitzer's secretaries is Alleyne Ireland, *An Adventure with a Genius* (1914; rev. ed. 1937). Julian S. Rammelkamp, *Pulitzer's Post-Dispatch* (1967), focuses on Pulitzer's early career, and George Juergens, *Joseph Pulitzer and the New York World* (1966), deals with the middle and late years and contains an excellent analysis of the appeal of the *New York World*. □

George Mortimer Pullman

George Mortimer Pullman (1831-1897) was an American industrial innovator who developed the railroad sleeping car and built a big business with it. He was one of the last industrialists to operate a company town.

George Pullman was born on March 3, 1831, in Brocton, N.Y., but his parents soon moved to Portland, N.Y. His upbringing in the Universalist Church greatly affected his later philosophy of labor. His formal education ended at the age of 14, and in 1845 he started work in a general store. After his father died, Pullman agreed to finish his father's contracts to move some homes in the path of an Erie Canal widening. Upon completion of that work in 1855 he moved to Chicago, where he entered the business of raising buildings onto higher foundations to avoid flooding because much of Chicago's land area was only a few feet above the level of Lake Michigan.

The idea of a sleeping car for railroads was not new, and various efforts had been made to construct and operate such cars before Pullman joined the field. He formed a partnership with Benjamin Field, who had the rights to operate sleepers on the Chicago and Alton and the Galena and Union railroads. Pullman remodeled two passenger cars into sleepers, using the principle of an upper berth hinged to the side of the car and supported by two jointed arms. Business grew slowly but steadily until the Civil War. In 1862 he went to the Colorado goldfields, where he operated a trading store and in his spare time continued to develop his sleeping car.

Returning to Chicago, Pullman and Field constructed the "Pioneer" sleeping car, which became a classic in rail history. Its initial trip conveyed Abraham Lincoln's widow from Washington to Springfield, Ill. Other railroads began to use the Pullman car. In 1867, the year of Pullman's marriage, the Illinois legislature chartered the Pullman Palace Car Company, which eventually became the world's largest such building concern. Initially, Pullman contracted for his cars; in 1870 he began construction in Detroit, although the headquarters remained in Chicago. The Pullman company always leased sleeping cars; it never sold them.

By 1880 Pullman had acquired land in the Calumet region of Chicago, where he constructed a new factory and a company town. Deeply disturbed by depressing urban conditions, he envisioned his town as a model of efficiency and healthfulness, though it was planned to return a 6 percent profit. The town cost over $5 million. A serious strike in 1894 marked the beginning of the separation of factory and town. Pullman died in Chicago on Oct. 19, 1897.

Further Reading

Pullman's life and work are discussed in Joseph Husband, *The Story of the Pullman Car* (1917); Stewart H. Holbrook, *The Story of American Railroads* (1947); August Mencken, *The Railroad Passenger Car* (1957); and Stanley Buder, *Pullman: An Experiment in Industrial Order and Community Planning, 1880-1930* (1967). □

Michael Idvorsky Pupin

The Serbo-American physicist and inventor Michael Idvorsky Pupin (1858-1935) is recognized for his contributions to telephony and telegraphy, his invention of electrical tuning, and his discovery of secondary x-ray radiation.

Michael Pupin was born on Oct. 4, 1858, at Idvor in Banat Province, a part of Austria (now of Yugoslavia) settled by Serbs in 1690. The son of illiterate but highly intelligent parents who sacrificed to give their son an education, Pupin soon left the village school to study at Pančevo and then at Prague. Following the death of his father, Pupin sailed to the United States in 1874. Arriving without funds or friends, he held farm and factory jobs, learned English, and in 1879 entered Columbia College.

Pupin subsequently became the first holder of Columbia's Tyndall fellowship in physics. By then he was pursuing his studies abroad, at Cambridge and Berlin, studying mathematical physics and physical chemistry. Receiving his doctorate in 1889, he returned to Columbia as an instructor in its new department of electrical engineering. Pupin combined effective teaching with a program of experimental research. His preliminary work and first publications dealt with electrical charges passing through gases and then with distortions in alternating currents and a general theory of wave propagation. This work led to his development of the electrical resonator (1893), later used in radio tuning, and then to the Pupin coils, inductance coils which when spaced properly along telephone circuits reinforced the vibrations and permitted long-distance calls (1894). Subsequently Pupin expanded upon this work, developing multiplex telegraphy and means to overcome static in wireless communications.

When Wilhelm Roentgen announced his discovery of x-rays in December 1895, Pupin made an x-ray tube and, within 2 weeks, discovered secondary x-radiation; he used

this discovery to make short-exposure x-ray photographs, a procedure of obvious medical importance later. The Bell Telephone Company acquired the rights to his line-loading coils in 1901, as did the Siemens and Halske Company in Germany, and long-distance telephony soon became a reality.

Concern over the people in his native land led Pupin to an increasingly active role in public affairs during the Balkan War and World War I, and he headed many philanthropic and humanitarian efforts on behalf of other Serbs. He was a popular and eloquent platform speaker and a skillful interpreter of scientific learning to laymen. Pupin published approximately 70 technical articles and reports during his lifetime, obtained 34 patents, and received many awards and distinctions. He died in New York City on March 12, 1935.

Further Reading

The best source on Pupin's life remains his charming and inspiring autobiography, *From Immigrant to Inventor* (1923), for which he received the Pulitzer Prize. His other major writings are *The New Reformation: From Physical to Spiritual Realities* (1927) and *Romance of the Machine* (1930). There is a short sketch of Pupin's work in Orrin E. Dunlap, Jr., *Radio's 100 Men of Science: Biographical Narratives of Pathfinders in Electronics and Television* (1944).

Additional Sources

Pupin, Michael Idvorsky, *From immigrant to inventor*, New York: Arno Press, 1980. □

Henry Purcell

The English composer and organist Henry Purcell (1659-1695) was the only great figure of English opera until recent times. In all his works he achieved a happy merger of English traditional styles with the new baroque principles from Italy.

Henry Purcell was probably born in Westminster, then a city separate from London. Son of Henry Purcell, Gentleman of the Chapel Royal and Master of the Choristers at Westminster Abbey, he learned early the fundamentals of his art. His parents lived in Great Almonry near the abbey, until his father died in 1664, at which time the family removed to nearby Tothill Street South. Young Henry was adopted by his uncle Thomas Purcell. Those proposing that Thomas was Henry's father uphold a theory that cannot be substantiated. The weight of the evidence still indicates that this Thomas was young Henry's uncle.

Very little is known of Purcell's schooling. The earliest official document bearing his name is the royal warrant for his dismissal from the Chapel Royal choir, dated Dec. 17, 1673, sometime after his voice had changed. In the Westminster School rolls a Henry Purcell, very likely the composer, is named as a scholar. Shortly after his dismissal from the choir, Henry was apprenticed to John Hingeston, Royal Keeper and Repairer of the Instruments. He also was paid small amounts as a copyist and for tuning the organ at the abbey. In 1677, upon the death of Matthew Locke, Purcell became a member of the Chapel Royal as composer-in-ordinary for the violins and in 1679 succeeded John Blow as organist at the abbey.

Shortly thereafter Purcell married Frances (?) Peters, who bore him six children, only two of whom survived infancy. By then Purcell had become one of England's most promising composers. In 1677 he set a beautiful and moving elegy to Matthew Locke ("Gentle Shepherds, ye that know") for which he may also have written the text. By the end of 1680 he finished not only almost all the elegant, deeply expressive fantasias and innomines but many of the trio sonatas and early songs as well. Stylistically all these were related to England's musical traditions but owed much to French and Italian models, as Purcell acknowledged in his trio sonatas published in 1683.

On July 31, 1682, Purcell's uncle Thomas died. The following year, perhaps merely as a formality, Purcell was required to take the sacrament of the Church of England in public, an event which may point to some suspicion that he had Papist sympathies. By then, though, he was firmly established as Charles II's chief composer. Among the best-known works from this period are the incidental music for Nathanial Lee's *Theodosius,* the Service in B-flat Major, the anthems "Rejoice in the Lord" and "They that go down to the sea in ships," and the song "Bess of Bedlam."

Purcell's first compositions for James II, who ascended the throne in 1685, reflect a change in style, as may be seen

in such works as the coronation anthem "My heart is inditing" and the ode "Why are all the muses mute?" Other differences in style, which in general reveal larger formal conceptions, are longer and more varied phrase constructions and evidence of greater attention to word illustrations and color contrasts. During the 3 years of James II's reign Purcell's reputation as a songwriter developed rapidly, and scarcely a collection or stage piece came out in London during this time without his participation.

Purcell was commissioned to supply music for the coronation ceremonies of William and Mary, which took place on April 11, 1689. Again a change in Purcell's music may be detected, for after the Glorious Revolution he turned to opera, to semiopera (a combined opera, stage play, ballet, and masque), and to more impressive sets of incidental music, showing a mastery of dramatic expression which no English composer ever surpassed.

Purcell began the new trend in 1689 with the opera *Dido and Aeneas,* which contains the moving lament "When I am laid in earth." He continued thereafter with at least one major dramatic composition each year. In 1690 he produced the heroic semiopera *Dioclesian* and in 1691 *King Arthur,* based on John Dryden's play; both operas relate topically to contemporary events. *The Fairy Queen* was produced in 1692, the incidental music for William Congreve's *The Double Dealer* in 1693, and the incidental music for *The Married Beau* in 1694. Purcell died while composing *The Indian Queen* in 1695, and his brother Daniel was asked to write the additional act.

During Purcell's last years he also wrote a great many other important works, including the *Ode to St. Cecilia* of 1692, six birthday odes for Queen Mary, the *Te Deum and Jubilate* in D Major, and a host of songs and dialogues. In addition, he found time to rewrite and revise portions of John Playford's *Introduction to the Skill of Music* (1694) and to carry out all his official duties as instrument repairer, organist, performer, and teacher.

Further Reading

The definitive single work on Purcell is Sir Jack A. Westrup, *Purcell* (1947), which provides a concise and perceptive account of the man and his music. A broader account of Purcell's life and times is in the projected three-volume work of Franklin B. Zimmerman, two volumes of which have been published: *Purcell's Musical Heritage: A Study of Musical Styles in Seventeenth Century England* (1966) and *Henry Purcell, 1659-1695: His Life and Times* (1967). For an analysis of Purcell's music see Zimmerman's *Henry Purcell, 1659-1695: An Analytical Catalogue of His Works* (1963). The best book on Purcell's stage music is Robert E. Moore, *Henry Purcell and the Restoration Theatre* (1961), which combines literary and musical insights in a fascinating study. For background, see Percy Young, *History of British Music* (1967).

Additional Sources

Campbell, Margaret, *Henry Purcell: glory of his age,* Oxford; New York: Oxford University Press, 1995.

Duffy, Maureen, *Henry Purcell,* London: Fourth Estate, 1994.

Dupre, Henri, *Purcell,* New York: AMS Press, 1978.

King, Robert, *Henry Purcell,* New York: Thames and Hudson, 1994.

Westrup, J. A. (Jack Allan), *Purcell,* Oxford; New York: Oxford University Press, 1995.

Zimmerman, Franklin B., *Henry Purcell, 1659-1695: his life and times,* Philadelphia: University of Pennsylvania Press, 1983. □

Robert Purvis

Robert Purvis (1810-1898) was a radical African American abolitionist and reformer as well as a prosperous gentleman farmer and businessman.

Robert Purvis was born on Aug. 4, 1810, in Charleston, S.C., of a free woman of Moorish ancestry and a wealthy abolitionist-oriented English cotton broker. In 1819 Robert's father established a school for colored children in Philadelphia at his own expense. There Robert obtained a sound education. He continued his studies at Pittsfield Academy and then at Amherst College.

Purvis became actively involved in the antislavery movement when William Lloyd Garrison, while visiting his home, unfolded plans for publishing the *Liberator*. Purvis became a regular contributor to this paper. In 1833 he was one of the founders of the American Antislavery Society and served as vice president. He also helped organize the Pennsylvania Antislavery Society, serving as president and member of the executive committee.

Only through the intercession of President Andrew Jackson did Purvis receive passports for himself and his bride to go abroad, where they met numerous opponents of slavery. Returning to the United States, Purvis single-handedly rescued Basil Dorsey from the court house in Doylestown, Pa., in 1836, just as the slave catchers appeared with the magistrate's warrant to return him to slavery. Purvis then escorted Dorsey to safety.

In 1838 Purvis published a pamphlet protesting the legislative proposal to disenfranchise African Americans in Pennsylvania. That year he further organized the Underground Railroad with agents, black and white, in Newbern, N.C., Baltimore, Md., and Wilmington, Del. He condemned the Dred Scott decision in the harshest terms and risked his life to publicly praise John Brown. He continually attacked the movement to colonize African Americans in Africa.

Purvis worked unremittingly to convince the U.S. government to place the Civil War on an antislavery basis and to establish a new union from which slavery would be excluded forever. He urged not only utilization of black soldiers but also appointment of black officers. He softened his antislavery stand only when Abraham Lincoln issued the Emancipation Proclamation, which Purvis felt recognized blacks as citizens. His antislavery work ceased with the passage of the 15th Amendment in 1870. In 1888 he presided at the semicentennial meeting of the Antislavery Society.

Purvis was also active in such organizations as the American Moral Reform Society, the Woman Suffrage Society, and the Committee of 100 for the Purification of Municipal Affairs in Philadelphia. As a gentleman farmer, he developed a showplace at Byberry and prizewinning livestock. He also owned a second farm and several pieces of real estate in Philadelphia, including mercantile property on Market Street. He died on April 15, 1898, in Philadelphia.

Further Reading

Biographical sketches of Purvis appear in Richard Bardolph, *The Negro Vanguard* (1959), and Wilhelmina S. Robinson, *Historical Negro Biographies* (1967). William Wells Brown reports personal impressions of Purvis in his *The Black Man: His Antecedents, His Genius, and His Achievements* (rev. ed. 1863). For commentary on Purvis's writings see Vernon Loggins, *The Negro Author: His Development in America* (1931). James M. McPherson, *The Struggle for Equality: Abolitionists and the Negro in the Civil War and Reconstruction* (1964), and Benjamin Quarles, *Black Abolitionists* (1969), discuss Purvis. □

Martin Puryear

Martin Puryear (born 1941) was one of the first African American artists to receive international recognition. His art was a fusion of cultures and of categories, such as sculpture, architecture, and craft. The result was an art that functions between "fine art" and "craft" and transcends national styles and topical issues.

Martin Puryear was born in Washington, D.C., on May 23, 1941. As an adolescent he showed an interest in nature by making detailed drawings of birds and insects, but he also demonstrated an aptitude for building functional objects, such as a guitar, a canoe, bow and arrows, and furniture. He entered Catholic University as a biology major but changed the emphasis of his studies to painting during his junior year. A favorite instructor there was Nell Sonneman, who presented art as a pursuit of truth through self-sacrifice. He graduated with a Bachelor of Arts degree in 1963.

Eager to travel, Puryear joined the Peace Corps and was assigned to a remote village in Sierra Leone, West Africa, where he taught biology, French, English, and art at the secondary school level. The village carpenters who made furniture for his classroom impressed him with the level of their craftsmanship. He especially admired their belief that true creativity can be achieved only through the mastery of one's craft.

Upon the completion of his two-year commitment to the Peace Corps in 1966, Puryear moved to Stockholm, Sweden, where he entered the printmaking program of the Swedish Royal Academy of Art. His choice of Sweden was prompted by his fascination for the Scandinavian landscape and modern furniture design. While there he undertook a long backpacking trip above the Arctic Circle through the Lapland of Sweden and Norway, during which he observed the traditional basketry and quillwork of the local residents. Back in Stockholm, he briefly apprenticed himself to the renowned cabinetmaker James Krenov, whom he admired as a knowledgeable, dedicated craftsman as well as for his skills and designs. Various aspects of his training and experience began to reinforce each other. He realized that the teachings of Sonneman and Krenov confirmed what he had observed in the carpenters of Sierra Leone. By combining his artistic impulses with his interest in craft, he recognized that construction was a legitimate way to make art. He returned to the United States in 1969 to study sculpture at Yale University.

After earning a Master of Fine Arts degree from Yale in 1971, Puryear taught at Fisk University in Nashville for two years, and then at the University of Maryland for four years. It was during this period that his career as an exhibiting artist blossomed. In 1972 he received his first one-person exhibition at the Henri 2 Gallery in Washington, D.C. While teaching at the University of Maryland and simultaneously maintaining a studio in Brooklyn, New York, he was awarded several grants, including a National Endowment for the Arts Individual Artist fellowship. In 1977 he was given a solo exhibition at the Corcoran Gallery in Washington, D.C., and received his first commission for an outdoor sculpture.

Unfortunately, that same year a fire in his Brooklyn studio destroyed many of his sculptures and tools. The following year he relocated his studio to Chicago, where he taught at the University of Illinois at Chicago. In 1979 he received a National Endowment for the Arts Planning Grant for Art in Public Places, which resulted in a number of major outdoor sculptures. Among his notable pieces are *The Black Circle* (1980, University of Illinois, Chicago); *Sentinel* (1982, Gettysburg College, Pennsylvania); and *Knoll* (1983, National Oceanographic and Atmospheric Administration, Seattle, Washington.) While the public sculptures were successful, his studio pieces are what brought him national and international recognition. "It is Puryear's combination of enigma and skill that makes him so strong an artist," wrote art critic Jonathan Goodman in 1995, reviewing two studio pieces, *Alien Huddle* and *No Title*. In 1984 the University Gallery of the University of Massachusetts at Amherst organized a ten-year retrospective exhibition that traveled to four other museums. In the same year Puryear had sculptures included in two important exhibitions at the Museum of Modern Art, New York: "An International Survey of Recent Painting and Sculpture" and "Primitivism in Twentieth Century Art: Affinity of the Tribal and the Modern." In 1984 he was also awarded a John S. Guggenheim Memorial Foundation grant, which enabled him to travel to Japan to study domestic architecture and gardens. He accepted an invitation in 1986 to be a visiting artist in residence at the American Academy in Rome. In 1989 he was awarded a MacArthur Foundation grant and also was the sole representative of the United States to the 1989 Sao Paolo Bienal, where he was awarded the grand prize; the following year he won the Skowhegan Award. In 1991 the Art Institute of Chicago organized a large exhibition of his work that trav-

eled to the Hirshorn Museum in Washington, D.C. and then nationally.

A member of the American Academy of Arts and Letters, Puryear's reputation increased in the 1990s. In 1991, he collaborated with musician Wynton Marsalis and playwright Garth Fagan in designing a dance production, "Griot New York." By 1997, he was living in upstate New York, continuing his teaching and art from there. He was a visiting artist at Penland School of Crafts in North Carolina in the spring of 1997; meanwhile, a major retrospective of his work was prepared for a European tour, opening in Madrid, then going to Sweden, the country where he once studied.

The emergence of Puryear's sculpture in the 1970s provided a welcome alternative to the waning minimalist styles of the previous decade. Like the minimalists, Puryear recognized the power of simple abstract forms, but he imbued his shapes with vaguely figurative references. Many of his hand-crafted constructions resemble man-made implements and structures, such as tools, vessels, or huts, and others are biomorphic, suggesting plants or animals; however, they all resist singular interpretations. In fact, duality is a recurring theme. His pieces may appear at once to be organic and geometric, natural and machine-like, massive yet transparent, random yet structured, crude yet elegant. For example, *Sanctuary* (1982), a sculpture consisting of a square wooden box anchored to a wall and connected to a wheel on the floor, reflects the artist's ambivalence between the stability of a permanent home and the liberation of mobility. Pertinent to this age of world travel and informed by his experiences, cultural adaptability is another important theme of Puryear's sculpture. Through his virtuoso craftsmanship, his sensitivity to his materials and borrowed forms, Puryear paid homage to the international craft traditions to which he was indebted. By learning traditional skills and understanding traditional methods, he sought to recover creative possibilities lost to our industrialized society.

Puryear's sculpture is in the collections of many major American museums, including the Art Institute of Chicago, Hirshorn Museum, the Museum of Modern Art and the National Gallery.

Further Reading

The most comprehensive publication on the artist and his sculpture is *Martin Puryear,* the 1991 exhibition catalogue by the Art Institute of Chicago, with essays by Neal Benezra and Robert Storr. It includes a concise chronology and an extensive bibliography. Another exhibition catalogue of the same title was published in 1984 by the University of Massachusetts, with essays by Hugh M. Davies and Helaine Posner. Two general surveys of contemporary art which include discussions of Puryear are Arnason, H.H., *History of Modern Art* (Third Edition, 1986) and Wheeler, Daniel, *Art Since Mid-Century: 1945 to the Present* (1991). More information is in Cummings, Paul, *Dictionary of Contemporary American Artists* (1994). A critique of a Puryear exhibition by Jonathan Goodman can be found in *ARTnews* (Sepember 1995). □

Edward Bouverie Pusey

The English clergyman and scholar Edward Bouverie Pusey (1800-1882) was one of the major figures of the Oxford Movement, which began at Oxford in 1833 to overcome the dangers threatening the Church of England.

Edward Pusey's lineage was noble. His father had inherited the estate of Pusey, in Berkshire, where Edward was born on Aug. 22, 1800. His childhood was calm and self-assured but isolated. He accepted his mother's High Anglican teaching and moved confidently toward a clerical vocation by way of Eton and Oxford. As a student, Pusey labored endlessly, reading for as much as 17 hours a day. He won a first-class degree at Christ Church, Oxford, and then in 1823 was elected a fellow of Oriel College, where he met John Keble and John Henry Newman.

Pusey then determined "to devote my life to the Old Testament," and he studied theology and Semitic languages at the universities of Göttingen and Berlin between 1826 and 1828. On his return his father permitted him to marry Maria Barker, whom he had loved for many years, and that same year Pusey was ordained. Late in 1828 he became regius professor of Hebrew at Oxford and was appointed canon of Christ Church. He also published a critical history of German theology.

Late in 1833 Pusey gravitated toward the Oxford Movement. He wrote tracts on the advantages of fasting (1834) and on baptism (1836) in the series *Tracts for the Times.* From the standpoint of public prestige, his adhesion to the Oxford Movement, Newman said, supplied it with "a position and a name." The movement was sometimes known as "Puseyism" throughout the later 1830s.

In 1836 Pusey began his influential editorship of the *Library of Fathers,* beginning with the works of St. Augustine, Ultimately 48 volumes in this series were published, and Pusey contributed several studies of patristic works.

When Newman withdrew from the Oxford Movement, Pusey became its leader. In 1843 Pusey, who had defended Newman's Tract No. 90, was charged with preaching heresy in a sermon on the Eucharist, "The Holy Eucharist, a Comfort to the Penitent." In secret proceedings of questionable fairness he was privately suspended from preaching at Oxford for 2 years. In 1845 he assisted in the establishment of the first Anglican sisterhood, and throughout the rest of his life he assisted in establishing Anglican orders. In 1846 Pusey claimed in his sermon "The Entire Absolution of the Penitent" that the Church of England possessed the right of priestly absolution, thus inaugurating the Anglican practice of private confession.

In his remaining years at Oxford, Pusey fought for Tractarian objectives but without major successes. He opposed the increasing secularization of the university, in which intellectual life was being segregated from a moral and spiritual base. He also worked for Christian unity, but he was defeated partly by the new assertions of Roman authority under the papacy of Pius IX. His sermon "The Rule of Faith" (1851) did, however, check English conversions to Roman Catholicism.

Pusey's private life exemplified the personal holiness that marked the Tractarians' purpose. His wife died of consumption in 1839, and his only son became a chronic invalid and a cripple. Only one child survived him. For Pusey these tragedies, and the public hostility he encountered, were spurs to greater penitence, humility, and submission. He practiced simplicity, self-denial, and works of charity.

Pusey's *Eirenicon* (3 parts, 1865-1870) was an attempt to find common ground for reuniting Roman Catholicism and the Church of England. Its publication caused much controversy, being answered by Newman. Pusey died at Ascot Priory, Berkshire, on Sept. 16, 1882.

Further Reading

The basic biography of Pusey is Henry P. Liddon, *Life of Edward Bouverie Pusey, D.D..* (4 vols., 1893-1897). A brief panegyric by Charles C. Grafton, *Pusey and the Church Revival* (1902), is useful as an explication of Anglo-Catholic theology. Newman's comments on Pusey are in his famous autobiography, *Apologia pro vita sua* (1864). Of the large literature on the Oxford Movement generally, an early and deeply sympathetic account by a disciple is Richard W. Church, *The Oxford Movement* (1897). Among the later histories are a broad and fair treatment by Yngue T. Brilioth, *The Anglican Revival* (1933), and Geoffrey C. Faber, *Oxford Apostles* (1933), a lively work full of psychological insight but not unfriendly. A useful anthology of primary readings is Owen Chadwick, ed., *The Mind of the Oxford Movement* (1960).

Additional Sources

Pusey rediscovered, London: SPCK, 1983. □

Aleksandr Sergeevich Pushkin

The Russian poet and prose writer Aleksandr Sergeevich Pushkin (1799-1837) ranks as the country's greatest poet. He not only brought Russian poetry to its highest excellence but also had a decisive influence on Russian literature in the 19th and 20th centuries.

Aleksandr Pushkin is Russia's national poet. He established the norms of classical Russian versification, and he laid the groundwork for much of the development of Russian prose in the 19th century. His work is distinguished by brilliance of language, compactness, terseness, and objectivity. His poetry is supremely untranslatable, and consequently Pushkin has had less influence on world literature than on Russian literature. He may be described as a romantic in subject matter and a classicist in style and form.

Pushkin was born on May 26, 1799, the son of a family of the middle nobility. On his father's side he was a descendant of one of the oldest lines of Russian nobility, and on his mother's side he was related to an Abyssinian, Abram Petrovich Hannibal, who had been kidnaped in Africa, brought to Constantinople, and sent as a gift to Peter I (the Great). Pushkin was brought up in an atmosphere that was predominantly French, and at a very early age he became acquainted with the classic works of 17th- and 18th-century French literature. Several of the important figures of Russian literature—including Nikolai Karamzin and Vasily Zhukovsky—were visitors to the Pushkin home during Aleksandr's childhood.

Between 1811 and 1817 Pushkin attended a special school established at Tsarskoye Selo (later renamed Pushkin) by Czar Alexander I for privileged children of the nobility. Pushkin was an indifferent student in most subjects, but he performed brilliantly in French and Russian literature.

Early Works, 1814-1820

After finishing school, Pushkin led the reckless and dissipated life of a typical nobleman. He wrote about 130 poems between 1814 and 1817, while still at school, and these and most of his works written between 1817 and 1820 were not published because of the boldness of his thoughts on political and erotic matters. In 1820 Pushkin completed his first narrative poem, *Russlan and Ludmilla*. It is a romance composed of fantastic adventures but told with 18th-century humor and irony. Before *Russlan and Ludmilla* was published in June 1820, Pushkin was exiled to the south of Russia because of the boldness of the political sentiments he had expressed in his poems. His "Ode to Liberty" contained, for example, a reference to the assassination of Paul I, the father of Czar Alexander I. Pushkin left St. Petersburg on May 6 and he did not return to the capital for more than 6 years.

South of Russia, 1820-1824

Pushkin spent the years 1820-1823 in various places in the Caucasus and in the Crimea, and he was at first charmed by the picturesque settings and relieved to be free of the intoxications and artificialities of the life of the capital. Subsequently, however, he felt bored by the life in small towns and took up again a life of gambling, drinking, and consorting with loose women. He was always short of money, for his salary in the civil service was small and his family refused to support him. He began to earn money with his poetic works, but these sums were seldom sufficient to permit him to compete comfortably with his affluent friends. In 1823 he was transferred to Odessa, where he found the life of a large city more to his liking.

The poet's life in Odessa in 1823-1824 was marked by three strong amorous attachments. First, he fell in love with Carolina Sobansky, a beauty who was 6 years older than he. He broke with her in October 1823 and then fell violently in love with the wife of a Dalmatian merchant, Amalia Riznich. She had many admirers and gave Pushkin ample cause for jealousy. Amalia, however, inspired some of Pushkin's best poems, such as "Night" and "Beneath the Blue

Sky of Her Native Land,'' and he remembered her to the end of his life. His third love was for the wife of the governor general, the Countess Eliza Vorontsov. She was a charming and beautiful woman. Vorontsov learned of the affair, and having no special liking for Pushkin he resolved to have him transferred from Odessa. He was aided in this endeavor by an unfortunate letter that Pushkin had written to a friend in which he had questioned the immortality of the soul. The letter was intercepted, and because of it Pushkin was expelled from the service on July 18, 1824, by the Czar and ordered to the family estate of Mikhailovskoye near Pskov.

Pushkin's poetic work during the 4 years that he spent in the south was rich in output and characterized by Lord Byron's influence, which can be seen in ''The Caucasian Captive'' (1820-1821), ''The Fountain of Bakhchisarai'' (1822), and ''The Gypsies'' (1824). These poems are mellifluous in verse and exotic in setting, but they already show the elements of Pushkin's classic style: measure, balance, terseness, and restraint.

Mikhailovskoye, 1824-1826

On Aug. 9, 1824, Pushkin arrived at Mikhailovskoye. His relations with his parents were not good. The father felt angry at his son's rebelliousness and on one occasion spread a story that his son had attempted to beat him. The family left the estate about mid-November, and Pushkin found himself alone with the family nurse, Arina Rodionovna, at Mikhailovskoye. He lived fairly much as a recluse during the next 2 years, occasionally visiting a neighboring town and infrequently entertaining old Petersburg friends. During this period he fell in love with a Madame Kern, who was married to an old general and who encouraged the attention of many men. Also at this time the nurse told Pushkin many folk tales, and it is generally believed that she imbued him with the feeling for folk life that manifested itself in many of his poems.

Pushkin's 2 years at Mikhailovskoye were extremely rich in poetic output. He completed ''The Gypsies,'' wrote the first three chapters of *Eugene Onegin,* and composed the tragedy *Boris Godunov.* In addition he composed many important lyrics and a humorous tale in verse entitled *Count Nulin. Boris Godunov* is a chronicle play. Pushkin took the subject from Karamzin's history, and it relates the claims of the impostor Demetrius to the throne of the elected monarch Boris Godunov.

Maturity, 1826-1831

After the end of his exile at Mikhailovskoye, Pushkin was received by the new czar, Nicholas I, who charmed Pushkin by his reasonableness and kindness. The Czar placed Pushkin under a privileged tyranny by promising him that his works would be censored by the Czar himself. The practical consequences of this arrangement were that Pushkin was placed under an honorable promise to publish nothing that was injurious to the government; in time this ''privileged'' censorship became increasingly onerous.

Pushkin continued his dissipated life after 1826 but with less gusto. Although he was still in his 20s, he began to feel the weight of his years, and he longed to settle down.

On April 6, 1830, he proposed to Nathalie Goncharova for the second time and was accepted. She came from a noble family that had fallen on hard times financially. The Goncharovs were dissatisfied with Pushkin's standing with the government and were unimpressed by his reputation as a poet. Pushkin had to ask for economic favors for the Goncharovs from the government, and he persuaded his father to settle an estate on him.

Pushkin's output in the years 1826-1829 was not so great as in the years 1824-1826, but it was still impressive. He continued to work on *Eugene Onegin,* wrote a number of excellent lyrics, worked on but did not finish a prose novel entitled *The Nigger of Peter the Great,* and wrote *Poltava,* a narrative poem on Peter the Great's struggle with Charles XII which celebrates the Russian victory over the Swedes. This poem shows the continuing development of Pushkin's style toward objectivity and austerity.

In the fall of 1830 Pushkin left the capital to visit a small estate by the name of Boldino, which his father had left him, with the intention of spending a few weeks there. However, he was blocked from returning to the capital by measures taken by the authorities because of a cholera epidemic, and he was forced to return to Boldino. During that autumn at Boldino, Pushkin wrote some of his greatest lyrics; *The Tales of Belkin;* a comic poem in octaves, ''The Little House in Kolomna''; and four small tragedies; and he virtually finished *Eugene Onegin.*

Eugene Onegin was begun in 1824 and finished in August 1831. This novel in verse is without doubt Pushkin's most famous work. It shows the influence in theme of Byron's *Don Juan* and in style of Laurence Sterne's novels. It is a ''novel'' about contemporary life, constructed in order to permit digressions and a variety of incidents and tones. The heart of the tale concerns the life of Eugene Onegin, a bored nobleman who rejects the advances of a young girl, Tatiana. He meets her later, greatly changed and now sophisticated, falls in love with her. He is in turn rejected by her because, although she loves him, she is married.

Pushkin's four little tragedies are models of spare, objective, and compact drama. The plays are short and vary in length from 240 to 550 lines. *The Feast during the Plague* is a translation of a scene from John Wilson's *The City of the Plague; The Stone Guest* is a variation of the Don Juan theme; *Mozart and Salieri* treats the tradition of Antonio Salieri's envy of Wolfgang Amadeus Mozart's effortless art and the injustice of Nature in dispensing her gifts; and *The Covetous Knight* has as its theme avariciousness and contains the famous monologue of the baron on his treasures.

The Tales of Belkin consists of five short stories: ''The Shot,'' ''The Snowstorm,'' ''The Stationmaster,'' ''The Undertaker,'' and ''The Peasant Gentlewoman.'' The stories are models of swift, unadorned narration.

Marriage, Duel, and Death, 1831-1837

After 1830 Pushkin wrote less and less poetry. ''The Bronze Horseman'' (1833) is considered by many to be his greatest poem. The setting is the great flood of 1824, which inundated much of St. Petersburg. The theme of the poem is the irreconcilable demands of the state and the individual.

The Golden Cockerel (1833) is a volume of Russian folktales. Pushkin's masterpiece in narrative is the short story "The Queen of Spades" (1834), about a gloomy engineer who is ruthless in his efforts to discover the secret of three winning cards. Mention should also be made of his *The History of the Pugachev Rebellion* (1834) and *The Captain's Daughter* (1837), a short novel about the Pugachev rebellion.

Pushkin married Nathalie Goncharova on Jan. 19, 1831. She bore him three children, but the couple were not happy together. She was beautiful and a favorite at court, but she was also somewhat uneducated and not free of vulgarity. She encouraged the attentions of Baron George d'Anthes, an exiled Alsatian Frenchman and a protégé of the minister of the Netherlands at St. Petersburg. Pushkin provoked D'Anthes to a duel on Jan. 26, 1837, and the duel took place the next day. Pushkin was wounded and died on January 29. There was great popular mourning at his death.

Many of Pushkin's works provided the basis for operas by Russian composers. They include *Ruslan and Ludmilla* by Mikhail Glinka, *Eugene Onegin* and *The Queen of Spades* by Peter Ilyich Tchaikovsky, *Boris Godunov* by Modest Mussorgsky, *The Stone Guest* by Aleksandr Dargomijsky, and *The Golden Cockerel* by Nicolai Rimsky-Korsakov.

Further Reading

Eugene Onegin is available in many translations. Recommended are those by Dorothea Prall Raddin and George Z. Patrick (1937) and by Vladimir Nabokov (4 vols., 1964); the Nabokov translation is accompanied by massive documentation. Among the excellent biographies of Pushkin are Ernest Simmons, *Pushkin* (1937), a full and readable account; Henry Troyat, *Pushkin: A Biography,* translated by Randolphe Weaver (1950), vivid and engrossing; and another work on Pushkin's life, David Magarshack, *Pushkin: A Biography* (1967). Walter N. Vickery, *Pushkin: Death of a Poet* (1968), is a work on the final days of Pushkin's life.

The most readable and informative review of Pushkin's works is Prince D. S. Mirsky, *Pushkin* (1926). Mirsky's *A History of Russian Literature* (2 vols., 1927) is recommended for general historical and literary background; this same work is available in a one-volume abridgment edited by Francis J. Whitfield (1958). □

Israel Putnam

Israel Putnam (1718-1790), American soldier, was a Revolutionary War general. Although known for his courage and energy in combat, he was an incompetent commander.

Israel Putnam was born in Salem Village, Mass., on Jan. 7, 1718. He had very little education and remained nearly illiterate all his life. In 1738 he married Hannah Pope and the following year moved to Connecticut, where he bought land and farmed successfully, soon becoming a man of substance. When the French and Indian War broke

out in 1756, Putnam was commissioned a lieutenant in the Connecticut militia and served throughout the conflict, rising steadily in rank until he reached a colonelcy by the time it ended in 1763. He fought in numerous engagements, earned a reputation for bravery and resourcefulness, and gained valuable military experience.

With the coming of peace, Putnam returned to farming and also operated a tavern. He took part in the developing conflict between England and the Colonies, helping organize the Sons of Liberty in 1765. He participated in the political life of Connecticut as a representative to the General Assembly in 1766 and 1767. In 1774 he headed the local Committee of Correspondence and accepted appointment as lieutenant colonel of a regiment of Connecticut militia. When the fighting began in the spring of 1775, Putnam entered active service and in June was appointed by the Continental Congress one of the four major generals under George Washington's command. It was not a wise appointment, for although Putnam was a good soldier and an inspiring and able leader, he did not have the qualities needed for planning major operations, commanding large units, or executing grand strategy.

Putnam was at Bunker Hill, at the siege of Boston, and in New York to plan the defenses there. He was in command at the Battle of Long Island in August 1776 until Washington's arrival, and that American defeat has been blamed by one historian on "the incapacity of Israel Putnam." In subsequent assignments his performance was no better. Washington ordered him to Princeton early in 1777, but Putnam delayed. He was then sent to command an

important post on the Hudson River, but in December 1777, after 7 months of inefficiency, he was removed. A court of inquiry convened to investigate his record in one action, but he was exonerated. It was clear, however, that he was unfit for a command. Washington sent Putnam to be chief of recruiting in Connecticut in 1779. In December of that year, a paralytic stroke ended his military career. He returned to his farm in Connecticut, where he died on May 29, 1790.

Further Reading

The best account of Putnam's career is William Farrand Livingston, *Israel Putnam, Pioneer, Ranger, and Major-General, 1718-1790* (1901). Two other biographies are useful: David Humphreys, *The Life and Heroic Exploits of Israel Putnam* (1835), and I. N. Tarbox, *Life of Israel Putnam ("Old Put"), Major-General in the Continental Army* (1877).

Additional Sources

Humphreys, David, *An essay on the life of the Honorable Major-General Israel Putnam,* New York: Garland Pub., 1977.
Niven, John, *Connecticut hero, Israel Putnam,* Hartford: American Revolution Bicentennial Commission of Connecticut, 1977. □

Pierre Puvis de Chavannes

Pierre Puvis de Chavannes (1824-1898) occupied a unique position in 19th-century French painting: he was one of the few academic painters whose work was deeply admired by the avant-garde artists of his day.

B orn in Lyons on Dec. 14, 1824, Pierre Puvis de Chavannes belonged to the generation of Gustave Courbet and Édouard Manet, and he was fully aware of their revolutionary achievements. Nevertheless, he was drawn to a more traditional and conservative style. From his first involvement with art, which began after a trip to Italy and which interrupted his intention to follow the engineering profession that his father practiced, Puvis pursued his career within the scope of academic classicism and the Salon. Even in this chosen arena, however, he was rejected, particularly during the 1850s. But he gradually won acceptance. By the 1880s he was an established figure in the Salons, and by the 1890s he was their acknowledged master.

In both personal and artistic ways Puvis's career was closely linked with the avant-grade. In the years of his growing public recognition, when he began to serve on Salon juries, he was consistently sympathetic to the work of younger, more radical artists. Later, as president of the Société Nationale des Beaux-Arts—the "new Salon," as it was called—he was able to exert even more of a liberalizing influence on the important annual exhibitions.

Puvis's sympathy to new and radical artistic directions was reflected in his own painting. Superficially he was a classicist, but his personal interpretation of that style was unconventional. His subject matter—religious themes, allegories, mythologies, and historical events—was clearly in keeping with the academic tradition. But his style eclipsed his outdated subjects: he characteristically worked with broad, simple compositions, and he resisted the dry photographic realism which had begun to typify academic painting about the end of the century. In addition, the space and figures in his paintings inclined toward flatness, calling attention to the surface on which the images were depicted. These qualities gave his work a modern, abstract look and distinguished it from the sterile tradition to which it might otherwise have been linked.

Along with their modern, formal properties, Puvis's paintings exhibited a serene and poetic range of feeling. His figures frequently seem to be wrapped in an aura of ritualistic mystery, as though they belong in a private world of dreams or visions. Yet these feelings invariably seem fresh and sincere. This combination of form and feeling deeply appealed to certain avant-garde artists of the 1880s and 1890s. Although Puvis claimed he was neither radical nor revolutionary, he was admired by the symbolist poets, writers, and painters—including Paul Gauguin and Maurice Denis—and he influenced the neoimpressionist painter Georges Seurat.

During his mature career Puvis executed many mural paintings. In Paris he did the *Life of St. Genevieve* (1874-1878) in the Panthéon and *Science, Art, and Letters* (1880s) in the Sorbonne. In Lyons he executed the *Sacred Grove,* the *Antique Vision,* and *Christian Inspiration* (1880s) in the Musée des Beaux-Arts. He painted *Pastoral Poetry* (1895-

1898) in the Boston Public Library. These commissions reflect the high esteem with which Puvis was regarded during his own lifetime. Among his most celebrated oil paintings are *Hope* (1872) and the *Poor Fisherman* (1881). He died in Paris on Oct. 10, 1898.

Further Reading

François Crastre, *Puvis de Chavannes* (1912), and Jean Laran, *Puvis de Chavannes* (1912), are biographical studies containing some reproductions of the paintings. Frank Gibson, *Six French Artists of the Nineteenth Century* (1925), includes a chapter on Puvis. A background study which briefly discusses Puvis is Jean Leymarie, *French Painting: The Nineteenth Century* (trans. 1962). □

Ernie Pyle

Ernie Pyle (1900-1945) was America's most beloved and famous war correspondent during World War II. His sympathetic accounts of the ordinary GI made him the champion of American fighting men.

Born in a little white farmhouse near Dana, Indiana, on August 3, 1900, to William C. and Maria Pyle, Earnest (Ernie) Taylor Pyle later wrote in one of his columns: "I wasn't born in a log cabin, but I did start driving a team in the fields when I was nine years old, if that helps any." He attended Indiana University for three and a half years, majoring in journalism because his classmates considered it "a breeze."

A few months before graduation in 1923 he quit college to take a job as a cub reporter on the *La Porte* (Indiana) *Herald-Argus*. Soon after, he was hired as a copy editor by the *Washington Daily News*. There he met Geraldine Siebolds of Stillwater, Minnesota. In 1926 they were married. Pyle quit his job, drew out his savings to purchase a Model-T Ford roadster, and the young couple began the first of their many driving trips together around the United States. Ending their vacation in New York City, Pyle went to work as a copyreader on the *Evening World* and on the *Evening Post*. In 1928 he returned to the *Daily News* as telegraph editor, then aviation columnist, and from 1932 to 1935 as managing editor.

Wearied of desk work, Pyle started writing pieces as a roving reporter for the Scripps-Howard chain of newspapers in 1935. In the next six years he and his wife, known to millions of readers as "that girl who rides with me," travelled over 200,000 miles "by practically all forms of locomotion, including piggyback," Pyle wrote in one of his columns in 1940. Visiting every country in the Western Hemisphere but two and crossing the United States some 30 times, "we have stayed in more than eight hundred hotels . . . flown in sixty-six different airplanes, ridden on twenty-nine different boats, walked two hundred miles, gone through five sets of tires and put out approximately $2,500 in tips." Each day's experience became material for a column: a Nebraska town on relief, old men with wooden legs,

a leper colony, Devil's Island, zipper-pants difficulties. Written simply and sensitively, like a letter to a friend back home, they revealed the world to millions of farm-bound and pavement bound Americans who could never make such journeys.

In the fall of 1940 Pyle flew to London to report the Battle of Britain. His vivid, grim accounts of England under Nazi German bombings tore at his readers' hearts, and the "little fellow"—I weigh 108 pounds, eat left-handed, am 28 inches around the waist, and still have a little hair left"— previously content to write about little things soon eclipsed the seasoned war correspondents in his cables back home. When American troops arrived in Europe, Pyle lived with them in Ireland; when they went into combat in Africa, his columns communicated all the hurt, horror, and homesickness the soldiers felt. Then Pyle marched with American troops in Sicily and Italy and landed with them in Normandy, France.

His warm, human stories about the GIs became a daily link between the fighting men and millions of American newspaper readers. His writings were read in some 300 newspapers in the United States like personal letters from the front. Throughout the war Pyle championed the common soldier; he spoke the ordinary GI's language and made it a permanent part of American folklore. His published collections of columns, *Here Is Your War* and *Brave Men,* quickly became best-sellers and were purchased by Hollywood as the basis for a motion picture on Pyle's wartime career entitled "GI Joe." Although his dispatches never glorified war, Pyle, more than any other correspondent, helped Americans to understand the true heroism and sacrifices of the GIs in battle.

In January 1945 Pyle went to report on the war in the Pacific. He did not relish going. He had already achieved fame and wealth. He had frequent premonitions of death—"I feel that I've used up all my chances, and I hate it. I don't want to be killed." But he journeyed across the Pacific to begin writing from foxholes again "because there's a war on and I'm part of it. . . . I've got to go, and I hate it." He landed in Okinawa with the Marines and trudged along the trails with the foot soldiers. On April 18, 1945, while riding a jeep toward a forward command post on the island of Ie Shima to cover the front-line combat, Ernie Pyle was hit by a Japanese machine-gun bullet in his left temple. He died instantly. Secretary of the Navy James V. Forrestal announced Pyle's death the next day, saddening the many Americans who eagerly read his column each day and all those servicemen who thought of him as their friend and spokesman. President Harry Truman best summed up Pyle's meaning to the World War II generation of Americans: "No man in this war has so well told the story of the American fighting man as American fighting men wanted it told. . . . He deserves the gratitude of all his countrymen."

Further Reading

Ernie Pyle's character and personality are clearly communicated in his writings: *Ernie Pyle in England* (1941), *Here Is Your War* (1943), and *Brave Men* (1944). His wartime reporting is analyzed in John Morton Blum, *V Was for Victory, Politics and American Culture During World War II* (1976) and in Richard R. Lingeman, *Don't You Know There's a War On? The American Home Front 1941-1945* (1970). In a title that highlights Pyle's work, David Nichols edited *Ernie's War: The Best of Ernie Pyle's World War II Dispatches* (1986). Biographical data appears in his obituary in the *New York Times* (April 19, 1945).

Additional Sources

Faircloth, Rudy, *"Buddy," Ernie Pyle, World War II's most beloved typewriter soldier,* Tabor City, N.C.: Atlantic Pub. Co., 1982.

Melzer, Richard, *Ernie Pyle in the American Southwest,* Santa Fe, N.M.: Sunstone Press, 1996. □

Francis Pym

The British statesman Francis Pym (born 1922) was foreign secretary during the Falkland Islands War of 1982.

Francis Leslie Pym was born on February 13, 1922, in Abergavenny, Monmouth County, Wales, into a family that had provided political leaders to Britain for centuries. One of his ancestors was John Pym, a leader of the parliamentary cause in the 17th-century civil war. When he entered the House of Commons for the first time in 1961, representing a Cambridgeshire district where his family had long been prominent, he was the fifth Pym to serve his

country there. His father, Leslie Ruthven Pym, was a member of Parliament who became Conservative Party whip as well as a wealthy real estate broker.

Brought up in a privileged background, Pym was educated at the traditional training grounds for the nation's ruling elite, Eton College, and at Magdalene College of Cambridge University. He entered the army in 1942 and served with distinction as an officer in the Royal Lancers in Italy and North Africa. After returning to civilian life in 1946, he entered the business world working for a department store chain in Birmingham and Liverpool. He married Valerie Fortune Daglish in 1949, and they had two sons and two daughters. In 1959 he entered politics, contesting Rhonda West as a Conservative, but he was defeated.

In 1961 he won his election from Cambridgeshire, beginning a parliamentary career that made him one of the most respected Conservatives of his era. He quickly gained office as assistant government whip from 1962 to 1964, and when the Labour Party ousted the Conservatives in 1964 Pym became an opposition whip (1964-1967) and then deputy chief whip for the opposition (1967-1970). An able parliamentarian with a talent for compromise, Pym was well placed to assume office when the Conservatives returned to power in 1970. Prime Minister Edward Heath chose him as parliamentary secretary to the treasury and government chief whip. He was in effect the floor manager for the government in the House of Commons, lining up the votes which the prime minister needed to get his programs enacted.

Pym found an assignment which not only tested his skills but also allowed him to work for something he strongly believed in—British entry into the European Economic Community (European Union). This was an issue which cut across party lines, and Pym managed to get the votes for passage. He had less success in his next assignment, as secretary of state for Northern Ireland from 1973 until the Heath government fell in 1974. In opposition again, Pym became his party's spokesman first on agriculture and then on Commons affairs and devolution (1976-1978) and foreign and commonwealth affairs (1978-1979).

Although Pym represented the more moderate and traditional wing of his party, he won the support of the right-winger who became Conservative leader in 1975, Margaret Thatcher. When she took office in 1979, Pym was passed over for foreign secretary, but he did win the position of secretary of state for defense. Thatcher's plans to cut back Britain's defense budget left Pym ill at ease and eventually led to his leaving the Defense Ministry in 1981 to become the leader of the House of Commons as well as chancellor of the duchy of Lancaster. In 1982, when the Falkland Islands War with Argentina began and Lord Carrington, the foreign secretary, was blamed for not heading off the trouble, Thatcher asked Pym to replace him.

As foreign secretary Pym not only had to deal with the Falklands and serve as a member of the prime minister's war cabinet, directing the conduct of the campaign, but he also had to handle a tense situation regarding Britain's contributions to the European Common Market. Thatcher gained immense public support for her role as a war leader, and as she headed towards a sweeping reelection victory in 1983 it became obvious that she intended to replace Pym with someone who represented her own kind of conservatism. During the elections Pym made a widely quoted comment that huge majorities were not good for governments. The prime minister publicly criticized him for this. When she won she dropped Pym from her government.

Pym was then free to speak his mind as an independent, and he began to elaborate on his criticisms of Thatcherism in 1984. He had always felt uneasy about the prime minister's monetarist economic policies which led to unemployment and what he felt caused unneeded suffering among the poor. In his speeches and in his book *The Politics of Consent* Pym explained why Thatcher's combative policies were at odds with the true Conservative approach. Pym's book gained support with some, while others claimed that it merely glossed over important topics—long on rhetoric and providing little substance. In May 1985, Pym launched an anti-Thatcher movement within the Conservative Party, the "Conservative Centre Forward," but this failed to attract the support of leading members of the party and was given little chance of success. In fact, Thatcher swept to an easy reelection victory in 1987, taking 43 percent of the vote in a three-party race. While his attempts to revamp the Conservative Party eventually fizzled, Pym accepted a peerage in 1987 for his lifetime service to his country, and was given the title Baron Francis Leslie Pym of Sandy.

Further Reading

Pym's book *The Politics of Consent* (1984) provides the best insights into his thinking. He is discussed in Alan Sked and Chris Cook, *Post-War Britain, A Political History* (1984), and in Peter Riddell, *The Thatcher Government* (1983). □

John Pym

The English statesman John Pym (1584-1643) led the House of Commons in the opening years of the English civil war.

John Pym was the son of a lesser landowner of Somerset. When he was a boy, Pym's views on religion were molded by his stepfather, Sir Anthony Rous, who was a devout Puritan. The defeat of the Spanish Armada was his first memory of public events, and the Gunpowder Plot occurred when he reached his majority. These high points of foreign and domestic Catholic aggression were determinants of Pym's public career. In 1599 he entered Oxford and in 1602 took up his legal studies at Middle Temple. He entered Parliament in 1614, probably in the interest of the Earl of Bedford. The earl's family had long favored the Pyms, and the 4th earl remained John Pym's patron until the earl's death in 1641.

In the Parliament of 1614 and again in 1621, Pym was most active in the matter of enforcing penalties against Catholics. He advocated an oath of loyalty by all Englishmen. A popular defense of English liberties was also a hallmark of Pym's political life.

After Charles I dissolved Parliament in 1629, Pym became treasurer of the Providence Company, which projected colonies in Connecticut and then on Providence Island (Isla de Providencia) off the coast of Central America. Although the company had religious and economic ends, its chief importance was as a political rallying point for the opposition during Charles I's personal government.

When Charles called Parliament in 1640, Pym was the most experienced leader of the Commons, and he immediately assumed leadership of that body. In the "Short" Parliament, Pym stressed the desire of the Commons for legal security, but when Parliament was summarily dissolved by the King, Pym keynoted the "Long" Parliament with a speech which stressed that the country was in danger because of its Catholic queen and its proto-Catholic clergy. It was an inflammatory call for the widest popular support for Parliament in a mortal struggle with the King. Pym's first order of business was the impeachment of the Earl of Strafford.

Charles went to Scotland in August 1641 in order to find evidence of the complicity of Pym and others in the 1638 Scots invasion of England. When Charles returned to England in November 1641, Pym faced his greatest trial as leader of the Commons. There was a wave of support for the King, and the rebellion of the Irish in October gave Charles an excuse to raise an army which might have destroyed

Parliament before it suppressed the Irish. Pym narrowly gained approval for the Grand Remonstrance, which recited the old faults of the King. Then, on Jan. 4, 1642, he maneuvered the King into making an unconstitutional entry into the House of Commons in order to arrest Pym and the other "Five Members." In that moment popular initiative returned to Pym and Parliament. They, not the King, were able to raise troops to suppress the Irish and prepare to meet the inevitable attempt of Charles to forcibly regain political mastery, which came on Aug. 14, 1642.

Pym secured the passage of the militia and assessment ordinances by Parliament despite their flagrant violation of strict legality. He also secured the passage of the unpopular excise tax to finance the parliamentary war effort and organized associations of counties to administer the war; Cromwell's Eastern Association became the most famous and effective of these. Politically, he was also able to keep persons of such diverse values as the Earl of Essex, Oliver Cromwell, and Oliver St. John steady in their combined defense of Parliament. Pym's last act was to arrange for the entry of the Scots into the war on the side of the hard-pressed parliamentary forces in September 1643. That alliance was sealed by the covenant which bound all Englishmen to support Parliament. With that final program of popular unity, Pym succumbed to cancer and was buried in Westminster Abbey on Dec. 15, 1643.

Further Reading

Jack H. Hexter, *The Reign of King Pym* (1941), is the best study. A standard biography of Pym is Sidney Reed Brett, *John Pym, 1583-1643: The Statesman of the Puritan Revolution* (1940).

Additional Sources

MacDonald, William W., *The making of an English revolutionary: the early parliamentary career of John Pym,* Rutherford N.J.: Fairleigh Dickinson University Press; London: Associated University Presses, 1982. ☐

Thomas Pynchon

The American novelist Thomas Pynchon (born 1937) is best known for *V., The Crying of Lot 49,* and *Gravity's Rainbow, Vineland,* and *Mason & Dixon,* complex fictions noted for their encyclopedic erudition and parodistic, labyrinthine plots.

Thomas Ruggles Pynchon, Jr. was born in Glen Cove, New York, on May 8, 1937, of a prominent family. Among Pynchon's ancestors were a 16th-century London high sheriff, a 17th-century Massachusetts Bay Colony patentee and treasurer who was also a founder of both Roxbury and Springfield, Massachusetts, and a 19th-century Trinity College president, after whom Pynchon was named by his father, Thomas Sr., an industrial surveyor in East Norwich, New York.

In 1953 Pynchon graduated from Oyster Bay High School, where he was class salutatorian and recipient of an English award at graduation. He matriculated at Cornell University, where he enrolled in engineering physics, transferring in his sophomore year into the College of Arts and Sciences. Pynchon's early academic interest and excellence in the sciences was evident later in his fiction, where scientific theories serve as suggestive and complex metaphors.

After his sophomore year Pynchon enlisted in the Navy for two years, returning to complete his B.A. in English at Cornell in 1959 "with distinction in all subjects." Among his teachers was Vladimir Nabokov, who was soon to become a famous novelist.

During his junior and senior years Pynchon had begun to write short stories that were later to be published in literary journals: "The Small Rain," "Mortality and Mercy in Vienna," "Entropy," "Lowlands," and "Under the Rose." Most of these can be found in a 1984 collection, *Slow Learner: Early Stories.* One other short Pynchon piece also deserves mention: "A Journey into the Mind of Watts," an article he published in the June 12, 1966, issue of the *New York Times Magazine.*

Although Pynchon's minor work received some popular and academic attention, his reputation rests largely on five major works: *V.* (1963), *The Crying of Lot 49* (1966), *Gravity's Rainbow* (1973), *Vineland* (1990), and *Mason & Dixon* (1997). After graduating from Cornell, Pynchon

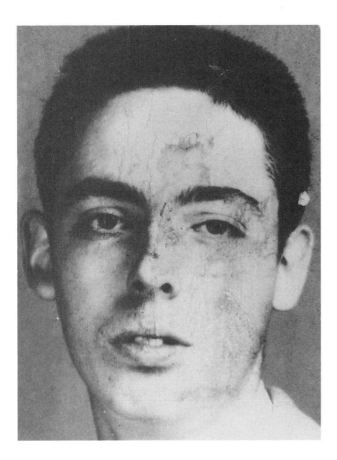

turned down a teaching offer there to work on *V.,* which he wrote in New York City, Seattle (where he worked for a time as an engineering aide for the Boeing Company), California, and Mexico. His efforts were rewarded when *V.* won the William Faulkner Foundation Award in 1963 as the best first novel.

A diffuse and discontinuous fiction, *V.* comprises two, essentially alternating, tales. The first, the picaresque adventures of Benny Profane, a passive drifter just discharged from the Navy who "yo-yos" from place to place principally in the eastern United States in late 1955 and 1956. The second, Herbert Stencil's imagined, sprawling, historical narrative of *V.,* the mysterious woman whom Stencil believes to be connected in some way to the 20th century's apocalyptic meaning and whose narrative ranges from 1898 Egypt to 1922 South-West Africa. The two narratives enclose a kind of polar vision of possibilities: the random disorder of Profane's present and the compulsive order of Stencil's past. Yet Pynchon's text refused to take itself seriously; both Stencil and Profane are comic, self-mocking characters, and their respective quest and non-quest function as parodies that ridicule such totalizing extremes.

Pynchon's second book, *The Crying of Lot 49,* won the Richard and Hilda Rosenthal Foundation Award of the National Institute of Arts and Letters. Unlike *V., The Crying of Lot 49* is a tightly plotted narrative focussing on a single protagonist, California housewife Oedipa Maas. Oedipa is named executrix of a former lover's wealthy estate and during the course of attempting to disentangle it is herself entangled in evidence of the apparent existence of a secret,

subversive postal organization named the Tristero. Oedipa's quest for the Tristero, whose origins date back to 16th-century Europe, becomes increasingly obsessive, and while the narrative implies that she may be paranoid, her search leads to encounters with a variety of equally obsessed, comic characters. At the end of the narrative Oedipa awaits definitive proof of the Tristero's existence at an auction, uncertain of the eventual outcome but having emerged from her previous insularity and ignorance.

Gravity's Rainbow may deservedly be called Pynchon's *magnum opus* and, along with *Moby Dick,* one of America's great fictions. The book is an impressive and bewildering labyrinth of characters and settings, plots and styles. Taking place primarily in England, France, and Germany near the end of World War II, *Gravity's Rainbow* traces the quest of American Tyrone Slothrop to learn the truth of his secret infant conditioning by scientist Laszlo Jamf of the German firm IG Farben. The central character of *Gravity's Rainbow,* however, is not Slothrop, nor is it even human. It is the inanimate German V-2 rocket, connected to Slothrop by virtue of his conditioning and fetishized by virtually all the book's characters. At the book's end Slothrop "scatters" as a character and a special V-2, the 00000, fails to escape gravity, killing a sacrificial German boy launched with it.

The literary importance of *Gravity's Rainbow* is beyond dispute. It shared the National Book Award for fiction with a collection of stories by I. B. Singer and won the Howells Medal of the National Institute of Arts and Letters and the American Academy of Arts and Letters (which Pynchon declined). *Gravity's Rainbow* was also nominated for but "lost" the Pulitzer Prize when the advisory board rejected the original committee's unanimous decision on the grounds that the book was "turgid," "overwritten," "obscene," and "unreadable." Despite the negative publicity, critics continued to associate it favorably with such books as *Ulysses* and have come to regard it with similar respect and admiration.

Nearly 17 years elapsed between the publication of *Gravity's Rainbow* and Pynchon's next novel, *Vineland.* On one level the title of this work alludes to America as it was discovered by Leif Ericson prior to the arrival of Columbus. It also refers to a fictitious county on the northern coast of California, the state's last uncharted wilderness. In the 1980s Vineland serves as a refuge for middle-aged veterans of the 1960s counterculture who have sought refuge from government repression. The novel focuses primarily on Prairie Wheeler's search for her long-lost mother, Frenesi Gates, a beautiful former member of a defunct radical group dedicated to exposing the corruption and hypocrisy of the Nixon administration. Although the novel contains many subplots and characters, combining elements of soap opera and political thriller, it is generally considered less ambitious in scope, thematic complexity, and historical range than Pynchon's earlier works.

Referred to as "the best 18th-century novel anyone has written in a long time," *Mason & Dixon* garnered wide critical praise when it was published in 1997. In addition to displaying Pynchon's patented multiple plots and encyclopedic knowledge in a dozen disciplines, it was generally recognized that this novel was at once darker and more humane than the novelist's previous work. The central narrative re-imagines the lives of two historical figures, astronomer Charles Mason and surveyor Jeremiah Dixon, who were hired by the Royal Society in 1764 to settle the boundary dispute between Maryland and Pennsylania and who created the famous Mason-Dixon line dividing the yet-to-be-born nation into North and South, free states and slave states. Appearing in the novel along with the real characters of George Washington, Ben Franklin, and Thomas Jefferson are a large cast of human, animal, and mechanical fictional characters, including a Chinese martial arts expert, a talking dog, and an amorous mechanical duck. Pynchon's most consciously literary novel, *Mason & Dixon* contains echoes of Kipling, Kafka, Lawrence, Conrad, Hawthorne, Melville, and Twain.

Rumored to live in California, Mexico, and most recently, New York City, Pynchon has remained reclusive and largely unknown, but his reputation as a significant American writer is assured.

Further Reading

Pynchon's celebrated reclusiveness was to a large extent effective; no biography of him exists, although Mathew Winston, ''The Quest for Pynchon,'' in George Levine and David Leverenz, editors, *Mindful Pleasures: Essays on Thomas Pynchon* (1976), does an admirable job in a critical vacuum. Two other general collections of essays are helpful: Edward Mendelson, editor, *Pynchon: A Collection of Critical Essays* (1978), and Richard Pearce, editor, *Critical Essays on Thomas Pynchon* (1981). Useful introductions to Pynchon and his work include Joseph Slade, *Thomas Pynchon* (1974); Douglas Mackey, *The Rainbow Quest of Thomas Pynchon* (1980); and Tony Tanner, *Thomas Pynchon* (1982). More rigorous critical analyses of Pynchon's texts are contained in William Plater, *The Grim Phoenix: Reconstructing Thomas Pynchon* (1978); David Cowart, *Thomas Pynchon: The Art of Allusion* (1980); Thomas Hill Schaub, Pynchon: *The Voice of Ambiguity* (1981); Peter Cooper, *Signs and Symptoms: Thomas Pynchon and the Contemporary World* (1983); and Molly Hite, *Ideas of Order in the Novels of Thomas Pynchon* (1983). □

Pythagoras

The Greek philosopher, scientist, and religious teacher Pythagoras (ca. 575-ca. 495 B.C.) evolved a school of thought that accepted the transmigration of souls and established number as the principle in the universe.

Born on the island of Samos, Pythagoras was the son of Mnesarchus. He fled to southern Italy to escape the tyranny of Polycrates, who came to power about 538, and he is said to have traveled to Egypt and Babylon. He and his followers became politically powerful in Croton in southern Italy, where Pythagoras had established a school for his newly formed sect. It is probable that the Pytha-

goreans took positions in the local government in order to lead men to the pure life which their teachings set forth. Eventually, however, a rival faction launched an attack on the Pythagoreans at a gathering of the sect, and the group was almost completely annihilated. Pythagoras either had been banished from Croton or had left voluntarily shortly before this attack. He died in Metapontum early in the 5th century.

Religious Teachings

Pythagoras and his followers were important for their contributions to both religion and science. His religious teachings were based on the doctrine of metempsychosis, which held that the soul was immortal and was destined to a cycle of rebirths until it could liberate itself from the cycle through the purity of its life. A number of precepts were drawn up as inviolable rules by which initiates must live.

Pythagoreanism differed from the other philosophical systems of its time in being not merely an intellectual search for truth but a whole way of life which would lead to salvation. In this respect it had more in common with the mystery religions than with philosophy. Several taboos and mystical beliefs were taught which sprang from a variety of primitive sources such as folk taboo, ritual, and sympathetic magic and were examples of the traditional beliefs that the Greeks continued to hold while developing highly imaginative and rational scientific systems.

An important underlying tenet of Pythagoreanism was the kinship of all life. A universal life spirit was thought to be present in animal and vegetable life, although there is no evidence to show that Pythagoras believed that the soul could be born in the form of a plant. It could be born, however, in the body of an animal, and Pythagoras claimed to have heard the voice of a dead friend in the howl of a dog being beaten.

The number of lives which the soul had to live before being liberated from the cycle is uncertain. Its liberation came through an ascetic life of high moral and ethical standards and strict adherence to the teachings and practices of the sect. Pythagoras himself claimed to remember four different lives. Followers of the sect were enjoined to secrecy, although the discussions of Pythagoras's teachings in other writers proved that the injunction was not faithfully observed.

Mathematical Teachings

The Pythagoreans posited the dualism between Limited and Unlimited. It was probably Pythagoras himself who declared that number was the principle in the universe, limiting and giving shape to matter. His study of musical intervals, leading to the discovery that the chief intervals can be expressed in numerical ratios between the first four integers, also led to the theory that the number 10, the sum of the first four integers, embraced the whole nature of number.

So great was the Pythagoreans' veneration for the ''Tetractys of the Decad'' (the sum of 1 + 2 + 3 + 4) that they swore their oaths by it rather than by the gods, as was conventional. Pythagoras may have discovered the theorem which still bears his name (in right triangles, the square on the hypotenuse equals the sum of the squares on the other sides), although this proposition has been discovered on a tablet dating from the time of the Babylonian king Hammurabi. Regardless of their sources, the Pythagoreans did important work in systematizing and extending the body of mathematical knowledge.

As a more general scheme, the Pythagoreans posited the two contraries, Limited and Unlimited, as ultimate principles. Numerical oddness and evenness are equated with Limited and Unlimited, as are one and plurality, right and left, male and female, motionlessness and movement, straight and crooked, light and darkness, good and bad, and square and oblong. It is not clear whether an ultimate One, or Monad, was posited as the cause of the two categories.

Cosmological Views

As a result of their religious beliefs and their careful study of mathematics, the Pythagoreans developed a cosmology which differed in some important respects from the world views of their contemporaries, the most important of which was their view of the earth as a sphere which circled the center of the universe. The center of this system was fire, which was invisible to man because his side of the earth was turned from it. The sun reflected that fire; there was a counterearth closer to the center, and the other five planets were farther away and followed longer courses around the center. It is not known how much of this theory was attributable to Pythagoras himself. Later writers ascribe much of it to Philolaos (active 400 B.C.), although it circulated as a view of the school as a whole.

The systematization of mathematical knowledge carried out by Pythagoras and his followers would have sufficed to make him an important figure in the history of Western thought. However, his religious sect and the asceticism which he taught, embracing as it did a vast number of ancient beliefs, make him one of the great teachers of religion in the ancient Greek world.

Further Reading

Pythagoras left no written works. A first-rate technical book, J. A. Philip, *Pythagoras and Early Pythagoreanism* (1966), separates the valid from the spurious among the legends that surround Pythagoras and his views. An excellent and thorough treatment of the evidence for his life and teachings is in W. K. C. Guthrie, *A History of Greek Philosophy* (3 vols., 1962-1969). A good account of Pythagoras and his followers is in Kathleen Freeman, *The Pre-Socratic Philosophers* (1946; 3d ed. 1953), and G. S. Kirk and J. E. Raven, *The Presocratic Philosophers* (1962). Briefer treatments of the Pythagoreans and the intellectual currents of their time are in the standard histories of Greek literature, such as Albin Lesky, *A History of Greek Literature* (trans. 1966), or in accounts of Greek philosophy, such as John Burnet, *Greek Philosophy* (1914). □

Pytheas

Pytheas (c. 380 B.C.-c. 300 B.C.), a Greek explorer from the city of Massalia in southern France, traveled all the way around Britain and wrote the first account of Scandinavia.

Pytheas was born in the Greek colony of Massalia on the south coast of France (now called Marseilles) in about 380 B.C. Sometime toward the end of the fourth century B.C., he was sent out by the merchants of his native city to find a route to the tin mines of southern Britain, which were the source of that valuable metal for all of Europe and the Mediterranean. The trade in tin was controlled by the Carthaginians (from the city of Carthage in present-day Tunisia), and the Greeks would have been glad to break their monopoly.

At that time, the Pillars of Hercules (the Straits of Gibraltar), the exit from the Mediterranean into the Atlantic, were controlled by the Carthaginians. So Pytheas either avoided them by going overland or he went during a time of Carthaginian weakness: possibly between 310-306 B.C. when Carthage was fighting a war with Syracuse in Sicily. In any case, he made it to the port of Corbilo at the mouth of the Loire River. From there he sailed to the island of Ouessant off the tip of Brittany.

Pytheas sailed from Brittany to Belerium (Land's End) in Cornwall, the southwestern tip of Britain, which was the source of tin. He described what he found: "The inhabitants of Britain who dwell about the headland of Belerium are unusually hospitable and have adopted a civilized manner of life because of their intercourse with foreign traders. It is they who work the tin, extracting it by an ingenious process. The bed itself is of rock but between are pieces of earth which they dig out to reach the tin. Then they work the tin into pieces the size of knuckle bones and carry it to an island that lies off Britain and is called Ictis (St. Michael's Mount, Cornwall); for at the time of ebb tide the space between this island and the mainland becomes dry, and they can take the tin in large quantities over to the island on their wagons."

From Cornwall, Pytheas sailed north through the Irish Sea between Britain and Ireland all the way to the northern tip of Scotland, probably going as far as the Orkney Islands. Along the way, he stopped and traveled for short distances inland and described the customs of the inhabitants. Beyond northern Scotland, Pytheas described another land called the "Island of Thule." (Ever since, the far northern extremes of the earth have had the poetic name of Thule: it is now given to the northernmost town in Greenland.) It is not clear whether Pytheas actually went to Thule or merely reports what he heard about it.

According to Pytheas, Thule is six days' sail north of Britain. In midsummer, the sun retires to its resting place for only two or three hours. The inhabitants lived on wild berries and "millet" (in this case, probably oats) and made mead (a drink) from wild honey. From his description, Thule was probably Norway in the present region of the city of Trondheim, although other locations have been suggested. North of Thule he was told of a land where the sea became solid and the sun never set in summertime. These reports seemed so crazy to the people of the Mediterranean world that his report was not believed and was ridiculed for years later.

From Thule, Pytheas sailed back to Britain and down its east coast and then crossed the North Sea to the North Frisian Islands off the coast of Germany and to the island of Heligoland, which he called Abalus. He said: "In the spring the waves wash up amber on the shores of this island. The inhabitants use it as fuel instead of wood . . . and also sell it to their neighbors the Teutons." From there Pytheas sailed back along the coast of Europe and returned home.

Further Reading

Py theas has generated more interest than any other of the ancient explorers. There are those who say that he is the first known explorer in the modern sense of the word. As a result, most histories of exploration have something to say about him, including: Fridtjof Nansen, *In Northern Mists: Arctic Exploration in Early Times*, 2 vols. (London: William Heinemann, 1911; reprinted, New York: AMS Press, 1969); M. Cary and E.H. Warmington, *The Ancient Explorers* (London: Methuen, 1929; reprinted in paperback, Baltimore, Md.: Penguin Books, 1963); Walter Woodburn Hyde, *Ancient Greek Mariners* (New York: Oxford University Press, 1947); Paul Herrmann, *Conquest by Man* (New York: Harper & Brothers, 1954); Björn Landström, *The Quest for India* (Garden City, N.Y.: Doubleday, 1964); Rhys Carpenter, *Beyond the Pillars of Heracles: The Classical World Seen Through the Eyes of Its Discoverers* (New York: Delacorte Press, 1966).

There is one recent monograph devoted to Pytheas: C.F.C. Hawkes, *Pytheas: Europe and the Greek Explorers* (Oxford: Oxford University Press, 1977). □

Q

Qaboos ibn Sa'id

Qaboos ibn Sa'id (born 1940), ruler of Arabia's strategically important Sultanate of Oman, defeated a Communist-inspired insurgency and guided an extensive socio-economic modernization of his once backward realm.

Qaboos ibn Sa'id headed Arabia's oldest reigning dynasty, the Al Bu Sa'id, rulers of Oman since 1744. Born on November 18, 1940, in Salalah, capital of Oman's southern province of Dhofar, he was the only son of Sultan Sa'id ibn Taymur, who died in 1972. His mother was daughter of a shaykh (sheik) of the Bayt Mu'ashani clan of Dhofar's dominant Qara tribe.

Until the mid-19th century Oman was a leading maritime state in the Indian Ocean and Arabian Gulf region. Then disaster overtook the country, and by the early 20th century its increasingly impotent rulers were dependent upon British support; its economy was stagnant and its society was disintegrating as many emigrated to more prosperous lands.

This decline was reversed only after Sultan Qaboos' father became ruler in 1932. By 1960, Sultan Sa'id had reasserted his dynasty's prestige and his personal absolutism by recovering his independence from British tutelage and establishing effective sovereignty over all Oman. Oil was discovered in the interior in 1964, but when Sa'id decided to restrict the kind of petroleum-driven modernization that was transforming the rest of eastern Arabia he provoked opposition that later brought his downfall. A rebellion, eventually taken over by Communist leadership, swept

Dhofar and, ultimately, conservative supporters of Al Bu Sa'id rule decided to oust Sultan Sa'id in order to save the dynasty. On July 23, 1970, a bloodless coup seated 29-year-old Qaboos ibn Sa'id on Oman's throne.

Little known when he became sultan, Qaboos had had few contacts with his countrymen during his childhood in Salalah. Sent to England in 1958, he spent two years in Suffolk preparing for Sandhurst, Britain's military academy, from which he graduated in 1962. A short stint with the British army in Germany was followed by several months studying local government with the Bedfordshire County Council and, finally, a world tour. But after Qaboos' return to Oman in 1964 his suspicious father denied the prince a responsible post and kept him confined studying Islamic law. Resenting his enforced isolation and fearing Oman's ominous drift, Qaboos regretfully joined the movement to oust his father after it received Britain's encouragement.

During the first seven years of Qaboos' reign he consolidated his personal ascendancy over Oman's political system, led his country irrevocably into socio-economic modernization, and regained control of Dhofar province. By the early 1970s this erstwhile guerrilla action had escalated into full-scale war. South Yemen and various Communist and radical Arab states aided the insurgents, while British, Jordanian, and Iranian troops helped the sultan, who diverted most of his oil revenues to military purposes and increased his army to 15,000 troops. Although minor skirmishing occurred as late as 1978, the war was virtually over when the sultan proclaimed victory in December 1975. Nevertheless, military expansion remained a high priority. By 1985 Oman's military mustered 24,000 well equipped troops, including air and naval units, plus 9,000 police and internal security units. In 1980 a cooperative Omani-American defense relationship was initiated. The United States

501

financed modernization of Omani military bases and enjoyed access to them in emergencies.

Sultan Qaboos' prestige soared after he won the Dhofar war. During the first year of his reign he shared power with his urbane, strong-willed uncle, Tariq ibn Taymur, but this ended when it appeared Tariq was becoming too powerful. The two were later reconciled, and Tariq's influence at the palace was emphasized in March 1976 when his daughter, Kamila, then 14, married Qaboos.

The Sultan's absolutism was always tempered by the influence of an oligarchy of advisers drawn from the ruling family, Omani businessmen, and influential British, American, and Arab experts. In 1981 the sultan appointed a State Consultative Council, a possible step toward democratization. Abandoning the isolationism of his father, he vigorously pursued an independent but staunchly pro-Western foreign policy. In a relatively short time, Qaboos brought about unprecedented prosperity to his country, and made Oman a leader among Arab nations. He sought the diverse aid from neighboring countries and the West necessary to tap Oman's natural resources and to improve his country's standard of living.

While post-1970 Oman witnessed fundamental socioeconomic change, the sultan tried zealously to preserve both the outward forms and the inner values of Oman's distinctive culture rooted in its Ibadi version of Islam. Initially, development concentrated on facilitating petroleum production and basic requirements such as ports, roads, hospitals, and schools. Economic diversification emphasizing private enterprise came later. Throughout all this growth, Qaboos strove to maintain the traditional character of his country, preserving ancient buildings and limiting tourism. Nevertheless, change had its price, including social dislocation, especially in rural areas, and some official corruption.

Once internal conflict and instability were quelled within his country, the Sultan sought to improve Omani relations abroad, not only with Gulf states but nations throughout the world. The Sultan constantly sought ways to improve long term peace and stability in the Middle East, taking steps that sometimes defied the traditional stance of Arab leaders. In 1981, he helped to form the Gulf Cooperation Council (GCC), an alliance between conservative Gulf countries to provide a joint security effort in the region. Later, he called for direct talks between Israel and Palestine to settle the Arab-Israeli conflict. In 1993, in the aftermath of the Gulf War, Qaboos signed the last of the border treaties with Oman's neighbors. Throughout his reign as sultan, Qaboos adopted a policy of peace, striving to improve Oman's prosperity through the security of the Gulf region.

Unsure and nervous in 1970, Sultan Qaboos was later known for his assurance, forceful speeches, and well groomed appearance. Dignified, soldierly, and somewhat withdrawn, he combined an appreciation for music and reading with a love of fast cars, horses, and well-appointed palaces. Sultan Qaboos has presided over an era of unprecedented change, continuing the transformation of Oman begun by his father and encouraging stability in the volatile Middle East.

Further Reading

Outside of brief official sketches there is no biography of Sultan Qaboos. Information is scattered among accounts in newspapers such as the *Times* (of London), the *New York Times,* and the *Christian Science Monitor,* as well as in works detailing Oman's recent history. Noteworthy among these are John Townsend's *Oman, The Making of a Modern State* (1977), J.E. Peterson's *Oman in the Twentieth Century* (1978), and Andrew Duncan's *Money Rush* (1979). □

Qianlong

Qianlong (1711–1899) was the emperor of China and an ideal Confucian ruler during the height of the last dynasty, the Qing (Ch'ing).

Qianlong (Ch'ien-lung, Hung-li) was born into the Aisin Gioro clan of the Manchu people, a semi-nomadic race living in Manchuria. During the closing years of the Ming dynasty (1368-1644), the Aisin Gioro clan, led by the great warrior Nurhaci (1559-1626), consolidated power in Manchuria and northern China. Weakened by corruption and economic decline, the Ming presented an irresistible target to the Manchus, and in 1644 they conquered the Ming capital at Beijing (Peking) and proclaimed the last of the Chinese dynasties, the Qing (Ch'ing; 1644-1911).

The Chinese political system was dominated by an all-powerful emperor who passed on the throne to his descendants. Each period occupied by one such family is termed a "dynasty." The Manchus had long lived in close proximity to the Chinese and understood Chinese culture and political practices. Because the Manchus could present themselves as Confucian rulers, and because the Ming had been so corrupt, the Manchus were accepted by the Chinese people as legitimate rulers.

The early Manchu emperors faced a number of significant problems, consolidation of their rule against Ming loyalists, and creation of political institutions which were acceptable both to the Chinese people and to the Manchu clans upon whose support the throne would depend for some time. The Manchus were fortunate in that the first several emperors were very capable men, strong in the warrior virtues of the Manchus and able to hold the throne, but intelligent enough to see the changes which were necessary to consolidate their rule. The fourth emperor (actually he was the second, but the Manchus proclaimed two of their early leaders emperors posthumously, to honor their achievements in preparing for the founding of the dynasty), the emperor Kangxi (K'ang-hsi; r. 1662-1722) was particularly capable. Kangxi lived a long life; he reigned for a longer period than any other Chinese emperor, the first of whom sat upon the Chinese throne in 221 b.c. During the reign of Kangxi, most of the outstanding problems of the

new dynasty were solved, the Manchus were fully accepted by the Chinese people, and the institutions which would bring China to its highest level of cultural and political achievement were created.

The Kangxi emperor, like all Chinese emperors, had a harem of wives and concubines. The harem was primarily a political institution which strengthened the throne by ensuring the support of the powerful families whose daughters were invited into the harem, all of whom hoped to become the mother of an emperor. These women sometimes numbered in the hundreds, and many of them rarely saw the emperor. But emperors often had a series of primary and secondary wives as well as numerous concubines. The Kangxi emperor had 56 children. He was succeeded by his son, the emperor Yong Zheng (Yung-cheng; r. 1723-35), father of Qianlong.

Qianlong's mother had entered the harem of the future Yong Zheng emperor in 1704 while Kangxi was still on the throne. Entering the harem at the age of 11, she was a member of the powerful Niohuru clan, which had been close to the Aisin Gioro clan since the days of Nurhaci. Such an early entry was not unusual as girls of good families were often raised in the harem. In 1711 at the age of 18, she gave birth to her son Qianlong, who grew up at the court of his grandfather, the Kangxi emperor.

It is difficult to ascertain the truth of many stories and tales which circulated at the court, most of which were intended to glorify the achievements of emperors, sometimes out of all proportion to reality. But it is evident that many of the stories told about the future Qianlong emperor were true, as he was a capable boy—both strong and intelligent. One such story said that while he was only 12 years old he accompanied the royal court on one of the favorite pastimes of the Manchus, a mounted hunt. The hunt was not only a recreation which permitted the Manchus to celebrate their roots as mounted archers, but it was also practice for war, requiring the coordination of thousands of men over vast distances as the game was driven for days to a selected area before the killing began. In this hunt, the 12-year-old Qianlong reportedly sat on his horse calmly while a bear charged him before an archer could kill it. Kangxi himself observed the incident and was genuinely impressed with the bravery of his grandson.

As emperors were very busy and often had many children, they rarely had a close relationship with their children. The young princes and princesses were educated by tutors and grew up in the imperial harem. Their relationship with their mother was usually a close and intimate one as the two shared not only the common bond between mother and child, but also common interests in the intensely political atmosphere of the royal court, riddled with rumors, gossip, and intrigue. Qianlong was particularly close to his mother and showered her with honors in his years as emperor, often going to unusual lengths to spend time with her, such as taking her on imperial trips which were designed primarily for her pleasure. Taken from C.B. Malone's book, *History of the Peking Summer Palaces under the Ch'ing Dynasty,* Qianlong's regard for her shows in this poem he wrote to commemorate a visit to a Buddhist temple which he had built for her:

> My mother's benevolent heart sincerely honors the doctrines of Buddhism. She is charmed with the scene, she claps her hands in devotion, and her face beams with joy, a joy which comes partly from what I have done for her.

One of the major problems facing the imperial institution was succession to the throne. While the emperor could in theory select any of his sons, the assumption was always that it would be the eldest son if he were capable. But for an emperor to name his successor before his own death invited trouble as cliques would invariably form around the future emperor and self-interested men would try to gain his ear. If an emperor lived for a long time, heirs might even grow impatient and plot to kill or imprison the emperor so that they might succeed him. But the alternative, to not name an heir, was hardly preferable as this option created the same cliques around all possible successors who were tempted to plot and intrigue against each other to clear their own way to the throne.

The Kangxi emperor, because he had ruled for more than 60 years, had a number of such problems and made and unmade several heirs. In his old age, these problems became critical, and he entered his decline without naming an heir. Qianlong's father seized the opportunity, organized supporters and shouldered aside other possible heirs, ascending the throne in 1723, though he cloaked his actions in Confucian respectability. Perhaps because of the problems of the Kangxi succession, Yong Zheng named his heir secretly and early: Qianlong. Raised in an unusually secure atmosphere (a series of early deaths of other children made him the obvious heir), Qianlong was systematically trained and educated from a young age to be the future emperor of China. He particularly loved the study of history, one of the foundations of Confucian learning. He was also interested in Western science, which had been brought to China by a series of Jesuit missionaries who hoped to win the soul of the Chinese emperor for Christianity. Including Jesuits among his teachers, Qianlong also had a high regard for Western technology.

The most important part of any emperor's education was the classical studies of Confucianism. Confucius (c. 551-479 b.c.) was an early Chinese philosopher who became the inspiration for later Chinese values and political institutions. Elite status in Chinese society depended in part upon a good foundation in the classical works of Confucianism, and all boys of good family were expected to be fully grounded in a study of them. Qianlong was an adept student and fully appreciated the importance of Confucian stereotypes in creating the public aspects of the imperial institution. He presented himself throughout his life as an ideal Confucian ruler who loved his parents, study, and Confucian wisdom, based his conduct on the values of the Confucian tradition; respected historical precedent; took a strong paternalistic interest in the welfare of the common man; and appreciated the fine arts of calligraphy, poetry, and painting. Harold Kahn, who has written the most com-

prehensive study of the monarchical institution under Qianlong, *Monarchy in the Emperor's Eyes,* argues that Confucian models were so strong that it is impossible to separate out the character of the Qianlong emperor from them: he made himself the ideal Confucian emperor.

Qianlong's father was a competent emperor who inherited the strong and stable foundation created by the Kangxi emperor. Furthering the process of improving upon the traditional Chinese political institutions, Yong Zheng created a stable and wealthy country. When he died in 1735, Qianlong succeeded him without incident.

Like that of all Chinese emperors, Qianlong's personal life was complex. He married before ascending the throne, to the Empress Xiao-Xian in 1727. She bore him a son who lived for only eight years. He took a second wife, a Manchu woman Ula Nara who bore him additional children. She broke with him in 1765 to become a Buddhist nun for reasons which are unclear. Ultimately fathering 17 sons and ten daughters by several wives and concubines, Qianlong does not seem to have been particularly close to any of his children save as the usages of the monarchy required. This is very much within the Confucian family tradition, where relationships between fathers and children are distant and frequently troubled.

Qianlong had a long and prosperous reign. His success was in part the result of the cumulative contributions of his predecessors. With the strong financial base created by the reforms of Kangxi and Yong Zheng, Qianlong was able to finance a series of military campaigns which saw the Chinese empire expand in all directions to reconquer lands claimed by earlier dynasties, raising the empire to its greatest extent. These campaigns included wars against Burma, Annam (Vietnam), Taiwan, Turkestan, the Zungars, and the Ghurka. His victories in the north against Turkestan and the Zungars were truly significant, bringing vast areas under Chinese control and destroying the power of the northern nomads, a constant threat to Chinese security. Although Qianlong sometimes claimed to be, like his forebears, a military genius, the evidence suggests that his ability lay in selecting and rewarding men with true military talent.

This military power was equalled by the brilliance of Chinese culture. Qianlong patronized poets and painters; his palaces became a series of great buildings stuffed with riches from all over the world, and resplendent in gilt, precious gems, and metals. In 1793, the British ambassador to the Chinese court, Lord McCartney—cited in Wakeman's study *The Fall of Imperial China*—wrote: (The buildings are) . . . furnished in the richest manner, with pictures of the Emperor's huntings and progresses; with stupendous vases of jasper and agate; with the finest porcelains and japan, and with every kind of European toys and sing-songs; with spheres, orreries, clocks and musical automatons of such exquisite workmanship, and in such profusion, that our presents must shrink from comparison.

Like the ideal Confucian monarch, Qianlong was a competent if uninspired poet who wrote over his lifetime hundreds, perhaps thousands of poems. He collected famous works of art and curios, and his collection, originally housed in the palace in Beijing, is now the heart of the collection of the world's greatest storehouse of oriental art treasures, The Palace Museum in Taipei, Taiwan.

But if he had the strengths of the ideal Confucian monarch, Qianlong also had his weaknesses. Confucianism was an extremely hierarchical and authoritarian system which permitted those with power to oppress those without it. The emperor of China was all-powerful, and as a result difficult to criticize or reproach. While he posed as a patron of scholarship and art, Qianlong also undertook a systematic purging of the Chinese literary corpus in 1773, setting censors to scrutinize all existing written works for their attitude toward the Manchu line and the rule of the emperors. Works deemed satisfactory were assembled into a great imperial collection which is still a major tool utilized by those studying China. But works deemed unsatisfactory were destroyed and their authors punished, in some cases executed or sold into slavery for some real or imagined slight of the dynasty.

Qianlong's administration, like that of previous emperors, also suffered from problems created by clique struggles and corrupt favorites who so enjoyed the protection of the emperor that they could abuse all accepted standards of ethical conduct. One of these men was Heshen (Ho Shen), a young and physically attractive Manchu guardsman at the palace who caught the emperor's eye in 1775. Qianlong was then 65. Heshen rose rapidly in the emperor's favor, some say, because the two enjoyed a homosexual relationship of the type not at all uncommon in Chinese history and culture. Whatever the nature of their relationship, Heshen took full advantage of it and placed his supporters in key positions at every administrative level in the empire. Heshen engaged in systematic theft and corruption at which he was so successful that at his death in 1799 his personal fortune was greater than the imperial treasury itself.

The Qianlong emperor, conscious as always of the necessity to respect tradition and his ancestors, decided that his own reign should not surpass in its length that of his imperial grandfather, the Kangxi emperor. In 1795, he decided upon an action almost without precedent in Chinese history and stepped down from the throne of his own accord, without threat or pressure, in favor of his son Jiaqing (Chia-ch'ing; r. 1796-1829). This created a very awkward situation however, as he kept the reins of power firmly under his own control, while Jiaqing was restricted to ceremonial observances, lacking real power. As Heshen continued to take advantage of Qianlong's support, the accumulated costs of military campaigns and a greatly enlarged army, coupled with the thefts of Heshen, seriously damaged the fiscal health of the country.

The imperial institutions do much to cloak the personal life of an emperor and it is particularly difficult to distinguish the fine line between bad judgment and senility in an aging emperor. We cannot be certain as to the cause of the problems of the last decade of Qianlong's rule. Some feel that he had grown senile and Heshen cleverly used that decline to increase his own depredations, others simply see the evil tendencies inherent in the Chinese imperial institutions carried to an extreme.

On February 7, 1799, Qianlong died. The direct causes were a severe cold, but he was simply old and infirm.

Jiaqing waited a scant five days before arresting and executing Heshen.

Qianlong was a talented and strong emperor, and he had inherited stable institutions, but the closing years of his reign saw the final decline of imperial China. China was soon to face a variety of challenges, from within as rapid population growth began to overwhelm traditional institutions, and from without, as the ambitious Western powers led by Great Britain began to cast covetous eyes on the wealth of the empire. During these gathering crises, the throne, like the Qianlong emperor himself, was isolated by custom and tradition, prevented by its own past successes from perceiving the need for rapid and revolutionary changes necessary to confront those challenges. It might be said that the strengths of the Qianlong emperor were his own: he was intelligent, diligent, and conscientious. His faults, perhaps, were those of the Confucian system. He lived and died the ideal Confucian monarch, the last which imperial China would ever see as it entered upon its final decline.

Further Reading

The standard biography of Qianlong in English is in Arthur W. Hummel, ed., *Eminent Chinese and the Ch'ing Period, 1644-1912* (2 vols., 1943-1944). A good study is Luther Carrington Goodrich, *The Literary Inquisition of Ch'ien-lung* (1935). Background material on Chinese foreign relations and trade can be found in Earl H. Pritchard, *The Crucial Years of Early Anglo-Chinese Relations, 1750-1800* (1936); John K. Fairbank, *Trade and Diplomacy on the China Coast* (2 vols., 1953; new ed., 1 vol., 1964); and John K. Fairbank, ed., *The Chinese World Order: Traditional China's Foreign Relations* (1968). Edwin O. Reischauer and John K. Fairbank, *A History of East Asian Civilization*, vol. 1: *East Asia: The Great Tradition* (1960), offers a general discussion of Chinese civilization, while Sven Hedin, *Jehol: City of Emperors* (trans. 1933), and Carroll Brown Malone, *History of Peking Summer Palaces under the Ch'ing Dynasty* (1934), treat specific aspects of the culture. See also Sir Edmund T. Backhouse and J. O. P. Bland, eds., *Annals and Memoirs of the Court of Peking* (1914).

Additional Sources

Hummel, Arthur W. *Eminent Chinese of the Ch'ing Period.* U.S. Government Printing Office, 1943.

Kahn, Harold L. *Monarchy in the Emperor's Eyes.* Harvard University Press, 1971.

Spence, Jonathan D. *Emperor of China.* Knopf, 1974.

Wakeman, Frederick A., Jr. *The Fall of Imperial China.* The Free Press, 1975.

Backhouse, E., and J. O. P. Bland. *Annals and Memoirs of the Court of Peking (from the 16th to the 20th century).* Houghton Mifflin, 1914.

Shuhan, Zhao, trans. *Inside Stories of the Forbidden City.* New World Press, 1986.

Spence, Jonathan D. *Ts'ao Yin and the K'ang-hsi Emperor.* Yale University Press, 1966. □

Salvatore Quasimodo

The Italian poet, translator, and critic Salvatore Quasimodo (1901-1968) was one of the chief exponents of Italian hermetic poetry.

Salvatore Quasimodo was born on Aug. 20, 1901, in Modica, Sicily, where his father was a stationmaster with the Italian railroads. After several moves throughout Sicily, the family in 1908 settled in Messina, where Quasimodo finished his education and remained until 1919. Subsequently he moved to Rome to study engineering at the Politechnical Institute but did not complete his studies. For some time he worked in different jobs until he moved to Reggio Calabria in 1926 as an employee of the Civil Engineering Board. Through Elio Vittorini, his brother-in-law, he was introduced to literary circles during a visit to Florence in 1929. Among others he met Eugenio Montale and Alessandro Bonsanti, the editor of *Solaria,* which in 1930 published his first poetry.

In 1931 Quasimodo was transferred to Imperia and, after a short interlude in Sardinia, eventually was assigned to duty in Milan. There he left his job in 1938 to become editor of the weekly *Tempo* until he was named in 1941 professor of Italian literature at the Giuseppe Verdi Conservatory of Music. Quasimodo was the recipient of several literary prizes, such as the Etna-Taormina in 1953 and the

Viareggio in 1958. In 1959 he was awarded the Nobel Prize for literature. Quasimodo died on June 14, 1968.

Quasimodo's poetics is characterized by a belief in the "magic of the word." Such an avowal eventually leads to the concept of an "absolute word" whose alliterative properties are stressed over its logical aspects. Quasimodo's later notion of the social potentialities of poetry does not necessarily indicate a break with his earlier manner but may be seen as a logical continuation, as he himself once said: "the words 'island' and 'Sicily' may be identified with my search for contact with the outside world." He refused to be associated with French symbolism, declaring that his work might better be seen in the tradition of "stilnovistic" poetry.

The goals of Quasimodo's poetics are already visible in his first collection of verse, *Acque e terre* (1930), in which the word no longer appears in a subordinate syntactic function but asserts its own immediate value. *Òboe sommerso* (1932), *Odore di Eucalyptus ed altri versi* (1933), and *Erato e Apòllion* (1936) are verse collections which are most characteristic of Quasimodo's hermetic approach, and it is here that his poetics of the absolute word is most clearly delineated and evident ("I divest myself by syllables," *Parola*). The themes are autobiographical, those of an odyssey and the search for a lost paradise. The almost realistic aspects of *Acque e terre* have disappeared; the technique of the analogies has become more daring; and the metaphors have become more tightened. The equilibrium between realistic and hermetic elements characteristic of the first collection is no longer existent.

Nuove poesie (1938) reiterates the old nostalgic feeling of *Acque e terre* for Sicily. Although retaining its hermetic aspects, the syntax has attained a higher degree of clarity, fusing with ease human elements with those of nature in a poised synthesis, as in the poem on Ilaria del Carretto. *Ed è subito sera* (1942), representing a stylistic and structural revision of all Quasimodo had written up to that time, arranged the poems in a chronological order and imparted the feeling of greater ease and of solutions that allowed a more detached attitude on the part of the reader.

The postwar collections *Giorno dopo giorno* (1947), *La vita non è sogno* (1949), and *Il falso e vero verde* (1956) seek a more direct relationship and dialogue with the reader, and Quasimodo himself referred to them as "poesia sociale." *La terra impareggiabile* (1958) is still oriented toward the social and dialogical approach, but it is somewhat weaker than the earlier collections.

Further Reading

A brief biography of Quasimodo is in Nobel Foundation, *Nobel Lectures: Literature, 1901-1967,* edited by Horst Frenz (1969). For general historical background see Carlo L. Golino, ed., *Contemporary Italian Poetry: An Anthology* (1962), and Eugenio Donadoni, *A History of Italian Literature* (1923; trans. and rev. ed., 2 vols., 1969). □

Matthew Stanley Quay

Matthew Stanley Quay (1833-1904) was a U.S. senator and Republican party boss in Pennsylvania. His political genius made "Quayism" a synonym for shrewd, even ruthless, politics in the "gilded age."

Matthew Quay was born on Sept. 30, 1833, in Dillsburg, Pa., the son of a Presbyterian minister. In 1850 he graduated from Jefferson College (now Washington and Jefferson) and in 1854 was admitted to the bar. He mastered several languages and boasted one of America's finest private libraries.

Quay's political career began modestly when, in 1856, he was elected prothonotary of Beaver County. His work in the gubernatorial election of 1860 gained the attention of state politicians. He served with distinction in the Civil War and won the Congressional Medal of Honor. In 1865 he was elected to the state House of Representatives.

Initially opposed to the state organization of Republican boss Simon Cameron, Quay turned from politics in 1867 to edit and publish the *Beaver Radical*. A twist in state politics brought him into the Cameron fold in 1872. The Cameron-Quay machine was as ruthless as the more famous Tweed organization of New York. As secretary of the Commonwealth of Pennsylvania (1872-1878, 1879-1881), Quay played a pivotal role in attempts to weld local organizations in Pittsburgh and Philadelphia to the state machine.

An especially blatant attempt to capture Philadelphia in 1878 by making him city recorder collapsed under public protest. Although implicated in a scandal in the state treasurer's office, he was elected state treasurer by an overwhelming margin in 1885. In 1888 Quay managed the presidential victory of Benjamin Harrison but broke with Harrison over distributing patronage. Intimate knowledge of his state, control of patronage, and insistence on party loyalty made Quay supreme in Pennsylvania. Shrewdly laconic, he knew, as one observer noted, "how to keep silent in fifteen languages."

Serving in the U.S. Senate (1887-1899, 1901-1902), Quay championed the protective tariff and little else. Controversy also marked his Senate career. When the Pennsylvania Legislature failed to fill his seat in 1899, the governor appointed Quay for a third term, only to have the Senate refuse to seat him. He was reelected in 1901. His public record, as with other bosses of the period, was no measure of his great influence within the national councils of his party. He was a partisan of minority rights, defending Indian tribes and opposing Chinese exclusion. His brand of politics, under attack when he died in 1904, helped nationalize American politics during years of rapid industrial and social change.

Further Reading

In the absence of a biography, Quay's own *Pennsylvania Politics: The Campaign of 1900* (1901) provides a sampling of his oratory and ideas. John Wanamaker, *Quayism and Boss Domination in Pennsylvania Politics* (1898), is a contemporary indictment by a Philadelphia merchant, one of Quay's chief opponents. Sylvester K. Stevens, *Pennsylvania: Birthplace of a Nation* (1964), and H. Wayne Morgan, *From Hayes to McKinley* (1969), discuss Quay in the context of state and national politics respectively.

Additional Sources

Kehl, James A., *Boss rule in the gilded age: Matt Quay of Pennsylvania*, Pittsburgh, Pa.: University of Pittsburgh Press, 1981. □

J. Danforth Quayle

J. Danforth Quayle (born 1947) became the second-youngest member of Congress in history when he was elected to the United States House of Representatives in 1976. He was the first person from the "baby boom" generation to win a spot on a national ticket and was the fifth youngest vice president ever elected in the United States.

Dan Quayle was born in Indianapolis on February 4, 1947. He was the son of James C. and Corinne Quayle and the grandson of Eugene Pulliam, the founder of Central Newspapers Inc., a national chain of conservative papers. Quayle received his secondary education in the publics schools of Huntington, Indiana, his hometown. In 1969 Quayle graduated from DePauw University, where he was a member of the Delta Kappa Epsilon fraternity. He attended law school at night at Indiana University, Indianapolis, and graduated in 1974. He was admitted to the Indiana Bar that same year. In 1972 Quayle married Marilyn Tucker, a fellow law student at Indiana University. The Quayles had three children—Tucker Danforth, Benjamin Eugene, and Mary Corinne.

After receiving his education, Quayle had very few jobs before running for public office. From 1969 to 1975, during law school, Quayle was a member of the Indiana National Guard. Also during law school he held several appointed positions in the Indiana state government. Afterwards, he worked as an associate publisher for the Huntington Herald press, a family owned paper, and founded Quayle and Quayle, a law office, with his wife. In 1976, with no political experience, he ran as a conservative Republican against Edward Roush, an eight-term incumbent Democrat, for a seat in the House of Representatives and won, becoming the second youngest representative in history. Quayle proved himself to be consistently conservative on all significant votes, enough so that the National Conservative Political Action Committee helped him in his bid for reelection, as they had in 1976. Much was made of Quayle's poor attendance record in the House during the 1978 campaign, but the bad press did not affect his popularity and he won by an overwhelming majority.

In 1980 Quayle ran for a seat in the Senate against another incumbent Democrat. This time his opponent was 18-year incumbent Birch Bayh, whom he also defeated.

Quayle had no difficulty winning reelection to the Senate in 1986. The term was to last until 1993 but his selection as the Republican Party's vice presidential candidate, and subsequent election, resulted in his resignation. In the Senate Quayle had again voted conservatively, especially in areas related to national defense. However, his votes did not always fall along party lines. The most significant example of his independence from the right was the Job Training Partnership Act of 1986, which he introduced with Senator Edward Kennedy in 1982. His bipartisan efforts sometimes put him at odds with the Reagan administration, but he was not concerned with the possible alienation of the administration.

On August 18, 1988, in New Orleans, George Bush announced that his running mate for the presidency would be Dan Quayle. The public, the media, and both conservative and liberal politicians were caught off-guard by Bush's selection. Outside of Indiana very few people had heard of Dan Quayle. The primary reasons that Bush selected Quayle as a running mate were Quayle's conservative reputation, his Midwest origin, his relative lack of prominence, and no doubt his young age and good looks.

However, Quayle also brought undesirable scrutiny from the media. During his speech at the GOP national convention Quayle made reference to his time spent in the Indiana National Guard during the Vietnam conflict, which made people wonder if he was dodging the draft. This investigation revealed that Quayle might have used his connections through family-owned papers to gain admittance to the Guard. The media then examined almost every facet of his life and career. Among the issues brought into question were Quayle's admission to the Guard and to law school (without the usual requirements) and his privileged lifestyle. These facts, compounded by several poorly handled speaking engagements, led some members of the GOP to express reservations about Quayle's appointment, but Bush never expressed any thoughts about replacing him. Despite the excessively negative media coverage the George Bush/ Dan Quayle ticket did very well, overwhelming the Michael Dukakis/Lloyd Bentsen ticket at the polls.

Once elected, Quayle was given several jobs by the president, most notably a trip to several South American countries to gather information about the war on drugs. After a short time, the media became less interested in the spectacle of Dan Quayle and he was left alone to perform his duties as the vice president. After two years of his first term in that office, many conservatives hailed Quayle as an excellent vice president and as a conservative who remains non-compromising in his political orientation.

Yet Quayle did not return to the White House after the 1992 election, as Bill Clinton's victory forced Bush out of office. Even though Quayle would no longer be the Vice President, his stint in politics and the public eye was not yet over. In 1994, he published a book entitled *Standing Firm.* Quayle announced in 1995 that he would not seek election in the Presidential race, citing family and personal reasons for his decision.

Further Reading

The only biography of Quayle is *The Making of a Senator: Dan Quayle,* by Richard F. Fenno Jr., published in 1989. Although widely covered in the media during the campaign, the best periodical sources on Quayle are political journals such as *Congressional Quarterly Weekly Reports* and the *National Journal.* □

Jacopo della Quercia

Jacopo della Quercia (1374-1438), an Italian sculptor and architect, was a major sculptural innovator of the Early Renaissance.

Documentation concerning Jacopo della Quercia is scant. He was born in Siena. In 1401 he entered the competition for the bronze doors of the Baptistery in Florence, along with Filippo Brunelleschi and Lorenzo Ghiberti (the winner). The panel Della Quercia submitted is lost. In 1406 he executed the marble tomb of Ilaria del Carretto in the Cathedral of Lucca, and 2 years later he was in Ferrara, where he carved the *Seated Madonna* (now in the Cathedral Museum).

The major sculptural cycle from Della Quercia's middle period is the Fonte Gaia in the square in front of the Palazzo Pubblico in Siena. (The present fountain is a replica; the dismantled marble fragments of the original are in the Palazzo Pubblico.) It was commissioned in 1409, but he did not begin work on it until 1414; it was completed in 1419. Featured in relief sculpture was the nearly life-sized Virgin and Child, Mary being the patron saint of Siena, while in niches on either side of a rectangular parapet were eight female personifications of the Virtues. The bodies no longer sit quietly, in the Gothic fashion, but twist and turn in powerful angles that show the new energy of the Renaissance.

In 1422 Della Quercia received payment for the wooden group of the Annunciation in the Pieve of S. Gimignano; the following year he finished the Trenta Altar in S. Frediano, Lucca. In 1425 he was commissioned to design the main portal of S. Petronio in Bologna, and he made trips to Verona, Venice, and Milan to acquire stone. Before the portal was completed, in 1438, the master received and executed in 1430 the commission for the bronze relief *Zaccharias Driven from the Temple* for the Baptistery font in Siena.

In 1436 Della Quercia was named master architect of the Cathedral in Siena. The next year the Signoria of the city intervened between him and the Bolognese, who claimed that the artist had not kept his promise to them. After a trip to Bologna he became ill, and he died in Siena on Oct. 20, 1438.

In the 10 well-preserved marble relief panels on either side of the portal of S. Petronio in Bologna, Della Quercia elevated the depiction of the human body, both nude and draped, to a level of inherent dignity, power, and beauty which was to be achieved by no other sculptor before Michelangelo. The panels tell the stories of the creation and fall of Adam and Eve and of Cain and Abel. Della Quercia abjured Ghiberti's delicately constructed nudes, and the voluptuous body of Eve in Della Quercia's *Temptation* was surely influenced by an ancient statue of Venus. It is clear that the noble male in his *Creation of Adam* was the prototype used by Michelangelo for his ceiling composition in the Sistine Chapel in Rome.

Further Reading

A fine scholarly study in English on the Fonte Gaia is Anne Coffin Hanson, *Jacopo della Quercia's Fonte Gaia* (1965). For general background see John Pope-Hennessy, *Italian Gothic Sculpture* (1955), and Charles Seymour, Jr., *Sculpture in Italy, 1400-1500* (1966). □

Gonzalo Jiménez de Quesada

Gonzalo Jiménez de Quesada (1509-1579) was a major Spanish conquistador. His conquest of the Chibchas brought one of the important American culture areas under Spanish rule.

Gonzalo Jiménez de Quesada was born at Cordova, probably of a converted Jewish family. He studied at a university, presumably Salamanca, and practiced law for several years before the Royal Audiencia of Granada. In 1535 Pedro Fernández de Lugo, newly appointed governor of Santa Marta on the Caribbean, offered Jiménez de Quesada the post of chief magistrate there, and he accepted.

When Lugo's large expedition reached Santa Marta, it found the infant colony in bad condition, with food scarce and disease prevalent. The governor's son, Alonso de Lugo, soon absconded to Spain with the first gold supply discovered, but the elderly Don Pedro remained hopeful. He sent Quesada, in whom he had discovered qualities of leadership, into the interior with most of the available manpower.

Conquest of the Chibchas

With about 800 men and several brigantines, Quesada ascended the Magdalena River with no precise objective. The ascent provided great hardships, as the men died rapidly of hunger, fever, snakebite, and the attacks of Indians and wild beasts. When Quesada reached the Opón, a Magdalena tributary, 9 months after leaving Santa Marta, he was near the semicivilized Chibcha (or Muisca) Indian country, rich in gold and precious stones. He had 166 men and 62 horses left with which to undertake the conquest.

Though the Chibchas had a warlike history, their conquest proved rather easy, as they seemed psychologically cowed by the Spaniards. Entering their land early in 1537, Quesada soon defeated and slew their most powerful chieftain, Zipa Bacatá, and took his city. He also made short work of the second in power, the Zaque of Tunja. By August 1538 Quesada had the plateau of Cundinamarca under fairly firm control. Next, Sebastián de Benalcázar from Popayán and Nikolaus Federmann from Coro in Venezuela brought their own expeditions to the Chibcha country, lured by reports of gold. Questions of jurisdiction arose, and the three decided to go together to Spain for a royal judgment.

Quesada proved slow in getting to the court and damaged his reputation by frequently gambling, being once arrested in Lisbon for gaming after hours. These delays caused the thieving Alonso de Lugo to be preferred over him—Don Pedro having meanwhile died—and Alonso received both Santa Marta and New Granada, as Quesada's conquest was called. Lugo went to Bogotá, but the general knowledge of his former misconduct and the corruption of his government forced him soon to leave.

Quesada left Spain and settled for some years in France and Flanders. In 1549, his fortune spent, and no longer young, he petitioned in Spain for some appointment in New Granada and received the title of marshal of Bogotá. He went there in 1550 and, despite his poverty, became the leading citizen of the area and was virtually governor de facto.

In 1569 Quesada led an expedition into the interior of South America in search of fabled El Dorado. It lasted 3 years and explored the tributaries of the Orinoco and Amazon, from which he and a few disappointed survivors returned. He died in 1579 and is said to have been a leper, but many skin ailments were then called leprosy and his disease cannot be diagnosed with certainty.

Further Reading

Biographies of Jiménez de Quesada are R. B. Cunninghame Graham, *The Conquest of New Granada, Being the Life of Gonzalo Jiménez de Quesada* (1922), and Germán Arciniegas, *Knight of El Dorado* (1939; trans. 1942). Each has some merits, yet neither is entirely reliable. Walker Chapman, *The Golden Dream* (1963), has a chapter on the Chibcha conquest. Jesús M. Henao and Gerardo Arrubla, *History of Colombia,* translated and edited by J. Fred Rippy (1938), provides reliable material on Quesada.

Additional Sources

Cunninghame Graham, R. B. (Robert Bontine), 1852-1936., *The conquest of New Granada: being the life of Gonzalo Jimenez de Quesada,* Boston: Longwood Press, 1978. □

Lambert Adolphe Jacques Quételet

The Belgian statistician and astronomer Lambert Adolphe Jacques Quételet (1796-1874) is considered the founder of modern statistics and demography.

Adolphe Quételet was born in Ghent on Feb. 22, 1796. When he finished secondary school at the age of 17, he took a job teaching mathematics in a secondary school. A professor of mathematics at the newly established University of Ghent influenced Quételet to study mathematics. In 1819 he received his doctorate in mathematics with a dissertation in which he claimed to have discovered a new curve. The work was heralded as an important contribution to analytic geometry.

That year Quételet was appointed to the chair of elementary mathematics at the Athenaeum, and shortly thereafter he was elected to membership in the Royal Academy of Sciences and Belles-lettres of Brussels. He wrote numerous essays in mathematics and physics, founded and edited a journal, delivered lectures on science in the Brussels Museum, and published introductory works in mathematics and natural science. In 1828 he became the first director of the Royal Observatory, a position held until his death on Feb. 17, 1874, in Brussels.

In Paris gathering technical knowledge for the building of the observatory, Quételet met a number of leading French scientists and mathematicians who were actively engaged in laying the foundations of modern probability theory. Although they were working in the natural sciences and mathematics, in the course of their studies some of them had occasion to analyze empirical social phenomena. What fascinated Quételet was the possibility of using statistics as an instrument to deal with social problems.

Quételet believed that statistical theory and research could be used to determine whether human actions occur with the expected regularity. If so, it would indicate that there are social laws which are as knowable as are the laws which govern the movements of the heavenly bodies. He thought that there were such social laws. He thus developed his famous notion of the "average man."

Quételet's concept of the average man was intended to be a construct of the mind or a model which would enable social "scientists" to express the differences among individuals in terms of their departure from the norm. This theory led to his "theory of oscillation." According to this hypothesis, as social contacts increase and racial groups intermarry, differences between men will decrease in intensity through a process of social and cultural oscillation, resulting in an ever-increasing balance and, eventually, international equilibrium and world peace. Thus, as Quételet saw it, the task of the academic and scientific communities in the immediate future was to develop a new social science, based on empirical observation and the use of statistics. This new science of "social physics" would discover the laws of society upon which human happiness depends. Quételet's subsequent works represent an attempt to formulate this new field of social physics.

To accomplish this goal, it was necessary to refine the techniques used in the collection of statistical data, since Quételet believed that through the analysis of such data empirical regularities or laws could be discovered. He was a moving force behind many of the governmental agencies and professional organizations involved in the gathering of statistical data, and he exerted an international influence on this area. His application of quantitative methods and mathematical techniques has been judged as anticipatory of the guiding principle of contemporary social science, especially his efforts to change statistics from a mere clerical function into an exact science of observation, measurement, and comparison of results.

Further Reading

Several of Quételet's major works are available in English translation. The best study in English of his significance is Frank H. Hankins, *Adolphe Quételet as Statistician* (1908), which includes a biographical sketch. See also George Sarton, *Sarton on the History of Science,* edited by Dorothy Stimson (1962), for the reasons why Sarton considers Quételet rather than Auguste Comte as the "founder of sociology," and Quételet's work *On Man and the Development of His Faculties* as "one of the greatest books of the nineteenth century." □

Francisco Gómez de Quevedo Y Villegas

The Spanish poet, satirist, novelist, and wit Francisco Gómez de Quevedo y Villegas (1580-1645) ranks as one of the major writers of Spain's Golden Age.

Francisco de Quevedo was born in Madrid to an aristocratic family and orphaned very young. He studied the humanities at the University of Alcalá and theology at Valladolid. He learned Latin, Greek, Hebrew, and several modern languages and became a classics scholar. He published his first poem at the age of 25. In 1613 he accompanied the Spanish viceroy, the Duke of Osuna, to Italy to serve as diplomatic adviser. Quevedo became involved in a political conspiracy in Venice in 1618 and was recalled to Madrid in disgrace and kept under house arrest.

Freed but unchastened, Quevedo engaged in acrid literary and political controversies. His adverse criticism of the government soon incurred the disapproval of the Conde-Duque de Olivares, who was the royal favorite, and Quevedo was imprisoned in León from 1639 until 1643. He went to Villanueva de los Infantes, where he died 2 years later.

Quevedo's name is used as the butt of jokes throughout the Spanish-speaking world. Because he always wore nose glasses, his name in the plural, *quevedos,* came to mean pince-nez.

In its manifold variety, Quevedo's writing dazzles the intellect. Quevedo the theologian produced about 15 books on theological and ascetic subjects, such as *La cuna y la sepultura* (1612; *The Cradle and the Grave*) and *La providencia de Dios* (1641; *The Providence of God*). Quevedo the critic and literary gadfly published *La culta latiniparla* (*The Craze for Speaking Latin*) and *Aguja de navegar cultos* (*Compass for Navigating among Euphuistic Reefs*), both aimed against Gongorism—the Spanish counterpart of euphuism.

Quevedo the satirist produced profoundly melancholy buffoonery and grotesque cosmic nonsense in *Los sueños* (1627; *Dreams*). He scourged doctors, tailors, judges, Genoese bankers, barbers, bores, poets, dramatists, and every age and sort of woman, spattering them with scatological humor. His books of political theory were products of many years of earnest thought and of his own political experience. Two of the most important are *La political de Dios* (1617-1626; *The Politics of the Lord*) and *La vida de Marco Bruto* (1632-1644; *The Life of Marcus Brutus*).

Quevedo the poet produced an enormous bulk of verse, much of it extremely witty and sarcastic—no few poems based on the subjects of metaphysical anguish, the brevity of beauty, the loss of love, inexorable time, and death. Quevedo the novelist is perhaps best known through his picaresque novel *La vida del buscón* (1626; *Paul the Sharper* or *The Scavenger*), in which he followed the usual episodic pattern of the picaresque novel, intermixing sardonic wit. In this novel he sought to entertain, to ridicule, and to hold up fraud and dishonesty to scorn, but he rarely moralized directly, as did other picaresque novelists of his time.

Further Reading

Translations of Quevedo into English are difficult to find. A translation of *El buscón,* entitled *The Scavenger,* was done by Hugh H. Harter in 1962. This volume contains an introduction expressly for the American reader. In 1963 the University of Illinois Press reprinted *Visions—As Translated by Sir Roger L'Estrange* from Quevedo's *Los sueños;* J. M. Cohen wrote the introduction, which contains significant comments on both L'Estrange and Quevedo. Charles Duff translated selections of Quevedo's work in *Quevedo: The Choice Humorous and Satirical Works* (1926). This volume includes the work of several translators and a study by Duff of the life and writings of Quevedo, with a list of English translations, none later than 1892. Quevedo's place in Spanish literature is discussed in Gerald Brenan, *The Literature of the Spanish People* (2d ed. 1953). For general historical background see Louis Bertrand and Sir Charles Petrie, *The History of Spain* (trans. 1934; rev. ed. 1952), and John Armstrong Crow, *Spain: The Root and the Flower* (1963). □

Manuel Luis Quezon

Manuel Luis Quezon (1878-1944) was the first president of the Commonwealth of the Philippines. He prepared the groundwork for Philippine independence in 1946.

Manuel Quezon was born on Aug. 19, 1878, to Lucio Quezon and Maria Molina, both schoolteachers, in Baler, Tayabas (now Quezon) Province, in Luzon. Manuel enrolled at San Juan de Letran College, after which he was appointed lecturer at the University of Santo Tomás. There he studied law, but his studies were interrupted by the outbreak of the Spanish-American War.

Quezon was considered "bright but lazy"; but when he joined the revolutionary forces of Gen. Emilio Aguinaldo during the revolution against Spain, Quezon displayed his fearless, bold, and quick-tempered style of fighting. He was promoted from private to major until, in 1899, he surrendered to the Americans, spent 6 months in jail, and then returned to Manila.

Early Public Offices

In 1903 Quezon passed the bar examination and set up practice in Baler. He gave up private practice to assume the post of provincial fiscal of Mindoro and later of Tayabas. In 1906 he was elected provincial governor. His campaign showed his native political wisdom when he sided with popular issues in a somewhat opportunistic manner. Often he abandoned consistency for the sake of pursuing what to his enemies was nothing but plain demagoguery.

In 1907 Quezon ran successfully as candidate for the Philippine Assembly on the Nacionalista party platform. In the Assembly he was elected floor leader, and Sergio Osmeña, his archrival, became Speaker of the House. Quezon served as resident commissioner in Washington, D. C. (1909-1916), where he became notorious as a romantic dancer, playboy diplomat, and shrewd lobbyist. He was instrumental in having a law revised so that Filipinos would form a majority in the Philippine Commission, the highest governing body in the Philippines. In February 1916 he cosponsored the Jones Act, which gave the Filipinos the power to legislate for themselves subject to veto by the

American governor general. With this act, Quezon returned home a hero.

In 1916 Quezon was elected to the Senate, and soon became its president. Here he began attacking Osmeña for the latter's theory of "unipersonal" leadership. Quezon's "collectivist" idea of leadership won in the 1922 election. Soon, however, the two warring factions of the Nacionalista party united in the Partido Nacionalista Consolidado, headed by Quezon, who then became president of the party.

In 1933 a bill providing for the future independence of the Philippines, the Hare-Hawes-Cutting Bill, was passed by the U.S. Senate. Quezon opposed the new law because "America would still hold military and naval bases in the Philippines even after the latter's independence, and, moreover, export duties regulated in the law would destroy both industry and trade." He was referring to what has since become the most troublesome cause of conflict between the Philippines and the United States: the right of jurisdiction over military bases and the special trade concessions given to landlords, compradors, and bureaucrat-capitalists with interests in export industries.

The real cause of Quezon's opposition to the law, apart from his objection to specific provisions, was the fact that it was identified with the Osmeña faction. Quezon led a mission to the United States to work for a bill generally similar to the Hare-Hawes-Cutting Law, the Tydings-McDuffie Law, known also as the Philippine Independence Act. This law provided for Philippine independence in 1946 and tax-free importation of Philippine products such as sugar, coconut oil, and cordage into the United States and the diplomatic negotiation of the military bases issue.

President of the Philippines

In September 1935, under the banner of a coalition party, Quezon was elected first president of the commonwealth, with Osmeña as vice president. Quezon's first act as chief executive was to push a national defense bill through the rubber-stamp unicameral legislature, which he controlled. This bill made him chairman of the Council for National Defense, with the chief of staff of the armed forces directly subordinate to him.

On Aug. 10, 1940, influenced by the growing Japanese imperialist encroachment, Quezon jammed through the National Assembly the Emergency Powers Bill, which vested him with dictatorial powers. Passed by a vote of 62 to 1, the bill gave Quezon the authority to change even the social and economic structure of the country: he was given the authority to require civilians to render service to the government, to outlaw strikes, to commandeer shipping and other transportation, to control fuel resources, to revise the educational system, and so forth.

In November 1941 Quezon was reelected president of the commonwealth. When the Japanese forces occupied Manila in 1942, Quezon and his Cabinet fled from the Philippines and set up an exile government in Washington in May 1942. Quezon died on Aug. 1, 1944, a year before the liberation of the Philippines.

Assessment of Quezon

Although Quezon lived through the most turbulent times in Philippine history, when the peasantry—who composed 75 percent of the people—was rebelling against social injustice and age-old exploitation, he failed to institute long-lasting reforms in land tenancy, wages, income distribution, and other areas of crisis. Essentially a politician who was both tactful and bullheaded, supple and compulsive, Quezon served mainly the interest of the Filipino elite, or ruling oligarchy (about 200 families), who owned and controlled the estates and businesses.

Quezon became a popular hero when he attacked the racist policies of Governor Leonard Wood with his declaration that he preferred ''a government run like hell by Filipinos to one run like heaven by Americans.'' Senator Claro M. Recto, a contemporary, pronounced the most balanced and acute judgment when he described Quezon as ''a successful politician . . . because he was a master of political intrigue. He knew how to build strong and loyal friendships even among political opponents, but he knew also how to excite envy, distrust, ambition, jealousy, even among his own loyal followers.''

Further Reading

The most authoritative source on Quezon's life is his autobiography, *The Good Fight* (1946). For his career and the historical circumstances surrounding it, the following are standard references: Carlos Quirino, *Quezon: Man of Destiny* (1935); Joseph R. Hayden, *The Philippines: A Study in National Development* (1942); Teodoro A. Agoncillo and Oscar M. Alfonso, *History of the Filipino People* (1960; rev. ed. 1967); Theodore Friend, *Between Two Empires: The Ordeal of the Philippines, 1929-46* (1965); and Teodoro A. Agoncillo, *A Short History of the Philippines* (1969).

Additional Sources

Enosawa, G. H., *Manuel L. Quezon: from Nipa house to Malacanan,* Manila?: M.L. Morato, 1993.
Quezon: thoughts and anecdotes about him and his fights, Quezon City?: J.F. Rivera, 1979.
Romulo, Carlos P., *The Philippine presidents: memoirs of,* Quezon City: New Day Publishers; Detroit, Mich.: exclusive distributors, Cellar Book Shop, 1988. □

Edith H. Quimby

A pioneer in the field of radiology, Edith H. Quimby (1891-1982) helped develop diagnostic and therapeutic applications for X rays, radium, and radioactive isotopes when the science of radiology was still in its infancy. Her research in measuring the penetration of radiation enabled physicians to determine the exact dose needed with the fewest side effects.

In addition to her accomplishments in the field of radiology, Edith H. Quimby worked to protect those handling radioactive material from its harmful effects. While a radiology professor at Columbia University, she established a research laboratory to study the medical uses of radioactive isotopes, including their application in cancer diagnosis and treatments. In recognition of her contributions to the field, the Radiological Society of North America awarded her a gold medal for work which ''placed every radiologist in her debt.''

Quimby was born on July 10, 1891, in Rockford, Illinois, to Arthur S. Hinkley, an architect and farmer, and Harriet Hinkley (whose maiden name was also Hinkley). The family—Quimby was one of three children—moved to several different states during Quimby's childhood. She graduated from high school in Boise, Idaho, and went on a full tuition scholarship to Whitman College in Walla Walla, Washington, where she majored in physics and mathematics. Two of her teachers at Whitman, B. H. Brown and Walter Bratton, were major influences in directing her toward a career in scientific research. After graduating in 1912, Quimby taught high school science in Nyssa, Oregon, and then went to the University of California in 1914 to accept a fellowship in physics. While in the graduate program there, she married fellow physics student Shirley L. Quimby. She earned her M.A. in 1915 and returned to teaching high school science, this time in Antioch, California. In 1919, when her husband moved to New York to teach physics at Columbia University, she went with him. The move to New York was a pivotal point in Quimby's

career, as she began working under Dr. Gioacchino Failla, chief physicist at the newly created New York City Memorial Hospital for Cancer and Allied Diseases. This began a scientific association that was to last forty years.

Quimby began studying the medical uses of X rays and radium, especially in treating tumors. At that time, physicians and researchers knew extremely little about this area; before Quimby's research, each doctor had to determine on a case-by-case basis how much radiation each patient needed for treatment. Quimby focused her attention on measuring the penetration of radiation so that radiotherapy doses could be more exact and side effects minimized. After several years of research, she successfully determined the number of roentgens (a now obsolete unit of radiation dosage) per minute emitted in the air, on the skin, and in the body. Her research on the effects of radiation on the skin was especially noteworthy to the scientific community, and her study was frequently quoted in the professional literature for many years.

From 1920 to 1940, Quimby conducted numerous experiments to examine various properties of radium and X rays. During this period she wrote dozens of articles for scientific journals, describing the results of her research and listing standards of measurement. In 1940 Quimby was the first woman to receive the Janeway Medal of the American Radium Society in recognition of her achievements in the field.

From 1941 to 1942, Quimby taught radiology courses at Cornell University Medical College. The following year she became associate professor of radiology at Columbia University College of Physicians and Surgeons, where she taught radiologic physics. While at Columbia, she and Failla founded the Radiological Research Laboratory. There they studied the medical uses of radioactive isotopes in cooperation with members of Columbia's medical departments. They focused their research on the application of radioactive isotopes (different forms of the same element whose unstable nuclei emit alpha, beta, or gamma rays) in treating thyroid disease, and for circulation studies and diagnosis of brain tumors. These inquiries made Quimby a pioneer in the field of nuclear medicine.

Quimby participated in other aspects of radiology research as well. She researched the use of synthetically produced radioactive sodium in medical research, and devoted considerable efforts to investigating ways to protect those handling radioactive substances from the harmful effects of exposure. Very early on, Quimby foresaw the potential for increased diagnostic and therapeutic use of atomic energy in medicine through radioactive isotopes.

In addition to her research and lecturing, Quimby worked on the Manhattan Project (which developed the atom bomb). She also worked for the Atomic Energy Commission, acted as a consultant on radiation therapy to the United States Veterans Administration, served as an examiner for the American Board of Radiology, and headed a scientific committee of the National Council on Radiation Protection and Measurements. A prolific writer, Quimby published a considerable amount of literature on various aspects of the medical uses of X rays, radium, and radioactive isotopes. She also coauthored a widely respected book entitled *Physical Foundations of Radiology*.

After her official retirement in 1960 as professor emeritus of radiology, Quimby continued to write, lecture, and consult well into the 1970s. She was a member of several radiology societies, including the American Radium Society, for which she served as vice president. In her nonprofessional life, Quimby was a member of the League of Women Voters.

On Quimby's death on October 11, 1982, at the age of ninety-one, Harald Rossi of Columbia University wrote in *Physics Today* that "all too often the creative achievements of scientific pioneers are overshadowed by further developments made by others or simply become anonymous components of accepted practice. Fortunately, Quimby's exceptional service to radiological physics was widely recognized."

Further Reading

New York Times, October 13, 1982, p. 28.
Physics Today, December, 1982, pp. 71–72. □

Willard Van Orman Quine

Willard Van Orman Quine (born 1908), American philosopher, is best known for his advocacy of the logical regimentation of ordinary language.

On June 25, 1908, W. V. Quine was born in Akron, Ohio. He earned the bachelor of arts degree *summa cum laude* in 1930 from Oberlin College. At Harvard University Graduate School he concentrated on logic under the supervision of Alfred North Whitehead. He received his doctorate in 1932. Quine then traveled to Vienna, Austria. He was there when the circle of logical positivist philosophers flourished, studied mathematical logic at Warsaw, and in Prague, befriended Rudolf Carnap, a leader of the logical positivist movement.

Quine's *A System of Logic* (1934) contributed significantly to the development of mathematical set theory. In 1936 he joined the Harvard faculty. His essay "New Foundations of Mathematical Logic" (1937) retained in principle Bertrand Russell's theory of types (a revision of set theory) but sought to avoid its complexities. Nevertheless, Quine's new theory had drawbacks. In *Mathematical Logic* (1940) he presented a superior system. His *Set Theory and Its Logic* (1963) traced relations between his own system of set theory and others.

Explaining Ontic Theory

Two articles, "Steps toward a Constructive Nominalism" (1947) and "On What There Is" (1948), represent Quine's widely considered doctrines in ontology. Ontology—in Quine's words, "ontic" theory—consists of assertions of existence. He made clear that accepted scientific theories allow for more than one ontic theory and that it is incorrect to seek to determine that one such ontic theory is true. He proposed a method for explaining the ontic importance of a theory, calling for formulation of the statements which a theory contains into symbolic expressions with existential importance. The primacy of mathematical logic in Quine's ontology is evident in his celebrated definition of being: "To be is to be the value of a variable."

A Reverse in Logic

Quine's ontology was originally nominalistic, maintaining that only particular individuals exist and that universals or abstract entities do not exist, except perhaps as linguistic symbols. In 1947 Quine denied the existence of abstract entities and proposed the construction of logical and mathematical systems without resort to such entities. In *Word and Object* (1960), however, Quine abandoned his earlier nominalism by acknowledging the existence of abstract entities. He contended that language consists of dispositions, acquired by conditioning, to respond acceptably to socially observable stimuli. His *Pursuit of Truth* (1990) also puts forth this argument.

Quine's main contribution to epistemology (the theory of knowledge), signaled by his article "Two Dogmas of Empiricism" (1951), was his denial of the validity of the analytic-synthetic distinction. According to this distinction, every statement in any system of knowledge is either synthetic or analytic. A synthetic statement is true or false as a matter of fact, and an analytic statement is true or false without reference to fact but with reference to meanings or formal rules within the language in which the statement is expressed. In challenging this central distinction in recent epistemology, Quine had a decisive impact on the field. He pointed out that the distinction was never made satisfactorily and, in fact, argued that it could not be made.

In 1955 Quine was appointed Edgar Pierce professor of philosophy at Harvard. President of the Association of Symbolic Logic (1953-1956), in 1957 he was elected president of the Eastern Division of the American Philosophical Association. In 1968 he inaugurated the John Dewey Lectures at Columbia University. In December 1971 he delivered the prestigious Carus Lectures before the American Philosophical Association. In 1996, Quine received the Kyoto Prize, one of Japan's most prestigious awards given by a private foundation. He was awarded the $460,000 prize in the category of creative arts and moral sciences.

Quine's philosophy at first seemed utterly fragmentary. Despite fundamental shifts in doctrine, however, his philosophy later assumed growing systematic coherence. Quine's publications include *From a Logical Point of View* (1953), *Word and Object* (1960), *Selected Logic Papers* (1966), *The Ways of Paradox* (1966), *Ontological Relativity and Other Essays* (1969), *Philosophy of Logic* (1970), and *Pursuit of Truth* (1990).

Further Reading

Quine's work is discussed in Donald Davidson and Jaakho Hintikka, eds., *Words and Objections: Essays on the Work of W. V. Quine* (1969). His importance is also analyzed in Neils Egmont Christensen, *On the Nature of Meanings: A Philo-

sophical Analysis (1961; 2d ed. 1965). A short biography of Quine is in Paul Kurtz, ed., *American Philosophy in the Twentieth Century* (1966).

Additional Sources

(Orenstein, Alex) *Willard Van Orman Quine,* Twayne Publishers, 1977.
(Quine, W. V.) *The Time of My Life: An Autobiography,* MIT Press, 1985.
(Honderich, Ted, ed.) *Oxford Companion to Philosophy,* Oxford University Press, 1995.
New York Times (July 1, 1996). □

Quin Shi Huang-Di

First emperor of the Qin Dynasty, Quin Shi Huang-di (259 B.C.-210 B.C.) unified China in 221 B.C. and turned the country into a centralized empire.

Before Qin Shi Huang (Ch'in Shih Huang-ti) unified China in 221 b.c., the country was torn apart by wars between the regional kingdoms. From the 8th century b.c., the rival principalities were constantly engaged in warfare during the later Zhou Dynasty. By 403 b.c., only seven major kingdoms remained, of which the Kingdom of Qin gradually became the strongest. These kingdoms continued their fighting until 221 b.c., when Qin's king, later known as Qin Shi Huang-di, defeated all the other kingdoms. His unification of China not only ended six centuries of wars but also started a centralized imperial system which was to last for over 2,000 years.

After his father's death, Qin Shi Huang acceded to Qin's throne in 247 b.c. He was only 13 years old. Lü Bu Wei, prime minister of the former king, continued to hold his position under the new king, who was now called Qin Wang Zheng (King Zheng of Qin). In 238 b.c., the ninth year of his kingship, King Zheng reached the age of 22, the legal age to rule the kingdom by himself. When he left for the old capital Yong for his coronation, Lao Ai, the Queen mother's lover, attempted a coup d'etat. Lao Ai's conspiracy was immediately discovered by King Zheng, who had him executed. Later, the king learned that his prime minister Lü Bu Wei was also involved in the attempted coup and banished Lü to Shu (today's Sichuan), which was a remote area at that time. Desperate, Lü committed suicide by poison in 235 b.c.

After the removal of Lü Bu Wei, King Zheng used the scholar Li Si as his major adviser in planning the conquest of China's six other kingdoms. Han, Zhao, and Wei were the three kingdoms directly to the east of Qin; beyond these were Yan in the north, Chu in the south, and Qi in between. King Zheng accepted Li Si's proposal to first launch frontal attacks upon Han, Zhao, and Wei, and then attack Yan and Chu, before finally taking over Qi for the final unification. Han, the weakest kingdom, was conquered in 230 b.c. In 228 b.c., Qin besieged Han Dan, the capital of the Zhao kingdom, and captured the king of Zhao. After Zhao's fall,

Qin presented a great threat to the kingdom of Yan. In the hope of preventing Qin's attack, in 227 b.c. the crown prince of Yan sent an assassin to kill King Zheng. After the attempt failed, the king of Yan killed the crown prince to make peace with Qin. In the five years between 225 b.c. and 221 b.c., Qin defeated and conquered the rest of the regional kingdoms and brought China to unification.

Following his triumph, King Zheng discussed with his ministers an appropriate title for the new ruler of China. Praising the King for his accomplishments, the court suggested the most respectable title of Ancient China: *Tai Huang*. But King Zheng, for his part, believed he incarnated the virtues and achievements of *San Huang Wu Di* ("Three Monarchs and Five Emperors," meaning all the great emperors of Ancient China). He, therefore, dropped *Tai* and added *Di* to *Huang* to form *Huang-di*, which can be translated as august emperor. Convinced he had established an eternal empire, of which he was the first emperor, he called himself, appropriately, Shi Huang-di, or the first emperor. Thus, King Zheng of Qin became Qin Shi Huang-di, or first emperor of the Qin Dynasty. With the conquest complete and the establishment of his emperorship, Qin Shi Huang began a series of reforms to consolidate his rule.

In the central government, the emperor was the highest ruler, followed by *San Gong Jiu Qing* (three *Gong* and nine *Qing;* the titles distinguishing their hierarchical status) who assisted the emperor in ruling the country. The three *Gong* were: (1) *Cheng Xiang,* or prime minister, the highest administrative official of the central government; (2) *Tai Wei,* the highest military officer who advised the emperor on military affairs (without, however, the power to move troops); and (3) *Yu Shi Dai Fu,* the general supervisor, who was to provide assistance to *Cheng Xiang* in his administrative work. In theory, the three *Gong* would exert checks on each other, while all power was concentrated in the hands of the emperor. Below the three *Gong,* there were nine *Qing,* whose major responsibilities included caring for the palace, the royal family, and the emperor.

For the local administration, Qin Shi Huang accepted Li Si's suggestion to abolish the old system of enfeoffment (feudalism) and establish a new system of administrative districts throughout the country. Qin Shi Huang divided the empire into 36 *Jun* (prefectures), under each of which were a number of *Xian* (counties). Under each county, were a number of *Xiang* (towns), under each town were a number of *Ting,* and under such *Ting* were 10 *Li,* the smallest rural administrative units. All the officials of prefectures and counties were appointed by the emperor with fixed salaries; their positions were not hereditary, and they were subject to recall or removal by the emperor. Most of the appointees were military officers who distinguished themselves in battles. This hierarchical system of administration achieved political unification and strongly reinforced the central government.

In order to prevent conspiracy, Qin Shi Huang ordered that all weapons belonging to civilians be gathered in the capital for melting down. From the meltdown, 12 "gold men" (bronze) were molded, each weighing 120 tons; they were placed in the front hall of his new palace. At the same time, Qin Shi Huang forced the 120,000 most powerful and wealthiest households in the empire to move into Xian Yang the capital, thereby, first, making the capital look prosperous and, second, making such powerful families easier to watch over. As for the old noble families of the conquered six kingdoms, Qin Shi Huang had some of them sent to Nan Yang and Ba Shu (southwest of China) from their native places, hoping that by forcing them to leave their hereditary lands, he was helping to reduce their power.

To tighten his rule of the empire, Qin Shi Huang also unified the code of laws, establishing laws regarding the responsibilities of government officials and punishment for the neglect of their duties. Officials at the basic levels, for example, were to report on time to county officials about agricultural and farming situations such as floods, droughts, storms, and insect pests. One law said that peasants were not allowed to drink liquor in "field huts"; if they did, they were punished. Criminal law enforcement was extremely cruel: the penalty for even small theft was cutting off the left foot or branding the face. The heaviest punishments included being torn apart by a chariot or the elimination of an entire family.

Prior to the unification, the writing of the same Chinese characters had varied in different regions of the kingdoms. Although all characters came from the script of the early Zhou Dynasty, known as the Large Seal Script, literature produced during the later Zhou Dynasty (known as the Period of Spring and Autumn and the Warring States, 770 b.c.-b.c.). brought about chronological and regional changes in the writing of Chinese characters. When Qin Shi Huang asked Li Si to help unify the script of Chinese language, Li Si and other scholars wrote a number of literary texts through which a new, simplified, standardized script, known as the Small Seal Script, was universalized throughout China.

Qin Shi Huang promoted the use of the reformed measuring system of his former kingdom, in which six feet equaled one *Bu* (Chinese double paces); 240 *Bu* equaled one *Mu;* and ten feet equaled one *Zhang.* In 221 b.c., a short imperial edict (of 40 Chinese characters) was promulgated on the unification of this measuring system, and it was required that all officially accepted measuring instruments must bear the edict's words.

In addition to writing and measuring systems, at the time of unification, different regions used different currencies. Qin Shi Huang reformed the currency system by declaring two types of currency: gold and copper. Gold was called upper currency, using *Yi* (24 ounces) as its unit, while copper was called the lower currency, which appeared in round coins with a square hole in the middle, each weighing a half *Liang* (half an ounce).

The second year after unification saw the beginnings of three major imperial highways, known as *Chi Dao.* With Xian Yang, the capital, as their center, the highways stretched northeast (reaching areas of the former kingdoms of Yan and Qi); southeast (reaching the former kingdoms of Wu and Chu); and north and south, about 800 kilometers (496 miles) with Wu Yuan (near today's Bao Tou in Inner Mongolia) at the northern end; and Ling Ling (in today's

Hunan province) at the southern end. These highways were 50 *Bu* (300 feet) wide with pine trees planted along the sides at intervals of three *Zhang* (30 feet). Remnants of *Chi Dao* survive today. With the total length of the Qin imperial highways stretching approximately 6,800 kilometers (4,216 miles), the completion of *Chi Dao* greatly increased the convenience of transporting troops and their supplies. In comparison, the total length of the Roman road system (ca. 150 a.d.) from Scotland to Rome and then to Jerusalem was about 5,984 kilometers (3,710 miles).

When Qin Shi Huang conquered the six kingdoms, he had specifications for all the palaces of the conquered kingdoms copied down so that they could then be rebuilt in the north of Xian Yang. But, thinking them too small, Qin Shi Huang proved dissatisfied with these palaces and so began the building of a new palace, called *A Fang Gong* in the southwest of Xian Yang. In his *General History of China,* Fan Wen-lan describes the grandeur of the palace's front hall:

500 Bu from east to west and 50 Zhang from north to south. It could hold 10,000 seats and flags of five Zhang height could stand in the Hall. . . . Magnetite was used . . . to detect people coming into the palace with hidden weapons.

It was estimated that more than 700,000 people worked on the palace, though Qin Shi Huang would not live to see its completion. His son, the second emperor, continued the building of the palace, but three years after his father's death Xiang Yu, a rebellious general, would enter the capital with his troops and set the palace on fire. *A Fang Gong* would burn for three months before falling in ashes.

Another large construction project undertaken by Qin Shi Huang was the building of the Emperor's tomb. Upon succession to the throne, Qin Shi Huang immediately began work on his mausoleum in Li Shan (black horse mountain). After the country's unification, over 700,000 corvée laborers (conscripts) were forced to work on the tomb which was more than 50 *Zhang* high with a radius of five *Li* (1.55 miles). There were palace halls in the tomb, providing seats for the hundred high officials. Mercury was used to create moving rivers and seas in the tomb. The inner tomb was protected by arrows that automatically discharged should anyone try to enter.

In 215 b.c., Qin Shi Huang sent General Meng Tian on an expedition to the north. In command of 300,000 troops, Meng Tian defeated the Xiongnu (Huns) and recovered the territories previously lost to them. According to *Shi Ji* (Historical Records), 34 counties were established in the recaptured areas, and a large number of people were sent there to cultivate the land. To prevent further attacks of Xiongnu, Qin Shi Huang began to repair and link up the old defensive walls built by the former kingdoms of Qin, Zhao, and Yan, beginning the world-famous construction of the Great Wall. Starting in the west in present-day Gansu province, the wall ended in the east in present-day Liaoning province. From east to west, it extended the length of 10,000 Chinese *Li* (over 1,400 miles). Tens of thousands of people were sent to build the wall, of whom more than half would die due to harsh living conditions and heavy labor.

In 214 b.c., Qin Shi Huang appointed Tu Sui as commander of 500,000 troops for the subjugation of areas in the south (today's Fujian, Guangdong and Guangxi). Tu Sui took over these areas without meeting much resistance. The newly conquered territories were divided into four prefectures, to which a large population of the Qin people were shifted to live with the native minorities. By this time, Qin Shi Huang had driven out the Xiongnu in the north and subdued minority tribes in the south, thereby greatly increasing and securing the whole empire.

Despite such methods of expansion and unification, the country remained far from intellectually unified. In 213 b.c., at Qin Shi Huang's birthday banquet in Xian Yang Palace, 70 scholars came forward to wish him longevity. One of them started to praise the emperor for his triumph over the rival kingdoms and the establishment of the new system of administrative districts throughout the country; but this praise induced a response from another scholar who thought that the new system of prefectures and counties was not as good as the old system of enfeoffment and that Qin Shi Huang should learn from the old dynasties. Remarked the scholar: "It's never heard that a government that does not model upon its predecessors ever lasts long." Li Si, now the Emperor's prime minister, refuted this fervently:

The five emperors never repeated each other; the three dynasties never inherited; they ruled by themselves not because they tried to be different but because times had changed. . . . Now the empire is established and all laws come from one source. . . . Men of letters should learn the laws. However, you scholars do not learn from the present but the past so as to criticize the present time and confuse the ordinary people.

Li Si's recommendation was that all books—except the history books about Qin—be burned. All the books of lyrics and the writings of the various schools of thought should be brought to governors of prefectures for burning; those who had these books and would not burn them within 30 days were to have their faces branded before being sent to labor for four years on the Great Wall. Those who dared to talk about these books were to be executed. Those who quoted the past to criticize the present were to be killed together with their entire families. Those who knew and did not report violations were to suffer the same punishment. The only books that were not to be burned were books on medicine, divination, and tree-planting. Qin Shi Huang approved of Li Si's plan and books were burned across the empire.

During the next year, 212 b.c., some Confucian scholars and magicians talked among themselves, criticizing the emperor of being power hungry, prone to kill and punish, and neglectful of intellectuals. When Qin Shi Huang learned of their dissent, he ordered a thorough investigation, during which the scholars blamed each other, rather than admitting to the criticisms. Finally, it was discovered that more than 460 scholars were involved. Qin Shi Huang ordered them all buried alive in the capital.

In 210 b.c., Qin Shi Huang made his fifth inspection tour around the country. When he reached a place called Sha Qiu (in today's Hebei province), he became seriously ill. Aware that he would soon die, he gave orders that his eldest son, Fu Su, should succeed him. But Zhao Gao, a favorite eunuch of the emperor and tutor of his second son, Hu Hai, changed the emperor's will. He issued a false edict ordering Fu Su to commit suicide and placed on the throne Hu Hai, who in three years lost the empire.

Meanwhile, the body of the first emperor was carried back to the capital. At his funeral, all the concubines who had not borne him sons were buried with him. Before they could escape, all the artisans who helped construct the emperor's tomb were also buried with him. In this way, the tomb was thought to be safe, because no one alive knew its secrets.

Further Reading

Guisso, R. W. L., et al. *The First Emperor of China.* Carol Pub Group, New York: Birch Lane Press; 1989.

Lang, Zhou. *Zhong Guo Li Dai Xing Wang Shi Tong Jian* (Rise and Fall of Each Dynasty in China). Wu Nan Publishing Company, 1985.

Twitchett, Denis, and John Fairbank, eds. *The Cambridge History of China.* Vol. 1. Cambridge University Press, 1986.

Yu-ning, Liu, ed. *The First Emperor of China.* White Plains, N.Y.: International Arts and Sciences, 1975.

Bodde, Dirk. *China's First Unifier: A Study of the Ch'in Dynasty as Seen in the Life of Li Ssu.* Hong Kong University Press, 1967.

Cotterell, Arthur, *The First Emperor of China: the Greatest Archeological Find of Our Time,* New York: Holt, Rinehart, and Winston, 1981.

Hsüe-chin, Li. *Eastern Zhou and Qin Civilizations.* Yale University Press, 1985.

Levenson, Joseph R. *China: An Interpretive History, From the Beginning to the Fall of Han.* University of California Press, 1969. □

Quintilian

Quintilian (ca. 35-ca. 99) was a Roman rhetorician and literary critic. His influence on rhetoric, literary criticism, and educational theory was profound.

Quintilian, or Marcus Fabius Quintilianus, was born at Calagurris in Spain, the son of a rhetorician. He studied mainly in Rome, under the orator Domitius After and perhaps the great grammarian Remmius Palaemon, among others. He then went back to Spain, probably as a teacher in his hometown, and returned to Rome in 68, the only certain date in his life. As a teacher of rhetoric, he became wealthy and famous from his lectures and was also an advocate in the law courts. Under the emperor Vespasian he was made a professor of rhetoric with a salary from the state. Among his pupils was Pliny the Younger.

At some time, probably in the early 80s, Quintilian married a very young woman. She died at the age of 18, after giving birth to two sons, who soon died as well. After 20 years of teaching, perhaps in 90, Quintilian retired and devoted himself to writing. Sometime after this, but before Domitian's death in 96, Quintilian was appointed by him as tutor to his two grandnephews; and through the influence of their father, Flavius Clemens, he received the insignia and privileges of a consul. The date of Quintilian's death is uncertain: Pliny the Younger, writing about 100, speaks of him in terms which suggest that he was already dead.

His Work

Only one work of Quintilian's has been preserved, the *Institutio oratoria* (On the Education of an Orator) in 12 books, composed about 92-96, the distillation of his long and successful career as a teacher. It treats of the education of an orator, beginning with the most elementary education. Book 1 sets the tone of the whole collection: it is moderate and practical, based on long experience with the actual behavior and psychology of children and careful attention to the smallest details of pedagogical practice. Book 2 treats of the more advanced education of the orator, and books 3 through 11 are more technical, dealing with the structure, argumentation, style, and delivery of orations.

Book 10 contains a discussion of the relative merits of the great Greek and Latin authors which has exercised a profound influence on subsequent literary criticism. Book 12 is based on a deeply moral conception of the importance of character as well as learning to the orator and of the

necessity for the style to be appropriate to the subject; it rounds out the work on an impressive note of grave dignity.

A complete text of Quintilian was rediscovered in the early 15th century. His educational aims, based on Cato the Elder's definition of an orator as "a good man, skilled in speaking," and looking toward the education of literate, humane, well-rounded, and useful citizens, were congenial to the ideals of the Renaissance.

Two further works, collections of declamations, survive under the name of Quintilian, but the fantastic nature of many of their subjects, an abuse specifically attacked by Quintilian, has led most scholars to dismiss them as spurious.

Further Reading

Two studies of Quintilian's life and work are Herbert Augustus Strong, *Quintilian, the Roman Schoolmaster* (1908), and George A. Kennedy, *Quintilian* (1969). Quintilian is discussed in John Wight Duff, *A Literary History of Rome in the Silver Age, from Tiberius to Hadrian* (1927); John W. H. Atkins, *Literary Criticism in Antiquity* (2 vols., 1934); Henri I. Marrou, *A History of Education in Antiquity* trans. 1956); and George M. A. Grube, *The Greek and Roman Critics* (1965). See also the introductions and notes to the editions of Quintilian's *Institutio oratoria*. □

Elpidio Quirino

Elpidio Quirino (1890-1956) was the second president of the Philippine Republic. During his administration, the Philippines passed through a period of revolutionary turmoil marked by widespread corruption, demoralization, economic crisis, and political terrorism.

Elpidio Quirino was born on Nov. 16, 1890, in Vigan, Ilocos Sur, the son of the warden of the provincial jail. Quirino taught school while studying at Vigan High School and then went to Manila, where he worked as junior computer in the Bureau of Lands and as property clerk in the Manila police department. He graduated from Manila High School in 1911 and also passed the civil service examination, first-grade.

After graduating from the College of Law, University of the Philippines, in 1915, Quirino served as law clerk in the Philippine Commission and then as secretary to Senate president Manuel Quezon. In 1919 Quirino won the post of congressional representative from the first district of Ilocos Sur. He opposed Sergio Osmeña, the leader of the Nacionalista party, and joined Quezon's Collectivista faction of the party. In 1925 Quirino was elected to the Senate. Quezon appointed him chairman of the Committee on Accounts and Claims and of the Committee on Public Instruction and to other important congressional bodies. In 1931 Quirino was reelected to the Senate. In the controversy surrounding the Hare-Hawes-Cutting Law of 1933, he sided with Quezon.

In 1934 Quirino became secretary of finance. He was also one of the drafters of the constitution approved on May 15, 1935. When the Philippine Commonwealth was inaugurated on Nov. 15, 1935, he held the position of secretary of finance (1935-1936) and then became secretary of interior (1936-1938). In 1941 he was elected as senator-at-large. When World War II broke out, Quirino refused to join the puppet government of José Laurel and became an underground leader of the Filipino resistance movement against the Japanese. He was captured and imprisoned by the Japanese military police in Ft. Santiago, and his wife, two daughters, and a son were murdered by the Japanese forces.

In 1945 Quirino became the leader of the majority in the Philippine Congress and then assumed the post of president pro tempore of the Senate. On the inauguration of the Philippine Republic in 1946, he occupied the post of vice president and first secretary of foreign affairs. In 1947 Quirino (who belonged to the class of landlords, compradors, and bureaucrat-capitalists) urged the adoption of the anomalous "parity amendment," imposed by the U.S. government in exchange for independence, war damage payments, and other loans.

When President Manuel Roxas died on April 15, 1948, Quirino succeeded him as president of the republic. For his weakness in tolerating rampant graft and corruption in his party, permitting immorality in the armed forces, and neglecting the impoverished plight of the majority of Filipinos, he was very unpopular, and in 1953 he was defeated by Ramon Magsaysay.

As president, Quirino was many times justly accused by Filipino nationalists of being extremely pro-American and even subservient to alien economic interests. To maintain peace and order for the sake of national unity, he granted amnesty to the Huk guerrillas on June 21, 1948; but this measure proved futile in solving the deep-rooted social injustice and exploitation inherent in the country's semifeudal economy. Although Quirino saw the need for increasing the appeal for loans from the United States and establishing controls to protect local Filipino industries and conserve natural resources, he failed to act vigorously and sincerely in implementing drastic agrarian reforms.

Quirino was elected president in 1949, when, according to historians and newspaper reports, widespread terrorism and violation of legal electoral processes occurred. He died on Feb. 29, 1956.

Further Reading

Standard references on Quirino's career and achievement include Sol H. Gwekoh, *Elpidio Quirino: The Barrio School Teacher Who Became President* (1949), and Hernando J. Abaya, *Betrayal in the Philippines* (1946) and *The Untold Philippine Story* (1967).

Additional Sources

Espinosa-Robles, Raissa, *To fight without end: the story of a misunderstood president,* Makati, Metro Manila, Philippines: Ayala Foundation, 1990.

Lopez, Salvador P., *Elpidio Quirino: the judgment of history,* Manila: President Elpidio Quirino Foundation, 1990.

Quirino, Carlos, *Apo Lakay: the biography of President Elpidio Quirino of the Philippines,* Makati, Metro Manila: Total Book World, 1987.

Romulo, Carlos P., *The Philippine presidents,* Quezon City: New Day Publishers; Detroit, Mich.: exclusive distributors, Cellar Book Shop, 1988. □

Horacio Quiroga

Horacio Quiroga (1878-1937) was a Uruguayan writer. His short stories are ranked among the best to emerge from Latin America.

Horacio Quiroga was born on December 31, 1878, in Salto, Uruguay, and died on February 19, 1937, in Buenos Aires, Argentina. Though born and raised in Uruguay, he spent most of his years in neighboring Argentina. His life was crammed with adventure and filled with recurrent tragedy and violence. When he was only a babe in arms his father was accidentally killed when a shotgun went off on a family outing. Later his step-father shot himself, and in 1902 Quiroga accidentally shot and killed one of his best friends and literary companions. In 1915 his first wife, unable to endure the hardships of life in

the jungle of northern Argentina where Quiroga insisted on living, committed suicide by taking a fatal dose of poison, leaving the widower with two small children to raise. Quiroga himself, when he realized he was incurably ill with cancer, took his own life.

His love affairs and marriages were also turbulent. He married twice, both times to younger women; his second wife, a friend of his daughter, was nearly 30 years his junior. The first marriage ended with his wife's suicide; the second, in separation. All this violence in his personal life undoubtedly explains a great deal about the obsession with death so marked in his work.

Quiroga's love of adventure and the attraction the jungle hinterland of northern Argentina held for him are also biographical details that have great impact on his writings. His first trip to Misiones province took place in 1903, when he accompanied his friend and fellow writer Leopoldo Lugones as photographer on an expedition to study the Jesuit ruins there. In 1906 he bought some land in San Ignacio, Misiones, and from then on divided his time chiefly between the hinterland and Buenos Aires. While living in the jungle Quiroga tried various experiments, such as distilling an orange liqueur. These endeavors ended in failure but provided him with good materials for his stories, as did all his activities there, such as building his bungalow, his furniture, and canoes and hunting and studying the wildlife of the region.

Quiroga began writing under the influence of Modernism, a literary movement which dominated Spanish Ameri-

can Literature at the turn of the century. Soon, however, he reacted against the artificiality of his first book in this mode, published in 1901, *Coral Reefs* (*Los arrecifes de coral*), a collection of prose poems and poetry, and turned to writing tales firmly rooted in reality, although they often emphasized the strange or the monstrous. Many of these early stories are reminiscent of Edgar Allan Poe, whose influence marked much of his work. "The Feather Pillow" ("El almohadón de pluma") is a good example of his expert handling of the Gothic tale. The effects of horror, something mysterious and perverse filling the atmosphere, are there from the beginning of the story, with a sensational revelation at the end.

For three decades in the early 20th century Quiroga continued writing and publishing stories in great quantity—his total output ran over 200—and many of them are of impressive quality. His several attempts at novels were relative failures. Among the various collections of his stories, two should be singled out as high points: *Stories of Love, Madness, and Death* (*Cuentos de amor, de locura, y de muerte*, 1917) and *The Exiled Ones* (*Los desterrados*), published in 1926. The splendid title of the first of these volumes sets forth his major themes and could properly be the heading for his entire work.

Quiroga also achieved great popularity with his *Jungle Tales* (*Cuentos de la selva*) in 1918, with its title reminiscent of Rudyard Kipling. This collection is made up of stories in a fable mold, with talking animals and usually an underlying moral. They are filled with humor and tenderness and are appropriate for children of all ages. Another of his celebrated tales, *Anaconda* (1921), describes a world of snakes and how they battle men and also one another. This long story moves at a slower pace than is usual in Quiroga's work and has a spun-out plot. Its reptilian characters are more compelling than believable, and the animal characterization, though good, is not quite as striking as in some of his shorter narratives.

If we examine Quiroga's stories carefully, we will find them full of vision concerning mankind. He had a sharp awareness of the problems besetting man on every side—not only the pitfalls of savage nature but also those referring to human relationships. Quiroga pointed out man's weaknesses and failings, but he also stressed the heroic virtues of courage, generosity, and compassion in many of his best stories.

All this rich human material is shaped into story form by a master craftsman. Quiroga was conscious of the problems involved in the art of the short story, and, like Poe, he wrote about them. He described his technique in what he called his "Manual of the Perfect Short Story Writer," which consists of ten commandments. Warnings stressing economy of expression are here; others are concerned with careful advance planning. His final suggestion for writing good stories is perhaps the best: "Tell the tale as if the story's only interest lay in the small surroundings of your characters, of which you might have been one. In no other way is *life* achieved in the short story." Quite rightly Quiroga emphasized here the word *life*, which lies at the core of his stories.

Usually Quiroga practiced the economy he preached in this manual. Feats of condensation are common, as in "The Dead Man," where he shows his powers in dramatic focus on a single scene describing a dying man, or in "Drifting," a stark story in which everything seems reduced to essentials, where the brief opening scene of a man bitten by a viper contains the germs of all that comes afterward. The language is terse, the situation of great intensity, the action straightforward and lineal. There is also much suggestion and implication, rather than outright telling, in his best work.

Quiroga did not seem to have a social axe to grind, although some of the most cutting social commentary in Spanish American fiction can be found in his stories, particularly those about the exploitation of the Misiones jungle lumberjacks, like "The Contract Workers" ("Los mensú"). Setting, as well as technique, is important to Quiroga because it is inseparable from the real, day-to-day experience of human existence. His feelings are bound up in place, especially in Misiones, where most of his best stories occur. He makes us feel the significance of this setting, the symbolic strength of the rivers and the hypnotic force of its snake-infested jungles.

Recognition for his mastery of the short story came to Quiroga fairly early in his career, and he continued to enjoy fame throughout his lifetime. In the Spanish-speaking world he is still much admired today, though the type of story he excelled at, in which man is pitted against nature and rarely if ever wins out, is no longer commonly composed in Latin America. Quiroga knew his trade inside and out, he was universal in his appeal and subjected his themes to dramatic form. He wrote tautly and described with intensity so that his stories would make their mark on the reader.

Further Reading

Quiroga is listed in such guides as *The Oxford Companion to Spanish Literature* (1978) and Foster and Foster, editors, *Modern Latin American Literature* (1975). For longer studies, see Jefferson Spell's chapter on Quiroga in *Contemporary Spanish American Fiction* (1944) or the excellent critical work in Spanish on his life and works by Emir Rodríguez Monegal, *The Exile: Life and Works of Horacio Quiroga* (*El desterrado: vida y obra de Horacio Quiroga*, 1968). Aside from scattered translations of Quiroga's stories in anthologies and the collection *South American Jungle Tales* (1959), there is available in English a book which includes a dozen of his best tales, *The Decapitated Chicken and Other Stories* (1976). □

Juan Facundo Quiroga

Juan Facundo Quiroga (1788-1835) was an Argentine caudillo who mastered a large part of northern Argentina for several years.

Juan Facundo Quiroga, often known as Juan Facundo, was born into a ranching family in La Rioja Province. Although his father was moderately wealthy, Juan had little formal schooling, learning only the basics of reading and writing. He spent most of his boyhood working on the family ranch, showing qualities of leadership and shrewdness. He left home in 1806, having gambled away the proceeds from his father's cattle sale.

Quiroga spent several years in and out of military service. He joined both cavalry and infantry units but disliked the discipline and regimentation of formal military life. Finally he was discharged—or he deserted—and returned home, where he was reconciled with his father.

From 1816, when he became a captain in the provincial militia, Quiroga began his rise in political and military affairs. By 1823 he was virtual dictator of La Rioja. Skilled in battle, of unflinching courage and daring ruthlessness, he had an almost mystical ability to command the absolute loyalty of his mounted troops.

From his power base in La Rioja, Quiroga extended his sway to surrounding provinces and was soon caught up in national politics. Argentina had declared its independence from Spain in 1816, but the nation's leaders could not agree on a permanent from of government. In 1826 Bernardino Rivadavia became president and attempted to establish a unitary system of government with control emanating from Buenos Aires. Quiroga joined other provincial *caudillos* in opposition and helped force Rivadavia's resignation in 1827. After a series of seesaw battles, Quiroga finally fragmented unitary forces in the interior of the country in 1831, and the various provinces became virtually independent.

Quiroga soon moved to Buenos Aires Province, where Juan Manuel de Rosas was trying to fasten his dictatorial hold. The two were never close, for Quiroga insisted that Argentina must have a truly national government, a concept Rosas always resisted. For more than a year the backwoods *caudillo* enjoyed the delights offered by the chief city of the nation and indulged his passion for gambling. Late in 1834 Rosas persuaded him to undertake a mission as mediator between quarreling provincial governors far in the interior. While returning from this assignment in 1835, Quiroga was killed in an ambush. The "Tiger of the Plains," champion of provincial autonomy, was a harsh man who lived in harsh times, when leadership was tested at the point of a lance and intellectual ability was valued less than raw courage. He gave northern Argentina a measure of stability in chaotic times, but he left no heritage of stable or progressive institutions, no base on which to build a greater Argentina.

Further Reading

Domingo F. Sarmiento, *Life in the Argentine Republic in the Days of the Tyrants: or, Civilization and Barbarism* (trans. 1961), viewing Quiroga as representative of the "barbarism," recounts his life and times in a sensational and anecdotal fashion. Frederick A. Kirkpatrick, *A History of the Argentine Republic* (1931), and Ricardo Levene, *A History of Argentina*, translated and edited by W. S. Robertson (1937), place Quiroga in the larger scope of Argentina's history.

Additional Sources

Sarmiento, Domingo Faustino, *Life in the Argentine Republic in the days of the tyrants: or, Civilization and barbarism*, New York: Gordon Press, 1976. □

R

Jean Joseph Rabearivelo

The Malagasy poet Jean Joseph Rabearivelo (1901-1937) was the first major French-language poet in Africa. Some of his most powerful poetry arose from the conflict between his intimacy with two cultures, Malagasy and French, and his estrangement from two societies, native and colonial.

Jean Joseph Rabearivelo was born on March 4, 1901, in Tananarive (Madagascar) into a noble family which had been impoverished as a result of the abolition of slavery by the French authorities soon after the colonial conquest in 1895. He left school at 13 in order to earn a precarious livelihood as proofreader in a local printing shop.

Tananarive in the early 1920s was a focus of intense literary and journalistic activity in the vernacular, and Rabearivelo was one of the first Malagasy poets to use the French language as his medium of literary expression. His early collections, *La Coupe de cendres* (1924), *Sylves* (1927), and *Volumes* (1928), were in the romantic-academic manner of such French 19th-century poets as appeared on the school curriculum in those days. But through his friendship with Pierre Camo—a French official who was also a minor poet—Rabearivelo became acquainted with contemporary symbolist poetry and managed to free himself of the shackles of conventional versification and diction. His best poems are to be found in *Presque-songes* (1934) and *Traduit de la nuit* (1935).

The poet's love of France, its language, and its literature was apt to take weird ritualistic forms. His wide reading in romantic and postromantic poetry had somehow driven him to the notion that poetic genius was inevitably associated with various forms of abnormality, such as reckless extravagance, chronic lack of money, almost permanent debauchery, ill health (usually tuberculosis), and suicidal tendencies. With pathetic conscientiousness, he was thus striving to mimic the most futilely morbid aspects in the lives of Balzac, Baudelaire, Verlaine, and a host of other, minor, if even more wildly aberrant, writers.

This ill-advised imitation of alien models was uneasily coupled with considerable pride in the literary achievements, oral and written, of Malagasy culture, even though, as a former aristocrat and a Frenchified intellectual, he felt some contempt for the illiterate masses. He was thus rejected by his more tradition-minded or nationalistic fellow citizens. As a native, he was also rejected by the local French society of petty traders and administrators. In his bulky diaries, which have never been edited in their entirety, he described his tragic predicament as that of a Latin mind under a black skin but also as that of a proud Malagasy eager to shed the Christian and Western disguise imposed upon him. His habit of wearing the traditional robe, the *lamba,* over his Westernstyle clothes illustrated this duality more than it could hide—let alone solve—it.

This dual allegiance and this dual rebellion imbue Rabearivelo's poetry. Although he mostly wrote in French, in part of his work he sought to bend the alien language to native themes, experiences, and even literary forms such as the *hainteny*. Aware of his uncommon gifts, yet confined to his underprivileged status, Rabearivelo found the best of his inspiration in an all-pervading, tragic sense of alienation, which finds adequate utterance in images of exile and death, rootlessness and sterility. He committed suicide on June 22, 1937.

Further Reading

There is no biography of Rabearivelo in English. Information on him is in Ulli Beier, ed., *Introduction to African Literature* (1967), and in Norman R. Shapiro, ed. and trans., *Negritude: Black Poetry from Africa and the Caribbean* (1970). □

François Rabelais

The French humanist, doctor, and writer François Rabelais (ca. 1494-ca. 1553) is acclaimed a master of the comic for his creations *Pantagruel* and *Gargantua*.

Unfortunately there are more legends than facts about François Rabelais The dates of his birth and death are only scholarly guesses. No record of his activities for long periods has survived. Most certainly born in the closing years of the 15th century, Rabelais consequently experienced a time of considerable ferment in the history of France's institutions and intellectual life. Unless one grasps the issues and the attitudes in this crisis, much of Rabelais's work is meaningless or subject to misinterpretation.

Central to the problems that faced Rabelais's contemporaries were the decline of scholasticism and the rise of humanist activity. (A humanist is defined here as a scholar of the language and literature of ancient times, including biblical research.) After the constructive work of St. Thomas Aquinas and Albertus Magnus, scholastic philosophy became increasingly dominated by the nominalists, who, in distinguishing between the realm of reason and the realm of faith, placed faith firmly beyond the reach of reason. As a consequence, a scholastic education evolved into an endless exercise of rational proof that displeased many believers who felt such training failed to respond to the spiritual side of man. Humanist inquiry completed the crisis of confidence in inherited institutions by revealing the great ignorance of many scholastics and the inaccuracy of their work. At the same time, the newly studied texts, such as Plato, and the reinterpreted texts, such as St. Paul, seemed more and more to offer the inspiration of which scholasticism had proved incapable.

During the first 30 years of the 16th century in France, the gamut of attitudes on such matters was great. Some merely studied ancient texts; others, like Lefèvre d'Étaples, brought their scholarly actions to bear on doctrinal questions without contemplating separation from the Church. Still others, like John Calvin, felt confronted by the necessity to form a new faith, a new church. All liberal minds felt disturbed by the evident disparity between, on the one hand, the sterility of scholastic pedagogy and the corruption of the Church and, on the other, the excitement in humanist studies and the vibrant faith of early Christianity.

Early Years

Rabelais's native land was the old province of Touraine, where his father, Antoine, practiced law. There is reason to believe that Rabelais was instructed according to scholastic methods. On March 4, 1521, he wrote a letter from the Franciscan monastery of Puy-Saint-Martin to Guillaume Budé, one of France's foremost humanists. Furthermore, in 1523 Rabelais's superiors confiscated his Greek books, and although the texts were returned, François soon left both his monastery and his order to become the secretary of Geoffroy d'Estissac of the Benedictines. He is next seen at Montpellier (1530), where he obtained a degree in medicine and taught the writings of Hippocrates and Galen from the original Greek text. In 1532 he settled in Lyons, where he was named physician at the Hôtel-Dieu and where, the same year, he published several works, including the first volume of his celebrated novel, *Horribles et espouventables faictz et prouesses de tres renommé Pantagruel, roy des Dipsodes.*

In addition to Rabelais's evident link with the humanists and his own scholarly accomplishments, certain critics have made much of his gradual separation from the monastery, implying that Rabelais's acts signify as well a separation from the Church (and religion). Nothing is more suspect. Rabelais wanted to study medicine, and this was not then possible if one remained a member of the regular clergy. If his books were seized, they were also returned, and the papal permission Rabelais received to change orders, too, intimates that he was far from being considered an errant atheist. Another papal authorization—this time to legitimize two children of Rabelais's (1540)—reveals that Rabelais could not recognize all the rules of monastic life, but this is not tantamount to saying that he could not recognize the tenets of the Church.

Pantagruel and Gargantua

Although *Gargantua* (1534) followed *Pantagruel* in order of publication, all modern editions place it at the beginning of the novel since the events it relates predate those of *Pantagruel*. The creation of *Gargantua,* the story of Pantagruel's father, attests to the success of the first volume. Rabelais, following the example of many medieval writers of *chansons de geste,* expands his material through a portrait of the hero's antecedents. The rapprochement with medieval literature is not gratuitous. In conception (the life and chivalric episodes of a family of giants) and execution (use of the vernacular, love of language, puns, mixture of popular and learned styles) the first two volumes of Rabelais's novel reflect practices well developed in medieval literature and known to Rabelais through the French and Italian chivalric romances, their parodies, and *Les Grandes et inestimables croniques du grand et énorme géant Gargantua.* Judging by the light and simple nature of Pantagruel, where traces of Rabelais's important themes are not always evident, it seems unlikely that the writer foresaw the volumes to follow or even the serious use to which his novel might be put.

It would also be incorrect to portray *Pantagruel* as devoid of any controversial material. It and *Gargantua* were signed by a pseudonym, Alcofrybas Nasier, an anagram of François Rabelais. The Sorbonne condemned both books. *Pantagruel* is not just Panurge's wild jokes or the fantastic war between the Dipsodes and Amaurotes. In portraying Pantagruel's adventures with legal cases and debating, Rabelais good-heartedly satirizes the bumbling "learned," so contemptible to the humanists. When Pantagruel visits the Library of Saint Victor, he finds such titles as *The Codpiece of the Law* and Béda's *Of the Excellence of Tripe.* If the first title is pure comedy, the second casts a satirical barb at Noël Béda, a conservative Catholic and notorious enemy of the reformers.

Contemporary religious questions keep reappearing and no doubt explain the Sorbonne's condemnation. Before a battle, Pantagruel promises God that if he is victorious, he will have God's word preached "purely, simply and wholly, so that the abuses of a host of hypocrites and false prophets will be eradicated from [his] land." Rabelais's sympathy with the reform could not be clearer. Mention should be made as well of Gargantua's letter to Pantagruel, in which the father contrasts the ignorance of his day with the new learning. It shows that the idea of a renaissance in France at this time was common among the humanists themselves.

There are striking contrasts between *Pantagruel* and *Gargantua*. Although both discuss religion and war, *Gargantua* gives these subjects an extended treatment in which Rabelais's serious thoughts direct the discussion instead of appearing sporadically as in *Pantagruel*. The reader first learns how Gargantua was taught by a (scholastic) theologian (changed in later editions to "sophist"). Gargantua studies those texts long discredited by humanist scholarship and proves his worth by learning to memorize texts backward. Under other sophists, he rises late, spends little time on studies or exercising but eats, drinks, and hears from 6 to 30 Masses. Then Gargantua receives a tutor schooled in the new humanist and religious thought. The tutor consults a doctor so that Gargantua's regime will benefit body as well as mind. The boy rises early and reads a page of the Scriptures. During the day not an hour is lost as the pupil strives to learn his lessons clearly and to absorb the great variety of skills required of a "renaissance man." There are limits to Rabelais's educational reform. He still emphasized memorization, and there can be no doubt about the continued importance of religion. His reform affects more the methods of education than its aims.

The battles against Picrochole are intended to show Rabelais's hatred of war. War is portrayed as interrupting more important pursuits, such as learning, and having an irrational basis. When Picrochole has been defeated, an entire chapter is devoted to Gargantua's treatment of the vanquished. His acts embody Christian charity. Only the King's evil minister and two instigators of the war receive a punishment (a very humanist punishment): they turn Gargantua's printing press!

The closing chapters of *Gargantua* are devoted to the Abbaye de Thélème, a utopian spot, where the motto is "Do What You Will." The phrase has been interpreted both as a frank statement of Rabelais's immorality and of his express confidence in the innate goodness of humanity. The text upholds neither interpretation. The rooms at Thélème have a chapel for worship, and Rabelais carefully enumerates those who are excluded from Thélème (hypocrites, lawyers, usurers, and jealous troublemakers) or invited (noble lords, ladies, and those who actively expound on the Scriptures). Religion is hardly absent from this abbey that also is not for everyone, and the inclusion of the aristocrat probably says more about Rabelais's association (a traditional one) of nobility of birth with nobility of soul than about his attitude toward original sin. In all three elements of *Gargantua*—education, war, Thélème—Rabelais's remarks are constructive and positive.

Later Life

Rabelais's continued association with the most able men of his time is attested to by trips he made to Rome in the party of Jean du Bellay (1534 and 1535) and by his presence at a dinner given for Étienne Dolet (1537). The same year he gave an anatomy lesson at Lyons. In 1546 he published the *Tiers livre des faictz et dictz héroïques du noble Pantagruel,* which Rabelais dared to sign with his own name and which the Sorbonne immediately condemned.

Firm traces of Rabelais now become increasingly difficult to find. The kindness of Jean du Bellay permitted him to visit Rome a third time, where he appeared definitely in 1548. That year saw published in Lyons a partial edition of the *Quart livre.* The full edition was printed in 1552. A fifth volume, called first *L'Isle sonante* in a truncated text of 1562 and then the *Cinquième livre* in a much enlarged printing of

1564, continues to bear, as it did then, the name of Rabelais, but its authenticity is yet to be confirmed. When, in January 1553, Rabelais signed away the rights to two ecclesiastical posts, he performed his last certain act.

Tiers livre and Quart livre

The *Tiers livre* contains much of Rabelais's most obscure writing. The romanesque battle scenes and the general hilarity of gigantic exploits no longer furnish him with a narrative line, although Pantagruel and Gargantua appear in the book. Even Panurge, the impish, amoral prankster of the first volume, shares the less funny and more disquieting quality of the *Tiers livre*, for which he provides a central theme. Panurge wonders whether he should marry and whether his wife will deceive him. The book enumerates all the efforts expended by Panurge to help him make a decision.

The complexity of the *Tiers livre* resides primarily in the portrait of Panurge. Pantagruel early states that Panurge must decide what is his will and act. If all else in life is fortuitous, man has his will and an obligation to use it. (Rabelais did not share John Calvin's views on predestination.) From this perspective the *Tiers livre* is a criticism of Panurge, who will not act and will not accept the advice given him. It has also been argued that much of the advice is open to discussion and that Panurge's final decision to consult the Dive Bouteille is a positive reaction before the need for self-knowledge. However one reads the *Tiers livre*, there is no missing its allusions to the gathering tensions in France after the reformers lost royal support.

The *Quart livre*, an account of Panurge's adventures on the voyage to the Dive Bouteille, contains the famous episode of Dindenault and his sheep, as well as Rabelais's final definition of *Pantagruélisme:* "a certain gaiety of spirit filled with contempt for fortuitous things." There is a chapter here devoted to the Papefigues (those who mocked the Pope). Their land was once rich and free. Its inhabitants are now poor, the subjects of the Papimanes (supporters of the Pope).

Later Pantagruel meets two groups of men, the Engastrimythes (ventriloquists) and the Gastrolates (adorers of the stomach). Rabelais specifically states that Pantagruel—generally so tolerant—"greatly detested them." In both cases there is a religious overtone. The Engastrimythes are prophets who fool the simple; the Gastrolates depict those enemies of the Cross who, in the words of St. Paul, have made Belly their God. By 1552, a mere decade before the outbreak of the religious wars, France had left far behind the optimism of the 1530s. Its evolution is well mirrored in the changing tones of Rabelais, who incorrectly but not unfortunately is remembered only as the jovial embodiment of Renaissance enthusiasm.

Further Reading

The most solid modern biography of Rabelais is Jean Plattard, *The Life of François Rabelais* (1930). Excellent studies of Rabelais's work include M. A. Screech, *The Rabelaisian Marriage* (1958); A. J. Krailsheimer, *Rabelais and the Franciscans* (1963); and Abraham C. Keller, *The Telling of Tales in Rabelais* (1963). Aspects of Rabelais's influence are well treated in Huntington Brown, *Rabelais in English Literature* (1933).

Additional Sources

Besant, Walter, Sir, *Rabelais,* Norwood, Pa.: Norwood Editions, 1978.
Frame, Donald Murdoch, *François Rabelais: a study,* New York: Harcourt Brace Jovanovich, 1977.
Henry, Gilles, *Rabelais,* Paris: Perrin, 1988.
Powys, John Cowper, *Rabelais: his life, the story told by him, selections therefrom here newly translated, and an interpretation of his genius and his religion,* London: Village Press, 1974. □

Isidor Isaac Rabi

The American physicist Isidor Isaac Rabi (1898-1988) pioneered in the development of precision atomic-and nuclear-beam measurements.

Isidor Rabi was born on July 29, 1898, in Rymanov in what was then Austria-Hungary. As an infant, he was brought to the United States, where his father engaged in the real estate business in New York City. Rabi attended Cornell University (1916-1919), obtaining a bachelor's degree in chemistry. Deciding to pursue graduate study in physics, he returned to Cornell (1922-1923) and then transferred to Columbia University, where in 1927 he obtained his doctoral degree. In 1926 he married Helen Newmark. The couple had two daughters.

Rabi studied in Europe (1927-1929), working with some of the most outstanding physicists. Otto Stern, with whom he remained for about a year, made the deepest impression on Rabi.

Work on Atomic and Molecular Beams

Immediately on his return to the United States, where he had accepted a position as lecturer in physics at Columbia, Rabi and his student V. Cohen exploited the atomic-and molecular-beam techniques Rabi had developed in Stern's laboratory. Together they proved that the sodium atom has four "hyperfine-structure" energy levels, which unambiguously fixed the "spin angular momentum" of its nucleus at a definite value, equal to 3/2 in units of $2\pi/h$. A few years later, by using beams of atomic hydrogen and deuterium, Rabi and his coworkers confirmed the surprisingly large value for the magnetic moment of the proton which Stern had found in 1933. It was during the course of this work that Rabi developed still another new method, the resonance method, that has since become the basis for all precision atomic-and molecular-beam measurements.

From the point of view of "pure physics," perhaps the most important measurements that have been made by exploiting Rabi's method have been those on the anomalous magnetic moment of the electron, the quadrupole moment of the deuteron, and the Lamb shift in hydrogen (which has become of great importance for the development of quan-

Atomic Energy Commission and served on the President's Science Advisory Committee and the United Nations Science Committee.

One of Rabi's most satisfying postwar achievements was his organization of a number of international United Nations Conferences on the Peaceful Uses of Atomic Energy. Like most physicists, he was deeply impressed by the awesome destructive power of the atomic bomb and worked unrelentingly to find means to ensure that the bomb would never be used again.

Communication is essential to understanding, and understanding is essential to unity: this was a major theme in Rabi's life, especially after the war. It applies not only to countries but also to intellectual disciplines. "What the scientist really desires," Rabi wrote, "is for his science to be understood, to become an integral part of our general culture, to be given proper weight in the cultural and practical affairs of the world. Like the poet, the scientist would rather be read than praised." According to Rabi, what people of all disciplines sorely require is wisdom: "Without it, knowledge is dry, almost unfit for human consumption, and dangerous in application.... Wisdom makes itself most manifest in the application of knowledge to human needs."

Granted his sincere search for unity, it is not surprising that Rabi, after holding the Higgins professorship of physics for seven years (1957-1964), became the first university professor at Columbia. This professorship is without ties to any particular department. The last subject Rabi lectured on before his retirement in 1967 was "The Philosophical and Social Implications of 20th Century Physics." Rabi explained to his Columbia students, in reference to atomic weapons, "just because we got their first doesn't mean that we should have the power of life and death over the whole world." Rabi died of a long-term illness on January 11, 1988 in New York City.

Further Reading

Rabi's brief *My Life and Times as a Physicist* appeared in 1960. Although Rabi did not deliver a Nobel lecture, a short biographical sketch of him appears in the Nobel Foundation, *Nobel Lectures in Physics* (3 vols., 1964-1967). See also Tina Nellie Levitan, *Laureates: Jewish Winners of the Nobel Prize* (1960). Norman F. Ramsey, *Molecular Beams* (1956), contains detailed technical information on Rabi's contributions to physics.

Additional Sources

(Rigden, John) *Rabi: Scientist and Citizen* Basic Books, 1987.
New York Times Biographical Service (January 1988).
Physics Today (October 1988).
Nature (March 10, 1988). □

tum electrodynamics). From the point of view of "practicality," Rabi's method has found numerous applications, for example, in the highly precise time measurements associated with "atomic clocks," in precise measurements of magnetic fields, and in the development of the laser, an exceedingly important and versatile instrument. For his atomic-and molecularbeam work and for his discovery of the resonance method, Rabi was elected to the National Academy of Sciences in 1940 and received the 1944 Nobel Prize.

War Work and Postwar Concerns

In 1937 Rabi achieved the rank of full professor at Columbia. Three years later he became associate director of the radiation laboratory at the Massachusetts Institute of Technology (MIT), recently established to develop microwave radar and related equipment for military uses. This work, which was closely related to Rabi's past researches and which relied heavily on British contributions, was eminently successful. In 1948 he received the United States Medal of Merit and the King's Medal for Service in the Cause of Freedom for his wartime efforts.

Rabi was executive officer of the physics department at Columbia (1945-1948), during which time he increased the strength of the department, especially in high-energy and microwave physics. He was also instrumental in establishing the Brookhaven National Laboratory on Long Island in 1945, and he started the movement that resulted in the large high-energy laboratory (CERN) in Geneva, Switzerland. He was the chairman of the General Advisory Committee of the

Yitzchak Rabin

Yitzchak Rabin (1922–1995) served his native Israel as chief-of-staff of the Israel Defense Forces, Minis-

ter of Defense, Prime Minister from 1974 to 1977, and again from 1992 to his death in 1995.

Yitzchak Rabin was born in Jerusalem in 1922, the son of Russian-Zionist pioneers Rosa and Nechemia Rabin. At the age of 14, intent on becoming a farmer, he entered the Kadoorie Agricultural School at Kfar Tabor, graduating in 1940. Plans to go on to college work in irrigational engineering at the University of California were disrupted by World War II, however. Rabin joined the Palmach, the commando unit of the Jewish underground army, the Haganah, which later became the nucleus for the Israel Defense Forces (IDF).

In the beginning of his brilliant military career Rabin took part in several operations behind the lines against the Vichy French in Syria and Lebanon in 1941 on behalf of the British and in defense of Palestine. By 1944 he had reached the rank of deputy battalion commander in the Palmach. After the war Anglo-Jewish cooperation ended as British opposition to Jewish independence intensified. Rabin himself was involved in anti-British underground activity, and at one point in 1946 he was caught and sentenced to six months in a detention camp. He was released in early 1947 in time to participate in the final struggle over Palestine.

Promoted to deputy commander of the elite Palmach, Rabin fought with distinction against the invading Arab forces during Israel's war of independence in 1948. He played a role in the defense of Jerusalem, helping to keep

open the vital supply road from Tel-Aviv and the coastal plain to the besieged city. In late 1948, now a colonel, he also fought on the southern front against Egypt. Then in the spring of 1949 Rabin served as military representative on the Israeli delegation to the Rhodes conference which resulted in a series of Arab-Israel armistice accords.

Having determined to pursue a military career, the post-1948 years saw Rabin advancing up the army hierarchy. He served successively as an armored brigade commander in the Negev, acting commander of the southern front (1949-1950), chief of tactical operations (1950-1952), head of the training branch (1954-1956), commanding officer of the northern front (1956-1959), and head of the manpower branch (1959-1960). During that period he was able to complete a year's study program at the British Staff College. Then from 1960 to 1963 Brigadier General Rabin filled two additional positions: deputy chief of staff and chief of the general staff branch. Finally, in January 1964 he was appointed chief-of-staff, remaining in that position until his retirement from the army in January 1968.

It was during his term of office as chief of staff that the 1967 Mid-East crisis occurred. Confronted by a military alliance of Egypt, Jordan, and Syria, the Israeli government authorized a preemptive war which began on June 6. Within six days the Israel Defense Forces, acting under Rabin's command and according to contingency plans drawn up under his instructions, had gained a spectacular victory. The Six Day War ended with Israel in control of the Sinai Peninsula, the Golan Heights, and all of the West Bank territories of Judea and Samaria up to the Jordan River. And Rabin found himself a national hero.

This newly-acquired prestige led to his being appointed Israel's ambassador to Washington in March 1968. During his time in the United States Rabin was involved intensely in various Middle East peace efforts—none of which was successful—and deepening American-Israel relations, especially in terms of U.S. military assistance to Israel during the Johnson and the Nixon administrations.

In March 1973 Rabin left the United States and returned to Israel in order to enter politics, joining the dominant Labour Party. The national elections that year were interrupted in the fall by the surprise Egyptian-Syrian attack. In the wake of the Yom Kippur War, in which Rabin had no official or military role, the elections were finally held in December 1973. Although Labour's parliamentary strength declined, Rabin gained a seat in the Knesset and was appointed minister of labor in the new cabinet headed by Golda Meir. However, the government lasted only a month due to Meir's decision to resign, which led to formation of a new government and selection by the Labour/Alignment of a premier-designate. In April 1974 the party's central committee turned to Rabin, entrusting him with the task of putting together a viable coalition, which he succeeded in doing by late May. The Rabin government was approved by the Knesset on June 3, 1974, making Rabin the fifth, and youngest, premier; he was also the first native-born Israeli to achieve that high position.

Rabin's stay in power only lasted until 1977 and was a troubled one from the outset. In the Knesset his fragile three-party coalition had only the barest majority—a single seat—meaning it could fall at any moment. Domestically, the Yom Kippur War's aftermath caused demoralization and created structural problems in the economy under the weight of the defense burden. Diplomatically the years 1974-1977 coincided with Henry Kissinger's shuttle diplomacy and efforts at pressuring Israel, thereby straining the U.S.-Israeli relationship. Nor did it help that sharp interpersonal rivalries within the cabinet further weakened the government's effectiveness. Finally, early in 1977 a coalition crisis led to the government's downfall. In the subsequent elections Labour and the Alignment were turned out of office; although re-elected to the Knesset, Rabin was soon replaced as party head by his arch-rival, Shimon Peres.

Nevertheless, upon formation of the National Unity government in September 1984, based on a unique power-sharing system of rotation between the Alignment and the Likud, Yitzchak Rabin was the agreed-upon candidate for the post of defense minister. Chosen to serve for the full four-year period, Rabin succeeded in improving his working relations with Prime Minister Peres and in gaining broad public confidence. He concentrated his efforts specifically on extricating the Israel Defense Forces from southern Lebanon, on reorganization plans for the defense forces, and on strengthening strategic cooperation with the United States.

Rabin's strong response to Palestinian insurrections gained him enough political support to make another bid to be prime minister in 1992. His victory came on promises of ending the conflict with the Palestinians. Secret talks with Palestinian Liberation Organization leader Yasser Arafat led to a conference in Oslo, Norway where an agreement was reached in 1993. In 1994, Rabin led negotiations with Jordan's King Hussein which led to peace between those two countries. In December 1994, Rabin was awarded the Nobel Prize for Peace, along with Foreign Minister Shimon Peres and PLO Chariman Yasser Arafat. On November 4, 1995, as he was departing a peace rally in Tel Aviv, Rabin was assassinated by a 27-year-old Jewish law student, Yigal Amir.

Further Reading

Robert Slater's *Rabin of Israel* (1993) is the most complete treatment of Rabin's life. A more personal perspective is offered in *Rabin: Our Life, His Legacy* (1997) by Leah Rabin, his wife. Rabin's own autobiography, *The Rabin Memoirs* (1979) and his book *Yitzhak Rabin Talks with Leaders and Heads of State* (1984) are the best sources of additional material. See also Bernard Reich, *Israel: Land of Tradition and Conflict* (1985). □

Rabindranath Tagore

Rabindranath Tagore (1861-1941) was a Bengali poet, philosopher, social reformer, and dramatist who came into international prominence when he was awarded the Nobel Prize for literature in 1913.

Rabindranath Tagore or simply Rabindranath as he is known in India, was born into an affluent and brilliantly talented Calcutta family on May 7, 1861. His grandfather Dwarkanath Tagore (1794-1846) had amassed great wealth through investment and speculation in coal mines, indigo, and sugar. Despite the fact that the family was an outcast Brahmin one, belonging to the group called *pirali brahman*—Brahmins who had been made ritually impure by sometimes forced contact with Moslems—the dynasty he founded gave Bengal and all of India some of its most prominent painters, poets, musicians, and religious leaders.

Family and Schooling

Dwarkanath's own views were iconoclastic; his wife left him, for example, because he had violated Hindu practice by eating meat. Rabindranath's father, Debendranath (1818-1905), was outstanding in fields of learning ranging from mathematics to ancient scripture and was a man of profound religious concern. He was one of the founders of the religious society called the Brahmo Samaj, which, confronted by Christianity, attempted to purge popular Hinduism of "idolatry" and to reconstruct the "pure monotheism" of classical Indian religion.

The house in which Rabindranath grew up was the home of a vast joint, or extended, family; there were sometimes as many as 200 Tagores living in the complex known as Jorasanko, in northern Calcutta. These included the painters Abinindranath and Gaganendranath and, among Rabindranath's own 11 elder brothers and sisters, the writer and philosopher Dvijendranath, the musician Jyotirindranath, and Bengal's first woman novelist, Svarnakumari Devi, who also edited a literary magazine.

With his father frequently away and his mother ill, Rabindranath was cared for in his early childhood largely by servants and teachers who confined him strictly, breeding in him, as he later wrote, a longing for the freedom of the outside world and a detestation of conventional and restrictive scholastic education. The boy showed unmistakable poetic talent, and as early as 8 he was urged by his brothers and cousins to express himself in poetry. This encouragement, which continued throughout his formative years, caused his talent to flourish. And when he was 11, his father took him on a trip to upper India and the Himalaya Mountains. Alone in the mountains, Debendranath instructed him in Sanskrit, English, and astronomy and taught him the ancient Hindu religious texts.

Such attention from his distinguished father, together with his own talent, brought him to the forefront of his extraordinary family. Rabindranath's first public recitation of his poetry came when he was 14 at a Bengali cultural and nationalistic festival organized by his brothers; his poem on the greatness of India's past, expressing sorrow at its present state, under British rule, was acclaimed. When he was 17, his brother Satyendranath, the first Indian ever admitted to the Indian civil service, took him on a trip to England; and the pattern of his life was established. These three elements occur throughout his life: a profound desire for freedom, both personal and national; an idea of the greatness of

Asia's, and especially India's, contribution to the world of the spirit; and poetry expressing both of these.

Social Consciousness

Although Rabindranath cherished freedom and had great pride in India and in Bengal, his gentle heart caused him to withdraw from the radical political activity with which many of his countrymen were trying to drive the British from their shores. Like Mohandas Gandhi, whom he knew well, Rabindranath abhorred terrorism; but he could not agree even with Gandhi on such political moves as boycott and burning of British-made goods. Rabindranath chose to express himself in other, more personal ways, such as resigning in 1919 the knighthood which he had received from the British crown and establishing a school and later a university at Shantiniketan, the ideals of which were education in a free atmosphere, in the open air, untrammeled by traditional restrictions, and the participation of students from all countries in common experience.

Rabindranath's social consciousness showed itself in many other ways as well. He spent many years as overseer of his family's vast estates in East Bengal and during that time worked hard for the betterment of the tenant farmers, being repaid by learning to know and love the songs and poetry of the people of the countryside; the folk arts of rural Bengal deeply influenced his own later work. And his experimental village called Sriniketan anticipated by many years the Village Development Program instituted by independent India and paralleled Gandhi's own experiments with the village as a viable economic and social unit.

Literary Fame

Rabindranath's ideas of Asia's unity, and later of the unity of the world, and his longing for personal freedom were both expressed in his continual and almost compulsive travel-to Japan, China, Europe, and the United States. In all of these places he lectured and wrote, and it was on one trip to England in 1912 that he fatefully found himself in the company of William Butler Yeats and Ezra Pound. He had prepared some prose versions of his Bengali collection of poems called *Gitanjali* (*Song Offerings*), religious poems for the most part of a lyrical and devotional sort very much akin to the songs of the ancient Hindu sect called Vaishnava. These he read to Yeats, who was entranced by them; and Pound, then representing Harriet Munroe's *Poetry* magazine of Chicago, cabled the editor to hold the next edition for the inclusion of some "very wonderful" poems by Tagore. *Gitanjali* was then published as a book, with an introduction by Yeats, and in 1913 came the Nobel Prize.

Rabindranath looked upon the award as a mixed blessing. In the years previous to its receipt he had retired more and more from the world to devote himself to writing, and he foresaw, correctly, that his peace would be disturbed by fame. He was beleaguered not only in his homeland, where the people, their pride rubbed raw by British dominance, suddenly saw him as a hero, but especially in the United States, where the atmosphere was right for the advent of a tall, handsome, whiterobed, and bearded wise man from the East. The reaction in India he greeted with disappoint-

ment; he saw his sudden prominence as nothing more than shallow chauvinism. And his reaction to the West's acclaim was confusion: he began to wonder whether India was as spiritual, and the West as materialistic, as he had thought. And this doubt was compounded by the fact that he had to look to the West for material support of his many projects, although he longed to live a simple life in the groves and fields of his "golden Bengal."

The deaths of almost all of his beloved immediate family in rapid succession, and painful illness, did not diminish Rabindranath's spirit. Until his death he remained a simple, tender man full of humor and love of life, deep in his sympathy, and strong in his ideals. His last poems, some of them dictated when he became too weak to hold a pen, show his love of nature and of man. He died on Aug. 7, 1941, in Calcutta.

Multifaceted Man

It would be a mistake to consider Rabindranath, as many, especially in the West, do, as only a poet. Late in his life he took up brush and ink, and his moody and often humorous wash drawings are a unique contribution to modern Indian art. Collections of essays like *The Religion of Man* and *Sadhana* (originally a series of lectures at Harvard) are thoughtful and provocative additions to the huge religious and philosophical literature of India. The essays in *Toward Universal Man* show him as a social and political theorist.

Such novels as *Gora, Seser kavita* (*Farewell My Friend*) and *Ghare baire* (*The Home and the World*) demonstrate not only Rabindranath's skill with the novel form but, even in translation, some of the innovations he brought to the Bengali novel: social realism, colloquial dialogue, light satire, and psychologically motivated plot development. His dramas, one of which was produced on Broadway as *The King of the Dark Chamber,* sometimes bordering on whimsy and fantasy, are often complex political or social commentary. His stories, some of the best of which are collected in translation under the title *The Housewarming and Other Stories,* range from ghost stories to lighthearted humor to scathing social satire to gentle warmth, the last being illustrated by the famous *Kabuliwalla* (*The Man from Kabul*).

An accomplished musician, Rabindranath was a vocal performer as well as composer. He developed a new style of vocal music which is called, after him, *Rabindra-sangit.* Never afraid to break the canons of the rigidly structured classical music of India, Rabindranath combined ragas (modes in the classical tradition strictly associated with time and place), brought in elements of the folk music of boatmen and wandering religious, mingled these with semiclassical forms of love songs, and drew from it all a unique style and form of music immensely popular on every level of Bengali society.

Themes of His Poetry

The words of the songs too were his own. Through them, in a way traditional to his culture but with a spirit unique to him, he expressed his love of God and man, his vision of the beauties of nature and the human heart, and his pride in his native land. The images he used were sometimes the old religious ones of the love between man and woman as representative of the love between man and God; sometimes they were the earthy images of the boatmen of the vast rivers or the country marketplace; and sometimes they were drawn from the complex life of Calcutta. They were always images which touched something deep in the hearts and memories of the Bengali people.

One of the aspects of Rabindranath's genius is his use of the Bengali language, for his musician's ear caught natural rhythms and his free mind paid little attention to classical rules of poetry. The forms he created were new; and even in the poetry which he intended to be read rather than sung, rhythms, internal rhyme and alliteration, and a peculiar sonorousness almost make the poems sing themselves. These are things that cannot even be suggested in translation. The translations of Rabindranath's poetry available in English are hardly representative of his total work. *Gitanjali*, on which his reputation in the West is largely based, shows nothing of the humor, for example, or intellectual rigor of which he was capable. Rabindranath's published work is largely, though not completely, contained in 26 substantial volumes.

It is sometimes said that Rabindranath was the last of the great traditional Indian poets. It is true that despite his independence of mind he looked for his inspiration to the past, to nature, and that his theme is man's relation to these and to God; he was never consumed with the complexities of psychology, as many poets who followed him in Bengal have been. He may have achieved his great and lasting popularity just because he was a poet of hope. Toward the end of his life he was stricken with horror by the Nazi march through Europe and Japan's ravages in China. And yet the keynote of his life was struck in such lines as these, from his collection called *Kaplana*:

"Even though slow and sluggish/ evening comes,/ and stops as with a gesture/ your song;/ even though you are alone/ in the infinite sky,/ and your body weary,/ and in terror you utter/ a silent mantra/ to horizons hidden by the veil-/ bird, O my bird,/ though it is darkening/ do not fold your wings."

Further Reading

A useful selection of Rabindranath's writings is Amiya Chakravarty, ed., *A Tagore Reader* (1961). *Rabindranath Tagore, 1861-1961: A Centenary Volume,* published by Sahitya Akademi (1968), contains translations of selected pieces, numerous and mostly adulatory essays by friends and critics, and reproductions of Rabindranath's art. Several biographies of Rabindranath are Marjorie Sykes, *Rabindranath Tagore* (1943); Krishna Kripalani, *Rabindranath Tagore: A Biography* (1962); and G. D. Khanolkar, *The Lute and the Plough: A Life of Rabindranath Tagore* (trans. 1963). Critical studies of his work include Sarvepalli Radhakrishnan, *The Philosophy of Rabindranath Tagore* (1918); John E. Thompson, *Rabindranath Tagore: Poet and Dramatist* (2d rev. ed. 1948); Benay G. Ray, *The Philosophy of Rabindranath Tagore* (1949); Sisirkumar Ghose, *The Later Poems of Tagore* (1961); and Stephen Hay, *Asian Ideas of East and West: Tagore and His Critics in Japan, China, and India* (1970).

Additional Sources

Dyson, Ketaki Kushari, *In your blossoming flower-garden: Rabindranath Tagore and Victoria Ocampo,* New Delhi: Sahitya Akademi, 1988.

Kripalani, Krishna, *Rabindranath Tagore: a biography,* Calcutta: Visva-Bharati, 1980.

Rabindranath Tagore: a 125th birth anniversary volume, Calcutta: Govt. of West Bengal, Dept. of Information & Cultural Affairs, 1988. □

Sergei Vasilievich Rachmaninov

Sergei Vasilievich Rachmaninov (1873-1943) was a highly successful Russian composer, an unrivaled pianist, and a distinguished conductor. "I have followed three hares," he once said. "Can I be certain that I have captured one?"

Sergei Rachmaninov was born in Novgorod on April 1, 1873, at the estate of his aristocratic, impoverished family. His paternal grandfather gave up his career in the army so that he could practice 5 hours a day; he was an amateur because at that time it was considered demeaning for men of his social class to be professional pianists. Sergei's parents were also musical, and his mother was his first piano teacher.

When Sergei was 9, his parents separated, and the mother and children moved to St. Petersburg. This was one of the most interesting and artistic cities in the world. The musical life centered on the conservatory, where Sergei was accepted as a student. He learned little from his teachers, so in 1885 his mother sent him to Moscow, Russia's other great musical and cultural center. He studied piano at the conservatory with Nicolai Sverev and lived at his teacher's house.

Rachmaninov became a fine pianist, but he was more interested in composing after he entered Anton Arensky's and Alexander Taneiev's classes. In 1892 Rachmaninov graduated in piano and also received the Gold Medal in composition, the conservatory's highest honor. His final project in composition, the one-act opera *Aleko,* was considered so outstanding that it received a professional production.

Diversified Activities

During the next 3 years Rachmaninov supported himself by teaching piano at two girls' schools, an occupation he did not enjoy. Among the pieces he wrote at this time was his Prelude in C-sharp Minor, which soon became one of the most popular piano pieces in the world. Its dark, "Russian" quality was irresistible, and it did more to make his name known than any of his other accomplishments.

In 1897 Rachmaninov's First Symphony was played in St. Petersburg; it was a fiasco, and the critics' reviews were merciless. The composer was aware of the symphony's weaknesses, and he became seriously depressed and unable to compose. He accepted an offer to become assistant conductor at an opera house but resigned after a year to conduct and play in London. Still suffering from a psychological block, he sought help from Nicolai Dahl, a physician who used hypnosis and suggestion to cure mental depression. The treatments were successful. In 1901 Rachmaninov completed his Second Piano Concerto, which he dedicated to Dahl. It had an immediate success and became one of the most frequently performed of all concertos. The concerto embodied the best traits of the composer's style, from the brooding sonorities of the opening chords, and the lyricism of the slow movement, to the brilliance of the third.

In 1902 Rachmaninov married his cousin, Natalie Satin, and continued his diversified activities. He found it difficult to follow his "three hares." He neglected composition when, in 1905, he became conductor at the Grand Theater Opera, a very important post in the musical life of Moscow. He soon resigned and moved to Dresden, Germany, to devote himself to composing. Two of his best works were completed in 1907: *The Isle of the Dead,* a tone poem; and the Second Symphony, whose high emotional level and colorful orchestration show a strong Tchaikovsky influence. By the time this symphony was composed, Debussy had written *La Mer,* Richard Strauss had written *Salome,* and Scriabin had written *The Poem of Ecstasy,* but Rachmaninov remained loyal to the ideals and idioms of late-19th-century romantic music.

In 1909 Rachmaninov visited the United States. He played the first performance of his Third Piano Concerto with the New York Symphony Orchestra and conducted the Boston Orchestra, as well as the New York Philharmonic. He was offered the post of conductor of the Boston Symphony but declined.

In 1910 Rachmaninov was named vice president of the Russian Imperial Music Society, which controlled all higher music schools in the country, including the conservatories in Moscow and St. Petersburg. He concentrated on improving the smaller provincial schools and established an important one in Kiev. All the while he was composing. Among his most important works were those for piano: Thirteen Preludes (1910), Six Études Tableaux (1911), and Nine Études Tableaux (1917). He wrote over 70 songs with piano accompaniment; *The Bells,* a choral symphony for soprano, tenor, and baritone (1913); and a Vesper Mass for boys' and men's voices (1913).

The Move to America

The turning point of Rachmaninov's life was the 1917 Revolution in Russia. He was in Moscow during the early uprisings, but he realized that it would be impossible to remain and accepted an invitation to play a series of concerts in Scandinavia. His family soon joined him, and they never returned to Russia. To support his family he became a concert pianist—something he never wanted to be. He rented a house in Copenhagen and started practicing to learn recital programs; up to this time he had played his own compositions almost exclusively.

In November 1918 Rachmaninov sailed for New York and began a career as a touring virtuoso. Each season was divided between the United States, England, and the Continent. Whenever he could, he would go to his house in Lucerne, Switzerland, where he enjoyed boating, driving his car, and composing. His Fourth Piano Concerto (1927), Third Symphony (1936), and Symphonoic Dances for Orchestra (1941) were not successful, but his *Rhapsody on a Theme by Paganini* for piano and orchestra (1934) became a favorite of pianists and audiences alike and soon rivaled the Second Concerto in popularity. With the outbreak of World War II he moved to Beverly Hills, Calif. He died there on March 28, 1943.

Rachmaninov's life was not a happy one. He thought of himself as a composer, but he was never able to devote himself entirely to composition. Furthermore, although some of his compositions achieved worldwide popularity, most of the critics condemned them for being old-fashioned and reactionary, and he felt that he was out of step with the times. He hated concertizing, and his standards were so high that he was rarely pleased with his playing. His "six and a half foot tall scowl," as his friend Igor Stravinsky called it, was famous.

Further Reading

Although Rachmaninov spoke disparagingly about the book by Oscar von Riesemann, *Rachmaninov's Recollections* (1934), it contains many interesting insights. Other biographies are Victor I. Seroff, *Rachmaninoff* (1950), and Sergei Bertensson and Jay Leyda, *Sergei Rachmaninoff: A Lifetime in Music* (1956). A critical analysis of each composition is in John Culshaw, *Rachmaninov: The Man and His Music* (1950).

Additional Sources

Bazhanov, N. (Nikolai), *Rachmaninov,* Moscow: Raduga, 1983.

Lyle, Watson, *Rachmaninoff: a biography,* New York: AMS Press, 1976.

Martyn, Barrie, *Rachmaninoff: composer, pianist, conductor,* Aldershot, Hants, England: Scolar Press; Brookfield, Vt., USA: Gower Pub. Co., 1990.

Matthew-Walker, Robert, *Rachmaninoff,* London; New York: Omnibus Press, 1984, 1980.

Norris, Geoffrey, *Rachmaninoff,* New York: Schirmer Books: Maxwell Macmillan International, 1994.

Piggott, Patrick, *Rachmaninov,* London: Faber and Faber, 1978. □

Jean Baptiste Racine

The French dramatist Jean Baptiste Racine (1639-1699), admired as a portrayer of man's subtle psychology and overwhelming passions, was the author of 11 tragedies and a comedy. His work is the greatest expression of French classicism.

Jean Racine was born in La Ferté-Milon and baptized there on Dec. 22, 1639. Both of his parents died within a few years, and the young Racine went to live with his paternal grandparents. There he was cared for by his grandmother and by his aunt, both of whom lived in close contact with the Jansenist convent of Port-Royal-des-Champs near Paris. Racine was educated in the schools of Port-Royal, receiving what was perhaps the best education available in his times. Sent on to the Jansenist-influenced school in Beauvais, Racine learned ancient Greek in addition to his other studies, before completing his education at Port-Royal and in Paris.

First Dramas

At some time before 1660 Racine entered the service of the Duke of Luynes in Paris, working as an assistant to a cousin who was the duke's steward. In his spare time Racine interested himself in poetry, made the acquaintance of Jean de La Fontaine, the poet and fabulist, and wrote an official poem, *La Nymphe de la Seine* (1660). He also wrote two tragedies, both refused by the theatrical troupes of the day and now lost. Apparently discouraged, Racine spent perhaps a year in Uzés preparing to enter the priesthood, but in 1663 he returned to Paris and to literature.

Racine was approached by the great comic writer and actor Molière, whose troupe wished to commission a tragedy, *La Thébaide,* to compete with one being put on by a rival troupe. Racine agreed to write such a tragedy according to Molière's instructions, and the play was first performed in 1664. Although it was indifferently received,

Molière requested another play from Racine. Racine's *Alexandre* (1665) was his first success in the theater.

French Theatrical Situation

During this period the French theater was influenced profoundly by the famous neo-Aristotelian precepts for good literature. Playwrights observed with ever greater severity the famous "three unities" of time, place, and action, and the principles of verisimilitude and theatrical *bienséance* (seemliness). Without renouncing the influence of Pierre Corneille, they nevertheless tended more and more to set their plays within a single stage decor, using fewer and fewer personages, simplifying their plots, and concentrating them in shorter texts. Contemporary playwrights thus presented less and less dramatic action, interesting themselves rather in the passions of their personages—and transforming the regular or "ruleconscious" theater of the 1630s and 1640s into the disciplined and passion-oriented classicist theater of the following decades. While Racine's *Thébaide* and *Alexandre* show both Corneillian and later classical tendencies, Racine expressed more purely classicist literary ideals in his third tragedy, *Andromaque.*

Andromaque and La Du Parc

Between the first performances of *Alexandre* and the first performances of *Andromaque* in 1667, Racine's way of life changed considerably. Apparently dissatisfied with Molière's production of his *Alexandre,* he secretly rehearsed the play with the actors of another troupe, who played *Alexandre* in competition with Molière in December 1665. The resulting theatrical scandal gave Racine the reputation of a devious and unscrupulous young man. As if to confirm this evil reputation, an ungrateful Racine also published a pamphlet against Jansenism, attacking his former teachers of Port-Royal. One year later Racine took as his mistress a notorious actress, Thérèse du Parc. It was apparently for "La Du Parc" that Racine wrote *Andromaque,* in which she played the title role.

The action of *Andromaque* takes place some years after the conclusion of the Trojan War. The play begins with the arrival of Oreste, the son of the Greek king Agamemnon, at the court of Pyrrhus, son of the Greek hero Achilles. Ostensibly, Oreste has come as the ambassador of all the Greeks to ask for the execution of Astyanax, son of the Trojan hero Hector, whom Pyrrhus is holding prisoner. In reality, however, Oreste has come to see Hermione, daughter of Helen of Troy, with whom he is in love. Hermione, however, is in love with Pyrrhus and indeed is engaged to marry him. Pyrrhus, however, is in love not with Hermione but with Andromaque, the disconsolate widow of Hector and the mother of Astyanax.

The rest of the tragedy turns less upon the action than upon the psychological interaction of these four personages, each of whom passionately and jealously loves someone who passionately loves someone else. When Andromaque rebuffs Pyrrhus, he threatens to carry out the Greeks' request and kill Astyanax. When Pyrrhus breaks off his engagement to Hermione and prepares to marry Andromaque, Hermione persuades Oreste to kill him. But when the unfortunate Oreste and his followers succeed in doing so, she repudiates him. Oreste goes mad and Hermione commits suicide, leaving Andromaque and Astyanax to initiate another round, some day, in the Trojan War against the Greeks.

Personal Characteristics

During the following years Racine retained his reputation for deviousness, ambition, and ingratitude. Through his mistress, La Du Parc, he came to know something of the shady side of court life. He may finally have secretly married La Du Parc, and after her death in mysterious circumstances in 1668 he was accused of poisoning her. Racine subsequently was compromised with the dead La Du Parc and others in the infamous "poison affair," and he may narrowly have escaped arrest. In any case, he took as his next mistress another actress, La Champmeslé. But during this period he also consolidated his reputation as the greatest playwright of his times, writing one comedy, *Les Plaideurs* (1668), and numerous tragedies for the Parisian stage.

Britannicus and *Bérénice*

In his succeeding tragedies Racine continued to explore passionate love and passionate jealousy. In *Britannicus* (1669) Racine shows the young Roman emperor Néron (Nero) torn between the wise counsel of his teacher Burrhus and the influence of his domineering mother, Agrippine. Jealously in love with Junie, who loves the young prince Britannicus, Néron finally poisons the latter, revealing himself as the tyrant so well remembered in Roman history. In *Bérénice* (1670) the Roman Senate demands that the emperor Titus renounce his plans to marry Bérénice, a ruler of a foreign state and thus politically suspect. The play proceeds with no action other than successive confrontations between the various personages. With the action essentially reduced to nothing, the play relies exclusively on the beauty of Racine's verse and his analysis of the passions of his personages. Although Racine's numerous enemies attempted to conspire against the play and although the elderly Corneille wrote a *Tite et Bérénice* to compete with it, Racine's play was a remarkable success, followed by *Bajazet* (1672), *Mithridate* (1673), *Iphigénie* (1674), and *Phèdre* (1677).

Racine's Masterpiece, *Phèdre*

When it became known that Racine was preparing a play on the subject of Phèdre, the Duchess of Bouillon and other friends of the aging Corneille apparently attempted to hurt Racine's play by commissioning another playwright, Nicolas Pradon, to write one on the same subject. Apparently based on a stolen copy of Racine's text, Pradon's *Phèdre et Hippolyte* opened in Paris only 2 days after Racine's play. The two works were the occasion of a bitter literary quarrel in which insulting sonnets and other writings were exchanged, but Racine's play eventually triumphed over its rival.

In Racine's *Phèdre,* Hippolyte, son of the absent King Thésée, states his intention of leaving his palace of Trézène in order to search for his father. Although at first it appears

he is ashamed of his love for Aricie, sister of some of his father's enemies, it soon becomes clear that he really wishes to avoid his stepmother, Phèdre. Phèdre is in love with Hippolyte and, in a memorable scene, declares her love for him. He at first pretends not to understand but finally can only flee her presence. When Thésée returns unexpectedly, Phèdre allows her nurse, Oenone, to accuse Hippolyte of making advances. In a rage Thésée asks the god Neptune to kill Hippolyte as he flees Trézène, hoping to marry Aricie and escape with her. Thésée learns his error too late to prevent the death of Hippolyte. Phèdre and Oenone commit suicide, leaving Thésée alone to pardon Aricie.

In *Phèdre,* as in Racine's other tragedies, critics have admired first the very refined, pure poetry of Racine's verse and second Racine's very incisive, though pessimistic, view of human psychology. A contemporary critic, Jean de La Bruyère, remarked that although tragedies on love and duty and heroic *gloire* had presented "man as he should be," Racine presented man as he really was. Man, as Racine presents him, often displays a sense of personal insecurity and self-doubt not unlike modern psychological "complexes." The Racinian character's self-doubt leads him—like Racine himself, as described by his enemies—to fight desperately and destructively to gain his ends, with inevitably tragic results. Some modern critics have ascribed this view, rather than to any Racinian observation of human nature, to the influence of Jansenism and its somber view of human helplessness before God. In any case, Racine has long been admired as one of the most perfect of French writers—that is, in another modern view, as the French writer who most successfully matches his poetic images to his psychology, his psychology to his plot, and his plot to the structure and neo-Aristotelian view of the tragedy, giving his plays a kind of total inner coherence unequaled in France's *grand siècle.*

Later Life

Yet in spite of Racine's genius—and almost as if he had written his sublime tragedies only to gain a place in society—he stopped writing tragedies after *Phèdre.* Six months after the premiere of *Phèdre,* Racine married. In October of the same year, 1677, he accepted a post as King Louis XIV's historiographer. At the same time, he announced his return to the Jansenist faith of his childhood. During the following years Racine lived comfortably and raised a family of seven children. As director of the French Academy, he eulogized his former bitter rival, Corneille, and published a new edition of his own works, from which he had removed remarks offensive to his enemies.

Although Racine apparently intended definitively to retire from the theater, he was persuaded by Louis XIV's morganatic wife Madame de Maintenon to write two more plays, of a slightly different character than his previous works. These were *Esther* (1689) and *Athalie* (1691)—tragedies written on specifically Christian themes and without any love interest, intended to be presented by the young ladies of Saint-Cyr, a girls' establishment protected by Madame de Maintenon. More and more a respectable citizen and favorite of the King in his later years, Racine died in Paris on April 21, 1699.

Further Reading

The best biography of Racine in English is Geoffrey Brereton, *Jean Racine: A Critical Biography* (1951). A penetrating analysis of Racine's dramaturgy, with an emphasis on structure and language, is Roland Barthes, *On Racine* (1963; trans. 1964). Other recent works in English on Racine are John C. Lapp, *Aspects of Racinian Tragedy* (1955), and Bernard Weinberg, *The Art of Jean Racine* (1963). A unique collection of critical essays is in Robert James Nelson, ed., *Corneille and Racine: Parallels and Contrasts* (1966), which includes essays from the 17th century to the present and constitutes a kind of history of literary criticism on the subject. More general studies are John Lough, *An Introduction to Seventeenth Century France* (1954), and Will G. Moore, *French Classical Literature* (1961). □

A. R. Radcliffe-Brown

The English anthropologist A. R. Radcliffe-Brown (1881-1955) pioneered the study of social relations as integrated systems. His analyses of kinship relations in Australia and in Africa have had a powerful influence on modern social anthropology.

Alfred Reginald Brown was born in Birmingham, England, in 1881. In 1926 he would add his mother's maiden name to his own, becoming famous as A. R. Radcliffe-Brown. Born into a family of modest means, he left school at 17 to work in the Birmingham library. On the urging of his brother, Brown began premedical studies at the University of Birmingham. Though he had aspired to a degree in the natural sciences, Brown was convinced by a Cambridge tutor to enter Trinity College as a student in the moral sciences. Among his Cambridge teachers was the psychologist W. H. R. Rivers, who had recently returned from the Torres-Strait expedition to Melanesia in the South Pacific—the first major anthropological expedition sponsored by Cambridge.

In 1906-1908 Radcliffe-Brown undertook his first field work in the Andaman Islands in the Indian Ocean, research which led in 1922 to the publication of his classic monograph *The Andaman Islanders*. His other major field research was a survey of different kinship systems among the aboriginal groups of Western Australia, undertaken in 1910-1912.

The rest of his professional life was taken up with teaching and writing theoretical papers. Over the course of three decades, Radcliffe-Brown held major teaching posts at the University of Capetown in South Africa, the University of Sydney in Australia, the University of Chicago in the United States, and Oxford University, where he was appointed to the first professorship in anthropology in 1937. In Sydney he founded the influential journal *Oceania*.

By force of personality and intellect, Radcliffe-Brown shaped the course of British anthropology throughout the decade of the 1940s. Whereas the influence of Bronislaw Malinowski, the other important British anthropologist of the time, was to set a high standard of field work and data collection, Radcliffe-Brown's influence was more theoretical. Malinowski had argued that cultural institutions had to be understood in relation to the basic human psychological and biological needs they satisfied. Radcliffe-Brown, however, stressed a "structural-functional" approach to social analysis which viewed social systems as integrated mechanisms in which all parts function to promote the harmony of the whole.

Here the influence of the great French sociologist Emil Durkheim was evident. Like Durkheim, Radcliffe-Brown thought that social institutions should be studied like any scientific object. The job of the social anthropologist was to describe the anatomy of interdependent social institutions—what he called social structure—and to define the functioning of all parts in relation to the whole. The aim of such analysis is to account for what holds a functioning society together.

This approach led Radcliffe-Brown to undertake somewhat abstract and clinical analyses of social institutions in the search for general social laws. Among his most famous analyses is that of "joking relationships" in tribal societies. In his famous essay "On Joking Relationships," published originally in 1940, he described an often noticed custom whereby certain individuals (often in-laws) are expected to engage in formalized banter. He proposed that one could only understand such strange customs by studying the specific joking relationships in the context of the total patterning of social relations in the society.

This highly formal approach to the study of social customs led Radcliffe-Brown to a number of other famous analyses. His early survey of Western Australian aboriginal societies, for instance, led to the first sophisticated account of complicated aboriginal kinship systems as a set of variations on a few structural themes. He was able to identify a set of relationships between kinship terminologies and marriage rules that made sense for the first time of the "structure" of aboriginal society. These studies are still the cornerstone of the social anthropology of aboriginal Australia.

In an early paper, "The Mother's Brother in South Africa," published in 1924, Radcliffe-Brown made sense of what had been thought to be isolated and peculiar customs observed in African societies whereby a boy has a special relationship with his maternal uncle (his mother's brother) that is distinct from his relationship with any other uncle or with his own father. Again, by examining this relationship in light of the total abstract pattern of kinship relations and the pattern of relations between different social groups, Radcliffe-Brown was able to show the structural-functional "logic" of an apparently irrational custom.

In yet another illuminating analysis, Radcliffe-Brown provided the basis of a coherent explanation of "totemism"—the set of associations between social groups and species of plants or animals. Radcliffe-Brown argued that totemic beliefs create solidarity between nature and human society. Nature was, through totemism, domesticated. Furthermore, Radcliffe-Brown insisted that oppositions between natural species of animals or plants served to symbolize differences between one social group and another. This approach to totemism, once again stressing analyzing specific social institutions in relation to their total encompassing social context, was a major advance in the understanding of such beliefs and paved the way for the more modern work of structuralists such as Claude Levi-Strauss.

Radcliffe-Brown's list of publications is not especially long. Yet in a series of powerfully argued papers he was able to transform the face of anthropology in his time. Throughout his career Radcliffe-Brown insisted that the proper aim of anthropology was the careful comparison of societies and the formulation of general social laws. When he went into anthropology exotic cultures were usually studied as collections of separable customs and cultural anthropology was the history of how such customs were "diffused" between cultures by borrowing or conquest. Radcliffe-Brown was a major part of a movement to understand human society as integrated systems, open to scientific analysis. This elegant and often abstract approach to social analysis has had its critics and its defenders. But Radcliffe-Brown's analysis of social patterns left an important mark on all of modern social anthropology.

Further Reading

The most influential of Radcliffe-Brown's essays have been published together under the title *Structure and Function in Primitive Society* (1952). The most informative account of Radcliffe-Brown's life and work is contained in the book *Anthropology and Anthropologists: The Modern British School* (1983) by Adam Kuper. Other extensive discussions of his impact on anthropology may be found in Marvin Harris, *The Rise of Anthropological Theory* (1968) and in David Bidney, *Theoretical Anthropology* (1967). □

Karl Bernardovich Radek

The Russian Communist leader and publicist Karl Bernardovich Radek (1885-1939) is best known for his brilliant and acerbic polemics. He was an outstanding apostle of internationalism.

Karl Radek was born Karl Sobelsohn in Lvov (then in Austrian Poland) to an Austrophile Jewish family. As a youth, he rejected his family's outlook and became involved in political agitation, moving to Switzerland in 1904. There he joined the left wing of Polish socialism, returning to Poland in 1905 to participate in revolutionary activity in Warsaw. After a brief prison term, Radek spent the next decade building his reputation, in both Poland and Germany, as a talented but volatile and often irresponsible journalist. His barbed comments so irritated leading Socialists that he was successively expelled from the Polish and German Socialist parties.

During World War I Radek returned to Switzerland, where he alternately collaborated with and contended with V. I. Lenin in the Zimmerwald Movement, an organization of antiwar Socialists. After the overthrow of the Czar in March 1917, Radek accompanied Lenin in the "sealed train" across Germany, but he was not allowed to enter Russia. He then spent several months in Stockholm organizing Bolshevik support among European Socialists, and after the Bolshevik coup in November 1917 he proceeded to Moscow. There he became responsible for foreign-language propaganda, accompanying Leon Trotsky to Brest Litovsk, where he propagandized German troops. At the end of 1918, after the collapse of the imperial regime in Germany, Radek returned to Berlin in order to help organize the German Communist party. Though he counseled against a German uprising, the "Spartacus" Putsch of January 1919 led to his incarceration for almost a year.

Upon his return to Moscow, Radek was assigned major roles in the Communist International (Comintern), where he enjoyed great influence, particularly in the German Communist party. His multilingual talents, his bizarre personal appearance—some of his contemporaries likened him to an ape—and his extraordinary sense of humor made him a great favorite of journalists in Moscow. From 1919 to 1923 Radek enjoyed considerable prominence both within and without Russia.

However, his political enemy Grigori Zinoviev used the collapse of the German revolution of 1923 to exclude Radek from the Comintern and high party posts. Under the influence of his new mistress, Larissa Reissner, Radek withdrew from party politics, and in 1925 he became rector of Sun Yat-sen University in Moscow. When Larissa died in 1926, Radek openly joined the Trotskyite opposition, with which he had long been identified; in 1927 he was expelled from the Bolshevik party and subsequently exiled to Siberia. In 1929 Radek renounced Trotsky and returned to Moscow to become once again a major publicist—for Stalin—although he never recovered his Comintern or party posts.

In 1936 Radek was one of the coauthors of the new Soviet constitution. However, later that year he was arrested for treason, and in a show trial in January 1937 Radek was sentenced to 10 years' imprisonment. Though rumors of his survival persisted, Radek apparently died in prison sometime in 1939.

Further Reading

The only biography of Radek is Warren Lerner, *Karl Radek: The Last Internationalist* (1970).

Additional Sources

Tuck, Jim, *Engine of mischief: an analytical biography of Karl Radek,* New York: Greenwood Press, 1988. □

Sarvepalli Radhakrishnan

Sarvepalli Radhakrishnan (1888-1975) was an Indian philosopher, statesman, and articulate interpreter of Hindu tradition to the West.

Radhakrishnan was born near Madras into a Brahmin family of orthodox Hindu persuasion. However, he was educated in Christian missionary institutions and was exposed both to routine religious criticisms of Hindu tradition and to the mainstream of Western philosophy. As his religious and philosophical sensibilities developed, he found himself more and more drawn to the values of the Vedanta. From the very first, he had felt himself imbued with a "firm faith in the reality of an unseen world behind the flux of phenomena." He was offended by the dogmatic and ill-informed criticisms leveled at Hindu culture by some of his teachers; and his sense of pride in his own tradition was deeply aroused by the eloquence of Vivekananda and Rabindranath Tagore.

The Idealist Thinker

Radhakrishnan resolved to explore his own tradition in fuller detail and wrote his master's thesis, *The Ethics of Vedanta* (1908), in part to refute the Western prejudice that the Vedanta simplistically affirmed the "illusory" (*maya*) nature of the world and lacked ethical content and power.

At the same time, Radhakrishnan found that he could not ignore the paralyzing superstitions which dominated Hindu social institutions and the life of the masses as integral features of their deepest religious commitments. He was encouraged by some of his more sensitive Western teachers to continue his research into Hindu philosophy in order to probe its innovative and universal potentials. He found much in Western philosophy—particularly in the idealists and the work of Henri Bergson—which was tangent to the Hindu and specifically Vedantic validation of mystical intuition and the spirituality of the universe.

Radhakrishnan was persuaded that philosophical enterprise must not simply provide rational verification and analysis but must give a profound and transforming insight into the spiritual content of existence in its personal and historical dimensions as an antidote to the dehumanizing values increasingly predominant in Western civilization. For Radhakrishnan, the unique strength of the Vedanta was its validation of personal spiritual striving for deeper penetration into the meaning of life itself.

Radhakrishnan combined this commitment with a humanistic focus on the need for social change and reform which he mediated in part by a reinterpretation of traditional Hindu religious forms and texts. His translation and interpretation of the *Bhagavad Gita* (Song of the Lord) strives to move traditional Hindu institutions (for instance, the caste system) in the direction of "democratic" values. He proved himself capable of performing this potentially awkward synthetic task by stressing the more profound aspects of Hindu philosophy which inherently transcend the provisional historical and social forms associated with normative Hinduism. Some of his other major works—*An Idealist*

View of Life and *Eastern Religions and Western Thought*—and his scholarly commentaries on Vedantic materials are also marked by a distinctive "this-worldly" humanism uniquely imbued with Vedantic mysticism.

There is an equally powerful psychological emphasis in much of Radhakrishnan's work on the therapeutic consequences of personality integration through intuition of the essential relation of the self to the sacred force from which all phenomena spring. And this he combines with a theory of history which affirms that its most important dimension is the evolution of human spiritual consciousness. Hindu mysticism and related techniques are, therefore, not modes of withdrawal from reality but are means for strengthening personal autonomy, active capacity for love, and conscious participation in the unfolding destiny of the universe.

This evolutionary historical perspective had a marked impact on Radhakrishnan's interpretation of the traditional doctrine of *Karma* (action—the law of ethical retribution). The individual is responsible not only for his own destiny within a static cosmology of personal transmigration but for the welfare of all men. Each person acts (or does not act) to promote future possibilities. In this way individual salvation is tied to the fate of mankind and the ultimate goal of the historical process itself. Although his concept of "true humanity" is deeply steeped in Vedantic teaching, he has several specific human models who embody his own commitment to reforms incorporating Western values within the deeper matrix of Hindu spirituality: they are Rabindranath Tagore, Mohandas Gandhi, and Jawaharlal Nehru. For Radhakrishnan, these paradigms of modern Indian creativity show an extraordinary ability to synthesize conflicting value systems by employing the pristine mystical and ascetic models which lie at the heart of Hinduism. It is with these men in mind that he asserts, "Man is not a detached spectator of a progress immanent in human history, but an active agent remolding the world nearer to his ideals."

Radhakrishnan's understanding of the role of the traditional yoga is also shaped by this commitment. Its aim is to provide a disciplined framework which facilitates the fulfillment of worldly obligations while continually reinforcing the universal search for spiritual perfection. The yoga renders the individual more capable of acting in the world and serving his fellowmen.

From Theory to Practice

Many of Radhakrishnan's writings seem to be "apologetic"—designed for popular consumption by Western readers; and he engaged in debates with Western theologians and philosophers who criticized Indian forms of spirituality. But the great bulk of his work is distinguished by a power clearly evident in the development of his own distinctive philosophy of life. His work as an educator and cultural ambassador to the West and his many public services to the Indian government are further evidence of his many talents. He served variously as professor of philosophy and religion at the universities of Mysore, Calcutta, and Oxford, and he had many teaching engagements at major universities in the United States. From 1949 to 1952 he was ambassador to the Soviet Union, returning to India to serve

for ten years as vice president of India and chancellor of Delhi University. He was also President of the United Nations Educational, Scientific, and Cultural Organization (UNESCO) from 1952-54. From 1962 to 1967 Radhakrishnan was president of India. He combined these activities with a continuing program of productive writing and lecturing, all of which made him a living embodiment of the values which he espoused. Radhakrishnan died on April 17, 1975 in Madras, India. The Indian Government ordered a week-long state of mourning.

Further Reading

Radhakrishnan's political writings have been collected and printed as *President Radhakrishnan's Speeches and Writings* (New Delhi, 1965). The most extensive volume on Radhakrishnan the philosopher, which also includes an autobiographical memoir, is Paul A. Schilpp, ed., *The Philosophy of Sarvepalli Radhakrishnan* (1952). Consult also C. E. M. Joad, *Counterattack from the East: the Philosophy of Radhakrishnan* (1933); S. J. Samartha, *Introduction to Radhakrishnan: The Man and His Thought* (1964); and the anniversary volume *Radhakrishnan: Comparative Studies in Philosophy Presented in Honour of His Sixtieth Birthday* (1951), edited by W. R. Inge and others.

Additional Sources

(Sarvepalli, Gopal) *Radharkrishnan, A Biography,* Unwin Hyman, 1989.
(McGreal, Ian, ed.) *Great Thinkers of the Eastern World,* Harper-Collins, 1995.
New York Times (April 18, 1975). □

Paul Radin

Paul Radin (1883-1959) was an American anthropologist and ethnographer who specialized in the ethnology of religion and mythology and the ethnography of Native Americans.

Paul Radin was born on April 2, 1883, in Poland, and in his early childhood lived in New York City. He received his bachelor's degree in 1902 at City College and after a short period abroad went to Columbia University to study history and anthropology under Franz Boas, receiving a doctorate in 1911. By studying with Boas at Columbia he joined a group of young scholars that became a major influence in the subsequent 4 decades of American anthropology. He did fieldwork among the Winnebago, the Ojibwa, the Fox, the Zapotec, the Wappo, the Wintun, and the Huave. Of these, the Winnebago were his specialty and provided him with material for numerous monographs and articles as well as many extensive examples for his more general writings.

One central theme ran through the greatest portion of Radin's work—the manner by which particular individuals respond to the vicissitudes of their immediate cultural environment. This theme is particularly evident in his three major works. Thus *Primitive Man as a Philosopher* (1927) cogently argues that reflective individuals are to be found quite as readily among primitives as elsewhere. In *Primitive Religion* (1937) he demonstrates that for any given culture the degree of religiosity to be found varies from indifferent to deep, depending on the proclivities and intelligence of the individual. The position of the individual was the explicit theme of *Crashing Thunder* (1926), for here Radin obtained, translated, and edited the autobiography of a member of the Winnebago tribe. This book was a landmark in American anthropology. It was the first and probably the best of a long line of similar autobiographical accounts of individual Indians that was published by subsequent anthropologists.

Other important works by Radin included the The Story of the American Indian (1927), *Social Anthropology* (1927), *The Method and Theory of Ethnology* (1933), *The Culture of the Winnebago, as Described by Themselves* (1949), and *The Trickster* (1956).

Radin never stayed at any one academic institution for more than a few years. He found the institutionalized aspect of intellectual life uncongenial and preferred to remain throughout his career an independent scholar. At various times he held posts at Berkeley, Mills College, Fisk University, Black Mountain College, Kenyon College, the University of Chicago, and, finally, Brandeis University, where he was made a Samuel Rubin professor and became head of the anthropology department. Radin died on Feb. 21, 1959.

Further Reading

An excellent biographical sketch of Radin is in Stanley Diamond, ed., *Culture in History: Essays in Honor of Paul Radin* (1960). Background studies are Robert H. Lowie, *The History of Ethnological Theory* (1937); H. R. Hays, *From Ape to Angel: An Informal History of Social Anthropology* (1958); and Marvin Harris, *The Rise of Anthropological Theory: A History of Theories of Culture* (1968). □

Pierre-Esprit Radisson

The French explorer and soldier of fortune Pierre-Esprit Radisson (ca. 1636-1710) is the most romantic and least known of all the famous explorers of the Canadian North and West. He was one of the originators of the Hudson's Bay Company.

Pierre-Esprit Radisson was born in France, but virtually no information survives concerning his early life. When still quite young, he somehow made his way to New France, where his half sister Marguerite lived. After her husband's death at the hands of the Iroquois, Marguerite married again. Her second husband, Medard Chouart Des Groseilliers, was to share much of the adventurous life of Radisson.

From his own sketchy account of his career, it appears that Radisson was captured by the Iroquois in the early 1650s, was adopted by an Indian family, and spent some 2 years traveling and hunting with his captors. He escaped in 1654, sailed to Amsterdam, and arrived back in Three Rivers late the same year. Apparently, Radisson remained in New France for the next 4 years, except for one more trip made to the Iroquois territory near Albany.

Radisson's first trip west was undertaken with his brother-in-law in 1659. They wintered southwest of Lake Superior in Sioux country. It was probably during this trip that the two men first heard of Hudson Bay and the treasure of beaver to be found in that area. In the spring Radisson and Des Groseilliers returned to Montreal laden with furs, most of which were promptly confiscated by corrupt officials. From this point on, patriotism played little part in the adventures of Radisson.

From 1662 to 1664 the two men operated from New England and tried—unsuccessfully—to reach Hudson Bay by sea. In 1664 they were persuaded to go to London. Their ship was captured by the Dutch, with whom England was then at war. After being put ashore in Spain, the two eventually turned up in London in time to witness the great fire and the ravages of the Black Death. They were able to interest some English merchants in the exploitation of the fur trade around Hudson Bay, with the assistance of a successful trip there by Des Groseilliers. Radisson remained in London and composed his Voyages. On May 2, 1670, the Hudson's Bay Company was formally chartered and began its long and generally prosperous career. For the next 15 years, Radisson and his brother-in-law served the company either in the bay or in the capital.

Pierre-Esprit Radisson (left)

In 1675 the two adventurers left the company, for reasons that are not at all clear, and resumed their French allegiance. It was not a rewarding transfer. Des Groseilliers settled in Three Rivers, and Radisson entered the service of the French navy and went campaigning in the Caribbean. He was back at Hudson Bay again in 1681 and was rejoined there by Des Groseilliers. They were successful in contending with the English for control of the territory around the Nelson River and in their trading ventures. But once again, they felt that rewards were unsatisfactory in the employ of the French. When his brother-in-law returned to Canada, Radisson turned up in the service of the Hudson's Bay Company once more, in 1684.

The company sent him back to the bay, where he succeeded in persuading the French at Ft. Nelson (which he had established) to abandon their allegiance and all their furs. Radisson made his last trip to Hudson Bay in late 1685 and remained there for 2 years, but he was unable to work in harmony with the other officers of the company. He returned to England and finally settled near London. Radisson married three times during his peripatetic life and was survived by several children.

Further Reading

The only reliable—and engaging—study of Radisson in English is in Grace Lee Nute, *Caesars of the Wilderness* (1943).

Additional Sources

Nute, Grace Lee, *Caesars of the wilderness: Medard Chouart, Sieur des Groseilliers and Pierre Esprit Radisson, 1618-1710,* St. Paul: Minnesota Historical Society Press, 1978, 1943. □